Gale Encyclopedia of E-Commerce

SECOND EDITION

VOLUME I

A–I

Laurie J. Fundukian

EDITOR

GALE
CENGAGE Learning®

Detroit • New York • San Francisco • New Haven, Conn • Waterville, Maine • London

GALE
CENGAGE Learning

Gale Encyclopedia of E-Commerce, Second Edition

Project Editor: Laurie J. Fundukian

Editorial: Tara Atterberry, Kristin Key, Jacqueline Longe, Brigham Narins, Jeff Wilson

Product Manager: Michele LaMeau

Indexing Services: Hawkeye Indexing

Composition: Evi Abou-El-Seoud

Manufacturing: Rita Wimberley

Product Design: Kristine Julien

Library of Congress Cataloging-in-Publication Data

Gale encyclopedia of e-commerce / Laurie J. Fundukian, editor; foreword by Miklos A. Vasarhelyi. -- 2nd ed.
p. cm.
Rev. ed. of: Gale encyclopedia of e-commerce / Jane A. Malonis, editor; foreword by Paula J. Haynes. c2002.
Includes bibliographical references and index.
ISBN 978-0-7876-9098-4 (hardback) -- ISBN 978-0-7876-9099-1 (v. 1) -- ISBN 978-0-7876-9100-4 (v. 2)
1. Electronic commerce--Encyclopedias. I. Fundukian, Laurie J.
HF5548.32.G35 2012
381'.17203--dc23 2012001401

Gale
27500 Drake Rd.
Farmington Hills, MI, 48331-3535

ISBN-13: 978-0-7876-9098-4 (set)
ISBN-13: 978-0-7876-9099-1 (vol. 1)
ISBN-13: 978-0-7876-9100-4 (vol. 2)

ISBN-10: 0-7876-9098-8 (set)
ISBN-10: 0-7876-9099-6 (vol. 1)
ISBN-10: 0-7876-9100-3 (vol. 2)

This title is also available as an e-book.
ISBN-13: 978-1-4144-9046-5
ISBN-10: 1-4144-9046-1
Contact your Gale, a part of Cengage Learning sales representative for ordering information.

Printed in Mexico
1 2 3 4 5 6 7 16 15 14 13 12

Gale Encyclopedia of E-Commerce

SECOND EDITION

Contents

Volume 2, J-Z

Highlights

This second edition of the *Gale Encyclopedia of E-Commerce (GEEC)* presents a comprehensive look at the topics and terms, companies, people, events, and legislation most relevant to the e-commerce industry. Designed for e-enterpreneurs and students performing industry research, as well as for individuals simply interested in understanding the industry more fully, *Gale Encyclopedia of E-Commerce* is an all-encompassing source of the information most critical to understanding the e-commerce industry.

Through 480 essays, readers will encounter a wide array of information on the terminology, players, people, and laws in the industry, including:

- Advanced Encryption Standard (AES)
- Advertising, Online
- Auction Sites
- Banking, Online
- Cyber Monday
- Mark Zuckerberg
- Business-to-Business (B2B) E-Commerce
- Business-to-Consumer (B2C) E-Commerce
- Cyberstrategy
- Digital Cash
- E-tailing
- Steve Jobs
- Global E-Commerce
- Internet Tax Freedom Act
- Novell Inc.
- Facebook
- Shipping and Shipment Tracking

- Web Site, Design and Set-up of
- Yahoo! Inc.
- YouTube

Essays offer a unique starting point for individuals seeking comprehensive information that can not be adequately conveyed through brief dictionary-like definitions. Put into context, the topics covered in these volumes are of both current and enduring interest. The history and changes of e-commerce has been noted in the updated original essays, and more than 50 new essays address things that did not exist ten years ago when the first edition was published.

ADDITIONAL FEATURES

- Contents are arranged alphabetically from A to Z across two volumes
- One enhanced multi-tiered Master Index simplifies accessibility
- Cross-references to help readers locate information
- Chronology and Timeline of the events critical in shaping the industry
- Further Reading section at the end of each essay provides source suggestions for further study, including URLs

Composed by business writers, under the guidance of an expert advisor, *Gale Encyclopedia of E-Commerce* represents a substantial contribution to general business reference. Students, scholars, and business practitioners alike will find a wealth of information in these new volumes.

Foreward

BIRTH OF THE INTERNET

During the cold war, the threat of nuclear attacks was ubiquitous. It was feared that such an attack on the area of Washington D.C. would bring the whole telecommunication network down. Moreover, the telephone network links and switching nodes were unreliable even without the nuclear attacks threat. There was a great need for a fail-proof network that would make traffic or communication rerouting possible. Even if one point failed, the traffic should switch routes, and the network should survive, regardless of the cause of failure. The United States Defense Advanced Research Projects Agency created in 1969 the first operational packet-switching network: ARPANet (Advanced Research Projects Agency Network), with the purpose of sharing information between the government and research institutions. First it consisted of four locations, soon to grow to 213 computer hosts in 1981. There were still several transmission protocols used until a new standardized internet protocol (TCP/IP) came to life in 1982. Access to the network expanded, and by the late 1980s and early 1990s, commercial Internet Service Providers (ISPs) began to appear. Among the first uses of this network came exchanging messages, such as e-mails and instant messages. Other services soon followed, including the World Wide Web, Voice over IP (VoIP), and two-way video conferencing.

EARLY DAYS OF THE INTERNET

Originally the data communicated between different locations was in the form of text. Many services started to emerge in addition to the transmission of text. In 1989, Tim Berners-Lee proposed a new protocol, HyperText Transfer Protocol (or HTTP), where Hyperlinks linked objects together, eliminating the need to enter text commands. A year later, he constructed the remaining tools he needed, such as the first web browser, web server, and even the first webpage. On August 6, 1991, a short description of Berners-Lee‘s project became the first publically available Web page. The World Wide Web was born. Navigating through pages and documents became easy, as it sufficed to click on a highlighted text (the hyperlink) to take you to another text. However, it was the development of Mosaic, the first web browser, that gave the World Wide Web the greatest boost. It became possible to link to objects other than text. If a hyperlink can lead to another text, why not lead to a picture, an audio or video file? Navigating the Web became simple and easy enough for the average user, not requiring specialized skills or knowledge.

EARLY DAYS OF E-COMMERCE

Until the mid-1990s, the use of the internet was restricted to researchers, academics, and of course the government, who provided most of the funding for the internet backbone until 1994. Businesses who wished to communicate with each other had to establish their own private networks. The early networks in the 1970s were used in financial transactions (Electronic Funds Transfer or EFT). Businesses then expanded the usage of their networks to allow for Electronic Data Interchange (EDI). Interconnected companies had the possibility of exchanging information and messages almost instantaneously. They could also conduct and complete transactions online, decreasing the time required to complete such transactions tremendously. An example is the first airline ticket reservation systems known as SABRE, developed by American Airlines. However, the advantages provided by these private networks were limited to large companies, such as banks and certain government agencies, which could afford establishing such networks.

It was not until 1994 when small to medium businesses were presented with a similar opportunity. The U.S. government removed commercial restrictions on the usage of the Internet, allowing such companies to take advantage of the existing Internet backbone. Small and medium sized companies saw the opportunity coming, and understood well that to take full advantage of the Internet would require the expensive steps of investing in technology and training their personnel. However, they found that even the minimum advantages they could gain from the Internet, such as e-mail services, could greatly enhance and improve their daily operations. Take e-mail services, for instance: firms can communicate with each other as well as with their customers in a much more convenient and efficient way. E-mails are fast and not affected by difference in time zones, making it possible to easily communicate with other users across the globe. These opportunities presented by the Internet appealed to both businesses as well as individual customers.

Although computers were available in almost all businesses for decades, the same could not be said about household users, who had little or. no experience in communicating electronically. After the commercial restrictions imposed on internet use by the U.S. government were lifted, and with the increase of ISPs and the affordability of personal computers, more household users gained access to the internet.

E-COMMERCE TAKES OFF

Until then, the only e-commerce transactions household users had encountered were mostly of the financial type, such as paying with a credit card or withdrawing money from an ATM. New doors were opening, and new services were emerging. Exchanging information with other individuals and businesses became possible. People learned about new web sites and services via advertisement as well as word of mouth. They began to access the internet looking for new information and services, and more importantly, they were able to do that according to their own schedules. To look for a book, users didn‘t need to wait until the local bookstore was open anymore; instead, they could simply visit its Web site, or even any bookstore‘s Web site anywhere in the world. Temporal and geographical limitations were practically eliminated. Businesses started to launch their Web sites, providing the customer with an easy and practical access to information about their products. Certain Web sites permitted the customer to complete transactions online. Additional services were surfacing, changing e-commerce from simply buying and selling products over the internet to e-Business. From just brochure-ware and order processing to pure online enterprises, passing by customer relation management, e-commerce was changing the way businesses operated.

As a consequence of e-commerce, prices of products and services became more transparent. Users know the market price of the desired product, and can decide whether to buy/sell or not based on this knowledge. The concept of bundling, or selling a basket of products or services instead of single items, became prevalent, with an enormous effect on competition. This is especially true for digital products where the cost of reproduction is minimal. Cable providers offer bundles that include voice, video, and internet together at prices much cheaper than individual products. Bundling also applies to software companies, where they offer suites of applications at slightly higher prices than a single product. It is noteworthy that these additional products/services have a negligible cost to the provider.

SECURITY CONCERNS

Due to the nature of information transmitted in online transactions, in addition to the open-nature of the Internet, several security issues emerged. When conducting a transaction with virtual stores as opposed to physical stores, you cannot verify the identity of the entity with whom you are dealing. How can we overcome such a hurdle? How can we make safe transactions in an untrusted environment? Online product purchases involve the exchange of financial information, such as account numbers and credit card information. Other personal services require the disclosure of personal information, such as home address and social security number. In the early days of e-commerce, when the number of players with access to the private networks was limited, it was easy to address the security concerns. But as the number of Internet users exploded, security concerns also increased. The business environment could not be trusted anymore. Even if the party from whom a customer is purchasing a product is trustworthy, the communication between the user and that company may still be unsecure.

Many electronic marketplaces act as intermediaries, connecting buyers and sellers. We might know and trust an electronic marketplace such as Amazon, but can we say the same about the seller it is connecting us to? Our information has to be forwarded to that seller as well. It is very important to have some techniques to ensure that only authorized people have access to our data. Many Web sites provide multiple levels of authentication to verify the users' credentials, such as the use of a security question on top of passwords. Moreover, most Web sites now use encrypted communication (which takes place in the background without the need of users' intervention) when transferring sensitive information. The security issues become more severe with certain products, especially the ones of a digital nature, such as music, software, and video. Intellectual property in these cases is the main product of value. The problem is that many products now fall under this category, from video streaming, to downloadable music and electronic books; consequently it is of great importance to provide the necessary means for protection against possible security attacks.

The concerns discussed so far take place when the company hosts its own servers. What about outsourcing, or contracting other entities to provide certain business functions for us? Many companies now outsource their payroll services, where the employees' information, sensitive as it is, is stored on the service providers' servers. It is necessary to ensure that such information is securely stored and maintained. Similar concerns are raised with cloud computing, when users (both individuals and businesses) take advantage of the resources provided by certain service providers. Are the systems used by the service providers secure? Can they withstand malicious attacks? In addition to that, is the service provider trusted not to use the data for unintended purposes? Ensuring the security of information in such a scenario is clearly more complicated.

PRIVACY CONCERNS

Whenever we visit a Web site, whether to look for information or to buy something, servers keep track of our visit, from the moment we enter that web site until the instance we exit it. This information is usually collected and analyzed in order to improve the quality of service provided. Consider the Web sites that provide recommendations of products and services. How can they manage to provide customers with relatively accurate recommendations? Simple: based on the information they collect about those customers as well as others, they create a profile for each user, and try to provide personalized experience.

Advertisement is not one size fits all anymore. The ads that a Web site shows an engineer may be different from those seen by a student. When seeking to rent a movie, such recommendation systems can suggest movies that are likely to appeal to the user. While the benefits from analyzing this data are obvious, privacy advocates raise an alarm. It is true that creating a profile to provide better services has its benefits, but what stops a malicious user from taking advantage of this information to do me some harm? Online services are spreading, leading to more users' information to be available online. Social networks, while providing means of communicating with friends and family, can cause privacy breaches when personal information falls into the hands of unintended parties. People may lose their jobs because of pictures they posted on their personal pages on social networks. It is up to the user to decide on the level of tradeoff between the benefits of personalization and the privacy requirements.

WHERE E-COMMERCE IS HEADED

Whether we are household users trying to make a purchase or a company looking to expand our business, we are involved in e-commerce, even if we don't realize that. In today's mobile and fast-moving world, e-commerce is a predominant reality. Every time someone buys an app for a mobile phone, an electronic transaction is conducted. Mobile users can (and do) use their devices to purchase products and make payments. Mobile services are flourishing, taking advantage of the ever-increasing sophistication of mobile devices to provide location-based and personalized services.

Firms have changed the way they conduct business due to the evolution of e-commerce and the development of new tools. E-commerce has also changed the customers' behavior, with all the information provided by the Internet and the possibilities of communicating with others, removing any geo-temporal restrictions. Even ISPs roles are changing: while the internet was previously government regulated, ISPs are now indulging in controlling and monitoring internet traffic, with the intent of improving the services they provide. E-commerce and the internet have become integrated in our daily transactions.

It only makes sense that people attempt to better understand the effects e-commerce has on their daily lives. Companies should also be interested in understanding the evolution of their business: where it was, how it changed due to the internet and e-commerce, and where it is going. In both scenarios, there is a need for a good and reliable source of information capable of answering questions such as: where did e-commerce come from? How it is affecting lives now? And where it is headed *Gale Encyclopedia of E-Commerce* describes various concepts and technologies that made e-commerce a reality and presents new e-commerce ideas and tools that are expected to further influence individuals as well as companies. The encyclopedia provides readers of different interests with the means to satisfy their curiosity and gain a better understanding of how to integrate of e-commerce in to their lives.

Hussein Issa
Ph.D. Candidate
Accounting Information Systems
Rutgers Business School, Rutgers University

Miklos A. Vasarhelyi
KPMG Professor of AIS
Director RARC, CarLab
Rutgers Business School, Rutgers University

Preface and User's Guide

PREFACE

Welcome to the second edition of the *Gale Encyclopedia of E-Commerce (GEEC).* Published in recognition of today's rapidly evolving business landscape, these volumes offer readers solid explanations of relevant concepts, issues, and terms, as well as profiles of pioneering companies, organizations, and individuals seen at the forefront of the e-commerce revolution. Readers new to the world of electronic business will find a wealth of basic information designed to answer their immediate questions and light their research path. Those already versed in the specifics of the New Economy will find essays constructed with useful background that lends richer context to their daily e-business interactions.

GEEC includes coverage of topics both far-ranging and finely focused. Into the former category might fall an overview of online business models, a general discussion of advertising in cyberspace, or a broad view of global internet security concerns. Within the latter category, readers can expect to find guidance on the ins and outs of designing a "storefront" or relaunching a Web site, the definitions of terms like disintermediation and Weblining, or Timothy Berners-Lee's take on the state of his brainchild, the World Wide Web. Among the people covered in *GEEC* are true pioneers (think Bill Gates, Steve Jobs, Gordon Moore, Robert Noyce, and Dr. Nicholas Negroponte) and, of course, many of the youthful visionaries who have made their way into the spotlight over the last few years, such as Mark Zuckerberg.

GEEC's coverage of firms that have in some way significantly impacted, or been crucially impacted by, the online revolution is not intended to be all-encompassing, but rather, our intention is to provide in these pages a strong sampling of companies that, as a whole, help to tell the stories, sometimes in colorful and dramatic ways, of the internet's influence on business practice and business culture. Mega-mergers, flash-in-the-pans, established bricks-and-mortars, and heroic survivors are all represented here. During the Gold Rush days of the 1800s, you didn't necessarily have to be a gold miner to benefit from the shiny substance unearthed from the ground. And so it is today; you don't have to be a computer manufacturer in order to reap the rewards, and to suffer the risks, of taking part in the internet economy. You just have to log-on, and go where you want the Web to take you. We invite you to open these volumes, and step into the dynamic and compelling world of e-commerce.

USER'S GUIDE

GEEC has been designed for ease of use. Comprised of two volumes, the essays are arranged alphabetically from A to Z by topic title throughout the set, and all essay titles are listed in full for easy perusal within the Table of Contents.

Included at the end of most essays are two special features: Further Reading sections, designed to reference quoted source material and to point readers toward suggested sources for further study, and See Also references, which refer the reader to essays of closely related interest elsewhere within *GEEC.*

At the back of the second volume is a list of suggested Books for Additional Reading, and the Master Index, a tiered, cumulative listing of thousands of citations with their corresponding volume and page numbers. The Master Index contains, specifically, alphabetical references to the following as mentioned within *GEEC* essays: important or unusual terms; names of companies, institutions, organizations, and associations; specific legislation; relevant court cases; key events; and names of prominent or historically important individuals.

ACKNOWLEDGMENTS

The editors gratefully acknowledge the counsel and helpful suggestions of our advisors.

John Surdyk
Faculty Associate: Management & Human Resources, Weinert Center for Entrepreneurship, Wisconsin School of Business

David P. Bianco, M.B.A., M.A.
Business author, editor, and consultant specializing in advertising, marketing, and public relations.

Marilyn M. Helms, D.B.A., CFPIM, CIRM,
Professor and Sesquicentennial Endowed Chair Division of Business and Technology Dalton State College

Thank you to foreword writer Hussein Issa, and his advisor Miklos A. Vasarhelyi of Rutgers University.

COMMENTS AND SUGGESTIONS

Comments and suggestions regarding the *Gale Encyclopedia of E-Commerce* are invited and encouraged. Please contact:

Managing Editor, Business, Research, Publications
27500 Drake Rd., Farmington Hills, MI, 48331-3535
Telephone: 1-800-877-4253
www.cengage.com

Chronology and Timeline

1904: The Fleming valve, the first vacuum tube, is patented by Sir John A. Fleming.

1905: Albert Einstein publishes the theory of relativity.

1915: The first transcontinental call, between San Francisco and NewYork, is placed by researchers working at AT&T.

1920: Czech author Karel Capek coins the word, robot.

1924: The Computing-Tabulating-Recording Company is renamed International Business Machines (IBM).

1934: Federal legislation is passed in the form of the Communications Act in an attempt to begin regulation of the telephone industry.

1939: The first digital computer prototype is created at Iowa State College by Clifford Berry and John Atanasoff. Hewlett-Packard is founded.

1941: Regular television broadcasting begins.

1947: Walter Brattain, John Bardeen, and William Shockley invent the first point-contact transistor at Bell Labs.

1948: Bell Labs unveils the transistor to the U.S. military and to the public at large.

1951: The UNIVAC 1, considered the first commercial computer, is sold to the U.S. Census Bureau by the Eckert and Mauchly Computer Co.

1956: Shockley, Bardeen, and Brattain win the Nobel Prize for their work on the transistor. IBM researchers unveil the first hard-disk drive.

1958: The U.S. Dept. of Defense creates the Advanced Research Projects Agency (ARPA). The first integrated circuit or "silicon chip" is invented.

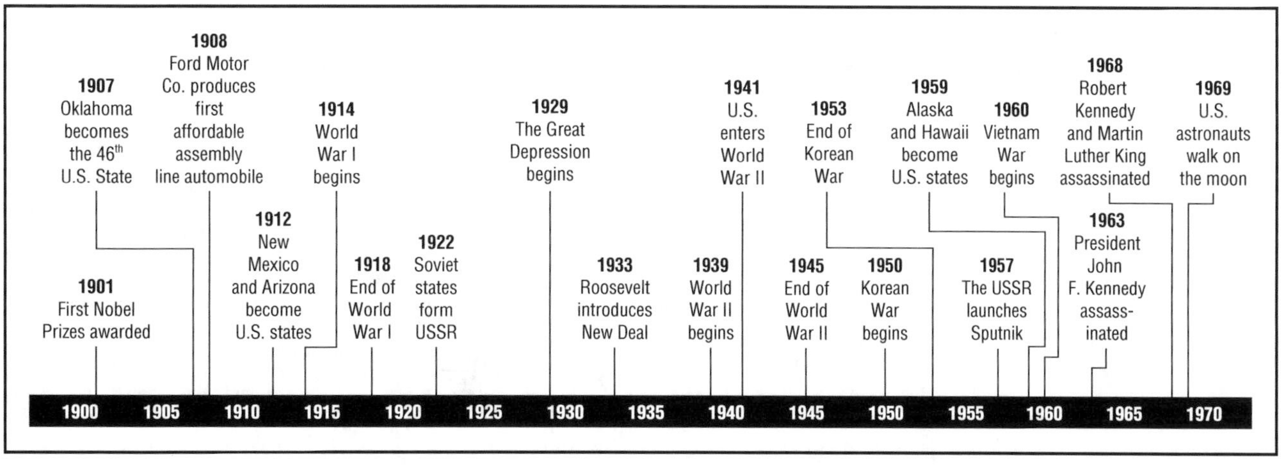

1962: Dr. J.C.R. Licklider defines the concept of global networking in a pioneering thesis at MIT, "On-Line Man Computer Communications."

1965: Moore's Law is espoused for the first time by Gordon Moore.

1968: Robert Noyce and Gordon Moore form the Intel Corp.

1969: ARPAnet is created.

1970: Glass fiber, precursor to the development of fiber optics, is created at Corning Glass.

1971: Intel creates the first microprocessor.

1972: The concept of electronic mail is introduced, as is the concept of open-architecture networking.

1974: Barcoded products appear in U.S. stores and cashiers begin using scanners.

1975: Bill Gates and Paul Allen form a partnership, naming their new business Microsoft.

1976: Steve Jobs and Steve Wozniak found Apple Computer Co. Cray Research, Inc. unveils the Cray-1, a supercomputer with revolutionary speed capabilities.

1981: IBM introduces its personal computer.

1982: The TCP/IP protocol is developed.

1983: Microsoft Word is unveiled, as is the Windows operating system. Time magazine chooses the PC as its 1982 "Man of the Year."

1984: Apple Computer Co. introduces the Macintosh.

1985: The National Science Foundation establishes NSFNET, an enhanced version of ARPAnet.

1986: Microsoft Corp. conducts its IPO.

1989: BITNET is born.

1990: Microsoft Corp. revenues exceed $1 billion. ARPAnet is decommissioned and shut down.

1991: The World Wide Web comes into existence as the National Science Foundation's decree that prevents commercial use of the Internet dissolves.

1993: Graphics-based Web browser Mosaic is released. The U.S. Justice Dept. begins its antitrust investigation into Microsoft Corp.

1994: The World Wide Web Consortium (W3C) is established.

1995: Amazon.com goes online for the first time. The National Science Foundation's financial support of the Internet is terminated.

2000: Technology stocks plummet in value as the dot-com shakeout takes hold. Internet startups are hit hard and many fold or merge.

2001: Time Warner and America Online (AOL) finalize their mega-merger.

2002: eBay acquires Paypal.

2003: Congress passes the Can-Spam act. iTunes is launched by Apple.

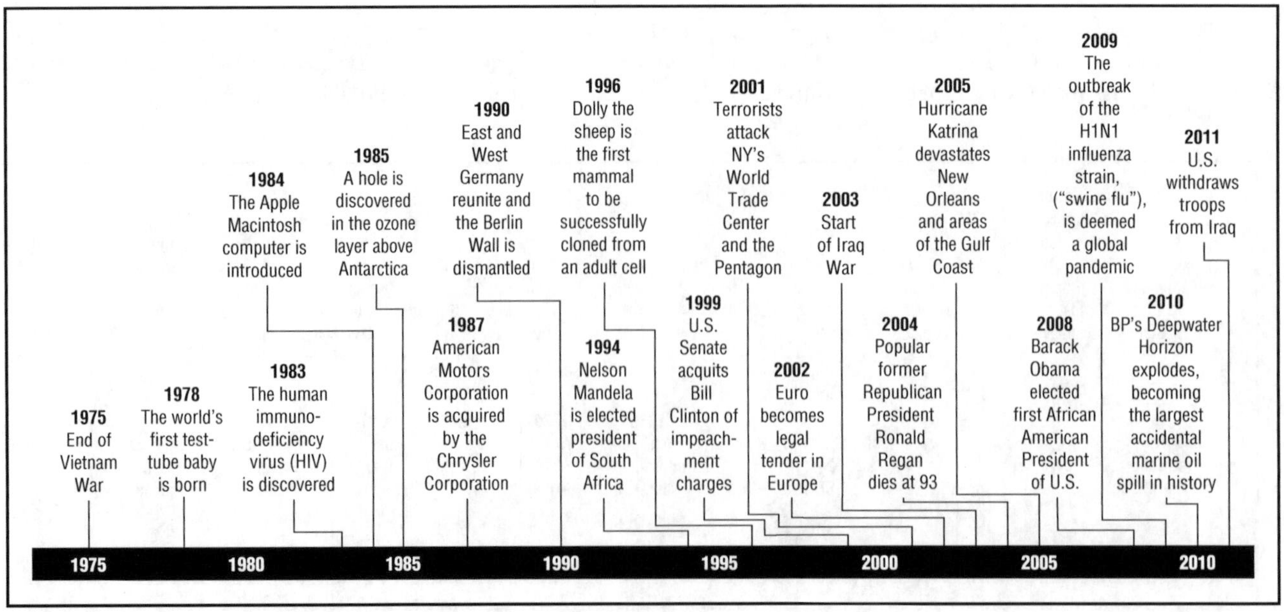

2004: The first platform for online B2B transactions in China is established (DHgate.com); Facebook, the massive social networking site founded at Harvard by Mark Zuckerberg, is launched.

2005: YouTube is launched. Web 2.0 makes web sites more interactive.

2006: Google starts its Google Checkouts service. Saddam Hussein is convicted of crimes against humanity, and is hung in Baghdad.

2007: The first iPhone is released by Apple. Broadband users in the U.S. reaches 200 million. California Democrat Nancy Pelosi becomes the first female Speaker of the House of Representatives.

2008: Groupon was launched in November 2008. Amazon launches TextBuyIt. Recession hits the U.S. and world.

2009: Yahoo and Bing team up against Google.

2010: Ebooks outsell physical books on Amazon.

2011: Steve Jobs dies at the age of 56. Skype is acquired by Microsoft. The world hits the milestone population of seven billion inhabitants.

A

24/7 REAL MEDIA INC.

24/7 Real Media Inc. is an advertising agency specializing in the Internet and interactive media. Headquartered in New York City, the company operates globally with 18 offices in 12 countries. Evolving since its founding in 1995, in the 2010s the company focuses on Internet advertising, offering its own network of Web sites to advertisers, as well as proprietary technologies that help publishers and clients track their advertising to gauge its effectiveness. The company is a subsidiary of international media conglomerate WPP.

As of 2012, the 24/7 Real Media network, called the Global Web Alliance, is composed of thousands of Web sites around the world, representing hundreds of millions of unique users each month. Through the combination of the Global Web Alliance and the 24/7 Real Media technology offerings, advertisers can target specific consumer groups and utilize a wide variety of Internet ads from the traditional banner page ads to videos. Clients also receive reports letting them see how effective their advertising is.

BEGAN OPERATIONS IN 1998

24/7 Media was formed in New York City by a merger of three companies involved in online advertising: Petry Interactive, Interactive Imaginations, and Katz Millennium Marketing. The formation of 24/7 Media was announced in December 1997, and the merger was completed in April 1998. David Moore, who was CEO of Petry Interactive, became 24/7 Media's CEO in February 1998. In its first year 24/7 Media raised $45.5 million through an initial public offering (IPO) in August 1998, with shares offered at $14 each. The company planned to grow through acquisitions and to challenge online advertising industry leader DoubleClick.

At its inception, 24/7 Media represented about 200 medium and large Web sites with a staff of 30 sales representatives. By the end of 1998 the company was operating three ad networks and representing thousands of mostly small and midsize Web sites as well as 100 to 200 major Web sites. During the year it acquired the CliqNow network of 75 financial, college, and travel-related sites from K2 Design for $4 million in cash and stock. In another acquisition, 24/7 Media purchased Intelligent Interactions, which developed an ad-serving product called Adfinity, for $7.7 million in stock.

Not all of 24/7 Media's efforts met with success. After the dot-com crash of the early 2000s, the company refocused its efforts on e-mail marketing, channeling a great deal of resources to this business segment. For example, in 2000 the company acquired Exactis.com Inc., a Denver-based e-mail marketing and communications firm, for $490 million in stock. Exactis reportedly sent out more than 10 million e-mail marketing messages a day and had highly scalable, precise e-mail delivery and advanced data mining systems. Following the acquisition 24/7 Mail had 23 million permission-based e-mail addresses under management.

In November 2000, 24/7 Media laid off about 200 workers, followed by another 100 layoffs in January 2001, which brought the company's workforce down to about 900. While it continued to maintain offices in Europe, Asia, and Latin America, 24/7 Media UK dropped about 25% of its client base to focus on top brands. The action marked a rethinking of the firm's strategy to gain the greatest reach in favor of representing only the strongest Web publishers. Also in 2001, the firm merged with Real Media Inc. and changed its name to 24/7 Real Media.

During the twenty-first century, 24/7 Real Media refocused on its core business in digital advertising and folded the e-mail marketing into its other capabilities.

24/7 GROWS THROUGH ACQUISITIONS

Beginning around 2003, 24/7 Real Media began a series of acquisitions that strengthened its position as a leader in Web advertising and service. The first acquisition in the series was the purchase of Insight First, a leading Web analytics firm, in January 2003. Insight First's technology was complementary to 24/7 Real Media's, and the company gained high-profile clients from the acquisition such as MTV, VH1, and Nickelodeon. In 2004 the company became one of the larger search engine marketing (SEM) companies worldwide with its acquisition of Decide Interactive. Decide Interactive's technology gave 24/7 Real Media new capabilities and advantages, such as paid search bid management tools, paid inclusion technology, and a stronger presence in the Asia-Pacific region. The technology, Decide DNA, allowed 24/7 Real Media's clients to manage thousands of keyword campaigns across search engines.

A joint venture between 24/7 Real Media and Dentsu of Japan further solidified the company's presence in the Japanese market. The partnership, which was signed in 2005, allowed Dentsu to sell 24/7 Real Media's SEM services to the Japanese market.

WPP BECOMES PARENT COMPANY OF 24/7 REAL MEDIA

By 2006 24/7 Real Media's partnership with Dentsu was so successful that the companies broadened it to include other Asian nations. 24/7 Real Media's success caught the eye of advertising giant WPP, an advertising company based in London, England. In 2007 WPP bought all shares of 24/7 Real Media's stock in a deal worth an estimated $649 million. The acquisition brought several advantages to both sides, with the most notable being the ability of WPP to bring many more clients to 24/7 Real Media, and 24/7 Real Media's ability to boost WPP's presence in digital marketing. 24/7 Real Media was folded into WPP's Digital Marketing group.

SEE ALSO *Advertising; Online.*

BIBLIOGRAPHY

24/7 Real Media Inc. "Company Overview." New York, 2011. Available from http://www.247realmedia.com/EN-US/us/company-overview.html.

Beale, Matthew. "24/7 Expands European Operations." *E-Commerce Times,* August 13, 1999. Available from http://www.ecommercetimes.com/story/993.html.

Brookman, Faye, et al. "The Biggest Players." *Crain's New York Business,* November 30, 1998.

Clark, Philip B. "Working 24/7 Entails Global Reach." *B to B,* July 3, 2000.

"Crunch Leaves Alley Firms Few Choices." *Crain's New York Business,* February 26, 2001.

Fineberg, Seth. "Dot-Com Sea Change Forces Ad Networks to Rethink Strategies." *Advertising Age,* September 25, 2000.

Frook, John Evan. "U.S. Firms Dominate Worldwide Ad Networks." *B to B,* November 20, 2000.

Maddox, Kate. "Ad Networks Adjust to Slowdown." *B to B,* April 2, 2001.

Virzi, Anna Maria. "24/7 Media Adds Services with Purchase of E-mail Marketing Firm." *Internet World,* March 15, 1999.

WPP. "About Us." London, UK, 2011. Available from http://www.wpp.com/wpp/about.

4G WIRELESS NETWORK

A 4G wireless network is the fourth generation of wireless technology developed for mobile high-speed broadband connectivity. Whereas the transition from 2G to 3G technology involved a shift from analog to digital transmissions, the move from 3G to 4G has been more subtle. While not as groundbreaking, 4G technology does promise higher quality and faster speeds of data transfer. A 4G wireless network gives consumers wireless broadband connectivity that facilitates improved video streaming and sound quality, IP-based voice systems, and gaming services for mobile devices at speeds that potentially meet or exceed those of wired transmissions.

Enhanced Internet data rates have generated new trends not only for the telecommunications market but also for mobile e-commerce in general. Smartphones equipped with 4G have particularly increased mobile e-commerce, as faster data streaming means that more consumers can use their phones for browsing and purchasing. Some apps for 4G-equipped mobile devices allow users to download coupons instantly for on-the-spot purchases, while others feature customer loyalty rewards. With 4G technology, consumers have more options than ever before for e-commerce transactions.

The International Telecommunication Union (ITU) coordinates the efforts of government, industry, and private sectors in the development of a 4G advanced global broadband international mobile telecommunications system, or IMT-Advanced. The standards platform supplied by IMT-Advanced allows for faster data access, unified messaging, enhanced roaming capabilities, and broadband multimedia. In December 2010, ITU's Radiocommunication Sector announced that it had completed an assessment of six systems for IMT-Advanced designation. The global 4G mobile wireless broadband technologies selected were LTE-Advanced and WiMAX-2.

WIMAX

The first type of 4G technology to appear on the market was WiMAX, short for "Worldwide Interoperability for Microwave Access." WiMAX is a broadband telecommunications technology based on the Institute of Electrical and Electronics Engineers (IEEE) standard 802.16. Considered a last-mile technology, WiMAX provides wireless broadband access in areas where DSL and cable are not available or are too expensive. WiMAX also offers an alternative to costly satellite Internet services for rural areas. Though theoretical maximum data transfer rates reach 75Mbps, actual transmission typically maxes out at around 45Mbps.

WiMAX provides both fixed and mobile non-line-of-sight service from a base station—mounted on a tower or tall building—to a subscriber device. While Wi-Fi coverage is measured in feet, WiMAX is measured in miles. Boasting connections four to ten times faster than 3G wireless, 4G WiMAX has the potential to replace Wi-Fi hotspots by offering coverage over metropolitan-sized areas. Another advantage over Wi-Fi is a reduction in interference caused by other devices, both wired and wireless. This benefit is a result of WiMAX's incorporation of advanced technologies new to cellular applications: Orthogonal Frequency Division Multiplexing (OFDM) and Multiple Input/Multiple Output (MIMO) smart antenna technology. By breaking down a signal into independent pieces, OFDM increases a signal's channel capacity. MIMO uses multiple antennas at both ends of a wireless connection to improve high-data bandwidth performance.

The WiMAX Forum—which would expand to include hundreds of technology companies, certification and testing laboratories, and software developers from all over the world—was established in 2001 for the purpose of marketing and promoting the 802.16 standard as a faster alternative to cable modems and DSL lines. Technology giant Intel Corporation was an early proponent of WiMAX, producing a WiMAX development card with an Intel chip that shipped to customers in 2004. This was two years before the WiMAX Forum officially revealed the first products to pass certification and interoperability testing for the fixed wireless broadband standard.

After several years of development, WiMAX finally debuted on the commercial front in 2008 through Sprint Nextel. Initially the service was used mostly by laptop wireless cards. Two years later, Sprint introduced its HTC EVO 4G cellular phone, the world's first 4G phone. Wireless high-speed Internet service provider Clearwire, the largest company to offer commercial WiMAX services in the United States, introduced WiMAX's next generation of wireless service, known as WiMAX-2 or Wireless-MAN-Advanced, in 2010. Although WiMAX was set to dominate the wireless network market, the technology soon faced a formidable competitor on the 4G wireless front: LTE.

LTE

In 2004 the Third Generation Partnership Project (3GPP) began developing Long Term Evolution (LTE) technology, a GSM-based wireless data standard with significantly faster download speeds of 100Mbps and upload speeds of 50Mbps. (GSM stands for Global System for Mobile Communications and is the primary method of cellular communications.) Referred to as the next generation in 4G cellular services, LTE bandwidth is scalable from 1.25 MHz to 10MHz. Like WiMAX, LTE incorporates Orthogonal Frequency Division Multiplexing and Multiple Input/Multiple Output technologies to counteract interference.

In 2007 Verizon and AT&T, the two largest mobile phone carriers in the United States, committed to introducing LTE networks on a national level. Verizon introduced its LTE service in 38 markets in December 2010, becoming the first major U.S. wireless carrier to offer commercial LTE services. In August 2011, AT&T began selling its first three LTE devices: the HTC Jetstream LTE tablet, the USB Connect Momentum 4G modem, and the Mobile Hotspot Elevate 4G. LTE technology developed in the early 2010s includes voice over LTE (VoLTE), which allows people to make calls and use smartphone applications at the same time.

Verizon expects to have its entire 3G network covered by 4G LTE by the end of 2013. Many experts predict that LTE will dominate the 4G mobile market by 2014, with more than 300 million subscribers as compared to WiMAX's 33 million. As LTE is expected to facilitate the creation of the first global mobile phone standard, manufacturers around the world are investing in the infrastructure required to support the technology. In 2011, China Mobile, China's largest mobile company, partnered with Verizon and Vodaphone, a London-based telecommunications operator, to study the efficacy of LTE as a single global standard. Deploying over 600 base stations in six cities around the world, the trial provides coverage for some 100 million subscribers. The industry anticipates that LTE-Advanced, a further evolution of LTE, will be commercially available in 2012.

Despite the buzz over LTE, the technology does have drawbacks. Although early subscribers will enjoy high-speed mobile broadband at first, data speeds will drop off as more users subscribe to LTE service. Experts warn that LTE will not live up to its potential until the Federal Communications Commission frees up more Advanced Wireless Services (AWS) spectrum. In addition, LTE-capable devices are still in developmental phases. Since LTE chips are large in comparison with other wireless hardware, some manufacturers in the 2010s have chosen to wait for smaller-scale chips so that their phones will look more like 3G models. Battery life is another concern because 4G connectivity and high-bandwidth data quickly drain power from standard batteries. As with LTE chips, batteries for LTE-enabled devices are bigger than traditional power sources, contributing to mobile equipment that is bulkier than that to which consumers have become accustomed.

SEE ALSO *Mobile Commerce: Smartphone; Wireless Fidelity Network.*

BIBLIOGRAPHY

Hansen, Kristena. "4G Wireless Technology: A Look at What's Ahead." *Los Angeles Times,* June 13, 2010. Available from http://articles.latimes.com/2010/jun/13/business/la-fi-4g-20100614.

International Telecommunication Union. "ITU Gobal Standard for International Mobile Telecommunications 'IMT-Advanced.'" Geneva, Switzerland, 2011. Available from http://www.itu.int/ITU-R/index.asp?category=information&rlink=imt-advanced&lang=en.

Mumford, Richard. "ITU Selects Next-Generation 4G Mobile Technologies." *Microwave Journal,* December 2010. Available from http://www.mwjournal.com/Journal/ITU_Selects_Next_generation_Mobile_Technologies/AR_10010.

Nolle, Tom. "Building the 4G Wireless Network: Exploring LTE Architecture and Services Drivers." *TechTarget,* September 2010. Available from http://searchtelecom.techtarget.com/feature/Building-the-4G-wireless-network-Exploring-LTE-architecture-and-services-drivers.

Reed, Brad. "4G Satellite Company Takes Aim at Cell Carriers; with Newly Acquired SkyTerra Network, Harbinger Capital Invests in 4G." *Network World,* March 30, 2010. Available from http://www.networkworld.com/news/2010/033010-skyterra-4g-satellite.html.

———. "LTE in 2011: Curb Your Enthusiasm." *Network World,* January 24, 2011. Available from http://www.networkworld.com/news/2011/012411-lte-verizon-att.html.

"What Is WiMAX?" WiMAX.com, September 22, 2011. Available from http://www.wimax.com/general/what-is-wimax.

Wilson, Richard. "MWC 2011: Will LTE Topple Wimax for the 4G Crown?" *Electronics Weekly,* February 8, 2011. Available from http://www.electronicsweekly.com/Articles/08/02/2011/50447/mwc-2011-will-lte-topple-wimax-for-4g-crown.htm.

ADAMS, RICHARD L.

Richard L. Adams, Jr., is the founder of UUNET Technologies, the first commercial Internet service provider (ISP). Among other things, Adams's accomplishments at the helm of UUNET include the invention of Serial Line Internet Protocol (SLIP), technology that allows personal computers to connect to the Internet via modems.

With a master's degree in computer science from Purdue University, Adams launched his career as a programmer for San Diego, California-based Science Application International Corp. He left in 1982 to accept a position as a data-gathering specialist with the Center for Seismic Studies, an outfit hired by the U.S. Department of Defense to develop technology for nuclear testing violation detection. It was there that Adams first encountered ARPAnet, precursor to the Internet. After hearing several individuals express their interest in using ARPAnet despite its high cost, Adams began toying with the idea of creating a nonprofit enterprise to offer moderately priced access to the fledgling network. He presented his plan to the Usenix Association, a Unix software users group to which he belonged, and secured $250,000 in funding.

In 1987, Adams formally established UUNET. Although the ISP initially offered services only to research institutes and universities, it was not long before Adams began expanding operations. The launch of AlterNet in 1990 marked UUNET's first foray into commercial service, as well as its conversion to a for-profit company. The firm's new focus on the corporate sector paid off a few years later when it landed the contract to carry Internet traffic for the Microsoft Network, beating out competitors like AT&T Corp. and MCI Communications Corp. As part of the deal Microsoft lent the company nearly $40 million to pay for the construction of additional networks.

Adams took UUNET public in 1995, in one of the largest technology public offerings to that date, and a year later agreed to a $2 billion buyout offer from MFS Communications, which was acquired by WorldCom shortly thereafter for $14 billion, one of the largest mergers in the corporate history of the United States at the time. Although he remained chairman and chief technology officer for a while, Adams eventually resigned and pursued other ventures.

After Adams departed from UUNET, John W. Sidgmore became chief executive officer of the company. Sidgmore had come on board in 1994 when Adams was looking for a seasoned executive to help him grow the firm.

In 2001, the name UUNET was dropped as the company became fully integrated into WorldCom. However, the name was briefly used in the mid-2000s as a brand name for wholesale ISP business of WorldCom. WorldCom changed its name to MCI in 2005, and MCI was acquired by Verizon in 2006. UUNET is part of Verizon Business and remained the backbone of that service in 140 countries. Verizon Business has over 130 data centers and 3,000 points of presence (areas with local phone line access) throughout the world.

WorldCom was caught up in an accounting scandal in 2002, as a result of which CEO Bernard Ebbers was convicted of fraud and conspiracy in 2005. The company was found to have falsified financial reports, costing investors billions. Ebbers was sentenced to prison, and Sidgmore, then still CEO of UUNet, took over as the leader of the entire company in 2002. As of 2011, the president and CEO of Verizon Telecom and Business, the unit that now includes UUNET, was Francis J. Shammo.

ADAMS AFTER UUNET

In addition to his work with UUNET Adams, along with his wife Donnalyn Frey, wrote multiple editions of a book published by technology publisher O'Reilly Media titled *!%@ A Directory of Electronic Mail Addressing & Networks.* Adams is also the author of the *Standard for Interchange of USENET Messages.*

After UUNET, Adams invested in restaurants in New York and the Washington, D.C. area. Adams also dabbled in commercial real estate development, purchasing 111 acres in Fairfax County for $37.5 million in 1997 through his company Fairview Property Investments. By the 2010s, some of this land had been converted into a commercial office park called Fairview Park. In 2011, tenants of this northern Virginia office park included General Dynamics, Northrop Grumman, and Computer Sciences Corporation.

In 2009, Adams won a court battle concerning who was the rightful owner of a 1776 copy of the Declaration of Independence. Adams had purchased the document in 2001 for $475,000. The State of Maine had argued that the document was the rightful possession of the town of Wiscasset, whose town clerk had kept the document in 1776. Clerk Solomon Holbrook, who died in 1929, kept the copy of the Declaration at his house, and in 1994 it was discovered among the remains of his daughter's estate, eventually ending up in Adams's hands. After the Virginia Supreme Court settled in Adams's favor, the State of Maine noted that it would pursue the matter no further.

SEE ALSO *Connectivity, Internet; Internet; Internet Access, Tracking Growth of; Internet and World Wide Web, History of the; Internet Service Provider (ISP).*

BIBLIOGRAPHY

Felberbaum, Michael. "Court: Virginia Man Owns 1776 Copy of Declaration." *Msnbc.com,* February 29, 2009. Available from http://www.msnbc.msn.com/id/29436312/#.TmomK9TAV8E.

"Fortune Visits 25 Cool Companies."*Fortune,* July 10, 1995.

Swisher, Kara. "Anticipating the Internet: Good Timing, Good Deal-Making and Good Luck Turned Rick Adams' UUNet into a Star." *Washington Post,* May 6, 1996.

Verizon Business. "About Us." Basking Ridge, NJ, 2011. Available from http://www.verizonbusiness.com/about/.

"Web Crawlers." *Forbes,* October 9, 2000.

"Web Masters." *Forbes.com,* October 11, 1999. Available from http://www.forbes.com.

ADHOCRACY

An adhocracy is an organization that lacks structure—the complete opposite of a bureaucracy. The term was popularized by futurist Alvin Toffler in his 1970 book *Future Shock.* This form of organization is common among advertising agencies and other creativity-based companies that want to encourage employees to think outside traditional molds. Start-ups often opt for such a structure as well because of its tendency to foster a team atmosphere. Characteristics of an adhocracy-type firm include taking risks and being flexible as new projects arise.

Not surprisingly, one e-company even chose to use the term as its name. Adhocracy LLC is an Internet-based marketing communications company consisting of advertising, communications, and Web professionals who work in a tele-computing atmosphere. The firm's creative teams provide advertising, Web design, direct mail, ideation (sometimes described simply as the development of ideas), cybercommerce, and market strategy services to clients ranging from start-ups to major national and international firms. It supports clients via offices in Dayton, Ohio; Simi Valley, California; New York City; Philadelphia; and Washington, D.C.

Adhocracy got its start in the 1990s when an ad hoc group of advertising professionals began to work on freelance projects together. The group noticed a strong demand within midsize companies for marketing communication services. This demand led the firm's managing partner and creative director Brooks Richey to develop an organization that utilized the skills of top-level advertising and communications professionals to offer marketing services.

Richey began his career at advertising industry titan Ogilvy & Mather, where he worked on major accounts like Sears and American Express. He also worked at other advertising and marketing firms including Ross Roy Group, UniWorld, the Lunar Group, Demaine Vickers & Associates, and the Garfield Group before starting Adhocracy. While at the Garfield Group he was the creative director in charge of several major accounts including BEA, ChannelWave, and Actinic.

The firm also provides Web design using both HTML and flash-based Web content, including streaming audio and video programming. It develops and creates Internet advertising programs and other marketing strategies that allow for maximum exposure on the Internet. Additionally, the company's team of professionals offers ideation and other marketing services. The company describes its strategy as "360 degree marketing" because it includes aspects of marketing not normally provided by other kinds of advertising and marketing firms, such as information technology support and software development. Materials on the firm's Web site explain the strategy this way: "Without ideas and vision, a marketing firm is no more than a glorified copy and print shop."

According to the firm's organizational chart it includes groups called both "the Know," also called the Nexus of Knowledge, and "the Know How." The Know group is a network of thinkers and strategists who take input and use that to develop ideas for clients, as well as a strategy for executing those ideas. The Know How group is in charge of implementation. It consists of professionals in a range of fields including public relations, design, multimedia, speech writing, viral marketing, technology and other disciplines that can put the ideas developed by the Know group into effect. Above both these groups are the key principals, and they are supported by assistants and project coordinators who oversee the day-to-day development of marketing plans and campaigns at the firm.

While the firm began by serving midsize clients, as of 2012, clients of Adhocracy include both larger national and international firms and small start-ups, including McDonald's Corp., MDI Products, Lutron, and Johns Hopkins University. The firm has won numerous awards for its advertising and marketing campaigns, including "The Best Awards" from *Advertising Age* magazine and several Addy awards given by the American Advertising Federation, a nonprofit industry association.

Richey, who continues to helm the firm, writes a regular blog about issues and current events called "Intellectual Bubblegum." Posts cover topics ranging from political issues to pop culture and media trends. In 2011, Richey's blog addressed issues such as Congresswoman Michele Bachmann's presidential campaign, the difficulty the media has in combating 9-11 conspiracy theories, and how to be successful using social media.

SEE ALSO *Knowledge Worker; E-Commerce Consultants.*

BIBLIOGRAPHY

"Adhocracy." *Encyclopedia of the New Economy.* Waltham, MA: Terra Lycos, 2001.

Adhocracy LLC. "About Us," 2011. Available from http://www.adhocracy.com/about-us.php.

Richey, Brooks. "Intellectual Bubblegum." 2010. Available from http://www.intellectualbubblegum.com.

Tovey, Roberta. "Best Firms More Alike Than Different—Around the Globe." Marketing Science Institute, 1997.

ADOBE SYSTEMS INC.

Adobe Systems Inc. is well known for its desktop publishing software products, including Photoshop, Illustrator, and InDesign. Manipulation of images by the company's Photoshop product is so widespread that the phrase "it's been photoshopped" is understood to mean the image has been processed and altered in some way by that program. Adobe also produces Acrobat (which allows people to view .PDF files), DreamWeaver (for Web site design), and Flash (which allows rich media such as video to be played), among many other offerings. Revenues for Adobe in 2010 were $3.8 billion, and the company had more than 9,000 employees.

EARLY HISTORY: WARNOCK AND GESCHKE

Adobe Systems Inc. was founded in 1982 by John Warnock and Charles Geschke. Less than two decades later, with annual sales exceeding $1 billion, Adobe was the third-largest PC software company in the United States. The firm emerged in the mid-1980s as a major force in desktop publishing and in the late 1990s as a leader in Web authoring tools and other Internet publishing technology.

Adobe's founders met at Xerox Corp. While earning his doctoral degree in electrical engineering at the University of Utah, Warnock worked for IBM Corp., as well as a handful of other technology companies. In 1980, he accepted a graphics research position at Xerox's new graphics and imaging lab, headed up by Geschke. Together Warnock and Geschke created the PostScript computer language, which conveyed to printers how electronic characters, lines, and digital images appear on paper. Dissatisfied with Xerox's limited interest in the new product, Warnock and Geschke decided to resign and establish a new company, Adobe Systems, as a vehicle for selling PostScript. Their printer language would soon fuel the desktop publishing industry's explosive growth, as well as the surging popularity of laser printers.

Adobe's first big break came when Geschke and Warnock convinced Apple Computer Inc. (now Apple Inc.) to use PostScript with its LaserWriter printer. As part of the deal, Apple purchased a 19% stake in Adobe. The first printer using the PostScript language was made available for sale in 1985. Texas Instruments Inc. began using PostScript in its IBM-compatible PCs in 1986. That year, Adobe conducted its initial public offering (IPO).

In 1987, Adobe launched its Illustrator design software program and expanded overseas by establishing Adobe Systems Europe. Soon thereafter, the company increased its international operations by founding a sales unit in the Pacific Rim. The acquisition of BluePoint Technologies, Nonlinear Technologies, and OCR Systems in the early 1990s marked the beginning of an expansion period. Along with seeking growth through acquisition, Adobe had already started licensing its PostScript software to printer manufacturers. In 1993, the firm also unveiled Acrobat, a software program that enabled users to create and view text, graphics, and photos within documents, regardless of whether they worked on a Macintosh or PC. Acrobat's portable document format (PDF) not only allowed for the transfer of files between incompatible systems, it also greatly simplified the electronic distribution of all sorts of documents.

MAJOR ACQUISITIONS

Adobe wanted to secure a desktop publishing application for its PostScript printing language. In 1994, it approached Aldus Corp., maker of PageMaker, the leading desktop publishing program for both Macintosh and Windows operating systems. A $450 million merger completed later that year secured Adobe's position as a leading PC software manufacturer among giants like Microsoft, Novell, and Lotus. The deal also positioned Adobe as a market leader in design and illustration software, image editing, and electronic document technology—areas that would prove essential to its emergence as a leader in Web publishing.

Adobe's second major acquisition—the $31.5 million purchase of Frame Technology Corp., maker of the Unix-based FrameMaker desktop publishing program—proved ill-fated. Adobe was unfamiliar with Frame's enterprise market, and the unit began to lose money soon after the transaction was completed in 1995. Consequently, Adobe's stock price plunged more than 50% to $33 per share in July 1996, compared to a high of approximately $74 per share earlier that year.

FOCUS ON INTERNET PUBLISHING

Depending on its acquisition of Web tools manufacturer Ceneca Communications to prove fruitful, Adobe shifted focus in 1996 to Internet publishing and converted the popular PDF into a Web format. Sales neared the $1 billion mark in 1997. Recessionary economic conditions in Japan undercut earnings in 1998, spurring Adobe to lay off roughly 10% of its management staff and place more emphasis on creating new products, particularly those that would help secure the firm's position as a key player in Web authoring tools. More than $207 million—roughly one-quarter of sales—was earmarked for research and development. The firm also hunted for strategic acquisitions like GoLive Systems Inc., a maker of Web development and design tools that it purchased early in 1999. The GoLive technology allowed Adobe to later launch its award-winning LiveMotion program, a graphics and animation manipulation software package for both novice and expert Web page designers.

By 2001, Internet publishing products accounted for more than 50% of Adobe's revenues. More importantly, Adobe's presence on the Internet was prolific. In the October 2000 issue of *Forbes* Elizabeth Corcoran wrote, "Pull up the Bridgestone/Firestone Web site to learn about defective tires and it tells you to use Adobe's free Acrobat Reader to see a graphical interpretation of the hieroglyphics on your tires' sidewalls." In fact, says Corcoran, more than 90% of all Web sites make use of Adobe's Photoshop software, while nearly three-fourths of all Web pages are designed with Adobe Illustrator.

ADOBE IN THE TWENTY-FIRST CENTURY

Throughout the 2000s Adobe Systems continued to focus its product offerings on software and technologies geared toward e-publishing across a variety of technology platforms. This led to steady sales growth throughout the first decade. Although the global recession of 2008 and 2009 did impact sales of the company's primary products such as Illustrator and Creative Suite, by 2010 sales of the latest version of Creative Suite, version 5, and its other popular products exceeded company expectations. By the second quarter of 2011, revenue had topped $1 billion.

Adobe's increase in sales has not all been organic. A few key acquisitions throughout its history have enabled the company to produce innovative and timely software and products. A few examples of these acquisitions include the December 12, 2005, stock purchase of leading competitor Macromedia in a deal valued at more than $3 billion. This acquisition led to the launch of more than a dozen new software products including Adobe Flash, Adobe Connect, and Adobe DreamWeaver. Additional key acquisitions include the 2009 purchase of Business Catalyst and the January 2011 addition of Demdex, which offered audience optimization software.

According to Adobe Systems, the company will continue to focus its efforts in areas where it is getting the most results. According to Adobe's 2010 annual report, effective in first quarter of fiscal 2011 the company realigned its products under six primary lines of business, which indicate the company's continuing focus on e-publishing and e-marketing. The six lines of business were as follows: creative and interactive solutions, digital media solutions, knowledge worker, enterprise, omniture (online marketing and Web analytics products), and print and publishing.

ADOBE AND APPLE

Since the 1990s, the relationship between Adobe Systems and Apple has been of vital importance to both companies. Throughout the print and publishing industry, Apple was considered the leading provider of hardware, with its designer-friendly operating system, and Adobe Systems worked hand-in-hand with the company to provide a number of software applications for Apple's products. However, in the twenty-first century, the relationship between the two leading companies has changed. As Microsoft provided more widely accepted design, Web, and publishing programs that competed with Adobe's, Apple depended less on Adobe. According to an article published in *CNET News,* while both companies acknowledge the importance of maintaining their relationship, each also realizes that it is less critical than in the early years. Examples of the changing relationship include Adobe's dropping of its support of Mac products like FrameMaker and several new Adobe products that were launched in Windows-only versions. However, Adobe released new products for the Apple iPad in May 2011, which indicates that this long-term relationship is in no danger of ending completely.

SEE ALSO *Electronic Publishing.*

BIBLIOGRAPHY

"Adobe and Allaire Join to Simplify Development of E-business; ColdFusion Extension for GoLive Is First of Many Joint Development Efforts." *Canadian Corporate News,* August 28, 2000.

Adobe Systems Inc. "Adobe Systems 2010 Annual Report." San Jose, CA, 2011. Available from http://www.adobe.com/aboutadobe/invrelations/pdfs/FY10_10-K_FINAL_Certified.pdf.

"Adobe and WebTrends Form Alliance to Provide E-business Intelligence for Adobe Web Applications." *Canadian Corporate News,* August 29, 2000.

Becker, David. "Apple, Adobe Drifting Apart." *CNET News,* March 30, 2004. Available from http://news.cnet.com/2100-1012-5181434.html.

Boeri, Robert J., and Martin Hensel. "Ecommerce Dilemma: Controlling What You Sell." *EMedia Magazine,* September 2000.

Corcoran, Elizabeth. "Go Forth and Publish." *Forbes,* October 2, 2000.

DeLong, Bradford J. "Why the Valley Is Here to Stay." *Fortune,* May 29, 2000.

Sheldon, AnnaMarie L. "Adobe Systems and Aldus." In *Cases in Corporate Acquisitions, Buyouts, Mergers, & Takeovers.* Farmington Hills, MI: Gale Group, 1999.

Wintrob, Suzanne. "Analyst Confident Adobe Will Rebound." *Computing Canada,* February 1, 1996.

ADVANCED ENCRYPTION STANDARD (AES)

The Advanced Encryption Standard (AES) is the U.S. government-sponsored, data-coding, algorithmic system designed to protect electronic information on hardware and software from security breaches. By providing a basic framework for coding and scrambling sensitive information, AES facilitates easy electronic data sharing and protection across a wide variety of platforms as well as across borders.

The predecessor to AES, the Data Encryption Standard (DES), was adopted in 1977. By the mid-1990s, DES had begun to show its age. As new, more intensive security needs arose as a result of the proliferation of the Internet and home computers, the National Institute of Standards and Technology (NIST), an agency of the U.S. Department of Commerce, announced in 1997 its plans to develop the Advanced Encryption Standard. When DES's five-year review came up in 1998, NIST reported that the 56-bit-key encryption was no longer capable of withstanding the kinds of attacks that would now threaten electronic data in the Internet world.

In short order, over a dozen groups were working on contenders for the new encryption standard, and NIST called for cryptographers all around the world to put the contestant algorithms to vigorous tests by applying various kinds of attacks. The contestants were judged on their performance in a number of areas, including speed, versatility (the encryption has to work across a variety of platforms, such as smart cards, satellite communications, and ATM networks, in addition to online information exchange), the amount of chip and memory space they consume, flexibility, and, of course, the strength of their security. In addition, the algorithms were to work with both hardware and software applications; DES, a product of its age, was geared more specifically toward hardware.

In October 2000, after three years spent wading through the various algorithms, the Department of Commerce finally declared the Rijndael system the winner. Developed by Joan Daemen of Proton World International and Vincent Rijmen of Katholieke Univiersiteit Leuven (Catholic University of Leuven) in Belgium, Rijndael is both much stronger and more flexible than its DES predecessor. While DES maintained an encryption key length of only 56 bits, the new AES was designed to support 128-, 192-, and 256-bit keys. Built on algebraic constructs, Rijndael undergoes a complex series of steps and operations to define, scramble, redefine, and mathematically encode data.

The AES specifications demanded that any standard adopted be available free of royalties anywhere in the world. The choosing of a Belgian model signaled the NIST's commitment to the internationalization of AES. (DES, by contrast, was developed under the purview of the U.S. National Security Agency.)

USE OF AES

AES became the standard for the federal government's computer systems after it was approved by the Commerce

Department in November 2001. In June 2003, the government released a statement saying the encryption standard was strong enough to be used for classified information. Since that time AES has also become popular as an encryption standard for commercial transactions in the private sector and has been used in other applications requiring security, such as online banking. File encryption and e-mail encryption are also commonly used applications for AES. Because of the open availability, AES is available to anyone who wants to use it, anywhere in the world. Free open source encryption programs such as TrueCrypt use the standard, as do proprietary programs such as Apple Inc.'s FileVault, which is found on Macintosh computers using the Panther operation system.

AES is also subject to an open review process by the cryptographic community, where cryptologists keep analyzing the standard, testing it, and searching for weaknesses as a way to improve its overall performance and security.

As a result of this open review process, researchers have conducted many tests on the security of the system since its adoption, and in the 2000s few flaws were found. In the first years after its inception most of the successful attacks were "s side channel attacks," which attack weaknesses in some of the various implementations of the standard but not the true cipher. Some actual weaknesses were identified in 2009, though the practical application of those for a hacker who wanted to break the code were deemed to be very limited.

In 2011, however, a team of researchers working for Microsoft Research—including Andrey Bogdanov, Dmitry Khovratovich, and Christian Rechberger—were able to develop a way to break AES's key much faster than experts had ever previously expected. However, even with this potential weakness it would require two billion years for a trillion computers testing a billion keys per second to recover a key, according to an August 2011 article in *Science Daily*. The article noted that current machines can only test 10 million keys per second. Due to the time and complexity of actually conducting the process to break the code, the practical application of this successful attack were effectively nil, the researchers pointed out. Still, the identification of such a weakness was an important development in the history of the AES and the ongoing quest for its security.

SEE ALSO *Computer Security; Cryptography, Public and Private Key; Data Encryption Standard (DES); Encryption.*

BIBLIOGRAPHY

"First Flaws in the Encryption Standard Used for Internet Banking Identified." *Science Daily*, August 17, 2011. Available from http://www.sciencedaily.com/releases/2011/08/110817075424.htm.

Harrison, Ann. "Advanced Encryption Standard." *Computerworld*, May 29, 2000.

———. "Feds Propose New Encryption Standard." *Computerworld*, October 9, 2000.

Hulme, George V. "Commerce Department Picks Rijndael Encryption Formula." *InformationWeek*, October 16, 2000.

Landau, Susan. "Designing Cryptography for the New Century." *Communications of the Association for Computing Machinery*, May 2000.

Loshin, Pete. "Cryptographic Turning Points." *Computerworld*, August 28, 2000.

ADVERTISING, ONLINE

During the early twenty-first century, the use of online advertisements evolved and varied according to company purposes. At first, advertising was used primarily to encourage Web traffic. Later, brand management and sponsorship also became important.

BANNER ADS

By the early 2000s, banner ads were in decline and losing favor. One problem had to do with click-through rates, a measure that advertisers used to help determine return-on-investment (ROI). By 2000, click-through rates had fallen to 0.3%, with business-to-business advertisers reporting average click-through rates around 0.5%. Advertisers who are focused on ROI typically use banner ads to drive traffic to their Web sites, though others use banner ads to increase consumer awareness of companies and products. Many banners use rich media effects to attract more attention. The more widely used and accepted rich media formats include HTML pull-down menus and forms, Java and JavaScript, Audio, Enliven (by @Home Network), Flash (by Macromedia), Jump Page, RealAudio (by RealNetworks), Shockwave (by Macromedia), Video, and VRML.

The key to successful banner advertising is proper targeting, which ensures that ads appear in contexts relevant to the target audience. Banner performance also can be enhanced by purchasing larger banners; this might involve purchasing what is called the "skyscraper" unit, which runs down the right-hand side of a Web page, in addition to the standard banner centered at the top of a page.

Effective use of banner ads also is dependent on profiling techniques. This technology became increasingly more advanced throughout the 2000s, and the costs of creating and placing banner ads also decreased, leading to a renewal of banner usage. However, even the best banners can suffer from bad placement. Automated systems, while very useful, can often make mistakes. An article on a defective product, for example, may call up a banner ad for the product itself in a mismatched effort to gain interest.

AD NETWORKS

The first Internet advertising network was created in 1996 by the newly formed Internet ad agency DoubleClick Inc. The DoubleClick Network began as a group of about 30 Web sites that the firm represented to advertisers. It was a model that other Internet advertising agencies would emulate. Over the course of its first five years DoubleClick expanded the network of Web sites it represented, segmented it to match the needs of Internet advertisers, and reorganized it to reflect changing market conditions. By April 2001, the DoubleClick Network represented nearly 1,500 Web publishers worldwide. It consisted of 16 different networks. Advertisers could purchase ad space on any individual country network, as well as in categories such as automotive, business, commerce, entertainment, technology, travel, and women and health.

By 2010, after changing hands several times, DoubleClick had come into the hands of Google, where it became part of the Google Ad Network, which was rated as the third-largest advertising network in the United States in 2010. (The Yahoo! Network and AOL Advertising were the two largest networks.)

While successful for basic advertising, ad networks began running into problems in the later 2000s as competition began to increase. In order to be successful, ad networks need to have a short turnaround, usually only a couple of days to produce and deliver an ad impression. This typically leaves out the possibility of advertisements that use rich media and other customer-winning features. The solution was a range of applications dedicated to helping ad networks, such as the 2011 Flite application, which allowed ad networks to rapidly search for key product data and quickly create interactive ads, especially for social networks.

By 2011, businesses were moving away from traditional mediums for message communication and focusing instead on newer areas, such as social networking. In *Marketing Weblog,* Carlos Saldana noted a study by eMarketer, which estimated that social networking would take up 10% of online advertisement spending in 2011. The focus on general merchandise marketing had not changed by the end of the 2000s, but real estate had moved to become the second-largest online advertiser, followed by the auto industry. When it came to search advertisers for Google, Amazon.com ranked number one in 2010, followed by other major marketing spenders like AT&T and Capital One.

MOBILE ADVERTISING

Between 2009 and 2011, the number of advertisers using mobile display ad strategies doubled, although it still accounted for only a few percentage points of the overall online advertising spending in the United States. Mobile ads can be part of a "push" strategy or a "pull" strategy. Ads that users download as part of other content rely on the user to "pull" them to their device. Other types of mobile ads can be sent to devices at unexpected times as part of a "push" strategy.

OUTLOOK FOR ONLINE ADVERTISING

Advertising in traditional media showed high efficacy in the late 2000s, which may have lessened business interest in online advertising. The growth of Internet user numbers and online purchasing was undeniable, however, so the field remained strong, and expectations were positive for the 2010s. At the end of 2010, an eMarketer report predicted double-digit annual growth for the industry up through 2014.

While technology remains at the center of strong online advertising, the ways in which it is used are expected to change. Previous attempts at linking ad impressions with viewed content were only partially effective. Businesses will require new tools that help manage not only content, but also context, so that their ads will appear next to relevant subject manner in a way that will drive sales. Of course, the proliferation of Internet ads also has the problem of consumers becoming more annoyed than impressed at online marketing. A potential solution in coming years is the adoption of more useful ads, with messages that communicate specific and useful data, especially local data like sports scores, weather information, and news updates as part of the ad itself.

Another expected solution to the backlash against ad prevalence is stricter ad and social networking control. Consumers will be more interested in participating in programs that keep their social networks and Web sites as clear of ads as possible, potentially with the help of government regulations.

Social networking itself is also expected to play a larger role in online advertising. By combining "like" buttons and linking options with their online ads, businesses can leverage social network use to spread the word about new products or promotions. Of course, it takes a strong, unique, and memorable ad to create social network buzz, so businesses may also increase their focus on ad quality instead of ad quantity.

Some businesses may start avoiding direct online advertising altogether, choosing instead to concentrate on branding videos and applications. Known as branded entertainment, these rich media objects provide users with the service or information they are looking for, with the business logo in clear sight or with the application clearly sponsored by the business so that advertisement is less obtrusive. As this occurs, it is expected that mobile advertisement will grow more popular, especially when it comes to video and other fields that have yet to reach their full potential.

Overall, added value may be the key trend for all online advertising. Consumers may begin to require ads to be worthwhile in order to pay any attention to them at all. Videos simply used as commercials viewed online are not expected to survive, and even inexpensive, simplistic advertisements may die out. In order to be truly relevant to consumers, businesses may need to apply innovative techniques to their strategies. Online videos can be effective advertisements if they are also sufficiently entertaining, and static ads can accomplish their purpose if they immediately fill a customer need based on accurate analysis.

SEE ALSO *Banner Ads.*

BIBLIOGRAPHY

Beltrone, Gabriel. "When Banner Ads Attack Are Publishers, Brands Safe from Mismatched Placements?" *Ad Week,* August 9, 2011. Available from http://www.adweek.com/news/advertising-branding/when-banner-ads-attack-133954.

Fineberg, Seth. "Dot-Com Sea Change Forces Ad Networks to Rethink Strategies." *Advertising Age,* September 25, 2000.

"Flite Introduces Cloud-Based Advertising for Ad Networks." *Dedicated Media,* June 8, 2011. Available from http://www.dedicatedmedia.com/news-and-events.asp.

Gimenez, Sylvia. "eValuating Online Advertising." *eMarketer,* February 28, 2001.

———. "These Ads Are on the House." *eMarketer,* March 2, 2001.

Gobry, Pascal-Emmanual. "Guess Who Google's Biggest Advertiser Is?" *Business Insider,* April 12, 2011. Available from http://www.businessinsider.com/google-biggest-advertiser-2011-4.

Jackson, Jonathan. "Advertising Unplugged." *eMarketer,* April 5, 2001.

Johansmeyer, Tom. "5 Predictions: Online Advertising in 2011." *Social Times,* December 17, 2010. Available from http://socialtimes.com/predictions-online-advertising-in-2011_b31711.

Marshall, Jack. "Top U.S. Online Ad Networks by Reach, September 2010." *Click Z,* October 12, 2010. Available from http://www.clickz.com/clickz/stats/1741917/online-networks-reach-september-2010.

Marshall, Matt. "Online Advertising Explodes to $31B, but Publishers Getting Squeezed." *Venture Beat,* June 8, 2011. Available from http://venturebeat.com/2011/06/08/online-advertising-explodes-to-31b-but-publishers-getting-squeezed.

"Online Advertising to Leap 14% in 2011; Video, Mobile, Particularly Strong." *Media Buyer Planner,* August 24, 2010. Available from http://www.mediabuyerplanner.com/entry/53862/online-advertising-to-leap-14-in-2011-video-mobile-particularly-strong.

"Real Estate Second-Biggest Online Advertiser." *Media Post,* May 20, 2011. Available from http://www.mediapost.com/publications/?fa=Articles.showArticle&art_aid=150939.

Rick, Christopher. "2011 Online Video Advertising Trends and Predictions – Part I – Branded, Interactive and Mobile." *Reel SEO,* 2010. Available from http://www.reelseo.com/2011-video-advertising.

Saldana, Carlos. "Trends in Online Advertising in 2011 in the United States." *Marketing Weblog,* January 23, 2011. Available from http://marketing.blogs.ie.edu/archives/2011/01/trends-in-online-advertising-in-2011-in-the-united-states.php.

"US Online Advertising Market to Reach $50B in 2011." *Marketing Charts,* January 22, 2008. Available from http://www.marketingcharts.com/interactive/us-online-advertising-market-to-reach-50b-in-2011-3128.

AFFILIATE MODEL

The affiliate (or click-through) model is a popular e-commerce relationship in which an online merchant agrees to pay an affiliate in exchange for providing an advertisement and link to the merchant's site. Each sale generated as a result of a customer "clicking through" from an affiliate to the merchant results in a small commission for the affiliate. The deal provides a stream of cash to affiliates and brings the merchant, which owns the affiliate network, a host of new traffic, cutting customer-acquisition costs and allowing it to target its desired audience.

Retailers may run their affiliate networks in-house or farm them out to third-party services that manage the networks, issue regular checks to affiliates, and address technical problems. The sales commission paid to affiliates generally falls between 5 and 7 %, according to *Forbes.* However, depending on the type of arrangement, the size of the firms, and the click-through rates, commissions can reach as high as 15%. The most common format for routing visitors to a merchant is the ubiquitous banner advertisement—electronic "billboards" that sprawl across Web pages. These provide merchants with virtual storefronts all over the Web rather than only on their own sites.

Amazon.com largely pioneered the affiliate model in 1996, when it began recruiting thousands of smaller Web sites to help generate new traffic to its online store. Amazon.com and other companies found willing partners among smaller e-businesses, content-based Web sites, and Web portals. Indeed, for several years banner ads were the lifeblood of most major Web portals, and many content sites depended heavily on click-through banners as well. By offering to route users to a merchant's Web site to spend money, affiliates stand to draw revenue by hopping on the coattails of the retailer's sales. However, a danger lurks in directing visitors away to another site. In that case, if the visitor chooses not to purchase anything from the retailer, the affiliate has potentially sent away its visitor, perhaps never to return.

Despite that fear, Amazon's affiliates program remains a major component of its sales strategy, and it works with several hundred thousand associates. In 2000, Amazon was granted a patent for some components of an affiliate program.

That same year, Google entered the affiliate marketing arena with the launch of Google AdWords, which provides advertising to Web sites on a pay-per-click, cost-per-thousand, and site-targeted basis. AdWords is currently the main source of revenue for the search engine company, bringing in $28 billion in 2010. eBay also uses affiliates through its eBay Partner Network, which pays commissions to other sites that are able to drive traffic to the site. Commissions are based on a variety of factors, such as the quality of the traffic, including whether or not the customer spends money on eBay.

TAXES AND THE AFFILIATE MODEL

Reports suggested that by the end of the first decade of the 2000s, affiliate marketing was losing ground, partly driven by the recession of 2008–2009 and a hefty dislike of banner ads by Internet users. Some affiliates also raised ire by using e-mail and blog spam to promote their affiliated products. Another issue was "search engine spam" which was a Web page, designed by an affiliate marketer and composed solely of product data feeds, which attempted to get a high ranking in search engine results.

Another major issue facing the industry was taxes. In 2008, the State of New York amended its sales tax law to permit the taxing of Amazon because the Web retailer had links to affiliates in New York. Amazon has challenged the tax in court, but the issue had not been resolved by 2011.

In July 2011, Amazon terminated its associates program in California, severing its relationship with 10,000 affiliates based there. The action was due to a law passed earlier that year that required out-of-state online sellers who had affiliates in California to collect sales tax on purchases made by state residents. Previously, only Internet stores that had actual physical locations in California were required to collect tax. In the wake of the law, Amazon was working to collect the 500,000 signatures required to put a referendum to recall the law on the ballot in February 2012.

Similar laws also caused Amazon to end its associates programs in Connecticut, Colorado, North Carolina, Arkansas, Rhode Island, and Illinois. The company has also threatened to terminate its business in other states where taxes on online purchases are being considered. As of 2012, these included Nevada, New Mexico, Missouri, Massachusetts, and Minnesota. Some states, such as Texas and Tennessee, were working with Amazon to develop plans that would preserve the relationships in those states by deferring or exempting the company from taxes in exchange for the construction of job-producing fulfillment centers.

In a 2011 online conference, chief executive officer Jeff Bezos stated that Amazon would continue to drop affiliates from the program in states that pass such laws. The issue needs to be resolved at a federal level, Bezos claimed, because existing tax laws do not take into account the Internet when determining how to collect taxes on interstate commerce.

SEE ALSO *Advertising, Online; Amazon.com; Banner Ads; Marketing, Internet.*

BIBLIOGRAPHY

Amazon.com, Inc. "Amazon Associates." Seattle, WA, 2011. Available from https://affiliate-program.amazon.com.

Andrews, Kelly J. "Art.com for the Masses." *Target Marketing,* October 1999.

Blankenhorn, Dana. "New Twists and Terms for Affiliates." *B to B,* July 31, 2000.

eBay Inc. "ebay Partner Network." San Jose, CA, 2011. Available from https://ebaypartnernetwork.com/files/hub/en-US/index.html.

Google. "Google Adwords." Mountain View, CA, 2011. Available from https://www.google.com/accounts/ServiceLogin?service=adwords&hl=en_US&ltmpl=regionalc&passive=false&ifr=false&alwf=true&continue=https://adwords.google.com/um/gaiaauth?apt%3DNone&error=newacct.

Green, Heather, and Ben Elgin. "Do E-ads Have a Future?" *Business Week,* January 22, 2001.

Maher, Rory. "Is the Affiliate Marketing Business Past Its Prime?" *Business Insider,* August 6, 2009. Available from http://www.businessinsider.com/is-the-affiliate-marketing-business-dead-2009-8.

Schoenberger, Chana R. "Don't Go There." *Forbes,* October 2, 2000.

Tedeschi, Bob. "To Cut Costs of Finding Consumers on the Internet, Online Merchants Pay Other Web Sites for Customer Referrals." *New York Times,* May 22, 1999.

Woo, Stu. "Amazon Battles States over Sales Tax." *Wall Street Journal,* August 3, 2011. Available from http://online.wsj.com/article/SB10001424053111904772304576468753564916130.html.

AGGREGATORS

The Internet is a vast sea of electronic information. However, to be of any value that information must be combined in ways that end-users find meaningful and useful, or in ways that bring buyers and sellers together in new ways. Aggregators, of which there are several kinds, play an important role in making this happen.

Web aggregators combine information—including sports scores; weather forecasts; articles from different newspapers, magazines, and trade journals; financial information; and even applications—and either display it for all to see or sell it to other companies through syndication for use on Web sites or corporate intranets. The format in which aggregators deliver information can vary and may include full text, HTML (hypertext markup language) links to headlines, rich media (pictures, video, and sound), and formats for wireless devices like mobile phones or personal digital assistants. These types of aggregators are sometimes called feed readers or really simple syndication (RSS) readers. Google Reader is an RSS reader released by Google in 2005 and usable on a range of devices, including smartphones. Yahoo Reader, the Drudge Report, and other Web sites can also act as aggregators, bringing together culled information from various sources that readers may be interested in.

Companies need information of this kind to make their Web sites interesting. By providing added value, visitors are likely to visit a site more often and stay longer when they do. By contracting with only one or two aggregators, companies can conveniently and cost-effectively obtain information from hundreds, or even thousands, of different sources. Companies like Mochila contract with many publications and Web sites and then provide that content to other sites, either on a per-piece basis or through a subscription model.

AGGREGATORS PROBLEMATIC TO OLD MEDIA

However, while news aggregators provide a service to consumers looking to follow and keep track of many sources of news and information, they also can be a threat to media companies. The aggregators benefit from the content created by the media companies, but the newspapers and magazines themselves may end up losing readers to the aggregators. In 2011, Stephens Media, a chain of newspapers based in Las Vegas, Nevada, was working with a specialized copyright infringement litigator firm, Righthaven LLC, to pursue lawsuits against bloggers and other types of aggregators who republish stories without permission, calling the practice a "parasitic business model." Other publishers were reportedly watching the company's litigation strategy closely.

Another type of aggregator brings large groups of buyers and sellers together in an online marketplace. A notable example would be craigslist, which brings together not only buyers and sellers but has areas devoted to jobs, real estate, personal ads, and others. Online auction site eBay could also be considered a type of aggregator, since it brings together a myriad of sellers and buyers who can conduct transactions through its system.

Another variant of aggregation involves small-business owners and consumers joining together to get better rates on things like long-distance telephone service. Group purchasing enables all of the individuals to get better rates than they could have obtained separately.

Some companies are taking this group purchasing one step further, by negotiating bulk deals with providers of goods and services and allowing individuals to purchase them at a discount. One of the largest providers of this service as of 2012 is Groupon, a company that allows members to purchase discounted goods and services through a group coupon system (hence the company's name). Businesses agree to provide the discounts because of the marketing benefits of introducing their business to so many new customers.

Some Web sites are designed to aggregate reviews of products or services to aid in purchasing decisions. In some cases, these sites use an algorithm to create a score based on reviews from around the Web. A popular example is Rotten Tomatoes, a Web site that aggregates movie reviews from Web sites and newspapers. Rotten Tomatoes was founded in 1999 by Senh Duong and in 2011 was purchased by Warner Bros. The site collects reviews and then rates them as either fresh, which means positive, or rotten, which means negative. The reviews are counted for a percentage score for the film overall. The system is so popular that information Web sites such as Wikipedia regularly include the overall score from Rotten Tomatoes when writing about current films.

Another type of aggregator, social network aggregators, work to simplify the experience of a user of multiple social network platforms by bringing together content from all of them into a single location. These aggregators can also help users consolidate their social networking profiles. Examples of these types of aggregators include Flock, Friendfeed, and Streamy.

SEE ALSO *Content Provider.*

BIBLIOGRAPHY

Alexander, Steve. "Aggregators." *Computerworld,* September 4, 2000.

Andrews, Whit. "Courting Retailers: Metasearchers Increasingly Cozy Up to E-commerce Sites?" *Internet World,* January 15, 2000.

Charski, Mindy. "Content Syndicators' New Aim: Bucks." *Interactive Week,* February 21, 2001.

"Content Aggregator." *Tech Encyclopedia,* February 20, 2001. Available from http://www.techweb.com/encyclopedia.

craigslist. "About craigslist." San Francisco, CA, 2011. Available from http://www.craigslist.org/about/.

DeMocker, Judy. "B-to-B Aggregators: Vertical Domination." *InternetWeek.com,* February 22, 2001. Available from http://www.internetwk.com/lead/lead020200.htm.

Funke, Susan. "New Web Site Content Options from New Content Aggregators." *Searcher,* July/August 2000.

Google. "A Quick Tour of Google Reader." Mountain View, CA, 2011. Available from http://www.google.com/intl/en/googlereader/tour.html.

Mochila, Inc. "About Mochila." New York, 2011. Available from http://www.mochila.com/about_mochila.html.

Pash, Adam. "3 Social Media Aggregators That Bring It All Together." *PC World*, August 3, 2009. Available from http://www.pcworld.com/article/169515/3_social_media_aggregators_that_bring_it_all_together.html.

Van Winkle, William. "Strength in Numbers." *Home Office Computing*, September 2000.

ALCATEL-LUCENT

The core businesses of Alcatel-Lucent, formerly two separate corporations—Alcatel and Lucent Technologies Inc.—includes mobile, fixed, Internet protocol, and optics technologies. Alcatel-Lucent supplies public and private communication systems and software to most of the world's largest communications network operators and service providers. Headquartered in Paris, it boasts operations in 130 countries and in 2010 reported revenues of EUR 16 billion. In 2011, Philippe Camus was chairman and Bernardus Verwaayen was CEO.

LUCENT TECHNOLOGIES INC.

Lucent Technologies Inc. was incorporated in November 1995 in the wake of AT&T's restructuring. AT&T sold 17.6% of Lucent to the public on April 10, 1996. The remaining 82.4% of Lucent was distributed to AT&T shareholders later in 1996. Lucent was the corporate descendant of AT&T's Western Electric manufacturing division that AT&T bought in 1881. Bell Laboratories also was made part of Lucent. Bell Laboratories is known as the inventor of the transistor, the communications satellite, the laser, the cellular phone, and electronic telephone switching. From the time it was founded until the time it was incorporated into Lucent, Bell Laboratories averaged one patent a day.

In its first nine months as a public company, Lucent reported revenue of $15.9 billion. From 1997 to 1999, Lucent spent $32 billion on some 30 acquisitions. Its largest acquisition during this period was Ascend Communications in 1999. Ascend was the leading manufacturer of ATM switches that were used by telephone carriers to link old voice circuits with new data lines. In 1999, Lucent also spent $1.5 billion to acquire Excel Switching Corp., which made telecommunications network switching products, and $1.5 billion on Kenan Systems Corp., which made customer service software.

Lucent continued to pursue acquisitions in 2000 as well as to sell off noncore businesses. It continued to divest its consumer products units, selling its consumer telephone manufacturing business in the United States to Hong Kong-based VTech Holdings for $113 million. Lucent's first major acquisition in 2000 was Ortel Corp. for $2.95 billion. Ortel developed opto-electronic components for cable TV networks and was a market leader for lasers that increased the bandwidth of existing cable networks. The acquisition strengthened Lucent's ability to build high-capacity networks for cable TV operators.

Other significant acquisitions in 2000 included Spring Tide Networks, a vendor of network switches and Internet protocol (IP) products, for $1.3 billion, and Hermann Technology Inc., a supplier of next-generation optical network devices, for $438 million.

Although Lucent was the leading vendor of power supplies in the United States and internationally, the company decided to put its power systems business up for sale in 2000. Lucent Power Systems generated revenue of $1 billion in the United States and $1.2 billion internationally. Late in 2000 it was sold to Tyco International Ltd. for $2.5 billion.

In March 2001, Lucent announced it was seeking buyers for its fiber and cable business unit, one of its core businesses. At the time Lucent was the second-largest producer of optical fiber in the world, behind Corning. The unit's revenue grew to nearly $2 billion in 2000. Alcatel SA made a bid for the fiber-optic business, then entered into talks with Lucent about a possible merger. At the end of May 2001, the *Washington Post* reported that Alcatel and Lucent were finalizing an agreement to merge, with Alcatel acquiring Lucent for $32 billion in stock. The next day it was announced that talks had collapsed, reportedly over issues of control. Lucent announced it would proceed with its own turnaround plan, which included laying off 10,000 workers and reducing annual expenses by $2 billion. Lucent subsequently sold its fiber-optic business to Furukawa Electric Co. of Japan for $2.5 billion, with Corning paying an additional $225 million for Lucent's interest in two joint ventures in China.

ALCATEL

On the other side of the Atlantic, La Compagnie Générale d'Electricité (CGE), the forerunner of Alcatel, was formed in 1898 as competition to AEG, Siemens, and General Electric. CGE became a leader in digital communications and is also known as the producer of the "TGV" (train à grande vitesse) high-speed trains in France. In the mid-1980s, CGE purchased the European telecommunications business of ITT Corporation and changed its name to Alcatel Alsthom.

In 1983, Alcatel Alsthom was one of the first foreign companies to establish a presence in China. In 1998, the company made a decision to concentrate fully on the telecommunications industry, divested itself of the activities of Alsthom, and changed its name to Alcatel.

THE MERGED COMPANY

Shareholders of Alcatel and Lucent Technologies agreed to Alcatel's $11 billion acquisition of Lucent in September

2006, paving the way for the merger of two rivals who had competed for years in the wireless and wired telecommunications markets. The consolidation of the two companies was seen as a merger of two equals. Alcatel, based in France, had strong ties with the European market, while Lucent Technologies, based in the United States, had strong ties with North American carriers.

Since the 2006 merger, Alcatel-Lucent has posted numerous quarterly losses and taken more than $4.5 billion in write-downs while watching its stock plummet by 50%. In the latter part of the 2000s, economic turmoil and tight credit conditions had an effect on all telecommunication companies, while foreign competitors such as China's Huawei stood ready to capture a share of the market.

In July 2008, *Bloomberg Businessweek* reported that shareholders were successful in ousting both Patricia Russo and the chairman of the board, Serge Tchuruk. Russo was replaced by Bernardus Verwaayen, formerly the vice chairman of Lucent Technologies' board in 1997. Phillipe Camus, a dual citizen of France and the United States, took over as chairman of the board.

At the end of 2006, Alcatel-Lucent purchased Nortel's UMTS radio access business. During 2007, the company acquired Canadian metro WDM networking supplier Tropic Networks, Inc.; enterprise services gateway products developer NetDevices; software company Tamblin; and the telecommunications consulting practice Thompson Advisory Group, Inc. In 2008, Alcatel-Lucent acquired Motive, Inc., a provider of service management software for broadband and mobile data services.

SEE ALSO *Optical Switching; Photonics.*

BIBLIOGRAPHY

Alcatel-Lucent. "Company Overview." Paris, France, 2011. Available from http://www.alcatel-lucent.com/aboutus/companyoverview.html.

"Back to the Drawing Board: Schacht Speeds up Lucent's Turnaround Effort." *Telephony,* June 11, 2001.

Bucholtz, Chris. "Avaya Takes Flight." *VARbusiness,* January 8, 2001.

Drozdiak, William, and Greg Schneider. "Lucent Merger Talks Collapse." *Washington Post,* May 30, 2001.

Feduschak, Natalia A. "Lucent Buys Ortel for $2.95B." *Multichannel News,* February 14, 2000.

Garretson, Rob, and John Schwartz. "For $4.75 Billion, Lucent Gets Tiny Va. Firm and a Big Idea." *Washington Post,* June 1, 2000.

"Loose Ends." *Orlando Business Journal,* July 27, 2001.

"Lucent: Suddenly, the Hole Is Even Deeper." *Business Week,* June 11, 2001.

Matlack, Carol, and Jennifer L. Schenker. "Alcatel-Lucent's Troubled Marriage." *Bloomberg Businessweek,* June 18, 2008. Available from http://www.businessweek.com/magazine/content/08_26/b4090056678890.htm.

Miller, Elizabeth Starr. "Download: Whale Watching." *Telephony,* February 26, 2001.

Reardon, Marguerite. "Shareholders Approve Alcatel, Lucent Merger." *CNET,* September 7, 2006. Available from http://news.cnet.com/Shareholders-approve-Alcatel%2C-Lucent-merger/2100-1037_3-6113357.html?tag=lia;rcol.

Schaff, William. "Reeling Lucent Pushes Spin-Off Despite Chilly IPO Market." *InformationWeek,* March 26, 2001.

ALLEN, PAUL

In 2010, *Forbes* ranked Paul Allen as the 17th-wealthiest person in the United States, with an estimated net worth of $12.7 billion. Allen was born in Seattle, Washington, on January 21, 1953, and attended Lakeside High School where he met Bill Gates. In 1975, after Allen left his programming job at Boston-based Honeywell, he and Gates cofounded Microsoft. Allen served as Microsoft's head of research and new product development. According to his Web page (ideaman.paulallen.com), Allen helped to engineer many of Microsoft's most successful products, including MS-DOS, Word, Windows, and the Microsoft Mouse.

Allen left Microsoft in 1983 to battle Hodgkin's disease and remained cancer free until he was diagnosed with non-Hodgkin's lymphoma in 2009. In 1985, he founded his own software company, Asymetrix (subsequently renamed Click2learn.com), and in 1986 established Vulcan Northwest Inc. and Vulcan Ventures. The latter is an investment capital firm, through which Allen has invested in high technology, e-commerce, media, and entertainment companies.

Allen was on *TIME* magazine's 100 Most Influential People in the World list in 2008 and 2009. His memoir, *Idea Man: A Memoir by the Cofounder of Microsoft,* was published by Portfolio Hardcover in 2011. He wrote the book after his second battle with cancer. In a May 2011 *McLean's* interview Allen commented: "I wanted to tell the story from my perspective. My side of the story had never been in print." Allen comments on his sometimes discordant relationships with Gates and Steve Ballmer, CEO of Microsoft as of 2011, including accusations that the pair discussed reducing Allen's financial stake in the firm after he was diagnosed with cancer the first time.

SPORTS AND MUSIC HOLDINGS

Allen's other interests include sports and music. His interest in the life and music of Jimi Hendrix led him to create the Experience Music Project in Seattle, which opened its doors in 2000. Following his passion for sports, Allen purchased the NBA's Portland Trail Blazers in 1988, and in 1988 and the NFL's Seattle Seahawks in

1997. Since 2006, he has been asking officials in Portland and Oregon to help finance the Trail Blazers, however, because the franchise continues to lose millions each year. He is also a part-owner of the Seattle Sounders FC, a Major League Soccer team.

INVESTMENTS

In 2000, Allen sold 58 million shares of his Microsoft holdings, worth more than $7 billion, and resigned from the company's board of directors. He retained some 200 million shares. The press speculated that Allen's connections with Microsoft were hindering his investment strategy, and selling the stock left him free to invest in Microsoft's competitors.

Allen's investments after leaving Microsoft were built around his vision of a "wired world," in which people are empowered by their connection to information and allowed to personalize it. To that end he has made numerous investments in a wide variety of companies, including technology and media firms. Allen was a substantial backer of the South Lake Union redevelopment project, an effort to make that Seattle neighborhood a hub for biotechnology with residential, office, retail and research space.

However, his technology investments suffered during the dot-com shakeout, and Vulcan cut back dramatically some of its investments in companies such as Pop.com, WebHouse Club, and others, shrinking his portfolio from 100 to 40 companies by 2004. Reports estimated that Allen lost at least a third of his Microsoft fortune in tech and media investments that took a downturn.

Allen also invests in social and political causes. In addition, Allen funded SpaceShipOne, a privately backed effort to put a civilian in suborbital space. The spaceplane completed its first manned private space flight in 2004. The project resulted in Allen and Burt Rutan winning the $10 million Ansari X Prize. Another project, Vulcan Productions, is a film company founded by Allen and his wife, Jody Allen. The company produces feature films, educational films, and documentaries.

In 2011, Allen gave his alma mater, Washington State University, the largest gift in that university's history when he donated $26 million to the School for Global Animal Health. That gift was one of many large donations he has given his alma mater and other schools in Washington State, where he continues to reside.

SEE ALSO *Gates, William (Bill); Microsoft Corp.; Microsoft Windows.*

BIBLIOGRAPHY

"About the Author." Seattle, WA: Vulcan, Inc. 2011. Available from http://ideaman.paulallen.com/TemplateMain.aspx?contentId=2.

Alsop, Stewart. "What's a New Economy without Research?" *Fortune,* May 15, 2000.

Baker, M. Sharon. "Allen's Interactive-Television Empire Gears Up." *Business Journal–Portland,* May 19, 2000.

Donohue, Steve. "Allen Answers ITV Queries." *Multichannel News,* December 4, 2000.

Greene, Jay. "The $12 Billion Education of Paul Allen." *Business Week,* May 3, 2004. Available from http://www.businessweek.com/magazine/content/04_18/b3881106_mz020.htm.

———. "Paul Allen's Book Is an Unabashed Bid for Computing Industry Credit." *CNET,* April 18, 2011. Available from http://news.cnet.com/8301-10805_3-20055156-75.html.

Kirkpatrick, David. "Are You Experienced?" *Fortune,* July 24, 2000.

———. "Why We're Betting Billions on TV." *Fortune,* May 15, 2000.

Moltzen, Edward F. "Eighteen: Paul Allen, the Money Man." *Computer Reseller News,* November 13, 2000.

"Net Leader Finds Reason to Retreat." *Internet World,* December 1, 2000.

"Paul Allen Leaves Microsoft Board." *Computer Weekly,* October 5, 2000.

Stross, Randall E. "This Keg's on Me, Fellas." *U.S. News & World Report,* November 13, 2000.

ALTAVISTA CO.

AltaVista—the name means "the view from above"—was a pioneering Web portal that offered Web pages, shopping, news, live audio and video, and community resources, including e-mail. AltaVista provided the first full-text search service in the world when it was created in 1995. However, its user base dwindled as Google's popularity increased, and the site was discontinued in 2011 by Yahoo!, its parent company since 2003.

AltaVista developed Babel Fish, the first machine translation service on the Web. AltaVista also let users search for photos, videos, and music through its index of more than 30 million multimedia objects. Other innovations included the first-ever multilingual search capacity on the Internet and the first search technology to support Chinese, Japanese, and Korean languages.

FOUNDING AND HEYDAY

AltaVista was created at the Palo Alto research laboratory of Digital Equipment Corporation (DEC). DEC's engineers devised a plan to store every word of every page on the entire Internet in a searchable index and then utilize DEC's new Alpha 8400 computers to extract relevant information from this body of knowledge.

When DEC was absorbed into Compaq Computer Corporation in 1998, AltaVista became a division of Compaq. Instead of selling AltaVista, Compaq invested more money in it. By the end of 1998 AltaVista had a user base of 12 million people and 32 million page views per day. With its core strength of extraordinary search technology that generated results faster than most other search engines, AltaVista's goal was to become one of the top five sites within three years. Its principal competitors at that time were Yahoo!, Excite, and Lycos. AltaVista was generating about $50 million a year in revenue, primarily from banner ads on its site.

In early 1999, Compaq spun AltaVista off into an independent company. Rod Schrock, senior vice president of Compaq's Consumer Product Group, was named president and CEO of AltaVista Co. Compaq added shopping capabilities to AltaVista in early 1999 with the $211 million acquisition of online retailer Shopping.com. Compaq also acquired Zip2 Corp., a company that specialized in providing directory and database services for newspapers. Zip2 Corp. organized content and advertising into an online, searchable format for 160 media partners. AltaVista planned to combine Zip2's directory and database features with the e-commerce capabilities of Shopping.com and to give local merchants access to the features of Shopping.com through the Web sites of their local newspapers. The *Houston Chronicle's* Houston4U. com Web site was showcased as an example of how AltaVista's local portals would work.

SALE TO CMGI INC.

With Compaq experiencing financial difficulties following its acquisition of DEC, AltaVista was sold to CMGI Inc. in mid-1999 for $2.3 billion. CMGI geared up for the 1999 holiday shopping season with a major redesign to the AltaVista site. Subject categories were introduced to help users narrow their searches. Additional online stores were integrated alongside Shopping.com, which had experienced a high level of complaints about late delivery of merchandise. Other new features included product reviews and comparative shopping.

The changes seemed to be working. According to Media Metrix, AltaVista was the eleventh-most-visited site in November 1999, up from fifteenth earlier in the year. In its December 1999 filing for an AltaVista initial public offering (IPO), CMGI claimed that AltaVista was the fifth-most-popular Internet search engine. However, changing market conditions in 2000 would prevent AltaVista from going public.

DOT-COM BUST AND THE RISE OF GOOGLE

AltaVista had never been profitable. For the six months ending January 31, 2000, it reported an operating loss of $542.9 million. There were substantial layoffs in 1999 and 2000, and the planned IPO was shelved in April 2000. In October 2000, CEO Rod Schrock stepped down, leaving the company to be run by president Greg Memo and chief financial officer Ken Barber.

The company beefed up its multimedia index, incorporated descriptions of search results, and revisited news sites several times a day to keep listings fresh. In 2002, AltaVista introduced the Prisma search technology, which helped users refine their search by suggesting related search terms. Meanwhile, Babel Fish was becoming the company's most popular offering. The free service translated text to and from English, Spanish, French, German, Portuguese, Italian, and Russian.

These innovations failed to keep AltaVista competitive in the aftermath of the dot-com downfall and the development of Google as the predominant search engine. Web site administrators had begun to complain that AltaVista, which once added new pages to its index quickly and at no charge, was giving more search prominence to businesses that paid to have their sites indexed. As a result, AltaVista (once regarded as having the freshest index updates) lost the trust of consumers seeking the most up-to-date and accurate results.

In 2000, Google introduced unobtrusive, text-based advertisements marketed with pay-per-click and keyword price bidding (a sales model, ironically, developed by future AltaVista parent and Yahoo! property Overture Services). Internet users flocked away from AltaVista's distracting banner ads and untrusted sponsored search results. Google quietly built a name for itself as a reliable search engine while the old search engines like AltaVista were busy rebranding themselves (with minimal success) as "portals."

Although AltaVista's valuation three years earlier had been $2.3 billion, Overture Services, Inc. (formerly Goto.com) acquired the company for $140 million in 2003. Later the same year, Yahoo! acquired Overture, and with it, AltaVista. Yahoo! also got Inktomi and AlltheWeb. Yahoo! had been Google's biggest licensing partner, incorporating the Google search results into the Yahoo! portal and giving Google lots of advertising in the process.

Yahoo! merged its new acquisitions into a new Yahoo! search engine with plans to go head-to-head against Google. It did not work. After several years of slipping everfurther behind in its race against Google, in 2009 Yahoo! announced a partnership to outsource search functionality to Microsoft's Bing. Though the AltaVista brand had essentially ceased to exist years before, in 2011 Yahoo! officially eliminated the division.

Many AltaVista innovations became standard features in Internet search technology. Still, through the uncertainty created with every makeover and ownership change, the insurmountable popularity of its biggest competitor (Google), and the unpredictable twists and turns of a new industry, AltaVista in the end proved unable to maintain its early dominance in the search industry.

SEE ALSO *Portals, Web.*

BIBLIOGRAPHY

"AltaVista Announcement Sparks UK Internet Access Price War." *Internet Business News,* March 2000.

"AltaVista Going Public." *San Francisco Business Times,* December 24, 1999.

"AltaVista Launches Prisma." *Pandia,* July 2, 2002. Available from www.pandia.com/sw-2002/22-altavista.html.

Andrews, Whit. "In Redesign, AltaVista Is Returning to Its Roots." *Internet World,* October 19, 1998.

Corcoran, Elizabeth. "Compaq Plans to Spin Off AltaVista." *Washington Post,* January 27, 1999.

Dodge, Don. "What Happened to AltaVista and Yahoo? From Innovator to Imitator to Forgotten." *Don Dodge on the Next Big Thing,* August 12, 2010. Available from http://dondodge.typepad.com/the_next_big_thing/2010/08/what-happened-to-altavista-and-yahoo.html.

Hansell, Saul. "Overture Services to Buy AltaVista for $140 Million." *New York Times,* February 19, 2003. Available from http://www.nytimes.com/2003/02/19/technology/19NET.html?pagewanted=all.

Liedtke, Michael. "Yahoo Comes Full Circle with Retreat from Search." *Seattle Times,* July 29, 2009. Available from http://seattletimes.nwsource.com/html/localnews/2009564994_apustecyahoosearch.html.

Schwartz, John. "CMGI Buys AltaVista from Ailing Compaq." *Washington Post,* June 30, 1999.

"Short History of Early Search Engines." *The History of SEO.* Available from www.thehistoryofseo.com/The-Industry/Short_History_of_Early_Search_Engines.aspx.

Zimmerman, Christine. "All the News That's Fit to Index." *InternetWeek,* March 26, 2001.

AMAZON.COM, INC.

Although Amazon.com built its reputation as an online bookstore, the Seattle-based company has pursued a strategy of offering a wide assortment of products, including books, electronics, toys, video, music, health and beauty, wireless phones, camera and photo, computer and video games, software, tools and hardware, lawn and patio, cars, auctions, and gifts.

Amazon.com went online in July 1995 and quickly set the standard for other e-tailers. The company changed the way people bought books by staying open 24 hours a day, seven days a week. It also developed its own user-friendly ordering system and provided reviews and other information about the books it sold that no traditional bookstore could match. Amazon.com's head start on other booksellers helped it to dominate the online book market; in 2010, sales were more than $34 billion.

Amazon.com was founded by Jeff Bezos. Bezos determined that books, videos, computer software and hardware, and CDs would be the easiest products to sell online. They were items that a customer did not necessarily need to see or handle before ordering, and they were easy to pack and ship. Without the physical space limitations of a brick-and-mortar store, Bezos realized that an online store could offer a wider selection of those items.

In the beginning, Amazon.com was aided by the established wholesale network for books that already existed. The company did not need a big inventory to start with. One reason Amazon.com chose Seattle, Washington, as its base was that it would be near the world's largest book wholesaler, which was based in Oregon. As years passed the company added more warehouses and storage facilities where necessary.

THE FIRST E-HOLIDAY SHOPPING SEASON: 1998

The fourth quarter of 1998 was the first holiday shopping season in the United States that had substantial retail sales over the Internet. The Boston Consulting Group estimated that American consumers spent about $4 billion buying goods and services online during the fourth quarter of 1998, and nearly $10 billion throughout the year. While that amounted to less than 1 % of all U.S. retail sales, e-commerce sales more than tripled from 1997. The same report estimated that more than eight million U.S. households made an online purchase during 1998.

In the fourth quarter of 1998 America Online (AOL) was the Internet's most popular shopping mall, but Amazon.com was the number one e-tailer. It sold a variety of books, CDs, videos, and gifts, including a selection of 185 toys. It also spent heavily on marketing and advertising—$29 on average to acquire a new customer.

By mid-1999, Amazon.com was valued at $22 billion, according to *Newsweek.* In two years its customer base had grown from 2 million to 11 million. Not only was Amazon the dominant bookseller, it had become the biggest music retailer on the Internet and was also becoming a source for toys and consumer electronics. Profits remained absent, however, eaten up by the ambitious expansion and marketing strategies of the company. This reabsorption of earnings eventually led to home improvement, software, and gift idea sections set up as part of the Amazon Web site.

Although management's strategy was aimed at achieving certain operating income levels rather than revenue growth, Amazon.com continued to lose money during the early 2000s. Fortunately, customer accounts continued to rise and certain departments, such as books and videos, began to see notable earnings.

Amazon.com also expanded internationally during this time, opening sites in France and Japan in addition to its existing sites in Germany and the United Kingdom. The Japanese-language site was launched in November 2000 and focused on books. Japan already was Amazon.com's largest export market, with nearly 200,000 Japanese customers ordering $34 million in products each year from the company's U.S.-based site.

A December 2000 report by Jupiter Media Metrix revealed the strength of Amazon.com's international appeal. It was the most visited e-tailer in Australia, Canada, the United Kingdom, and the United States. In addition, Amazon.com was among the top five online retailers in Brazil, Denmark, France, and Japan. In the United Kingdom the company actually ranked first and second, with its U.K. site attracting 1.75 million unique visitors in November, while its U.S. site attracted 993,000 visitors. The U.S. site reported 1.22 million visitors during November from Canada and 461,000 from Australia.

As well as being the one of the largest e-tailers, Amazon.com also become one of the largest online advertisers, spending more than any other American business on online advertisement with a focus on primary sites with high traffic. While direct marketing was a part of this strategy, brand recognition was also important in the early stages of business growth as Amazon.com attempted to associate itself with consumer-oriented e-commerce across many different industries.

Perhaps Amazon.com's most important partnership of 2000 was its online joint venture with Toys 'R' Us, which had been struggling to develop its own online strategy. For the 2000 holiday shopping season, Amazon.com and brick-and-mortar retailer Toys 'R' Us joined forces to create Toysrus.com. The alliance was announced in August 2000, with the newly created Toysrus.com to select and purchase the toys using its parent company's clout, while Amazon.com would run the store on its Web site, ship the products, and handle customer service. The venture played to the strengths of both companies and the joint site was used more frequently than any rival during the holidays following its creation.

FOCUSED ON PROFITABILITY

By 2002, Amazon.com was able to post a net profit of $5 million, the first time the company could show positive net earnings after a net loss of $545 million the previous year. The profit was due both to continued growth, a strong holiday season, and an aggressive strategy to cut costs in order to improve product performance. In one quarter alone the company cut its operating costs in half, allowing for price drops and a higher volume of sales that finally put it over the top. However, the road to reach profitability was long, and Amazon.com still had around $2 billion in debt to pay off.

TECHNOLOGICAL SHIFTS

For Amazon, the mid-2000s were a period of recovery from the dot-com bust and a slow move toward growth and profitability for its shareholders. However, by 2006 and 2007, technology had changed so much that Amazon began new and ultimately model-changing projects to stay at the forefront of online sales and value offerings.

While iTunes would eventually offer strong digital download sales for music, video, and movies, Amazon also attempted to expand in this area with the Amazon Unbox in 2006, a service that let customers buy and download movies or television shows directly to their computers or entertainment systems. The next year the Amazon MP3 store was introduced. These new ventures helped bring in additional revenue for the company and also provided the necessary platforms for a key change: moving from selling other company products to selling Amazon-based products. The most notable product was the Amazon Kindle, an e-reader.

The Kindle become the highest-selling product of Amazon.com by 2009 and positioned the company for even greater success in the e-commerce world. Not only was the Kindle useful because it worked well with the Kindle store Amazon offered online, but Amazon was also one of the first companies to create a workable, consumer-friendly e-reader while offering downloadable books at acceptable prices. This eventually led to Amazon holding 90% of the American e-book market in 2009.

While competitive e-readers were eventually developed by Apple and Barnes & Noble, the Kindle had a significant head start, and Amazon was experienced enough to handle the shift from physical to digital products. In 2010, sales for Kindle books outpaced sells for hardcover books for the first time. By 2011, Kindle sales had grown larger than both hardcover and paperback books, and the newest version of the Kindle was available for $114. Amazon also began offering cloud-computing music features such as "music lockers" that allowed users to store their tracks online instead of on their own computers.

FUTURE PLANS

As the 2010s began, Amazon started to channel more of its earnings into expansion and operations once again. While Amazon traditionally does not disclose its future plans and product releases outside of its own advertising channels, rumors in 2011 pinpointed a potential multipurpose tablet slated for later release. The tablet would be an evolution of the Kindle that would allow for color viewing, Amazon MP3 support, and the viewing of movies and shows bought from the Amazon store.

The company also continued its expansion into cloud computing by offering and maintaining key services in its Amazon Web Services. Past clients included Pfizer, Netflix, and a vast array of business start-ups that wanted to use applications run on Amazon servers to manage various aspects of their businesses. While Amazon had previously invested in data centers on a global level to meet the demand, cloud computing was still a relatively unexplored option in 2010 and 2011. The company ran into issues with technical problems on its servers that kept its client businesses from operating in 2011, leading to worries that such Web services were not as dependable as they could be.

SEE ALSO *Bezos, Jeff.*

BIBLIOGRAPHY

"All Boxed In." *TIME,* September 4, 2000.

"Amazon.com Inc." *New York Times,* August 17, 2011. Available from http://topics.nytimes.com/top/news/business/companies/amazon_inc/index.html.

"Amazon.com's Profits Tumbles More Than Expected." *Huffington Post,* April 26, 2011. Available from http://www.huffingtonpost.com/2011/04/26/amazoncom-profit-tumbles_n_854050.html.

"Amazon in New E-tail Deals." *Puget Sound Business Journal,* January 28, 2000.

"Amazon Posts a Profit." *CNN Money,* January 22, 2002. Available from http://money.cnn.com/2002/01/22/technology/amazon.

Bishop, Todd. "Amazon.com's New Tablet Would Be the Anti-iPad." *Geek Wire,* May 3, 2011. Available from http://www.geekwire.com/2011/amazons-tablet-challenge-apples-ipad-shining-flashlights-eyes.

Enos, Lori. "Amazon Ranked as Net Ad Champ." *E-Commerce Times,* December 14, 2000. Available from http://www.macnewsworld.com/story/6059.html.

"Inside the First E-Christmas." *Fortune,* February 1, 1999.

Lohr, Steve. "Amazon's Trouble Raises Cloud Computing Doubts." *New York Times,* April 22, 2011. Available from http://www.nytimes.com/2011/04/23/technology/23cloud.html.

Macaluso, Nora. "Amazon and Toys 'R' Us Take E-holiday Prize." *E-Commerce Times,* January 2, 2001. Available from http://www.ecommercetimes.com/story/6398.html.

Reid, Calvin. "Amazon.com in Pact to Take Over Borders.com." *Publishers Weekly,* April 16, 2001.

Saliba, Clare. "Report: Amazon Smashed E-tail Competition in January." *E-Commerce Times,* February 14, 2001. Available from http://www.ecommercetimes.com/story/commerce/7511.html.

"We Have Lift-off." *Economist (US),* February 3, 2001.

"Wired for the Bottom Line." *Newsweek,* September 20, 1999.

AMERICAN NATIONAL STANDARDS INSTITUTE (ANSI)

A private, nonprofit organization that works to coordinate voluntary standards, the American National Standards Institute (ANSI) is the hub of all standards-related policy decisions in the United States. It is the primary U.S. body that coordinates the efforts of industry, consumer, and governmental standards developers, and it is the sole organization that accredits other U.S. standards organizations. With offices in New York City and headquarters in Washington, D.C., ANSI's mission is to boost the competitiveness of U.S. business and the American quality of life by ensuring the U.S. voluntary standardization system is well coordinated and promoted. Therefore, ANSI sees to it that U.S. businesses and industries maintain an adequate performance level for products, services, and processes, ideally keeping in mind the range of affected interests.

ANSI has played an important role in U.S. commerce for many years. It was founded in 1918 by a coalition of five engineering societies and three government agencies. The organization generates funding through its membership, which consists of private and public sector members, including individual companies, organizations, governmental agencies, institutions, and international organizations.

Mainly a service to the U.S. private sector and its position in the global economy, ANSI also works closely with governmental organizations. ANSI often coordinates its efforts with the National Institute of Standards and Technology (NIST), an agency of the U.S. Department of Commerce's technology administration. A key area of activity is conformity assessment. Through its accreditation process, ANSI oversees the moves made by manufacturers and others to incorporate voluntary standards. ANSI confers the "American National Standard" (ANS) designation upon those organizations that meet its basic guidelines of due process, openness, balance, and consensus in setting and meeting the organization's voluntary standards.

ANSI does not, however, actually write or implement standards. Rather, the organization acts as a consensus-generating facilitator between various groups devoted to developing standards specific to their areas of concern. In this way, ANSI eschews a top-down approach to standards development, leaving the various sectors with autonomy in creating standards appropriate to the conditions they face. ANSI simply seeks to ease the standards into use with an eye toward a holistic look at U.S. competitiveness and quality-of-life issues.

ANSI ON THE WORLD STAGE

ANSI is the U.S. affiliate of the International Organization for Standardization (ISO), of which it is a founding member and one of the five permanent members of the governing ISO Council. ANSI also is a member of the International Accreditation Forum (IAF) and the International Electrotechnical Committee (IEC). Additionally, ANSI champions the adoption of U.S.-based standards on the international scene, and when appropriate, aims to incorporate international standards in the United States.

There is a perpetual tension surrounding the nationalistic character of standards, whereby individual nations insist on autonomy in setting their own standards.

Conversely, the internationalization of standards carries some of the same complications to the next level. Nations sometimes disagree when one nation tries to impose its standards as the global ones, thereby attaining a state of hegemony and other advantages. In the late 1990s, European organizations increasingly introduced new standards that some in the United States feared would undermine U.S. competitiveness in the global marketplace. ANSI and related organizations thus recognized the need to produce a more systematic and responsive U.S. standardization environment.

While renewing support for the established U.S. standards-writing principles—which cherish open participation by all interested parties and easy access to the status and progress of standards writing—ANSI called for a 12-step program to be undertaken in the United States. Its purpose was to give the nation a unified voice and a quick, fair, and workable standards-writing and implementation process for competing in the global marketplace. The steps involved included integrating several elements into the writing process. Among these were the environmental, health, and safety concerns of affected parties; a greater awareness and consideration of consumer concerns; and coordinated efforts with industries in other countries. In December 2000, ANSI and NIST signed a memorandum of understanding (MoU) that aimed to further the National Standards Strategy by increasing communication between the two organizations and private and public interests in the United States. Moreover, the MoU shored up the recognition of ANSI as the sole international representative of U.S. standards interests.

ANSI AND THE INTERNET

Before e-commerce, ANSI already was involved in standardizing processes for computers. For instance, the well-known C programming language was approved by the ANSI committee, thereby ensuring that most C compilers were compatible with each other, regardless of the vendor. Additionally, ANSI established a range of standards for both electronic and electrical components and interactions, and set the standards for a range of communications protocols, including those for fiber-optic data transmission.

As the Internet opened up in the early 1990s and e-commerce became an increasingly important social and economic phenomenon, ANSI again kicked into high gear to coordinate the virtually wide-open move to develop protocols and standards. With the Internet and e-commerce speeding the pace of development and change, there grew increasing calls for a speeding of the standards-setting process. For instance, developments in the methods of online payments have been crucial to the development and expansion of e-commerce, and it has been crucial that the speed and security of such payments keep pace with the speed of the Internet in general. In that spirit, ANSI oversaw the development of uniform standards for electronic signatures, which facilitate the employment of e-checks for online payment. These standards set guidelines for the generation, verification, and security of electronic signatures.

In the early 2000s, the ANSI-accredited ASC X12 Committee focused on pan-industrial business standards for Extensible Markup Language (XML), a hypertext meta-language allowing for the definition of Web-based information, design, and communication. The committee based its standards-writing on the Electronic Business XML (ebXML) initiative, which is designed to facilitate the business-to-business e-commerce market. The standards aim to coordinate a set of business "objects," valid across national boundaries, which define elements of online transactions.

In the late 1990s, ANSI joined 24 other standards organizations worldwide in calling for the development of international e-commerce standards, mainly to protect consumers. These proposals included measures to ensure the reliability of merchants and to safeguard privacy and the security of financial information. At the ISO's Committee on Consumer Policy (COPOLCO) meeting in May 2000, COPOLCO presented evidence that consumers, for lack of confidence in these areas, often were hesitant to engage in online commerce. Thus, the development of such standards was of great concern to consumers and businesses alike. The lack of standardization in an area with such rich opportunities provided business groups with a vital stake in contributing to and facilitating an e-commerce standardization process.

The result of the COPOLCO meeting was the creation of the E-Commerce Consumer Standards Solutions Forum, which centered worldwide discussion on the implementation of international standards for the online marketplace. The ultimate goal was increased consumer acceptance of and involvement in e-commerce, aided by multilateral governmental agreements, domestic regulations, standards created and implemented through the normal domestic and international channels, consumer education and outreach, and other approaches.

DEVELOPMENTS IN THE TWENTY-FIRST CENTURY

At the start of the twenty-first century, ANSI developed and published the first guidelines of its kind, the *National Standards Strategy for the United States.* In theory, this provided a reliable, market-driven process for standards creation that all types of businesses in the country could utilize. Since the U.S. Congress estimated in 2005 that private-sector standards and government technical regulations directly affected at least $7 trillion of world trade in 2003, the importance of standards was clear.

Another trend noted by ANSI that occurred in the 2000s was toward developing standards for processes, systems, and personnel rather than just technology and manufacturing. This occurred in response to the continued evolution of the U.S. economy from manufacturing-based to service- and technology-based. Examples of this movement include standards panels that are working on (or overseeing) standards on homeland security, identity theft and identity management, nanotechnology, and health care information technology.

In 2003, ANSI began offering accreditation to organizations that provide certification of personnel so that people in specific occupations could be recognized for their skills and abilities in different states and nations. For example, in 2009, ANSI accredited Microsoft Corporation's certification process for Microsoft Certified IT Professionals, both as enterprise administrators and server administrators. ANSI also accredited the Institute of Hazardous Materials Management certification for Certified Hazardous Materials managers and practitioners. And in 2005, ANSI revised its National Standards Strategy, publishing new guidelines called the *United States Standards Strategy* (USSS). The USSS introduced a new focus on working together as consortia to develop standards that are applicable across the globe. ANSI works closely with the World Wide Web Consortium, the International Organization for Standardization, and the U.S. Chamber of Commerce.

By the early 2010s, the focus on personnel certification and global standards was continuing to guide the organization's programs. Organizations that provide personnel certification and that have been accredited by ANSI as of 2012 include Board of Certified Safety Professionals, Association of Professionals in Business Management, and Cardiovascular Credentialing International.

BIBLIOGRAPHY

"About ANSI: Overview." Washington, DC: American National Standards Institute, 2011. Available from http://www.ansi.org/about_ansi/overview/overview.aspx?menuid=1.

"Implementation of the U.S. National Standards Strategy and Coordinated Efforts in International Standardization Play Key Roles in Revised MoU Between ANSI and NIST." Washington, DC: American National Standards Institute, February 2001.

"ISO COPOLCO and the Euro Commission Establish On-Line Forums for E-commerce Discussions." Washington, DC: American National Standards Institute, August 2000.

Lyford, Richard. "Developing Standards for Storage Area Networks," *Computer Technology Review*, October 1999.

Murphy, Patricia A. "Building an Internet Payments Platform." *Bank Technology News*, September 2000.

Nailen, Richard L. "As the World Turns, Standards Writing Gets More Complex." *Electrical Apparatus*, December 2000.

Zuckerman, Amy. "Hot Global Standards and Testing Trends." *World Trade*, October 2000.

ANALOG

Information can be presented in one of two formats, analog or digital. The main difference between the two involves continuity. Analog information is representative of the way events or phenomena unfold in the real world. Mechanical wristwatches are an excellent example because the hands of a watch display every possible point in time as they unfold, including the very smallest fractional units, in a smooth, continuous, uninterrupted fashion. Other examples of analog devices are thermometers and speedometers, the measurements on which correspond directly to conditions in the real world. By comparison, digital devices are only able to display information in finite units (10 degrees versus, for example, 10.0625 degrees).

Although the majority of computers are digital machines, meaning that they process information in a binary format of zeros and ones (0, 1, 10, 11, 100, 111, and so on), analog computers do exist. They are used for simulating real-world systems in the fields of hydraulics, electronics, nuclear power, and so forth. Through the use of a component called an operational amplifier, these devices create complicated mathematical expressions that companies and scientists use to make more informed decisions.

ANALOG COMPUTING

The world's oldest analog computer was developed in Ancient Greece, around 80 BCE. Experts believe that the Antikythera mechanism, named after the Greek island nearest to the shipwreck on which it was discovered in 1901, was intended to predict eclipses. The Antikythera mechanism possesses a complex array of gears, and it was not until the fourteenth century in Europe that devices of similar complexity, such as astronomical clocks, were produced.

Study of the Antikythera mechanism was funded, in part, by Hewlett-Packard. In 2005, the computer supplier sent a team to the National Archaeological Museum in Athens to use advanced reflectance imaging techniques, which led to successive discoveries regarding the uses of the mechanism. Based upon the inscriptions on the device, it was thought to have been used to help determine the ideal timing for the Greek precursor to the Olympic Games. Calculations were displayed on a wheel that was cranked manually. Dials connected by complex arrays of gears would turn and be interpreted visually with an uncanny degree of precision.

While some analog devices still are used in the 2010s, digital electronic devices are more prominent by an overwhelming margin, although some people in various industries (such as sound recording) still maintain that analog is superior in terms of quality.

SEE ALSO *Digital.*

BIBLIOGRAPHY

The Antikythera Mechanism Research Project. "Project Overview." Wales, UK, 2011. Available from http://www.antikythera-mechanism.gr/project/overview.

"Digital and Analog Information." *The PC Guide,* May 9, 2001. Available from http://www.pcguide.com/intro/works/computDigital-c.html.

Freeth, Tony. "Decoding an Ancient Computer: Greek Technology Tracked the Heavens." *Scientific American,* November 30, 2009. Available from http://www.scientificamerican.com/article.cfm?id=decoding-an-ancient-computer.

Massey, Howard. "Analog vs. Digital." The International Association of Electronic Keyboard Manufacturers, May 12, 2001.

"The Mathematics of Computing." *The PC Guide,* May 9, 2001. Available from http://www.pcguide.com/intro/works/computMath-c.html.

ANDREESSEN, MARC

Marc Andreessen first made his mark by developing breakthrough Internet browser software, first with Mosaic and then with Netscape Navigator, and he cofounded Netscape Communications Corp. with Jim Clark. After Netscape was acquired by America Online and Sun Microsystems, Andreessen served as AOL's chief technology officer for about six months. He left AOL in September 1999, and the following month announced the formation of Loudcloud Inc., a new e-commerce services company that built complicated Web sites and infrastructure, while providing a range of support services. Loudcloud survived the dot-com bust, weathering numerous ups and downs until changing its name to Opsware and being sold to Hewlett-Packard for $1.6 billion in 2007. By that time, Andreessen also had cofounded Ning, a social media platform generator, and started venture capital firm Andreessen Horowitz with long-time partner Ben Horowitz two years later.

EARLY LIFE

Andreessen was born in Iowa in 1972 and grew up with his parents in the small town of New Lisbon, Wisconsin. He took an early interest in computers, writing his first program on a school computer when he was in the sixth grade. The program was designed to complete his homework assignments for him, but it was promptly lost when a school staff member unknowingly turned off the power supply to the building. The next year his parents bought him his own computer, a TRS-80 from Radio Shack. Marc taught himself BASIC, a programming language known for its simplicity, so he could create video games for his new computer.

After graduating from high school, Andreessen attended the University of Illinois at Champaign-Urbana. It was while working at the university's National Center for Supercomputing Applications (NCSA) that he became interested in the Internet. At the NCSA he worked with master programmer Eric Bina to develop an interface for the World Wide Web that would integrate text, graphics, and sound. In 1993, the NCSA team completed an interface called Mosaic and made it available for free over the Internet. More than two million copies of the browser were downloaded in the first year, and Mosaic was responsible for a ten-thousandfold increase in Web users over a period of two years.

Andreessen graduated from college in 1993 and took a job with California-based Enterprise Integration Technologies, which made Internet security enhancement products. However, one day he received an e-mail message from Jim Clark, a former associate professor of computer science at Stanford University. Clark was something of an entrepreneur, having founded Silicon Graphics Inc. He had heard of Andreessen and Mosaic. After pushing around a number of possibilities, Andreessen ventured the idea that "We could always build a Mosaic killer—build a better product and build a business around it." The two decided to combine Andreessen's technical know-how with Clark's business expertise to launch their own company in 1994.

NETSCAPE COMMUNICATIONS CORP.

At first the new company was called Mosaic Communications Corp. However, the NCSA, which held the copyright to Mosaic software, objected, and the company was renamed Netscape Communications Corp. Andreessen, then 22 years old, became Netscape's vice president of technology, or chief technology officer (CTO). His job was to make the Web browser Mosaic faster and more interactive, which leveraged many of the skills he came to be known for, namely quick, innovative, abstract thinking. At the same time, he was insulated from day-to-day management, which even he admitted (in an interview with *Wired*) that he would not be good at. Later, when he cofounded Loudcloud, he ceded the position of chief executive officer (CEO) to Ben Horowitz, explaining, "I would hate the job and I wouldn't be particularly good at it. I can contribute more if I don't have to be consistent. I am free to drive everyone crazy with new ideas and impatience. I'm happy to push people right to the edge."

Andreessen persuaded several NCSA team members to join him at Netscape, and soon the company released its new browser. While the development team wanted to call it Mozilla, short for Mosaic Killer, the company's marketing executives insisted on calling it Netscape Navigator.

Like Mosaic before it, Netscape Navigator was distributed for free on the Internet and quickly became very popular. The development of a downloadable browser and its introduction in October 1994 removed a significant technological hurdle for people seeking to go online; *E-Commerce Times* considered it one of the ten key moments in the making of e-commerce. It was Netscape's browser that established the brand name, and that name soon became well known, prompting computer users to try other Netscape products. Soon, the company was profitable, and on August 9, 1995, made its initial public offering (IPO). On the first day of the IPO, Netscape's shares opened at $7 and closed at $29 after reaching a high of $36. In one day, Andreessen, who had worked at NSCA for $6.85 an hour, achieved a net worth of more than $50 million. By the end of 1995 his shares were worth $171 million.

For some time, Netscape enjoyed little or no competition for its browser. It was clear, however, by 1997 that Netscape was losing market share to Microsoft, which had introduced a competing browser—Internet Explorer 2.0—in 1995, followed by Explorer 3.0 in 1996. Andreessen, as Netscape's executive vice president in charge of product development, oversaw a staff of 1,000 tasked with staying ahead of the software giant. The most serious blow to Netscape's market position occurred when Microsoft brought out Internet Explorer 4.0 in September 1997 and bundled it with its Windows operating system. Netscape began to lose money, and by April 1998 Microsoft had captured some 40% of the browser market, while Netscape's share had shrunk from around 80% to 60%.

Andreessen refocused Netscape toward enterprise software for corporate intranets and electronic commerce in an effort to develop new sources of revenue. Before the year was over, however, America Online and Sun Microsystems announced they would jointly acquire Netscape's assets for $4.2 billion. Sun took over Netscape's intellectual property and the continuing development of its products, while America Online got Netscape's popular Web portal Net Center and other assets. After the acquisition was completed in 1999, Andreessen became AOL's chief technology officer and worked from an office at AOL's headquarters in Virginia. Andreessen soon got restless, and he resigned in September 1999.

LOUDCLOUD, NING, AND ANDREESSEN HOROWITZ

The next month Andreessen announced the formation of a new company called Loudcloud Inc., which would provide technology, infrastructure, and services to Internet companies and e-commerce Web sites. The company was cofounded by Andreessen, who would serve as chairman, and Ben Horowitz, who became president and CEO. Getting the company off the ground was not a difficult task, considering Netscape's recent success and Andreessen's charisma.

Loudcloud officially opened for business in February 2000 with seven customers and $68 million in venture capital financing. Yet the company, even with its prescient ideas about cloud computing, experienced difficulties. In late 2002, it reached a low point, with shares selling at 40 cents apiece. Nonetheless, five years later, after switching names to Opsware and making a number of versatile shifts in the new marketplace, the company was purchased by Hewlett-Packard (HP) for $1.6 billion. Though it was not a business success of the same degree as Netscape, the idea behind Loudcloud continued to define the Internet in 2011, as quickly growing companies turned to cloud software and software as a service (SaaS) as the new horizon of electronic commerce.

Before the HP-Opsware deal, Andreessen had turned some of his attention to Ning. Ning was based on an idea that was similar in concept to Loudcloud but focused on social media networks. The company offered modules via cloud software and storage space that would allow businesses or individuals to create their own social network Web pages. Loudcloud had been focused on the same principle of not only tapping into a market by supplying a product, but also controlling the market by using technology to drastically reduce the time and funding required for production. In essence, it was a strategy to become a supplier of suppliers. With cloud technology, Ning would facilitate the production of social media sites and allow clients to become producers.

In 2009, Andreessen shifted from entrepreneur to a venture capitalist, cofounding a venture capital firm with Horowitz called Andreessen Horowitz. In the early 2010s, the firm has investments in a variety of prominent social media companies, including Facebook, Twitter, and Groupon.

SEE ALSO *Clark, Jim; Netscape Communications Corp.*.

BIBLIOGRAPHY

Andreessen, Marc. "An Update from Ning Chairman & Co-Founder Marc Andreesseen." *Ning*, Palo Alto, CA, March 15, 2010. Available from http://www.ning.com/blog/author/pmarca.

Barnett, Emma. "Ning Chief: Businesses Need to Reclaim Their Online Identities and Go Social." *Telegraph*, August 29, 2011. Available from http://www.telegraph.co.uk/technology/social-media/8673637/Ning-chief-Businesses-need-to-reclaim-their-online-identities-and-go-social.html.

Byron, Christopher. "Netscape Founder Offers a New Cash-Burning Dot-Com." *Los Angeles Business Journal*, February 26, 2001.

Chandrasekaran, Rajiv. "Netscape's Boy Wonder Looks Beyond the Browser." *Washington Post*, March 25, 1997.

Elmer-DeWitt, Philip. "How the Internet Was Tamed." *TIME*, September 26, 1994.

Henry, Shannon. "Andreessen to Start New Firm." *Washington Post,* October 27, 1999.

Herhold, Scott. "Netscape Co-Founder to Launch Start-Up as Talent Exodus Continues." *Knight-Ridder/Tribune Business News,* October 26, 1999.

Hill, Jonathan. "Marc Andreessen and Ben Horowitz." *Internet World,* October 15, 2000.

Kaplan, David A. "Nothing but Net." *Newsweek,* December 25, 1995.

"The Last Days of Net Mania." *Business Week,* April 16, 2001.

Nash, Kim S. "Hey! Don't Call It a Browser." *Computerworld,* October 21, 1996.

"A New Electronic Messiah." *Economist (U.S.),* August 15, 1995.

"A Pioneer Once More." *Business Week,* February 28, 2000.

Sheff, David. "Crank It Up." *Wired,* August, 2000. Available from http://byliner.com/david-sheff/stories/crank-it-up.

Sliwa, Carol. "Andreessen Targets Web Outsource Model." *Computerworld,* September 25, 2000.

Tetzeli, Rick. "What It's Really Like to Be Marc Andreessen." *Fortune,* December 9, 1996.

Tetzeli, Rick, and David Kirkpatrick. "Marc Andreessen: 'The Concept of Being Always On Is a Very Powerful One.'" *Fortune,* October 9, 2000.

ANGEL INVESTORS

In a sense, angel investing has been around as long as business itself. Traditionally, before an entrepreneur even created a sound or promising business plan or prototype to attract seed money from institutional investors, he or she would seek initial start-up funds from a wealthy patron. Angels provide entrepreneurs with the early-stage seed money needed to get on their feet, while venture capital (VC) firms tend to steer their money toward firms that are in the later stages of early development, closer to an initial public offering (IPO). In addition, angels put their own money into companies, unlike venture capitalist firms, which pool funds and invest them in a manner similar to mutual funds.

Risk is an inherent component for angels. Besides backing entrepreneurs that are not yet attractive enough for VC funds, angels also eschew other investment safeguards, such as Federal Deposit Insurance Corp. (FDIC)-insured accounts. With excess money at their disposal, angels more or less take a chance when handing checks over to entrepreneurs, albeit not without an often-heavy hand in guiding the development process. And even in the fairy-tale dot-com boom of the late 1990s and early 2000s, the risk was very real; roughly nine out of ten angel investments proved to be washouts. However, the high yield of winners makes the field what it is. Thus, angels tend to approach their investments as though they were buying lottery tickets; it takes only one success to hit it big, and that one easily pays for all the others.

Different angels have different styles. While some bring in lawyers to negotiate deals and demand a great deal of say in company development, others are more relaxed and hands-off. Some specialize in greasing the wheels between entrepreneurs, banks, and investors, while other angels concentrate almost exclusively on seeking out new entrepreneurs, giving little attention to how things progress. Hands-off angels work on the idea that one big winner will pay for the less-sound investments. There also are those philanthropic angels who, with money to spare, throw it behind valuable and socially redeemable projects out of altruistic motives.

ANGELS AFTER THE DOT-COM FALL

After the dot-com bubble burst in the early 2000s, angel investments took a steep plunge. By 2002, the $40 billion market had declined to roughly $15.7 billion in investments. At that time, according to the Venture Capital Center, total investments were dispersed among 36,000 entrepreneurial endeavors, a number that suggested angels were spending about half the money they had spent in 2001 but were spending it on 75% of the number of investments. Roughly 40% of investments were in software, with life sciences (excluding biotech) comprising another 14% of the total.

Angel investing suffered from a number of problems throughout the 2000s. Internet businesses had lost assurance of returns in software, but no other fields had gained sufficient attention to warrant mass investment. In addition, many angel investors had lost or nearly lost their investments. In response, the field consolidated, regrouped, and invested more conservatively. A number of angel organizations were formed in order to pool resources and share risk. Whereas in 2000 there were 150 angel clubs in the United States, by 2010 there were over 330 angel groups in the Angel Capital Association alone. The association had been formed in 2004 to "support the growth, financial stability and investment success of its member angel groups." Many individual member groups shared a similar philosophy but for their individual members. Some of these angel groups would focus on a particular geographical area or industry in order to specialize.

Angels also found their role shifting, as different expectations were placed upon them. They were more conservative, and their time was therefore in shorter supply. During the global recession of 2008–2009, many angel organizations began to charge initial payments, either for services, seminars, or to review business plans. Maverick Angels, one such group, charged $495 for training and $1,000 for introductions to potential investors, apiece. Angel funding was also requested by more than just entrepreneurs. In an interview with the *New York Times,* the managing partner of Vantage Group and the founder of a number of angel organizations, John May, stated: "We're seeing a new kind of applicant, distressed properties.... Companies that may have had their loan called or credit line reduced with the words 'through no fault of your own' are looking to angels."

In 2010, the angel investment portfolio had shifted drastically in terms of industry and risk. According to the Center for Venture Research, health care, medical services, and equipment took the majority of funding, with 30% of investments. Software and biotechnology were approximately tied for second and third place, with 15% apiece. Ventures had reached a much higher level of stability, with half of angel exits resulting in profit, though the margin was variable. Total investments were also up from the previous year, reaching $20.1 billion. Roughly two-thirds of funding went to companies that had already passed the start-up stage and were in the early and expansion stage. Nonetheless, the Center for Venture Research projected more spending on start-ups in following years.

SEE ALSO *Financing, Securing.*

BIBLIOGRAPHY

Angel Capital Association. "ACA Mission & Leadership." Overland, KS, 2011. Available from http://www.angelcapitalassociation.org/about-aca.

Center for Venture Research. "Full Year 2002 Angel Market Analysis Report." Durham, NH: University of New Hampshire, Whittemore School of Business and Economics. Available from http://wsbe.unh.edu/cvr-analysis-reports.

Colkin, Eileen. "Pennies from Heaven Keep on Falling." *InformationWeek,* January 29, 2000.

Darrow, Barbara. "Touched by an Angel." *Computer Reseller News,* April 17, 2000.

Flanagan, James. "Angel Investors Become a Little Less So." *New York Times,* August 19, 2009. Available from http://www.nytimes.com/2009/08/20/business/smallbusiness/20edge.html.

Fox, Loren. "Another Face for Venture Capitalism." *Upside,* October 1999.

Gordon, Joanne. "Wings." *Forbes,* October 30, 2000.

Helyar, John. "The Venture Capitalist Next Door." *Fortune,* November 13, 2000.

Sohl, Jeffrey. "The Angel Investor Market in 2010: A Market on the Rebound." Durham, NH: University of New Hampshire, Whittemore School of Business and Economics, Center for Venture Research, April 12, 2011. Available from http://www.unh.edu/news/docs/2010angelanalysis.pdf.

Van Osnabrugge, Mark, and Robert J. Robinson. *Angel Investing: Matching Startup Funds with Startup Companies.* San Francisco: Jossey-Bass, 2000.

AOL, INC.

AOL began as America Online in the 1990s and quickly rose to prominence as a major supplier of Internet services. The company has gone through several iterations, first as America Online, then as AOL Time Warner after a major 2000 merger, and finally simply AOL, Inc., after the large split and spin-off in 2009 that again separated the two companies. In the early 2010s, AOL continued to focus on a variety of Internet services and applications.

HISTORY OF AMERICA ONLINE

America Online's roots go back to 1985, when Steve Case and Jim Kimsey founded Quantum Computer Services. Quantum provided online services for users of Commodore computers, then a popular brand of home computers. Two years later Quantum began providing online services for Apple Computer, Inc.'s operating system and developing software for both the Macintosh and the Apple II. After that Quantum grew quickly and was soon providing online services and related software for other companies, including Tandy Corporation and computer industry leader IBM Corp.

Quantum's costs were high, and it quickly ran through its capital. In 1991, Quantum was renamed America Online, with Case taking Kimsey's place as CEO and Kimsey becoming chairman of the company. AOL held its initial public offering in March 1992 and raised $66 million, with shares initially selling for $1.64.

At that time, the two leaders in providing online services were Prodigy and CompuServe. Case focused on achieving market dominance and pursued a strategy that included forming alliances with companies that would benefit AOL. He dropped membership prices below that of the major competitors and shipped out huge quantities of software diskettes to potential customers, offering them a free trial period using the AOL service. These marketing efforts paid off in rapid membership growth for AOL, and by the end of 1993 the company had more than 600,000 subscribers.

AOL was the subject of two takeover attempts in 1993, one from Microsoft cofounder Paul Allen, the other from Microsoft head Bill Gates. Allen, who had already left Microsoft, acquired a 24.9% interest in AOL and attempted to secure a seat on its board of directors. Both takeover attempts were thwarted by Case and AOL, eventually prompting Microsoft to develop its own online service, the Microsoft Network.

Key acquisitions in late 1994 helped AOL provide its subscribers with access to the World Wide Web, a part of the Internet that was quickly becoming popular because of its open platform and ease of use via graphical browsers like Netscape. Until this time AOL was essentially a closed network that offered subscribers access only to its own content providers, vendors, and other AOL subscribers. Content agreements with the *New York Times, TIME,* NBC, and others had expanded AOL's content, but it was an essential part of the company's strategy to become a gateway to the Internet. This strategy was facilitated by the acquisition of Advanced Network Services, Inc., which built fiber optic networks to support Internet access. This was followed by the acquisition of BookLink Technologies and the Global Network Navigator, which enabled AOL customers to browse the Internet using graphic browsing software from BookLink. Later, in 1996, AOL would reach agreements with Netscape and Microsoft, who were competing heavily in the browser market, to use their browsers.

AOL began to grow more rapidly as it added new content providers and gave its subscribers greater access to the public Internet. In March 1995, AOL's subscriber base reached two million, and by August 1996 the company had six million subscribers. In October 1996, AOL introduced flat-rate service for a monthly fee of $19.95. In 1996, Bob Pittman, founder of MTV and considered a successful brand-builder, was hired to improve AOL's customer service and strengthen AOL's brand among consumers. After Pittman reduced AOL's subscriber growth to a sustainable level and improved the company's customer service reputation, he was promoted to president and chief operating officer. Case gave up his title of president and remained chairman and CEO.

By 1997, AOL had 9 million subscribers. During the year it gained 2.6 million CompuServe subscribers, which it continued to operate as a separate business. AOL's stock rose 600% in 1998 and even more in 1999. This infusion of market capital gave it the power to make more and bigger acquisitions. In November 1998, AOL announced it would acquire Netscape Communications Corp. for $4.2 billion in stock, about 10% of AOL's market value. Included in the acquisition were the Web browser Netscape Navigator and Netscape's Web portal, Netcenter. A third party to the acquisition was Sun Microsystems, which agreed to pay $350 million over three years to license Netscape's software, while AOL agreed to purchase $500 million worth of servers from Sun. The Sun-Netscape alliance adopted the brand iPlanet to market the next generation of Netscape Web and application servers. During 2000, AOL recast Netscape Netcenter as a business professional's portal, and in Fall 2000 AOL unveiled its new Netscape Netbusiness service, which was designed to help small businesses build Web-based storefronts and engage in business-to-business e-commerce.

In January 2000, AOL announced its bid to acquire Time Warner Inc. for approximately $165 billion in stock, with the exact value to be determined by the stock prices of both firms after the acquisition was finalized. By that point AOL alone had four major lines of business: the Interactive Services Group, the Interactive Properties Group, the AOL International Group, and the Netscape Enterprise Group.

THE AOL TIME WARNER MERGER

When AOL announced its intention to acquire Time Warner, AOL's stock was near its all-time high. In the month following the announcement AOL's stock lost about 30% of its value. The announcement caused Time Warner's stock to rise nearly 50% before settling back some 20% off its peak.

In addition to requiring the shareholders' approval at both companies, the merger had to pass regulatory approval from the European Union, the Federal Trade Commission (FTC), and the Federal Communications Commission (FCC). While the merger was being reviewed, both companies undertook actions that would appease regulators. Both promised they would not block other Internet service providers or content providers from using their distribution system. In March 2000, AOL announced it would pay up to $8.25 billion to buy out German media conglomerate Bertelsmann AG's interest in AOL Europe and AOL Australia, a move to allay fears that Bertelsmann and AOL Time Warner would pool their interests to undermine other competitors. Bertelsmann, whose holdings included book publishers and record labels, was considered a competitor to Time Warner, particularly in the music business.

Several companies that were opposed to the merger joined together to lobby U.S. regulators to impose strict limits on the proposed company's business practices. Leading the group was the Walt Disney Co., which benefited from the keyword shortcut of "Disney" on the AOL service and also ran its Disney Channel over several Time Warner cable franchises. Disney proposed that regulators split AOL Time Warner into two companies, one for handling content and the other for handling distribution. In May 2000, the National Association of Broadcasters went on record with the FCC opposing the merger and asked the FCC to require that AOL Time Warner not discriminate against properties they did not own. SBC Communications Inc. also joined the opposition to the merger, expressing concern about AOL Time Warner's interlocking business relationships with competing telephone carriers such as AT&T-Media One and Bell Atlantic-GTE (later reconfigured as Verizon).

Following a lengthy FCC hearing in July, Time Warner announced an agreement in August with Juno Online Services Inc. that gave the Internet service provider (ISP) access to Time Warner's cable subscribers. The agreement was Time Warner's first with an unaffiliated ISP and allowed Juno to offer its services to cable subscribers. As part of the deal the two companies would split the Internet access subscription revenue from the service.

The FTC gave its approval to the merger on December 14, 2000. Focusing on Time Warner's vast cable television network, the FTC required that Time Warner open its cable lines to ISPs that competed with AOL, in effect turning Time Warner's privately owned system into a kind of public channel for Internet access, much in the way telephone systems were treated under the telecommunications regulatory reforms of the middle and late 1990s. In addition to the agreement with Earthlink, AOL Time Warner was required to make deals with two other competing ISPs within 90 days of making AOL available to Time Warner subscribers in large markets. Such deals would also require the approval of the FTC. The FTC requirements were to remain in effect for five years.

FCC approval, with some additional conditions, quickly followed in January 2001. The value of the merger was estimated at approximately $110 billion, with AOL's stock trading at about half of its value at the time the merger was originally announced. The new company began business with about 88,500 employees. Prominent figures from both companies were chosen for the executive team, but some favor was given to the acquirer, AOL. Steve Case became chairman of the new company, while Time Warner's chairman Gerald Levin was named CEO. Ted Turner was named vice chairman; however, within a year he was forced out of that role in a board reshuffling.

ROCKY MERGER

By 2009, the merger was still the largest of its kind in American history, but the online landscape had utterly changed and the differences between the two companies were seen as irreconcilable. The deal was supposed to cement the future of online activity by eventually taking the place of traditional media channels and allowing for nearly unlimited untapped potential. Unfortunately, the companies were simply too different in operations and business modeling. With too much focus placed on selling Web connectivity and not enough on platform, communication, and design work, problems rose quickly. The AOL model that had worked in the 1990s began to falter in the 2000s as more and more companies offered increased competition, including services like e-mail and chatting without the need for a full subscription or fees.

As a result, the merger led to job losses, desperate tapping of company funds, the elimination of many company retirement accounts, and investigations by the Securities and Exchange Commission (SEC) and Justice Department. By 2009, the companies had split apart again, and the AOL division was known simply as AOL, Inc. once more. Combined, the total value of the two now-separate corporations was only a seventh of what it had been at the time of the merger.

NEW PROJECTS AND ACQUISITIONS IN THE 2000s

While the merger with Time Warner was seen as an example of one of the worst tech partnerships, AOL faced additional struggles as the 2000s progressed. Following the dot-com bust, company advertising revenues plummeted. New technology soon made cable and direct phone Internet connections the most efficient way of using the Internet, rapidly taking business away from the dial-up focus that had been AOL's specialty for years. The company peaked at 27 million subscribers in 2002 and started slowing down in growth. Google, Yahoo!, and social networking sites all began offering services for free that AOL had been charging for since the early days of widespread Internet use. In the struggle to change its business model accordingly, the company began losing vast portions of its revenue.

The next several years marked both the beginning and the downfall of major AOL projects. While AOL bought MapQuest in 1999 and cornered the market on online mapping for a short time, by 2004 Google had developed Google Maps, which swiftly took over the lion's share of the market. Seeing the success of MySpace and the rise of Facebook, the company attempted to start AIM Pages as a social network of its own, but the project was unsuccessful. In 2006, AOL committed itself to free content for all users, but in the process released private search records and faced both public anger and a lawsuit. Ad revenue growth began falling markedly behind even the industry average, and by 2007 more than 2,000 layoffs were planned for the company.

The AOL solution to these problems appeared to be acquisitions. While AOL had a previous habit of buying start-ups and smaller service providers, it continued the expensive habit even after revenues began dropping. In 2004, it bought Advertising.com, and in 2007 it purchased Third Screen Media for $105.4 million (as well as Tacoda and Quigo). In 2008, it purchased the British social network Bebo. In the 15 months after the Time Warner spin-off, AOL bought 14 more businesses for more than $600 million. Both Patch.com and Going.com were acquired in 2009, as well as MMAFighting.com. In 2010, the company acquired StudioNow for $36.5 million, the mobile networking business RallyUp with its popular iPhone application, the video content syndication network 5min, the tech blog TechCrunch ($40 million), and many others.

A trend began to emerge with these purposes: a desperate bid to catch up to the Internet giants that had overtaken AOL years ago and become, not a service provider, but a key content provider. The acquisitions culminated in the merger with the Huffington Post, one of the largest news Web sites in the United States, for which AOL paid $315 million, the largest deal since the infamous Time Warner agreement.

The deal showed a key change for AOL's business focus. Arianna Huffington, the owner of the Huffington Post, agreed to take control of AOL editorial content, creating a new combined corporation known as the Huffington Post Media Group. With Huffington spearheading national, local, and financial news operations in addition to other media ventures like Moviefone, she became the new face of AOL. The Huffington Post was a private company, and Huffington admitted to posting a profit for the first time in 2010, but it was growing compared to the shrinking state of AOL and offered strength for AOL's new editorial focus.

As the merger went ahead, it was difficult to say whether the new company would be able to secure profits. In 2010, ad revenue was down 29% for AOL compared to 2009, and the company had to sell the social network Bebo for 1/85th of what it originally acquired it for in 2008. However, the other acquisitions left the company with room to develop in the future, and Tim Armstrong, the CEO governing the Huffington Post merger, promised a new era for the Internet corporation.

SEE ALSO *Case, Stephen.*

BIBLIOGRAPHY

"AOL LLC.'s Acquisitions." *New York Times,* May 9, 2011. Available from http://topics.nytimes.com/top/news/business/companies/aol/index.html.

Arango, Tim. "How the AOL-Time Warner Merger Went So Wrong." *New York Times,* January 10, 2010. Available from http://www.nytimes.com/2010/01/11/business/media/11merger.html?pagewanted=all.

Bercovici, Jeff. "Will Huffpo Join AOL's $11.4 Billion History of Bad Ideas?" *Forbes,* February 7, 2011. Available from http://www.forbes.com/sites/jeffbercovici/2011/02/07/will-huffpo-join-aols-11-3-billion-history-of-bad-deals.

Gunther, Marc. "Understanding AOL's Grand United Theory of the Media Cosmos." *Fortune,* January 8, 2001.

Halonen, Doug. "Kennard FCC's Last Act—AOL Merger OK'd." *Electronic Media,* January 15, 2001.

Peters, Jeremy W. "Betting on News, AOL Is Buying the Huffington Post." *New York Times,* February 7, 2011. Available from http://www.nytimes.com/2011/02/07/business/media/07aol.html.

Rockwood, Kate. "You've Got Problems!" *Fast Company,* April 1, 2008. Available from http://www.fastcompany.com/magazine/124/youve-got-problems.html.

Sandberg, Jared. "Net Gain." *Newsweek,* December 7, 1998.

"A Short History of AOL.'s Acquisitions." *CNBC,* 2011. Available from http://www.cnbc.com/id/41461459/A_Short_History_of_AOL_s_Acquisitions.

Sullivan, John, and Michael Robuck. "AOL and Time Warner." *Boardwatch Magazine,* February 2001.

Swisher, Kara. *AOL.com: How Steve Case Beat Bill Gates, Nailed the Netheads & Made Millions in the War for the Web.* New York: Crown Publishing, 1999.

APPLE INC.

Apple Inc., once known primarily for its Macintosh personal computers (PCs), including the colorful iMac, has since expanded its influence across a wide spectrum of media by introducing revolutionary products such as the iPod, the iPhone, and the iPad. As a result, the company changed its name; once called Apple Computer, it is now simply known as Apple. Although Apple's share of the worldwide PC market had dwindled to less than 3% by 2001, just a decade later, thanks to its innovative products and marketing approach, including opening hundreds of retail stores nationwide and in other countries, Apple was considered a leading global technology company and one of the most innovative in the world.

Much of Apple's success was attributed to cofounder Steve Jobs, who resigned as CEO of Apple on August 25, 2011, due to his battle with pancreatic cancer. Jobs died in early October, and there was concern that as a result of his death, the company's ability to design and introduce innovative new products may be seriously impaired.

EARLY HISTORY

Stephen G. Wozniak and Steven P. Jobs founded Apple Computer Co. in April 1976. The partners launched operations by making and selling a computer circuit board, dubbed the Apple I. The machine had no keyboard, case, sound, or graphics. Computer retailing chain Byte Shop ordered 50 Apple I units a month later, and Jobs used his parents' garage as a temporary manufacturing site. Mike Markkula, a former marketing executive for both Intel Corp. and Fairchild Semiconductor, paid $250,000 for a 33% stake in Apple and helped Jobs to create a long-term business plan. In 1977, the firm unveiled the Apple II—the first PC to offer color graphics capacity. The new machine also included a keyboard, power supply, case, and 4KB of standard memory. That year, the company's sales reached $1 million.

Apple's earliest venture into online technology came in 1978 when it began offering Apple II users a telephone-based connection service to Dow Jones. Just two years after its inception, the company became one of the fastest-growing companies in the United States. Sales grew tenfold, and the firm's dealer network grew to include roughly 300 distributors. Employees were required to give up their typewriters in favor of PCs in 1979. The firm also released the Apple II Plus, which offered 48KB of memory, and the first Apple printer, known as the Silentype. In an effort to tap into the school market, Apple established the Apple Education Foundation. Sales of the Apple II jumped 40%, reaching 35,000 units, and the company's employees totaled 250.

In 1980, Apple released the Apple III, its most advanced machine to date. Boasting a new operating system, a built-in disk controller, and four peripheral slots, the Apple III was priced at $3,495—nearly double the price of its predecessors. To bolster international sales, Apple constructed a manufacturing plant in Ireland

and a European support center in the Netherlands. EDUNET, an online network serving professionals in higher education and research fields, adopted the Apple II as its network access PC. Apple also established Apple Seed, a computer program designed to promote computer literacy among elementary and high school students. That year, the firm conducted its initial public offering (IPO), selling 4.6 million shares at $22 apiece. At that time, employees exceeded 1,000. With a dealer network of 800 distributors in the United States and Canada, and another 1,000 distributors overseas, Apple had the farthest reach of any major player in the computer industry.

In 1981, Apple established offices in both France and England. Of the firm's 40 new product releases that year, the most notable were the Apple Language Card, which increased the compatibility of Apple II machines with programs written in languages such as Pascal and Fortran; the IEEE-488 interface card, which allowed Apple II units to work with more than 1,400 scientific and technical instruments; and Profile, a 5MB hard disk. In 1982, Apple became the first PC company to attain sales of $1 billion. Competition intensified as more than 100 companies started manufacturing PCs. Apple unveiled its dot matrix printer that year. In 1983, Apple introduced the Apple IIe and Apple III Plus PCs; the ImageWriter printer and other peripheral devices; and AppleWorks, a suite of products including word processing, spreadsheet, and database software. The firm was ranked 411th on the *Fortune* 500 list.

ADVENT OF THE MACINTOSH

Apple shipped its blockbuster Macintosh machine in 1984, after first advertising it on television during the Super Bowl. Initial versions of the Macintosh retailed for $2,495, while the more powerful Macintosh 512KB was priced at $3,195. That year, the firm established the Apple University Consortium, which included 24 major colleges and universities that collectively agreed to use the Macintosh for educational programs and to spend $61 million over a three-year period. Other product releases included 300- and 1200-baud modems, the Scribe printer, and the Apple IIc. By the year's end, more than 400,000 Apple IIc machines had been sold.

The LaserWriter printer—priced at roughly $7,000—made its debut in 1985, as did the AppleTalk Personal Network. Northern Telecom and Apple began working together to connect Macintosh computers via telephone lines. An inventory glut prompted the firm to shut down manufacturing plants for one week. The firm also permanently closed three of its six plants and laid off 20% of its workforce, roughly 1,200 employees. As a result, Apple posted its first-ever quarterly loss, and Jobs resigned to start a new computer venture. The AppleLink telecommunications network went online that year, connecting Apple employees, dealers, and suppliers to Apple information libraries, as well as to each other via e-mail.

By 1986, more than 200,000 AppleTalk local area computer networks were in place. Internationally, Apple had extended its reach to 80 countries. Earnings rebounded, growing 151% to reach a record high. The following year, new product releases included desktop communications products, such as the AppleTalk PC Card and the AppleShare file server, as well as an updated version of Apple IIe and the next generation of Macintosh PCs. Apple also founded Claris, an independent software manufacturer.

The late 1980s were marked by a series of strategic alliances with other leading technology firms. The firm worked with Texas Instruments to integrate Macintosh II with Texas Instruments' Explorer Lisp coprocessor board. The joint venture with Texas Instrument proved to be one of Apple's largest value-added reseller agreements for the Macintosh line. That year, Apple filed suit against Microsoft Corp. for allegedly using the "look and feel" of the Macintosh operating system as the basis for its increasingly popular Windows platform. Apple's lawyers requested that Microsoft either pay royalties or simply stop selling Windows. Net income exceeded $400 million on revenues of roughly $4 billion.

In response to intense competition, Apple reduced its prices in 1990 and introduced a series of low-cost Macintosh PCs. The following year, it shipped several low-cost printers. Apple also asked the Federal Communications Commission (FCC) to allow computers to send and receive information over radio waves. The FCC granted permission for this type of electronic communication, and the decision fostered the development of a new class of data communications known as Data Personal Communications Services.

In 1991, in an effort to steal market share back from Microsoft, IBM and Apple forged an alliance to develop a new operating system that would make computers easier to use and also increase compatibility between IBM and Apple machines. By then, roughly 90% of worldwide PCs used Microsoft's Windows platform, and Apple had broadened its litigation against Microsoft. However, a judge ruled in favor of Microsoft in 1992 after deciding that the appearance of the Macintosh operating system was not protected by Apple's copyrights. Apple appealed the decision, but the Supreme Court refused to hear Apple's case.

In 1993, Apple ranked as the world's second-largest PC maker, behind Microsoft. Sales exceeded $7 million, and employees totaled roughly 15,000. The following year, the firm unveiled its PowerPC microprocessor. In the mid-1990s, sales began to slow and inventory mounted, prompting Apple to cut its prices by up to 25%. Management shakeups also plagued the firm. Market share tumbled to 3.2% in 1997, and Apple posted a $1.1 billion loss. The firm then purchased NeXT Software Inc. from original Apple founder Steve Jobs, who agreed to serve as an advisor to Apple. Shortly thereafter, Jobs was reinstated as Apple's CEO.

INTERNET STRATEGY

The iMac, a PC designed to make Internet access as straightforward as possible, was launched in 1998. Available in a variety of bright colors, the iMac housed its monitor and hard drive in a single unit. The new machine's popularity boosted the performance of Apple, which earned $309 million in its first profitable year since 1995. In 1999, Apple released a laptop version of the iMac called the iBook.

The iMac was a key component of Jobs's strategy to gain Internet dominance by offering an easy-to-use machine along with a series of free Internet services known as iTools. These iTools included 20MB of online storage space, content filters for parents, e-mail and greeting card services, and a World Wide Web site rating system called iReview. In addition to the new machines and free services, Apple also released a new operating system, Mac OS X, in 2001.

APPLE AND INNOVATION

By the early 2000s, Apple had switched its focus from computers to other forms of communication. It revolutionized the music industry with the introduction of the iPod in late 2001. The iPod, a portable media player, allowed consumers to store nearly all of their favorite music in a single device that could be taken anywhere. The iPod was able to drive much-needed additional revenue to the company in two ways: sales of the iPod itself and sales of music for the iPod through the iTunes store, an online retail outlet. The enormous success of the iPod led to the development of several competing products, but none had the market presence and staying power of the original iPod.

Next, the company turned to another communications platform, the cellular phone. While other companies introduced their smartphones, Apple's iPhone was an immediate and uncontested market success. The iPhone was one of the first phones that allowed users to access the Internet, receive and send e-mails, and serve as a multiple media player. Originally, AT&T was the only cellular service provider that offered the iPhone, but by 2011 it was also available through Verizon. This led to another retail outlet for Apple, the App Store, which launched in 2008 and sold hundreds of thousands of downloadable applications designed for the iPhones.

NEW FRONTIERS AND CHALLENGES

By 2010, Apple's iPad was revolutionizing the mobile device industry. The iPad, a product that took the tablet PC industry by storm, is a touch screen device that allows users to read e-books, view movies, listen to music, play games, and access the Web. It can also run apps, purchased through the App Store, bringing in more sales and revenues to the company. Close to three million iPads were sold in the first few months of its launch.

In the early 2010s, Apple also offered Apple TV, which gave Apple device users a way to purchase and download TV shows, movies, music, and more directly from Apple. It partnered with Netflix so that Apple device users can download and watch their Netflix picks instantly. This is a change in philosophy from remaining a stand-alone provider.

Apple planned to continue its goal of innovating and predicting market trends and needs by launching a new product at the end of 2011 called iCloud. iCloud will allow users to store their music, videos, documents, photos, and most other files all in one location and download them to any of their Apple devices. These products are possible because of Apple's iOS, originally the operating system of the iPhone, which has since become an exclusive operting system for all of Apple's mobile devices. iOS cannot be licensed to other software developers, which has led to extensive criticism of the company. However, by 2010, the company was allowing third-party developers such as Flash to develop apps for Apple iOS-powered devices.

Another significant source of revenue for the company is its iAd offering. Application providers can have a share of the ad revenue generated by joining the iAd network. Advertisements appear as an application is opened. BMW, Best Buy, Nissan, and Target are all companies that have purchased advertising through iAd.

While the company still sells its brands of personal computers, its focus in the 2010s is clearly on leading the personal communication device industry and continuing to offer innovative products for this industry. It is unclear whether the death of Steve Jobs will have a significant impact on the company, but with 2011 revenue of $108 billion and profit of $26 billion, Apple is clearly doing quite well for the time being.

SEE ALSO *Jobs, Steven; Wozniak, Stephen.*

BIBLIOGRAPHY

"Apple Computer Inc." In *Notable Corporate Chronologies.* Farmington Hills, MI: Gale Group, 1999.

Apple Inc. "Annual Report 2010." Cupertino, CA, October 27, 2010. Available from http://investor.apple.com/secfiling.cfm?filingID=1193125-10-238044&CIK=320193>.

"Apple Incorporated." *New York Times,* November 15, 2011. Available from http://topics.nytimes.com/top/news/business/companies/apple_computer_inc/index.html.

"Apple Stronger, Not Out of the Woods." *Microprocessor Report,* March 29, 1999.

Bethoney, Herb. "Rumors of Apple's Death Are Greatly..." *eWeek,* April 23, 2001.

Deutschman, Alan. "Despite Recent Stock Slip, Jobs Isn't Finished With Apple." *Computer Reseller News,* October 16, 2000.

Haddad, Charles. "Steve Jobs's New Lesson Plan." *BusinessWeek Online,* March 28, 2001. Available from http://www.businessweek.com/bwdaily/dnflash/mar2001/nf20010328_888.htm.

"Steve Jobs' Apple Gets Way Cooler." *Fortune,* January 24, 2000.

APPLICATION SERVICE PROVIDER (ASP)

An application service provider (ASP) is a company that delivers and manages software applications and computer services from a remote data center to multiple users, though the term is now somewhat outdated. In concept, ASPs aim to serve some of the same functions for their clients as software as a service (SaaS) companies did after cloud computing began to take hold.

In the late twentieth century, companies typically accessed an ASP's applications and services over the Internet, through a virtual private network (VPN), or through dedicated lease lines. A wide range of both applications and communications and infrastructure capabilities were available from ASPs. Among the most commonly used types were enterprise applications, including enterprise resource planning (ERP), customer relationship management (CRM), supply management, human resources, and financial management. When it came to information technology (IT) and network infrastructure, ASPs offered delivery of network services, complex mission-critical hosting, software and hardware provisioning, infrastructure integration and support services, business continuity services, network management and administration services, and managed VPNs. ASPs also delivered network-based access to processing power and remote data storage facilities.

In addition to calling themselves ASPs, some were known as managed (or management) service providers (MSPs), network service providers (NSPs), netsourcers, total service providers (TSPs), and software rental companies. A full-service provider (FSP)—also known as a total service provider—is an ASP that offers a wide range of Web-based information technology services, such as planning and creating a Web presence, software applications, and Web hosting and maintenance. Business service providers (BSPs) are similar to ASPs in that they provide customers with application packages over networks. However, BSPs differ from ASPs in that they tend to tailor software packages to a customer's needs and offer back-office solutions for processes like payroll and bookkeeping. A management service provider (MSP) provided the personnel to manage and administer IT services for other companies, thus saving clients the need to have their own administrative personnel.

ASPs evolved from simply hosting Web services to building and managing e-commerce and platforms. They handled e-commerce issues such as security, registration, and payments, and also provided Internet-based technologies. ASPs could provide communications platforms for messaging, voicemail, IP fax, and hosted collaboration platforms, as well as portals that offered such services as free Web e-mail, contact management, and calendaring.

By hosting these services for other businesses, ASPs enabled smaller businesses to benefit from high-priced software packages and systems without having to purchase them. Larger companies tended to use ASPs for outsourcing, while smaller businesses with low budgets used them to gain access to high-end enterprise computing that would be too expensive to purchase. Whatever the size of the client company, using ASPs allowed businesses to focus their resources on their core competencies rather than on their information systems (IS) and information technology, two fundamental advantages that remained true for purchasers of cloud computing software in the 2010s.

ASPS DEVELOP TO SAAS, IAAS, AND PAAS

Many experts predicted that ASPs would break out in 2000 and that sales would skyrocket. According to the Gartner Group, companies spent $2.7 billion on ASPs in 2000 and were expected to increase spending to anywhere from $16 billion to $22.7 billion by 2003, suggesting a massive overhaul of the IT services industry. However, the transition was more difficult to achieve than anticipated. ASPs did not eliminate many IT requirements. Companies would still be required to support their own data, infrastructure, and platforms, rendering ASPs as merely useful, not necessary.

After the advent of cloud computing in 2005 and over the latter half of the 2000s, the market gradually developed ways to provide information systems' needs, ranging from software and storage to platforms and infrastructures. Services companies in IT would often offer a number of these functions in conjunction. They were called either software or storage as a service (SaaS), platform as a service (PaaS), or infrastructure as a service (IaaS). Alternatively, clients could opt for in-premise delivery for some or all of these features. Many companies offering these services would constrain themselves to one particular purpose, such as customer relations management (CRM).

Even with all of these technological advances, SaaS dominated the market with only $10 billion in revenues in 2010, according to a Gartner report, falling short of predictions forecasted for seven years prior. CRM was the largest constituent of the SaaS market, claiming $3.2 billion in 2010 revenues. Just behind CRM was content, communications, and collaboration (CCC) sales, with $2.8 billion. The market for cloud computing business solutions was expected to grow significantly, due to emerging nations and a stronger international economy. Emerging countries were expected to be particularly enticed by SaaS because, experts presumed, old IT systems were not already in place to warrant integrations with new software. Therefore, none of the up-front costs that companies in Europe, the United States, and Japan faced were expected to cause lag in developing countries.

However, two years before, market analysts had been incredibly optimistic regarding the near future of cloud computing. Merrill Lynch optimistically forecast international revenues of $95 billion by 2013. Google, Dell, Microsoft, and Hewlett-Packard were purchasing cloud computing centers across the globe.

Others were more skeptical. Reliability was the major problem with cloud computing, especially for large enterprises. According to an industry report by *Bloomberg Businessweek,* even brief outages could mean massive loss, which would make chief information officers (CIOs) skeptical of relying on external networks for crucial processes. Upgrading and integrating with old technology was also still an unresolved issue, which would mean slow, consistent growth rather than the quick outbreak many experts predicted.

SEE ALSO *Hosting Services; Scalability; Software.*

BIBLIOGRAPHY

"ASPs: Setting Off a Sea of Change." *CIO,* October 1, 2000.

King, Rachael. "How Cloud Computing Is Changing the World." *Bloomberg Businessweek,* August 4, 2008. Available from http://www.businessweek.com/technology/content/aug2008/tc2008082_445669.htm.

"Research and Markets: Key SaaS, PaaS and IaaS Trends Through 2015 Business Transformation via the Cloud." *Business Wire,* January 24, 2011. Available from http://www.businesswire.com/news/home/20110124005842/en/Research-Markets-Key-SaaS-PaaS-IaaS-Trends.

"SaaS Revenue to Reach $12.1 Billion This Year." *Business CloudNews,* July 7, 2011. Available from http://www.businesscloudnews.com/software-as-a-service/458-saas-revenue-to-reach-121-billion-by-end-of-year-.html.

Semilof, Margie. "ASP Group Boosts Its Membership." *Computer Reseller News,* July 5, 1999.

"The Value of Opting for an ASP." *CIO,* October 1, 2000.

ARPAnet

Dr. J. C. R. Licklider is one of a number of individuals credited with coming up with the idea of the Internet, though the Internet required collaboration among teams of individuals in order to be brought into reality. In November 1962, the Defense Advanced Research Projects Agency (DARPA) had hired Licklider to oversee how best to use emerging computer technology. Licklider looked beyond the mathematical uses of computer technology and saw its potential for facilitating communication between institutions and between individuals. He had written a number of memos about a "Galactic Network," in which he expounded upon the potential of connecting computers and users all over the world.

When he came to DARPA in November 1962, Licklider impressed one of his colleagues, Massachusetts Institute of Technology (MIT) researcher Lawrence Roberts, with the idea. Leonard Kleinrock, also at MIT, convinced Roberts of the ability of data packets to be used for communication, as opposed to circuits, convincing the researcher that the Internet could be created. Roberts then published a paper on what he called the ARPAnet in 1967.

Considered the predecessor of the Internet, ARPAnet was established by DARPA in 1969 to allow for the transfer of data between various institutes of research. It was a project commissioned by the U.S. Department of Defense. Some have claimed that ARPAnet was intended to provide messaging capabilities to the government in the event of nuclear war. Proponents of this theory point to Paul Baran, a researcher at RAND Corporation, who suggested packet switching as a solution to the threat of nuclear conflict. Although he did collaborate with some of the DARPA team members, his research had no official ties to their project. Bob Taylor, overseer of ARPAnet, commented, "the creation of ARPAnet was not motivated by considerations of war." No evidence has suggested that the Department of Defense intended to use ARPAnet as a failsafe communication network.

HARDWARE AND PROTOCOLS

ARPA began formally moving forward on its plan to create a Wide Area Network (WAN) in 1967. After deciding to use Interface Message Processors (IMPs) to connect host computers via telephone lines, ARPA began looking for a contractor able to create the underlying network needed to connect the IMPs. Bolt, Beranek and Newman, the Cambridge, Massachusetts-based research and development outfit that Licklider left when he began working for ARPA, successfully bid on the project. The final piece of technology needed—the protocol, or set of standards that would actually allow the host sites to communicate with one another—was developed internally by the Network Working Group.

The first three organizations connected by ARPAnet were the University of California at Los Angeles (UCLA), the Stanford Research Institute, and the University of Utah. Via ARPAnet's Network Control Protocol (NCP), users were able to access and use both computers and printers in other locations and transport files back and forth between computers. Ironically, one of the most important developments in ARPAnet technology, a more sophisticated network code known as Transmission Control Protocol/Internet Protocol (TCP/IP), also established the groundwork for what would one day supersede ARPAnet. TCP/IP replaced NCP in 1983, allowing ARPAnet to be connected with a variety of other networks that had since been launched. This group of networks evolved into what later became known simply as the Internet.

Several other key technologies emerged from various efforts to tweak ARPAnet. For example, e-mail capabilities, first introduced by Ray Tomlinson, were added to ARPAnet in 1971. Online discussion groups sprang up a short while later from address lists of e-mail users with common interests. Although the U.S. Department of Defense disbanded ARPAnet in 1990, its effects on online communications in the late twentieth and early twenty-first centuries were immeasurable.

SEE ALSO *History of the Internet and WWW.*

BIBLIOGRAPHY

Hauben, Michael. "History of ARPANET." 2001. Available from http://www.dei.isep.ipp.pt/~acc/docs/arpa.html.

Internet Society. "Brief History of the Internet." Reston VA, 2011. Available from http://www.isoc.org/internet/history/brief.shtml.

Martin, Richard. "Present at the Creation: An Oral History of the Internet." *PreText Magazine,* March 1998.

National Museum of American History. "Birth of the Internet: ARPANET: General Overview." Washington, DC: Smithsonian Institution, 2001. Available from smithsonian.yahoo.com/arpanet2.html.

RAND Corporation. "Paul Baran and the Origins of the Internet." Santa Monica, CA, 2010. Available from http://www.rand.org/about/history/baran.html.

Winder, Davey. "Top Ten Internet History Myths." *PC Pro,* August 26, 2011. Available from http://www.pcpro.co.uk/features/369490/top-ten-internet-history-myths.

AT&T INC.

AT&T Inc. is one of the world's leading communications service providers. AT&T Mobility is the second-largest wireless firm in the United States, behind Verizon Wireless. AT&T also sells local phone, Internet, and digital television services, the latter primarily under the U-verse brand. In 2010, sales were more than $124 billion and the company employed approximately 265,000 people.

EARLY HISTORY

Alexander Graham Bell and two partners created the Bell Telephone Co. in 1877 with plans to begin marketing the newly invented telephone. Bell Telephone licensee New Haven District Telephone Co. developed the world's first telephone exchange and issued the world's first telephone directory one year later.

After a series of mergers and acquisitions, American Bell became the sole manufacturer of Western Union equipment. The firm diversified into long-distance telephone operations with the formation of American Telephone and Telegraph Co. (AT&T) in 1885. American Bell hoped its new subsidiary would be able to create a widespread national telephone network before several of its patents expired in 1893.

Shortly after its inception, AT&T began building its first long-distance telephone line, which would connect New York City to Philadelphia, Pennsylvania. In 1888, after several blizzards in the northeastern United States destroyed long-distance lines, AT&T began looking into underground cable options. Two years later, American Bell began upgrading its one-wire circuits to two-wire circuits to allow for long-distance transmissions. Within two years, these two-wire, or metallic, circuits connected roughly 12% of American Bell's 240,000 customers. When Bell's original telephone patent expired in 1893, several competitors emerged, prompting lawsuits by AT&T, which strove to retain its monopoly in the long-distance market. Busy with this litigation, AT&T eventually lost substantial market share to rivals in the West and Midwest.

AT&T's network comprised more than 2.2 million telephones in 1905. Although that number rose to more than 3 million in 1907, the firm struggled with public relations problems, low employee morale, and mounting debt. These problems prompted management to begin taking over competitors, rather than engaging in litigation against them. The firm also started to cut prices, discount bond prices in an effort to generate fresh capital, and bolster its research and development arm. In 1913, faced with charges of unlawful conspiracy to monopolize the long-distance market in the Northwest, AT&T agreed to sell previously purchased Western Union assets and to allow competing local telephone service providers to use its long-distance lines.

AT&T AND THE GOVERNMENT

During World War I, AT&T supplied phone service to the U.S. military. The firm also put in place a communications system of radios, telephones, and telegraph lines in France for use by American forces. In 1918, President Wilson nationalized the U.S. phone network, promising that rates would fall under public control. However, expenses related to wartime activities prompted AT&T to raise prices, and U.S. citizens began calling for the government to release control of the phone system. By then, AT&T operated a network of roughly ten million telephones. Mounting public pressure prompted the government to privatize AT&T in 1919. Two years later, AT&T linked Key West, Florida, and Havana, Cuba, via its first submarine cable. After the government began allowing telephone company mergers in the early 1920s, AT&T launched an expansion effort that was fueled by several acquisitions. AT&T spun off its research and development arm as Bell Telephone Laboratories in 1925. The new firm was funded by both AT&T and Western Electric.

In 1934, the U.S. government created the Federal Communications Commission (FCC) to regulate the interstate telephone industry. The FCC launched an investigation of AT&T's competitive practices the following year. By then, the firm controlled 83% of U.S. phones and 98% of long-distance cables. Officials also were concerned about its Western Electric subsidiary, which held a 90% share of the nation's telephone equipment market. With assets of $5 billion, AT&T was the largest company in the United States.

World War II granted AT&T a reprieve from the antitrust investigation. However, the FCC did force the firm to cut prices then. By the war's end, long-distance telephone calls had started to take the place of letter writing in American society as the most common means of communication. The FCC's investigation heated up again in 1949, prompting the U.S. attorney general to file suit against AT&T for violating antitrust laws. Although the attorney general's recommendation included separating AT&T and Western Electric, the two firms managed to remain united by agreeing to several limitations. For example, AT&T was restricted to providing common carrier service, while Western Electric was limited to supplying equipment to AT&T and fulfilling government contracts. The complex litigation was formally resolved in 1956.

AT&T, the British Post Office, and the Canadian Overseas Telecommunications Corp. put in place the first transatlantic telephone cable in 1955. Two years later, AT&T and Western Electric landed a contract to build an early warning radar system for the U.S. military. AT&T also created a new subsidiary, named Bellcom, to manufacture communications equipment for the U.S. space program. The firm launched a $2.6 billion infrastructure overhaul in 1960. Developments during the early part of the decade included the first wide area telephone service, which allowed customers to pay a flat fee for unlimited long-distance calls; Centrex, which allowed offices to maintain their own automatic switching exchange; and Telstar, AT&T's first satellite. The firm also created Comsat to oversee its U.S. satellite communications operations and began offering touch-tone service for the first time. By mid-decade, AT&T had established the seven-digit phone number as standard throughout North America. The installation of electronic switching equipment allowed for an increased volume of calls. Employees totaled roughly one million.

AT&T's legal battles continued in the mid-1970s when both Microwave Communications Inc. (MCI) and the U.S. Department of Justice filed two suits against the telephone giant, alleging both monopoly and conspiracy to monopolize the telecommunications industry. Six years later, a jury found AT&T guilty in the MCI suit and ordered AT&T to pay damages of $1.8 billion. A jury eventually reduced those damages to $37.8 million in an appeal. In 1982, AT&T and the U.S. Department of Justice settled their landmark antitrust suit when AT&T agreed to sell off its regional operating companies, which would become unregulated, competing businesses. As part of the agreement, AT&T created American Bell Inc. as a separate, unregulated subsidiary to sell equipment and services. AT&T was allowed to once again pursue nontelecommunications ventures, a freedom that would enable it to enter the computer market.

BREAKUP AND COMPETITION

Plans for the breakup of AT&T were formalized in 1983, and the firm began spinning off BellSouth, Bell Atlantic, NYNEX, American Information Technologies, Southwestern Bell, U.S. West, and Pacific Telesis as regional phone service providers. Although AT&T retained control of its long-distance services, it was no longer protected from competition. Once the divestitures were completed, AT&T reorganized its remaining operations into two units; its communications unit managed the long-distance network, and its technologies unit manufactured and sold telecommunications equipment.

Within a year of its reorganization, AT&T had started pursuing markets across the globe in anticipation of increased domestic competition. Along with establishing a regional headquarters in Brussels, Belgium, for operations in Europe, the Middle East, and Africa, AT&T also began to forge joint ventures with overseas companies. Its share of the U.S. long-distance market fell in 1987 to 76%, compared to 91% just four years earlier. AT&T laid off 16,000 workers and took a one-time $6.7 billion network modernization charge, which resulted in a $1.7 billion loss in 1988.

When government regulators allowed AT&T to match the lower long-distance rates of competitors MCI Communications Corp. and Sprint Corp. in 1989, profits rebounded to $2.7 billion, their highest point since the 1984 spin-offs. In 1991, AT&T diversified into computers for the first time when it bought NCR Corp. for $7.4 billion, becoming the fourth-largest U.S. and seventh-largest worldwide computer maker. The firm entered the cellular telephony market in 1993 by paying $12.6 billion for McCaw Cellular. The NCR unit was renamed AT&T Global Information Solutions in 1994.

MOVE TO CABLE AND INTERNET MARKETS

To promote its image as a leading technology developer and content provider, AT&T launched a Web site, with various online services, in 1995. The Telecommunications Act of 1996, which essentially deregulated the U.S. telecommunications industry, allowed local and long-distance phone companies, Internet firms, and cable businesses to begin competing in each other's markets. AT&T took advantage of the legislation almost immediately, launching WorldNet, an Internet service provider (ISP), in March. By November, WorldNet had secured roughly 425,000 subscribers. Other leading telecommunications firms began announcing billion-dollar mergers. While consolidation in the industry already had been happening on a limited basis prior to February 1996, the act opened up unprecedented cross-market penetration opportunities. To prepare itself for such deals, AT&T split into three separate entities in December. The firm retained its communications operations; consolidated the Bell Laboratories equipment manufacturing operations into a new public company, called Lucent Technology; and spun off its struggling computer operations, which had lost roughly $4 billion over the previous five years.

In 1997, AT&T added two electronic catalogs—one for residential customers and one for small business clients—to its Web site. Plans to allow e-commerce transactions to take place on the site were launched by the newly formed AT&T Interactive Group. The firm also began marketing its first virtual private network (VPN) service to corporations in December. Earlier in the year, C. Michael Armstrong had replaced Robert Allen as CEO. Wanting to reduce his firm's reliance on the increasingly competitive long-distance market, particularly since attempts to penetrate the computer market had failed, Armstrong orchestrated the $11.3 billion purchase of Teleport Communications Group—a local phone service for businesses owned by cable operators Tele-Communications Inc. (TCI), Cox Enterprises, and Comcast—in 1998. That year, in a deal valued at $10 billion, AT&T and British Telecommunications PLC agreed to merge their international operations to form WorldPartners.

Believing that local telephone, cable, and Internet services would converge into one giant industry in the near future, AT&T also began eyeing cable and Internet firms. Almost immediately after taking over as CEO, Armstrong had approached TCI, attracted to its broadband Internet services and cable operations. They announced a $48 million merger agreement in June 1998 and received Justice Department approval in January 1999. When the $59 billion deal closed in March, AT&T changed TCI's name to AT&T Broadband & Internet Services. The firm then began working on upgrading TCI's infrastructure to allow for integrated local telephone, cable television, and broadband Internet services.

AT&T became the largest U.S. cable carrier when it paid $58 billion for MediaOne Group Inc. in the middle of the year. However, stock prices began to plummet when several analysts criticized the firm for underestimating the cost and complexity of transforming cable networks into local telephone and Internet pipelines.

In 2001, AT&T agreed to purchase bankrupt ISP NorthPoint Communications Inc., including its digital subscriber line (DSL) services. Although the firm's WorldNet ISP had grown rapidly to 1.1 million subscribers by mid-1998, its growth in 1999 and 2000 had been stagnant.

AT&T IN THE 2000S

In 2000, the volume of data traffic on the AT&T network grew larger than the voice traffic, and this trend would continue to grow with the adoption of 3G and similar data elements in telecommunications. This growth began to delineate the data packages necessary for wireless services versus other services, and by 2001 AT&T had completed the spin-off of AT&T Wireless, which became an independent company. That same year Comcast purchased AT&T Broadband.

After the dot-com bust, the market for telecommunications began to pick up speed again and started changing rapidly. Not only were there service improvements thanks to new technology, but entirely new markets were beginning to open up. AT&T, after its lengthy term of acquisitions, began turning toward new frontiers to keep up. It created an intelligent optical network to help repair service problems using advanced algorithms. It also developed VoiceTone, an automated answering service for network customer service that could read and respond to human voices.

These new investments drew the attention of other businesses, and in 2005 SBC Communications (one of the spun-off regional Bell companies) agreed to purchase AT&T for $16 billion. SBC intended to combine its total services and become the primary communucations provider in the United States. As part of the deal, the name of the new company was changed to AT&T Inc.

By 2006, there were only a few major telecommunication services left in the United States. Sprint bought Nextel in 2005, and this was followed by the acquisition of MCI by Verizon. In 2006, AT&T acquired BellSouth and merged its services with the AT&T brand. By 2008, only Sprint, T-Mobile, Clearwire, Verizon, and AT&T remained in the field, although Clearwire was essentially a division of Sprint, which held majority shares in the company.

During this period of major consolidation, the wireless market grew rapidly for both Internet capabilities and mobile phones. Smartphones, which needed dedicated data transfer streams for online connectivity, became common across the United States. For much of the 2000s the 3G data format was used for mobile devices, but as 2010 approached companies began to unveil newer, faster standards, which were prematurely named 4G, a moniker that eventually stuck and became the new marketing thrust of all U.S. telecom giants.

THE IPHONE

In the midst of these changes, AT&T sought a way to differentiate itself from the crowd. Cingular had by this time purchased AT&T Wireless, and AT&T had in turn purchased Cingular, reabsorbing its wireless service capabilities, so it was ready for the mobile market. In 2007, Apple approached both AT&T and Verizon for a potential partnership over service provision for the iPhone. AT&T took the contract, which began an immensely lucrative but rocky relationship as the Apple iPhone become one of the most popular smartphones available, using the AT&T network exclusively. The two companies had difficulty seeing eye to eye on the data plans, since AT&T was primarily interested in cost savings and revenue while Apple had the maneuverability to focus on features and customer usage habits, but after a tricky first year the partnership continued throughout several iterations of the iPhone. After years of rumors, however, by 2011 Apple was also offering the iPhone with Verizon services as well to give consumers an additional choice.

By the end of the 2000s, mobile and broadband services were the focus of the industry, and consolidation had almost reached its limit. In 2011, AT&T solidified plans to purchase T-Mobile from Deutsche Telekom, which would have left only the big three: AT&T, Verizon, and Sprint, all in fierce competition. However, the U.S. government blocked the completion of the acquisition later that same year, citing the reduction in overall competition that it would create.

The primary telecom companies did not always compete directly against one another. In late 2010, AT&T, T-Mobile, and Verizon Wireless joined in a partnership to create Isis. The Isis venture was designed to be a mobile payments service, competing with similar services by offering merchants a way for customers to pay quickly in both brick-and-mortar and online storefronts. By the middle of 2011, the venture refocused its goals and, instead of competing with major services like Visa and MasterCard, it decided to go more behind the scenes with its Mobile Wallet initiative. The Wallet was designed to be usable by card issuers, major company brands, and merchants, with Isis also offering banks the ability to use the venture as a trusted service manager for the transactions. Isis goals set its first launch for 2012.

SEE ALSO *Broadband Technology; Connectivity, Internet.*

BIBLIOGRAPHY

"AT&T Corp." In *Notable Corporate Chronologies.* Farmington Hills, MI: Gale Research, 1999.

AT&T Inc. "Milestones in the AT&T History." Dallas, TX, 2011. Available from http://www.corp.att.com/history/milestones.html.

Cheng, Jacqui. "AT&T Offers Unlimited Mobile to Mobile Calling to Any Number." *Ars Technica,* February 2011. Available from http://arstechnica.com/gadgets/news/2011/02/att-offers-unlimited-mobile-to-mobile-calling-even-to-non-att-numbers.ars.

Clark, Sarah. "Isis Sets Out Its New NFC Strategy." *NFC World,* May 24, 2011. Available from http://www.nfcworld.com/2011/05/24/37652/isis-sets-out-new-nfc-strategy.

Davis, Stephania H. "Interact with Us: AT&T Enhances Its Online Offering." *Telephony,* November 24 1997.

Higgins, John M. "AT&T for Sale?" *Broadcasting & Cable,* December 4, 2000.

Kastre, Michael. "The Inevitable Demise of 'Ma Bell.'" *Multi-channel News,* February 26, 2001.

McCracken, Harry. "A Brief History of the Rise and Fall of Telephone Competition in the US, 1982–2011." *Technologizer,* March 20, 2011. Available from http://technologizer.com/2011/03/20/att-buys-t-mobile.

Mermigas, Diane. "The Wheels Are Turning at AT&T." *Electronic Media,* March 5, 2001.

Rawson, Chris. "The History of Apple and AT&T's Marriage of Convenience." *The Unofficial Apple Web Log (TUAW),* July 20, 2010. Available from http://www.tuaw.com/2010/07/20/the-history-of-apple-and-atandts-marriage-of-convenience.

"A Tangled Family Tree." *Wall Street Journal,* March 30, 2011. Available from http://online.wsj.com/article/SB10001424052748704471904576229250860034510.html.

Wooley, Scott. "Mike Strikes Back." *Forbes,* December 13, 1999.

ATTENTION ECONOMY

The term "attention economy" was used in the late 1990s and early 2000s to describe the economic period that followed, in succession, the agricultural economy, the industrial economy, and the information economy. On the heels of the information economy, according to proponents of the attention-economy concept, human attention has become the scarcest resource amidst the swirl of information constantly bombarding consumers. The proliferation of communication media—television, radio, telephone, print, wireless communications, and the Internet—and their expanding and overlapping reach, creates a situation in which audiences are easily distracted. In order to gain and hold consumers' attention in such an environment, marketers must offer messages that audiences find meaningful and significant. Thus, products and services must be sold and marketed not just on their merits of utility, cost savings, and enjoyment, but with a thick layer of symbolic packaging and narratives that confer meaning in order to capture consumers' attention and money. In short, the attention economy privileges and emphasizes context over content.

On a less abstract level, the attention economy describes a state in which, on a Web site, the content, product, or service being offered is important but hardly sufficient. Rather, as a way of getting visitors to stay at a site and spend money, the site must feature an attractive image and user interface designed to augment the feelings and images the merchant wants them to harbor.

A central characteristic of the attention economy, according to Esther Dyson—a prominent commentator on Internet matters and the woman who coined the phrase—is the relative end of economic scarcity and general fulfillment of human needs. In the attention economy, she contends, consumers generally are free of want for life's necessities and comforts. This sets the stage for one of the primary challenges that e-commerce merchants face in their marketing strategies. Essentially, what marketers compete for is the attention of otherwise fulfilled customers.

Michael Erard elaborated on Dyson's comments by positing in a 2009 article for *Design Observer* that prices of information commodities could be inversely adjusted to the brain power necessary to consume them; in other words, pricing would be attention-based. For instance, items that require long attention spans would be cheaper, while items requiring short attention spans would command luxury prices.

DEVELOPMENT OF THE ATTENTION ECONOMY

Prior to the universal embrace of the Internet, attention was—at least for media producers—easily measured by such criteria as circulation and ratings. A newspaper worked to boost circulation and subsequently justify charging higher advertising rates. Likewise, a TV station saw its ratings increase, enabling it to charge its advertisers more to reach its larger audience. The advent of the Web considerably changed those metrics for the attention economy. "The value of attention began eroding once Web traffic entered into it, since the monetization of attention—audience—is so much harder online," wrote Jon Fine in *Businessweek.* Fine further contended that social media networks like Twitter represented an endpoint of sorts in the decline in the value of attention. While such networks are seductive, they produce no profit for users who garner thousands—even millions—of followers.

The evolution of social media throughout the late 2000s continued to redefine exactly what "attention economy" meant to businesses and consumers. Some skeptics have criticized social media for creating a vehicle for devaluing attention. Writer Mahendra Palsule suggested that sharing something on a social network is essentially asking followers for their attention. The attention every item gets depends on how many items one shares: share too many, and each shared item's value goes down; share too few, and it reduces the baseline value. The best way to increase reputation and influence (not to mention attention value), wrote Palsule, is to share information that is valuable to followers. That, in turn, requires a "brutal and ruthless evaluation."

Amidst an increasingly sophisticated advertising and entertainment culture, along with perpetual connectivity to media and a vast wealth of information at people's fingertips, the race to capture, hold, and channel people's attention continues to gain momentum. Individual businesses and the greater economy count attention among the scarcest resources. Thus, attention has become a nexus of competition and strategy. Firms have begun to develop new ways of measuring and testing attention in order to harness it for economically beneficial ends. Meanwhile, the public's already fragmented attention continues to be divided into ever more potential revenue streams. Even so, writer and marketing expert Seth Godin suggested that it can be all too easy to overlook the attention economy. "Attention is a bit like real estate, in that they're not making any more of it," Godin wrote in 2011. "Unlike real estate, though, it keeps going up in value."

SEE ALSO *Cyberculture.*

BIBLIOGRAPHY

Davenport, Thomas H., and John C. Beck. "Getting the Attention You Need." *Harvard Business Review,* September/October 2000.

———. *The Attention Economy: Understanding the New Currency of Business.* Boston, MA: Harvard Business School Press, 2001.

Erard, Michael. "A Short Manifesto on the Future of Attention." *Design Observer,* August 12, 2009. Available from http://observatory.designobserver.com/entry.html?entry=10297.

Fine, Jon. "Twitter and (Not) Monetizing the Attention Economy." *Businessweek,* March 31, 2009. Available from http://www.businessweek.com/innovate/FineOnMedia/archives/2009/03/twitter_and_the.html.

Godin, Seth. "Paying Attention to the Attention Economy." *Seth Godin's Blog,* July 5, 2011. Available from http://sethgodin.typepad.com/seths_blog/2011/07/paying-attention-to-the-attention-economy.html.

Howard, Henry. "Capturing' Attention.'" *Home Textiles Today,* February 2000.

Palsule, Mahendra. "Role of Curation in the Attention Economy." *Skeptic Geek,* March 21, 2010. Available from http://www.skepticgeek.com/socialweb/role-of-curation-in-the-attention-economy.

Roberts, Kevin. "Brand Identity 2000: Redefining the World." *Advertising Age,* November 29, 1999.
Sviokla, John. "The Attention Economy." *Industry Standard,* March 6, 2000.

AUCTION SITES

Online auctions have proven very popular with consumers and businesses alike. They offer many benefits to both buyers and sellers. Online auctions offer buyers the promise of lower prices for merchandise and collectibles (although spirited bidding for desirable items may drive up prices beyond what they would have been in a fixed price environment). Online auctions have virtually unlimited geographic reach, bringing together buyers and sellers from almost anywhere in the world. Initially, collectibles were the dominant type of merchandise sold at online auctions. By the 2010s, there were relatively few items that were not sold through one of hundreds of online auction sites.

While eBay dominates the online auction market and has a dominant presence on the Web, as of 2012 there are hundreds of auction sites, many of them specialized. For example, there are online auction sites specifically for antiques, guns, motorcycles, and cars. According to NetTop20.com, the top five auction sites as of 2012 are eBay, uBid, Bidz.com, Auctions at Overstock.com, and Amazon.com Auctions.

BUSINESS-TO-CONSUMER AUCTIONS

Businesses also sell goods and services through auction sites. Small businesses use auction sites such as eBay and Amazon.com Auctions not only to sell merchandise but also to build their brand and reputation. Online auctions also give businesses an outlet for selling excess inventory that would have remained in their warehouse. Other uses that businesses find for auction sites include test marketing new products to see if they will sell. Occasionally, bidders will drive up the price of items to a level well above what was expected.

Most auction sites post feedback on how well sellers perform. While positive feedback can enhance a seller's reputation, a few negative comments from a small number of buyers have the potential to tarnish a seller's name. In order to ensure positive feedback, sellers must devote more resources to providing high levels of customer service. Auction shoppers tend to be value-oriented and have high expectations for service.

Businesses that use auction sites to list their merchandise must also be prepared to devote time to posting their listings, answering a large volume of e-mail, and managing functions such as billing, shipping, and payment collection. Some of the larger auction sites provide tools to help with some of these chores, and there are even businesses that specialize in providing auction management services to small businesses in the form of Web-based tools. For instance, Vendio (formerly AuctionWatch.com) promotes itself as "The Complete Auction Management Solution" and offers a range of services for online merchants.

In the early years of auction sites, selling items to the highest bidder without running a credit check on them left sellers open to the risk of nonpayment. As a result, most sites now require buyers to register with the site, and sellers can specify what forms of payment they accept. Only those forms of payments can be used to purchase that item. On eBay, checks, money order, and bank wire transfers are not acceptable forms of payment.

A MATURING INDUSTRY

By 2008, the online auction business had reached maturity, and the growth of leading sites like eBay had begun to decline. In fact, according to a report published by the online publication *Slate,* the online auction industry was past its prime as the number of new buyers drawn to online auction sites peaked around this time. In order to generate additional new sales, eBay changed its pricing structure so that it did not cost as much to list items for sale, and fees were only charged when items sold. The result was a 19% increase in the number of auctions at the site. By 2011, eBay had diversified its business, acquiring other companies such as GSI Commerce, which works with large companies to launch e-commerce Web sites. For example, Dollar General contracted with GSI commerce for the construction of its e-commerce site.

Online auctions will continue to evolve, and according to NetPlaces.com, there are some trends expected throughout the 2010s. One trend is the development of a universal auction registration clearinghouse, which means that once buyers or sellers register at this particular site, they are registered with all auction sites, and their feedback scores would travel with them from site to site. Another trend that is expected to continue is the specialization of sites, with people less likely to buy items from the larger sites and more likely to turn to sites that are specific to the item they wish to purchase.

SEE ALSO *Amazon.com; eBay.*

BIBLIOGRAPHY

eBay Inc. "eBay News." San Jose, CA, 2011. Available from http://www.ebayinc.com/news.
Ensell, Steve, and Si Dunn. "The Future of Online Auctions." *Netplaces.com,* March 7, 2001. Available from http://www.netplaces.com/online-auctions/where-to-go-from-here/the-future-of-online-auctions.htm.
Frey, Bruce. *Online Auctions! I Didn't Know You Could Do That.* Alameda, CA: Sybex, 2000.
"Going, Going, Gone." *Business Week,* April 12, 1999.

Goldsborough, Reid. "Internet Auctions Examined." *Link-Up,* November 2000.
Hunt, Justin. "You've Got to Be Bidding." *Internet Magazine,* December 1999.
Matlin, Chadwick. "eBay's Identity Is Going, Going." *Slate,* July 17, 2008. Available from http://www.source.ly/108hr#.To2_jXFViHk.
O'Loughlin, Luanne, et al. *Online Auctions: The Internet Guide for Bargain Hunters & Collectors.* New York: McGraw-Hill, 2000.
"Online Auctions Are Taking Off." *InfoWorld,* February 8, 1999.
"Online Auction Sites Review." *TopTenReviews.com,* 2011. Available from http://online-auction-sites.toptenreviews.com.

AUGMENTED REALITY

Augmented reality (AR) refers to an electronic image that appears as an overlay over another image that a consumer is viewing. Early demonstrations of augmented reality occurred during television broadcasts of sports events. An important game feature, such as the first down line in a football game, could be clearly displayed to viewers by adding an overlay image. Overlays also held potential for marketers, as they could also be used to mark the location of a business on a map, or display the fastest way to get to the business.

Augmented reality can be difficult to implement. Displaying the overlay over an image that is constantly updated is challenging, because the location of the overlay must be rapidly recalculated. *Popular Mechanics* reported that displaying the first down line added an extra $25,000 to the cost of broadcasting a football game, and the broadcaster had to bring another trailer to carry the augmented reality equipment.

EARLY AUGMENTED REALITY

The aerospace industry was one of the first sectors to use augmented reality systems. Boeing developed one of these systems as a tool to help it train its airplane technicians during the 1990s. These early augmented reality devices were worn over a technician's face and were designed to display reference information automatically when the technician looked at an airplane part. This meant the pilot would not have to spend time searching for the correct manual, according to *Scientific American.*

Augmented reality was also popular in the medical field in the 2000s. One of the major challenges involved with surgery was that the surgeon could not easily see many of the patient's internal organs. In an article for the technology blog *ReadWriteWeb,* Chris Cameron pointed out that because an augmented reality system can display an image of the organs outside of the patient's body, a surgeon can make smaller incisions, which helps patients recover faster from their operations. Some hospitals also used augmented reality systems as a training tool that familiarized medical students with the layout of a patient's internal organs.

In both the aerospace and medical sectors, the costs of a mistake were high, and purchases of expensive, high-tech equipment were frequent. Marketers had considered the use of augmented reality in other sectors, but it was an expensive technology that offered few obvious benefits. In the late 2000s, as mobile devices became more common, more useful applications for augmented reality started to appear.

MOBILE DEVICES

Cell phones provided a consumer platform for augmented reality in 2009. Cell phones typically contained internal cameras, allowing their user to capture an image that could hold the overlay. Cell phone users also frequently carried their phones with them throughout the day, which was more convenient than carrying a visor, goggles, or other dedicated augmented reality device. Many cell phones supported consumer apps, which were convenient for a user to download.

The killer app for augmented reality was location-based services. Previously, a traveler could access business reviews on the Web, but looking up the information mid-journey was inconvenient, just like looking for the product manual was inconvenient for the airplane technician. *Bloomberg Businessweek* reported that Apple's iPhone was one of the first devices that popularized augmented reality, using restaurant reviews. iPhone users could simply point their cell phone at a restaurant as they walked along the street and see what other Web site viewers had to say about the quality of the restaurant's food, its pricing, and its menu selection.

Augmented reality on cell phones also offered a platform for other retailers. A department store could now provide an experience that surpassed a competitor's mirror and dressing room. A customer could use augmented reality to try on mascara, a new dress, or lipstick, and she could send a virtual image to her friends with her cell phone. Augmented reality also had potential for optometrists and hair salons. A customer could even check out a new look before visiting a retail store. *Tec Trend Africa* reported that one of the main benefits of TryLive, a cell phone and Web app from the AR firm Total Immersion, was that it offered a virtual dressing room for Web merchants who could not offer a physical dressing room.

SEE ALSO *Killer Applications; Smartphone.*

BIBLIOGRAPHY

"Augmented Reality: The Past, Present and Future." *Tec Trend Africa,* 2011. Available from http://www.tectrendafrica.com/2011/07/03/augmented-reality-the-past-present-and-future.

Cameron, Chris. "How Augmented Reality Helps Doctors Save Lives." *ReadWriteWeb,* June 2, 2010. Available from http://www.readwriteweb.com/archives/how_augmented_reality_helps_doctors_save_lives.php.

Greenemeier, Larry. "New Computer Graphics Systems Give Reality a Convincing Makeover." *Scientific American,* October 2, 2009. Available from http://www.scientificamerican.com/article.cfm?id=augmented-reality.

King, Rachael. "Augmented Reality Goes Mobile." *Bloomberg Businessweek,* November 3, 2009. Available from http://www.businessweek.com/technology/content/nov2009/tc2009112_434755.htm.

Sawers, Paul. "Augmented Reality: The Past, Present, and Future." *The Next Web,* July 3, 2011. Available from http://thenextweb.com/insider/2011/07/03/augmented-reality-the-past-present-and-future.

St. John, Allen. "The Tech Behind the Football's Broadcast-Only First Down Line." *Popular Mechanics,* December 18, 2009. Available from http://www.popularmechanics.com/outdoors/sports/4301993.

AUTHENTICATION

When consumers attempt to withdraw money from a bank, or obtain passports for international travel, they are required to provide one or more forms of identification that authenticate who they are or prove their identity. These situations usually involve face-to-face encounters with other people. But e-commerce occurs on the Internet, where a general atmosphere of anonymity pervades. In general, it is possible to do a wide variety of things online without divulging one's identity. However, when it comes to engaging in financial transactions and building trust between buyers and sellers, the issue of authentication is just as important online as it is offline. Put simply, parties engaging in transactions and attempting to access closed systems must be able to prove that they are indeed who they say they are.

Security is a cornerstone of e-commerce, as it helps alleviate fears consumers and businesses may have about conducting transactions online. Authentication must occur prior to authorization, which allows entry and access to a system, and fulfills three critical functions: it ensures confidentiality, maintains data integrity, and provides nonrepudiation (making it difficult for entities to deny involvement in electronic transactions).

AUTHENTICATION METHODS

A wide variety of methods, used alone or in combination, are employed to authenticate online entities of businesses or individuals. User names and passwords are perhaps the most basic means of authenticating users. Someone wishing to gain access to privileged information, such as bank account data or credit card information, is required to enter a user name, which is normally not secret, as well as a secret password consisting of varying character combinations of letters or numbers.

Large online merchants like Amazon.com and eBay require user accounts to authenticate customers using user name/password combinations. However, such accounts are still vulnerable to phishing (masquerading as a trustworthy entity to obtain personal information online). Therefore, merchants often verify additional factors such as whether a user's IP address matches the one associated with his or her user account. Personal identification numbers (PINs), digital certificates, biometrics, RSA SecurID tokens, and CAPTCHAs (Completely Automated Public Turing Test to Tell Computers and Humans Apart) are other common methods by which users are authenticated in the early 2010s. Biometrics, an emerging technology, involves a range of equipment—including voice recognition software, retina scanners, fingerprint readers, and cameras—that identify unique physical characteristics. Such devices can be installed on both laptops and desktop computers. As described by Mandy Andress in *Information Security,* "SecurID tokens are essentially one-time passwords for user authentication and can be used to authenticate to a Windows domain. The time-synchronized SecurID card has an LCD screen that shows a string of numbers that changes every minute." Along with a PIN number, such numeric strings are used together when users attempt to gain access to certain systems.

CAPTCHA is a program used by many Web sites to ensure that human users rather than automated computer systems gain access. A CAPTCHA generates distorted text that a user has to retype into a field in order to gain access to a site or utilize some kind of online functionality. If the text is improperly entered, access or functionality is typically denied.

As threats to online user privacy have grown, businesses have developed innovative authentication protocols, including two-factor authentication required by many financial institutions. Typically, when a consumer logs into his bank account via his home computer, for example, the bank will recognize the computer and approve access. However, if that user logs into the account from a new computer or an office workstation, the bank will require answers to a series of questions. A second transaction-level authentication is then often utilized when finishing a transaction such as wiring money out of an account. For instance, a banking institution may use a CAPTCHA to authenticate the user prior to finalizing such a financial transaction. The extra level of authentication prevents malware from sending transactions on a user's behalf.

Despite the proliferation of authentication tools in e-commerce, consumer adoption has been sporadic at best, according to Taher Elgamal in *Dark Reading.* E-commerce fraud is far more prevalent than instances of fraud in physical transactions, wrote Elgamal, due perhaps to the lack of user authentication in online payments. Elgamal suggested that the lack might stem from the cost associated with implementing user authentication. As such, efforts were pursued throughout the 2000s to consolidate authentication in the e-commerce sector. Identity Ecosystem (IE), one such effort, was a "trust directory" technology that endeavored to enable consumers and merchants to rely on one "identity service provider" to provide the data necessary to complete online transactions.

However, IE faced its share of obstacles on the road to widespread implementation. Merchant adoption was far from guaranteed, implementation costs conflicted with business priorities, and the return on investment for curbing fraudulent activities remained negligible. Nonetheless, IE was supported by federal and industry groups as a potentially effective method for improving online authentication and user privacy.

SEE ALSO *Biometrics; Computer Security.*

BIBLIOGRAPHY

Andress, Mandy. "Reach Out and ID Someone." *Information Security,* April, 2001.

"CAPTCHA: Telling Humans and Computers Apart Automatically." Pittsburgh, PA: Carnegie Mellon University, 2010. Available from http://www.captcha.net.

Elgamal, Taher. "User Authentication in E-commerce." *Dark Reading,* September 29, 2010. Available from http://www.darkreading.com/blog/227700809/user-authentication-in-e-commerce.html.

Mercator Advisory Group. "Trekking to Find the Holy Grail: E-commerce Identity and Authentication." Maynard, MA, January 2011. Available from http://www.mercatoradvisorygroup.com/images/MRC%20WHITEPAPER.pdf.

Saliba, Clare. "EU Signs Off on E-signature Initiative." *E-Commerce Times,* August 1, 2001. Available from http://www.ecommercetimes.com/story/12431.html.

AUTHORIZATION AND AUTHORIZATION CODE

Credit cards are the main method consumers use to pay for goods and services when engaged in e-commerce transactions. In general, businesses and consumers obtain credit cards by applying for varying lines of credit from one of the many card-issuing banks located throughout the world. Although the process of using a credit card may appear to be simple to an end-user, many steps are involved when a transaction takes place. These steps involve several different entities including merchants, the acquiring banks that handle credit card transactions for them, acquiring processors, card-issuing banks, and cardholders.

AUTHORIZATION PROCESS

Authorization is the process by which card-issuing banks ultimately verify to merchants that cardholders have enough credit to cover purchases. This process often is handled by acquiring processors, which act on behalf of merchants' acquiring banks, and is just one part of the larger card processing system. Card processing typically begins when the card information is processed by manual entry, card imprinter, point-of-sale terminal, or virtual terminal. Some banks have begun to offer cardless authorization within their ATM networks. For instance, a user can download a digital application to his or her mobile phone and, using a mobile personal identification number (MPIN), withdraw money instantly. The MPIN acts as an authorization code to complete the transaction.

Authorization is a very important step in a credit card transaction because it determines whether or not a purchase will be allowed. If a cardholder's attempt to use his or her credit card is denied because of insufficient credit or any other reason, the acquiring processor returns a denial code to the merchant. If the credit card usage is allowed, the merchant receives an authorization code. Codes normally range from two to six digits and correspond specifically to each transaction. Authorization codes cause card-issuing banks to hold funds (which are immediately deducted from the cardholder's credit limit) until they are actually received at a later time (usually the end of the business day) by the merchant.

An authorization response can include an electronic approval or decline, as well as a response pending more information that requires the merchant to contact a toll-free authorization phone number. Other responses might include "hold card" (a request to remove the card from circulation); "waiting for line" (indicating phone lines are busy); and "code 10 operator" (indicating that the transaction may be suspicious or fraudulent). Once authorization is complete, approved transactions are batched and submitted for funding. The issuer, or financial institution that issued the card, pays the merchant, and then the cardholder is billed.

PREAUTHORIZATION

Some merchants preauthorize a credit or debit card before a purchase is made. Gas stations in particular preauthorize cards for a certain amount of money prior to allowing a customer to pump gas. Many such companies preauthorize $1 for gas purchases to ensure each card is active. However, some preauthorize for significantly more, an issue that has created some controversy among consumers. According to *MSN Money,* British Petroleum preauthorizes $75 for debit and credit card gas purchases. Large preauthorizations such as these can be risky for debit cardholders in particular, since debit cards deduct money from the user's bank account regardless of whether it is used in a debit or credit capacity. The issuing bank will block out that amount of money in the checking account for up to 72 hours, long after the batch transaction has been approved. That can lead to bounced checks, although customers who address the problem with their banks will typically (but not always) be refunded the amount bounced. Credit card companies have used preauthorization for years in a variety of capacities, such as hotel and car rental.

SEE ALSO *Merchant Model; Transaction Issues.*

BIBLIOGRAPHY

Bank of America. "Processing Basics to Accept Credit Cards." Charlotte, NC, 2011. Available from http://corp.bankofamerica.com/public/public.portal?_pd_page_label=merchant/contact/processing-basics.

Klemow, Jason. "Credit Card Transactions via the Internet." *TMA Journal,* January/February 1999.

Sarang, Bindisha. "Now Withdraw Cash at an ATM without Using Your Card." *Live Mint,* September 1, 2011. Available from http://www.livemint.com/2011/09/01210147/Now-withdraw-cash-at-an-ATM-wi.html?h=B.

Solomon, Christopher. "Hosed at the Gas Pump—by Your Debit Card." *MSN Money.* Available from http://articles.moneycentral.msn.com/Banking/BetterBanking/HosedAtTheGasPumpByYourDebitCard.aspx.

Wells Fargo. "Authorizations." San Francisco, CA, 2011. Available from https://www.wellsfargo.com/biz/merchant/service/manage/authorization.

Wilson, Ralph F. "Unraveling the Mysteries of Merchant Credit Card Accounts for Web Commerce." *Web Commerce Today,* August 15, 1997. Available from http://www.wilsonweb.com/articles/merch-cc.htm.

AWARDS, WEB

The evolution of Web sites from bland depositories of information to sophisticated and user-friendly entities of conscious design carried with it a growing tendency to recognize the achievements of intelligent, artistic, and useful Web design practices with awards. There were countless Web awards in the early 2010s, ranging from the relatively anonymous to the highly prestigious. Awards were sponsored by established organizations and followed by pundits and Web aficionados alike. In addition, many magazines issued awards for excellent Web achievements in fields of interest to their readers. In the early 2010s, some of the most recognized Web awards included the Webbies and the Web Marketing Association's WebAward Competition.

Some awards programs focus on one particular element of Web design. For instance, the Dope Awards showcase leading Flash designers in the industry. Mashable's Open Web Awards: Social Media Edition is an online voting competition that honors innovations in Web technology and achievements in the social media segment. Winners typically include a range of companies and developers, from the obscure to the ubiquitous. Manhattan User's Guide (Best Local Blog), Pandora (Best Mobile Music Site or App), and Angry Video Game Nerd (Best Online Video Web Series) are among the many winners in the Mashable contest. Other award programs infamously highlight less savory aspects of the online world. RankMyHack lists hacking claims and gives points to hackers based on the reputation of the targeted Web site.

THE GROWTH OF WEB AWARDS

According to Mic Miller's "A History of Web Awards" in *Awards Scoop,* Web awards had their genesis in 1994 with the Best of the Web Awards program established by Brandon Plewe of the State University of New York at Buffalo. The winners were announced in May of that year at the First International Conference on the World Wide Web in Geneva, Switzerland. A spate of other awards sprang up in the mid-1990s, usually presenting digital badges or medals to Web sites judged excellent by the awards' criteria. Soon, Web designers shifted their design strategies from attempting to impress their loosely affiliated peers in the design community to chasing after specific awards recognized by large swaths of the Web population.

THE WEBBY AWARDS

Perhaps most widely known are the Webby Awards, presented by the International Academy of Digital Arts and Sciences (IADAS). Based in San Francisco, IADAS was founded two years after the Webbies began, sprouting from the original awards' judging academy, and its members were generally recognized leaders in fields related to electronic media. The Webbies is the annual ceremony at which the academy bestows awards on sites in various categories and for various criteria of excellence. In general, the Webbies aim to honor those sites that are most likely to make Web surfers want to visit and provide the best overall browsing experience.

In 2011, the Webbies covered more than 100 categories, including interactive advertising, online film and video, and mobile and "apps." The Webbies recognize excellence in technical and artistic achievement, as well as outstanding individual contributions and achievements. The IADAS selects all nominees, but for each category two awards are bestowed: the Webby (presented by the academy) and the People's Voice Award (voted by the online public). The Webbies draw celebrity power, as well. The 2011 ceremony—featuring performance art, film, video, and animation—was hosted by actress Lisa Kudrow.

OTHER WEB AWARDS

The Web Marketing Association's WebAward Competition recognized the best Web sites in 96 industries. The annual competition fetes individuals and organizations responsible for developing interesting and effective Web sites. Sites are submitted for evaluation by a panel of expert judges, based on criteria including design, innovation, content, technology, and interactivity. Scores range from 0 to 70 points; a score of 60 or greater earns the Outstanding Website WebAward.

The Favourite Website Awards billed itself as the most visited Web site award program online, with more than 140 million site visits as of mid-2011. Established in 2000, the English organization culls submissions from around the world to select progressively designed Web sites, and showcases a site of the day and site of the month. Likewise, the Awwwards recognize and promote leading developers, designers, and Web agencies worldwide. The program engages an international jury that evaluates each site on a scale of 1 to 10 based on design, creativity, usability, and content.

The Best of the Web awards program spotlights the top ten state, county, and city Web sites throughout the country. Sites are judged on innovation, functionality, and efficiency. In 2011, Arkansas' official Web portal took top honors in the state category; Seattle won the city category; and Stearns County, Minnesota, was honored in the county category.

SEE ALSO *Web Site Basics; Web Site Design and Set-up; Web Site Usability Issues.*

BIBLIOGRAPHY

"About the Webby Awards." San Francisco, CA, 2011. Available from http://www.webbyawards.com/about.

Awwwards. Available from http://www.awwwards.com.

Dope Awards. Maidstone, UK. Available from http://www.dopeawards.com.

Favourite Website Awards. "Introduction." Litlington, UK, 2011. Available from http://www.thefwa.com/about.

Golden Web Awards. Available from http://www.goldenwebawards.com.

Heaton, Brian. "2011 Best of the Web Award Winners Announced." *Government Technology,* September 1, 2011. Available from http://www.govtech.com/e-government/2011-Best-of-the-Web-Award-Winners-Announced.html.

Mashable. "Open Web Awards: Social Media Edition." New York, 2010. Available from http://mashable.com/owa.

"New Website Awards Points to Google, Mozilla, Nasa Hackers." *CBR Online,* August 23, 2011. Available from http://security.cbronline.com/news/new-website-awards-points-to-google-mozilla-nasa-hackers-230811.

Web Marketing Association. "Why WebAwards." Available from http://www.webaward.org/whywma.asp.

"Welcome to the World Best Website Awards!" Melbourne, Australia: World Best Websites, 2011. Available from http://www.worldbestwebsites.com.

B

BALLMER, STEVE

When Steve Ballmer assumed the CEO position at Microsoft Corp., he filled the shoes of Bill Gates—the world's richest man at that time and most famous software mogul. Ballmer took over at the start of 2000, in the thick of the government's antitrust lawsuit against the company. A longtime friend and number-two man to Gates, Ballmer was tapped as CEO to smooth over Microsoft's transition to a postlitigation phase by streamlining the company's internal bureaucracy and freeing Gates to concentrate on a future vision for the company.

HISTORY

Born in 1956, Ballmer grew up near Detroit, where his father was a manager for Ford Motor Co. Ballmer and Gates first met when the two were classmates at Harvard University. His college days were highlighted by managing the football team and working on the *Harvard Crimson* newspaper as well as the university literary magazine. According to the *Wall Street Journal,* Ballmer and Gates often played poker and even skipped a graduate economics class for a whole semester. They convened a few days prior to the final exam to cram the material; Ballmer later recalled getting a 97 on the test, while Gates got a 99. While Gates famously dropped out to start Microsoft, Ballmer stayed on to graduate with degrees in mathematics and economics before accepting a job as an assistant product manager at Procter & Gamble. Prior to starting at Microsoft, Ballmer attended Stanford University's Graduate School of Business (although he did not finish).

After Gates lured him to Microsoft, Ballmer started in the sales department in 1980 and spent many years managing the company's relationship with high-tech giant IBM. While Gates focused on business strategy and technology, Ballmer oversaw the development of the Windows operating system, which would become the company's premier product and cash cow. Among his many roles with the company, Ballmer served as Microsoft's first business manager and expanded international operations. In 1998, Gates named Ballmer president of the company, and his appointment to CEO followed less than two years later.

LEADING MICROSOFT

One of Ballmer's responsibilities was overhauling Microsoft's image in the face of its contentious legal difficulties. The company's inherently centralized management structure led to internal breakdowns in the late 1990s. During this challenging period, Ballmer was insistent about the company's innocence. Additionally, Ballmer announced the next phase in Microsoft's technological evolution, that of transforming Windows products into a fundamentally new kind of operating system that would be spread throughout the Internet and all machines connected to it.

Notorious for his bombastic and hard-headed management style, along with an easygoing and affable personal demeanor—features that distinguished him from Gates—Ballmer was widely viewed as the logical and perfect choice to succeed Gates amidst the company's difficulties in the late 1990s. Meanwhile, managing the ambitions and difficulties of Gates paid off handsomely; in 2011, *Forbes* listed Ballmer as the 46th-richest man in the world and 16th richest in the United States.

The leadership transition between Gates and Ballmer was not without tension. In 2008, news reports emerged that the two engaged in a power struggle after Gates relinquished the CEO title but retained the role of chairman. "Things became so bitter that, on one occasion, Mr. Gates stormed out of a meeting after a shouting match in which Mr. Ballmer jumped to the defense of several colleagues," according to the *Wall Street Journal.* Their conflict, in many ways, froze the company's strategic decisions as board members tried to perpetuate a truce between the two leaders. Ballmer, attempting to assert himself in his new CEO role, clashed with Gates, who reportedly would undermine Ballmer in front of other executives. As executives and the board became increasingly concerned, Ballmer and Gates eventually settled on a plan that would see Gates fully transition out of leadership and enable Ballmer to assume his managerial duties.

Following Gates' departure, Ballmer made quick work of restructuring Microsoft to give executives more decision-making power. He promoted employees with general management experience into positions that were previously held by technology-centric executives. Ballmer additionally took a stronger role in dealing with the company's ongoing litigation, acting more conciliatory than Gates previously had.

In the late 2000s, Ballmer steered Microsoft in a more diverse direction. While the company maintained its Windows operating system, the company experimented in mobile devices that reflected the technology industry's general shift away from desktop personal computers. In the face of software competition like the wildly popular iPhone and Android operating systems, Ballmer and Microsoft had their work cut out for them. The company additionally introduced Bing, a search engine meant to rival Google.

Some shareholders voiced disenchantment with Ballmer's performance, criticizing him for allowing other companies to gain a lead in search, wireless communications software, tablet devices, and social networking. Nonetheless, as late as 2011, Microsoft had enormous cash reserve and stable stock prices with Ballmer at the helm.

SEE ALSO *Allen, Paul; Gates, William (Bill); Microsoft Corp.; Microsoft Network (MSN); Microsoft Windows.*

BIBLIOGRAPHY

Bank, David. "How Steve Ballmer Is Already Remaking Microsoft." *Wall Street Journal,* January 17, 2000.

Clarke, Gavin. "Ballmer Garnishes Bing 2.0 with iPhone 'Stomp.'" *The Register,* September 11, 2009. Available from http://www.theregister.co.uk/2009/09/11/ballmer_iphone_bing_win_7_ad.

Greene, Jay. "Ballmer-Bashing Fund Manager Ups Microsoft Stake." *CNET,* August 16, 2011. Available from http://news.cnet.com/8301-10805_3-20093054-75/ballmer-bashing-fund-manager-ups-microsoft-stake.

Guth, Robert A. "Gates-Ballmer Clash Shaped Microsoft's Coming Handover." *Wall Street Journal,* June 5, 2008.

Ignatius, David. "A Kinder, Gentler Microsoft?" *Washington Post,* May 7, 2000.

Markoff, John. "Microsoft's Chief Settles into His Best Friend's Old Job." *New York Times,* January 15, 2000.

Microsoft Corp. "Steve Ballmer." Redmond, WA, March 1, 2008. Available from http://www.microsoft.com/presspass/exec/steve/?tab=biography.

Rigby, Bill. "Microsoft Lines Up Its Big Swing at Tablets." *Reuters,* September 7, 2011. Available from http://www.reuters.com/article/2011/09/08/us-microsoft-tablets-idUSTRE78708X20110908.

Rooney, Paula. "Steve Ballmer: Citizen Microsoft." *Computer Reseller News,* November 13, 2000.

Schlender, Brent. "The $100 Billion Friendship." *Fortune,* October 25, 1999.

"Steve Ballmer." *Forbes,* March 2011. Available from http://www.forbes.com/profile/steve-ballmer.

BANDWIDTH MANAGEMENT

Bandwidth management refers to the process of optimizing the bandwidth that carries traffic over networks. Bandwidth—the amount of data transferred over a communication channel in a specific amount of time—can be controlled by bandwidth management tools, which often are referred to as traffic or packet shapers. These tools enable network managers to control communications by allowing high-priority traffic to utilize more bandwidth than something given a lower priority status. Business-critical applications, including e-commerce transactions, are dependent upon successful bandwidth management.

The need for bandwidth management has significantly increased since the mid-1990s as more information is transferred over the Internet in increasingly diverse formats. Key factors that led to its development include:

- the growing number of new users added to networks
- the popularity of streaming media applications, which allow users to listen to radio stations or view movies via the Internet
- the development of peer-to-peer protocols, such as BitTorrent and Gnutella, for sharing very large files over the Internet
- business movement from mainframes to personal computers
- the rise of e-commerce applications
- the growing use of virtual and cloud computing

As online traffic and the demand for media-rich and e-business applications has grown, any network without successful bandwidth management tools in place can experience severe bottlenecks or slowdowns.

Controlling bandwidth is important for Internet service providers (ISPs), application service providers (ASPs), hosting service providers (HSPs), and other networked enterprises. ISPs, for example, can pinpoint how much bandwidth each member is using for billing purposes to ensure an adequate amount of bandwidth is allocated for such transactions. For ASPs and HSPs, bandwidth management can ensure that critical software applications and solution-based operations have network resources available. Wide-area networks, intranets, and extranets use bandwidth management to control network traffic and ensure that business-critical applications have the necessary resources.

BANDWIDTH MANAGEMENT TOOLS

Instead of adding additional bandwidth to networks to solve bottleneck problems—a short-term solution that is rather costly—network managers use bandwidth management tools such as packet and traffic shapers to control bandwidth allocation. These tools identify and prioritize packets that carry information through networks. For instance, when university networks experienced problems in the late 1990s and early 2000s as students began using campus resources to share music via Napster, network administrators avoided purchasing more bandwidth or restricted access to their sites by using tools that would slow access to sites like Napster, thus giving priority to academic requests on the network.

These tools also enable network managers to identify network traffic patterns, establish priorities, optimize application performance, and allocate resources. Bandwidth shaping tools, such as PacketShaper, optimize bandwidth by categorizing network traffic based on application, protocol, subnet, and URL, allowing managers to prioritize requests on the network. These tools also analyze networks to determine efficiency and bandwidth allocation; allowing IT managers to control traffic and optimize critical application performance. For example, to give online businesses the ability to allocate more bandwidth to e-commerce transaction traffic than to less important applications.

Other bandwidth management tools, such as Cisco's Bandwidth Quality Manager, allow users to determine areas of greatest network congestion, set targets across the network, and program thresholds for generating triggered event traces and alerting the network manager for performance degradation before it affects application users. This type of product is sometimes called an auto-shaper, because the management software uses algorithms to analyze usage patterns and predict where the highest traffic will occur. The management software then allocates traffic priority based on these predictions.

The rise of peer-to-peer protocols also has meant that network managers need to develop policies for shaping and managing traffic more effectively. Rate-shaping tools allow network managers to set a base rate at which traffic can flow through the network; set a limit on the rate of traffic from different users; and borrow bandwidth from one user or group of users to apply to other users.

Another development in bandwidth management since the early 2000s is the increasing number of people who need to manage their bandwidth at home. Households with multiple users, including those playing online multiplayer games, streaming music and video, and using Voice over Internet Protocol (VoiP) and Skype, may need to manage their personal bandwidth. Several companies have developed bandwidth management tools for PCs. Downloadable tools such as Antamedia Bandwidth Manager Lite and Crysnet Bandwidth Manager allow home PC users to monitor and control easily the bandwidth of multiple PCs and apply rules for prioritizing particular IP addresses, ports, or network interfaces. These tools are also useful for small businesses with just a few computers. At the same time, some large companies have begun developing their own private networks in order to speed data transfer and increase the bandwidth available to the company.

Open source bandwidth management also grew throughout the 2000s. These free programs, such as IPCop and SmoothWall, are designed to run on any PC and may be especially useful for users in the developing world. For example, the m0n0wall program operates as a commercial router and can be run without a hard drive. It allows traffic shaping and port filtering, and provides firewall protection with minimum use of memory, making it useful for small companies with limited funds for upgrades. Bandwidth management is also becoming an interest of the nonprofit sector. The Kenya Education Network Trust is developing an open source toolkit to allow affordable and easy-to-use bandwidth management for users in areas with limited bandwidth.

As the number of Internet users continues to increase, and demand for media-rich and peer-to-peer applications rises, bandwidth management will continue to play a role in network management. However, finding a management solution is not always an easy task. While there are many tools on the market, the continual evolution of technology, including e-commerce applications, can make network management a tough chore.

SEE ALSO *Application Service Provider (ASP); Bandwidth; Broadband Technology; Internet Service Provider (ISP); Multimedia; Streaming Media.*

BIBLIOGRAPHY

"Bandwidth Management." In *Techencyclopedia.* Point Pleasant, PA: Computer Language Co., 2001. Available from http://ubm.computerlanguage.com/host_app/search?cid=C008000&def=62616e647769647468206d616e6167656d656e74.htm.

Barnes, Cecily. "Schools, Businesses Restrain Bandwidth Hogs." *CNET,* February 15, 2001. Available from http://news.cnet.com/2100-1023-252661.html.

Blue Coat Systems Inc. "PacketShaper." Sunnyvale, CA, 2011. Available from http://www.bluecoat.com/products/packetshaper.

F5 Networks. "Bandwidth Management for Peer-to-Peer Applications." Seattle, WA, December 2007. Available from http://www.f5.com/pdf/white-papers/rateshaping-wp.pdf.

Hunter, Philip. "The Perennial Problem." *Communicate,* February 2001.

Jude, Michael, and Nancy Meachim. "Bandwidth Management and the Profit Thing." *Network World ASP Newsletter,* May 17, 2000.

Liebmann, Lenny. "Bandwidth Management Evolves." *Planet IT News,* August 9, 2000.

Murph, Darren. "Bigfoot Brings Killer Bandwidth Management to Laptops via Wireless N Module." *Engadget,* May 1, 2011. Available from http://www.engadget.com/2011/03/01/bigfoot-brings-killer-bandwidth-management-to-laptops-via-wirele.

"New Bandwidth Management Techniques Boost Operating Efficiency in Multi-Core Chips." *Science Daily,* May 25, 2011. Available from http://www.sciencedaily.com/releases/2011/05/110525120048.htm.

Sperling, Ed. "Solving the Bandwidth Problem." *Forbes,* January 4, 2010. Available from http://www.forbes.com/2009/12/31/wireless-internet-bandwidth-technology-cio-network-telecom.html.

BANKING, ONLINE

When the "clicks-and-bricks" euphoria hit in the late 1990s, many banks began to view Web-based banking as a strategic imperative. The attractions of online banking for banks are fairly obvious: diminished transaction costs, easier integration of services, interactive marketing capabilities, and other benefits that boost customer lists and profit margins. Additionally, Web banking services allow institutions to bundle more services into single packages, thereby luring customers and minimizing overhead.

A mergers-and-acquisitions wave swept the financial industries in the mid- and late 1990s, greatly expanding the customer base of many banks. Following this, banks looked to the Web as a way of maintaining their customers and building loyalty. In 1994, Stanford Federal Credit Union became the first financial institution to offer online internet banking services to all of its members.

A number of different factors are causing bankers to shift more of their business to the virtual realm. Among these are electronic billing; the validity of e-signatures, approved by Congress in 2000; account aggregation (whereby a customer's entire range of financial relationships are coalesced on a single Web site); and the move in the wake of the Financial Services Modernization Act to create one-stop shopping for financial services. A 2011 survey by the American Bankers Association found that 62% of Americans preferred to bank online.

Online banking encompasses both the Web-based operations of established brick-and-mortar banks as well as Internet-only banks. The latter offer several perks, including higher interest rates on checking accounts, higher yields on certificates of deposit, and electronic billing free of charge. However, Web-only banks suffer from several drawbacks, such as the inability to provide local business loans and other regionally based services, a lack of ATM machines, and security concerns.

THE EVOLUTION OF ONLINE BANKING

While prototypic PC banking systems were first developed in the 1980s, the online banking industry really took off with Microsoft Corp.'s home banking network, introduced in 1994. By 1997, some 4.2 million U.S. households did their banking on the Internet. For several years, online banking was synonymous with computers, but today Internet-based financial transactions are increasingly conducted with cell phones and other wireless devices. In 2010, more than 29 million Americans accessed their bank account wirelessly.

Another important development in online banking came with PayPal, established in 2000. PayPal allows users to transfer money securely to other people or to a bank account online. PayPal was purchased by eBay in 2002, and by 2011, the company processed $27.4 billion in payments. In 2011, Bank of America, JPMorgan Chase, and Wells Fargo launched a competitor to PayPal called clearXchange, to allow account holders of those banks to transfer money to another account holder online or wirelessly, simply by sending an e-mail or entering a phone number.

The first Internet-only bank was Security First Network Bank, which was established in 1995. Although Security First was bought out three years later, it demonstrated that the Internet-only model was viable. By 2011, there was a wide choice of FDIC-insured, Internet-only banks, including ING Direct, FNBO Direct, SmartyPig, and Everbank. Internet-only banks provide ATM access through networks such as the Allpoint network, and some offer round-the-clock phone assistance.

SECURITY CONCERNS

Online banking is fraught with difficulties. Leading this list is consumer confidence in the ability of banks to protect financial information from hackers and cyberthieves. This concern has not diminished over time, as thieves have adapted new ways of using online banking to steal money. One of the most popular scams is phishing—setting up a

Web site that duplicates a bank site and then sending customers e-mails asking them to log on to their accounts. The customers enter their passwords onto the fake site and the thieves then empty their account. Another technique used by cyberthieves is to embed spyware or Trojan horse programs onto users computers, allowing them to record the user's keystrokes and steal their passwords. A survey by Gartner found that as much as $3.2 billion may have been stolen using phishing attacks in 2007 alone. Over the three year, a single Trojan horse, called Sinowal Trojan, was used to steal money from more than 300,000 online bank accounts.

To counter fraud, banks have begun using measures such as texting users every time an online transaction takes place, and issuing security devices that generate a separate security code for each transaction. Banks and law enforcement consistently warn consumers of the latest online banking scams, but the battle between scammers and security continues. In 2010, the Anti-Phishing Working Group identified more than 126,000 fake Web sites created to steal users' banking information.

Despite the ongoing security concerns related to online and wireless banking, the sheer convenience of online banking means it will probably continue to grow in usage. Online banking has allowed the rise of social banking, where individuals loan money to others at an agreed rate of interest, or invest in businesses privately, using online facilitation Web sites.

SEE ALSO *Electronic Payment; Recurring Payment Transactions.*

BIBLIOGRAPHY

Barbato, Frank. "8 Online Banking Trends for 2011." G+, January 3, 2011. Available from https://www.gplus.com/commercial-banking/insight/8-online-banking-trends-for-2011-52068.

Barret, Larry. "Online Banking Security a Concern for Most: Survey." "eSecurity Planet," November 12, 2010. Available from http://www.esecurityplanet.com/trends/article.php/3912941/Online-Banking-Security-a-Concern-for-Most-Survey.htm.

Bielski, Lauren. "Online Banking Yet to Deliver." *ABA Banking Journal,* September 2000.

Block, Sandra. "Banks Offer Cash Transfers via Cell Number, E-mail Address." *USA Today,* May 26, 2011. Available from http://www.usatoday.com/money/industries/banking/2011-05-25-banks-cash-transfer-cell-email_n.htm.

Condon, Mark. "The Shape of Things to Come." *Credit Union Magazine,* January 2001.

Engen, John R. "Banking on the Run." *Banking Strategies,* July/August, 2000.

Fox, Susannah. "Online Banking 2005." Washington, DC: Pew Internet & American Life Project. February 9, 2005. Available from http://www.pewinternet.org/Reports/2005/Online-Banking-2005.aspx.

Hamlet, Clay. "Community Banks Go Online." *ABA Banking Journal,* March 2000.

Hernandez, Jr., Louis. "The Boom Beneath the Bust: Internet Strategies to Win—Banks Need to Know How to Maneuver Within Cyberspace." *Banking Wire,* October 4, 2001.

Monahan, Julie. "In the Out Door." *Banking Strategies,* November/December 2000.

Robinson, Teri. "Internet Banking: Still Not a Perfect Marriage." *InformationWeek,* April 17, 2000.

Salazar, Carolyn. "How Dangerous Is Online Banking?" *MSN Money,* January 28, 2009. Available from http://articles.moneycentral.msn.com/Investing/StockInvestingTrading/how-dangerous-is-online-banking.aspx.

Salkever, Alex. "Online Banking: The Nightmare." *Business Week,* October 9, 2000.

Skousen, Mark. "Online Banking's Goodies." *Forbes,* June 12, 2000.

BANNER ADS

Ever since their debut on the HotWired site in October 1994, banner ads have been a leading format for online advertising. They also have been a disappointment for advertisers and Web site publishers alike. They have been blamed, perhaps unfairly, for everything from the high rate of failure of content-based Web sites (which are dependent on advertising revenue) to invasion of privacy.

Banner ads come in a variety of sizes and are measured in pixels. According to Nielson, the most popular size in 2010 was the 300-by-250 medium rectangle size, followed by the 728-by-90 "leaderboard" size. These two sizes also perform the best, with click-through rates of 0.37% and 0.27% in 2010.

The total average click-through rates on banner ads have fallen from an average of around 2% in 1997 to 0.2% in 2010. A click-through rate of 0.2% means that for every 1,000 people who visit a site, only two will click on the ad. Despite this poor return, banner ads still accounted for 23% of the total spending on online advertising in 2010.

HOW BANNER ADS WORK

Banner ads were developed to serve three basic functions: build brand awareness; sell a product or service; and drive traffic to an advertiser's Web site. In order for advertisers to make effective use of banner ads, they need to establish goals for their ad campaigns and determine whether they want to build brand awareness, sell something, or drive traffic to their Web sites.

Advertisers may purchase advertising space for their banner ads on individual Web sites, but most advertisers work through an ad agency or network. Networks such as DoubleClick Inc. and FlyCast represent groups of Web sites and sell advertising on them, in addition to offering other services to advertisers. Advertisers are charged for banner advertising using one of two models. Under the CPM (cost per thousand impressions) model, rates are based on the number of viewers. The more popular CPA (cost per action) model charges advertisers only when a click-through is made on their banner ad.

Another option is to join an affiliate network, such as Commission Junction (cj.com) or Link-Share (Linkshare.com). Through affiliate programs, Web sites select banner ads they believe are appropriate to display on their site. The affiliate network then keeps track of click-throughs and pays the Web site a commission on each click-through instance. Banner exchange programs, such as LinkBuddies (Linkbuddies.com), offer the ability to trade banner ads.

TARGETING AND TRACKING

Banner ads have the potential to offer unlimited targeting, tracking, and measurability. Tracking and measuring the performance of banner ads allow advertisers to analyze and select the best performing ads for each placement. Targeted banner advertising means serving the appropriate ad to a specific type of user based on a user profile. Rather than contextual advertising, where ads are delivered based on the content of the Web page itself, targeting is behavior-based, so that banner ads are placed based on the viewer's previous actions. This may involve knowing what Web pages the viewer has visited recently, as well as whether or not they made a purchase, signed a registration form, or took other similar actions.

Tracking and targeting banner ads became more controversial, starting around 2007, as social networking sites (and other sites) began to share and sell more information to advertisers. In 2011, Facebook pioneered a system using deep packet inspection for targeting banner ads in real time. Deep packet inspection involves examining data for key words as it passes through an inspection point. This allowed Facebook to monitor real-time conversations on the site and place ads related to these conversations. For example, if a user posts that they are thinking about going on a ski trip, banner ads for ski holidays may immediately pop-up on their page. Privacy groups, such as Privacy International, are particularly concerned that deep packet inspection and similar information mining techniques have the potential to allow the theft of personal information on a large scale. In 2011, U.S. senators John Kerry and John McCain introduced the Commercial Privacy Bill of Rights Act to force all sites to require an opt-in consent for the collection and use of personal information.

Despite falling click-through rates and privacy concerns, advertisers and Web sites continue to improve their targeting methods for banner ads. In 2009, software became available to allow the display of banner ads on cell phones. In 2011, companies began to target banner ads at their existing or previous customers, placing banner ads on whatever sites they happened to be looking at. The effectiveness of these types of targeted banner ads remains to be seen.

SEE ALSO *Advertising, Online; Affiliate Model; Marketing, Internet; Privacy: Issues, Policies, Statements.*

BIBLIOGRAPHY

"Banner-Ad Blues." *Economist (US),* February 24, 2001.

Callahan, Sean. "Banner Believers Endure Season of Disenchantment." *B to B,* October 23, 2000.

Claburn, Thomas. "The Banner Ad Is Dead. (OK, Not Really)." *Ziff Davis Smart Business for the New Economy,* March 1, 2001.

Coster, Helen. "Cellphones: The New Billboards." *Forbes,* July 14, 2009. Available from http://www.forbes.com/2009/07/15/mobile-marketing-cmo-network-mobilemarketing.html.

Freedman, David H. "The Future of Advertising Is Here." *Inc.,* August 1, 2005. Available from http://www.inc.com/magazine/20050801/future-of-advertising.html.

Holahan, Catherine, and Robert D. Hof. "So Many Ads, So Few Clicks." *Bloomberg Businessweek,* November 12, 2007. Available from http://www.businessweek.com/magazine/content/07_46/b4058053.htm.

Interactive Advertising Bureau (IAB). "Internet Ad Revenues Break Records, Climb to More Than $12 Billion for First Half of '10." October 12, 2010. Available from http://www.iab.net/about_the_iab/recent_press_releases/press_release_archive/press_release/pr-101210.

Nielson. "Most Popular Ad Sizes." Milpitas, CA, 2011. Available from http://www.adrelevance.com/intelligence/intel_dataglance.jsp?flash=true&sr=89654.

Randall, Neil. "Profiting: Adding an Affiliate Program Links Site Content to Product Sales." *PC Magazine,* February 20, 2001.

Schwartz, Matthew. "Online Ads Enter the Next Generation." *B to B,* March 5, 2001.

Vlahos, Christopher J. "The Internet Banner Ad Now Exists in Survival Mode." *Business First—Columbus,* April 27, 2001.

BARNESANDNOBLE.COM

Barnesandnoble.com, a wholly owned subsidiary of Barnes & Noble Inc., is an online bookstore. In 2011, Barnesandnoble.com had more than one million titles in stock, in addition to other offerings such as magazines, toys, games, MP3s, and DVDs. In 2009, the company launched its "Nook" e-reader, a competitor to Amazon's Kindle device, Apple's iPad, and other e-book readers.

The parent company's brick-and-mortar chain enjoys the largest market share of any bookstore in the United States, operating 705 bookstores in 50 states and the District of Columbia in 2011. The company's textbook branch, Barnes & Noble College Booksellers, operated 636 stores at colleges and universities. In 2010, the company employed about 40,000 people.

EARLY DAYS

Barnes & Noble entered the world of online bookselling in March 1997 as the exclusive bookseller on America Online (AOL). Two months later the company set up its own Web site for online purchases, Barnesandnoble.com. Sales at Barnesandnoble.com doubled in each of 1997's first three quarters, and reached $11.9 million that year. In addition to being the exclusive bookseller on AOL, the online bookseller also reached an agreement with Microsoft to be the exclusive bookseller on three of its Web sites: MSNBC, Microsoft Investor, and Expedia. All of the Microsoft Web sites attracted millions of visitors daily. By the end of 1998, Barnesandnoble.com was the exclusive English language bookseller on Microsoft's MSN.com and its global network of Web portals.

REORGANIZED WITH NEW INVESTOR: 1998

Barnesandnoble.com was reorganized in 1998 when German media conglomerate Bertelsmann AG agreed to invest $200 million in the online bookseller for a 50% interest. Barnesandnoble.com became a limited liability company (LLC) in order to operate online retail bookselling operations. As a result of Bertelsmann's investment, the bookseller postponed its planned initial public offering (IPO). For 1998, Barnesandnoble.com reported sales of $61.8 million and a net loss of $83.1 million.

In March 1999, together with Bertelsmann, Barnes & Noble announced it would spin off Barnesandnoble.com as a public company, selling 15% to 20% of the company's stock to the public. In May 1999, Barnesandnoble.com went public with an initial stock price of $18 per share. Following the IPO, Barnes & Noble and Bertelsmann each owned about 41% of Barnesandnoble.com, with the public holding the remaining 18%.

In 1999, Barnesandnoble.com faced a patent infringement suit raised by rival online bookseller Amazon.com. Amazon.com had received a patent on its technology for streamlining the purchase process, which it called 1-Click. Its suit claimed that Barnesandnoble.com's Express Checkout system violated its patent. When a federal judge issued an injunction against Barnesandnoble.com to stop using the technology until the suit was settled, the company had to introduce a new online ordering technology to its Web site. The terms of the settlement, reached in 2002, were never disclosed to the public.

In 2002, Stephen Riggio—brother to Leonard Riggio, who had purchased the fledgling bookstore in 1971 and run it up to that point—was named CEO of Barnes & Noble, with Leonard Riggio moving to its chair.

THE DIGITAL REVOLUTION

Amazon.com introduced the first e-reader, a portable tablet computer designed specifically for reading electronic books, in 2007. Two years later, Barnes & Noble responded with the Nook. Like the Kindle, the Nook featured an "E-Ink" display and wireless connectivity, but added a color touch screen, access to books purchased on other devices, and a "lending" feature. Barnesandnoble.com launched the NOOK Bookstore as part of an aggressive digital strategy. It also acquired Fictionwise, another e-book seller, in 2009.

Barnes & Noble put itself up for sale in 2010, as the demand for e-books rose while traditional brick-and-mortar bookstores suffered. Despite earlier talks of mergers and buyouts, key competitor Borders shut its doors and laid off more than 10,000 employees in 2011—the liquidation of its stock meant temporarily slumping sales for Barnes & Noble, and it was not clear how Borders' closing would affect Barnesandnoble.com in the long haul.

Barnes & Noble also changed CEOs that year, promoting William Lynch from president of Barnesandnoble.com. The move signified a heightened emphasis on the company's digital strategy. According to *USA Today,* Lynch helped launch the Nook and its complementary bookstore, and the company was "counting on the technology to boost sales and ward off intense competition from online retailers, discount stores and rival e-readers such as Amazon.com's Kindle." Stephen Riggio stayed on as vice chairman.

In the early 2010s, Barnes & Noble was pinning increasing hope on Barnesandnoble.com as digital book sales rose while sales in stores dropped. Billionaire Ron Burkle, who held 19% of company stock, engaged in a long proxy battle with the company and its chair, blaming management for its flagging brick-and-mortar business—a fight he lost in 2010 when Barnes & Noble blocked his attempt to purchase further shares.

In 2011, Liberty Media, owned by another billionaire (John Malone), was considering acquiring 70% of Barnes & Noble if chairman and 30% stockholder Leonard Riggio would agree to the deal. Liberty Media valued Barnes & Noble at about $1 billion and was banking largely on the success of Barnesandnoble.com and the Nook.

Barnes & Noble introduced the All-New Nook in 2011, which boasted a long battery life, relatively small size, and features such as a color touch screen and e-mail program. The All-New Nook connects to Barnesandnoble.com's wirelessly.

SEE ALSO *Amazon.com Inc.; E-books.*

BIBLIOGRAPHY

Barnes & Noble Inc. "Barnes & Noble History." Lyndhurst, NJ, 2011. Available from http://www.barnesandnobleinc.com/our_company/history/bn_history.html.

"Barnes & Noble Names Website Head William Lynch as CEO." *USA Today,* March 18, 2010. Available from http://

www.usatoday.com/money/companies/management/2010-03-18-barnes-and-noble-execs_N.htm.

"Barnes & Noble Sees Revenue of $9 Billion in Fiscal 2014." *Publishers Weekly,* June 29, 2010. Available from http://www.publishersweekly.com/pw/by-topic/industry-news/financial-reporting/article/43685-barnes–noble-sees-revenue-of-9-billion-in-fiscal-2014.html.

"Bertelsmann AG." *Brandweek,* October 12, 1998.

De La Merced, Michael J. "Barnes & Noble Keeps Mum on Liberty Bid as Loss Widens." *New York Times,* June 21, 2011. Available from http://dealbook.nytimes.com/2011/06/21/barnes-noble-keeps-mum-on-liberty-bid-as-loss-widens.

De La Merced, Michael J., and Julie Bosman. "Calling Off Auction, Borders to Liquidate." *New York Times,* July 18, 2011. Available from http://dealbook.nytimes.com/2011/07/18/borders-calls-off-auction-plans-to-liquidate.

Duvall, Mel. "Amazon Files against B&N." *Inter@ctive Week,* October 25, 1999.

"How Barnes & Noble Misread the Web." *Business Week,* February 7, 2000.

McCracken, Harry. "Your First Look at Nook: The Technologizer Review." *Technologizer,* December 6, 2009. Available from http://technologizer.com/2009/12/06/nook-review.

Milliot, Jim. "BN.com Grabs Majority Stake in Enews." *Publishers Weekly,* April 16, 2001.

———. "Books Accounted for 93 Percent of BN.com Sales in 1999." *Publishers Weekly,* April 17, 2000.

Murphy, Chris. "Barnesandnoble.com Seeks to Close Book on Losses." *InformationWeek,* February 14, 2000.

Nawotka, Edward. "BN.com Replaces Amazon as Featured Bookseller on Yahoo!" *Publishers Weekly,* September 25, 2000.

———. "BN.com, Microsoft in Multimillion-Dollar Deal." *Publishers Weekly,* December 14, 1998.

Woollacott, Matthew. "Patent Lawsuit: 'One-Click' Dispute Rages On in Court." *InfoWorld,* February 19, 2001.

BASIC

BASIC stands for Beginner's All-Purpose Symbolic Instruction Code, a computer programming language known for its simplicity. Many students first learn BASIC before moving on to more complex languages like Fortran and C++. Thomas Kurtz, professor of mathematics at Dartmouth College, and John G. Kemeny, chairman of the Mathematics Department at Dartmouth, developed BASIC, which is one of the easiest high-level programming languages to learn. They created it so that students could write programs for the General Electric, or GE-225—a mainframe, time-sharing computer system.

BASIC was first developed as a compiled language, one which is translated into machine language prior to execution. However, because BASIC was never copyrighted or patented, all sorts of variations cropped up, including versions that were interpreted, or translated into statements that executed individually. In the mid-1970s, Harvard student Bill Gates and Honeywell employee Paul Allen used an interpreted version of BASIC when they created a language for Altair, the world's first personal computer (PC). When Gates and Allen moved back to Seattle, the former grade school classmates began customizing BASIC for use with other platforms. Their efforts eventually led to the founding of Microsoft Corp.

Other early PC developers also preferred interpreted versions of BASIC, mainly because such versions allowed more computer memory to remain free. Computer manufacturers like IBM, Hewlett-Packard, and Digital Equipment Corp. used interpreted versions of BASIC in the read-only memory (ROM) of their machines. By the mid-1980s, technology companies including RadioShack Corp., Apple Computer, Inc., and Intel Corp. had written their own versions of BASIC. The American National Standards Institute (ANSI) began circulating Standard BASIC in 1988, but the number of versions of BASIC continued to grow, and by 2011 there were more than 150 versions of the programming language in existence.

VISUAL BASIC

In 1992, Microsoft created Visual BASIC for use with Microsoft Windows applications. This is an object-oriented version of the language that uses "drag and drop" to allow programming without needing to type in all the code for common objects such as buttons and scrollbars. Visual BASIC became popular among small businesses who wanted to create custom applications easily, as well as among amateur game developers. Real BASIC, first released in 1998, allowed Macintosh users to create compiled applications easily. Versions of Real BASIC using the same source code became available for Linux and Microsoft Windows in 2005. Open source projects such as OpenOffice.org have also developed BASIC programs and applications that allow creation of custom spreadsheets, macros, word processing, and presentation applications.

One of the original advantages of BASIC was its ease of use, which allowed children to create simple programs for themselves and provided a useful introduction to computer programming. BASIC also taught creative thinking and a deeper understanding of computer technology. In order to allow people to develop these skills, some versions of BASIC (such as Chipmunk BASIC) were developed as free, downloadable cross-platform interpreters. These allowed PC and Apple users to develop and run simple BASIC programs using a traditional command-line console programming environment.

Despite its limited uses, the simplicity of BASIC, and its open source code, may ensure that it remains a useful tool in the 2010s. New versions of the programming language are being developed all the time, and new uses are being found for it. In 2011, a version of BASIC for the iPad and iPhone became available for sale through the Apple iTunes store, allowing a new generation of programmers to cut their teeth on BASIC.

SEE ALSO *C (Programming Language); Programming Language.*

BIBLIOGRAPHY

"BASIC." In *Webopedia.* Darien, CT: Internet.com, 2001. Available from http://www.webopedia.com/TERM/B/BASIC.html.

"BASIC." In *Techencyclopedia.* Point Pleasant, PA: Computer Language Co., 2001. Available from http://www.techweb.com/encyclopedia.

Brin, David. "Why Johnny Can't Code." *Salon,* September 14, 2006. Available from http://www.salon.com/technology/feature/2006/09/14/basic.

"Chipmunk Basic." Ronald H Nicholson, Jr. & HotPaw Productions, 2011. Available from http://www.nicholson.com/rhn/basic/.

Hudson, Daniel P. "A Brief History of the Development of BASIC." Available from http://www.phys.uu.nl/~bergmann/history.html.

"Interpreter." In *Webopedia.* Darien, CT: Internet.com, 2001. Available from http://www.webopedia.com/TERM/I/interpreter.html.

Neuberg, Matt. *Real Basic: TDG.* 2nd ed. O'Reilly Media, 2001.

BERKMAN CENTER FOR INTERNET & SOCIETY

The Berkman Center for Internet & Society is a high-profile, multidisciplinary, interfaculty initiative at Harvard University that brings together leading thinkers, policy makers, technologists, and businesses involved with the Internet, law, and society. The group describes its operations as follows: "Our mode—entrepreneurial nonprofit—embraces our pursuit of scholarly research in the manner and spirit of an academic think tank, anchored by the diverse collaborative and individual work of our faculty and fellows." Housed within the law school, the center boasts a broad array of contributing members, which spans the university. This interdisciplinary approach allows the organization to maintain appraisal of the development of the Internet from multiple viewpoints, such as economics, engineering, and the social sciences. Moreover, the center serves as an open forum where representatives from industry, government, academia, science, and interest groups can debate and collaborate. The center operationalizes relevant issues by starting project groups, which often publish their research for mass consumption through reports, seminars, and other delivery methods via the center's Web site. These include discussing the direction of the Internet as it pertains to continued business development and global competitiveness; working toward a consensus in the creation of e-business infrastructures and strategies; negotiating concerns and goals for U.S. and international Internet policies regarding trade, regulation, taxation, and technological development; and speculating on the many ways in which the Internet could positively and negatively influence human life.

CONFERENCE ORIGINS

Before the group gained a physical base in the law school, it was a conference. The first meeting of the Harvard Conference on Internet & Society was called to order in May 1996, at the dawn of the e-commerce age and before the economic boom fueled largely by the Internet and its related technologies. As a result, the general tenor of the conference centered on the novelty and promise of the Internet, including great speculation about the direction it would take and its place in history. Harvard University president Neil Rudenstine chimed in with a talk comparing the development of the Internet and its potential for research and information sharing with the modern university library infrastructure that emerged at the end of the nineteenth century.

By contrast, the 1998 gathering took place right in the middle of the dot-com boom. Companies and policy makers alike were focused on the way to most vigorously embrace the Internet and turn it into a competitive tool. U.S. president Bill Clinton's Internet policy adviser, Ira Magaziner, issued a broad outline of the president's strategy for the Internet and information technology, noting that the boom in IT innovation was largely responsible for much of the country's mid-and late 1990s economic prosperity and charging the private sector with taking the lead in the development of the digital economy. Magaziner outlined that the general tendency of U.S. government was toward self-regulation of the Internet by the private sector rather than the top-down regulation favored by many European countries.

At the same meeting, top executives from IBM, Oracle, Sun Microsystems, Microsoft, and other major industry players contributed their thoughts on how the Internet and related information technologies not only were opening up new business channels via the emergence of e-commerce but were also transforming the ways in which old and new businesses alike operate. Esther Dyson, one of the noted public intellectuals of the digital age, weighed in with her notion that small companies were going to be the primary engines of innovation in the Internet era.

While optimism and the drive for new business opportunities were the thrust of the 1998 conference, it was not short on negativity. The most obvious target was Microsoft Corp. At the time, Microsoft was at the outset of its investigation by the U.S. Justice Department for alleged antitrust violations. Heads of rival companies in the Internet business took turns taking Microsoft to task for what they saw as heavy-handed business tactics.

When the 2000 conference rolled around, it lacked the feeling of boundless optimism, particularly related to the possibilities of e-commerce, that characterized earlier meetings. Scheduled just after the precipitous decline of the NASDAQ stock market and in the midst of the massive e-commerce shakeout, the meeting took place during a time of relative uncertainty for Internet companies. So instead of a focus on business opportunities and speeches from leading Internet players, the 2000 conference was geared more heavily toward issues of public policy, social uses of the Internet, and politics. Odes to the financial gold mines waiting to be discovered on the Internet were barely visible. The conference primarily concentrated on how the Internet was transforming human social life via alterations in business practices, policy, law, technology, and education. The ability of the Internet to allow political parties to quickly disseminate personalized information during campaigns was widely discussed, as was the Internet's utility as a campaign fund-raising vehicle. Keynote speaker and Internet pioneer Mitch Kapor, the founder of Lotus Development Corp., took the opportunity to decry the excessive commercialization of the Web and its attendant "strip mall" feel. In place of an online shopping medium, Kapor called for enhanced emphasis on the Internet's original purpose: to facilitate greater communication, networking, and understanding throughout the world.

The Harvard Conference also served other, less lofty purposes as well. Companies used the conference as a platform for public relations and marketing by showcasing new products and hyping new business models. Individuals and firms sometimes took to settling personal scores through thinly veiled jabs, underscoring some of the political overtones of the event. But the common, recognized purpose of the Harvard Conference on Internet & Society was to seek out a positive development scheme for the Internet. Such contentious social issues as the digital divide and the commercialization of the Internet were assessed, argued, and theorized, with an eye toward forming a general policy framework in which the Internet could develop for the greatest overall benefit to society, consistent with the various interlocking interests the attendees represented.

PROJECTS

This primary sociopolitical focal point earned the Berkman Center recognition, advancement, and funding. The MacArthur Foundation provided a number of large grants, increasing in size during the 2000s. One of these was a $4 million gift in late 2007, which was to celebrate and support the organization in its second decade of scholarship and thought. The following May, the center was raised to its current status within Harvard University as a university-wide, interfaculty initiative. Although the new status was merely an extension of the powers that the organization previously held, William Fisher, faculty director, commented on the benefits of the new recognition: "While the Berkman Center has always been to some extent an interdisciplinary enterprise, this institutional change will increase sharply the methodological range of our work and the diversity of the faculty, fellows, and students we enlist to do it."

The recognition was a boon for the program, allowing the Berkman Center to spread its network. The Global Network Initiative, a Berkman project begun in 2009, was a collaborative effort of those entities involved in information and communication technologies (ICT) to facilitate privacy and freedom of expression online. Human rights organizations (such as the World Press Freedom Committee), private companies (such as Google and Yahoo!), academics (such as representatives from Harvard University's Center for Democracy & Technology), as well as academics from other universities around the globe met to take collective action to produce a global organization capable of defending rights of expression on the Web.

Among its new projects taken up in 2011, the Berkman Center added Distributed Denial of Service (DDoS) to its growing list of initiatives, due to the increasing prevalence of this type of cybercrime and the insufficiency of the law to punish it. (DDoS is an attack on a Web site designed to make it unusable for a period of time.)

SEE ALSO *Cyberculture; Digital Divide; Global E-Commerce Regulation.*

BIBLIOGRAPHY

Benkler, Yochai, Rob Faris, Urs Gasser, Laura Miyakawa, and Stephen Schultze, "Next Generation Connectivity." Berkman Center for Internet & Society. Cambridge, MA, February 15, 2010. Available from http://cyber.law.harvard.edu/publications/2010/Next_Generation_Connectivity.

"Berkman Center Receives $4M gift from MacArthur Foundation." *Harvard Gazette,*, November 29, 2007. Available from http://news.harvard.edu/gazette/story/2007/11/berkman-center-receives-4m-gift-from-macarthur-foundation.

Bradner, Scott. "The Web as Luther, the Net as Widener." *Network World,* June 10, 1996.

"Harvard Elevates Study of Technology and Society." *Harvard Gazette,* May 15, 2008. Available from http://news.harvard.edu/gazette/story/2008/05/harvard-elevates-study-of-technology-and-society.

Kaplan, Karen. "Harvard Conference on Internet and Society: At Highbrow Event, Low Blows for Microsoft." *Los Angeles Times,* June 1, 1998.

Katz, Frances. "Internet Access, Microsoft Top Harvard Agenda." *Atlanta Journal and Constitution,* May 31, 1998.

———. "The Party's Over." *Atlanta Journal and Constitution,* June 25, 2000.

Machlis, Sharon. "Crystal Balls Focus on Internet and on E-commerce at Harvard Confab." *Computer World,* June 1, 1998.

O'Reilly Associates, eds. *The Harvard Conference on the Internet & Society.* Cambridge, MA: Harvard University Press, 1997.

"Research." Cambridge, MA: Berkman Center for Internet & Society. 2011. Available from http://cyber.law.harvard.edu/research.

Weil, Nancy. "Group to Manage Domain Names." *InfoWorld,* June 8, 1998.

BERNERS-LEE, TIMOTHY

Tim Berners-Lee is founder and director of the World Wide Web Consortium (W3C). His greatest invention draws numerous comparisons to Gutenberg's printing press because it brings information and tools, formerly reserved for a select few, to the masses. Sitting at a tiny cubicle in a physics laboratory in Switzerland, the reclusive, soft-spoken Berners-Lee gave birth to the World Wide Web and helped transform the economic, cultural, and social realms of the modern world. Moreover, he insists that the Web he originally created was only the beginning. "The glorified television channel you see today," Berners-Lee proclaims, "is just part of the plan."

EARLY LIFE

Born in London in 1955, Timothy J. Berners-Lee is the son of two mathematicians who worked on the first commercially sold computers. A physicist by training, he did his pioneering work at the Centre Europen de Recherche Nucleaire (European Laboratory for Particle Physics, or CERN), the Geneva-based physics laboratory, as a contract programmer. His proposal to develop an interactive, universal interface for use on the Internet—the project that would become the World Wide Web—was twice rejected at CERN until he put the lab's 10,000-name phone book into his programming language as a prototype to show the Web's possibilities. His prototype, designed to function in a "brain-like way" but also to track and connect all the random associations that are often buried in the brain, was called Enquire Within Upon Everything. In just two months, he gave the Pentagon-funded, technical-user-oriented communications program known as the Internet a human face, ready for global use. Bypassing the need for large centralized registries, he developed uniform resource locators (URLs), as well as hypertext transfer protocol (HTTP) for transferring data to and from any connected computer. He also designed the lingua franca of the Web: Hypertext Markup Language (HTML). Thus, the World Wide Web was born in 1991, at which point he gave it all away for free and began devoting his time to promoting its wider use.

In 1994, Berners-Lee left CERN for a position at the Laboratory for Computer Science at the Massachusetts Institute of Technology (MIT), where he founded the World Wide Web Consortium, a loose-knit collection of Web, hardware, and software firms as well as other interested parties. The W3C's primary mission was to oversee the Web's development (although it is not a governing body), and in large part the consortium worked to stave off proprietary battles over standards and protocols. The W3C and Berners-Lee were both instrumental in the fight to keep the Web free and nonproprietary.

Berners-Lee continued to push the Web's development forward, particularly through his pioneering work on Extensible Markup Language (XML), a metalanguage that focuses on the conceptual meaning of Web content, rather than simply on page formatting. XML allows for two-way communication between Web servers so as to facilitate more comprehensive treatment of content and transactions. According to Berners-Lee, XML will be the driving force in creating the next step in the Web's evolution—the Semantic Web, or Web 3.0.

Broadly, the Semantic Web is Berners-Lee's vision for a system that will perform the more mundane tasks of human interactions and transactions, leaving the actual thinking to humans. With dramatically enhanced ability to define objects in cyberspace, the XML-driven Semantic Web promises vastly more powerful and accurate search engines that will make the Web more navigable and a less dizzying mess of information. True to its name, the Semantic Web is intended to make reading and interpreting Web content easier for computers by increasing their recognition of context and their ability to make logical inferences. It will also allow more direct communication between machines and will free individuals to concentrate on more involved and creative thinking. This is a crucial step in what Berners-Lee sees as the creation of a Web that acts as cells within a global brain.

Throughout the first decade of the twenty-first century, the Semantic Web saw slow but inexorable progress as Berners-Lee and W3C began to develop protocols, definitions, and technical standards that would allow the markup language behind each Web page to be cross-referenced to convey added meaning. Berners-Lee gives an example of how a Web 3.0 site that announces a conference would work. Users could click on a link that would transfer the date and time of the conference to a PDA, while the address is sent to the their GPS, and the names of other attendees are transferred to the their e-mail address book.

In December 2004, Berners-Lee became a professor in computer sciences at the University of Southampton, United Kingdom. In 2006, he helped to launch the Web Science Trust, a multidisciplinary research body dedicated to guiding the future use and design of the Web. In 2008, he started the World Wide Web Foundation, a nonprofit body dedicated to funding and coordinating the further development of the Web. Berners-Lee was given a knighthood in 2004 for services to the Internet.

Berners-Lee's vision includes a Web that can help humans to create a fairer and better world through greater interconnectivity. He envisions the Web allowing people to make connections they may not have dreamed of, through greater and more efficient access to more data. In a 2011 interview with John Naish of the *New Statesman,* Berners-Lee said that he felt his greatest achievement was in creating the Web as an open platform, and his greatest fear is the loss of Internet freedom. Although he could have made billions from his invention, Berners-Lee has committed himself, and the foundations he works with, to pushing for the continued openness and decentralization of knowledge and resources. His vision of the Web is of an all-encompassing democratic force for global civilization, in which business issues are dominated by their social implications. While his claim that the Web will serve as the vehicle for the next stage of human civilization may at first sound grandiose, the possibility grows closer every day.

SEE ALSO *HTML (Hypertext Markup Language); History of the Internet and World Wide Web; World Wide Web Consortium (W3C); XML (Extensible Markup Language).*

BIBLIOGRAPHY

Berners-Lee, Tim. "Long Live the Web: A Call for Continued Open Standards and Neutrality." *Scientific American,* November 22, 2010. Available from http://www.scientific american.com/article.cfm?id=long-live-the-web.

Berners-Lee, Tim, James Hendler, and Ora Lassila. "The Semantic Web." *Scientific American,* May 17, 2001. Available from http://www.scientificamerican.com/article.cfm?id=the-semantic-web.

Berners-Lee, Tim, and Mark Fischetti. *Weaving the Web: The Original Design and Ultimate Destiny of the World Wide Web by Its Inventor.*San Francisco: HarperCollins, 1999.

Lee, Mike. "Top 10 Most Influential People: No. 1—Tim Berners-Lee." *Network Computing,* October 2, 2000.

Lohr, Steve. "Its Creator Seeks an Even Wider Web" *Bits* (blog), *New York Times,* September 15, 2008. Available from http://bits.blogs.nytimes.com/2008/09/15/its-creator-seeks-an-even-wider-web.

Luh, James C. "Tim Berners-Lee." *Internet World,* January 1, 2000.

Naish, John. "The NS Profile: Tim Berners-Lee." *New Statesman,* August 15, 2011. Available from http://www.newstatesman.com/scitech/2011/08/berners-lee-web-world-internet.

Owens, Ross. "E-business Innovators: Tim Berners-Lee; XML." *InfoWorld,* October 9, 2000.

Port, Otis. "How the Net Was Born—and Where It's Headed." *Business Week,* November 1, 1999.

Quittner, Joshua, and Frederic Golden. "Network Designer: Tim Berners-Lee." *Time,* March 29, 1999.

Reinbach, Andrew. "Sidestepping Bureaucracy in the Web's Next Iteration." *U.S. Banker,* February 2000.

Reiss, Spencer. "St. Tim of the Web." *Forbes,* November 15, 1999.

Shannon, Victoria. "A 'More Revolutionary' Web." *New York Times,* May 23, 2006. Available from http://www.nytimes.com/2006/05/23/technology/23iht-web.html?_r=1.

Woolnough, Roisin. "Meet the Man Who Invented the Web." *Computer Weekly,* November 30, 2000.

BERTELSMANN AG

German publishing giant Bertelsmann AG is a large international media company with four primary divisions: television (RTL Group), book publishing (Random House), magazine publishing (Gruner + Jahr), and media services (Arvato). Its corporate arm comprises administration and investments, which include music rights company BMG. The company's core markets are in Western Europe and the United States.

Bertelsmann has acquired and divested a number of companies and initiatives over the years, in line with its strategy to strengthen core businesses while positioning itself in promising growth markets. The company has attempted to adapt to the rapidly changing nature of the digital world by marketing existing products through new channels as well as offering complementary services.

EARLY HISTORY

Carl Bertelsmann began working as a bookbinder in his hometown of Gutersloh, Germany, in 1819. The bookbinder's initial work consisted of printing and binding hymnals for nearby churches. In 1835, Bertelsmann incorporated his business as C. Bertelsmann Verlag. Bertelsmann died in 1850, leaving his son Heinrich a sizable inheritance and control of the family business. *Missionsharfe* (Missionary Harp) was first published in 1853 and became Bertelsmann's first best seller with a circulation of more than two million copies. The firm's early success encouraged Heinrich to began expanding beyond religious books to publish historical works and even novels.

Friederike Bertelsmann, Heinrich's daughter, married Johannes Mohn in 1881. Heinrich had no male heirs, so the Mohn family inherited the business upon his death in 1887. In an effort to increase production at a minimal cost, Mohn expanded Bertelsmann's internal printing operations.

STAIN OF HITLER

While the truth did not surface until 2002, when a Bertelsmann-appointed commission revealed it in an 800-page report, Bertelsmann had strong ties to the Nazi regime. Until the report was publicized, Bertelsmann claimed to have been shut down by the Nazis in 1944 not due to war shortages but for publishing anti-Nazi propaganda—a lie the company used during its 1998 takeover of U.S. publishing giant Random House. In reality, Bertelsmann profited during Hitler's reign by publishing texts with a clear anti-Jewish bias. It also used Jewish slave labor in its Latvian and Lithuanian operations, and Heinrich Mohn (Friederike and Johannes son) was found to have made donations to the Nazi *Schutzstaffel,* or SS. The company later apologized for its Nazi involvement and subsequent cover-up, telling the BBC that the "values of Bertelsmann then are irreconcilable with the company today."

After the war, Reinhard Mohn, grandson of Johannes Mohn, set about rebuilding the company. In 1950, he launched Bertelsmann Lesering, a book club that granted bargains and other perks to members. The club's rapid success—it amassed one million members in less than four years—set the stage for additional growth. Bertelsmann bought a small portion of Gruner + Jahr, a publishing company based in Hamburg in 1969, and ten years later upped its stake to nearly 75%. Bertelsmann also entered the American book publishing arena by purchasing a controlling stake in thriving U.S. paperback publisher Bantam Books. The company also ventured outside of book publishing for the first time by acquiring the Arista record label from Columbia Pictures.

GLOBAL GROWTH AND DIVERSIFICATION

A string of acquisitions during the 1980s vaulted Bertelsmann to a leadership position among global media and communication companies. For example, Bantam became a wholly owned subsidiary of Bertelsmann in 1981. The firm also added to its U.S. holdings with the $475 million purchase of Doubleday, a leading U.S. book publisher, in 1986. The deal gave Bertelsmann control of the well-known Dell paperbacks line, along with various book clubs and retail stores. To supplement its growing music holdings, Bertelsmann bought 75% of RCA's record division for $330 million, instantly becoming the world's third-largest recording company. *Fortune* magazine ranked Bertelsmann as the world's largest publishing company in 1991.

Further diversification came in 1993 when Bertelsmann and TeleCommunications Inc. (TCI) forged a joint venture to establish a cable television channel for music and video distribution in the United States. The 1995 purchase of a minority stake in America Online (AOL) marked Bertelsmann's first Internet venture. The $50 million investment turned into a $5 billion windfall and established the groundwork for Bertelsmann's future alliances with AOL and its later move into the e-commerce arena.

Late in 1997, Advance Publications Inc. began negotiating its sale of Random House with Bertelsmann. At the time, the $1.4 billion deal was the largest in industry history. It was finalized in July of the following year, leaving Bertelsmann with control of nearly one-third of all hardcover bestsellers and half of the leading paperback books in the United States.

FOCUS ON E-COMMERCE

Although Bertelsmann had dabbled in various online ventures in the mid-1990s, it was not until a few years later that a concrete e-commerce plan emerged. In 1998, the firm paid roughly $200 million for a 50% stake in Barnesandnoble.com to shore up its position in the U.S. online book industry and launched its own retail book site, BOL.com, to compete with Amazon.com in Europe. The new Bertelsmann eCommerce Group, or BeCG, bought online music retailer CDNOW and joined forces with music indexing site Napster in 2000 despite widespread controversy over alleged copyright infringement regarding the technology that allowed Napster users to exchange songs for free. It was a regrettable move: Bertelsmann extended Napster roughly $85 million in credit, only to settle four lawsuits from music labels, all accusing Bertelsmann of aiding Napster's copyright infringement, over the next several years. Bertelsmann paid $130 million to the National Music Publishers Association, $60 million to Universal Music, $110 million to Warner Music at $110 million, and an undisclosed amount (thought to be between $50 million and $150 million) to EMI.

Also in 2000, Bertelsmann dismissed CEO and chief new media architect Thomas Middelhoff after shareholders disagreed with the company's direction. Gunter Thielen replaced him and immediately began cutting unprofitable operations from the company, many of them in the e-commerce arena. The same year, the head of BeCG, Andreas Schmidt, resigned. He had played a key role in the deal with Napster. Operations of the e-commerce group shifted to Bertelsmann's Direct Group, which handled book clubs, online shops, brick-and-mortar bookstores, and publishing.

The company sold its 37% stake in Barnesandnoble.com to Barnes & Noble Inc. in 2003.

In 2004, Bertelsmann embarked on a partnership with Sony in Japan, creating Sony BMG Music Entertainment. The merger, according to the *New York Times,* served as "an example of the perils of joint ventures. It suffered early on from feuding between Sony and Bertelsmann, much revolving around its first chief executive,

Andrew R. Lack." Former chief of BMG Rolf Schmidt-Holtz replaced Lack in 2006, and while he increased cooperation between the partners he could not prevent the partnership's failure to monetize media assets online. Sony and Bertelsmann unraveled the joint venture in 2008, with Sony buying Bertelsmann's 50% stake for $900 million—much less than the $1.6 billion Bertelsmann had once hoped to get for its half.

Bertelsmann has continued to retreat from e-commerce as it has built up its traditional service businesses. It disbanded the Direct Group division in 2011 after several years of selling off online books sales clubs. "As part of our strategy to improve the growth profile of Bertelsmann, we have gradually sold off Direct Group's international operations since 2008," said Bertelsmann chairman and CEO Hartmut Ostrowski. "We reached another milestone with the divestment of the businesses in France, after having sold a number of other businesses earlier. The decision to reorganize the remaining Club businesses completes the scale-back of Direct Group, and thus concludes a large strategic task."

SEE ALSO *Napster.*

BIBLIOGRAPHY

Andrews, Robert. "EMI, Bertelsmann Settle; Put Napster Dispute to Rest." *PaidContent.org,* March 27, 2007. Available from http://paidcontent.org/article/419-emi-bertelsmann-settle-put-napster-dispute-to-rest.

"Bertelsmann Admits Nazi Past." *BBC News,* October 8, 2002. Available from http://news.bbc.co.uk/2/hi/business/2308415.stm.

Bertelsmann AG. "Bertelsmann at a Glance." Gütersloh, Germany, 2011. Available from http://www.bertelsmann.com/Investor-Relations/Bertelsmann-at-a-Glance.html.

"Bertelsmann AG." In *Notable Corporate Chronologies.* Farmington Hills, MI: Gale Group, 1999.

"Bertelsmann Completes Acquisition of CDNOW." *PR Newswire,* September 1, 2000.

"Bertelsmann Selling E-commerce Assets." *InternetNews.com,* September 2, 2002. Available from http://www.internetnews.com/ec-news/article.php/1455471/Bertelsmann+Selling+ECommerce+Assets.htm.

"Bertelsmann—Under E-construction." *Economist,* June 10, 2000.

Christman, Ed. "BMG Owner Investing in Book Net Site." *Billboard,* October 17, 1998.

Ewing, Jack. "Bertelsmann: Building a Video Napster." *BusinessWeek Online,* February 5, 2001. Available from http://www.businessweek.com/bwdaily/dnflash/feb2001/nf2001025_932.htm.

Gibney, Frank. "Middlehoff's Vision: The Bertelsmann Boss Pulls Off a Shocking Deal with Renegade Napster. And He's Just Warming Up." *TIME International,* November 13, 2000.

Hu, Jim. "Bertelsmann's E-commerce Chief Resigns." *CNET News,* November 28, 2001. Available from http://news.cnet.com/2100-1023-276281.html.

Kesgin, Tayfun, Howell Llewellyn, et al. "Bertelsmann in Online Alliance." *Billboard,* May 27, 2000.

Kontzer, Tony. "BMG's Man on the Move—Andreas Schmidt Plays a Part in the Music Industry's Digital Awakening." *InformationWeek,* January 1, 2001.

Landler, Mark. "Sony and Bertelsmann End Their Partnership in Music." *New York Times,* August 5, 2008. Available from http://www.nytimes.com/2008/08/06/business/worldbusiness/06music.html.

"The Man Who Would Be Cool—Face Value: Thomas Middlehoff, Napster's Music-Industry Ally." *Economist,* March 10, 2001.

O'Leary, Siobhan. "Rethinking Book Club Biz, Bertelsmann Disbands 'Direct Group'." *Publishing Perspectives,* June 15, 2011. Available from http://publishingperspectives.com/2011/06/rethinking-book-club-biz-bertelsmann-disbands-direct-group.

BEYOND.COM

Over the last 20 years, two different firms have held the name Beyond.com.

THE FIRST BEYOND.COM: 1994–2002

Beyond.com, which went out of business in 2002, was considered an e-services pioneer. The company designed, built, and managed e-stores for companies like Symantec Corp. and Inprise/Borland. The firm set itself apart from other e-commerce service providers by offering back-end services, such as product distribution, along with more traditional Web page design services. Thanks to its eStore 3.0 system, Beyond.com was able to construct an online store in less than four weeks. The firm also sold software online to government agencies and, on a lesser scale, to individuals. In September 2000, Deloitte and Touche ranked Beyond.com as tenth on its Silicon Valley Technology Fast 50 list, which evaluates the fastest-growing technology firms in California's Silicon Valley based on revenue growth. The rapid fall of Beyond.com illustrates the fate of many once-promising technology firms when the dot-com bubble burst.

Founded in 1994 by former Egghead executive William McKiernan, Beyond.com was first known as Software.net. After running his upstart firm for roughly four years, McKiernan convinced Mark Breier to leave his post as director of marketing at Amazon.com to head up operations at Beyond.com. Beyond.com also acquired General Services Administration (GSA) authorization, allowing it to sell software to the U.S. government as an authorized provider. Beyond.com established a separate Government Systems Group to sell software to the federal government. In 1999, the online software retailer was selling 45,000 software titles (nearly 5,600 of which could be downloaded via the Internet), had more than one million customers, and had annual sales of more than $37 million. Despite its status as a leading online software vendor, in 1999 Beyond.com lost nearly as much money as it made.

Recognizing that competition was only going to become more fierce in the online retail software market, Breier and his management team opted early in 2000 to shift Beyond.com's focus to the business-to-business (B2B) market by establishing an eStores division and offering e-commerce services such as constructing and operating e-stores. Believing this new aim was beyond the scope of his expertise, Breier relinquished control of daily operations to C. Richard Neely Jr., who served as interim CEO until the firm hired Ron Smith in June 2000.

Throughout 2000 and 2001, Beyond.com created a suite of extensive e-commerce services offered via the firm's eStores. Services included the actual construction and management of e-stores, from customer screening to order fulfillment, and eStores clients could also opt for eMarketing Solutions, which included tactics for increasing and retaining site traffic, such as eBanner, eCoupon, ePartners, eChannels, and BeDirect Mail. In August 2001, Beyond.com launched an Internet mall. The company's clients could place their eStores in the online mall and Beyond.com would receive commissions for purchases made through the mall.

Although Beyond.com reported a 50% rise in its eStores' revenue in the third quarter of 2001, and a 44% increase in government sales, the company was competing with Amazon.com, which had turned a profit in 2001, and the rapidly growing eBay. Unable to secure additional capital to continue operations, Beyond.com announced in January 2002 that it was filing for Chapter 11 bankruptcy. Beyond.com reached an agreement with e-commerce outsourcing company Digital River for the sale of its assets and clients' contracts for $3.5 million in cash and $7.5 million in Digital River stock.

Digital River was eventually forced to back out of the agreement to buy Beyond.com's Government Systems business, due to a failure to meet all of the closing conditions of the sale. Instead, Digital River purchased Beyond.com's eStores business for $4 million in stock, and the company's Government Systems Group was sold to Softchoice Corporation for $3.3 million in cash.

Digital River CEO Joel Ronning stated in a 2002 *eCommerce Times* interview that although Beyond.com's technology was sound, the company had suffered a failure in execution and leadership, compounded by frequent turnover among top executives. According to Ronning, the e-commerce industry was not willing to support a "second- or third-place player." The bursting of the dot-com bubble meant there were few investors for a loss-making online businesses.

THE SECOND BEYOND.COM: 2005–

Although the original Beyond.com completed its bankruptcy and went out of business in 2002, the name has since been taken by a Philadelphia-based career network. PhillyJobs.com was founded in 1998 as a free jobs board for the Philadelphia area. Seeing the need for an expanded service, PhillyJobs expanded to provide recruitment software used by employers and recruitment agencies. By the end of 1998, the company had changed its name to 4Business Network.

In 2001, the 4BusinessNetwork changed its name again, to Artemis HR, and acquired the 4Jobs.com domain. This become the 4Jobs Career Network, a hub for national job search and listings. The site developed its own software to allow applicants to apply for jobs directly via the 4Jobs Web site, and also licensed its software to other online job search sites. These sites were then linked vertically to the 4Jobs network. The 4Jobs network expanded to include more than 2,000 job search sites by 2004, when Artemis HR acquired MegaJobSites.com. The following year, Artemis rebranded itself and became Beyond.com. Acquisitions of TechCareers.com and JobAnimal.com followed, in 2007, giving Beyond.com a large presence in the Canadian market. In 2009, Beyond.com also acquired Matthews Career Centers, which operated a network of local job sites, such as SeattleJobs.com. *Forbes* named Beyond.com as the 11th most popular job search site in 2009, with 1.3 million unique visitors.

Capitalizing on its success in creating job search networks, Beyond.com signed a deal in 2010 making it the U.S. partner for the Network, an international job board network. Beyond.com became the exclusive U.S. member of the Network alliance. Later in 2010, Beyond.com acquired Orbius, a social Web site platform. Orbius operates as a type of "Facebook for small business," allowing businesses to create their own networking communities.

Although 2011's Beyond.com has no connection with the previous company using the name, it continues the work of creating e-communities begun by its namesake and predecessor.

SEE ALSO *Digital Economy; E-commerce Solutions; E-tailing.*

BIBLIOGRAPHY

Berman, Phyllis. "Hat Trick." *Forbes,* May 3, 1999.

"Beyond.com Acquires Orbius." *BusinessWire,* October 6, 2010. Available from http://eon.businesswire.com/news/eon/20101006005247/en.

Beyond.com. "Company History and Milestones." King of Prussia, PA, 2011. Available from http://about.beyond.com/history.

"Beyond.com Launches eStores in Germany and France for McAfee.com, Expanding Physical Product Distribution Capabilities." *Business Wire,* March 1, 2001.

"Beyond.com Named Silicon Valley's Tenth Fastest Growing Company by Deloitte & Touche." *Business Wire,* September 22, 2000. Available from http://www.thefreelibrary.com/Beyond.com+Named+Silicon+Valley%27s+Tenth+Fastest+Growing+Company+by...-a065381314.

Campbell, Scott, and David Jastrow. "E-commerce Pioneer Goes Beyond Software Sales." *Computer Reseller News,* June 12, 2000.

Grant, Elaine X. "Beyond.com Files for Bankruptcy" *E-Commerce Times,* January 25, 2002. Available from http://www.ecommercetimes.com/story/16004.html.

Kary, Tiffany. "Digital River Pulls Back on Beyond Deal." *CNET,* February 11, 2002. Available from http://news.cnet.com/2100-1017-834009.html.

Marcus, Miriam. "The Best Way to Find (and Fill) a Job Online." *Forbes,* May 26, 2009. Available from http://www.forbes.com/2009/05/26/job-seeking-websites-entrepreneurs-human-resources-monster.html.

"Ronald S. Smith—Beyond.com." *Wall Street Transcript,* September 4, 2000. Available from http://www.twst.com/ceos/bynd1.html.

Softchoice. "Softchoice Completes Acquisition of Beyond.com's Government Systems Group." Toronto, Ontario, Canada, July 31, 2002. Available from http://www.softchoice.com/about/press/2002/28.

BEZOS, JEFF

Jeff Bezos is the founder and CEO of Amazon.com, one of the largest online retailers. While Amazon.com became profitable in the early 2000s, its first several years were marked by growth but a lack of profitably as Bezos kept advertising and operating costs high. This led many to wonder if Bezos had a plan with long-term potential. Eventually, however, technology and marketability caught up with Amazon.com and allowed the e-commerce giant to begin turning a profit and then, through its products like the Kindle e-reader, successfully grow earnings.

LAUNCHING AMAZON

After graduating from Princeton University with degrees in electrical engineering and computer science, Jeff Bezos began working on Wall Street. Banker's Trust hired him to develop electronic fund management systems. Eventually, he left to begin working for hedge fund firm D.E. Shaw & Co., where he became the youngest senior vice president. Despite his success, the 30-year-old Bezos left his job at Shaw in 1994 to pursue his dream of creating an Internet retailer. He moved to Seattle, Washington, and began working on a business plan that would allow him to capitalize on what many analysts were predicting to be explosive growth in Internet use.

After researching 20 different products he believed could be sold via the Internet, including magazines, CDs, and computer software, Bezos settled on books, guessing that this sizable market, with its wide range of purchase choices, would be well served by electronic searching and organizing capabilities. Books also were relatively inexpensive, and Bezos concluded that consumers would be more likely to make their first purchase online if the risk was minimal. In addition, the small size of most books made for easier distribution. Bezos liked the fact that market share was distributed among many leading publishers. Industry leader Barnes & Noble held less than 12% of the $25 billion book retailing market, and Bezos believed this market fragmentation left room for fledgling companies.

Bezos decided to set up shop in Seattle, where he would be close to the warehouse of Ingram, a leading U.S. book distributor, as well as a large pool of technology professionals. He hired four employees and began working in the garage of his new home to build the software that would operate his online site. Although he initially planned to call his new business Cadabra, Bezos eventually settled on Amazon.com, believing the name of the largest river in the world conveyed Amazon's potential to reach vast numbers of customers. In July 1995, Bezos launched Amazon.com, a World Wide Web site that offered books at low prices and allowed visitors to search for books by author, title, subject, or keyword. Once a customer placed an order, Amazon requested the title or titles from the appropriate publisher, which shipped them to Bezos' home. At first, Bezos packaged the orders himself and took them to the post office. Typically, customers received their books within five days of placing an order. Books were shipped to all 50 states and 45 countries throughout the world.

In October, three months after its inception, Amazon achieved its first 100-order day. Shortly thereafter, the site became so busy that the beep heard at the office each time a customer completed an order was turned off because its tone became continual. Throughout Amazon's first year, Bezos worked to continually update the site to increase its user friendliness and customer service options. Many of these options also were designed to garner repeat business for Amazon. For example, customers could choose to sign up for e-mail messages that would let them know when their favorite author released a new title.

GROWING AMAZON

During Amazon's second year of operation, Bezos began to look for ways to increase the firm's growth. One of his first moves was to create the "associates" program in July 1996. This program allowed individual Web site owners and operators to offer links to Amazon from their sites. The associates then received a commission any time a visitor clicked on those links and bought books. To help fund future acquisitions, Bezos secured $10 million in capital from Kleiner Perkins Caufield & Byer in exchange for a minority stake in Amazon and a seat on the board. Advertising efforts included banner bars on some of the most heavily trafficked Web sites, as well more traditional plugs in print sources likely to be perused by book lovers. By the end of 1996, Amazon employed 110 people and its book database had grown to include more than one million titles. According to Bezos, the breadth of its offerings was key to the site's success, along with the fact that most books were discounted between 10% and 30%.

INITIAL PUBLIC OFFERING

In May 1997, although it had not earned a profit, Amazon went public, listing its shares for $18 apiece on NASDAQ. In less than a year those shares were worth nearly $100, and Bezos was on his way to becoming a billionaire. Bezos planned to use some of the funds from the offering to enhance Amazon's distribution arm. In October, Amazon became the Internet's first retail operation with one million customers. To commemorate this milestone, Bezos himself personally delivered the site's one-millionth order to a customer's home in Japan. The firm's name recognition was bolstered further when Vice President Al Gore spent a day answering customer service calls. Bezos forged alliances with America Online Inc. and Yahoo! Inc., both of which resulted in Amazon's promotion on these high-traffic sites. Growing 20% to 30% each month, sales at Amazon neared the $150 million mark, and book offerings grew to roughly 2.5 million.

The associates program reached 30,000 members in 1998. Bezos then oversaw the launch of Amazon.com Advantage, a program designed to promote the sales of independent authors and publishers. In April, the firm expanded internationally and also diversified into online video sales when it acquired the U.K.-based Internet Movie Database. Two months later, after Bezos decided to expand Amazon's product line with CDs, he unveiled Amazon Music, which offered more than 125,000 music titles online. In December 1998, more than 1 million new customers shopped online at Amazon for holiday gifts. Customers exceeded 6.2 million, securing Amazon's position as the number three U.S. bookseller, behind Barnes & Noble and Borders.

In 1999, Amazon secured its ten-millionth customer. Expanding his site's offerings even further, Bezos created Amazon Toys and Amazon Electronics. He also launched Amazon zShops, which permitted manufacturers to offer products for sale on Amazon. Bezos conducted a $1.25 billion bond offering to fund an acquisition spree that included stakes in Drugstore.com, HomeGrocer.com, Pets.com, Gear.com, and Della.com. This move later proved costly as several of the smaller dot-com businesses went bankrupt, and Amazon was left with nearly $2 billion in debt.

Eventually, Bezos divided Amazon's offerings into virtual stores that focused on merchandise like software, video games, gifts, and hardware. Customers also were able to sign up for a wish list service. By the end of 1999, Amazon had shipped 20 million items to 150 countries across the globe. Bezos was named "Person of the Year" by *TIME* magazine. According to United Press International, Bezos earned the award because his "vision of the online retailing universe was so complete, his Amazon.-com site so elegant and appealing that it became from day one the point of reference for anyone who had anything to sell online."

BUSINESS VALUES

During his growing of Amazon, Jeff Bezos adopted what he called the Six Core Values. These values were attitudes and goals that he used to concentrate Amazon operations on what he believed mattered most. First came Customer Obsession, his term for outstanding customer service. Next, Ownership helped to frame accountability practices, Bias for Action avoided wasting time, and Frugality helped control costs. He also included a High Hiring Bar to ensure the best employees possible worked for Amazon, and Innovation to keep the company exploring new ways to offer online value to customers. These values were at least partially responsible for Amazon surviving the dot-com bust that brought so many other online companies down.

In the 2000s, Amazon sales continued to grow and profits became more dependable as larger numbers of people turned to online shopping, and transportation methods became more cost effective. By 2006, Amazon was bringing in more than $10 billion in revenue, and profits were continuous. No serious competitors rose to challenge it, and even other large online stores like BarnesandNoble.com could not compete in the years to come. Bezos, however, was increasingly interested in exploring the frontiers of technology. After investigating the possibilities behind e-ink (an electronic technology designed to resemble the appearance of ink on printed paper) and the future of the book industry that Amazon had built its business on, Bezos began diverting more funds toward operations once again. By 2007, the company had not only created a way to sell digital music through Amazon MP3s, but also come out with the first version of the Kindle e-reader.

Bezos quickly increased profits with Kindle sales through a successful early-entry strategy. By the time

Apple had come out with the iPad and Barnes & Noble had developed an e-reader for competition, Bezos had already cornered 95% of the market in the United States. (Europe and other areas had a longer history with e-ready devices.) When faced with the new devices, Bezos simply cut costs and started releasing new versions with increased capabilities, color, and wireless features. By 2010, Kindle and e-book sales were generating $2.38 billion annually, with more sales of e-books than physical books on the Amazon Web site.

SPACE TRAVEL

By the late 2000s Bezos was sufficiently wealthy to start investigating other investment activities. The 47-year-old CEO's value was estimated at $18.1 billion in March 2011. The 2011 *Forbes* list of the world's billionaires placed him at number thirty, due to a 50% spike in Amazon stock between 2010 and 2011, courtesy of the increased success of the Kindle.

In 2011, Bezos donated $10 million to a local Seattle history museum project designed to help note the role Seattle played in the rise of many successful companies, including Microsoft, Costco, and Boeing. The year also saw a $19.5 million investment from Bezos to nuclear technology projects being created and researched by General Fusion of Canada. A third project in 2011 saw Bezos giving $43 million for the construction of a 10,000-Year Clock being built in Texas.

However, few of Bezos' projects have captured the interest of the public like Blue Origin, the aerospace company founded and funded by Bezos in an attempt to commercialize space travel. Bezos started Blue Origin in 2004 with a research campus on the outskirts of Seattle and grew the venture continually over the years, developing a private rocket-launching facility in West Texas. After receiving funding from NASA the company started testing rocket vehicles like the New Shepard for the potential of multipassenger space flights at competitive prices for the public. While the beginning of the 2010s saw other competitors around the world start their own space ventures as NASA pulled out of the exploration and design sector, Blue Origin has remained one of the best funded out of all the space projects thanks to Bezos's personal interest.

SEE ALSO *Amazon.com, Inc.*

BIBLIOGRAPHY

"Amazon Paddles Along." *Chain Store Age Executive,* March 2001.

"Amazon.com Chief Honored by Time." *United Press International,* December 20, 1999.

"An Amazonian Survival Strategy: The E-tailer Is Long on Web Savvy, Short on Profits." *Newsweek,* April 9, 2001.

Appelbaum, Alec. "Amazon's Juggling Act." *Money,* March 1, 2001.

Brooker, Katrina. "Beautiful Dreamer." *Fortune,* December 18, 2000.

Cook, John. "Bezos Donates $10M to Seattle History Museum, Creating New Center for Innovation." *GeekWire,* August 17, 2011. Available from http://www.geekwire.com/2011/bezos-donates-10m-seattle-history-museum-create-center-innovation.

———. "Jeff Bezos Touts the Power of Long-Term Thinking, Budgets $42M for 10,000 Year Clock." *GeekWire,* July 26, 2011. Available from http://www.geekwire.com/2011/jeff-bezos-celebrates-longterm-thinking-budgets-42m-clock-ticks-10000-years.

Eads, Stephani. "Will Jeff Bezos Be the Next Tim Koogle?" *BusinessWeek Online,* March 12, 2001. Available from http://www.businessweek.com/bwdaily/dnflash/mar2001/nf20010312_979.htm.

"From Zero to 10 Million in Less Than Four Years: Amazon.com to Pass E-commerce Milestone Today." *PR Newswire,* June 7, 1999.

Hazleton, Lesley. "Jeff Bezos: How He Built a Billion-Dollar Net Worth Before His Company Even Turned a Profit." *Success,* July 1998.

Hof, Robert D. "Jeff Bezos." *BusinessWeek Online,* May 15, 2000.

"Jeff Bezos Biography." Academy of Achievement, 2010. Available from http://www.achievement.org/autodoc/page/bez0bio-1.

Lamm, Greg. "How Bezos, Ballmer and Allen Rank on 2011 Forbes Wealthiest List." *TechFlash,* March 10, 2011. Available from http://www.techflash.com/seattle/2011/03/bezos-ballmer-allen-on-forbes-list.html.

Martin, Michael H. "The Next Big Thing: A Bookstore?" *Fortune,* December 9, 1996.

Pollowitz, Greg. "Jeff Bezos Goes Nuclear." *National Review,* May 5, 2011. Available from http://www.nationalreview.com/planet-gore/266588/jeff-bezos-goes-nuclear-greg-pollowitz.

Prior, Molly. "Amazon, TRU Web Site Proves Successful Online Model." *DSN Retailing Today,* January 22, 2001.

Scally, Robert. "The Force That's Altering E-tail, One Category at a Time." *DSN Retailing Today,* May 8, 2000.

Schaff, William. "Insight into Technology Investing—Amazon's Profit Potential Is Growing, but It Still Isn't a Sure Bet." *InformationWeek,* April 16, 2001.

BIOMETRICS

Biometrics is a field of security and identification technology based on the measurement of unique physical and behavioral characteristics. Physical identifiers include fingerprints, retinal patterns, facial structure, and DNA profiling. Behavioral identifiers include keyboard dynamics, gait, and voice recognition. To verify an individual's identity, biometric devices scan certain characteristics and compare them with a stored entry in a computer database. While the fingerprint identification can be traced to the fourth century, automated biometric systems have been used since the 1960s. Automated fingerprint-based identification systems were standardized by the Federal Bureau of Investigation (FBI) in the late 1960s and spread throughout law enforcement by the mid-1970s. Since then, other biometric technologies have been used in highly sensitive institutions such as defense and nuclear facilities, health care facilities, and other commercial industries that require user authentication.

HOW BIOMETRICS WORKS

Biometrics systems are used for identity verification and simple identification. Identity verification biometric systems require two forms of input: the biometric input along with a personal identification number (PIN). Upon receiving the PIN, the computer accesses its stored database and locates the biometric template for that individual. The computer scans the two biological features looking for differences and, if it produces an exact match, verifies the individual's identity and grants access. In a simple identification system, on the other hand, the computer receives no cues from PINs or access cards and scans its entire database of biometric templates looking for a match. As a result, these systems must be more powerful.

TYPES OF BIOMETRIC SYSTEMS

Fingerprint- and palm-based biometric systems scan the dimensions, patterns, and topography of fingers, thumbs, and palms. The most common biometric in forensic and governmental databases, fingerprints contain up to 60 possibilities for minute variation, and extremely large and increasingly integrated networks of these stored databases exist. The primary disadvantage of fingerprint identification systems is that up to 5% of fingerprint recognition systems cannot provide sufficient resolution because of fingerprint erosion caused by manual labor or chemical use.

Like the fingerprint, a palmprint is distinctive. However, it has other unique geometric properties, such as width, length, and surface area. In addition, the palm contains three principal lines unique to each person, often known commonly as "the heart line, the life line, and the head line." These features require minimal storage space for identity verification systems. Also advantageous is the fact that a palm's principal lines are distinctive and stable. That is, they remain intact throughout a person's life.

Facial Recognition Facial recognition systems vary according to the features they measure. Some look at the shadow patterns under a set lighting pattern, while others scan heat patterns or thermal images using an infrared camera that illuminates the eyes and cheekbones. These systems are powerful enough to scope out the minutest differences in facial patterns, even between identical twins. The hardware for facial recognition systems became commercially available in the 1990s and is relatively inexpensive.

Eye Scans There are two main features of the eye that are targeted by biometric systems: the retina and the iris. Each contains more points of identification than a fingerprint. Retina scanners trace the pattern of blood cells behind the retina by quickly flashing an infrared light into the eye. Iris scanners create a unique biological bar code by scanning the eye's distinctive color patterns. Eye scans tend to occupy less space in a computer and thus operate relatively quickly, although some users are squeamish about having beams of light shot into their eyes.

Deoxyribonucleicacid (DNA) The most precise recognition systems are DNA-based systems. DNA is the nucleic acid containing genetic coding for all living beings. Except for identical twins, DNA patterns are absolutely unique. DNA profiling was developed by Sir Alec Jeffreys in 1984. Detecting DNA involves isolating a fragment of DNA at a recognizable portion of the chain and visually reproducing it with ink blots. DNA testing can be done using blood, semen, saliva, and hair. However, DNA testing can be problematic if it is contaminated by those that handle the specimen. In addition, DNA recognition has raised privacy and discriminatory issues, restricting its use in forensic applications.

Voice Verification Although voices can sound similar and can be consciously altered, the topography of the mouth, teeth, and vocal cords produces distinct pitch, cadence, tone, and dynamics that give away would-be impersonators. Widely used in phone-based identification systems, voice-verification biometrics also is used with personal computers.

Keystroke Dynamic A biometric system that is tailor-made for personal computers, keystroke-dynamic biometrics measures unique patterns in the way an individual uses a keyboard—such as speed, force, the variation of force on different parts of the keyboard, and multiple-key functions—and exploits them as a means of identification.

FUTURE BIOMETRIC SYSTEMS

The challenge to commercialize traditional biometric systems involves consumer resistance because of privacy concerns as well as the fact that such systems can be cost-prohibitive. Researchers continue to create new methods for biometric use in attempts to overcome these barriers.

An electrocardiogram (ECG) is a technique that measures the contraction of the heart muscle using electrical impulses. These electrical impulses have been found to be distinct to an individual. The advantages of using an ECG is that data storage is minimal for authentication. However, methods for data collection are inconvenient, and the body's motion affects the results.

Photoplethysmographic (PPG) signals are measurements of red blood cell movement in the heart. The measurements are taken using infrared optical sensors. While not quite as specific as fingerprint or DNA identification techniques, the measurement of four unique features identify individuals with a 94% accuracy rate. The PPG signal can be collected simply with a fingertip sensor. When used in combination with other biometric methods, PPG signals show promising application.

FEARS OF MISUSE AND LOSS OF PRIVACY

With the increasing demand for and applications of biometric devices come ethical and legal questions and concerns. Chief among these considerations is privacy. The storing of such intimate biological detail in large networks sparks fear of privacy invasion, as well as possibilities for misuse. Such fears have hampered the biometric industry's movement into new markets, particularly in the United States where concern for privacy is markedly high. Just how far a business or government has the right to look into the identities of individuals in the name of security was a matter that began to draw serious attention from government, industry, and various organizations in the twenty-first century.

The banking and medical industries have been the primary focus for privacy legislation. The government regulated personal medical information under the Health Information Technology for Economic and Clinical Health (HITECH) Act. Passed in 2009, HITECH requires companies to secure data adequately and notify individuals affected when data may have been compromised. The Gramm-Leach-Bliley Act (GLBA) of 1999 similarly governs banking and financial transactions. Both industries have found market uses for mass storage of personal information to enhance services to customers and increase worker efficiency. The trend toward increased centralized electronic data storage raised awareness of the sensitivity of private data becoming known to criminal elements, which became the catalyst for these laws.

However, concern for citizen privacy has also prevented the government from implementing measures meant to protect the United States from terrorism. The U.S. government has not followed the international trend of issuing national biometric identification cards. The national ID card would link to a national identity register (NIR) where biometric information such as fingerprints, iris scans, and other data would be stored. The national ID card could be used to access medical data when traveling, identify criminals, and prevent illegal immigration. In November 2008, the British government began issuing national ID cards to foreign nationals and planned to do so for British citizens on a voluntary basis. While U.S. public opinion has so far prevented a similar measure, the Real ID Act of 2005 gives the U.S. government the authority to issue national ID cards. As of 2012, the United States had not yet issued national ID cards, perhaps due to the estimated price tag of $17 billion.

THE BIOMETRICS MARKET

As biometric technologies have grown more sophisticated and affordable, they have found ever more markets to penetrate. Governmental applications remained the most common by 2011, as governments sought to safeguard their sensitive computer networks. But the private sector was adopting the technology at an accelerating rate.

In 2000, many industry experts believed biometrics manufacturers would find great profit in the expansion of e-commerce. However, by 2006, less than 7% of U.S. financial institutions had implemented biometric applications. Smart cards, outfitted with embedded microprocessor chips that could store biometric data as well as PINs, could only be read by a smart card reader. These applications were yet to become standard by 2011, due in part to the 2008–2009 recession in the United States that hit the banking industry especially hard. Instead of making the investment to equip customers with card readers, credit card companies and banks slashed budgets to stay afloat.

Meanwhile, the health care industry found that automated systems created substantial advantages such as information sharing and increased accuracy of medical records. This necessitated the industry deploying authentication solutions for employees. As electronic health records become prevalent in the industry, a new awareness for patient privacy introduces the need for reliable electronic security. Fingerprint biometrics allows authorized personnel to access centralized medical databases, reducing the need for duplicate records and forgotten passwords and PINs.

While biometric authentication for access to financial data has yet to take off as of early 2012, access to physical assets has increasingly involved biometric applications. Products that utilize biometric authentication systems are personal mobile devices, automobiles, and child protection services. The popular iPad and iPhone devices utilizing fingerprint identification were introduced at the Allscripts Client Experience (ACE) in August 2011. FIST Enterprises specializes in using fingerprint technology to prevent auto theft. In addition, companies use biometric technology for employees, allowing access to workstations, safes, and other company assets.

SEE ALSO *Authentication; Computer Ethics; Computer Security; Privacy: Issues, Policies, Statements; Computer Ethics; Computer Security; Privacy: Issues, Policies, Statements.*

BIBLIOGRAPHY

"Bank Security: Bodily Functions." *Economist,* July 12, 2008.

Bankston, Karen. "Biometrics: Toys or Tools?" *Credit Union Management,* January 2001.

"Biometric Keys to Networks, PCs Finally Come Alive." *Security,* September 1, 2000.

"Biometrics, Smart Cards on the Rise." *Information Security,* June 2000.

Bruno-Britz, Maria. "Back to the Future: Banks Are Revisiting Biometrics, Study Says." *IBank Systems + Technology,* March 2006, 16.

"Casefiles: Colin Pitchfork—First Murder Conviction on DNA Evidence Also Clears the Prime Suspect." *Forensic Science Service,* December 14, 2006.

"Children's Clinics Implements Fingerprint Biometrics for Secure Access to Electronic Health Records." *TMCnet.com,* August 26, 2011. Available from http://www.tmcnet.com/usubmit/2011/08/26/5732855.htm.

"An Evolving Biometrics Market." *ID World,* November 1999.

Hammel, Benjamin. "Are Digital Certificates Secure?" *Communications News,* December 15, 2000.

McGarr, Michael S. "Tuning in Biometrics to Reduce E-commerce Risk." *Electronic Commerce World,* February 2000.

Ma, Ting, Yan Zhang, and Yuang-Ting Zhang. "Biometrics." In *Wiley Encyclopedia of Biomedical Engineering,* edited by Metin Akay. Vol. 1, 537–48. Hoboken, NJ: Wiley, 2006.

"The Measure of Man." *Economist,* September 9, 2000.

O'Shea, Timothy, and Mike Lee. "Biometric Authentication Management—Biometric Authentication Systems Are Being Integrated into Desktop Systems." *Network Computing,* December 27, 1999.

Pepe, Michele. "Buzz about Biometrics." *Computer Reseller News,* November 27, 2000.

BIONOMICS

Bionomics is a field of economic thought. It breaks from previous economic philosophy by situating economics as an extension of biology and ecology. Proponents of bionomics, such as its founder Michael Rothschild, reject what they describe as the idea of the economy as a mechanistic process and instead view the economy as an "evolving ecosystem." Adherents interpret all participants and elements in an economy as organisms acting naturally and organically in a complex web of relationships, some cooperative and some competitive.

HISTORY OF THE STUDY OF BIONOMICS

Bionomics takes as its metaphor the natural evolutionary process in which participants seek to survive in a complex and changing environment, working toward ever-greater levels of complexity and efficiency. Thus, bionomics interprets economic phenomena as autonomous; the economy essentially runs itself. In his book *Bionomics: The Economy as Ecosystem,* Rothschild insists that all the technological information available in modern books, on the Internet, in journals, and in people's brains forms the basis of modern life in the same manner in which DNA constitutes the basis of biological life. This concept applies only to capitalism, which is viewed as a natural and spontaneous system, as opposed to socialism, which proponents of bionomics view as a belief system.

Bionomics suggests that governments should do as little as possible to interfere with what it interprets as a natural, organic process. Thus, bionomics discourages government regulations, redistributive tax schemes, and other measures to plan, control, or fix the economy. Markets are viewed as the optimal means to achieve economic efficiency and societal improvement.

CRITICISM OF BIONOMICS

Critics view bionomics as an elaborate apologia for right-wing politics and as replicating some of the uglier manifestations of social Darwinism beneath a guise of ecological and biological science. Some, such as economist Paul Krugman, go so far as to accuse bionomics of failing to grasp either traditional economics or natural evolution. And while bionomics criticizes governmental action for impeding rather than nurturing technological development, debunkers point out that nearly all high-tech industries in which the United States is competitive—including biotechnology, computers, the Internet, and electronics—were heavily subsidized, protected, and developed directly and indirectly through governmental intervention. Despite such criticism, bionomics won strong support from powerful groups and individuals, including the libertarian think tank the Cato Institute and former Speaker of the House Newt Gingrich.

By 2000, the study of bionomics had fallen out of favor, as its champions moved to new endeavors after the technology bust of the late 1990s created distrust of theories such as bionomics. Specifically, the assumption that traditional economic theory fails to account for technological change has been strongly challenged. According to Paul Krugman, "Bob Solow . . . got the Nobel Prize for his work on technological change, in particular for his demonstration that technology, not capital accumulation, historically has been the main driving force in economic growth." However, one facet of bionomics does resonate with both economists and scientists; in particular, economists largely agree with the notion that government intervention in the economy rarely has the intended effect.

BIBLIOGRAPHY

Borsook, Paulina. *Cyberselfish: A Critical Romp Through the Terribly Libertarian Culture of High-Tech.* New York: Public Affairs, 2000.

Dyson, George B. *Darwin among the Machines: The Evolution of Global Intelligence.* New York: Basic Books, 1998.

Huber, Peter. "Telecom Undone—A Cautionary Tale." New York: Manhattan Institute for Policy Research, January 2003. Available from http://www.manhattan-institute.org/html/_comm-telecom.htm.

Kakutani, Michiko. "Silicon Valley Views the Economy as a Rain Forest." *New York Times,* July 25, 2000.

Krugman, Paul. "New-Age Market Theory Is Bio-Babble: Pseudo-Economics Meets Pseudo Evolution." *Ottawa Citizen,* November 1, 1997.

Prime, Eugenie. "The Spider, the Fly, and the Internet." *Econ-tent,* June/July 2000.

Rothschild, Michael. *Bionomics: The Economy as Ecosystem.* New York: Henry Holt, 1990.

"Welcome to the Bionomics Institute." San Rafael, CA: The Bionomics Institute, 2011. Available from http://www.bionomics-institute.org.

BITNET

Ira Fuchs and Greydon Freeman founded the Because It's Time Network (BITNET) on May 5, 1981. Used mainly in academia, BITNET quickly became one of the world's largest networks, eventually connecting more than 500 U.S. and 1,400 international universities and research institutions by allowing for the electronic transfer of messages and files. Although BITNET itself had become obsolete by the mid-1990s, its development was important to the growth and popularity of the Internet and, in particular, e-mail.

As director of the City University of New York's (CUNY) computing center, Fuchs recognized that liberal arts scholars would benefit from a messaging network similar to ARPAnet, a U.S. Department of Defense network that had been used by mathematics and physics researchers since its inception in 1969. Fuchs began discussing his idea with Freeman, one of the heads of technology development at Yale. Recognizing that most campuses already were equipped with the remote spooling communications system (RSCS) built into IBM computers, Fuchs and Freeman began researching ways to use RSCS to allow messages and files to pass back and forth between universities. The network structure they came up with—which simply required a mainframe system, a modem, and a phone line—was based on NJE, a communications protocol developed and used by IBM.

In March 1981, Fuchs and Freeman established a group of computing center directors from several universities in the northeastern United States. The organization began operating as the managerial board for BITNET, which was formally launched when CUNY and Yale were connected less than two months later. More than 150 campuses were linked via BITNET over the next three years. BITNET networks soon emerged in Europe as the European Academic and Research Network, in Asia as Asia Net, and in Canada as NetNorth. Much of the international expansion was funded by IBM, as was the construction of a central office known as BITNET Network Information Center.

BITNET AND NEW TECHNOLOGIES

Several new supplemental technologies sprang up for BITNET, the most long-lasting of which was LISTSERV, developed by Eric Thomas in 1986. Mailing list software that served as both a list manager and a file server, LISTSERV allowed BITNET users to send e-mail messages to a single list address with multiple recipients. Messages sent to a LISTSERV address were then automatically routed to everyone on the mailing list. Eventually, LISTSERV evolved into well-known commercial mailing list server software, sold by L-Soft International, that was compatible with other platforms like Unix.

In 1991, Transmission Control Protocol/Internet Protocol (TCP/IP) technology became the Internet standard, prompting BITNET's managerial board to merge BITNET with CSnet, a struggling TCP/IP network. The newly merged entity, known as the Corporation for Research and Educational Networking (CREN) created BITNET II, which relied on TCP/IP for message and file transfers. BITNET founder Ira Fuchs became the president of the Board of Trustees.

While new technologies started out as a complement to BITNET's application, they eventually led to its obsolescence. BITNET was undeniably an important precursor to the Internet. However, the Internet grew beyond BITNET's purpose into an unexpected household consumer good. As users and providers realized the potential applications of the Internet, usage exploded. Users demanded ease of use, faster access, and inexpensive storage space. Software providers and broadband cable companies met these demands and offered ever more applications such as entertainment, online education, and stock trading. BITNET, used for communication and academic research, became archaic in short order.

DISSOLUTION

BITNET/CREN's membership peaked in 1992, reaching 1,400 members across 49 countries. However, CREN ended its support for BITNET II in 1996. Although used by some academic institutions, BITNET II failed to achieve the popularity of the original BITNET network. The proliferation of broadband connectivity allowed the Internet to become a vastly superior product. Instead of transferring data, the service BITNET was created for, users could access data on any server connected to the Internet without using their own storage space. This effectively made BITNET obsolete, although it was still used for data transfer of private documents.

CREN's mission was to support higher education and research organizations with information technology services and communication tools. CREN offered digital and Web certificate services to secure data transmissions. CREN also offered Webcasts such as TechTalk, which featured IT experts. Finally, CREN established business alliances for the purpose of addressing technology issues for higher-education issues.

However, membership dwindled by the turn of the century, as member businesses used CREN's services less and less. On January 3, 2003, members voted to dissolve CREN. On December 3, 2004, all services for BITNET II were closed.

Founder Ira Fuchs continued his work to utilize technology for academic research. He went on to become vice president for computing and information technology at Princeton University and the chief scientist of JSTOR, a company that archives scholarly journals. In 2000, Fuchs became the vice president and program officer for research in information technology at the Andrew W. Mellon Foundation. In 2010, Fuchs reduced his professional workload but continued to serve on a number of boards for companies interested in technology and data archival.

SEE ALSO *ARPAnet; Connectivity, Internet; History of the Internet and World Wide Web.*

BIBLIOGRAPHY

CREN. "CREN Members to Vote on Closing." Washington, DC, December 5, 2002. Available from http://www.cren.net/press_release.html.

Grier, David Alan, and Mary Campbell. "A Social History of Bitnet and Listserv, 1985–1991." In *IEEE Annals of the History of Computing* 22, no. 2 (April-June 2000): 32–41. Available from http://www.computer.org/portal/web/csdl/doi?doc=doi/10.1109/85.841135.

Katz, Richard N. "Archimedes' Lever and Collaboration: An Interview with Ira H. Fuchs." *EDUCAUSE* 36, no. 2 (March/April) 2001. Available from https://net.educause.edu/ir/library/pdf/erm0120.pdf.

Mackie, Christopher J. "Collaboration for a Positive-Sum Outcome: An Interview with Ira H. Fuchs." *EDUCAUSE* 46, no. 3 (May/June 2011). Available from https://net.educause.edu/ir/library/pdf/ERM1132.pdf.

BLOOMBERG L.P.

Bloomberg L.P. is among the world's leading financial information, news, and media companies. Along with selling real-time financial data to banks, investment firms, government agencies, and other institutions, the firm operates news bureaus throughout the world, publishes magazines, produces radio and television shows, and manages one of the most frequently visited financial information sites.

EARLY HISTORY

When Harvard Business School graduate Michael Bloomberg was fired from Salomon Brothers Inc. in October 1981, he began to explore the idea of establishing his own business. Bloomberg had worked in equity trading and sales for Salomon Brothers, where he was eventually named general partner. It was while working for the securities trader that Bloomberg first saw the need among Wall Street firms for a more sophisticated method of gathering and analyzing information.

In March 1982, Bloomberg sold off his Salomon Brothers stock and used the fresh capital to create Innovative Market Systems (IMS). He hired a team of computer programmers to begin developing an electronic information system that would grant users access to real-time securities market data via a desktop terminal. In December of that year, Merrill Lynch became IMS's first customer by ordering 20 terminals on the condition that IMS not market the machines to any Merrill Lynch competitors for five years. Impressed by the technology's potential, Merrill Lynch also bought a 30% stake in IMS for $30 million.

IMS launched the Portable Bloomberg machine in 1984. By pointing out that increased sales would up the value of Merrill Lynch's stock in IMS, Bloomberg convinced Merrill Lynch to lift the five-year sales restriction, freeing IMS to begin widespread marketing of its terminals at a price of $1,500 per month for a single terminal, and $1,000 per month for additional machines. IMS focused on marketing its technology to pension funds, central banks, mutual funds, insurers, and other "buy side" firms. Bloomberg changed his company's name to Bloomberg L.P. in 1986 and increased its user base by selling terminals to securities underwriters, trading firms, and other "sell side" firms for the first time.

International expansion efforts heated up in 1987 when the firm opened offices in both London and Tokyo. Global growth continued in 1989 with the launch of an office in Sydney, Australia. An office in Singapore opened in 1990. Bloomberg moved into Germany in 1992 by establishing a unit in Frankfurt and established a Hong Kong office in 1993. Eventually, the company established units in Brazil and India, and by the end of the 1990s, its customers spanned more than 100 countries.

Technological developments throughout these years also fueled the firm's growth. For example, a new securities trading feature allowed the firm to launch the Bloomberg Trading System in 1988—an electronic bond trading system that made the company a player in the electronic commerce arena before the term e-commerce had even been coined. The firm also launched the Bloomberg Traveler, which allowed subscribers to access Bloomberg information from remote locations. The 10,000th Bloomberg terminal was installed in 1990. Enhancements such as color monitors and video training materials, as well as e-mail and multimedia capabilities, came in the early 1990s.

GROWTH VIA NEW MEDIA OUTLETS

In 1991, the firm diversified into a new industry when Bloomberg hired former *Wall Street Journal* writer Matthew Winkler as the editor-in-chief of Bloomberg's Business News, a Washington, D.C.-based upstart news service that would cover the financial aspects of politics, business, general news, and sports. The news service eventually allowed Bloomberg to complete with the likes of Bridge Information, Dow Jones, Knight-Ridder, Reuters, and other news wires that served the world's largest newspapers and magazines.

That year, in what many would later call one of his most astute maneuvers, Bloomberg convinced the *New York Times* to publish Bloomberg Business News articles with the Bloomberg byline in exchange for providing the newspaper with a free terminal. (It was not until January 1, 1999, that Bloomberg began charging a monthly fee for the terminals it had been giving away to newspapers and magazines.) By 1992, Bloomberg had secured a similar deal with every major newspaper in the United States, essentially guaranteeing name recognition among financial news readers for his company.

Bloomberg began capitalizing on that name recognition almost immediately by venturing into other types of media. It acquired radio station WNEW, based in New York City, for $13.5 million, and changed its call letters to WBBR, which stood for Bloomberg Business Radio. The company also began publishing the *Bloomberg Magazine,* and in 1994 launched a new Sunday insert magazine called *Bloomberg Personal.* That publication's initial circulation of roughly six million marked it as one of the largest magazine launches in business.

The company moved into television when it aired its first episode of the Bloomberg Forum, a television show that consisted of interviews with corporate executives. In January 1994, Bloomberg Information Television, a 24-hour financial news service produced by Maryland Public Television and distributed by DirecTV, made its debut. In 1995, to allow subscribers to access the television service from their terminals, Bloomberg began wiring each terminal for compatibility with DirecTV satellite dishes. Bloomberg Information Television was launched in Europe that year. By then, Bloomberg Business News had expanded to include more than 330 reporters in 56 bureaus, and the firm had installed its 50,000th terminal.

IMPACT OF THE INTERNET

Although Michael Bloomberg believed that the financial information increasingly made available for free on the Internet was too unreliable and served too broad an audience to pose any real threat to his service, the firm launched its own Web site at the end of 1995. Due in large part to the Bloomberg name recognition, it quickly became one of the world's most heavily trafficked Internet sites. As with its traditional service, Bloomberg offered a wide-ranging combination of both financial data and news and general news on its site. However, the highly condensed data targeted a mass market and did not compete with Bloomberg's fee-based service. According to Bloomberg himself in a *AsiaPulse News* article in 2000, "The Internet is not fast and reliable enough for professionals. It is for the man on the street."

Unlike most of its competitors, Bloomberg did not race to use the Internet as a commerce vehicle. The company kept key features like the Bloomberg Trade Book and its fixed-income security trading network, launched in 2000, off the Internet, preferring to focus sales on its own terminal units. As the 2000s progressed and Bloomberg began to expand and diversify, this insular approach would ease up a little, but the business remained focused on its own hardware long after other financial institutions had moved to a Web-based business model. Surprisingly, Bloomberg remained successful despite the changes, in part because of the dedicated purposes of its terminals and in part because it had cornered the financial data market so completely in the 1990s.

GROWTH AND ACQUISITIONS

After weathering the dot-com bust in the early 2000s (which spared most of the financially focused and well-established Bloomberg clients), the company began to see steady, strong growth along with the rest of the investment market. Between 2004 and 2007, Bloomberg averaged a 13% growth rate each year. The company began expanding via acquisitions of other financial services, such as Brainpower NV in 2006 and New Energy Finance in 2009.

The late 2000s market crisis resulting from an overreliance on risky mortgage-backed securities and investment deals caused a slowdown in the previously high Bloomberg growth rates, in part due to the fall of so many financial moguls. Lehman Brothers alone used 3,500 Bloomberg terminals for its business. This setback slowed revenue growth to only a few percentage point annually until 2010, when the company began to pick up steam once again, albeit in a slightly different direction.

Bloomberg programs increased in complexity and services following their initiation in the late 1990s and early 2000s. As 2010 approached, investors were able to map their portfolios graphically using Bloomberg applications and use new analytics to calculate counterparty risk. This helped maintain the strong financial worker market core that Bloomberg depended on for much of its profit.

However, Bloomberg also moved with the times, especially when it came to new media options and the decline of traditional media and newspaper outlets. The company started an important and fundamental change. Michael Bloomberg himself was serving as mayor of New York for his third term in 2011 when the company appointed Daniel Doctoroff as CEO, while chairman Peter T. Grauer remained in the same position. Doctoroff admitted plans to lead the company into more general news service offerings to leverage the more common needs of online users. Not only did the company continue acquiring other financial organizations such as the Bureau of National Affairs ($990 million, in 2011), but it also started hiring employees who had lost positions in traditional print media like the *Wall Street Journal* and *Fortune* magazine. It also worked to acquire broader news services like *BusinessWeek*, which it bought for $5 million in 2009. It also continued to grow globally, opening offices in Ecuador and Abu Dhabi.

By 2011, Bloomberg had 300,000 financial professionals using its proprietary network and employed 12,900 people worldwide, with a presence in 72 countries. The company also released its first iPad app in 2011, the Bloomberg BusinessWeek+, designed to rely content from the print issue of *BusinessWeek* to tablet computer users. Notably, the program was designed in-house by Bloomberg publishers.

SEE ALSO *Bloomberg, Michael.*

BIBLIOGRAPHY

Berman, Dennis. "What's Hot in the Newsrooms: Bloomberg's 'Free Lunch' Is Over." *BusinessWeek Online*, October 12, 1998. Available from http://www.businessweek.com/bwdaily/dnflash/oct1998/nf81012g.htm.

"Bloomberg Anticipates No Threat from Internet." *AsiaPulse News*, June 29, 2000.

"Bloomberg L.P." In *Notable Corporate Chronologies*. Farmington Hills, MI: Gale Group, 1999.

"Bloomberg LP Appoints Daniel L. Doctoroff as CEO." *Bloomberg*, July 12, 2011. Available from http://www.bloomberg.com/news/2011-07-12/bloomberg-lp-appoints-daniel-l-doctoroff-as-ceo.html.

"Bloomberg LP M&A History." *Alacra Store*, 2011. Available from http://www.alacrastore.com/mergers-acquisitions/Bloomberg_L_P-1021175.

Clifford, Stephanie and Julie Creswell. "At Bloomberg, Modest Strategy to Rule the World." *New York Times*, November 14, 2009. Available from http://www.nytimes.com/2009/11/15/business/media/15bloom.htm?pagewanted=all.

Guerra, Anthony. "Bloomberg Aims to Simplify Straight-Through Processing." *InformationWeek*, December 18, 2000.

Harding, James, and Peter Thal Larsen. "Companies & Finance the Americas: Hot Debate Over Bloomberg's Future Is Political Issue." *Financial Times*, March 13, 2001.

Kover, Amy. "Why the Net Could Be Bad News for Bloomberg." *Fortune*. October 12, 1998.

McMeekin, Tara. "Bloomberg Tuned in to Readers." *News & Tech*, May 3, 2011. Available from http://www.newsandtech.com/magazines_and_more/article_72ac7ed6-75d4-11e0-8604-001cc4c03286.html.

Moukheiber, Zina. "Open—A Little: In an Age of Open Systems, Mike Bloomberg Only Reluctantly Separated His Data from His Terminals. Is He Resisting a Tidal Wave?" *Forbes*, December 16, 1996.

O'Leary, Mick. "Bloomberg Empire Takes On the Web." *InformationToday*, November 1, 1998.

Thompson, Amy. "Bloomberg Agrees to Buy Bureau of National Affairs for About $990 Million." *Bloomberg*, August 25, 2011. Available from http://www.bloomberg.com/news/2011-08-25/bloomberg-agrees-to-buy-bureau-of-national-affairs-for-about-990-million.html.

BLOOMBERG, MICHAEL

Michael R. Bloomberg is the founder and majority owner of Bloomberg L.P., one of the world's largest financial information, news, and media companies. Considered an industry mogul by most accounts, Bloomberg is known for parlaying his financial information services upstart into a billion-dollar media giant that competes with the likes of Dow Jones, Knight-Ridder, and Reuters. Despite Bloomberg's initial reluctance to compete on the Internet—a medium he viewed as targeting a much more general audience than the one his company served—his firm's Web site, launched in 1995, became one of the most frequently visited financial information sites on the Internet. In 2001, Bloomberg resigned as chairman of his firm and ran successfully for the office of mayor of New York City.

A native of Boston, Massachusetts, Bloomberg graduated from Johns Hopkins University in 1964 with a bachelors degree in electrical engineering. Two years later, he earned an MBA from Harvard Business School. He spent many of the early years of his career working in equity trading and sales for securities trader Salomon Brothers Inc., where he eventually achieved general partner status and headed up the development of an in-house computerized financial system. Salomon Brothers fired Bloomberg in October 1981. He sold his Salomon Brothers stock and used the proceeds and severance to found his own company.

Five months later, he established Innovative Market Systems (IMS) and put together a team of computer programmers to develop something he believed Wall Street sorely needed: a computerized information system that would grant subscribers, mainly Wall Street firms, access to real-time securities market data via a desktop terminal. In 1983, Bloomberg and his partners unveiled the first such machine to Merrill Lynch, which agreed to order 20 terminals and pay $30 million for a 30% stake in the fledgling information provider. Bloomberg's timing proved fortuitous. Ready for electronic access to the kinds of financial information Bloomberg offered, other major firms began signing up for the terminals. Bloomberg changed his company's name to Bloomberg L.P. in 1986.

One of Bloomberg's savvy moves in growing his company was convincing the *New York Times* to publish Bloomberg Business News articles with the Bloomberg byline in exchange for providing the newspaper with a free terminal. By 1992, Bloomberg had secured a similar deal with every major newspaper, virtually guaranteeing his firm's name recognition among financial news readers.

By the end of the 1990s, Bloomberg was publishing magazines and producing radio and television shows. The company also operated a Web site with live broadcasts and an electronic trading vehicle, and made its information available over mobile devices. By placing real-time financial data at the fingertips of securities investors, Bloomberg played an instrumental role in the industry's increasing reliance on online mediums.

FROM MOGUL TO MAYOR

Bloomberg turned to a political career in 2001. Although still a majority owner of Bloomberg L.P., he surrendered leadership to Peter Grauer and Lex Fenwick. While Bloomberg had been a registered Democrat for most of his life, he ran for mayor of New York City as a Republican on the 2001 ballot. He won the election, using $73 million of his own fortune for the campaign. Bloomberg's political platforms classify him as a fiscal conservative, although he takes a more liberal stand for social issues, such as abortion rights, gay marriage, and immigration. He is credited with balancing New York City's $6 billion budget, although he did so with tax increases. His first term focused on reforming public education. By 2009, Bloomberg's efforts resulted in reduced in-school crime, increased graduation rates and test scores, and measured accountability for both faculty and students.

In 2005, Bloomberg won a second term by a wide margin with a political stance that appealed to Democrats and Independents as well as his own Republican party. Indeed, the Independent Party of New York held a phone campaign to recruit volunteers to reelect Bloomberg, In addition, several well-known New York Democrats supported Bloomberg. Bloomberg's second term was marked by a 35% decrease in overall crime. In 2007, Bloomberg again switched his political party affiliation from Republican to Independent to more closely represent his ideology.

Known for bold actions, Bloomberg ran for a third term after successfully lobbying to change the city's term limits from two to three consecutive four-year terms. Bloomberg won the election with 51% of the vote. His third term will end in 2013.

Bloomberg's popularity and success as mayor can be attributed to some of the same things that drove his success as an entrepreneur. He uses statistical approaches to measure results of the city's management. He promotes accountability, allowing autonomy among his staff.

PHILANTHROPY

Bloomberg contributes his time and resources to causes he supports. The *Chronicle of Philanthropy* ranked him as the second most generous person in America. In 2010, he donated almost $280 million to 970 charities. He supports health initiatives, funding art education, and environmental responsibility. Bloomberg asserts that his parents instilled the desire to give back, and that doing so inspires others to do the same.

Named as one of *TIME* magazine's 100 Most Influential People, Bloomberg's financial success is easily measured. As of March 2011, his net worth totaled $18.1 billion, and *Forbes* ranked him among the top twenty richest Americans. His initiatives as New York City's mayor include measurable reductions in crime and increased public education quality. As a philanthropist, Bloomberg has donated more than $1.6 billion. In 2011, there was ample speculation about what Bloomberg would do when his third term as mayor of New York City was completed. He has denied that he will run for president or governor of New York, and his company's success without him at the helm may deter him from taking the reins again. A philanthropic endeavor seems likely, as does another start-up.

SEE ALSO *Bloomberg L.P.; Bloomberg U.S. Internet Index.*

BIBLIOGRAPHY

"About Mike Bloomberg." MikeBloomberg.com, 2011. Available from http://www.mikebloomberg.com/index.cfm?objectid=E689D66F-96FD-E9F6-B1AF64B8DAE78A69.

"Bloomberg Anticipates No Threat from Internet." *AsiaPulse News,* June 29, 2000.

"Bloomberg Steps Down." *United Press International,* March 6, 2001.

Dolan, Kerry A. "Bloomberg for Sale?" *Forbes,* September 18, 2000.

"Making the Grade." *New York Post,* October 19, 2009. Available from http://www.nypost.com/p/news/opinion/editorials/item_puJ8zClrMf7ihNWM7X9nyI.

Pasanen, Glenn. "Mayor's Legacy: Educational Improvements and Poverty Reduction, or Bold Budgeting and Economic Development?" *Gotham Gazette,* September 2006. Available from http://www.gothamgazette.com/article/finance/20060907/8/1964.

Spiro, Leah Nathans. "In Search of Michael Bloomberg." *BusinessWeek Online,* May 5, 1997. Available from http://www.businessweek.com/1997/18/b352532.htm.

"World's Billionaires: Michael Bloomberg." *Forbes,* March 2011. Available from http://www.forbes.com/profile/michael-bloomberg/.

BLOOMBERG U.S. INTERNET INDEX

The Bloomberg U.S. Internet Index is a benchmark for U.S. Internet companies that have a market capitalization greater than $250 million. It is owned and operated by Bloomberg L.P., a leading business publisher with scores of products relating to business news, statistics, and analysis. Among the companies tracked by the index are Web retailers of all varieties, Web-based advertising firms, content providers, Internet software vendors, Web portals, networking equipment companies, and other Internet-based service providers. The index weighs companies by their market capitalization, with the minimum capitalization set at $250 million. Among the major companies tracked by the index are Google, Priceline.com, and Amazon.com.

As e-commerce grew in the mid-1990s and the slate of new dot-com start-ups began turning investors into millionaires, interest grew in the specific tracking of Internet-based companies' stock market performance. Bloomberg began tracking these stocks in its own index on December 31, 1998, when the index was set at a base value of 100. Skyrocketing more than 250% in its first year, it far outpaced the growth of other major benchmarks such as the Standard & Poor's 500. However, the dot-com shakeout and larger tech-market bust in spring of 2000 that sank the NASDAQ index took the Bloomberg U.S. Internet Index with it. By the end of 2000, the index had fallen from its peak of $2.9 trillion to $1.2 trillion.

AFTER THE DOT-COM BUST

After 2002, successful IPOs were not necessarily ones that fit the profile of the Bloomberg U.S. Internet Index. Start-up companies were more along the lines of broader-based tech companies than companies with services exclusively tied to the Internet. For example, companies such as Samsung, Verizon, and Apple depend on the Internet to distribute their products, but Internet-based services are not their only product or service. One exception was Google, which went public in 2003, raising more than $1.5 billion.

The Bloomberg U.S. Internet Index began a slow ascent after hitting bottom in October 2002. Internet companies with more credible business models went public. Navteq Corp. went public in 2004, raising $880 million. In 2006, Spark Networks earned $259 million with its IPO, and Pandora, an online radio company, went public in 2011. In the early 2010s, other companies' investors are watching closely for IPO announcements are Facebook (scheduled for 2012), Twitter, Skype, Kayak Software, and Demand Media.

Due to its narrow definition (one that includes only Internet companies in the United States), the Bloomberg U.S. Internet Index is not widely quoted in financial news. Instead, the NASDAQ 100 Technology Sector Index, the Dow Jones U.S. Technology Index, and the S&P Global 1200 Information Technology Index are more popular measurements of the U.S. and global technology sector.

SEE ALSO *Bloomberg, Michael; Bloomberg L.P.; Volatility.*

BIBLIOGRAPHY

Baldwin, Clare, and Alina Selyukh. "LinkedIn Share Price More Than Doubles in NYSE Debut." *Reuters,* May 19, 2011. Available from http://www.reuters.com/article/2011/05/19/us-linkedin-ipo-risks-idUSTRE74H0TL20110519.

Bloomberg L.P. "Commodities News." New York, 2011. Available from http://www.bloomberg.com/news/commodities.

Kelly, Kate. "Facebook IPO Valuation Could Top $100 Billion." *CNBC,* June 13, 2011. Available from http://www.cnbc.com/id/43378490/Facebook_IPO_Valuation_Could_Top_100_Billion_Sources.

Mitchell, Ian. "Have Dotcoms Had Their Day?" *Computer Weekly,* November 16, 2000.

Ovide, Shira. "LinkedIn: Biggest Internet IPO Since Google." *Deal Journal* (blog), *Wall Street Journal,* May 18, 2011. Available from http://blogs.wsj.com/deals/2011/05/18/linkedin-biggest-internet-ipo-since-google.

Primack, Dan. "10 Largest Internet IPOs Since Google." *Fortune,* May 17, 2011. Available from http://finance.fortune.cnn.com/2011/05/17/10-largest-internet-ipos-since-google.

BLUETOOTH

Bluetooth, which was first developed by the Scandinavian telecom Ericsson as a universal telecommunications standard, took its name from Harald "Bluetooth" Gormsson, a Viking king who unified much of Scandinavia in the tenth century by expanding his kingdom across all of Denmark and taking over Norway. Bluetooth was meant to become a unified wireless protocol that mobile devices, laptops, and many other consumer devices could use to communicate with each other. Bluetooth was always developed as a wireless protocol, unlike earlier network protocols that were designed to send messages along cables.

BLUETOOTH DEVELOPMENT

Ericsson's employees first proposed the idea of Bluetooth in 1994. To develop the protocol further, Ericsson formed a Bluetooth standards group in 1998, which many large technology companies in the United States, Europe, and Japan quickly joined. This standards group made the specifications for Bluetooth devices visible to everyone on its Web site, but the technology itself was not free to use. A manufacturer still had to pay licensing fees to the Bluetooth standards group before its Bluetooth device could be sold to consumers. The group tested and registered each new Bluetooth compatible product, and unregistered products could not be marketed with the Bluetooth trademark.

By 1999, the Bluetooth standards group had completed the first version of the standard, announcing Bluetooth 1.0. The *Bluetooth SIGnal* announced that a thousand companies had joined the Bluetooth standards group, although complications with device compatibility testing would prevent the launch of any Bluetooth-compatible products until 2000. Bluetooth also had to change its logo, which was originally based on a Viking warship, as this image looked like a symbol owned by the Dutch media firm VNU (which later merged with Nielsen). The new logo combined runes for H and B, adding a reference to the Viking king as well as the unification potential of Bluetooth technology.

BLUETOOTH IN CARS

In 2002, Bluetooth technology started appearing as an option on luxury cars. The remote communication capabilities of a Bluetooth device were very convenient in a compact environment in which a tangled cable would be a major concern. Most cars did not come with Bluetooth capability, so car shops began offering Bluetooth upgrades for older vehicles. *CNN* reported that vehicle regulations were also driving the growth of the automotive Bluetooth market, as many jurisdictions were starting to prohibit drivers from using cell phones in their vehicles. These laws mainly punished drivers for holding their cell phones while on the road, and the Bluetooth devices could operate hands-free.

Security was a growing concern with Bluetooth devices. Eavesdropping tools potentially allowed nearby hackers to listen to conversations on Bluetooth devices inside other drivers' cars. Direct messages to another driver's phone were also possible with these tools, which had the potential to facilitate harassment. The *New York Times* reported in 2005 that other vehicle-based phone systems, including OnStar and TeleAid, shared these vulnerabilities. Also, a thief, using the network location software on his own Bluetooth device, could detect a Bluetooth-capable phone that a driver had left inside his car and then break into the car and steal the driver's phone.

BLUETOOTH CHALLENGES

By 2009, the need for Bluetooth had become less apparent. Bluetooth had advertised a personal local area network (LAN) on a remote device, without the need for cable connections. Traditional wireless LAN technology had caught up, and Wi-Fi Direct was introduced as a standard that offered the transfer rates of a home wireless network on a mobile platform and a better range than Bluetooth, according to *PC World*.

The Bluetooth 4.0 standard included three specifications, allowing higher-end Bluetooth devices to compete with newer Wi-Fi technology while expanding Bluetooth technology into new markets. The high-speed specification offered features that were comparable to Wi-Fi Direct, such as normal home-based network speeds and improved range. The classic specification ensured reverse compatibility with earlier Bluetooth devices. The low-power specification was meant for products such as heart rate monitors that were relatively small and could not hold a large battery, according to *CNET*. The Bluetooth 4.0 low-power specification lacked reverse compatibility, which had always been one of Bluetooth's main selling points, although cell phones and other Bluetooth 4.0 capable devices with larger batteries retained their reverse compatibility by switching between all three specifications to send messages.

SEE ALSO *Mobile E-commerce; Wireless Fidelity.*

BIBLIOGRAPHY

Berger, Ivan. "Miss Manners Wouldn't Approve: Snoops Bug the High-Tech Car." *New York Times*, August 14, 2005. Available from http://www.nytimes.com/2005/08/14/automobiles/14BLUE.html.

Blasdel, Justin, and Kian Pokorny. "The Future of Bluetooth Technology." Lebanon, IL: McKendree University, April 16, 2004. Available from http://faculty.mckendree.edu/kian_pokorny/Course_Pages/CSI490/Senior%20Projects.htm.

Heikkila, Pila. "Bluetooth Option for Car Phones." *CNN*, December 13, 2002. Available from http://articles. cnn.com/2002-12-13/tech/yourtech.carphones_1_bluetooth-technology-nick-hunn-mobile-phones?_s=PM:TECH.

"Issue No.2." *Bluetooth SIGnal*, September 1999.

Paul, Ian. "Wi-Fi Direct vs. Bluetooth 4.0: A Battle for Supremacy." *PC World*, October 26, 2010. Available from http://www.pcworld.com/article/208778/wifi_direct_vs_bluetooth_40_a_battle_for_supremacy.html.

Quan, Michael. "Bluetooth." Berkeley, CA: Letters & Science Computing Resources, University of California, October 3, 2011. Available from http://lscr.berkeley.edu/advice/using/bluetooth.

Whitney, Lance. "Bluetooth 4.0 Spec Gets Finalized." *CNET*, April 21, 2010. Available from http://news.cnet.com/8301-1035_3-20003029-94.html.

BOOLEAN OPERATOR

Boolean operators are used to search data sets for information efficiently. Boolean operations consist of three operators: "AND," "OR," and "NOT." These operators are often used to eliminate unnecessary results, include additional information, and maximize the relevancy of the search. By entering them in the form of a search query, these operators specify the parameters of a search. For example, someone searching for information about surfing in California might enter the following query to target their search: "Surfing AND California". By using the "AND" operator, the search will only include results that contain the words California and surfing, not results that include only one of the two terms. If the individual were interested in results about California, surfing, or California and surfing, the following query could be used: Surfing OR California. Finally, if someone wanted information about surfing, but specifically *not* about surfing in California, the NOT operator could be used as follows: Surfing NOT California.

Boolean operators are a fundamental component of a kind of algebra called Boolean Logic, named after English mathematician George Boole (1815–1864). Boolean Logic is a system that expresses logical statements using mathematical formulas. Boolean Logic boils down all values to one of two states: true or false. This closely mirrors the binary approach digital computers use to interpret and process information, whereby commands are converted to sequences of either zeros or ones. The millions of transistors found on a computer's microprocessor are always in one of two states (on or off). These two states, which are represented by ones and zeros, respectively, correspond to Boolean Logic.

BOOLEAN LOGIC AND THE INTERNET

While Boolean logic was introduced as an effective search tool for Internet surfers, users noted that the logic sometimes returned flawed results. In addition, novice users found the queries confusing. One of the first providers of "plain English" logic was Ask Jeeves from Berkeley, California, in 1996. Founded by David Warthen and Garrett Gruener, Ask Jeeves was a database of common questions that filtered common Internet searches into a database to find a match. For example, a person who might search for "the tallest building in the United States" would find a better match on Ask Jeeves than it would with a browser using Boolean logic. Another such company was named Neuromedia Inc., which used advanced search technology called "bots" that analyzed questions and provided answers from a proprietary database. Ask Jeeves eventually changed its name to Ask.com in 2005. In 2011, it attracted over 90 million users monthly. Neuromedia closed its doors in 2000.

Another approach to facilitating easier browsing searches was to enhance the programming logic for Boolean operators. Called "Implied Boolean Logic," web programmers coded logic so that users do not need to use the specific operators "AND," "OR, " or "NOT." In this way, common English phrases use Boolean logic without the user's required knowledge of the operations. Symbols are used to represent Boolean logical operations. For example, Implied Boolean logic assigns the operator "AND" to a space. A search for "blue mittens" returns results for "blue AND mittens." Similarly, an Internet search that says, "Tell me about hyperactivity in kids" automatically returns the results for "hyperactivity AND kids." Another example of implied Boolean logic is the following: "Tell me photography without film"; this would imply "photography NOT film."

Some Internet browsers offer "Search Form Terminology," allowing users to perform advanced searches, choosing Boolean operators from drop-down menus. These advanced search engines are popular with libraries and news Web sites.

BIBLIOGRAPHY

Abate, Tom. "Search Tools Multiply/They Make It Easier to Find Answers." *San Fransisco Chronicle,* December 1997.

"Boolean Expression." *Webopedia,* May 25, 2001. Available from http://www.webopedia.com/TERM/B/Boolean_expression.html.

"Boolean Logic." *Webopedia,* May 25, 2001. Available from http://www.webopedia.com/TERM/B/Boolean_logic.html.

"Boolean Logic." *Tech Encyclopedia,*. May 25, 2001. Available from http://www.techweb.com/encyclopedia/.

"Boolean Searching on the Internet." *Internet Tutorials.* Available from http://www.internettutorials.net/boolean.asp.

Morton, Douglas. "Refresher Course: Boolean AND (Searching OR Retrieval)." *Online* 17, no. 1 (January 1993): 57–59.

BRAND BUILDING

The key to a successful brand lies in delivering value to the customer. Brands offer customers a promise, a set of values that will motivate them. This requires understanding customer needs and fulfilling company promises. Sometimes this insight has been lost on e-businesses, in particular, which have spent millions of dollars on e-brand building programs, motivated by speed rather than quality.

There are many benefits to having a recognized brand. A strong brand is regarded as an important asset that can enable a company to build stronger relationships with its customers and give it a measure of strategic control. A strong brand cuts through clutter in a fragmented marketplace and keeps a firm's products from becoming commodities. It can affect investment decisions and a firm's market capitalization.

Brand building is multidimensional, the result of a cumulative effort affected not only by advertising but customer service, product development, and the myriad of new features and abilities created by online enterprise. Companies need to determine what is important to their customers and recognize that different customers have different preferences. Factors such as low price, high quality, broad selection, and personal service figure into customer preferences and brand building. One group of online customers may prefer high quality, a reputable brand, and the lowest possible price. Another group may prefer speed, convenience, and a high level of functionality and interactivity when shopping online.

USING THE WEB FOR BRAND BUILDING

Brands originally came into existence to identify the creator of a product or service and create some type of competitive advantage. The Internet has the potential of helping companies use their brands to create new sources of competitive advantage through content richness, interactivity, and targeting. Internet-related investments in brand building include using the Web as a way to manage customer relationships and cross-sell. Customer service has always been a key element in building a brand. In e-commerce, the Internet has raised the importance of customer service and accelerated the time frame in which companies have to provide superior service to their customers.

MORE THAN BRAND AWARENESS

Critics of large advertising expenditures for brand building point out that awareness is only one aspect of creating a strong brand. More significant to a brand's strength is the underlying business and how it relates to its customers. Brands simply cannot be invented overnight. A strong brand is the result of creating a promise to consumers—one that is clear and memorable—and then creating a history of fulfilling that promise.

What does good customer service look like for online companies that would like to build a brand? Since information online is available in such a wide variety of styles and from so many sources, customer service is actually beginning to split from brand construction as a whole. Since customers can access company information through increasingly complex platforms and purchase products or services in so many ways, direct customer service is taking second place to brand formation.

SOCIAL MEDIA REVOLUTION

By the late 2000s social media had become a major tool for brand building. The sense of community and easy, fast-paced sharing of information that social media engendered was well fitted to spreading and solidifying brands. While some sites, such as MySpace, had declined in use, other sites like Facebook and Twitter increased rapidly in use. In addition to these general sites a vast number of blogs, forums, and social networks sprang up dedicated to particular topics and industries. Online businesses found themselves with a lot of room to expand into the social media world but without any clear guidelines for doing so.

At first, the results were mixed. Social media is primarily a consumer- and community-driven movement, which meant that business actions were often unwanted, especially traditional marketing messages. The hard sell and push of conventional marketing often had the opposite of the intended effect when inserted into social media communication. Eventually, marketing strategy caught up with the movement and began to develop more effective ways to reach customers through social constructs. This new strategy was closely associated with the rise of the importance of the brand and seeing the brand as a relationship with the customer, a reputation based on many different facets.

By the early 2010s, social media brand management had settled down into several different areas. On their own Web sites, companies focused on blogs and forums where they could direct personal messages toward interested customers and answer particular questions. On affiliate or similar Web sites, companies used interlinking and reciprocal references to boost awareness through soft partnerships. Companies formed extensive profiles on Twitter, Facebook, LinkedIn, Google+, and similar social network sites to raise brand awareness and broadcast advertising messages to strengthen the brand, building excitement by leveraging well-known value offerings. The category of social objects was also developed: a social object was a particular media message—such as a section of text, a video, or an image—that could be easily broadcast on many different social media levels at the same time. These social media objects were especially well fitted for carrying branding effects and influencing viral marketing.

BRAND MONITORING

Online brand management is much more useful when companies can see what customers are actually thinking about a brand in real time. These types of analytics were not available in the past, but by the late 2000s they had become increasingly common and useful tools for even small businesses. A crop of customizable applications became available to accomplish tasks, such as automatically searching Twitter and organizing all current Tweets regarding a particular product, company, or brand. Other programs did the same thing, but (like Google Alerts) supplied news articles, comments from other social networks, blog posts, and other information, all updated in real time. This allowed companies to track how a change in the brand was being received and what types of problems or questions needed to be addressed to continue building a strong and powerful brand.

BUILDING REPUTATION

Brand management comes down to building reputation, and despite the digital changes in communication, that goal remains the same. The way customers looked at reputation, however, began to change. One of the most noticeable examples occurred in expectations regarding company voice and communication style. Previous marketing initiatives were designed to win customers over and convince them of product superiority. However, with the rise of social media, one-sided marketing messages began to show a company in a detrimental light. Two-way communication became a pillar of brand building, and businesses were expected to take comments, respond to questions, ask advice, and interact with customers like they belonged to the same community.

However, social media and the rise of so many different channels with which to communicate a brand have also raised a few stumbling blocks. Logos have always been central to branding. Color, design, and taglines are some of the primary building blocks of all brands. Some rules remained the same: effective logos were ultimately simple and appealing to the target audience. Red was still associated with energy and competition, and green still evoked nature and prosperity. However, traditional brand building only needed to worry about creating a single logo design for ads, with possibly a few different versions in different sizes for packaging and additional marketing features. In the highly developed online world, logos became more complex to distribute. Companies had to decide how the logo should be used on blogs, social network profiles, Twitter backgrounds, embedded social objects, and other aspects of brand management. Some companies chose to use the same logo throughout, while others chose more general brand concepts with a simple logo that could be used in some circumstances but replaced with a color or image in other cases. In the end, brand management became more about flexibility and communication than about enforcing a particular reputation.

SEE ALSO *Advertising, Online; Affiliate Model; Banner Ads; Marketing, Internet; Promoting the Web Site.*

BIBLIOGRAPHY

"5 Brand Building Tips for Your Business Website." *Blogotechblog,* August 16, 2011. Available from http://www.blogotechblog.com/2011/08/brand-building-tips-for-business-Web site.

Berger, Warren. "After Ads That Shouted, Dot-Com Survivors Try Quieter, Cheaper Spots." *New York Times,* February 28, 2001.

Elliott, Stuart. "Betty Crocker: Can She Cook in Cyberspace?" *New York Times,* December 13, 2000.

Gilbert, Jennifer. "Running on Empty." *Advertising Age,* November 6, 2000.

Greenberg, Paul A. "Keep the Faith, Net Advertisers!" *E-Commerce Times,* January 15, 2001. Available from http://www.ecommercetimes.com/story/6699.html?wlc=1316287346.

Lang, Benjamin. "10 Ways for Entrepreneurs to Build Brands Online." *Mashable,* May 25, 2011. Available from http://mashable.com/2011/05/25/entrepreneur-brand-building.

Macale, Sherilynn. "14 Must-Haves for Your Online Personal Brand Building Toolkit." *Social Media,* August 30, 2011. Available from http://thenextweb.com/socialmedia/2011/08/30/14-must-haves-for-your-online-personal-brand-building-toolkit.

Moon, Michael. *Firebrands!: Building Brand Loyalty in the Internet Age.* New York: McGraw-Hill Professional Book Group, 2000.

Pierce, Andrew, and Eric Almquist. "Brand Building May Face a Test." *Advertising Age,* April 9, 2001.

"Online Brand Building." *SAE Business,* July 5, 2011. Available from http://www.sae-business.com/blog/2011/05/online-brand-building.

Regan, Keith. "What Makes a Good Online Brand Name?" *E-Commerce Times,* May 4, 2001. Available from http://www.ecommercetimes.com/story/9396.html.

———. "The X10 Question: Traffic without Dollars?" *E-Commerce Times,* June 14, 2001. Available from http://www.ecommercetimes.com/story/11248.html.

Shanes, Cory. "What Do You Mean I Have to Optimize It Too?" *Building Brand Online,* June 26, 2011. Available from http://buildingabrandonline.com/social-media-search-engine-optimization.

Solis, Brian. *Engage!* Hoboken, NJ: John Wiley and Sons, 2010.

Strahler, Steven R. "Going to the Next Level." *Crain's Chicago Business,* September 18, 2000.

Sweeney, Terry. "Advertisers Seek More Bang for Their Web Bucks." *InformationWeek,* October 2, 2000.

"When E-brands Fail: Building New Brand Value with Old Brand Tricks." *Chief Executive (U.S.),* May 2001.

BRIN, SERGEY

Sergey Brin is cofounder of Google, one of the most successful dot-com companies in history. Brin, along with cofounder Larry Page, has changed the way the world uses the Internet by revolutionizing the search engine. As president of technology at Google, Brin directs special projects and is responsible for the development of new products. With a net worth of approximately $16.7 billion each, Brin and Page shared 15th place on the *Forbes* 400 Richest Americans list in 2011.

FAMILY BACKGROUND

Brin was born in Moscow, Russia, on August 21, 1973, and came from a family background rich in science and technology. His great-grandmother studied microbiology at the University of Chicago before returning to Russia, and his grandfather was a math professor in Moscow. Brin's mother, Eugenia, who had graduated from the School of Mechanics at Moscow State University, worked as a civil engineer. With a doctorate in mathematics, Brin's father, Michael, was an economist at the Soviet State Planning Committee, an agency that instituted economic national plans according to objectives outlined by the Communist Party.

A Russian-Jewish family, the Brins immigrated to the United States when their son was six to escape anti-Semitism in Russia. They moved to Adelphi, Maryland, and Michael began teaching math at the University of Maryland, while Eugenia was employed as an analyst at NASA's Goddard Space Flight Center.

The young Brin was intrigued by computers, playing games and working on a Commodore 64, an early personal computer, that he had received for his ninth birthday. Like his father, Brin was also captivated by the world of numbers. He was so advanced in math that his middle school brought in a special teacher for him, but he always felt that he learned much more at home than at school.

Brin attended the University of Maryland, taking many graduate-level courses while still an undergraduate. David A. Vise, in his book *The Google Story,* quoted Brin as saying, "I got a lot of attention, a lot of one-on-one. I was better prepared than peers from MIT and Harvard." Brin spent his summers working at Wolfram Research, designing a code analysis and extraction tool for the Mathematica source code, and at General Electric Information Services, where he developed both a macro language library that could be embedded into any application and a graphical front end for a C++ file transfer program. At the University of Maryland Institute for Advanced Computer Studies, Brin created a system of parallel algorithms for image processing, as well as a 3-D graphics program for flight simulation. When he was 19, Brin graduated from the University of Maryland with honors in math and computer science.

RESEARCH

The recipient of a National Science Foundation fellowship, Brin entered graduate school at Stanford University, studying computer science. He also collaborated with other students and professors on various projects, including one focused on molecular biology and another dealing with the automated detection of copyright violations. With Professor Rajeev Motwani, Brin established a new research group, Mining Data at Stanford (MIDAS). Brin explored the potential of data mining—taking large amounts of data, analyzing it for patterns, and extracting useful relationships—for organizing the vast information on the Internet.

In 1995, Brin met Larry Page during a student orientation at Stanford. Page, a computer engineer, was interested in applications for the links that were returned when an Internet search was conducted. Page enlisted the help of Brin in extracting relevant data from large amounts of information on the World Wide Web. Together, they set out to create a search tool that would find the most relevant Web pages first. The two men designed an algorithm that, according to the *Encyclopedia of World Biography,* "analyzed the 'back links' in a hypertext document, or how many times other sites linked to it—the more links, the higher the relevancy of the page." Page named the link-rating system PageRank.

It soon became apparent to Brin and Page that they could build a full-scale search engine using their algorithm. The result was BackRub, so named because it had the ability to analyze the back links of Web pages. In 1997, Brin and Page decided to change the name of the search engine to Google, based on the word "googol," a mathematical term for the number one followed by 100 zeros. Brin and Page believed that this large number was an appropriate representation of the huge amount of World Wide Web data they were attempting to organize.

GOOGLE INC.

Working out of their dorm rooms—Brin's served as the business office, Page's as the data center—Brin and Page introduced Google to students, faculty, and administrators at Stanford. The search engine was an immediate success, and the pair began their own search for investors or buyers. After being rejected by such companies as Yahoo!, AltaVista, and Excite, Brin and Page concentrated on improving Google by adding enhanced features. In 1998, Brin created the first Google logo, block letters in primary colors with an exclamation point at the end, imitating Yahoo! The next year, Brin had the idea of decorating the logo for certain holidays, and the Google doodle was born.

Brin and Page found their first financial backer in August 1998, prompting them to establish Google Inc. as a legal corporation on September 7, 1998. Brin was president, and Page served as CEO. Preparing to commercialize Google on a large scale, Brin elected to take a leave of absence from the Stanford doctorate program. His decision proved wise, as he and Page were able to evaluate and adjust their business plan to accommodate their new search engine that had quickly surpassed all competition. By mid-2000 Google was handling some 15 million search queries per day. Within four years, that number had grown to 200 million.

Instead of devastating Google, the dot-com bust of 2001 gave the young company an opportunity to hire technology experts who had lost their jobs. Brin and Page appointed a new CEO, Eric Schmidt, former chief technology officer at Sun Microsystems. Schmidt, they believed, had the experience and business savvy to prepare Google to go public. When Google completed its initial public offering in August 2004, Brin and Page became billionaires overnight. The entrepreneurs, however, were recognized for more than their financial gain. They received the Marconi Prize for their lasting contributions to human progress in the field of information technology, along with the Academy of Achievement's Golden Plate Award.

Throughout the 2000s, Brin remained an integral part of Google's success as a leader in technology. He and Page introduced several popular services, including Gmail, Google Maps, Google Apps, and Google Earth. Google expanded into the mobile device industry with the release of its Android open source mobile platform in 2008. (By October 2011, that sector of the company was bringing in around $625 million per quarter, mainly through online-search advertising.) Google launched Google Chrome OS in 2009, at which time Brin commented that the technology of Chrome and Android would most likely converge at some point. Other mobile device technology included the Google Wallet, which allows consumers to use their phones as wallets. Brin's role in this kind of product development was emphasized when Page was reinstated as CEO in April 2011.

SEE ALSO *Google Inc.; Page, Larry.*

BIBLIOGRAPHY

Academy of Achievement. "Sergey Brin & Larry Page." Washington, DC, January 21, 2011. Available from http://www.achievement.org/autodoc/page/pag0int-1.

Chapman, Mike. "Media Entrepreneurs of the Decade." *Brandweek,* December 14, 2009.

"Compute This: Google Chrome OS and Google Android OS." *Searcher,* May 2010. Available from http://www.infotoday.com/searcher/may10/LiveLinks_Mattison_0510.htm.

"Larry Page and Sergey Brin Biography." *Encyclopedia of World Biography.* Available from http://www.notablebiographies.com/news/Ow-Sh/Page-Larry-and-Brin-Sergey.html.

Scott, Virginia. *Google.* Westport, CT: Greenwood Press, 2008.

Vise, David A. *The Google Story.* New York: Bantam Dell, 2005.

BROADBAND TECHNOLOGY

Broadband technology refers to a high-speed, high-bandwidth connection to the Internet. The greater bandwidth of a broadband connection allows for more data to be transmitted at higher speeds than a conventional telephone line. Broadband connections are always on.

Broadband technology includes cable modem and digital subscriber line (DSL) connections to the Internet as well as a number of alternative technologies. DSL technology uses ordinary copper telephone lines to deliver a high-bandwidth connection to the Internet, with typical data transmission speeds ranging from 512 Kbps to 2 Mbps (millions of bits per second). However, a number of technological breakthroughs in the 2000s brought significant increases in speed to high-end DSL connections. Verizon's FiOS boasted access speeds over 100 Mbps, for example.

Cable modems are among the most popular broadband connection for consumers. Alternative broadband technologies, mostly used by businesses, include leased lines, frame relay, fiber optics, asynchronous transfer mode (ATM), T1 and T3 lines, and integrated services digital network (ISDN). High-speed Internet access is also available through satellite services, although the number of subscribers remains small in comparison to cable modem and DSL subscribers.

RISE OF BROADBAND

A May 2011 report from the Pew Internet & American LifeProject portrayed a steep upward trend in broadband adoption by the American public throughout the 2000s. In 2000, under 40% of U.S. adults had accessed the Internet, with less than 5% having broadband access. One decade later, over 60% had Internet access, and more than 95% of those with access had broadband capacity.

Nonetheless, the United States lagged behind many other countries in broadband connectivity. Of the 30 most tech-savvy countries in the world, the United States fell in the middle of the pack, regarding most areas of importance. A Berkman Center for Internet & Society report published international broadband rankings, in which the United States was ranked in categories, such as:

- penetration per 100 (15th)
- household penetration (15th)
- 3G penetration, Telegeography (19th)
- Wi-Fi hotspots per 1,000,000 (9th)
- maximum advertised speed (9th)
- average advertised speed (19th)
- average speed (11th)
- median download (11th)
- median upload (5th)
- median latency (17th)
- price for low speeds (9th)
- price for medium speeds (19th)
- price for high speeds (18th)
- price for next generation speeds (19th)

Furthermore, the future of U.S. broadband connectedness looked mediocre. Consequently, a growing number of organizations began to advocate for international broadband competitiveness. The Economist Intelligence Unit, a research division associated with the *Economist* magazine, created a government broadband index (gBBi), which was intended to measure governmental plans to facilitate and support a countrywide network. Components that impacted the gBBi score included goals for speed, coverage, time-to-completion, efficacy of proposed regulations in the production of a competitive broadband market, and the amount of funding required for the achievement of target objectives, with the latter counting in inverse proportion to score. This meant that the more money a government proposed to use to accomplish broadband achievements, the less highly it would score (out of 5 points).

- South Korea (4.4)
- Japan (4.3)
- Singapore (4.2)
- Sweden (4.1)
- Finland (4.1)
- Estonia (4.0)
- France (3.9)
- Spain (3.7)
- Denmark (3.6)
- Australia (3.4)
- New Zealand (3.0)
- United States (3.0)
- Italy (2.9)
- United Kingdom (2.7)
- Germany (2.6)
- Greece (2.4)

Government facilitation of widespread broadband services was deemed necessary for two reasons. First, international consensus suggested that Internet usage was directly correlated to a number of important cultural and economic touchpoints, such as human development and financial prosperity. Therefore, it was important for broadband access to be available to as many households as possible, at affordable rates. Second, there was a growing discrepancy between broadband access in urban versus rural areas. Private enterprises do not have sufficient incentive to lay the infrastructure necessary to connect many rural areas, and this hampers widespread development of the Web in rural areas.

WHAT DO BROADBAND CONSUMERS WANT?

By 2011, 78% of adult Americans reported using the Internet, and 92% of these used search engines to find information. Seventy-six percent looked for news, and 71% watched video from a streaming source. While a dial-up connection would be sufficient for the first two activities, streaming video was difficult for anything but broadband connections to handle.

There is conflicting data as to whether or not broadband users will ever be interested in next-generation services, and whether they are prepared to pay for them. In general, fairly large segments of online users have some interest in premium services, but only a small percentage say they are willing to pay extra for them. In the 2010s, many people felt that download speeds of 100 Mbps were unnecessary, and most people would not pay for services they did not need. However, there was a high likelihood that 100 Mbps would go even further to connect international populations and facilitate the exchange of an increasingly complex array of data.

BROADBAND FOR BUSINESSES

Broadband connections offer several benefits to business enterprises. Broadband facilitates greater information flow and communication within the organization as well as with clients and suppliers. It also enables companies to use rich media, such as streaming video and audio, to communicate with employees, while video conferencing can save on travel expenses. In addition, a growing portion of enterprise software was available on the cloud. In order to use these software as a service (SaaS) applications, companies required faster connection speeds, in accordance with the amount of data exchanged between the company network and the application provider. SaaS was expected to become increasingly prevalent in the 2010s, as broadband coverage increased and more versatile, innovative solutions were devised.

SEE ALSO *Bandwidth Management; Connectivity, Internet.*

BIBLIOGRAPHY

Berkman Center for Internet & Society. "Next Generation Connectivity." Cambridge, MA, February 16, 2010. Available from http://cyber.law.harvard.edu/pubrelease/broadband.

"Full Speed Ahead: The Government Broadband Index Q1 2011." London: Economist Intelligence Unit, 2011. Available from https://www.eiu.com/public/topical_report.aspx?campaignid=broadband2011.

Pew Internet & American Life Project. "Trend Data." Washington, DC, 2011. Available from http://www.pewinternet.org/Static-Pages/Trend-Data/Home-Broadband-Adoption.aspx.

"Verizon Files Lawsuit Against FCC's 'Net Neutrality' Rules." *Computer Business Review,* October 3, 2011. Available from http://telecoms.cbronline.com/news/verizon-files-lawsuit-against-fccs-net-neutrality-rules-031011.

BROKERAGE MODEL

Whether a company sells products or services to consumers, other businesses, or both, there are many different ways to approach the marketplace and make a profit. Business models, of which the brokerage model is simply one, are used to describe how companies go about this process. They spell out the main ways in which companies make profits by identifying a company's role during commerce and describing how products, information, and other important elements are structured. Just as there are many different industries and types of companies, there are many different kinds of business models. While some are simple, others are very complex. Even within the same industry, companies may rely on business models that are very different from one another, and some companies may use a combination of several different models.

Some long-established business models have been adopted on the Internet with varying degrees of success. Among these are mail-order models, advertising models, free-trial models, subscription models, and direct marketing models. Other business models originate with the Internet and e-commerce and focus heavily on the movement of electronic information. These include digital delivery models, information barter models, freeware models, and the brokerage model.

THE BROKERAGE MODEL

At the heart of this model are third parties known as brokers, who bring sellers and buyers of products and services together to engage in transactions. Normally, the broker charges a fee to at least one party involved in a transaction. While many brokers are involved in connecting consumers with retailers, they also may connect businesses with other businesses or consumers with other consumers. A wide variety of different scenarios or business configurations fall under the banner of a brokerage model. These include everything from Web sites posting simple online classified ads and Internet shopping malls (Web sites that sell products from a variety of different companies) to online marketplaces, online auctions, aggregators, and shopping bots. According to the Organisation of Economic and Co-operative Development (OECD), e-commerce intermediaries represented over $97 billion in online sales in 2008. These figures continued to rise through the economic recession of 2008–2009, though at a reduced rate.

Some brokers simply focus on fulfillment between buyers and sellers. Travel agents like Travelocity.com and Priceline.com are examples of this approach. An online marketplace is an example of brokers with a business-to-business focus. These entities bring large groups of commercial buyers and sellers together online. Online marketplaces existed for many different industries, ranging from the food and beverage industries to consumer packaged goods and interior design. The costs for participating in an online marketplace varied. In some cases, participating companies (suppliers, purchasers, or both) were required to purchase special software from a third party. Third parties also levied different charges for making transactions, joining the network, updating catalogs of available products, and so on. Electronic markets recorded $400 billion in transactions in 2008, roughly 7% of wholesale trade in the United States, according to the OECD.

Aggregators are brokers that bring business owners or consumers together to get better rates on services like long-distance telephone service. The key concept is group purchasing, which enables individual businesses or consumers to get better rates than they could obtain on their own. Metamediaries are another kind of broker. These entities, which include online shopping malls, not only bring interested parties together, they also provide different services related to the actual transaction, such as billing or order tracking.

By the 2010s, the brokerage model of online business proved itself to be one of the most effective and useful ways for businesses to make money online. The OECD identified seven primary areas to which brokerage-model businesses could potentially add value. These are infrastructure, information processing and organization, social exchange, aggregation of supply and demand, facilitation of market action, trust, and communication between buyers and sellers, specifically regarding the needs and wants of both parties.

As a facilitator of social exchange and information, third-party advertising became an even greater potential source of revenue for brokerage-model firms. By 2009, approximately 10% of advertising spending was diverted to online operations, an 11% growth in a single year. Companies such as eBay, Amazon.com, and Priceline.com were in a good position to capitalize on this increased interest.

SEE ALSO *Aggregators; Community Model; Infomediary Model; Manufacturer Model.*

BIBLIOGRAPHY

Bambury, Paul. "A Taxonomy of Internet Commerce." *First-Monday* 3, No. 10 (October 5, 1998). Available from http://firstmonday.org/htbin/cgiwrap/bin/ojs/index.php/fm/article/view/624/545.

Levy, Ari, and Roben Farzad. "Priceline's Winding Path to Success." *Bloomberg Businessweek,* June 18, 2010. Available from http://www.msnbc.msn.com/id/37767385/#.Tr1KqvFViHk.

McDowell, Dagen. "Dear Dagen: Business Models Explained." *The Street,* September 13, 1999. Available from http://www.thestreet.com/story/782926/1.html.

Organisation for Economic Co-operation and Development. "The Economic and Social Role of Internet Intermediaries." Paris, France, April, 2010. Available from http://www.oecd.org/dataoecd/49/4/44949023.pdf.

Rappa, Michael. "Business Models on the Web." *Digital Enterprise,* January 17, 2010. Available from http://digitalenterprise.org/models/models.html.

Rayport, Jeffrey F. "The Truth About Internet Business Models." *Strategy & Business,* Third Quarter, 1999.

Schneider, Ivan. "R2-D2 Meets 401(k)." *Bank Systems & Technology,* November, 2000.

Schwartz, Ephraim. "Web Bots Enhance Self-Service Experience." *InfoWorld,* February 7, 2000.

Timmers, Paul. "Business Models for Electronic Markets." *Electronic Markets,* April 1998. Available from http://www.docstoc.com/docs/38528956/Business-Models-for-Electronic-Markets.

Van Winkle, William. "Strength in Numbers." *Home Office Computing,* September 2000.

BUFFETT, WARREN

An extremely high-profile investor, Warren Buffett's investment success made him the richest man in the world in 2008. Worth about $39 billion in November 2011, according to *Forbes,* Buffett remained the third-richest man in the world and one of the very few of his class to attain such fortune solely on the strength of stock investments. The chairman of Omaha, Nebraska-based Berkshire Hathaway, Buffett has been known to refer to his annual stockholders' meeting as a "Woodstock weekend for capitalists." Accordingly, the event draws investors from around the world who flock to hear his sermon. Buffett's awe-inspiring success and cult-like status spawned a potpourri of investment-related Web sites, magazine stories, and books, many offering advice on how to "invest like Warren Buffett." The fawning, sometimes almost worshipful attitude of some of Buffett's followers earned him the affectionate nickname, the "Sage of Omaha."

Equally famous as his astronomical investment success was his notorious sourness toward the new economy and dot-com mania. Buffett and his legions of followers are well known for eschewing the trendy and faddish in stock investment. Buffett in large part built his reputation by attracting like-minded investors, who were in it for the long term rather than for quick speculative profits. His method ignores macroeconomic trends and Wall Street tips and wisdom, focusing instead on companies that boast significant market share and growth potential, but with low earnings and depressed valuation. In short, he looks for solid, strong companies that will put together sound earnings over the long term. The naysayers who view this strategy as quaint, or as a fossil of a bygone age in an era of tip- and rumor-based day trading, more often than not end up coming to see his moves as conventional market wisdom.

While his favored established firms' stocks tumbled in the late 1990s, the dot-com mania swept the markets, producing a surge of new investment hotshots and poking holes in the aura of mystique that surrounded the Buffett legend. By 2000, however, dot-coms were in trouble, and once again Buffett came out ahead of the pack. Even after e-commerce stabilized somewhat in the 2000s, Buffett preferred to leave Internet companies to his friend, Mr. William Gates III, and stick with one of the pillars of his investment program: only invest in what you know. Rather than diverting his attention into a field that was wholly different from the companies already under his control, the billionaire expanded his reach from insurance and textiles into energy and electric cars.

THE SAGE'S STORY

Born in Omaha in 1933, Warren Edward Buffett showed a very early affinity for remembering and calculating numbers. According to a profile in the online magazine *Salon,* the young Buffett was marking the board at his father's brokerage and purchasing his first stock at age 11. Within three years, Buffett used his paper route savings to dive into real estate, purchasing 40 acres of farmland and leasing it to a tenant farmer.

He came across the highly regarded investment tome *The Intelligent Investor,* by Benjamin Graham, as a senior at the University of Nebraska and was strongly influenced by the investment principles therein. Graham was a famous skeptic of Wall Street trends, encouraging so-called value investors to seek out "cigar butts"—those firms that Wall Street had all but abandoned but which could still be lit up for a few good puffs of stock activity. Buffett's first investment success came in 1951, when he threw $10,282 into the auto insurance firm Geico. Just a year later, he pulled out for $15,259. In 1952, the 21-year-old Buffett began offering his own classes on investing, selling his course via an advertisement in a local Omaha newspaper.

After a few years working and studying with Graham, Buffett began to feel constrained by the former's strict rules of value investment. Instead of picking up nearly lifeless companies cheaply, Buffett began to experiment with buying stocks of still vigorous but undervalued companies. In 1956, Buffett began an investment partnership on the seed money provided by himself, his sister, his neighbor, and his lawyer. The following year, a local couple who had attended his class invested $100,000 into the partnership. Buffett's earliest believers, known as the Berkshire Bunch, amassed enormous fortunes over the years by putting money behind the young investment guru's ideas. In Omaha alone, according to *Forbes,* more than 30 families accumulated at least $100 million in Berkshire Hathaway stock.

In 1962, Buffett began purchasing shares of Berkshire Hathaway, a struggling textile manufacturer in New Bedford, Massachusetts. Three years later he controlled the entire company. Berkshire's book value per share registered nearly 25% compound annual gains through the rest of the century, according to Credit Suisse First Boston Corp. By the end of the 1960s, finding good bargains few and far between, Buffett dissolved the investment partnership, returning his investors' money. From this point, he concentrated on Berkshire, which at first functioned primarily as a textile company with a small investment operation. Before long, however, investments were Berkshire's bread and butter, and Buffett returned to his practice of picking up depressed companies. There were many such firms by the early and mid-1970s, after the 1960s stock rally gave out and inflation set in, making cheap stocks plentiful.

Buffett's bold moves and foresight helped him weather the tough economic climate of the late 1970s, and despite the tremendous market crash in 1987, Berkshire finished that year in much better shape than the year before. His head-scratching investments in companies such as Coca-Cola proved ingenious, with their brand-name recognition and untapped international potential.

Once viewed basically as an investment fund, acquisitions of insurance firms, such as Geico and General Reinsurance, through the 1990s transformed Berkshire Hathaway primarily into an insurance company in which the investment portfolio happened to be managed by one of the world's most famous investors. By the end of the 1990s, insurance accounted for more than 70% of Berkshire's revenues. Buffett came to believe that his company's greatest strength lay in purchasing companies outright rather than simply picking established stocks at the right stages of their valuations.

Buffett's attraction to the insurance industry was fairly logical. Since policyholders pay their premiums up front, while the firms pay out claims later, the company can be used as a strong investment catalyst. With a constant stream of revenue coming in, the insurers have a gap of time in which they have a good deal of money to invest before the claims are actually paid. This was Berkshire's strength, using the premium money to invest in Buffett's favored brands of undervalued stock.

His methods of investing and strategizing were extremely out of fashion and against the grain in the dot-com explosion of the late 1990s. In 1999, Buffett experienced his first down year in a decade, with Berkshire's per-share book value underperforming the S&P 500 index for the first time in 20 years. At the time, the judgmental pronounced his insistence on investing in firmly established, proven businesses out of date for the much-heralded, dot-com-heavy new economy. Instead of investing in the dot-com bubble, Buffett pumped his money into the MidAmerican Energy Holdings Company. For a brief period, the billionaire's investment strategy was regarded as a traditional, conservative approach. In 2000, however, Buffett appeared to have the last laugh, as reality weighed down the dot-com mania and the high-tech stock bubble burst. Buffett's portfolio, meanwhile, bounced back as investors ran to established companies, and once again pundits and analysts were praising the far-sighted wisdom of Buffett.

The 2000s brought in another 50% increase to Buffett's fortune. While a significant portion of gains were attributable to the quick-fire investments Buffett was known for, the billionaire also continued to build a global empire. Strategic acquisitions during the decade included another energy company, PacifiCorp, for slightly under $10 billion in 2005. This came during a period of consolidation in the energy industry, according to *Businessweek.* PacifiCorp was in dire straits when the acquisition took place, which undoubtedly gave Buffett a prime deal. Bleeding from debt, the Western energy company did not have the resources to upgrade its facilities. In addition, the company was dependent upon hydroelectric energy sources, and a period of decreased precipitation forced PacifiCorp to purchase some of its energy on the wholesale market. Berkshire's deep pockets were able to turn the company around while capitalizing on Utah's increasing energy needs, thereby solidifying Buffett's expansive energy empire.

Three years later, the billionaire seemed to change his own tune with the purchase of one-tenth of BYD, a Chinese electric car company. Not only was the foreign investment a large step over the Pacific Ocean, it was a step into technology and therefore a risky investment by comparison to the other businesses in Berkshire Hathaway's menagerie. There were enough familiar elements in BYD to satisfy Buffett's need for understanding. After all, neither energy nor cars were new areas for the businessman. In fact, his electric company MidAmerican acquired Constellation Energy earlier in the same year, adding another 9,000 megawatts of power to its foothold in the U.S. energy market. However, the seeming diversion from the Buffett plan caused a stir among investors, who crowded to get their feet in the door of BYD.

SEE ALSO *Volatility.*

BIBLIOGRAPHY

Atlas, Riva. "Warren Buffetted." *Institutional Investor,* January 2000.

Bary, Andrew. "What's Wrong, Warren?" *Barron's,* December 27, 1999.

Berman, Dennis K. "Going on Safari with Warren Buffett." *Wall Street Journal,* March 1, 2011. Available from http://online.wsj.com/article/SB10001424052748704615504576172722252292438.html.

Bradsher, Keith. "Hertz to Begin Renting Electric Cars in China." *New York Times,* August 23, 2011. Available from http://www.nytimes.com/2011/08/24/business/global/hertz-to-begin-renting-electric-cars-in-china.html.

Carter, Adrienne. "Warren Buffett's Current Passion." *Bloomberg Businessweek,* May 25, 2005. Available from http://www.businessweek.com/bwdaily/dnflash/may2005/nf20050525_1710_db016.htm.

"For the Buffett Faithful, Time Paid Off." *Forbes,* October 12, 1998.

"Gallery: The Richest People on the Planet." *Forbes,* November 2011. Available from http://www.forbes.com/profile/warren-buffett.

Kadleck, Daniel. "Berkshire's Buffett-ing." *TIME,* October 25, 1999.

Kanter, Larry. "Salon Brilliant Careers: Warren Buffett." *Salon,* August 31, 1999. Available from http://www.salon.com/1999/08/31/buffett.

Kover, Amy. "Warren Buffett: Revivalist." *Fortune,* May 29, 2000.

Lenzer, Robert. "The Berkshire Bunch." *Forbes,* October 12, 1998.

BUNDLING

Bundling is the process of combining multiple products or services and selling them as a single package. Most major telecommunications and computer technology firms bundle at least some of their products and services. In some cases, both products and services are bundled together. For example, cell phone service providers often offer a free or drastically reduced phone in exchange for signing a long-term service contract. E-commerce site builders bundle page design software and online traffic monitoring tools with e-marketing services. Online content providers like the *Wall Street Journal Online* offer subscriptions that not only include access to an online version of a publication, but also accounts with other online publications, the ability to retrieve archived articles, real-time stock quotes, stock tracking services, and more.

The Telecommunications Act of 1996 deregulated the communications industry in the United States, allowing broadcasting, cable, wireless, and telephone industries to compete in one another's markets for the first time and opening up a host of new bundling opportunities. Cable television companies began bundling their traditional cable service with high-speed Internet access, as did telephone companies. Bundling these services can often provide a great deal for the consumer. Many providers offer a one-year $99-a-month start-up plan that typically includes premium television service, standard-speed broadband Internet service, and telephone service with advanced calling features. When the year is up, customers can often negotiate good deals to resign. Bundling telecommunications services is less likely to be a good deal if the customers' needs are more basic, such as basic cable television or no need for long-distance calling.

Another common practice is bundling software. Bundled software, or bundleware, is the practice of grouping several related games or other software into a single package. One example of this is Microsoft Office, which bundles Word, Excel, PowerPoint, and One Note into one package. Microsoft Office is also often included in an even larger software bundle when consumers purchase new PCs. The Microsoft Office software is often bundled with an operating system (usually the latest version of Windows), as well as some form of antivirus software. The online gaming industry often bundles software to allow users access to a game and all of its expansions. One example of this is Blizzard Software's "Battle Chest" series which includes its popular Diablo II, StarCraft, and Warcraft gaming series. New gaming systems for home use are often sold in bundles, too. In 2011, the Playstation Move was sold as a bundle that, in addition to the system itself, included motion controllers, a camera peripheral, and the multiplayer game, *Sports Champions.*

In the 2010s, bundling has suppliers offering assembled bundles of hardware and software, making large-scale computing easier and less expensive for customers. The shift to packaging hardware and software together was behind some large business deals in 2009 and 2010 that formed partnerships between Hewlett-Packard and Microsoft, as well as Cisco Systems and EMC.

One particularly noteworthy example of bundling was Microsoft's inclusion of its Internet Explorer browser with its Windows 95 operating system in the mid-1990s. The move allowed the firm to compete with browser rival Netscape, but some critics believe it worked a bit too well. It resulted in an antitrust investigation conducted by the U.S. Department of Justice that eventually made its way to court. A judge ruled that Microsoft must offer a version of Windows 95 unbundled from Internet Explorer, although that verdict was later overturned on appeal. The litigation sparked by the bundling continued, however, and in 2000 Microsoft was found guilty of monopolistic practices and ordered to split into two companies, a ruling that was also appealed. Eventually, Microsoft agreed to a settlement giving full access to its systems, records, and source codes for five years. The

Department of Justice (DOJ) felt this would give other PC manufacturers the opportunity to adopt non-Microsoft software of their own in order to create more competition. However, the DOJ did not require Microsoft to change any of its code, and it did not prevent it from tying other software with Windows in the future. Full access to Microsoft was extended beyond the five-year mark but was allowed to expire in May 2011.

SEE ALSO *Microsoft Corp.*

BIBLIOGRAPHY

Arnst, Catherine. "The Coming Telescramble: Deregulation Is Launching a $1 Trillion Digital Free-for-All." *Business Week,* April 8, 1996.

Buckman, Rebecca. "Looking Through Microsoft's Window." *Wall Street Journal,* May 1, 2000.

Dix, John. "The Future Is Bundles, Even for DSL." *Network World,* October 23, 2000.

Lohr, Steve. "Bundling Hardware and Software to Do Big Jobs." *New York Times,*. February 8, 2010. Available from http://www.nytimes.com/2010/02/08/technology/08blue.html.

Schwartz, Evan I. "Turning Surfers Into Subscribers." *Mediaweek,* October 30, 2000.

Tessler, Joelle. "DOJ Antitrust Settlement with Microsoft to Expire." *USA Today,* May 12, 2011. Available from http://www.usatoday.com/tech/news/2011-05-12-microsoft-antitrust-settlement_n.htm.

U.S. Department of Justice. "Information on the United States v. Microsoft Settlement." Washington, DC, 2003. Available from http://www.justice.gov/atr/cases/ms-settle.htm.

BUSINESS MODELS

The advent of e-commerce in the mid-1990s brought with it many new ways of doing business. Some were viable and others were not. While the number of ways to conduct business electronically is vast, only a handful of business models—methods by which businesses generate revenue—proved worthy enough to survive the dot-com fallout of 2000. Several variations exist within each model, and many firms attempt to meld models to increase profitability.

MERCHANT MODEL

Perhaps the most well-known e-commerce business model, Internet-based merchandising is what comes to mind for many when the subject of e-commerce is raised. One of the most successful online merchants using this model, Amazon.com, began operating as a business-to-consumer (B2C) Internet company by selling books online from a database that exceeded one million titles by the end of 1996. Amazon's wide selection, along with its practice of discounting books by 10% to 30%, were key factors in its success. The firm developed one-click shopping technology, which allowed returning shoppers to purchase an item with a single click.

Amazon.com has adapted its business model to incorporate some aspects of a multisided platform as well, which allowed the company to succeed where many other dot-coms failed. The site was not only a merchant—it was an intermediary, hosting other book resellers in its database (see brokerage model below). On the one end, the site provided an easy-to-search database of books for buyers. On the other, it offered sellers cheap entrance to a heavily trafficked distribution channel. As a facilitator of exchange, the site gained networking properties, which it built into its platform by enabling customer reviews. This participative network platform not only gave customers trust in exchanging money over the Web, it also meant that each purchase added value to the site.

Wal-Mart adopted a similarly hybrid pure merchant approach to its online operations, using customer reviews to add trust and create a customer network. However, Wal-Mart took physical possession of the products it sold. As such, on the spectrum between merchants and multisided intermediaries, it fell even closer to the pure merchant business model than Amazon.com, which implemented plans closer to the brokerage model.

ADVERTISING MODEL

This model relies on advertising to make money. To attract users to its site, once-leading Web portal Yahoo! offered things like free e-mail, extensive content, and travel services. Unlike many other dot-com start-ups, Yahoo! actually was able to parlay advertising dollars into profitability. However, eventually Yahoo! proved too reliant on other dot-com upstarts for advertising revenue. When these fledgling ventures were forced to curtail spending, Yahoo! began looking to traditional brick-and-mortar companies. However, many of these firms also were cutting costs, and quite often the dollars earmarked for online advertising were the most vulnerable to cuts. Eventually, the firm recognized that it needed to reduce its reliance on advertising, which accounted for roughly 85% of sales in 2000. Yahoo! altered its business model when it began offering fee-based services like online bill paying to consumers and fee-based services like e-store management to corporate clients. While Yahoo! is still in business in the early 2010s, its influence in the world of e-commerce has dramatically waned.

INFORMATION MODEL

Several online ventures focus on the sale of information. For example, *Consumer Reports Online* offers access to its product ratings and reports for a fee. To draw more readers, firms in this market sometimes offer a limited amount of free content but charge a subscription for access to premium content. Quite often, sites like these also rely on advertising to make money.

BROKERAGE MODEL

Like Amazon.com, eBay is another pure-play Internet company, meaning that it conducts business solely on the Internet. However, instead of using the retailing model employed by Amazon, the firm uses a brokerage format that brings sellers and buyers together. The world's largest online auction site, eBay was founded by Pierre Omidyar in 1995 as Auction Web, a site that allowed sellers to list descriptions of items for sale, require a minimum bid, and set an auction's length between three and ten days. When the auction expired, the highest bidder was able to purchase the object for the bid price, providing the minimum had been met. The buyer and seller were responsible for handling payment and delivery. As site traffic grew, Auction Web began charging a small fee, basing it on the final price of each object sold. Because the auctioning process was automated, overhead costs were kept to a minimum and the site achieved profitability quickly.

BUSINESS-TO-BUSINESS SERVICES

As an increasing number of companies integrated e-commerce distribution channels in the 2000s, the market for online business solutions also grew. Data became more complex and from disparate sources, such as real-world sales and online purchases. A number of companies, such as SAP, IBM, SAS, Oracle, Microsoft, and others developed business intelligence (BI) software, which was offered as programs and platforms. These integrated, stored, and in many cases provided analytics software that supported the decision-making process. BI platforms could be installed onsite, as was often the case prior to 2005. With the rise of cloud computing in the latter half of the 2000s, however, more BI platforms became available as Web-based portals and applications.

SEE ALSO *Affiliate Model; Brokerage Model; Community Model; Infomediary Model; Manufacturer Model; Merchant Model; Subscription Model; Utility Model.*

BIBLIOGRAPHY

Cornelius, Thomas. "The Rise of the Online to Offline Commerce Network." *Business Insider,* September 27, 2011. Available from http://articles.businessinsider.com/2011-09-27/tech/30203204_1_groupon-connectivity-open-graph.

Elkind, Peter. "The Hype Is Big, Really Big, at Priceline." *Fortune,* September 6, 1999.

Hagiu, Andrei. "Merchant or Two-Sided Platform?" *Review of Network Economics* 6, no. 2 (2007), doi: 10.2202/1446-9022.1113. Available from http://www.bepress.com/rne/vol6/iss2/3.

Levine, Daniel S. "Survey Tells Tale of Dot-Com Survivors Gaining New Lives." *Sacramento Business Journal,* June 15, 2001.

Olavsrud, Thor. "Ten Leading Business Intelligence Software Solutions." *Datamation,* May 5, 2010. Available from http://itmanagement.earthweb.com/entdev/article.php/3880336/Ten-Leading-Business-Intelligence-Software-Solutions.htm.

Organisation for Economic Co-operation and Development. "The Economic and Social Role of Internet Intermediaries." Paris, France, April, 2010. Available from http://www.oecd.org/dataoecd/49/4/44949023.pdf.

Rappa, Michael. "Business Models on the Web." *Digital Enterprise,* January 17, 2010. Available from http://digitalenterprise.org/models/models.html.

Sweat, Jeff. "Well-Tailored E-commerce." *InformationWeek,* April 16, 2001.

"We Have Lift-Off; Amazon, Yahoo! and eBay Grow Up." *Economist,* February 3, 2001.

BUSINESS PLAN

A business plan is a document written by an individual or group of individuals interested in launching a new business. Along with helping to determine whether or not an idea can be transformed into a functional company, a business plan is also used to secure capital and recruit executives. Business plans may also be written by existing companies that are considering a major change to their operations and want to explain and offer projections of the planned effects of the changes for investors and others.

Business plans do not need to follow a specific format, and businesses are not required to have one. During the dot-com mania of the late 1990s, several analysts began to criticize the many Internet-based ventures operating without a formal business plan, as well as the business investors pouring funding into these upstarts. In the early part of the twenty-first century Internet companies began to develop more formal business plans as a way to secure funding and establish themselves as legitimate business ventures. In addition, the Internet also proved to be a resource for small businesses and start-ups looking for information on model business plans and how to write one.

TARGET MARKET

Most business plans cover both the existing size and the anticipated growth rate of the market they are targeting. Business plans also quite often include descriptions of potential customers, including their gender, age, level of education, marital status, how they make purchases, and the reasons behind those purchases. Discussions of target market also provide information on the history of the market, as well as various trends within the market.

While e-commerce entrepreneurs planning to target an emerging market might be unable to produce historical data, they might be able to make comparisons with related markets. Although Amazon.com founder Jeff Bezos was unable to analyze the online consumer book industry—which for all practical purposes did not exist prior to Amazon's launch—while creating his business plan, he was able to examine the traditional book industry. In fact, it was only after researching 20 different products that he believed could be sold via the Internet—including magazines, CDs, and computer software—that Bezos settled on books, guessing that this sizable market, with its wide range of purchase choices, would be well served by the electronic searching and organizing capabilities of the Web.

MARKETING TACTICS

An explanation of how customers will be made aware of products and services is another key feature of most business plans. Often discussed are advertising mediums—including print, television, and the Internet—as well as pricing strategies, major promotions, and any guarantees or warranties that might be used to attract customers.

DISTRIBUTION

Business plans describe the channels through which customers will obtain products and services, including retail stores, catalogs, and Web sites. In the case of Amazon.com, the ease of distribution was a key concern for Bezos, who believed the small size of most books would facilitate easy shipping. Another of his decisions related to distribution was location. Liking its proximity to the warehouse of Ingram, a leading U.S. book distributor, Bezos chose Seattle, Washington, as his base of operations. According to Bezos' plans, upon receipt of an order, he could request the title or titles be shipped to his home, where he would package the order and take it to the post office. Using this process, customers would receive their books within five days of placing an order, and Bezos could ship books to all 50 states and 45 countries throughout the world, an incredibly broad market for an upstart.

Netflix, Inc., a successful e-commerce company that mails DVDs or provides streaming movies and other content to subscribers, is another company that had a unique distribution system as part of its business plan. Prior to Netflix's launch, most people rented DVDs and videos at a store, so the way Netflix intended to distribute its products was unusual enough to merit being highlighted in a business plan.

COMPETITION

Analysis of competition is an essential component of most business plans. This section tends to cover the strengths and weaknesses of rivals and includes information about their market share, profitability, and pricing strategies. Prior to choosing books as Amazon's initial focus, Bezos analyzed his competition and realized that market share was distributed among many leading book publishers. In fact, at the time, industry leader Barnes & Noble held less than 12% of the $25 billion book retailing market. This market fragmentation, Bezos believed, left room for upstarts. He also planned to gain a competitive advantage over traditional book retailers by offering a wider selection and undercutting prices by 10% to 30%. Successful brick-and-mortar firms drawing up business plans for new online ventures might also include a discussion of how their established customer base and distribution outlets affords them an advantage over rivals only operating online.

TRADEMARKS AND LICENSES

The steps a business has taken or will take to gain protections like trademarks and licenses are also relevant to many business plans. In the case of businesses engaged or planning to engage in e-commerce, domain name registration plans may also be included.

MANAGEMENT

Résumés of any managers or board members recruited by the time the plan is completed can be included in the business plan, as well as discussion of how they can help the business succeed. The section might also include a listing of the desired qualifications for positions that remain vacant, an explanation of how candidates will be recruited, and an organizational chart that details chain of command and the roles that will be played by various executives.

The lack of a strong management team has been identified as one of the most common problems with a business plan, despite the obvious need for good leadership. Entrepreneurs may not have the contacts or the ability to find a high-quality management team, and they may not have the required leadership skills themselves. Because of this, many investors may be interested in knowing as much as possible about the current management team and how experienced managers will be recruited in the future.

NECESSARY FINANCING

Most business plans also set forth how much capital is needed to sustain operations for five years. According to statistics from the Small Business Administration, about half of new businesses will fail in that period of time, and failure rates are similar across U.S. states and industries. A major reason for many business failures is an inadequate amount of capital to keep the company going until it reaches profitability. A business plan will usually detail the dollar amount needed as well as the company's intended plan for securing the needed funding, such as selling off a portion of the company to private investors or conducting an initial public offering (IPO).

EXECUTIVE SUMMARY

Most business plan experts recommend that entrepreneurs write a two- or three-page executive summary that will be placed at the beginning of the business plan. The summary gives readers a thumbnail sketch of the contents of the entire plan. It briefly describes the type of business detailed in the plan, as well as what need the business is meeting. The more concise and compelling the executive summary, the more likely readers will be to examine the remainder of the plan.

SEE ALSO *Financing, Securing.*

BIBLIOGRAPHY

Barker, Emily. "The Bullet-Proof Business Plan." *Inc.,* October 1, 2001.

Hawk, Ken. "10 Weeks to a Business Plan." *Catalog Age,* July 1997, 189.

Klein, Karen E. "Building Your Business Plan: Where to Begin, Part 1." *BusinessWeek Online,* June 20, 2000. Available from http://www.businessweek.com/smallbiz/0006/sa000620.htm?scriptFramed.

Mullins, John W. "Why Business Plans Don't Deliver." *MIT Sloan Management Review,* June 22, 2009. Available from http://sloanreview.mit.edu/executive-adviser/2009-2/5121/why-business-plans-dont-deliver.

Regan, Keith. "New Rules for Writing an E-Business Plan." *E-Commerce Times,* October 30, 2001. Available from http://www.ecommercetimes.com/story/14347.html.

U.S. Small Business Administration. "Frequently Asked Questions." Washington, DC, 2011. Available from http://web.sba.gov/faqs.

BUSINESS-TO-BUSINESS (B2B) E-COMMERCE

Internet-based business-to-business (B2B) e-commerce is conducted through company Web sites but also industry-sponsored marketplaces and through private exchanges set up by large companies for their suppliers and customers.

Business-to-business (B2B) e-commerce is significantly different from business-to-consumer (B2C) e-commerce. While B2C merchants sell on a first-come, first-served basis, most B2B commerce is done through negotiated contracts that allow the seller to anticipate and plan for how much the buyer will purchase. In some cases B2B is less a matter of generating revenue than of making connections with business partners.

B2B E-COMMERCE QUANTIFIED

The Internet was always an attractive place for businesses to contract and supply one another, but B2B e-commerce went through several stages of development. In the late 1990s, the common method was electronic data interchange (EDI), which more than half of manufacturers surveyed used. By the early 2000s the Internet was more common than basic EDI methods, but growth was still relatively slow, especially when it came to profits. Proprietary networks were simply more customizable, useful, and comfortable than trying to conduct business through online portals.

Companies began to discover that B2B e-commerce required a significant investment in infrastructure, with Web sites needing significant work on marketing, infrastructure, and e-procurement fronts. However, spending and revenue predictions for the sector were very high in the early 2000s, since analysts in large part assumed that B2B e-commerce was still in an early adoption stage and would grow quickly in coming years, becoming more of a necessity. These predictions proved increasingly accurate throughout the 2000s.

For a period of time, B2B e-commerce entered a limbo phase, where smaller suppliers waited to see what e-commerce network large companies set up, and larger suppliers waited to see if the market would accept an online B2B venture. Companies hesitated to build sites dedicated to the process, since the Internet still appeared to be a largely consumer-based sector. However, several factors helped the industry to break out of this phase. First, EDI methods were getting old and showing increased signs of incompatibility. They were expensive, difficult to manage, and could be slow. Creating Web sites for managing supplier relationships began to look faster and cheaper. Cost management was helped by the proliferation of new business applications and programming designed to give even small businesses access to B2B tools online.

The first-generation B2B e-commerce Web sites were difficult for customers to use. Problems included too many Web pages to click through, distracting and unhelpful content, difficulty signing up for online service, and difficulty researching products. In these first stages, Web sites tended to be simple models where sellers would list their offerings in online product catalogs and take orders, often on a one-on-one basis. In May 2001, Accenture, a large consulting firm, released a study of B2B buyers that categorized them into five types:

1. traditionalists (28%), who were principally brand sensitive but also valued customer service and good prices
2. eService Seekers (23%), for whom customer service was the most important

3. price sensitives (21%), for whom value lay in the price
4. eSkeptics (17%), who valued brand above all
5. eVanguard (17%), who were comparison buyers

B2B FOR SMALL BUSINESS

Recognizing that 28 million small U.S. businesses represented a lucrative market, Internet portals serving consumers added B2B features. Yahoo! Small Business debuted in August 1998 and provided content, services, and commerce opportunities. In March 2000, the portal launched Yahoo! Business-to-Business Marketplace, which allowed businesses to search for products and services across industries. In January 2001, it created three Yahoo! Industry Marketplaces for IT hardware, IT software, and electronics. AOL Time Warner went after the small-business market through its subsidiary Netscape, which introduced its small-business portal Netbusiness in September 2000. Microsoft's entry was bCentral, a small-business portal that was launched in October 1999.

The dot-com bust of the early 2000s did not help the market during this beginning phase. Poor customer service also had a negative effect on B2B e-commerce, according to a May 2001 study by Jupiter Media Metrix. In terms of responding to e-mail inquiries, the study found that only 41% of B2B companies responded to customer e-mails within six hours, and only half of those responses were deemed satisfactory. Approximately 64% answered e-mail inquiries within 24 hours, and 29% said they never responded. As a result, there was a lack of confidence in e-mail as a customer service channel.

IMPROVEMENT

B2B models began to change and accommodate new online factors. The conventional listing of products, prices, and services was replaced with a much more lively type of interaction. Companies began to experiment with digital versions of auctions and trade shows where companies could show what goods they had and accept views and bids for suppliers. In this new phase, large numbers of buyers and sellers converged, leaving one-on-one transactions to only a portion of the market. By dealing with many potential partnerships at the same time, even more money was saved on transaction costs.

Eventually, the online market evolved in three separate types of B2B exchange models. The first model was primarily controlled by buyers. In this case, buyers gathered either formally or informally through Web site portals to list their requirements and accept incoming bids from suppliers. The second category was a similar arrangement but in reverse. Organizations higher up on the supply chain offered their products and interacted with buyers that visited the online community that they created. The third category was a hybrid version made possible primarily by the growth of online functions, where a third party created a business based on matching business buyers and sellers for a fee.

EXCHANGE GROWTH

By the mid-2000s, portal sites where large numbers of companies interacted together were common. Private exchanges were only private in that they required authorization to enter, but still took place in online environments. Predictions became highly positive again, and the Gartner Group forecasted $7.29 trillion in global revenue from B2B sales in 2004. Part of this rapid growth was due to the increase in international partnerships, which were also made possible by the advent of online technology. The Internet became a flexible enough tool that businesses could start taking advantage of its market-reaching capabilities. With a single Web site or one profile created on an exchange, companies could reach exponentially more potential suppliers or distributors than they would have been able to otherwise. Online trade fairs became common, with nominal fees required for digital booths and with numerous third-party companies offering to help complete transactions. As invoices, data logs, inventory systems, and order tracking also became available online, the need for physical interaction became increasingly remote.

By 2010, the marketing mix had utterly changed. According to Circle Research, this was the first year that (on average) digital B2B marketing overtook traditional marketing in terms of spending. By this time, online opportunities had become so varied that most industries felt the need to participate. Most B2B marketing budgets were devoted to online industry events and tradeshows or online magazines and other trade publications. New categories, however, were also appearing on budgets, such as expenses for online video, search engine marketing (SEM) and search engine optimization (SEO), e-mail marketing, and social media.

By the 2010s, the market had accepted B2B transactions from company Web sites and e-procurement sites, as well as specialized industry portals and brokering sites. Another category of online site arose simply to provide information on industries and where potential suppliers could be found or searched for. Predictably, software companies started to capitalize on this change by offering increasingly complex programs to search and manage B2B relationships. In 2011, IBM advertised its WebSphere Commerce program to deliver digital content to client businesses and show both inventory available and order status to buyers in one package. Analytics, customization, and cross-channel management were common features in such software.

International B2B revenues also increased rapidly as digital channels became more accessible. In China alone, B2B revenues rose more than 40 percent between 2010 and 2011, with much of the revenue provide by smaller companies that were able to use online portals to find overseas buyers.

NEW B2B ONLINE FEATURES

In the early 2010s, B2B e-commerce had stabilized and companies started experimenting with improvements to systems. The rise of social media, for example, proved a catalyst for some relatively new B2B sites across the Internet. Forums became a common tool to exchange information between buyers and suppliers in informal ways. Chatting between representatives became a standard option for quick conversations. Also, social networks (especially those oriented toward a particular industry) became places where buyers could discuss sellers and provide informal advice, suggestions, and reviews. Sellers could do the same for other organizations, and before long reputation management became a key part of mastering B2B e-commerce.

With digital content becoming even easier to create and spread, image and video use became much more common throughout exchanges. Web sites devoted to B2B opportunities became easier to navigate, and many companies worked on educating viewers so they would have fewer questions and understand the value of product offerings or the specific needs of the organization. Companies started to experiment with quizzes, online representations of customizable products, and advanced search tools for finding the desired product type. These were all tools that once existed solely in the B2C realm.

SEE ALSO *Business-to-Consumer (B2C) E-Commerce; Electronic Data Interchange (EDI); Vortals.*

BIBLIOGRAPHY

"B2B (Business2Business or Business-to-Business)." *Search CIO,* 2011. Available from http://searchcio.techtarget.com/definition/B2B.

Enos, Lori. "The Biggest Myths about B2B." *E-Commerce Times,* June 22 and 25, 2001. Available from http://www.ecommercetimes.com/story/11327.html.

Grygo, Eugene, et al. "B-to-B Players Retrench." *InfoWorld,* April 9, 2001.

IBM. "B2B E-Commerce Software." Armonk, NY, 2011. Available from http://www-01.ibm.com/software/genservers/commerce/b2bdrp.

Mahoney, Michael. "Dell B2B Marketplace Unplugged." *E-Commerce Times,* February 7, 2001. Available from http://www.ecommercetimes.com/story/7303.html.

Regan, Keith. "Boring Old B2B Steals E-Tail's Thunder." *E-Commerce Times,* March 9, 2001. Available from http://www.technewsworld.com/story/8053.html.

———. "Study: Customer Service Lapses Hurt B2B." *E-Commerce Times,* May 16, 2001. Available from http://www.technewsworld.com/story/commerce/9771.html.

"Retail Exchanges Have Only Tapped Tip of the Iceberg." *DSN Retailing Today,* June 18, 2001.

Richards, Luke. "Making Sense of the B2B Marketing Mix." *Econsultancy,* September 1, 2011. Available from http://econsultancy.com/us/blog/7949-making-sense-of-the-b2b-marketing-mix.

Rodenberg, Rachel. "Trends in B2B Ecommerce for 2011 and Beyond." *Ecommerce Insights,* June 21, 2011. Available from http://www.info.insitesoft.com/Insite-Software-Blog/bid/64618/Trends-in-B2B-Ecommerce-for-2011-and-Beyond.

Saliba, Clare. "Study: B2B Exchanges Need to Supply More Services." *E-Commerce Times,* May 24, 2001. Available from http://www.technewsworld.com/story/9990.html.

Sanborn, Stephanie. "Reverse Auctions Make a Bid for Business." *InfoWorld,* March 19, 2001.

Srikanth, A. "E-Commerce: A B2B Guide." *Hindu Business Line,* May 28, 2000. Available from http://www.thehindubusinessline.in/businessline/iw/2000/05/28/stories/0728g101.htm.

Taddonio, Linda. "The Tremendous Transformative Powers of B2B E-Commerce." *E-Commerce Times,* June 1, 2011. Available from http://www.ecommercetimes.com/rsstory/72561.html?wlc=1314897754.

Tedeschi, Bob. "Why Purchasing Agents Turned Out to Be Hard to Herd." *New York Times,* February 28, 2001.

Yan, Hao. "China's B2B E-Commerce Q1 Revenue Hits 2.9b Yuan." *China Daily,* April 21, 2011. Available from http://usa.chinadaily.com.cn/business/2011-04/21/content_12370911.htm.

BUSINESS-TO-CONSUMER (B2C) E-COMMERCE

Business-to-consumer (B2C) e-commerce has woven itself into the fabric of business and consumer relations. While the Internet started by being a facilitator in the B2C transaction process, it soon began engendering new channels of doing business altogether. This allowed businesses to expand their markets, grow their customer bases, and explore innovative ways of producing and delivering products or services.

GROWTH

The 1998 holiday season represented the first "e-tail Christmas" for U.S. consumers. Online consumers spent an estimated $4 billion during the fourth quarter of 1998 for goods and services, including travel, and nearly $10 billion for the year, according to the Boston Consulting Group. For the first time, online retailer Amazon.com surpassed $1 billion in annual sales as a result of the 1998 holiday shopping season.

The next year marked an even greater success for online retailers, with big gains over the previous year. Jupiter Communications (now Jupiter Research) estimated total holiday Internet sales at $7 billion, while PC Data Online reported online holiday sales of $5 billion.

One of the biggest problems online shoppers have faced, particularly during a holiday rush, is late delivery of merchandise. This was a serious problem in the early years of e-commerce, and in 1999 the Federal Trade Commission (FTC) received a large volume of complaints from customers of online companies like Macys.com and Toysrus.com. After penalties, refunds, and warnings, e-tailers began to plan more efficiently for the holiday seasons, forming partnerships with delivery services and developing transportation models.

During 2000, the stock prices of many top online retailers fell dramatically as the stock markets in general, and technology firms in particular, suffered a broad and protracted sell-off amid investor concerns about future growth and general economic conditions. The E-Commerce Times Stock Index fell 82% from the end of 1999 through the end of 2000. The year 2000, as a result, was also the year of the dot-com shakeout, with many e-tailers going out of business. An estimated 150 dot-coms folded during the year, including Boo.com, Toysmart.com, Petstore.com, Living.com, Pop.com, WebHouse Club, Eve.com, Pets.com, MotherNature.com, and Garden.com.

UNDERLYING STRENGTH

Despite difficulties, during 2000 online shopping continued to rise. Growth was attributed to new shoppers as well as to more spending by established customers. During the year online retailing received greater support from offline retailers who wanted to add new distribution channels and shore up their revenues. Strong ties to established brands in 2000 helped the growth of "bricks and clicks," further integrating traditional retailing with online channels.

The categories of online retailers with the strongest growth were mail-order firms, automobile companies, and online bookstores. Mail-order companies and traditional retailers showed faster growth than pure-play e-tailers. Their strong performance was attributed to having infrastructures in place, such as distribution, customer relation, and billing systems, as well as having recognizable brands. Consumers also appeared more comfortable making online purchases: repeated Internet use and knowing other people who bought online reduced concerns about security and Internet fraud.

Estimates of the amount spent online during all of 2000 varied considerably. In January 2001 Activ-Media Research reported that online shopping in 2000 reached $56 billion, with sales during the holiday season of about $9 billion. That compared to an estimated $3.5 to $4.5 billion spent during the 1999 holiday season. Factors contributing to the surge in online holiday spending included better order processing systems and more effective marketing promotions. Some 57% of all consumer-oriented Web sites had e-commerce capabilities, while an additional 36% provided presale information and postsale support without actually taking orders.

PURE PLAYERS

Most pure-play e-tailers had little concern for profits when they first launched. They focused on acquiring market share, spending to gain new customers, and building their brands. They succeeded in driving traffic to their Web sites, but their margins were not enough to achieve profitability. As a result, many pure-play e-tailers went out of business in the wake of the dot-com shakeout of 2000. Others faced cash shortages and needed to raise funds to cover their cash-burn rate and lack of profitability. In order to meet these challenges, companies like Amazon.com and Buy.com began cutting labor, operating expenses, and other costs in an effort to produce real earnings. For Amazon.com, 2002 became the first year with significant profits, leading to a surge in profit throughout the 2000s, hampered by the recession of 2008–2009 but with a rebound by the beginning of the 2010s.

BRICKS-AND-CLICKS

A study in the early 2000s by McKinsey & Co. revealed that more than 75% of the best-performing e-tailers were online cousins of traditional retailers. Bricks-and-clicks had the benefit of existing brands, established marketing and distribution arrangements, and an installed information technology base. The study found that e-tailers that sold clothing and apparel did the best in terms of gaining revenue from customers, with an average 21% operating margin.

Bricks-and-clicks also had the ability to bring the Internet into their traditional stores. In-store kiosks with Web access allowed consumers to research potential purchases online, then find the merchandise they wanted in the store. Brick-and-click bookseller Barnes & Noble took steps in 2001 to integrate its online bookselling with its stores. For example, the company allowed customers who purchased books online the convenience of being able to return them to a Barnes & Noble bookstore.

As the 2000s progressed, several key trends began to develop. Web site hosting and creation became more common and less costly. A wide variety of security and payment options were developed for customers, and e-tailers began to have increased advantages over storefront-bound competitors. This caused many brick-and-mortar companies to pour even more funds into developing strong Web sites. By 2011, Barnes & Noble had survived the collapse of major competitor Borders and harsh marketing conditions due in large part to its extensive online segment. In the same year Amazon.com reported more digital sales of books for e-readers than printed books, hardcover and paperback combined.

EXPANSION IN THE 2000s

As the 2000s continued and the rise of online business began to stabilize, growth expanded beyond the well-developed market in the United States. Europe began to embrace an e-tailer culture first, with growth concentrated in the United Kingdom, Germany, and France. But by 2010, markets had also begun to grow in Italy, the Netherlands, Spain, and smaller sectors throughout the continent. Emerging markets in Latin America, India, and China created a rising middle class that had enough income to afford computers and Internet access, which meant a growing e-commerce demand. The advent of digital music, books, and videos made it all the easier for consumers to depend on online resources for their goods, especially in entertainment industries.

While the recession led to a slowdown in overall economic growth from 2007 to 2009, many e-tailers belonged to industries that were able to bounce back with relative ease. By 2010, B2C e-commerce sales worldwide had grown 25% since 2009. Sales between 2009 and 2013 were expected to double globally, according to IMR World, with growth concentrated in Latin America and Eastern Europe. In countries like Switzerland, B2C e-commerce revenue grew by as much as 50% between 2009 and 2010. The United Kingdom, Germany, and France still accounted for more than 70% of online sales in Europe, but potential was high for greater and more diverse growth.

The improvement seen in 2010 e-commerce was felt around the globe, but some industries profited more than others. The strongest e-commerce markets for consumers were apparel, electronics, general merchandise, and media, followed by food and drug industries and a variety of specialty brand businesses.

KEYS TO PROFITABILITY

As e-tailers sought to achieve profitability by cutting costs and spending less to gain customers, the ability to generate positive gross margins became a significant factor in e-tail success. Another critical factor was driving traffic to the Web site and generating a high conversion rate, turning at least 10 to 15% of those visitors into customers.

Information quickly became key in the battle to win customer loyalty. By 2010, e-tailers had developed complex strategies to deliver key information to customers in ways that were both easy to find and understand. Data on product availability, use, and similar needs often proved a tipping point in winning sales, so online info-pages, rating systems, and guides became powerful tools. However, technology also had a pivotal role to play, especially when it came to the rise in mobile users seen in the latter 2000s. This meant that retailers anxious to capitalize on the more immediate mobile sales opportunities had to create user-friendly apps for smartphones, tablet computers, and similar devices. Making a mobile-optimized Web site that was both attractive and simple to use proved a challenge, especially if businesses wanted to offer the same choice of goods. Delivering engaging and consistent user experiences with the rise of multiple channels was a key investment area in 2011 for B2C e-commerce.

The result was the growth of varied customer features and services designed to make buying online a better experience. E-tailers, with major companies like Amazon.com often leading the way, began offering detailed recommendations, reviews, and popular items, saving past consumer behavior and using complex metrics to offer discounts and promotions for items that might also capture interest. Customization for more complex items, like computers, became a standard online option. Portals like craigslist and eBay, once primarily intended for consumer-to-consumer (C2C) content, became hospitable environments for businesses as well, especially small online companies looking for inexpensive channels through which to sell their goods. With the availability of online selling, channel conflict became an issue in highly developed markets: manufacturers and service providers began offering their goods or service packages directly to consumers via Web sites instead of using traditional distributor channels, reworking the common business models of some industries.

By the 2010s, the Internet had become a very social place. Social networks, forums, blogs, and wikis became standard and were soon primary sources of information regarding products and services, even before data provided on e-tailer Web sites. In 2011, user experience was rated as a top investment area for B2C e-commerce, and this usually meant work in the social media field. Companies started to create their own profiles and blogs to better answer customer questions and provide information for online promotions. Marketing became a two-sided concept, with response and follow-up becoming key steps in the advertising process. E-tailers found themselves managing not only information on their own site, but ratings and opinions given on sites from Yelp to Facebook, where users could pass information onto each other more quickly than searching for data on a company Web site.

SAFETY ISSUES

Another dominant area of concern for e-tailers continued to be security. When entering personal information online, there was always a danger of identity theft and the loss of previous financial data. Mobile sales only increased these dangers, since the wireless transmission of data was even more open to infiltration. Trust swiftly became a major consumer issue, and statements of privacy and security started making appearances on major sales sites as e-tailers tried to prove their safety.

Responses to the problem approached the issue on several levels. Credit card data, some of the most vulnerable financial information, was hidden in e-wallets that could be taken offline when not in use. Payment systems sprang up to offer electronic checks, online accounts, and credit authorization so that an intermediary could offer some fund protection. However, these systems created by outside vendors often came with a cost per transaction, and forming proprietary systems required significant investment and planning, leading to the continued challenge of matching security with cost management.

SEE ALSO *Business-to-Business (B2B) E-commerce; Business Models.*

BIBLIOGRAPHY

"B2C Global E-Commerce Overview 2011." *IMR World,* 2011. Available from http://www.imrg.org/ImrgWebsite/IMRG Contents/Files/IMRG_B2C_global_ecommerce_2011_ Summary.pdf.

Cuneo, Alice Z. "Retailers Stress Bricks over Clicks." *Advertising Age,* September 25, 2000.

Davis, Jessica, and Dan Neel. "Pure-Play E-tailers Retrench." *InfoWorld,* February 5, 2001.

"E-commerce Definition and Solutions." *CIO,* March 6, 2007. Available from http://www.cio.com/article/40298/ E_Commerce_Definition_and_Solutions?page=1& taxonomyId=3055.

"Electronic Commerce Security: An Introduction for Everyone." *MSEN,* 2009. Available from http://www.msen.com/~chad/ ecomm_sec.html.

Enos, Lori, and Elizabeth Blakey. "Portals Turn Eyeballs into E-commerce." *E-Commerce Times,* July 20, 2000. Available from http://www.technewsworld.com/story/3824.html.

"European E-commerce to Reach 323 Billion Euros in 2011." *Marketing Charts,* August 9, 2007. Available from http:// www.marketingcharts.com/direct/european-e-commerce-to-reach-323-billion-euros-in-2011-1239.

Hampton, Jennifer M. "U.S. Fines E-tailers $1.5M for Late Holiday Deliveries." *E-Commerce Times,* July 27, 2000. Available from http://www.technewsworld.com/story/3883.html.

"Inside the First E-Christmas." *Fortune,* February 1, 1999.

Jerome, Marty. "E-commerce." *Ziff Davis Smart Business for the New Economy,* December 1, 2000.

Johnson, Brenna. "Why B2C eCommerce Named User Experience the #1 Investment Area for 2011." *Endeca,* February 1, 2011. Available from http://ebusinessfacets.endeca.com/2011/02/b2c-ecommerce-user-experience-1-investment.

Mahoney, Michael. "Report: Brick-and-Clicks Now E-tail Model." *E-Commerce Times,* December 20, 2000. Available from http://www.ecommercetimes.com/story/commerce/ 6207.html.

———. "Report: North American E-commerce to Grow 46 Percent in 2001." *E-Commerce Times,* May 3, 2001. Available from http://www.technewsworld.com/story/9440.html.

Saliba, Clare. "New Data Confirms $10B+ E-holiday." *E-Commerce Times,* January 17, 2001. Available from http:// www.technewsworld.com/story/6785.html.

Schulz, Rick. "Retailers Bring the Internet Inside to Compete Effectively." *DM News,* January 15, 2001.

"Solution Overview." *EZMCOM,* 2009. Available from http:// www.8i.com.my/ezmcom/solutions_portal.jsp.

"The Straight Dope on Web Retailers." *Fortune,* February 21, 2000.

"The User Experience within an Advancing Multichannel World." *Transaction Age,* April 8, 2011. Available from http://www.transactionage.com/2011/04/08/the-user-experience-within-an-advancing-multichannel-world.

Weisman, Jon. "The Making of E-commerce: 10 Key Moments." *E-Commerce Times,* August 22, 2000. Available from http://www.ecommercetimes.com/story/4085.html.

BUY.COM INC.

Buy.com offers millions of consumer goods online, including computers, software, office products, wireless products, electronics, books, videos, games, music, and sports. In 2010, Buy.com became a subsidiary of Japanese e-tailer Rakuten, which acquired it to expand its presence globally.

INITIAL REACTIONS WERE SKEPTICAL

Buy.com's original business model was not designed to make money on its margins the way traditional retailers have done, but to generate a profit by selling advertising on its Web site. By selling merchandise at, near, or even below cost, Buy.com hoped to attract enough eyeballs to make consumer goods manufacturers want to advertise on its Web site. It was a revolutionary business model, and one that founder Scott Blum hoped would make Buy.com the fastest-growing company in U.S. history.

Barely two months after the Buy.com Web site was launched, *Fortune* magazine described it as a "seemingly crazy new model" and compared it to a Web site selling dollars for 85 cents. If Buy.com proved to be successful, the magazine argued, it would demonstrate that it was possible to build a brand completely on price. It also would have revolutionary implications for Internet retailing.

Buy.com originally was BuyComp.com, a discount seller of computer products founded in October 1996 by Scott Blum. BuyComp.com was selling about $1 million worth of computer products a day when it changed its name to Buy.com in November 1998. The name change reflected the wider range of products the company would sell. With $60 million in venture capital financing from Japanese software distributor Softbank, Buy.com was able to acquire SpeedServe, the Internet division of Ingram Entertainment that sold videos, DVDs, books, and computer games. Almost immediately the company launched a consumer advertising campaign that included national TV spots and print advertising. Buy.com offered videos and DVDs through a new subsite of Buy.com called BuyVideos.com, thereby establishing a pattern it would follow of creating specialty stores for new product lines. To prepare for the addition of new specialty stores, Buy.com purchased the rights to more than 2,000 domain names beginning with the word "buy."

If Buy.com's business model was to work, the company had to offer the lowest prices on the Internet. To accomplish this Blum spent more than a year perfecting search agents that would automatically scan the Web for the lowest prices on products he was selling. The company also did not carry any inventory, instead having wholesalers ship products directly to Buy.com's customers. The company got off to a fast start. For 1998, it posted sales of $125 million. By February 1999, it was selling about $2 million worth of merchandise a day, and for 1999 it reported total revenue of nearly $600 million.

EXPANSION, CUSTOMER COMPLAINTS MARKED FIRST YEAR

During 1999, Buy.com added an online music store that featured every title on the Billboard 200 for $9.95, excluding two-CD and box sets. In mid-1999, Buy.com redesigned its Web site to allow customers to buy products from its different specialty stores with one shopping cart. Specialty stores in operation included Buycomp.com for computer hardware and software, Buyvideos.com, Buygames.com, and Buybooks.com.

While Buy.com was hoping to gain customer loyalty on the basis of price, it was falling short in the area of customer service, according to some complaints. Protest sites with names like BoycottBuy.com began to appear, criticizing the company's customer service. A survey by ResellerRatings.com that was published in *Sm@rt Reseller* reported that more than 60% of online shoppers felt the company's sales staff was neither knowledgeable nor easy to deal with. More than 80% said exchanges were not handled professionally, and only about half said they would recommend Buy.com to a friend.

One area of consumer concern was the company's billing practices. Buy.com would book orders and bill the customer's credit card even if the item ordered was not in stock at its distributor, Ingram Micro. If the order went unfilled, then Buy.com would credit the customer's account—in some cases days or even weeks after the order was placed. When Buy.com's advertised price for a Hitachi monitor was mistakenly listed $400 below the company's intended price, it refused to deliver the monitors at the incorrect price. That resulted in a class-action lawsuit on behalf of customers who ordered the monitor, and the initial ruling in the case went against Buy.com.

All of this was especially troubling to Buy.com's new CEO, Gregory Hawkins, who joined the company from Ingram Micro. To smooth things over, Hawkins invited a group of unhappy customers to the firm's Orange County headquarters in Aliso Viejo, California, and promised to hire customer service representatives to improve the firm's customer transactions. Before the end of the year, founder Scott Blum resigned as chairman and director. Hawkins became chairman, CEO, and president.

IPO RAISED $182 MILLION IN 2000

Buy.com's initial public offering (IPO) took place in February 2000. The company sold 14 million shares at $13 each, raising approximately $182 million. Investors quickly bid the price up to $35 on the first day of trading before closing at $25.12 a share. Investor interest appeared to be unaffected by Buy.com's failure to turn a profit. Although revenue for 1999 increased nearly fourfold to $296.8 million, the company's loss for the year was $130.2 million, compared to a loss of $17.8 million in 1998. The company never regained the stock price it reached on the first day of its IPO.

Buy.com expanded in several ways in 2000 with varying degrees of success. Through an alliance with United Airlines it opened a full-service airline ticket booking service called Buytravel.com. The site offered discounted fares and rates from United, fares from about 500 other airlines, and other travel-related services. including hotels and car rentals. However, Buytravel.com only operated from February to November 2000 before it was shut down.

The company also expanded internationally by opening Web sites in the United Kingdom and Australia. Both sites were accessible from Buy.com's home page. However, Australian operations were discontinued in November 2000, and the company's operations in the United Kingdom were sold to Britain's department store group, John Lewis Partnership, in March 2001.

THE BUBBLE BURSTS

After continued struggles to raise capital and become profitable, the company entered 2001 with a new management team. Chairman and CEO Gregory Hawkins and chief financial officer (CFO) Mitch Hill resigned in February 2001. Donald Kendall, former chairman and CEO of PepsiCo and a Buy.com board member, was appointed chairman. James Roszak was named interim

CEO, and Robert Price joined the firm from PairGain Technologies as president and CFO.

In 2002, the company decided to expand beyond selling electronics, movies, and music and add other goods, including books, which was part of a bid to attract customers away from the rapidly expanding Amazon.com. Buy.com also started a print magazine, called *BuyMagazine,* that was later converted to a digital-only publication. Buy.com filed paperwork with the U.S. Securities and Exchange Commission for a second IPO in 2005, but the offering was postponed due to market conditions.

In 2006, Neel Grover was appointed CEO of Buy.com. Prior to that appointment, Grover had served as president. Before joining Buy.com, Grover worked as a general partner with ThinkTank Holdings, a private equity management company. Also in 2006, Greg Girardi was named chief operating officer and general counsel. Girardi had been general counsel for the company since October 2003.

Buy.com's business model continued to evolve. In 2007, a newly revamped Web site added Buy.tv, a video channel for product and vendor reviews. The new site also added third-party vendor partners who could sell products through the Buy.com site, with customers only needing to use one account to make purchases. This marketplace setup was similar to Amazon.com's relationship with its vendor partners. By 2010, the company was working with thousands of partners, offering millions of products.

BUY.COM AND EBAY

In 2008, Buy.com forged a deal with online auction retailer eBay that allowed the company to sell its electronics, videos, and other items at fixed prices on eBay without paying the same level of fees that other sellers were charged. This move angered some of eBay's small vendors who felt they could not compete with Buy.com's copious listings on eBay and the larger company's ability to offer perks like free shipping that led to higher feedback ratings. The move had industry observers suggesting that eBay was shifting away from its previous online auction model, which favored smaller vendors, toward more relationships with larger fixed-price sellers, similar to Amazon.com's marketplace.

By 2011, Buy.com was selling millions of products, many of them through eBay, in a wide range of categories, including electronics, computers, computer software, cell phones, books, toys, games, home décor, baby items, jewelry, fragrance, shoes, and apparel, among others.

In May 2010, Japanese online retailer Rakuten announced plans to aquire Buy.com for $250 million. The move was Rakuten's first foray into the U.S. market, though the company was an Asian online powerhouse with operations in Taiwan, Thailand, and China as well as Japan. After the acquisition, Buy.com implemented a 45-day return policy and a Rakuten Super Points program to reward frequent loyal shoppers with points that could be used on purchases in the future.

SEE ALSO *eBay Inc.*

BIBLIOGRAPHY

Buy.com. "Buy.com Executive Biographies." Aliso Viejo, CA, 2011. Available from http://www.buy.com/toc/executive-biographies/15791.html.

———. "Buy.com Milestones." Aliso Viejo, CA, 2011. Available from http://www.buy.com/toc/buy-com-milestones/15787.html.

———. "Buy.com Reports Biggest Sales Day in History on Cyber Monday." Aliso Viejo, CA, November 29, 2010. Available from http://www.buy.com/corp/toc_feature.asp?loc=68951.

Chen, Christine Y. "All I Want for Christmas Is a Pulse." *Fortune,* November 27, 2000.

"The Everything Website." *Fortune,* December 7, 1998.

Foster, Ed. "Dubious Marketing Ploys at Buy.com Expose the Seamy Side of E-commerce." *InfoWorld,* May 3, 1999.

Gurley, J. William. "The Lowest Prices on Earth." *Fortune,* January 11, 1999.

Hardy, Quentin. "The Death and Life of Buy.com." *Forbes,* January 21, 2002. Available from http://www.forbes.com/forbes/2002/0121/086.html.

Hibbard, Justin. "Buy.com: How Soon We Forget." *Business Week,* January 25, 2005. Available from http://www.businessweek.com/the_thread/dealflow/archives/2005/01/buycom_how_soon.html.

"I-Way Bumps." *Business Week,* May 15, 2000.

Milliot, Jim. "Buy.com Hopes to Net $138 Million in Public Offering." *Publishers Weekly,* November 8, 1999.

Nee, Eric. "Meet Mister Buy.com (Everything)." *Fortune,* March 29, 1999.

Panettieri, Joseph C. "Customer Boycott Bites Buy.com." *Sm@rt Reseller,* April 5, 1999.

Sacirbey, Omar. "Buy.com Signals E-tailings Long Farewell?" *IPO Reporter,* February 7, 2000.

Stone, Brad. "Buy.com Deal with eBay Angers Sellers." *New York Times,* July 14, 2008. Available from http://www.nytimes.com/2008/07/14/technology/14ebay.html.

Vogelstein, Fred. "Whoa! Has Buy.com Got a Deal for You!" *U.S. News & World Report,* February 15, 1999.

C

C (PROGRAMMING LANGUAGE)

C is a high-level programming language that is used to develop many kinds of software, including applications that are used during e-commerce. High-level programming languages are much closer to human language than machine language, through which computer hardware accepts commands. High-level languages eventually get translated to machine language, which is numeric (consisting mainly of zeros and ones). C allows programmers to manipulate the main elements—bytes, bits, and addresses—that influence the way a computer functions.

C is often used for system programming, including implementing operating systems and embedded system applications. C uses an array of programming applications. One example, and one of its biggest applications, is the UNIX operating system. By using C, programmers were easily able to place UNIX on new computers. C also made it much easier for programmers to customize and improve UNIX.

Although it is a high-level language, C is capable of controlling the computer on which it operates at a low level, much like assembly language—a form of computer language that resides between machine languages and high-level languages. This enables programs written in C to perform in a very stable manner. Its mix of high-and low-level capabilities make C ideal for a wide variety of different uses. Additionally, compared to other programming languages C enables programs to be written in smaller formats that require less memory. Finally, perhaps one of the most popular features of C is its portability—a characteristic that lies at the heart of its creation.

C was created in 1972 by Ken Thompson and Dennis Ritchie, researchers at AT&T's Bell Labs in Murray Hill, New Jersey, who also invented the UNIX operating system (a program used to operate computer systems). After creating UNIX, the two programmers needed to enable it for use on many different kinds of computers. Improving upon a language called B that Thompson had developed, they created C to accomplish this task. By doing so, they created the first portable operating system, and UNIX became the first major program to be written in the C language. According to *C Programming* by Augie Hansen, C went through a long period of development before it was released in Brian Kernighan and Dennis Ritchie's 1978 book *The C Programming Language.* Later, the American National Standards Institute (ANSI) developed a standardized version of the language to make it more acceptable for international use.

In the early 2000s, an enhanced version of C called C++ was widely used by programmers for just about every kind of program imaginable, especially on Windows and Macintosh systems. Developed at Bell Labs by Bjarne Stroustrup, C++ was effective for creating games, interpreters, spreadsheets, word processors, project managers, and more. In addition to the features of C, C++ contained many improvements, and it supported object-oriented programming (OOP)—techniques that allowed programmers to increase efficiency and reduce complexity.

Another revision came in 1999 and was known as C99. C99 offered many new features. Historically, embedded C programming required nonstandard extensions to the C language in order to support more in-depth features such as fixed-point arithmetic and multiple distinct memory banks. In 2008, the C Standards Committee set out to correct this by publishing a technical report extending the language to address these issues by providing a common standard for all implementations to adhere to.

Despite the extensions, problems remained with C99. Some of the mandatory C99 features proved difficult to implement in some platforms. Some features were questioned and were not embraced by the C community. In 2007, work began on another revision to completely replace the standard C (C99). C1X is set to fix some of these problems and also make C more compatible with later versions of C++. It will also make some of the mandatory features of C99 optional, giving vendors more freedom in choosing the set of features that they have to support.

C1X is set to offer many new features, such as support for multiple threads of execution including an improved memory sequencing model. If all goes well, C1X could become the new standard C sometime in the 2010s.

SEE ALSO *BASIC; COBOL; FORTRAN; Programming Language; UNIX.*

BIBLIOGRAPHY

Appleman, Daniel. *How Computer Programming Works.* Berkeley, CA: Apress, 2000.

Benito, John. "C – The C1X Charter," June 29, 2007. Available from http://www.open-std.org/jtc1/sc22/wg14/www/docs/n1250.pdf.

"C." *Techencyclopedia,* March 7, 2001. Available from http://www.techweb.com/encyclopedia.

"C." *Webopedia,* March 27, 2001. Available from http://www.webopedia.com/TERM/C/C.html.

Computer Languages. Alexandria, VA: Time-Life Books, 1986.

"The C Programming Language." December 7, 1999. Available from http://groups.engin.umd.umich.edu/CIS/course.des/cis400/c/c.html.

"C Programming Language History." *Living Internet.* Available from http://www.livinginternet.com/i/iw_unix_c.htm.

Kalev, Danny. "A Tour of C1X." *InformIT,* August 5, 2011. Available from http://www.informit.com/guides/content.aspx?g=cplusplus&seqNum=551.

"Learn C/C++ Today." *Cyberdiem,* January 30, 2001. Available from www.cyberdiem.com/vin.

Parlante, Nick. "Essential C." Stanford CS Education Library, 2003. Available from http://cslibrary.stanford.edu/101/EssentialC.pdf.

"Status of C99 Features in GCC 4.6." GNU Compiler Collection, April 25, 2011. Available from http://gcc.gnu.org/gcc-4.6/c99status.html.

Walls, Douglas. "C1X Is Coming." *Douglas Walls' Blog,* March 24, 2011. Available from http://blogs.oracle.com/dew/entry/c1x_is_coming.

CALL CENTER SERVICES

Call center services, sometimes more accurately referred to as contact services, manage the interaction between consumers and company customer service or sales operations. Such services can be handled by the company internally or outsourced to third-party providers. Call or contact services are typically of three types: technical helpdesk services, outbound telemarketing services, and inbound call center services.

OUTSOURCING OF CALL CENTERS

Outsourcing of call center operations by companies has increasingly become the norm, due largely to the lower cost of outsourcing such operations to developing countries. Labor costs, which account for up to 60% of call center operating expenses, is the primary reason for outsourcing to foreign-based operations. India, the most popular destination for outsourcing, offers a number of advantages other countries have not been able to equal thus far, including a well-educated and large workforce and the use of the latest technology. However, cost of operation in India has been increasing rapidly in the 2010s, and other low-cost competitors are gaining ground. Other countries with growing call center operations include the Philippines, Malaysia, and China.

CALL CENTERS AND THE WEB

Since the late 1990s Web-enabled call centers have adapted to the increased migration of both retail and business-to-business customer interaction to the Web by offering consumers both telephone and online service contacts. Most companies now link their call centers to their Web sites in order to provide advanced customer service options. These centers have added e-mail, instant chat, and other Web-based services such as interactive voice response (IVR), a service that allows consumers to speak to service representatives over the Web from a variety of enabled devices. Some call centers even offer video services, which enable online customers to see the representative with whom they are in contact.

Consumers report that the options available through a multichannel call center operation significantly reduce response time, as well as improving rapport between customer and service agent. Businesses find the capacity and scalability of these operations also give them more options, including around the clock operation, peak volume support, and higher first-call resolution rates.

TRENDS IN CALL CENTER SERVICES

As a rapidly evolving industry, call center services are sensitive both to the needs of their business clients and the new opportunities that technology affords to improve their offerings. Some of the trends appearing in call services in the early 2010s include:

- Improved customer experience—Companies are increasingly demanding better customer interaction, even if it means increased cost.

- Hosted Services—Companies are migrating to hosted services at double-digit annual rates, and the largest contact centers are experiencing the fastest growth.
- Social Media—In 2010, over 30% of companies support some form of social media customer interaction. Social media benefits are widely touted by companies as helping provide better service, driving sales, and improving customer loyalty.
- Texting or SMS—Inbound interactions with contact centers are growing quickly in this segment, with a 25% increase in activity between 2009 and 2010.
- Proactive Contact—65% of companies indicate they intend to increase their proactive value-added customer contact through outbound call center activity.

The call and contact center market will continue to evolve and adapt to changes in the expectations of both consumers and businesses. Increasing penetration of wireless Web technologies and social media are expected to strongly influence interaction between customer and businesses throughout the 2010s and beyond.

SEE ALSO *Customer Relationship Management (CRM).*

BIBLIOGRAPHY

Convery, Anna. "Call Center Data." *DestinationCRM.com,* May 1, 2007. http://www.destinationcrm.com/Articles/Web-Exclusives/Viewpoints/Call-Center-Data-47952.aspx.

"Why India?" Princeton, NJ: Flatworld Solutions Inc. 2011. Available from http://www.outsource2india.com.

Wilde, Candee. "Web-Enabled Call Center Services Promise to Let Service Providers Put On Quite a Show—Assuming They Don't Drop the Ball." *CMP Media,* June 26, 2000.

Zaibak, Omar. "Contact Center Trends in 2011."*Customer1 Blog,* September 27, 2010. Available from http://www.customer1.com/blog/contact-center-trends-2011.

CAN-SPAM

Passed on December 8, 2003, the Controlling the Assault of Non-Solicited Pornography and Marketing Act of 2003, also known as the CAN-SPAM Act of 2003, was an attempt by the U.S. government to regulate e-mail marketing. It controls commercial e-mail, defined by the law as "an electronic message for which the primary purpose is commercial advertisement or promotion of a commercial product or service (including content on an Internet Web site operated for a commercial purpose)." The intention of the CAN-SPAM Act is to limit spam, or unsolicited bulk e-mail or electronic junk mail. Marketing anything from weight-loss solutions to penny stocks to pornography, these unwanted solicitations clog inboxes.

More than simply annoying, some spam e-mails carry viruses embedded in them, while others attempt to trick people into giving out their personal information, which can result in unauthorized charges or identity theft. According to a *Network World* report by Carolyn Duffy Marsan, around 15 billion spam messages were sent every day in 2003 alone, and close to 75% of adult users of computers supported legislation that would make mass spamming illegal.

MAIN PROVISIONS

The CAN-SPAM Act prohibits the use of false or misleading transmission information in commercial e-mail. The "To," "From," and "Reply to" lines must disclose the identity of the person or business that initiated the message. Some spammers disguise the origin of a commercial e-mail by relaying or retransmitting the message through multiple computers, so the law stipulates that the routing information of the message, which includes the originating domain name and e-mail address, must be accurate. In addition, subject headings must truthfully reflect the content of the message, and marketers must clearly indicate that the message is an advertisement or solicitation. If an e-mail contains sexually oriented material, warning labels have to appear in both the subject and message.

Besides including a valid physical postal address for the sender, a commercial e-mail must provide recipients with a functioning e-mail address or other Internet-based way to respond. The CAN-SPAM Act prohibits hijacking, or registering for multiple e-mail or online user accounts for the purpose of transmitting unlawful commercial e-mail messages. The person or entity sending the message must offer recipients the opportunity to "opt out," or decline to receive further commercial e-mails. The law gives senders ten business days to honor an opt-out request. Once this is received from a person, his or her e-mail address cannot be sold or transferred to any other marketers.

Congress charged the Federal Trade Commission (FTC), the Federal Communications Commission (FCC), and the U.S. Department of Justice with enforcing the CAN-SPAM Act. After the law was put into effect, those in noncompliance faced fines of up to $250 per spam e-mail. Aggravated violations, such as dictionary attacks (using automated means to generate possible e-mail addresses by combining names, letters, or numbers into numerous variations) or harvesting (using automated means to obtain e-mail addresses from a Web site or online service operated by another individual or entity that had previously provided clients with a notice stating that e-mail addresses would not be sold or transferred) carried higher penalties, including time in prison.

In the year following the enactment of the CAN-SPAM Act, Internet service providers filed hundreds of civil lawsuits against spammers.

WIRELESS DEVICES

The CAN-SPAM Act was expanded to include Commercial Mobile Radio Service (CMRS) providers that send Mobile Service Commercial Messages (MSCMs) to subscribers' wireless devices. The law defines an MSCM as "a commercial electronic mail message that is transmitted directly to a wireless device that is utilized by a subscriber of commercial mobile service…in connection with such service." In March 2005, the Federal Communications Commission (FCC) effected a ban on sending unwanted commercial e-mail and text messages to wireless devices without express prior authorization. Congress emphasized that users of wireless devices could be charged by their mobile carriers for time spent accessing, reviewing, and deleting unwanted e-mail.

The FCC's ban does not include transactional or relationship messages, which are notices regarding a transaction a consumer has agreed upon. Examples of such messages are warranty information about a purchased product or statements about an existing account. For a message to be covered by the 2005 rules, it must use an Internet address that includes an Internet domain name. Short messages, typically sent from one mobile phone to another, do not use the Internet and therefore are not subject to the CAN-SPAM Act. Additionally, e-mail forwarded from a person's computer to his or her wireless device are not covered, nor are noncommercial messages, such as political ads.

NEW RULE PROVISIONS: 2008

In May 2008, the FTC announced four new rule provisions under the CAN-SPAM Act in order to clarify the legislation. As stated by the FTC in "FTC Approves New Rule Provision under the CAN-SPAM Act:"

- An e-mail recipient could not be required to pay a fee, provide information other than his or her e-mail address and opt-out preferences, or take any steps other than sending a reply e-mail message or visiting a single Internet Web page to opt out of receiving future e-mail from a sender.
- The definition of "sender" was modified to make it easier to determine which of multiple parties advertising in a single e-mail message is responsible for complying with the act's opt-out requirements.
- A sender of commercial e-mail can include an accurately registered post office box or private mailbox established under United States Postal Service regulations to satisfy the act's requirement that a commercial e-mail display a valid physical postal address.
- A definition of the term "person" was added to clarify that CAN-SPAM's obligations are not limited to natural persons.

EFFECTIVENESS OF THE LAW

Since its inception, the CAN-SPAM Act has been the subject of much criticism. Antispam activists claim that the law has helped spammers because recipients are responsible for opting out of unsolicited e-mail by contacting each sender, as opposed to making senders obtain opt-in permission before they transmit unwanted marketing messages. Critics argue that the CAN-SPAM Act is not enforced, as demonstrated by the fact that the number of spam messages increases every year. The billions of spam e-mails sent every day cost corporations and Internet service providers in the United States alone billions of dollars. One of the biggest complaints about the CAN-SPAM Act is that it does not allow individuals to bring suit against spammers. Only state agencies or Internet service providers can initiate legal action.

Industry analysts hold that despite its shortcomings, the CAN-SPAM Act was a success because, wrote Marsan, "it defined spam, it prompted legitimate e-mail senders to improve their online marketing, and it led to several high-profile convictions of spammers in conjunction with other fraud laws." By giving legitimate companies a framework for how use e-mail appropriately in online marketing, the CAN-SPAM Act has improved e-commerce. Perhaps most importantly, it has made consumers more aware of how to protect themselves.

SEE ALSO *E-Mail; Misinformation Online.*

BIBLIOGRAPHY

Fair, Lesley. "A Common Sense Look at CAN-SPAM." Washington, DC: Federal Trade Commission, Bureau of Consumer Protection, September 2011. Available from http://business.ftc.gov/documents/common-sense-look-can-spam.

Federal Communications Commission. "Petition for Reconsideration Filed by Cingular Wireless, LLC of the Commission's CAN-SPAM Order Denied." Washington, DC, March 22, 2007. Available from http://transition.fcc.gov/cgb/policy/canspam.html.

———. "Rules and Regulations Implementing the Controlling the Assault of Non-Solicited Pornography and Marketing Act of 2003; and Rules and Regulations Implementing the Telephone Consumer Protection Act of 1991." Washington, DC, March 25, 2005. Available from http://transition.fcc.gov/cgb/policy/canspam.html.

———. "Spam: Unwanted Text Messages and E-mail." Washington, DC, September 20, 2011. Available from http://www.fcc.gov/guides/spam-unwanted-text-messages-and-email.

Federal Trade Commission. "Court Stops Spammers from Circulating Unwanted Sexually-Explicit E-mails." Washington, DC, January 11, 2005. Available from http://www.ftc.gov/opa/2005/01/globalnetsolutions.shtm.

———. "FTC Approves New Rule Provision under the CAN-SPAM Act." Washington, DC, May 12, 2008. Available from http://www.ftc.gov/opa/2008/05/canspam.shtm.

Gross, Grant. "CAN-SPAM Law Seen as Ineffective." *Computerworld,* December 27, 2004. Available from http://www.computerworld.com/s/article/98559/CAN_SPAM_law_seen_as_ineffective.

Marsan, Carolyn Duffy. "CAN-SPAM: What Went Wrong?" *Network World,* October 6, 2008. Available from http://www.networkworld.com/news/2008/100608-can-spam.html.

Office of the Comptroller of the Currency. "Controlling the Assault of Non-Solicited Pornography and Marketing Act of 2003." Washington, DC, March 30, 2006. Available from http://www.occ.gov/news-issuances/bulletins/2006/bulletin-2006-14a.pdf.

CANNIBALIZATION

Cannibalization refers to the business process whereby engaging in one activity or practice necessarily eats into another activity or practice. Cannibalization can take place within a firm, between businesses, or across industries.

Throughout the growth of e-commerce in both business-to-business and business-to-consumer marketing, the issue of sales channel cannibalization has been an area of significant concern for companies moving from an exclusively brick-and-mortar to a "bricks-and-clicks" business model. Also, existing brick-and-mortar companies must manage the impact of newly arrived Web-based competitors, and what competitive cannibalization might occur to their business channel as a result.

CANNIBALIZATION IN EXISTING COMPANIES

Companies that are heavily invested in existing sales channels do not wish to see this investment destroyed by their efforts to utilize the new technological opportunities afforded by establishing a Web presence. On the other hand, the potential synergistic opportunities afforded by establishing a Web-based sales channel—including cost savings and market expansion and differentiation—are often too significant to be ignored.

The sources of multichannel synergy include having a common customer and marketing base, as well as the ability to share value in other operations, from management to infrastructure costs. These competing and conflicting values have resulted in a number of colossal failures and a few successes in the realm of Web-based business channel transition.

To avoid potential intracompany channel cannibalization, the process of Web channel integration must be handled carefully. Management must be explicit in aligning company goals to prevent internal conflict. Cross-channel cooperation should be incentivized to take advantage of the strengths each channel can bring to the company's operations and bottom line. For example, the Web channel can provide significant benefit to the traditional sales channel by offering customers the opportunity to research products online without utilizing employee time in the process. Then, when customers enter the store, they are familiar with the product and ready to buy. Quantifying these benefits is difficult, and management must be open to these synergistic and often intangible effects.

Cannibalization from New Competition Cannibalization of traditional marketing channels by the advent of e-commerce has had sweeping effects on many industries through the beginning of the 2010s.

Retailing has been one area in which the impact has been most keenly felt. There are numerous examples of e-commerce cannibalization in the retail sector, none more graphic than the rise of Amazon.com. Initially, Amazon.com took advantage of the compactness and lack of brand differentiation of book sales to cannibalize its brick-and-mortar competition. Traditional firms, such as Borders, were too slow to respond to the e-commerce challenge. Borders, in an attempt to isolate the internal conflict a multichannel operation might produce, outsourced its Web channel operations to others. From the late 1990s through the early 2000s, Borders saw its sales increasingly cannibalized by competitors who transitioned earlier and more completely to multichannel operations. Finally, in 2011, Borders was forced to file for bankruptcy. Meanwhile, Amazon.com has continued expanding its product offering and become the king of Internet retailing.

Benefits of Cannibalization Despite the harshness of the term, cannibalization is sometimes viewed as a good, or at least necessary, business practice. In these cases, the implementation of new operations or new business channels at the expense of existing ones is seen as unavoidable. When the channel transition that must occur starts to take place, the best strategy can be to use the old channel to support the new one during the transition period. During the early years of online business operations, many companies deliberately cannibalized their existing sales operations in order to strengthen their Web-based brand presence. The alternative was often to be completely squeezed out of the game by more Internet-savvy competitors.

In the early 2010s, the rise of Web 2.0 initiatives and social marketing are threatening to produce a new wave of cannibalization, this time within the e-commerce channel itself. A new platform for e-commerce is rising on sites such as Facebook, Twitter, and MySpace. Utilizing the interactive qualities of this growing format, marketers need to devise new ways of capturing and holding an audience for their products and services. In this new environment collaboration and participation are the new approach to building brand and product identity.

Mobile computing is another platform having ramifications as yet not completely understood. Significant cannibalization effects are being felt as people switch from notebook to tablet computers and from basic cellphones to smartphones. Both of these transitions will have significant rollover effects on existing e-commerce channels.

In view of the fast-paced change that naturally occurs in the evolution of a new technology like e-commerce, it is likely cannibalization will continue to be a significant force throughout the 2010s, as both businesses and consumers adapt to this transformational business model.

SEE ALSO *Channel Conflict/Harmony; Channel Transparency.*

BIBLIOGRAPHY

"Cannibalization and Channel Conflict." Witiger.com, March 28, 2011. Available from http://www.witiger.com/ecommerce/cannibalization.htm

Christman, Ed. "Retail 'Cannibalization' by Net Sales Seen." *Billboard,* August 21, 1999.

Cuneo, Alice Z. "Cannibalization Is the Buzzword and the Consumer Is King, but the Day-to-Day Pressure to Cut Costs Will Squeeze Store Chains." *Advertising Age,* September 20, 1999.

Lehmann, R. J. "Is Your Web Site Stealing Your Readers?" *Folio,* September 15, 2000.

———. "Learn E-business—or Risk E-limination." *Business Week,* March 22, 1999.

Paczkowski, John. "Tablet Cannibalization on the Rise in 2011." *AllThingsD.com,* February 8, 2011. Available from http://allthingsd.com/20110208/tablet-cannibalization-on-the-rise-in-2011.

Steinfield, Charles. "Understanding Click and Mortar E-commerce Approaches." *Journal of Interactive Advertising* 2, no. 2, (Spring 2010): 1–10. Available from http://jiad.org/article19.

CARD-ISSUING BANK

Card-issuing banks are the originators of credit cards issued to consumers. In the early 2010s, bank-issued credit cards were still the most frequent means of payment for e-commerce acquired services or goods, constituting nearly 90% of such payments. When a consumer uses a credit card to purchase a product or service, a merchant bank, or merchant service provider (MSP), obtains approval from the card-issuing bank at the time of the transaction. In this case, a merchant is an e-commerce business that accepts credit or debit cards in exchange for goods or services.

E-commerce merchants must establish an e-commerce merchant account with a merchant bank, or MSP, in order to process transactions and obtain cash from credit card purchases. A merchant also must utilize online credit card processing software in order to accept credit or debit cards as a method of payment on the World Wide Web.

A basic e-commerce credit card transaction, referred to as a card-not-present (CNP) transaction, begins when a consumer selects goods or services on a merchant's Web site and fills out a merchant commerce application.

Due to threats associated with online credit card use, merchants utilize a protected security protocol for transmitting personal data over the Web, usually Secure Sockets Layer (SSL). Once a payment request is made it is relayed through the payment gateway to the merchant bank, which is also connected to a network of card-issuing banks. The merchant bank or MSP then sends the request to the card-issuing bank, which issues either an approval or denial code and sends a message back to the merchant bank, which forwards the action to the merchant. This entire process takes only a few seconds.

A consumer's credit card is not charged at the time of purchase. However, the card-issuing bank does put a hold on the card for the transaction amount. A merchant's batch—all of the credit card transactions that took place during a specific timeframe—typically are settled at the end of the business day. The consumer's credit card is charged and the merchant bank receives the funds, in a transaction known as an interchange, from the card-issuing bank. Those funds are then placed into the merchant's bank account.

THIRD-PARTY PROCESSING

New or small e-commerce companies often utilize a variation of this method, called third-party processing. The third-party processor typically connects through an additional secure payment gateway to a merchant bank or MSP, sharing its expenses. Such third-party processors often represent a large number of merchants sharing one secure merchant bank relationship. This type of transaction processing is excellent for low-volume e-commerce operations that need to minimize transaction processing costs.

An evolving technology in the bank-issued card category is the so-called smart card. Smart card demand exceeded five billion in annual card shipments in 2010 and was growing rapidly in the early 2010s. The smart card contains an embedded memory or processor chip which stores or transacts data. Special electronic readers, which are connected to a computer system, are employed to read the card data. Smart cards can bring significant added value to the e-commerce payment chain in the form of several added features, including:

- Convenience—Smart cards can carry personal information, thereby eliminating forms in e-commerce transactions and minimizing transaction time.
- Control—Smart cards can minimize or control expenditures by instituting automatic limits.
- Loyalty program tracking—Smart cards can act as repositories of loyalty program information across multiple vendors, dispensing awards when earned.
- Micropayments—Small payments can sometimes be made without triggering credit card transaction fees.
- Added security—Smart cards allow for two-factor authentication, a major benefit in eliminating many wireless Internet security threats.

The expanding use of transactions over wireless networks poses a significant threat to the security of e-commerce, given the ease with which such data can be intercepted. The added reliability and security features of the smart card are considered extremely useful to the continued growth and evolution of e-commerce in general and to wireless e-commerce payment system in particular.

Whatever technological innovations occur in e-commerce payments systems in the coming years, card-issuing banks will likely continue to play an important role in the payment processing chain.

SEE ALSO *Authorizaton and Authorization Code; Chargeback; Electronic Payment; Interchange and Interchange Fee.*

BIBLIOGRAPHY

"The Difference Between Merchant Accounts, Payment Gateways, and Third Party Processors." London: GSPAY, 2011. Available from http://www.gspay.com/the-difference-between-merchant-accounts,-payment-gateways-and-third-party-processors.php.

"Smart Card Overview." *Smart Card Basics,* 2010. Available from http://www.smartcardbasics.com/smart-card-overview.html.

CARSDIRECT.COM

CarsDirect.com was founded as an online direct auto buying company, but by 2011 it had evolved into a broad-based e-commerce and online media company called Internet Brands, which in addition to selling cars also provided online access to home loans, real estate, and other goods and services. By diversifying, the firm was able to outlast other online auto buying services also founded during the Internet boom, such as Microsoft CarPoint's Drive-Off.com subsidiary and CarOrder.com of Austin, Texas. Internet Brands went public in 2007 but was bought out by a private equity group in September 2010.

SUCCESSFUL TEST LED TO NATIONAL MAY 1999 LAUNCH

CarsDirect.com was created at the Internet incubator Idealab, which also developed such Internet companies as eToys.com and GoTo.com. Cofounders were Bill Gross, founder of Idealab, and Scott Painter, who became CarsDirect.com's CEO. At the time CarsDirect.com was founded in Culver City, California, in late 1998, it was a bold step to try and sell autos and trucks directly to consumers through a Web site. Existing auto buying services, such as Autoweb.com and Autobytel.com, did not sell cars themselves. Rather, they referred prospective buyers to brick-and-mortar dealers, who paid them for the referrals. Other auto Web sites, such as AutoTrader.com, worked more like a newspaper classified section, offering ads from individuals who had cars for sale.

CarsDirect.com began selling vehicles over the Internet through a test program launched in December 1998. Loan and lease financing for customers was provided by Bank One Corp., which partnered with CarsDirect.com to form CD1Financial.com, an Internet auto lending and leasing company. The outlook for online car-buying services was favorable, according to Forrester Research, whose report noted that two million people researched their new car purchases online in 1998. Forrester projected that 17,000 people would buy their cars online in 1999, a figure that was projected to increase to 470,000 households by 2003, representing $12 billion in online sales.

CarsDirect.com's test proved successful. It sold 277 cars in April 1999, and in May the company launched its national Web site. It had received about $30 million in financing from several sources, including Idealab, which held a 40% stake in the company, and Michael Dell's venture capital firm MSD Capital LP. In the two months following its official launch, CarsDirect.com sold more than $1.5 million worth of vehicles a day, making it the fastest-growing company developed by Idealab. It obtained vehicles from a network of 1,200 dealers.

To purchase a vehicle, prospective customers would use a series of pull-down menus at the company's Web site to select their cars and choose their options. In the final step, customers chose a method of financing their purchase.

AIMED TO BE A BRAND LEADER

Five months after its national launch, CarsDirect.com began building its brand with a $20 million advertising campaign for the fourth quarter of 1999. The company hoped the campaign would help boost sales from more than 1,000 cars a month to more than 2,500 by the end of the year. According to Media Metrix, CarsDirect.com received 215,000 unique visitors in August 1999. Comparatively, referral site Autoweb.com received 731,000 visitors, and Autobytel.com received 1.1 million. By November, the company was selling more than 1,400 vehicles a month. As part of its brand-building efforts, CarsDirect.com announced a three-year deal to sponsor a NASCAR Winston Cup race at the Las Vegas Motor Speedway.

Also in the fourth quarter, CarsDirect.com named Robert Brisco as its new CEO, with former CEO and cofounder Scott Painter moving to vice chairman. Brisco was 36 years old when he joined CarsDirect.com. Formerly he was president of the theme park and entertainment complex Universal Studios Hollywood and CityWalk. At one time, Brisco also worked as an advertising and marketing executive at the *Los Angeles Times.* He joined CarsDirect.com just after the company had raised $280 million in financing. Brisco planned to use the new investment capital to improve customer service and build the firm's brand. He told the *Los Angeles Business Journal,* "We want to make this the best retail experience consumers have ever had." Brisco also announced plans to expand the company's network of 1,700 dealer partners.

SURVIVED DOT-COM SHAKEOUT OF 2000

By the time Brisco took over as CEO, CarsDirect.com had figured out how to price its vehicles without losing money on every sale. Initially, its policy was to price vehicles at invoice plus 1%. That resulted in underpricing by about $1,500 per vehicle. CarsDirect then changed its policy to make deals at market prices. The company found that some high-demand vehicles could be sold at a much higher premium over invoice. By the end of 1999, the company was breaking even on its vehicle sales. It expected much of its revenue would come from the finance, leasing, insurance, and warranty products it could sell along with each vehicle. Dealers would participate by earning incremental income and handling trade-ins.

In early 2000, CarsDirect.com began offering extended service contracts, which added $800 to $900 to the cost of a vehicle. The company also improved its Web site by adding live online customer service technology that helped shoppers fill out forms and complete the purchase process. In March 2000, CarsDirect forged an alliance with competitor Autoweb.com in an effort to capture a larger share of online automotive buyers. The two companies planned to develop a direct new car buying service on Autoweb.com that would enable consumers to receive a fixed price on vehicles and conduct the entire purchase process online.

CarsDirect.com, as well as the entire online auto business, suffered through several speed bumps in 2000, some more serious than others. At least two consumer-based studies offered negative assessments of the online auto business. They included one by CNW Marketing/Research, which showed that eight different Web sites, including CarsDirect.com, routinely published inaccurate pricing information. An evaluation of five sites by *Consumer Reports* found that in many cases potential customers did not receive requested price quotes within two days. Oftentimes, the quotes were for vehicles other than those consumers requested. Meanwhile, established brick-and-mortar dealers were lobbying state legislatures to further restrict online auto sales, which already were prohibited in 11 states. Additional opposition was coming from the Big Three automakers, which warned their dealers not to sell cars to online brokers. For its part, CarsDirect.com noted that it was not a broker, did not intend to buy dealerships, and was not violating any dealer franchise agreements with the automakers.

CarsDirect.com planned to go public in 2000 and filed for an initial public offering (IPO) in May 2000. It planned to raise $175.2 million through its IPO. However, as the market for Internet IPOs shriveled during the year, CarsDirect.com scrapped its IPO plans in December. It was one of 27 companies that withdrew their registration statements for IPOs. Although CarsDirect.com lost $144 million in the previous 15 months, the company announced it had developed plans to be a profitable, long-term player. As a private company, it had raised more than $300 million in private equity financing since its inception. That included a mid-2000 investment from the Penske Automotive Group, which bought a 10% interest in CarsDirect.com for $17 million. As a result, all 117 Penske-owned dealerships would display their inventory on CarsDirect.com's Web site. By this time CarsDirect.com had 2,500 licensed franchised dealers in its network. Following the investment by Penske, Roger Penske replaced Scott Painter on CarsDirect.com's board of directors, and Painter subsequently left the company to start a new company called Direct Ventures.

The end of 2000 and early 2001 saw an industry downturn for online auto sales. CarsDirect.com reduced its workforce by 12% in November, laying off about 90 of its 750 employees. On February 15, 2001, Microsoft CarPoint shut down its DriveOff.com subsidiary.

A CHANGE OF FOCUS

The company began to transition away from its founding as an auto retailer in 2005, with the goal of becoming a diversified Internet platform offering a wider variety of products to consumers. In February of that year, the company acquired a mortgage technology platform and two mortgage Web sites, BestRate.com and LoanApp.com, from Myers Internet Inc. These acquisitions, along with the company's existing loan Web sites LoanStore.com and CheckInterestRates.com, positioned CarsDirect.com for a broader role in the online marketplace.

As a reflection of its expanding platform, the company changed its name to Internet Brands, Inc., in June 2005. The renamed firm continued to make acquisitions, including the July 2007 purchase of Jelsoft Enterprises and vBulletin Solutions, which produced vBulletin, an Internet forum software. Other acquisitions included home improvement, health, travel, and other Web sites that provided goods and services to consumers.

In October 2007, Internet Brands announced plans to raise money via an IPO. The initial plan was to sell 9.57 million shares in a range of $10 to $12 per share; however, a failure to price led the company to amend its prospectus with the U.S. Securities and Exchange Commission to say it intended to cut the size and price of its IPO, and instead sell 6 million shares at $8 each. Some commentators at the time said that the diverse nature of Internet Brand's Web sites and software subsidiaries made it difficult for potential investors to see the synergies within the company.

In the wake of the economic recession of 2008–2009 the company decided to go private in 2010 through a merger agreement with an affiliate of the private equity firm Hellman & Friedman Capital Partners VI. The deal, valued at $640 million, provided stockholders of the company with $13.35 for each share of common stock. The offer was 46.5% more than the closing price of the stock prior to the announcement of the acquisition. At the time, the largest shareholder was Idealab, which entered into a voting agreement with Hellman & Friedman for the merger. Idealab owned 19% of the outstanding stock of the company at the time and had a voting power of 64%.

By 2011, Internet Brands owned more than 100 Web sites with over 79 million unique visitors each month, and was a leader in vertical markets. CarsDirect remained one of its key properties, and in 2011, the site introduced a new design that incorporated more research capabilities, a car pricing insider blog, and expanded access to used cars through CarsDirect partners.

BIBLIOGRAPHY

Couretas, John. "CarsDirect Tops Online Buying List from Gomez." *Automotive News,* September 20, 1999,

"Dot-Coms to Dot-Bombs." *Automotive News,* January 22, 2001.

Edgerton, Jerry. "Cars: Smart Strategies for Shopping Online." *Money,* October 15, 2000.

Harris, Donna. "Greenlight.com CEO Steps Down; CarsDirect.com Founder Leaves." *Automotive News,* August 14, 2000.

Internet Brands, Inc. "Our Story." El Segundo, CA, 2011. Available from http://www.internetbrands.com/the-company.

"Internet Brands IPO Cuts Size and Price of IPO." *Reuters,* November 16, 2007. Available from http://www.reuters.com/article/2007/11/16/internetbrands-ipo-idUSWNAS276420071116.

Sieroty, Chris. "Wheeling through Cyberspace." *Los Angeles Business Journal,* February 19, 2001.

Smith, Jennifer. "Brisco Has Plans for Investment Money at CarsDirect.com." *Los Angeles Business Journal,* November 22, 1999.

Taub, Daniel. "Firm Proves People Are Ready to Buy Cars on the Web." *Los Angeles Business Journal,* August 23, 1999.

Taulli, Tom. "Internet Brands' Bland IPO." *BloggingStocks,* November 19, 2007. Available from http://www.bloggingstocks.com/2007/11/19/internet-brands-bland-ipo.

Wang, Andy. "CarsDirect Closes Near-Record Equity Placement." *E-Commerce Times,* November 16, 1999. Available from http://www.ecommercetimes.com/story/1755.html.

Wauters, Robin. "Private Equity Firm Acquires Internet Brands in $640 Million Deal." *Tech Crunch,* September 20, 2010. Available from http://techcrunch.com/2010/09/20/private-equity-firm-acquires-internet-brands-in-640-million-deal.

CASE, STEPHEN M.

Stephen M. Case (1958–) was the cofounder of a small online service provider in 1985, which was renamed America Online (AOL) in 1989. AOL was the first Internet-based company to be listed in the *Fortune* 500. Case developed a business model that allowed his firm to reach revenues of nearly $7 billion by the end of the century, at which time he orchestrated a merger with Time Warner. Case continued to serve as the new company's chairman, but the dot-com fallout led to a plummeting stock value. He retired as chairman in 2003 and left the board two years later.

Case established the investment firm Revolutions LCC prior to his retirement from AOL Time Warner, and as of 2011 he continued to serve as CEO and chairman of Revolutions. Due to Case's business background and work with the Case Foundation, established with his wife in 1997, President Obama appointed him as co-chair of the National Advisory Council on Innovation and Entrepreneurship in 2010 as well as founding chairman of the Startup America Partnership the following year.

COFOUNDER OF QUANTUM COMPUTER

A native of Hawaii, Case earned his bachelor's degree in political science at Williams College. He launched his career as a marketing manager at Procter & Gamble, where he developed brands of different health and beauty products. In the early 1980s, he joined Pizza Hut and began developing new types of pizza for the chain. Well before personal computers became commonplace in American homes, Case went online, using a service known as the Source. In 1983, he began working in the marketing department of Control Video, which ran an online service for Atari users. As Atari began to falter, James Kimsey was named CEO of Control Video, and Case was promoted to marketing director.

When Control Video went bankrupt, Case and Kimsey secured $2 million in financial backing for a new venture. In May 1985, the pair established Quantum Computer Services Inc. and began offering Q-Link, a modem-based online service, to Commodore personal computer (PC) users. In 1987, the same year that IBM and Sears launched the Prodigy online service, Quantum achieved profitability for the first time on total sales of $9 million. The firm launched PC-Link for IBM-compatible PCs and AppleLink for Macintosh PCs the following year. Competition continued to heat up when CompuServe acquired the Source in 1989.

HEAD OF AOL

In October 1989, AppleLink was renamed America Online, which included games, e-mail, and real-time chat capabilities. Case was named president in 1990. He consolidated operations to focus on IBM-compatible and Macintosh computer markets and upped the firm's subscribers base via intense marketing efforts, such as giving AOL software away for free and partnerships with media firms. On the verge of the launch of a PC-version of AOL, Case opposed a buyout by CompuServe in 1991. After AOL went public in 1992, Case was appointed CEO, while Kimsey remained chairman of the board until his retirement in 1997.

After convincing his board to turn down a buyout offer from Microsoft in 1993, Case forged content deals with media firms like Knight-Ridder and CNN. He also steered AOL's development of a version of its online service for the Windows platform. In response to predictions that the World Wide Web would render online services like AOL obsolete, Case decided in 1994 to develop a gateway, AOL.com, to offer subscribers a link to the Internet from AOL. That year, the number of AOL members exceeded one million for the first time.

STEERING AOL'S SUCCESS

Case took his firm international with service in Germany, and subscribers tripled to three million in 1995. He entered Canada, France, and the United Kingdom the following year. Through cross-marketing deals with Microsoft, AT&T, Apple, Sun Microsystems, Hewlett-Packard, and Netscape Communications, Case positioned AOL as the leader in online services. A new e-commerce strategy led to online retailers like Amazon.com agreeing to sell their merchandise on AOL, and revenues surpassed $1 billion. Membership grew to more than 10 million subscribers after AOL entered Japan in 1997.

AOL's meteoric rise to dominance certainly was not glitch-free, however. For example, the firm became the target of a class-action lawsuit regarding its billing practices in the mid-1990s. Also, a technical snafu in August 1996 shut the service down for 19 hours. When the firm launched a $19.95 per month flat-fee program later in the year, with no limits on usage, it was ill-prepared for the crush of increased traffic it received. Users trying to get online became increasingly frustrated by busy signals, and eventually representatives from 36 state attorneys general offices met to address the issue, resulting in costly refunds to subscribers.

Despite being lambasted for AOL's troubles, Case stuck to his strategy of offering a user-friendly, comprehensive online service to an increasing number of subscribers. With the technical snags behind him, Case oversaw two major acquisitions in 1998: instant messaging firm ICQ and rival CompuServe Inc. AOL paid a staggering $10 billion to add Netscape Communications to its growing list of holdings in 1999. The following year, AOL began offering online access to wireless consumers and also purchased MapQuest.com.

DEPARTURE FROM AOL TIME WARNER

At the beginning of the new decade, Case made a bold move designed to cement AOL's future position as a leading Internet player. He orchestrated one of the largest mergers in media industry history—the $165 billion union of AOL and entertainment giant Time Warner Inc. to form AOL Time Warner Inc. Case's vision for AOL incorporated video and sound that would turn PCs into high-end televisions, and this merger gave AOL access to Time Warner's cable-television empire and high-speed Internet connections. Case relinquished his role of CEO to Gerald Levin, the head of Time Warner, but remained chairman of the board of the combined company AOL Time Warner.

The ill-timed merger was finalized just prior to the dot-com bubble bursting. When AOL Time Warner's 2001 financials were released, a staggering goodwill impairment of $54 billion was a record-setting write-down, due to the stock's significant devaluation. This prompted Levin to step down, with Richard Parsons appointed as the new CEO. In the three years after the merger was announced, AOL Time Warner's stock plummeted roughly 80%. The declining value of AOL led to a $100 billion loss for the year, which set a record in corporate history. This led to Case's retirement as chairman of the board at the onset of 2003, although he stayed on as a director until October 2005.

PHILANTHROPIST AND CEO OF REVOLUTION

In 1997, Steve and his wife Jean established the Case Foundation to "create and support initiatives that leverage new technologies and entrepreneurial approaches to drive innovation in the social sector and encourage individuals to get involved with the communities and causes they care about." Case also became involved in a brain cancer cure initiative when his brother Daniel was diagnosed with brain cancer in 2001 and died the following year. Together with their daughter-in-law Stacey Case, Steve and Jean founded Accelerate Brain Cancer Cure. As of 2011, the nonprofit had invested more than $15 million in research, and Steve continued to serve as its chairman.

Case cofounded the investment company Revolution LLC in April 2005 before retiring from AOL Time Warner's board. As the father of five children, he continued his interest in the health care industry with the creation of Revolution Health Group. Following the division's launch of RevolutionHealth.com in May 2007, it purchased CarePages.com and HealthTalk.com, invested in SparkPeople.com, and signed an affiliate deal with online retailer Drugstore.com. In October 2008, the Revolution Health Network merged with Everyday Health Inc. By 2011, Everyday Health was providing health services across a broad portfolio of more than 25 Web sites. Through Revolution's other three divisions, Case continued to invest in high-growth consumer companies, early-stage technology companies, and real estate and hospitality businesses.

Amidst a U.S. economic slump, President Obama formed the National Advisory Council on Innovation and Entrepreneurship in July 2010. Case was appointed as one of three co-chairs on this council, which would advise the president on ways to foster entrepreneurship and create jobs. To further this initiative, President Obama appointed Case as founding chairman of the Startup America Partnership, which was formed at the beginning of 2011 to provide start-ups with resources and strategic guidance. During the year, companies like Intel and IBM jointed the partnership, which targeted information technology and other high-growth, job-creating industries.

SEE ALSO *AOL; Internet Access, Tracking Growth of; Internet Service Provider (ISP).*

BIBLIOGRAPHY

Bulik, Beth Snyder. "Steve Case, a Man with a Medical Mission." *Advertising Age,* March 17, 2008. Available from http://adage.com/article/print-edition/steve-case-a-man-a-medical-mission/125728/.

Clifford, Catherine. "Obama, Big Business to Aid Entrepreneurs." *CNN,* January 31, 2011. Available from http://money.cnn.com/2011/01/31/smallbusiness/startup_america_launch/index.htm.

Gilbert, Jennifer. "Steve Case." *Advertising Age,* April 17, 2000. Available from http://adage.com/article/news/steve-case/58724.

Hernandez, Christina. "At the Case Foundation, Bringing Tech Entrepreneurialism to Philanthropy." *SmartPlanet,* October 21, 2010. Available from http://www.smartplanet.com/blog/pure-genius/at-the-case-foundation-bringing-tech-entrepreneurialism-to-philanthropy/4735.

Pellegrini, Frank. "What AOL Time Warner's $54 Billion Loss Means." *Time,* April 25, 2002. Available from http://www.time.com/time/business/article/0,8599,233436,00.html.

Swartz, Jon. "America (Online) the Beautiful." *Forbes,* April 4, 2000. Available from http://www.forbes.com/2000/04/04/feat.html.

Vise, David A. "Case Quits as Time Warner Director." *Washington Post,* November 1, 2005. Available from http://www.washingtonpost.com/wp-dyn/content/article/2005/10/31/AR2005103100414.html.

CDNOW INC.

Founded in 1994, CDNow Inc. was an early pioneer in the online retail business. The German media conglomerate Bertelsmann AG added the then-public company to its expanding Internet operations in 2000. In the wake of the dot-com fallout, Bertelsmann refocused on its book and music club business. As part of the company's exit from its e-commerce businesses, Bertelsmann struck a deal with Amazon.com to begin handling the fulfillment of CDNow's orders as well as other operations for the site. (Bertelsmann eventually sold its direct-to-consumer businesses in 2008.) As of early 2012, CDNow.com was no longer operating, although Amazon.com linked to its music offering through CDNow.net.

RAPID GROWTH AS A DOT-COM START-UP

After having difficulty locating information about various musicians in the retail music stores he frequented, Jason Olim dreamed up the idea of selling CDs on a Web site that also would house a database of the information typically found in a music encyclopedia. Jason recruited his twin brother Matthew, a Columbia University astrophysics student, to write the code for the site. In August 1994, with $20,000 in capital, the partners launched CDNow from their parents' basement in Fort Washington, Pennsylvania. Visitors to the virtual store could search its database for any CD or artist and make a purchase with a credit card. To facilitate order fulfillment, Olim forged agreements with several warehouses, which shipped purchases directly to customers.

Within a year, sales at CDNow had reached $2 million. Following the addition of RealAudio sound samples that allowed site visitors to listen to various song samples from a CD before making a purchase, revenues jumped to $6.3 million in 1997. Content offerings were enhanced with music reviews from leading music magazines as well as articles submitted by freelance writers. By the end of its third full year of operation, CDNow had become the leading music retailer on the Internet, with sales of $17.4 million and a market share of roughly 33%.

The Olim brothers took their firm public in 1998, selling shares for $16 each. They also launched My CDNow, allowing visitors to customize their shopping experience based on their musical preferences, and began selling customized CDs. In March 1999, CDNow merged with rival N2K Inc., and N2K's Musicblvd.com site was integrated with CDNow.com. Sales rose to $147 million; however, the company lost $119 million that year. In hopes of achieving profitability, the company expanded into selling music downloads and movies.

MERGER WITH BERTELSMANN

Despite CDNow's rapid growth, Amazon.com surpassed CDNow in music sales in 2000. A survey completed by Forrester Research Inc. ranked CDNow fourth—behind Amazon.com, Barnesandnoble.com, and Buy.com—on its list of the best music Web sites, citing poor customer service, unreliable delivery, and technology glitches as common problems faced by users of CDNow. However, the survey complimented CDNow on its buyers' guides, which helped users to select merchandise.

A merger deal with club-based music and video seller Columbia House, announced in July 1999, fell through in March 2000. This prompted speculation that the dot-com fallout and CDNow's resulting stock price plunge had soured the deal. Others pointed to CDNow's $30 million debt and lack of profitability—it had lost roughly $200 million since its inception—as reasons for the nixed plans, which caused share prices to tumble 28%. Columbia House coowners Sony Corp. and Time Warner Inc. still invested $51 million in CDNow. However, reports that the firm might run out of cash by September pushed stock to a record low of $3.50.

CDNow initiated cost-cutting measures in 2000 in an attempt to raise new capital and stay in business. These efforts paid off in July, when international media giant Bertelsmann agreed to purchase the firm for roughly $117 million, or $3 per share. Bertelsmann's e-commerce efforts had been formally launched in 1998 when Thomas Middelhoff took over as CEO and chairman. At this time, the firm bought half of Barnesandnoble.com for $200 million and created its own online retail book site to take on Amazon.com in Europe. CDNow's founders believed that Bertelsmann's market reach would allow their firm to better compete with Amazon.com.

In October, Bertelsmann merged CDNow into its newly formed Bertelsmann e-Commerce Group, headed by former AOL Europe executive Andreas Schmidt. Jason Olim was named chairman of CDNow, which began operating as a wholly owned subsidiary of DirectGroup Bertelsmann. CDNow saw its video sales double by early 2001 after expanding its video offerings to more than 70,000 titles and adding content such as film reviews and best-seller lists to its Video Shop.

INTEGRATION WITH AMAZON.COM

In May 2001, Bertelsmann continued its acquisition strategy with the purchase of MyPlay, a site that allowed users to upload, store, and manage their digitized music collections. Two months later, the Bertelsmann e-Commerce Group formed a new music services division to focus on music distribution in the United States. Based in New York City, the BeMusic business unit included BMG Direct record club, CDNow, and MyPlay. However, with the unexpected departure of e-Commerce Group chief executive Andreas Schmidt in November of that year, the BeMusic site never made it to fruition.

A month following the appointment of Gunter Thielen as the new CEO and chairman of Bertelsmann in August 2002, the company began to divest its e-commerce businesses in Europe. Although the firm originally stated that this would not impact BeMusic, Bertelsmann announced the shutdown of MyPlay, and a multiyear deal was struck with Amazon.com, Inc., to take over operations of CDNow. At this time, Amazon.com was selling music, DVDs, videos, books, and other consumer products.

Before the year ended, Amazon.com launched CDNow.com as a syndicated store and continued to sell similar items at Amazon.com. Although details of the agreement were not disclosed, the business model of its syndicated stores program was to own the inventory, set prices, and be responsible for fulfillment and customer service. In return, Bertelsmann would earn a commission on product sales. Other Web sites that Amazon.com operated in this fashion included Virginmega.com, Borders.com, and Waldenbooks.com.

SEE ALSO *Amazon.com.*

BIBLIOGRAPHY

"Bertelsmann Buys CDNow." *CNNMoney,* July 20, 2000. Available from http://money.cnn.com/2000/07/20/deals/bmg_cdnow.

Borrego, Anne Marie. "Online Music Retailer Faces the Realities of the Internet Economy." *Inc.,* January 1, 2001. Available from http://technology.inc.com/2001/01/01/online-music-retailer-faces-the-realities-of-the-internet-economy.

Cox, Beth. "Bertelsmann Loses E-commerce Exec." *Internet News,* November 28, 2001. Available from http://www.

internetnews.com/ec-news/article.php/929851/Bertelsmann+Loses+ECommerce+Exec+.htm.

Kane, Margaret. "Amazon, CDNow Make It Official." *CNET,* December 4, 2002. Available from http://news.cnet.com/2100-1023-976008.html.

Philips, Chuck. "Time Warner and Sony to Buy Net Retailer CDNow." *Los Angeles Times,* July 14, 1999. Available from http://articles.latimes.com/1999/jul/14/business/fi-55755.

CHANGE, MANAGING

In the 1990s, e-commerce was the holy grail of business, with every type of traditional brick-and-mortar enterprise finding it necessary to adopt some sort of e-business strategy, whether or not there were effective business reasons for doing so. The dot-com world boomed, then busted, and then became a ubiquitous part of everyday life. Businesses have had to adapt to the changes this ever-developing technology has wrought, with even the largest companies with the deepest pockets forced to go through many iterations of their e-commerce approach before finding success.

While some of the predictions about the success of dot-com entities of the 1990s ultimately failed to come true, the Internet has become a dominant force in many businesses, and a powerful venue for exchanging information as well as for buying and selling products and services. According to the Information Technology and Innovation Foundation (ITIF), the global economic benefits of the commercial Internet were $1.5 trillion by 2010.

E-commerce is no longer just the sale of goods and services over the Internet; it also encompasses developing and marketing products. In some cases, the products themselves are virtual and only exist online, such as tools used in an online game or access to content in an online publication. Customers have high expectations about their Web experience and will abandon companies that are difficult to deal with over the Internet.

MANAGING THE DEVELOPMENT OF AN E-BUSINESS STRATEGY

When businesses first began the shift from a traditional brick-and-mortar enterprise to a "click-and-mortar" entity, the change typically started with the formation of the e-business strategy itself, often a time-consuming and labor-intensive process. Many steps are involved in creating an effective business approach, and many levels of management are typically involved. The enterprise had to first decide on the goals it wished to achieve by implementing an e-business plan. Management needed to decide why the company was going online and what benefits the Internet could provide. The company also had to decide if it was going to target existing customers or try to attract new ones. The enterprise also needed to select target markets and advertising methods, decide what it would be promoting online, identify its competitors, and be in tune with conditions in its selected markets.

While these steps were no doubt important, managing the change that goes along with creating a new business strategy was often difficult, and even overlooked. According to a study done by Deloitte and Touche in 2000, 70% of online retailers surveyed at that time did not have an e-commerce strategy. Many simply had established a Web site to test demand for their product or service on the Internet. The study did find that those who took the time to develop a strategy were outpacing their competition.

By 2011, most businesses had acknowledged the importance of implementing e-commerce into their operation. According to Linda Taddonio, in a June 2011 *E-Commerce Times* article, "The development and adoption of e-commerce strategies for established businesses has become a given over the past few years. It seems appropriate to say that we have crossed a line where the question of, 'Should a business have an e-commerce strategy?' has been replaced with, 'When will a business have an e-commerce strategy?' or even with, 'How many e-commerce sites can be leveraged as a part of the overall strategy?'."

MANAGING STAFFING ISSUES

In order to successfully manage an e-business strategy, the enterprise must also have an employee base that is open to change. These employees must be adaptable to new technology and able to learn new skills. Major decisions management must make as its strategy develops and evolves include deciding whether or not to use existing staff, hire new information technology (IT) employees, create new departments, or outsource e-business-related tasks to specialized outside companies. Employees, as well as the enterprise as a whole, must also learn how to interact with customers, suppliers, and colleagues by utilizing new communication methods, such as Twitter or text messaging.

Staffing issues can also be a major snag in implementing an e-business strategy. As Internet technology evolves, employees must be trained to keep up, and the executives in charge of the strategy must have enough knowledge to keep the plan evolving. In order to manage quickly evolving e-business development, enterprises need to have employees in place who can work effectively in a fast-paced, changing environment.

As Zack Urlocker put it in an August 2011 article in *E-Commerce Times,* "Customers expect to get service at any time of the day or night and assume that customer service teams will keep a history of all interactions." Urlocker also noted that social media Web sites such as Facebook allow a disgruntled customer the opportunity to publicize a poor experience to the point where it can snowball into a major public relations disaster.

MANAGING INTEGRATION AND NEW CUSTOMER RELATIONSHIPS

Providing high levels of customer service is key to integrating an e-business strategy successfully. As of September 2009, according to ITIF, an estimated 1.7 billion of the world's 6.7 billion citizens, or 25.6%, were on the Internet, representing a 380% increase over 2000. In some parts of the world, the number of Web shoppers has increased dramatically, such as Western Europe, which saw an 85% increase in dot-com shoppers between 2004 and 2009.

While some of the largest and most successful e-commerce companies were built online from the ground up, such as Amazon.com and Netflix, there are also brick-and-mortar companies that have been able to translate their business model into strong e-commerce initiatives. According to a list of the top 500 business-to-consumer Web retailers, published by *Internet Retailer,* companies such as Office Depot, Wal-Mart, and Sears were among the top ten.

SEE ALSO *Integration.*

BIBLIOGRAPHY

Abraham, Jack. "Commerce 3.0: Online Research, Offline Buying." *E-Commerce Times,* August 13, 2011. Available from http://www.ecommercetimes.com/story/73066.html.

Atkinson, Robert D., Stephen J. Ezell, Scott M. Andes, Daniel D. Castro, and Richard Bennett. "The Internet Economy 25 Years After .Com: Transforming Commerce and Life." Washington DC: The Information Technology & Innovation Foundation, March, 2010. Available from http://www.itif.org/files/2010-25-years.pdf.

Hof, Robert D. "What Every CEO Needs to Know About Electronic Business." *BusinessWeek Online,* March 10, 1999. Available from http://www.businessweek.com/1999/99_12/b3621002.htm.

Regan, Keith. "Toys "R" Us Wins Right to End Amazon Partnership." *E-Commerce Times,* March 3, 2006. Available from http://www.technewsworld.com/story/49188.html.

Speigel, Robert. "Report: 70 Percent of Retailers Lack E-commerce Strategy." *E-Commerce Times,* January 26, 2000. Available from http://www.ecommercetimes.com/story/2335.html.

Taddonio, Linda. "The Tremendous Transformative Powers of B2B E-commerce." *E-Commerce Times,* June 1, 2011. Available from http://www.ecommercetimes.com/story/The-Tremendous-Transformative-Powers-of-B2B-E-Commerce-72561.html.

"The Top 500 List." *Internet Retailer,* 2010. Available from http://www.internetretailer.com/top500/list.

Urlocker, Zack. "Managing the Customer Service Revolution." *E-Commerce Times,* August 22, 2011. Available from http://www.ecommercetimes.com/story/73119.html.

CHANNEL CONFLICT/ HARMONY

Channel conflict has long been an issue when businesses establish multiple sales and distribution channels to the same group of customers. Examples include a manufacturer that has a direct sales force but also sells through distributors, or a merchant that sells through company stores as well as other retailers. When companies also use the Internet to sell directly to customers, they have to contend with channel conflict with existing intermediaries in their distribution network. This is because e-commerce often eliminates the role of these intermediaries, referred to as disintermediation, in the sales process. To create channel harmony, e-commerce companies are challenged to integrate the online sales channel with existing distributors or retailers in a way that builds customer loyalty and achieves revenue objectives. Merchants that operate strictly online are not without their share of channel conflict, which can occur between e-tailers.

CHANNEL CONFLICT FROM DISINTERMEDIATION

As access to the Internet became widespread, drastically lower transaction costs and higher margins for merchants made Internet-based direct customer sales irresistible. However, the ease of implementing e-commerce was far easier for some companies than others. Dell Computer, which exclusively sold computers directly to consumers, is widely regarded as the premier early adopter of disintermediation. Thus, for Dell, it was an easy transition to begin selling online. However, the same was not true for other computer companies, which had to alleviate channel conflict that arose with existing resellers that were now competing against the manufacturer for the same business.

Besides computers, online brokerages, online travel, books, music, and auctions were the early adopters of e-commerce. Brand strength was another key criteria in the successful adoption of an e-commerce strategy. For example, Estee Lauder did not rely on traditional channels to generate product awareness about its cosmetics, unlike Mary Kay. Clothing manufacturers like Nike and Levi Strauss, with strong brand awareness among consumers, appeared to be ideal candidates for setting up an online shop that sold directly to consumers. However, when Levi Strauss forbade retailers to sell its merchandise online, it had to contend with backlash from its retailer network that caused the company to exit e-commerce and allow its two top retailers to take over selling Levis and Dockers online.

It is a widely known fact that conducting business online is far cheaper than selling through human contact, either face-to-face or by phone. What many manufacturers soon found, however, was that although the sales came easily through e-commerce, the profits did not. For example, selling to 10 wholesalers (who in turn sold and shipped to many retailers) may cost far less than selling directly online to thousands of customers. The logistics of warehousing, inventory management, shipping, and customer service can quickly count against the higher profits from online ordering. Therefore, businesses had the challenge of incorporating e-commerce in a way that minimized channel conflict and met financial objectives.

DUAL-CHANNEL HARMONY

A business than begins to sell directly to customers online often must continue to rely on existing resellers or risk dwindling sales. Resellers may be necessary for adequate market penetration or to create brand awareness. Additionally, resellers may perform valuable functions, such as educating customers, gathering market information, and providing customer service after the sale. Therefore, a business must look for ways to appease its resellers before implementing an e-commerce strategy that will minimize the channel conflict.

In a dual-channel distribution network, one proven strategy is to offer different product lines. For example, carpet manufacturers have long used private labeling to sell the same products to retailers in the same geographic region. Private labeling makes it difficult for a consumer to walk into two stores, locate the same product, and compare pricing. Mattress manufacturers use a similar strategy with their major retailers. When Compaq Computer began to sell directly to consumers via the Internet (no doubt to better compete against the success of Dell Computer), the firm launched a new line of computers specifically for this market. Consequently, the computers being sold through resellers could not be purchased online.

Allowing the distribution network to add value to online sales is another method often used to appease distributors. IBM took this approach by directing buyers to distributors for assembly services. However, as a business sees its Internet sales increase, the distributors may be increasingly challenged to prove they add immediate value and justify their role in the supply chain. Additionally, traditional distributors are competing against a whole new crop of distributors that rose up to handle logistics and other tasks specifically for dot-coms.

Other strategies seek to minimize channel conflict by continuing the traditional role of resellers. One such selling scheme allows resellers to continue to market the product, but the buyer is directed online to place the order. Consequently, the reseller is paid a commission for each referral. Another selling scheme allows resellers to order online but relies on the distribution network to fulfill the order. Travelocity used this approach by allowing travel agents to continue to provide the ticketing function for flights that consumers booked online. Circuit City allowed customers to reserve products online, but they had to pick up the merchandise at a local store, which appeased the company's retailers. It is interesting to note, however, that Circuit City went out of business in 2009, with all physical locations closing. In the early 2010s, the brand existed only online.

CHANNEL HARMONY FOR RETAILERS

More and more consumers are using the Internet to make buying decisions, especially with the ease of getting online via smartphones. The Home Depot, for example, recognized that nearly half of its shoppers visit their Web site before stopping in a local store. In a 2011 interview with *Internet Retailer,* Hal Lawton, president of Home Depot Online, said the company's "goal is that there is zero channel conflict with a consumer." The retail chain tries to achieve this by compensating store managers based on combined Internet and in-store sales.

Similarly, Nordstrom tries to blend click-and-mortar into one idyllic shopping experience. This retailer's Web site allows consumers looking for a particular item to search its more than 100 store warehouses. Retailers like the Gap and J. Crew are using Twitter and other social media channels to notify customers about sales. Retailers are also directing consumers to their Web sites after a sale to complete a survey. This presents an opportunity to provide customer service as well as cross-sell the retailer's whole product line.

SEE ALSO *Cannibalization; Channel Transparency; Disintermediation.*

BIBLIOGRAPHY

Demery, Paul. "Manufacturer Calloway Golf Takes a Swing at Resolving Channel Conflict." *Internet Retailer,* June 14, 2007. Available from https://www.internetretailer.com/2007/06/14/manufacturer-callaway-golf-takes-a-swing-at-resolving-channel-co.

Egner, Bob. "The Secret of E-Commerce Success: Many Channels, One Brand." *E-Commerce Times,* August 30, 2010. Available from http://www.ecommercetimes.com/rsstory/70715.html.

Enright, Allison. "How Home Depot Provides Consistency In-store and Online." *Internet Retailer,* February 15, 2011.

Available from http://www.internetretailer.com/2011/02/15/how-home-depot-provides-consistency-store-and-online.

Gilbert, Alorie, and Beth Bacheldor. "The Big Squeeze." *InformationWeek,* March 27, 2000. Available from http://www.informationweek.com/779/channel.htm.

Greenberg, Paul A. "Manufacturers Beset by E-Commerce 'Channel Conflict.'" *E-Commerce Times,* January 7, 2000. Available from http://www.ecommercetimes.com/story/2248.html.

LeClaire, Jennifer. "Phase Two for E-Commerce." *E-Commerce Times,* August 1, 2002. Available from http://www.ecommercetimes.com/story/18840.html.

Sidhu, Inder. "Clicks and Mortar Integration: Where Retail Excellence and Relevance Come Together." *Forbes,* November 19, 2010. Available from http://www.forbes.com/sites/indersidhu/2010/11/19/clicks-and-mortar-integration-where-retail-excellence-and-relevance-come-together.

Tsay, Andy, and Narendra Agrawal. "Channel Conflict and Coordination in the E-commerce Age." *Production and Operations Management* 13, no. 1 (Spring 2004): 93–110. Available from http://www.poms.org/journal/2004-01-Tsay.pdf.

Zetlin, Minda. "Channel Conflicts." *Computerworld,* September 25, 2000. Available from http://www.computerworld.com/s/article/51004/Channel_Conflicts.

CHANNEL TRANSPARENCY

Channel transparency refers to the expectation that e-commerce will mimic the experience of buying through traditional channels, be it sales representatives, retail stores, or catalogs. For example, customers loyal to a certain retailer expect to have the same shopping experience online as they are accustomed to in stores. When a business achieves channel transparency, the customer's task of finding, purchasing, receiving, and returning products and services using the Web are nearly interchangeable with other methods. By creating harmony between the various channels used to reach the same customers, e-commerce can increase sales and profit margins.

SEAMLESS INTEGRATION OF E-COMMERCE

Channel transparency is a major goal of businesses struggling to remain competitive, as customers more and more seek quick, easy, and cheap means of finding, purchasing, and receiving products and services using the Web. Channel transparency seeks to make purchasing and service processes familiar for customers no matter where they occur. Ideally, customers should be able to conduct research on a smartphone, make their purchase in a store, and receive customer service through a call center, where each channel supports the others. To minimize channel conflict from e-commerce, the focus of executives should be on the end result of the merged channels, rather than which channel makes the sales transaction. This means making sure the necessary resources and personnel are allocated in all channels, and the right people are compensated for sales through a blended channel.

Achieving channel transparency entails understanding just what customers want and value in their dealings with companies. This knowledge can help a company leverage the strengths of its various channels. For example, do customers want to conduct research online but buy in-store to avoid shipping, or do they want to stop in a store to get expert advice and then order later online? Often the creation of channel transparency involves going deep into a company's infrastructure and updating or overhauling entire systems in order to create a single system that can harmonize operations and partner relationships to achieve transparency. This investment, in fact, is one of the chief obstacles click-and-mortar companies face in striving for channel transparency. Nonetheless, creating a seamless, integrated relationship with customers across all channels is one way for companies to gain a competitive edge.

INTEGRATION OF THE MOBILE CHANNEL

The increase in popularity of mobile devices has given rise to a whole new shopping process. According to a study conducted of 1,500 shoppers in January 2011, more than half use a smartphone while shopping. Customers are using smartphones while in a store to research product information, read reviews, and compare prices. Added convenience can be added with advanced applications that allow consumers to conduct a visual search based on what an item looks like or compare prices online simply by scanning the product's bar code with their phone's camera. As mobile devices break down barriers between channels, retailers are under pressure to remain competitive and provide consistent pricing throughout a given geographic area.

Another example of how mobile devices are being integrated into the shopping process is the use of coupons. Distributing coupons via e-mail is a common practice used by retailers to reward loyal customers. More and more retailers are accepting coupons on a mobile device, rather than requiring consumers to remember to print out the coupon and bring it with them to a store. This allows for a transparent operation between online promotions and in-store purchases.

More and more retailers are migrating toward mobile apps that permit consumers to place orders online. After launching its mobile app, Amazon.com announced this channel had generated $1 billion in sales in a 12-month period. No doubt many of these transactions were made while the customer was in a retail store. These results are a rallying cry to other retailers to develop mobile apps that emulate buying through other channels in order to effectively compete against this giant e-tailer. However, the challenge is overcoming the security issues of mobile transactions compared to computer-based ordering.

SEE ALSO *Channel Conflict/Harmony; Disintermediation.*

BIBLIOGRAPHY

Kats, Rimma. "Mobile-Enabled Price Transparency Is a Challenge for Retailers." *Mobile Commerce Daily,* April 18, 2011. Available from http://www.mobilecommercedaily.com/2011/04/18/mobile-enabled-price-transparency-is-a-challenge-for-retailers.

Quinton, Brian. "Smartphones Get Heavy Use During Shopping: Study." *Chief Marketer,* March 28, 2011. Available from http://chiefmarketer.com/mobile/smartphones-heavy-use-0328bq/?cid=nl_cm_mobile#.

Regan, Keith. "How the Bricks Conquered the Net." *E-Commerce Times,* March 6, 2003. Available from http://www.technewsworld.com/story/16631.html.

Schuman, Evan. "The Hidden E-Commerce Sales." *eWeek,* June 18, 2007. Available from http://www.eweek.com/c/a/Enterprise-Applications/The-Hidden-ECommerce-Sales.

Siwicki, Bill. "Amazon's Mobile Milestone Is a Signal to Other Retailers, Experts Say." *Internet Retailer,* July 23, 2010. Available from http://www.internetretailer.com/2010/07/23/amazons-mobile-milestone-signal-other-retailers.

CHARGE-BACK

When consumers are dissatisfied with a transaction in which a credit card was used, or if their credit card number was used without authorization, it is possible to request a charge-back from the credit card company in order to receive a credit for the amount of the purchase. Since e-commerce sales transactions occur without the merchant seeing an actual credit card or customer signature, the opportunity for illegal use of a credit card is higher. Additionally, since online shoppers are buying goods sight unseen, there is a higher chance that the consumer will be dissatisfied with the product. Therefore, the incidence of charge-backs is likely to be higher with online transactions.

THE CHARGE-BACK PROCESS

Merchants who deal with consumers face-to-face use a variety of steps to ensure a cardholder's legitimacy, including verification of the person's signature. When these precautions are taken, the bank that issued the credit card normally is responsible for any charge-backs due to fraud. However, when transactions take place without an actual card being presented to the merchant, as in e-commerce, the merchant is liable for fraud-related charge-backs.

In the event that an unauthorized charge appears on a credit card statement, the cardholder should immediately contact the credit card company to report the possible fraud. If the charge does appear to be fraudulent, the credit card company will freeze the account and look into the matter. At this point, to avoid a charge-back the seller must provide evidence that the cardholder participated in the purchase. If the purchase was made without the cardholder's authorization, the credit card company will charge-back the amount. (Federal law states that the consumer's maximum liability for unauthorized charges is $50 per credit card.)

Charge-backs may also occur when a consumer is dissatisfied with the goods or service received in an online transaction. If a resolution cannot be reached by contacting the seller's customer service department, the consumer's next course of action is to file a dispute with the issuer of the credit card used in the transaction. Generally, consumers have up to 180 days to initiate a dispute. At this point, the burden of proof rests on the e-commerce company to provide evidence that the goods were delivered according to expectation or that the service was rendered properly to avoid a charge-back.

When a business does incur a charge-back, the credit card company debits the merchant's or service provider's account and credits the consumer's credit card account for the amount of the purchase. Typically, the business must also pay a charge-back fee to the credit card company. A charge-back is particularly costly for a business when high-value goods are shipped after an unauthorized transaction, because the business loses the sale and the tangible goods.

PREVENTING CHARGE-BACK FRAUD

Online fraud is a major concern for companies engaging in e-commerce. Merchants that process a high volume of Internet transactions, especially for jewelry, electronics, and other high-value merchandise, are at a greater risk of incurring charge-backs due to unauthorized credit card use. Geographic location of the buyer also correlates to frequency of charge-backs. According to a 2009 study by CyberSource, merchants that accept international orders are at a higher risk for credit card fraud. New York City, Miami, and Los Angeles were identified as the U.S. cities with the highest fraud risk.

To reduce costly charge-backs, an e-commerce company should implement an internal fraud-management system or outsource the task to a security services provider. Such a system monitors purchase transactions, assigns a risk score, and flags suspicious activity for further review by fraud-prevention staff before the goods are shipped. According to articles published by *Internet Retailer,* a year after outsourcing fraud detection to a security services provider, 1-800-Flowers.com experienced a 63% reduction in charge-backs, and Bodybuilding.com experienced an 85% drop in charge-backs. A spokesperson from 1-800-Flowers.com stated that the new system also resulted in fewer fraud attempts, most likely due to its new reputation as a "site that's difficult to defraud."

SEE ALSO *Electronic Payment; Fraud, Internet; Recurring Payment Transactions; Transaction Issues.*

BIBLIOGRAPHY

Demery, Paul. "Bodybuilding.com Pushes Down Its Chargeback Rate." *Internet Retailer,* April 7, 2011. Available from http://www.internetretailer.com/2011/04/07/bodybuildingcom-pushes-down-its-chargeback-rate.

———. "How 1-800-Flowers Cust Back Online Fraud." *Internet Retailer,* December 21, 2010. Available from http://www.internetretailer.com/2010/12/09/how-1-800-flowers-cuts-back-online-fraud.

Ensight Merchant Services. "Assessing Charge Back Risk." Hackensack, NJ. Available from http://www.ensightmerchantservices.com/Charge-Back-Risk.html.

Federal Trade Commission. "Avoiding Credit and Charge Card Fraud." Washington, DC, August 1997. Available from http://www.ftc.gov/bcp/edu/pubs/consumer/credit/cre07.shtm.

Stambor, Zak. "Web Merchants Say International Fraud Rates Fell to 2% in 2009, Study Says." *Internet Retailer,* February 22, 2010. Available from http://www.internetretailer.com/2010/02/22/web-merchants-say-international-fraud-rates-fell-to-2-in-2009.

Visa. "Charge Back Cycle." San Francisco, CA. Available from http://usa.visa.com/merchants/operations/chargebacks_dispute_resolution/chargeback_cycle.html.

"What Is a Chargeback?" *Consumerist,* April 9, 2007. Available from http://consumerist.com/2007/04/what-is-a-chargeback.html.

CHILDREN AND THE INTERNET

More than any other group, children have been a center of controversy on the Internet. American youth access the Internet for school, communication, shopping, and recreation. Children's relationship with the Internet has attracted the attention of Internet providers, marketers, advertisers, teachers, lawmakers, and public interest groups. The Internet's role in education, the online collection of children's personal information, and the nature of the material available on the Web, raise a host of controversial issues, including freedom of access to information, regulation of Web site content, and invasion of children's privacy, along with broader issues of social equality, education, and the regulation of business.

CHILDREN, DEMOGRAPHICS, AND THE INTERNET

By 2011, 80% of children age 5 and under who used the Internet in the United States did so at least weekly. While television use remained the highest form of media for the age group, multimedia data from online connections had grown quickly. More than 60% of children under the age of 3 watched videos online. For the 8 to 18 age group, 20% of their video content was streamed from an online source, especially from mobile sources. Of course, converging technologies also made it increasingly difficult to tell the difference between watching television and using the Internet. A 2010 study showed that more than a third of children between 2 and 11 used both types of media at the same time.

MARKETING TO CHILDREN ONLINE

Since advertisers believe brand preferences are set by age 12, merchandisers are anxiously probing this market and devising new methods to tap its potential. Specialized market research firms have emerged that conduct information gathering via online focus groups, surveys, and chat sessions. Most companies integrate purchasing options into all areas of their Web sites, and many advertisers seek visibility on well-known children's sites.

Online marketing targeted at children has stirred parental concerns, especially about the saturation that can be achieved by a constant bombardment of ads. Parents worry about their inability to supervise children's online purchases, about children's fiscal responsibility, and about marketers' aggressive invasion of children's privacy. In response to such concerns, marketers have focused on generating ways to allay parental fears. Sites such as DoughNET, RocketCash, and iCanBuy offered "digital wallets" funded by a specified cash amount that draws, much like debit cards, on a savings account to prevent children from overspending. Other sites permit parents to stipulate where their kids can shop.

ONLINE PORNOGRAPHY

Children's ever-increasing Net access, much of it unsupervised, has generated concerns beyond those about target marketing. Many parents worry about children's exposure to inappropriate Web site content, such as excessive violence and pornography.

In addition to accessing online pornography, children also may be its subjects. The FBI and U.S. Customs Service cooperate with foreign governments on international investigations of child pornography sites. However, servers located in countries that lack treaties with the United States are often difficult to shut down.

PRIVACY

Many marketers use the Internet to compile market research profiles of preadult Net surfers. They may elicit sought-after information with the promise of some form of compensation. A study by the Annenberg Public Policy Center found that two-thirds of children polled would supply the names of their favorite stores when offered a "great free gift," while 40 percent would volunteer details concerning family cars, their allowances, and family political opinions. Thus, children serve as sources of information about not only their own, but also their family members' purchasing and lifestyle habits. Concerns over such practices center on the fact that children are far less guarded than adults. Hence, the possibility for abusing minors' privacy runs high.

Proponents of greater safeguards for children's online privacy argue that personal information gathered online aids marketers in further targeting a highly vulnerable audience. Children may expose themselves to dangers when they post personal information on Facebook or elsewhere. An FBI and Department of Justice study determined that child predators utilize such online information.

As social network use among children became common throughout the 2000s, focus was also placed on the policies those social networks used. In Europe, the European Commission responsible for Digital Agenda recommended that all social networks have their profiles set automatically to private, where only friends could see the information unless otherwise specified. Rating systems, regulatory and awareness agencies, and events like the annual Safer Internet Day were all created in order to educate people on privacy, especially for children.

Social media and the increased number of channels for communication also created the need for additional parental controls for operating systems. For example, Apple created white lists, or approved lists for correspondence in Mail, IM, Web sites, and applications that may be used by children, requiring permission from a parent for any correspondence with someone not on the list. The number of third-party solutions that provided similar features also rapidly increased, including browsers like BumperCar and KidsBrowser.

CHILDREN'S PROTECTION ACTS

The findings of the Federal Trade Commission (FTC) led the U.S. Congress to pass the Children's Online Privacy Protection Act (COPPA) in 1999. The act mandated that the FTC produce rules to govern the online compilation and use of personal information from children under 13. Web site operators must provide notice and obtain "verifiable parental consent" before they can gather or disclose information from children. Web sites must alert parents about their policies concerning children's personal data, and site operators must remedy situations when a child's information has been disclosed. If a parent requests it, the operator is required to describe the personal information collected from the child.

COPPA restricts enticing children to disclose personal information through contests or prizes. However, it does not provide parents or children a private right of action. It also shields Web sites from liability if they can demonstrate a good faith effort to remedy prior disclosure of a child's personal information. Under the FTC's rule, businesses may implement self-regulatory "safe harbor" programs by submitting guidelines to the FTC for approval. Many smaller Internet businesses protested COPPA, stating that compliance costs would be impossible to manage. They argued that parental compliance forms would discourage traffic to lesser-known sites and many children would access teen- or adult-oriented sites to circumvent parental compliance altogether.

In 2001, COPPA was replaced in many forms by the updated CIPA, or Children's Internet Protection Act, as well as the Neighborhood Children's Internet Protection Act (NCIPA) which went into effect at the same time. The acts placed limitations on what Internet-based funding could be used by certain organizations such as libraries and educational institutions. It required these organizations to update their filtering capabilities and audit their current safety policies, especially when it came to data that was harmful to minors. Such harmful data was defined in clear detail.

The United States was not the only nation where such movements were being developed. In 2008, the Child Online Protection initiative began as part of the effects of the Global Cybersecurity Agenda. The initiative was designed to help provide clear standards and child online safety actions for participating countries.

Some bills were more controversial. For example, in 2011 federal legislation titled the Protecting Children from Internet Pornographers Act was introduced. The bill required, among other things, that Internet service providers keep a list of customer IP addresses for at least a year. Privacy groups lobbied against the bill, claiming that it interfered with user rights to privacy and that there was already sufficient evidence available to prosecute child pornography offenders. In July 2011, the bill had been approved by the U.S. House Judiciary Committee but had not yet become law.

INDUSTRY SELF-REGULATION AND FILTERING SOFTWARE

Congressional legislation was not the only vehicle to regulate children's Internet interactions. The industry voluntarily launched several self-regulatory practices concerning children. In 1998, the Online Privacy Alliance (OPA), a coalition of industry groups, was formed to tackle Web-related privacy concerns. Among its measures were proposed online privacy guidelines governing the online collection of personal data, and guidelines protecting children's privacy.

TRUSTe, a nonprofit organization, certifies that its members have disclosed their online information-collection practices. In return, members display a seal verifying program participation. The Better Business Bureau Online sponsors a similar effort. Members must inform users of their collection practices, supply data security, submit to periodic monitoring, and use encryption for the receipt and transfer of sensitive information. Skeptics counter that industry self-regulation does not guarantee compliance or enforcement of programs. Moreover, few Web providers participate in seal programs.

Filtering software was another protective measure Web sites could use to safeguard children. Such software shields children from objectionable Web sites and protects children's privacy by screening incoming and outgoing text. Specific terms prompt outgoing screening and block sensitive information from being sent to the provider. In 2011, some of the top products included Net Nanny, PureSight, and CYBERsitter. Remote management and reporting features were common in these products, allowing parents to manage and filter their home computers from any location with Internet access. Another notable new feature was the ability to keep track of social network profiles and posts for Web sites like Facebook and Twitter.

LIBRARIES

Libraries face particular challenges concerning children's access to the Internet. Though voters and the courts have favored a lack of restrictions in the interests of intellectual freedom, many groups call for mandatory filtering of the Internet in schools and public libraries. Some libraries require parental agreement forms before granting children Internet access. Others mandate that youngsters be accompanied by a parent when using computers. Still others install filtering software on computers utilized by children.

Although they serve as protective measures, strategies such as filtering also carry disadvantages. Although "objectionable" terms can be blocked, filters may prevent students from conducting research on legitimate topics such as medical advances or disease. A student, for example, might not be able to conduct online searches regarding AIDS transmission or breast cancer, if such filtering were in place.

SEE ALSO *Digital Divide; Higher Education, E-Commerce and Global E-Commerce Regulation; Legal Issues; Privacy: Issues, Policies, Statements; Profiling.*

BIBLIOGRAPHY

American Library Association. "The Children's Internet Protection Act." Chicago, 2011. Available from http://www.ala.org/ala/issuesadvocacy/advocacy/federallegislation/cipa/index.cfm.

Anderson, Pat. "Child's Play." *Marketing Week.* September 9, 1999.

Anthony, Barbara, and Thomas Cohn. "Putting Parents Back in Charge of Kids' Privacy." *Computerworld,* May 15, 2000.

Chen, Christine Y. "Chasing the Net Generation." *Fortune,* September 4, 2000.

Cheng, Kipp. "Wee Web." *Brandweek,* May 3, 1999.

Chilik Wollenberg, Yvonne. "Do You Know What Your Kids are Saying About You Online." *Medical Economics.* October 23, 2000.

Chordas, Lori. "A New Generation in the Cross Hairs." *Best's Review,* February 2001.

Crockett, Roger O. "Forget the Mall. Kids Shop the Net." *Business Week,* July 26, 1999.

Demner, Dina. "Children on the Internet," College Park, MD: University of Maryland, April 2001. Available from http://otal.umd.edu/uupractice/children.

Hertzell, Dorothy. "Don't Talk to Strangers: An Analysis of Government and Industry Efforts to Protect a Child's Privacy Online." *Federal Communications Law Journal* March 2000.

Holton, Lisa. "The Surfer in the Family." *American Demographics,* April 2000.

Kaste, Martin. "Child Pornography Bill Makes Privacy Experts Skittish." *NPR,* August 24, 2011. Available from http://www.npr.org/2011/08/24/139875599/child-pornography-bill-makes-privacy-experts-skittish.

"Internet Filter Software Review." *Top Ten Reviews,* 2011. Available from http://internet-filter-review.toptenreviews.com.

"Internet Safety for Children." The X Lab, 2011. Available from http://www.thexlab.com/faqs/internetsafetychild.html.

"ITU Child Online Protection." Safer Internet Day, 2011. Available from http://www.saferinternetday.org/web/itu/my-home/-/blogs/sid-2011:-working-to-make-the-internet-safer-for-children-and-adolescents;jsessionid=FACA0DA6F2E9641621BC3B7FE2CC0B13.

Jezzard, Helen. "Is the Internet Beyond Control?" *Information World Review,* June 2000.

Kessler, Sarah. "Children's Consumption of Digital Media on the Rise." *Mashable,* March 14, 2011. Available from http://mashable.com/2011/03/14/children-internet-stats.

Kroes, Neelie. "Safer Internet Day 2011: Protecting Children Online." *Europa,* February 8, 2011. Available from http://europa.eu/rapid/pressReleasesAction.do?reference=SPEECH/11/73&format=HTML&aged=0&language=EN&guiLanguage=en.

Kwak, Mary. "Fair Play?" *Inc.* March 14, 2000.

Leonard, Bill. "After Generations X and Y Comes Generation I." *HRMagazine,* January 2000.

Long, Tim. "On the Road to a Safe Net for Kids." *Computer Reseller News,* August 14, 2000.

Marmer Solomon, Charlene. "Ready or Not, Here Comes the Net Kids." *Workforce,* February 2000.

Martens, Ellin. "A Laptop for Every Kid." *Time,* May 1, 2000.

Minkel, Walter. "Dealing with the Filtering Stigma." *Library Journal,* Spring 2000.

——. "Young Children and the Web: A Boolean Match, or Not?" *Library Journal.* January 2000.

Pepe, Michele. "Safety Net for Young Surfers." *Computer Reseller News,* December 6, 1999.

Radcliff, Deborah. "Vigilante Group Targets Child Pornography Sites." *Computerworld,* January 17, 2000.

Rogers, Michael, and Norman Oder. "School Net Logs Case Hits Snag." *Library Journal,* January 2001.

Ross, Sid. "Clicks for Kids." *Adweek.* January 8, 2001.

Smith, Ellis. "Comcast Offers Cheap Internet to School Children." *Times Free Press,* September 2, 2011. Available from http://www.timesfreepress.com/news/2011/sep/02/comcast-offers-cheap-internet-school-children.

Symonds, William C. "Wired Schools." *Business Week,* September 25, 2001.

CHURN

In business, churn most often refers to loss of customers, but it can also mean employee turnover. Churn is particularly important to service industries, such as telecommunication or software as a service (SaaS), where it is easy for customers to leave one firm and go to a competitor. The churn rate is quantified as the percentage of customers that are lost during a given time period, such as one year. It is calculated by dividing the number of customers that leave during the time period by the total number of customers at the start. Churn is a crucial business metric to track because it provides insight into pricing, customer service, and competition. It is also important for a business to estimate future churn rates as well as differentiate voluntary churn from involuntary, which is typically due to an inability to pay or a move. Some industries, such as mobile telecommunications, have higher churn rates than others. Overall, service providers that charge an ongoing fee should strive to have lower churn year-to-year compared to competitors.

THE COST OF CHURN

A high churn rate is costly for several reasons. First, the cost of acquiring a new customer is high, as a firm has the cost of running advertising or promotions and paying a salesperson. There are also costs associated with setting up a new account. Second, the inability to maintain customer loyalty makes for poor public relations, as a business is not likely to acquire new customers through positive word-of-mouth. Companies that are not proactive in identifying unhappy customers and addressing problems before a customer is ready to leave may have to cut prices to entice a customer to stay. All of these expenses result in lower profit margins. Churn can go from bad to worse if a company decides to cut customer service to improve profits.

Involuntary churn due to an inability to pay is particularly costly for a business that loses a customer and does not get paid. Although prepaid subscriptions may be less profitable than postpaid, a company will not have as many problems with unpaid bills. Additionally, implementing more stringent credit requirements upfront is a way to reduce the likelihood of involuntary churn from the inability to pay.

In an industry that relies heavily on customer service, a high attrition rate for customer service representatives can be particularly costly. If a company is continually hiring and training new customer service people, this will have a negative impact on customer service. Consequently, customers who experience poor customer service are more likely to churn. A business facing high costs associated with both hiring and acquiring new customers will have greater difficulty achieving profitability.

A company that implement a major change, such as a price increase, should predict how it will increase churn. Sometimes the bottom line profits will actually improve from such a change, thus justifying the higher churn rate. For example, Netflix announced a 60% price increase in July 2011 for customers who received one DVD at a time and streaming video. Although angered customers churned, the revenue per remaining customer was set high enough to offset the loss of customers.

MINIMIZING CHURN

One strategy for minimizing churn is to attract loyal customers in the first place. Promotional campaigns should be aimed at acquiring new customers that are less likely to switch to a competitor. For a business with solid customer service, these are likely customers that value service more than price. Consequently, a customer lured away from a competitor based solely on pricing, such as a free 30-day trial period, is more likely to switch again. Certain characteristics may also make for more loyal customers. In the mobile telecom industry, for example, research has shown that older, married homeowners tend to be more loyal than young, single renters.

A key component of a low churn rate is understanding what makes customers loyal. According to an article in *Information Management,* there are three factors that measure loyalty of telecom customers: the extent to which customers engage in revenue-generating activities, the length of time as a customer, and the extent to which customers use the full range of products/services offered. Both existing and former customers should be segmented to predict which are likely to churn in the future. The company can then improve service or offer financial incentives to reduce the churn rate. Rewards programs or bundled services at a price customers want to pay are ways to add value that are not easy for a customer to give up.

SEE ALSO *Loyalty.*

BIBLIOGRAPHY

Dignan, Larry. "Netflix's Pricing Backlash: Follow the Money, Churn Rate." *ZDNet,* July 13, 2011. Available from http://www.zdnet.com/blog/btl/netflixs-pricing-backlash-follow-the-money-churn-rates/52295.

Hughes, Arthur Middleton. "Churn Away." *Direct,* March 1, 2008. Available from http://directmag.com/crm/marketing_churn_away.

Kumar, Shailendra. "Understanding the Relationship Between Loyalty and Churn." *Information Management,* October 2005. Available from http://www.information-management.com/specialreports/20051018/1039409-1.html.

Wilson, Carol. "Forrester: Stop Churn Before It Happens." *Connected Planet,* January 22, 2009. Available from http://connectedplanetonline.com/residential_services/news/offer ing-consumer-education-0122.

CISCO SYSTEMS, INC.

Electronics, networking, and computer technology company Cisco Systems of San Jose, California, had more than 73,000 employees and over $40 billion in 2010 annual revenue. The company's core business is as a major manufacturer of Internet infrastructure as well as other products that allow people to access the Internet and help companies manage Web sites. The company is listed on numerous major financial indices, including the Dow Jones Industrial Average, the S&P 500 Index, the NASDAQ 100 Index, and others.

In addition to the network architecture products that the company is known for, Cisco has also expanded to provide a range of other products for businesses and consumers, such as phones and security cameras, mainly through a long series of acquisitions in the 1990s, 2000s, and beyond.

EARLY HISTORY

Two Stanford University computer scientists—married couple Leonard Bosack and Sandra Lerner—established Cisco Systems in December 1984. The new company began marketing the internetworking technology Bosack had developed while at Stanford to universities, research centers, and government agencies. The following year, Stanford asked Cisco for $11 million in licensing fees, arguing that Stanford held rights to Bosack's technology since it had been developed at the university. Stanford accepted a settlement of $150,000 and free products and support services in 1986. That year, Cisco became one of the first networking technology firms to develop a router, a device linking a number of local area networks (LANs), compatible with Transmission Control Protocol/Internet Protocol (TCP/IP).

Cisco's first chief executive officer was Bill Graves, who served until 1988. In that year, John Morgridge took the post, which he held until 1995 when he was succeeded by John Chambers, though Morgridge remained the company's chairman until 2006. Chambers joined Cisco in 1991 as the senior vice president of worldwide sales and operations, after stints at Wang Laboratories and IBM. He became CEO in 1995 and chairman in November 2006.

Bosack and Lerner exited the company in 1990, after Lerner was fired and Bosack quit in protest. Bosack later served in leadership roles at other technology companies, and is CEO of XKL LLC (as of 2012). Lerner went on to found Urban Decay cosmetics.

IPO AND EARLY GROWTH

Sales reached $1.5 million in 1987, and Cisco began marketing its networking products to businesses with offices in a wide range of locations. To fund future growth, Cisco conducted its initial public offering (IPO) in 1990. Sales that year grew to $70 million and more than doubled in 1991 to $183 million. Pacific Bell began purchasing the bulk of its routers from Cisco in 1992. New product developments that year included integrated services digital routers, as well as upgrades to fiber distributed data interface (FDDI) and token ring technologies. International expansion was launched via an original equipment manufacturer (OEM) agreement with British Telecom, and Cisco also started to market its routers to U.S. long-distance providers. After revenues surged to $340 million, *Forbes* ranked Cisco number two on its list of the fastest-growing companies in the United States.

When the development of asynchronous transfer mode (ATM) technologies threatened to render router technology obsolete in 1993, Cisco developed routers that could assist ATM transmissions. International expansion continued with the establishment of Cisco Systems HK Ltd. in Hong Kong and new units in Europe, Japan, and Australia. AT&T Corp. and StrataCom agreed to work with Cisco to foster compatibility among rival protocols.

GROWTH VIA ACQUISITION

Cisco launched an acquisition spree in 1993, paying $100 million for Crescendo Communications, creator of copper distributed data interface technology. Setting the stage for how future acquisitions would be integrated into existing operations, Cisco retained Crescendo head Mario Mazzola and all of his employees. Success with this purchase prompted Cisco to continue paying for companies with products and services in high-growth areas, rather than spending money on research and development to create its own products.

U.S. Robotics and Cisco inked a technology-sharing alliance in 1995. By the following year, Cisco's routers were considered an integral part of the Internet. Making its largest purchase to date, Cisco paid roughly $4 billion for Stratacom Inc. in 1996. The firm also paid $100 million for Nashoba Networks, a maker of token-ring network hubs; $79 million for NetSys Technology Inc., a networking technology vendor; and $220 million for Granite Systems, a manufacturer of gigabit Ethernet technologies. As a result, Cisco ended up owning plants manufacturing three rival Ethernet switching systems.

CONDUCTING BUSINESS VIA THE INTERNET

The 1997 purchases of Ardent Communications Corp. and Global Internet Software Group elevated Cisco to the number one spot among worldwide networking equipment makers, with an 80% share of the Internet router market. That year, the firm sold nearly $1 billion worth of networking equipment via its Web site, one of the earliest business-to-business sites to prove successful. By 1998, Internet sales accounted for more than 40% of Cisco's $3.6 billion in annual revenues, which grew 44% from the previous year. (Earnings jumped 55% over the same time period.) According to a March 1998 article in *InternetWeek,* Cisco's Web site went well beyond simply allowing clients to place orders and make payments. It explained: "The site provides online documentation, order updates, design tools, and help-desk support. Cisco delivers the tools to cut the time required for negotiating contracts, determining pricing, calculating lead times, checking on status and verifying shipment dates." In December, the firm established its Internet Business Solutions Group after clients began asking Cisco for helping with setting up their own Internet-based business ventures.

The acquisition spree continued in 2000, when Cisco paid $5.7 billion in stock for ArrowPoint Communications Inc., a maker of network switches, and completed 19 additional purchases. By then, Internet sales accounted for roughly 80% of Cisco's total revenues. The firm's continued success selling its technology via the Web fueled the growth of its Internet Business Solutions Group, whose clients included Lands' End, the Gap, and Wal-Mart.

Cisco served as a model of e-business efficiency. Its accounting practices were so automated that the firm was able to operate with several hundred fewer accountants than other firms its size. A mere 4 auditors handled Cisco's travel and expense reports, compared to the roughly 40 auditors employed by comparable firms. Also, more than 90% of customer service requests were taken care of on the firm's Web site. Productivity gains in 1999 allowed Cisco to save $825 million, and savings the following year reached $1.35 billion. In April 2000, Cisco achieved a market capitalization of $550 billion, surpassing both Microsoft and General Electric as the world's most highly valued company.

Despite its continued success, Cisco also found itself vulnerable to competition from smaller, more nimble rivals. The firm saw its market share for Internet-only traffic routers, known as "core" routers, fall from 80% in 2000 to 69% in 2001, due mainly to competition from Juniper Network, which developed an Internet traffic router in 1996 that was faster than any of Cisco's offerings. Hoping to speed its diversification efforts, in 2000 Cisco funneled considerable resources into developing its acquired telecommunications equipment operations.

THE DOT-COM BUST AND THE RECESSION

When the U.S. economy buckled later in 2000, many of the young businesses that were Cisco's customers began to slow spending, and in several cases they simply declared bankruptcy. Consequently, Cisco saw a large portion of its orders dissolve virtually overnight. To make matters worse, the firm had spent the last several months beefing up its inventory in an effort to fill customer orders more quickly. As a result, Cisco announced its intent to take a one-time $2.5 billion charge to write off its inventory glut. The company also cut roughly 8,000 jobs in March 2001, which amounted to nearly 17% of its workforce.

Acquisitions ground to a near halt as Cisco executives pondered how to best prepare the firm for an anticipated economic rebound. Looking to the future, several analysts believed the firm would make a major strategic shift by paring down noncore operations and increasing internal research and development efforts. Other observers criticized the company for not anticipating the effects of the downturn the way some competitors had and continuing to forecast profits that were not in line with overall industry expectations during the downturn.

However, unlike other tech companies that succumbed to bankruptcy during the financial downturn, Cisco rebounded as a leaner company. Chambers began rebuilding the company with a focus on cost-cutting and operating discipline. The company wrote down inventory, continued layoffs, and severely curtailed plans for future acquisitions. Cisco also cut partnerships with resellers and suppliers as part of its bid to cut costs, and by 2003, it had returned to profitability.

After making a single acquisition in 2001, a $181 million deal for Allegro Systems, Cisco came back into the game as its fortunes rebounded and continued to make dozens of deals during the 2000s, including several sizable ones. In 2002, the company spent $2.5 billion to buy Andiamo Systems, a data storage company. And in 2006, the company bought Scientific-Atlanta, a manufacturer of cable television, telecommunications technology, and broadband, for $6.9 billion. Other major acquisitions include WebEx, a web conferencing company, Tandberg, a video conferencing firm, and Starent Networks.

However, Cisco's fortunes took another downturn after the recession of 2008–2009. As the economy struggled, and federal and local governments cut costs, many of the company's largest customers, including public sector clients such as public universities and hospitals, cut back dramatically on purchases of new equipment. This caused sales to decline for the Internet architecture giant.

In May 2011, Chambers announced plans to cut costs by $1 billion, including cutting 6,500 jobs worldwide. Of that number, 2,100 were employees who took an early retirement program.

Part of the restructuring was to narrow the company's focus, including dissolving its Flip video camcorder business. Analysts called the moves "unfortunate" but necessary if Cisco wanted to regain its competitive role in the industry.

SEE ALSO *Business-to-Business (B2B) E-Commerce; Internet Infrastructure.*

BIBLIOGRAPHY

Carey, Peter. "A Start-Up's True Tale." *San Jose Mercury News,* December 1, 2001. Available from http://pdp10.nocrew.org/docs/cisco.html.

"Cisco Fractures Its Own Fairy Tale." *Fortune,* May 14, 2001.

Cisco Systems, Inc. "Annual Report." San Jose, CA, 2010. Available from http://www.cisco.com/web/about/ac49/ac20/ac19/ar2010/letter/index.html.

———. "Frequently Asked Questions." San Jose, CA, 2011. Available from http://investor.cisco.com/faq.cfm.

"Cisco Systems Inc." In *Notable Corporate Chronologies.* Farmington Hills, MI: Gale Group, 1999.

Goldblatt, Henry. "Cisco's Secrets." *Fortune,* November 8, 1999.

Hardy, Quentin. "Cisco Kidding?" *Forbes,* May 14, 2001. Available from http://www.forbes.com/forbes/2001/0514/052.html.

Kopytoff, Verne G. "Profit Slides on Soft Sales, but Cisco Stays Upbeat." *New York Times,* August 10, 2011. Available from http://www.nytimes.com/2011/08/11/technology/ciscos-profit-falls.html.

Metz, Rachel. "Cisco Layoffs: Tech Giant to Shed Thousands of Employees." *Huffington Post,* July 18, 2011. Available from http://www.huffingtonpost.com/2011/07/18/cisco-layoffs-thousands-employees_n_902180.html.

Moazami, Mohsen. "The Web's Largest Store." *Chain Store Age Executive,* August, 2000.

Nee, Eric. "Cisco: How It Aims to Keep Right on Growing." *Fortune,* February 2, 2001.

Walsh, Brian. "Best Site for Business-to-Business Commerce." *InternetWeek,* March 9, 1998.

Yang, Dori J. "Cisco's Spectacular Slide from Stardom." *U.S. News & World Report,* April 16, 2001.

CLARK, JAMES (JIM) H.

James H. (Jim) Clark is an entrepreneur who founded three influential technology companies in the 1980s and 1990s. He is perhaps best known for his role as cofounder of Netscape Communications Corporation, a graphical interface web browser that *Fortune's* Adam Lashinsky claims "set the technological, social, and financial tone of the Internet Age." Long before his days at Netscape, Clark created Silicon Graphics, the pioneer of three-dimensional computer graphics technology. Clark's third brainchild, Healtheon, grew into a leading health industry Web site offering health information to consumers, as well as electronic transaction processing for medical facilities and physician groups.

3-D GRAPHICS

While a computer science professor at Stanford University in the late 1970s, Clark developed the Geometry Engine, a three-dimensional graphics chip. In 1981, he resigned from his position at Stanford to start his own business for developing and marketing the chip. Clark formally launched Silicon Graphics a year later. The new firm offered the first three-dimensional terminal, called the IRIS 1000, in 1983. Clark chose IRIS as the terminal's name to reflect his technology's focus on appealing to the sense of sight. In 1984, Clark developed IRIS 1400, the industry's first three-dimensional workstation, which sold for $75,000. Recognizing his limitations as a manager, Clark appointed Edward McCracken, a former executive at Hewlett-Packard, as president of Silicon Graphics.

Clark incorporated his company in 1986. At that time, Silicon Graphics was the leading maker of high-end three-dimensional workstations, which it marketed mainly to technical and scientific organizations. In 1987, Clark and his engineers added reduced instruction set computing (RISC) chips to the company's terminals. The Personal IRIS, the first personal graphics workstation to hit the market, was shipped in 1988, as was the IRIS POWER Series of compatible multiprocessing workstations. To generate capital for new product development, Clark divested 20% of Silicon Graphics' stock to Control Data for roughly $68.5 million. He also licensed the IRIS Graphic Library to IBM Corp. in an attempt to entice software vendors to develop programs that would run on Silicon Graphics workstations. By the early 1990s, Silicon Graphics had made its way to the *Fortune* 500, and sales had reached $550 million. Software programs available for Silicon Graphics workstations totaled more than 1,400. Increasing tension with McCracken prompted Clark to leave his firm in 1994.

THE RISE OF WEB BROWSERS

Clark then considered investing his earnings into an interactive television venture. However, after meeting

22-year-old Marc Andreessen—who had developed the Mosaic graphic user interface (GUI) program for World Wide Web browsing with a group of fellow University of Illinois students—Clark saw the potential for a commercial Web browsing software program. Clark and Andreessen agreed to launch Mosaic Communications Corporation in April 1994 with $3 million of Clark's money along with additional venture capital from investor John Doerr. A few months later, the University of Illinois claimed they had rights to the name Mosaic, since the technology was developed when Andreessen had worked there. Clark and Andreessen changed the name of their enterprise to Netscape Communications and christened its proprietary Web browser "Netscape Navigator."

In October 1994, Clark and Andreessen offered AT&T executive Jim Barksdale a seat on Netscape's board. Three months later, they talked him into running Netscape. Although the firm was not yet profitable, Clark encouraged his colleagues to take the company public. His instincts paid off on August 9, 1995, in a very lucrative initial public offering (IPO). On the day of the IPO, Clark's 20% stake in Netscape was worth $663 million. Soon, Netscape Navigator was serving roughly 80% of the Web's browser market.

Aware of competitors, engineers worked to improve Navigator. In February 1996, Netscape Navigator Version 2.0 debuted. The technology incorporated JavaScript, software that, among other things, allowed nonprofessionals to create their own Web sites. By October 1996, users had downloaded some 45 million Netscape browsers, and revenues had soared from $85 million in 1995 to $346 million. That success was short-lived, however, thanks to Microsoft's launch of its Internet Explorer browser.

Though he left the day-to-day operations to other Netscape employees, Clark continued to be an integral part of Netscape as it battled Microsoft in what became known as the "browser wars." Unlike Netscape, Internet Explorer was free to use. By 1997, Microsoft's Internet Explorer, bundled with the Windows 95 operating system, had reduced Netscape's browser market share by nearly 50%. When Netscape filed a complaint alleging that Microsoft's strategy of bundling Explorer with Windows 95 was anticompetitive, the U.S. Department of Justice ruled that Microsoft must offer a version of Windows 95 unbundled from Internet Explorer. Although that decision was later overturned in an appeal, the litigation sparked an investigation of Microsoft's alleged monopolist tactics. In 2000, the computer industry giant was found guilty and ordered to split into two companies, a verdict which Microsoft immediately appealed.

HEALTH CARE MANAGEMENT

Even as Clark enjoyed the success of Netscape, he had his sights set on a new enterprise. To help streamline what he perceived to be a bureaucratic and highly inefficient health care industry, he launched Healthscape, a virtual health care network, in 1996. The firm's first product, an Internet-based system that automated enrollment in health plans for insurance companies and large employers, flopped. Clark had to work hard to reassure his investors that the company, renamed Healtheon, was still a lucrative idea. Recognizing that he needed someone with experience in marketing computer services, Clark brought in a new CEO, Mike Long, in 1997. Long shifted Healtheon's focus to physician groups, believing that they would be more likely to embrace new technology than giant insurance companies.

According to *Fortune* columnist Julie Creswell, it was Microsoft that helped spark Healtheon's growth. "When Healtheon learned that Microsoft was on the verge of investing $100 million in an Atlanta online health start-up called WebMD, Clark and Long foresaw a battle they wanted to avoid. Instead of fighting Microsoft, they made a deal valued at $6.5 billion to merge Healtheon and WebMD." The deal with WebMD proved lucrative. Consumers already used the site to gather reputable medical information. While Healtheon could continue to devise ways to automate information processing procedures for health care providers, WebMD would be able to take advantage of the advertising potential a growing base of online visitors offered. Healtheon, like Silicon Graphics and Netscape, attracted numerous investors. When Healthon reached a market capitalization of over $1 billion, Clark had the distinction of being the first entrepreneur to establish three multibillion-dollar technology companies.

OTHER VENTURES

Clark's involvement with Netscape essentially ended in November 1998, when American Online (AOL) agreed to pay roughly $4.2 billion for Netscape. When news of the deal became public, stock prices skyrocketed. Clark invested some of his profits into other ventures that year, including photography Web start-up Shutterfly and MyCFO Inc., an Internet-based financial management services firm. After resigning as chairman of Healtheon/WebMD in 2000, Clark sold MyCFO to Harris Private Bank in 2002.

In 2003, Clark decided to try his hand at real estate development. Partnering with Tom Jermoluk, former CEO of Excite@Home, Clark founded Hyperion Development Group in Miami, Florida. He also made headlines for his philanthropy, particularly when he donated $150 million—the largest single contribution in the school's history—to Stanford University for the construction of the James H. Clark Center for Biomedical Engineering in Sciences. Clark's gift enabled Stanford scientists and engineers to pursue studies in biomedicine, a field that included stem cell research. However, federal restrictions against embryonic stem cell research in the early 2000s led Clark to withdraw $60 million of his pledge in protest.

Clark voiced his dissent again in 2007 when he resigned as chairman of Shutterfly three months after the company's IPO, writing in a letter attached to the company's 8-K, "As a technologist, I feel there is little that I can offer to guide what has become a manufacturing company." Furthermore, he criticized the constraints imposed by the Sarbanes-Oxley Act, passed by Congress in 2002 in an effort to restore investor confidence and prevent abuses in corporate financial practices, on his role in the company as both chairman and primary investor. Clark began selling his shares in the company in 2008, offloading a total of 1.4 million shares by April 2009. After Shutterfly, Clark chose not to be involved in business pursuits. Instead, he chose to focus on philanthropy and environmental activism. One project he funded was a nonprofit organization that worked to increase people's awareness of issues involving the world's oceans.

SEE ALSO *Andreessen, Marc.; Microsoft Corp.; Netscape Communications Corp..*

BIBLIOGRAPHY

Byrnes, Nanette. "Jim Clark—Clipped Wings at Shutterfly." *Bloomberg Businessweek,* January 22, 2007. Available from http://www.businessweek.com/magazine/content/07_04/b4018051.htm.

Creswell, Julie. "What the Heck Is Healtheon?" *Fortune,* February 21, 2000.

Dunlap, Charlotte. "5 Biggest Investors: Jim Clark—The Man with the Midas Touch—Integral to the Launch of Three Billion-Dollar Start-Up Companies." *Computer Reseller News,* September 20, 1999.

Lashinsky, Adam, Oliver Ryan, and Patricia Neering. "The Birth of the Web." *Fortune,* July 25, 2005. Available from http://money.cnn.com/magazines/fortune/fortune_archive/2005/07/25/8266639/index.htm.

Lewis, Michael. *The New New Thing: A Silicon Valley Story.* New York: W. W. Norton, 1999.

Little, Candace M. "The Super Highway Facing the Digitized World Full Speed Ahead." *Utah Business,* June 2010. Available from http://www.thefreelibrary.com/The+super+highway+facing+the+digitized+world+full+speed+ahead.-a0230885637.

"Netscape Pioneers Back Startup." *The Business Review,* November 12, 2001. General OneFile (A80605752).

Taft, Darryl K. "The Men Who Took Down Microsoft." *Computer Reseller News,* June 26, 2000.

CLOUD COMPUTING

By the late 2000s online technology had progressed to the point where software could be easily uploaded through servers and accessed by any user with the necessary clearance and connection speed. Online businesses took advantage of this opportunity to provide applications that did not need to be permanently installed on local hardware, but instead accessed through Internet connections whenever and wherever needed. This was the beginning of the cloud computing industry.

The term "cloud computing" appears to have originated with some basic textbook examples of the Internet, which often portrayed the Internet as a cloud-like shape in which various components floated. It was an ideal metaphor for the new branches of products and services, which could be offered by businesses through online connections. By 2011, it was possible to offer an entire virtual server or a virtual data center through a cloud.

DEVELOPMENTAL HISTORY

The concept of cloud computing began originally with John McCarthy, who in the 1960s predicted the need for computers to be organized as a public utility. The idea continued sporadically until the early 1990s, when it was reborn as grid computing, a system where computer power was relayed where needed in the same way an electrical grid worked. Before long, providers and new online businesses began to realize that data could be distributed in a similar way.

The 1990s also saw the rise of Virtual Private Networks, or VPNs, in the telecommunication industry. VPNs were based on the allocation of resources to the proper areas for the most efficient result possible, a complex form of load balancing. Developers began to realize that, if they could allow data to flow efficiently from servers, it would be possible for many activities to be completed within an online framework. The primary problems were speed and space, but rapidly evolving technology began to offer solutions.

COMMERCIAL INTEREST

In 1998, the company VMware was founded: the business focused on software that made virtualization possible. Virtualization, or using the Internet for tasks once relegated to console-bound programs and separated hardware, was considered an important precursor to cloud computing and eventually a step into cloud computing acceptance. Companies soon found the advantages in accessing computer profiles, data logs, and document applications through Internet connections from any computer station. In 1999, Salesforce.com became one of the first acknowledged adopters of cloud computing technology. The e-tailer used cloud computing to offer enterprise applications for businesses through a basic Web site interface.

Throughout the early 2000s virtualization and basic forms of cloud computing developed. Amazon.com was one of the first to launch a platform offering more advanced cloud capabilities to interested businesses in

2006, known as Amazon Web Services through what was dubbed the Elastic Compute Cloud. Amazon.com had been working on this project for years to help solve its internal scalability issues and quickly realized its profitability. Throughout the 2000s Amazon.com continued to update its Web Services, offering more efficient data or product management applications.

Around the same time, the first payment systems for cloud computing had become standardized. While users were used to paying providers a monthly fee for their Internet service with some variation in data limitations, the same model did not work for cloud computing services. Instead, cloud providers charged for usage time (by the hour) for licensing fees and for gigabytes stored in provider servers.

GROWING APPLICATIONS

While Amazon.com was instrumental in commercializing cloud computing, especially for businesses, Google was responsible for bringing the concept to a larger audience with Google Docs. An amalgam of Google Spreadsheets, the acquired software Writely, and the acquired XL2Web product, Google Docs was released in 2007. It offered the no-charge ability to read a variety of different documents in an online environment and became very popular amongst individual users. By 2010, it worked with all file types and provided a free gigabyte of storage. In 2008, Google released the Google App Engine, which allowed users to have their apps run on Google infrastructure but without the full access that Amazon.com allowed.

By 2008, cloud computing products were becoming increasingly common. Virtualization software like VoIP (Voice over Internet Protocol) for business phone networks had become widely accepted. The Eucalyptus platform was introduced and was an open-source tool for creating and running private clouds. OpenNebula, released soon after, offered similar services.

In 2009, Microsoft joined the game with its Windows Azure project. In 2010, VMware continued to be a major player through its Cloud Foundry offering, an open-source platform as a service tool that allowed users to build, deploy, and run their cloud apps through Java, Ruby, and other major development formats. Amazon.com made news by offering a VM Import tool as part of its Web services that allowed users to run a VMware virtual machine. Analysts predicted this was only the beginning of the complex solutions cloud computing could offer.

ISSUES AND TRENDS

As cloud technology entered the 2010s and continued to evolve, problems with widespread application emerged. One issue was space. Cloud computing worked as long as the provider had excellent servers with a significant amount of room for new data. Microsoft, for example, ran hundreds of thousands of physical servers in six data centers worldwide by 2010. But smaller companies could not hope to compete with those numbers and could not support anywhere near the same number of clients. The solution was private clouds, or services that businesses created in-house and offered through their own servers so that all employees on the intranet could use them.

Another issue was security. Many users were content to run their simple applications through a cloud but worried that their data could be lost or stolen. Cloud computing by nature does not have the same security that a physical program bound to a single computer has. Cloud protection was frequently based on provider server security, out of the hands of clients. Not only was data theft possible, but a server malfunction could put entire clouds offline for multiple businesses. While uses for the technology grew, developers realized that even more work was necessary to keep service quality high.

SEE ALSO *Software; Web 2.0.*

BIBLIOGRAPHY

Babcock, Charles. "Top 5 Cloud Computing Predictions for 2011." *Information Week,* January 8, 2011. Available from http://www.informationweek.com/news/smb/hardware_software/228801016?pgno=1.

Bartels, Angela. "Open Cloud Computing: History of Open Source Coding and the Open Cloud." *Rack Space,* June 8, 2011. Available from http://www.rackspace.com/cloud/blog/2011/06/08/open-cloud-computing-history-of-open-source-coding-and-the-open-cloud.

"Cloud Computing and Google Docs." *CloudTweaks,* December 18, 2011. Available from http://www.cloudtweaks.com/2010/12/cloud-computing-and-google-docs.

"A History of Cloud Computing." *CloudTweaks,* February 9, 2011. Available from http://www.cloudtweaks.com/2011/02/a-history-of-cloud-computing.

"The History of Cloud Computing." *MSDN UK Team Blog,* July 26, 2011. Available from http://blogs.msdn.com/b/ukmsdn/archive/2011/07/26/the-history-of-cloud-computing.aspx.

Sullivan, Tom. "Cloud Computing–A Brief History." *EarthLink Cloud,* September 22, 2011. Available from http://www.earthlinkcloud.com/2011/09/cloud-computing-%E2%80%93-a-brief-history.

CNET NETWORKS INC.

CNET Networks Inc. was founded in 1993 by Shelby Bonnie and Halsey Minor as a new media company designed to provide technology and e-commerce news and information across several media, including the Internet, television, radio, and print. It was acquired in a $1.8

billion deal in 2008 by CBS Corp. and its properties became part of CBS Interactive, the television network's online content subsidiary.

CNET Networks is particularly notable in the world of Web-based firms because it was one of the earliest Internet ventures to become profitable.

Despite the CBS acquisition, the CNET name continues to live on, primarily through the technology Web site Cnet.com, which acts as the online portal to the operations of the former CNET Networks. The main CNET Web site publishes articles, reviews, and blog posts about consumer electronics and other types of technology, and also provides software downloads, how-to information, and links to other CNET Web sites like CNET.TV. CNET has over 80,000 free downloads of software patches, games, mobile apps, and other types of software. The site also provides access to Cnetshopper.com, an online tool for finding the best price from e-commerce retailers that was founded in 1998.

Another CNET property, CNET.TV, began by producing technology-themed television shows for various TV channels, such as the Sci-Fi Channel and the USA Network. In the 2010s, CNET.TV provides on-demand videos and shows, including original content, via the Web.

CNET Content Solutions, formerly known as CNET Data Services, plays a central role in providing information that drives computer and electronics sales and distribution channels. In 2011, CNET Content Solutions had content on more than five million technology products in 15 languages and worked with over 2,100 e-commerce partners, including CDW, Computacenter, Dabs.com, Dell, Hewlett-Packard, Insight, Microsoft, OfficeMax, PC World Business, and Tech Data.

FOUNDED IN 1992 BY HALSEY MINOR

CNET Inc. was founded in San Francisco in 1992 by 27-year-old Halsey Minor, who led the company as its chairman and CEO until 2000. In March 2000 CNET's vice chairman Shelby Bonnie succeeded Minor as CEO, with Minor remaining as chairman. In 2001, Bonnie became chairman and CEO, with Minor becoming chairman emeritus. As a managing director of venture capital firm Tiger Management in 1992, Bonnie was the first major investor in CNET. In 1993, he became the company's third employee and was its chief financial officer and chief operating officer. Prior to founding CNET, Minor was an investment banker and publisher.

By 1994, the company was attempting to launch a new cable network, C\NET: The Computer Network. It planned to start with a single show, called C\NET Central, that would run for several hours over a weekend. The start-up cable network received a significant investment from Microsoft cofounder Paul Allen in 1994, and in 1995, USA Networks became a minority investor. At the time a competing computer channel, Jones Computer Network, reached 1.5 million homes, and Microsoft was planning to launch the PC Channel in association with cable operator Tele-Communications Inc. (TCI). USA Networks agreed to show C\NET programming on its USA and Sci-Fi cable channels.

The president of C\NET Networks was Kevin Wendle, who was an original member of the Fox Broadcasting team and an Emmy Award-winning producer. In 1995, the network was developing two shows in addition to "C\NET Central." One was to be called "The Web" and focus on the Internet, while the other would consist of multimedia software and product reviews. The company also began developing a Web site that would be a leading source of information about computer technology and digital media. By mid-1995, C\NET Online had more than 43,000 registered users. Its lead advertisers were Hewlett-Packard, IBM, and MCI. The demand for online advertising was such that CNET created a separate department to provide data to potential advertisers. Within four months the number of employees working on the Web site increased from 6 to more than 85.

The national exposure that resulted from the weekly airing of C\NET Central on the USA and Sci-Fi channels helped to boost traffic at CNET's Web sites. The company's flagship Web site was CNET Online (Cnet.com), which was getting nine million hits a day in mid-1996. It offered technology news, game reviews, technical support, bulletin boards, and product reviews, as well as an online radio component that delivered audio. Visitors to CNET Online also could view C\NET Central's studio. In addition to CNET Online, the company also operated Shareware.com, an archive of more than 170,000 free software titles, and Search.com, a Web site that gathered search engine programs that indexed Web sites.

NEW ONLINE PROPERTIES

CNET went public in 1996. Later that year the company added more Web sites and scaled back plans to operate a 24-hour cable channel, deciding instead to stick with limited cable TV programming and to focus on the Internet. CNET's newly launched Web sites included News.com, a source of technology news; Download.com, a library of software demo titles; and BuyDirect.com, a site that allowed registering, purchasing, and downloading software.

In 1997, CNET launched Snap! Online, a combined online service, directory, and tutorial. Challenging America Online, which then had 12 million subscribers, Snap!

included a comprehensive CD-ROM tutorial for first-time Internet users. The free service also organized Internet content into channels for news, sports, entertainment, and other topics. In 1998, Snap! attracted a $5.9 million investment from NBC, which had an option to acquire a 60% interest in the Web portal for an additional $38 million.

CNET continued to develop its e-commerce strategy in 1999 with the acquisition of NetVentures Inc. and its ShopBuilder (Shopbuilder.com) online store creation system for $12 million. It planned to help resellers of unbranded computer systems, or "white boxes," build their own online stores and benefit from CNET's marketing clout. In August 1999, CNET began Store.com, a store-hosting service for small and midsize merchants.

In early 1999, CNET began providing online computer buyer guides to America Online. Around this time CNET reorganized its Web sites into an efficient e-commerce platform. Shopper.com, News.com, Builder.com, and Computers.com were reconfigured into ten content areas. The company's main page, Cnet.com, focused on searching and included archived articles, editors' picks, the Snap portal, searches from Inktomi, and links to retailers. In May 1999, CNET strengthened its search engine capabilities by acquiring Sumo Inc., an Internet Service directory, for $29 million in stock. Later in 1999, CNET acquired Internet search firm SavvySearch Ltd. for $22 million.

CNET stepped up its branding efforts in 1999 as well. The company started out the year with an advertising budget for a national branding campaign estimated at $40–$45 million. Then, putting growth before profits, CEO Halsey Minor announced in mid-1999 he would spend $100 million on advertising to build CNET's brand and make it synonymous with technology. The new national branding campaign featured the tagline: "CNET: The source for computers and technology."

ACQUISITIONS AND MERGERS: 2000

CNET continued to be active in broadcast media in 1999 and 2000. In fall 1999, CNET News.com debuted on CNBC, and the company launched the CNET Investor Channel. In January 2000, CNET formed an alliance with AMFM Inc. to create CNET Radio, the first U.S. all-tech radio format. That same month CNET spent $700 million to acquire comparative shopper mySimon.com. In March, the company changed its name from CNET Inc. to CNET Networks Inc.

In July, the merger of two major technology portals, CNET and ZDNet, was announced, with CNET acquiring Ziff-Davis Inc. With 16.6 million unduplicated users, CNET Networks became the eighth-largest Internet property, according to Media Metrix. The sale of Ziff-Davis Inc. and ZDNet to CNET was completed in October for approximately $1.6 billion. Earlier in the year Ziff-Davis Inc., ZDNet's parent company, had sold its Ziff-Davis Publishing business, which included computer magazines *PC Magazine, PC Computing,* and *PC Week.* Also not included in the sale to CNET was ZDTV, which had been sold to Paul Allen's Vulcan Ventures. In addition to the Web portal ZDNet.com, CNET gained *Computer Shopper* magazine, the SmartPlanet online service, and an equity stake in Red Herring Communications. Japanese software giant Softbank Corp., which owned 50% of Ziff-Davis, would have a 17% interest in the new company.

However, in 2001 Ziff-Davis Media reached a deal with CNET and ZDNet to buy back some of the URLs it had lost in the 2000 acquisition, and ZDNet itself was redesigned as a publication for business executives.

The company appeared committed to making more acquisitions in the 2000s. In April it acquired a 90% interest in the technology industry research firm TechRepublic Inc. from the Gartner Group for $23 million. In 2004, CNET acquired Webshots, a leading photography Web site, in a $70 million deal, but later sold the property to American Greetings for only $45 million.

CNET experiments with other media faltered in the early 2000s. In 2001, it expanded its a technology-themed radio talk program to air on a San Francisco radio station (KNEW 910 AM), WBPS 890 AM in Boston, and XM Satellite Radio through an arrangement with radio powerhouse Clear Channel. However, the shows did not attract a large enough audience and they were canceled in 2003.

In March 2007, CNET Networks rolled out BNET, a news and technology information site geared towards business professionals. The site included various content for business professionals in all areas of their lives, as well as white papers, case studies, blogs, and other media.

CEO DEPARTS OVER STOCK OPTIONS ISSUE

In 2006, CNET announced that Shelby Bonnie, one of the cofounders of the company and its chairman and chief executive officer, had resigned. Neil Ashe, who had been the head of corporate strategy and development, took over as CEO, and Jarl Mohr became chairman.

The resignation came about after a committee appointed by CNET's board of directors found that some stock options had been backdated. While the company determined that Bonnie and other executives had not engaged in any deliberate wrongdoing, they were still held responsible and Bonnie stepped down. The incident occurred during a period when dozens of companies were being accused of backdating stock options in order to give employees a greater payout. Bonnie went on to found Whiskey Media, another online media company.

ACQUISITION BY CBS INTERACTIVE

In 2008, after fighting off an attempt by a consortium of investment funds led by hedge fund Jana Partners to take over CNET's board of directors, the company agreed to an acquisition by CBS.

Under the terms of the deal, CBS agreed to pay $11.50 a share, which was a 44% increase over the closing price of CNET's stock before the deal was announced, for a total value of $1.8 billion. CBS hired Quincy Smith, formerly an investment banker specializing in media and technology, to lead the interactive unit in 2006.

Since the acquisition CNET has worked within the framework of CBS Interactive, combining its technology and business-focused content and data with CBS's other Web sites that cover entertainment, sports, and news. CBS Interactive is led by Jim Lanzone, formerly the CEO of Clicker.

BIBLIOGRAPHY

Andrews, Whit. "NBC Buys into CNET's Web Hub, Snap." *Internet World,* June 15, 1998.

Atwood, Brett. "C Net Sets Sights on Cable-TV Market." *Billboard,* April 6, 1996.

Chandrasekaran, Rajiv. "Free New Service Aims to Make Direct Internet Access Easy as AOL." *Washington Post,* September 23, 1997.

"CNET Goes for Broke." *Business Week,* July 12, 1999.

"CNET Pulls Plug on Radio Program." *Silicon Valley/San Jose Business Journal,* January 16, 2003. Available from http://www.bizjournals.com/sanjose/stories/2003/01/13/daily60.html.

"CNet's Paper Chase."; *Forbes,* June 3, 1996.

"CNET Spins a Wider Web." *Business Week,* March 27, 2000.

"CNET, Ziff-Davis Revise Content Deal." *CNET News,* January 14, 2001. Available from http://news.cnet.com/CNET,-Ziff-Davis-revise-content-deal/2110-1023_3-251452.html.

"Halsey Minor's Major Plans." *Business Week,* July 26, 1999.

Kane, Margaret. "CBS to Buy CNET Networks." *CNET News,* May 15, 2008. Available from http://news.cnet.com/8301-10784_3-9944882-7.html.

Musil, Steven, and Jeff Pelline. "CNET Buys Rival Ziff-Davis for $1.6 Billion." *CNET News,* July 19, 2000. Available from http://news.cnet.com/2100-1023-243338.html.

Paul, Franklin. "Activist CNET Shareholder Drops Proxy Fight." *Reuters,* June 19, 2008. Available from http://www.reuters.com/article/2008/06/19/us-cnet-idUSN1932010620080619.

Schwartz, Matthew. "CNET Networks Rolls Out BNET, Web Site Targeting Managers." *B to B Online,* March 1, 2007. Available from http://www.btobonline.com/apps/pbcs.dll/article?AID=/20070301/FREE/70301001/1078#seenit.

Steinert-Threlkeld, Tom. "Electronoclast: If You Can't Beat 'Em." *Inter@ctive Week,* July 24, 2000.

Strauss, Robert. "Networked TV: Cable Shows Take the Lead in Connecting Viewers to Computers." *Washington Post,* February 12, 1997.

"Tech Sites Merge as Net Eats Computer Publishing." *Communications Today,* July 20, 2000.

COBOL

One of the oldest programming languages still in active use, COBOL (COmmon Business Oriented Language), was designed to run a variety of business applications on both mainframe computers and desktop systems manufactured by different companies. It is one of the first high-level computer languages, meaning that it is much closer to human language than the machine language through which computer hardware accepts commands. High-level languages eventually get translated to a primary, numeric machine language consisting of zeros and ones. As its name implies, COBOL was intended to be "common," or nonproprietary. This meant that the programming language was compatible among different kinds of computers from different manufacturers.

COBOL has several advantages. One is the language's ability to process data. It is especially valuable when simple processes—such as calculating percentages or performing basic addition and subtraction—must be applied to large batches of information. Another one of COBOL's strengths is its simplicity. Due to the fact that it is very readable and easy to understand, it is difficult to hide malicious or destructive computer code within COBOL and easy to spot and correct programming errors. Finally, because COBOL is capable of running on many different kinds of computers, it is portable.

DOMINATING THE INDUSTRY

COBOL was developed by members of the Conference on Data Systems Languages (CODASYL), a consortium comprising representatives from industry, major universities, and the U.S. government charged with creating a standardized business language that could be used on a wide variety of computers. Released in 1959, COBOL was based on a prototype created by computer programmer Grace Murray Hopper. Early applications for COBOL included payroll and budget management, along with property tracking. COBOL was quickly adopted by several federal agencies, as well as the private corporate sector. (FORTRAN, another high-level computer language, was developed for scientists and engineers in the 1950s.) After its initial release, COBOL was updated several times. The first update occurred in 1962 and included such improvements as a report-writing feature that made the language especially popular.

COBOL was the mainstay of commercial business data processing applications throughout the 1970s and 1980s, and the American National Standards Institute (ANSI) issued COBOL standards revisions in 1974 and 1985. When the software business emerged as an industry in the mid-1970s, COBOL was the leading language used for applications, most of which were accounting and statistical programs. Compatibility among machines became more important in the 1980s as the number of computer manufacturers grew, along with the variety of models being produced. Even as other programming languages entered the market, namely C++, an object-oriented language, COBOL dominated.

In the 1990s, COBOL was challenged by Java, a programming language designed for use on the Internet, especially for interactive Web sites. However, since huge amounts of code already existed in COBOL, the majority of government and business entities stuck with COBOL for their business applications. As the twentieth century drew to a close, it was estimated that approximately 80% of the 300 billion lines of computer code used around the world was in COBOL. Programmers at the time focused on the Y2K bug, a software glitch that caused a widespread panic. People all over the globe were afraid that computers—and everything run by computers, from air travel to banking to online stores—would fail when the year changed from 1999 to 2000 because COBOL programming used two numbers instead of four to indicate the year. Although some computer applications were affected at the time, major problems were averted.

ADAPTING TO THE FUTURE

The early 2000s saw an increased demand in COBOL due to e-commerce integration. According to Jim Duggan, vice president of Gartner Group, as quoted by msnbc.com, "The driving force is older bricks-and-mortar companies such as Barnes & Noble that have a huge installed base of company applications, written mostly in COBOL, which must be integrated with the Web storefronts." Growing numbers of technology companies offered custom-written Web-based COBOL applications for e-commerce needs, including online public stores, ordering tools, and inventory management. Many companies allowed customers to access data, such as the part number and price of an item, on mainframe computers running COBOL programs. Finding ways to enable COBOL to interface with hypertext markup language, used to create pages on the World Wide Web, became increasingly important.

By the mid-2000s most new COBOL programs were written to support applications that already existed on a mainframe computer. Critics said that COBOL was an antiquated technology. While it remained effective for batch operations, they claimed, it did not facilitate Web-based front ends or interactive applications. Nonetheless, despite competition from other programming languages, such as Visual Basic, Java, and JavaScript, COBOL remained the second most used programming language in 2006, reported Robert L. Mitchell in *Computerworld.* However, this was due in large part to the fact that many companies considered replacing COBOL to be too expensive and too difficult.

The future of COBOL appeared to be secure in the 2010s. The ubiquitous programming language continued to be used for business transactions conducted all over the world. According to a Micro Focus article, there were still around 220 billion lines of COBOL code in active use in January 2011. As an example, the article pointed out that "COBOL systems are responsible for transporting up to 72,000 shipping containers, caring for 60 million patients, processing 80% of point-of-sales transactions, and connecting 500 million mobile phone users." With such a pervasive presence, COBOL was expected to be in use for many years to come.

SEE ALSO *C (Programming Language); FORTRAN; Programming Language; UNIX.*

BIBLIOGRAPHY

Anthes, Gary. "Cobol Coders: Going, Going, Gone?" *Computerworld,* October 9, 2006. Available from http://www.computerworld.com/s/article/266228/Cobol_Coders_Going_Going_Gone.

Copeland, Lee. "Webifying Mainframe Apps: Lessons from the Field." *Computerworld,* January 3, 2000. Available from http://www.computerworld.com/s/article/40501/Webifying_Mainframe_Apps_Lessons_from_the_Field.

"E-commerce Could Give New Boost to COBOL." *msnbc.com,* January 26, 2000.

Glass, Robert. "COBOL—a Contradiction and an Enigma." *Communications of the ACM,* September 1, 1997.

Hall, Mark. "Save CBL, Don't ABBRVI8." *Computerworld,* April 28, 2008. Available from http://www.computerworld.com/s/article/317221/Save_CBL_Don_t_ABBRVI8.

Micro Focus. "COBOL Futures: The Next 50 Years." Rockville, MD, September 1, 2011. Available from http://www.microfocus.com/downloads/cobol-futures-the-next-50-years-93996.aspx.

Mitchell, Robert L. "Cobol: Not Dead Yet." *Computerworld,* October 9, 2006. Available from http://www.computerworld.com/s/article/266156/Cobol_Not_Dead_Yet.

Nickerson, Robert C. *Fundamentals of Structured COBOL.* New York: HarperCollins, 1991.

Radcliff, Deborah. "Moving COBOL to the Web—Safely." *Computerworld,* May 1, 2000. Available from http://www.computerworld.com.au/article/95628/security_alert_moving_cobol_web_safely/#closeme.

COMMERCE ONE/ PERFECT COMMERCE

A pioneer in e-commerce in the late 1990s, Commerce One facilitated business-to-business (B2B) e-commerce exchanges that allowed companies to do business via the World Wide Web or other electronic platforms. The idea behind these exchanges, or marketplaces, was to cut costs for all parties involved by creating a single place where buyers, sellers, distributors, and suppliers could complete commerce transactions. Commerce One exchanges, based on the firm's Market Site Portal software, offered auction capabilities, which let clients collect offers for their merchandise to get the best possible prices. Similarly, reverse auctions allowed businesses to solicit competitive bids for products and services they were interested in purchasing. Commerce One's BuySite procurement software suite was geared more toward creating private supply chain sites for individual companies. This technology also allowed buyers to view various supplier catalogs online and complete secure transactions electronically.

BUSINESS MODEL

Founded in 1994 as DistriVision Development Corp. by Tom Gonzales and his son, the firm first focused on selling office automation software to banks. By the time Mark Hoffman, cofounder of Sybase Inc., was named president and CEO of DistriVision in 1996, the company had also moved into multimedia catalog development. Hoffman secured more than $7 million in financial backing and brought in new managers, some from Sybase, to steer DistriVision's transformation into Commerce One the next year, creating a firm that sold products and services for B2B electronic commerce. Judith Mottl wrote in *InternetWeek,* Hoffman's "idea was to use DistriVision's supply-chain software to move the procurement process to the Web, linking buyers and sellers to a circle of exchanges and marketplaces that would automate, simplify, and speed business-to-business transactions."

Commerce One made its money by licensing its software, levying service and network charges, and retaining a stake (typically 50%) in the exchanges it created. Market Site Portals cost anywhere from $500,000 to more than $2 million, depending on the amount of work involved in putting catalogs online, creating search engines, and training employees. Once the site was up and running, the company or companies operating the exchange charged those who used the site—suppliers, distributors, sellers, and buyers—a fee for each transaction completed. Commerce One received a portion of each of these fees. For these fees to amount to profits for Commerce One, suppliers had to be willing to complete a high number of transactions at these sites. Therefore, in an effort to promote B2B marketplace use across the globe, the company also required its Market Site Portal clients to join the Global Trading Web, which by mid-2000 linked 58 B2B online marketplaces.

RAPID GROWTH

The company went public in 1999. It experienced intense growth that year, reaching sales of $33 million, up from $2 million the previous year. The number of employees grew from roughly 500 to 1,300 over the same time period. Lending credibility to the upstart was its ability to sign on customers like automobile maker General Motors, which ended up holding a 20% stake in Commerce One, and BellSouth, a telecommunications firm. Commerce One also was busy forging partnerships with firms like Microsoft. In fact, Commerce One was one of the few e-commerce upstarts to use Microsoft's Windows operating system, rather than Unix, as its main platform. Since Microsoft was looking for ways to extend its reach into electronic commerce, Commerce One's decision to use Windows was of particular importance to the software giant.

At its peak in early 2000, Commerce One was worth over $20 billion, with its proprietary Supplier Relationship Management (SRM) software bringing in all of the company's revenue for the year. With approximately 4,000 employees in 80 offices worldwide, Commerce One planned to build a 780,000-square-foot campus in Dublin, Ireland, to serve as its headquarters. That year, Commerce One concentrated on the development of more than 100 commerce exchanges for its clients.

Faced with increased competition from rivals Oracle Corp. and Ariba Inc., Commerce One continued to develop new technology and forge deals that would increase the comprehensiveness of its suite of products. For example, the firm formed a licensing joint venture with Germany's SAP AG, a leading developer of software applications that allowed enterprises to manage their resources electronically. In September, Commerce One unveiled an upgrade to its auction software that expanded the number of languages and currencies it supported. It also allowed related items to be grouped together for an auction that accepted bids for the entire grouping, as well as for individual items.

One of Commerce One's largest exchange projects in 2000 was Covisint, the online marketplace for the worldwide automotive industry launched by Ford Motor Co., General Motors, and DaimlerChrysler. By December, Ford and GM each ended up with a 7% stake in Commerce One, while Commerce One received a 2% stake in Covisint. However, the B2B exchange model, like many others, would not live up to promises of significant savings.

FINANCIAL UPHEAVAL

In September 2000, Commerce One paid $1.4 billion for AppNet, Inc., a provider of end-to-end Internet professional services. With AppNet's solutions capabilities, Commerce One expected to reduce the time to bring e-marketplaces online. The acquisition, however, was not well received by many investors. *Information Age* reported that the deal "raised eyebrows: not just because Commerce

One was paying well above the market value but because the purchase pitched the company directly against some of its services partners." To many analysts, this deal marked the beginning of the end.

Almost all e-marketplaces and B2B e-commerce companies took a hit in the early 2000s due to an economic downturn that led to the dot-com bust of 2001. Commerce One was no exception, and it sank rapidly. During one quarter in 2001, the company lost $2 billion. Critics charged that Commerce One reacted too slowly to the industry's decline by not laying off employees early enough and by hanging onto its expensive Silicon Valley real estate too long. In May 2002, COO Dennis Jones left the company, followed by CFO Peter Pervere, and Hoffman was left to reevaluate Commerce One's future. SAP, no longer confident in Commerce One's financial viability, withdrew from its merger deal, leaving the foundering company with no capital. By mid-2002, Commerce One stock was trading at less than one dollar.

Hoffman made a last-ditch effort in 2003 to rescue Commerce One by turning away from e-marketplace offerings and becoming a Web services company. Through a new product called Conductor, Commerce One provided software that linked internal systems with external partners. Unfortunately, Conductor was in direct competition with similar products from IBM and BEA Systems Inc. that had been on the market longer. In December 2003, Covisint terminated its relationship with Commerce One, and it sold the B2B exchange and Web portal to Compuware Corp. in February 2004.

BANKRUPTCY AND RESURRECTION

It became clear to Hoffman in early 2004 that Conductor would not be able to pull the company out of its financial hole. "At that time," reported Eric Lai in the *San Francisco Business Times,* "Hoffman brought on two funds, ComVest Investment Partners of New York and DCC Ventures of Minneapolis. Rather than taking shares in the firm, the funds became its largest creditors. That allowed ComVest and DCC to acquire the long-neglected SRM division." In October 2004, Hoffman resigned as CEO, and Commerce One declared bankruptcy. Two months later, 39 Internet-related patents owned by the company were bought by JGR Acquisitions for $15.5 million in a bankruptcy court auction.

Filing Chapter 11 bankruptcy gave Commerce One the opportunity to start fresh as Commerce One LLC, a privately held company backed by ComVest and DCC. Mark Pecoraro, who had worked for Hoffman at Sybase, was named CEO, and 30 employees were hired. Concentrating on SRM software, Commerce One LLC attracted both new and former customers in 2005.

Within a year, Commerce One had attracted the attention of the world's largest supplier of on-demand SRM solutions, Perfect Commerce Inc. Perfect Commerce, which provided connectivity to trading partners through the Open Supplier Network (SM) (OSN(SM)), boasted more than 500 clients and 165,000 users and had offices in the metropolitan Kansas City area, Texas, California, Nevada, and France. Perfect Commerce acquired Commerce One in February 2006, integrating all of Commerce One's operations under the name Perfect Commerce, led by CEO Sandy Kemper.

SEE ALSO *Business-to-Business (B2B) E-commerce; Platforms.*

BIBLIOGRAPHY

"Commerce One Completes Its Final Transaction." *Information Age,* December 10, 2006. Available from http://www.information-age.com/article-archive/291346/commerce-one-completes-its-final-transaction.thtml.

Gilbert, Alorie. "A Second Act for Commerce One." *CNET.com,* July 16, 2002. Available from http://news.cnet.com/A-second-act-for-Commerce-One/2008-1082_3-944197.html .

Greene, Jay. "Microsoft's Little Bro." *BusinessWeek Online,* December 11, 2000. Available from http://www.businessweek.com/2000/00_50/b3711044.htm?scriptFramed.

Gross, Grant. "Commerce One Patents Auctioned for $15.5 Million." *NetworkWorld,* December 13, 2004. Available from http://www.networkworld.com/news/2004/121304commerceone.html.

Lai, Eric. "Commerce One Rises from Dot-ashes." *San Francisco Business Times,* March 5, 2005. Available from http://www.bizjournals.com/eastbay/stories/2005/03/07/story1.html.

Mottl, Judith N. "Commerce One Rides Internet Wave—Supply Chain Software Provider Benefits from Growing Demand for Internet Exchanges." *InternetWeek,* May 15, 2000.

"Perfect Commerce Acquires Commerce One." *PR Newswire,* February 7, 2006. Available from http://www.prnewswire.com/news-releases/perfect-commerce-acquires-commerce-one-55231257.html.

"Q&A with Commerce One's Mark Hoffman." *BusinessWeek Online,* December 11, 2000. Available from http://www.businessweek.com/2000/00_50/b3711049.htm.

Riggs, Brian. "Wide Open E-commerce." *LAN Times,* August 1997.

COMMODITIZATION

Commoditization is the dilution of a market sector's internal differentiation and competitive nuances in favor of a mass market where price alone determines consumer behavior. In simpler terms, a product or service is considered commoditized when it becomes widely available and is interchangeable with that of another company. The industry's mode of competition thus moves away from product or service innovation and toward alternative methods of building value.

As industries mature, barriers to market entry gradually erode, competition intensifies, and the market becomes saturated, forcing prices downward. In the eye of the consumer, there is increasing parity among a market sector's products and services, and building customer loyalty becomes all the more challenging for companies. As a product or service within a market sector reaches the commoditization point, the perceived distinction between brands vanishes altogether, and customers base their purchasing decisions solely on price. This in turn leads to a pricing war that wreaks havoc on profit margins. To combat commoditization, companies generally seek out new operating models, bundle services to add value, or diversify or specialize their products in order to capture a niche market within a broader market. If all else fails, firms may simply cut realized or potential losses by exiting the market.

COMMODITIZATION IN THE DIGITAL AGE

The Internet's impact on commoditization was monumental. Initially, the Internet allowed companies to avoid commoditization of their products and services by opening new areas of competition. For fear of losing market share to rivals quicker to adapt, companies shifted their business plans very rapidly in an effort to be among the first to capitalize on the possibilities afforded by the Internet.

In the 1990s and 2000s, companies were able to distinguish themselves and stay a step ahead of industry commoditization by augmenting their brick-and-mortar operations with online operations. What resulted was another form of commoditization that was accelerated by the emergence of the World Wide Web as a medium of commerce that made transactions, comparison shopping, and bidding both quick and virtually effortless.

Besides influencing how the general business sector operated, the Internet revolutionized commoditization in the area of information technology. Analysts agreed that computer hardware commoditized in the 1980s due to, according to technology consultant Rob Landley, "the rise of PC clones replacing integrated proprietary systems with interchangeable parts available from multiple sources." From that point, the rate at which information technology evolved was closely matched by the speed of product and service commoditization. When an innovative new product or service was hyped as the next great thing, it soon reached its peak price. Competitors then began to offer copycat products or services, driving down prices and sparking a war of innovation in which engineers developed new, technologically advanced features in an effort to differentiate their products or services from clones.

After a while, consumers lost interest in those "new and improved" features, and sales dropped. What followed was a new product that stole most of the market—the replacement of videocassette recorders by DVD players, for example—and drove the original product or service out of the market completely. E-commerce expedited the entire process.

Commoditization had always been a point of contention in economic systems, and e-commerce encouraged even more debate in the twenty-first century. Traditionally, how commoditization was dealt with largely depended on the nature of the industry and the mode of competition therein. Commoditization was less likely to affect markets that required more capital investment to enter, such as heavy manufacturing. Yet even those industries were challenged by burgeoning online marketplaces. In the ever-changing field of information technology, prudent companies, wrote Mitch Halpern and Vas Vasiliadis, would "create (and regularly revise) action plans to deal with loss of exclusivity granted by patents or intellectual property" in order to deal with commoditization, which inevitably happened with all high-tech products and services. As it had since its inception, the Internet continued to play a significant role in commoditization as consumers not only researched, but also purchased more products and services online.

SEE ALSO *Channel Conflict/Harmony; Channel Transparency.*

BIBLIOGRAPHY

Boomer, Gary L. "Boomer's Blueprint: Avoid Commoditization, Increase Value." *Accounting Today,* November 27, 2007. Infotrac.

Carr, Nicholas G. "IT Doesn't Matter.'" *Harvard Business Review* 81, no. 5 (May 2003): 41–49.

Glen, Paul. "IT Leaders: Master the Upcoming Culture Change." *Computerworld,* August 23, 2010. Available from http://www.computerworld.com/s/article/350900/IT_Leaders_Master_the_Upcoming_Culture_Change.

Halpern, Mitch, and Vas Vasiliadis. "Combating 'Technology Commoditization.'" *Intellectual Property & Technology Law Journal* 21, no. 4 (April 2009): 5–7.

King, Julia. "Businesses Weigh Pros and Cons of Web Marketplaces." *Computerworld,* March 13, 2000. Available from http://www.computerworld.com/s/article/41772/Businesses_Weigh_Pros_and_Cons_of_Web_Marketplaces.

Landley, Rob. "The Commoditization Argument for Open Source." Landley.net, August 30, 2011. Available from http://www.landley.net/writing/stuff/commodity.html.

Schmerken, Ivy. "The Challenge: Coping With Commoditization." *Wall Street & Technology,* December 14, 2000. Available from http://www.wallstreetandtech.com/articles/14704647.

Surowiecki, James. "The Commoditization Conundrum." *Slate,* January 30, 1998. Available from http://www.slate.com/articles/arts/the_motley_fool/1998/01/the_commoditization_conundrum.html.

COMMUNICATION PROTOCOLS

In order for e-commerce to take place, computers must be able to communicate with one another. To do so, they must use a language format and rules that each machine understands. Protocols, which can reside in either software or hardware, are the means by which this communication occurs. Protocols ensure that each device understands exactly how information will be sent and received. They define the format in which data will be communicated; whether it will be transmitted in a steady stream or at irregular intervals; the speed in which it will be sent; whether data will be transmitted between two devices at the same time (full duplex) or alternately in turns (half duplex); whether data will be compressed, or reduced into a smaller format during transmission. Protocols also provide a means of ensuring that data sent from one device arrives intact on the receiving end.

OPEN SYSTEMS INTERCONNECT MODEL

The Open Systems Interconnect Model (OSI), created by the International Standards Organization in 1974, provides a solid framework for understanding how communication protocols work. As its name suggests, OSI is a model, not a type of computer program or an actual device. The model was designed so that many different kinds of computer systems could exchange data in a seamless, universal process. The OSI Model divides computer networks into seven different layers: physical, data link, network, transport, session, presentation, and application. Each layer plays a different role in the transmission of information. Many different kinds of protocols can be involved at each layer, and individual protocols can be involved in more than one layer of the model.

The *physical layer* resides at the bottom of the OSI Model. It deals exclusively with the transmission and reception of electronic or mechanical signals (which contain bits of information) between two mediums. This level includes the actual cables and hardware involved in the communication process.

When data is sent over a local area network (LAN)—a network of computers and servers in a specific area, such as within a company—it is often done in packets or chunks known as frames, which conform to the type of network involved. At the *data link layer,* bits of information are changed into frames, such as Ethernet frames. Ethernets are one very common type of way of accessing LANs with PCs and Macintosh computers.

At the *network layer,* the most efficient pathway for the transmission of information between a sender and receiver is determined. This includes different points, called nodes, on the networks involved. At this level, data from one network is relayed to other networks via devices called routers.

Unlike the first three levels of the OSI Model, which are concerned with the movement of information from one node to another, the *transport layer* is responsible for determining the overall integrity of a message. In other words, this level determines that data sent arrives intact on the receiving end. This level also ensures that data is received in a timely manner and in the correct order or sequence. End-to-end communication between the sending and receiving sources is possible at this level. From the transport layer on, the focus is on how information moves between processes or programs, instead of nodes or points on a network.

The *session layer* is where communication links between two network stations originate. They are also managed, and terminated, at this layer. The timing, direction (one-way or two-way), and flow of a connection are controlled at this level. According to *Tech Encyclopedia,* this layer is sometimes unused, particularly when the steps at this level occur at the transport layer.

The translation of data—which includes encryption, decryption, and presentation—is determined at the *presentation layer.* This layer is responsible for taking data from many different systems and putting it into a format that can be read by computers on a network. Like the session layer, the presentation layer is not always used by all protocols.

Finally, the *application layer* involves the management of interactions between users and programs, or between two programs. At this level, files are opened, closed, transferred, and written. Additionally, e-mail messages are sent.

TCP/IP

There are scores of different communication protocols. Those that work behind the scenes as people engage in e-commerce are used on the Internet. In order for networks to share data, the Internet relies on a collection of protocols often referred to as the TCP/IP model, short for Transmission Control Protocol/Internet Protocol. They are used when information is transmitted between a host computer (the one containing information) and the remote users that obtain information from the host. The TCP/IP model can be compared to the OSI model. However, beyond physical networks, it relies upon only four layers to send and receive information: data link, network, transport, and application.

Among the most recognizable TCP/IP protocols are Hypertext Markup Language (HTML), used for creating documents that can be linked together with hypertext; Hypertext Transfer Protocol (HTTP), used by computers to transfer hypertext documents and other chunks of information over the Internet; Domain Name System (DNS), which ties the name of computers or networks to specific addresses; File Transfer Protocol (FTP), used for transferring files between computer systems; Point-to-Point Protocol (PPP), which allows a host computer to link directly with a network; and World Wide Web (WWW), which allows users to graphically view a system of hypertext documents, or Web pages.

WIRELESS PROTOCOLS

The widespread introduction of wireless communication in the 1990s changed the way business was conducted around the globe. Instead of being tied to an office, people could search the Internet, check e-mail, access company files, and send faxes using a wireless handheld device. In 1997, four major mobile phone providers—Ericsson, Motorola, Nokia, and Unwired Planet—came together to create a standard known as Wireless Application Protocol (WAP). At the time, customers could access some Internet content via their phones, but each cellular service provider had a different kind of communication protocol. For instance, WAP drew from Unwired Planet's Handheld Device Markup Language (HDML) and Handheld Device Transport Protocol (HDTP), Nokia's Smart Messaging Specification, and Ericsson's Intelligent Terminal Transfer Protocol (ITTP). In the end, WAP used what became known as Wireless Markup Language (WML). WAP became available to the public on September 15, 1997, while other vendors were allowed to integrate it into their products without paying future royalty fees.

With WAP, handheld wireless devices had faster data transfer rates, and users could navigate a Web page more easily. After a user turned on the device and opened the minibrowser, the device searched for service by sending out a radio signal. A connection was made with a service provider, which enabled the user to select a Web site to view. Next, the device sent a request to a gateway server using WAP. The gateway server retrieved data from the Web page through HTTP, which was then encoded in WML and sent to the wireless device. The user could then view the version of the Web site that had been created for handheld wireless devices—typically text-only or low-graphic.

With technological advances came new communication protocols. One of these was the General Packet Radio Service (GPRS), which became commercially available in the early 2000s. Supporting a wide range of bandwidths, GPRS maintained a continuous connection to the Internet and ran at a speed of up to 114 KB per second, as opposed to the 9.6 KB offered by other communication protocols. GPRS worked by storing data in packets or bundles that were transmitted across the mobile network. Any device with GPRS capability could run remote applications over a network, interface with the Internet, and function as a wireless modem for a computer. GPRS began to be phased out in the mid-2000s as 3G and 4G smartphones flooded the wireless market. Communication protocols for these devices included Enhanced Data GSM Environment (EDGE), Universal Mobile Telecommunications Service (UMTS), Wideband Code-Division Multiple Access (WCDMA), High-Speed Downlink Packet Access (HSDPA), Evolution Data Maximized (EVDO), and International Mobile Telecommunications Advanced (IMT-Advanced).

In the 2010s, companies explored the potential of wireless sensor network (WSN) technologies in smart meters and home area networks. According to an article in *Appliance Design,* "Significant communication protocols in contention for control of these applications include ZigBee, Z-Wave, Bluetooth LE, Powerline, IEEE 802.15.1, and Wi-Fi. It is most likely that all protocols will be used in different implementations within the sector, with the underlying common requirement being the ability to connect via Internet Protocol." With this sensor node technology, consumer electronics, appliances, and other devices for the home could be interconnected through two-way networks. As with other communication protocols, WSN worked through different layers of a network stack. Different classes of WSN protocols included: address-free protocols, commonly data dissemination protocols by which data was sent directly from a source node to all other nodes in the network; name-based protocols, in which nodes were explicitly named; and MAC protocols, which remained active long enough for communication to transpire between other sensor nodes before shutting off radio communication. Computer science experts expected that decreasing costs in the manufacture of sensor nodes would lead to large-scale WSN in a number of fields, including medical, industrial, and environmental monitoring, as well as surveillance and military operations.

SEE ALSO *HTML (Hypertext Markup Language); Three Protocols, The.*

BIBLIOGRAPHY

"ABI Research Rolls Out Mobile Devices Connectivity Study." *TMCnet.com,* August 9, 2011. Available from http://www.tmcnet.com/usubmit/2011/08/09/5692224.htm.

Callaway, Edgar H. *Wireless Sensor Networks: Architectures and Protocols.* Boca Raton: CRC Press, 2004.

"Communications Protocol." In *Tech Encyclopedia,* September 2, 2011. Available from http://www.techweb.com/encyclopedia.

Kessler, Gary C. "An Overview of TCP/IP Protocols and the Internet." Garykessler.net, November 9, 2010. Available from http://www.garykessler.net.

Loshin, Pete. *TCP/IP Clearly Explained.* San Diego: Academic Press, 1997.

Naugle, Matthew. *Network Protocols.* New York: McGraw Hill, 1999.

"OSI Model." *Tech Encyclopedia,* September 2, 2011. Available from www.techweb.com/encyclopedia.

Taaffe, Joanne. "Mobile Phone Makers Work on Standard: Wireless Application Protocol Would Help Prevent Market Fragmentation." *InfoWorld,* July 7, 1997.

"WTRS: IP Connectivity Key to Smart Metering and Home Area Networks." *Appliance Design,* July 2011. General OneFile (A261738941).

COMMUNITY MODEL

The community model is a method of developing an online presence in which several individuals or groups are encouraged to join and participate in ongoing interaction designed around a common purpose. Web communities, or virtual communities, are not only a way for like-minded people to come together online, they also are an increasingly important element of business plans. The late 1990s and early 2000s saw the cropping up of countless new Web communities facilitating one-to-one, one-to-many, many-to-one, and many-to-many lines of communication and cooperation.

Communities utilize electronic tools such as forums, chat rooms, e-mail lists, message boards, and other interactive Internet mechanisms, which are usually tailored to the particular community. Ideally, such communities are as interactive as possible, creating the greatest level of synthesis between their various offerings. Thus, the discussions that take place in the forums can be linked to content elsewhere on a Web site, while the company or community host can generate new content based on discussions that take place between community members.

TYPES OF COMMUNITY

Broadly, the community model comes in two basic varieties: those centered on relationships and those centered on tasks. The former typically are informal, grassroots-oriented communities that revolve around shared interests, ideas, topics, and goals. In these communities, the development of relationships is the primary goal. To maximize member involvement, community sites must offer maximum degrees of interactivity and personalization. For example, Facebook offers space and tools for members to set up their own Web sites and establish virtual communities within the broader Facebook community. Task-centered communities generally are more structured and impersonal. The relationships established or augmented online are a means to a mutual end, such as enhanced profits. More specifically, Web communities are established between business partners, between businesses and their customers, between different groups of customers, within companies, and between individuals and groups devoted to particular topics.

In business-to-business (B2B) relationships, the community model provides all community members with the ability to share and check electronic invoices, communicate and exchange funds on secured networks, and resolve problems quickly and openly. Internet communities offer exceptionally streamlined workflow processes between and within companies, where the functionality of key tasks is integrated and synthesized. This necessitates less personnel, paperwork, and software, and boosts efficiency, thereby minimizing operating costs and enhancing profit margins.

Web communities allow companies to use the Web to open up new channels for customer support and outreach, advertising, sales, ordering, distribution, and communication. In the field of customer service, the online community is often viewed as a vital step in creating consistent and seamless service across all kinds of media, mirroring the call center as a vehicle for quick service but going beyond it in the level of interactivity. For instance, companies may encourage their users to access the Web to receive customer support in an online forum, in which they can seek advice from a company expert and interact with other customers. In this way, customers are encouraged to become part of a coherent community tied to the company, thereby creating added value and boosting customer loyalty. This built-in source of customer feedback can be extremely valuable, allowing companies to take proactive measures to improve products and customer service. It also enables firms to further personalize their sites and build customer profiles that can be utilized for later advertising and product development. In addition, companies can take advantage of such features to monitor their customers' needs and values, and modify their products and services accordingly. Finally, such arrangements can lighten the burden on company support staff, as customers are encouraged to get and offer help to other customers.

Communities were increasingly popular within companies in the twenty-first century. Linking employees to each other and to managers, intrabusiness Web communities facilitate communication within and across departments and divisions, enhance coordination of strategies starting from the bottom up (rather than mandating them from the top down), and provide a forum for training programs, employee grievances, conflict resolution, and socializing. Furthermore, as *Sloan Management Review* pointed out, intrafirm online communities are an excellent way to encourage and foster voluntary employee participation and initiative, which are crucial concerns among employers.

COMPONENTS OF A COMMUNITY

The infrastructure of an online community consists of hardware, software, design elements, and an interface. All of these characteristics, analysts point out, are best tailored to the specific needs of the community; no one formula is appropriate for every community. Ultimately, communities must revolve around their members, not their features. While the tools available for Web communities are often highly attractive, hosts must keep in mind that the tools must fit the community, not the other way around, or the purpose of the model is lost. In general, a community must grow organically from the genuine needs and desires of the members themselves, and will gradually take shape over time as the community grows.

SOCIAL NETWORKS

The development of community model Web sites has become one of the most active areas for business and e-commerce development in the twenty-first century. An area of rapid growth in the community model has been social networking sites. These sites provide people the ability to connect to other people along a common area of interest, from personal friendship to similar professional interests, hobbies, and even romance. Social networking sites include the prominent Facebook, Twitter, and LinkedIn Web sites. A host of other social and professional networking communities are also online and typically represent a specific demographic, such as divorce, dating, and cancer communities. Each community has different needs, allowing businesses to focus products and services directly at a specific community.

Businesses often enter these social networking communities via blogs, Web banners, and as active participants in forums with the goal of building a "virtual community" in association with the Web site, such as Facebook. Companies may also have their own social network Web page, which helps them gain credibility with the online community, foster employee relationships, and build a forum for communication with customers. The theory behind the community model and the creation of virtual communities is that people who visit these sites are more inclined to fall in with the norms of that particular community, including their consumer behavior.

Another approach beyond direct advertising is to link social networking sites of individuals or groups to a company's associated products or sponsors. In the case of Facebook, the Web site began to feature a direct link between sharing on Facebook and revenue generation at e-commerce sites. By 2011, 18 of the top 25 e-commerce sites used Facebook features such as Facebook Connect or the "Like" button, which allows a user to share the content of a company's Facebook page with other friends on Facebook. When the user clicks the "Like" button on a site, a story will appear in the user's friends' "News Feed" and include a link back to the company's Web site.

According to a *New York Times* article by Miguel Helft, the Giantnerd.com Web site for outdoor gear "saw a doubling in revenue generate[d] from Facebook within two weeks of adding the Like button" to its Facebook page. In the case of American Eagle Outfitters, users referred by Facebook spent an average of 57% more on the site. The virtual community model is also typically associated with other Internet business models, such as the Amazon.com Web site. Although Amazon.com is primary an e-shop, its design include facilities for users to ask questions of authors and artists or to submit reviews, which makes it much like a virtual community.

A rising concern in all e-commerce, which also applies to the community model, is maintaining a company's reputation and avoiding online brand abuse, such as a type of blackmail by cybercriminals that threaten to slur corporate reputations. According to *Financial Director* contributor Robert Jacques, "Gartner [an IT analyst] advised a three-pronged strategy: companies must understand the role that reputation plays in social and commercial relationships, ensure that PR and marketing staff have a reputation management strategy and, finally, educate staff about the importance of maintaining the company's good name in cyberspace."

SEE ALSO *Business Models; Channel Conflict/Harmony; Channel Transparency; Virtual Communities.*

BIBLIOGRAPHY

Brenner, Ev. "Virtual Communities in the Business World." *Information Today,* December 2000.

Chaudhury, Abhijit, Debasish N. Mallick, and H. Raghav Rao. "Web Channels in E-commerce." *Communications of the Association for Computing Machinery,* January 2001.

Helft, Miguel."Facebook Promotes Social E-commerce." *Bits* (blog), *New York Times,* April 6, 2011. Available from http://bits.blogs.nytimes.com/2011/04/06/facebook-touts-social-e-commerce.

Jacques, Robert. "The Darkness Within." *Financial Director,* April 29, 2010.

Marks, Andrew. "E-maintenance Management." *Chain Store Age,* May 2000.

Philbin, Tamara. "Old-Line to Online." *Association Management,* December 2000.

Williams, Ruth L., and Joseph Cothrel. "Four Smart Ways to Run Online Communities." *Sloan Management Review,* Summer 2000.

Wonnacott, Laura. "To Create a Community, Look to a Good Platform and Examine the Needs of Your Customers." *InfoWorld,* April 3, 2000.

COMPETITION

The concept of competition is well known in the fields of economics. In everyday usage, it also connotes a kind of positive, creative energy that fuels markets. As mainstream use of the Internet grew through the 1990s, so did competition among the industry's many players. Hordes of upstart companies that became known as dot-coms emerged. They competed aggressively with one another, and with traditional industry leaders, to gain dominance in market niches such as online discount travel services and online product evaluation services. Competition was particularly intense in the online services sector between America Online (AOL) and rivals like Compuserve and Prodigy, and in the personal computer (PC) industry as players like Dell Computer Corp. used the Internet to challenge the dominance of larger competitors in the 1990s. For example, in the case of Dell, one of the company's most important moves in its quest for PC market share was to begin selling its PCs and related equipment on the Internet in 1996. Customers were able to place their orders on Dell's Web site as easily as they had done via the telephone. In 1997, roughly one-third of the orders Dell received were being placed on the Internet. More importantly, the majority of these online customers were new to Dell.

NEW BUSINESS MODEL

The phenomenal growth of the Internet and e-commerce has fostered a new business model not only for computer and Internet-based companies but also for retailers of all kinds. Relationships between a business and its customers are no longer as dependent on geographical location as they once were. Also, the fact that consumers now have instant access to a wealth of information via the Web has resulted in the decline of a competitive advantage based on a business's sharing of information and consumer education in a personalized way. This development has produced a shift in power from the supplier to the consumer.

There are numerous instances of how e-commerce changed the competitive landscape. A prime example is the big-box stores that began to dominate the marketplace in the 1980s. By stocking a wide variety and quantity of products at prices small retailers could not compete with, big-box stores such as Home Depot and Toys"R"Us put many smaller retailers, such as mom-and-pop hardware stores, out of business. However, the rise of e-commerce gave consumers a virtual big-box store that featured the convenience of not having to leave the home to shop and the ability to shop and compare prices and products among a wide range of competitors. Online e-commerce giants such as Amazon.com have led to stronger competition for consumers in nearly all product areas and have contributed to financial crises in stores such as the book and CD seller Borders, which declared Chapter 11 bankruptcy in 2011.

A prime example of the changing competitive landscape is Blockbuster, a once successful video rental business. Blockbuster was slow to recognize the value of e-commerce. As a result, another company, Netflix, developed an online video rental business that used the U.S. mail to deliver movies quickly to customers. As Netflix grew, Blockbuster and other video rental stores started to decline, eventually leading Blockbuster to declare Chapter 11 bankruptcy in 2010. Many thought that Blockbuster's strong brand recognition, customer expertise, and a sophisticated management of inventory would allow it to transition easily to the Web. However, as James Surowiecki wrote in the *New Yorker,* "Blockbuster's huge investment, both literally and psychologically, in traditional stores made it slow to recognize the Web's importance: in 2002, it was still calling the Net a 'niche' market." As a result, Blockbuster entered the online rental market too late to overcome Netflix.

BIG VERSUS SMALL

E-commerce and the growth of the Internet as a shopping resource has also allowed small and home-based businesses that once had no presence on the Web to establish an online presence, thereby enabling them to compete with larger retailers. Small business have embraced e-commerce, which gives many of them a worldwide presence. A survey of small businesses in January 2011, conducted by Network Solutions, LLC, and the University of Maryland's Robert H. Smith School of Business, showed that approximately 56% of small businesses had Web sites, up 10% from the year before. In addition, small business were also turning to social Internet media, such as Facebook and LinkedIn, to establish a competitive presence. According to the survey, 31% of small businesses in the United States had a social media presence by 2011, compared to 24% the previous year and only 12% two years earlier.

Despite small businesses' newfound ability to compete in e-commerce, size still matters on the Internet as larger companies are able to collect more information about potential consumers and negotiate more favorable deals with partners, which allows them to use that leverage to further their dominance. As a result, larger e-commerce businesses still consider other larger corporations and businesses as their primary competitors. As the 2008–2009 economic downturn affected all businesses, including e-commerce, competition increased among major e-commerce giants, such as eBay and Amazon.com. The two companies once considered their businesses complementary but by 2008 found themselves growing in direct competition. Amazon.com began to court small online vendors and recruit them to its Web site, making it more like the one-time auction-based eBay. In turn, eBay began to emphasize the traditional fixed-price approach to sales of both new and old merchandise, thus becoming more like Amazon.com.

COOPERATION VERSUS COMPETITION

Internet companies in Silicon Valley have also begun turning to a philosophy of cooperation in addition to the traditional free-market economy built on competition. The philosophy is based on the idea that innovation is collaborative and that the market place for online products is rapidly expanding to the point that it is almost limitless. "Businesses that focus on the process of free-wheeling creation—rather than squashing the competition—gain dominance and profit," wrote Greg Ferenstein for the *Washington Post.*

Google is a primary example of the cooperative approach. Although Google has developed applications such as Gmail and Google Maps, the company does not focusing on locking users into using its products. Part of the reason that Google and other Internet businesses give away Internet products is that they help to support the company's own innovations. For example, Google developed Body Browser, now called Google Body, an interactive, three-dimensional approach to exploring the human body. Instead of charging for the service, Google provides it free, hoping that hospitals, medical centers, and academic medical centers will pay premium advertising rates to get the attention of someone looking into certain aspects of the human body, such as the heart and cardiovascular disease, who may also be seeking medical help.

The success of Silicon Valley's approach, in which companies both compete and cooperate, has drawn the attention of governments throughout the world as they look to support their own tech centers and better understand the balance between competition and cooperation. "The allure of cooperative economics is that it might not just be good for individual businesses but also build industries and even economic communities," wrote Ferenstein for the *Washington Post.*

SEE ALSO *AOL; Apple Computer Inc.; AT&T Competitive Advantage; Co-opetition; Dell Computer Corp.; Differentiation; Hewlett-Packard Co.; Microsoft Corp.; Netscape Communications Corp.; Sun Microsystems.*

BIBLIOGRAPHY

Ferenstein, Greg. "In a Cutthroat World, Some Web Giants Thrive by Cooperating." *Washington Post,* February 19, 2011. Available from http://www.washingtonpost.com/wp-dyn/content/article/2011/02/19/AR2011021902888.html.

Jacobs, April. "Businesses Warm to Internet PC Sales." *Computerworld,* December 29, 1997.

Koprowski, Gene. "AOL CEO Steve Case." *Forbes,* October 17, 1996.

Network Solutions, LLC. "The State of Small Business Report: January 2011 Survey of Small Business Success," February 9, 2011. Available from http://www.networksolutions.com.

Simons, John. "Steve Case Wants to Get America Online." *U.S. News & World Report,* March 25, 1996.

Stone, Brad. "Amid the Gloom, an E-commerce War." *New York Times,* October 12, 2008. Available from http://www.nytimes.com/2008/10/12/business/12giants.html?pagewanted=all.

Surowiecki, James. "The Next Level." *New Yorker,* October 18, 2010. Available from http://www.newyorker.com/talk/financial/2010/10/18/101018ta_talk_surowiecki.

COMPETITIVE ADVANTAGE

Competitive advantage has to do with a company's ability to outdo competitors, either by improving upon what competitors are currently doing or by doing something completely different in a way that proves successful. Being able to implement an e-commerce plan that improves sales or cuts costs might give one retailer a competitive advantage over another. At the same time, being the first to come up with a new e-commerce business model, or a unique twist on an existing model, might also allow an upstart to gain an early competitive advantage.

According to Dena Waggoner, in the *Encyclopedia of Management,* "The strongest competitive advantage is a strategy that cannot be imitated by other companies. Competitive advantage can also be viewed as any activity that creates superior value above its rivals."

A prime example of an upstart gaining an early competitive advantage by being first-to-market with a new business model is eBay.com, the world's largest online auction site, with more than 86 million active users and roughly 8,000 product categories. Although rivals like Yahoo! and Amazon.com attempted to gain market share from eBay by launching their own auction sites, eBay's ability to gain critical mass gave it the competitive edge it needed to stave off its rivals. Despite Amazon.com's attempt to lure customers with guarantees of product quality and Yahoo!'s offering of commission-free auctions, eBay attracted more sellers than any other auction site simply because it had the most buyers.

Dell Computer Corp. was able to use the Internet to trim costs and boost sales, both of which were becoming increasingly difficult to do in the nearly saturated personal computer (PC) market of the late 1990s. Hoping to gain a competitive advantage, the firm started to sell PCs via the Internet in 1996. It became possible for customers who previously had placed custom orders via the telephone to place them on Dell's Web site. Customers could select configuration options, get price quotes, and order both single and multiple systems. The site also allowed purchasers to view their order status, and it offered support services to Dell owners. Within a year, Dell was selling roughly $1 million worth of computers a day via the Internet. Even more importantly, nearly 80% of the online clients were new to Dell. With the more automated Web-based PC purchasing process, Dell found itself able to handle the growing sales volume without having to increase staff drastically. Cost savings also were achieved as the firm's phone bill began shrinking. Dell's business model, which allowed for easy tracking of customer purchases, also allowed the firm to keep inventory at a minimum.

EXPANDED MARKETS

As the use of the Internet for business purposes has grown in the twenty-first century, e-commerce has fundamentally changed the economy and the way business is conducted. One of the most important aspects of e-commerce is that it can impact sales and marketing efforts immediately. For example, when a neighborhood store or home-based consulting service goes online, it suddenly expands its ability to reach a national and international base of potential customers. Furthermore, the Internet enables a business to operate a "store" that is open 24 hours a day, seven days a week.

According to a 2005 survey conducted by IPSOS and commissioned by PayPal, the Internet proved to be a minimal extra "expense." Rather, according to the survey, 64% of the small businesses that sold online reported that the Internet increased their revenues or sales, while 48% felt the Internet aided in expanding their geographic reach in the United States. Furthermore, 73% of the businesses noted they saved money by decreasing administrative costs, including the need to expand their sales force.

The overall view is that entrepreneurs who go online establish a more level playing field with larger competitors. The smallest online retailer, for example, can be equally attractive and as functional as larger big-box stores, such as Wal-Mart and Home Depot, without having to have a physical presence in every town or on every street corner. E-commerce has proven to have several competitive advantages over brick-and-mortar retail organizations, especially in terms of having to pay exorbitant rents and fixed overheads, even when sales are down. Establishing an online storefront has allowed many businesses to reduce such operating costs and compete effectively with their brick-and-mortar competitors.

A prime example of gaining a competitive advantage using e-commerce has been the bookselling industry, which has been at the forefront of establishing business models to seek competitive advantage through the Internet. Amazon.com was one of the first movers in this new business approach and patiently developed a business model in virtual markets that allowed it to build a significant lead in the market and sustain a competitive advantage over the years. Establishing itself as a leader in the bookselling industry required ongoing reassessment of operations as Amazon.com saw its competitive advantage eroded by a combination of debt financing and new competition from rivals. As a result, Amazon.com, which is the world's largest online retailer and one of the biggest booksellers in the United States, expanded its online business to include other products from CDs and movies to toys, furniture, clothing, and groceries. Nevertheless, Amazon.com, which went public in May 1997, did not make a profit until 2002.

Although Amazon.com's stocks suffered during the dot-com bust that began in 2000, by 2007 the company's profits began to show an upswing, largely due to more and more consumers using the Internet and a growing trust in e-commerce. Amazon.com also developed a reputation for convenience of shopping, a broad selection of products, and good prices. In 2007, the company furthered its competitive advantage by expanding its product base to include selling its own products with the introduction of the Kindle, an electronic book reader that could download electronic books. Despite other companies, such as Sony, also selling electronic book readers, the Kindle has proven to be the industry leader, with Amazon.com offering users the opportunity to buy almost any book, any time, anywhere. By May 2009, Kindle was the company's largest-selling product, with Amazon building a 90% share of the American e-book market due to its wide range of books available electronically and the ability to offer heavily discounted standard prices. On July 19, 2010, Amazon announced that for the previous three months Kindle book sales had outnumbered sales of hardcover books. This growth continued, and by May 2011 Kindle books were outselling both hardcover and paperback books.

SOCIAL MEDIA

Another developing strategy used by e-commerce companies for competitive advantage has been to leverage online social media to advantage for themselves and their customers. "Building a truly interactive social media community within an e-commerce platform is important as it creates a more efficient retail environment where customer opinions, relevant content, and product information are freely distributed," noted Gabe Dennison in an article for the *Adotas* Web site. The growth of the smartphone business has also led to another approach for competitive advantage in e-commerce. Companies are developing mobile e-commerce (m-commerce) sites that target younger customers and bypass issues of investing in specific platforms, such as Apple or Android. This approach allows companies to reach as many smartphone users as possible.

Overall, the competitive advantages of e-commerce are due to three factors. First, e-commerce removes location and availability restrictions because customers can access the "store" and its products from anywhere as long as they have Internet access, thus expanding a company's market reach. Second, e-commerce reduces time and money spent by reducing the costs needed to complete traditional business procedures, such as the cost of rent and direct mail advertising. Finally, e-commerce allows a business to heighten its customer service by providing more effective communications with its customers and offering highly customizable services.

SEE ALSO *Dell Computer Corp.; eBay; Mobile Commerce; Social Media.*

BIBLIOGRAPHY

"Amazon.com Inc." *New York Times Business Day,* September 28, 2011. Available from http://topics.nytimes.com/top/news/business/companies/amazon_inc/index.html?scp=1&sq=Amazon.com%20Inc&st=Search.

Dennison, Gabe. "Social Media and E-commerce Go Hand in Hand." *Adotas,* February 5, 2010. Available from http://www.adotas.com/2010/02/social-media-and-e-commerce-go-hand-in-hand.

"Exploring E-commerce." *Entrepreneur,* December 5, 2005. Available from http://www.entrepreneur.com/article/81238.

Govidarajan, Vijay. "Strategic Innovation: A Conceptual Road-Map."*Business Horizons,* July 2001.

Melendez, Tony. "It's Too Late for 'Wait and See' Approach in E-commerce Arena."*Houston Business Journal,* October 6, 2000.

Waggoner, Dena. "Competitive Advantage." In *Encyclopedia of Management,* edited by Marilyn Helms. 4th ed. Farmington Hills, MI: Gale Group, 2000.

COMPUTER CRIME

Computer crime includes traditional criminal acts committed with a computer, as well as offenses that lack any parallels with noncomputer crimes. The diversity of offenses renders any narrow definition unworkable. The U.S. Department of Justice (DOJ) broadly defines computer crimes as "any violations of criminal law that involve a knowledge of computer technology for their perpetration, investigation, or prosecution." The aggregate annual losses to businesses and governments are estimated to be in the billions of dollars.

Cybercrimes are frequently grouped into three categories. The first are those in which the computer comprises the "object" of a crime and in which the perpetrator targets the computer itself. This includes theft of computer processor time and computerized services. The second category involves those in which the computer forms the "subject" of a crime, either as the physical site of the offense or as the source of some form of loss or damage. This category includes viruses and related attacks. The third category includes those in which the computer serves as the "instrument" used to commit traditional crimes in cyberspace. This encompasses offenses like cyber-fraud, online harassment, and child pornography.

Though teenage hackers and underage, e-fraud perpetrators have captured headlines, no "typical" cybercriminal exists. Perpetrators also commit cybercrimes for a variety of reasons. Motives range from a desire to showcase technical expertise, expose vulnerabilities in computer security systems, retaliate against former employers, or sabotage government computer systems.

According to a 2010 Internet Crime report by the Federal Bureau of Investigation (FBI), the top three most reported complaints regarding cybercrime were the non-delivery of payment or merchandise, scams where the FBI itself was impersonated, and identity theft. An average of 25,000 complaints per month had become common, which served not only as potential leads but also as valuable data in the tracking of computer crimes. By 2010, the FBI had learned that most victims were males between 40 and 50 years of age (at least, this was the group that filed the most complaints) and by far the state with the most complaints was California.

The Norton Cybercrime Report 2011 listed the cost of yearly computer crimes at $388 billion globally, more than the black market for marijuana, cocaine, and heroin combined. Mobile threats in particular rose 42% between 2009 and 2010, and the report showed that men between the ages of 18 and 31 were the most likely to be targeted.

Company reaction to computer crimes is often mixed. While companies understand that crime can affect both them and their customers, decreasing revenue due to suspicion and lack of trust, solving crime problems can create costs that many businesses are not willing to pay. In a 2010/2011 report by the Computer Security Institute, only 15.9% of commercial respondents said they offered new security services to their customers following a computer-based attack.

TYPES OF COMPUTER CRIMES

Virus programs infect computer files by inserting copies of themselves into those files; they are spread from host to host when users transmit infected files by e-mail, over the Internet, across a company's network, or by disk. Related problems include worms, which can travel within a computer or network without a user transmitting files; trojan horses, which are disguised as innocuous files but which, once activated, can steal users' login names and passwords, thus facilitating identity theft; and logic bombs, programs activated by a specific event.

Other widely publicized computer crimes involved online fraud, such as stock scams and securities fraud via the Internet. Theft of online content also is common, and the Internet has made the distribution of information obtained in identity thefts, such as a person's name or social security number, much quicker and easier. The dissemination of child pornography online also has garnered widespread public and law-enforcement attention.

SOCIAL NETWORKS, MOBILE DEVICES, AND COMPUTER CRIMES

The rise of social media and the prevalence of social networking by the late 2000s did little to change the approach that cybercriminals took when trying to extort or steal money, but it did add to the channels available to them. Tools used in interactive social sites became common targets for cybercrimes. For example, in 2008 Trend Micro Security found more than 400 phishing kits targeting social network, video sharing, and VoIP sites. These phishing scams were designed to lead customers to fraudulent Web sites that would then steal personal information. Phishing and vishing (phishing via voice messages) are dangerous forms of crimes because they can appear legitimate and fool victims into releasing financial information of their own accord. Many phishing schemes even hide themselves in fraudulent offers to stop phishing attempts by e-mail.

Mobile devices had also become a common target for computer crimes by the late 2000s. In a 2011 study of e-crime, 92% of companies surveyed said they believed the greatest threat was born by smartphones and computer tablets. These mobile devices must use wireless technologies in order to access the Internet, technologies that have inherently fewer security features than physical online connections. In the beginning, mobile crimes relied on simple premium rate frauds, but by 2011 they had advanced into two-way communication possibilities between the user and a criminal operator via malware.

Other advances, like cloud computing, posed issues of the their own. While businesses were able to keep the majority of their programs on desktops and similar devices, security issues could be addressed through careful monitoring of online access and maintenance of intranets. In contrast, cloud computing requires the use of applications supplied by outside servers, which significantly raises the potential of security hazards and criminal targeting.

ANTI-CYBERCRIME LEGISLATION

Early federal statutes that addressed computer crimes included the Copyright Act, the National Stolen Property Act, mail and wire fraud statutes, the Electronic Communications Privacy Act, the Communications Decency Act of 1996, and the Child Pornography Prevention Act (CPPA) of 1996. Congress recognized computer-related crimes as discrete federal offenses with the 1984 passage of the Counterfeit Access Device and Computer Fraud and Abuse Law, which was revised four times in the following decade. This law narrowly protected classified U.S. defense and foreign relations information, files of financial institutions and consumer reporting agencies, and access to governmental computers.

Congress enacted another major anti-cybercrime law in 1996, the National Information Infrastructure Protection Act (NIIPA). NIIPA broadened the scope of protection offered by the Computer Fraud and Abuse Law by covering all computers attached to the Internet and, therefore all computers used in interstate commerce. It also criminalized all unauthorized access of computer files in order to transmit classified government information; intentional access of U.S. department or agency nonpublic computers without permission; and accessing protected computers, without or beyond authorization, to defraud and obtain something of value.

The Copyright Act covers computer-related copyright infractions, such as software piracy. The act provides criminal remedies for any intentional infringement of a copyright perpetrated for commercial advantage or private financial gain. Given the ease and anonymity of nearly identical reproductions made of online intellectual property, such as software, digitized text, and audio and visual files—and the ability to disseminate those copies worldwide—many see copyright as an increasingly costly cybercrime offense. Traditional exceptions to copyright privileges, such as "fair use" and the "right of first sale," may be eroded under evolving copyright protection laws in cyberspace. Digital intellectual property rights also are regulated by the No Electronic Theft Act of 1996, which criminalizes the electronic reproduction and dissemination of copyrighted material.

The National Stolen Property Act (NSPA) has been extended to cover the fraudulent transfer of funds online, as well as the theft of tangible hardware. The courts have determined that federal mail and wire fraud statutes, which outlaw the use of interstate wire communications or the mail to defraud persons of money or property, also can apply to computer-aided theft.

The problem of online child pornography spawned several laws intended to block the online transmission of pornographic material to minors. Congress passed the Communications Decency Act of 1996 (CDA, also Title V of the Telecommunications Act of 1996), which prohibited the transmission of "indecent," "patently offensive," and "obscene" material to minors over the Internet.

However, the Supreme Court invalidated certain sections of the CDA in *Reno v. American Civil Liberties Union,* stating that they infringed the First Amendment protection of free speech.

In response, Congress passed the Child Online Protection Act, which penalized any commercial Web site that allowed children to access content that was "harmful to minors." By summer 2001, this act was challenged on First Amendment grounds in a U.S. circuit court. The Internet's role in the production and dissemination of child pornography also is addressed by the Child Pornography Prevention Act of 1996, intended to criminalize the production, distribution, and reception of computer-generated sexual images of children. The CPPA has survived constitutional challenges in court.

Regulations were increased and modified over time. By 2011, Congress was considering the Protecting Children from Internet Pornographers Act, a bill that raised key concerns among privacy activists. Although initially approved by committee, the bill required providers to hold IP addresses for up to a year to make following up on criminal leads easier for investigators. This sparked concerns that such information could also be used in actions that violated key privacy rights in the United States.

Also in 2011, the White House drafted a new bill that would give the Homeland Security Department increased oversight over computer networks managed by civilian agencies, as opposed to primarily military organizations. The bill was part of an effort to increase the overall cyber security of America and develop key methods of defending against cyberterrorism.

ENFORCEMENT AGENCIES

Despite the relative infrequency of cybercrime prosecutions to date, the U.S. government has backed numerous initiatives to encourage and invigorate prosecution efforts. In 1995, the FBI launched its "Innocent Images" probe to track down online child pornography. The FBI also organized the Infrastructure Protection and Computer Intrusion Squad (ICPIS) in Washington D.C., which constitutes a national investigative body and resource on cybercrime. The FBI's InfraGard program fosters cooperation between federal law enforcement officials and the private sector. InfraGard maintains a secure Web site so businesses can alert law enforcement agencies about suspicious network activity or attacks.

The DOJ addresses computer crime through its Computer Crime and Intellectual Property Section (CCIPS), founded in 1991. Among other duties, CCIPS enforces the NET Act and collaborates with assistant U.S. attorneys around the country to target cybercrimes. Other sections of the DOJ's Criminal Division target e-crime within their areas of particular concern, such as fraud, child exploitation and obscenity, terrorism, and violent crime.

The Electronic Crimes Task Force (ECTF) forms a central clearinghouse dedicated to computer-related crimes for all local, state, and national law enforcement. Based in New York City, it is headed by the U.S. Secret Service and cooperates with selected partners from private industry. ECTF has successfully cracked large drug cartels, organized crime groups, and individual hackers. The ECTF also generated the precedent for e-mail wiretapping when it arrested 44 members of the John Gotti Jr. crime group for telecommunications fraud.

The DOJ, FBI, Department of Defense, and members of business also cooperate in the National Infrastructure Protection Center (NIPC), created in 1998 to aid in the enforcement of existing anti-cybercrime laws and to foster cooperation among public and private sector prosecution efforts. The NIPC focuses on identifying viruses, issuing warnings, and locating cybercriminals.

Another government and industry collaboration is the Computer Emergency Response Team (CERT) Coordination Center, dedicated to detecting, disseminating information about, and disabling computer viruses. CERT, part of the Software Engineering Institute (SEI), a publicly and privately funded research and development center, was founded in 1988.

In 2003, a restructuring led to a partnership between the FBI and the National White Collar Crime Center to create the IC3, the Internet Crime Complaint Center. It remained a key hub of complaint and crime data gathering throughout the 2000s, accepting information on a wide variety of computer crimes, from hacking and extortion to identity theft and economic espionage.

COMPUTER CRIME TRENDS

Computer crime trends are influenced by both new technologies and social movements. For the former, new ways to access devices digitally almost always provide new illegal channels as well. This is seen in the fast-flux technique, developed in the latter 2000s to allow domain-name-server switches to operate more efficiently by using peer-to-peer networking, load balancing, proxy redirection, and similar advancements. Unfortunately, this also allowed phishing Web sites to remain active and "hide" more easily by moving throughout the fast-flux processes.

As computer crimes have become more advanced, they have also become more specific. In 2008, crimes began to focus on large corporations and agencies, seeking out pertinent targets like personal information or financial data that could be used for profit, a trend that continued into the 2010s.

Social activism also began to play a role in computer crimes. By 2011, groups like Anonymous and LulzSec had committed cybercrimes using a combination of shared hacking techniques and the anonymity that online communication provided. PayPal, for instance, was targeted by the groups after it stopped processing payments to WikiLeaks, an organization being investigated for similar crimes. A crime sweep in 2011 for members of the groups spanned the United States, the United Kingdom, and the Netherlands.

SEE ALSO *Children and the Internet; Computer Fraud and Abuse Act of 1986; Computer Security; Data Mining; Fraud, Internet; Intellectual Property; Legal Issues; National Information Infrastructure Protection Act of 1996; National Infrastructure Protection Center; Privacy: Issues, Policies, Statements; Safe Harbor Privacy Framework; Viruses; Worms.*

BIBLIOGRAPHY

Albanesius, Chloe. "Cyber Crime Costs $114B Per Year, Mobile Attacks on the Rise." *PC Mag,* September 7, 2011. Available from http://www.pcmag.com/article2/0,2817,2392570,00.asp.

Brooke Paul. "DDoS: Internet Weapons of Mass Destruction." *Network Computing,* January 8, 2001.

Chen, Christine, and Greg Lindsay. "Viruses, Attacks, and Sabotage: It's a Computer Crime Wave." *Fortune,* May 15, 2000.

Chin, Woo Siew. "Insight into Cyber Terrorism." *New Straits Times,* October 3, 2001.

"Cloud Computing and Mobile Devices Lead to an Increase in Cyber Crime." *Lets Byte Code,* September 7, 2011. Available from http://letsbytecode.com/security/cloud-computing-and-mobile-devices-lead-to-an-increase-in-cyber-crime.

"CSI Computer Crime and Security Survey 2010/2011." New York: Computer Security Institute (CSI), 2011. Available from http://gocsi.com/survey.

"Cybercrime: Community Accession to an International Convention." *European Report,* March 21, 2001.

"Cybercriminals Reinvent Methods of Malicious Attacks." Computer Crime Research Center, July 11, 2008. Available from http://www.crime-research.org/analytics/3451.

Fletcher, Charlie. "ID Thievery Is on the Rise." *Catalog Age,* June 2000.

Gantz, John. "Take a Bite Out of Crime on the Web." *Computerworld,* February 19, 2001.

Gittlen, Sandra. "World Organizations Urge Sharing of Security Info." *Network World,* October 23, 2000.

Godwin, Mike. "Save the Children." *American Lawyer,* August 2001.

Grosso, Andrew. "The Promise and Problems of the No Electronic Theft Act." *Communications of the ACM,* February 2000.

"HR 1981: Protecting Children from Internet Pornographers Act of 2011." GovTrack.us, 2011. Available from http://www.govtrack.us/congress/bill.xpd?bill=h112-1981.

Internet Crime Complaint Center (IC3). "About Us," 2011. Available from http://www.ic3.gov/default.aspx.

Miller, Jason. "White House Draft Bill Expands DHS Cyber Responsibilities."*Federal News Radio,* April 14, 2011. Available from http://federalnewsradio.com.

Munro, Neil. "Cybercrime Treaty on Trial." *National Journal,* March 10, 2001.

Neeley, DeQuendre. "Justice Department Report Arouses Concerns." *Security Management,* May 2000.

Nicholson, Laura, Tom Shebar, and Meredith Weinberg. "Computer Crimes." *American Criminal Law Review,* Spring 2000.

Oreskovic, Alexei. "FBI Warns of Digital-Crime Wave from Eastern Europe." *Industry Standard,* March 11, 2001.

Radcliff, Deborah. "A Case of Cyberstalking." *Network World,* May 29, 2000.

———. "Crime in the 21st Century: The New Field of Computer Forensics." *InfoWorld,* December 14, 1998.

Rapaport, Richard. "Cyberwars: The Feds Strike Back." *Forbes,* August 23, 1999.

Rawlinson, Kevin. "London Teenager Arrested in International Cybercrime Raids." *Independent,* July 21, 2011. Available from http://www.independent.co.uk/life-style/gadgets-and-tech/news/london-teenager-arrested-in-international-cyber crime-raids-2317867.html.

Shrimsely, Robert. "'Cybercrime' Covered by Extended Law on Terrorism." *Financial Times,* February 20, 2001.

Spiegel, Peter. "U.S. Cybercops Face Global Challenge as World Gets Wired Up." *Financial Times,* October 25, 2000.

Taylor, Rob. "Australia Unveils Cybercrime Laws to Combat Global Threat."*Reuters,* June 21, 2011. Available from http://www.reuters.com/article/2011/06/22/us-australia-cybercrime-idUSTRE75L0C520110622.

Thibodeau, Patrick. "European Cybertreaty Raising Concerns." *Computerworld,* December 11, 2000.

U.S. Department of Justice. Federal Bureau of Investigation (FBI). "Internet Crime Tends." Washington, DC, February 24, 2011. Available from http://www.fbi.gov/news/stories/2011/february/internet_022411/internet_022411.

Verton, Dan. "FBI Completes Cybercrime Program Rollout." *Computerworld,* January 15, 2001.

———. "National Security Threatened by Internet, Studies Say." *Computerworld,* January 1, 2001.

COMPUTER ETHICS

Computer ethics refers to the ways in which ethical traditions and norms are tested, applied, stretched, negotiated, and broken in the realm of computer technology. As computers brought about dramatically enhanced power of communication and data manipulation, new ethical questions and controversies were forced to the forefront of contemporary ethics debates. While ethics is concerned with codes of behavior, the arena of computer technology has created many uncertainties that make the establishment of such clear codes an often daunting task.

The more dramatic abuses of computer technology, such as major Internet hackings of company Web sites and online theft of credit card numbers, achieve a high profile. While there are few uncertainties about such cases, these are only the most visible examples of far more prevalent phenomena. Most cases are more subtle, frequent, and tied to the everyday workings of ordinary, law-abiding citizens. Due to the rapid pace of technological change, novel situations arise with great frequency, which can prove dangerous when these fields and practices are mixed with business and sensitive information.

The sheer scope of computer usage, spanning nearly every part of daily life and work, from medical records and social networking to online banking and national defense systems, makes the untangling of ethical considerations all the more important, as unchecked ethical violations in one area can have severe repercussions throughout a wider system. On the personal level, individuals may run into ethical difficulties in considering what other activities they are facilitating by performing their particular functions via computer. Unfortunately, the speed of computer innovation has usually far outpaced the development of ethical norms to guide the application of new technologies.

INFORMATION EVERYWHERE

The sheer volume of data available to individuals and organizations heightens the concern over computer ethics. No firm, for instance, can forego the opportunity to take advantage of the wealth of data and data manipulation afforded by modern information technology and telecommunications. The competitive nature of the economy provides an incentive to beat competitors to certain advantageous practices so as to capitalize on those advantages. The trick, then, is for organizations to devise ethical principles that allow for the greatest level of innovation and competitive strategy while remaining within the bounds of acceptable societal ethics. Likewise, businesses need to coordinate codes of ethics to avoid having their own information systems compromised and putting themselves at a disadvantage.

E-commerce, in particular, creates a host of new ethical considerations, particularly in the area of marketing. The level of personal information and detail that can be accumulated about an individual—thanks to the conversion of integrated databases, polling and purchasing data, tracking consumer behavior online, and other computer-based data—poses rather serious questions about an individual's rights to personal privacy in the digital spectrum. The easy collection and exchange of personal consumption patterns and interests over the Internet, while highly desirable to many firms, makes civil libertarians queasy. More broadly, those concerned with computer ethics ask to what extent information perceived as a public good ought to be transformed into a marketable commodity.

Of course, computer activity that is legal is not necessarily ethical. (In fact, when the first computer crime was reported in 1966—a programmer modifying a system so his checking account would not appear overdrawn—there were no laws covering the incident.) For example, the invasion of employee privacy via the monitoring of computer-based communications and other computer activity, while generally held to be legal, nonetheless poses serious ethical dilemmas. In addition, computers and related technology greatly depersonalize information and communication and allow for enhanced anonymity, which in turn can lead to diminished barriers to unethical behavior.

While the field of computer ethics dates to 1950, information technology and computer professionals began seriously considering the long-term effects of computer ethics in the late 1980s. They recognized the need to organize professionally through such bodies as the Association for Computing Machinery, the International Information Systems Security Certification Consortium, and the Institute of Electrical and Electronics Engineers to devise professional codes of conduct. However, the increasing proliferation of powerful computers in the hands of nonprofessionals widens the scope of potential problems.

Public interest groups such as the Computer Ethics Institute have made attempts to draw out basic guidelines for ethical computer behavior applicable throughout society. In that spirit, the institute formulated the "Ten Commandments of Computer Ethics," a list of basic dos and don'ts for computer use. Several professional associations have attempted to devise computer ethics codes. The code devised by the Association for Computing Machinery, for instance, included specific instructions that it is "the responsibility of professionals to maintain the privacy and integrity of data describing individuals," and that clear definitions for the retention and storage of such information and the enforcement thereof must be implemented for the protection of individual privacy.

"Ethical issues of information technology are already a normal part of our everyday life and media discussions," Professor Bernd Stahl of De Montfort University Leicester told *Database and Network Journal* in 2011. As technology continues to spread, he added, it will "raise a large number of ethical questions that we currently do not even think about."

COMPUTER ETHICS IN THE WORKPLACE

The bulk of the scholarly literature on computer ethics focuses on ethical issues in the workplace. Companies and organizations are continually confronted with ethical challenges and violations that require resolution either through clarifying internal policy, internal disciplining and enforcement, or litigation, depending on the nature and severity of the violation. But in addition to the obvious financial vulnerabilities of unethical computer use—such as compromised financial data, employee theft, and a battered public image—the organization's attempts to solve the problems internally can rack up significant costs as well. John D'Arcy, an informational technology professor at Notre Dame, estimated a June 2011 hacking attack at Sony caused more than $172 million in damages, amounting to "major financial and reputational damage." NewsCorp. shut down its financially successful *News of the World* tabloid in 2011 after a scandal that included e-mail and telephone hacking. The U.S. government was embarrassed in 2010 after a member of the military released diplomatic cables to WikiLeaks, causing an international incident and straining global relations.

There is a legislative history to the enforcement of ethical behavior in the business world and incentive for companies to implement and enforce their own codes of ethics. Regulations to protect citizens' privacy are covered in legislation ranging from the Federal Privacy Act of 1974 to HIPPA (medical records) in 1996 and the Sarbanes-Oxley Act of 2002. Sarbanes-Oxley and the Dodd-Frank Wall Street Reform and Consumer Protection Act of 2010 specifically addressed business ethics in corporate America, including computer-related issues. The USA Patriot Act of 2001 expanded federal agencies' access to electronic records as they investigated global terrorism.

However, legislation and the courts cannot always solve these issues. The ongoing legal battles against online pirating of movies, records, and other entertainment media has done little to slow the proliferation of free file sharing and downloads. The *Journal of Retailing and Consumer Services* reported in March 2011 that free online music "threatens the very survival of the record industry as we know it." While legitimate sites like Apple's iTunes have revolutionized how music is distributed, there are a large number of younger consumers who have a "cultural expectation" that they should be able to access music for free. The report notes that the same technologies that make it easier to sell music around the world also make music piracy easier.

PRIVACY

Aside from obvious criminal activities, subtler forms of computer activity can pose ethical problems. For instance, the use of company computer equipment by employees for personal activities has been vigorously debated, but no clear answers have been formulated that can apply in all organizations. Most employees who use computers maintain an e-mail account and regularly check their mail at work. Generally, this is essential since internal company communications often are transmitted via e-mail. However, employees also may receive personal e-mail at the same account and spend their time at work using the company computer to send and receive personal messages.

New technologies allowed not only for the monitoring of e-mail communications, but also for other Internet activity such as social network sites, chat rooms, and even Web browsing. While companies may well wish to make sure their employees are using their time for company purposes, the monitoring of Web traffic strikes many as an ethical lapse, particularly since the reasoning behind visiting a Web site cannot always be determined simply by knowing that an individual went there. This problem extended far beyond the company setting. Fears over governmental or private monitoring of individuals' activities on the Internet opens up an entire range of serious ethical concerns. Since the context of a certain kind of communication or site visitation may be unknown to outside monitors, there is a significant possibility of misunderstanding, misinterpretation, and misuse of such acquired data.

The conflict between personal privacy and company surveillance of e-mail communications and other computer activity was one of the most widely publicized computer ethics controversies in the early twenty-first century. While companies argue that the monitoring of their own systems to ensure their appropriate use and the beneficial use of company time is necessary to maintain competitiveness, the moral right to personal privacy was continually asserted.

SOCIAL MEDIA

The emergence of social media has also raised new concerns about privacy and ethical behavior in general. An article by James Hyatt in *Business Ethics* noted that Facebook, Twitter, blogs, and other online media are "making a hash of once-resolved issues and creating all kinds of new dilemmas." Hyatt noted that irate consumers and bloggers can "snipe away" with impunity at a business or professional online, damaging reputations with or without cause. Employers vetting job applicants routinely search online for personal information about prospective hires (and sometimes existing employees). Medical students, journalists, lawyers and members of the U.S. Armed Forces are among those who have been targeted by highly publicized social media policies.

COMPUTER ETHICS AS EDUCATION

Computer ethics is a growing concern on college campuses, with more programs arising to address the issue. The *American Journal of Business Education* noted that more programs are addressing computer ethics among information technology professionals. However, with computers used across virtually all industries and professions, the need for ethics education is also universal. For example, The Project Management Institute (PMI) has added professional ethics to curriculum for certifying professional project managers. The *Journal of Teacher Education* reported that teacher programs have lagged behind other ethics courses for medical, legal, and business schools. These and other studies emphasize that more ethics training is needed to address the complex requirements of the computer age.

SEE ALSO *Computer Ethics Institute; Privacy: Issues, Policies, Statements.*

BIBLIOGRAPHY

Bush, Victoria D., Beverly T. Venable, and Alan J. Bush. "Ethics and Marketing on the Internet: Practitioners' Perceptions of Societal, Industry, and Company Concerns." *Journal of Business Ethics,* February, 2000.

"Business Ethics and Leadership: Sarbanes Oxley Act." Los Angeles, CA: Josephson Institute of Ethics, 2011. Available from http://josephsoninstitute.org/business/blog/tag/sarbanes-oxley-act.

Brooks, Rochelle. "The Development of a Code of Ethics: An Online Classroom Approach to Making Connections Between Ethical Foundations and the Challenges Presented by Information Technology." *American Journal of Business Education* 3, no. 10 (October 2010): 1.

Chapla, Shannon. "ND Expert: Hackers Cause Sony Major Financial, Reputational Damage." *Notre Dame News,* June 7, 2011. Available from http://newsinfo.nd.edu/news/22193-nd-expert-hackers-cause-sony-major-financial-reputational-damage.

Computer Ethics Institute. "What Is CEI?" Washington, DC, 2011. Available from http://www.computerethicsinstitute.org/aboutcei/whatiscei.html.

Harned, Patricia. "After the Debacle: How News Corp. Can Rebuild Trust." *Huffington Post,* July 25, 2011. Available from http://www.huffingtonpost.com/patricia-harned/after-the-debacle-how-new_b_909160.html.

Hyatt, James. "The Ethics of Social Media – Part I: Adjusting to a 24/7 World." *Business Ethics,* December 14, 2010. Available from http://business-ethics.com/2010/12/14/the-ethics-of-social-media-part-i-adjusting-to-a-24-7-world.

"The Ethics of Social Media Part II: Playing by New Rules." *Business Ethics,* November 11, 2010. Available from http://business-ethics.com/2010/11/19/the-ethics-of-social-media-part-ii-playing-by-new-rules.

International Information Systems Security Certification Consortium, Inc. "About (ISC).^{2}" Vienna, VA, 2011. Available from https://www.isc2.org/aboutus/default.aspx.

Kerschberg, Ben. "Your Ethical Legal Duties When Using Wireless (Wi-Fi) Networks." *Forbes,* May 5, 2011. Available from http://www.forbes.com/sites/benkerschberg/2011/05/05/your-ethical-legal-duties-when-using-wireless-wi-fi-networks.

Miller, Seumas, and John Weckert. "Privacy, the Workplace, and the Internet." *Journal of Business Ethics,* December 2000.

Pierce, Margaret Anne, and John W. Henry. "Judgments About Computer Ethics: Do Individual, Co-worker, and Company Judgments Differ? Do Company Codes Make a Difference." *Journal of Business Ethics,* December, 2000.

"PMI's Code of Ethics and Professional Conduct." Newtown Square, PA: Project Management Institute, 2011. Available from http://www.pmi.org/About-Us/Ethics/Code-of-Ethics.aspx.

"Tackling the Hidden Dangers of Tomorrow's Technology." *Database and Networking Journal* 41, no. 2 (April 1, 2011): 10.

Warnick, Bryan, and Sarah Wilverman. "A Framework for Professional Ethics Courses in Teacher Education." *Journal of Teacher Education* 62, no. 3 (May 1 2011): 273.

Warr, Richard, and Mark Goode. "Is the Music Industry Stuck between Rock and a Hard Place? The Role of the Internet and Three Possible Scenarios." *Journal of Retailing and Consumer Services* 18, no. 2 (March 2011): 126.

Weinstein, Bob. "Right and Wrong on the Net: In New Frontier, Educators See Need to Teach Ethics to the Young." *Boston Globe,* January 14, 2001.

COMPUTER ETHICS INSTITUTE

The Computer Ethics Institute (CEI) is a prominent organization dedicated to the promotion of ethical computer use in the United States. Its primary function is to study, publicize, and coordinate the intersection of information technology innovations, business interests, regulations and other public policies, and ethics. The organization was founded in 1985 by the Brookings Institution, IBM, the Washington Consulting Group, and the Washington Theological Consortium, and was originally known as the Coalition for Computer Ethics. In 1992, the coalition changed its name and incorporated as a research, education, and policy study group.

CEI includes among its ranks members of the various computer science and information technology professions, corporate representatives, industry organizations, and academic and public policy groups. Thus, CEI positions itself as a forum in which diverse interests can pool their knowledge and resources to identify and remedy ethical difficulties that arise along with the development and proliferation of advanced computer technology.

One of the organization's hallmarks is its "Ten Commandments for Computer Ethics":

1. Thou shalt not use a computer to harm other people.
2. Thou shalt not interfere with other people's computer work.
3. Thou shalt not snoop around in other people's files.
4. Thou shalt not use a computer to steal.
5. Thou shalt not use a computer to bear false witness.
6. Thou shalt not use or copy software for which you have not paid.
7. Thou shalt not use other people's computer resources without authorization.

8. Thou shalt not appropriate other people's intellectual output.
9. Thou shalt think about the social consequences of the program you write.
10. Thou shalt use a computer in ways that show consideration and respect.

Recognizing that not all legal computing activity is in fact ethical, the CEI drew up the list of ethical commandments in part to elicit conversation about computer ethics, and it has since become a widely cited general code for computer ethics in the United States. As of 2012, CEI's "Ten Commandments" has been translated into 21 languages worldwide. "Computer ethics begin where the fingers meet the keyboard," Patrick Sullivan, executive director of CEI once noted in a *Human Rights Forum* Web site article. "But ethics are more than a philosophical concern. They are directly relevant to managers and system operators, for whom computer technology presents ethical problems ranging from e-mail privacy and worker monitoring to employee use of corporate resources."

CAMPAIGNS AND CONFERENCES

In the early 1990s, CEI also joined the National Computer Security Association to jointly run the National Computer Ethics and Responsibilities Campaign (NCERC) to foster computer ethic awareness and education. "The campaign is not promoting any approach, 'code of conduct' position, or recommendation other than the need to raise awareness of the positive and negative consequences of the analog-to-digital shift and of the fact that tools and resources exist to help people make intelligent, informed choices about how best to develop, manage, and use information technology" noted the authors of *Rights and Responsibilities of Participants in Networked Communities.*

CEI began holding national conferences in 1986 that featured discussions focused on issues in computer ethics. For example, in 2003, CEI held an invitation-only event for government agencies, corporations, and scholars. The event, titled "Balancing Civil Liberties and National Security in the Post-9/11 Era: The Challenge of Information Sharing," provided an overview of various technologies for securing the nation in matters of information integration, electronic communication interception, and public surveillance. Another issue addressed by CEI in 2004 focused on the media's role in the security versus liberty debate. A conference was attended by reporters, columnists, and scholars to discuss creating a framework for balancing security and liberty in the government's use of information technologies for data integration and information sharing.

In 2007, CEI's officers voted to establish a new agenda for the institute, including raising an endowment that would allow CEI to achieve its ongoing and future goals, which included instructions for K-12 education and developing a case study repository. Also in 2007, CEI held a conference titled "Information Sharing: The Good, the Bad, and the Ugly." The conference focused on the impediments to maximizing information technologies' benefits and information sharing as it was being practiced in the federal government.

SEE ALSO *Computer Ethics.*

BIBLIOGRAPHY

Denning, Dorothy Elizabeth Robling, and others. *Rights and Responsibilities of Participants in Networked Communities.* Washington, DC: National Academies, 1994.

Goldsborough, Reid. "Computers and Ethics." *Link-up,* January/February, 2000.

"Historical Timeline." Washington, DC: Computer Ethics Institute, 2011. Available from http://computerethicsinstitute.org/aboutcei/historicaltimeline.html.

"Introducing Ethics into the Computer World." *Human Rights Forum,* 2004. Available from http://www.theta.com/goodman/ethics.htm.

COMPUTER FRAUD AND ABUSE ACT OF 1986

The Computer Fraud and Abuse Act (CFAA) of 1986 is federal legislation aimed at curtailing computer crime. It especially applies to interstate crimes that fall under federal jurisdiction. The act was designed to strengthen, expand, and clarify the intentionally narrow Computer Fraud and Abuse Act of 1984. It safeguards sensitive data harbored by government agencies and related organizations, covering nuclear systems, financial institutions, and medical records.

The act forbids interference with any federal-interest computer system or any system that spans across state lines. Obviously, the act assumed greater importance as the Internet, World Wide Web, and e-commerce grew in prominence. The law prohibits the unauthorized access of any computer system and the obtainment of classified government information. More specifically, it specifies three categories of unclassified information: information belonging to a financial institution, credit card issuer, or consumer reporting agency; information from a department or agency of the United States; and information from any computer deemed "protected," or used exclusively by a financial institution, the U.S. government, or used in interstate or foreign commerce or communication. In addition, the act aims to safeguard computer system integrity with specific prohibitions against computer vandalism. This includes the transmission of a virus or similar code intended to cause damage to a computer or system; unauthorized access that causes damage recklessly; or unauthorized access of a computer from which damage results, but where malicious intent may not be present.

For purposes of prosecution, the law focuses its attention on the actual damage done to computer systems and the specific economic losses stemming from an act of computer fraud or abuse. For instance, while possession of a code for a computer virus cannot be prosecuted under the law, the loading of such a virus onto a network would be criminal under the Computer Fraud and Abuse Act. Violators are prosecuted for knowingly or recklessly damaging such systems, and can be punished with prison sentences as long as 20 years and fines reaching as high as $250,000. Prosecutors under the law, however, often face the difficult challenge of proving that the defendant knowingly inflicted the damage, thereby establishing intent.

AMENDMENTS

The CFAA has been amended several times over the years, including a 1994 amendment that allowed civil actions to be brought under the statute in addition to criminal court actions. On October 25, 2001, the United States Patriot Act was signed into law and focused on enhancing the ability of the United States to withstand terrorist action. The law included an amendment to the CFAA by addressing the concept of "damage" in an effort to define better what constituted damage and loss in computer hacking. As statutorily defined in the Patriot Act, loss is "any reasonable cost to any victim, including the cost of responding to an offense, conducting a damage assessment, and restoring the data program, system, or information to its condition prior to the offense, and any revenue lost, cost incurred, or other consequential damages incurred because of interruption of service." As a result, a person could be prosecuted not only for actual damage that occurred but simply for deliberately attempting to cause damage.

In 2008, the CFAA was amended once again by the Identity Theft Enforcement and Restitution Act, which enhanced several aspects of the CFAA. One subsection of the act enables charges to be brought against people who conspire to commit a criminal offense, not just those who commit or attempt to commit an offense. It also broadened the CFAA's scope by eliminating the requirement that forbidden access involve an interstate or foreign communication, thus allowing authorities to address computer hacking crimes that focus on computers that are located within the same state. Furthermore, the amendment eliminated the need for a plaintiff's loss to be more than $5,000 and made it a felony for causing damage to ten or more computers. Overall, the amendments to the CFAA have broadened the act to extend far beyond hacking. "The law now criminalizes computer use that 'exceeds authorized access' to any computer," noted Orin S. Kerr in an article for the *Wall Street Journal*.

BROADENING SCOPE AND PENALITIES

In May 2011, the administration of President Barack Obama asked the U.S. Congress to consider making further wide-ranging changes to the CFAA. A major component of the administration's proposal was to make unauthorized access of a computer a felony instead of a misdemeanor and include a three-year minimum sentence for anyone attacking critical infrastructure. The administration was also seeking to update prison sentences for hacking to be more in line with current guidelines for committing mail or wire fraud, thus changing the maximum 5-year sentence for hacking to a 20-year maximum sentence.

In September 2011, the U.S. Congress began debating the requested changes to the CFAA, with some Congress members expressing concern that the changes proposed by the administration might lead to all computer-related crimes becoming federal offenses. They pointed out that it is not unusual for routine computer use to exceed "authorized access." The Justice Department, however, has argued that "terms of use" violations for Web sites and breaches of workplace computer-use policies do fall under exceeding authorized access. This issue raises a number of problems, including potentially giving power to anyone setting up a public Web site to criminalize any computer use of their Web site that they deem inappropriate.

Several cases related to terms-of-use issues have already been heard in courts, including a 2009 case in which the Justice Department prosecuted someone for breaking the social networking site MySpace.com's "terms of service" agreement by posting false profile information. Another case prosecuted by the Justice Department involved an employee violating workplace policies concerning the limited use of the company's computers for legitimate company business only. According to the Justice Department, any other use exceeded authorized access by the company and was liable to criminal prosecution.

SEE ALSO *Computer Crime; Fraud, Internet.*

BIBLIOGRAPHY

American Civil Liberties Union. "Text of the USA PATRIOT Act." New York, April 3, 2003. Available from http://www.aclu.org/national-security/text-usa-patriot-act.

Cantos, Lisa, Chad Chambers, Lorin Fine, and Randi Singer. "Internet Security Legislation Introduced in the Senate." *Journal of Proprietary Rights,* May 2000.

Conley, John M., and Robert M. Bryan. "A Survey of Computer Crime Legislation in the United States." *Information & Communications Technology Law,* March 1999.

Doyle, Charles. *Cybercrime: An Overview of the Federal Computer Fraud and Abuse Statute and Related Federal Criminal Laws.* Washington, DC: Congressional Research Service. December 27, 2010. Available from http://www.fas.org/sgp/crs/misc/97-1025.pdf.

Kerr, Orin S. "Should Faking a Name on Facebook Be a Felony?" *Wall Street Journal,* September 14, 2011. Available from http://online.wsj.com/article/SB10001424053111903285704576562294116160896.html.

Montana, John C. "Viruses and the Law: Why the Law Is Ineffective." *Information Management Journal,* October 2000.

Schwartz, Mathew J. "Treat Hackers as Organized Criminals, Says Government." *InformationWeek,* September 9, 2011. Available from http://www.informationweek.com/news/security/government/231601078.

COMPUTER SECURITY

Computer security encompasses a wide range of technological issues. Computer security professionals work to combat hacking, which includes illegally accessing, manipulating, or destroying private information contained in computer networks. Computer security efforts typically involve the use of a combination of passwords, data encryption applications, virus detectors, and firewalls (hardware or software products that filter all information passed between a private intranet and other intranets or the Internet). Along with preventing hacking, computer security systems also offer detection programs, which allow network managers to determine if a security breach has happened and pinpoint the effects of the breach. Such trends as the rapid growth of the Internet, social networking sites, and cloud computing have accelerated the need for computer security solutions.

HISTORY OF COMPUTER SECURITY PROBLEMS

The issue of computer security first arose in the 1970s as individuals began to break into telephone systems. As technology advanced, computer systems became targets as well. The Federal Bureau of Investigation (FBI) made one of its first arrests related to computer hacking in the early 1980s. A group of hackers known as the 414s, named after their area code in Milwaukee, Wisconsin, were indicted for attacking 60 different computer systems including the Los Alamos National Laboratory and the Memorial Sloan-Kettering Cancer Center. Computer security breaches like these became increasingly commonplace throughout the 1980s, prompting the passage of the Computer Fraud and Abuse Act. The new legislation allowed more stringent punishments to be levied against individuals caught illegally abusing computer systems. Although a multitude of hackers were brought to justice, many continued to operate, including one who successfully pilfered $70 million from the First National Bank of Chicago. Eventually, the Computer Emergency Response Team was established by the U.S. government to research the increasing number of computer security breaches. Nevertheless, computer hacking continued to spread. In 2011, a group of hackers known as "LulzSec" attacked Sony Corporation, causing an estimated $172 million in damages and gaining access to the personal data of more than 100 million customers.

Along with growth in hacking activity came the spread of computer viruses. When computer companies like IBM Corp. and Symantec Corp. began researching ways to detect and remove viruses from computers, as well as ways to prevent infection in the first place, virus writers began developing more elusive viruses. These viruses are spread through e-mail attachments, infected software disks, Web sites, and other means.

Computer security gaps were exposed at many major corporations and governmental bodies—including AT&T Corp., Griffith Air Force Base, NASA, and the Korean Atomic Research Institute—during the 1990s. For example, an attack on AT&T's network caused the firm's long-distance service to temporarily shut down. A study conducted by the Computer Security Institute in 1995 determined that one in every five Web sites had been hacked.

As the amount of commerce handled via the Internet grew, so did the number of malicious attacks. In July 2011, Google disclosed that hackers had infected some two million computers with a virus that diverted users from their normal Google searches.

However, the threat is not confined to large companies. Small businesses must also protect their systems against viruses and hackers that can destroy data, mine mailing lists, or steal customers' credit card and bank account numbers. While large corporations have sophisticated computer monitoring systems in place, the rising use of computer systems in small and midsize companies is making them a more attractive and frequent target for hackers, the *Washington Post* reported. The report cited a 2010 survey by the National Federation of Retailers, which showed that most small retailers were not aware of the threat to their companies and about half had not even reviewed their security practices. Small businesses and individuals are also often targeted by global criminals who use technology to steal from their victims. *Wired* magazine profiled a small Romanian town nicknamed "Hackerville" for its high number of cybercriminals, as well as the San Francisco man who headed the world's largest online credit card fraud network before his arrest.

Governments have attempted to respond to computer security issues but innovative hackers often manage to stay ahead of the laws and lawmen trying to rein them in. In 1998, the U.S. Department of Justice created the National Infrastructure Protection Center, charging it with the task of safeguarding domestic technology, telecommunications, and transportation systems from hackers. Other agencies, such as the FBI, the Secret Service, and the Department of Homeland Security have also formed units that focus on computer-based crimes and threats. Legislation such as the Computer Security Act of 1987 and USA Patriot Act of 2001 attempted to further address the growing threats of cybercrime and terrorism. Most U.S. states have also enacted their own computer security laws.

Computer security has also been a significant international problem. MSNBC reported that the government of the People's Republic of China has been linked with Chinese criminals who attacked the French and British treasuries, Google, and leading defense contractors in the United States. However, China also claimed it was the target of 480,000 Trojan horse attacks in 2010. A report by the country's National Computer Network Emergency Response Team also stated that some 35,000 Chinese Web sites had been hacked during 2010.

TYPES OF COMPUTER SECURITY PROBLEMS

As the need for high levels of computer security became increasingly apparent to business owners, many began to earmark additional dollars for security technology and for staff to oversee security measures. By then, the most popular form of attack was the denial-of-service (DoS), which simply overloads a network system until it crashes. *Network World* noted that distributed DoS attacks (DDoS), which are attacks by multiple compromised systems on a single target, have continued through the early twenty-first century, knocking out such sites as WordPress, CNN, Facebook, and Visa. The attacks are expensive to undertake and seldom bring a financial payback for the hackers, so DoS campaigns are generally attributed to political motivations or personal grudges.

Mail bombs behave in the same manner. However, they target a network's mail server with the goal of shutting down e-mail service by overloading the system. Hackers targeting networks may also attempt to gain access to secure areas containing sensitive data, such as credit card numbers or social security numbers. A security breach of this type can cause serious damage to a business or institution since data files can be not only copied, but also deleted.

COMPUTER SECURITY PROGRAMS

The first major computer security program was developed late in the 1970s, when three Massachusetts Institute of Technology (MIT) graduates created RSA encryption technology. The data-scrambling program eventually was used in leading computer platforms such as Microsoft Windows and well-known software applications like Quicken and Lotus Notes. Computer security primarily remained a governmental concern throughout the 1970s and 1980s. The rise of corporate networks, along with the growth of e-commerce, prompted more widespread concern about computer security in the 1990s.

Companies using computers began linking them together via networks in the 1980s. Many of those networks were then linked to the Internet in the 1990s, and to home computer networks by the early 2000s. Companies with many geographically dispersed offices were able to use the Internet to link networks and allow employees to work from home as telecommuters. Similarly, those with employees on the road could grant off-site workers access to the intranet. In fact, according to *PC Week* writer Jamie Lewis, one of the Internet's most important benefits to businesses was its ability to "simplify the often expensive and complex tasks of giving remote users access to corporate networks and of linking remote sites."

Another major boon of the Internet revolution, the rise of e-commerce, also brought with it major security headaches. To make a purchase online, shoppers were normally required to input their credit card numbers. Eventually, even tax returns became something consumers could transmit via the Internet. To protect this sensitive data, companies began seeking sophisticated security systems. Most online merchants began using data encryption programs, such as Secure Sockets Layer (SSL), to protect personal information transmitted over the Web. These types of technologies are often incorporated into online banking sites and electronic payment processors such as PayPal.

The most popular method of computer protection among home computer users is antivirus software. Companies including Symantec Corp. and Norton offer antivirus applications that scan every file on a disk or on a computer's hard drive for infected material, alerting users if corrupted files are found. To keep pace with the continual development of new viruses, many computer security software firms prompt users to periodically download from their Web sites software upgrades which recognize newer viruses. Firewalls, once mainly used for computer networks, also have become popular with home users, particularly those who operate wireless computer networks.

Many computer industry experts believe that avoiding all hacking activity is nearly impossible. However, analysts cited by *eWeek* in early 2011 predicted that global network and data security spending would increase from the $6 billion reported in 2010 to $10 billion by

2016. The rise in cloud computing, along with greater health care and financial services spending online, was expected to continue driving computer security spending for the foreseeable future.

SEE ALSO *Computer Crime; Cryptography, Public and Private Key; Encryption; Hacking; Viruses; Worms.*

BIBLIOGRAPHY

Bhattacharjee, Yudhijit. "Welcome to Hackerville: the Romanian Cybercriminal Hotspot." *Wired,* February 7, 2011. Available from http://www.wired.co.uk/magazine/archive/2011/03/features/welcome-to-hackerville?page=all.

Chapla, Shannon. "ND Expert: Hackers Cause Sony Major Financial, Reputational Damage." *Notre Dame News,* June 7, 2011. Available from http://newsinfo.nd.edu/news/22193-nd-expert-hackers-cause-sony-major-financial-reputational-damage.

Cortez, Dana. "Computer Security Vital to Small Businesses; Watch Out for Malware, Experts Say." *Redding Record Spotlight,* August 13, 2011. Available from http://www.redding.com/news/2011/aug/13/computer-security-vital-to-small-businesses.

Fowler, Geoffrey, and Ben Worthen. "Hackers Shift Attack to Small Firms." *Wall Street Journal,* July 21, 2011. Available from http://online.wsj.com/article/SB10001424052702304567604576454173706460768.html.

Greene, Tim. "The DDoS Hall of Shame." *Network World,* March 5, 2011. Available from http://www.networkworld.com/news/2011/030611-ddos-hall-shame-wordpress.html.

Kan, Michael. "China Hit by 480,000 Trojan Horse Attacks in 2010." *NetworkWorld,* August 10, 2011. Available from http://www.networkworld.com/news/2011/081011-china-hit-by-480000-trojan.html.

Lewis, Jamie. "VPNs: Fulfilling the Internet's Promise." *PC Week,* June 1, 1998.

Poulsen, Kevin. "The Card Master: Why Max Butler Crowned Himself King of a Global Online Fraud Network." *Wired,* March 2011. Available from http://www.wired.co.uk/magazine/archive/2011/03/features/the-card-master?page=all.

Rashid, Fahmida Y. "Network-Security Spending to Double to More Than $10B by 2016: Analysts." *Eweek,* January 12, 2011. Available from http://www.eweek.com/c/a/Security/Network-Security-Spending-to-Double-to-More-than-10B-by-2016-Analysts-544757.

Trigaux, Robert. "A History of Hacking." *St. Petersburg Times,* 2000.

Tsukayama, Hayley. "Google Warns about PC Virus." *Faster Forward* (blog), *Washington Post,* July 21, 2011. Available from http://www.washingtonpost.com/blogs/faster-forward/post/google-warns-about-pc-virus/2011/07/21/gIQAEhL1RI_blog.html.

"U.S. Government and Industry Coming into Closer Alignment on Information Security Priorities and Solultions, Finds Survey of Government Chiefs." *PRWeb,* May 9, 2011. Available from http://www.prweb.com/releases/2011/5/prweb8400643.htm.

COMPUWARE CORP.

Compuware Corp. makes and sells software that allows clients to test and debug corporate mainframe systems. It also offers a suite of system management tools, which have become increasingly important to companies conducting business electronically. Compuware's services include systems integration and capacity testing. Compuware also offers Web site design and creation and related e-business services. One of the firm's goals is to offer comprehensive e-commerce services and solutions to its clients. In 2011, the firm made almost $930 million in revenue and employed approximately 4,400 people.

EARLY HISTORY

Along with partners Thomas Thewes and Allen Cutting, Peter Karmanos Jr. founded Compuware Corp. in 1973. Based in Southfield, Michigan, the company offered professional data processing, computer installation help, and a team of programming consultants willing to take on short-term projects. Compuware operated on the premise that its technical services allowed clients to spend more time running their business, rather than dealing with technology concerns. Four years later, the firm unveiled its first software product, Abend-AID. The fault diagnosis tool made the jobs of programmers easier by examining corporate mainframe systems for errors and offering suggestions for alterations. Abend-AID's success prompted the firm to establish a separate software division.

In 1978, Compuware established an office in the northeastern United States. A year later, the company developed an interactive analysis and debugging software program called MBX Xpediter/TSO, which eventually won an International Computer Program (ICP) award. Sales exceeded $1 million in 1983. That year, Compuware shipped File-AID, a data management software line for IBM and IBM-compatible mainframe computers. The firm created its first automated testing tool, MVS PLAYBACK, in 1986. The following year, Abend-AID received an ICP award, and Compuware expanded internationally for the first time by purchasing European distributors. By the end of the decade, sales had grown to roughly $100 million. Software brought in 65% of that total, while services accounted for 30%.

In an attempt to shore up its position in the interactive analysis and debugging industry, Compuware acquired Centura Software in 1990. The firm created its first personal computer (PC) software product in 1991 by developing a PC version of File-AID. However, most of Compuware's new products continued to focus on improving the performance of large corporate mainframes. Other product releases included database manager DBA-XPERT and Pathvu/2, an interactive analysis and debugging program for the OS/2 platform. In 1992, the firm completed its initial public offering.

MOVE INTO E-COMMERCE SOFTWARE AND SERVICES

In the mid-1990s, Compuware acquired Uniface Holding B.V., a client/server software producer based in the Netherlands, and CoroNet, a management systems software maker based in Los Altos, California. Compuware then renamed CoroNet's software EcoS-COPE and merged it into its EcoSystems software line to increase the comprehensiveness of its network management tools, including those related to e-business. The firm continued its plan of growth via acquisition with the 1996 purchase of London-based automated software testing products and services provider Direct Technology Ltd. and the 1997 purchase of NuMega Technologies Inc., one of the world's largest manufacturers of error detection and debugging software for Windows and Java systems.

As mainframe computers—what Compuware's software attempted to debug and enhance—were losing ground to Internet-based networks, the firm shifted gears in the late 1990s. It devised a plan to spend a few years preparing firms for the Y2K transition and then retain many of those same firms by offering them e-commerce services and solutions once the transition was complete. In 1997, to position itself as an authority on the impending Y2K transition, Compuware published *Millennium,* a newsletter about the effects the year 2000 could have on the computer industry. Sales exceeded $1 billion for the first time that year. *Millennium* was published online in 1998.

To augment its growing base of e-commerce holdings, Compuware purchased CACI Products Co. in 1999. The firm integrated CACI's application capacity planning tools into its EcoSystems suite, allowing clients to better manage the performance of their e-commerce applications. Although Compuware was ultimately successful in its efforts to become a leading Y2K consultant for companies operating mainframe systems, it soon found that it had overestimated the number of clients who would be looking to move into e-commerce early in 2000, and underestimated the amount of time it would take to train its Y2K specialists to function as e-commerce consultants. As a result, the firm failed to meet earnings forecasts for the first time in several quarters, and stock prices tumbled by roughly 80% in 2000.

In 2000, Compuware turned two of its acquisitions—Montreal-based Nomex Inc., a provider of Web design and development services, and Kansas City-based Internet consulting services provider BlairLake Inc.—into digital development centers (DDCs). The DDCs were designed to offer full-scale e-commerce services to clients wishing to undertake e-business ventures. A third DDC was soon opened in Farmington Hills, Michigan, at the firm's headquarters complex. The purchase of Optima, an e-business performance measuring software developer, further increased Compuware's e-commerce holdings.

In 2002, Compuware's Predictor software program, a wide area network (WAN) provisioning and capacity planning tool and key component of the company's Vantage performance management suite, was named "Best Network Application and Operating Software Product" at the Networking Industry Awards. The following year, the company celebrated its 30th anniversary by completing construction on its new world headquarters building in downtown Detroit, Michigan. The company also launched its Compuware Application Reliability Solution (CARS) in 2003 to provide users with greater control over application delivery.

BUYING COMPANIES AND EXPANDING SERVICES

In February 2004, Compuware announced that it had paid $7 million to buy Covisint LLC, an Internet venture first developed in 2001 by General Motors, Ford Motor Co., and Daimler-Chrysler. The automotive companies wanted a secure business-to-business online marketplace where auto manufacturers and suppliers could conduct business with each other. Although Covisint soon began offering additional services for customers using its exchange, the enterprise struggled to gain popularity. The problem stemmed from the automakers, who had invested more than $500 million in the venture but disagreed about what services to offer. Nevertheless, Covisint continued to add applications and services and eventually turned a profit the year prior to Compuware purchasing the company. According to *NetworkWorld.com* contributor Ellen Messmer, Peter Karmanos, then Compuware's chairman and CEO, "wanted to acquire Covisint because he's confident its e-commerce portal products and services can grow from roughly $20 million per year to $100 million over the next few years."

Covisint, which provides collaborative portal, identity management, and data exchange services, went on to broaden its customer base beyond the car industry to include industries such as health care and oil and gas. The company successfully reinvented itself as a health care portal beginning in the state of Michigan in 2005 when it worked with health care provider Blue Cross Blue Shield of Michigan. The result was a statewide health care portal that featured services such as medical records, electronic reporting and e-prescribing, benefits information, and claim submissions.

Compuware also acquired the privately held Gomez company, a leader in Web application experience management, for $295 million in 2009. The purchase resulted in

Compuware becoming one of the world's leading software as a service (SaaS) infrastructure management provider. "The idea, [Compuware President Bob] Paul said, is that an IT administrator will be able to view, from a single dashboard, the performance of ERP applications running in his company's data center, the performance of an E-commerce Web site, and the quality of a Cloud-based provider's service," wrote *InformationWeek* contributor Mary Hayes Weier.

ENTERING THE CLOUD

In 2010, Compuware launched CloudSleuth, a partner-driven cloud community built specifically to spotlight the performance of the cloud's "federated infrastructure." Cloud computing is a global application platform that provides organizations access to plug into a network of shared configurable computing resources, including networks, servers, storage, applications, and services. Compuware's CloudSleuth also allowed active members to take part in forums and discussions about solving common cloud-related issues.

Overall, by 2011, Compuware had 7,100 customers around the world. Its clients included 46 of the top 50 *Fortune* 500 companies and 12 of the 20 most visited Web sites in the United States. In addition to application performance management and Covisint's information systems for secure communications and collaboration, Compuware's computing solutions included portfolio management, mainframe solutions, and Uniface, which is a mainframe application development environment. Compuware also offered professional services in areas such as mobile computing and IT portfolio management.

SEE ALSO *Business-to-Business (B2B) E-Commerce; E-Commerce Solutions; Software.*

BIBLIOGRAPHY

"Compuware Acquires E-commerce Services Company." *PR Newswire,* May 10, 2000.

"Compuware Acquires Web Development Services Company." *PR Newswire,* February 15, 2000.

Compuware Corp. "History." Farmington Hills, MI, 2011. Available from http://www.compuware.com/about/company-history.html.

"Compuware Corp." In *Notable Corporate Chronologies.* Farmington Hills, MI: Gale Group, 1999.

"Compuware Extends Fault Management to E-business Applications." *PR Newswire,* January 5, 2001.

"Compuware Lauded for E-business Application." *Graphic Arts Monthly,* January 2000.

"Covisint: New Identity." *Information Age,* February 25, 2006. Available from http://www.information-age.com/article-archive/288691/covisint-new-identity.thtml.

Kahn, Jeremy. "Growth Elixirs May Be Risky: There Are Lots of Ways to Make a Business Sprout. Some of Them Can Be Positively Suicidal. Just Look at What Happened to Four of the Fastest-Growing Companies on Last Year's List." *Fortune,* September 4, 2000.

Macvittie, Lori. "Web Performance Monitoring Is Critical to EBusiness—Performance Monitoring Tools Will Help You Get to the Bottom of Those Nagging Problems." *InformationWeek,* November 13, 2000.

Mcconnell, John. "Better Monitoring Tools Good for E-biz." *InternetWeek,* April 3, 2000.

Messmer, Ellen. "Compuware to Acquire Covisint B2B Exchange." *NetworkWorld,* February 5, 2004. Available from http://www.networkworld.com/news/2004/0205covisint.html.

Weier, Mary Hayes. "Compuware to Acquire Gomez for $295 Million." *InformationWeek,* October 7, 2009. Available from http://www.informationweek.com/news/software/app_optimization/220301463.

Zeichick, Alan. "Network Crystal Ball—EcoPredictor Forecasts Effects of WAN Traffic Growth." *InternetWeek,* March 19, 2001.

CONNECTIVITY, INTERNET

The term "Internet connectivity" refers to the way people are hooked up to the Internet, and may include dial-up telephone lines, always-on broadband connections, wireless devices, and mobile computing access through laptops, notebook computers, smartphones, and PC tablets. A study by Nielsen/NetRatings covering the year 2000 found that more than 85% of home-based users connected to the Internet with ordinary telephone modems, with adoption just beginning for newer technologies such as wireless access and such broadband connections as DSL (digital subscriber line), ADSL (asymmetrical DSL), and cable modems. However, by 2010, only 10% of adults in the United States used dial-up access, according to a study by the Pew Internet and American Life Project, while 66% had a broadband connection in their homes. CITA, the wireless industry trade association, reported that in December 2010, 26.6% of households in the United States were wireless-only. Another study by Internet World Stats found 78.3% of the North American population were Internet users, as of March 31, 2011.

Since the early days of the Internet, connectivity for the typical user has improved markedly, with greater speeds for data transmission and wider bandwidth to accommodate special services such as audio and video. In the consumer market, the first improvements were made in dial-up telephone connections, with modems increasing in speed from 14.4 Kbps to 56 Kbps. Internet providers later added high-speed dial-up, which used special acceleration servers to increase download speeds up to seven times faster than conventional dial-up.

However, with the growth in popularity of the World Wide Web and its ever-expanding stock of multimedia content, the need for more bandwidth and higher transmission speeds created new demand in households and small businesses for broadband alternatives, which until that time were common only in large corporations, universities, and government agencies. The telecommunications industry responded with high-speed DSL connections over telephone and cable lines; 3G and 4G mobile networks; direct-to-satellite transmission networks; and a variety of other solutions to improve online connection speeds and capacities.

CONNECTIVITY AND COMMERCE

By the early 2000s, Internet connectivity had become vital to many industries. For example, *Wisconsin Ag Connection* reported that 62% of farms in the United States had Internet access by 2011.

The "digital divide" that sees wealthier Americans obtaining access to high-speed Internet connectivity more frequently than low-income populations is also a concern in developing countries. According to a study by the Maplecroft consulting firm, in countries like India, more affluent residents and an emerging middle class are embracing modern communication technologies more quickly than less wealthy sectors of the population. Programs to address the lack of connectivity are underway in a number of developing countries. For example, the government of Tonga, in the South Pacific, announced a $34 million program backed by the World Bank and the Asian Development Bank (ADB) to provide high-speed broadband to 100,000 citizens via an underwater optic fiber cable. "This critical link will connect Tonga firmly with the rest of the world, generating huge economic opportunities from early 2013," said Haruhiko Kuroda, ADB president.

BROADBAND CONNECTIVITY

Although broadband technology offered high-speed Internet access, consumers were initially slow to adopt it. While the greater bandwidth of a broadband connection allowed for more data to be transmitted at higher speeds than a conventional telephone line, most consumers were unwilling to pay $40 or more a month for broadband services that would enable them to view streaming media better or download Web pages faster. However, the widespread use of the Internet and mobile devices for personal, educational, and business applications soon led to broader adoption of broadband technologies around the world.

The Federal Communications Commission's 2011 International Broadband Data Report noted that the United States ranked 12th out of 33 countries for fixed broadband adoption and 9th out of 29 nations for mobile broadband. The Internet site WebSiteOptimization.com cited statistics indicating there were more than two billion Internet users worldwide, with Europe leading the world in Internet usage, fixed broadband penetration, and mobile broadband in 2010. However, the Internet World Stats site noted the United States has the largest broadband market.

WIRELESS CONNECTIVITY

Wireless connectivity to the Internet was still in its infancy in the early 2000s, but exploded during the following decade with the development of new protocols, specifications, and next-generation technologies. While most personal computers could access virtually any Web site, early wireless devices could not because wireless systems used a different method of encoding Web content. Typically, wireless devices were used to retrieve e-mail and obtain a range of news, sports, stocks, weather, and local information. However, technical advances and the growth of Web sites built specifically for mobile computer gave cell phones greater access to more Internet information. Apple's introduction of the iPhone, and the subsequent Google-backed Android operating system, added thousands of mobile applications that further increased the size of the wireless connection platform. The growth of "hot-spots"—wireless connection points that first gained popularity at Starbucks stores and spread to restaurants, airports, and other public places—also spurred the growth of wireless computing in the early twenty-first century.

Competition among cell phone providers also fueled growth in wireless, due to less expensive data plans, more bundled services, and more affordable mobile connectivity, according to the Organisation for Economic Co-operation and Development (OECD). The group reported that wireless broadband subscriptions among its member countries had reached half a billion by December 2010. Fixed broadband hit 300 million subscriptions for the same period. While wireless subscriptions grew by 10% from June to December 2010, OECD added, fixed broadband dropped to 6% during that period.

SEE ALSO *Bandwidth; Bandwidth Management; Broadband Technology; Wireless Fidelity (Wi-Fi) Network.*

BIBLIOGRAPHY

"The Benefits of Broadband – June 2011 Bandwidth Report." Ann Arbor, MI: Website Optimization LLC, June 2011. Available from http://www.websiteoptimization.com/bw/1106.

Carter, Adrienne. "Wireless Trading, Version 1.0." *Money,* October 1, 2000.

———. "Picking up the Connection Pace." *eMarketer,* February 13, 2001.

CTIA. The Wireless Association. "Wireless Quick Facts." Washington, DC, December 2010. Available from http://www.ctia.org/advocacy/research/index.cfm/aid/10323.

Committee on Wireless Technology Prospects and Policy Options, National Research Council. *Wireless Technology Prospects and Policy Options.* Washington, DC: National Academies Press, 2011.

Dowd, James. "Comcast to Provide Discounted Internet Access, Computers to Low-Income Memphis." *Commercial Appeal,* August 11, 2011. Available from http://www.commercialappeal.com/news/2011/aug/11/comcast-provide-discounted-internet-access-compute.

Federal Communications Commission. "International Broadband Data Report." Washington, DC, May 20 2011. Available from http://www.fcc.gov/reports/international-broadband-data-report-second.

Fleishman, Glenn. "The Web, without Wires, Wherever." *New York Times,*February 22, 2001.

"India Still Hungry for Internet Access." *Memeburn,* August 15, 2011. Available from http://memeburn.com/2011/08/india-still-hungry-for-internet-access.

Internet World Stats. "Usage and Population Statistics." Bogota, Colombia, August 2011. Available from http://www.internetworldstats.com.

"Maplecroft Ranking Highlighting the 'Digital Divide' Reveals India Lagging Behind Brazil, Russia and China." Bath, UK: Maplecroft, March 30, 2011. Available from http://maplecroft.com/about/news/digital_inclusion_index.html.

"More Farmers Using Computers, Internet." *Wisconsin Ag Connection,* August 15, 2011. Available from http://www.wisconsinagconnection.com/story-national.php?Id=1716&yr=2011.

Organisation for Economic Co-operation and Development. "Broadband Portal – Press Release." Paris, France, December 2010. Available from http://www.oecd.org/document/4/0,3746,en_2649_34225_42800196_1_1_1_1,00.html.

Pepe, Michele. "Forging the Wireless Pipeline." *Computer Reseller News,* March 5, 2001.

Pew Research Center. "Home Broadband 2010." Washington, DC, August 11, 2010. Available from http://www.pewinternet.org/Reports/2010/Home-Broadband-2010.aspx.

———. "Smartphone Adoption and Usage." Washington, DC, July 11, 2011. Available from http://www.pewinternet.org/Reports/2011/Smartphones.aspx.

———. "Updated: Change in Internet Access by Age Group, 2000–2010." Washington, DC, September 10, 2010. Available from http://pewinternet.org/Infographics/2010/Internet-acess-by-age-group-over-time-Update.aspx.

Rufino, Pia. "Tonga to Gain Broadband Internet Access." *FutureGov,* August 16, 2011. Available from http://www.futuregov.asia/articles/2011/aug/16/tonga-gain-broadband-internet-access.

Sartain, Julie. "Internet2 Turns 15. Has It Delivered on Its Promise?" *Network World,* April 11, 2011. Available from http://www.networkworld.com/news/2011/041111-internet2.html.

U.S. Department of Commerce. Bureau of the Census. "E-Stats." Washington, DC, May 26 2011. Available from http://www.census.gov/estats.

Verizon Wireless. "Verizon Wireless Launches Its 4G LTE Network in Johnstown and Altoona, Pennsylvania Tomorrow." Basking Ridge, NJ, August 17 2011. Available from http://www.verizonzone.com/verizon-wireless-launches-its-4g-lte-network-in-johnstown-and-altoona-pennsylvania-tomorrow.

Wendland, Mike. "Speedy Internet2 Makes Wildest Dreams Tame." *Detroit Free Press,* May 10, 2001.

CONSUMER TO CONSUMER

Consumer-to-consumer (C2C) Web sites allow an individual to arrange financing for a project without the involvement of a traditional intermediary. These sites are very useful for funding small-scale projects. For example, several fans of a musician can each pledge a small amount to help the musician produce his or her album, which frees the musician from dependence on signing a contract with a studio. This can also be described as crowdsourcing project funding, or crowdfunding, as the artist collects pledges from many end consumers instead of arranging a deal with a single client.

STEPHEN KING

One of the first examples of a C2C funding scheme on the Internet was Stephen King's Web publishing experiment in 2000. King had previously worked with established publishers, who arranged book advances and helped market his books to consumers. Under the C2C model, King made an offer directly to his readers. Each reader who downloaded a chapter of the novel from King's Web site could decide whether to pay for a chapter of the new novel. If an acceptable percentage of readers contributed, King would release the new chapter online.

One factor that led to the development of the C2C funding model was piracy. Authors and publishers were concerned that the introduction of e-books would allow any reader to download new novels without paying the artist to create them. Piracy was already common in the computer software and music sectors. By asking end consumers to pay for a novel before he wrote it, King believed that the piracy issue could be eliminated. The crowdsourcing model also offered a way to make annoying and intrusive digital rights management software unnecessary. An artist would not need to worry about consumers sharing his work because he had already received his desired compensation.

Many readers were already familiar with King's books. This model showed great potential for an established artist, but artists who were not already widely known still had to take on additional promotional responsibilities because they could not rely on a publisher.

C2C WEB SITES

By the mid 2000s, Web sites that helped artists with the promotion challenges of the C2C model started to appear. Artistshare was one of these new music labels. Unlike a traditional music label, musicians had to finance all of the costs of producing their music, but they got to keep a much higher percentage of their earnings. The main weakness of these music sites was that the musicians still had to cover their upfront costs. The *New York Times* reported that one jazz musician spent $87,000 to create her album.

The release of Kickstarter in 2009 offered a solution to this issue. Instead of the artist creating the work of art first, and then asking customers to make a pledge, Kickstarter operated under a model that was similar to Steven King's model. Artists told their fans how much money they expected for their work, and then these fans could each make a contribution. If the artists reached their goal, they distributed the work to their fans. Some artists set up several pledge brackets, offering additional perks for fans who offered larger pledges.

Kickstarter added a feature that protected an artist's fans. After fans pledged a contribution, they were not required to pay until other fans advanced enough contributions to meet the artist's goal. According to a *Wired* article, the goal that the artist set was a minimum funding level, and some artists collected more than the initial payment they requested.

CONTROVERSIES

Artistshare filed a patent application in 2003 that gave it the rights to the crowdfunding model. After Artistshare attempted to use its patent to get Kickstarter to pay licensing fees, Kickstarter responded by asking a court to invalidate Artistshare's patent, claiming that several music Web sites were using the crowdfunding model when the patent was awarded.

Another controversy arose from the terminology that Kickstarter used. Calling the fans' payments pledges suggested that they were voluntary payments. This was misleading, because artists were using the Kickstarter payments as an alternative to receiving royalty payments from a traditional intermediary, and the pledge model made some artists feel like they were panhandling for spare change.

As Kickstarter and other sites became more popular, established retailers started to market their own products on these sites. This was controversial because these sites were meant to help individual artists make direct sales to consumers. A corporate retailer had other ways of financing its inventory. *Wired* reported that Kickstarter's managers received many requests to list corporate projects in 2011 but rejected these projects to maintain the site's original purpose.

SEE ALSO *Business-to-Consumer (B2C) E-commerce.*

BIBLIOGRAPHY

Adler, Carlye. "How Kickstarter Became a Lab for Daring Prototypes and Ingenious Products." *Wired,* March 18, 2011. Available from http://www.wired.com/magazine/2011/03/ff_kickstarter/all/1.

Coyle, Diane. "Stephen King Spooks Publishing's Middlemen." *Independent,* July 25, 2000.

Kaplan, Fred. "MUSIC: D.I.Y. Meets N.R.L. (No Record Label)." *New York Times,* July 4, 2004. Available from http://www.nytimes.com/2004/07/04/arts/music-diy-meets-nrl-no-record-label.html?pagewanted=all&src=pm.

Masnick, Mike. "Crowdfunding Patented; Kickstarter Threatened, Asks Court to Invalidate." *Techdirt,* October 5, 2011. Available from http://www.techdirt.com/articles/2011 1005/14504316226/crowdfunding-patented-kickstarter-threatened-asks-court-to-invalidate.shtml.

CONTENT PROVIDER

According to PCMag.com, the term "content provider" refers to "an organization or individual that creates information, educational or entertainment content for the Internet, CD-ROMS, or other software-based products. A content provider may or may not provide the software used to access the material." The first content providers were entities such as America Online (AOL), which provided content to users for a subscription fee. However, over time, many providers began to offer some or all of their information services free of charge. Unlike e-commerce sites, whose user traffic ideally generates sales, content providers tend to derive revenue from sources such as banner ads and other forms of advertising and syndication. Some content providers purchase and aggregate industry-specific information from sources such as LexisNexis. Many news content providers, such as Dow Jones, Hoover's, and LexisNexis also furnish archival content for users.

PAYING FOR CONTENT

The most common business model for early online content providers was the click-through model, which focused on click-through rates. However, this did not provide a reliable measure of responses to an advertisement, since getting visitors to visit a site did not necessarily lead to sales. While the bulk of content providers derived a substantial proportion of their revenues from banner advertisements, the utility of those ads was increasingly questioned in the early 2000s as firms realized the ads were too often ignored.

In the 2010s, one growth area for content providers was mobile phone operations, with providers supplying users with relevant information connected to location-based services such as malls, restaurants, and entertainment venues. Many content providers expected that customers would adjust to paying per-usage fees for such content, since they were already paying for cellular phone service.

TYPES OF CONTENT PROVIDERS

Junta 42 reported that according to Joe Pulizzi, founder of the Content Marketing Institute, and author of the e-book *Content Marketing Playbook 2011—42 Ways to Connect with Customers,* content can be categorized in six ways: long-form content, short-form content, periodicals, community engagement, content sharing, and event-driven content. Pulizzi also pointed out that content providers bring people who are actively seeking something, whether it is information, insight, or solutions to their problems. Apart from the content providers previously listed, provider companies include journalists, small content shops, custom publishers and content agencies. They supply text and graphics of articles or interviews, new developments, news stories, and so forth, making the publication or site appealing and useful to its visitors.

SHIFTING ATTITUDES

Traditional ways of doing business are changing as new digital technologies are introduced and consumers demand continuous access to high-quality content. Cross-platform access to content at any time and any place is becoming the norm. The digital world is making the consumer experience better by offering wider and more immediate distribution. Webcredible, a digital consultancy, suggested in a 2011 report that there was a trend away from the passive consumption of content and toward active information-seeking behavior. People are less likely to prefer receiving news via packaged material, written by professional journalists. Social networking tools such as Twitter and Facebook news pages allow mainstream news to reach people without them having to seek it out. Mobile devices also allow people to receive relevant content while on the move. Tablet devices and smart phones are both interactive and popular means of news consumption.

An ever-changing digital market place is forcing content provider companies to transform their business. They must have a well-planned integrated transformation strategy and execute it effectively. Content providers need to understand consumers and deliver what they want. It is essential that companies continue to optimize and innovate content, and investigate opportunities as they emerge. For companies to survive and grow, they must also exploit new technologies and platforms, and be prepared to exploit new channels in an integrated way.

BIBLIOGRAPHY

"The Accenture Global Content Study 2008." Accenture, 2008. Available from http://www.accenture.com/us-en/Pages/insight-media-entertainment-global-content-study.aspx.

Agnew, Marion. "Syndicators Spin Out More News for Web Sites: Online Content Providers Offer Information from a Variety of Sources." *InformationWeek,* February 26, 2001.

Albiniak, Paige. "Do Not Pass Go." *Broadcasting & Cable,* November 6, 2000.

Cholewka, Kathleen. "Opting into the Wireless Web." *Sales and Marketing Management,* January 2001.

"Content Provider." *PCMag.com,* 2011. Available from http://www.pcmag.com/encyclopedia_term/0,2542,t=content+provider&i=40275,00.asp.

"The Future of Online Content: An International Perspective." Webcredible, March 2011. Available from http://www.webcredible.co.uk/user-friendly-resources/white-papers/content.pdf.

"Internet Content Providers." Austin, TX: Hoover's, 2011. Available from http://www.hoovers.com.

Lee, Chris. "Adapt or Die, Content Providers Warned." *New Media Knowledge,* May 12, 2011. Available from http://www.nmk.co.uk/article/2011/5/12/adapt-or-die-content-providers-warned.

McElligott, Tim. "Taking Over-the-Top Through the Middle." *B/OSS,* April 28, 2010. Available from http://www.billingworld.com/articles/2010/04/taking-over-the-top-through-the-middle.aspx.

Szabo, Gabor and Bernardo A. Huberman. "Predicting the Popularity of Online Content." *Communications of the ACM* 53, no. 8 (August 2010): 80–88. Available from http://www.hpl.hp.com/research/idl/papers/predictions/predictions.pdf.

"What Types of Content Provider Companies Are Available?" *Junta 42.* Available from http://www.junta42.com/cmu/content-provider/what-types-of-content-provider-companies-available.aspx.

CONVERGENCE

In the field of e-commerce and information technology, convergence typically refers to media convergence, and especially to the combination of television, telecommunications, and the personal computer into a single box that would deliver high-speed Internet access, traditional television programming, and interactive services. However, as of mid-2011, one-box systems were as much vision as they were a reality. While there were services and hardware offered that came close, such as Apple and Google TV, consumers did not respond to technological developments as quickly as expected, and the industry was divided between traditional television businesses and IT companies entering media.

CONSUMERS SLOW TO ACCEPT MEDIA CONVERGENCE

Convergence has been an industry-driven rather than a consumer-driven phenomenon. Companies such as Microsoft, Time Warner Inc., and Apple have invested heavily in developing iTV platforms. General consumers, on the other hand, have been less than enthusiastic. Although this changed somewhat in the 2000s, it was clear that convergence was not simply a technological issue; it also was a matter of culture, lifestyle, and economics.

During the 2000s, technology became more approachable for the general consumer, and convergence hardware became easier to use. Consumers appear to be integrating the personal computer into their home life but more slowly than anticipated. After a number of innovations—such as Apple TV, tablets like the iPad, and increasingly sophisticated smartphones—which streamlined user experience, consumers began to accept nontraditional sources of visual media. Netflix, a hybrid company that originally disseminated DVDs through the mail, experienced increasing success through 2011 by offering movies streamed over the Internet. By 2011, the company accounted for 24.71% of Internet traffic, according to a report from Sandvine, reported by Leslie Horn in *PCMag.* This was accounted for, in part, by the number of distribution channels the company used to reach consumers, which included Apple TV, Microsoft's Xbox 360, Google TV, and tablets. A study by Convergence Consulting Group demonstrated that 600,000 people switched off cable television and began using Internet content providers in 2009. This was barely a scratch to the $84 billion television provider industry, but networks worried that the trend would continue to gain momentum.

OBSTACLES TO CONVERGENCE

As more people began to use the Internet in their daily lives, competition increased between television and Web-based companies, making it difficult for consumers to meet their media demands through a single distributor. On the one hand, cable companies formed a coalition among television channels and media suppliers, including ABC, Fox, and NBC. The group created Hulu, a Web site that streamed television for free, with commercials sparsely placed throughout programs. In 2011, Hulu released Hulu Plus, which offered increased services for an $8 monthly subscription fee. Hulu Plus exceeded expectations, gaining 875,000 paid subscriptions by June, according to *MediaBeat.* When Google TV was launched in 2010, the Hulu coalition, CBS, and Viacom all blocked access. Such actions illustrate another central problem with convergence: large businesses who feel that convergence might erode their profitability or make their business models obsolete often do whatever they can to prevent such convergence from happening.

SEE ALSO *Broadband Technology; Connectivity, Internet; Home Networking.*

BIBLIOGRAPHY

Berger, Robin. "TV and Web Can Already Get Together." *Electronic Media,* January 22, 2001.

"The Big iTV Five." *Variety,* January 15, 2001.

Cheng, Kipp. "AOL-Time Warner Deal Hastens Convergence." *Mediaweek,* January 17, 2000.

Cheredar, Tom. " Not Too Shabby: Hulu Nears a Million Paid Subscribers." *MediaBeat,* July 6, 2011. Available from http://venturebeat.com/2011/07/06/not-too-shabby-hulu-nears-a-million-paid-subscribers.

"Convergence." *Whatis?.com,* July 25, 2001. Available from http://whatis.techtarget.com/definition/0,,sid9_gci211837,00.html.

Greenberg, Daniel. "AOLTV: Tuning in to Channel Zero." *Washington Post,* December 8, 2000.

Horn, Leslie. "Report: Netflix Is Largest Source of Internet Traffic in North America." *PCMag,* May 17, 2011. Available from http://www.pcmag.com/article2/0,2817,2385512,00.asp.

Jenkins, Henry. "Convergence? I Diverge." *Technology Review,* June 2001.

"Please Stand By." *Economist,* November 30, 2010. Available from http://www.economist.com/blogs/babbage/2010/11/streaming_television.

Schonfeld, Erick. "Estimate: 800,000 U.S. Households Abandoned Their TVs for the Web." *TechCrunch,* April 13, 2010. Available from http://techcrunch.com/2010/04/13/800000-households-abandoned-tvs-web/.

CO-OPETITION

Co-opetition, a term combining the words "cooperation" and "competition," refers to the arrangement between competing firms to cooperate on specific projects or in certain areas of business for mutual benefit, even while remaining competitors in general. The players enter into the agreement with the expectation that the isolated cooperation will lead to greater overall returns for each firm. The term was coined in the early 1990s by Raymond J. Noorda, the founder of Novell Corp., and gradually achieved prominence, particularly in the dot-com economy.

A number of factors contributed to the rise of co-opetition in the late 1990s and 2000s, including the accelerating breakthroughs in information and communication technologies and the development of internal and external networks by most major companies. The layers of interconnectedness, channel conflict, and novelty involved in e-commerce pushed the term co-opetition to the forefront of business strategy. For example, bitter rivals Microsoft Corp. and IBM entered into an arrangement whereby Microsoft agreed to supply its Windows NT operating systems to IBM for use in the latter's personal computers and workstations. Each firm recognized that greater overall margins would result from the temporary alliance.

When the rush of information technology met e-commerce, co-opetition grew dramatically. This often occurred in complex webs of interconnecting relationships between several firms that operated in similar areas and competed and cooperated with each other simultaneously. On the Internet, companies entering the new e-commerce arena from different angles and with different strategies often saw that creating strategic alliances to forge new online markets, and sharing sales channels and information in certain e-market areas, was a mutually beneficial strategy.

Co-opetition creates something of a paradox because it brings together both common and conflicting interests under one arrangement. The separation of these two kinds of interests is crucial if the goals of the co-opetitive strategy are to be reached. A chief concern of partners in a co-opetitive arrangement, for instance, is secrecy. Usually, such relationships call for a degree of information exchange and mutual access to potentially sensitive data. In these cases, the participating companies must walk a fine line to negotiate between their competing objectives. On the one hand, a degree of openness and mutual trust is necessary if the arrangement is to bear the desired fruit. On the other hand, neither company wishes to give more to the other firm than the arrangement calls for, and neither wants to end the deal in a relatively weakened competitive position. Thus, the management of information flow between firms engaging in co-opetition is among the most difficult tasks companies face and requires shrewd but diplomatic execution.

The trend toward co-opetition continued in the 2000s and 2010s. In order to offer a more streamlined user experience, hardware and software companies benefited either from collaboration or merger. The former was the case when Google and Intel announced their alliance in the mobile devices market. According to *VentureBeat,* 2011 was the perfect time for joining forces, as "Google now needs fast chips because it has purchased Motorola's phone business. And Intel's major partner, Nokia, has shifted away from the Intel-co-developed MeeGo operating system to Microsoft's Windows Phone 7." The two companies announced the co-opetitive effort at the Intel Developer Forum.

In a field as volatile as IT, the timing for co-opetitive efforts is often delicate, and even the most stalwart alliances could dissolve into conflict. In these cases, the confidentiality and trust forced by collaboration was often forfeited. Longtime partners Hewlett-Packard (HP) and Oracle began to experience friction with Oracle's acquisition of Sun Microsystems in 2009, which provided Oracle with a different access point to the hardware industry, undermining the company's reliance on HP to breach the market. After the companies began to compete in earnest for the same customers, there was an increasing amount of friction. The next two years devolved into accusations of breaches of secrecy, underhanded tactics, secret alliances, and petty squabbles. Though co-opetition clearly is a complex undertaking, the advantages it offers frequently are too enticing to ignore.

SEE ALSO *Competition.*

BIBLIOGRAPHY

Bengtsson, Maria, and Soren Kock. "'Coopetition' in Business Networks—to Cooperate and Compete Simultaneously." *Industrial Marketing Management,* September 2000.

James, Keith. "Sometimes, It Pays to Sleep with the Enemy." *Business Times* (Singapore), March 16, 1999.

Kobielus, James. "Oracle's Sun Acquisition Accelerates Push into Data Warehousing Appliances." *Information Management,* April 22, 2009. Available from https://secure.information-management.com/blogs/oracle_sun_aquisition_data_warehousing_appliance-10015337-1.html.

Loebecke, Claudia, Paul C. Van Fenema, and Philip Powell. "Co-opetition and Knowledge Transfer." *Database for Advances in Information Systems,* Spring 1999.

Manring, Audrey Y. "Net Markets Gather B-to-B Momentum." *Informationweek,* November 20, 2000.

Rosoff, Matt. "Oracle Blasts HP In New Court Filing." *Business Insider,* August 30, 2011. Available from http://www.businessinsider.com/oracle-blasts-hp-in-new-court-filing-2011-8.

Takahashi, Dean. "Intel and Google Announce Their Alliance around Android and Smartphones." *VentureBeat,* September 13, 2011. Available from http://venturebeat.com/2011/09/13/intel-and-google-announce-their-alliance-around-android-and-smartphones-video.

CREATIVE COMMONS

The Creative Commons was developed as a response to restrictive copyright licenses. Movies, books, music, and other creative works could typically not be shared with other consumers legally, although illegal sharing was common. To stop illegal file sharing, media end-user licensing agreements became more and more restrictive. Some artists wanted to promote a license that established fewer restrictions, so they could build on each other's work. The traditional alternative, releasing a work into the public domain, was not acceptable to these artists. A public domain work could be used by a business to develop a new work that was subject to a restrictive copyright agreement, and the original artist might not receive credit for his work.

ESTABLISHMENT OF THE CREATIVE COMMONS

The Creative Commons was established in December 2001. Lawrence Lessig, a law professor at Stanford and Harvard, served as the chairman of the organization. The Creative Commons project was considered part of the Open Source movement, but it was designed to offer an artist more flexibility than existing open source licenses, such as the GNU General Public License (GPL). Some artists wanted to share their work with the public without allowing other artists to create derivative works, and other artists simply wanted to receive credit if their work was used in another project. The Creative Commons wrote up six licenses, which allowed an artist to select the most appropriate license to use for his or her project.

The first Creative Commons licenses were released in December 2002. According to *eWeek*, the new licenses received relatively little attention from artists until 2004, when several large news organizations started to promote the project. The availability of multiple licensing options helped the project gain popularity. Some artists used several Creative Commons licenses for the same work. An artist could grant a nonprofit organization the right to use the work for free with one license, while charging a corporation royalty fees under another license. Writing even a single copyright license was difficult for many artists, let alone several.

Another challenge for artists was finding the Creative Commons works. A search engine could find a relevant work of art, but search engines originally did not offer the ability to search by copyright status. A Creative Commons press release reported that Yahoo! had implemented this feature in March 2004, and Google followed with its own Creative Commons search option in November 2005.

ADOPTION

The Creative Commons license quickly gained popularity with academic researchers. The *Michigan State Law Review* reported that the Public Library of Science (PLoS) established new Creative Commons journals in biology and medicine that gained academic researchers prominent exposure in much less time than traditional, copyright-restricted academic journals.

Wikipedia also adopted a Creative Commons license, ShareAlike. According to Creative Commons, ShareAlike was the version of the license that matched the philosophy of the GNU project best. As with GPL software, the public could alter Wikipedia entries and use them in business ventures, but the ShareAlike licensing terms also applied to all derivative works. GNU argued that some other Creative Commons licenses that banned commercial use and banned modifications by other artists violated the spirit of the Open Source project.

Flickr also became a prominent source of Creative Commons images. This social photo-sharing site allowed an artist to choose the license that would apply to her work, and many artists chose the Creative Commons license. *ReadWriteWeb* reported that in October 2011 Flickr was hosting more than 200 million images that had Creative Commons licenses.

By 2011, Creative Commons licensing had spread to videos on the Internet. YouTube announced that it would allow its users to select a Creative Commons license when they uploaded a video. According to *Wired*, YouTube also formed partnerships with several news organizations to ensure that Creative Commons video footage would be available for its users to work with, including C-SPAN and Al-Jazeera.

SEE ALSO *Digital Millennium Copyright Act; Intellectual Property.*

BIBLIOGRAPHY

Carroll, Michael W. "Creative Commons and the New Intermediaries." *Michigan State Law Review* 45, (Spring 2006). Available from http://papers.ssrn.com/sol3/papers.cfm?abstract_id=782405.

Creative Commons. "About the Licenses." Mountain View, CA, 2011. Available from http://creativecommons.org/licenses.

Garlick, Mia. "Google Advanced Search Allows CC-Customized Searching." Mountain View, CA: Creative Commons, November 4, 2005. Available from http://creativecommons.org/press-releases/entry/5692.

George, Philip. "The Role of Free and Open Source Software in Digital Literacy Education." Bowling Green, OH: Bowling Green State University, Spring 2011. Available from http://www.bgsu.edu/cconline/pg_cco%20article/intro.html.

Gustin, Sam. "Google Rolls Out Creative Commons YouTube Licenses." *Wired*, June 2, 2011. Available from http://www.wired.com/epicenter/2011/06/youtube-creative-commons.

Kirkpatrick, Marshall. "One Thing Facebook Can Never Do: Flickr Hits 200m Creative Commons Photos." *ReadWriteWeb*, October 5, 2011. Available from http://www.readwriteweb.com/archives/one_thing_facebook_can_never_do_flickr_hits_200m_c.php.

Nolan, Chris. "Creative Licensing Scheme Grabs Artists Attention." *eWeek*, September 29, 2004. Available from http://www.eweek.com/c/a/Government-IT/Creative-Licensing-Scheme-Grabs-Artists-Attention.

CRYPTOGRAPHY, PUBLIC AND PRIVATE KEY

Cryptography—called "crypto" by its practitioners—is the study of codes and ciphers and their use to protect information. Cryptography has existed, in one form or another, since the ancient Greeks began toying with methods for encoding with mathematics. In the modern period, cryptography was utilized mainly in wartime to protect sensitive military information, and in the high-stakes and secretive world of diplomacy and spying.

For years, computer-based cryptography was almost exclusively used by the U.S. National Security Agency

(NSA) for coding and decoding sensitive information and messages during the Cold War. For many years after private-sector computer scientists began working on cryptography, the government fought such efforts out of concern for national security. Cryptographers, however, were wary of government monopolization of the technology, which raised fears of a "Big Brother" capable of snooping into the private lives and communications of its citizens.

This door was opened in 1975 by Massachusetts Institute of Technology graduate Whitfield Diffie and Stanford University professor Martin Hellman. The two were searching for a way to share encrypted messages between two people who did not know each other, and thus could not have devised their own scrambling formula beforehand. The Diffie-Hellman algorithm that resulted was the birth of contemporary public-key cryptography, the dominant cryptographic infrastructure used on the Internet.

Cryptography assumed a whole new significance with the development of e-commerce in the mid-1990s. Perhaps the biggest roadblocks to e-commerce were consumer fears over privacy and the security of their financial and personal information. As a consequence of this concern, cryptography was of central importance to the growth of the Internet economy.

Encryption is the scrambling of text-based messages into unrecognizable code via a complex mathematical algorithm. Only those with the correct "key" are able to encrypt or decrypt such a message in a given cryptographic system. The key is a set of specific parameters, based on the algorithmic encryption formula, that act to lock and unlock the coded information. The formula typically consists of a long string of bits, sometimes more than 200 digits long. The more digits involved and the more complicated the algorithmic equation used to generate the code, the more difficult the hacker's job in breaking it.

The two basic infrastructures used in cryptographic systems are public key and private key. While early computer systems used private-key cryptography almost exclusively, by the late 1990s and early 2000s the tide was shifting in favor of public-key cryptography. The dominant encryption standards were testament to the sea of change. The original Data Encryption Standard (DES), a private-key algorithm developed by the NSA, was being phased out due to its lack of flexibility and a level of security that could no longer withstand sophisticated modern attacks, not to mention the limited use of private-key systems in e-commerce. In its place came Triple DES (3DES) and the public-key Advanced Encryption Standard (AES). 3DES was a method of encryption that applied three DES keys in a single encryption. AES was even more difficult to break. DES was a 64-bit key, meaning that there were 64 ones or zeros in each key. Eight of these values were predetermined, so DES was really a 56-bit encryption. Developed by cryptographers Joan Daemen and Vincent Rijmen, AES used either a 128-bit, 192-bit, or 256-bit code. Since each byte of data would multiply the number of possible combinations by two, AES was vastly more complex. It is considered, for both practical and extremely impractical purposes, impossible to break.

PRIVATE-KEY CRYPTOGRAPHY

Private-key, or symmetric, encryption systems employ a single common key, possessed by those on both sides of the transaction, to both lock and unlock a message. Private keys are generally smaller, meaning they contain less bits of information, and as a result compute more quickly than do public keys. However, that also means they are more vulnerable to attack than are public keys.

Since private-key cryptography involves a series of one-to-one transactions, the concern over secrecy is paramount. For example, if a firm maintained a private-key infrastructure with several thousand clients, the company would need to ensure the secrecy of several thousand separate keys, and the opportunity for compromised security escalates. Thus private-key encryption can pose difficulties, especially over large networks of individuals, simply because key management can become a headache that costs a good deal of time and effort to manage.

PUBLIC-KEY CRYPTOGRAPHY

Public-key, or asymmetric, cryptography involves two separate keys: both a private key maintained by a single entity and a public key available to any user over a network. A central authority, such as an online bank, broadcasts its public key, enabling any client to send encrypted messages to that destination. Only that original authority, however, can decrypt the communications using its private key, thereby securing the information from hackers and other unauthorized onlookers. As the usage of these keys is spread over such a wide network of people, they typically contain a greater number of information bits to make the code more difficult to crack.

Due to its simple availability to large numbers of people, public-key encryption was considered the favored infrastructure for e-commerce in the early 2000s. Digital signature technology, for instance, relies on the public-key infrastructure. The 2000 passage of the Electronic Signatures in Global & National Commerce Act opened the floodgates for public-key cryptography as never before by creating legal parity between handwritten signatures and digital signatures. In turn, this was a major boon to a whole range of new and established forms of e-commerce, particularly in the financial services industries. The leading public-key encryption scheme used in e-commerce was Secure Sockets Layer (SSL), originally developed by Netscape.

The primary vehicle by which transactions and messages are encrypted using public-key cryptography is the digital certificate. Digital certificates are issued by a central authority and contain the user's name and e-mail address, an expiration date, and the authority's name. Digital certificates are stored on the user's computer or, increasingly, on a smart card or a central server accessible over the Internet.

The complexity of the public-key infrastructure stems from the management of a hierarchy of different certificate authorities and central servers, along with the level of individual customization involved in using a digital certificate on a personal computer or smart card. But once a public-key infrastructure is in place and a sound key management system has been implemented, the rewards can be astounding, particularly for those e-commerce firms engaged in the transfer of massive amounts of sensitive information, as in online banking. In business-to-business operations, public-key cryptography also can lead to efficiency gains. With the security afforded by digital certificates, companies can allow each other mutual access to internal company network infrastructures, greatly streamlining the transaction processes between business partners.

THE CRYPTOGRAPHIC OUTLOOK

The future of Secure Sockets Layer (SSL) as the standard for public encryption was uncertain in 2011. In two famous cases, hackers had broken into certificate authorities' systems and forged false certificates, enabling them to gain users' private log-in information. In one case, where Certificate Authority (CA) DigiNotar's system had been breached, perpetrators had issued themselves certificates for organizations as notable as the Central Intelligence Agency, the Israeli Secret Service, and others, according to *PCWorld.* At the time, there were hundreds of CAs around the globe, any one of which could have posed an easy target, and some people, such as computer security researcher Moxie Marlinspike, pointed out some of the significant weaknesses of the SSL system. Even if a CA such as DigiNotar were hacked, users could not effectively respond because if they chose to reject DigiNotar's certificates, then they would be cut off from those sites using DigiNotar authentication, which would often mean a significant quadrant of the Web would become unavailable. While the system was difficult to break into, there were no safeguards in the event of a security breach.

As might be expected, the search for ever-more impenetrable encryption systems was certain to continue in the 2010s. Essentially, the development of such cryptography technologies and the increasing sophistication of hackers and code-breaking systems is an ongoing virtual arms race between those using cryptography to enhance security and those using cryptography to compromise security.

SEE ALSO *Advanced Encryption Standard (AES); Computer Security; Data Encryption Standard (DES); Digital Certificate; Digital Certificate Authority; Digital Signature; Digital Signature Legislation; Encryption.*

BIBLIOGRAPHY

Arden, Michelle, and Bradley Palmer. "Enabling Secure Applications with a Public-Key Infrastructure." *Security,* May, 1999.

Crowe, David. "Cutting-Edge Security." *Wireless Review,* January 1, 2001.

Danielyan, Edgar. "Goodbye DES, Welcome AES." *Internet Protocol Journal* 4, no. 2 (2001). Available from http://www.cisco.com/web/about/ac123/ac147/archived_issues/ipj_4-2/goodbye_des.html.

Fratto, Mike. "Top 10 Technologies: Cryptography—Lock and Key for a Safer Net." *Network Computing,* October 16, 2000.

Harrison, Ann. "Basically Uncrackable." *Computerworld,* January 19, 2000.

Kerner, Sean Michael. "Who Do You Trust with SSL?" *eSecurity Planet,* August 5, 2011. Available from http://www.esecurityplanet.com/news/article.php/3938211/Who-Do-You-Trust-with-SSL.htm.

Kerstetter, Jim. "Web Encrytpers." *Business Week,* February 19, 2001.

Levitt, Jason. "In Keys We Trust." *InformationWeek,* June 14, 1999.

Levy, Stephen. "Crypto." *Newsweek,* January 15, 2001.

Rothman, Mike. "Public-Key Encryption for Dummies." *Network World,* May 17, 1999.

Schultz, Keith. "Network Infrastructure: SSL in the Driver's Seat." *Internetweek,* November 13, 2001.

Udo de Haes, Andreas, "Hackers Forge Certificates to Break into Spy Agencies." *PCWorld,* September 4, 2011. Available from http://www.pcworld.com/article/239497/hackers_forge_certificates_to_break_into_spy_agencies.html.

CUBAN, MARK

Mark Cuban, the cofounder of Dallas-based firm Broadcast.com and owner of the National Basketball Association's Dallas Mavericks, was among the most high-profile, outspoken, and wealthiest dot-com moguls of the late 1990s and early 2000s. Broadcast.com built its fortune by taking established media outlets online and streaming their signals over the Internet on the Broadcast.com Web site in exchange for promotion on the firm's television or radio stations. Cuban positioned his company as adding value to traditional media outlets by offering them an online presence. Despite its success and its leadership in the online streaming media market,

Broadcast.com was one of the many dot-com sensations that failed to turn a profit despite its sizeable splash. Although Broadcast.com remained in the red, Cuban struck it rich when his former partner Yahoo! Inc. purchased the company in 1999 for $5.7 billion. This enabled Cuban to purchase the NBA Dallas Mavericks in 2000. (The Mavericks won their first NBA title in 2011.)

EARLY HISTORY

A Pittsburgh native born in 1958, Cuban's background in computers was modest, to say the least. He took only one computer course at Indiana University, where he majored in business, and failed because of poor typing skills, according to a profile in *Broadcasting & Cable.* Nonetheless, after graduation in 1981 he found a job with Mellon Bank as a computer systems integrator in Pittsburgh. After moving to Dallas, Cuban was fired from a job as a computer software salesman despite strong sales skills, because, according to Cuban, he was not interested in sweeping floors. However, Cuban felt his experience was strong enough to start his own firm, a computer networking outfit called MicroSolutions, which proved a modest success; he sold the firm to CompuServe for $3 million after seven years.

Streaming media and Cuban's love of basketball first merged in 1995 when he and his friend Tony Wagner affixed a phone line to a personal computer in order to watch the Indiana Hoosiers. They shopped their idea around on the message boards at America Online and were impressed by the level of interest. Inspired, they decided to launch a new firm called AudioNet to connect users to their favorite hometown sports teams over the Internet.

In 1998, they renamed the firm Broadcast.com and took it public. The clients rolled in; at the time of the sale to Yahoo!, Broadcast.com reached more than 60 million U.S. Internet users with its streaming media packages. While Wagner left the new partnership within a year of Yahoo!'s takeover, Cuban maintained 2% of Yahoo!'s shares. Cuban's main pursuit, however, was to live up to the life he had earned as a hotshot dot-com entrepreneur. He purchased the Dallas Mavericks for $280 million and made himself one of the NBA's most visible and outspoken owners.

Thoroughly steeped in the high-speed competitive atmosphere of e-commerce, in 1999 Cuban told *Broadcasting & Cable* that "Business is like a game and the stock price and the money is the scorecard. The whole idea is to win." By any measure, Cuban had his share of victory. In 1999, *Forbes* ranked Cuban seventh on its list of the richest people in America involved in the Internet, with a net worth of $1.2 billion.

After selling Broadcast.com to Yahoo!, Cuban negotiated the purchase of a $40 million jet from Gulfstream, placing him in *The Guinness Book of World Records* for the largest purchase conducted online. As reported in an interview with *BusinessJet Traveler,* Cuban sent an e-mail to Gulfstream to communicate his prospective interest and set up a test flight for his pilot. When his pilot related his positive impression of the jet's capabilities, Cuban immediately set up payment and made the purchase.

The billionaire also placed two other planes into his airline menagerie, each of which was considered a marvel in its own right. After buying the NBA's Dallas Mavericks, the billionaire increased the team's perks with the purchase of a Boeing 757. Built to be comfortable for players over seven feet tall, the airplane was equipped with a weight room, medical facilities, a conference room, and other "necessities." Although the purchase was controversial (as many of the choices made by the billionaire were), Cuban cited strategic reasons for the plane, saying, "the ability to be comfortable, get rest, and have enough room for basic treatment of physical problems gives us a competitive advantage. I came up with the strategic vision for the airplane, but not the details."

The Mavericks were not the only business controlled by Cuban, who also cofounded HDNet in 2001, a visual media broadcasting company that was the first national network to use a high-definition, 1080i signal. HDNet comprised two channels, HDNet and HDNet Movies, the latter of which converted 35 millimeter films to high-quality, digital information. In 2006, Cuban picked up Dan Rather for "Dan Rather Reports," a news program, which was nominated for 12 Emmy awards, winning twice. Cuban picked up his own recognition for HDNet as well, receiving honorable mention at the Clio Awards in 2009.

Cuban's aggressiveness brought fame, fortune, and success, but it also made him a number of enemies. Ross Perot Jr., the millionaire from whom he had purchased the Mavericks, continued to file small claims against his companies and holdings. More significantly, the Securities and Exchange Commission (SEC) filed insider trading charges against him. The SEC claimed that Cuban had sold his significant share of Momma.com after receiving confidential information about an additional private offering from the CEO of the company. Allegedly, upon hearing that his share of the company was to become diluted by additional investors, Cuban lost his temper at the CEO and sold his stock the next day. When the additional round of investment was conducted, Momma.com's stock dropped, saving Cuban $750,000. Initially, the court decided in favor of Cuban, but an additional round of appeals was still pending in 2011.

SEE ALSO *Streaming Media; Yahoo!.*

BIBLIOGRAPHY

Bauder, David. "Dan Rather Nearing 5 Years at HDNet and 80." *Boston.com,* August 22, 2011. Available from http://articles.boston.com/2011-08-22/ae/29915331_1_hdnet-hard-edged-field-reports-airs.

Cassavoy, Liane. "Three Minutes with Mark Cuban." *PCWorld,* September 2, 2004. Available from http://www.pcworld.com/article/117430/three_minutes_with_mark_cuban.html.

Doyle, T.C. "The Cuban Story: From Neighborhood VAR to Internet Czar." *VAR Business,* October 25, 1999.

Gallagher, Leigh. "Take Back Your Poils." *Forbes,* October 9, 2000.

Kindley, Mark. "Mark Cuban: A Success Story You Can Relate To." *VAR Business,* October 25, 1999.

Newcomb, Peter, and Erika Brown. "The Forbes 400: Web Masters." *Forbes,* October 11, 1999.

Pope, Steven. "Mark Cuban." *Business Jet Traveler,* June 1, 2010. Available from http://www.bjtonline.com/people/center-stage/s/p/1/article/mark-cuban-2408.html.

Rathburn, Elizabeth A. "Crusader for Convergence." *Broadcasting & Cable,* October 18, 1999.

———. "Cuban: Embrace the Web." *Broadcasting & Cable,* October 4, 1999.

Scannell, Kara, Leslie Eaton, and Stephanie Simon. "SEC Calls a Foul on NBA's Cuban, Alleges Insider Trades in Web Firm." *Wall Street Journal,* November 18, 2008.

CUSTOMER RELATIONSHIP MANAGEMENT (CRM)

Customer relationship management (CRM) refers to the type of enterprise software that is designed to improve a company's interaction with its customers and thereby increase revenue from sales. In addition to offering the potential to increase revenue, CRM can also reduce the cost of supporting customers. CRM has the ability to move any transaction to the lowest cost channel possible and still satisfy customer needs.

CRM can provide a complete view of all customer relationships, taking into account all points of customer contact and the different media through which customers interface with the enterprise. CRM systems give companies the ability to track customer interaction across a range of channels, from e-mail to call centers. CRM can also provide the customer data required to conduct personalized marketing campaigns, elements of which might include offers tailored to an individual visiting a company's Web site, dynamically served-up Web pages for different users, and personalized e-mail offers and announcements.

CRM covers a range of products and vendors. It is often fragmented, with no single package delivering complete functionality, according to *Bank Systems & Technology* magazine. Among the technologies included in a CRM environment are sales force automation (SFA), customer analytics, real-time marketing solutions, customer behavior modeling, and real-time decision making. CRM technology is designed to allow the customer to view, access, and interact with the complete set of services offered by the enterprise.

Different components of CRM relate to the different goals of customer acquisition, customer retention, and improved customer value. SFA and marketing applications are designed to help a company acquire more customers and convert prospects into customers. Data warehousing and analytical tools, along with customer service applications for call center and contact center management, help companies retain customers through improved communications and customer relations. CRM applications that can help improve customer value include marketing automation and campaign management software for cross-selling and up-selling. Data warehousing and analytical tools are also available to improve customer value.

SOME CRM VENDORS

As CRM became more popular, the advancements made by customer service providers became more competitive in nature. Companies began to find value in mergers and acquisitions. Salesforce.com, headed by Marc Benioff, became a mainstay of the industry throughout the 2000s, and in 2011 the company acquired Radian6, a social media monitor and provider, for $326 million. This move was designed to help connect popular public social networks with the private Chatter, the social network available only for the Salesforce.com enterprise.

As Oracle continued growing, it also found success in mergers. In fact, since the creation of the original company in 1977, CEO Larry Ellison has spearheaded the acquisition of 70 tech companies. In 2011, the company was completing a deal to buy the Art Technology Group (ATG) for $1 billion. ATG was a provider of e-commerce software and helped supplement the presence in the online market that Oracle was aiming for.

CRM AND SOCIAL MEDIA

Online communication and social networks have both had impact on CRM strategies and providers. The late 2000s saw the rise of Facebook, YouTube, Twitter, and innumerable blogs in the social sphere, diffusing the power of marketing and communication among consumers. CRM quickly adopted social media strategies as part of its overall systems. On the back end, social media allowed CRM systems to quickly collect ready-made information on what customers were saying about promotions, products, and brands. On the front end, social media provided key ways for companies to enter into real conversations with customers, sending messages, replying to comments, linking to blogs, and sharing information through the Web in ways that were not possible for traditional customer service. As customers began communicating with each other more frequently, developing opinions, ratings, and reviews of products beyond what the company provided, brand management became an increasingly important part of CRM. Indeed, by the 2010s there were few aspects of business that CRM did not touch, from the customization of products to management of price strategies.

MARKET FOR CRM

As the 2000s progressed, CRM became a more common term, and online businesses began making plans for adopting full, and increasingly complex, CRM strategies. The e-tailers that survived the dot-com bust emerged stronger, as did those that survived the recession of 2008–2009. In the early 2010s, the CRM market began to explore several new, key methods of combining customer service management and e-commerce.

One major addition to the market was mobile CRM tools. Since mobile commerce and mobile networking began growing exponentially, e-commerce companies found it to their advantage to make mobile features and mobile analytics part of the CRM systems. In 2011, Sugar Mobile, for example, let customers interact with data when logging and sorting calls on their phones. Salesforce.com came out with Salesforce Mobile to compete with other CRM providers. The same year, Resco MobileCRM gave users the ability to access and share accounts on the popular Microsoft Dynamics CRM program. SAP, the well-known provider of enterprise resource planning software (a broader form of CRM incorporating primary business operations) released SAP Business ByDesign as a mobile version of their software, targeted specifically at small to midsize companies.

The focus on small and midsize companies was another important development of the 2000s, when it became clear that CRM was no longer only for corporate behemoths. Providers began to offer customized solutions for smaller companies, ways to build interdepartment teams for CRM projects, and methods to change internal controls and audit procedures to account for CRM. Small businesses found that it was easier to begin a slow adoption of CRM practices, focusing only on one department or type of service, then quickly expand and involve CRM training with their other customer service coaching for incoming employees.

Changes in pricing also brought CRM within reach of smaller businesses. In 2010, Microsoft announced that the new price for its Microsoft Dynamics CRM Online was $34 per user, per month, for the first year of service. This promotion put the price well below any other CRM packages at that time and caused other providers to reconsider their own pricing strategies.

CRM AND CONSUMER EXPECTATIONS

As consumers became more Internet-savvy in the 2000s, they also expected higher levels of quality and service. Chat functions became increasingly common. Accuracy and readability became key components of CRM strategies, since customers primarily encountered companies through information on Web sites, profiles, and blogs. Businesses began hiring content creators full time to manage their "voice" and style in order to give customers fully accurate data in a tone that matched their brand and the image they wanted to create. The online ordering process, with its sharp increase in payment options, also became an important test factor in determining successful online CRM.

EVALUATING CRM PERFORMANCE

CRM is more than a matter of having the right technology. It requires the support of a well-developed business plan. Perhaps the biggest cause of CRM project failures is not the technology but the lack of a clear-cut business plan that includes a method for measuring the success of a CRM solution. Companies tend to use customer satisfaction as a metric for performance, but cost savings can also be important and ultimately more useful, since focusing only on customer satisfaction can lead to losses because of redundant spending. A balanced evaluation that takes into account both tangible and intangible results works best when analyzing CRM. Of course, goal orientation also plays a major role. Customer retention is a measurable metric and often a goal of companies adopting new CRM processes. Increase sales revenue is a ubiquitous goal that can be attached to CRM practices, albeit indirectly.

Companies behind on data management techniques can also use CRM systems to update their databases and create new ways of managing data and data capacity for their companies. Other businesses prefer to set strategic goals like cross-selling, linking customer activities and profiles, and making customer management seamless across all departments.

CRM HORIZONS

While e-commerce became a mainstay for CRM strategies, brick-and-mortar organizations were also able to increase their own participation. New forms of CRM began edging toward combining online and storefront channels, allowing customers to order online but pick up items at a store for maximum convenience. The overarching goals of CRM also had their share of changes. Social CRM, the support of social and environmental issues to further customer engagement and seek goals beyond increased sales, became popular in the latter 2000s.

SEE ALSO *Business-to-Consumer (B2C) E-Commerce; Mass Customization.*

BIBLIOGRAPHY

"The 2011 CRM Influential Leaders." *Destination CRM,* August 2011. Available from http://www.destinationcrm.com/Articles/Editorial/Magazine-Features/The-2011-CRM-Influential-Leaders-76463.aspx.

Apicella, Mario. "Are You Being Served?" *InfoWorld,* July 16, 2001.

Bucholtz, Christopher J. "Successful CRM Champions Start Small, Thing Big, Act Fast." *E-Commerce Times,* September 8, 2011. Available from http://www.ecommercetimes.com/story/Successful-CRM-Champions-Start-Small-Think-Big-Act-Fast-73242.html.

Chiem, Phat X. "Special Report: Revolution Gives Way to Evolution." *B to B,* February 19, 2001.

Clark, Philip B. "The ROI of CRM." *B to B,* June 11, 2001.

"Customer Relationship Management." *InfoWorld,* April 16, 2001.

Leon, Mark. "CRM." *InfoWorld,* July 16, 2001.

Morgan, Jacob. "What Is Social CRM?" *Social Media Examiner,* November 3, 2010. Available from http://www.socialmediaexaminer.com/what-is-social-crm.

Morphy, Erika. "Microsoft Stirs Up CRM Market with Price-Cut Strategy." *E-Commerce Times,* October 14, 2010. Available from http://www.ecommercetimes.com/story/71033.html.

Schmerken, Ivy, et al. "Technology Makes Convergence a Reality." *Bank Systems & Technology,* May 2001.

Seybold, Patricia. *The Customer Revolution.* New York: Crown Publishing Group, 2001.

Ueland, Sig. "17 Mobile Apps for Customer Management." *Practical Ecommerce,* May 5, 2011. Available from http://www.practicalecommerce.com/articles/2763-17-Mobile-Apps-for-Customer-Management.

Walia, Sandeep. "Ecommerce Trends for 2011." *Ignify,* February 14, 2011. Available from http://blog.ignify.com/2011/02/14/ecommerce-growth-and-trends-for-retailers.

CYBER MONDAY

Black Friday, the day following Thanksgiving, was first considered a day of deals and promotions in the United States in the 1980s. Since many retailers depended on the holiday season in order to make a significant portion of their profits, Black Friday became associated with economic metrics and advertising alike. In 2005, however, a newly trending day entered the season as well: Cyber Monday, the Monday following Black Friday.

Several things kept Cyber Monday from being lumped together with the Black Friday weekend, in addition to its separate branding initiative. First, the deals offered focused primarily on e-tailers and online commerce in general. Second, Cyber Monday traditionally specialized in electronic goods, especially computer devices.

By the start of the 2010s Cyber Monday had become an institution for American shoppers who had become accustomed to shopping online for their Christmas needs. While Cyber Monday still brought in only a fraction of the sales of Black Friday, and the extended weekend was still dwarfed by the shopping days around Christmas, the new shopping day was growing in popularity and sales were seeing steady increases. E-commerce companies began to find they could offer a wider variety of promotions with Cyber Monday than storefront-bound shopping days could contain.

BEGINNINGS

Cyber Monday, like Black Friday, only began to be popularized as a result of marketing campaigns designed to draw attention to the deals offered by major companies. The primary difference was in speed of acceptance. For decades Black Friday was a negative term used to describe the crowding and irritation of the shopping days after Thanksgiving, although the term was ultimately redeemed through marketing efforts in the 1980s. Cyber Monday, however, began as a marketing initiative and quickly grew to prominence within only a few years.

The first use of the term was in 2005, when Shop.org used the phrase in a press release remarking on the increased online sales and shopping the Monday after Black Friday. The National Retail Foundation seized on the term and used to begin publicizing particular online deals in an effort to set the day apart.

The goal was to make Cyber Monday the most lucrative day for e-commerce in the season, and it came at an ideal time for the online industry. Internet speeds had reached the point where online shopping was quick and effective. Americans had adopted online purchasing and had become comfortable doing so at home or at the office, providing extra shopping time. E-tailers had created business models with efficient transaction methods and easy ways for customers to find what they were looking for on Web site stores. The first Cyber Monday of 2005 generated more than $486 million in sales.

DEVELOPMENT

While it took a couple years for Cyber Monday to become widely known, a variety of e-tailers jumped on the chance to offer separate, specialized deals of their own. In 2006, Cyber Monday pulled in $608 million in revenue. Between 2008 and 2009, sales rose by 14% and customers bought nearly 30% more products online. Sales rose to $883 million in 2009. By 2010, an estimated 85% of online retailers offered an online deal for the day, up from 43% in 2006.

It was no surprise that online-oriented and electronic goods were the most popular sellers. The Amazon.com e-reader, Kindle, was one of the best-selling products in Cyber Monday 2009. Best Buy and Barnes and Noble also developed major promotional plans for the day, as did Overstock.com, Blue Nile, and many other corporations dependent on online sales. Not only did Cyber Monday help make them extra profits, but the expected effect also tended to increase company stocks prices around the day.

EVOLUTION AND PITFALLS

In 2010, Cyber Monday made news again by breaking the $1 billion mark in sales, making $1.028 billion, a 16% increase from 2009. E-tailers had become so comfortable with the day that they were customizing deals in anticipation. Best Buy began to combine online deals with in-store deals, both for Cyber Monday promotions. Amazon.com, traditionally one of the biggest winners in Cyber Monday, continued to evolve its Lightning Deals, online discounts that only applied for a few minutes at a time and generated increased customer interest in the site.

Following its success, Cyber Monday began to run into several issues by the late 2000s. Companies eager to jump on the bandwagon began to offer Cyber Monday deals that were no different from the promotions they had been using before. Fake e-mail confirmations began a wave of scams that took advantage of Cyber Monday buying. Some deals promising easy returns or free shipping managed to insert unexpected fees in the buying process and disappointed consumers.

One of the primary difficulties that Cyber Monday began facing by 2010 was the ease at which companies could offer deals. As promotions were offered at earlier and earlier times, some Wall Street analysts, such as Brian Sozzi, who was quoted in an article by Agustino Fontevecchia in *Forbes,* believed that Cyber Monday would again be absorbed into Black Friday and cease to have any separate relevance. To prevent this development, companies like Amazon.com began strict policies of offering deals that began at midnight on Sunday and not before.

SEE ALSO *Amazon.com; Marketing, Internet.*

BIBLIOGRAPHY

Fontevecchia, Agustino. "Black Friday Bleeds into Cyber Monday as Retailers Roll into December." *Forbes,* November 29, 2010. Available from http://www.forbes.com/2010/11/29/black-friday-overview-markets-equities-monday.html.

"History of Cyber Monday." *Cyber Monday 2011,* 2010. Available from http://www.cybermonday2011.com/2009/11/history-of-cyber-monday.

Kavilanz, Parija. "Cyber Monday: A Lot of Clicking and Shopping." *CNN Money,* December 1 2009. Available from http://money.cnn.com/2009/12/01/news/economy/cyber_monday_shopping.

Lentz, Jon. "Retailers Hope Cyber Monday Keeps Shoppers Buying." *Reuters,* November 29, 2010. Available from http://www.reuters.com/article/2010/11/29/usa-retail-cyber monday-idUSN2920136820101129.

Mayerowitz, Scott. "Cyber Monday: Myth and Reality." *ABC News,* November 26, 2007. Available from http://abcnews.go.com/Business/ChristmasCountdown/story?id=3905931&page=1.

Saba, Michael. "Cyber Monday: A Brief History." *Paste Magazine,* November 30, 2009. Available from http://www.pastemagazine.com/articles/2009/11/cyber-monday-a-brief-history.html.

"Scope Out These Cyber Monday Deals." *CBS News,* November 27, 2010. Available from http://www.cbsnews.com/stories/2010/11/27/earlyshow/living/parenting/main7094179.shtml.

Van Grove, Jennifer. "Cyber Mondey Makes History: Online Spending Exceeds $1 Billion." *Mashable,* December 1, 2010. Available from http://mashable.com/2010/12/01/cyber-monday-2010-spending.

CYBERCULTURE: SOCIETY, CULTURE, AND THE INTERNET

Few technologies in human history rival the Internet in terms of the speed with which it was adopted and the range of its impact. The spread of the Internet has been compared to the advent of the printing press, which, like the Internet, greatly enhanced the availability of information and the rate of its reproduction. Many have commented on the Internet's ability to transform business and the broader economy, but perhaps an equally profound change is being felt throughout society and culture, where the Internet and the World Wide Web are transforming how people live and interact. The Internet's influence generates a range of reactions from different people, ranging from idealism to cynicism, but however it is received, there is no denying that it has led to dramatic shifts in such areas as interpersonal interaction, work culture, relations to time, expectations of speed and convenience, networking between individuals and groups, and even use of language.

The word "cyberculture" is used in a variety of ways, often referring to certain cultural products and practices born of computer and Internet technologies, but also to specific subcultures that champion computer-related hobbies, art, and language. In the 1970s, cyberculture was the exclusive domain of a handful of technology experts, including mathematicians, computer scientists, digital enthusiasts, and academics, devoted to exchanging and promoting ideas related to the growing fields of computers and electronics. These early cyberculturists sometimes advanced a view of the future guided by the progressive and beneficial hand of technological change. Yet following the commercialization of the Internet and the World Wide Web in the mid-1990s, cyberculture took on a new life, and computer and information technologies took the dynamics of culture and social relations in dramatically new directions.

The Internet became even more pervasive in the early years of the twenty-first century, with more than two billion users around the world in March 2011, according to Internet World Stats. The same source showed 245,000,000 Internet users in the United States in March 2011, including more than 151,350,260 using the Facebook social media platform, as of June 2011. Faster download speeds and the spread of mobile technology helped expand the usage of social networks; photo, music, and video sharing platforms; virtual gaming; hyper-local news sites (e.g., Patch.com) and shopping offers (e.g., Groupon.com); and online storefronts for retailers.

INFLUENCE OF THE WEB

The Internet touches many parts of life in advanced industrial societies, and its influence is growing in developing countries as well. Everything from shopping, paying bills, and playing the stock market to news gathering, family interaction, romantic courtships, job hunting, medical consulting, and play all take place in cyberspace—activities that before the mid-1990s took place in more traditional settings. The Internet profoundly influences what and how children learn, the vocabulary employed in daily conversation, the way people coordinate their schedules and work habits, and perceptions of distance and time. With the ability to jump from China to Brazil to Los Angeles within a minute via videoconferencing or online telephone systems, and with e-mail offering lightning-fast communication, the Web has taken the advancements of the telephone several steps further toward bridging physical distances between people, not to mention time. For that matter, the Internet is a 24-hour-a-day operation, and thus consumers are no longer confined by store hours or locally available inventories to go shopping.

Internet and cyberculture enthusiasts come from all shades of political persuasion. Conservatives applaud the Internet's subversion of state functions such as taxation and regulatory interference with the free activity of commercial interests. Liberals applaud the Internet's capacities to network disenfranchised groups and coordinate efforts toward greater social equality. Social media played a key role in organizing the protests during the "Arab Spring" political upheaval in 2011 as well as in the London civil riots later that year.

But if cyberculture has been hailed by all shades of political opinion, it is also criticized by as broad a spectrum. Social conservatives rail against the excessive openness of the Internet and its attendant capacity to spread materials and ideas they find indecent or morally or socially unacceptable, while left-leaning advocates warn against the excessive commercialization of the Internet and its tendency to transform social needs and relationships into personalized consumer needs, fracturing social solidarity. Terrorist organizations such as al-Qaeda have also used Web sites, blogs, and social media to organize their campaigns, as have international criminal organizations. With so much complexity around the implications of cyberculture, it is safe to say that arguments for and against Internet practices are not drawn along clear political lines.

INTERNET ADDICTION

The lure of the online world has also raised concerns about Internet addiction, which was first identified as a growing problem in 1996 by Dr. Kimberly Young, founder of the Center for Internet Addiction. The ease of Internet access and the anonymity of the virtual world can draw in persons who already have compulsive behaviors, such as gamblers. United Press International reported in 2010 that Florida college students were twice as likely to be compulsive gamblers than the general population, with online poker cited as the main cause of the growing problem.

However, the Internet itself can also be addictive. A 2011 study by behavorial research group Intersperience, as reported by *International Business Times,* found that for many people, "giving up Internet technology for even one day was like an addict trying to quit smoking or drinking." The study suggested that "withdrawal from the Internet is how smokers feel when they haven't had a cigarette in a considerable amount of time." Another 2011 study by the online security company Webroot claimed that social networking is a form of Internet addiction which was being exploited by cybercriminals.

THE INTERNET AND WORK CULTURE

The Internet has greatly changed the nature of work in connected segments of the world. For instance, work increasingly is performed outside of the traditional work place—a central office or factory—and more often in homes and other remote locations. The most cybercultured companies, moreover, more or less do away with the physical models of work, and are little more than interconnecting networks rather than physical, hierarchical organizations. Telecommuting allows workers to adjust their schedules to their own convenience and perform work in the comfort of their home offices. Various studies cited by SuiteCommute show improvements of productivity for home-based workers of 15% to 40%, with IBM Canada showing improvements of up to 50%. (Globally, up to 43% of IBM employees telecommute, saving the corporation more than $100 million in real estate costs alone.)

CYBERPERSONALITIES AND VIRTUAL COMMUNITIES

The anonymity afforded by the World Wide Web is another crucial element of cyberculture. Individuals routinely create screen names and, in some cases, online personalities that may or may not diverge from the ones they project in the physical world. Again, this feature could be either a blessing or a curse. On the one hand, the anonymity offers space for individuals who may feel ostracized or isolated to access information and take part in communities that may be practically off limits in the physical world. On the other hand, critics note that the anonymity simply fosters a culture of mischief in which individuals may indulge in social behaviors online that would be unacceptable in face-to-face interaction, and perhaps even illegal or subversive activities. Using avatars and other forms of alternative identities also tempts many people to be dishonest, such as lying about personal details, or posting out-of-date photographs of themselves (or even using another person's image).

The early 2000s witnessed extensive growth in virtual communities. Second Life, the first major online virtual world to move beyond gaming into creating an alternative world, received considerable media hype around 2007. The platform and its virtual marketplace attracted a number of major brands, including Coca-Cola, Limited Express, American Apparel, and Toyota. The *Washington Post* reported that online entrepreneurs selling virtual items to Second Life's 770,000 users spent more than $567 million in 2009, a 65% increase over the prior year. Second Life itself reported annual revenues of $100 million in 2011. Second Life also provided a platform for medical education and remote patient care. However, by 2011, publications such as *Technology Review* were reporting that Second Life had not met the heavy expectations that were placed upon it in its early years. "Seekers of the next big thing had moved on to the richer fields of Facebook and Twitter and Apple i-gadgets," the publication stated.

Indeed, many of the Second Life features that were innovative in the early 2000s were commonplace in the broader-based social media sites like Facebook, Twitter, and LinkedIn that took off in the middle of the decade. The virtual communities pioneered by Second Life had become a staple in social networking and gaming sites. Online storefronts had been adopted by eBay, Amazon.com, and other major Web-based retailers. And as those platforms drew more followers, the advertising dollars flowed to those sites as well.

By 2010, Facebook was the dominant platform for cyberculture and social networking. In 2011, Facebook claimed 750 million active users around the world, moving it easily past the older MySpace as the top site worldwide. Facebook was embraced not only by the general public—which used it for staying in touch with friends and family, planning high school reunions, and sharing personal stories—but by companies that wanted to market to attractive demographic groups. Facebook, which launched in 2004 as a way for Harvard University students to connect, had annual revenues estimated at $2 billion by 2011. However, Google, the Internet search giant, had begun to challenge Facebook for social networking dominance with the 2011 launch of its own Google+ network.

One of the leading beneficiaries of Facebook's rapid growth was Zynga, a company that makes social network-based games such as FarmVille, CityVille, and MafiaWars. Zynga had $850 million in revenues and 270 million active users in 2010, with virtually all its business coming through its partnership with Facebook.

Companies like Second Life and Zynga make much of their income through virtual transactions: selling items that players use in their games. Zynga games are free, so the company makes most of its money by selling virtual tractors to FarmVille players, for example. Research firm Javelin Strategy and Research defined virtual goods as including both "virtual currency as well as other intangible objects purchased for use in online games or communities." Javelin also stated, "The virtual goods market has experienced significant growth in recent years, with growth projected to increase from $0.6 billion in 2009 to $2.4 billion in 2012 in the U.S. alone."

SEE ALSO *Community Model; Facebook Inc.; Virtual Communities.*

BIBLIOGRAPHY

Baker, Liana B. "Zynga Draws Fewer Paid Players Than Expected." *Reuters,* August 11, 2011. Available from http://www.reuters.com/article/2011/08/11/us-zynga-idUSTRE77A6RL20110811.

Bockmier, Zack. "Zynga Likely to Benefit from Facebook-Google+ Competition." *Seeking Alpha,* August 17, 2011. Available from http://seekingalpha.com/article/287885-zynga-likely-to-benefit-from-facebook-google-competition.

Bournellis, Cynthia. "Cyberculture–Focus On Human Needs." *Electronic News,* July 20, 1998.

Center for Internet Addiction. Bradford, PA, 2011. Available from http://www.netaddiction.com.

Dibell, Julian. "Serious Games: The Online World of Second Life Seemed Like the Next Big Thing, Only to Be Written Off." *Technology Review (Cambridge)* 114, no. 1 (January 2011): 74.

"Google+ and Facebook." *Live Trading News,* August 19, 2011. Available from http://www.livetradingnews.com.

"Internet Addiction: Study Says Internet Is Like Cigarettes." *International Business Times,* July 27, 2011. Available from http://www.ibtimes.com/articles/187931/20110727/internet-addiction-study-says-internet-is-like-cigarettes.htm.

Internet World Stats. "Usage and Population Statistics." Bogota, Colombia, August 2011. Available from http://www.internet worldstats.com.

Mitchell, Jon. "Second Life Makes $100M a Year in Revenue." *ReadWriteWeb,* August 8, 2011. Available from http://www.readwriteweb.com/archives/second_life_makes_100m_a_year_in_revenue.php.

"The PC Is a Cruel Mistress: How Computers Affect Quality of Life." *Canadian Business,* September 18, 2000.

"Productivity." St. Louis, MO: SuiteCommute, 2011. Available from http://www.suitecommute.com/research-and-statistics/statistics/productivity.

Rosenwald, Michael S. "In the Virtual World, Making Actual Millions." *Washington Post,* March 8, 2010. Available from http://www.washingtonpost.com/wp-dyn/content/article/2010/03/07/AR2010030703524.html.

"Second Life Lessons." *Business Week,* November 27, 2006. Available from http://www.businessweek.com/magazine/content/06_48/b4011413.htm.

"Social Networking Is an Exploitable Internet Addiction Says Webroot." *InfoSecurity,* August 19, 2011. Available from http://www.infosecurity-magazine.com/view/20213/social-networking-is-an-exploitable-internet-addiction-says-webroot-.

Tilley, Julie, and Brian Kaihoi. "Virtual Worlds: A New Universe for Education, Patient Care and More." *PT in Motion* 3, no. 6 (July 1, 2011): 16.

"Virtual Currency and Social Network Payments–The New Gold Rush: How Emerging Virtual Transactions Will Alter the Payments Landscape Forever." Pleasanton, CA: Javelin Strategy and Research, June 29, 2011. Available from http://www.researchandmarkets.com/research/53ccd0/virtual_currency_a.

Walmsley, Andrew. "Facebook Dominates, but (. . .)." *Marketing,* August 3, 2011. Avalable from http://www.market ingmagazine.co.uk.

CYBERSPACE

Cyberspace refers to the online world that is formed by computer systems and networks. The word was coined by author William Gibson in his science fiction novel *Neuromancer* (1984). The term gained currency in the mid-1980s as a definition of the virtual world that existed due to the advent of the Internet, which in its earliest form was a community that shared ideas and information.

E-COMMERCE

The rising popularity of e-commerce has made it nearly impossible to go online and enter cyberspace without encountering a barrage of advertising and commerce information. For instance, when the search engine Yahoo! was first introduced, no shopping links appeared on its home page. By the early 2000s, this had changed, and Web surfers using the site to search for information saw a list of online stores pop up, offering products related to their search. Similarly, Google, through its AdWords and AdSense features, allows businesses to pay in order to raise their value on the Search Engine Results Page (SERP). These campaigns accounted for 96% of Google's approximate $30 billion in revenue in 2010. This revenue rose in accordance with the number of people browsing for items online.

From November to mid-December 2000, online spending more than doubled over the same time period in the previous year, reaching $8.7 billion. By 2010, online spending accounted for $43 billion in the fourth quarter, an 11% jump over 2009. In the same year, 84% of people using the Internet made purchases online, which was a 6% rise over the previous year. Since almost any cyberspace visitor was a potential customer, it became increasingly worthwhile for companies to set up shop in cyberspace.

To protect the growing numbers of online consumers and merchants, e-commerce legislation known as cyberlaw emerged. Similar to laws in the real world, cyberlaw deals with topics such as the protection of copyrights, business transactions, electronic payment systems, prosecution of cybercrime, and privacy. This type of legislation continues to develop in response to the evolution of cyberspace, commercial and otherwise. In 2010, the Berkman Center for Internet & Society at Harvard University considered Distributed Denial of Service (DDoS) attacks to be a potential area of concern in future years. DDoS attacks became increasingly prevalent at the end of the 2000s, particularly as a device for social networks, governments, and competitors to damage the Internet presence of target organizations, such as independent media, human rights, or private businesses.

The most common DDoS attacks were conducted by a large number of computers, which would all attempt to access a target's Web site simultaneously, continuing to request access for hours to render the Web site temporarily unavailable. Some of the most notable attacks in 2010 targeted the Motion Picture Association of America, the Recording Industry Association of America, the British Photographic Industry, PayPal, Visa, and MasterCard. These attacks through cyberspace were conducted by groups of people responding to actions taken by the target organizations. Such vigilante tactics were, as of early 2012, not punishable by cyberlaw, illuminating one new area that would require lawmakers' attention in the years to come.

SEE ALSO *Cyberculture: Society, Culture, and the Internet; History of the Internet and World Wide Web (WWW); Virtual Communities; Virtual Communities.*

BIBLIOGRAPHY

Barham, Richard. "Quest for Harmony in Cyberspace." *The Banker,* August 2000.

Colin, Robert, and Lori Enos. "Report: 85 Percent of Net Surfers Shop Online." *E-Commerce Times,* May 31, 2000. Available

from http://www.ecommercetimes.com/story/3440.html?wlc=1316908450.
comScore. "comScore Reports Record-Breaking $43.4 Billion in Q4 2010 U.S. Retail E-Commerce Spending, Up 11 Percent vs. Year Ago." Reston, VA, February 4, 2011. Available from http://www.comscore.com/Press_Events/Press_Releases/2011/2/comScore_Reports_Record-Breaking_43.4_Billion_in_Q4_2010_U.S._Retail_E-Commerce_Spending.
Cyber-Geography Research. "What Is Cyberspace?" 2001. Available from http://personalpages.manchester.ac.uk/staff/m.dodge/cybergeography/what_cyberspace.html.
Enos, Lori. "Study: E-holiday Spending Doubled." *E-Commerce Times,* December 27, 2000. Available from http://www.ecommercetimes.com/story/6306.html.
Google, Inc. "Form 10-K." Mountain View, CA, 2011. Available from http://investor.google.com/documents/20101231_google_10K.html.
Regan, Keith. "These Are the Web's Good Old Days."*E-Commerce Times,* June 2, 2000. Available from http://www.ecommercetimes.com/story/3463.html.
Zuckerman, Ethan, Hal Roberts, and Jillian C. York. "Distributed Denial of Service Attacks Against Independent Media and Human Rights Sites." Cambridge, MA: The Berkman Center for Internet & Society at Harvard University, 2010. Available from http://cyber.law.harvard.edu/events/luncheon/2011/01/zuckerman_roberts.

CYBERSQUATTING

The bane of companies, organizations, brand names, and celebrities, cybersquatting is the practice of registering the name of a company, trademark, brand, or person as a domain name for a Web site in hopes of misleading users to one's own site by using a well-known name. The top-level domain (TLD), the highest level of the Uniform Resource Locator (URL) such as *sitename.com* or *sitename.org,* is the portion of the Web address that companies covet most. Companies generally prefer the URL that will be easiest to remember and thus more recognizable to the visitor. Cybersquatters attempt to beat the company, individual, or organization to the punch in registering that domain. Failing that, squatters may try closely related alternatives, such as adding a hyphen or a single letter to the domain name to lure inattentive users. At times cybersquatters have registered these names in hopes of selling them back to their namesakes at a handsome profit, but U.S. court rulings and laws have curtailed these activities.

Businesses fear that cybersquatting exploits and erodes their brand identities. The domain-name registration system does not prevent users from selecting a registered trademark as a domain name. In essence, if a particular name or variation of a name has not been registered already, almost anyone can register it for a small fee. Given the ease of acquiring names, the strategy of cybersquatters is to route traffic to their sites from unsuspecting followers of another brand or identity, thereby generating an audience for themselves. The most malicious form of cybersquatting happens when squatters take a certain brand or identity and associate it with negative or offensive materials, for example, routing a children-related domain name to a pornographic Web site.

Cybersquatters may have a variety of intentions. The most common goal is to hold the domain hostage, so to speak, and name a ransom price at which the squatter hopes to sell it to the company, trademark holder, organization, or individual. Cybersquatters also simply try to attract visitors to their Web sites by exploiting a popular name, either to expand the audience for their own message or product or to boost their advertising revenue.

Relief from cybersquatting came with the Anti-Cybersquatting Consumer Protection Act (ACPA), passed in 1999, which was designed specifically to curtail the registration of domain names that used others' trademarks or trade names. The law covers unregistered trademarks and individual names as well. ACPA applies to all TLDs, covering the three most common suffixes, known as generic top-level domain names (gTLDs), *sitename.com, sitename.net,* and *sitename.org,* as well as all country-code top-level domain names (ccTLDs), such as *.ca* for Canada and *.fr* for France. Prior to ACPA, victims of cybersquatting had little recourse, and many ended up paying the exorbitant fees demanded by squatters to purchase their own names. Since cybersquatters can be prosecuted under ACPA, the law has generally made cybersquatting less profitable, though it has hardly stamped out the practice.

The Internet Corporation for Assigned Names and Numbers (ICANN) is the official body charged with monitoring the allocation of domain names. In December 1999, ICANN unveiled a standard procedure for settling name disputes, the Uniform Domain Name Dispute Resolution Policy (UDRP). ICANN's procedure determines the plausibility of the cybersquatting claims using three tests. First, it verifies that the domain name is identical or confusingly similar to the trademark. Then, it determines whether the domain name owner maintains a legitimate interest in the name. Finally, ICANN judges whether or not the domain owner acted in bad faith.

UDRP had been proposed by the World Intellectual Property Organization (WIPO), according to the organization's Web site. The WIPO was formed in 1994 as a body that would facilitate private-party alternative dispute resolution (ADR) for international commercial disputes. It was, then, in a perfect position to arbitrate disputes of cyberproperty.

In addition to suing under ACPA, after 2000 companies suffering from cybersquatters were provided with one more recourse—filing UDPRs with WIPO. WIPO would process disputes for $1,500 per domain name, and if the dispute was deemed valid, then WIPO would force the illegal registrant to turn over the domain name. Disputes were often processed in under two months. For example, in 2009 LEGO filed a widely reputed dispute with WIPO over the misuse of the domain name *freelegoporn.com* and won.

In addition to litigation, individuals, firms, and organizations have a number of strategies at their disposal to combat cybersquatting. The most common is to simply register, as quickly as possible, other similar domain names, such as those with and without hyphens or with commonly used initials. Many companies and individuals have even gone so far as to register or purchase the domain names of possible "gripe sites," also known as cyberbashers. During the 2000 U.S. presidential campaign the Web site George-Bushsucks.com routed curious visitors to the official George W. Bush campaign site. Chase Manhattan and other large companies engaged in similar preemptive strikes against cyberbashers and squatters.

But for some companies, such as Verizon Communications Inc., preemptive strikes proved inadequate. The company fought a long, hard fight with cybersquatters; in 2009, Sarah Deutsche, vice president, reported the company had reclaimed, "9 million new visitors, just from [domain] names we've managed to get back." The company had also bought up more than 10,000 domains in self-defense, but cybersquatters continued to harass the company's organic traffic. With little recourse, the company began suing, under ACPA, the companies that were feeding off its site, as it noticed that some companies were setting up high quantities of sites. By incurring severe penalties on the businesses that were doing significant portions of the damage, Verizon managed to curtail the propagation of unwanted sites.

Cybersquatting initially receded in the first half of the 2000s. After UDRP and ACPA provided a means to combat the practice, WIPO recorded fewer and fewer cases. From 1,857 cases in 2000, the numbers had dropped to 1,557 and 1,207 in 2001 and 2002, respectively. After 2004, however, cases began to rise again, and by 2010 there were 2,696 disputes filed on 4,370 domain names, a new record. The rise in activity could be attributed, in part, to the rise of Google, as affiliate marketers were able to make money by rerouting traffic from their fake domains to the real corporate entity they were posing as. In this dark twist of fate, corporations would pay Google for bringing visitors to their site, and Google would pay the cybersquatters for "advertising."

It is likely that 2012 will be another big year for the "industry," as ICANN announced a new slew of domain name extensions to be added. The company hoped to dissuade cybersquatters by attaching a hefty price tag for the service: $185,000 for the extension and a $25,000 annual fee. In effect, this would raise the penalty payment to the level of a significant lawsuit. If ICANN proceeded with its plan, losing a domain extension would come to mean $185,000, thereby making extensions untenable for illegal entities. In turn, clients would be able to see immediately whether they had been directed to a legitimate or illegitimate site simply by looking at the extension.

SEE ALSO *Domain Name; ICANN; Uniform Resource Locator (URL).*

BIBLIOGRAPHY

Brown, Marc E. "Don't Pay Off a Cybersquatter." *Electronic Business,* March 2000.

Copeland, Lee. "Cyberbashers Proliferate." *Computerworld,* February 21, 2000.

"ICANN Call It What I Want." *Economist,* September 9, 2000, 74.

Lesser, Lori E. "'Cybersquatting' Law Aids in Pirate Prosecutions." *Journal of Property Rights,* January 2000.

Miller, Amy. "Will ICANN Domain System Thwart Cybersquatters?" *Law Technology News,* July 26, 2011. Available from http://www.law.com/jsp/lawtechnologynews/PubArticleLTN.jsp?id=1202506481767 &slreturn=1 &hbxlogin=1.

Mitchell, Robert. "Domain-Name Wars: Rise of the Cybersquatters." *PCWorld,* June 25, 2009.

Plave, Lee J. "Franchisors Brandish Pair of Powerful Weapons in the War on Cybersquatters." *Franchising World,* September/October, 2000.

Railo, Matt J. "Protecting Brands Online: Practical Considerations in the Fight Against Cybersquatting." *Intellectual Property & Technology Law Journal,* December 2000.

Ulanoff, Lance. "ICANN's New Domain Policy Resets the Web." *PCMag.com,* June 20, 2011. Available from http://www.pcmag.com/article2/0,2817,2387270,00.asp.

WIPO. "Cybersquatting Hits Record Level, WIPO Center Rolls out New Services." Geneva, Switzerland, March 31, 2011. Available from http://www.wipo.int/pressroom/en/articles/2011/article_0010.html.

D

DATA ENCRYPTION STANDARD (DES)

Highly sensitive digital information is often the target of computer hackers, international spies, and criminals. In order to protect such information, in 1977 the National Security Agency (NSA) and the National Bureau of Standards (NBS) adopted the Data Encryption Standard (DES) to protect sensitive, unclassified, nonmilitary digital information from unauthorized access. Encryption is the intentional scrambling or masking of digital data to protect it from compromise.

DES utilized symmetric-key (or private-key) encryption, in which the sender and receiver of a message share a single, common key that is used to encrypt and decrypt the message. The key is a string of digits that has been generated by a complex mathematical algorithm, or formula. Private-key encryption differs from public-key encryption, which utilizes two keys—a public key to encrypt messages and a private key to decrypt them. Private-key systems are simpler and faster, but their main drawback is that both parties must somehow exchange the key in a secure manner. Public-key encryption avoids this problem because the public key can be distributed in a nonsecure way, and the private key is never transmitted. In the former case, secrecy is shared between only two users, whereas in the latter, the public key is a more or less an "open secret." Thus, public-key encryption requires many more bits to rival private-key systems' level of protection.

Although the NSA usually supervises development of governmental encryption systems, its hesitation over creating such a system for public use led to an open call for the system's design. Ultimately IBM produced a 56-bit key algorithm that became DES. Controversy arose over the extent to which DES-encrypted products could be exported outside the United States, since federal regulations govern export of encrypted items. Security considerations led the U.S. government to limit the export of encryption systems to those of 40 bits or less. Since DES employed 56 bits, most products incorporating DES could not be exported, despite a report on national encryption policy issued by the National Research Council in 1996 that called for a relaxation of export regulations.

DES underwent its most serious challenge in 1998, and failed. The Electronic Frontier Foundation (EFF) constructed a custom-designed machine, which broke open a DES-encrypted code in 56 hours. Subsequent tests, conducted on 100,000 PCs networked with the EFF machine, reduced the time required to 22 hours. This procedure resulted in the lifting of the U.S. restrictions on exporting DES-encrypted products.

DES's efficacy under continuous surveillance was reassessed every five years after its inception. The 1998 EFF crack-through concluded that DES' Achilles heel was its short key length. DES's versatility also was limited because it worked only in hardware, and the explosion of the Internet and e-commerce led to much greater use and versatility of software than could have been anticipated by DES's designers.

As DES's vulnerabilities became apparent, the National Institute of Standards and Technology (NIST) opened an international competition in 1997 to find a permanent replacement for DES. To be christened the Advanced Encryption Standard (AES), the replacement would be operable into the twenty-first century. NIST recommended a minimum key length of 128 bits and sought to guarantee that encrypted files would continue to be secure even after AES was eventually phased out. In addition, the algorithm had to implement public-key cryptography and work with key sizes of 128, 192, and 256 bits. Flexibility also was a premium concern of AES' designers. AES had to function with eight-bit processors, smart cards, ATM networks, high-definition TVs, voice-recognition systems, and satellite communications. Finally, it had to be available internationally on a nonexclusive, royalty-free basis.

RIJNDAEL

By 2000, Rijndael, an algorithm, was chosen as the DES replacement. Designed by Joan Daemen and Vincent Rijmen, the new AES would stymie all of the code-cracking strategies known at the time. Differential, truncated differential, square, interpolation, and linear attacks would not work on either software or hardware encrypted with AES. In fact, the best-known decoding attempt would be to automatically input every possible combination. At a rate of 50 billion combinations per second, this process would require billions of years. This was true for the 128-bit key, which was the smallest bit-size and easiest to crack.

Shortly after the creation of AES, DES became relatively easy for hackers to break. According to *ComputerWorld,* a 2004 computer system could crack a DES encryption within two or three hours. The system would not need any advanced math to do so but would be able to accomplish this feat simply by positing every possible permutation of the encryption key.

In 2004, the NIST moved for withdrawal of Federal Information Processing Standard (FIPS) certification from DES. Once accepted, old systems, software and hardware, needed to be replaced because they were not adaptable to new encryption key types. The new wave of encryption spread across corporations, consumer trends, and governments.

Ultimately, DES was a testament to the pace of technological change in the late twentieth century. It was considered to be adequately powerful and impenetrable in its day. However, the cracks in DES widened into gaping holes as cryptographic and computer technology developed, and as the Internet and other networked systems heightened the need for flexible and durable encryption.

ENCRYPTION AND SMARTPHONES

By 2011, encryption was brought to mobile apps. A German computer engineer, Karsten Nohl, proved that consumers needed protection by hacking into a number of well-known companies' telecommunications feeds. He and his assistant only needed to use a combination of free apps to do so. The news quickly spread that, according to Nohl, two companies did not even encrypt their data, while a number of other companies provided weak resistance. This was particularly true for general packet radio service (GPRS) networks, which had been implemented in 2000. However, according to the *New York Times,* even the more modern 3G networks would often reroute customers to GPRS, in many cases sacrificing security to do so.

SEE ALSO *Advanced Encryption Standard; Cryptography, Public and Private Key; Encryption; Hacking.*

BIBLIOGRAPHY

Anthes, Gary H., and Patrick Thibodeau. "IT & the Feds: The Five Years." *Computerworld,* June 14, 1999.

Danielyan, Edgar. "Goodbye DES, Welcome AES." *Internet Protocol Journal,* 4, no. 2 (2001). Available from http://www.cisco.com/web/about/ac123/ac147/archived_issues/ipj_4-2/goodbye_des.html.

Harrison, Ann. "Advanced Encryption Standard." *Computerworld,* May 29, 2000.

———. "Cryptographers Urge Review of Standard." *Computerworld,* August 23, 1999, 4.

———. "Encryption Standard Finals." *Computerworld,* August 16, 1999, 6. Available from http://www.computerworld.com.au/article/22593/encryption_standard_finals/#closeme.

———. "Feds Propose New Encryption Standard." *Computerworld,* October 9, 2000.

Hulme, Geroge V. "Commerce Department Picks Rijndael Encryption Formula." *InformationWeek,* October 16, 2000.

Landau, Susan. "Designing Cryptography for the New Century." *Communications of the ACM,* May 2000.

Loshin, Pete."Cryptographic Turning Points." *Computerworld,* August 28, 2000.

Mearian, Lucas, and Patrick Thibodeau. "Encryption Mandate Puts Strain on Financial IT." *ComputerWorld,* August 4, 2003. Available from http://www.computerworld.com/s/article/83685/Encryption_mandate_puts_strain_on_financial_IT.

Messmer, Ellen."Crypto Proposal Faces Long Journey." *Network World,* October 16, 2000.

O'Brien, Kevin J. "Hacker to Demonstrate 'Weak' Mobile Internet Security." *New York Times,* August 9, 2011. Available from http://www.nytimes.com/2011/08/10/technology/hacker-to-demonstrate-weak-mobile-internet-security.html.

Roberts, Paul. "NIST Says Data Encryption Standard Now 'Inadequate'." *ComputerWorld,* July 29, 2004. Available from http://www.computerworld.com/s/article/94910/NIST_says_Data_Encryption_Standard_now_inadequate_.

Yasin, Rutrell. "U.S. Picks AES Encryption Spec: Belgian Formula Seen Overcoming DES's Vulnerability to Hackers and Hardware Requirements." *Internetweek,* October 9, 2000.

DATA INTEGRITY

Information is what gives power to the Web and e-commerce. In a matter of minutes, consumers are able to research, compare, and purchase products and services online. This availability of information has created more discriminating consumers and has put increased pressure on retailers to offer competitive prices. Understandably, the accuracy or integrity of data is very important during e-commerce.

SOURCES OF FAULTY DATA

The integrity of data can be compromised in a variety of ways, including malicious proprietors, human mistakes, and technical error. Unfortunately, like accurate information, faulty, inaccurate, or misleading information also travels freely on the Internet, and consumers and companies alike have been negatively affected by it.

Fraudulent business schemes account for a significant amount of erroneous information on the Web. Sellers often make faulty or exaggerated claims about products and services that sometimes do not exist. According to Nua Internet Surveys, a study by the Worldwide E-Commerce Fraud Prevention Network found that 50% of businesses in the United States saw online fraud as a significant problem. Ten percent of those companies ranked online fraud as their "most significant problem." Among those surveyed, half had experienced losses between $1,000 and $10,000, and 19% in excess of $100,000.

Some schemes were easy to achieve and highly pernicious. In 2011, a wave of businesses were wrongfully reported to be closed on Google Places, according to the *New York Times.* Many of these business owners did not become aware of the problem until weeks after the crime, and therefore lost customers who believed their enterprises had shut down. At that time, the Google system was based upon good faith.

INTERNET CRIME COMPLAINT CENTER

In the 2000s, Internet fraud diversified, matured, and became increasingly consumer-focused. Online auctions were among the leading areas of e-commerce fraud in the early 2000s, comprising 71.2% of complaints registered with the U.S. Internet Crime Complaint Center (IC3). The IC3 was the organization responsible for harboring complaints, issuing referrals to appropriate organizations and disseminating information regarding current trends in Internet fraud. The organization registered more than 20,000 complaints in its first six months of existence. Sixty-four percent of the complaints involved auction fraud.

Over the course of the decade, attacks became less predictable and more numerous. In 2010, there were 303,809 complaints, or an average of 25,332 complaints per month. Auction fraud took less than 6% of total cases reported, whereas nondelivery of payment/merchandise ranked first, with 14.4% of reports. FBI-related scams comprised 13.2%, and identity theft was listed with 9.8% of total reports. Target profiles had also become more evenly distributed among age groups, with approximately one-fifth of cases reported by persons from each of four age groups: 20–29, 30–39, 40–49, and 50–59.

ENSURING DATA INTEGRITY

Although there is no universal way to ensure the integrity of data, and technical errors are bound to occur from time to time, consumers and companies alike are able to take measures to protect themselves. Common sense and critical evaluation were essential first lines of defense for both parties. For consumers, measures could be taken to verify the identity of a Web site's owner. Secure certificates issued by companies like VeriSign were means of doing this in the 2000s. Secure sockets layer (SSL) certificates would be issued by any Certification Authority (CA), of which there were roughly 650 by 2011. SSL certificates issued by any one of these companies would be recognized by users' Web browsers. However, the system had its flaws. In 2011, there were two major breaches in Internet security, when hackers were able to break into two CAs, Comodo and DigiNotar, and issue fraudulent certificates for their own use. According to *PCWorld*, perpetrators were able to steal user login information, intercept communications, and purvey other vital information accessible by the user. When news came out in August of the breach, users were furious, in part because there was nothing they could do but hope their accounts would not be targeted.

Proponents of changing the system, such as security researcher Moxie Marlinspike, claimed that SSL certification did not allow users to adjust quickly to security breaches, such as those with Comodo and DigiNotar. While any user could choose what CAs to trust, rejecting a popular CA would mean that some Web sites would become unavailable. Therefore, users were likely to continue accepting CAs from Comodo and DigiNotar, despite the possibility that their information could be unsafe.

SEE ALSO *Digital Certificate; Fraud, Internet; Misinformation Online.*

BIBLIOGRAPHY

"Auction Sites Generate Most Complaints." NUA Internet Surveys, March 8, 2001.

Bloomberg, Jason. "Shopping Carts and Data Integrity." *EarthWeb,* April 27, 1999. Available from http://www.developer.com/tech/article.php/1024811/Shopping-carts-and-Data-Integrity.htm.

"Data Integrity." *Webopedia,* May 3, 2001. Available from http://www.webopedia.com/TERM/D/data_integrity.html.

Fitzpatrick, Michele. "The Fight for Data Integrity." *Chicago Tribune,* July 7, 2000.

Goldsborough, Reid. "Information on the Net Often Needs Checking." *RN,* May 1999.

Internet Crime Complaint Center. "2004 Internet Fraud Crime Report." United States, 2011. Available from https://www.ncjrs.gov/App/publications/Abstract.aspx?id=210759.

———. "2010 Internet Crime Report," 2011. Available from http://www.ic3.gov/media/annualreport/2010_ic3report.pdf.

Kendis, Randall. "DataIntegrity—Who Cares?" *Chain Store Age Executive with Shopping Center Age,* April 1998.

Lemos, Robert. "Time for a Better Web of Trust?" *Darkreading,* August 8, 2011. Available from http://www.darkreading.com/advanced-threats/167901091/security/attacks-breaches/231300428/time-for-a-better-web-of-trust.html.

Segal, David. "Closed, Says Google, but Shops' Signs Say Open." *New York Times,* September 5, 2011. Available from http://www.nytimes.com/2011/09/06/technology/closed-in-error-on-google-places-merchants-seek-fixes.html.

Tyburski, Genie. "Honest Mistakes, Deceptive Facts." *Legal Assistant Today,* March/April, 2000.

Udo de Haes, Andreas. "Hackers Forge Certificates to Break into Spy Agencies." *PCWorld,* September 4, 2011. Available from http://www.pcworld.com/article/239497/hackers_forge_certificates_to_break_into_spy_agencies.html.

Wallace, Bob. "Data Quality Moves to the Forefront." *Informationweek,* September 20, 1999.

"Worldwide E-commerce Fraud Prevention Network: U.S. Firms Concerned about Online Fraud." NuaInternet Surveys, April 10, 2001.

DATA MINING

Data mining is the practice of ferreting out useful knowledge from the wealth of information stored in computer systems, databases, communications records, financial and sales data, and other sources. A staple of the so-called information economy, data mining has evolved into a standard—and often requisite—business practice, and is often as valuable to firms as their underlying products or services. With competition heating up and making use of the mountains of new information technologies, those most able to exploit data mining to derive insights for use in a business model or strategy are often those with a competitive edge.

Data mining combines expertise in data analysis with sophisticated pattern-searching software to crunch diverse mountains of data and churn out information designed to capture market share and boost profit margins. As the sheer wealth of information available escalated through the 1990s and 2000s, such techniques assumed paramount importance. The focus of data mining is on organizing data and identifying patterns that translate into new understandings and viable predictions. Companies thus try to use data mining to discover relationships between data and phenomena that ordinary operations and routine analysis would otherwise overlook, and thereby identify squandered opportunity, redundancy, and waste.

Data mining combines features of various disciplines, particularly computer science, database management, and statistics, to map low-level data into more advanced and meaningful forms. In its truest form, data mining is part of the broader knowledge discovery from data (KDD) process, although the terms are often used interchangeably. KDD refers to the entire process of data warehousing, organization, cleansing, analysis, and interpretation. Colloquially, however, data mining stands for this entire process of deriving useful knowledge, using computational systems, from massive amounts of data. According to Forrester Research, predictive analytics and data-mining solutions bring together business intelligence, enterprise data warehousing, and many other platforms and tools that drive planning and operational decisions.

Data-mining software systems are generally based on a combination of mathematical algorithms designed to seek out and organize information by variables and relationships. For instance, one common algorithm is called recursive partitioning regression (RPR). RPR processes all the variables chosen for a particular set of data and parses them for their explanatory power, that is, for the degree to which they account for variations in the data. In sifting through customer profiles, for example, the algorithm would isolate information such as personal incomes, education levels, sex, and so on.

DELINEATION OF DATA MINING

The data-mining process is divided into three stages: data preparation, data processing, and data analysis. In the first stage, the data to be mined is selected and cleared of superfluous elements in order to streamline mining. In the second stage, the data is run through the algorithms at the heart of data mining, and characteristics and variables are identified and categorized, thereby transforming the data into broader, more meaningful pieces of information. In the final stage, the extracted information is analyzed for useful knowledge that can be applied to a business strategy.

Data-mining software was first developed in the late 1960s and 1970s as a way of tracking consumer purchasing habits. Over the years, the application of data mining extended beyond retail to encompass larger-scale business practices and was combined with advances in database management, artificial intelligence, computers, and telecommunications to constitute extremely powerful tools for knowledge extraction. The early 2000s saw a broad range of predictive analytic software that provided increasingly more sophisticated data mining solutions for companies of all sizes. In particularly, the use of Predictive Model Markup Language (PMML) made it easier and more efficient to share mined data between different types of statistical programs, systems, and platforms.

Traditionally, data mining was used primarily for categorized information; in other words, techniques and tools were designed to find relationships and patterns in masses of data that were already segmented into different categories via structured databases, such as a customer's age and residence. Later techniques greatly expanded the power of data mining by allowing for mining of unstructured text documents, such as e-mails, customer requests, and Web pages. In this way, data mining applies structure to loosely organized data and highlights valuable information that might otherwise be missed. This technique, known as text mining, creates a database of words that can be categorized and a sophisticated search engine to seek out those words and related alternatives. The National Centre for Text Mining has been established at the University of Manchester in the United Kingdom to provide text-mining services for the academic world.

Many times the first step toward data mining is building a data warehouse, a vast electronic database to contain and organize the wealth of information collected. Without a data warehouse, companies lack the infrastructure to mine useful knowledge out of the data available. Like word processing programs and computer operating systems, data mining has grown more user-friendly and graphics-based as its application has spread throughout society to less technically inclined users. Software programs increasingly feature visualization techniques to dramatize specified data, relationships, and patterns.

Data mining has become a crucial component of customer management. The most common form of data mining begins with the accumulation of various kinds of customer profiles. These can take the form of simple names and addresses derived from other firms' customer lists and used for purposes of mass mailing, or they can constitute more sophisticated and comprehensive reports on consumer tastes and buying habits. Over time, firms amass great quantities of customer profiles through their own sales and through arrangements with other firms, and apply data-mining techniques to sift through them for clues as to how to adjust their strategies.

Whether to attract, service, or maintain customers, businesses position data mining at the cornerstone of customer relations. Using advanced data-mining techniques, companies can determine what level of spending can be expected from a particular customer, the range of his or her tastes, the customer's likeliness to churn (i.e., leave), and a range of other information useful for customer relations. In these ways, companies are better able to assess the value of its individual customers, and adjust its resources accordingly. More broadly, they can derive comprehensive information on demographic patterns, like distinctions in purchasing patterns between age groups, income levels, and ethnic backgrounds, to discover additional retention and cross-selling possibilities. In this way they can segment their customer bases into specialized marketing focuses. By shifting outreach, advertising, and service resources to effectively capitalize on their diverse clientele, firms can realize cost savings, better conversion rates, and higher margins.

In the e-commerce world, data mining carries an additional range of benefits. In particular, as e-commerce merchants worked to create the maximum amount of value out of what the Web has to offer, they moved to personalize products and services. The extraction of personal information allowed by data mining greatly facilitated this process. By plugging data-mining analysis into customer-service databases and their Web applications, companies can tailor products and services to accord with individual customers' habits and preferences, thereby maximizing value.

The software industry responsible for data-mining programs was enjoying solid sales growth in the late 2000s and early 2010s. The market research firm International Data Corp. (IDC) estimated that the market for business analytic application software and solutions (including data mining) would grow by 7% annually through 2014, "with even greater growth expected over the next ten years." IDC also found the global business intelligence tools market grew from $7.8 billion in 2008 to $8.9 billion in 2010. The top five business analytics vendors were SAP, IBM, SAS, Oracle, and Microsoft in 2010.

PREDICTIVE MODEL MARKUP LANGUAGE

The introduction of PMML has been a major factor in the growth of data mining. PMML is a standard for statistical and data-mining models developed by the Data Mining Group, a consortium of more than 20 vendors and other organizations. In announcing Version 4.0 of PMML in 2007, the group stated, "The idea behind the product is to make it 'straightforward' to develop a model on one system using one application, and deploy the model on another system using another application." The group claimed PMML saved organizations months of work to integrate and deploy data-mining models across platforms. PMML uses Extensible Markup Language (XML) to create common structures and documents that can then be read by other applications.

The uses of data mining go beyond market research and product planning. Retailers combating employee fraud examine data from automated sales transactions to pinpoint cashiers who may be stealing from the company. Data mining can also aid criminals; *SC Magazine* reported that AT&T sued two Utah men in 2011 who allegedly used data mining to steal customer data, costing the company $6.5 million.

However, data mining is not restricted to corporations. Data-mining techniques are also used by governments to tackle security issues and by medical researchers seeking new treatments from existing drugs. The *New York Times* reported that data-mining techniques have been applied to analyze propaganda practices by the Confederacy during the U.S. Civil War and to study the British criminal justice system by analyzing records from the Old Bailey court in London.

However, the broad expansion of data-mining practices has also run into some ethical and legal challenges. In 2011, the U.S. Supreme Court overturned a Vermont law that tried to limit the marketing approach called "detailing," wherein pharmaceutical companies mine data about individual physicians' prescription tendencies to help them pitch new drugs to those doctors. *Computerworld* reported that data-mining tools can also draw incorrect conclusions if the information being examined is not consistent, the tools are not used correctly, or the user does not analyze the results properly.

SEE ALSO *Customer Relationship Management; Database Management.*

BIBLIOGRAPHY

Akst, Jef. "Data Mining for New Treatments." *The Scientist,* August 18, 2011. Available from http://the-scientist.com/2011/08/18/data-mining-for-new-treatments.

Bell, Stephen. "Law Commission against Data Mining Regulation." *Computerworld New Zealand,* August 15, 2011. Available from http://computerworld.co.nz/news.nsf/news/law-commission-against-data-mining-regulation.

Cohen, Patricia. "As the Gavels Fell: 240 Years at Old Bailey." *New York Times,* August 17, 2011. Available from http://www.nytimes.com/2011/08/18/books/old-bailey-trials-are-tabulated-for-scholars-online.html.

Data Mining Group. "PMML 4.0: General Structure of a PMML Document." Chicago, IL, August 2011. Available from http://www.dmg.org/v4-0-1/GeneralStructure.html.

Drew, James H., D.R. Mani, Andrew L. Betz, and Piew Datta. "Targeting Customers with Statistical and Data-Mining Techniques." *Journal of Service Research,* February 2001.

Greenhouse, Steven. "Shoplifters? Studies Say Keep an Eye on Workers." *New York Times,* December 30, 2009. Available from http://www.nytimes.com/2009/12/30/business/30theft.html

"IDC Finds Demand for Business Analytics Software and Solutions Growing as End Users Become More Aware of the Technology's Benefits." Framingham, MA: International Data Group, October 7, 2010. Available from http://www.idg.com/www/pr.nsf/ByID/IDGC-8MBQTH.

Kobielus, James. "Advanced Analytics Predictions for 2010." *Forrester Blogs,* December 15, 2009. Available from http://blogs.forrester.com/business_process/2009/12/advanced-analytics-predictions-for-2010.html.

———. "The Forrester Wave: Predictive Analytics and Data Mining Solutinos, Q1 2010." Cambridge, MA: Forrester Research, February 4, 2010. Available from http://www.forrester.com/rb/Research/wave%26trade%3B_predictive_analytics_and_data_mining_solutions%2C/q/id/56077/t/2.

Le Beau, Christina. "Mountains to Mine." *American Demographics,* August 2000.

Liddy, Elizabeth D. "Text Mining." *Bulletin of the American Society for Information Science,* October/November 2000.

Liptak, Adam. "Drug Makers Win Two Supreme Court Decisions." *New York Times,* June 24, 2011. Available from http://www.nytimes.com/2011/06/24/business/24bizcourt.html?pagewanted=all.

Masi, C. G. "Data Mining Can Tame Mountains of Information." *Research & Development,* November 2000.

Moscaritolo, Angela. "AT&T Sues Two Over Scheme to Steal Customer Data." *SC Magazine,* August 17, 2011. Available from http://www.scmagazineus.com/att-sues-two-over-scheme-to-steal-customer-data/article/209763.

National Centre for Text Mining. "Welcome to NaCTeM." Manchester, UK, 2011. Available from http://www.nactem.ac.uk.

Nelson, Robert K. "Of Monsters, Men and Topic Modeling." *Opinionator* blog, *New York Times,* May 29, 2011. Available from http://opinionator.blogs.nytimes.com/2011/05/29/of-monsters-men-and-topic-modeling.

Palace, Bill. "Data Mining: What Is Data Mining?" Los Angeles, CA: University of California, Anderson School of Management, 1996. Available from http://www.anderson. ucla.edu/faculty/jason.frand/teacher/technologies/palace/datamining.htm.

Reitsma, Reineke. "Trends That Will Shape Market Research in 2011: Organization, Technology and Social." *Forrester Blogs,* December 20, 2010. Available from http://blogs.forrester.com/reineke_reitsma/10-12-20-trends_that_will_shape_market_research_in_2011_organization_ technology_and_social.

Stedman, Craig. "Data Mining for Fool's Gold." *Computerworld,* December 1, 1997.

DATA WAREHOUSING

Data warehousing refers to the organization and assembly of data created from day-to-day business operations. Data warehousing enables a user to retrieve data from online transaction processing (OLTP) and online analytical processing (OLAP), and allows for the storage of that data in a format that can be read and analyzed. The integrated information, which is stored in a data warehouse, can be analyzed and queried to help management make more informed business decisions.

The idea of data warehousing dates back to the early 1980s. At that time, a popular system that utilized the concept of data warehousing was the relational database, which was run on minicomputers and used for OLTP functions. Quite often, relational database systems operated networks such as automated teller machines. As technology continued to advance, several key factors—including changing business trends, the evolution of the global economy, enterprise resource planning (ERP), business process reengineering (BPR), increased focus on customer needs, and the rise of e-business—led to the development of data warehouses in the 1990s.

Run on powerful client/server networks, not only can data warehouses read OLTP, they are equipped to translate OLAP as well. The development of data warehousing enabled companies to gather several types of information concerning business transactions, as well as important analytical data. In *Contract Professional Magazine,* Pam Derringer wrote that as a knowledge tool, "data warehousing restructures massive volumes of unorganized data into new formats that can be queried for answers to individual questions or sliced and diced for analytical trend reports."

DATA TYPES

Two important types of information in data warehousing are operational and informational data. Operational data—the data businesses use on a day-to-day basis—is stored, retrieved, and updated by an OLTP system. This type of data normally is stored in a relational database. Informational data is operational data that has been manipulated and summarized, and is what makes up a data warehouse. In the process of data warehousing, informational data is created from operational data and systems by using transformation or propagation tools. This process is necessary to ensure that the information can be retrieved in an easy and time-efficient manner. Multidimensional analysis, or OLAP, is the desired result of data warehousing. It allows a user to analyze large amounts of data regarding things like sales, products, time periods, and geographies. The multidimensional data structure, or data warehouse, allows for the storing and analyzing of such data.

Another component to data warehousing is metadata, which is made up of technical data and business data. Technical data is used by system administrators and contains information about the data warehouse itself. Business data, on the other hand, is what an analyst might be searching for in order to forecast sales or predict trends. Data mining tools are then used to interpret data and find patterns within the information. For example, a retail company might use data warehousing and data mining to find relationships in purchasing patterns and to gather information about its customers.

Implementing a data warehouse structure within a company can be a costly and time-intensive process. These barriers have led to the development of data marts, data warehouse appliances, and on-demand business intelligence software—smaller versions of data warehouses that are more specialized to serve a specific department, cover a specific topic, or cater to midsize and small companies. Traditional data warehouses are measured in terabytes and petabytes, whereas the more compact data marts are measured in terabytes. Smaller companies, with more limited budgets, often opt for these types of data structure because their data sources are not as varied.

Each year, as the billions of dollars spent online for products and services increases, businesses are turning to advanced data management solutions to analyze information, make forecasts, look for trends, identify shopper characteristics, and control inventory. This has increased the demand for data warehousing and, therefore, increased competition between solution-based companies. According to a Gartner report, in the early 2010s Teradata, Oracle, and IBM were the biggest names in the industry.

By the 2010s, data warehousing clients could pick and choose services, hardware, and software from a variety of vendors. According to *InformationWeek,* "Historically customers choose the database first and the hardware second, but appliances are blurring those lines." Appliances are built for specific functions within a business. Designed to integrate easily with existing business intelligence tools, these appliances were another possible solution for large companies in need of adding to existing data warehousing structures.

CLOUDS OF DATA

Cloud technology played an increasingly significant part in the data warehousing industry, adding volatility to an already fast-paced field. For example, data firm Greenplum announced an "Enterprise DataCloud" initiative in 2009 to enable large enterprises, with data warehousing and data mart structures, to connect their various databases with a single infrastructure, accessed via a cloud application. Theoretically, this would optimize costs for large enterprises that were expanding. According to analyst Curt Monash, Greenplum was offering a valuable service, as centralized data warehousing was extremely limiting for large enterprise.

One year later, Greenplum was acquired by EMC, a key player in the industry that had been a major storage-systems provider. The acquisition repositioned EMC to offer integrated data warehousing appliance and cloud/virtualization solutions. The 2010 Gartner report on the industry expected consolidation of the market to continue, as well as increasing demand for cloud-based services.

SEE ALSO *Cloud Computing; Database Management; Information Management Systems.*

BIBLIOGRAPHY

"2004 DM Review 100 Numerical Ranking." *DM Review,* 2004. Available from http://www.netezza.com/media/2004/DMReview_top100.htm.

IBM Corp. "Data Warehousing Concepts for AS/400." Armonk, NY, 2000.

Derringer, Pam. "Data Warehousing: The Next Boom?" *Contract Professional Magazine,* 2000.

Eckerson, Wayne W. "Ten Rules for Building an Intelligent Business for the E-world." Seattle, WA: The Data Warehousing Institute, 2000.

Henschen, Doug. "Gartner Ranks Data Warehousing Leaders." *InformationWeek,* February 10, 2011. Available from http://www.informationweek.com/news/software/info_management/229215658.

———. "HP's Half-Step Back into Data Warehousing." *InformationWeek,* February 16, 2011. Available from http://www.informationweek.com/news/software/info_management/229218795.

Kanaracus, Chris. "Greenplum Spins 'Enterprise Data Cloud' Vision." *PCWorld,* June 8, 2009. Available from http://www.pcworld.com/businesscenter/article/166305/greenplum_spins_enterprise_data_cloud_vision.html.

Moye, Joe, and Dave Upton. "Data Warehousing 101." *Strategic Finance,* February 2001.

Schroeck, Michael. "Data Warehousing: The Past 10 Years Have Been Quite a Ride." *Information Management,* February 2001. Available from http://www.information-management.com/issues/20010201/3007-1.html.

SAP. "SAP Solutions for Small Businesses and Mid-Size Companies." Newton Square, PA, June 8, 2009. Available from http://www.sap.com/solutions/sme/index.epx.

DATABASE MANAGEMENT

Database management refers to the process of storing and manipulating the information housed in a database. Databases can be as simple as the electronic address books used by individuals to keep track of e-mail recipients or as complex as electronic library systems or online flight reservation systems. Typically, some sort of query system allows users to gain access to specific information in a database. For example, electronic library systems often are designed to accept queries such as "a = author name," "t = title," and "s = subject." Therefore, the query "title = War and Peace" would retrieve all database entries which contained "War and Peace" in the title field. The tools used to actually manage databases are grouped together into database management systems (DBMSs). Several types of DBMSs exist, including those designed for personal computers (PCs), as well as those running on large mainframe systems.

HISTORY OF DATABASE MANAGEMENT

Although various rudimentary DBMSs had been in use prior to IBM Corp.'s release of Information Management System (IMS) in 1966, IMS was the first commercially available DBMS. IMS was considered a hierarchical database, in which standardized data records were organized within other standardized data records, creating a hierarchy of information about a single entry. In the late 1960s, firms like Honeywell Corp. and General Electric Corp. developed DBMSs based on a network data model, but the next major database management breakthrough came in 1970 when a research scientist at IBM first outlined his theory for relational databases. Six years later, IBM completed a prototype for a relational DBMS.

In 1977, computer programmers Larry Ellison and Robert Miner cofounded Oracle Systems Corp. Their combined experience designing specialized database programs for governmental organizations landed the partners a $50,000 contract from the Central Intelligence Agency (CIA) to develop a customized database program. While working on the CIA project, Ellison and Miner became interested in IBM's efforts to develop a relational database, which involved Structured Query Language (SQL). Recognizing that SQL would allow computer users to retrieve data from a variety of sources and sensing that SQL would become a database industry standard, Ellison and Miner began working on developing a program similar to the relational DBMS being developed by IBM. In 1978, Oracle released its own relational DBMS, the world's first relational database management system (RDBMS) using SQL. Oracle began shipping its RDBMS the following year, nearly two years before IBM shipped its first version of DB2, which would become a leading RDBMS competing with the database management applications of industry giants like Microsoft Corp. and Oracle. Relational databases eventually outpaced all other database types, mainly because they allowed for highly complex queries and could support various tools which enhanced their usefulness.

In 1983, Oracle developed the first portable RDBMS, which allowed firms to run their DBMS on various machines including mainframes, workstations, and personal computers. Soon thereafter, the firm also launched a distributed DBMS, based on SQL-Star software, which granted users the same kind of access to data stored on a network they would have if the data were housed in a single computer. By the end of the decade, Oracle had grown into the world's leading enterprise DBMS provider with more than $100 million in sales.

It was not long before DBMSs were developed for use on individual PCs. In 1993, Microsoft Corp. created an application called Access. The program competed with FileMaker Inc.'s FileMaker Pro, a database application initially designed for Macintosh machines.

IMPACT OF THE INTERNET ON DATABASE MANAGEMENT TECHNOLOGY

The rise of the Internet prompted the development of many new database management system features. These were designed to enable clients to take advantage of Internet-based opportunities such as e-commerce, which emerged in the late 1990s.

Database management giants like Oracle had begun tailoring their products to the Internet in the mid-1990s. For example, the firm's Web-enabled Oracle Express Server 6.0, launched in 1996, offered online data analysis functionality on both the Internet and corporate intranets. Oracle began to restructure itself around its Internet operations in 1998 when it released Oracle 8i, a version of its flagship database management product that allowed firms to manage all of their database functions on the Web. Oracle continued to develop new Internet-based technology in 2000. In May, the firm launched its E-Business Suite, as well as the Oracle 9i DBMS, which included an application server allowing users to run e-commerce applications related to their databases. The new product also offered file and document management, e-mail, Web server, and message queuing features.

By then, both Microsoft and IBM had begun to pay more attention to the DBMS market, recognizing its importance to the increasingly Web-based information technology industry. Microsoft began discussing plans to upgrade its SQL Server to support extensible markup language (XML), the language used to create Web documents, in 1997. According to an October 2000 article in *InformationWeek,* "XML is one of the primary areas that all the major database vendors have scrambled to embrace. Why is XML so important? XML facilitates communications between systems that normally don't speak the same language. Because of its self-describing nature, XML provides a way to pass information between dissimilar systems with some level of confidence that it will be properly interpreted on the other end. Direct XML support in the database means there is no need for any other tool to translate data from an external provider into something that can be used immediately." As a result, XML support, which included the ability to store, manage, index and search XML documents, was seen as increasingly necessary for DBMSs.

MANAGING BIG DATA WITH CLOUD COMPUTING AND NOSQL

With the success of Web sites such as Google, Amazon.com, eBay, Twitter, and Facebook came an emphasis on the scalability of database management systems. As of May 2010, the YouTube video collection required 600 terabytes of space, according to *InformationWeek.* This data was constantly being updated and accessed, making it almost impossible to house the data under any DBMS using Structured Query Language (SQL). As a result, Internet companies increasingly purchased DBMSs that did not use SQL. According to *InformationWeek,* "A big reason for this movement, dubbed NoSQL, is that different implementations of Web, enterprise, and cloud computing applications have different requirements of their databases. Not every app requires rigid data consistency, for example." Firstly, the data was distributed over thousands or even millions of users, rather than existing in a single data warehouse. Secondly, users of these Web sites unpredictably added, deleted, and changed information, requiring an entirely different set of characteristics from those used for internal operations.

By 2010, there were markets for both SQL and NoSQL DBMSs. There are two sets of standards of compliance for DBMSs. Businesses running customer relations management software and other critical functions required their DBMSs to comply with "ACID" standards—atomicity, consistency, isolation, and durability. However, companies like Facebook and Amazon, as well as many mobile apps, prioritized "BASE" standards—basically available, soft state, and eventually consistent. These qualities allowed for chaotic flow of data into and out of networks consisting of millions of users. In order to provide BASE standards, NoSQL DBMSs segmented data through a process called sharding. Sharding a database would split the data into an array of networks, whereas relational databases required the data to be shared via a single network.

Another reason for apps' reliance on NoSQL boiled down to simple economics. Many apps implemented data from a number of disparate sources. Sometimes, they would draw on thousands of servers to provide their basic functions. Using SQL-based DBMSs meant paying per-processor licensing fees, whereas NoSQL server software did not cost anything. Access was made possible via cloud services, which allowed companies to avoid fees entirely.

Despite these economics, analysts predict a continued market for SQL DBMSs. For business services such as customer relations management, relations databases were necessary for their consistency, isolation, and ability to manipulate data. Relational databases would continue to play an important role in database management systems. At the same time, companies would have the option of using NoSQL as well, particularly when their business model was reliant on high user volume.

SEE ALSO *Data Mining; Data Warehousing; IBM Inc.; Information Management Systems; Oracle Corp.*

BIBLIOGRAPHY

Borysowich, Craig. "An Overview of Database Management Systems." *Toolbox.com,* April 10, 2007. Available from http://it.toolbox.com/blogs/enterprise-solutions/an-overview-of-database-management-systems-15615.

Ferrill, Paul. "Databases That Focus on the Net." *Information-Week,* October 9, 2000.

"IBM vs. Oracle: It Could Get Bloody." *BusinessWeek Online,* May 28, 2001. Available from http://www.businessweek.com/magazine/content/01_22/b3734104.htm.

Korzeniowski, Paul. "Microsoft Delivers Knockout Punch." *VARbusiness.* October 1, 2001.

North, Ken. "The NoSQL Alternative." *InformationWeek,* May 22, 2010. Available from http://www.informationweek.com/news/development/architecture-design/224900559.

Ogbuji, Uche. "Choosing a Database Management System." *IBM developerWorks,* July 2001. Available from http://www.ibm.com/developerworks/webservices/library/ws-dbpick/index.html.

Ricadela, Aaron, and Rick Whiting. "Microsoft Introduces SQL Server 2000." *InformationWeek,* December 20, 1999.

Zicari, Roberto V., ed. *On NoSQL Technologies.* ODBMS.org, December 2009. Available from http://www.odbms.org/download/OnNoSQL.pdf.

DAY TRADING

As one of the new economy's most popular pastimes, day trading generated intense emotions from supporters and detractors alike, and the practice was the source of much controversy. Sometimes referred to with derision as "recreational trading," day trading is a form of stock market activity in which investors, known as day traders, make blitzkrieg runs on several stocks for the purpose of generating very quick gains but without an eye toward long-term returns. The logic behind day trading holds that the rapid buying and selling of securities in response to very incremental movements can generate quick profits that result in tremendous savings over time. The concept gained popularity in the late 1990s, dropped off substantially after the Internet bubble burst in 2000, but continued to have some practitioners even after the 2008 stock market collapse.

The practice is premised on the idea that markets are not completely efficient. Therefore, small profits can be made by trading in expectation of tiny, incremental movements in stock. Day traders move in to capitalize on the market's corrections. Repeated often enough, these small transactions can escalate into hefty profits by the end of a day's trading, at which point day traders generally liquidate their entire portfolios. Since companies may issue announcements and company news after a day's trading has closed, day traders do not generally want to hold onto stocks overnight, since their line of work entails making split-second buy and sell orders before others can beat them to it.

DAY TRADING'S ROLLER-COASTER RIDE

Day trading got its start in the early 1990s, according to *Institutional Investor,* when a New Yorker named Harvey Houtkin began monitoring the delays between breaking news events and the adjustment of prices by certain dealers. Using the Nasdaq's Small Order Execution System, Houtkin made a name for himself by exploiting those delays to make a profit. By doing so, he opened the floodgates to hordes of new independent traders making connections to exchanges. In addition, these activities engendered the momentum that would evolve into the e-brokerage boom and the emergence of new trading media like electronic communications networks (ECNs).

Day trading made a splash in the late 1990s as the U.S. bull market seemed to defy gravity, and news accounts lauded the new economy. Additionally, the Internet opened new lines of business and gave birth to the dot-com stock craze while also lowering the costs of trading. All of these factors enticed new entrants into the field of stock trading. In order to compete with the traditional NASDAQ market makers without paying hefty, profit-reducing fees, day traders began to create their own electronic trading networks, such as Island ECN, to provide a space for buyers and sellers to trade and share real-time market information. As day trading grew more mainstream, the major online trading houses increasingly assumed the capabilities of the larger brokerages. They developed the technological means to scan several securities markets simultaneously, locate the best prices on given securities, and then purchase them instantaneously.

The day-trading binge was cradled by the can't-miss buzz surrounding dot-com stocks in the late 1990s. Paradoxically, this was a buzz that day trading helped to sustain. The most sensational stories told of middle-level office workers making millions by trading on their lunch breaks, or quitting their jobs to trade full time and retire at age 30.

In all, however, the hype surrounding day trading tended to inflate individuals' expectations, often with drastic effects. While there was, indeed, no shortage of success stories, they were in fact an unrepresentative sample. The North American Securities Administrators Association (NASAA) reported in 1999 that 77% of all day traders wound up losing money, while the average profit of the winners was a mere $22,000 over a period of eight months.

Following the dot-com and tech-market bust in Spring 2000, day trading was widely seen as a passing fad, and in large part the novelty was just that. But day trading never went away completely.

FOREIGN DAY TRADING

Day trading washed up on European shores several years after it dominated American business headlines. However, with it came the lessons of the American phenomenon. As a result, day trading took hold more slowly and more subtly than it had in the United States, gaining gradual acceptance in Europe, Asia, Australia, and other parts of the world. The *New York Times* reported that small investors in Japan turned to day trading after their stock market struggled for years with sluggish growth. The same publication also reported in late 2010 that up to 10,000 people in China were engaged in speculative day trading during the overnight hours when American markets are still open. The day traders included college students hired by trading firms from North America who were hiring inexpensive labor to flip stocks on major New York-based exchanges.

THE IMPACT OF DAY TRADING

Among professional money managers, day trading was widely perceived as a form of gambling engaged in by uninformed amateurs. Media reports such as a 2009 broadcast by *CBS News* compared day trading to compulsive gambling, pointing to the aforementioned study commissioned by NASAA that more than 70% of day traders lose money. A 2011 paper in *Gaming Law Review and Economics* made a similar argument, stating, "The risks, behaviors, and fates of many online day-traders are eerily similar to, if not indistinguishable from, those of online gamblers." Another report in the *Motley Fool* was even more blunt, stating, "Day trading isn't gambling—it's riskier than gambling."

While the high profile of day trading declined during the stock market turmoil of the first decade of the twenty-first century, the practice still continued around the world. *Money* magazine reported in July 2011 that there were 610,000 persons online who traded shares at least four times each month. While this number was 40,000 fewer than the same-day-trading statistic for 2008, it showed there were still plenty of speculative investors in the marketplace. (In fact, there was enough interest in the approach for the magazine to run several articles with pointers on becoming a successful day trader.) A December 2010 article in the *New York Times* noted that several day traders were still making a sizeable income from the market, or by providing paying subscribers with help in learning the ropes. The report noted that the social networking site Twitter has proven to be a natural platform for exchanging information in the rapid-fire world of day trading. Still, the article added, studies showed that only about 1% of day traders turned a profit on a consistent basis.

SEE ALSO *Volatility.*

BIBLIOGRAPHY

Barber, Brad, Yi-Tsung Lee, Yu-Jane Liu, and Terrance Odean. "Do Day Traders Rationally Learn about Their Ability?" Berkeley, CA: University of California, Haas School of Business, October 2010. Available from http://faculty.haas.berkeley.edu.

Barboza, David. "Day Trading, Conducted Overnight, Grows in China." *New York Times,* December 10, 2010. Available from http://www.nytimes.com/2010/12/10/business/global/10daytrade.html?pagewanted=all.

Fackler, Martin. "Small Investors in Japan Jump In." *New York Times,* November 7, 2008. Available from http://www.nytimes.com/2008/11/07/business/worldbusiness/07yen.html?pagewanted=all.

Futrelle, David. "Let Us Now Praise the Day Traders." *Money,* October 1999.

Griefner, Rich. "Day Traders: Dumber Than Ever." *Motley Fool,* May 11, 2010. Available from http://www.fool.com/investing/general/2010/05/11/day-traders-dumber-than-ever.aspx.

Maiello, Michael. "Day Trading Eldorado." *Forbes,* June 12, 2000.

Millman, Gregory J. "The Dawn of European Day Trading." *Institutional Investor,* December 2000.

"Profits by the Hour; It May Sound Scary So Here's What You Need to Know to Be a Successful Day Trader." *Money,* July 2011. Available from http://www.money.cnn.com.

Rose, I. Nelson. "How Securities Trading Became Legally Not Gambling." *Gaming Law Review and Economics* 15, no. 5 (May 2011): 249.

Salter, Philip. "Four Skills for Trading When Volatility Is High." *City A.M.,* August 9, 2011. Available from http://www.cityam.com/wealth-management/four-skills-trading-when-volatility-high.

"The Seduction of Day Trading." *CBS News,* February 11, 2009. Available from http://www.cbsnews.com/stories/1999/10/25/48hours/main67937.shtml.

Segal, David. "Day Traders 2.0: Wired, Angry and Loving It." *New York Times,* March 28, 2010. Available from http://www.nytimes.com/2010/03/28/business/28trader.html?pagewanted=all.

Sorkin, Andrew Ross. "An Addition to the List of Tax Loopholes." *New York Times,* July 11, 2011. Available from http://dealbook.nytimes.com/2011/07/11/an-addition-to-the-list-of-tax-loopholes/.

Stone, Robert, and Ashley R. Lyman. "Trading with A Day Job: Can Automated Trading Strategies Be Profitable?" *Journal of Business & Economics Research* 5, no. 10 (2007).

U.S. Securities and Exchange Commission. "Day Trading." Washington, DC, 2011. Available from http://www.sec.gov/answers/daytrading.htm.

———."Day Trading: Your Dollars at Risk." Washington, DC, 2011. Available from http://www.sec.gov/investor/pubs/daytips.htm.

Vines, Stephen. "Crash Course for Investors." *South China Morning Post,* August 15, 2011. Available from http://www.scmp.com.

DELL INC.

Dell Inc. is the third-largest personal computer (PC) vendor in the world behind Hewlett-Packard (HP) and Lenovo. Dell has worked to diversify its revenues portfolio throughout the 2000s and into the 2010s, expanding its services branch and acquiring companies in data storage and cloud software. In 2010, total revenues reached roughly $61.5 billion, and employees exceeded 43,000.

EARLY HISTORY

University of Texas freshman Michael S. Dell began selling IBM-compatible computers from his dorm room in 1984. Using parts he purchased at wholesale prices, Dell built the machines to closely resemble IBM models and then sold them to PC users looking to avoid the prices typically charged by computer retailers. Realizing that the $80,000 per month he brought in could easily be transformed into a full-fledged business, Dell left school and founded Dell Computer Corp. in April 1984. Believing that more experienced computer users would likely recognize the value his custom-built machines offered, Dell began placing advertisements in computer magazines. Customers used an 800 number to place orders; Dell would ship via mail upon completion. Dell used no middleman, and the firm's direct sales model allowed it to price machines significantly lower than competing PC vendors.

Dell quickly found itself a leader in mail-order PC sales. Revenues of $6 million in 1985 ballooned to nearly $40 million the following year. Realizing that he needed help managing the company's growth, Dell recruited several marketing managers from competitor Tandy Corp., as well as investment banker E. Lee Walker to serve as president. Dell himself served as CEO. In 1987, Dell began expanding its manufacturing facilities. The firm also created a national customer support center and started offering on-site setup, maintenance, and repair services for Dell products. An office in the United Kingdom marked the firm's initial foray into international sales. Dell also published its first catalog.

The firm's new marketing team began peddling Dell products to larger businesses. It also expanded Dell's sales force and increased advertising expenditures. Believing his firm was moving too far away from its initial direct selling model, Dell began criticizing his marketing executives for spending too much on advertising and using traditional marketing tactics. By the end of 1987, most of the executives from Tandy had either been asked to leave or had left on their own. Dell reorganized to improve its customer services in 1988. The firm also launched three new PC models, opened an office in Canada, began offering a leasing option, and increased its emphasis on targeting larger clients, such as governmental entities, corporations, and educational institutions. That year, Dell completed its initial public offering, selling shares for $8.50 each.

To better compete with Japanese PC firms that were lowering their prices, Dell began working to upgrade its machines. To this end, Dell hired former IBM Corp. engineer Glenn Henry in 1989, charging him with the task of overseeing product development. The firm also became one of the first to create file servers that used the Unix platform, and began working to incorporate Intel Corp.'s 486 microprocessor into its computers as soon as the chip was released. Dell also began selling several new dot matrix printers manufactured by Epson. Corporations accounted for 40% of the firm's 1990 revenues, which reached $546 million. Despite twofold sales growth, profits plunged by 64%, which Dell blamed on the higher research and development costs and a surplus inventory of memory chips. The firm began using retail outlets for the first time that year after reaching a sales agreement with Soft Warehouse Inc., a U.S. computer retailer. International growth continued with the construction of a manufacturing plant in Ireland and offices in France, Italy, and Sweden.

INTENSE GROWTH

Believing that its selling model was as important to the company's success as the products it sold, Dell devoted considerable resources to training its customer service staff, requiring all employees to complete a six-week training program—which covered how to answer questions, resolve complaints, take orders, and help clients select the best options for their computing needs—before allowing them to answer the phones. Customer complaints were aired in weekly staff meetings, which focused on how to best resolve issues. These efforts paid off in 1990 when J.D. Powers & Associates ranked Dell number one in its first customer satisfaction survey regarding PC makers. That year, the firm moved into 6th place among the largest U.S. PC manufacturers, compared to 22nd in 1989.

In 1991, Dell unveiled its first notebook PC, hoping to become a major player in the burgeoning market. International growth continued at a rapid pace. Subsidiaries were established in Belgium, Finland, Luxembourg, Norway, and Spain; a customer support center was set up in the Netherlands; sales offices opened in Ireland and Belgium; and a direct marketing and on-site service program launched in Mexico. To enhance its industry-leading customer service practices, Dell became the first PC maker to install applications software free for its clients.

Unlike many of its competitors, Dell actually benefited from the recessionary economic conditions of the early 1990s. Although corporate and consumer belt tightening was not severe enough to prevent PC users from making purchases, it did prompt many PC shoppers to seek discounted options for the first time. Consequently, Dell's customer base continued to swell. However, with the firm's success came increased competition from companies trying to imitate its direct sales model. One such copycat rival, Gateway 2000, replaced Dell as the leading U.S. PC direct seller in 1992. That year, Dell implemented a program that reduced on-site service call response time to less than four hours. The firm also created its Professional Services Capabilities Unit, which facilitated communication among Dell's systems integrators, network integrators, and consultants across the globe. Subsidiaries opened in Poland, the Czech Republic, and Switzerland. Sales grew to $890 million, and in 1992 Dell was listed as a *Fortune* 500 company for the first time.

By the end of 1993, Dell had become the world's fifth-largest PC maker with sales of more than $2 billion. To counter the deep discounting tactics of Compaq Computer Corp., Dell launched Dimensions by Dell, a new series of low-cost PCs. Competitors like Compaq found it difficult to compete with Dell because the direct seller's operating costs were only 18%, roughly half those of a traditional PC seller. Dell was able to achieve these operating costs in large part because it operated with a minimal inventory. Customers told Dell exactly what machine they wanted before Dell made it, eliminating the guesswork faced by PC makers who were selling their machines through retail outlets. In 1995, Dell's share of the worldwide PC market reached 3%.

IMPACT OF THE INTERNET

Dell's direct sales model was ideally suited to a medium like the Internet. Dell began selling its PCs and related equipment via the World Wide Web in 1996. Customers were able to place their order on Dell's Web site via a process similar to the one used when they called Dell on the phone. The firm's Internet store allowed users to choose configuration options, solicit price quotes, and place orders for single or multiple systems. The site also allowed purchasers to view their order status and offered support services to Dell owners. Within a year, Dell was selling roughly $1 million worth of computers a day via the Internet, and nearly 80% of the online clients were new to Dell. Since the Web helped to automate the PC purchasing process, Dell found itself able to handle the growing sales volume without having to drastically increase staff. By the end of 1997, nearly one-third of the orders received by Dell were being placed on the Internet.

According to a 2001 profile of Michael Dell in *Business-Week Online,* Dell "was e-business before e-business was cool. During the boom in technology spending, he used the Internet to reach out to customers and sell $50 million worth of computers a day." However, the Internet served as more than just a powerful sales medium for Dell in the late 1990s. The growing number of Internet users also fueled the server market, which Dell had started targeting in 1996, hoping to lessen its dependence on decreasingly expensive PCs. The following year, Dell also diversified into workstations. By 1998, servers were bringing in 16% of Dell's total sales, which topped $12 billion. One year later, Dell was second only to Compaq Computer Corp. in U.S. server sales. That year, when competitors once again began cutting PC prices, Dell responded with its first PC under $1,000. Sales nearly doubled to $25.3 billion, and stock prices surged roughly 140% for the fourth consecutive year.

As the PC industry continued to decelerate in 2000, Dell started repositioning itself as an Internet technology provider, increasing its focus on servers and also moving into the storage systems market. The firm also started selling a variety of Internet services such as wireless access to the Internet and Web hosting. In April 2001, Dell moved ahead of Compaq Computer to become the world leader in PC sales.

Despite Dell's success in the PC price wars, several analysts criticized the firm, pointing out that more than half of Dell's sales still came from the deteriorating PC market. Furthermore, the firm's efforts in 2000 to develop an Internet PC called WebPC had dissolved when the firm realized it would not be able to develop the technology without charging a relatively high price for it. In the past, Dell had been known more as a marketer of technology developed by other firms than a technology developer itself. Dell's attempt to develop a machine for the relatively new Internet appliance market marked a shift in direction for the firm, which continued through 2011.

DELL LEAVES DELL, COMES BACK

At first, the company seemed to flounder as it lost focus. In 2004, Michael Dell stepped down as CEO, ceding the position to Kevin Rollins. The founder remained on the board, as chairman. Three years later, the company was investigated by the Securities and Exchange Commission for allegedly receiving roughly $1 billion in excess microchip rebates from Intel in exchange for neglecting to implement the more advanced technology of Intel's competitor, AMD. Intel faced antitrust claims, while Dell settled the case, paying $100 million. In the same year, HP surpassed the company in sales, and Kevin Rollins resigned. Michael Dell was reinstated as CEO in January 2007.

Initially, Dell had made its name by synthesizing the products of other companies, packaging, and distributing it more effectively than its competitors. By 2011, it had begun to master the art of innovation through acquisition.

The game was the same, except rather than purchasing computer parts, the company was purchasing technology. According to a Reuters report, Dell was looking for acquisitions in the $1 to $5 billion range, and analysts saw a trend toward cloud software and services. In 2008, EqualLogic was acquired, while other cloud software companies, Boomi and InSite One, were purchased in 2010. The company projected that by 2015, its storage sales would total around $5 billion, while services would generate roughly twice that amount in revenue.

SEE ALSO *Dell, Michael.*

BIBLIOGRAPHY

Brown, Eryn. "First: Could the Very Best PC Maker Be Dell Computer?" *Fortune,* April 14, 1997.

"Can Michael Dell Escape the Box?" *Fortune,* October 16, 2000.

"Dell Computer Corp." In *Notable Corporate Chronologies.* Farmington Hills, MI: Gale Group, 1999.

Dell Inc. "Fiscal Year 2011 in Review." Round Rock, TX, 2011. Available from http://content.dell.com/us/en/corp/d/secure/fy-11-year-in-review.

DiCarlo, Lisa. "Dell Expands Net Plans." *PC Week,* April 28, 1997.

Gibbs, Lisa. "Is Dell's Ride Over?" *Money,* November 1, 2000.

Gupta, Poornima. "Dell to Keep Up Acquisitions, Sustain Margin Growth." *Reuters,* June 29, 2011. Available from http://www.reuters.com/article/2011/06/29/us-dell-idUSTRE75S35R20110629.

Jacobs, April. "Businesses Warm to Internet PC Sales." *Computerworld,* December 29, 1997.

Lewis, Scott M. "Dell Computer Corp." In *International Directory of Company Histories.* Vol. 9. Detroit, MI: St. James Press, 1994.

"Michael Dell." *BusinessWeek Online,* May 14, 2001. Available from http://www.businessweek.com/magazine/content/01_20/b3732667.htm.

Mulqueen, John T. "Round Two for Dell's Web Site." *InternetWeek,* December 15, 1997.

Popovich, Ken, and Mary Jo Foley. "Dell Remains Committed to Pricing Strategy." *eWeek,* April 9, 2001.

"Rebooting their Systems: Two Giants Prepare for a World No Longer Dominated by the PC." *Economist,* March 10, 2011. Available from http://www.economist.com/node/18332916.

"A Revolution of One; Face Value: Michael Dell, a Lone Revolutionary." *Economist,* April 14, 2001.

Shook, David. "The Winner of the PC Price Wars: Dell." *Business Week Online,* May 1, 2001. Available from http://www.businessweek.com/bwdaily/dnflash/may2001/nf2001051_655.htm.

Vance, Ashlee. "State Accuses Intel in an Antitrust Suit." *New York Times,* November 4, 2009. Available from http://www.nytimes.com/2009/11/05/technology/companies/05chip.html.

DELL, MICHAEL

Michael S. Dell is the founder, CEO, and chairman of Dell Inc., one of the largest personal computer (PC) vendors in the world. Dell has served his firm—which boasted sales in excess of $61.5 billion and employed more than 43,000 individuals in 2010—since its inception in 1984. For the majority of his tenure, he acted as CEO but relinquished the position from 2004 to 2007. He acted as chairman in the interim.

While Dell Inc. still sells PCs primarily, Michael Dell has worked to move his firm into the more lucrative Internet-based server and storage markets since the late 1990s, and in the 2000s he positioned his company as an IT services provider. He retains a 12.7% stake in the company, with 243,349,682 shares as of March 21, 2011.

COLLEGE BEGINNINGS

While a student at the University of Texas, Dell began selling IBM-compatible computers from his dorm room. He bought parts at wholesale prices, constructed the machines on his own, and sold them to bargain PC shoppers. The success of his venture prompted Dell to quit school in April 1984 and establish his own business, Dell Computer Corp., with $1,000 in capital. Dell advertised his low-cost, custom-built PCs in computer magazines, targeting savvy PCs users. Customers were able to call a toll-free number to place orders, and Dell shipped completed PCs directly to customers. What set Dell's firm apart from competitors was his practice of direct selling. The elimination of middlemen allowed Dell to price his computers well below market prices.

To facilitate his firm's rapid growth, Dell hired investment banking executive E. Lee Walker as president in 1986. The following year, he launched an expansion of manufacturing facilities and developed a national customer support center. Dell also began offering on-site services for Dell products. International expansion was initiated by the creation of an office in the United Kingdom. The firm also published a catalog for the first time and expanded its sales force. In 1988, Dell took his company public, offering 3.5 million shares at $8.50 each. Dell's firm also began offering leasing options to customers and furthered international expansion by establishing units in Canada and West Germany. In 1989, Dell became one of the first firms to license the UNIX trademark from AT&T Corp. However, record sales were marred by a 64% plunge in earnings, which Dell blamed on higher costs and an inventory glut.

Early in the 1990s, Dell intensified international expansion, overseeing the establishment of various operations in Ireland, Italy, Sweden, Poland, the Czech Republic, Belgium, Finland, Spain, Norway, Luxembourg, the Netherlands, and Mexico. Dell was the first personal computer manufacturer to offer applications software installation as a free standard service option. Copycat competitor Gateway usurped Dell as the top direct seller of PCs in the

United States in 1992. To express his determination to reduce expenses at his firm, Dell reduced his pay by 5%.

Sales exceeded $2 billion in the mid-1990s. By then, Dell had grown into the world's sixth-largest desktop PC maker. The firm's success was due in large part to its ability to use the Internet to take and fill customers' orders quickly and inexpensively. According to a May 2001 *BusinessWeek Online* article, "Michael Dell was e-business before e-business was cool. During the boom in technology spending, he used the Internet to reach out to customers and sell $50 million worth of computers a day." Dell's business model, which allowed for easy tracking of customer purchases, also allowed the firm to keep inventory at a minimum.

Wanting to reduce his company's reliance on PCs—which were being discounted by many rivals—Dell pushed his firm into the server market in 1996. Within two years, servers accounted for 16% of the company's $12 billion revenue, and within three years, Dell was second only to Compaq Computer Corp. in U.S. server sales. In 1999, when competitors began cutting PC prices further, Dell responded with its first PC under $1,000. That year, *Business Week* listed Michael Dell among its top 25 managers for the third consecutive year. Stock grew roughly 140%, a rate it had maintained for the previous four years.

As the PC market slowed in 2000, Dell began working to reposition his firm as a provider of Internet technology, focusing on servers and storage systems similar to those offered by Sun Microsystems Inc. The firm also began offering various Internet services such as Web hosting and wireless access to the Internet. Sales growth slowed nearly 10% to 38.5%, and stock prices began to falter, prompting Dell to reduce his bonus by 36%. Despite these troubles, Dell dethroned Compaq Computer as the leader in PC sales in April 2001. That year, *Chief Executive* magazine named Dell CEO of the Year, adding to his list of previous awards, which included *PC* magazine's Man of the Year and *Inc.* magazine's Entrepreneur of the Year.

CEDES CEO POSITION

In the 2000s, despite its success, Dell's company was not immune to the vagaries of the rapidly changing IT industry, and a string of problems and repositioning tactics weakened the company's hold on the PC market. In 2004, Michael Dell ceded his position as CEO to Kevin Rollins, preferring the position of chairman from which to run the company. Internally, there was not a significant difference in how the company was run when the change took place. Rollins gradually increased the day-to-day responsibilities of his position, while Michael Dell relaxed control, still making strategic decisions but allowing Rollins to carry them out. Company operations did not suffer a significant shock. Three years later, however, after the company suffered a number of setbacks, Rollins resigned as CEO and board member, and Michael Dell resumed his position as CEO.

The 2000s saw the company diversify its revenue portfolio by expanding into storage and IT services. Vertical expansion strategies of this type were quickly becoming a trend, though Dell's company did not appear to be as effective in implementing them as others. Various up-and-coming PC suppliers, such as Acer and Hewlett-Packard, gained ground on the international leader. As Dell gobbled up companies in data storage, HP focused on the PC market, first outperforming Dell in the last quarter in 2003 and then breaking out with a clear lead in 2006.

Dell Inc. also suffered collateral damage from an antitrust lawsuit filed against longtime supplier Intel. Allegedly, in 2005 Dell received large "incentives" for continuing to purchase chips that were inferior to a competitor's. The incentives, totaling $1 billion, were included in the company's quarterly report to investors, tallied up as revenue. According to the *New York Times,* after Dell finally switched to competitor AMD's chips, approximately $600 million of the chip rebates disappeared. Rather than take the case to court, Dell settled with the Securities and Exchange Commission for $100 million in 2010. This was a slap on the wrist for a company earning more than $61 billion in sales, but the damage to Dell's reputation was incalculable.

By fiscal year 2011, the company was third in the international PC makers' market. Over the course of the 2000s, Dell's company had slipped behind Hewlett-Packard and Acer to claim just 12% of the market, and stock prices had dropped. However, some analysts believed Dell was better positioned than its rivals, pointing to the company's revenue portfolio, which had diversified considerably, stretching out of the low-margin PC market.

With investors and the media still dubious about the future of his business, in 2011 Michael Dell took the opportunity to purchase an additional $150 million in stock, bringing his share to 12.7%.

SEE ALSO *Dell Inc.*.

BIBLIOGRAPHY

"Can Michael Dell Escape the Box?"*Fortune,* October 16, 2000.

"Dell Computer Corp." In *Notable Corporate Chronologies.* Farmington Hills, MI: Gale Group, 1999.

Dell Inc. "Fiscal Year 2011 in Review." Round Rock, TX, 2011. Available from http://content.dell.com/us/en/corp/d/secure/fy-11-year-in-review.

———. "Michael S. Dell." Round Rock, TX, 2011. Available from http://content.dell.com/us/en/corp/d/bios/michael-dell-bio.aspx.

Gupta, Poornima. "Dell to Keep Up Acquisitions, Sustain Margin Growth." *Reuters,* June 29, 2011. Available from http://www.reuters.com/article/2011/06/30/us-dell-idUSTRE75S35R20110630.

"Michael Dell." *BusinessWeek Online,* May 14, 2001. Available from http://www.businessweek.com/magazine/content/01_20/b3732667.htm.

"Rebooting Their Systems: Two Giants Prepare for a World No Longer Dominated by the PC." *Economist,* March 10, 2011. Available from http://www.economist.com/node/18332916.

"A Revolution of One—Face Value: Michael Dell, A Lone Revolutionary." *Economist,* April 14, 2001.

Shook, David. "The Winner of the PC Price Wars: Dell." *BusinessWeek Online,* May 1, 2001. Available from http://www.businessweek.com/bwdaily/dnflash/may2001/nf2001051_655.htm.

Spooner, John. "Michael Dell Steps Down as Dell CEO." *Silicon.com,* July 16, 2004. Available from http://www.silicon.com/technology/hardware/2004/07/16/michael-dell-steps-down-as-dell-ceo-39122316.

Vance, Ashlee. "State Accuses Intel in an Antitrust Suit." *New York Times,* November 4, 2009. Available from http://www.nytimes.com/2009/11/05/technology/companies/05chip.html.

Williams, Grace. "Michael Dell's $150 Million Buy." *Barron's,* March 21, 2011. Available from http://online.barrons.com/article/SB50001424052970204582404576214990233626596.html.

DENIAL-OF-SERVICE ATTACK

Hackers have been known to place programs onto networked computers that create high volumes of dubious requests or messages, resulting in an interruption of network service. This practice is called a denial-of-service (DOS) attack. When more than one networked computer is used to flood a network with phony traffic, the practice is called a distributed denial-of-service attack (DDOS) and many of the computers used in the attack, dubbed botnets, are hijacked without their owner's knowledge.

There are different types of DOS attacks, including teardrop attacks, infrastructure attacks, buffer overflow attacks, smurf attacks, and those caused by computer viruses. The motivations behind the attack are many, but some are inspired by political movements or protests, some derive from individual discontent, and many involve criminal activity. Some DOS attacks are pure online vandalism, while others may be a cyber tactic in a confrontation between nations.

FORMS OF ATTACK

Depending on their type, DOS attacks work in different ways. For example, infrastructure attacks involve situations where service is impaired due to a physical, real-world assault on cabling or other equipment used for network operations. Smurf attacks involve a utility called pinging. Normally, this utility is used to verify the existence and operation of a host computer (such as a Web server used to host a Web site). A signal is sent to the host, and a reply requested. Smurf attacks involve hackers spoofing, or using a phony reply address (the target for the DOS attack), and requesting that the reply be broadcast to multiple points within the target's network, causing a spike in dubious traffic. Regardless of the means, the ultimate objective of most DOS attacks is to prevent networks from working properly by overloading them with more traffic than they were designed to handle.

Although they can happen accidentally, DOS attacks normally are caused intentionally. Much like computer viruses, the consequences of DOS attacks are real, resulting in lost revenue for companies, frustrated consumers and companies who want to purchase goods and services, and sometimes damaged computer files. To make matters worse, tracking down attackers can be very difficult. Most e-commerce attacks are targeted at large businesses, according to *Inc. Technology,* rather than small online ventures. The emergence of DOS threats in the late 1990s and early twenty-first century made international headlines and posed a threat to the growing e-commerce business sector. Some of the most well-known names in the relatively new venture were targeted, according to *Inc. Technology,* and in one three-week period in February 2001 some 13,000 DOS attacks were recorded.

Unfortunately, attacks continued in subsequent years, often growing more sophisticated in nature. In 2004, *Computerworld* magazine offered practical advice to businesses on surviving a DOS attack, noting that the Internet was a "dangerous place," where hackers had "ever-more-powerful tools" at their disposal.

As of 2011, there no were no proven ways to stop DOS attacks from happening. However, several organizations began to develop or offered solutions that were able to provide varying degrees of relief. Captus Networks offered equipment that detected traffic surges and held them back while it attempted to differentiate between legitimate and bogus messages. Captus's solution also was able to check spoofed addresses used in smurf attacks and either deny illegitimate traffic or send it to another location for investigative analysis.

Mazu Networks, a company with ties to the Massachusetts Institute of Technology (MIT), developed similar technology that, according to *Network World,* could "identify traffic characteristics of distributed denial-of-service attacks and communicate that information to the ISPs, Web-hosting centers or Web server owner via a private network. The devices would be able to take active response measures, such as filtering and tracing the attack, and gathering forensics." Moreover, in November 2000 an industry group was created to work toward a solution and develop cooperation between ISPs, who play central roles in the attacks. DOS attacks were an especially pressing issue as e-commerce developed and businesses became exposed to fraud and liability issues.

Over the next decade a pattern began to emerge as hackers found ways to circumvent security measures, prompting network operators to adopt new security procedures which, in turn, created a new challenge for hackers. The decade was a series of technological battles in the DOS war. In 2004, those defending networks from attacks had several tools at their disposal, according to *Computerworld,* including firewalls, mitigation devices that cleaned up incoming traffic, server configuration adjustments, and techniques like black-holing that simply blocked all traffic, both good and bad, when an attack was detected. Software giants like Microsoft offered numerous patches and software solutions to users to address DOS and DDOS issues.

However, hackers were agile and attacks continued, prompting a group of security experts to ponder in a *NetWorld* chat if the battle would ever be won, particularly as hackers were turning more and more to DDOS attacks utilizing unsuspecting Internet users. The failure of consumers to update software and use antivirus programs allowed hackers to hijack computers, and the ever-widening bandwidth available to hackers to set up large botnets prompted *NetWorld* to conclude that the cycle would continue because new methods used to thwart attacks were constantly being met with new ways to attack.

RISE OF BOTNETS

One of the most famous DDOS attacks utilizing botnets was detailed by *Wired* magazine in 2007. The attack, believed to have come from Russia, targeted an entire country, Estonia, shutting down its electronic infrastructure including banks, media, and servers. "This was the first time that a botnet threatened the national security of an entire nation," an Estonian official told *Wired.* In 2008, the security company Symantec reported it was detecting 75,158 bot-infected computers a day, a 31% jump from the previous year, according to *Business Week.* By the next year, 2009, security experts reported they were seeing a large growth in botnet attacks which led, in turn, to a price war among underground hackers, with prices dropping from $100 a day to around $30 to $50 to rent a botnet in some Russian forums, according to *Computerworld.*

The number of botnets with more than a million hijacked computers had grown from about a half dozen in 2007 to dozens by 2009, according to *Business Week,* and renting 10,000 hijacked computers a day from a criminal enterprise cost as little as $200 a day. The number of daily attacks had doubled, also. Governments had to update legal codes to address DOS attacks. In 2006, the United Kingdom outlawed DOS attacks, making them a criminal activity after a 2005 case exposed a loophole in the law. A judge found there was no criminal culpability for a man who had sent five million e-mails to his former employer, causing the employer's server to crash, according to *CNET.*

The costs of a DOS attack can be enormous for business. A 2011 Hewlett-Packard study, cited by *CNET,* found the median cost of cybercrime to 50 organizations, both public and private, surveyed was $5.9 million a year, and ranged from $1.5 million to $36.5 million. The most expensive cybercrime was a DOS attack, and some lasted up to 18 days.

DOS and DDOS attacks have played a role on the world stage, also. In 2008, a DDOS attack was launched against servers in Georgia as the small country became embroiled in a border dispute with Russia. Millions of requests shut down the country servers, a cyberattack that was later followed by real gunfire, as noted in the *New York Times.* During Iran's unsuccessful "green revolution" in 2009, leaders urged Iranians to attack the regime with a DDOS. Another notable attack took place in 2010 when supporters of WikiLeaks bombarded MasterCard after the credit card company said it would not process donations to the WikiLeaks cause. The DDOS not only crippled MasterCard but also took the Swedish prosecution authority offline as punishment for charging WikiLeaks founder Julian Assange with raping two Swedish women, according to the *Guardian* newspaper.

With the growing popularity of social media like Twitter and Facebook, DOS and DDOS attacks spread to those realms. A botnet attack on Twitter brought down the service in 2009, according to *Business Week.* Hackers were targeting Georgy Jakhaia, a Russian dissident known online as Cyxymu who was critical of the central government, but the attack was so powerful it brought down the whole Twitter network and slowed LiveJournal and Facebook, where Cyxymu also posted. In an increasingly connected world, it was clear proof that the threat of DOS and DDOS attacks aimed at either a narrow target or a countrywide one had not diminished, despite the development of tactics and technology to address the issue.

SEE ALSO *Computer Crime; Computer Security; Hacking.*

BIBLIOGRAPHY

Addley, Esther, and Josh Halliday. "Operation Payback Cripples Mastercard Site in Revenge for WikiLeaks Ban." *Guardian,* December 8, 2010. Available from http://www.guardian.co.uk/media/2010/dec/08/operation-payback-mastercard-website-wikileaks.

Davis, Joshua. "Hackers Take Down the Most Wired Country in Europe." *Wired,* August 21, 2007. Available from http://www.wired.com/politics/security/magazine/15-09/ff_estonia?currentPage=all.

"Denial of Service." *SearchSoftwareQuality.com,* 2011. Available from http://searchsoftwarequality.techtarget.com/definition/denial-of-service.

Duffy, Jim. "Has Progress Been Made in Fighting DDoS Attacks?" *NetworkWorld,* December 9, 2010. Available from http://www.networkworld.com/news/2010/120910-wikileaks-ddos-attacks.html.

Espiner, Tom. "U.K. Outlaws Denial-of-Service Attacks." *CNET,* November 10, 2006. Available from http://news.cnet.com/U.K.-outlaws-denial-of-service-attacks/2100-7348_3-6134472.html.

Froutan, Paul. "How to Defend Against DDoS Attacks." *Computerworld,* June 24, 2004. Available from http://www.computerworld.com/s/article/94014/How_to_defend_against_DDoS_attacks.

Lowensohn, Jerome. "Study: Cybercrime Costs on the Rise from Last Year." *CNET,* August 2, 2011. Available from http://news.cnet.com/8301-1009_3-20087069-83/study-cybercrime-costs-on-the-rise-from-last-year/?tag=mncol;2n.

Markoff, John. "Before the Gunfire, Cyberattacks." *New York Times,* August 12, 2008. Available from http://www.nytimes.com/2008/08/13/technology/13cyber.html?em.

McMillan, Robert. "With Botnets Everywhere, DDoS Attacks Get Cheaper." *Computerworld,* October 14, 2009. Available from http://www.computerworld.com/s/article/9139398/With_botnets_everywhere_DDoS_attacks_get_cheaper.

Messmer, Ellen. "Start-Ups Go on Attack vs. Denial-of-Service Threat." *Network World,* June 18, 2001.

———. "Start-ups Vie to Defeat DoS Attacks." *Network World,* February 5, 2001. Available from http://www.networkworld.com/archive/2001/116394_02-05-2001.html.

Protalinski, Emil. "Microsoft Releases Beta Tool for Fighting DoS Attacks." *Ars Technica,* June 2008. Available from http://arstechnica.com/microsoft/news/2009/02/microsoft-releases-beta-tool-for-fighting-dos-attacks.ars.

Riley, Michael. "On the Internet, Nobody Knows You're a Robot." *Businessweek,* September 15, 2011. Available from http://www.businessweek.com/magazine/on-the-internet-nobody-knows-youre-a-robot-09152011.html.

Shachtman, Noah. "Activists Launch Hack Attacks on Tehran Regime." *Wired,* June 15, 2009. Available from http://www.wired.com/dangerroom/2009/06/activists-launch-hack-attacks-on-tehran-regime.

Stuart, Anne. "Can You Prevent a Denial-of-Service Attack on Your Website?" *Inc. Technology,* January 1, 2007. Available from http://technology.inc.com/2007/01/01/can-you-prevent-a-denial-of-service-attack-on-your-website.

U.S. Department of Homeland Security. US-CERT. United States Computer Emergency Readiness Team.

"Understanding Denial-of-Servce Attacks: National Cyber Alert System." Washington, DC. Last modified November 4, 2009. Available from http://www.us-cert.gov/cas/tips/ST04-015.html.

DIFFERENTIATION

In terms of e-commerce, differentiation is, simply, how one company sets its e-commerce products and services apart from those offered by competitors. In some cases, the differentiation might be in name recognition. As online shopping began to take hold at the end of the twentieth century, it seemed likely that established brand names would be key to attracting online customers. In a world filled with Internet start-ups, the familiarity of a name like Hewlett-Packard or Microsoft likely would be an important distinction to some customers looking to purchase e-commerce technology and services. A study of fashion and style customers shopping online found they were buying online the same brands they knew and trusted in the offline marketplace, according to the *E-Commerce Times.* But as e-commerce grew and online shoppers gained access to a wide world of goods, other factors came into play and differentiation became key in a crowded online marketplace.

EARLY PROBLEMS

Simply having a familiar name was not sufficient, and large offline retailers often struggled with establishing a successful online presence. In 2000, according to *CNET,* noted brands like Walt Disney and Levi Strauss left the online arena. National U.S. toy store chain Toys"R"Us had a lackluster online launching and stepped back to reassess its approach. A decade later, the toy store chain had an effective online strategy that included offering customers the ability to order online and pick up at a local store—a tactic that had been adopted by other giant retailers, including Wal-Mart, which launched same-day pickup in mid-2011.

The merging of online and offline stores, pricing, product functionality, and the comprehensiveness of services like free shipping and free returns became common areas where Internet-based businesses sought to differentiate from competitors. Web site design also was key. The proliferation of e-commerce sites required businesses to stay abreast of the latest search technologies and to design sites that were not only easy to use but that provided good customer service. A survey of online shoppers in 2007 found for that the third year in a row, nine out of ten shoppers had experienced a problem with an online transaction, according to *Marketing Charts.* Differentiation for e-commerce sites meant not only attracting customers, but also ensuring their online experience, both browsing and ordering, was successful.

Differentiation in a fast-changing e-commerce environment has proved easier for some segments of the marketplace than others. Writing in *Techcrunch*, Jamie Murray-Wells, the founder of Glasses Direct in the United Kingdom, suggested in 2009 that the first wave of e-commerce saw the successful establishment of a marketplace for books, travel, and DVDs, what he called "generic products." The second wave, he suggested, was the sale of high-end and personalized products like jewelry, cosmetics, fitted clothes and—citing his own business—eyewear. Selling those products online required businesses to differentiate by using various tools, Murray-Wells wrote, including providing consumers in-depth background information, online customer service, and online tools that allowed customers to visualize themselves in the product. Another vital component was the successful creation of an emotional connection to the product.

Personalization and interaction were key to a successful e-commerce site, according to Ivan Lim, writing in *PowerRetail.com*, and the lack of those qualities were cited as the failure of several major Australian retailers to be successful in the e-commerce arena in 2011. Good design, ease of navigation, and plenty of product choices were simply not enough in the evolving e-commerce marketplace to drive online sales. Both major stores and small businesses were being challenged in a widening global marketplace to find new ways to differentiate, including the development of new approaches like the Facebook app developed by New Zealand fashion store Farmers which allowed potential customers to mix and match clothes from its online catalog and share the visual results with friends, according to Lim.

Despite a worldwide recession that took hold in 2008, e-commerce continued to grow, and *Smashing Magazine* noted that sophisticated online consumers wanted online shopping to be quick and easy but also satisfying aesthetically. Sophisticated Web site designs, many of them visually stunning or beautiful, were providing that experience, the magazine noted; among its winners were online sites for Godiva chocolates, Harry Winston diamonds, and Narwhal Company's wallets made from recycled ties—evidence of the growing diversity of online products.

SEE ALSO *Business Models; Competition; Competitive Advantage.*

BIBLIOGRAPHY

Colkin, Ellen. "Net Stocks Tracked." *InformationWeek*, February 22, 1999.

"Consumers Remain Intolerant toward Ecommerce Site Failures." *Marketing Charts*, September 19, 2007. Available from http://www.marketingcharts.com/direct/consumers-remain-intolerant-toward-ecommerce-site-failures-1693.

Enright, Allison. "Wal-Mart Takes Same Day Pick-Up National." *Internet Retailer*, March 10, 2011. Available from http://www.internetretailer.com/2011/03/10/wal-mart-takes-same-day-pick-national.

Futrelle, David. "The Internet Index Mania: There Are Many Benchmarks, but Few Measure Anything Meaningful." *Money*, November 1, 1999.

Hajsaleh, Khalid. " Differentiate or Die: 5 Techniques to Set an E-commerce Site Apart from Competition." *SearchEngine Journal.com*, July 30, 2007. Available from http://www.searchenginejournal.com/differentiate-or-die-5-techniques-to-set-an-e-commerce-site-apart-from-competition/5395.

Hillebrand, Mary. "Study: E-commerce Brand Names Trump Clever Marketing." *E-Commerce Times*, February 8, 2000. Available from http://www.ecommercetimes.com/story/2456.html.

"How Glasses Direct Took a High-Street Business to the Internet. " *BizGene*, February 11, 2011. Available from http://www.bizgene.com/1554989/how-glasses-direct-took-a-high-street-business-to-the-internet.

Lim, Ivan. "Five Reasons Big Australian Retailers Struggle with E-commerce." *PowerRetail*, March 31, 2011. Available from http://www.powerretail.com.au/insights/five-reasons-big-australian-retailers-struggle-with-e-commerce.

May, Julie. "35 Beautiful E-commerce Websites." *Smashing Magazine*, January 22, 2010. Available from http://www.smashingmagazine.com/2010/01/22/35-beautiful-and-effective-ecommerce-websites.

Murray-Wells, Jamie. "E-commerce—Is the Next Wave About to Break?" *Techcrunch*, May 26, 2009. Available from http://eu.techcrunch.com/2009/05/26/e-commerce-is-the-next-wave-about-to-break.

Rains, Julie. "6 Ways to Differentiate Your E-commerce Website." *American Express Open Forum*, March 10, 2010. Available from http://www.openforum.com/idea-hub/topics/money/article/6-ways-to-differentiate-your-ecommerce-website-1.

Sandoval, Greg. "Is Toys 'R' Us Headed for E-commerce Sidelines?" *CNET*, August 18, 2000. Available from http://news.cnet.com/Is-Toys-R-Us-headed-for-e-commerce-sidelines/2100-1017_3-244654.html.

"Siteseeing." *Computer Weekly*, January 13, 2000.

Weintraub, Arlene. "E-commerce Crusader." *Businessweek Online*, June 5, 2000. Available from http://www.businessweek.com/2000/00_23/b3684047.htm.

DIGITAL

In the field of computing, information can be conveyed in digital or analog formats. Continuity is the differentiating factor between the two. For example, digital devices are only able to display information in finite units (10 degrees versus 10.0625 degrees), while analog devices display information that corresponds more precisely to real-world phenomena. Digital watches display time in measured increments while analog watches show time unfold continuously through the circular movement of mechanical hands.

Although analog computers are used for simulating real-world conditions in a variety of fields, including nuclear power and electronics, the majority of computers, including those used for e-commerce, are digital machines. They process information in a binary format of zeros and ones (0, 1, 10, 11, 100, 111, and so on). Accordingly, while the software programs used during e-commerce—including Web browsers and database programs—are written in high-level programming languages like C++ and Java that closely resemble human grammar, they eventually are converted to commands consisting of ones and zeros that a computer's hardware can accept and understand. Digital computers function through four essential components: an input-output device; a control unit; main memory; and an arithmetic-logic unit.

DIGITAL MUSIC

The difference between analog and digital information can be shown in the audio recording process. Analog devices record sound waves directly onto magnetic tape, whereas digital devices take the same wave, convert it to a sequence of ones and zeros, and store it for future use. When played back, the numbers are converted into electronic signals resembling the original sound wave. Digital information, including computer software programs, word processing documents, digital audio, and digital video, can be duplicated an infinite number of times without a loss in quality or integrity; the numeric expressions of zeros and ones remain the same throughout time. In comparison, the quality of analog information, such as songs recorded on magnetic tape, deteriorates with successive generations as copies are made.

The advent of digital devices, notably sound recorders and cameras, led to an ongoing spirited debate in the first decade of the twenty-first century over which technology was best—digital or analog. The various merits of each were argued with vigor, with some music aficionados claiming that analog recordings had better sound quality, while professional photographers discussed the merits of fast-disappearing traditional film over digital images.

The debate not only centered on production quality, but also price. Some digital products continued to cost more than analog devices, hearing aids being just one example. Some critics of digital devices faulted their design and lack of the tactile quality found in analog products, which often had dials rather than digital push buttons or keys. Writing in *Popular Mechanics* in 2009, Glenn Harlan Reynolds reminisced about the tactile quality of car radios and the ability to fine tune or control volume with a dial on an analog radio. He praised the "quasi-analog dial" of the iPod for its tactile appeal. But the rise of digital products over analog products continued, prompting the commonplace usage of the term "digital age" to apply to the last decade of the twentieth century and the beginning of the twenty-first.

The online magazine, the *Daily Beast,* captured the growing influence of digital technology in daily lives in a chart in 2010. From 2000 to 2010, the number of blogs on the Internet rose from 12,000 to 141 million; Google searches went from 100 million a day to 2 billion daily; text messages rose from 400,000 to 4.5 billion; e-mails rose from 12 billion daily to 247 billion a day worldwide; and the number of songs downloaded from Apple's iTunes store went from zero to 10 billion.

The digital age also became a global phenomenon. In 2000, cheap $50 black-and-white analog televisions were being exported by China to Sub-Saharan Africa, according to the *Economist,* sparking a market for local news and regional programming. Within a decade, the magazine reported, the lower costs of digital technology over traditional land-based systems made cellphone usage ubiquitous, not only in the Sub-Saharan region, but throughout the African continent, where in 2011 there were an estimated 84 million mobile phones with some measure of Internet connectivity. That made the cellphone the "computer of choice" for many Africans.

In the United States, the use of digital technology in television broadcasting had a significant impact on the U.S. consumer and the broadband marketplace in the 2000s as television stations began broadcasting their signals digitally in 2009. The move to all-digital broadcasting, according to the Federal Communications Commission, freed up parts of the broadband spectrum for public safety communications channels and allowed some of the spectrum to be auctioned for advanced wireless services. The digital signals gave consumers improved picture and sound quality. The move also allowed broadcasters to multicast, sending both high definition (HD) or standard definition (SD) simultaneously. (The move to digital required owners of analog television sets to acquire a signal converter box, and the U.S. government subsidized the cost for many consumers.)

By the second decade of the twenty-first century, digital devices dominated personal entertainment, including MP3 players, iPods, iPads, tablets, and e-readers for books. Everyday appliances also had digital components, from timers on slow cookers to alarm clocks. Sony's DASH alarm clock radios included Internet radio, photo albums, weather maps and, of course, an alarm clock, but one equipped with a digital readout, not an old-fashioned analog clock face.

SEE ALSO *Analog: Global E-Commerce: Africa.*

BIBLIOGRAPHY

"Back Story: How the Digital Revolution Changed Our World." *Daily Beast,* 2010. Available from http://www.thedailybeast.com/newsweek/features/2010/by-the-numbers-how-the-digital-revolution-changed-our-world.html.

"Digital." *Webopedia,* 2001. Available from http://www.webopedia. com/TERM/D/digital.html.

"Digital." *Techencyclopedia,* 2001. Available from http://www.techweb.com/encyclopedia.

"Digital and Analog Information." *PC Guide,* 2001. Available from http://www.pcguide.com/intro/works/computDigital-c.html.

"Digital Computer." *Encyclopedia Britannica,* 2001. Available from http://www.britannica.com/EBchecked/topic/163278/digital-computer.

"Digital Hearing Aids vs. Analog Hearing Aids." *HearingAids101,* 2011. Available from http://www.hearingaids101.com/digital_vs_analog.aspx.

"Digital Revolution Makers of Mobile Devices See a New Growth." *Economist,* April 7, 2011. Available from http://www.economist.com/node/18529875.

Federal Communications Commission. "What Is DTV?" Washington, DC, 2011. Available from http://www.dtv.gov/whatisdtv.html.

"Introduction to Digital Photography: Differences Between Analogue and Digital." *Canon Infobank,* 2011. Available from http://cpn.canon-europe.com/content/education/infobank/introduction_to_digital_photography/differences_between_analogue_and_digital.do.

Guttenberg, Steve. "Digital vs. Analog Audio: Which Sounds Better?" *CNET,* April 21, 2011. Available from http://news.cnet.com/8301-13645_3-20055650-47.html.

Massey, Howard. "Analog vs. Digital." The International Association of Electronic Keyboard Manufacturers, May 12, 2001.

"The Mathematics of Computing." *PC Guide,* May 9, 2001. Available from http://www.pcguide.com/intro/works/computMath-c.html.

"Portable Digital Devices." *TWICE: This Week in Customer Electronics,* 2011. Available from http://www.twice.com/channel/Portable_Digital_Devices.php.

Reynolds, Glenn Harlan. "Bring Back Our Knobs: Analog vs. Digital." *Popular Mechanics,* October 2009. http://www.popularmechanics.com/technology/gadgets/news/4213770.

Richtel, Mark, and Jenna Wortham. "Rabbit Ears Perk Up for Free HDTV." *New York Times,* December 5, 2010. Available from http://www.nytimes.com/2010/12/06/business/media/06rabbitears.html?ref=digitalandhighdefinitiontelevision.

DIGITAL CASH

Digital cash, or electronic money, consists of encrypted data that serves as an electronic substitute for regular hard currency. It can exist in the form of a cash Internet transaction, a monetary value stored on a smart card or accessed via a smartphone. Developing from the electronic money used in bank transactions, currency exchanges, credit cards, and automatic tellers, by the twenty-first century digital currency was evolving rapidly. Applications, or "apps," and "widgets" were developed to serve as money transfer mechanisms, allowing consumers to pay for goods and services or transfer cash between accounts simply by waving a smartphone screen equipped with a near field communication (NFC) chip at another phone or device similarly equipped.

A HISTORY OF DIGITAL CASH

In a sense, digital cash has been around for years in the form of the automated clearinghouse (ACH), automated teller machines (ATMs), point-of-sale debit cards, and credit card networks. Coded subway and phone cards functioned as a type of electronic cash and later were expanded to allow consumers to use the smartcards to purchase items other than bus and subway tickets. In 1996, the U.S. government initiated a campaign to create a universal, all-electronic payment system to decrease the nearly 70 billion paper checks Americans write each year. The effort was instigated by the Financial Services Technology Consortium (FSTC), which was composed of members of the banking and information technology industries. In 1998, the U.S. Treasury Department sponsored a pilot program to test the workability of paying participating federal contractors with e-checks. More than $2.5 million was paid out during the test period.

The use of e-check technology became ubiquitous for government entities and large businesses, and in 2010, the U.S. Treasury announced a new rule requiring all benefit payments to be made either by direct deposit to a bank account or with the use of a Direct Express card. This new rule eliminating paper checks would take effect in March 2013, but not all efforts to eliminate paper checks were successful. The Payments Council, a financial consortium governing banking transactions in the United Kingdom, announced in 2010 it would seek the elimination of all paper checks, or cheques as they are known there. However, opposition among some of the council's 600 stakeholder groups prompted the organization to say the 2018 date was a goal, not a mandate, and paper cheques would continue to be valid as long as customers asked for them.

Analysts began to see the potential for digital cash as the use of the Internet grew in the late 1990s, but many of the first versions of emoney—including CyberCoins and CyberCash, which appeared in the early 1990s—eventually folded. They often worked like online gift certificates, whereby consumers bought a certain amount of digital cash and then redeemed it at participating online vendors. These versions failed to win consumer acceptance because of doubts about their validity, the limited venues where the cash could be spent, and the need to install special software just to use the products.

The second generation of e-cash appeared in the late 1990s. Related to technologies such as electronic checks (e-checks) and embedded-chip smart cards, digital cash systems transferred monetary amounts over the Internet on open networks and utilized public-key cryptography to protect the content of the messages being relayed over the system. Later developments in digital cash permitted users to transfer cash via e-mail once they established an online account with a provider permitting payment at online vendor sites. Customers therefore avoided usage fees and merchants avoided the 1% to 2% transaction costs associated with credit card transactions. This e-cash did not require software downloads, and some versions also allowed cash withdrawals at ATMs.

Credit card payments continued to account for more than 90% of all Web site purchases, compared to only 25% of offline sales at the beginning of the twenty-first century, but security concerns prompted the developers of digital cash to develop new technologies that diminished fraud and boosted consumer confidence. A major player in the digital cash revolution was PayPal. The company announced in 2001, as part of its planned initial public offering (IPO), that it had brought its fraud rate down to less than 0.5%. It also chose to use the Secure Sockets Layer encryption that was built into most browsers, rather than more complicated software, the "digital wallets" used by competitors, according to *Technology Review.* PayPal emerged a big winner in the digital cash marketplace, and others like CyberCash, DigiCash, First Virtual, and many other "micropayment" companies like MilliCent fell by the wayside. They were victims of the complicated software that consumers found cumbersome, or the lack of markets where micropayments could be useful.

Digital cash usage also got a boost in the first decade of the twenty-first century with the adoption by several major urban transit systems of reloadable cash cards like London's Oyster card and Hong Kong's Octopus card. The cards were expanded for other uses in the Netherlands under the Chipknip electronic money system, allowing consumers to use them for small purchases while avoiding the potential exposure to fraud when using a debit card linked to a large bank balance, or a credit card with a substantial credit line.

RISE OF ONLINE SHOPPING

Online shopping gained wide acceptance in the first decade of the twenty-first century. The Pew Research Center found 54% of respondents in a 2009 poll said online shopping was a change for the better, with 15% disagreeing and the rest having no opinion or being neutral on the question. According to a U.S. Census report on e-commerce, issued in 2011, an analysis of sales from 2004 to 2009 found retail e-sales had increased at an annual average growth of 18.1%, compared to 2.2% for total retail sales. As a total percentage of all retail sales, e-commerce sales were 4%, $145 billion, in 2009, compared to 3.6% of total sales in 2008. While the discount department store held first place, as it had since 1997, the Internet came in second among Christmas shoppers, according to Deloitte's 2010 shopping survey, and 71% of respondents said they would likely spend some of their Christmas budget on the Internet.

One of the biggest boosts to internet holiday shopping came in the mid-2000s with the creation of Cyber Monday, now a phenomenon in several countries around the world. While traditional shopping venues relied on Black Friday, the day after the Thanksgiving holiday, to kick start the shopping season, online retailers devised their own kick-off event and dubbed it Cyber Monday. Promoted by Shop.org, an association for online retailers, Cyber Monday was a success and was described by *Businessweek* as masterful marketing. Consumers spent $925 million online over the 2005 Thanksgiving holiday, up 24% from the year before, according to comScore Networks, as reported in the *New York Times.*

Digital cash usage was not just limited to the developed world. In Africa, cellphone companies developed M-Pesa, launched in Kenya and utilized to send cash via a secure transaction to an individual or business. The BBC reported it cost $1 to send or receive money using the system in Kenya. Using a SIM card, loaded with funds at a kiosk or store, the sender could relay the funds using a PIN number to a recipient who could then visit an M-Pesa store and retrieve the hard currency, or use the funds as digital cash. The system became popular in Africa, where some $93 million is sent from migrants working outside the continent to family members back home. M-Pesa also was launched successfully in Afghanistan.

The use of digital cash helped open up vast new online retail opportunities in booming, emerging markets like China. In 2009, China's online market sales increased by an astounding 93.7% over 2008 with sales of some 248 billion yuan ($39 billion). *eMarket* reported analysts estimated China's online sales would top 1000 billion yuan ($157 billion) by 2013.

The development of so-called "wave and pay" technology for smartphones and preloaded cards also began to grow more popular in 2010. While the cards still required occasional verification with a PIN, some smartphone transactions did not, allowing the data connection to serve as verification. Near field communication (NFC) allowed phones or cards to be waved in front of scanning devices in a quick motion. The NFC technology was tied to a specific device. London's *Telegraph* pondered in 2011 whether the NFC technology could spell the end of cash and cited a survey reporting that 42% of British smartphone users wanted to use their phones as a digital wallet. Google obliged in September 2011, launching Google Wallet, an easy-to-use application that allowed consumers to type their credit or debit card information into a smartphone for swipe purchases at NFC devices. Consumers also could set a time limit from one minute to two hours for the PIN activation to remain in effect; after that time, reentry of a PIN was required.

PayPal also unveiled a smartphone widget in 2011 that allowed two PayPal account holders to simply tap their NFC-enabled phones together and instantly transfer cash. However, *Wired* magazine also noted that PayPal was not putting all its eggs in the NFC basket and had acquired Zong, a mobile payments company that allowed consumers to add purchases to their wireless phone bill. Zong utilized a similar model dubbed Isis, created by three major U.S. mobile companies in 2010 (T-Mobile, Verizon, and AT&T).

RISKS AND LIMITATIONS

Digital cash systems pose unique risks for both online merchants and consumers, including questions about security, the ability to safeguard users' privacy, susceptibility to counterfeiting, and suitability as a medium for online fraud. All of these generated fears among e-commerce merchants over increased legal liability. While traditional monetary systems combat fraud by using closed networks that block unauthorized access to the system, the open networks along which e-cash payments are transmitted often lacked adequate safeguards against fraudulent access. Therefore, they must utilize elaborate encryption methods to code the information in such a way that only authorized parties can read it. Digital cash has become more secure, but it also continues to attract fraudsters. It also generates some new challenges, as *Nova Online* noted in its series on making money. Digital cash can be hard to trace, posing opportunities for money launderers and tax evaders. It also allows for quick global transactions that have advantages in commerce, but this also gives criminals a way to move money quickly out of reach of authorities.

SEE ALSO *Cryptography, Public and Private Key; Digital Wallet Technology; Fraud, Internet; Privacy: Issues, Policies, Statements.*

BIBLIOGRAPHY

Barbaro, Michael. "Online Sales Take Off on 'Cyber Monday'." *New York Times,* November 30, 2005. Available from http://www.nytimes.com/2005/11/30/technology/30iht-cyber.html?scp=12&sq=cyber%20monday&st=cse.

"Cash Advanced: Google Wallet Is Tomorrow's Billfold." *Wired,* September 19, 2011. Available from http://www.wired.com/reviews/2011/09/gwallet.

"China Online Shopping Rapidly Develops in 2010." *eMarket Services,* July 7, 2011. Available from http://www.emarketservices.com/start/News/International/news/China-Online-Shopping-Market-Rapidly-Develops-in-2010.html?xz=0&cc=1&sd=1&ci=3607.

"Deloitte's 25th Annual Holiday Survey." New York: Deloitte, 2010. Available from http://www.deloitte.com/view/en_US/us/Industries/Retail-Distribution/consumer-spending/d5b052bb0bdac210VgnVCM3000001c56f00aRCRD.htm.

Bielski, Lauren. "New Wave of E-money Options Hits the Web." *ABA Banking Journal,* August 2000.

"E-cash 2.0." *Economist,* February 19, 2000.

"Follow the E-money." *Foreign Policy,* September/October 2000.

Hof, Robert D. "Cyber Monday, Marketing Myth." *Businessweek,* November 29, 2005. Available from http://www.businessweek.com/bwdaily/dnflash/nov2005/nf20051129_9946_db016. htm.

Isaac, Mike. "PayPal Brings Wireless Cash Transfers to Android Phones." *Wired,* July 13, 2011. Available from http://www.wired.com/gadgetlab/2011/07/paypal-android-nexus-s.

Kuykendall, Lavonne. "The Online Challengers." *Credit Card Management,* November 1999.

"Leaders: Cash Remains King." *Economist,* February 19, 2000.

McAndrews, James. "E-money and Payment System Risks." *Contemporary Economic Policy,* July 1999.

Menn, Joseph. "'Wave and Pay' Technology for iPhone 5." *Financial Times,* January 25, 2011. Available from http://www.ft.com/cms/s/2/0a835462-28c0-11e0-aa18-00144feab49a.html#ixzz1DpmitClQ.

Mitchell, Lori. "E-cash Aims to Ease Security—and Privacy-Concerned Shoppers." *InfoWorld,* August 2000.

Mwakugu, Noel. "Money Transfer Service Wows Kenya." *BBC News,* April 2, 2007. Available from http://news.bbc.co.uk/2/hi/africa/6510165.stm.

Nocera, Joseph. "Easy Money." *Money,* August 2000.

Payments Council. "Payments Council to Keep Cheques and Cancels 2018 Target." London, July 12, 2011. Available from http://www.paymentscouncil.org.uk/media_centre/press_releases/-/page/1575.

"Public Looks Back at Worst Decade in 50 Years." Pew Research Center for the People & the Press, Washington, DC, December 21, 2009. Available from http://pewresearch.org/pubs/1447/worst-decade-major-technological-communications-advances.

Puffer, Brad. "Digital Cash: Secrets of Making Money." *Nova Online,* August 2002. Available fromhttp://www.pbs.org/wgbh/nova/moolah/digitalcash.html.

Ridgway, Nicole. "Down to the Wire." *Forbes,* November 13, 2000.

Schwartz, Evan I. "Digital Cash Payoff." *Technology Review,* December 2001 Available from http://www.technologyreview.com/business/12696.

Sherman, Lauren. "Mobile Shopping's First Christmas," *Businessweek,* November 19, 2009. Available from http://www.businessweek.com/lifestyle/content/nov2009/bw20091117_316474.htm.

U.S. Department of Commerce. Bureau of the Census. "Measuring the Electronic Economy." Washington, DC, May 2011. Available from http://www.census.gov/econ/estats.

"U.S. Online Holiday Shopping Season Reaches Record $32.6 Billion for November-December Period, up 12 Percent vs. Year Ago." *comScore.com,* January 10, 2011. Available from http://www.comscore.com/Press_Events/Press_Releases/2011/1/U.S._Online_Holiday_Shopping_Season_Reaches_Record_32.6_Billion_for_November_December_Period.

"U.S. Treasury Electronic-Benefit Campaign Gears Up as Checks Dwindle." *Digital Transactions,* September 8, 2011. Available from http://www.digitaltransactions.net/news/story/3194.

Warman, Matt. "'Wave and Pay' Mobile Phone Spells End for Cash." *Telegraph,* September 14, 2011. Available from http://www.telegraph.co.uk/technology/samsung/8527049/Wave-and-pay-mobile-phone-spells-the-end-for-cash.html.

DIGITAL CERTIFICATE

Digital certificates are digitally encrypted storage vehicles for transporting personal information, especially digital signatures, over the Internet. VeriSign, a major certificate authority (a security company that issues certificates) compares them to a driver's license or passport. For most consumers, though, the certificates play no overt role in their daily use of the Internet as Web browsers act as the traffic cop, demanding an electronic wave of the license or passport in the background. Only when a certificate is questionable or untrusted does the individual consumer become aware of the process, and then a pop-up alert usually appears with a warning that the site where the user is headed is untrustworthy.

CERTIFICATES A BOON TO E-COMMERCE

The appeal of digital certificates in e-commerce is obvious. They greatly enhance the security and speed of online transactions, making the Internet's instantaneous sales and communications possibilities more viable. In the early 2000s, digital certificates were a primary means for the advancement of Web-based commerce. They validate the user at the point of purchase, streamlining the transaction process by eliminating the need for third-party validation. The information contained in the certificate includes the user's name and e-mail address, expiration data, a serial number, and the name of the certificate authority that issued the certificate. Institutions and businesses also encourage their employees and officials to use personal digital certificates to verify the authenticity of their e-mails.

Digital certificates were developed by Salt Lake City-based Zions First National Bank in conjunction with the American Bankers Association. The organizations launched a pilot program with the U.S. Social Security Administration in the late 1990s in which hundreds of companies filed their Social Security reports online using digital certificates. The tremendous success of the program opened the door for wider interest and application. In summer 2000, President Bill Clinton signed into law, using a digital certificate, the Electronic Signatures in Global & National Commerce Act. This legislation heralded a turning point, particularly for online banking, which had been forestalled by concerns over the security and authentication of online financial transactions. By making these digital signatures legally binding and secure, Web-based banking began to finally begin fulfilling its tremendous promise.

The early 2000s witnessed a flurry of new technologies aimed at facilitating the wider application and integration of digital certificates, such as Web forms designed to accept certificates. Other developments included storage space for digital certificates in secure central directories.

Digital certificates generally are stored as files on personal computer Web browsers and are protected by personal identification numbers (PINs), thereby verifying that communications come from particular users. However, some imperfections are implicit. For instance, a digital certificate essentially authenticates the computer, not the individual using it. While users of digital certificates typically safeguard their machines with layers of personal verification for use, in addition to the PIN, certificates stored on computers are nonetheless susceptible to hackers. One highly touted solution to this difficulty was the augmenting of digital certificates with biometric technology, which verifies identity via personal characteristics such as fingerprints, retina, or voice. So-called two-layer authentication utilizing a biometric token adds an additional level of protection to digital certificates stored on an individual computer or laptop.

CONCERN ABOUT CERTIFICATES

With the widespread use of digital certificates and their value in e-commerce, it perhaps was inevitable that fraud would become a paramount issue for online businesses throughout the first decade of the twenty-first century. By the early 2010s, there was growing concern that the very nature of digital certificates and their reliance on sometimes vulnerable algorithms was a critical flaw in the system. In 2009, a survey by *Netcraft* revealed that 14% of valid third-party SSL certificates were issued using the MD5 algorithm which had previously been shown to be at risk of being used to produce fake certificates. As *Netcraft* pointed out, digital certificate security was a "moving target" as a newer algorithm, SHA1, also showed weaknesses. The digital certificate authorities were being tested to come up with stronger, less vulnerable algorithms in a world that was becoming more reliant on their product.

In 2011, the Electronic Frontier Foundation, a digital rights and privacy advocacy group, voiced its concerns about the widening reliance on digital certificates, pointing out that a single e-commerce transaction using a Web server could involve 1,500 certificates. Meanwhile, while securing individual computers remained key, hackers were focusing on a much broader target: the certificate issuing authorities. Security concerns escalated in 2011 when an Iranian hacker, calling himself "Comodohacker," claimed to have stolen digital certificates for 531 sites from DigiNotar, a Dutch certificate authority. The certificates included those owned by Facebook, Mozilla, Yahoo, Android, Twitter, and Skype, according to India's *The Hindu* newspaper, which also reported national intelligence services had also been affected. Security experts, quoted by *InfoWeek,* suggested digital certificate technology was becoming too unwieldy and vulnerable.

While the most commonly used Web browsers continued to monitor digital certificate status and issue frequent security updates, managing multiple digital certificates had become a challenge for businesses as the increasing number of mobile applications and cloud-based service boosted their digital certificate usage, *eWeek.com* reported in 2011. In response to the challenge, Symantec, the largest digital certificate authority in 2011, announced the formation of a cloud-based Certificate Intelligence Center designed to help organizations manage their digital certificates and respond quickly to any attack.

SEE ALSO *Digital Certificate Authority; Digital Signature; Encryption.*

BIBLIOGRAPHY

Bielski, Lauren. "Digital Certificates Get Mobilized by 'E-Sign Act.'" *ABA Banking Journal,* September 2000.

Bright, Peter. " Another Fraudulent Certificate Raises the Same Old Questions about Certificate Authorities." *Ars Technica,* August 2011. Available from http://arstechnica.com/security/news/2011/08/earlier-this-year-an-iranian.ars

Connolly, P. J. "Digital Certificates Are Gaining Ground in Business." *InfoWorld,* October 16, 2000.

Eckersley, Peter. "Iranian Hackers Obtain Fraudulent HTTPS Certificates: How Close to a Web Security Meltdown Did We Get?" San Francisco, CA: Electronic Frontier Foundation, March 23, 2011. Available from https://www.eff.org/deeplinks/2011/03/iranian-hackers-obtain-fraudulent-https.

"Google Issues Warning to Iranian Gmail Users." *The Hindu,* September 13, 2011. Available from http://www.thehindu.com/sci-tech/article2449951.ece.

Hammell, Benjamin. "Are Digital Certificates Secure?" *Communications News,* December 2000.

Harrison, Ann. "Digital Certificates." *Computerworld,* August 14, 2000.

Koller, Mike, and Rutrell Yasin. "Security Gets Some Legs: Digital ID Systems No Longer Hold Users Captive to a Single Browser, PC or Location." *Internetweek,* December 11, 2000.

Musthaler, Linda. "Combine Biometrics and Token Technologies for More Secure Laptops." *NetworkWorld,* February 25, 2008. Available from http://www.networkworld.com/newsletters/2008/0225techexec1.html.

O'Donnell, Anthony. "Security on the Internet: Who Goes There?" *Insurance & Technology,* January 2001.

Perera, Rick. "USB Tokens Offer Pocket-Sized Security." *PCWorld,* March 15, 2002. Available from http://www.pcworld.com/article/89263/usb_tokens_offer_pocketsized_security.html.

Phipps, Colin. "14% of SSL Certificates Signed Using Vulnerable MD5 Algorithm." *Netcraft,* January 1, 2009. Available from http://news.netcraft.com/archives/2009/01/01/14_of_ssl_certificates_signed_using_vulnerable_md5_algorithm.html.

Rashid, Fahmida Y. "Symantec Launches Cloud-Based SSL Certificate Management Service." *eWeek.com,* September 12, 2011.Available from http://www.eweek.com/c/a/Security/Symantec-Launches-CloudBased-SSL-Certificate-Management-Service-205222.

Schwartz, Matthew J., "Are Digital Certificates Doomed?" *Information Week,* September 6, 2011. Available from http://informationweek.com/news/security/vulnerabilities/231600829.

Streeter, Bill. "Will Banks Have a Role in E-commerce? It's a 'Cert'ainty." *ABA Banking Journal,* September 2000.

VeriSign, Inc. "Introduction to Digital Certificates." Dulles, VA, 2011. Available from http://www.verisign.com.au/repository/tutorial/digital/intro1.shtml#step1.

DIGITAL CERTIFICATE AUTHORITY

Certificate authorities were at the hub of many e-commerce developments in the early 2000s and became vital in e-commerce as consumers became ever more reliant on the Internet for commercial transactions and personal communication. One of the greatest impediments to the widespread adoption of online commerce was the fear among many consumers and businesses of the security risks involved in sending financial or other information over the Internet. Certificate authorities aimed to alleviate such fears by acting as guarantors of the authenticity and security of online transactions. To accomplish this, they issued digital certificates, or encrypted electronic packages carrying information that authenticates its sender.

Digital certificates employ a public-key infrastructure. A public code, or key, can be used by anyone to encrypt a message to a given authority. However, only that authority can decrypt the message using its private key. Only the combination of the private key and the public key can authenticate a user's identity or a transaction using a digital certificate. Digital certificates, in turn, were the primary vehicles for digital signatures, which played an enormous role in the burgeoning e-commerce world of the 2000s. Certificate authorities maintain the private key and therefore serve as the trusted agents behind these encrypted transactions. Certificates then carry an authority's stamp of approval wherever they travel, and recipients refer to that authority as the mark of trust to ensure that the given information is secure and the identity of the sender is sound. The authority legally binds an individual, or at least an individual computer, to a particular public key, and certifies that the certificate holder is officially recognized by a trusted third party.

Some certificate authorities are run by large corporations or institutions for their internal and external communications and transactions, but the ever-widening utilization of the Internet by consumers and small businesses sparked the development of commercial certificate authorities. For example, VeriSign, based in Mountain View, California, was a commercial authority that dominated the industry in the late 1990s and early 2000s. According to *Slate* magazine, the major certificate authorities like VeriSign, Equifax, and Thawte benefitted from the confidence expressed in them by browser creators Internet Explorer and Netscape Navigator. In 2004, Go Daddy Inc., a major player in the domain registration and Web hosting marketplace, began selling Secure Sockets Layer (SSL) certificates through its Starfield Technologies subsidiary. The three major SSL certificate authorities vying with Go Daddy mid-decade, according to *Netcraft,* included GeoTrust, The Comodo Group, and VeriSign, which had absorbed Thawte. (In 2010, VeriSign, the largest certificate authority, according to *Netcraft,* sold its SSL and trust services to Symantec Inc.) Netcraft's annual survey gave VeriSign a 38% share of the market with around half a million certificates in use.

AUTHORITY SERVICES

Certificate authorities determine the conditions of a certificate contract, including the duration of its activity, the breadth of privileges it affords, and the obligations of the certificate holder. Certificates usually are issued for one year, although the duration can vary widely. Most authorities are wary of issuing certificates for longer periods because of concerns over long-term security in light of developing technology, the aversion to risk stemming from the trust of individual holders, and the desire to reap continued income from issuing new certificates. Certificates also can be revoked before their expiration date using a certificate revocation list (CRL)—a list digitally signed and issued by the certificate authority that signals to recipients of digital certificates that a given user is no longer validated by the authority.

The certificate authority relationship extends beyond the one-to-many relationship between the authority and its certificate holders. Within a public-key infrastructure, certificate authorities are organized hierarchically, so that each authority lower in the hierarchy maintains a parent authority to verify its public key. This relationship becomes particularly crucial in business-to-business Internet transactions, in which companies need to share secured information using digital certificates for verification. In such cases, the coordination and interoperability between certificate authorities is important to facilitate smooth interaction. The management of multiple certificates creates headaches and uses up valuable resources for a company. Thus, creating authority hierarchies in which certificate validity is smooth throughout various levels was considered an optimal business solution.

Moreover, authorities provide a mechanism for built-in fraud control, in that companies and individuals can trace the path of certificate authorities through which a transaction moved to determine where any mischief may have taken place. Upon discovering abuse of the certificate, the authority can immediately revoke the offending user's certificate. However, since certificate authorities are the trustees of signature security on the Internet, ensuring their own physical, personnel, and network security is a premium concern.

When digital signatures were officially recognized as legally binding by the passage of the Electronic Signatures in Global and National Commerce Act in 2000, the function of certificate authorities in the e-commerce world was taken up a few levels. More and more transactions began to take place over the Internet, including Web-based banking, making the secure validation of such transactions critical. Stringent security measures and protocols became even more crucial to the certificate authorities as online commerce and communication flourished thanks to mobile and cloud-based technologies.

The early major certificate authorities like VeriSign enjoyed "near-monopoly profits," as *Slate* magazine dubbed them, thanks to the blessings of the then-dominant browsers, Netscape and Internet Explorer. The major authorities continued to have the biggest footprint in the marketplace, but as the Web widened and global interactions increased, the number of certificate authorities grew to meet the demands placed on the process by local laws and accreditation requirements. In 2011, Safari and Firefox trusted over 60 certificates authorities by default, and Microsoft software trusted more than 100. But the ever-growing list of trusted certificate authorities and their granting of trust to numerous organizations, including large companies and government agencies, raised questions of both privacy and security. The Electronic Frontier Foundation (EFF), a digital rights advocacy group, questioned whether such trust and empowerment opened a "secret back door" to the Internet, according to *Slate.*

As the number of certificates and the number of authorities issuing them grew throughout the first decade of the twenty-first century, it was matched by a growing number of hackers whose attacks on various commercial and government sites also grew. Unbeknownst to their owners, hackers often used hijacked computers in a wide network dubbed a botnet. It became vital that individual computer owners maintained virus software and updated their browsers with security measures regularly in order to combat these botnet invasions by hackers.

Most certificate authorities, according to the EFF in 2011, did a good job guarding privacy and providing consumers and companies with a secure e-commerce environment. But a growing concern was the structure and sheer size of the system. A single transaction on a Web server, or an e-mail exchange, could involve literally 650 authorities and some 1,500 certificates. The widening use of certificates, and the growth in the number of certificate authorities, became a concern in the wake of successful attacks in 2010 and 2011 as hackers stole certificates, enabling them to pilfer passwords, read e-mail, access bank and credit card accounts, or redirect users to a site set up for criminal purposes.

The vital role played by the digital certificate authorities made them a key target in the developing cyberwars. In 2011, there were reports of attacks on U.S. defense contractors from servers in China, and an Iranian hacker took aim at two authorities, Comodo and DigiNotar. There was speculation that the attack was in response to cyber efforts aimed at disabling Iranian nuclear development through the use of a virus. The hacker, who professed to be a loyal follower of the Iranian regime, stole certificates, compromising major sites like Facebook and Google. The cyberattack on DigiNotar, a Dutch company, had a major effect on government agencies in the Netherlands, according to the *Los Angeles Times,* throwing the country into chaos and prompting one government official to pronounce that only pen, paper, and fax machine were a secure way to communicate with the government. Many commentators said the attack had all the hallmarks of a government-sanctioned attack and predicted this type of attack would be a typical tactic in twenty-first century cyberwarfare. Writing in *Ars Technica* in August 2011, analyst Peter Bright opined: "The absolute trust given to certificate authorities, and the susceptibility of that trust to abuse, has long been considered a problem. … The certificate authorities remain a weak link in the entire public key infrastructure, and though cryptographic systems can be created that reduce this possibility, the scheme we have remains firmly entrenched, regardless of its flaws."

SEE ALSO *Cryptography, Public and Private Key; Digital Certificate; Digital Signature; Digital Signature Legislation; Encryption.*

BIBLIOGRAPHY

Albanesius, Chloe. "Apple Blocks DigiNotar Certificates." *PCMag.com,* September 9, 2011. Available from http://www.pcmag.com/article2/0,2817,2392733,00.asp.

Andress, Mandy. "Multivendor PKI the Key to Smooth E-business Communications." *InfoWorld,* May 29, 2000.

Bradner, Scott. "Are You Usefully Certifiable?" *Network World,* August 16, 1999.

Bright, Peter. " Another Fraudulent Certificate Raises the Same Old Questions about Certificate Authorities." *Ars Technica,* August 2011. Available from http://arstechnica.com/security/news/2011/08/earlier-this-year-an-iranian.ars.

Dilanian, Ken. "Cyber-Attack in Europe Highlights Internet Risks." *Los Angeles Times,* September 9, 2011. Available from http://articles.latimes.com/2011/sep/09/world/la-fgw-cyber-attack-20110910.

Eckersley, Peter. "Iranian Hackers Obtain Fraudulent HTTPS Certificates: How Close to a Web Security Meltdown Did We Get?" San Francisco, CA: Electronic Frontier Foundation, March 23, 2011. Available from https://www.eff.org/deeplinks/2011/03/iranian-hackers-obtain-fraudulent-https.

"Go Daddy Now an SSL Certification Authority." *Netcraft,* March 12, 2004. Available from http://news.netcraft.com/archives/2004/03/12/go_daddy_now_an_ssl_certificate_authority.html.

Harrison, Ann. "Digital Certificates." *Computerworld,* August 14, 2000.

Hurley, Hanna. "Certificate Authorities Move In-House." *Telephony,* September 13, 1999.

Jackson Higgins, Kelly. "Outsourcing PKI Is an Option to Building One." *Informationweek,* November 6, 2000.

McMillan, Robert. "After Digital Certificate Hack, Mozilla Seeks Reassurances." *PCWorld,* September, 8, 2011. Available from http://www.pcworld.com/businesscenter/article/239699/after_digital_certificate_hack_mozilla_seeks_reassurances.html.

O'Brien, Danny. "The Internet's Secret Back Door." *Slate,* August 27, 2010. Available from http://www.slate.com/id/2265204/.

Poynter, Ian. "In Pursuit of Validation." *Network World,* February 26, 2001.

"Symantec Buys Large Share of SSL Market." *Netcraft,* March 20, 2010. Available from http://news.netcraft.com/archives/2010/05/20/symantec_buys_large_share_of_ssl_market.html.

Zetter, Kim. "DigiNotar Files for Bankruptcy in Wake of Devastating Hack." *Wired,* September 20, 2011. Available from http://www.wired.com/threatlevel/2011/09/diginotar-bankruptcy/#more-30141.

DIGITAL DIVIDE

In the beginning, the Internet, and particularly the World Wide Web, was extolled as a powerful force toward the democratization of information and, ultimately, of politics and economics. This was the idealistic vision of the Web's founder, Tim Berners-Lee. By placing such a wealth of information and opportunity at individuals' fingertips, the Web, according to its most ardent supporters, was to act as the great societal leveler. While some aspects of that vision may have leaked through, most observers note that the technology has taken a very different course, and has led to what is popularly known as the digital divide.

Both in the United States and on the global level, the gulf between those individuals, families, organizations, and businesses that enjoy access to the Internet and those that do not constitutes the digital divide.

MAPPING THE DIGITAL DIVIDE

Discussion of a gap between the Internet haves and have-nots formally began with the publication of "Falling Through the Net," a report issued by the National Telecommunications and Information Administration (NTIA) of the U.S. Department of Commerce in 1995. At first associated primarily with racial disparities, the general tenor of the discourse gradually broadened to include a wider array and matrix of social indicators, particularly those related to class.

The Department of Commerce in late 2000 reported that 12.7% of Americans earning less than $15,000 per year had access to the Internet in their homes, compared with 77.7% of those making more than $75,000 a year. The *Journal of Housing and Community Development* noted that racial divisions intersected with income levels; 23% of African Americans and Hispanics combined maintained home Internet access, while 46% of Caucasians were connected at home.

LIBRARIES

Libraries started to offer computers that had Internet connections to the public, providing an alternative to people who could not afford to purchase their own hardware. A 2002 Colorado State Library study showed that the existence of public Internet access was the main reason that people were traveling to the library, and about a third of library visitors had no other method of accessing the Internet. The library Internet service was very important because it was available free, and other alternatives such as copy centers and coffee shops typically rented out Internet services based on the amount of time that a customer spent using the Internet. About a third of the survey respondents were using the library computers to find work.

ACCESS TRENDS

In 2003, the Federal Reserve Bank of San Francisco released a report on the digital divide. It found that a majority of Asian and white respondents had home Internet access, while about a third of African American and Hispanic respondents had access. There was a very strong correlation between both family income and family education levels and Internet access, as about 80% of respondents who had either a graduate degree or earned more than $75,000 a year had home internet service, while only about 20% of respondents who had less than a high school education or earned less than $15,000 had home Internet service. Many respondents who lacked home Internet service did obtain such service through work or school, so about 50% of the respondents with the lowest incomes or the least education still had some type of access to the Internet.

WORLD INFORMATION SUMMIT

Although Internet access was at that point available to most Americans, there were still more than a billion people throughout the world who were not connected, many of whom earned very low wages. In 2003, the United Nations announced that it would hold a conference on the Information Society, emphasizing the difficulties that the rural poor had obtaining access to the Internet. The summit focused on making information about modern agricultural techniques widely available through Internet technology, because many of the rural poor were subsistence farmers.

CHILDREN

Another factor that influenced the digital divide was whether children lived in a household. A New Zealand report showed that having any children present increased the likelihood of home Internet access, and the effect was stronger if the household included more than one child. Internet access was also more widespread in households with two adults present.

EXPANDING ACCESS

Pew Research Center conducted a survey in 2005 and found that access to the Internet at home had increased among most demographic groups of Americans, and more than two-thirds of Americans were online. Americans older than 65 were the only age group in which most respondents did not have Internet access, with only 26% going online, while 84% of the 18 to 29 group had used the Internet. Pew also found that there were very few respondents who had recently been introduced to the Internet, and about four-fifths of respondents had been using the Internet for at least four years. The racial access gap had also shrunk, dropping to a 13% difference between African American and white survey respondents.

DESCRIBING THE DIVIDE

The digital divide is more complicated than simply determining whether an individual has access to the Internet. High-speed connections are important for many services, such as video streams, but high-speed access is not always available, especially in rural locations. Awareness is also important. An individual needs additional knowledge about the Internet to look up scientific research or organize political groups, such as the ability to decide whether a report is trustworthy.

WIRELESS ACCESS

The price of computers dropped throughout the 2000s, and by the middle of that decade, new computers were available for a few hundred dollars. Internet service was still a major issue, as it involved a regular monthly bill which could be $50 a month for broadband service. To help their lower-income residents access the Internet, cities including Philadelphia started to build public access wireless networks which allowed anyone who was within range of the transmitters to connect to the Internet without paying a monthly bill. Another benefit of a free public network (according to Forrester Research) was that, like any utility, a cable or DSL subscription typically requires the subscriber to provide evidence of a satisfactory credit history, which can be challenging for low-income households.

SOCIAL NETWORKS

Social networks, which were gaining prominence during the mid-2000s, helped reduce the digital divide. Social networks were a major draw for students, and the University of Minnesota reported that 77% of students in a 2008 survey were using social networks. Although the students were using the social networks mainly for entertainment purposes, the researchers noted that the students were learning important communication and creative techniques.

WIRELESS REGULATIONS

In the United Kingdom, regulators decided to improve access to rural residents by extending the range of the existing wireless towers. By allowing wireless towers to double their power and send out a four-watt signal, each tower could serve a larger area. A telecommunications firm would not have to pay to construct new towers in locations that had relatively few customers.

HEALTH CARE ACCESS

The digital divide also affected the health care industry. A 2009 *Amednews* article reported that hospitals that cared for poor patients were less likely to have modern information technology. The federal government allocated additional funds to help these hospitals set up electronic medical records and other services.

CELL PHONES

In 2010, the *New York Times* reported that some demographic groups that were less likely to own computers were more likely to own other devices which could access the Internet, such as cell phones. However, the article concluded that the digital divide was still present, because cell phones have fewer capabilities than a laptop, and many of these cell phone users did not own laptops.

NATIONAL BROADBAND

By the beginning of the 2010s, most Americans could obtain Internet access, although a few rural areas still suffered from low-quality connections. The *Washington Post* reported that a federal survey showed that 10% of rural residents still did not have the opportunity to subscribe to high-speed Internet service. In 2011, the Obama administration was considering a national broadband initiative that would expand broadband coverage to almost all communities in the nation, which would cost a total of $18 billion.

SEE ALSO *Children and the Internet; Social Media.*

BIBLIOGRAPHY

Albrecht, Karl, and Ronald Gunn. "Digital Backlash." *Training & Development,* November 2000.

Armstrong, Anne A. "Missing the Boat." *Government Executive,* August 2000.

Blanks Hindman, Douglas. "The Rural-Urban Digital Divide." *Journalism and Mass Communications Quarterly,* Autumn 2000.

Brustein, Joshua. "Mobile Web Use and the Digital Divide." *Bits* (blog), *New York Times,* July 7, 2010. Available from http://bits.blogs.nytimes.com/2010/07/07/increased-mobile-web-use-and-the-digital-divide/.

Chanda, Nayan. "Asian Innovation Awards: The Digital Divide." *Far Eastern Economic Review,* October 19, 2000.

Chon, Kilnam. "The Future of the Internet Digital Divide." *Communications of the ACM,* March 2001.

"Damning the Digital Divide." *America's Network,* October 1, 2000.

"The Digital Divide." *CMA Management,* July/August 2000.

Ebenkamp, Becky. "Divide and Culture." *Brandweek,* January 29, 2001.

Fattah, Hassan. "The Digital Divide—Politics of a Real Problem?" *MC Technology Marketing Intelligence,* September 2000.

Federal Reserve Bank of San Francisco. "Is There a Digital Divide?" December 26, 2003. Available from http://www.frbsf.org/publications/economics/letter/2003/el2003-38.html.

Foley, Kathleen. "Deeds, Not Words, Will Fix the Digital Divide." *InformationWeek,* March 26, 2001.

Food and Agriculture Organization of the United Nations (FAO). "Rural Digital Divide Distancing Development, FAO Warns." Rome, Italy, December 10, 2003. Available from http://www.fao.org/english/newsroom/news/2003/26167-en.html.

Fox, Susannah. "Digital Divisions." Pew Internet and American Life Project, October 5, 2005. Available from http://www.pewinternet.org/Reports/2005/Digital-Divisions.aspx.

Gomolski, Barb. "Web Users Get Special Deals: Is It the Digital Divide or Just Good Business Sense?" *InfoWorld,* February 26, 2001.

Hecht, Ben. "Bridging the Digital Divide." *Journal of Housing and Community Development,* March/April 2001.

Hoffman, Thomas. "Leaders: Education Key to Bridging Digital Divide." *Computerworld,* September 11, 2000.

Kang, Cecilia. "Survey of Online Access Finds Digital Divide." *Washington Post,* February 17, 2011. Available from http://www.washingtonpost.com/wp-dyn/content/article/2011/02/17/AR2011021707234.html.

Kim, Michael C., and Dennis A. Steckler. "Leaping the Digital Divide." *Best's Review,* February 2001.

Lach, Jennifer. "Crossing the Digital Divide." *American Demographics,* June 2000.

Lipke, David J. "Dead End Ahead?" *American Demographics,* August 2000.

Melymuka, Kathleen. "Dabbling at Diversity." *Computerworld,* December 11, 2000.

Moe, Tammi, and Keith Curry Lance. "Colorado Public Libraries and the 'Digital Divide'." Colorado State Library Library Research Service, October 2004. Available from http://www.lrs.org/documents/DD_2002/DD_report_revised_oct_2004.pdf.

Nagel, David. "Digital Divide? What Digital Divide?" *The Journal,* June 23, 2008. Available from http://thejournal.com/articles/2008/06/23/digital-divide-what-digital-divide.aspx.

Olsen, Stefanie. "Will the Digital Divide Close by Itself?" *Bits* (blog), *New York Times,* October 30, 2009. Available from http://bits.blogs.nytimes.com/2009/10/30/will-the-digital-divide-close-by-itself/.

O'Reilly, Kevin B. "Digital Divide Emerges at Hospitals Serving Poor Patients." *Amednews,* November 23, 2009. Available from http://www.ama-assn.org/amednews/2009/11/23/prsb1123.htm.

Rombel, Adam. "The Global Digital Divide." *Global Finance,* December 2000.

Statistics New Zealand. "New Report Sheds Light on Digital Divide." Wellington, New Zealand, March 5, 2004. Available from http://www2.stats.govt.nz/domino/external/pasfull/pasfull.nsf/52ed0cdd657e68f54c256568000e2235/4c2567ef00247c6acc256e4d00094f38?OpenDocument.

Vehovar, Vasja, et al. "Methological Challenges of Digital Divide Measurements." *Information Society,* 22, (2006): 279–90. DOI: 10.1080/01972240600904076. Available from http://www.intramis.net/tis_articles/Methodological_Challenges.pdf.

Wallman, Kathleen M. H. "Counting Down the Top Ten." *America's Network,* March 1, 2001.

"Will Philly Close Digital Divide By 2006?" Cambridge, MA: Forrester Research, January 20, 2005. Available from http://blogs.forrester.com/adm/05-01-20-will_philly_close_digital_divide_2006.

"Wireless Power Limit Doubled to Bridge Digital Divide." *The Register,* June 6, 2007. Available from http://www.theregister.co.uk/2007/06/06/wireless_power_limit_raised/.

DIGITAL ECONOMY

In June 2000, the U.S. government issued the *Digital Economy 2000* report, a follow-up to its previous *Emerging Digital Economy* reports published in 1998 and 1999. The report was based on research conducted by the Council of Economic Advisors (CEA), the Congressional Budget Office (CBO), the Federal Reserve, and outside economists. It announced that information technology (IT) industries were responsible for at least 50% of increased U.S. productivity rates, which grew at an annual rate of 1.4% from 1973 to 1995, and 2.8% thereafter. Although IT industries only accounted for an 8.3% share of the U.S. economy by 2000, they generated roughly 30% of overall U.S. economic growth. Electronic commerce (e-commerce) led growth throughout the new digital economy.

Digital Economy 2000 identified several significant IT-related business and economic trends. In general, businesses turned ever more frequently to the Internet to boost efficiency by shifting supply networks and sales online and relying on networked systems to streamline internal procedures. The resulting improvement in productivity led to lower inflation and higher real wages. However, the report indicated that this still was an emerging trend.

GROWTH OF IT WORKERS

The number of workers in the software and computer services industries rose from 850,000 in 1992 to 1.6 million in 1998. By 1998, there were 7.4 million workers in IT-related positions nationwide, or about 6% of the total U.S. workforce. Hiring of the most highly skilled employees, such as systems analysts, programmers, and computer scientists, rose by nearly 80% to about 1 million positions during the same period. IT salaries averaged $58,000 a year, 85% higher than the average for the private sector.

By the second decade of the twenty-first century, there were many more millions of workers in the IT industry, and the industry itself had segmented into several sectors. For example, the U.S. Census Bureau's breakdown of IT and computer-related business sectors numbered 28 in 2007. The growing number of IT workers both in the United States and around the world reflects the increasing number of people turning to e-sources on a daily basis. According to e-Week.com, one trend that is becoming dominant in the digital economy of the twenty-first century is the preference of employers to hire more technically skilled employees. This was evident in figures reported by the U.S. Bureau of Labor Statistics that the telecommunications and data processing industries lost more than 47,000 jobs in August 2011, while 13,700 professional IT jobs were added during the same month. It was the 15th consecutive month the IT sector added jobs rather than losing them.

INTERNET ACCESS IN THE DIGITAL ECONOMY

Worldwide, approximately 304 million people had Internet access by 2000. In contrast, only 3 million people around the globe had similar access in 1994. Most of the growth occurred outside of the United States and Canada, which for the first time totaled less than half of those with online access. However, the number of American Web users still rose by 40%. In most other areas of the world, Internet access at least doubled. Access in Africa showed a 136% increase; Asia and the Pacific, 155%; Europe, 108%; the Middle East, 111%; and South America, 102%. By 2006, there were 1 billion people across the globe who had access to the Internet, according to a report published by Miniwatts Marketing Group, and according to a report published by the U.S. Census Bureau, as of 2009 there were 1.8 billion Internet users in the world.

According to data published by the U.S. Census Bureau, by 2007–2008, e-commerce had gained widespread use in most industries. For example, e-commerce accounted for more than 40% of total shipments in industries such as beverage and tobacco manufacturing, textile mills and products, petroleum and coal products manufacturing, and transportation equipment manufacturing.

The digital economy is also spawning a whole new sector of Web-based jobs, especially for workers in developing countries, according to a report by *info* Dev, an arm of the World Bank Group. The report, published on April 7, 2011, noted that the virtual economy is worth $3 billion and employed more than 100,000 people. Some of these people earn a living by completing online tasks on video games for wealthy clients who do not have the time to play but wish to improve their character profiles on the games. Other tasks these workers complete are transcribing handwritten documents and classifying products on an online shopping Web site or catalog. One participant of this trend is Amazon.com, which hires workers to delete duplicate pages on its e-commerce site.

SEE ALSO *Digital Divide.*

BIBLIOGRAPHY

Beattie, Andrew. "Market Crashes: The Dotcom Crash." *Investopedia.* Available from http://www.investopedia.com/features/crashes/crashes8.asp#axzz1XkY8QZkS.

Eddy, Nathan. "IT Employment Opportunities Persist Despite Weak Job Market: Foote Partners." *eWeek.com,* September 6, 2011. Available from http://www.eweek.com/c/a/IT-Management/IT-Employment-Opportunities-Persist-Despite-Weak-Job-Market-Foote-Partners-116872.

Haskins, Walaika. "Super Economy." *PC Magazine,* August 1, 2000.

"Jobs of the Future." *Economist,* April 7, 2011. Available from http://www.economist.com/blogs/schumpeter/2011/04/digital_economy.

Mason, Paul. "'Boom is IT-Driven' Say US Economists." *Computer Weekly,* June 15, 2000.

Strassmann, Paul. "Fuzzy Math in D.C." *Computerworld,* January 8, 2001.

U.S. Department of Commerce. "Background for Digital Economy 2000 Report." Washington, DC: GPO, 2000.

U.S. Department of Commerce. Bureau of the Census. *Digital Economy 2000.* Washington, DC: GPO, June 2000.

———. "Key Global Telecom Indicators for the World Telecommunication Service Center: 2005–2009." Washington, DC: GPO, 2011.

———. "U.S Manufacturing Shipments–Total and E-commerce Value." Washington, DC: GPO, 2000.

DIGITAL ESTATE PLANNING

Digital estate planning refers to the management of the digital valuables of deceased users. While traditional estate planning is used to plan for the disbursement of property, accounts, and tangible assets, digital estate planning is used instead to preserve or manage the information users have stored online. Taxes may not be involved and digital information may not even count as assets from an accounting perspective, but users often amass messages, photographs, videos, and slideshows, all dear to survivors but all stored in remote servers.

Users rarely consider what death may do to their accounts. According to 2011 reports, 375,000 Facebook users die each year. Traditionally, photographs and letters were physical objects that could be shared and inherited. The same is not true of online social profiles, photo books, and blogs that may be password protected or closed after death, separating family members from mementos and creating legal issues with copyrighted material. Digital estate planning seeks to create a solution through financial strategy and the streamlining of user policies when it comes to inheritance or holding data. While this has generated a new industry for some markets in the late 2000s, other markets remained closed or wary of the trend.

PERSONAL MANAGEMENT OF DIGITAL ESTATES

A significant portion of digital estate planning consists of actions the user takes before death. One of the easiest ways to prepare for death or incapacitation is to tally all online accounts and prepare information agents, executors, and family members. A user should begin by taking inventory of an online presence, moving through all online applications and recording any Web site domain name ownership, music playlists, online videos, and online magazine subscriptions. These accounts should then be listed with their respective passwords and prepared for agents or executors.

Of course, there are also any social media profiles users have, and any online accounts they use to manage utilities or investments. These also have their own passwords, which should be collected for family. Hardware like wireless networks and software like security programs can also come with passwords that survivors will need to know after death.

COMMON NOTICES

While gathering passwords is helpful, digital assets and data are often controlled by the terms of individual social media sites which users sign up for. This can create a myriad of potential legal issues that executors must keep in mind.

Facebook, one of the most popular social networks, has a memorialize function that goes into effect once an account user has died, making notification an important step for protecting Facebook information. The memorialization option restricts the account to confirmed friends and allows messages to be posted on the account in remembrance. The account is closed when next of kin makes a formal request. LinkedIn follows similar rules but removes all messaging functionality.

Twitter offers to remove an account permanently or offer family members help in saving a backup of public tweets, which helps prevent future issues with spammers retweeting useless messages on the account of someone who is deceased.

Some regulations are fairly lax, such as the Google regulations, which allow continued access to all features until someone with the authority to shut down the account logs on and deletes the account in the conventional way. Otherwise, family members must send documented proof of the death and relation to the user to Google in order shut down the account. Yahoo! and other e-mail providers often close accounts after three to six months without use, including Yahoo! Flickr accounts used to store photographs.

For online game companies like Second Life or World of Warcraft, details can vary based on the agreements. Second Life does not allow virtual land licenses to be claimed through the right of survivorship or similar dispositions. Other agreements may specifically allow disposal through inheritance.

DIGITAL EXECUTORS

The term digital executor describes online companies that sprang up to address the issue of digital estate planning. These companies ensure that all digital account information is properly collated and passed on. Entrustet, for example, allows users to create a list of online accounts, memberships, passwords, and computer-based files with security protection. This involves nominating a legal digital executor and incorporating digital assets into a will, trust, or other method of disposal, but users can ensure that friends and family members are able to receive any important files or access information desired. Users can also upload particularly important files to a separate Entrustet account for preservation.

Legacy Locker and DataInherit are similar sites. Legacy Locker offers a digital version of a safety deposit box to hold all passwords and allows the user to assign a beneficiary for each account and store scanned documents on Legacy Locker space. DataInherit has similar services and emphasizes the notification of family members upon death to avoid confusion.

DEVELOPMENT AND ROADBLOCKS

While digital estate planning had become a common concept by the 2010s, several issues were still keeping the industry from fully developing. A major issue was the nature of the market itself. Demographically, in the 2010s the people most in need of the service were those in their 60s and 70s, but these were also the people who were the least likely to contact a digital executor.

Even those involved in online activities may not be willing to take the digital estate planning step. Avoidance is a common American issue when it comes to any type of estate planning. Only a third of Americans had a will in 2011, and distrust of online security was a growing concern among many markets. On the side of government legislators and legal professionals, the concept remains relatively new compared to traditional estate planning. With so little legal dispute and inspection of the digital estate process, there had not been a chance by 2011 to create a significant body of legal rulings or government bills on the issue. States and federal authorities alike, however, were expected to begin creating regulations on the issue as applicability continued to grow.

SEE ALSO *Facebook; Virtual Communities.*

BIBLIOGRAPHY

"5 Reasons Digital Estate Planning Hasn't Caught On . . . Yet." Annandale, VA: The Zucker Law Firm PLLC, July 30 2011. Available from http://estateplanninginfoblog.com/2011/07/5-reasons-digital-estate-planning-hasn%E2%80%99t-caught-on-%E2%80%A6-yet.

Boys, Brian. "Digital Estate Planning." *Oast & Hook,* September 23, 2011. Available from http://oasthook.com/resources/elder-law-newsletter/387-digital-estate-planning.html.

"Digital Assets: Estate Planning for Online Accounts Becoming Essential." Annandale, VA: The Zucker Law Firm PLLC, December 13 2010. Available from http://estateplanninginfoblog.com/2010/12/digital-assets-estate-planning-for-online-accounts-becoming-essential-part-i.

Entrustet. "How Entrustet Helps Consumers." Madison, WI, 2011. Available from https://www.entrustet.com/help-consumers.

Kwong, Justin. "Digital Estate Planning." *Virtual Navigator,* January 11, 2011. Available from http://virtualnavigator.wordpress.com/2011/01/11/digital-estate-planning.

"Overview Data Inheritance." Zurich, Switzerland: DataInherit, 2011. Available from http://www.datainherit.com/en/why_data_inheritance/overview_data_inheritance.html.

Walker, Rob. "Cyberspace When You're Dead." *New York Times,* January 5, 2011. Available from http://www.nytimes.com/2011/01/09/magazine/09Immortality-t.html?pagewanted=all.

Legacy Locker. "Your Legacy Locker." San Francisco, CA, 2011. Available from http://legacylocker.com/features/locker.

DIGITAL MILLENNIUM COPYRIGHT ACT

The Digital Millennium Copyright Act, often abbreviated to DMCA, is a comprehensive piece of federal legislation designed to focus on many of the issues raised by the exchange of digital information on the Internet. It fostered a foundation for behavior, a platform for analyzing new issues, and an area of contention for the 2000s and early 2010s. Among its chief applications were laws regarding digital copyrights, copyright liability for specific parties, and fees for the use of copyrighted information.

CREATION

The DMCA was enacted in 1998 by the United States Congress and signed into law by President Clinton. At this stage the act had several different goals. Foremost among them was the desire to update laws for a new world, a United States after the Information Revolution. This was one reason that the DMCA was so far-reaching and contained some of the most drastic copyright law reform seen in the United States.

The federal government also had its eye on treaties and standards being created through the World Intellectual Property Organization. Realizing that global business and the international online exchange of information would be inevitable, the United States decided to pass the DMCA proactively in order to meet many of the standards being set forth through the new treaties. However, not all of the DMCA was immediately enforced. Several parts were phased in or adjusted over several years, so the law was not fully applicable until the early 2000s.

MAJOR POINTS

The DMCA focused on several major points that were expected to become vital issues in the coming years. Many of the details of the act were designed to prevent digital piracy through criminalizing certain acts, such as circumventing the antipiracy measures that many types of commercial software contained. The act also made it illegal to manufacture or sell code-cracking devices that could be used for hacking and copying protected software (exemptions were made for encryption research and security processes). The act ensured that some organizations, especially nonprofit archives and similar institutions, would be spared from some unnecessary portions of the antipiracy laws when sharing data.

The act also addressed infringement liability, detailing who would be held responsible for breaking these new laws in the online world of providers, users, and intermediaries. Internet service providers were not held liable for transferring information per their contract requirements, even if that information contained illegally copied information. However, these same providers were required to remove material from user Web sites that appeared to infringe on current copyright, creating what became known as "takedown notices" for users.

The DMCA did help create a primary body of legislation for settling online issues, but as the 2000s progressed, issues continued to develop. Despite the act's specifications, enforceability became a problem for the U.S. government, and piracy continued to grow in online circles, both domestically and internationally. Pirating software and security measures entered a technology race that the government had limited influence in, though the DMCA did help to clarify the issue.

By the start of the 2010s, online information creation and sharing became so common that it was difficult for many providers to keep track of what was protected through copyrights and what was not. In the tension that occurred between organizations trying to enforce the DMCA and bloggers, posters, or Web site users preferring a more *laissez-faire* attitude, the takedown notices became a notorious, oft-used tool.

SPECIAL CIRCUMSTANCES: HIGHER EDUCATION

Just as the federal government showed it understood the position of Internet providers in DMCA liability laws, other organizations were also granted special treatment known in the act as safe harbor. Notably, the act addressed the difficulties of universities and other centers of higher education. Higher education organizations supplied Internet access to students, but the act ensured that they would not be held liable for piracy or other copyright infringement created by the students.

In order to qualify for this provision, centers of higher education had to follow the standards set the DMCA. Colleges were required to inform the general college community of its rights and responsibilities when it came to protected online information. Compliance with DMCA regulations was often made a part of college guidelines, actions that became increasingly important as the 2000s progressed and file share software use among students grew more common.

SPECIAL CIRCUMSTANCES: WEBCASTING

The DMCA also updated laws regarding the use of copyrighted material, allowing for online use in specific cases. Webcasting, or streaming radio broadcasts, songs, and videos fell under the purview of updated regulations. An emphasis was placed on music and radio, creating licensing fees that Webcasters had to pay to record companies in order to stream music on their Web sites. This meant that Webcasters which used "ephemeral copies" on their servers had to pay for permission to publish these copies online.

Royalty rates became a matter of agreement between the copyright owners and the Web services using the license. In the event of a disagreement, a Copyright Arbitration Royalty Panel (CARP) could be convened. In 2002, a CARP produced a report that based marketplace rates on the contract between the Recording Industry Association of America and Yahoo!, which was at that time a major Webcaster. This agreement stipulated a rate of 14 cents for each transmitted performance and 0.07 cents for each retransmission.

SEE ALSO *Intellectual Property; World Intellectual Property Association.*

BIBLIOGRAPHY

"The Digital Millennium Copyright Act." Los Angeles: UCLA Online Institute for Cyberspace and Policy, 2001. Available from http://gseis.ucla.edu/iclp/dmca1.htm.

"Digital Millennium Copyright Act Policy." Phoenix, AZ: University of Phoenix, 2011. Available from http://www.phoenix.edu/about_us/regulatory/consumer-information/digital-millennium-copyright-act-policy.html.

"DMCA–99 Resources." Washington, DC: EDUCAUSE, May 2011. Available from http://www.educause.edu/Resources/Browse//31236.

"DMCA and the Higher Education Opportunity Act." Boone, NC: Appalachian State University, 2011. Available from: http://support.appstate.edu/dmca.

U.S. Copyright Office. "Summary of the Determination of the Librarian of Congress on Rates and Terms for Webcasting and Ephemeral Recordings." Washington, DC, 2002. Available from http://www.copyright.gov/carp/webcasting_rates_final.html.

DIGITAL SIGNATURE

The legally binding electronic autographs known as digital signatures were among the key technologies that made the Internet a forum for commerce beginning in the early 2000s. They not only verify an individual's identity but also guarantee the validity of the information attached to the signature, be it a credit card number, an order form, or a written document. Digital signatures significantly reduce the costs of conducting business over the Internet.

Digital signatures usually are transported in digital certificates—encrypted electronic packages sent as e-mail attachments and increasingly used with Web forms. Digital certificates are assured by trusted third parties called certificate authorities, which issue certificates and act as a guarantor of their validity. Digital certificates generally contain more comprehensive data than digital signatures, including company information, the certificate's expiration date, and so on.

Using techniques from the field of cryptography, digital signatures are generated by applying a mathematical formula, or algorithm, to scramble the information into a string of digits. This ensures that only those with the correct keys—those who will make use of the signature, either for signing or for verification—can unscramble them. Only the holder of the private key—the one whose signature it is—can actually sign a document with that digital signature, while anyone with the public key can verify that it came from that individual. Moreover, digital signatures are bound to the document to which they are applied, and cannot be illicitly copied and transferred to another document. Therefore, signatures help not only to ensure legal validity but security as well. While digital signatures are not immune from criminal mischief, they certainly are more difficult to forge than handwritten signatures. Their use over a public-key encryption system greatly fortifies digital signatures from attack by malicious hackers.

Digital signatures did not originate with e-commerce. The basic principle behind digital signatures—electronic validation of a user's identity over computer networks—has been used for years, most notably with automatic teller machines (ATMs) and other systems that utilize a personal identification number along with another piece of information, such as a magnetic identification card. In the early days of e-commerce, the phrase "digital signature" was loosely defined. It could, for instance, even refer to a handwritten signature that had been scanned into an electronic format. However, such methods, which were extremely prone to forgery, rarely were considered legally binding and failed to win widespread support as a safe and viable means of validating transactions.

On June 30, 2000, President Bill Clinton signed into law—using a digital signature—the Electronic Signatures in Global and National Commerce Act, or E-Sign. This act, which went into effect on October 1 of that year, officially conferred the same legal status on digital signatures as handwritten signatures. The U.S. government, meanwhile, mandated that all federal agencies accept digital signatures by October 2003.

The widespread use of digital signatures was held in check in the early 2000s due to the disparate software programs used to validate digital certificates. Since various software programs exist and often are tailored to different organizations, the technological infrastructure that allows for seamless, wide-ranging transactions was far from complete. Moreover, certificate authorities each maintain their own rules of certificate issuance, validation, and revocation. Therefore, legal responsibility and authentication frequently was muddled outside of a small, contained network.

E-SIGNATURES VERSUS DIGITAL SIGNATURES

By the 2010s, electronic signatures were becoming more commonplace, especially in e-commerce and business-to-business transactions. However, confusion reigned over whether e-signatures or digital signatures were the more legally binding choice. According to a report by Forrester Research, the definition of e-signatures is quite broad and can mean any digital response used to signify a signature, such as an electronic sound, symbol, or click. Digital signatures, on the other hand, use the encryption methods and algorithms already described to ensure an authentic signature. As a result, although e-signatures are also frequently used, digital signatures are the more secure choice.

By 2006, there were one billion people across the globe who had access to the Internet, according to a report published by Miniwatts Marketing Group. With the increasing globalization of businesses and e-commerce, digital signature use is also increasing, and that trend is expected to continue throughout the 2010s. The use of digital signatures has been identified as a key component of success for companies in developing and emerging economies that wish to increase their presence globally, according to a paper published by the nonprofit foundation Diplo. While digital signatures have been legally recognized in the United States, Japan, and Europe, developing nations must also recognize digital signatures if they are to become a ubiquitous presence in the global marketplace.

SEE ALSO *Cryptography, Public and Private Key; Digital Certificate; Digital Certificate Authority; Digital Signature Legislation; Encryption.*

BIBLIOGRAPHY

Ceniceros, Roberto. "Digital Signatures Mean Better Security Online." *Business Insurance,* December 4, 2000.

de Almeida, Guilherme Alberto Almeida, Alfonso Avila, and Violeta Boncanoska. "Promoting E-commerce in Developing Countries." Internet Governance and Policy Discussion Papers. Available from www.diplomacy.edu/poolbin.asp?IDPool=454.

Edfors, Patty. "Your John Hancock Goes Digital." *Communications News,* December 2000.

"E-Signatures to Take Hold Slowly, Report Says." *Bank Systems & Technology,* February 2001.

Gelbord, Boaz. "Signing Your 011001010: The Problems of Digital Signatures." *Communications of the ACM,* December 2000.

Hallenborg, John C., and Orla O'Sullivan. "Not By Software Alone." *U.S. Banker,* February 2001.

Hammar, Sven. "PKI Enables Digital Signatures." *Network World,* October 30, 2000.

Nagel, Bill. "E-signatures Q&A: Legalize It." Cambridge, MA: Forrester Research, December 2, 2009. Available from http://www.echosign.com/static/Forrester%20Research%20-%20%20eSignatures%20QandA%20-%20Dec%2009.pdf.

Stephens, David O. "Digital Signatures and Global e-Commerce: Part I—U.S. Initiatives." *Information Management Journal,* January 2001.

DIGITAL SIGNATURE LEGISLATION

Legislators and business leaders long recognized that the passage of digital legislation was of central importance to the development of e-commerce. However, for several years Republicans and Democrats in the U.S. Congress haggled over what should be included in such a bill. In the meantime, several states passed their own legislation allowing some forms of digital signatures to be legally binding in certain situations. When a major piece of national legislation went into effect in 2000, it was heralded as a giant step toward the harmonization of interstate and international laws, and was expected to help propel e-commerce forward in the early 2000s.

The most sweeping digital signature legislation on the books in the early 2000s was the Electronic Signatures in Global and National Commerce Act, popularly known as the E-Sign Act. President Bill Clinton signed the act into law on June 30, 2000, and it became effective on October 1 of that year. Under E-Sign, digital signatures used in interstate and foreign commerce assumed the same legally binding status as handwritten signatures. The act defined electronic signature broadly as any "electronic sound, symbol, or process attached to or logically associated with a contract or other record and executed or adopted by a person with the intent to sign the record." This flexibility allows the legislation to remain valid through the course of technological development. It was expected to open the way for a flood of financial transactions over the Internet, from securing loans to transferring money between accounts to closing home sales.

Significantly, under the act no individual is required to use a digital signature in any situation, nor is any business compelled to accept them. However, once parties agree to make use of digital signatures, then all parties are bound to recognize the signatures as legally binding. In short, the act bars discrimination against a signature for the sole reason that it is electronic.

Prior to E-Sign, almost every state had at least one law on the books that validated electronic signatures in some situations, while 20 states had signed onto the Uniform Electronic Transactions Act (UETA), which recognized digital signatures as legally binding for contracts. However, in adopting UETA, several states made their own modifications that progressively eroded the uniformity of the law. For example, Utah's Digital Signature Act of 1995 tended to favor electronic signatures using digital certificates over public key encryption systems. Effectively, E-Sign facilitated the harmonization between such laws and took national what many states had already allowed.

In addition, E-Sign includes provisions for electronic record keeping. It allows electronically stored records to be considered legally valid, provided they accurately convey the information in the original record and are freely accessible to all involved parties in a form that can be accurately reproduced. As long as these conditions are met, the record keeper fulfills the legal obligation to retain records in their original form.

E-Sign is a self-executing law. Thus, it makes no provisions or requirements for a state or federal regulatory agency to adopt or enforce its measures. Regulatory actions that involve aspects of E-Sign are permissible only if the regulations remain consistent with E-Sign, do not issue any requirement that a record be in paper form, remain technology neutral, and confer no unreasonable costs on the use of electronic signatures.

E-Sign charges the secretary of commerce with promoting the use of digital signatures in international transactions and the harmonization of signature standards. For these efforts, the act refers to the Model Law on Electronic Commerce as its basis, which was adopted by the United Nations Commission on International Trade Law. By the time E-Sign went into effect, many European countries already recognized digital signatures. Japan, meanwhile, began officially recognizing them in April 2001. Therefore, with its heavy emphasis on international commerce, E-Sign placed the United States on the same playing field as the most developed countries.

GLOBAL ADOPTION OF DIGITAL SIGNATURES

Most countries had developed and enacted legislature legalizing digital signatures by the end of the first decade of the twenty-first century. Some notable legislation includes the Uniform Electronic Commerce Act of Canada, enacted in 2000; The Electronic Communications Act of 2000 in the United Kingdom; the EU Directive for Electronic Signatures of 1999; and the Electronic Signature Law of the People's Republic of China, which was enacted in 2004. Other countries that have enacted digital signature legislation include Brazil, India, the Russian Federation, and South Africa. These pieces of legislation, for the most part, provide details about what constitutes a legally valid digital signature, and under what circumstances it may be able to be obtained.

RESULTS OF ADOPTION OF DIGITAL SIGNATURES

One consequence of worldwide digital signature legislation has been its adoption in a variety of business transactions. A study conducted by Parag Shiralkar and Bindiganavale S. Vijayaraman noted that digital signature technologies were developed and used primarily in business-to-business transactions in the early 2000s.

In most countries, legal challenges arising from digital signatures has been minimal. However, in the United States, there has been an increasing number of lawsuits filed as the result of companies not being able to prove that customers had agreed to all terms of a transaction. For example, in 2004, one customer filed a class-action law suit against the retail store Best Buy when she used an electronic signature pad, agreeing to accept what she was told was a free subscription for *Sports Illustrated,* only to be charged for the subscription six months later. Best Buy claimed the offer details, including the fact that the customer would receive six free issues before she would begin to be charged for them, appeared on the screen prior to her signing. However, Best Buy was unable to verify that it provided the information on-screen.

New legislation or court decisions may also impact the political landscape. In May 2011, software company Verafirma sued San Mateo County in California for not accepting the electronic signature on a legislative initiative in 2010. The 1st District Court of Appeal in San Francisco was asked to decide whether e-signatures will be allowed on petitions, and Verafirma, the company developing specific software for political use, continued its legal battle to have electronic signatures accepted.

SEE ALSO *Cryptography, Public and Private Key; Digital Certificate; Digital Certificate Authority; Digital Signature; Encryption.*

BIBLIOGRAPHY

Bishop, Shaun. "San Mateo County Involved in Court Fight Over E-signatures." *San Francisco Examiner,* March 2, 2011, Available from http://www.sfexaminer.com/local/bay-area/2011/03/san-mateo-county-involved-court-fight-over-e-signatures.

de Almeida, Guilherme Alberto Almeida, Alfonso Avila, and Violeta Boncanoska. "Promoting E-commerce in Developing Countries." Internet Governance and Policy Discussion

Papers. Available from www.diplomacy.edu/poolbin.asp?IDPool=454.

Edfors, Patty. "Your John Hancock Goes Digital." *Communications News,* December 2000.

Glover, K. Daniel. "John Hancock Goes Digital." *Financial Executive,* March/April 2001.

Harrell, Ron. "Electronic Signatures Will Change Business Practices." *American Agent & Broker,* February 2001.

Kromer, John. "The ABCs of the E-Sign Act for Community Banks." *Community Banker,* January 2001.

McElligot, Tim. "Pen Pals." *Telephony,* January 1, 2001.

Montana, John C. "The Electronic Signatures in Global and National Commerce Act: A Sea Change in Electronic Records Law." *Information Management Journal,* January 2001.

Nagel, Bill. "E-signatures Q&A: Legalize It." Cambridge, MA: Forrester Research, December 2, 2009. Available from http://www.echosign.com/static/Forrester%20Research%20-%20%20eSignatures%20QandA%20-%20Dec%2009.pdf.

Shiralkar, Parag, and Bindiganavale S. Vijayaraman."Digital Signature: Application Development Trends in E-business." *Journal of Electronic Commerce Research* 4, no. 3 (2003): 94–101.

Witt, Amanda M., and Jon A. Neiditz, "Case Law on Electronic Signatures and the Enforceability of Electronic Transactions." *InfoLaw Notes,* May 15, 2008, Available from http://www.nelsonmullins.com/DocumentDepot/ACC1.pdf.

Wright, Benjamin. "Technology File: Laws Guide Uniformity for E-signatures." *Credit Union Executive Journal,* November/December 2000.

Zinkewicz, Phil. "Sign on the Dotted Line," *Rough Notes,* December 2000.

DIGITAL WALLET TECHNOLOGY

Digital wallets are small electronic packages that automatically supply information such as credit card numbers and shipping addresses for use in conducting Internet transactions. Also known more broadly as Internet payment services, they provide a means by which customers may order products and services online without ever entering sensitive information and submitting it via e-mail or the World Wide Web, where it is vulnerable to theft by hackers and other cybercriminals. Digital wallets thus allow consumers to make online purchases easily and securely, safeguarding the privacy of purchasing habits and financial information alike.

Traditionally, digital wallets were stored on the desktops of personal computers. By the early 2000s new digital wallets were compatible with wireless and other mobile devices, and were more often stored on a central server owned by a digital wallet vendor or Internet service provider (ISP).

Digital wallet vendors maintain relationships with online merchants in a manner similar to those between credit card companies and brick-and-mortar stores. The digital wallet vendor either charges a commission to the retailer on every purchase involving the vendor's wallet, or merchants pay the vendor a flat fee for accepting the vendor's wallet in their transactions. In turn, businesses and customers mutually agree to use the products, software, and services of a particular digital wallet vendor, which then acts as an intermediary for all transactions between the firm and its customers. In this way, customers need not transmit credit card numbers for each transaction. Instead, they send the purchase order to the wallet vendor, which simply charges it to the customer's account.

USING DIGITAL WALLETS

Digital wallets were heralded as one of the technological innovations that would help fulfill the promise of ultimate shopping convenience afforded by e-commerce. While online shoppers need not wait in long lines or sit in traffic to make their purchases, the long and often convoluted form-filling process required in order to make a purchase online using a credit card number kept e-commerce from achieving the prominence that e-merchants had counted on.

With digital wallets, customers could forego the process of filling out lengthy order forms each time they made an online purchase. Rather, they could simply activate the wallet to automatically and securely fill out the required information fields, including the customer's name, credit card number and expiration date, and billing and shipping information.

Typically, digital wallets also allow customers to store preferences for Web sites and purchases, thereby allowing the merchants that support the wallet to personalize their offerings and notify the customer of special sales and new products. Moreover, when the digital wallet enters the required information in its appropriate fields, it automatically encrypts the data.

THE PUNCTUATED EVOLUTION OF DIGITAL WALLETS

Digital wallets first emerged in the mid-1990s with a great deal of hype but to a lukewarm public reception. The earliest wallets required customers to download the digital wallet vendor's software and store it on their desktops. This method largely inhibited customers from warming to the technology. Downloads generally were viewed with some skepticism by analysts, since they tended to limit overall distribution. Slow connection speeds exacerbated the problem, since customers tend to grow frustrated and abort downloads if they take an excessively long time to complete.

Another impediment to digital wallet penetration was customer awareness. In 1999, according to the research firm Bizrate.com, only 58% of online purchasers were even familiar with digital wallets, while only one-fourth understood their capabilities. In addition, the sheer glut of digital wallet offerings in the late 1990s—issued by merchants, software vendors, credit card firms, banks, and other outfits—led to customer confusion, not to mention frustration stemming from the lack of compatibility between all these wallet packages.

Several online retailers, including Amazon.com, created their own versions of digital wallets for use only on their sites to encourage repeat purchases. After the first purchase, when a customer filled out an entire order form, he or she only needed to click a button to repeat the entire order-filling process automatically. However, only a small number of very large firms had the clout to make such an investment worthwhile.

In 2000, Forrester Research released the results of a survey of online merchants. The merchants were asked why digital wallets had failed to attain prominence. Sixty-two percent of U.S. e-merchants felt there simply was too little customer demand, while 54% reported that digital wallets were not a priority. Twenty-seven percent thought the market was too immature, another 27% could not see any benefits in adopting the technology, and 19% thought that digital wallets would result in the loss of customer relationships.

Digital wallet vendors increasingly aligned with credit card issuers, whose massive marketing clout was expected to further the wallets' cause. The popular American Express Blue credit card was packaged with American Express's own digital wallet to facilitate use of Blue on the Internet. Meanwhile, Visa and MasterCard spent 1999 and 2000 in vigorous competition to align with wireless software and hardware vendors with an eye toward capitalizing on the expected boom in digital wallet use.

By the early 2000s, digital wallets were undergoing a mild renaissance. The models developed at that time abandoned software downloads altogether, opting instead for digital wallet systems that worked directly with ISPs and other telecommunications firms.

Moreover, the details of purchases were not generally shared directly with the ISP or other intermediary—only the connection to use the digital wallet was routed through these agents. In this way, consumer fears of privacy invasion were somewhat eased, as the information was shared only with a company with whom they already entrusted the data. Meanwhile, in an effort to hang on to market share in an increasingly competitive market, ISPs often pitched their Internet payment services options to their customers as an added value of their offerings.

CHALLENGES IN THE EARLY 2000s

Despite the improvements and the increasing competition, digital wallet technology still was largely a novelty by the early 2000s, and it was uncertain how well vendors could turn such systems into a widespread force in the e-commerce world. Vendors were very conscious of their market's less-than-glorious history. Digital wallets were more often referred to as Internet or Web-based payment systems by the early 2000s, in large part to disassociate the products from their rather unsuccessful predecessors in the mid- and late 1990s. One challenge was to adapt Internet payment systems to tap into the vibrant business-to-business market. By the early 2000s, most digital wallet systems were designed for the business-to-consumer market.

Customer awareness, or lack thereof, was an irritatingly persistent problem. According to Biz-Rate.com, in 2001 only 38% of online shoppers understood how digital wallets worked, 25% knew about digital wallets but were unfamiliar with how they worked, and 37% of online buyers had never heard of digital wallets at all. Meanwhile, only 22% of online shoppers had actually used a digital wallet at least once, and a mere 5% used them frequently. This last figure, in fact, was equal to the percentage of customers who had used digital wallets at least once and swore they would never use one again. Such results clearly were a concern to vendors and merchants alike.

PAYPAL

Although many major banks and chain retailers were setting up digital wallet services, a start-up firm, PayPal, gained control of the online cash transaction market. Founded as Confinity in 1999, the company originally planned to handle cash transactions via mobile devices. However, since the mobile device cash transfer market was not yet well developed, but there was significant demand for a secure cash payment system on the Internet, Confinity decided to focus on Internet transactions instead. The Confinity founders, Peter Thiel and Max Levchin, sold the company to Elon Musk's X.com in 2000. Under Musk, PayPal grew quickly, as the service allowed a merchant to transfer cash to an account even if the account owner had not yet registered with PayPal, providing a strong incentive for a potential client to register, according to *Funding Universe.*

COMPETITION WITH PAYPAL

After PayPal entered the market, it quickly became dominant. Another reason for PayPal's rapid growth was that it offered clients the opportunity to transmit large amounts of money each day, and competitors such as Citibank were not willing to authorize these major transactions because they were concerned about security. Citibank tried to buy PayPal, but PayPal refused its offer and accepted a bid from eBay instead in late 2002. Citibank shut down its c2it digital wallet in early 2003 because it lacked market share, and eBay closed its own Billpoint digital wallet service, concentrating its resources on PayPal.

NEAR FIELD TECHNOLOGY

As mobile devices became more widespread, companies continued to test mobile cash transfer technology that used these devices. One major research area was near field technology, which used a scanner that read a radio frequency identification (RFID) tag to complete a transaction. Tag reading technology had already been introduced on toll roads, subway passes, and other types of mass transit, typically using a device that scanned a card or sticker so a commuter did not need to remember to carry exact change. The *MIT Technology Review* reported that mass transit authorities in Frankfurt, Germany, tested mobile cash transfer technology using cell phones in April 2006.

ISIS NETWORK

In November 2010, the major telecommunications firms AT&T, Verizon, and T-Mobile announced a joint venture, the Isis Network. The Isis network was designed to streamline retail purchases for consumers, because it would track loyalty programs and discounts as well as handling the cash exchange, reducing the number of cards that a customer had to carry in his wallet. The telecommunications firms planned to launch the Isis Network in 2012.

PAYPAL STRATEGY IN THE 2010s

Although PayPal had more than 100 million customers by 2010, most of them were using its Internet services, and payment systems that used mobile devices were becoming much more popular. *Tech Crunch* reported that PayPal was buying companies that controlled mobile transaction technology during 2011, because its executives predicted that mobile devices would be widely used to pay for goods at physical retail stores and restaurants by 2015.

ONLINE GAMING

Visa was also working on a digital wallet system in 2011, and one of the core components of its strategy was online gaming. In an online game that allows a player to purchase in-game items, a digital wallet is very helpful, because the use of a digital wallet allows the player to rapidly buy an item that changes the course of the game. *Venturebeat* reported that Visa bought Playspan, which handles in-game purchases for many large media companies, in 2011 at a price of $190 million. Visa also planned to offer its digital wallet service to physical retail stores and other merchants.

SQUARE REGISTER

Square, a digital wallet provider, expanded its services to offer additional software utilities for merchants. In May 2011, Square introduced Register, which performs basic inventory analysis using the sales data that the digital wallet system collects, such as reporting the number of cups of soda that a convenience store has sold at the end of the day. Although many established retailers already have computer systems that collect this type of information, a digital wallet service can help a casual vendor who does not have access to a sophisticated inventory control system.

GOOGLE

Google also announced a digital wallet in 2011, including additional features to compete with the hot start-up Groupon, which helped local businesses offer coupons to their customers. Google designed Wallet for mobile devices, so a customer could see a deal while traveling and immediately claim the discount, which was intended to be more convenient than printing out a coupon at a home computer and then traveling to a store. Google formed a partnership with Sprint, the major telecommunications firm that was not a member of the Isis project, and Mastercard, Visa's competitor, to offer its Wallet service.

DRAWBACKS

The main benefit of a digital wallet is its convenience, as the service can be slightly more expensive than a standard credit card transaction. According to *Consumer Reports,* the Square and PayPal services are the most expensive, while Google and Visa charge their regular fees. A digital wallet may also have fewer protections against fraudulent charges than a credit card or debit card offers, depending on the service contract. Payment systems that add charges to a customer's phone bill are considered especially risky.

IMPLEMENTATION

Although several telecommunication firms, internet companies, and credit card processors were introducing digital wallet technology in 2011, the widespread adoption of digital wallets in mobile commerce was still limited in the United States because the services relied on near field technology. According to a Reuters report, near field technology can only be used if a cell phone has a RFID chip installed, and most cell phones that were available in the U.S. market in 2011 did not have this RFID chip. Widespread adoption will require digital wallet vendors to convince consumers to replace their cell phones, which could be challenging because the poor economy in the early 2010s was encouraging consumers to cut their expenses.

INTERNATIONAL MARKET

Digital wallets were widespread in Europe, Japan, and South Korea during the 2000s, and they were also in use in Africa. Some cell phone subscribers in developing countries did not have access to traditional bank accounts or credit cards, so a digital wallet service was the most convenient way to make a purchase. Vodacom, a large African telecommunications company, offered a digital wallet service called M-pesa. Vodacom customers could deposit, transfer, and withdraw money from their m-pesa account as an alternative to traditional banking.

SEE ALSO *Digital Cash; Digital Certificate; Digital Certificate Authority; Electronic Payment; Internet Payment Provider.*

BIBLIOGRAPHY

"The Answer to Internet Debit Payments?" *Electronic Payments International,* February 29, 2000.

Austen, Ian. "A Chilly Welcome for Digital Wallets." *New York Times,* November 4, 1999.

Brewin, Bob. "MasterCard, Visa Vie for Wireless Victory." *Computerworld,* April 3, 2000.

Bryant Quinn, Jane. "Opening Soon: The Digital Wallet." *Washington Post,* December 5, 1999.

Collett, Stacy. "IBM Unveils 'Easier' Digital Wallet Tool." *Computerworld,* September 20, 1999.

Courter, Eileen. "Wait & See." *Credit Union Management,* August 2000.

"The Digital Wallet Soon to Be in Every Pocket." *Reuters,* June 1, 2011. Available from http://blogs.reuters.com/mediafile/2011/06/01/digital-wallet-every-pocket.

Eaton, Kit. "Google's NFC-Powered Digital Wallet: Room for Your Shopping Lists, Credit Cards ... and Complete Trust." *Fast Company,* May 26, 2011. Available from http://www.fastcompany.com/1755490/google-shopping-wireless-wallet-nfc-payment-nexus-smartphones.

Ehrenman, Gayle. "Internet Trivia: Folks May Be Shopping Online, but They're Sticking to Traditional Forms of Payment." *Internetweek,* February 5, 2001.

Fitzgerald, Michael. "Your Digital Wallet." *MIT Technology Review,* August 24, 2006. Available from http://www.technologyreview.com/read_article.aspx?ch=specialsections&sc=personal&id=17355.

Gross, Grant. "Verizon, AT&T, T-Mobile Form Joint Digital Wallet Venture." *Computer World,* November 16, 2010. Available from http://www.computerworld.com/s/article/9196783/Verizon_AT_T_T_Mobile_form_joint_digital_wallet_venture.

Gustin, Sam. "Square 'Register' Aims to Squeeze Out the Cash Register." *Wired,* May 23, 2011. Available from http://www.wired.com/epicenter/2011/05/square-register.

"Hidden Costs in Cell Phone and Digital-Wallet Payment Services." *Consumer Reports,* August 2, 2011. Available from http://pressroom.consumerreports.org/pressroom/2011/08/survey-finds-americans-not-clamoring-to-pay-with-cell-phones-just-yet-yonkers-ny-while-americans-are-still-using-plenty.html.

"Industry Proposes New 'Digital Wallet' Standard." *Graphic Arts Monthly,* August 1999.

Kiesnoski, Kenneth. "MasterCard Eyeing Voice-Activated Wallet." *Bank Systems & Technology,* June 2000.

Kiesnoski, Kenneth, and Bob Curley. "Digital Wallets: Card Issuers Seek to Ease Web Shopping." *Bank Systems & Technology,* October 1999.

Lavonne, Kuykendall. "No Small Change." *Internet Retailer,* May 2000.

Oberndorf, Shannon. "The Promise of Digital Wallets." *Catalog Age,* November 1999.

Rao, Leena. "PayPal VP: Supporting Payments in the Physical World Is Critical For PayPal." *TechCrunch,* July 11, 2011. Available from http://techcrunch.com/2011/07/11/paypal-vp-supporting-payments-in-the-physical-world-is-critical-for-paypal.

Schwartz, Jeffrey. "e-Commerce Leaders Agree on Standard Checkout Spec." *Internetweek,* June 21, 1999.

Short, Sharon Gwyn. "Beyond Digital Wallets: Internet Payment Services as E-commerce Boom or Bust." *Econtent,* April/May 2000.

Steiner, Ina. "Another One Bites the Dust: PayPal Competitor C2it to Close." *ECommerceBytes.com,* September 30, 2003. Available from http://www.auctionbytes.com/cab/abn/y03/m09/i30/s01.

Takahashi, Dean. "Visa Unveils New 'Digital Wallet' for Electronic Commerce." *Venture Beat,* May 11, 2011. Available from http://venturebeat.com/2011/05/11/visa-unveils-new-digital-wallet-for-electronic-commerce.

Taneja, Sunil. "Digital Wallets Ease E-business." *Chain Store Age,* September 1999.

Vodacom. "M-PESA: Changing Lives in a Changing World." London, 2011. Available from http://enterprise.vodafone.com/products_solutions/finance_solutions/m-pesa.jsp.

Walker, Christy. "Digital Wallets." *Computerworld,* July 5, 1999.

DISCUSSION FORUMS

Online discussion forums, also known as World Wide Web forums, bulletin boards, or message boards, emerged in the mid-1990s and allowed Internet surfers to post and respond to messages on the Web. Since that time, discussion forums have become increasingly popular. They cover a wide variety of topics ranging from sports, health, and business, to current events, finance, and entertainment.

EARLY HISTORY

The idea for Web-based discussion forums stemmed from newsgroups that used the Usenet system. Developed in 1979, Usenet operated as a bulletin board system and it was supported by UNIX machines. As technology advanced, discussion forums were developed to operate on the Web rather than on a UNIX-based system. Along with newsgroups, discussion forums also were similar to Internet chat. Both discussion forum and chat technologies allowed Web surfers to communicate online. Discussion forums used asynchronous communication, however, which differed from chat in that it allowed its users to post and respond to messages from any computer at any time rather than requiring all chatters to be logged on simultaneously.

Over time, discussion forums become increasingly user friendly. Forums typically arranged messages by thread—topic, date, and time—and allowed users to respond to a certain message or create a new message, or thread, of their own. In order to become part of a forum, many sites required Web surfers to register for a user ID and password. These forums also typically had a set of rules that discouraged malicious or inappropriate language and reserved the right to block any users that abused the forum. Certain discussion forums also had moderators, who viewed messages before they were posted in order to ensure they met the site's standards.

Discussion forums have been used by a wide variety of organizations, including businesses and educational institutions. For example, many college professors began utilizing these forums as a teaching tool in the late 1990s. Students were encouraged to use specific forums set up by the college or professor to discuss class topics. The largest group of discussion forum users, however, was made up of individuals seeking information. Countless discussion forums emerged for these users in the mid-1990s.

By 2001, more than 300,000 Web forums were listed by an index published by Forum One Communications Corp. Search engine Yahoo! also operated discussion forums on a wide variety of topics, allowing its users to post and respond to messages. In addition, many traditional businesses integrated discussion forums into their sites. According to a Forrester Consulting research report, businesses traditionally used discussion forums as a means of gaining customer or client feedback on specific products and services and on the company as a whole. Nonprofit organizations began using discussion forums to gain support for the organization or cause. Nonprofits representing health conditions were also able to use discussion forums to provide health care and emotional support to people diagnosed with that particular disease.

THE EFFECT OF SOCIAL NETWORKS ON DISCUSSION FORUMS

Throughout the 2000s, social network sites like Facebook, MySpace, Twitter, and others, captured millions of users. These sites could also be used as discussion forums and for online chatting. According to the Forrester Research report "Social Networking in the Enterprise: Benefits and Inhibitors," by the 2010s discussion forum usage had decreased due to the increased use of social networks. The report noted that due to social networks, such discussion forums that still existed were much more focused, driving conversation on a very specific topic, and integrated within a company's or organization's bigger picture or overall online presence.

Virginia Heffernan noted this decline in her opinion piece published in 2011 on the *New York Times* Web site. Heffernan cited the decline of posts on one of her favorite discussion boards, AltDotLife, which averaged 20,000 to 24,000 posts per month in 2008 and 2009, and was down to less than 10,000 posts per month. Users agreed that they were going to Facebook for the same types of discussions they used to have on AltDotLife. In his response to this apparent decline of discussion forums, Joe Ewaskiw, public relations manager for Internet Brands, the company that publishes vBulletin software products for forums, stated that forums will continue but will focus on more specific topics and groups of people. In a comment that appeared in response to Robert Niles' article in *Online Journalism Review,* Ewaskiw wrote, "Out of all your friends on the 'big' social networks, you probably won't find too many who are interested in constantly and obsessively discussing your favorite obscure hobby. So there's still very much a place for quality message boards with a defined purpose."

Another concern for general or personal discussion forum groups by the 2010s was funding. During the early 2000s, forums could count on large Internet advertisers to help bring in advertising dollars. By the end of the 2000s, these same advertisers were asking to have their ads blocked from discussion forums due to the potential of being associated with sites that contained inappropriate content. Discussion forms not connected with a business or organization had to ask for voluntary contributions from users to keep the forum operating or discover other means of support, such as selling sponsorships.

SEE ALSO *Community Model; Virtual Communities.*

BIBLIOGRAPHY

Cashel, Jim. "Top Ten Trends for Online Communities." *Online Community Report,* July 2001. Available from http://www.knowledgeboard.com/item/1090.

Heffernan, Virginia. "The Old Internet Neighborhoods." *New York Times,* July 10, 2011. Available from http://opinionator.blogs.nytimes.com/2011/07/10/remembrance-of-message-boards-past/?ref=opinion.

Niles, Robert. "The 'Decline of Online Message Boards' Doesn't Have to Happen." *Online Journalism Review,* July 13, 2011.

Available from http://www.ojr.org/ojr/people/robert/201107/1992.

Shickles, Steve. "Can Forums Still Make Money?" *Sitepoint,* August 12, 2007. Available from http://www.sitepoint.com/can-forums-still-make-money.

"Social Networking in the Enterprise: Benefits and Inhibitors." Cambridge, MA: Forrester Research, June 2010. Available from http://www.cisco.com/en/US/prod/collateral/ps10680/ps10683/ps10668/soc_nw_en_tlp.pdf.

DISINTERMEDIATION

In the business world, third parties, like distributors, traditionally served as links between the consumers and manufacturers or providers of goods and services. Such middlemen also played important roles in the business-to-business sector, connecting companies with various suppliers of parts, components, and raw materials. Disintermediation occurs when third parties are eliminated from the supply chain, allowing direct links between buyers and sellers.

DISINTERMEDIATION, PROS AND CONS

Disintermediation has several advantages. In addition to giving consumers simpler and more direct access to goods and services, it can also mean lower prices, because supply chains are streamlined and the fees charged by distributors and logistics providers are eliminated or sharply reduced. The advent of e-commerce made it possible for many companies to begin selling directly to consumers, some of whom had never done so before.

While the potential to sell directly via the Internet was appealing because of the potential for greater profits, it also had several drawbacks. First, disintermediation caused tension between many companies and their business partners, including salespeople, rep firms, distributors, dealers, and retailers. Due to this tension, industry trade associations like the National Automotive Dealers Association and the Wine Wholesalers Association took steps to preserve their roles. For instance, they worked to make it impossible for wineries to sell wine online, or for automobile manufacturers like Ford and Chrysler to bypass local dealers and sell cars directly to consumers.

Another drawback to disintermediation was that some companies failed to identify the kind of infrastructure required for handling fulfillment online. Fulfillment, the act of filling and shipping orders received from customers, is different on the Internet because high volumes of smaller orders are often received. This stands in contrast to traditional fulfillment involving large shipments of product to distributors or retail chains. Successful online fulfillment requires responsive, integrated back-end processes in areas like accounting, customer service, marketing, and shipping. This makes it possible to offer customers real-time information about available products, shipping and order confirmations, problem notifications, and more. Having a fancy Web site to accept orders simply was not enough, which many companies eventually discovered to their dismay.

EXAMPLES OF DISINTERMEDIATION AND ITS IMPACT

Disintermediation has had varying degrees of impact on different industries. One industry in which the Internet has caused noteworthy disintermediation is health care. Before the World Wide Web, local health care providers often served as a primary resource for individuals with questions or concerns about health issues. Furthermore, a doctor's opinion was accepted with little or no question. The explosion in online information had a significant impact on consumers who were thirsty for health care information, spurring them to seek answers about health care from various Web sites instead of from local professionals.

The Internet also helped to render patients better informed. Just as automobile consumers, armed with information obtained through online research, went to local dealers armed with information about the price and reliability of vehicles, health care consumers began investigating health issues and possible treatments prior to visits with physicians. This was beneficial for patients in many cases. In addition to large numbers of articles, online communities and support groups made it possible for people suffering from diseases to share information and strategies about treating and coping with their conditions.

Disintermediation in the health care industry had downsides as well. Among the negative factors was the questionable reliability and integrity of some of the sources from which the information was obtained. In some cases, information was old, outdated, or simply inaccurate. Objections also arose from many physicians who felt their professional skills and authority were being second-guessed. In *Health Management Technology,* Peter J. Plantes, MD, explained: "While disintermediation has fueled the growth of e-commerce in many industries, it can have negative consequences for health systems. Removing the local healthcare organization and their physicians from the healthcare equation decreases patients' identification, reliance and access to local resources and healthcare options that can best meet their needs. For healthcare organizations and their physicians, disintermediation erodes the local patient base and creates roadblocks to reaching physicians, and can be in opposition with outreach and integration strategies."

By the early 2000s, disintermediation had infiltrated a wide array of industries. In the packaged goods and toy industries, companies like Nabisco and Mattel sold a percentage of their products directly. In the computer industry, Dell Computer sold directly on an exclusive basis. As a consequence of the company's overwhelming success in the early 2000s, Dell is an excellent example of how disintermediation can work. The company built computers on demand for both individual consumers and organizations. A large percentage of Dell's direct orders came via the World Wide Web.

The disintermediation caused by e-commerce has affected long-established business channels. Although some third parties have been eliminated altogether, many continue to survive because their services bring real value to the business world. Still other companies have been created as online intermediaries, and they are thriving. Examples include travel Web sites where consumers can shop for and purchase airline tickets and hotel stays. Travelocity, Orbitz, and Priceline.com are all examples of these types of intermediaries that sprang up as a result of e-commerce.

INDUSTRIES IMPACTED AND THE RESULTS

Although in the early 2000s many predicted the Internet would eliminate most middlemen through disintermediation, as of early 2012 this was far from true. Some industries have been hit hard by disintermediation, while some have remained untouched, and others have actually gained intermediary companies. For example, one industry that has been dramatically impacted by disintermediation is the video rental industry. By the end of the first decade of the twenty-first century, consumers had many choices when it came to renting, buying, and watching movies and television shows. In addition to the online movie rental company Netflix, computers, digital television systems, and digital game systems allowed consumers to instantly order and download or stream videos of all kinds. As a result, major retail chain Blockbuster Video filed for bankruptcy in 2010. By then, many other DVD rental stores had already closed or followed suit.

Another industry that has felt the effects of disintermediation by the early 2010s is the music industry. For decades, record labels served as the intermediary between performers and their fans, recording and selling their music and providing publicity and other services. By the 2010s, more successful recording artists were recording their own music and selling it directly to consumers through their Web sites.

On the other hand, some industries have seen the rise of a new group of Internet-based intermediaries. Prime examples include the new and used car industries and the legal industry. People interested in purchasing a used car, for example, can get a complete history of any accidents the car has been in through Carfax.com. When it comes to the legal industry, the Internet has opened many opportunities. Traditionally when a company wanted to incorporate, an attorney was almost always involved to file all the necessary paperwork. It could prove a lengthy and expensive process. In the 2010s, these same companies can go to Web sites like LegalZoom, which helps companies file basic paperwork, or Nolo, which provides the forms for companies to do the work themselves. Even the U.S. government provides the forms online so that companies do not always need the assistance of an attorney.

SEE ALSO *Channel Conflict/Harmony; Fulfillment Problems; Order Fulfillment.*

BIBLIOGRAPHY

Berghel, Hal. "Predatory Disintermediation." *Communications of the ACM,* May 2000.

Campbell, Anita. "Trend of Anti-disintermediation or Personalized Services?" *Small Business Trends,* October 1, 2005. Available from http://smallbiztrends.com/2005/10/trend-of-anti-disintermediation-or.html.

"Consumer Direct Sales to Explode." *Web Trend Watch,* July 14, 1999.

Kador, John. "New Economy Rules for Recruiting." *InfoWorld,* July 3, 2001.

Keenan, William Jr. "E-commerce Impacts Channel Partners." *Industry Week,*July 19, 1999.

Plantes, Peter J. "Disintermediation: The New Competitor." *Health Management Technology,* September 2000.

"Progressive Policy Institute: Middlemen Hampering Ecommerce." Global Technology Forum, February 1, 2001. Available from http://www.ebusinessforum.com/index.asp?layout=rich_story&doc_id=2187&categoryid=&channelid=&search=retailers.

Rodgers, Denise. "Who's Afraid of Disintermediation?" *Catalog Age,* August 2000.

St. John, Caryna. "The Rise of Disintermediation in the Music Industry." *Helium,* September 5, 2011. Available from http://www.helium.com/items/2085023-the-rise-of-disintermediation-in-the-music-industry.

DISPUTE RESOLUTION

As with any form of commerce, disputes between two parties engaged in e-commerce arise. By 2009, more than 1.5 billion people, nearly 25% of the world's population, were accessing the Internet. Consumers and businesses from across the globe used the Internet to order goods and services. This led to the ever-increasing need for online dispute resolution (ODR), as some companies did not always deliver as expected, or consumers had complaints.

By the 2010s, the most popular shopping sites like Amazon, eBay, and similar sites had developed their own dispute resolution policies, tools, and procedures. In most cases, parties are asked to try to work out their differences directly. When that does not occur after a designated period of time, the parties have the option of involving a mediator who works for the Web site. In some cases, the Web site does not offer its own dispute resolution process, and a consumer may seek dispute resolution services regarding a complaint it has with an online business. One option for such an individual is BBBOnLine. The Council of Better Business Bureaus (BBB), an advocate for fair and ethical business practices, decided to broaden its scope to include e-commerce in the summer of 1996, when it founded BBBOnLine Inc. to operate as the Better Business Bureau of the World Wide Web.

As of 2012, the BBBOnLine continues to serve as a place where online shoppers can look to see if companies they are considering doing business with have registered complaints or disputes. The BBBOnLine offers a database that consumers can access to get information about online companies. The BBB also developed a code of business practices, including an online standard. If companies provide documentation that they comply with these standards, they are able to display the BBB Accredited Business Seal on their Web sites. According to the BBBOnLine, there were more than 141,000 Web sites displaying the seal by 2011.

Online dispute resolution continued to evolve throughout the first decade of the twenty-first century. By the 2010s, three primary ODR methods had developed. The first method used computer software to manage the dispute. An example of this is when a consumer on a large shopping site does not receive an order. The consumer can file a dispute online, and software automatically notifies the seller of the dispute. The seller is able to enter its information online, and the software either makes a decision and communicates it to both parties, or it simply manages the process by giving the parties a specific number of days to resolve the dispute. If that does not happen, an arbitrator or mediator gets involved.

The second method for ODR is for both parties to use online channels to communicate directly about the dispute, either unassisted or through a mediator. If a mediator is used, both parties must agree to abide by the mediator's decision. The use of an arbitrator is the third most common means of dispute resolution. In this method, a trained person, who in some cases may be a specialized attorney, hears both sides of the dispute and makes a decision.

By the 2010s, ODR was highly prevalent in the e-commerce industry. According to an article published by ITBusiness.ca, eBay and PayPal handle a combined total of 60 million disputes each year.

ISSUES WITH DOMAIN NAMES

Those seeking dispute resolution regarding Internet domain names, or site addresses, can turn to the Internet Corporation for Assigned Names and Numbers (ICANN), a nonprofit organization that oversees domain name distribution, as well as the assignation of other identifiers that differentiate one Web site from another. ICANN replaced IANA (Internet Assigned Numbers Authority), a government entity that had been created by the Internet Society and Federal Network Council to handle the assignment of domain names and other Internet protocol. The Clinton administration had decided in July 1997 that the increasing number of clashes surrounding domain name ownership warranted the creation of a standard international policy regarding domain name assignation and dispute resolution procedures. This led the U.S. Department of Commerce to facilitate the creation of ICANN, a private, nonprofit association run by Dr. Jon Postel, in 1998.

By the 2010s, ICANN coordinated the naming of Web sites across the globe. Between January 2012 and April 2012, individuals, companies, government entities, and nonprofit organizations could apply for Generic Top Level Domain names through ICANN. These are not the same as regular domain names, as they include the ability to add a different extension from the .com, .org, and so forth that are currently in use. In theory, using customer extensions will allow more in-depth marketing and branding on the Web to occur.

SEE ALSO *ICANN (Internet Corp. for Assigned Names and Numbers).*

BIBLIOGRAPHY

Council of Better Business Bureaus. "About Us." Arlington, VA, 2011. Available from http://www.bbb.org/us/About-BBB.

Enos, Lori. "Consumer Watchdog Unveils Net Conduct Code." *E-Commerce Times,* October 25, 2000. Available from http://www.ecommercetimes.com/story/4636.html.

Goyal, Monica. "Online Dispute Resolution Saves Firms Time and Money." ITBusiness.ca, July 28, 2011. Available from http://blogs.itbusiness.ca/2011/07/online-dispute-resolution-saves-firms-time-and-money.

Internet Corporation for Assigned Names and Numbers (ICANN). "About." Marina del Rey, CA, 2011. Available from http://www.icann.org/en/about.

Kao, Chi-Chung. "Online Consumer Dispute Resolution and the ODR Practice in Taiwan–A Comparative Analysis." *Asian Social Science* 5, no. 7 (July 2009): 113–25. Available from http://www.ccsenet.org/journal/index.php/ass/article/view/2977/2744.

"Online Dispute Resolution." Berkman Center for Internet & Society at Harvard University. Available from http://cyber.law.harvard.edu/olds/ecommerce/disputestext.html#odr.

"SquareTrade to Serve as eBay's Exclusive Provider of Online Dispute Resolution." *Business Wire,* August 2, 2000.

DISTRIBUTED SYSTEMS

The Internet consists of an enormous number of smaller computer networks which are linked together across the globe. No one central computer is responsible for the Internet's performance, or for the sea of available information that people obtain from it every day. Rather, this performance and information is distributed among and affected by millions of individual entities (individuals, companies, and organizations) and devices (routers, servers, workstations, desktop computers, and other pieces of the Internet's infrastructure). In this sense, the Internet is a distributed system.

This same principle applies to smaller computing environments used by companies and individuals who engage in e-commerce. For example, employees at a large company may use a software application to enter customer data into a database. Rather than being directly installed on each user's computer, this software application is more often installed on one server and shared among hundreds or thousands of users via a network. Applications used in such distributed environments often are object-oriented programs, and the parts (objects) they consist of can be located on one or more machines and accessed by many users as needed. Additionally, even though different parts of a program may be located on different machines, to users it appears as if the application were running right from their computer.

The general concept of distributed systems grew in popularity and prominence along with the evolution of computer technology. When companies began using computers for the first time, large mainframe systems, and later minicomputers, were used to solve complicated business problems and perform difficult computing tasks. Computers became tools for performing calculations and analyzing different combinations of variables that were virtually impossible, or which would be too time-consuming, for humans to do. Since that time, such operations have become increasingly decentralized, and networks of smaller distributed systems, working collectively, have been applied to modern-day information-processing challenges.

The SETI Institute is one example of how an organization has used distributed computing in this way. SETI is "an institutional home for scientific and educational projects relevant to the nature, distribution, and prevalence of life in the universe." SETI scans radio frequencies from space in an attempt to discover communications from extraterrestrial life forms. Through the organization's SETI@home program, individuals with computers and Internet access were able to help SETI by loading a special screen saver onto their computers. The screen saver connected to SETI while computers were not being used, retrieved data from SETI, analyzed it for signs of life, and reported back to SETI. The alternative to this approach was for SETI to obtain an expensive supercomputer to perform analyses, which was beyond its financial means.

Distributed computing not only allows otherwise idle computing resources to be used, it also allows data to be distributed more efficiently. For example, companies that offer software or various forms of content downloads on the Internet can address potential traffic overload issues by distributing downloadable data at strategic Internet locations instead of forcing the world's users to download it from only one source.

BITTORRENT

This paradigm was taken a step further in 2001, when Bram Cohen designed a new protocol for downloading files. Called BitTorrent, the protocol allowed for users to download a single file from an entire network—rather than a single file-holder—simultaneously. Prior to BitTorrent, if only one computer had the desired file in its entirety, then that computer's upload speed was the fastest that file could be sent. On early file-sharing programs, such as Napster and Limewire, the person uploading (or ceder) would become a bottleneck, and enormous queues would accumulate for popular files. BitTorrent would, in essence, fragment the file into a multitude of pieces. Once any one of these pieces was completely sent to another user in the network, that user would be able to start uploading that piece of the file to other users in the network. The protocol managed the process to optimize the dissemination of data. By 2011, BitTorrent exchange was estimated to be responsible for 27%–55% of international Internet traffic, according to Mozy, a data storage company and subsidiary of EMC Corporation. BitTorrent sites were in many ways a new kind of social network, arranged to facilitate the transmission of information.

By 2008, there had been so many changes to the structure and protocols of the Internet that analysts began calling it Web 2.0. Although experts, according to *ComputerWeekly.com,* could not agree precisely on what Web 2.0 was, it was generally agreed that cloud computing was a large component. Cloud computing can be seen as another version of distributed network, one in which applications and data can be accessed from multiple points within a network. Prior to cloud computing, Web sites would typically upload their content to a site visitor, then disconnect from the visitor. Cloud computing involved significantly more interaction between visitor and site. Content could be added in real time, and visitors could communicate with the site. With increasing amounts of bandwidth available, these communications became more and more robust, until companies could offer applications online, not for download but for use on their Web sites.

Even software that was extremely complicated, such as business-to-business customer relations management (CRM) software, was being offered as an application in 2011. These are called software as a service (SasS), infrastructure as a service (IaaS), and platform as a service (PaaS), to designate the variety of functions these apps can perform. Businesses, rather than purchasing hardware and installing it at their physical location, could rent data storage space and access to analytics software "on the cloud." Whereas the dream of the Internet as connecting the globe under one, vast distributed system was not new, the realization of that dream moved forward in the early 2010s as a result of cloud computing.

BIBLIOGRAPHY

"About Us." Mountain View, CA: The SETI Institute, July 15, 2001. Available from http://www.seti.org/page.aspx?pid=234.

"Clash of the Clouds." *Economist,* October 15, 2009.

Langley, Nick. "Web 2.0: What Does It Constitute?" *ComputerWeekly.com,* February 11, 2008. Available from http://www.computerweekly.com/Articles/2008/02/28/229337/Web-2.0-What-does-it-constitute.htm.

Mozy. "A History of BitTorrent." Seattle, Washington, 2011. Available from http://mozy.com/infographics/a-history-of-bittorrent/.

Shankland, Stephen. "Buddy, Can You Spare Some Processing Time?" *CNET.com,* September 1, 2000. Available from http://news.cnet.com/2100-1001-245266.html.

Talbot, David. "Collective Computing." *Technology Review,* May 2001.

World Wide Web Consortium (W3C). "WC3 Mission." New York, 2011. Available from http://www.w3.org/Consortium/mission.

———. "W3C Web Services Standards Approved as ISO/IEC International Standards." New York, September 6, 2011. Available from http://www.w3.org/2011/07/wspas-pr.html.en.

DISTRIBUTION

The manner in which commercial goods are distributed has evolved throughout history. Long ago, consumers directly traded physical goods and services. Eventually, different forms of physical currency, such as coins and paper money, were added to the mix. Increasingly sophisticated methods of communication played an important role in the evolution of distribution. As *Purchasing* explained, "In the past, to communicate needs, buyers used couriers, which evolved to using water, rail, and air as each new transportation mode came into being. For critical needs, telegraph replaced the horse followed by phone, telex, fax, private networks and, finally, the Internet."

The Internet, and later the World Wide Web, gave birth to e-commerce. For the first time in history, it was possible for buyers and sellers to communicate instantly with one another, regardless of physical location, and make arrangements regarding the exchange of goods and services. While it was relatively simple to enable online payments, the part of the transaction involving the movement of goods was another matter. Physical goods still had to be transported in some manner. On the other hand, digital goods could be transported as quickly as online payments.

DIGITAL GOODS

Digital goods, also known as soft goods or virtual goods, exist in an electronic format. Digital goods normally include different varieties of information, including text documents, audio, and video. The vast majority of computers used by the public, and by those engaging in e-commerce, are digital devices. At their most basic level, digital computers understand and process information in a binary format of zeros and ones (0, 1, 10, 11, 100, 111, and so on). The programming languages used to create software like Web browsers, databases, word processors, and spreadsheets are written in formats closely resembling human grammar that ultimately are converted to a computer's machine language of ones and zeros.

One of the advantages of digital goods is their minimal storage requirements. Unlike compact discs and paper books, large amounts of digital goods can be stored on magnetic media like a computer's hard drive. This requires less physical storage space for buyers and sellers alike. Digital goods also are perpetual. This means that text documents, computer software, digital audio, and digital video can be preserved without fear of deterioration from environmental conditions that might affect physical goods over long periods of time. Additionally, digital goods can be duplicated infinitely with each copy retaining the exact properties of the original, without a loss in quality. While this is an advantage in one regard, it also is a weakness because digital goods can be easily pirated and distributed illegally.

SECURITY

Once a consumer pays for digital goods, which are normally received in the form of a downloadable file, it is possible for the recipient to make endless copies of the file and redistribute them for profit or for free. This obviously damages the original seller's profit potential. One area where this kind of fraud has cost manufacturers is software. Pirates are well known for duplicating software applications that cost many hundreds of dollars in stores and selling them at lower costs via online auctions or other means.

Obviously, law enforcement agencies prosecute pirates for copyright violations and online fraud. However, this problem presented a serious roadblock for companies looking to sell digital goods via e-commerce in the early 2000s. While companies like the *Wall Street Journal* were able to sell information with little concern over privacy (the information quickly becomes outdated), piracy was a more serious threat for companies selling digital goods like books or audio, which had much longer life spans.

Copyright infringement became an even greater problem, particularly for audio and video, after the creation of BitTorrent protocol in 2001. This new facilitator of file sharing drastically reduced the amount of time for downloading files, making the process more convenient and widespread. Moreover, it was extremely difficult to prosecute for illegal use. Torrent files were essentially files divided into a multitude of small pieces. Users would download a single piece from a file and immediately be able to upload that data to other users. The onus of responsibility for file sharing, then, was dispersed equally among the entire network of users, who all partook equally in copyright infringement.

Authorities eventually tried to make an example of the facilitators of file exchange. One of the most famous cases, taking place between Swedish Web site the Pirate Bay and a number of allegedly cheated American companies, including Warner Brothers and MGM, ended in less than one year of jail time for each of three administrators associated with the site and roughly $6.5 million in fines to split between them. Considering the massive amount of copyrights the site had flaunted, this was a small figure. While some were optimistic that the case would serve as an example for other BitTorrent facilitors and decrease BitTorrent piracy, two years later, in 2011, an estimated quarter-to-half of Internet exchange was comprised of BitTorrent activity, according to a Mozy report.

Traditional media sources countered BitTorrents with a two-pronged strategy. First, companies increased security measures for authentic files. In addition to permanent copyright notices called digital watermarks, which serve as means of identifying when illegal distribution has occurred, several measures were developed to safeguard these kinds of goods during distribution. These involved limiting what people were able to do with digital content after a file was downloaded. For example, digital music files were created which only played on the computer to which they were downloaded. Another was a system that allowed digital goods to be transferred between media with the condition that they were removed from the system they were copied from, leaving only one copy. InterTrust Technologies Corp. was one company offering technology like this. It offered solutions in the area of digital rights management to content providers, service providers, application builders, and others. Its technology ensured that organizations could "release digital information and profitably benefit from it throughout its full lifecycle by persistently protecting it, implementing a wide variety of business models, monitoring usage, and getting paid."

Consequently, a number of authentic, online outlets were created, giving users the option of purchasing music, video, and e-books from a trusted source. In addition, companies, such as Apple, Amazon.com, and other online media distributors focused on convenience and increasing user experience. Amazon.com, for instance, patented its one-click purchase option, while Apple added mobile devices, such as the iPod, iPad, and iPhone, all of which integrated easily with its iTunes music store. Rather than attempting to prosecute copyright infringement, companies simply joined the crowd of online activity and endeavored to beat copyright infringers at their own game.

In general, the strategy worked. Netflix originally used mail delivery as its primary distribution channel, but after the company amped up its online video streaming services, its revenues increased from $1.3 billion to $2.1 billion between 2008 and 2010. Apple's iTunes music store experienced a similar influx of customers over the same period, doubling from $200 million to $400 million in revenues per month. BitTorrent activity continued, so piracy and illegal file sharing still existed. However, private companies had also found the growing mass of online media consumers, as well as the distribution channels that appealed to this demographic.

SEE ALSO *Fulfillment Problems; Order Fulfillment; Shipping and Shipment Tracking.*

BIBLIOGRAPHY

Bell, Gordon. "A Personal Digital Store." *Communications of the ACM,* January 2001.

Bulkelely, Michael. "Machines Talk to Machines."*Purchasing,* December 22, 2000.

Cheng, Jacqui. "Appeals Court: Pirate Bay Admins Still Guilty, Now With Higher Fines." *ArsTechnica,* November 26, 2010. Available from http://arstechnica.com/tech-policy/news/2010/11/appeals-court-pirate-bay-admins-still-guilty-now-with-higher-damages.ars.

Dediu, Horace. "The App Industry vs. the Music Industry." *Asymco,* June 15, 2011. Available from http://www.asymco.com/2011/06/15/the-app-industry-vs-the-music-industry.

"Digital and Analog Information." *PC Guide,* May 9, 2001. Available from http://www.pcguide.com/intro/works/computDigital-c.html.

"Going Straight." *Economist,* April 5, 2001.

Hane, Paula J. "Qpass Teams With Virage for Video-Content Solution."*Information Today,* November 2000.

Mozy. "A History of BitTorrent." Seattle, Washington, 2011. Available from http://mozy.com/infographics/a-history-of-bittorrent/.

Netflix Inc. "Form 10-K." Los Gatos, CA, April 19, 2011. Available from http://ir.netflix.com.

Schull, Jonathan. "Infonomics 101: A Map of the Information Economy." *Inform,* February 1999.

DOMAIN NAME

A domain name identifies an Internet Protocol (IP) address, or series of addresses, on the Internet. Each site on the Internet is assigned a series of 11 or 12 numbers, known as an IP address. Addresses are translated via a Domain Name System (DNS) server into domain names, which simply are the names assigned to the numbers. The main reason for the DNS is to make Internet addresses easier to remember. For example, 134.167.21.147 is the IP address for the domain name techcorps.org, the Internet site for an organization known as Tech Corps. The .org suffix is considered a top-level domain (TLD) for organizations such as nonprofit associations. This is an example of a generic top-level domain (gTLD). Other common gTLDs include .edu for educational institutions, .gov for governmental bodies, .com for companies, .mil for military organizations, and .net for network administrators. Internet sites operating in countries other than the United States attach two-letter country-code top-level domains (ccTLDs), such as .ca for Canada and .jp for Japan, to the ends of their domain names. To secure a domain name, those wishing to create an Internet site simply must verify that the domain name they desire is not in use, via a firm such as Checkdomain.com, and then pay a fee to register that name.

In 1995, the number of domain names registered totaled roughly 100,000. By the spring of 1999, more than 7 million domain names had been registered. That number jumped to 28.2 million by the end of 2000. By the second quarter in 2011, there were over 215 million registered domains, according to Verisign. As the level of domain name registration intensified, issues such as the unapproved use of trademarked names arose, prompting calls for legislation dealing with domain name registration. In 1997, the Clinton administration started pushing for the creation of international policy standards regarding the assignment of domain names and the resolving of disputes over domain name rights. At the directive of the U.S. Department of Commerce, Dr. Jon Postel founded Internet Corporation for Assigned Names and Numbers (ICANN) in 1998. ICANN is a U.S.-based, private, nonprofit association overseeing Internet infrastructure issues, including addressing protocol and dispute resolution. It replaced the government-operated IANA (Internet Assigned Numbers Authority), a unit of the Internet Society and Federal Network Council that had been handling the assignment of domain names and other Internet protocol parameters. The organization's primary goal is to promote "a stable, secure, and unified global Internet."

DOMAIN NAME DISPUTE RESOLUTION

One of ICANN's first tasks was to begin developing an international dispute resolution policy for domain name disagreements. The resulting Uniform Domain Name Dispute Resolution Policy (UDRP) stipulated that entities using one of the three most common top-level domains—.com, .net, and .org—must resolve any trademark-based domain name squabbles via litigation, arbitration, or formal agreement before a registered name could be transferred or canceled. All registrants are required to adhere to the UDRP, and those who register for a domain name also must accept the terms of the UDRP. By signing a subscriber agreement, registrants declare that, as far as they know, their domain name, as well as the way in which it will be used, in no way violates trademark law. They also agree to participate in a dispute resolution proceeding in the event of a complaint. In 1999, the organization approved two domain name dispute resolution service providers: World Intellectual Property Organization (WIPO) and National Arbitration Forum. The following year, ICANN selected two more dispute resolution services providers: eResolution and CPR Institute for Dispute Resolution. Of these, WIPO became the leading organization in domain name dispute resolution.

In the late 1990s, pop singer Madonna was one of several celebrities to file a complaint over the use of a trademarked name in a domain name by an unauthorized agent. Madonna alleged that Dan Parisi used her name to attract viewers to his pornographic Web site Madonna.com. According to an October 2000 article in *E-Commerce Times,* Madonna was required to demonstrate that "the domain name registered by Parisi was identical or confusingly similar to a trademark or service mark in which Madonna has rights; Parisi had no legitimate interests in respect of the domain name; and the domain name had been registered and used in bad faith." Since Parisi could not satisfactorily justify his use of the word "Madonna" in his domain name, a three-member panel of WIPO came to the conclusion that the defendant was using the trademarked name to lure Internet users into visiting his site in hopes of finding information related to Madonna. As a result, WIPO judged in favor of Madonna in October 2000 and ordered Parisi to transfer the domain name rights to the entertainer.

Offering additional legal options to U.S.-based trademark holders is the Anti-Cybersquatting Consumer Protection Act, a federal law passed by the U.S. Congress in 1999. Those found guilty of cybersquatting—attempting to use a trademark in a domain name to profit from it, either by capitalizing on name recognition or by selling the domain name to the trademark holder at an elevated price—can be fined up to $100,000 in damages. According to the April 2001 issue of the *San Diego Business Journal,* the act "differs from the Uniform Dispute Resolution Process (UDRP) in that it is a court proceeding, rather than an administrative proceeding, and is U.S. law rather than internationally enforced policy."

DISPUTES CONTINUE

While these options for domain name dispute resolution seemed to work in the early 2000s, illegal activity and claims increased substantially toward the end of the decade. WIPO, for example, had 2,696 cases in 2010, compared to 1,857 cases in 2000. It was clear that despite reforms in domain name policy, which gave legal bodies tools to deal with cybersquatting, more was needed. Analysts proposed that ICANN's strategy to auction private domain name extensions might help to alleviate some of the most significant problems for high-traffic, brand-name companies. With an entire extension for private use, experts reasoned that it would be easier for traffic to discriminate between real company Web pages and those of imposters. Thereby, the success of cybersquatters would be reduced. ICANN's proposal was set to go into effect in January 2012.

DOMAIN NAME DISTRIBUTION AND REGISTRATION

Along with developing dispute resolution policies, one of ICANN's primary roles is to oversee the distribution of Internet domain names and the assignment of IP addresses. In the 2000s, ICANN expanded the number of available gTLDs. In 2000, .aero, .biz, .coop, .info, .museum, .name, and .pro were added. In 2004, .asia, .cat, .mobi, .tel, and .travel were added. However, in 2011, of the 215 million registered domains, almost 100 million used the .com extension. CcTDLs comprised approximately 40 million of the total.

During the same time period, domain name registration globalized. In 2010 alone, 13 new members were added to ICANN's Governmental Advisory Committee, which served in an advisory role for ICANN's public policy decisions. In addition, internationalized domain names were introduced, which provided extensions in scripts other than the Western alphabet. Domain name extensions in Chinese, Arabic, and other scripts were added, among others, serving the group's main purpose of supporting a more globalized Web.

ICANN is a large, private organization. It claimed $65 billion in revenue in 2010, a $5.5 billion increase from 2009. More than 90% of the organization's income came from domain-name registry and registrar transactions. In 2011, ICANN announced it planned to continue to open up the domain name market by offering private extensions. Under the plan, any extension could be created, such as .mcdonalds, for $200,000, with $25,000 in annual upkeep. Analysts, such as Lance Ulanoff of *PCMag,* predicted that this tactic would deter illegal domain name registrations, but it would create another area of contention for corporations. While private corporation names would not be contested, he expected that more general names, such as .money, would be highly sought after and fought over.

SEE ALSO *Cybersquatting; Dispute Resolution; ICANN (Internet Corp. for Assigned Names and Numbers); URL (Uniform Resource Locator).*

BIBLIOGRAPHY

"DomainMonopoly's Days are Numbered." *Reuters,* April 12, 1999.

"Domain Name." In *Webopedia.* Darien, CT: Internet.com, 2001. Available from http://www.webopedia.com/TERM/D/domain_name.html.

Hoisington, Michael J. "A Perfect Domain Name Within a Business's Reach." *San Diego Business Journal,* April 2, 2001.

ICANN. "Annual Report 2010." Marina del Rey, CA, June 10, 2011. Available from http://www.icann.org/en/annualreport.

———. "New Generic Top-Level Domains–Frequently Asked Questions." Marina del Rey, CA, June 10, 2011. Available from http://newgtlds.icann.org/applicants/faqs/faqs-en.

———. "Uniform Domain-Name Dispute-Resolution Policy." Marina del Rey, CA, 2001. Available from http://www.icann.org/en/udrp/udrp.htm.

"ICANN." In *Techencyclopedia.* Point Pleasant, PA: Computer Language Co., 2001. Available from www.techweb.com/encyclopedia.

"ICANN." In *Webopedia.* Darien, CT: Internet.com, 2001. Available from http://www.webopedia.com/TERM/I/ICANN.html.

Mahoney, Michael. "Madonna Wins Domain Name Dispute." *E-Commerce Times,* October 17, 2000. Available from http://www.ecommercetimes.com/story/4560.html.

Posnock, Susan T. "Conquering Cybersquatters." *Folio: the Magazine for Magazine Management,* April 2001.

"Scramble for New Internet Domains Begins." *United Press International,* June 22, 2001.

Ulanoff, Lance. "ICANN's New Domain Policy Resets the Web." *PCMag.com,* June 20, 2011. Available from http://www.pcmag.com/article2/0,2817,2387270,00.asp.

Verisign. "Domain Name Industry Brief." Mountain View, CA, August 2011. Available from http://www.verisigninc.com/en_US/why-verisign/research-trends/domain-name-industry-brief/index.xhtml.

WIPO. "Cybersquatting Hits Record Level, WIPO Center Rolls out New Services." Geneva, Switzerland, March 31, 2011. Available from http://www.wipo.int/pressroom/en/articles/2011/article_0010.html.

DOT-COM

At the most basic level, "dot-com" is simply a colloquial term born of the suffix appended to Uniform Resource Locators (URLs), as in www.companyname.com. However, the term has come to stand for a variety of phenomena. By the early 2000s it stood for Internet-based businesses, the business craze born of the outlandish stock boom these companies enjoyed and exacerbated, a certain type of unorthodox business model, and even an era of contemporary economics.

The opening of the Internet to commerce in the 1990s unleashed a flurry of new business possibilities, and no one seemed to know just where it would all land. Still, a palpable sense of optimism was in the air. In many ways, dot-com companies were widely seen as being removed from the "real world." On a literal level, this removal referred to their virtual presence in cyberspace, remote from the brick-and-mortar economy. Figuratively, dot-com firms were famously immune—until the tech-market stock bubble burst in spring 2000—from traditional forms of valuation and the importance of tried-and-true business fundamentals.

The speed and extent of the dot-com boom in the late 1990s helped propel this seeming immunity of dot-com companies from such old economy staples as sound business strategies, plans for long-term value and profitability, and attention to macroeconomic warning signs. Dot-coms defied all market logic through the end of the decade, and the flow of cash into the Internet industry seemed nearly endless. The soaring stock prices seemed to lend weight to dot-com entrepreneurs' claims that this was, indeed, a new economy in which the old rules no longer applied.

Valuations were a consistent mystery, with companies registering market values in the hundreds of millions of dollars without ever turning profits. As *Business Week* pointed out, when Yahoo! Inc.'s market value came in at an astronomical $1 billion in 1997, sober investors might have been wise to disbelieve it. However, had they done so they would have missed out on a massive three-year run that would have generated a fortune.

APRÈS LE DÉLUGE

The tech-market stock bust in early 2000 set off a massive dot-com shakeout, and the Web was littered with sunken Internet companies. Meanwhile, the cultural tone shifted away from dot-com euphoria and toward a more tempered attitude about e-commerce. At least 210 dot-coms closed their doors in 2000. An approximated $5 trillion was lost, according to the *Observer.* Meanwhile, the dot-com bust had many holdouts sneering at broken dot-com investors, saying "I told you so."

Even while the conservatively minded sneered, some tech companies survived the boom and bust. Amazon.com, Google, and Yahoo! are a few famous examples. Although it was clear that Information Technology (IT) had run rampant with investors' pocketbooks, this did not deter investments in companies that added real value to world commerce, even when these companies were not immediately profitable (such as Amazon.com, which did not turn a profit until 2002).

As another example, Google was created without a plan for how it would make revenue. It received funding for the value its Web browser planned to add to online commerce. PageRank, the concept of valuating Web sites by the number of sites that linked to them, was the result of an academic project by Sergey Brin and Lawrence Page. PageRank gave Google a significant competitive advantage over other Web browsers. More than this, the search engine made it significantly easier for Internet users to find reputable Web sites, thereby increasing the popularity and value of the Web.

It took time for Google's algorithm to create its own market, but it did. In 2004, 30% of Web users visited Google once per week, and by 2006, the company generated $10 billion in revenues. In 2010, that figure had risen to $30 billion. Approximately 95% of revenues were generated from advertising, through the Google AdWords and AdSense campaign. Whereas the dot-coms that had failed during the bust of 2000 and 2001 had gathered investments and posted revenues for unremarkable products and services, Google had the product before it was a company.

In 2011, 10 years after the dot-com collapse, dot-com businesses were still feeling the impact of that bust. In a *New York Times* interview with Netscape cofounder Marc Andreessen, he pithily described the economic valuation of IT firms: "I'm certainly not an investment adviser, but on a 30-year basis, these things are *cheap.* If you compare how big industrial companies like GE are valued compared with big tech companies like Microsoft, Cisco, Google and Apple, tech stocks have never been valued more poorly in comparison. . . .This bubble talk is about everybody being unbelievably psychologically scarred from 10 years ago."

SEE ALSO *Cyberculture: Society, Culture, and the Internet; New Economy; Shake-out, Dot-com.*

BIBLIOGRAPHY

"Getting Over the Dot-Con." *Business Week.* December 11, 2000.

Goldman, Andrew. "Bubble? What Bubble?" *New York Times,* July 7, 2011. Available from http://www.nytimes.com/2011/07/10/magazine/marc-andreessen-on-the-dot-com-bubble.html?_r=1&scp=1&sq=Bubble?%20What%20Bubble?&st=cse&gwh=C80644937F3165F0D75BAAF48E4B814B.

Google. "Google 2010 Annual Report." Mountain View, CA, January 20, 2011. Available from http://investor.google.com.

"How Google Works." *Economist,* September 16, 2004. Available from http://www.economist.com/node/3171440.

Johnson, Bobbie. "When the Dotcom Bubble Burst the Ideas Didn't Just Float Away." *Observer,* March 14, 2010. Available from http://www.guardian.co.uk/business/2010/mar/14/dotcom-bubble-aftermath.

"Leaders: Is There Life in E-commerce?" *Economist,* February 3, 2001.

Mullaney, Timothy J. "Gone but Not Forgotten." *Business Week,* January 22, 2001.

Wilder, Clinton. "Success: Opiate of Dot-Com Elite." *Informationweek,* February 12, 2001.

DOW JONES INTERNET INDEX

Since its inception in February 1999, Dow Jones and Co.'s Dow Jones Internet Index has served as a benchmark for the stock performance of U.S.-based Internet companies. Companies listed on the index must use the Internet to garner at least 50% of their annual sales, must have operated as a public company for a minimum of three months, and must have a market capitalization (the full value, expressed in dollars, of all outstanding shares) averaging $100 million or more over three months. A company's stock also must average a closing price of roughly $10 per share or greater, and it must be traded frequently enough to offer liquidity, which allows investors to buy and sell without major disturbance.

Dow Jones established the Dow Jones Internet Index in response to the intense trading of Internet stocks that took place in the late 1990s. The Internet stock craze began in the mid-1990s when a few upstarts found themselves boasting billion-dollar market valuations soon after their initial public offerings (IPOs). For example, when Netscape conducted its IPO in 1995, its stock price jumped 108% in a single day. Less than a year old, Yahoo! was valued at almost $1 billion after it completed its IPO in 1996. The stock of online auction site eBay jumped more than 900% within three months of its 1998 IPO. The following year, an unprecedented 240 Internet-based firms went public. Dow Jones decided to create its Internet Index early in 1999 because, as stated by Dow Jones Indexes managing director Michael A. Petronella in *Information Today,* "Internet stocks have rapidly become among the most volatile, popular sectors of the equities market. This has led to the need for an Internet benchmark that can be the standard Internet stock measurement tool for all investors."

The firm divided its Internet Index, which consisted of 40 stocks, into two subindexes: the Services Index and the Internet Commerce Index. Companies originally listed on the Services Index included America Online Corp., Netscape Communications Corp., and other entities like Internet service providers and Internet access providers. America Online was later removed from the index when it merged with Time Warner, because the bulk of its revenues were attributed to the non-Internet operations of Time Warner. The Internet Commerce Index included companies engaged in some form of Internet-based e-commerce, such as book e-tailer Amazon.com and online stock trader E*Trade Group Inc.

By the end of 1999, the Dow Jones Internet Index had grown 167% since its inception. However, that meteoric rise was soon interrupted by what became known as the dot-com fallout. Between May 1999 and May 2000, the Internet Index grew only 3.1%. By October 2000, more than 60% of Internet upstarts were trading below their initial IPO price. Companies that had once been listed on the Dow Jones Internet Index at a price-to-earnings ratio of more than 300—meaning that the firm could have been sold for 300 times what it secured in earnings—found their stock prices plummeting as investors, no longer willing to overlook poor earnings or a lack of profitability, began dumping shares. Many of the firms that had yet to earn a profit folded, and even those that had achieved profitability, such as Yahoo! Inc., saw stock prices nosedive. In fact, Yahoo!'s stock, which had reached a high of $237.50 per share in January 2000, was hovering around $20 per share in early 2001.

E-COMMERCE AFTER THE CRASH

The postbubble tech industry was slow and steady in its recovery. This was fueled in large part by a gradual proliferation of e-commerce. The 2000 fiscal year closed with e-commerce retail sales comprising just 0.5% of total retail sales. The following year saw an increase to roughly 1%, and by the end of 2004, approximately 2% of total sales in the United States were conducted online. That figure doubled again by 2011, with e-commerce accounting for 4.6%. Market capitalization had risen to $371.9 billion, and annualized total returns on investments since the index's beginning were estimated at 17.71%, overall.

In September 2011, the 15 companies on the Dow Jones Internet Commerce Index were Priceline.com, Inc. (PCLN); WebMD Health Corp. (WBMD); Google Inc. (GOOG); Salesforce.com, Inc. (CRM); Amazon.com, Inc. (AMZN); eBay, Inc. (EBAY); Netflix, Inc. (NFLX); Expedia, Inc. (EXPE); Blue Nile (NILE); Constant Contact Inc. (CTCT); Yahoo! Inc., (YHOO); E*Trade Financial Corporation (ETFC); Concur Technologies, Inc. (CNQR); Ameritrade Holdings Corp. (AMTD); and Monster Worldwide, Inc. (MWW).

SEE ALSO *Shake-Out, Dot-com; Volatility.*

BIBLIOGRAPHY

"AOL-Time Warner Merger Will Trigger Changes in Dow Jones Internet Indexes." *Business Wire,* January 2, 2001.

CME Group Index Services. "Dow Jones Internet Composite Index." Chicago, 2011. Available from http://www.djindexes.com.

———. "Dow Jones Internet Composite Index Fact Sheet." Chicago, 2011. Available from http://www.djindexes.com.

Colkin, Eillen."Net Stocks Tracked." *InformationWeek,* February 22, 1999.

"Dow Jones Indexes Launches Internet Index." *Information Today,* April 1999.

"Dow Jones Internet and Technology Sector Indexes Become Now Tradable Through New Exchange-Traded Funds; Total Assets Linked to Dow Jones Internet Indexes Top $240 Billion." *Business Wire,* May 18, 2000.

Futrelle, David. "The Internet Index Mania: There Are Many Benchmarks, but Few Measure Anything Meaningful." *Money,* November 1, 1999.

Henssler, Gene W. "Past Year a Great Lesson." *Georgia Trend,* February 2001.

Johnson, Patrice D. "On Internet Time." *Money,* December 1, 2000.

"Markets Stagger; Google Buys; H-P Pivots." *Wall Street Journal,* August 20, 2011. Available from http://online.wsj.com/article/SB10001424053111903596904576514322139330938.html.

Wang, Zhu. "Technological Innovation and Market Turbulence: The Dot-com Experience." *Review of Economic Dynamics* 5, no. 1 (2007): 78–45.

DUE DILIGENCE

In general business terms, due diligence refers to the scrutiny used by an individual or a group of individuals considering making a purchase of some sort. Those conducting due diligence do so to determine the degree of risk associated with a particular course of action, such as funding an initial public offering (IPO) or an investment. In the case of an acquisition or merger, the attorneys or accountants working for the purchasing party conduct due diligence when they examine the financial status, competitive position, and management practices of the business under consideration, as well as the legality of the deal. When upstarts and established companies seek funding, one of the main reasons they complete detailed business plans is to assist lenders in conducting due diligence. It is the responsibility of the lenders, however, to verify the data contained in such a document.

In the late 1990s, the dot-com bubble, which continued to grow as highly publicized predictions of astronomical growth in e-commerce began to saturate mainstream media outlets, prompted many venture capitalists considering an investment in a young Internet upstart to relax due diligence standards. The highly successful IPOs of firms like Netscape Communications Corp., Amazon.com, and eBay fueled the investment community's desire to move dot-com upstarts toward IPOs as quickly as possible, despite the fact that obtaining profitability would, in all likelihood, take many years. Venture capitalists tended to overlook the fact that most of these new businesses were based on unproven business models. The examination of things such as the likelihood of long-term success, the experience of executives, and the integrity of financial forecasts became increasingly relaxed. According to an article in the April 2001 issue of *Oregon Business,* "Many investors, fearful of missing out, seemed to skip the traditional drawn-out due diligence and hardly paused before infusing startups with capital to get a piece of the dot.com action. The message was clear: strike now or taste dust." Formal business plans for dot-com, if they were submitted at all, tended to be much shorter and less detailed than their traditional counterparts. In fact, a March 2000 study of 300 e-commerce businesses in California revealed that most launched operations with no business plan in place.

This lack of planning eventually caught up with many of the fledgling firms when shareholders began pressuring some of them to achieve profitability. When dot-com stocks began tumbling in 2000, funding sources evaporated in a hurry. Many upstarts, which had relied on the availability of additional capital for expansion, had no choice but to close their doors, a phenomenon which drove the stock prices of the remaining Internet players down even further. Recessionary economic conditions compounded the problem, and dot-com investors sustained major losses. As a result, venture capital funding by the middle of 2001 was less than half of what it had been during the first half of 2000. In the third quarter of 2001, only 540 companies had raised $6.7 billion in venture capital funds, compared to the 1,634 companies that raised $23.9 billion during the third quarter of 2000. Although investors willing to pour capital into Internet-related ventures still existed, the level of scrutiny to which they subjected their applicants substantially increased. As stated in an October 2001 article in *Puget Sound Business Journal,*"The venture community is witnessing a return to stricter investment criteria, more thorough due diligence and tighter term sheets. . .venture capital funds can no longer rely upon abundant capital, frothy IPO markets, and a carnivorous mergers and acquisitions market to mitigate lax investment practices."

DUE DILIGENCE IN THE 2010s

When hot Internet companies (such as Zynga and Groupon) began to garner much attention for proposed IPOs in the early 2010s, many wondered if the lesson from the earlier dot-com bubble would be remembered or forgotten. There was a new litmus test for investment opportunities, which helped to keep investments grounded in reality. If a company's business plan proposed to add real value, then it would be considered as a potential investment opportunity. However, determining long-term value was particularly difficult in IT. Robin Greenwood of the Harvard Business School pointed out that while some of the new, successful companies of the tech boom added value to e-commerce (such as Facebook), others were more questionable. Groupon and LivingSocial, for example, two companies that offered their users coupons based upon geographical location and other user preferences, were more likely to experience difficulty in the future. Competition was underestimated before the dot-com bust, and competition could drive down the companies' profit margins. Even though the value-added litmus test gave investors a useful due diligence strategy, the unpredictability of e-commerce continued to confuse valuations of long-term profitability.

However, there were other reasons the early 2010s tech boom could remain manageable, at least in the United States, with one reason being this particular boom was not confined to any one country. In China, for example, internet start-ups were valuated much more highly, on average, than they were in the United States (by $15 or $20 million, on average). Internet start-up Rovio, in Finland, managed to raise $42 million in funding based on the success of a mobile app game, Angry Birds, which had taken off in 2010. With a global investment trend, the *Economist* stated there was an increased likelihood that a country other than the United States would cause the bubble to burst first.

SEE ALSO *Initial Public Offering (IPO); New Economy; Shake-Out, Dot-com.*

BIBLIOGRAPHY

"Back to Basics." *Oregon Business,* April 2001.

Blakey, Elizabeth. "Tech VC: Looking Back While Looking Ahead." *E-Commerce Times,* May 31, 2001. Available from http://www.technewsworld.com/story/9858.html.

Garbade, Michael J. "The Key Differences in VC Financing of IT Startups in the U.S., UK, Germany and France." *Business Insider,* May 25, 2011. Available from http://articles.businessinsider.com/2011-05-25/tech/30074330_1_vc-financing-investment-startups.

Greenwood, Robin. "Consumers Win. Investors Lose." *New York Times,* April 1, 2011. Available from http://www.nytimes.com/roomfordebate/2011/03/30/are-we-heading-for-another-tech-bubble/consumers-win-investors-lose.

"The New Tech Bubble." *Economist,* May 12, 2011. Available from http://www.economist.com/node/18681576.

Simpson, Tom. "Investing Today versus During the Dot-Com Boom." *Puget Sound Business Journal,* October 5, 2001.

Walsh, Mark. "Wary Angel Investors Answer Fewer Prayers; Due Diligence Replaces 'Just Do It'; Entrepreneurs Scramble for Funds." *Crain's New York Business,* June 18, 2001.

E

EARTHLINK INC.

Historically, EarthLink Inc. has been one of the largest Internet service providers (ISPs) in the United States. Following its merger with MindSpring at the turn of the century, EarthLink served more than 4.8 million consumers and small businesses. Based in Atlanta, Georgia, the company offers its members dial-up access; broadband access through digital subscriber line (DSL), cable, or satellite; Web hosting; and other related services. The company's Internet access services to residential customers are provided through contracts with third-party network service providers. Due to these contracts expiring by 2013 and increased competitive factors, EarthLink is in the process of transforming from an ISP for residential customers (nearly three-quarters of EarthLink's revenue was from residential customers in 2010) into an IT infrastructure and managed services provider to businesses and carriers. To this end, the company began a series of acquisitions to expand into managed voice, integrated voice and data, and cloud hosting services.

EMERGENCE AS A LEADING ISP

EarthLink Network was founded in 1994 by Sky Dayton after he secured $100,000 in funding from investors Reed Slatkin and Kevin O'Donnell. In 1995, the firm teamed up with Netscape Communications Corp. in a deal that provided EarthLink members with Netscape's Navigator, an Internet browser. Dayton also launched EarthLink Software, an innovative package that set up computers for Internet access. In August of that year, EarthLink broadened its service area dramatically when it signed a deal with UUNET Technologies. The alliance allowed EarthLink to use UUNET dial-up access numbers to provide national service in 98 U.S. cities. The company also became the first ISP to offer unlimited dial-up access for a flat rate of $19.95 per month, allowing members to surf the Web without time constraints.

EarthLink continued its expansion and in July 1996 partnered with PSINet to offer dial-up access across the United States and Canada. The firm also teamed up with industry giant Microsoft Corp. and began distributing Microsoft's Internet Explorer browser to members. EarthLink, in turn, was included on Microsoft's Windows 95 operating system desktop. Along with capturing a large portion of individual accounts, the company also began to focus on providing services to businesses as well. In late 1996, it began to offer nationwide integrated services digital network (ISDN) and frame relay services, which provided higher-speed access to the Internet. In January 1997, EarthLink went public with a membership of nearly 300,000 North American-based individuals and businesses.

GROWTH VIA STRATEGIC ALLIANCES AND EXPANDED SERVICES

In February 1998, EarthLink teamed up with Sprint Corp. in a deal that combined the two companies' Internet services and gave Sprint a stake in EarthLink. It also positioned EarthLink as a major player in the Internet services market and gave the firm access to Sprint's large customer base. By April, EarthLink had signed on its 500,000th member.

Through strategic alliances with Apple Computer, Packard Bell, and NEC Ready Computers; EarthLink became the default ISP on the computers manufactured by these companies just in time for the 1998 holiday season. The partnerships secured more member sign-ups than any other marketing promotion in EarthLink's history to date. Finally, an agreement with CompUSA, a major U.S. computer retailer, secured EarthLink as the chain's official ISP and also gave EarthLink access to CompUSA's customers and exposure in the store's promotional materials. By the end of 1998, EarthLink's customer base had reached one million.

The following year, EarthLink continued lucrative partnerships with computer manufacturers as well as expanding its service offering. In March 1999, EarthLink launched TotalCommerce, which offered small businesses the opportunity to set up online storefronts. This augmented the firm's Click-n-Build Web site creation tool that allowed members to build Web pages. Utilizing Sprint's DSL network, EarthLink began offering its customers high-speed access options. It also teamed up with UUNet to offer nationwide DSL access to consumers—the first such offering in the industry.

MERGER WITH MINDSPRING

EarthLink entered the new millennium with a mission of becoming the largest ISP in the world. To facilitate this, EarthLink merged with MindSpring Enterprises, an ISP formed in 1994 by Charles Brewer. After the $1.3 billion deal was completed, EarthLink—which formally changed its name from EarthLink Network to EarthLink Inc.—served more than three million members and operated as the second-largest ISP in the United States. A few months later, EarthLink broadened its subscriber base once again with the purchase of OneMain.com, a leading ISP that served 762,000 dial-up, broadband, and Web hosting members in rural and suburban areas. Building upon that deal, EarthLink partnered with Hughes Network Systems in November 2000 to offer high-speed satellite broadband services to those in rural areas.

Despite EarthLink's position as the second-largest ISP in the country at the turn of the century, its membership base of 4.8 million was still far behind America Online's (AOL) nearly 29 million users. Believing broadband services were essential to remaining competitive in the ISP industry, EarthLink forged a deal with Time Warner at the end of 2000. The agreement, which allowed EarthLink to deliver high-speed Internet services over Time Warner's cable lines in 39 markets, occurred after rival AOL had announced plans to merge with Time Warner.

EXPANSION OF BUSINESS SERVICES THROUGH ACQUISITION

In 2004, EarthLink became the first major ISP to offer its broadband users a voice solution as an alternative to traditional telephone service. In 2004, EarthLink expanded into virtual private networks and managed data networks for businesses with the acquisition of New Edge Networks. Cardi Prinzi became president of this wholly owned subsidiary in 2009, following several other changes in key management. Rolla Huff became CEO in 2007 after CEO Garry Betty succumbed to cancer. Huff also assumed the role of chairman when founder Sky Dayton retired in 2009. Joseph Wetzel became the company's president in 2010.

Managment changes aside, EarthLink's 2000s decade was primarily defined by an eroding subscriber base, particularly for dial-up access. EarthLink's membership was down to 1.6 million in 2010, and revenues were cut in half from a high of $1.4 billion in 2003. As EarthLink did not own Internet infrastructure, it was dependent on long-term contracts with Level 3 Communications for the bulk of its dial-up access, and agreements with Time Warner Cable, Comcast, AT&T, and others for its cable and DSL access. All of these contracts were to expire over the next three years. The future of EarthLink's primary business, as an ISP for residential customers, looked fairly bleak.

Therefore, EarthLink embarked on a strategy to expand its business services, which accounted for only 26% of sales, through a series of acquisitions. The purchase of ITC Deltacom for $524 million at the end of 2010, which operated a fiber-optics network in 14 states, gave EarthLink its first ownership of Internet infrastructure. At this same time, the company announced the acquisition of One Communications for $370 million, which provided telecommunication services in the Upper Midwest, the Northeast, and Mid-Atlantic regions. ITC Deltacom and One Communications remained wholly owned subsidiaries of EarthLink.

EarthLink continued its acquisition strategy in 2011 with the purchase of Logical Solutions, a cloud hosting services firm, and Saturn Telecommunication Services Inc. (STS Telecom), which operated a hosted Voice over Internet Protocol (VoIP) platform in Florida and Georgia. The company planned to use STS Telecom's expertise to rollout a hosted VoIP product nationwide. To better market its expanded services offering, the company launched a new EarthLink Carrier division to focus on wholesale customers and an EarthLink Cloud division to focus on managed services. EarthLink Carrier incorporated New Edge Networks' wholesale segment, Deltacom's fiber-optics network, and One Communications' carrier business. To add to the EarthLink Cloud business, the company acquired Business Vitals in May 2011. Based in Columbia, South Carolina, this information technology and security solutions provider added a secure data center to EarthLink's fiber optic network as well as a client base in 10 countries.

SEE ALSO *Bandwidth; Broadband Technology; Connectivity, Internet; Internet Access, Tracking growth of; Internet Service Providers (ISPs); UUNet.com.*

BIBLIOGRAPHY

EarthLink Inc. "EarthLink's History." Atlanta, GA, 2011. Available from http://www.earthlink.net/about/corp/history.faces.

Farmer, Melanie Austria. "ISPs MindSpring, EarthLink to Merge." *CNET,* September 23, 1999. Available from http://news.cnet.com/2100-1040-252668.html.

Hillebrand, Mary. "EarthLink Broadens Base, Buys OneMain.com." *E-Commerce Times,* June 9, 2000. Available from http://www.ecommercetimes.com/story/3524.html.

Kopytoff, Verne. "EarthLink to Buy PeoplePC for $10 Million/Deal Adds More Than 500,000 Subscribers to 4th Biggest ISP." *SFGate,* June 11, 2002. Available from http://articles.sfgate.com/2002-06-11/business/17547080_1_nick-grouf-peoplepc-garry-betty-earthlink-earthlink-spokesman.

Macaluso, Nora. "Time Warner Deal Boosts EarthLink." *E-Commerce Times,* November 21, 2000. Available from http://www.ecommercetimes.com/story/5436.html.

eBAY

eBay was founded in 1995 by Pierre Omidyar, who wanted to set up an auction site for sellers of obscure and collectible items. After the site proved popular, eBay was incorporated in May 1996. All of the inventory, ordering, shipping, and payments were handled by sellers and buyers who registered on the eBay site. The company's revenue came from commissions on items that were sold and from listing fees.

In 1998, Margaret C. "Meg" Whitman became eBay's CEO, joining the company after working at FTD Inc., Walt Disney Co., and Hasbro Inc. eBay was both popular and profitable, having transformed auctions into highly charged classified ads. Last-minute bidding frenzies were common on the timed auctions. By providing feedback from buyers and sellers, eBay had succeeded in establishing an online community.

After Whitman joined eBay, she revamped the site to make it easier for users to participate. She sought ways to make it safer for customers to purchase items. Whitman revamped the payment process by allowing customers to use credit cards instead of personal checks or money orders. She also began expanding eBay beyond its core model of collectibles. eBay acquired art auctioneer Butterfield & Butterfield in 1999 and used the Los Angeles area as a test market for local auctions of items that were difficult to ship, such as cars and furniture.

PUBLIC COMPANY IN 1998

In September 1998, eBay went public with an initial public offering (IPO) that raised more than $60 million. Potential investors were attracted by the fact that eBay would not have any money invested in inventory. Items that were auctioned over eBay remained the property of the seller, who received payment directly from the buyer. At no point would eBay take possession of an item to be sold or payment for an item. Sellers paid eBay a small commission for listing items, from $.25 to $2 per item. They could pay an additional $50 for additional promotion on the eBay site. When an item was sold, eBay received a percentage ranging from slightly more than 1% to 5% of the selling price.

According to the company's 1998 IPO prospectus, revenue for 1997 totaled $5.7 million. Net sales for the first half of 1998 were $14.9 million, with gross profits of $13.2 million. Earnings from operations for the first six months of 1998 were $2.8 million, and the company managed to earn net income of $348,000. During that period the number of registered users increased from 340,000 to more than 850,000. At the time of the IPO, founder and chairman Pierre Omidyar owned 42% of the company, and venture capital firm Benchmark Capital had a 21.5% interest after investing $5 million.

GROWTH AND EXPANSION: 1999–2001

Throughout 1999 and 2000 eBay grew by adding new categories, forming strategic partnerships, and making acquisitions. Following the acquisition of Kruse International in May 1999, eBay launched a new automotive category later in the year. Kruse was an Indiana-based automotive auction house that sold some 130,000 collectible cars each year through more than 40 events. That same month eBay also acquired Billpoint, a company that facilitated person-to-person credit card payments over the Internet. In March 2000, eBay formed a strategic partnership with Wells Fargo & Co. to develop an online person-to-person payment platform. The partnership involved Wells Fargo taking a 35% equity interest in Billpoint. Later in 2000, eBay and Wells Fargo launched Electronic Check, a new payment option for eBay buyers and sellers.

In January 2001, eBay launched eBay Premier, a new site for art, antiques, and rare collectibles. The site grew out of the previously existing eBay Great Collections site and was the result of the connections eBay had made in the art world. At the time eBay was reported to be the number one online auctioneer in the United States, the United Kingdom, Germany, Canada, and Australia. It also operated sites in France and Japan.

At the end of January 2001 eBay raised its listing fees. The announcement came after Yahoo! Auctions began charging listing fees after being a free auction service since its inception. The fee increases on eBay were the company's first since December 1996.

In March 2001, eBay announced an alliance with Microsoft that would integrate eBay's auction marketplace into selected Microsoft Web sites. Other new partnerships included an alliance with Artnet.com that made Artnet.com's fine art pricing database available to eBay Premier customers. An alliance with Eppraisals.com gave eBay users access to professional art and antiques appraisers. During the second quarter eBay expanded offerings on Half.com, adding millions of new items across four main categories: computers, consumer electronics, sporting goods, and trading cards. eBay's fixed-price formats, such as Buy it Now, also performed well. Buy it Now enabled buyers to instantly buy an auction item.

eBay was one of the first Internet companies to achieve profitability and figure out how to make online auctions work. It was the first company to enter the online auction market, after which it experienced rapid growth. By mid-2001 eBay held a clear leadership position and its name was a household word. With online auction sales increasing 149% in May 2001 to $556 million, eBay accounted for more than 65%, according to a study by Nielsen/NetRatings and Harris Interactive.

PAYPAL ACQUISITION: 2002

Buying PayPal was a logical step for eBay, because about a quarter of the winning bidders on its site were using PayPal to transfer funds to make their purchases. Only about two-fifths of bidders were using electronic payments in 2002, according to *CNET,* and eBay wanted to encourage buyers to use rapid electronic payments instead of slower methods such as mailing checks. eBay and PayPal had previously been rivals in the electronic payment market, but this deal ended the rivalry as eBay shut down Billpoint, its competing electronic payment service.

eBay was now listing many products that were not available at retail stores, including parts that the National Aeronautic and Space Administration (NASA) needed for its shuttles. Shuttles used computer systems that were considered obsolete by office supply stores, because these older systems had been thoroughly tested for potential weaknesses. In 2002, the *New York Times* reported that NASA purchasing agents were buying these older model computer parts in eBay auctions, because hardware manufacturers such as Intel were no longer producing chips using 20-year-old designs.

CRAIGSLIST

In 2004, Craigslist was growing rapidly because it allowed many sellers to list products on an online marketplace free, unlike eBay, which charged for its listings. eBay responded by purchasing slightly more than a quarter of craigslist's stock, which did not trade on public markets. Initially, both companies were satisfied with the new partnership, but craigslist managers became unhappy when eBay tried to assert a greater level of control over the craigslist site. After craigslist rebuffed eBay's attempts to buy the rest of the craigslist stock, eBay decided to establish a competing site, Kijiji, which initially operated outside the United States but entered the U.S. market in 2007, according to *ABC News.* craigslist filed a lawsuit against eBay, claiming that the decision to launch Kijiji violated the terms of the acquisition agreement.

SKYPE PURCHASE: 2005

In 2005, eBay made another major acquisition, buying the Internet telecommunications company Skype for $2.6 billion. The synergy between eBay and Skype was not as obvious as it was in the craigslist or PayPal deals, so the purchase seemed unusual to many investors. The BBC reported that analysts were asking why eBay bought Skype, because eBay could simply license the Skype communications technology at a lower price if it needed a better system to help its vendors communicate with customers, or even construct a new Internet telecommunications network without spending $2.6 billion. The deal reduced eBay's 2005 earnings, which also annoyed investors. The Skype deal did diversify eBay's streams of revenue, as eBay could now earn money from the ads on the Skype Web site in addition to collecting its auction and cash transfer commissions.

INTERNATIONAL SALES PROBLEMS 2006

eBay showed listings to bidders that included vendors throughout the world, which was annoying some vendors on its local sites, especially in Canada and Britain. In 2006, eBay responded to these vendor complaints by changing the way search results displayed items in Canada, placing vendors who were located in the same nation first and announcing that the change could reduce shipping times. British vendors were also angry because eBay was not charging its usual listing fees to Chinese vendors in an attempt to quickly boost its market share, stated *Ecommerce Bytes.*

WHITMAN LEAVES: 2008

CEO Meg Whitman announced her departure in 2008, after serving as CEO since 1998. The company continued to show strong performance, earning $7.6 billion in revenue in 2007. PayPal and Skype showed especially good results, as Skype improved its revenue by 76%, and PayPal reported 35% higher revenue than it had earned in 2006, according to *Direct Marketing News.* eBay announced that John Donahoe, who had previously headed eBay's Marketplaces, would become the new CEO after Whitman left in March 2008.

Although Skype continued to earn money for eBay, it was not providing the benefits to eBay's other divisions that eBay had expected, so eBay decided to sell Skype. eBay sold about 70% of Skype in the first exchange, receiving $1.9 billion, which was considered a loss for eBay because it had paid additional money, about $530 million, in earnings incentives to Skype's founders in the 2005 sale. eBay's second exchange, in which it sold its remaining 30% stake in Skype to Microsoft for $2.5 billion, made its ownership of Skype profitable overall, reported *GigaOM.*

MOBILE COMMERCE

eBay initially entered the mobile market with its acquisition of PayPal. By the early 2010s, eBay had gained a larger foothold in the mobile marketplace, reporting $2 billion in total sales for 2010 and projecting $4 billion in sales for 2011, according to *Mobile Marketer.* PayPal continued to handle many of these online transactions. eBay had also released applications for several mobile devices, so bidders were using its Android and Blackberry apps to shop on the eBay Web site. Liane Yvkoff reported in *CNET* that bidders were buying high end luxury cars through eBay's mobile auctions, including the Mercedes SR McLaren, which sold for $240,001. eBay also announced that each month, three or four bidders typically purchased a Ferrari using its mobile site.

eBay reported better earnings in the first two quarters of 2011, reaching a new high in the second quarter, when the company collected $2.7 billion in revenue. After expenses, this was the first quarter in which eBay reported more than a billion dollars of income, reported *VentureBeat.* CEO John Donahoe was confident about eBay's future success, announcing that his 2015 target was $15 billion in yearly revenue.

SEE ALSO *Auction Sites; Business-to-Consumer (B2C) E-Commerce; Omidyar, Pierre; Yahoo! Inc..*

BIBLIOGRAPHY

Ashman, Anastasia. "Two Auction Players Launch eBay Infrastructure." *Internet World,* February 21, 2001.

"Auction Brawl." *Business Week,* June 4, 2001.

"Auction Nation." *TIME,* December 27, 1999.

Broad, William J. "For Parts, NASA Boldly Goes . . . On eBay." *New York Times,* May 12, 2002. Available from http://www.nytimes.com/2002/05/12/us/for-parts-nasa-boldly-goes-on-ebay.html.

Daphne. "eBay's 'Voices' Program." *eBay,* April 2003. Available from http://pages.ebay.com/community/chatter/2003Apr/InsideeBay.html.

"eBay's Bid for Fixed Prices." *Business Week,* June 26, 2000.

Enos, Lori. "Can Anyone Catch eBay?" *E-Commerce Times,* June 19, 2001. Available from http://www.ecommercetimes.com/story/11349.html.

Fehd, Amanda. "eBay Goes Public with craigslist Complaint." *USA Today,* May 1, 2008. Available from http://abcnews.go.com/Technology/story?id=4773116&page=1.

Kane, Margaret. "eBay Picks Up PayPal for $1.5 Billion." *CNET,* July 8, 2002. Available from http://news.cnet.com/2100-1017-941964.html.

Kelley, Megan. "PayPal Strong in eBay Second Quarter Earnings, New Product on the Way." *VentureBeat,* July 20, 2011. Available from http://venturebeat.com/2011/07/20/paypal-ebay-payments-q2.

Mahoney, Michael. "eBay Beats Street, Raises 2001 Expectations." *E-Commerce Times,* July 20, 2001. Available from http://www.ecommercetimes.com/story/12156.html.

Malik, Om. "For eBay, the Bet on Skype Pays Off. Finally!" *GigaOM,* May 10, 2011. Available from http://gigaom.com/2011/05/10/for-ebay-the-bet-on-skype-pays-off-finally.

Regan, Keith. "eBay Storefronts Arrive." *E-Commerce Times,* June 11, 2001. Available from http://www.ecommercetimes.com/story/11140.html.

Ressner, Jeffrey. "Online Flea Markets." *TIME,* October 5,1998.

Robinson, Blake. "Google Scores eBay International Advertising Deal." *TechCrunch,* August 28, 2006. Available from http://techcrunch.com/2006/08/28/google-scores-ebay-international-advertising-deal.

Saliba, Clare. "eBay Jumps into Newspaper Classifieds." *E-Commerce Times,* May 4, 2001. Available from http://www.ecommercetimes.com/story/commerce/9495.html.

Sausner, Rebecca. "Report: Yahoo! Retains Online Ratings Crown." *E-Commerce Times,* May 1, 2001.

Schwartz, Vira Mamchur. "Bidding, Buying as Lifestyle." *Folio: The Magazine for Magazine Management,* December 1, 1999.

Steiner, Ina. "eBay Canada Changes Search to Favor Canadian Sellers." *eCommerce Bytes,* June 23, 2006. Available from http://www.auctionbytes.com/cab/abn/y06/m06/i23/s01.

Todé, Chantal. "eBay's 2007 Sales Up, Whitman's Successor Named." *Direct Marketing News,* January 24, 2008. Available from http://www.dmnews.com/ebays-2007-sales-up-whitmans-successor-named/article/104510.

Tsirulnik, Giselle. "eBay CEO Says Mobile Sales Will Reach $4B By Year-End." *Mobile Marketer,* April 29, 2011. Available from http://www.mobilemarketer.com/cms/news/commerce/9833.html.

Virzi, Anna Maria. "eBay Buys Major Auto Auction House." *Internet World,* May 24, 1999.

Wang, Nelson. "Auction Site eBay Files to Go Public with $64M IPO." *Internet World,* July 27, 1998.

Ward, Mark. "Portal Bid Drives eBay Skype Deal." *BBC,* September 12, 2005. Available from http://news.bbc.co.uk/2/hi/business/4238258.stm.

"We Have Lift-Off: Amazon, Yahoo! and eBay Grow Up." *Economist (US),* February 3, 2001.

"Wired for the Bottom Line." *Newsweek,* September 20, 1999.

Yvkoff, Liane. "Fancy a Ferrari? Rev Up eBay Motors Mobile App." *CNET,* February 3, 2011. Available from http://reviews.cnet.com/8301-13746_7-20030552-48.html.

E-BOOKS

An electronic book, or e-book, is a book that is accessed electronically via a personal computer (PC), a specially designed e-book reader, a tablet, or smartphone. Users download the text from an Internet site after paying; however, many companies distribute e-books freely, using them as promotional material. Depending on the technology used, e-book purchasers are able to highlight, bookmark, and annotate specific passages as well as search an entire document.

Despite many bold predictions in the late 1990s that e-books would soon render paper publications obsolete, e-book sales remained weak in the early 2000s, with total sales struggling to achieve more than $5 million per fiscal quarter. Three main issues—incompatible formats, difficult-to-use reading devices, and uncertainty surrounding copyright laws—plagued the industry by undercutting both supply and demand. In the latter half of the 2000s these main issues were addressed. Tablets and smartphones made the technology more convenient, while technology improved the reading experience. The ePub file format, as the first industry standard, made e-books more widely accessible, while apps had made reading electronic material extremely convenient. It was possible to read e-books by any publisher on most devices and access purchased material from multiple devices. As a result, e-books were on the sharp rise by 2010, claiming approximately $100 million in sales per quarter.

ADVENT OF E-BOOK TECHNOLOGY

Although the concept of electronic publishing had existed for several decades, it was not until the summer of 1998 that specific devices for reading e-books, as well as e-books themselves, became available at the retail level. Both NuvoMedia Inc. and Softbook Press Inc. developed e-book readers at that time. Designed to offer users an experience as close to reading a print book as possible, the NuvoMedia Rocket eBook's screen was roughly the same size as a page in a traditional paperback book. Specific buttons allowed users to select either a landscape or portrait format, view the next or previous page, and pull down various menu options. The hardware appliance was designed to allow users to download texts from various online sites. While the Softbook reader offered many of the same features as the Rocket, its screen was nearly double in size, and the only way to import texts was to use a telephone line or Ethernet connection to link to a Softbook Press information center. In 1999, the two firms sold a total of roughly 10,000 e-book readers and offered less than 5,000 titles. Gemstar International Group Ltd. paid $400 million to buy both NuvoMedia and Softbook Press in January 2000, planning to use advertising campaigns and licensing agreements to generate a higher demand for the e-book readers.

That same month, Barnesandnoble.com and Microsoft announced their intention to work together to develop an e-book reader for PCs. Another e-book hardware maker, Glassbook, revealed plans to do the same. Popular author Stephen King released a new novella as an e-book in March, in conjunction with publisher Simon & Schuster. However, problems with security measures allowed Internet users who had paid for the book to download multiple unauthorized copies. Publishers continued experimenting with e-book technology despite such problems. In fact, Simon & Schuster also began publishing novels by Mary Higgins Clark as e-books in May 2000. The first Spanish language e-book made its way online in June. Two months later, Stephen King circumvented traditional publishers by offering a new novel, *Ride the Bullet,* on the Internet for $1 per chapter. More than 40,000 readers downloaded the first chapter within 15 hours of its release. At roughly the same time, Adobe Systems Inc. acquired Glassbook, and in November Franklin launched its palm-sized reader known as eBookman.

SUPPLY AND DEMAND PROBLEMS

By the autumn of 2000, roughly 25,000 e-book reading devices had been sold, a number much lower than many analysts had predicted. Despite sluggish sales, several industry pundits cited the success of King's online novel as an indication that e-books were finally finding a mainstream audience. Andersen Consulting predicted that e-book sales would exceed $2.3 billion by 2005, compared to less than $5 million in 2000. The company's predictions turned out to be optimistic. Consumers, producers, and lawmakers would require a longer timeline to solve the problems arising from publishing companies, lawmakers, and technology.

The e-book industry contended with limited supply. E-book availability was growing at a much slower pace than e-book reading device makers had anticipated. In March 2001, the number of e-books compatible with the industry's leading platform—Gemstar's RocketBook—had only reached a few thousand. Afraid that e-book sales might undercut traditional sales—particularly on new blockbuster releases likely to make the bestseller lists—many publishers only offered electronic versions of classics like *Moby Dick, The Iliad,* and *Romeo and Juliet.*

Concerns regarding the impact e-book sales would have on traditional sales represented only a minor problem for the industry, however. Three others factors contributed more significantly to the supply and demand problems experienced within the e-book industry. One of the most pressing problems had to do with incompatible formats. By the end of the twentieth century, three main e-book players had emerged as industry leaders: Gemstar, Adobe, and Microsoft. According to a November 2000 article in the *Atlantic Online,* the fact that each firm was trying to position its format as the industry standard undercut the e-book industry as a whole. "E-books are software, and the future of reading is presently being held hostage in a computer 'standards war' where competing companies try to ensure that their proprietary technology becomes the toll-taker at the gate. Most publishers and retailers now offer every e-book title in at least two incompatible formats, sometimes three, and it may not stop there." Uncertain as to which format would eventually dominate the industry and hesitant to commit to a format that might soon be rendered obsolete, many publishers entered the e-book industry more slowly than they otherwise might have. At the same time, and for similar reasons, consumers balked at the idea of paying hundreds of dollars for an e-book reading device that could read only one format.

A second reason e-book readers were not selling well as the twentieth century came to an end had to do with the technology itself. The e-book reading devices simply were unable to compete with the convenience of a print book. Readers used to stuffing a paperback into a beach bag or setting a novel on the edge of the tub were unwilling to do the same with an expensive electronic device. Also, many e-book readers were difficult to read in the bright sun, some had to be held at a certain angle for optimal viewing, and all ran on a battery that required recharging.

Third, at the same time that book lovers proved reluctant to give up the convenience and familiarity of print books for the increased functionality offered by electronic readers, many publishers proved reluctant to make a significant investment in e-book technology due to concerns over copyright issues. While new laws like the Digital Millennium Copyright Act, which made it illegal to make or sell products designed to skirt copyright laws, had been put in place to help protect copyright holders, publishers remained uncertain as to how to best protect copyrighted material offered electronically. In addition, those unwilling to publish electronic versions of their copyrighted books also worked to prevent other companies from doing so. For example, when RosettaBooks secured permission from authors such as Kurt Vonnegut and Robert Parker to publish electronic versions of their books, Random House, copyright holder of the traditional print books written by those authors, filed suit. The litigation, formally launched in February 2001, ended in a settlement that set an important precedent for future copyright law. Random House secured some royalties from Rosetta's sales, while RosettaBooks received the go-ahead to distribute Random House titles.

THE E-BOOK INDUSTRY TAKES OFF

Over the course of the 2000s, the most limiting problems faced by e-books were either dealt with or reduced, leaving room for significant growth in sales. Technology had improved; the groundwork for copyright law had been established, and the file format problem was no longer an issue for users. Although the industry, by 2010, had yet to meet Andersen Consulting's prediction for 2005, a number of factors pointed to significant growth potential throughout the 2010s. Among these was the double-digit growth in sales, which had begun in 2008 and continued through 2010. The third quarter in 2010 saw $120 million in revenue, approximately ten times the money received in the same quarter only two years prior.

The file format wars had come to a halt in 2007, with the production of ePub, a standardized e-book file format, by the International Digital Publishing Forum (IDPF), in collaboration with renowned companies and organizations, such as Adobe, Barnes & Noble, World Health Organization, HarperCollins, Educational Testing Service, DAISY Consortium, and others. Publishing companies, such as Apple, could use the format but still encrypt the data with DRM software, disabling users from distributing files themselves.

Better e-book readers also aided sales. The Amazon Kindle debuted in 2007, and the Apple iPad appeared two years later. Both of these devices had distinct advantages; as an Amazon.com product, the Kindle was promoted by the largest online bookstore in the world, and this gave the device a very large and receptive initial audience. The iPad followed the iPhone and iPod, two Apple devices that consumers seemed to treasure for style and status as much as for technological utility. Along with the Nook (released by Barnes & Noble in 2009), consumers had a multitude of e-book readers to choose from with advanced graphics and wireless connectivity options.

As a consequence of these improvements, at the end of 2010 Amazon announced that e-book sales surpassed regular book sales for the first time.

SEE ALSO *Electronic Publishing.*

BIBLIOGRAPHY

Chenoweth, Emily. "Psst. Hey Little Girl, Wanna Try an E-book?" *Inside.com,* May 9, 2001.

Falcone, John P. "Kindle vs. Nook vs. iPad: Which E-book Reader Should You Buy?" *CNET,* June 27, 2011. Available from http://news.cnet.com/8301-17938_105-20009738-1/kindle-vs-nook-vs-ipad-which-e-book-reader-should-you-buy.

Garber, Joseph R. "Publish and Perish." *Forbes,* October 16, 2000.

Gelles, David. "Walls Close in on E-book Garden." *Financial Times,* January 29, 2010. Available from http://www.ft.com/

cms/s/0/a00ad6f8-0d0b-11df-a2dc-00144feabdc0,s01=1.html#axzz1f2p8WO9N.

International Digital Publishing Forum. "Industry Statistics." Seattle, WA, 2011. Available from http://idpf.org/about-us/industry-statistics.

Kafka, Peter. "Horror Story." *Forbes,* August 21, 2000.

Lombreglia, Ralph. "Exit Gutenberg?" *Atlantic Online,* November 16, 2000. Available from http://www.theatlantic.com/past/docs/unbound/digitalreader/dr2000-11-16.htm.

Manes, Stephen. "Electronic Page-Turners." *Forbes,* May 28, 2001.

Runne, Jen. "Why eBooks are Sputtering." *eMarketer,* March 14, 2001.

Wood, Christina. "The Myth of E-books." *PC Magazine,* July 1, 2001.

E-BUSINESS SERVICE PROVIDER (EBSP)

Late in the 1990s, businesses were scrambling to establish an Internet presence to increase visibility. E-business service provider (eBSP) companies emerged to help businesses in this endeavor, particularly smaller businesses unable or unwilling to hire their own technology specialists. EBSPs were considered Internet consultants, or e-consultants, which helped businesses quickly design and implement a Web site. As dot-coms began to emerge, eBSPs enjoyed high-flying success as the go-to companies for creating online storefronts.

Following the dot-com bust in 2000, the pool of smaller companies that needed eBSPs suddenly evaporated, while larger businesses that had established expensive Web sites were reevaluating the expense. As capital spending on technology continued to soften, so did the demand for Internet consultants. Instead, executives wanted enterprise consultants that could integrate a virtual business into their existing business. Consequently, many of the smaller eBSPs failed to survive the rapid drop in revenues, while others were swallowed by their larger competitors.

DOT-COM DARLINGS DWINDLE

Founded in late 1997, Scient Corp. was one of the original eBSPs. The firm's early marketing tactics centered around the slogan, "It takes courage to be legendary." Advertising campaigns aimed at potential clients stressed the advantages of being the first to utilize new e-business technology as well as the disadvantages of being left behind. These efforts paid off as the firm landed several contracts not long after its creation. In addition to securing business from fledgling Internet ventures like Wineshopper.com, furniture e-tailer Living.com, PlanetRx Inc., and ePhysician, the firm also helped to launch sites such as Chase Online for Chase Manhattan Corp. For its fiscal year ending in March 2000, Scient had achieved $156 million in revenue and had grown to more than 1,100 employees.

Approximately two weeks later, the NASDAQ meltdown occurred. As investors began to shy away from dot-com startups, eBSPs like Scient watched their client base shrink. In August 2000, rival iXL Enterprises Inc., which had been selected to revamp Web sites for big-name clients like Home Depot and FedEx the year prior, was the first to announce a layoff of 350 employees. It would be forced to cut another 850 jobs later in the year. According to an article published by *CNET,* "many companies have started to focus on selling services to larger, more traditional companies. But because these types of projects typically take longer to complete, analysts have said that earnings growth will not be as steep."

Viant Corp. and Razorfish were among the other e-business pioneers that had successfully targeted large customers, but were forced to announce layoffs after the shockingly disappointing third-quarter results. Newly formed MarchFirst Inc., which resulted from the merger of USWeb/CKS and Whittman-Hart Inc. in July 2000, was forced to cut 1,000 jobs just four months later. Amid the layoffs, MarchFirst and others shifted the focus to the most profitable customers, rather than the dot-coms that had brought the combined companies' initial success.

Although Scient dodged the initial wave of layoffs, the firm was forced to lay off 460 employees. Also troubling was the fact that Living.com and other dot-coms it had helped build had folded, while others were on the verge of collapse. In an attempt to survive the dot-com fallout, Scient and iXL agreed to merge in 2001. Like many pure-play eBSPs, the newly merged Scient would not recover and was forced to file for bankruptcy in July 2002. The assets were purchased by SBI Group, which acquired Razorfish the following year. (As one of the lucky firms to survive, Razorfish has existed as a subsidiary of Publicis Groupe since 2009.)

POWERHOUSES PERSEVERE

IBM was the first of the major computer manufacturers to recognize e-business service as a highly lucrative market. IBM's strategy to become a one-stop solution provider had refocused the company as a global services consulting business, and services had become the most rapidly growing portion of IBM's operations. By 1998, services revenue had doubled from the time Louis Gerstner had taken over five years prior and now accounted for nearly 30% of total revenue. One strategy used by IBM and others was to partner with an established consulting firm. IBM formed an alliance with Ernst & Young in March 1999, and Cisco Systems Inc. teamed up with the computer consulting firm of Electronic Data Systems

(EDS) in the same month. In February 2000, Microsoft Corp. announced an alliance with KPMG.

IBM's focus on Internet services paid off, as its e-business grew to $3 billion in 1999 and $5.2 billion in 2000. Part of the firm's success was due to its nationwide network of 25 e-Business Innovation Centers. These centers were staffed by e-business experts in interactive design, Web use analysis, portal personalization, data mining technologies, and other areas that helped businesses migrate to the Internet. According to an article by Matthew Hicks published in *eWeek* in December 2000, one disadvantage of eBSP startups was that large customers viewed them "as good partners for individual Web projects but not necessarily for long-term engagements."

In the 2010s, EBSPs still exist, but in a form much different from a decade ago. Instead of a small firm creating Web sites for other companies, business service providers in the early 2010s are more likely to be a unit (within a much larger company or division) that offers a suite of marketing and related services across a range of sales platforms.

SEE ALSO *E-Commerce Solutions; IBM Inc.*.

BIBLIOGRAPHY

Cirillo, Rich. "VARBusiness 500: Back to Business." *CRN,* June 13, 2002. Available from http://www.crn.com/news/channel-programs/18828501/varbusiness-500-back-to-business.htm;jsessionid=46Jrl0Jp-h0MBeYCYs+vzg**.ecappj03.

Hammonds, Keith. "Scient's Near-Death Experience." *Fast Company,* January 31, 2001. Available from http://www.fastcompany.com/magazine/43/scient.html.

Hicks, Matthew. "Rough Waters Ahead." *eWeek,* December 11, 2000. Available from http://www.eweek.com/c/a/IT-Management/Rough-Waters-Ahead.

Junnarkar, Sandeep. "E-business the Next Frontier for Big Blue." *CNET,* June 20, 2000. Available from http://news.cnet.com/E-business-the-next-frontier-for-Big-Blue/2100-1017_3-242129.html.

Kane, Margaret. "Scient Files for Chapter 11." *CNET,* July 17, 2002. Available from http://news.cnet.com/Scient-files-for-Chapter-11/2100-1017_3-944377.html.

Loomis, William R. "What Now for E-business Services?" *CNET,* May 3, 2001. Available from http://news.cnet.com/What-now-for-e-business-services/2010-1071_3-281451.html.

Mand, Adrienne. "All About E: New IBM Site Targets E-business Market." *Adweek,* February 15, 1999. Available from http://www.adweek.com/news/advertising/iq-news-all-about-e-new-ibm-site-targets-e-business-market-27410.

Mayo, Dean. "E-business Has Far to Go to Live Up to Its Hype." *CRN,* September 14, 2000. Available from http://www.crn.com/news/channel-programs/18811355/e-business-has-far-to-go-to-live-up-to-its-hype.htm.

"Rebuilding the Garage." *Economist,* July 13, 2000. Available from http://www.economist.com/node/5938.

E-COMMERCE CONSULTANTS

E-commerce consultants help companies develop an e-commerce strategy. This involves elements such as understanding the e-marketplace, assessing where a firm can find its niche, implementing the right internal and external networks, and acquiring the correct software and equipment. E-commerce consultants shape how companies relate to the world online and integrate the image they project on the Internet with that of their brick-and-mortar operations. The field developed in the 2000s, splitting off into a number of specializations, such as software and hardware solutions, IT consulting, infrastructure and network support, and Internet marketing.

Companies, ranging from old economy stalwarts to young hopefuls, often lack either the internal knowledge or resources necessary to devise and implement a successful e-business strategy. A comprehensive and effective e-commerce strategy can make or break a company's online prospects. Moreover, the lightning pace of technological development is often too fast for companies, concerned with their core business operations, to keep up with.

As a result, the market for e-commerce consulting was booming. According to International Data Corporation, $26 billion of systems integration, $36 billion of IT outsourcing, and $9 billion of IT education was purchased in the United States in 2010.

INDUSTRY ORGANIZATION

The nature of e-commerce consulting contracts can vary considerably. Some consultants are brought in merely for short-term planning. In this case, they simply may offer guidance or play devil's advocate en route to mapping out a broad direction for e-commerce strategies. Such consulting operations typically are conducted on an hourly basis and last a very short time, from several days to several months. Other contracts amount to more comprehensive partnerships in which a consultancy agrees to handle e-commerce strategies and concerns as they arise over the long term, meeting new challenges as they present themselves. In such contracts, firms essentially outsource an essential component of their business to a consultancy. These agreements can last for years, or indefinitely through the lifetime of the client company.

Consultants usually start by running several days of workshops with company leaders to map out where the firm currently stands and where it wants to go, and to grasp the challenges involved in getting the firm online in a competitive manner. In this way, consultants can pare down the project to keep it within the scope of the company's and the consultant's practical reach.

Unfortunately for the industry, when the bottom fell out of the dot-com market in early 2000, companies severely retrenched their e-business consulting budgets, culminating in massive layoffs at e-commerce consultancies. The larger, diversified consultancies were able to manage without too much difficulty, but the smaller firms devoted to e-commerce consulting found themselves without the experience necessary to shift into new areas, and many were forced to shut down. After the market began to regroup and firms continued with their e-commerce strategies—albeit without the enthusiasm that characterized the late 1990s dot-com craze—the field began to expand again. The industry as a whole, however, gravitated toward established *Fortune* 1000 companies and away from riskier dot-com start-ups.

In 2002, IBM completely changed the nature of the industry with its acquisition of Pricewaterhouse Coopers (PwC). Initially attracted to the knowledge base and methods of the consultancy firm, the company integrated PwC's specific industry templates and expertise in the construction of its Global Business Services Division, which immediately brought in $184 million in profit in 2003, according to *Bloomberg Businessweek.* Industry templates were frameworks that had allowed PwC consultants to devise quick and effective solutions for vertical industries. The company added to the template database, and in 2011 planned to merge the methodology with real-time data, with the goal of streaming effective solutions even while acquiring new data.

SEE ALSO *Forrester Research.*

BIBLIOGRAPHY

Fisher, Susan E. "E-business Strategy Boom." *Upside,* October 1999.

Gallagher, Terry. "The War for E-commerce Talent." *Consulting to Management,* May 2000.

Glater, Jonathan D. "A High-Tech Domino Effect: As Dot.com's Go, So Go the E-commerce Consultants." *New York Times,* December 16, 2000.

Hamm, Steve. "IBM Roars into Business Consulting." *Bloomberg Businessweek,* April 14, 2009. Available from http://www.businessweek.com/technology/content/apr2009/tc20090414_322525.htm.

Jastrow, David. "Ushering In the 'E' Millennium." *Computer Reseller News,* December 20/December 27, 1999.

King, Charles. "IBM Research Drives Services Innovation." *E-Commerce Times,* August 9, 2011. Available from http://www.ecommercetimes.com/story/73034.html.

Levinsohn, Alan. "SEC and Accountants Cut a Deal on Audit Rules." *Strategic Finance,* December 2000.

Lieb, Rebecca. "Search Industry Poised for Double-Digit Growth." *Econsultancy,* March 25, 2010. Available from http://econsultancy.com/us/blog/5649-search-industry-poised-for-double-digit-growth.

Little, Gard. "IDC's Worldwide Services Taxonomy, 2011." Framingham, MA: International Data Corporation, March 2011. Available from http://www.idc-mi.com/getdoc.jsp?containerId=226877.

Mateyaschuk, Jennifer. "Consulting Firms Tap Stock Market." *InformationWeek,* October 18, 1999.

Noguchi, Yuki. "A Tough Time for Consultants: Cost-Cutting Dot.Coms Start to Shun Advice from Experts." *Washington Post,* December 4, 2000.

Stimpson, Jeff. "Brave New E-world." *Practical Accountant,* March 2000.

E-COMMERCE SOLUTIONS

E-commerce solutions are the products and services that help a company conduct business electronically. The range of available e-commerce solutions is vast, including those that allow traditional businesses to design, create, and operate World Wide Web sites. Some solutions focus on a specific problem. For example, a company selling its wares via a World Wide Web site might purchase a bandwidth management solution in an effort to allocate more resources to actual commerce transactions than to other applications. Similarly, an electronic merchant that wants to improve the online checkout process for its clients might turn to a specialized vendor for a shopping cart solution.

As the needs of those engaged in e-commerce have grown more complex, however, the demand for more comprehensive solutions has intensified. As a result, many e-commerce solutions providers now focus on offering a suite of products and services designed to meet multiple needs and solve various problems. E-commerce solutions providers have moved away from simply managing transactions, expanding their offerings into other areas such as customer relationship management.

E-COMMERCE SOLUTION PROVIDERS

Computer hardware and services giant IBM Corp. began working to recreate itself as an e-business services provider in the mid-1990s. The firm's push into e-business began as early as June 1995, with the purchase of Lotus Development Corp. The acquisition was meant to bolster IBM's position in the computer software market, as well as allow IBM to offer integrated e-mail, data processing, and Internet services to clients via Lotus Notes messaging software. Within two years, services had become the fastest-growing operating unit at IBM, and the firm began working to sell itself as an e-business solutions provider. Central to the firm's e-business services was its WebSphere server software, which IBM used to support the e-commerce initiatives, including retail Web sites, of clients. The WebSphere Commerce Suite 4.1 package, launched in 2000, included Web development tools and customer categorizing functions that allowed e-business to sharpen future marketing efforts.

IBM expanded its e-commerce services throughout the 2000s by purchasing other services providers, including a major 2010 deal in which it paid $1.4 billion to AT&T for Sterling Communications. Sterling Communications was a company that provided logistics support to retail stores, creating software that managed inventory replenishment, customer orders, and other supply chain functions. Since IBM already had a strong brand and sizable customer base with WebSphere, it merged Sterling Communications into its WebSphere division.

IBM also bought Unica to improve the marketing capabilities of its e-commerce services, and Coremetrics to improve its statistical analysis, in 2010. Combining the strengths of each acquired company, IBM announced an improved e-commerce service in 2011. According to *Information Week,* the combined IBM package was more convenient for its clients because Unica had offered its services at the physical facilities of its clients, while Coremetrics was Internet-based, which made it difficult for clients to integrate both of these marketing and statistical packages into their own systems.

Hewlett-Packard Co. Founded in 1938, Hewlett-Packard Co. (HP) is second only to IBM Corp. among the world's largest computer firms. Along with manufacturing and marketing computers and printers, HP also sells Web-based hardware, software, and services. In 1997, the firm released an Internet Solutions line, creating the Internet Applications Systems Division to oversee its new products. Two years later, the firm restructured its offerings into three divisions: information tools, infrastructure for these tools, and e-services.

The HP 9000 Superdome server, which allowed different operating systems to run at the same time, was at the core of HP's quest to become the leading computer system supplier for Internet-based enterprises. The firm began marketing its new release to major dot-com businesses in September 2000. HP's purchase of e-business tools maker Bluestone Software Inc. in January 2001 allowed the firm to launch 25 software products the following month, including the Netaction e-services development and implementation suite and the OpenView e-services systems management suite. A few months later, HP added 19 Internet server appliances to its growing line of e-business solutions.

HP followed a path similar to IBM, in that it started as a hardware provider and then moved into e-commerce later. In 2011, CEO Leo Apotheker decided to change HP's strategic goals, focusing more on providing business services than manufacturing computer hardware. Computer hardware was becoming a commodity, and the company's profit margin on its line of personal computers was decreasing. Apotheker decided to sell HP's personal computer division and acquire the British data analysis firm Autonomy. In his blog on *ZDNet,* Denis Howlett explained that the PC division only brought in about a sixth of HP's operating income, although it collected more than a third of the company's total revenue. By contrast, Autonomy had a much healthier operating margin, at 41%, even though it had just bought Iron Mountain, which managed digital archives. The transaction was expensive for HP, with a valuation of around $10 billion.

While Apotheker had decided to sell the PC division and purchase Autonomy, he was ousted by the board of HP in 2011 before he had served a full year. Former eBay CEO Meg Whitman was appointed in September to replace him. Although Whitman stated she would continue with Apotheker's strategies, uncertainty swirled within the company as a result of the rapid executive turnover.

Oracle Corp. Oracle became the largest player in the customer relationship management (CRM) market when it purchased Siebel Systems in 2005. The acquisition cost Oracle $5.85 billion, reported the *New York Times.* The Securities and Exchange Commission allowed this merger because there were several other large companies in this market, such as SAP, Salesforce, and Microsoft. After Oracle completed its purchase, it continued to market the Siebel CRM package, as well as marketing its other CRM solutions, On Demand, PeopleSoft and E-Business Suite. The Siebel purchase helped Oracle move toward a subscription-based pricing model for CRM, which was becoming more popular with its customers. In 2010, Oracle announced that it planned to merge its CRM offerings and create a new CRM package, Oracle Fusion. *Enterprise Apps Today* reported that Fusion could operate as either an Internet-based service, stand-alone software, or a hybrid, depending on customer preferences.

In 2010, Oracle improved its mobile e-commerce capabilities with its purchase of the Art Technology Group (ATG), at a price of $1 billion. ATG provided the Catalyst service, which was designed to make it simple for a retailer to set up applications to serve mobile customers. A 2010 *GigaOM* article explained that Oracle wanted to make sure that it had e-commerce solutions available to cover multiple sales channels, especially mobile, because Oracle expected mobile sales to grow rapidly during the 2010s.

Salesforce A former Oracle executive, Marc Benioff, founded Salesforce to provide customer relationship management services in 1999. Salesforce provided its services under subscription arrangements instead of selling stand-alone software packages, claiming that this pricing model was useful for a company that might be skeptical about making a large upfront payment for a software package that it might not decide to use. A client also did not need to purchase and maintain enterprise hardware to set up its e-commerce services. In a *CRN* interview, Benioff stated that the Salesforce strategy was successful even in the poor market after the dot-com collapse, and might even have countercyclical benefits, as corporations were less willing to buy expensive hardware and software while the economy was bad.

As social networks expanded, marketers were interested in using social networks to gain potential customers, and concerned about rumors that users were spreading on these networks. To help its clients improve their images on social networks, Salesforce bought Radian6 in March 2011, which tracked messages across a variety of platforms such as Facebook and Twitter, helping marketers respond quickly to customer concerns, according to *Venturebeat.* Salesforce also offered social networking features in its own e-commerce package through its Chatter service, which offered additional social tools such as the opportunity to track and recommend topics to its clients.

Zoho Zoho competes with its much larger rivals by offering budget e-commerce services through a subscription service. Reviewing Zoho's CRM Professional Edition for *PC Mag,* Jamie Lendino explained that Zoho's basic CRM package was free in 2010. Adding additional features to an account raised the monthly subscription fee, and this could bring the price into the $30 range that competitors charged for their CRM packages.

SEE ALSO *E-business Service Provider (eBSP).*

BIBLIOGRAPHY

Berqowitz, Gadi. "Commerce Server 2009 Overview." *Gadi Berqowitz' Blog,* January 9, 2011. Available from http://blogs.microsoft.co.il/blogs/gadib/archive/2011/01/09/commerce-server-2009-overview.aspx.

Brock, James R. "WebSphere Keeps the World of E-commerce Turning." *InfoWorld,* March 5, 2001.

Bull, Katherine. "Mark Hoffman: Changing the Face of the Digital Exchange Industry—Commerce One CEO Believes Digital Exchange Growth Depends on Supplying Both Software and Services." *InfoWorld,* July 3, 2000.

Conner, Deni. "Hewlett-Packard Unveils Bevy of Internet Appliances." *Network World,* April 23, 2001.

Corcoran, Elizabeth. "Oracle: Walking the Talk." *Forbes,* January 8, 2001.

Cox, John. "Oracle Eats Its Own E-business Dog Food." *Network World,* July 17, 2000.

Egusa, Conrad. "Salesforce Acquires Radian6 for $326M to Boost Social Offerings." *Venturebeat,* March 30, 2011. Available from http://venturebeat.com/2011/03/30/salesforce-buys-radian6.

"Firstsource Connect Customized Portals for the Web Marketplace." *PC World,* March 2001.

Flynn, Laurie J. "Oracle to Pay $5.85 Billion for Siebel." *New York Times,* September 13, 2005. Available from http://www.nytimes.com/2005/09/13/technology/13oracle.html.

Fontana, John. "Microsoft Relies on BizTalk Server 2000." *Network World,* December 18, 2000.

Frook, John Evan. "Big Blue Boosts Ad Spending 21 Percent to Spread E-business Message to the Web-Challenged." *Business Marketing,* December 1, 1999.

Fulton III, Scott M. "Microsoft Dynamics AX 2012 Dips Its Toes in the Cloud, Carefully." *ReadWriteCloud,*September 8, 2011. Available from http://www.readwriteweb.com/cloud/2011/09/microsoft-dynamics-ax-2012-dip.php.

Gladwin, Lee C. "Borders Turns to Amazon for Outsourcing." *ComputerWorld,* April 16, 2001.

Greenmeier, Larry. "How HP Carves Out the Magic—Hewlett-Packard Wants to Expand Its Service Offerings into the Product-Agnostic World of E-business." *InformationWeek,* November 13, 2000.

Hatlestad, Luc. "Q&A: SalesForce Founder Marc Benioff." *CRN,*April 30, 2003. Available from http://www.crn.com/news/channel-programs/18822493/q-a-salesforce-founder-marc-benioff.htm;jsessionid=O+leg9GlOmuT-givExZbKg**.ecappj02.

Henschen, Doug. "Inside IBM's Coremetrics-Unica SaaS Marketing Markup." *InformationWeek,*July 20, 2011. Available from http://www.informationweek.com/news/software/bi/231002187.

"Hewlett-Packard Buys Bluestone in E-business Bid." *News-bytes,* October 16, 2000.

Howlett, Dennis. "Making Sense of HP's Autonomy Acquisition." *Irregular Enterprise* (blog), *ZDNet,* August 19, 2011. Available from http://www.zdnet.com/blog/howlett/making-sense-of-hps-autonomy-acquisition/3345?tag=mantle_skin;content.

IBM. "IBM Agrees to Acquire Sterling Commerce from AT&T for $1.4 Billion." Armonk, NY, May 24, 2010. Available from http://www-03.ibm.com/press/us/en/pressrelease/31742.wss.

Jastrow, David. "Internet Resellers Alter Web Strategies." *Computer Reseller News,* June 21, 1999.

Kim, Ryan. "Oracle to Buy ATG. Follows Money to Mobiles." *GigaOM,* November 2, 2010. Available from http://gigaom.com/2010/11/02/with-atg-buy-oracle-will-follow-the-money-to-mobiles.

Lendino, Jamie. "Zoho CRM Professional Edition." *PCMag,* June 14, 2010. Available from http://www.pcmag.com/article2/0,2817,2365023,00.asp#fbid=xb2DGBORABl.

Meister, Frank, Jeetu Patel, Joe and Fenner. "E-Commerce Platforms Mature." *InformationWeek,* October 23, 2000. Available from http://www.informationweek.com/809/ecom.htm.

Moschella, David. "IBM: Your One-Stop E-Commerce Shop?" *Computerworld,* October 27, 1997.

Robb, Drew. "Oracle CRM Buying Guide." *Enterprise Apps Today,* September 12, 2011. Available from http://www.enterpriseappstoday.com/crm/oracle-crm-buying-guide.html.

Roush, Wade. "Borrowing a Page from Facebook and Ning, Broadvision Bets the Company on the 'Social Business

Cloud'." *Xconomy,* November 9, 2010. Available from http://www.xconomy.com/san-francisco/2010/11/09/borrowing-a-page-from-facebook-and-ning-broadvision-bets-the-company-on-the-social-business-cloud/.

ECONOMIES OF SCALE

In manufacturing, the term "economies of scale" refers to the reduction of average production costs over the long term as a result of boosted output. The attractiveness of building economies of scale lies in the fact that they allow firms to pass their cost savings on to customers in the form of lower prices, thereby undercutting competitors without damaging profit margins and heightening barriers to market entry for smaller firms. For an e-commerce site, economies of scale can be achieved as a business grows by reducing costs associated with creating and running a Web site, fulfilling orders, and resolving customer service issues.

A BALANCING ACT

As economists note, bigger does not always mean better. Business analysts coined the term "diseconomies of scale" to describe those conditions in which expanded production actually contributes to rising production costs and declining productivity. Usually, this is caused by excessive bureaucratization within an organization and the use of too many people in the production process, which entails more training to bring people up to speed and winds up using time and money inefficiently. Diseconomies of scale can also occur from quality control issues resulting from increased production.

During the online sales cycle, diseconomies of scale occur when an e-commerce site does not meet customer expectations in ordering and fulfillment, resulting in lost sales opportunities. For example, during the peak holiday season, the technology that e-tailers have in place may not be sufficient to keep up with the traffic load from users. One popular method for balancing traffic load is to create a mirror site. This alternate server contains the same information as the original but can help balance a high volume of ordering. A mirror site also serves as a backup in the event of a disaster at one datacenter location.

LEVERAGING TECHNOLOGY

An e-commerce company may look for ways to achieve economies of scale by sharing its technological innovations. When e-commerce was first emerging, companies had no option but to build their own platform, which created a barrier to entry for many. Amazon.com, for example, spent $160 million on its Web site and technology in 1999. To recoup these costs, Amazon.com began to leverage its technology by expanding its product line beyond books through acquisitions and alliances. By 2002, consumers could buy apparel, electronics, and a wide range of products through its Amazon Marketplace program.

Amazon.com also developed programs to further leverage its existing technology by offering e-commerce services to other e-tailers. Through its Merchant program, retailers like Toysrus.com, Babiesrus.com, and Target could sell their products through Amazon.com but handle all fulfillment activities. In return, Amazon.com received a commission on each sale. Another strategy used by Amazon.com was to integrate its technology with another Web site. In this case, consumers were directed to a site like Borders.com, Waldenbooks.com, or CDNow.com, where Amazon.com's e-commerce services, features, and technologies were implemented. Under this arrangement, Amazon.com also handled fulfillment and customer service and received the revenue, while the owner of the Web site was paid a commission.

CLOUD COMPUTING

Cloud computing is growing in popularity as a way for e-commerce businesses to achieve economies of scale in maintaining an online storefront. Although a business can operate or have a third party operate its own private cloud, the greatest cost savings are achieved from outsourcing to a public cloud or through providers such as Amazon.com and Salesforce.com. According to the National Institute of Standards and Technology (NIST), cloud computing can be broken down into three levels of service. Software as a Service (SaaS) gives a business the ability to access the provider's software. Platform as a Service (PaaS) allows a business to develop its own applications using the provider's tools and application programming interface. Infrastructure as a Service (IaaS) allows a business to run arbitrary operating systems and applications. In all three models, the service provider incurs costs associated with the infrastructure for processing, storage, networks, and other fundamental computing resources.

Public cloud computing allows a business to harness the power of a large datacenter (e.g., fast wide-area networks and powerful servers) without any capital investment in technology. The cloud computing service provider charges the business for just the resources it uses. These costs are much lower than if the business operated a private cloud because the cost of ownership is much lower for a large datacenter. According to a Microsoft white paper published in November 2010, a cloud with 100,000 servers lowers the cost of ownership by approximately 80% compared to a cloud with only 1,000 servers. This is due to a lower cost for electricity, less infrastructure labor, and greater buying power for hardware and software upgrades.

In addition to massive upfront and ongoing cost savings, the flexibility of cloud computing offers many other economic benefits. As customer demand on an e-commerce site rises and falls throughout the day, from season to season, or from changes in the industry, the business only pays for what resources it uses. It does not have to worry about predicting what computer resources it might need to meet rising customer demand and bring that new capacity online in a timely manner. Nor will the business incur costs associated with the burden of unused resources during periods of lower customer demand. By correlating the cost of operating an e-commerce site directly with the volume of ordering, a business can prevent diseconomies of scale from having more computing resources than it needs.

SEE ALSO *Amazon.com; Cloud Computing; Economies of Time.*

BIBLIOGRAPHY

Dignan, Larry. "Microsoft Riffs on Cloudonomics: Economies of Scale Favor Public Cloud Computing." *ZDNet,* November 12, 2010. Available from http://www.zdnet.com/blog/btl/microsoft-riffs-on-cloudonomics-economies-of-scale-favor-public-cloud-computing/41610.

Kharif, Olga. "Will Apple Benefit from the iphone Price Cut?" *Bloomberg Businessweek,* September 7, 2007. Available from http://www.businessweek.com/the_thread/techbeat/archives/2007/09/will_apple_bene.html.

Microsoft. "The Economics of the Cloud." Redmond, WA, November 2010. Available from http://www.microsoft.com/presspass/presskits/cloud/docs/The-Economics-of-the-Cloud.pdf.

National Institute of Standards and Technology. "The NIST Definition of Cloud Computing (Draft)." Gaithersburg, MD, January 2011. Available from http://csrc.nist.gov/publications/drafts/800-145/Draft-SP-800-145_cloud-definition.pdf.

ECONOMIES OF TIME

In comparison to a brick-and-mortar outlet, the premise behind every e-commerce site is to gain, "economies of time." Automation reduces the number of steps and people involved in many business processes. Whereas a floor salesperson typically deals with only one customer at a time (this is certainly true at checkout), that same person in an e-commerce situation might be able to respond to the queries of multiple online shoppers at the same time. As a result, in theory the efforts of staff can be refocused on further improvements that can lead to additional economic benefits.

STREAMLINED OPERATIONS

E-commerce changes the way operational tasks are conducted. Productivity per capita, or productivity per person, increases when tasks that were previously conducted using manual labor are automated. For example, the steps in a purchasing transaction typically include locating the right product for the customer, providing or negotiating pricing, invoicing or processing payment, and arranging delivery. Each of these steps incurs costs that tend to increase as a function of time and distance. E-commerce simplifies and accelerates the exchange of information, so it takes less time for an employee to complete them as well as allows some tasks to occur simultaneously without human interaction at all.

In an online business-to-business marketplace, companies are able to link their systems with those of suppliers, distributors, and manufacturers. One example of how companies can increase efficiency are automated procurement systems that track inventory levels and replenish supplies automatically from suppliers, thereby freeing staff to focus on more valuable tasks. The challenge is setting up compatible systems that can exchange information with business partners and training employees to use these systems. Once in place, a business should be able to achieve economies in time by needing fewer people to manage the supply chain.

FASTER ACCESS TO INFORMATION

The Internet also provides e-commerce businesses faster access to information, both upstream to suppliers and downstream to customers. By knowing the location of a shipment, order variances, and production and inventory levels, the business is better able to manage its supply chain. By capturing information about customers using the Web site, the business is able to create more targeted marketing programs and be more responsive to the needs of customers. For example, an e-commerce site that enables customers to check the status of shipments or initiate contact through online chat requires less manpower and allows issues to be resolved in a more timely manner.

One challenge of e-commerce is meeting the expectation of customers. According to an article published in *E-Commerce Times,* "a Web site must fulfill four distinct needs: availability, responsiveness, clarity, and utility." Although a business may be able to achieve economies of time through automation, customers also expect a Web site to be easier than other methods of ordering, as well as easier than using a competitor's site. An automated ordering process for the customer might include locating products, comparing features and prices, placing the order, paying, and arranging method of delivery. If any of these steps are difficult and the customer becomes frustrated, the business risks losing customers. Ultimately, e-commerce can only improve the bottom line if it truly streamlines business processes and customers are happy with the system.

SEE ALSO *Economies of Scale.*

BIBLIOGRAPHY

Chan, Claribel. "Electronic Commerce." *Stanford Journal of International Relations* 1, no. 3 (Spring 1999). Available from http://www.stanford.edu/group/sjir/1.2.05_chan.html.

Choppy, Ralph. "Supply Chain Performance: Beneath the Tip of the Iceberg." *E-Commerce Times,* August 3, 2010. Available from http://www.technewsworld.com/story/70540.html.

Loosley, Chris. "When Is Your Web Site Fast Enough?" *E-Commerce Times,* October 12, 2005. Available from http://www.ecommercetimes.com/story/46627.html.

Wenninger, John. "Business-to-Business Electronic Commerce." *Current Issues in Economics and Finance* 5, no. 10 (June 1999). Available from http://www.ny.frb.org/research/current_issues/ci5-10.pdf.

E-GOVERNMENT WEB PRIVACY COALITION

In June 2000, representatives from ten state and local governments as well as four private-sector technology companies—facilitated by a California-based subsidiary of the e-government technology leader National Information Consortium (NIC)—formed the e-Government Web Privacy Coalition. At that time, the issue of self-regulation of privacy by commercial Web sites was coming to the forefront, and the government was also being scrutinized for the privacy and security of its online information. The purpose of the coalition was to debate e-government privacy and security issues. The coalition no longer exists, but in subsequent years, policies like the e-Government Act of 2002 were enacted "to provide enhanced access to government information and services in a manner consistent with laws regarding protection of personal privacy, national security, records retention, access for persons with disabilities, and other relevant laws."

BACKGROUND ON ITS FORMATION

At the dawn of the twenty-first century, state and local governments began to make sizable investments in e-government systems. Constituencies increasingly demanded that basic governmental information and citizenship services be made available over the Internet, as they were at the federal level, and thus vendors flocked to the booming market for state and local government information technology. Local governments thus began reengineering and Web-enabling their systems to provide their constituents with portal-based integrated systems, alleviating the need for individuals to keep track of many different electronic contact points within government.

While citizens increasingly demanded electronic government services, there existed the fear—similar to that with online shopping—that with the convenience came a price of potentially compromised privacy and security. Just days before the coalition was formed, the Federal Trade Commission (FTC) and consumer groups had asked Congress for stronger privacy regulation after a survey revealed only 20% of commercial Web sites were adhering to standards of fair information practices. Obviously, the government needed to ensure its Web sites were in compliance before it could require the same from the private sector. A few months later, the General Accounting Office used the FTC's survey methodology and found the government's Web efforts were indeed lacking. Only 3% of the 65 sites surveyed were providing adequate privacy, and all of the 24 agencies surveyed had computer security weaknesses.

Among the specific issues the e-Government Web Privacy Coalition planned to address were public-key infrastructure and other encryption schemes, digital signatures, and network and infrastructure security. The coalition's mission was to protect citizens and their sensitive data by constructing an environment in which electronic data could flow freely and securely between governments and citizens in a safe network. If e-government was to fulfill its potential, according to the coalition, citizens needed to feel comfortable that their participation in an online democracy was accompanied by the requisite level of privacy and security.

The group maintained two stated goals. The first was to devise and disseminate methods and processes by which standards could be achieved to promote confidentiality, privacy, and "the preservation of the public trust." The second was to build itself into an independent organization leading the development and guidance of e-government via voluntary certification programs for e-government portals and other applications. Certification was marked with a privacy seal, awarded only to those e-government portals and applications that met the privacy standards and protocols enacted by the coalition.

COALITION MEMBERS

While the coalition's policies primarily were driven by its public-sector representatives, the involvement of private companies was intended to facilitate a smooth, cooperative relationship between governments and the companies that would need to adopt the standards and protocols the coalition set. The original private-sector members were Cisco

Systems Inc., Compaq Computer Corp., Digital Signature Trust Co., and Oracle Corp., all of which were invited by NIC Technologies Inc. based on their record of developing comprehensive privacy systems.

In addition, the Progress & Freedom Foundation (PFF) was selected as an advisor to the coalition. The PFF was founded as a nonprofit organization in Washington, D.C. in 1993. This think tank was devoted to studying the digital revolution and advocating limited government until it closed its doors on October 1, 2010.

NIC Technologies, formerly SDR Technologies Inc., was acquired by NIC the month before the coalition was formed. NIC was founded as Kansas Information Consortium in 1992, when it received the contract to create an Internet portal for the state of Kansas. By 2000, NIC's subsidiaries had contracts with 12 other state governments. Although the e-Government Web Privacy Coalition did not last long and made no significant impact while it did exist, NIC continues to build online services for federal, state, and local government agencies. As of 2010, NIC managed the official Web sites for 23 states.

SEE ALSO *Cryptography, Public and Private Key; Privacy: Issues, Policies, Statements; Safe Harbor Privacy Framework.*

BIBLIOGRAPHY

Hu, Jim, and Melanie Austria Farmer. "Study: Government Web Sites Weak on Privacy, Security." *CNET*, September 12, 2000. Available from http://news.cnet.com/Study-Government-Web-sites-weak-on-privacy,-security/2100-1023_3-245604.html.

Keegan, Daniel. "Technology and Gov Leaders to Debate E-gov Privacy." *Federal Computer Week*, June 5, 2000. Available from http://fcw.com/articles/2000/06/05/technology-and-gov-leaders-to-debate-egov-privacy.aspx.

Mariano, Gwendolyn. "FTC, Consumer Groups Fight for Privacy Control." *CNET*, May 25, 2000. Available from http://news.cnet.com/FTC,-consumer-groups-fight-for-privacy-control/2100-1023_3-241116.html.

NIC Inc. "NIC and eGovernment History." Olathe, KS, 2010. Available from http://www.egov.com/AboutNIC/Pages/History.aspx.

The Progress & Freedom Foundation. "Our Mission." Washington, DC, November 2011. Available from http://www.pff.org/about/.

Symonds, Matthew. "The Next Revolution." *Economist*, June 22, 2000. Available from http://www.economist.com/node/80746.

U.S. Department of Justice. Office of Justice Programs. Justice Information Sharing. "Federal Statutes." Washington, DC. Last modified April 8, 2010. Available from http://it.ojp.gov/default.aspx?area=privacy&page=1287.

ELECTRONIC COMMUNICATIONS NETWORKS (ECNS)

Electronic communications networks (ECNs) are computerized trading systems through which buyers and sellers of stocks and other securities have their orders matched via instant digital transactions.

Sustaining liquidity is a primary concern of ECNs, especially smaller networks. If there are too few investors placing limit orders, there would be no exchange. This gives ECNs a significant incentive to expand, either by enticing dealers to the network, or by shipping orders to external markets where prices are better. This latter solution increased the comparative value of ECNs and increased intermarket exchange. It also served as the principal reason for the consolidation of the ECN market and its eventual acquisition by traditional exchanges.

Initially, ECNs were most threatening to the NASDAQ exchange. The NYSE, with its layers of complex rules and regulations regarding the trading of large-capitalization securities, has been much more resistant to encroachment by ECNs. By early 2001, ECNs accounted for a hefty 35% of all NASDAQ trading volume, and in 2005, that figure had risen to 40% of total trading being conducted in the two major ECNs, Archipelago and Instinet.

With the technology to compete against the NYSE and NASDAQ but lacking in infrastructure, Instinet and Archipelago were acquired by NASDAQ and NYSE, respectively, in 2005. From 2005 to 2011, both stock exchanges upgraded their computerized trading systems, offering better and better exchange times, as well as increasing efficiency.

THE DEVELOPMENT OF THE ECN INDUSTRY

The earliest precursor to the modern ECN was Instinet Corp., founded in 1969 by Reuters Group PLC as a venue for institutional investors to trade after regular trading hours. Thus, Instinet was more of a private system that catered to established investors rather than to the more wide-open customer base served by later ECNs.

On the heels of a NASDAQ trading scandal in the mid-1990s—in which market makers were accused of conspiracy to skim profits by refusing to carry out unprofitable orders and by filling orders at prices that did not meet buyers' expectations—the Securities and Exchange Commission (SEC) issued new order handling rules in 1996, requiring all market makers to publish their orders on NASDAQ. Alternatively, the SEC allowed market makers to publish on an ECN that would subsequently list the order on the NASDAQ Level II quotation system. As a result of this ruling, the activities of the exclusive electronic trading networks like Instinet were forced into public view, and the modern ECN industry was born.

The emergence of major ECNs coincided, happily enough, with the day-trading phenomenon of the late 1990s. This worked out perfectly for ECNs, since day traders typically were nontraditional investors with no solid roots in, or relationships with, the large brokerages. Instead, day traders were looking for quick and cheap ways to place a flurry of orders and reap a quick profit. Thus, the market conditions were ripe for new investment vehicles like ECNs to grab a piece of the action. One of the biggest ECNs, Island ECN Inc., was majority-owned by the online brokerage Datek Online Holdings Corp., which was deeply entrenched in day trading.

DUKING IT OUT WITH THE EXCHANGES

By the turn of the twenty-first century, ECNs were generating heavy enough trading volume to make the customary exchanges, such as NASDAQ and NYSE, extremely nervous. Indeed, several leading ECNs even filed with the SEC to acquire exchange status themselves, which set off a small war with the traditional exchanges. When ECN giant Archipelago Holdings LLC merged with the Pacific Stock Exchange to create the first ECN-exchange hybrid, it was able to function simultaneously as an exchange and trade stocks through NYSE. Island and NexTrade Holdings Inc. followed a similar path, and as they moved closer to regulatory approval the major exchanges, particularly NASDAQ, took arms in defense. Upon assuming exchange status, ECNs would enjoy direct access to the National Market System linking all stock exchanges, while having their quotations listed alongside those of other exchanges across the nation.

In 2001, NASDAQ attacked Archipelago's ambitions, complaining to the SEC that such moves were anticompetitive. At first blush, this complaint from a system that trafficked 2 billion shares per day against an ECN that moved 100 million daily shares looked incongruous, but it was in fact indicative of the exchanges' fear of ECNs' potential—particularly that of NASDAQ, which was the most immediately threatened.

EXCHANGES ACQUIRE ECNS

With more and more trading taking place online, speed of information delivery and exchange was a critical differentiating factor, and Instinet and Archipelago had technological advantages that were extremely desirable to the traditional stock exchanges, according to *InformationWeek.* In addition, the two major ECNs represented quick ways to increase market share. When NASDAQ acquired Instinet, it gained roughly 5% of the market. The deal was made only two days after NYSE acquired Archipelago Holdings Inc. It was pointed out that NYSE had more to gain with Archipelago, as it had yet to design a competitive ECN of its own. In 2009, four years after the deal, NYSE had reduced the time of its transactions to five milliseconds, from one-third of a second in 2007.

SEE ALSO *NASDAQ Stock Market.*

BIBLIOGRAPHY

"Cents and Sensibility." *Money,* September 2000.

Der Hovanesian, Mara, and Emily Thornton. "Tough Times in Electronic Trading." *Business Week,* October 23, 2000.

"ECNs Poised to Take Off." *Wall Street & Technology,* July 2000.

Gogoi, Pallavi. "Behind NASDAQ's Hissy Fit." *Business Week,* March 5, 2001.

James, Sylvia. "From Trading Floor to ECN." *Information World Review,* June 2000.

Jovin, Ellen. "Fair Trades: Enthusiasts Say ECNs Level the Playing Field for Traders, but Many Others Remain Skeptical." *Financial Planning,* June 1, 2000.

Marlin, Steve. "Nasdaq Buying Instinet Group, Setting Up E-trading Showdown with NYSE." *InformationWeek,* April 22, 2005. Available from http://www.informationweek.com/news/161501151.

Mehta, Nina. "Nasdaq May Inherit NYSE Floor That Greifeld Sought to Bury." *Bloomberg Businessweek,* April 4, 2011. Available from http://www.businessweek.com/news/2011-04-04/nasdaq-may-inherit-nyse-floor-that-greifeld-sought-to-bury.html.

Minkoff, Jerry. "Market & Exchanges: ECNs Adapting to Rapidly Changing Environment." *Web Finance,* February 28, 2000.

NYSE Euronext. "NYSE Cuts Order-Execution Time to 5 Milliseconds from 105." New York, July 1, 2009. Available from http://www.nyse.com/press/1246442836537.html.

Radcliff, Deborah. "Trading Nets Give Exchanges a Run for Their Money." *Computerworld,* December 18, 2000.

Stoll, Hans R. "Electronic Trading in Stock Markets." *Journal of Economic Perspectives* 20, no. 1 (2006): 153–174.

Vinzant, Carol. "Do We Need a Stock Exchange?" *Fortune,* November 22, 1999.

Weinberg, Neil. "The Big Board Comes Back from the Brink." *Forbes,* November 13, 2000.

ELECTRONIC DATA INTERCHANGE (EDI)

Electronic data interchange (EDI) is the electronic exchange of business information—purchase orders, invoices, bills of lading, inventory data and various types of confirmations—between organizations or trading partners in standardized formats. EDI also is used within individual organizations to transfer data between different divisions or departments, including finance, purchasing, and shipping.

When the focus of EDI centers on payments, especially between banks and companies, the term financial EDI (FEDI) is sometimes used. Along with digital currency, electronic catalogs, intranets, and extranets, EDI is a major cornerstone of e-commerce overall.

Two characteristics set EDI apart from other ways of exchanging information. First, EDI only involves business-to-business transactions; individual consumers do not directly use EDI to purchase goods or services. Secondly, EDI involves transactions between computers or databases, not individuals. Therefore, individuals sending e-mail messages or sharing files over a network does not constitute EDI.

BEFORE THE INTERNET

While the concept of e-commerce did not receive widespread attention until the 1990s, large companies have been using EDI since the 1960s. The railroad industry was among the first to adopt EDI, followed by other players in the transportation industry. By the early 1980s, EDI was being used by companies in many different industry sectors. In the beginning, companies using EDI transferred information to one another on magnetic tape via mail or courier, which had many drawbacks including long lead times and the potential for a tape to be damaged in transit. During the 1980s, telecommunications emerged as the preferred vehicle for transferring information via EDI.

INTRODUCTION OF INTERNET-BASED EDI

By the early 2000s, the Internet was playing a larger role in EDI. It became possible for companies to translate EDI files and send them to another company's computer system over the Internet, via e-mail or file transfer protocol (FTP). As it was an open network and access was not terribly expensive, using the Internet for EDI was more cost effective for companies with limited means. The low cost associated with open EDI also meant that more companies could participate. This was important because the level of value for participants often increased along with their number. However, this also presented a dilemma for large companies who had invested a considerable sum in traditional EDI systems.

In March 2000, an e-marketplace called the World-Wide Retail Exchange (WWRE) was established. It allowed suppliers and retails in various industry sectors—including retail, general merchandise, food, and drugstores—to conduct transactions over the World Wide Web. After one year of operation, the WWRE had 53 retailer members with combined annual turnover of $722 billion.

Wal-mart Announces Edi Project: 2002 In the early 2000s, most businesses were still using value-added networks (VANs), which transmitted messages across private networks that were controlled by the VAN provider. Internet-based EDI had been considered unreliable because companies were concerned that the risks of network outages and security breaches were too high on public networks. Wal-Mart decided that the cost savings it could obtain by using public networks instead of a VAN made a switch worthwhile, because it would no longer have to pay fees to a VAN provider. *Network World* reported that Wal-Mart purchased Isoft EDI software and announced that it was building its own network in November 2002. Although Wal-Mart was not charging its suppliers licensing fees to use the Isoft software, it did require its suppliers to pay $300 per year to cover the support costs.

Edi Provider Market 2003 Isoft had not been well known in the EDI industry before it gained Wal-Mart as a customer, according to an article by Alorie Gilbert in *CNET.* VAN providers such as Sterling Commerce and Global Exchange Services realized that many retailers would follow Wal-Mart's switch to Internet-based EDI, and developed their own plans to enter this market. Wal-Mart's decision also benefited many small software companies which had suffered from the effects of the dot-com crash, because major retail suppliers were upgrading their own systems so that they could continue to sell to Wal-Mart.

IBM LEAVES THE MARKET: 2004

IBM had been one of the main VAN providers, but in 2004, it decided to sell its VAN division. IBM believed that EDI would become less important in the future, and it would gain a better return in the electronic commerce market by investing its resources in its WebSphere software. IBM unloaded both its VAN services division and its Internet-based EDI division in the sale to Francisco Partners. Francisco Partners was a venture capital firm that owned the VAN provider GXS. By combining IBM's EDI divisions with its own GXS services, Francisco Partners gained control over most of the EDI market in the United States. *Network World* reported that Francisco Partners had also decided to switch its current VAN customers over to Internet-based EDI services, although many customers were still resisting the transition because of the reliability advantages that a private network offered.

EDI FORMATS

There were still many competing EDI formats during the 2000s, although some formats were more widespread in certain regions. EDIFACT was designed to serve as an international EDI standard by the United Nations Economic Commission for Europe (UNECE). Most

American organizations, including businesses and government institutions, were using ASC X12, an EDI format developed by the American National Standards Institute (ANSI), while EDIFACT was common in European nations. Both ASC X12 and EDIFACT were older formats that had gained widespread acceptance before the use of Internet-based EDI, and newer competitors such as XML-based EDI and Universal Business Language (UBL) were also becoming more popular.

EDIFACT EDIFACT had been designed as a standard that covered all types of industries throughout Europe. Since this standard was established while VANs were common, message sizes were a concern for many businesses, as VAN providers typically charged fees that were based on the volume of the data that they delivered for their clients. To conserve costs, companies set up groups that established EDIFACT subsets for each industry. For example, chemical manufacturers established the Chemical Industry Data Exchange (CIDX), and hospitals formed the European Medical Electronic Data Interchange Association (EMEDI), according to *Tripcom.* These industry-specific EDIFACT subsets were also known as EDIFACT implementation guidelines.

EDI Managed Services Although the VAN provider could handle the transmission of documents to many other companies after a company uploaded them to the network, the uploading process itself was difficult for many firms. A company needed to convert the documents that it held on its own databases into a standard EDI format such as EDIFACT or ASC X12, which required translation software, and it needed to convert the EDI documents that it received back into a legible format. As buyers started to ask their suppliers to provide more detailed information about their products, managing an internal EDI network became more difficult for these suppliers. Larger EDI providers such as GXS started offering complete EDI outsourcing services, offering to translate automatically the documents that were stored in a company's databases into any format that a business partner required, including EDI formats which were widely used in foreign countries.

EDI AND CLOUD-BASED SERVICES

In the early 2010s, some companies were phasing out EDI and switching to the cloud to handle their purchasing arrangements. One major problem with EDI was that a large company might have several hundred suppliers, and arranging an individual trading partner agreement with each supplier was time-consuming. Companies were also starting to purchase more raw materials from suppliers that were located in distant nations, extending the length of their supply chains, while attempting to implement just-in-time practices to reduce their inventory stockpiles. A 2011 Wharton School of Business article reported that decreasing technology costs were also a factor in the switch away from EDI, because cloud-based purchasing systems were now more cost effective for more retailers.

Cloud-based EDI services were also available as an alternative to the older value-added networks in 2011. *EBN* reported that some managers remained concerned about the reliability of cloud-based EDI systems, but a survey showed that these cloud-based systems suffered fewer outages than the VAN networks that the respondents were using. Companies that managed their own EDI networks reported the worst results in the survey, reporting frequent outages. Even short outages in an EDI network can be an issue, because a company that implements just-in-time practices needs access to product tracking information throughout the delivery process. For example, if a delivery truck is caught in traffic for several hours, the company may need to arrange an alternate supplier if it keeps low inventory stocks.

GXS BUYS INOVIS: 2010

GXS continued to buy EDI providers, acquiring Inovis in 2010. Although these EDI providers primarily operated in the United States, the British government still reviewed the merger because of its antitrust potential. Although the merger further strengthened GXS' dominance of the VAN sector, the VAN-based EDI industry itself was starting to decline because corporations were switching to other EDI delivery methods (such as managed services) where GXS was less dominant, stated the British Office of Fair Trading.

Other large technology firms, such as IBM and Oracle, also signaled their intent to compete more aggressively in the EDI market. IBM bought Sterling Commerce in 2010, reentering the EDI market in which it had been a very strong competitor for many years before its exit in 2004, as it saw potential in EDI once again. Oracle provided EDI through its arrangement with E2Open.

SEE ALSO *Business-to-Business (B2B) E-commerce; Intranets and Extranets.*

BIBLIOGRAPHY

Bednars, Ann. "GXS to Inherit IBM's EDI Business." *Network World,* November 1, 2004. Available from http://www.networkworld.com/news/2004/110104ibmvan.html.

"E-commerce Growth Prospects Remain Strong." *Corporate EFT Report,* January 17, 2001.

Federal Reserve. "Fundamentals of Financial EDI." Federal Reserve Bank Services, February 14, 2011. Available from http://www.frbservices.org.

Foxvog, Doug, Juan Pablo Palacios, and Elena Pasluru Bontas Simperl. "Analysis of EDIFACT and Other Standards."

TripCom, October 16, 2006. Available from http://www.tripcom.org/docs/del/Tripcom-D71.pdf.

Gilbert, Alorie. "Wal-Mart Project Boon for Software Makers." *CNET,* August 14, 2003. Available from http://news.cnet.com/2100-1017_3-5064075.html.

Karpinski, Richard. "The Future of EDI." *Planet IT,* March 3, 1999.

Koegler, Scott. "EDI Downtime: Internal Vs. External Services." *EBN,* September 14, 2011. Available from http://www.ebnonline.com/author.asp?section_id=1306&doc_id=233374.

Kosiur, David. *Understanding Electronic Commerce,* Seattle: Microsoft Press, 1997.

Kumar, Ram, and Connie Crook. "Educating Senior Management on the Strategic Benefits of Electronic Data Interchange." *Journal of Systems Management,* March/April 1996.

Moozakis, Chuck. "No Longer E-biz Misfits." *InternetWeek.com,* March 3, 1999. Available from http://www.internetwk.com/lead/lead100200-1.htm.

Office of Fair Trading. "Completed Acquisition by GXS of Inovis." London, July 14, 2010. Available from http://www.oft.gov.uk/OFTwork/mergers/decisions/2010/gxs.

Shim, Jae K., Anique A. Qureshi, Joel G. Siegel, and Roberta M. Siegel. *The International Handbook of Electronic Commerce.* New York: AMACOM, 2000.

"Supply-Chain Management: Growing Global Complexity Drives Companies into the 'Cloud'." Philadelphia, PA: Wharton School of Business, January 12, 2011. Available from http://knowledge.wharton.upenn.edu/article.cfm?articleid=2669.

Tiernan, Bernadette. *E-tailing.* Chicago: Dearborn Financial Publishing Inc. 2000.

Wilson, Tim. "Wal-Mart Cuts the VAN out of EDI." *Network World,* September 23, 2002. Available from http://www.networkworld.com/newsletters/asp/2002/01560820.html.

ELECTRONIC FRONTIER FOUNDATION

Electronic Frontier Foundation (EFF) is a nonprofit civil liberties group formed to ensure that communication in a digital world receives the same protection as other forms of speech. In addition to preserving freedom of online communication, many EFF cases sought to protect digital privacy, defend online fair use, and promote innovation. As the EFF seeks to leverage the approximately $3 million it receives in donations from members and corporations, the organization only litigates cases that are class action or that could benefit the greater good in how case law is being applied to technology. EFF also uses its advisory attorneys and experts to influence policy making relating to technology. Through the official EFF Web site and other sites it has launched, the organization also seeks to educate the public about their digital rights.

DEFENDER OF CIVIL LIBERTIES

Established in July 1990, EFF initially was funded by private contributions from Mitchell Kapor and Apple Computer Inc. cofounder Steve Wozniak. Kapor founded EFF with John Perry Barlow and John Gilmore, and they raised contributions from a wide constituency. One of the first legal cases in which the foundation intervened involved a game manufacturer that was the target of the Secret Service's nationwide investigation into data piracy. Without warning, the government had seized company computer equipment owned by Steve Jackson and deleted critical company e-mail before the computers were returned. EFF won the case, which set the precedent that e-mail deserved the same protection as other forms of speech.

A second case had EFF defending freedom of information published online, when the U.S. government charged Craig Neidorf, a University of Missouri student who edited the electronic newsletter *Phrack World News,* with crimes that he did not knowingly commit. Kapor discussed the foundation's interest in these cases in an EFF press release, explaining: "It is becoming increasingly obvious that the rate of technology advancement in communications is far outpacing the establishment of appropriate cultural, legal, and political frameworks to handle the issues that are arising. And the Steve Jackson and Neidorf cases dramatically point to the timeliness of the Foundation's mission. We intend to be instrumental in helping shape a new framework that embraces these powerful new technologies for the public good."

LANDMARK CASES

In 1998, the U.S. Congress passed the Digital Millennium Copyright Act (DMCA), which was aimed at preventing the circumvention of antipiracy protection on CDs. It also limited the liability of Internet service providers (ISP) for transmitting copyrighted material but required them to remove material from Web sites that appeared to be an infringement. In 2003, EFF published a white paper outlining the ways in which the DMCA was being used by the entertainment and software industries to prevent what it considered fair use of purchased electronic media.

EFF spent the 2000s waging many battles against the entertainment industry, often involving unfair applications of the DMCA. For example, in 2009, EFF prevailed in a case against the American Society of Composers, Authors and Publishers' (ASCAP) claim that music ringtones were a copyright infringement. In that same year, EFF successfully defended YouTube in a lawsuit filed by Viacom claiming the Web site was liable for copyright infringements by users.

EFF has been involved in numerous cases with companies that have sought to apply the DMCA in ways that restricted the use of property owned by consumers. In 2009, EFF won three exemptions against the DMCA. Following the ruling by the U.S. Copyright Office, consumers had the right to unlock a cell phone in order to use it with another network provider, "jailbreak" an iPhone so that it could be used with applications other than those offered at the iTunes App Store, or use footage from a DVD to create an original video for noncommercial use.

EFF has also fought many battles against the U.S. government and large corporations, especially when the EFF believes these institutions have used their power to infringe on the privacy of ordinary citizens. In August 2011, EFF appeared before the U.S. Circuit Court of Appeals to argue against the dismissal of two intertwined class-action cases two years prior. EFF had filed the first case, *Hepting v. AT&T,* on behalf of the telecom's customers in January 2006, after a news story broke about the surveillance of AT&T customers at the request of the U.S. National Security Agency (NSA). Nearly two years later, EFF filed *Jewel v. NSA* to challenge the actions of the NSA in making the request.

MEMBER OF THE GLOBAL NETWORK INITIATIVE

Governments forcing ISPs to disclose personal information about users was an international issue in which EFF became involved. In order to continue their business interests in China in 2006, the companies Google, Microsoft, and Yahoo! had been pressured by the Chinese government in ways the firms considered to be censorship. Consequently, the three companies began to formulate a code of conduct, along with EFF and other civil society organizations. At the end of 2008, the Global Network Initiative (GNI) was formally launched as a nonprofit organization to help information and communications technology companies ensure their policies and practices did not infringe upon international users' rights of freedom of expression and privacy. Specifically, the two main goals of the GNI were preventing governments from forcing ISPs to disclose personal data about political activists and preventing governments from censoring information.

The GNI was incorporated in the United States in February 2010. A year later, the GNI was being criticized for its inability to attract other big Internet companies with global users, such as Facebook and Twitter. One issue was the considerable costs companies must incur to participate in the GNI. According to an article by Larry Downes published in *Forbes,* "corporate members must establish formal procedures for dealing with key human rights issues and for responding to government requests for private information or to limit freedom of expression. They must also submit to regular assessments of how well the company is complying with its own policies, conducted by outside assessors accredited by GNI." In the 2010s, it remains to be seen whether the GNI will have significant influence in changing the laws of oppressive governments.

EFF's leadership includes Shari Steele, who assumed the role of executive director in 2000, and John Buckman, founder of two online companies—Magnatune and Bookmooch. Two of EFF's cofounders—John Perry Barlow and John Gilmore—continued to serve on the board, as of 2012. Most of the organization's staff of approximately 35 employees are based at the headquarters in San Francisco, but the organization also has an office in Washington, D.C.

SEE ALSO *Cyberculture: Culture, Society, and the Internet; Kapor, Mitchell; Privacy: Issues, Policies, Statements.*

BIBLIOGRAPHY

Downes, Larry. "Why No One Will Join the Global Network Initiative." *Forbes,* March 30, 2011. Available from http://www.forbes.com/sites/larrydownes/2011/03/30/why-no-one-will-join-the-global-network-initiative.

Electronic Frontier Foundation. "2006 Annual Report: EFF Timeline." San Francisco, CA, 2007. Available from http://www.eff.org/files/eff-2006-annual-report.pdf.

———. "EFF Legal Victories." San Francisco, CA, 2011. Available from http://www.eff.org/victories.

———. "A History of Protecting Freedom Where Law and Technology Collide." San Francisco, CA, 2011. Available from http://www.eff.org/about/history.

———. "NSA Multi-District Litigation." San Francisco, CA, July 1, 2009. Available from http://www.eff.org/cases/att.

———. "Unintended Consequences: Five Years Under the DCMA." San Francisco, CA, March, 2003. Available from http://www.eff.org/wp/unintended-consequences-five-years-under-the-dmca.

Global Network Initiative. "Inaugural Report 2010," 2011. Available from http://www.globalnetworkinitiative.org/cms/uploads/1/GNI_annual_report_2010.pdf.

ELECTRONIC INCOME-TAX FILING

Electronic filing of taxes enables professional tax preparers and most taxpayers to submit tax returns to the Internal Revenue Service (IRS) and some state agencies via computer modem. Taxpayers have various options for filing their taxes electronically. They can use special tax software to prepare their returns, and then transmit the completed forms electronically to an authorized intermediary who will forward them to the IRS. They also can take a completed paper form to an authorized intermediary for transmission, or have an authorized preparer complete their taxes and transmit them. As of 2012, qualifying taxpayers could also transmit their completed tax forms to the IRS directly via the Internet.

A number of online services committed to easing e-filing came into being during the late 2000s. Services such as TurboTax and H&R Block E-File enabled taxpayers to file their tax returns through secure online channels that bypassed the risks associated with sending them via e-mail. A taxpayer typically was required to pay an upfront cost to use the software, and then pay an additional e-filing fee. E-filing was additionally available not only to individual taxpayers but also to certain businesses, nonprofit organizations, and charitable institutions.

In 1986, the IRS reported about 25,000 electronic tax returns. In 2010, more than 116 million of 230 million total federal income tax returns were filed electronically. Seventy percent of all individual income tax returns were e-filed in 2010.

HISTORY

By the time the IRS introduced electronic filing during the 1986 tax year, more taxpayers had begun preparing their returns on personal computers. The agency's main idea was to cut its own costs of processing returns. Every year thousands of temporary employees had to be hired to sift through mountains of tax returns, and then check and enter the data by hand into IRS computers. E-filing eliminated much of that human labor.

E-filing was tested in three cities in 1986 and proved so successful it was expanded to four more cities the following year. In 1988, the program included 14 states. From the beginning, e-filers did not submit returns directly to the IRS. They were transmitted to an IRS-authorized private agent, usually an established tax firm, which transmitted them to a regional IRS office. Intermediaries usually charged a fee, anywhere from $25 to $75, for e-filing returns. One attraction of the service for taxpayers was the promise of a refund check in as few as two weeks. To sweeten the deal, the tax firms sometimes offered, for another fee, "refund anticipation loans"—a check for the expected refund issued as soon as the return was sent to the federal government. Following the e-submission of a return, taxpayers affixed their signature to a paper form and mailed it to the IRS separately.

In 1993, the IRS approved commercial software for the 1040PC—a tax form that could be filled out on a PC, printed, and then mailed to the IRS. This helped trim IRS costs because of the higher accuracy compared to older methods. By the end of the 1990s, tax returns could be submitted to authorized businesses for further transmission using a software package approved by the IRS.

ADVANTAGES AND DISADVANTAGES

E-filing provides many advantages to taxpayers. Quick processing means refunds are received much sooner, particularly if they are deposited directly into a bank account. Errors are reduced at both ends and e-tax preparation software can sometimes suggest deductions, review returns for data that could lead to an audit, or even download W-2 and 1099 forms. Federal and state returns can sometimes be calculated together. In addition, a majority of forms are available electronically. However, e-filing has disadvantages as well. About 22% of e-filers had their e-signatures rejected for some reason in 2010. Between the cost of software and finding an authorized agent, e-filing can cost more than mailing a traditional paper return. However, the IRS offered a FreeFile program to qualifying taxpayers. FreeFile allowed any taxpayer with less than $58,000 in annual income to file online for free directly to the IRS. The service additionally supported some state tax returns, also at no cost to the taxpayer.

In the late 2000s the IRS endeavored to tackle many of the issues obstructing efficient e-filing for consumers. A 2009 Government Accountability Office report recommended the agency "develop and document a strategy to prevent and resolve errors causing electronically filed returns to be rejected." To meet these challenges, the IRS began to require practitioner and self-select personal identification numbers and mandated e-signatures on individual income tax returns, among other efforts.

Perhaps the most serious downside of e-filing for most taxpayers was the question of the security of their personal and tax data. The IRS has taken steps to improve its computer security. In 2010, the service mandated six new security, privacy, and business standards in regard to consumer information that would be collected, processed, and stored by online providers of tax returns. The standards came on the heels of the Gramm-Leach-Bliley Act, which required financial institutions to explain their information-sharing activities to customers as well as safeguard sensitive data. They included:

1. Extended validation SSL certificate: Online tax return providers shall possess a valid Extended Validation Secure Sockets Layer (certificates that give Web browsers information that identify the organizational identity of another Web site).
2. External vulnerability scan: E-filing providers shall work with third-party vendors to scan their networks for vulnerabilities.
3. Information privacy and safeguard policies: E-filing providers shall have printed data privacy and safeguard policies that are consistent with government and industry guidelines, as well as maintain a license/accreditation seal from an accepted consumer protection and privacy vendor.

4. Protection against bulk filing of fraudulent income tax returns: E-filing vendors shall utilize technology that protects their sites from fraudulent bulk filing.
5. Public domain name registration: E-filing providers shall register their Web domain names with a registrar located in the United States and accredited by the Internet Corporation for Assigned Names and Numbers.
6. Reporting of security incidents: E-filing providers shall report security incidents to the IRS as soon as possible and no later than the next business day following the incident's confirmation.

SEE ALSO *Digital Signature.*

BIBLIOGRAPHY

Abramson, E. M. "IRS Flirts with Concept of Electronic Filing." *Washington Post,* August 18, 1986.

Barker, Jeff. "IRS Urged to Make Filing Easier; Technology Could Aid Taxpayers, Deconcini Says." *Arizona Republic,* March 8, 1993.

Beaupre, Becky. "Despite Kinks, Millions Will E-file 2000 Taxes." *Chicago Sun Times,* March 18, 2001.

Erb, Kelly Phillips. "10 Questions to Ask Before Paying for Add-On Tax Preparation Services." *DailyFinance,* March 9, 2011. Available from http://www.dailyfinance.com/2011/03/09/10-questions-to-ask-before-paying-for-add-on-tax-preparation-ser.

Federal Trade Commission. Bureau of Consumer Protection. "Gramm-Leach-Bliley Act." Washington, DC. Available from http://business.ftc.gov/privacy-and-security/gramm-leach-bliley-act.

Fogarty, Thomas A., "Taxes: How E-filing Options Stack Up." *USA Today,* February 11, 2000.

Granelli, James S. "Hitting the Return Key; Tax Filing by Computer Means You Can Get Your Refund Faster." *Los Angeles Times,* October 18, 1988.

Luther, Jim. "IRS Expands Use of Computerized Tax Returns; Electronic Filing to Be Available Next Year to Professional Preparers in 14 States." *Washington Post,* June 10, 1987.

Meyer, Gene. "E-Z Tax Filing; The Internet Makes It Cheaper, Faster for Some to Fill Out Their Form 1040." *Kansas City Star,* February 6, 2000.

Reid, T. R. "Form 1040 Would Never Be Missed; IRS Might Let Taxpayers File by Computer, Instead." *Washington Post,* April 14, 1985.

U.S. Department of the Treasury. Internal Revenue Service. "IRS Releases 2010 Data Book." Washington, DC, March 14, 2011. Available from http://www.irs.gov/newsroom/article/0,,id=237393,00.html.

———. "E-file Rejects." Washington, DC, June 2011. Available from http://www.irs.gov/pub/irs-utl/8_panel.pdf.

———. "Information for E-file." Washington, DC, August 10, 2011. Available from http://www.irs.gov/efile.

———. "IRS E-file Security, Privacy and Business Standards Mandated as of January 1, 2010." Washington, DC, December 8, 2010. Available from http://www.irs.gov/efile/article/0,,id=201195,00.html.

Waggoner, John. "Electronic Filing Is Perfect but Far From Popular; Agency's Low Tech Can't Keep Up." *USA Today,* March 26, 1990.

Weston, Liz Pulliam. "IRS Considers Plan That Could Allow Marketing Pitches." *Los Angeles Times,* August 15, 2000.

———. "Lax Security Found in IRS Electronic Filing System." *Los Angeles Times,* March 15, 2001.

ELECTRONIC PAYMENT

In the world of e-commerce, electronic payment most commonly refers to the use of a credit or debit card by a consumer to purchase a product or service online. For online merchants to accept credit or debit card numbers as payment, they must use online credit card processing technology that processes payments via online platforms such as the World Wide Web. To alleviate consumer concerns regarding the risk involved in using credit and debit cards online, most online sites use secure electronic transaction specifications that help to protect personal information like credit card numbers.

Like traditional merchants, online businesses also must work in conjunction with an acquiring bank in order to process transactions and obtain cash from credit card purchases. For example, once a consumer at an e-tailer like Threadless.com inputs his or her credit card information as payment, the online merchant uses real-time online processing software to send the information to the acquiring bank. Once the acquiring bank receives the request, it seeks credit card authorization from an acquiring processor, which handles credit card processing, billing, reporting, and settlement services. The acquiring processor transmits the request to the card-issuing bank—the bank that issued the credit card to the consumer—which either responds with an approval or denial code. The acquiring processor then sends the code to the merchant. Despite its complexity, this entire process typically is completed in less than 15 seconds.

E-BILLING

During the late 1990s, a phenomenon known as electronic bill presentment and payment (EBPP) began to grow in popularity. EBPP is a process that allows businesses to bill clients and secure payment via the Internet. Invoices typically are transmitted by an e-mail message that includes a link to an online payment service provider's Web page, which houses more detailed billing information and allows payees to make an electronic payment with a single click. The most popular online payment service provider is CheckFree Corp., which makes money by charging transaction fees to the billing companies. The National Automated Clearing House Association (NACHA) predicted that by 2016, e-bills would be more widely used than traditional paper bills as consumers become more comfortable with security issues and as business-to-business enterprises increase their use of such technology.

In the United States, the Automated Clearing House (ACH) was the chief electronic network for electronic financial transactions. The ACH network worked as a batch-processing, store-and-forward system. A financial institution received transactions throughout the day and processed them at a later time in batch mode. Since ACH transactions were accumulated and sorted by destination for transmission, the process was significantly faster than using paper checks. ACH transactions included direct deposit of payroll, direct payment of consumer bills, business-to-business payments, e-commerce payments, and federal payments. According to NACHA, the entity that governed the ACH network, ACH transactions rose 3.44% in 2010 to more than 19 million.

The proliferation of smartphones and tablet devices in the late 2000s led to innovative developments in e-billing. Not only could consumers rely on their desktop computers to go completely "paperless," devices like the Apple iPhone enabled them to make electronic payments on the go. Along with the devices came software applications (apps) that could be downloaded to the device and used to process electronic payments.

In addition, businesses increasingly adopted mobile payment processing as an alternative to traditional credit and debit transactions. For instance, Starbucks introduced its Starbucks Card Mobile, a system that allowed customers to use their smartphones to pay for their coffee by scanning two-dimensional bar codes. The advent of near field communication (NFC) further simplified electronic payment transactions by enabling consumers to conclude payments with two smartphones in close proximity to each other. NFC worked by engaging a short-range, low-power communications protocol between two devices. One device acted as the initiator, using magnet induction to create a radio-wave field that the second device could detect. Users could tap their phones against an NFC-enabled payment terminal to complete an electronic payment transaction.

VULNERABILITIES

While electronic payments were in widespread use by the early 2010s, the technology was vulnerable. Hackers and others interested in unlawfully gaining access to user information, including bank accounts, could do so with relative ease. The Federal Trade Commission offered a number of ways consumers could recognize and avoid such fraud:

- Secure browser—Use a secure browser with encryption software that scrambles purchase information sent over the Internet.
- Privacy policies—Determine if a Web site will share consumer information with other parties.
- Shipping policies—Double-check disclosures about a site's shipping and refund policies.
- Personal information—Consumers should not disclose their personal information unless they know who collects it and for what purposes.
- Payment information—Consumers should only give payment information to parties they know and trust.
- Keep records—Consumers can avoid potential problems by keeping good records of online transactions, as well as checking e-mail for merchant contacts.
- Review statements—Consumers should review their monthly credit card and bank statements for potential errors.

SEE ALSO *Authorizaton and Authorization Code; Card-Issuing Bank; Charge-back; Interchange and Interchange Fee.*

BIBLIOGRAPHY

"EBPP." In *Webopedia.* Darien, CT, 2001. Available from http://www.webopedia.com/TERM/E/EBPP.html.

"EBPP." In *Techencyclopedia,* Point Pleasant, PA, 2001. Available from http://www.techweb.com/encyclopedia.

Federal Trade Commission. Bureau of Consumer Protection. "Facts for Consumers." Washington, DC, March 2003. Available from http://www.ftc.gov/bcp/edu/pubs/consumer/tech/tec01.shtm.

Greenberg, Paul A. "One Year Ago: CheckFree Acquires TransPoint for $1B+." *E-Commerce Times,* February 14, 2001. Available from http://www.ecommercetimes.com/story/7402.html.

National Automated Clearing House Association. "Introduction to NACHA." Herndon, VA. Available from http://www.nacha.org/c/aboutus.cfm.

Nosowitz, Dan. "Everything You Need to Know About Near Field Communication." *Popular Science,* March 1, 2011. Available from http://www.popsci.com/gadgets/article/2011-02/near-field-communication-helping-your-smartphone-replace-your-wallet-2010.

Van Grove, Jennifer. "How Starbucks Is Paving the Way for Mainstream Mobile Payments." *Mashable,* June 28, 2011. Available from http://mashable.com/2011/06/28/starbucks-mobile-pay-tech.

ELECTRONIC PRIVACY INFORMATION CENTER

Founded in 1994, the Washington, D.C.-based non-profit Electronic Privacy Information Center (EPIC) serves as a clearinghouse to disseminate information concerning the protection of Internet users' privacy. Its founder and executive director, Marc Rotenburg, created the organization to address perceived Internet privacy violations committed by both the government and businesses that operate Web sites.

EPIC's Web site includes Internet privacy news, the organization's newsletter, details on pending legislation, and other items (books, lectures) concerning "emerging privacy and civil liberties issues." The site's privacy section includes information about securing online privacy in the workplace, eliminating spam and junk mail, and protecting one's Social Security number. Finally, the site furnishes an annotated listing of relevant organizations, print publications, national and international Web sites, privacy tools, and electronic newsgroups.

POLICY INITIATIVES

EPIC makes frequent use of the Freedom of Information Act (FOIA) in its online privacy litigation. Among its targets have been the Federal Bureau of Investigation, National Security Agency, Federal Trade Commission, the State Department, and the Department of Commerce. EPIC has used similar tactics against members of online industries. For example, it filed several federal complaints against the online social media firm Facebook arguing for stronger user privacy protections. The center spoke out against the company's use or proposed use of facial recognition software, user phone numbers, home addresses, and user location tracking, among other efforts. Facebook reined in many of its initiatives as a result of the complaints. For instance, the company adopted a limited opt-in mechanism for its advertising system.

Other EPIC targets included airport body scanners. The center obtained technical specifications and vendor contracts for the scanners in an effort that eventually led to a Congressional investigation and hearings. EPIC recommended suspending the controversial program.

As evidenced in its work regarding Facebook and airport body scanners, EPIC's work spanned a range of industries. In the late 2000s, the center urged the Supreme Court to protect the privacy of cell phone text messages and urged an update to Constitutional safeguards for mobile devices. It also recommended—to Secretary of State Hillary Clinton—the establishment of an international convention on privacy protection and urged the federal government to create privacy safeguards for users of cloud-based government services.

EPIC additionally engaged online search portal Google on a variety of fronts. It appeared in federal court to argue in favor of the privacy rights of users of Google Books, and monitored that company's Google Street View project. The latter began in 2007 as an effort to photograph and catalog location information for addresses around the world. EPIC, among other consumer groups, filed a complaint with the Federal Communications Commission over the project's privacy implications (namely, that the company was obtaining vast amounts of Wi-Fi data from receivers concealed in its Street View vehicles).

Other EPIC endeavors included extending safeguards in the Children's Online Privacy Protection Act, urging federal agencies not to exempt themselves from the Federal Privacy Act, and organizing a conference, "The Public Voice: Global Privacy Standards for a Global World."

POST-9/11

In the wake of the terrorist attacks of September 11, 2001, EPIC became increasingly involved in public privacy advocacy, particularly in the arenas of public surveillance cameras and e-mail tapping. Two-thirds of Americans said they would not mind sacrificing some privacy in the fight against terrorism, according to a 2011 poll conducted by the Associated Press and NORC Center for Public Affairs Research. However, 54 percent indicated they would choose civil liberties when faced with the options of either preserving their rights or protecting people from terrorists. While Americans were surprisingly willing to accept new surveillance techniques after September 11, 2001, EPIC executive director Rotenberg said in 2011 that citizens felt less inclined to support such measures a decade later.

SEE ALSO *Electronic Frontier Foundation; Privacy: Issues, Policies, Statements.*

BIBLIOGRAPHY

Agiesta, Jennifer. "Poll: OK to Trade Some Freedoms to Fight Terrorism." *Associated Press,* September 6, 2011. Available from http://www.google.com/hostednews/ap/article/ALeqM5gBaK0p622wltcxOYy-OUf-TMqAbQ?docId=26bb3fd43ba6461b80a86faedb2f3c22.

Awe, Susan. "Electronic Privacy Information Center." *Library Journal,* October 1, 2000.

Electronic Privacy Information Center. "2010 EPIC Brochure." Available from http://epic.org/epic/2010_EPIC_Brochure.pdf.

———. "About EPIC." Washington, DC, 2011. Available from http://epic.org/epic/about.html.

Harrison, Ann. "Privacy Group Critical of Release of Carnivore Data." *Computerworld,* October 9, 2000.

Harrison, Ann, and Kathleen Ohlson. "Advocates: Sites Still Don't Protect Privacy." *Computerworld,* January 3, 2000.

Stepanek, Marcia. "Marc Rotenberg." *Business Week,* May 15, 2000.

Weiss, Todd. "Bush Faces His First Privacy Challenge." *Computerworld,* January 22, 2001.

ELECTRONIC PUBLISHING

Electronic publishing refers to the publication of books in an electronic format, which a reader can then view on a laptop, tablet computer, or electronic reading device. Electronic publishing was slow to take off because of the flaws of early electronic readers, but it became much more popular with the introduction of Amazon's Kindle, Barnes and Noble's Nook, and Apple's iPad. By 2011, e-books made up a major share of publishers' revenue. The Association of American Publishers reported that American publishers had earned $387.9 million from e-book sales during the first five months of the year, out of $2,967.5 million in total book sales in that time. This placed the e-book market second only to the adult paperback market, which had sales of $473.1 million for the period. E-book sales were expected to continue rising rapidly during the 2010s, while print book revenues were expected to shrink.

EARLY ELECTRONIC BOOK PUBLISHING: 1998–2001

Electronic books, or e-books, became available at the retail level in 1998. That year, e-book readers—the lightweight, paperback book-sized electronic devices used to display e-books—were released by NuvoMedia Inc. and Softbook Press Inc. Both readers allowed users to highlight, bookmark, and annotate specific passages, and to search an entire document. Many e-books also were accessible via a standard personal computer (PC). NuvoMedia and Softbook sold a total of roughly 10,000 e-book readers in 1999. At the time, less than 5,000 titles were available electronically.

At roughly the same time, Barnesandnoble.com and Microsoft began working on their own e-book reader for PCs, and another e-book hardware manufacturer, Glassbook, disclosed similar plans. Via an agreement with publisher Simon & Schuster, celebrated author Stephen King released a new novella as an e-book that spring.

However, by the end of the year, only 25,000 e-book reading devices had been sold, and e-book sales were less than $5 million. Along with sluggish demand, the e-book industry was also forced to deal with limited supplies. E-book availability was growing at a much slower pace than e-book reading device makers had anticipated. In March 2001, the number of e-books compatible with Gemstar's RocketBook—the industry's leading platform—had reached only a few thousand. Concerned that e-book sales might undermine print sales, particularly on new releases likely to make the best-seller lists, many publishers were only willing to offer electronic versions of classics like *Moby Dick* and *Romeo and Juliet.*

Incompatible formats posed another problem for the e-book industry. By the end of 2000, each of the three e-book industry leaders—Gemstar, Adobe, and Microsoft—was working to position its format as the industry standard. This left many publishers leery about committing to any single format, and many decided to wait and see which format proved dominant before investing in the e-book industry. For the same reason, consumers resisted spending money on e-book reading devices, most of which could read only one format.

Copyright issues also proved daunting to many publishers. Despite legislation like the Digital Millennium Copyright Act—which made the manufacture or sale of products designed to dodge copyright laws illegal—many publishers were unsure how to go about protecting copyrighted books offered electronically. At the same time, publishers unwilling to release electronic versions of their copyrighted books also worked to prohibit other companies from doing so.

TABLET PC: 2002

In November 2002, Microsoft announced that its e-book reader project was complete, and Tablet PCs were now available. Tablet PCs used Microsoft's Reader software, which allowed users to both read books on these devices and write on the tablets with an electronic pen. *Publishing Trends* reported that the Tablet PCs were originally priced at around $2,500, which could be too expensive for many customers, but Microsoft planned on initially marketing the Tablet PCs to wealthy customers who wanted early access to new technological trends.

Sales grew throughout 2003, although competing software formats were still delaying widespread e-book adoption. Established publishers remained relatively unconcerned. Although e-books were heavily hyped during the dot-com bubble, analysts' predictions that e-books would replace print had not materialized. A December 2003 *Canadian Printer* article reported that it was difficult to determine the total amount of e-book revenue that was earned in 2003, because the initial industry survey reported values for both the retail and publishing businesses, and some companies were active in both sectors. However, the total revenue from e-book sales was still under $10 million for the first six months of 2003.

Publishers also reported gradually increasing revenues for 2004, as more recent fiction books became available. Dan Brown's fiction books were popular, including the year's best-selling e-book, *The Da Vinci Code,* as well as his books *Angels and Demons* and *Deception Point,* reported the International Digital Publishing Forum.

ACADEMIC EBOOKS: 2005

In 2005, higher education institutions started offering e-books to their students. These books were pitched as a way for students to conserve money, because the e-books had lower list prices than print texts. These academic e-books were controversial because the student would lose access to the e-book after the class was over, which prevented the student from reselling the book, a common practice among university students. *CNET* reported that the e-book format also made it much more difficult for a student to share a book with his fellow students, because the book could only be accessed on a single reader.

NEW PRODUCTS

The widely anticipated November 2007 launch of the Kindle by Amazon.com introduced a device that showed major improvements over its predecessors. The *Daily Beast* reported that the Kindle weighed less than a pound, had a battery that could run for 30 hours, and clearly displayed text on its small screen. Unlike many earlier e-readers, the Kindle was also equipped with mobile communication technology, which was a major factor in its success. Amazon.com had arranged deals with major news publishers so the Kindle could download and display articles that covered current events, as well as serving as an e-book platform. Its $399 introduction price was much lower than earlier e-readers that had cost thousands of dollars.

E-book sales grew much more rapidly after the introduction of the Kindle, while print sales were falling. Barnes and Noble needed a strategy that would help it compete with the Internet-based Amazon.com, which was dominating the market with its Kindle. As the Kindle used proprietary formats and did not allow readers to share e-books, the Barnes and Noble's Nook included a sharing option that a publisher could authorize. The Kindle had a relatively utilitarian appearance, so the Nook included cosmetic improvements, such as a color touchscreen. The Nook was initially priced at $260, although by this point the Kindle was also available at this price. *Wired* reported that Barnes and Noble had also integrated the Nook with its physical stores, including mobile communication technology that allowed a Nook user to browse through Barnes and Noble's offerings while he or she was inside a retail store.

Unlike the Nook and the Kindle, Apple's iPad was not designed to serve solely as an e-reader. An iPad is a tablet computer that is larger and heavier than a dedicated reader, offers additional storage capacity and graphics display capabilities, and comes with a higher price tag. The iPad also runs Apple's mobile applications, one of which, iBooks, allows it to function as an e-reader. The iPad was marketed toward Apple enthusiasts who were willing to pay higher prices for a better reading experience. *Mashable* reported that the initial $499 price for the basic iPad was comparable to the Kindle DX at $489, and it included features which this high-end version of the Kindle did not offer.

E-PUBLISHING IN THE 2010s

Amazon.com issued a press release in May 2011 stating that its Kindle book sales had been outpacing its sales of traditional books in the United States since the beginning of April. The preference for Kindle books was even greater in the United Kingdom, where Amazon announced that its e-books had accounted for more than twice as many sales as print books during the period.

Google planned to expand its search offerings by allowing its users to search through the texts of printed books, so it hired employees who traveled to libraries, scanned those book collections with electronic readers, and then uploaded the documents to Google's Web site. Google believed that it was safe from copyright infringement because the books that it was scanning had copyrights that had already expired. When the Authors Guild, a trade organization that represents writers, found its writers' protected works on the site, it organized other publishers and filed a class-action lawsuit against Google, which Google agreed to settle for $125 million. As part of the settlement agreement, Google agreed to establish an online royalty payment system for writers (similar to the royalty system that the music industry used) which allowed authors to collect royalties when readers purchased access to their books through Google's Web site.

This settlement was later blocked by a federal judge, according to the *Washington Post,* because it would automatically consider authors to be members of the royalty arrangement unless they told Google that they objected, and the Authors Guild was working on a new settlement with Google that was expected to be announced in September 2011.

In 2011, Amazon.com looked toward the online video rental industry to develop a new publishing model, announcing that it planned to offer e-book rentals under a subscription service. Subscribers would gain the right to check out and read the books in Amazon.com's library while their subscription was current. This model had been successfully implemented by music publishers, according to *CBS News,* but some book publishers were worried that it could eat into their paperback sales and damage their relationships with retailers who operated brick-and-mortar bookstores.

SEE ALSO *Amazon.com; Barnesandnoble.com; E-Books; E-Zines.*

BIBLIOGRAPHY

Amazon.com. "Amazon.com Now Selling More Kindle Books Than Print Books." Seattle, WA, May 19, 2011. Available from http://phx.corporate-ir.net/phoenix.zhtml?ID=1565581&c=176060&p=irol-newsArticle.

"Authors Sue Universities, Say Unauthorized Online Books Being Scanned for Use." *Washington Post,* September 12, 2011. Available from http://www.washingtonpost.com/local/education/authors-sue-universities-say-unauthorized-online-books-being-scanned-for-use/2011/09/12/gIQADY6vNK_story.html.

Blount Jr., Ray. "$125 Million Settlement in Authors Guild vs. Google." Authors Guild, October 28, 2008. Available from http://www.authorsguild.org/advocacy/articles/member-alert-google.html.

Borland, John. "Coming to Campus: E-books with Expiration Dates." *CNET,* August 9, 2005. Available from http://news.cnet.com/2100-1025_3-5825301.html.

Brady, Diane. "Six Parties a Night? It's a Living." *BusinessWeek Online,* April 3, 2000. Available from http://www.businessweek.com/archives/2000/b3675163.arc.htm.

Catone, Josh. "4 Reasons the Kindle Is Dead, 4 Reasons It's Not."*Mashable,* January 27, 2010. Available from http://mashable.com/2010/01/27/kindle-dead-ipad.

Earnshaw, Aliza. "Making Money's the Big Challenge Online." *Business Journal* (Portland, OR), August 3, 2001.

Garber, Joseph R. "Publish and Perish." *Forbes,* October 16, 2000.

Hendley, Nate. "Seeing Through the E-book Threat." *Canadian Printer,* December 2003. Available from http://www.natehendley.com/writing/nh_sample4.html.

Kafka, Peter. "Horror Story." *Forbes,* August 21, 2000.

Katz, Amanda. "How We Read Now." *Boston.com,* July 17, 2011. Available from http://articles.boston.com/2011-07-17/yourtown/29784807_1_e-books-book-sales-e-reader.

Levy, Steven. "The Future of Reading."*Daily Beast,* November 17, 2007. Available from http://www.thedailybeast.com/newsweek/2007/11/17/the-future-of-reading.html.

Lombreglia, Ralph. "Exit Gutenberg?" *Atlantic Online,* November 16, 2000. Available from http://www.theatlantic.com/past/docs/unbound/digitalreader/dr2000-11-16.htm.

Manes, Stephen. "Electronic Page-Turners." *Forbes,* May 28, 2001.

Ngak, Chenda. "Amazon Might Add E-book Lending Service That's Sort of Like Netflix." *CBS News,* September 12, 2011. Available from http://www.cbsnews.com/8301-501465_162-20104791-501465.html.

Peek, Robin. "Jump-Starting Electronic Books." *Information Today,* March 2000.

Sporkin, Andi. "Paperback and E-books Rank #1, #2 in Trade Market While K-12 School Curriculum Market Shows Growth in AAP Publishers' May 2011 Report." Washington, DC, Association of American Publishers, July 21, 2011. Available from http://www.publishers.org/press/41.

"Tablet PC, the E-book Savior?"*Publishing Trends,* December 2002. Available from http://www.publishingtrends.com/2002/12/tablet-pc-the-ebook-savior.

"Top Selling eBooks of 2004 Announced." International Digital Publishing Forum, January 12, 2005. Available from http://old.idpf.org/pressroom/pressreleases/2004bestsellers.htm.

Van Buskirk, Eliot. "Barnes & Noble's Shiny, Sharing-Friendly 'Nook' E-book Reader." *Wired,* October 20, 2009. Available from http://www.wired.com/epicenter/2009/10/barnes-noble-unveils-nook-ebook-reader-again.

Wood, Christina. "The Myth of E-books." *PC Magazine,* July 1, 2001.

ELLISON, LAWRENCE J. (LARRY)

Lawrence J. (Larry) Ellison is founder and CEO of Oracle Corp., one of the world's largest software companies. Serving as CEO since the firm's inception in 1977, Ellison steered its initial growth as a database software maker and its eventual move into e-commerce. In late 2011, he owned 22% of Oracle's stock, which has made him one of the richest men in the world.

START OF ORACLE

Ellison cofounded Oracle with fellow computer programmer Robert N. Miner in Belmont, California. The partners used their combined experience in specialized database program design to convince the Central Intelligence Agency (CIA) to hire them to build a $50,000 customized database program. It was while working for the CIA that Ellison recognized the potential profit in IBM's efforts to develop a relational database, using Structured Query Language (SQL), that would allow users to pull corporate data from various sources. Ellison and Miner beat IBM to the market by nearly two years when they launched Oracle RDBMS, the world's first relational database using SQL, in 1978.

When Ellison took Oracle public in 1986, the firm had become one of the fastest-growing software companies in the world, as well as the world's leading database management software maker. The 10-year-old company had $55 million in annual revenues and 450 employees at that time. (Twenty years later, Oracle had 65,000 workers and revenues exceeding $15 billion.)

Ellison began to focus his firm on the Internet in 1998. According to *Business Week Online* columnist Sam Jaffe, "Back then, some experts argued that the database software market Oracle dominates would quickly erode as companies found cheaper and simpler ways of managing their data on the Web. Instead the opposite happened—after CEO Larry Ellison ordered an 'Internetization' of his company." Not only did Oracle begin manufacturing products that allowed users to manage data from the World Wide Web, it also began using this e-business technology to streamline its own operations. It was this shift in direction that allowed Oracle to outperform many of its competitors through the end of 2000.

ORACLE IN THE 2000S

Beginning in 2004, Ellison grew Oracle largely through a strategy of acquiring direct competitors and complementary products. The company spent $25 billion in three years to support that strategy. From its inception through September 2011, Oracle had acquired 75 companies valued at $400 billion and had a market capitalization of $146.5 billion. Major deals included the 2010 acquisition of Sun Microsystems for $7.4 billion; $10.3 billion for PeopleSoft in 2005 (which included the J.D. Edwards software line); $5.85 billion in 2006 for Siebel Systems; $3.3 billion in 2007 for Hyperion; and $8.5 billion in 2008 for BEA Systems.

The acquisitions of PeopleSoft and Siebel systems in particular helped launch a period of software industry consolidation. While Oracle began with a focus on databases, it has relied heavily on acquisitions as it expanded further into enterprise resource planning (ERP), customer relationship (CRM) and supply chain management (SCM), application development, enterprise collaboration, and middleware software.

By 2007, Oracle had already become the third-largest software company by revenues, trailing only Microsoft and IBM. As analysts wondered what software companies were left to buy, Oracle branched into hardware with its 2010 Sun Microsystems acquisition. Sun built its reputation as a provider of server hardware during the boom times of the dot-com era, later developing the popular Java programming language that is easily portable across multiple operating platforms. IBM had been expected to acquire Sun but IBM reportedly did not offer terms that appealed to the Sun board of directors, providing an opening for Oracle. The Sun deal represented a reversal in strategy for Ellison, who in 2003 had called a possible Oracle-Sun deal "a bad idea." He also told Oracle stockholders that fall, "I don't think Oracle should be in the hardware business, so I don't think you'll see us buying any hardware companies."

ORACLE IN THE 2010s

By 2011, Oracle began to cut back on its acquisitions, focusing on smaller niche deals rather than large blockbuster mergers. The reduced strategy was partially a reaction to the poor economic climate and partly driven by a need to focus on integrating the Sun Microsystems acquisition. However, Oracle was widely expected to eventually resume its deal-making tradition—particularly after adding Mark Hurd, the former CEO of Hewlett-Packard and a long-time Ellison friend, as Oracle copresident in 2010.

During the twenty-first century, Ellison usually ranked in the Top 10 on the annual *Forbes* list of the world's richest people. He ranked fifth in 2011 with an estimated net worth of $39.5 billion. He is one of the highest-paid executives in the United States. Although his salary at Oracle was only $1, Ellison received $960 million from 2005 to 2010 alone by exercising Oracle stock options. Ellison also reportedly plans to give 95% of his wealth to charity.

Ellison invested heavily to support his sporting interests, tennis and sailing. He paid $100 million in 2009 to acquire the BNP Paribaas Open tennis tournament. The tournament was close to being sold and moved overseas from its longtime home in California before Ellison stepped in and kept the major competition in the United States. According to his *Forbes* profile, Ellison also spent $100 million on a 10-year campaign to win the America's Cup yachting competition, which he captured in 2010.

SEE ALSO *Database Management; Oracle Corp.*

BIBLIOGRAPHY

Bergman, Ben. "Oracle CEO Ellison Saves Tennis' BNP Paribas Open." *National Public Radio,* March 18, 2011. Available from http://www.wbur.org/npr/134646327/Oracle-CEO-Ellison-Saves-PNP-Paribas-Tennis-Tournament.

Brodkin, Jon. "Oracle's Larry Ellison Sailing Team Wins America's Cup." *Network World,* February 16, 2010. Available from http://www.networkworld.com/news/2010/021610-larry-ellison-americas-cup.html.

Cox, John. "Oracle Eats Its Own E-business Dog Food." *Network World,* July 17, 2000.

Jaffe, Sam. "Oracle: A B2B Rebirth That Few Foretold." *BusinessWeek Online,* April 6, 2000. Available from http://www.businessweek.com/ebiz/0004/es0406.htm.

Kanaracus, Chris. "Oracle Moves Away from Big Acquisitions." *InfoWorld,* May 24, 2011. Available from http://www.infoworld.com/d/the-industry-standard/oracle-moves-away-big-acquisitions-956.

"Larry Ellison." *Forbes,* March 2011. Available from http://people.forbes.com/profile/larry-ellison/60466

"Larry Ellison Profile." *Forbes,* March 2011.

"Lawrence J. Ellison." Washington, DC: Academy of Achievement, 2011. Available from http://www.achievement.org/autodoc/page/ell0bio-1.

Skillings, Jonathan. "Oracle to Buy Sun in $7.4 Billion Deal." *CNET,* April 20, 2009. Available from http://news.cnet.com/8301-1001_3-10223044-92.html.

Slywotzky, Adrian. "Four Lessons from Larry: Ellison Was Late in Reshaping Oracle for the Net. But When He Did It, He Did It Fast. Here's How." *Fortune,* March 5, 2001.

E-MAIL

Electronic messages sent over a network are known as e-mail. Users may send messages to a single recipient or to a group of several recipients anywhere in the world. In many cases, messages are transmitted along high-speed data communications networks in a matter of seconds. Once a message is received, a user may view it, save it, delete it, or forward it to other recipients. E-mail programs consist of two main components: the store-and-forward messaging system and the send-and-receive interface, which is what a user sees when working with an e-mail program. The text itself usually is in ASCII format and sent via Simple Mail Transfer Protocol (SMTP). Advances in technology like Multipurpose Internet Mail Extensions (MIME) allow e-mail users to attach files—including graphics, audio files, word processing documents, spreadsheets, and even executable programs—to their messages for recipients to open on their machines.

HISTORY

The first e-mail message was sent by Ray Tomlinson in 1971. Tomlinson came up with the idea for e-mail when he was working for Bolt Beranek and Newman, a Cambridge, Massachusetts-based research and development outfit. The firm was contracted in 1968 by the U.S. Department of Defense to construct ARPAnet, a network that would allow the government to have messaging capabilities in the event of nuclear war. To create his e-mail program, Tomlinson used a rudimentary file transfer protocol known as CYPNET along with SNDMSG, an electronic messaging system that allowed users of a single machine to leave messages for each other on that machine. He decided to use the @ (pronounced "at") symbol to identify messages that were going to be sent along the network to another machine. When Tomlinson sent his new e-mail program to other ARPAnet users, who loaded it onto their computers, e-mail essentially was born. However, it was not until years later that Tomlinson and his colleagues recognized just how widespread e-mail could become as a communications tool for educational, social, and commercial endeavors.

The Internet, which eventually replaced ARPAnet, had an immeasurable impact on e-mail technology. Although Internet-based e-mail programs emerged in the 1980s, most simply allowed local area network (LAN) users to communicate with one another. It was not until the 1990s that e-mail truly began to evolve into the open communications system it is today.

E-MAIL IN THE 2010s

According to the Radicati Group, the number of global e-mail accounts was 2.9 billion in 2010, the majority of which were free or low-cost consumer accounts. Three-quarters of e-mail accounts belonged to consumers, and the balance to corporate users. The Asia/Pacific region accounted for the largest concentration of the world's e-mail accounts (47%), followed by Europe (23%), North America (14%), and the rest of the world (16%).

This method of quickly and easily communicating with large numbers of people is not without complications. One major issue for many e-mail users is the amount of unsolicited advertisements, commonly known as spam, they receive. Many companies and individuals purchase huge mailing lists of e-mail addresses from various information sources and send unwanted advertisements or solicitations to recipients. In some cases these advertisements are legal, and in other cases they are not, but the senders are quite often very difficult to trace. Many proprietary e-mail programs, such as those offered to workers by an employer, include filtering technology that helps to block spam. Users of freely available Internet-based mail services, such as Yahoo! and Hotmail, are more likely to receive spam. Fighting spam can be a considerable expense for many corporations. A typical 1,000-member company may spend as much as $3 million a year to manage spam, according to the Radicati Group.

Another problem inherent in an open communication system like e-mail is the ease with which viruses (or malware) can be spread via e-mail message attachments. Many virus programs are disguised as attached files from colleagues or friends. Once they are unwittingly opened by a recipient, the virus reads the recipient's address book and forwards the virus on to each user in that address book. As the e-mail looks as though it was sent by the victim of the virus, the likelihood that future recipients will open the disguised virus is quite high. An entire industry of malware-blocking software manufacturers has risen out of the need to prevent spam and viruses. In August 2011, nearly 200 million network attacks were blocked, 64 million Web-borne viruses were prevented, and 258 million malicious programs were detected and neutralized on user computers, according to Kaspersky Lab.

MOBILE TECHNOLOGY

The proliferation of smartphones and electronic tablet devices in the late 2000s made sending and receiving e-mail possible from practically anywhere in the world, assuming a cell phone or satellite connection was available. This development carried weighty implications for e-mail technology, as smartphone shipments were anticipated to surpass personal computers in the 2010s. In 2010, 85% of smartphone users checked their e-mail on their devices. Some 35% made at least one purchase from an e-mail sent via smartphone, and nearly all smartphone users accessed the same e-mail account on their devices as they did on their computers, according to ExactTarget.

Even while e-mail has penetrated virtually all sectors of modern society, it nonetheless faces new challenges from social networking tools like Facebook and Twitter. Users of these social media tools often rely more on communicating through their networks than on e-mail to stay in touch. According to comScore's *2010 U.S. Digital Year in Review,* usage of Web-based e-mail declined 1.5% between 2009 and 2010, to 11% of time spent in online leisure activities. Conversely, search portals commanded the highest share of time spent (20.2%), followed by social networking (14.4%) and entertainment (12.6%). "As communication platforms and devices continue to proliferate, the usage of Web-based e-mail has begun to decline, particularly among younger segments of consumers who are increasingly shifting towards instant messaging, social media, and mobile communications," according to the report.

SEE ALSO *ARPAnet; E-mail Marketing; History of the Internet and World Wide Web (WWW).*

BIBLIOGRAPHY

Campbell, Todd. "The First E-mail Message." *PreText,* March 1998.

comScore. *2010 U.S. Digital Year in Review.* Reston, VA, February 7, 2011. Available from http://www.comscore.com/Press_Events/Presentations_Whitepapers/2011/2010_US_Digital_Year_in_Review.

"E-mail." *Webopedia,* 2001. Available from http://www.webopedia.com/TERM/E/e_mail.html.

"E-mail." *Techencyclopedia,* 2001. Available from http://www.techweb.com/encyclopedia.

"E-mail or Email." *NetLingo,* 2006. Available from http://www.netlingo.com/word/e-mail-or-email.php.

Gostev, Alexander. "Monthly Malware Statistics: August 2011." Kaspersky Lab, September 8, 2011. Available from http://www.securelist.com/en/analysis/204792190/Monthly_Malware_Statistics_August_2011.

The Radicati Group. "Email Statistics Report, 2010." Palo Alto, CA, April 2010. Available from http://www.radicati.com/wp/wp-content/uploads/2010/04/Email-Statistics-Report-2010-2014-Executive-Summary2.pdf.

Stewart, Morgan. "Statistics for Email Use on Smartphones." *ExactTarget Blog,* July 30, 2010. Available from http://blog.exacttarget.com/blog/morgan-stewart/statistics-for-email-use-on-smartphones.

Vicom Technology Ltd. "A Brief History of Email." Kirkland, WA, 2001. Available from http://www.vicomsoft.com/learning-center/history-of-email/.

E-MAIL MARKETING

The term e-mail marketing covers a wide range of e-mail used to deliver commercial messages. It includes e-mail newsletters that deliver news, information, or content that people have specifically requested. These newsletters typically contain advertising messages targeted to the interests of the newsletters' readers. At the other end of the e-mail marketing spectrum is unsolicited bulk e-mail, often referred to as "spam."

When e-mail became a part of people's daily routine, using it as a marketing medium became an opportunity that marketers could not afford to ignore. According to a mid-2011 Pew Internet survey, 92% of adult Internet users send or read e-mail, and 66% do so on a daily basis. Another survey conducted in 2011 estimated there were 3.1 billion e-mail accounts worldwide, with that number estimated to swell to 4 billion by 2015. According to the Pew survey, e-mail is still the most popular online activity in 2010, as it has been for over a decade, with e-mail use outstripping search engine use by 7%.

eMail Marketing Reports reported that e-mail message volume increased from 536.3 billion annually in 2000 to 294 billion every day in 2010.

E-MAIL MARKETING VS. OTHER DIRECT MARKETING METHODS

Marketers have found that e-mail marketing is often cheaper and more effective than traditional direct marketing methods. A 2010 study by Direct Marketing Association determined the return of investment (ROI) for e-mail campaigns was $42.08 for every dollar spent, second in value only to organic search engine optimization (SEO). A 2009 survey of industry executives found 80% indicated their e-mail marketing channels were performing strongly with almost 40% finding e-mail to be their most effective advertising channel. Shop.org conducted a survey in 2009 which determined that retailers found "email is the most mentioned successful tactic overall." Furthermore, while many advertising methods were showing declining productivity during the recession of the late 2000s, e-mail marketing was still recording improved results according to *Opt-n News.* With such high marks for effectiveness, it is not surprising that expenditures for e-mail marketing rose worldwide from $1.3 billion in 2001 to $13.4 billion in 2009.

E-mail succeeds for a variety of reasons. When properly used it is more targeted and data driven than many traditional forms of advertising. Furthermore, it also builds customer relationships and supports sales efforts through complementary marketing channels. E-mail campaigns are often better able to use technology to capture and track customer responses, thus providing marketers with the metrics needed to learn more about their customers' buying behavior, allowing them to refine and update customer profiles for future communications. The flexibility of e-mail marketing also makes it possible to change an offer quickly, if for example, a special discount does not bring in the desired level of customer traffic.

Businesses wanting to conduct e-mail marketing campaigns can choose from accessing packaged e-mail marketing software or outsourced e-mail marketing services. A company can combine one or both of these technologies with its own customer database to deliver personalized messages based on one or more database attributes and specific e-mailings can be targeted to customer groups based on past purchase and response behavior.

Opt-in e-mail campaigns, in which recipients have asked to receive information, are conducted to achieve different objectives. They can be used to prospect for new customers outside of a company's established customer base. The low cost of e-mail makes it possible to test market new products and services more quickly and inexpensively. E-mail marketing campaigns also are used to drive traffic to a company's Web site.

OPT-IN AND OPT-OUT METHODS

"Opt-in" and "opt-out" are two kinds of privacy mechanisms that have been adapted to e-mail marketing. With the opt-in method, consumers must actively agree to receive commercial e-mail messages, usually by clicking a box or making some other type of positive response. Under this system, consumers only receive commercial e-mail messages after they have expressly given their permission. Therefore, opt-in e-mail lists consist only of e-mail addresses for individuals who have given their permission to receive commercial e-mail messages. Double opt-in means that, after giving their permission, consumers must also send in a confirming e-mail.

Under the opt-out method, consumers are given the option of not receiving any further promotional e-mails after they have already received one. Under this system, messages are sent to individuals until they ask to be removed from the mailing list. A similar system, known as passive consent or negative opt-in, allows marketers to add consumers to their lists if they do not click or unclick a checkbox on a Web page in order to avoid receiving commercial e-mail.

BEST PRACTICES IN E-MAIL MARKETING

Overuse of low-quality unsolicited e-mail marketing campaigns are sighted by 55% of marketers as a serious threat to the e-marketing industry. Everyone, executive decision makers in particular, complains about e-mail boxes groaning with unsolicited or "spam" messages. As a result, ISP services have installed sophisticated filters to screen out much of this undesirable traffic, sometimes deleting even desired messages. Therefore, the bar to achieve e-mail marketing success is continually being set higher, with more sophisticated techniques continually being required to improve sales.

All e-mail marketing campaigns attempt to drive higher the most frequently cited industry metric, "customer conversion rate," and specific practices which accomplish this are closely tracked. For example, while some e-mail marketing techniques have declined in effectiveness, opt-in systems providing regular e-mail newsletters are still one of the most valuable techniques used in e-mail marketing. Opt-in lists are highly targeted and many online suppliers of these lists can make a good living from such a list containing as few as 5,000 e-mail addresses. Users have developed sophisticated methods of approaching their clients, such as sending only relevant textual ads closely tied to the area of interest covered by the newsletter.

Some owners of large e-mail lists do not attempt to sell any products through their lists directly; instead, they use the list to drive traffic to their Web sites where users can click on advertising displayed adjacent to the news content.

Other practices which produce improved e-mail marketing revenue include:

- "cross-selling," where buyers are sent a message postpurchase regarding related products
- "marketing integration," combining e-mail sales efforts with other channel operations
- use of personalized welcome messages to new opt-in subscribers
- effective analysis of buyer metrics, such as click through rates, to guide future performance

One report found that closely tracking buyer analytics can bring 9 times the sales and 18 times the profits realized by using untargeted e-mail marketing methods.

NEW FRONTIERS FOR E-MAIL MARKETING

Higher processor and internet server speeds have permitted increasing complexity in e-mail marketing. One emerging innovation is the use of Flash technology, a technique which allows steaming video clips and animation to be embedded in marketing e-mails. Since almost 100% of Internet users, and increasing numbers of 3G and 4G mobile device users, have Flash players, the use of Flash has become a means to construct an e-mail advertising campaign that stands out from conventional competition. Flash can be an excellent format for getting a message across quickly; the old adage "a picture is worth a thousand words" is even more true for animation. Frequent uses for Flash technology include product demonstrations or introductions of key company personnel.

E-mail or digital couponing is an area of expanding growth for e-marketing. A fragile world economy has led to a resurgence of interest in this traditional marketing technique. A growing list of online and e-mail coupon marketing now complements the traditional "cut and clip" providers. Leaders in this field include Coupons.-com, SmartSource.com, and Redplum.com.

Group buying is an area of exploding e-marketing growth. Using viral marketing concepts and social media Web sites, companies such as Groupon.com allow buyers to purchase goods at a special discount once a certain number of transactions are accumulated. This method encourages buyers to socialize the deal through e-mail or other social messaging, thus "advertising" the item or service through a network of friends or acquaintances. Facebook is fast becoming a mecca for such marketing techniques, including retail giants like Wal-Mart. Wal-Mart launched its own group buying concept on Facebook called "Crowdsaver," which requires a minimum number of participants (often 5,000) to lock the price of an item available on Walmart.com.

Unquestionably the biggest opportunity to come in e-mail marketing since the rise of the internet is the rapid spread of mobile Internet devices. Coupon and other marketing outlets have not overlooked the marketing value of this new segment of users. Wireless coupons or advertisements can arrive in a variety of forms on this dynamic new environment. From sending coupons via instant or text messages to utilizing the GPS capabilities of wireless devices to deliver advertisements to customers while they walk past an advertiser's outlet, the opportunities for point of sale and targeted marketing represent new opportunities for e-mail and instant message advertising.

REGULATING E-MAIL MARKETING

By 2001, spam was regulated by a patchwork of state laws, some of which were more effective than others. The Coalition Against Unsolicited Commercial E-Mail (CAUCE), an organization that lobbies for federal anti-spam legislation, found that state laws generally were ineffective at stopping spam. CAUCE noted that states must be careful to avoid violating the interstate commerce clause of the U.S. Constitution, which prevents states from placing an undue burden on interstate commerce. These concerns often resulted in weak or no state legislation of commercial e-mail.

In 2003, the U.S. Congress passed the CAN-SPAM Act, signed into law by President George W. Bush in December of that year. CAN_SPAM established the first national guidelines for the distribution of e-mail advertising and pornography, to be enforced by the Federal Trade Commission. The initial act, and subsequent modifications, allows for the commercial promotion of products or services via e-mail provided they adhere to three basic compliance rules. Under the law, marketers generally must provide means by which receivers may opt-out of e-mail solicitations; meet standards of honesty and accuracy regarding the content of e-mail advertisements; and comply with restrictions on the broadcast method and means of targeting such advertisements. Certain types of messages, such as political and religious communications, were exempt from the legislation. The act did not regulate the communication companies have with established customers, or those who inquire about a company's products or services.

CAN-SPAM makes violations of its rules a misdemeanor offence for most minor transgressions like misleading header lines. A higher level of legal violation called an "aggregated offense" was established for more serious transgressions, such as sending viruses or worms through e-mail communications. In the first year under the law, some studies showed spam e-mail use was down about 10%, but in the early 2010s the effect of the law has widely been considered minimal in the operation of e-mail marketing.

SEE ALSO *Advertising, Online; Business-to-Business (B2B) E-Commerce; Business-to-Consumer (B2C) E-Commerce; E-Mail.*

BIBLIOGRAPHY

Baxter, Alex. "Getting In on the Ground Floor: Digital Couponing and Group Buying." *Minonline.com,* 2011. Available from http://www.minonline.com/minsiders/Alex-Baxter/Getting-in-on-the-Ground-Floor-Digital-Couponing-and-Group-Buying_15653.html.

"Email Marketers Report Success Despite Lagging Economy." *Opt-inNews.com,*2009. Available from http://www.optinnews.com/marketers_report_success.html.

Enos, Lori. "Washington State's Highest Court Upholds Anti-Spam Law." *E-Commerce Times,* June 8, 2001. Available from http://www.ecommercetimes.com/story/11103.html.

Hardigree, Steve. "Opt-In E-mail as Prospecting Source." *DM News,* May 21, 2001.

Iron Mountain. "Can Spam Act: Requirements for Commercial Emailers." Mountain View, CA. Available from http://www.mimosasystems.com/articles/can-spam-act-requirements-for-commercial-emailers.html.

Joffe, Rodney. "Merge/Purge of E-mail Addresses." *DM News,* February 5, 2001.

Melissa. "How Effective Is Email Marketing?" Morristown, NJ: Optimum7, March 11, 2010. Available from http://www.optimum7.com/internet-marketing/direct-marketing/how-effective-is-email-marketing.html.

Regan, Keith. "Walking the Line Between E-mail and Spam." *E-Commerce Times,* April 17, 2001. Available from http://www.ecommercetimes.com/story/8966.html?wlc=1316556953.

Schwartz, John. "Marketers Turn to a Simple Tool: E-Mail." *New York Times,* December 13, 2000.

"U.S. Small Businesses to Spend $2.2 Billion on E-mail Marketing by 2005 According to The Kelsey Group."

PRNewswire, May 22, 2001. Available from http://www.prnewswire.com/news-releases/us-small-businesses-to-spend-22-billion-on-e-mail-marketing-by-2005-according-to-the-kelsey-group-71912257.html.

ENCRYPTION

The Internet is an open and interconnected system that can be both a boon and a hazard to businesses and consumers. On one hand, it makes the act of shopping, comparing, and purchasing extraordinarily quick and convenient. On the other hand, with so many people able to access information and potentially misuse it, there are justified fears about transferring sensitive information, such as credit card numbers and purchasing habits, over the Internet. E-commerce encryption was developed to minimize these hazards so that the benefits of e-commerce can be enjoyed in a more secure manner. Encryption is the scrambling of sensitive information, such as credit card numbers, personal information, legal documents, confidential records, and even personal communications, in such a way that only authorized persons or organizations are able to decipher it.

The main elements of an encryption system are:

- the plain text (unencrypted message)
- the cipher or algorithm (the mathematical rules for how the plain text is to be combined with the key)
- the key (a string of numbers)
- the cipher text (the final encrypted message)

While crude methods of data encryption have existed since the fifth century BCE, modern encryption typically involves processing information with one or more mathematical algorithms, such that it is unintelligible to anyone without the decryption key.

In the early years of e-commerce, frequent incidents of cyberfraud were widely reported and led to a decline in consumer confidence in e-commerce. Fully 37% of e-shoppers in 2005 reported they had stopped engaging in e-commerce out of fear of identity theft. With hundreds of billions of dollars on the line, the e-commerce industry needed to find a relatively foolproof means to prevent spoofing, data alteration, and unauthorized disclosure of sensitive information, particularly credit card numbers, which constitute the payment method used in over 90% of e-commerce transactions.

The pillars of a safe e-commerce transaction are built around four principles:

1. authentication—is the person or organization the customer is dealing with legitimate?
2. integrity—is the data being transferred between the two parties free of tampering?
3. nonrepudiation—prevents either party from denying they ever made or received the particular message
4. privacy

POPULAR ENCRYPTION TECHNOLOGIES

Countless encryption schemes are used throughout the world for commerce, communication, and other purposes. Two types of encryption systems, symmetrical and asymmetrical, offer protection that is secure and simple enough for e-commerce transactions. Symmetrical encryption, or "private key encryption," uses a common key held by all parties to a transaction for encryption and decryption. Asymmetrical encryption, sometimes called "public key encryption," involves the use of more than one key, thus offering greater protection, and has proven over the years more cost effective and secure than its alternative for most types of e-commerce. In asymmetrical encryption, the public key is used to encrypt the message, and a second private key is used for decryption of the message. This system is more secure because knowing how to translate one key does not infer knowing how to translate the other.

An effective public key infrastructure (PKI) involves a "certificate authority (CA)", often a third party, which maintains private key security, and thus prevents unauthorized decryption of online data. RSA, the encryption algorithm common used in PKI, is based on the product of two large prime numbers, which is sufficiently challenging to common methods to prevent unauthorized decryption, especially considering the separate use of public and private keys.

As successful as PKI has been, it has its shortcomings. Public key encryption requires costly computation with data hashing capabilities for additional security. Critics have maintained that PKI is either unnecessary or does not solve the essential problem of guaranteeing a secure transaction, questioning the trustworthiness of CA vendors as a critical weakness. Digital signatures are also still considered vulnerable to cyberattack, enabling, for example, a third party to pose in some circumstances as the original message sender.

Secure Sockets Layer (SSL), a public-key encryption scheme widely used in client-to-server applications, is a Web mainstay for e-commerce transactions. Identified in commercial software by the small gold lock symbol that appears upon loading a Web page secured by SSL, the scheme was employed for the transmission of personal identification numbers (PINs), credit card information, and passwords, among other things. However, SSL suffers from its complex computation system, and cybercriminals, exploiting a weakness in the algorithm used by SSL, have been able to forge authentication certificates.

Another popular encryption technology is Pretty Good Privacy (PGP), developed by Phil Zimmerman and released in 1991. PGP was hailed for its easy-to-use format and strong encryption, and has become the most widely used encryption technology by individuals. Initially used primarily for e-mail transfer encryption, uses for the technology have expanded to cover full desktop and file transfer protection protocols. PGP has been shown, in a variety of criminal investigation cases worldwide, to be unbreakable even by such high-level cryptoanalysis as is possessed by agencies such as the Federal Bureau of Investigation. Current owners of PGP, well-known antivirus software producer Symantec Corp., frequently releases new versions of the technology as weaknesses in the algorithm are discovered. PGP is the technology used to encrypt messages for the popular RIM Blackberry family of mobile devices. Addition versions have been developed for Windows and Mac-OS systems.

CUTTING-EDGE ENCRYPTION SCHEMES

In the early 2010s, one of the areas of concern in encryption management has arisen as a result of increasingly sophisticated mobile devices having access to nonpublic, secured computer networks, or "managed environments." Many of these devices have all the capabilities, and vulnerabilities, of desktop or laptop computers. By 2011 only a few of these devices have the necessary clearance to operate securely in sensitive environments. Blackberry 3G and 4G devices have such capabilities and have been approved for accessing secure data. Other phones are not so well protected. This includes the popular iPhone, which famous hacker Charlie Miller claimed (in 2009) he could hack with a text message from anywhere in the world. In response, software companies have developed software that can wipe the memories of these devices remotely, should they be lost or stolen. However, it is also important to educate users about the vulnerabilities of these devices and a few precautions that need to be taken, including being wary of open Wi-Fi networks, shutting off Bluetooth devices when not in use, and avoiding phishing e-mails or suspicious Web sites.

SEE ALSO *Advanced Encryption Standard (AES); Cryptography, Public and Private Key ; Data Encryption Standard (DES); Digital Certificate; Digital Certificate Authority; Digital Signature; Digital Signature Legislation; Electronic Frontier Foundation* .

BIBLIOGRAPHY

Black, Tricia E. "Taking Account of the World As It Will Be: The Shifting Course of U.S. Encryption Policy." *Federal Communications Law Journal,* March 2001, 289.

Diana, Alison. "Benchmarking Encryption Technology." *E-Commerce Times,* August 12, 2003. Available from http://www.technewsworld.com/story/security/31311.html.

Dugan, Sean M. "e-Business Innovators: Phil Zimmerman, Security." *InfoWorld,* October 9, 2000, 64.

"Electronic Security Technology Roadmap." *Power Engineering,* November 2000, 37.

Gingrich, Newt. "Bush Faces Two Top IT Challenges." *Computerworld,* January 15, 2001.

Harrison, Ann. "Web Outpaces Crypto Rules." *Computerworld,* April 10, 2000. Available from http://www.computerworld.com/s/article/44361/Web_Outpaces_Crypto_Rules_ .

Landau, Susan. "Designing Cryptography for the New Century." *Communications of the ACM,* May 2000.

Levy, Steven. "An Unbreakable Code?" *Newsweek,* March 5, 2001.

"Security and the Basics of Encryption in E-commerce." Cambridge, MA: Berkman Center for Internet & Society at Harvard University. Available from http://cyber.law.harvard.edu/ecommerce/encrypt.html.

"Voltage Security Unveils Encryption Technology." *Finextra,* April 27, 2011. Available from http://www.finextra.com/news/announcement.aspx?pressreleaseid=38933.

Zetlin, Minda. "Cell Phones: A Security Risk to Your Business?" *Technology Inc.com,* March 22, 2010. Available from http://technology.inc.com/2010/03/22/cell-phones-a-security-risk-to-your-business-2.

ENTERPRISE APPLICATION INTEGRATION (EAI)

Enterprise application integration (EAI) is the process of allowing two or more enterprise systems to operate as one. Most EAI offerings include software, hardware, and services. Often, EAI systems are used to integrate incompatible systems—such as an older system in which a major investment has already been made, commonly referred to as a legacy system, and a newer application, such as a customer resource management (CRM) system—within a single business. However, EAI systems are also used with increasing frequency to integrate the enterprise systems of various companies to allow business transactions between enterprises to take place electronically. As the systems integration field has matured, EAI has evolved from its original stand-alone status into a component of other enterprise-oriented offerings, most frequently business process management (BPM).

TYPES OF EAI

A highly complex process, EAI can take place at many levels within an enterprise system. For example, disparate databases can be linked to allow for information sharing between the databases. In addition, two or more applications can be integrated to allow for either data or business processes to be shared among the applications. In this case, an EAI package could link a World Wide Web site to a company's existing inventory management system to allow for real-time inventory updating. The most comprehensive form of EAI, a common virtual system, integrates all elements of an enterprise so that they operate as a single application—even including mobile applications.

The need for EAI arose in the 1980s as many companies that had already used information technology (IT) to automate various business processes began to recognize that the integration of these applications could, among other things, increase efficiency and improve accuracy within business processes. According to Internet portal ITtoolbox.com, "many corporate IT staff members attempted to redesign already implemented applications to make them appear as if they were integrated. Examples include trying to perform operational transaction processing (associated with enterprise resource planning (ERP) system functionality) on systems designed for informational data processing." ERP systems, which integrated accounting, human resources, distribution, manufacturing, and other back-end processes—those business procedures that do not directly involve customers—grew in popularity throughout the early 1990s as most major corporations began upgrading their mainframe systems with the new client/server-based ERP systems developed by industry leaders like SAP AG, PeopleSoft Inc., and J.D. Edwards & Co. To make these systems compatible with their legacy systems, businesses turned to EAI vendors for integration solutions.

Another factor fueling the growth of the EAI industry was the growing popularity of e-commerce, which required the integration of front-end business processes—those which involve interaction with clients, such as CRM and online sales—with back-end functions like inventory management. Although many leading ERP vendors began working to incorporate these front-end processes into their systems, several new companies focused specifically on EAI emerged as well. For example, Vitria Technology, Inc., was founded in Sunnyvale, California, in 1994. Four years later, the firm shipped its blockbuster BusinessWare integration server, which linked the existing IT systems and applications of enterprises like Sprint Corp., AT&T, Blue Cross/Blue Shield, and Deutsche Bank with the Internet. Firms could also use BusinessWare to link all sorts of disparate systems within their enterprise.

Another EAI vendor, Fairfax, Virginia-based webMethods, Inc., was founded in 1996 to create a business-to-business (B2B) integration tool based on the Internet's extensible markup language (XML). The firm conducted its initial public offering (IPO) in early 2000; by then, its client base included the likes of SAP, Eastman Chemical, Lucent Technologies, and Dell Computer Corp. WebMethods was acquired in 2007 by Software AG for $546 million. Also founded in 1996 was CrossWorlds Software Inc., an integration tools and services provider based in Burlingame, California, whose clients included Nortel Networks and Caterpillar. IBM Corp. paid $129 million for CrossWorlds in October 2001 in an effort to add EAI functionality to its WebSphere application server suite.

The early EAI leader, San Jose, California-based BEA Systems, Inc., was founded in 1995 by Bill Coleman, Ed Scott, and Alfred Chuang. In early 1996, the partners decided to acquire Tuxedo, a transaction processing application, from Novell, Inc. It was this purchase that formed the core of BEA's online transaction processing (OLTP) software, which would later fuel its rise to dominance in the EAI industry. ERP giant PeopleSoft agreed to bundle BEA Tuxedo with its major product releases later that year. BEA also released Jolt, its first Java-based program, which allowed users to move business applications to the Internet.

To gain access to an application server, BEA acquired WebLogic in 1998. In February 1999, BEA eLink, which formed the EAI component of future releases of WebLogic, was shipped. The new EAI program included adapters for integration with SAP and PeopleSoft ERP systems, as well as older legacy systems. BEA Systems, along with PeopleSoft and J.D. Edwards, were acquired by Oracle Corp. between 2005 and 2008.

EAI IN THE 2010s

Since EAI solutions can help companies integrate their existing systems, such as ERP and CRM, as well as allow businesses to integrate their systems with Web-based operations, the need for EAI solutions will likely continue to grow. For example, the firm WinterGreen Research forecast that the global integration software market would grow from $4.6 billion in 2006 to $11.5 billion by 2013. Also, a 2010 Gartner survey indicated BPM spending (a category that includes EAI solutions) was expected to grow 20% annually for the near future.

As the Gartner statistics indicate, the early years of the twenty-first century saw a blurring of the former distinctions between EAI and other software markets. The EAI approach of integrating various applications came to be seen as part of the larger disciplines of BPM (which emphasized how business processes work together, not simply integrating existing systems) and service-oriented architecture (SOA, which takes an even higher view of computer system architecture before EAI or BPM). In his article for the SOA Institute titled "EAI, BPM, and SOA," Sandeep Arora stated that EAI is "a subset of what a BPM system offers." He explained, "Traditionally, the focus of EAI was data and data change. EAI connected applications around data." He continued, "BPM leverages the application connectivity aspect of EAI but changes the focus to process."

EAI's importance was also increased by the rise of the Internet, increased delivery of Web-based products and services, and the growth of cloud computing. (Cloud computing, also known as SaaS [software as a service] refers to organizations replacing their local servers with Web-based servers that deliver services and store products on remote servers accessed through the Internet.) Arora wrote that the universal connectivity provided by the Internet provides an ideal match between EAI, BPM, and Web services. Similarly, Joe McKendrick stated in a 2010 article for *ZDNet* that SOA, enterprise architecture, BPM, cloud computing, and other disciplines seemed to be in the process of merging into subsets of the same, larger approach to computer systems design and implementation. Dave Linthicum, in a 2011 article for *InfoWorld* titled "How to Integrate with the Cloud," noted that integration technology allows enterprise systems to share data more easily through SaaS.

By late 2011, some of the early EAI pioneers (such as BEA, PeopleSoft, webMethods and CrossWorlds) were still providing integration products following their acquisitions by larger players like IBM and Oracle. Other major EAI applications available at that time included IBM's WebSphere, Integration Designer, Sterling Commerce, Cast Iron, and other EAI offerings; Microsoft BizTalk; Tibco Active Matrix; SAP Business Suites; and Adeptia Integration Suite. Newer companies included Boom!, which offered a cloud-based EAI solution, and JitterBit, developer of an open-source EAI product.

SEE ALSO *Cloud Computing; Integration.*

BIBLIOGRAPHY

Arora, Sandeep. "EAI, BPM and SOA." Westboro, MA: SOA Institute, December 9, 2005. Available from http://www.soainstitute.org/articles/article/article/eai-bpm-and-soa.html.

"EAI Overview." ITtoolbox.com, 2001.

"Enterprise Application Integration (EAI) Market Opportunities, Strategies and Forecasts, 2007 to 2013." Lexington, MA: WinterGreen Research, Inc., April 2007. Available from http://www.wintergreenresearch.com/reports/EAI%20 2007.html.

Gold-Bernstein, Beth. "EAI Market Segmentation." *EAI Journal,* July 1999.

Gonsalves, Antone. "Value of EAI Grows as Integration Needs Expand." *InformationWeek,* May 28, 2001.

Hohpe, Gregor. "Enterprise Integration Patterns." Available from http://www.eaipatterns.com.

Jones, Teresa. "Survey Analysis: BPM Spending Expected to Grow Significantly in 2011." Stamford, CT: Gartner Group, February 17 2011. Available from http://www.gartner.com.

Kanaracus, Chris. "Oracle Moves Away from Big Acquisitions." *InfoWorld,* May 24, 2011. Available from http://www.infoworld.com/d/the-industry-standard/oracle-moves-away-big-acquisitions-956.

Linthicum, Dave. "How to Integrate with the Cloud." *InfoWorld,* April 27, 2011. Available from http://www.infoworld.com/d/cloud-computing/how-integrate-the-cloud-714.

McKendrick, Joe. "SOA's Next Act: EA? EAI? Cloud? BPM? All of the Above?" *ZDNet,* October 8, 2010. Available from http://www.zdnet.com/blog/service-oriented.

Parkes, Clara. "Business Snapshot: EAI." *Enterprise Systems Journal,* November 2001.

Vitria Technology. "About Vitria/Company." Fallbrook, CA, September 2011. Available from http://www.vitria.com/company.

ENTERPRISE RESOURCE PLANNING (ERP)

Enterprise resource planning (ERP) systems integrate accounting, human resources distribution, manufacturing, and other back-end processes—those that do not directly involve customers—for businesses of all sizes. ERP systems have also evolved to include front-end processes—those that involve customers—such as customer relationship management (CRM), supply chain management, and e-commerce. Traditionally, ERP installation was a large project, requiring integration services for up to one year. This period was designed to facilitate the business' shift from its old practices to the more efficient model that ERP software would support.

In the early 1990s, most major corporations began upgrading their mainframe systems with the new client/server-based ERP systems developed by industry leaders like SAP AG, PeopleSoft Inc., and J.D. Edwards & Co. The 2000s saw, first, consolidation of the industry, with PeopleSoft's acquisition of J.D. Edwards & Co., followed by Oracle's acquisition of PeopleSoft. This left the $25 billion market split between SAP AG and Oracle Corp. for the latter half of the 2000s.

The industry faced a potential overhaul in the 2010s, requiring adaptation and acquisitions. First, as the World Wide Web began to replace client/server platforms, ERP firms had begun working to enable their technology to operate via the Web. The rise of cloud computing in the 2000s presented other possible spin-off versions of traditional ERP integration. Software as a Service (SaaS), which enabled subscription to Web-accessible ERP software, became available. This option was often cheaper; however, industry professionals were skeptical that cloud technology would succeed in ousting the need for consulting services entirely.

IMPACT OF THE INTERNET AND THE CLOUD ON ERP SYSTEMS

According to an October 2000 article in *Internet Week,* what companies like SAP, J.D. Edwards, and PeopleSoft were doing entailed "the Webification of enterprise resource planning software, a migration long promised but only recently realized. The core ERP applications, which until recently meant back-office functions such as accounting, human resources, payroll, and fulfillment among others, are expanding to embrace strategic functions such as e-business relationships (EBR), supply chain management (SCM) and e-commerce services." According to many industry experts, however, adding front-end applications and Web functionality to their products only scratched the surface of what ERP vendors would need to do to stay afloat in constantly shifting e-business landscape.

Innovation and acquisition were the two principles of the ERP leader in the 2000s. SAP spent increasing percentages of its revenues on research and development, reaching 13.9% in 2010. In the same year, the company acquired Sybase. In part, this acquisition was aimed at the data management, synchronization, encryption, and mobile messaging services technology that Sybase encapsulated. Another important consideration was the company's workforce, which was incorporated into SAP's U.S.-based R&D operations. Other acquisitions in the same year included German firm and SAP partner TechniData, which was a supplier of product safety as well as environment solutions.

Innovation became a necessity for ERP companies, and cloud software was the next horizon of development. In 2011, SAP featured a number of "on demand" software offerings, including SAP Carbon Impact OnDemand, which was designed to help clients alleviate their carbon footprint. The company had also expanded into e-procurement, with SAP Sourcing OnDemand, as well as Cloud-Based Decision Making, and a number of other new programs. Some of these were designed to be integrated with previous installations of SAP Business software, while others were designed with particular functions in mind that would anticipate a new need businesses would face.

However, in 2011 services and software giant IBM Corp. entered the fray by collaborating with an ERP software company, Infor. According to *Forbes,* Infor was the fourth-largest ERP company in 2011, behind SAP, Oracle, and Microsoft. The company had single-handedly consolidated the second tier of ERP providers, with an aggressive string of acquisitions throughout the 2000s, spending $4.4 billion between 2004 and 2008. Partnering with IBM, the leading IT consulting firm in the world, had the potential to bring them into direct competition with the three industry leaders.

Although cloud computing had become a trend in IT innovation, many experts remained skeptical as to its usefulness to ERP. Whereas some services, such as e-procurement, were oriented to facilitating transfer of external information and exchange, ERP was an internal process that required significant integration between new and old software/systems. In fact, a series of case studies had concluded that the five major aspects of successful ERP integrations were all service-oriented. In addition, issues arising from proper adoption of SaaS solutions, such as data fragmentation, had been documented, creating a need for services to be provided with cloud-based applications either by the ERP provider or by an additional integration firm.

SEE ALSO *Cloud Computing; Customer Relation Management (CRM).*

BIBLIOGRAPHY

Borck, James R. "Enterprise Strategies: ERP Faces Rocky Road." *InfoWorld,* May 14, 2001.

Brown, Carol V., and Iris Vessey. "Managing the Next Wave of Enterprise Systems: Leveraging Lessons from ERP." *MIS Quarterly Executive* 2, no. 1 (2003): 65–77.

Chiem, Phat X. "ERP Vendors Make Move from Back Office to Front." *B to B,* February 19, 2001.

Mullin, Rick. "ECM: Where ERP Meets the Web." *Chemical Week,* April 25, 2001.

RP, Srikanth. "Cloud Computing Is Driving the Next Wave of Data Fragmentation." *InformationWeek,* May 3, 2011. Available from http://m.informationweek.in.

SAP. "Management Report." Weinheim, Germany, 2010. Available from http://www.sapannualreport.com/2010/en.

Stevens, Tim. "ERP Explodes." *Industry Week,* July 1, 1996.

Trefis Team. "IBM Adds ERP Specialist Infor to its Deep Bench." *Forbes,* August 9, 2011. Available from http://www.forbes.com/sites/greatspeculations/2011/08/09/ibm-adds-erp-specialist-infor-to-its-deep-bench.

ENTERPRISE SERVER

As the number of businesses adopting e-business strategies continued rising into the new millennium, technology firms began offering a host of hardware and software options designed to meet enterprise needs. These offerings, enterprise servers among them, were developed to give companies a competitive edge by providing high-performance infrastructures, as well as control over growing networks and Internet operations.

In a basic client/server relationship, the server acted as the host computer that stored information and was shared by clients within a network. The client, another computer or remote device, could retrieve information from the server. The term server also referred to the software that allowed the transfer of information to take place.

EARLY SERVER SPECIALIZATION

As technology advanced and businesses began using computers for a variety of tasks, different types of servers were developed to manage different types of resources. For instance, file servers were used to store files, printing servers were used to manage printers on a network, network servers evolved to handle traffic within a network, and database servers were developed to control information and process database queries. Application servers, most often used by enterprises with both intranet and Internet operations, performed data processing tasks that allowed up-to-date information to be delivered to clients. Application servers typically linked to Web servers, which enabled content to be transferred over the Internet. Web servers would receive a request from a Web browser, retrieve the stored Web page, and then process the request so the page could be viewed via the browser.

Enterprise servers emerged in the late 1990s as businesses began looking for solutions that could manage their e-business infrastructures and networks. The focus turned from servers that benefitted one department or application and more toward computers that provided services across the enterprise (be it a company, institution, or government agency). As demand for these types of servers increased, technology firms began developing products that could manage growth; provide flexibility in selecting, creating, and utilizing applications; provide security; and insure reliable performance.

Designed to benefit the organization as a whole, enterprise servers were developed as enhanced servers involved in a multitude of tasks including Web development, content management, and data processing. Enterprise servers also could manage many aspects of a company's network, acting as file, printing, network, database, application, and Web servers. The sale of these servers was targeted toward businesses needing to become Web-enabled in order to begin conducting commerce on the Internet.

By the early 2000s, IT managers in search of enterprise servers had many options. Technology firms including IBM, Hewlett-Packard (HP) and Microsoft all offered versions of enterprise servers. Microsoft also offered enterprise servers under the name .NET Enterprise Servers. IBM's zSeries was developed to manage data and transaction processing. The firm touted the product as the first "e-business" enterprise server for its performance and application management capabilities.

In 2000, the enterprise server industry slowed, due in part to the dot-com bust and the lagging economy. According to statistics from industry analyst International Data Corporation (IDC), server spending hit its bottom point in mid-2000, then resumed steady growth to its global peak of $13.9 billion in revenues in the second quarter of 2008. However, the recession which began later that year again cut into spending on servers and other systems requirements. According to IDC and technology research firm Gartner, shipments and revenues had rebounded to $13.2 billion by mid-2011 but still lagged behind the levels reached before the 2008–2009 recession. IDC noted that most of the server sales growth was coming from Asia by 2011, while the United States and Europe markets were below their sales and unit levels of 2008.

SERVING THE CLOUD

Experts said cloud computing was responsible for most of the growth reported in the early 2010s. In cloud computing, companies store data, access programs, and share other resources on outside vendors' servers rather than buying and maintaining their own hardware. The trend meant that fewer individual companies were buying their own servers, while cloud computing firms were buying larger numbers of servers to provide services for their clients.

At the same time as enterprise servers began shifting from individual companies to cloud computing, the server industry itself went through a period of consolidation in the years following the dot-com crash. Compaq was acquired by HP for $25 billion in 2002, with HP phasing out the Compaq brand several years later.

By 2010, the main companies supplying servers were Microsoft, IBM, HP, and Sun Microsystems. IBM and other mainframe computer companies generally supplied larger server platforms. Smaller systems were available from companies like HP, Sun, and Microsoft (through its Windows 2000 package)—although over the years, those formerly small systems grew to become more and more powerful. By 2011, Microsoft dominated the enterprise server market. IDC reported Windows Server represented 71% of enterprise server shipments in the second quarter of 2011, with revenues totaling $5.9 billion and a 45.5% share of the total global revenue. The remaining enterprise server market was divided among Unix, Linux, mainframe, and other platforms.

SEE ALSO *E-commerce Solutions; Hewlett-Packard Co.; IBM Inc.; Microsoft Corp.*

BIBLIOGRAPHY

Brodkin, Jon. "Despite Enterprise Dominance, Microsoft Struggles in Web Server Market." *Ars Technica,* September 16, 2011. Available from http://arstechnica.com/business/news/2011/09/despite-enterprise-dominance-microsoft-struggles-in-web-server-market.ars.

Burt, Jeffrey. "Oracle Hardware Focus Stays on High End of Server Business." *Eweek,* September 21, 2011. Available from http://www.eweek.com/c/a/IT-Infrastructure/Oracle-Hardware-Focus-Stays-on-High-End-of-Server-Business-832392.

Linthicum, Dave. "How to Integrate with the Cloud." *InfoWorld,* April 27, 2011. Available from http://www.infoworld.com/d/cloud-computing/how-integrate-the-cloud-714.

Lynn, Samara. "Will Windows 8 Be Bigger Hit on Server Side?" *PC Magazine,* September 22, 2011. Available from http://www.pcmag.com/article2/0,2817,2393410,00.asp.

Morgan, Timothy Prickett. "Server Sales Up, but Great Recession Lingers." *The Register,* September 7, 2011. Available from http://www.theregister.co.uk/2011/09/07/idc_gartner_server_spending_analysis/.

"SUSE Linux Enterprise Server Selected for Use with SAP HANA." *PR Newswire,* September 14, 2011. Available from http://www.prnewswire.com/news-releases/suse-linux-enterprise-server-selected-for-use-with-sap-hana-129823738.html.

Wittman, Art. "The Yin and Yang of Enterprise Computing." *Network Computing,* September 1998. Available from http://www.networkcomputing.com/916/916colwittmann.html.

"Worldwide Market for Enterprise Server Virtualization to Reach $19.3 Billion by 2014, According to IDC." *Business Wire,* December 6, 2010. Available from http://www.thefreelibrary.com/Worldwide+Market+for+Enterprise+Server+Virtualization+to+Reach+$19.3...-a0243648374.

E-PROCUREMENT

Procurement is the process whereby companies purchase goods and services from various suppliers. These include everything from indirect goods like light bulbs, uniforms, toilet paper, and office supplies, to the direct goods used for manufacturing products. Procurement also involves the purchase of temporary labor, energy, vehicle leases, and so forth. Searching, sourcing, negotiating, ordering, receipt, and review are all parts of procurement.

Companies negotiate discount contracts for some goods and services, and buy others on the spot. Procurement can be an important part of a company's overall strategy for reducing costs. Historically, the individuals or departments responsible for purchasing a company's goods and services relied on various methods for doing so. The most basic included placing orders via telephone, fax, or mail. Electronic procurement methods, generally referred to as e-procurement, enabled the procurement process to unfold in a faster, more efficient manner, and with fewer errors. These methods include electronic data interchange (EDI), e-tendering, online marketplaces or e-marketplaces, e-auction, e-catalog, and various blends of these methods. According to the *Journal of Public Procurement,*, the field is considered a subset of e-commerce.

Although traditional methods are gradually being replaced by more efficient, e-procurement systems, the process of streamlining operations with technology met with unexpected difficulties in the 2000s. There were a number of notable failures in the public sector in the United States and the United Kingdom. These failures, coupled with the expensive nature of e-procurement products, slowed growth. The global recession of 2008–2009 was a boon for e-procurement, as decreasing revenues forced companies to cut operating costs rather than expand. Large businesses and governments, attracted to the potential benefits of added efficiency, attempted to stimulate growth. With a global trend toward efficiency and sustainability, the market for e-procurement continued to develop.

ELECTRONIC DATA INTERCHANGE

Since the 1960s, many large companies have relied on electronic data interchange (EDI) for the procurement of goods. EDI deals more with the way information is communicated during procurement than it does with the act of linking buyers and suppliers. By definition, EDI is the electronic exchange of business information—purchase orders, invoices, bills of lading, inventory data, and various types of confirmations—between organizations or trading partners in standardized formats. EDI also is used within individual organizations to transfer data between different divisions or departments, such as finance, purchasing, and shipping. Two characteristics set EDI apart from other ways of exchanging information. First, EDI only involves business-to-business transactions; individual consumers do not directly use EDI to purchase goods or services. Secondly, EDI involves transactions between computers or databases, not individuals. Therefore, individuals sending e-mail messages or sharing files over a network does not constitute EDI.

For companies using the Internet as the electronic medium (referred to as open EDI), a language called extensible markup language (XML), similar in some respects to hypertext markup language (HTML), allows users to share information in a universal, standard way without making the kinds of special arrangements EDI often requires.

Online auctions were another tool companies used to procure goods and services for both contract and spot buys. A number of factors were critical to the success of online auctions, including the kind of bidders involved, the number of bidders, and the length of the bidding periods. Although it is not directly part of the auction, online negotiation also can be a factor if the auction involves complicated elements like delivery and support. As technology advanced, online auctions, which would automatically pair the cheapest suppliers with buyers, became more prominent. The technology was provided by IT consulting firms, such as IBM.

PROS AND CONS

Along with all of the positives, there also are disadvantages to e-procurement. Suppliers often complained that e-transactions gave increased leverage to the purchaser, while purchasers struggled to sort through the wide array of products offered. E-commerce sites often relied on product reviews, written by consumers who had purchased the product, to make the purchasing process more dependable. There were also substantial problems with public e-procurement in the early 2000s. The U.S. General Services Administration's services, which had been upgraded to implement cutting-edge technology, were criticized as unreliable. Meanwhile e-procurement systems in South Carolina, Massachusetts, and Indiana were either abandoned before completion or shut down. The United Kingdom opted not to implement its trial e-Tendering system, while New Zealand found the technology much more complex than anticipated.

Despite the limitations and unexpected difficulties, the European Commission continued its interest in e-procurement as a potential source of efficacy, publishing a green paper in 2010 that called for the continued adoption of e-practices. Hopes that 50% of total procurement would be achieved through electronic means by 2010 had been thwarted. By that time, only 5% of the EU's public procurement was being conducted by automated systems. Nonetheless, the commission saw an opportunity to cut costs and save paper. The green paper stated: "The technology is now mature. Successful e-procurement platforms are well-established in many regions and Member States. Traffic through these systems has reached a critical mass and is growing strongly. There is an opportunity to disseminate best practice and correct shortcomings in the EU legal and policy environment which might otherwise stifle these developments."

SEE ALSO *Auction Sites; Business-to-Business (B2B) E-commerce; Electronic Data Interchange (EDI).*

BIBLIOGRAPHY

Banham, Russ. "Procurement Made Easy." *World Trade,* October 2000.

Carr, David. "Ariba Discovery Helps Buyers Find Suppliers." *Information Week,* March 23, 2011. Available from http://www.informationweek.com/thebrainyard/news/social_networking_private_platforms/229400183.

Copacino, William. "Auctions Expand E-procurement Menu." *Logistics Management & Distribution Report,* January 2001.

Dwyer, John. "Who's Afraid of the Big, Bad E?" *Works Management,* January 2001.

"E-commerce Growth Prospects Remain Strong." *Corporate EFT Report,* January 17, 2001.

European Commission. "Green Paper: On Expanding the Use of E-procurement in the EU." Brussels, Belgium, October 18, 2010. Available from http://ec.europa.eu/internal_market.

Gilbert, Alorie. "E-procurement for Smaller Users." *InformationWeek,* November 27, 2000. Available from http://www.informationweek.com/814/baworks.htm

———. "E-procurement: Problems Behind the Promise." *InformationWeek,* November 20, 2000. Available from http://www.informationweek.com/813/eprocure.htm.

KishorVaidya, A. S., M. Sajeev, and Guy Callender. "Critical Factors that Influence E-procurement Implementation Success in the Public Sector." *Journal of Public Procurement,* 6 (2006): 70–99.

Welty, Terry. "Beware the Pitfalls of Internet Procurement." *Communications News,* March 2000. Available from http://findarticles.com/p/articles/mi_m0CMN/is_3_37/ai_60498431/

E-TAILING

Electronic retailing, or e-tailing, refers to the practice of selling goods and services over an electronic medium like the Internet. Many traditional brick-and-mortar firms like Toys"R"Us and Barnes and Noble also sell their wares via Web sites. Other companies, such as Amazon.com, rely solely on the Web to conduct business. While books, CDs, and computer software and hardware are the most common goods sold by e-tailers, clothes, cosmetics, perfume, plants, toys, and other types of merchandise have also made their way to the Web. Nearly 80% of the U.S. population was online by 2011; 27% of the world population was online during the same year, according to the World Bank. With Internet use continuously gaining momentum in developed nations and emerging markets alike, e-tailing was posed to experience similar gains.

HISTORY

One of the first and most well-known e-tailers, Amazon.com got its start in 1995. Because the business-to-consumer (B2C) model was relatively new and unproven then, Amazon.com had to develop its own architecture and manage its own site. As online shopping grew in popularity—accounting for $3 billion in consumer spending in 1997 and $7.1 billion in 1998—technology vendors like IBM moved into e-commerce and began offering to build and even oversee sites for companies wanting to launch an e-tailing venture.

Several e-tailing blunders occurred during the 1999 holiday shopping season. For example, Toysrus.com found itself ill prepared to handle an unexpected surge in orders and failed to deliver shipments by Christmas day that year. Some analysts believed that the resulting dip in consumer confidence did not bode well for the future of online sales. However, as sites continued to address issues important to consumers, such as the security of online payment via credit card, an increasing number of consumers continued to make online purchases.

TWENTY-FIRST CENTURY E-TAILING

E-tailing flourished throughout the first decade of the twenty-first century, as consumers increasingly shifted their shopping patterns online. Especially during the recession of the late 2000s, e-tailing showed itself to be a more robust sales medium than traditional sales vehicles. E-tail sales totaled $165 billion in 2010, a nearly 15% increase from the prior year and representing 4.2% of all retail sales, according to the U.S. Commerce Department. Between 2002 and 2009, e-tail sales grew an average 18% per year, compared to 2% for total retail sales, according to the Census Bureau. Clothing and clothing accessories represented the leading merchandise category for e-tail sales. Like traditional retail operations, e-tailing was sensitive to seasonal fluctuations. In 2010, e-tailing enjoyed a strong fourth quarter, thanks in large part to robust holiday sales.

AMAZON.COM AND NEW RIVALS

While Amazon.com dominated the e-tailing sector during the first decade of the twenty-first century, brick-and-mortar retailers raised competitive pressures against the market leader. Traditional retailers and consumer products manufacturers found new opportunities online as budget-conscious consumers looked to the Web to maximize their spending power. Procter & Gamble, Mattel, and Columbia Sportswear were among the many firms to make significant investments in their e-commerce sites and become noteworthy rivals to pure e-tailers like Amazon.com. "There's a wide variety of folks that have been historically considered manufacturers that are now positioning themselves as retailers," Sally McKenzie, an e-commerce consultant, told *Bloomberg Businessweek* in 2010. "It's harder and harder for their products to stand out. The Web is a phenomenal opportunity to assert their brand authority."

As such, direct sales of consumer-brand products became one of the fastest-growing segments of e-tailing in the late 2000s, rising nearly 13% in 2009 alone, according to Vertical Web Media. Sales were just one component of Web sites, however. Traditional retailers increasingly found value in Web-based tools for engaging customers in meaningful ways. For instance, toymaker Mattel's online store enabled customers to make purchases while simultaneously playing games with other customers and friends. Part of the drive to sell online has been the growing popularity of private-label brands, according to *Bloomberg Businessweek.* Wal-Mart added dozens of new products under its Great Value brand, while Target sold groceries under its Archer Farms label. The recession of the late 2000s also pushed more consumers to shop online, where bargains were comparatively easier to find. Despite the proliferation of niche sites, Amazon.com remained an undisputed market leader thanks to its wide range of products and efficiencies in warehousing and shipping.

As the sector experienced rapid growth, e-tailing businesses were increasingly pressured to operate reliable Web sites. According to consulting firm the E-tailing Group, nearly 30% of online merchants did not test their Web site features in 2011. "Few companies fully take advantage of testing's ability to improve shoppers' online experience and increase conversion rates," according to *Internet Retailer.* "Testing generally includes. . .recording which site features and tweaks attract more consumers and sales."

As e-tailing became increasingly competitive, site owners sought new ways to lure online consumers. E-tailers did this by listing their products on third-party sites like Google Shopping, improving page load speeds, and building a presence on social media networks like Facebook and Twitter. Getting consumers' attention was a significant challenge for e-tailers, some of whom successfully implemented audio and video messages into their Web sites to engage visitors.

SEE ALSO *Business-to-Consumer (B2C) E-commerce; Electronic Payment.*

BIBLIOGRAPHY

Bonisteel, Steven. "Online Retailing Only in 'Second Inning'—Global Report." *Newsbytes,* February 6, 2001.

Brookman, Faye. "E-sales Surge Despite Flaws." *Discount Store News,* January 25, 1999.

Donegan, Priscilla. "The State of Cybershopping." *Grocery Headquarters,* May 2000.

Enright, Allison. "E-commerce Sales Rise 14.8% in 2010." *Internet Retailer,* February 17, 2011. Available from http://www.internetretailer.com/2011/02/17/e-commerce-sales-rise-148-2010.

Falla, Jane M. "Business-to-Consumer E-commerce: What Is(n't) the Problem?" *e-Business Advisor,* August 2000.

Galante, Joseph. "Levi, P&G, Mattel Tackle E-tailing." *Bloomberg Businessweek,* March 4, 2010. Available from http://www.businessweek.com/technology/content/mar2010/tc2010034_952664.htm.

Manes, Stephen. "If You Buy It Online, Will It Come?" *Computerworld,* January 31, 2000. Available from http://www.computerworld.com.au/article/80818/full_disclosure/#closeme.

Moore, Stefany. "On-Site Testing Is a Must, the E-tailing Group Says." *Internet Retailer,* February 15, 2011. Available from http://www.internetretailer.com/2011/02/15/site-testing-must-e-tailing-group-says.

Prince, C. J. "Etail's Big Comeback." *Chief Executive,* July 2000.

Remis, Andrew. "12 Solutions to Ecommerce Sites' Biggest Marketing Challenges." *HubSpot Blog,* December 3, 2010. Available from http://blog.hubspot.com/blog/tabid/6307/bid/7234/12-Solutions-to-Ecommerce-Sites-Biggest-Marketing-Challenges.aspx.

U.S. Department of Commerce. Bureau of the Census. "E-commerce 2009." Washington, DC, May 26, 2011. Available from http://www.census.gov/econ/estats/2009/2009reportfinal.pdf.

The World Bank. "World Development Indicators." Washington, DC. Available from http://data.worldbank.org/data-catalog/world-development-indicators?cid=GPD_WDI.

eTOYS, INC.

eToys was established in 1997 by Edward "Toby" Lenk, a former vice president of corporate strategic planning for Walt Disney Co., to provide a simplified shopping experience for toys and other children's merchandise. The company's Web site, eToys.com, launched in October 1997 and let consumers browse for products based on age group and price range. Customers also could access detailed product descriptions, including lists of safety features, which were unavailable to shoppers at toy stores. As Lenk told *Inc.,* "We take two days of shopping and compress it into 15 minutes. That must be worth something."

For four holiday shopping seasons eToys was indeed worth something. In the end, however, the company ran out of money and had to close its online doors. Several factors contributed to its demise, especially the dot-com shakeout of 2000 that severely limited the company's access to capital. Hardly alone in its plummet, several other online toy retailers also went out of business in 2000. Perhaps the final nail in eToys's coffin came when Amazon.com and Toys 'R' Us teamed up to create the number one online Web site for toys, which cut into eToys' holiday revenue at a crucial time in 2000. Nonetheless, as the first online toy retailer, eToys was an important e-commerce player.

EMULATED AMAZON.COM'S ONLINE MODEL

eToys aimed to emulate Amazon.com, which was launched in 1995, by providing a Web site where customers could search among a large selection of items, order them online, pay by credit card, and receive delivery in a short period of time. In its first year eToys—which was headquartered in Santa Monica, California, and had a nearby warehouse—generated awareness for its site through marketing relationships with America Online and Yahoo!, among others. It established relationships with about 350 toy manufacturers, including all of the major ones, and offered some 8,000 products, some of which were stored in its warehouse. The company's initial financing included more than $10 million that Lenk raised from venture capital firms, former Disney colleagues, and other sources. In March 1998, the company acquired Toys.com, which was operated by Web Magic Inc.

SPENT HEAVILY TO GAIN CUSTOMERS

Throughout its four-year history eToys seemed unconcerned with turning a profit. The company lost $2.3 million in its first fiscal year ending March 31, 1998, and another $15.3 million in the nine months ending December 31, 1998. Its goal was to acquire customers, and it spent heavily to do so. With venture capital running out, the company turned to the public equity markets and held its initial public offering (IPO) in May 1999. Eight percent of the company was offered to the public. Shares began trading on the NASDAQ on May 20, 1999, at $20 a share, raising $166 million for eToys. The stock rose as high as $85 on the first day of trading and ended the day around $76.50, giving eToys a market value of $7.8 billion, more than the $5.6 billion market value of Toys 'R' Us.

Around this time the company acquired BabyCenter Inc. (which it sold off at the end of 1999), and outsourced its e-commerce order fulfillment to Fingerhut Companies Inc. In July, eToys began selling children's books, offering some 80,000 titles, and its acquisition of BabyCenter expanded the company's demographic to infants and toddlers. Based on its 1998 performance, eToys had become the brand to beat in merchandise for children up to age 12. In 1999, it faced increased competition from Toys 'R' Us, as well as from Amazon.com, which added a toy section in July 1999. Other competitors included KB Toys, a subsidiary of Consolidated Stores Corp., and Wal-Mart Stores Inc., the largest U.S. toy seller.

eToys attempted to distinguish itself from its competitors in several ways. One was the depth of its product offerings—15,000 items compared to Toys 'R' Us's 10,000. The company also focused on offering services that its competitors could not match, such as putting personalized gift tags on each item and offering multiple wrappings, a gift registry that parents could protect with a password, a wish-list feature for kids, and a spare parts and repair service for toys. The company also had a compelling product bundling strategy, whereby no item was treated as a single entity. Rather, toys were bundled with books and videos, for example, and customers could select which items they wanted to include in their bundle.

In August 1999, eToys expanded its marketing relationship with America Online by committing to a three-year, $18 million agreement that made eToys the premier retailer of children's products on several AOL channels, including Shop@AOL, AOL Families Channel, AOL.com, Netscape Netcenter, and CompuServe. The company's national print and television advertising campaign, which launched in October, was expected to cost $20 million. eToys also expanded into the United Kingdom for the 1999 holiday season, opening a U.K. Web site in October and stocking some 5,000 items at a British warehouse.

WALL STREET NOT IMPRESSED WITH STRONG HOLIDAY SALES

Although eToys's holiday sales for the quarter ending December 31, 1999, more than quadrupled to $107 million, the company reported a quarterly loss of $62.5 million, compared to a loss of $8.2 million for the same quarter in 1998. Responding to the news, Wall Street sent eToys's stock down to around $17 a share at the end of January 2000. eToys attributed its losses to the high cost of fulfilling orders, due mainly to its outsourcing arrangement with Fingerhut. eToys planned to bring its order fulfillment in-house for 2000, opening a new warehouse in Virginia to service the eastern United States and expanding its Southern California facility.

As Wall Street continued to punish tech and e-commerce stocks, eToys's stock price fell to around $6 a share in April 2000. Both *Fortune* and *Los Angeles Business Journal* reported that some analysts thought eToys would have difficulty making it through the next Christmas. The company had about $220 million in cash and liquid assets, and in June it raised another $100 million through a direct placement of convertible preferred stock to private equity funds and a group of investors. Analysts felt that eToys needed to raise another $100 million to continue operating until it could turn a profit.

HOLIDAY SALES SHORTFALL LED TO OPERATIONS CRISIS

With everything riding on its holiday sales, eToys faced an operations crisis even before December 25 rolled around, when it reported that its holiday sales would be around $120 million to $130 million, well below the projected $210 million to $240 million. That meant the company would run out of operating cash three months sooner than expected. Wall Street sent the company's stock below $1 a share for the first time, giving eToys a market value of just $37 million. The biggest factor affecting eToys's holiday performance was the online joint venture between Amazon.com and Toys"R"Us, which dominated holiday sales with 123 million visitors during the holiday season, compared with 21.12 million visits to eToys.

From there it was all downhill for eToys, which could not raise capital under those market conditions. In January, it closed its European operations and laid off 700 workers in the United States, representing 70% of its workforce. The company also quit delivering to Canada, closed its two distribution centers, and finally announced that it had sent layoff notices to its remaining 293 employees. The company planned to file for Chapter 11 bankruptcy protection and cease operations by April 2001.

SUBSEQUENT OWNERS

In October 2001, *E-Commerce Times* reported that a former rival, KB Holdings, had acquired the remaining assets of eToys and its Web site for a combined total of almost $5 million. The Web site was resurrected in time for the 2001 holiday season, and eToys began operating as a division of KB Holdings' children's division, KBKids.com.

In 2008, KB Toys filed for bankruptcy for the second time—the first time was in 2004—citing debts of $500 million and assets of a similar amount. Most of its assets, including eToys.com, were purchased by D.E. Shaw, a New York-based hedge fund and majority shareholder in the Parent Company, another Internet retailer of children's products.

The *New York Times* reported in December 2008 that the Parent Company, along with nine of its subsidiaries, including eToys.com, was also filing for bankruptcy, a victim of the economic recession. In February 2009, *BusinessWire* ran a press release from Toys"R"Us describing its acquisition of the e-commerce sites eToys.com and BabyUniverse.com and the parenting resource site, ePregnancy.com from the Parent Company. In the release, Toys"R"Us commented, "This acquisition provides the company with a unique opportunity to broaden its web-based portfolio through the addition of these three well-established online destinations for parents and families."

SEE ALSO *Amazon.com Inc.*.

BIBLIOGRAPHY

Brinsley, John. "eToys: Stock Went from Hot to Shot." *Los Angeles Business Journal,* April 10, 2000.

Enos, Lori. "eToys to File for Bankruptcy." *E-Commerce Times,* February 27, 2001. Available from http://www.ecommercetimes.com/story/7772.html.

"eToys Files for IPO." *InformationWeek,* February 22, 1999.

"eToy Story." *Business Week,* January 10, 2000.

Gorchov, Jolie. "Pundits Point to eToys as Dot-Com Dud." *Los Angeles Business Journal,* April 24, 2000.

Guglielmo, Connie. "Medium of Exchange: E-Com in Toy-land." *Inter@ctive Week,*October 4, 1999.

———. "Medium of Exchange: Toy Story 2000." *Inter@ctive Week.* October 9, 2000.

Leiby, Richard. "The Fine Art of Compromise." *Washington Post,* December 31, 1999.

Macaluso, Nora. "Amazon and Toys 'R' Us Take E-holiday Prize." *E-Commerce Times,* January 2, 2001. Available from http://www.ecommercetimes.com/story/6398.html.

———. "eToys Site Back in Business." *E-Commerce Times,* October 18, 2001. Available from http://www.ecommercetimes.com/story/14237.html.

Mahoney, Michael, and Jon Weisman. "The Last Days of eToys." *E-Commerce Times,* March 7, 2001. Available from http://www.ecommercetimes.com/story/7978.html.

Pereira, Joseph. "eToys Investors Claim Conflict at Law Firm." *Pittsburgh Post-Gazette.com,* July 25, 2005. Available from http://www.post-gazette.com/pg/05206/543481-28.stm.

Regan, Keith. "eToys Fires Staff, Sets April Shutdown." *E-Commerce Times,* February 6, 2001. Available from http://www.ecommercetimes.com/story/7275.html.

Rosenbloom, Stephanie. "Parent Company, a Retailer, Files for Bankruptcy." *New York Times,* December 29, 2008. Available from http://www.nytimes.com/2008/12/30/business/30shop.html.

"This Toy War Is No Game." *Business Week,* August 9, 1999.

Trager, Louis. "Toy Market's Batteries Die." *Inter@ctive Week,* June 26, 2000.

Walker, Leslie. "Market Punishes eToys for Losses." *Washington Post,* January 28, 2000.

Weisman, Jon, and Elizabeth Blakey. "Embattled eToys Slashes 700 Jobs." *E-Commerce Times,* January 5, 2001. Available from http://www.ecommercetimes.com/story/6485.html.

"With Early-Bird Web-Site and Portal Deals, Former Disney Executive Seeks to Preempt Toys 'R' Us." *Inc.,* October 1998.

E*TRADE FINANCIAL CORP.

E*Trade Financial Corp. started as a basic online investment company in the early 1990s and grew over time to offer a full range of financial services. By the latter 2000s, it had become one of the largest investment Web sites for the average investor interested in casual funding options. By 2010, the company had over 3,000 employees with 28 branches located across the United States. While E*Trade started by offering the ability to invest in basic stocks, it has since expanded into offering a variety of investor tools.

In 2011, E*Trade gave its customers the chance to buy stocks, options, mutual funds, bonds, and futures, with the ability to buy into initial public offerings (IPOs). It divided funds into both national and international options so investors could choose a focused or hybrid area portfolio. On the banking side, the company offered its own checking account for subscribers, with no charge for those who kept more than $5,000 in the account. This checking option was one of the few parts of the E*Trade offering that was Federal Deposit Insurance Corporation (FDIC) insured. The business also gave customers the ability to invest in a number of individual retirement accounts (IRAs), including IRAs for youth and education savings accounts.

E*Trade followed up these basic offerings with a number of online tools designed to give its customers more control over their finances and a broader number of choices for what to do with their funds. The company came out with Quick Transfer, a tool investors can use to access their accounts at any time and move money between E*Trade accounts or between E*Trade and outside institutions, for a maximum of $100,000 per day. Investors could also choose to use a retirement calculator to plan out what types of funds they wanted to use and how to use them. Also in 2011, E*Trade introduced a community beta test, a social media tool for its subscribers to use, allowing them to exchange market tips, investment ideas, and allocation information. For more straightforward research, the business also provided a section for market reports and breaking news.

ONE OF THE FIRST ALL-ELECTRONIC BROKERAGES

E*Trade Securities was founded in 1992 in Palo Alto, California, as a subsidiary of Trade*Plus, but its online trading technology was in use as early as 1983. Trade*Plus was a service bureau founded in 1982 by Bill Porter, a physicist and inventor with more than a dozen patents. The company provided online quote and trading services to Fidelity, Charles Schwab, and Quick & Reilly. When Porter asked himself why he had to pay a broker hundreds of dollars for stock transactions, he realized that someday everyone would have computers and use them to buy and sell stocks and other securities. It was not until 1992 that Porter launched E*Trade Securities, one of the first all-electronic brokerages. At first E*Trade offered online investing services through America Online and CompuServe. From 1993 to 1995, E*Trade made Trade*Plus the fastest-growing private company in Silicon Valley, according to a survey by the *Business Journal.* E*Trade's lowest trading fee was $19.95, and in 1994 sales from Trade*Plus and E*Trade reached $10.9 million. In 1996, E*Trade began Internet trading with the launch of Etrade.com.

By 1996, E*Trade had evolved organizationally from an entrepreneurial type of company to one with a more well-defined corporate structure. In March 1996, Porter turned over his CEO duties to Christos Cotsakos while remaining as chairman. Cotsakos was a decorated Vietnam

War veteran with 19 years of experience with Federal Express and 5 years at A.C. Nielsen Co., where he was co-CEO, chief operating officer (COO), president, and a director. Under Cotsakos's leadership, E*Trade would become a public company and one of the leading online financial services companies. In April 1996, the company opened a second facility in Rancho Cordova, near Sacramento. Its goal was to duplicate operations there, so there would never be any lost connections with clients. In August, the company went public as E*Trade Group Inc. with an initial public offering (IPO). By the end of December 1996, E*Trade had 112,800 customer accounts, up three times from the previous year.

In 1997, E*Trade raised additional capital through a secondary offering. During the year, the company launched E*Trade Canada, its first international venture, as well as its Mutual Fund Center, which initially offered some 3,500 funds. Revenue for the year was $142.7 million, and the company was profitable with net income of $13.9 million.

In 1999, E*Trade's brand-building expenditures and temporary moratorium on profits paid off. The company's revenue climbed to $621.4 million for fiscal 1999 ending September 30, with a reported net loss of $54.4 million. Much of the revenue was used to build one of the strongest brands in online financial services and to fuel new product development and diversification. The launch of Destination E*Trade in September 1998 helped the company to gain one million net new active accounts in fiscal 1999. E*Trade was receiving an average of $52 million in deposits every business day, compared to an average of $20 million the previous year. Customer assets increased 154% to $28 billion. Market share, as measured by online trades per day, rose from 10% of the market to 15%, and Opinion Research Corp.'s Internet Brand Study ranked E*Trade as the fourth-most-recognized e-commerce brand, behind Amazon.com, eBay, and Priceline.com. The company also expanded its Mutual Fund Center, offering more than 5,000 funds and introducing four E*Trade proprietary funds.

THE NEW MILLENIUM

E*Trade's revenue diversification strategy was designed to reduce the company's reliance on online trading volume as a primary source of revenue. Planned diversifications included Internet banking, the IPO market, stock plan management services for corporations, and venture capital funds. The company's pending acquisition of Telebanc Financial Corp., which operated the leading Internet bank, signaled E*Trade's entry into Internet banking. Announced in mid-1999, the acquisition of Telebanc closed in January 2000. E*Trade Bank was launched in April 2000, and wireless banking and brokerage services were first offered by E*Trade in October 2000.

In 2003, the company reported revenues of $1.4 billion, an increase of about 2% over the previous year. The increase in revenue was due primarily to a 30% increase in banking revenues. The United States contained E*Trade's largest customer base and represented approximately 92% of revenues in 2003.

THE "MILKAHOLIC" AFFAIR

During the Super Bowl game of 2007, E*Trade introduced an online and television commercial featuring a talking baby sitting in front of a Web cam discussing financing and investing in an adult voice. The commercial was popular and returned the following year, together with a Facebook page, updates on Twitter, and outtake videos on YouTube.

In March 2010, actress Lindsay Lohan filed a lawsuit against E*Trade alleging that one of the baby characters, named "Lindsay," invoked her "likeness, name, characterization, and personality" without her permission and therefore violated her privacy. "Lindsay," the baby character, was referred to in the commercial as a "milkaholic." Lohan sued for $50 million in compensatory damages and $50 million in exemplary damages, and demanded that E*Trade cease using the advertisement.

Lohan and E*Trade came to an undisclosed settlement in September 2010, according to the news service Reuters.

DEALS, ACQUISITIONS AND MERGERS

In 2003, the company changed its name from E*Trade Group Inc. to E*Trade Financial Corporation. In the same year, the Toronto Dominion Bank (TD Bank) considered merging its TD Waterhouse discount brokerage firm with E*Trade, but the two sides could not agree over control of the new entity.

In 2005, E*Trade attempted to acquire Ameritrade, at the time the second largest U.S. discount broker. However, Ameritrade purchased TD Waterhouse instead. Also in 2005, E*Trade Financial acquired Harrisdirect, a former discount brokerage service of the Bank of Montreal, and Brown & Company, a discount brokerage service of J.P. Morgan.

In 2007, E*Trade Australia was acquired by the Australia and New Zealand Banking Group Ltd. (ANZ), one of the largest companies in Australia and New Zealand and a major international banking and financial services group headquartered in Melbourne, Australia. With the exception of Hong Kong and Singapore, this effectively ended E*Trade's local market trading in Asia. Local market trading is the situation in which non-U.S. investors trade in non-U.S. stocks.

In July 2011, the *Wall Street Journal* reported the possibility of TD Ameritrade Holding Corporation acquiring E*Trade Financial Corporation, although a subsequent report noted that TD Ameritrade was "lukewarm" to the idea in light of the possible price and the size of E*Trade's mortgage portfolio.

SEE ALSO *Day Trading; TD Ameritrade Holding Corp.; Volatility.*

BIBLIOGRAPHY

Ahmed, Azam. "Citadel Turns up Heat on E*Trade." *New York Times,* July 25, 2011. Available from http://dealbook.nytimes.com/2011/07/25/citadel-turns-up-heat-on-etrade.

Australia and New Zealand Banking Group Ltd. "About Us." Melbourne, Australia, 2011. Available from http://www.anz.com/about-us.

"E*Trade Caves in to Citadel, Hires Goldman." *Reuters,* August 5, 2011. Available from http://www.reuters.com/article/2011/08/08/etrade-citadel-idUSN1E7771UX20110808.

E*Trade Financial Corp. "A Growth Company in a Growth Market." New York, 2011. Available from https://us.etrade.com/e/t/home/aboutus.

———. "Products and Services." *E*Trade,* 2011. Available from https://us.etrade.com/e/t/home/productservices.

Fernandes, Lorna. "ETrade Seeking Security in Sacto." *Business Journal,* April 8, 1996.

Gerlach, Douglas. "Special Report." *PC World,* February 1999.

Gunn, Eileen. "Huge Growth for E-brokers." *Internet World,* May 3, 1999.

Kerr, Deborah. "Number One: A Second-Thought Success." *Business Journal,* October 23, 1995.

Philbin, Brett. "Ameritrade, E*Trade, Posted Record Trading Volume Monday." *Wall Street Journal,* August 4, 2011. Available from http://online.wsj.com/article/BT-CO-20110810-718693.html.

Rusli, Evelyn M. "Citadel Storms E*Trade." *Forbes.com,* November 29, 2007. Available from http://www.forbes.com/2007/11/29/etrade-citadel-update-markets-equity-cx_er_1129markets20.html.

Schifrin, Matthew. "E-warning." *Forbes,* February 22, 1999.

Stempel, Jonathan. "Lohan Settles E*Trade Milkaholic Suit." *Reuters,* September 20, 2010. Available from http://www.reuters.com/article/2010/09/21/us-lindsaylohan-etrade-idUSTRE68J4JU20100921.

Swett, Clint. "California-Based ETrade Takes Huge Gamble with Online Stock Trading." *Knight-Ridder/Tribune Business News,* June 17, 1998.

EUROPEAN COMMISSION'S DIRECTIVE ON DATA PRIVACY

In October 1995, the European Commission issued a parliamentary directive on data protection (Directive 95/46/EC) that contained comprehensive guidelines for safeguarding the privacy of Internet users. The guidelines addressed the collection, storage, retrieval, and dissemination of personal data that could be gathered and transferred over the Web. The directive was aimed at the European Union (EU) member states and constituted one of the strongest statements regarding the protection of online users' privacy rights in the international Internet forum. The EU followed that initial directive with several others that expanded its scope to include mobile telecommunications, the use of computer cookies, site privacy "opt-in" policies, and related topics.

The directive, which took effect in the fall of 1998, created a standardized framework for online privacy rights for citizens of all EU member states. It set out minimum standards that the Internet privacy legislation of each EU member nation must meet. For example, it prohibits the processing and collection of personal data unless the user consents to such an activity. In addition, data considered to be of a particularly sensitive nature—such as that concerning political or religious beliefs, racial or ethnic origin, or sexual preference—cannot be gathered at all, except in cases where the individual user has explicitly agreed, or where pressing medical or legal circumstances mandate it. Finally, the transfer of personal data outside of the EU can only occur if the recipient demonstrates it will provide an "adequate" level of protection for the individual's privacy consistent with the directive's standards. The acceptability of non-EU data recipients is gauged by the industry rules and security measures taken to be the standard in the recipient's country. Under the directive, individual EU citizens may sue for breach of privacy.

Critics of the directive—prominent among them government officials and multinational companies in the United States—feel that the EU approach is too restrictive, and that by privileging user privacy it stifles both economic enterprise and free expression on the Web. In contrast to mandated legislation, American online marketers have argued for industry self-regulation. The United States worked to establish this through the Safe Harbor Privacy Program, which requires that participating organizations voluntarily provide proof to the U.S. Department of Commerce that they have "reasonable data protections" in place. In July 2000, the European Commission ruled that the American Safe Harbor Privacy Principles met the protection standards outlined by the commission directive. According to those standards, Safe Harbor certification can be earned by becoming a member of a self-regulatory program that follows Safe Harbor guidelines; by developing an internal privacy policy that meets those guidelines; or by submitting to an administrative, regulatory, or statutory body or law that provides an acceptable level of data protection.

If such practices satisfy the standards of the EU directive, compliant organizations are exempt from prosecution for violating the directive's guidelines when they transfer personal data into or out of any EU member country. In the United States, the first Safe Harbor program was put into place in 2000. U.S. companies were initially slow to embrace the terms of the agreement, although it did gain wider acceptance and participation during the first decade of implementation. As more U.S. multinational companies expanded their e-commerce and related operations to the Internet, they adopted measures compliant with both the U.S. privacy directive and a similar law adopted by Switzerland.

AMENDMENTS

The EU also amended and expanded the original directive (95/46/EC) with additional privacy directives. The first was 2002/58/EC on Privacy and Electronic Communications (also referred to as the E-Privacy Directive), effective on July 12, 2002. This directive was a response to the rapid expansion of mobile communication devices across Europe and around the world. The directive spells out privacy regulations governing cellular phones, smartphones, and other mobile devices. The E-Privacy Directive addresses secure traffic, privacy, security, spamming, electronic cookies, and related concerns in the use of digital devices.

In 2009, the EU began drafting further revisions to the existing policy directives. Known as Directive 2009/136/EU, the proposal was drafted in 2010 and the enabling legislation introduced in 2011. The directive was in the process of being adopted and implemented in late 2011.

According to the Electronic Privacy Information Center, the latest EU Data Protection Directive contains numerous "proposals on how to modernize the EU framework for data protection rules." Goals of the directive include strengthening the rights of individuals; enhancing the free flow of information; more effective enforcement of privacy rules; and "ensuring high levels of protection for data transferred outside of the European Union."

The 2009 Directive had been controversial but was expected to eventually gain EU approval. In the United States, witnesses and legislators at Congressional hearings in September 2011 expressed concerns that the EU rules were too restrictive. As each EU member nation implements its own laws to comply with EU directives, business leaders testified, it can be difficult to comply with the various local regulations.

The new directive has also drawn fire within the EU. Some politicians feel it is too restrictive and invasive, while other parties such as consumer groups claim current protection policies are not effective and not well enforced.

SEE ALSO *Global E-Commerce: Europe; Privacy: Issues, Policies, Statements; Safe Harbor Privacy Framework.*

BIBLIOGRAPHY

Eggerton, John. "Hill Looks at EU Privacy Directives." *Broadcasting & Cable,* September 15, 2011. Available from http://www.broadcastingcable.com/article/473911-Hill_Looks_at_EU_Privacy_Directives.php.

Electronic Privacy Information Center (EPIC). "EU Data Protection Directive." Washington, DC, September 2011. Available from http://epic.org/privacy/intl/eu_data_protection_directive.html.

Fienberg, Howard. "Hobbled by Murphy's Law?" *Research,* September 16, 2011. Available from http://www.research-live.com/features/hobbled-by-murphys-law?/4006019.article.

Gillin, Donna. "Safe Harbor Principles for the European Privacy Directive Are Finalized." *Marketing Research,* Winter 2000.

Hunton & Williams LLP. "European Parliament Meeting Offers Update on Review of EU Data Protection Directive." *Privacy & Information Security Law Blog,* March 16 2011. Available from http://www.huntonprivacyblog.com/2011/03/articles/european-union-1/european-parliament-meeting-offers-update-on-review-of-eu-data-protection-directive/.

Johnson, Mark. "As Seen from Europe: A Very Public War Over Privacy." *Global Finance,* January 2001.

"Leading Privacy Law Experts Examine Impact of New EU Cookie Rules on Online Marketing." *PR Newswire,* September 13 2011. Available from http://www.prnewswire.com/news-releases/leading-privacy-law-experts-examine-impact-of-new-eu-cookie-rules-on-online-marketing-129758283.html.

Ozimek, Jane Fae. "EU Data Retention Directive 'Flawed, Unlawful'." *The Register,* April 16, 2011. Available from http://www.theregister.co.uk/2011/04/18/eu_data_retention_directive.

Thibodeau, Patrick. "Big Companies Shy Away from Safe Harbor Accord." *Computerworld,* February 19, 2001.

U.S. Department of Commerce. "Welcome to the U.S.- EU and U.S.-Swiss Safe Harbor Frameworks." Washington, DC, September 2011. Available from http://export.gov/safeharbor/index.asp.

EVANS, NANCY

Nancy Evans is cofounder and was editor-in-chief of iVillage Inc., one of the Web's largest content sites and the leading online service for women. Visitors to the site totaled more than 30 million each month during 2011, ranking it as the largest content-driven community for women.

iVillage targets women between the ages of 25 and 54 with channels such as Pregnancy & Parenting, Health, Entertainment, Beauty & Style, Food, Home & Garden, and Love & Sex. iVillage users can converse with online experts on a variety of subjects, participate in support and discussion groups, read frequently asked questions and answers on a wide range of topics, take quizzes, post links to their own Web sites, enroll in giveaways, and purchase goods and services. Membership in iVillage is free. The site garners its revenues via advertising and sponsorships and also from taking a percentage of the profits of products sold online at iVillage.

An English literature graduate from Skidmore College, Evans launched her publishing career as an editor for *Harper's Weekly.* She left that position to serve as contributing editor for *Glamour,* where she oversaw book reviews and featured editorials for the magazine. In 1985, Book-of-the-Month Club hired Evans as editor-in-chief and vice president. Two years later, she moved to Doubleday, serving as both president and publisher until 1991. With partner Jann Wenner, Evans founded and managed *Family Life* magazine in the early 1990s.

In June 1995, Evans helped former Time Warner executive Candice Carpenter (now Carpenter Olsen) create iVillage.com. As president and editor-in-chief, Evans was responsible for developing the site's content, including that available on iVillage's first two networks, About Work and Parent Soup. Evans continued to oversee the addition of new content to the site throughout the late 1990s and early 2000s.

The company went public in March 1999, with shares jumping from an initial $24 to more than $100 during the first two days of trading. In 2001, iVillage merged with rival Women.com, which gave the Hearst Corporation a 25% stake in iVillage. However, iVillage stock fell below $1 per share in 2002 following the bursting of the Internet bubble.

On July 25, 2003, iVillage announced that Evans had resigned as editor-in-chief and as a member of the company's board of directors to pursue other interests. She stated, "It's been a glorious eight years—defying the odds to create a platform of lasting consequence for women, working with the most wonderful colleagues on the planet, and serving the millions of women who inspire and delight. But boy is it time to move on to do a few more things from what iVillage women call the 'forever' projects list." Kelly Gould, a seven-year veteran at iVillage, was named as the new editor-in-chief.

In 2006, iVillage hired investment bankers to put the company up for sale. NBC Universal bought iVillage for $600 million, or about $8.50 per share.

Since leaving iVillage, Evans has worked as an independent professional in the publishing industry in the New York area. This has included writing the foreword for books such as the 2009 *The Parent Soup A-to-Z Guide to Your Toddler.*

SEE ALSO *Carpenter, Candice; iVillage.*

BIBLIOGRAPHY

Flinn, John, and Laura Rich. "Nancy Evans & Candice Carpenter: iVillage Is Building Virtual Communities for Grown-Ups to Call Home on the Internet." *ADWEEK Eastern Edition,* September 23, 1996.

Hansell, Saul. "NBC Buys a Web Site for Women." *New York Times,* March 7, 2006. Available from http://www.nytimes.com/2006/03/07/business/media/07place.html.

"iVillage Co-Founder and Editor-in-Chief Departs." *PR Newswire,* July 25, 2003. Available from http://www.prnewswire.com/news-releases/ivillage-co-founder-and-editor-in-chief-departs-70836502.html.

iVillage Inc. "About iVillage." New York, 2011. Available from http://www.ivillage.com/about-ivillage/8-a-257165.

Mack, Ann. "iVillage Co-Founder Resigns." *ADWEEK,* July 29, 2003. Available from http://www.adweek.com/news/advertising/ivillage-co-founder-resigns-66059.

Post, Tom. "It Takes More Than an Ivillage." *Forbes,* February 22, 1999. Available from http://www.forbes.com/forbes/1999/0222/6304112s1.html.

EXCITE

Excite, founded in 1994 by students at Stanford University and initially called Architext, went public in 1996 with the launch of its initial public offering (IPO). Excite's early success, ranking fifth in 1996 among Internet portals, was attributed to its search engine being one of the first to go beyond simple keyword search by developing full concept search capability. Excite used this advantage to propel its Web portal and search engine service to become one of the most recognizable names in the early years of the Internet.

EXCITE, 1996–1998

Before the end of 1996 Excite had added a broad array of information and services to its search engine to encourage Web users to make the site their default home page. Among these offerings were City.Net, an information service covering major U.S. and international cities, along with a variety of reviews, news, directories, and other references. Despite these dynamic new offerings, a late 1996 article in *Fortune* noted that, of all the leading Internet search engines, Excite appeared to be in the most precarious financial position at the end of that year. The company's stock had also lost about two-thirds of its value since its initial offering. Additionally, the firm had spent $30 million of its dwindling capital on acquisitions, partnerships, and advertising by the end of 1996.

As Internet usage surged in 1997, other Internet search engines were earning higher advertising revenue than Excite. For the third quarter Yahoo! reported a $1.6 million profit on revenue of $17 million, while Excite continued to operate at a loss. Excite continued to soldier on despite its economic shortcomings, and in a 1998 review of 11 Web portals by *PC Magazine,* Excite was rated "the best portal on the Web." The magazine noted that Excite offered excellent personalization tools, a search feature that anticipated what a person was looking for, and a sense of community.

EXCITE@HOME, 1999–2001

Excite continued to struggle financially until 1999, when high-speed Internet access provider @Home acquired the Excite Network for $6.7 billion. At the time of the acquisition Excite could boast of 20 million registered users. @Home, for its part, had 330,000 subscribers signed up for its high-speed Internet access service. @Home also had cable distribution agreements in place reaching 60 million homes. However, since many of those systems had not yet been upgraded to offer high-speed Internet access, @Home was available to only about 13 million homes at the beginning of 1999.

This acquisition, like many during the high-octane era of the early Internet, was fueled by a consolidation boom which led to @Home paying a premium value for access to Excite's customer base, thus catapulting Excite's market valuation into the stratosphere. Other portal consolidations were taking place as well, including the acquisition of Netscape Communications by America Online and Walt Disney Co.'s investment in Infoseek Corp.

Following the acquisition, the new company now called Excite@Home, had about 1,200 employees and company executives revenues of about $2 billion by 2002. George Bell, formerly CEO of Excite, became the new president of Excite@Home.

Excite@Home planned to move forward on three fronts. First, the company wanted to grow its narrowband Internet service, which had more than 28 million regular users. Second, it intended to expand the @Home subscriber base, in part by targeting registered Excite users who lived in areas where @Home's cable partners already had upgraded their systems. Third, the company planned to develop new programming opportunities for the exclusive use of its @Home broadband customers.

Over the next two years Excite@Home also pioneered or acquired a number of e-commerce services offered over its growing web portal. iMall, an early Web shopping portal, was acquired for $425 million in stock. With iMall, Excite@Home offered to set up Web shopping stores for merchants in as little as one day. Part-owner of iMall, First Data Corporation also partnered with Excite@Home to offer credit card transaction capability over the company's Web site.

In October 1999, the company launched Work.com, a service for business professionals and their companies. It was the first step of the company's initiative to develop a business portal through its business-to-business (B2B) division, @Work. In December 1999, Excite@Home acquired electronic greeting card site Blue Mountain Arts for $780 million and also launched a new consumer site, Excite Photo Center, where users could upload, download, store, edit, and print high-resolution photos. By the beginning of 2000 Excite@Home ranked third among Internet search engines in terms of unique visitors, behind Yahoo! and Lycos.

Unfortunately, the company's plan to expand its installed base of high-speed users failed when the inventory of potential homes far exceeded the company's ability to install its service. In many cases consumer demand, fueled by the company's marketing efforts, exceeded the cable operators' ability to service that demand. Furthermore, Excite@Home was involved in an increasingly fierce competition with telephone operators and America Online to build a critical mass of subscribers. This competition led to extravagant offers to subscribers, predicated on the belief that eventually the revenue from these new subscribers would justify the high initial acquisition cost. In one such promotion, Excite@Home offered three months of free service to convert AOL subscribers.

Events began to come to a head in 2000 when Excite@Home lost $7.44 billion, compared to a $1.5 billion loss for 1999. Post-first-quarter filings in 2001 by majority shareholder AT&T and by Excite@Home revealed the company's precarious financial position, attributable to shrinking online advertising revenues and a costly investment in its high-speed cable modem subscriber base. In 2001, the company planned to focus its European strategy on the United Kingdom and Italy, where there were better prospects for growth, and it closed its operations in France, Germany, and Spain. However, by the end of the year independent auditors were expressing doubt about the company's capacity to continue operations.

A further blow came when the Comcast and Cox cable companies both terminated their exclusive high-speed Internet access agreement with the company and opened their systems to other high-speed providers. With its stock trading at a 52-week low of less than $1 a share, and the company being forced to sell off its greeting card operation for a fraction of its purchase price, the company was forced to declare bankruptcy by the end of 2001.

EXCITE, 2001 AND BEYOND

At the end of 2001, following the collapse of Excite@Home, a start-up company called iWon.com began designing a site along the lines of the now defunct Excite site. Eventually, iWon.com and Infospace combined to buy the domain and brand of Excite. iWon.com, capitalizing on the high name recognition of Excite, subsequently changed its name to Excite Network and continued to operate the portal until 2004.

In 2004, fellow Web portal search engine operator Ask Jeeves, later known as Ask.com, acquired Excite Network and continued to operate the Web portal until 2005, when Ask Jeeves was acquired by Barry Diller's media company Interactive Corporation (IAC).

In 2011, still owned by IAC, Excite was part of IAC's Mindspark Interactive Network Inc., a collection of Internet B2B and B2C brands. Mindspark's strategy is to improve sites and products while recognizing and developing new strategic opportunities. Excite.com continues to distinguish itself from other Web portals by providing a highly customizable interface, easy-to-use Webmail platform, address book, and content supplied by over 100 leading providers.

In the year ending December 2010, Excite's parent company IAC had revenues of $1.64 billion, with total assets of $3.44 billion. The search portion of IAC's revenues—attributable to Excite and Ask.com—was approximately $1 billion, a 28% rate of revenue growth year-over-year. Search revenues are derived from advertising and partner product sales.

SEE ALSO *AT&T Corp; Netscape Communications Corp.; Portals, Web.*

BIBLIOGRAPHY

"@Home IPO Zooms." *Broadcasting & Cable,* July 14, 1997.

"AT&T Sings Broadband Blues." *Communications Today,* April 23, 2001.

Brady, Mick. "Excite's Free Online Stores an Overnight Hit." *E-Commerce Times,* July 14, 2000. Available from http://www.ecommercetimes.com/story/3780.html.

Conlin, Robert. "iMall Snapped Up by Excite@Home for $425 Million." *E-Commerce Times,* July 13, 1999. Available from http://www.ecommercetimes.com/story/768.html.

"Excite Search Engine and Web Portal." ThinkbizSolutions.com. Available from http://www.thinkbizsolutions.com/seo_sem_glossary/excite.html.

Fernandes, Lorna. "Internet Search Engines Are on a Roll." *Business Journal,* November 17, 1997.

Ferranti, Marc, and Mary Lisbeth D'Amico. "@Home Buys Excite for $6.7B." *Computerworld,* January 25, 1999.

IAC. "About Excite." Excite.com. Available from http://www.excite.com.

———. "Excite." New York, 2011. Available from http://www.iac.com/Our-Businesses/Excite.

"IAC Reports 2011 Q2 Results." *PRNewswire,* July 27, 2011. Available from http://www.prnewswire.com/news-releases/iac-reports-q2-results-126240113.html.

"Internet Service Provider Excite@Home May Not Survive." *Knight-Ridder/Tribune Business News,* August 21, 2001.

Krantz, Michael. "Start Your Engines: Excite and Yahoo, the Two Leading Web-Search Sites, Race to Remake Themselves into 'Portals.'" *Time,* April 20, 1998.

Leger, Jill. "Excite." *PC Magazine,* September 1, 1998.

Mermigas, Diane. "High-Speed Slowdown: Excite@Home Growth Outpacing Cable's Capacity." *Electronic Media,* August 2, 1999.

Needle, David. "Fast Growth, Fast Friends." *PC Magazine,* September 22, 1998.

Spooner, John. "Excitable Boy." *Adweek Eastern Edition,* July 7, 1997.

Stapleton, Paul. "Excite@Home." *Boardwatch Magazine,* May 2000.

Tedesco, Richard. "Excite's New Engine Points at Yahoo's Pole Position." *Broadcasting & Cable,* July 29, 1996.

"Top Search Sites." *PC Magazine,* May 9, 2000.

Wang, Andy. "Excite@Home Goes to Work.com." *E-Commerce Times,* September 30, 1999. Available from http://www.ecommercetimes.com/story/1325.html.

E-ZINES

E-zines are magazines published electronically, most often on the Internet. The terms e-zine and Webzine typically refer to the same thing. Initially, a "zine" referred to a niche magazine targeting a small, unique market. However, as the number of mainstream publications that made their way to the Web grew throughout the 1990s and 2000s, the term e-zine grew to encompass both niche and mainstream magazines that were published via the Internet. In addition to online content, most e-zines offer interactive features, such as the ability to search current and archived articles for a particular topic or keyword. Many also house message boards, which allow readers to respond to articles. Some e-zines rely solely on advertising to make money, others charge subscription fees, and many rely on both revenue sources.

EARLY ADOPTERS

One of the most well-known e-zines, *Slate,* is owned by the Washington Post Co. Roughly five million unique readers log on to *Slate*—which covers news, politics, and culture—each month. The e-zine was created in 1996 by Michael Kinsley, a former *New Republic* senior editor and cohost of CNN's political commentary program, *Crossfire.* The site includes Build Your Own Slate, a site personalization feature, and a discussion forum known as the Fray. Along with traditional banner bars, *Slate* relies on larger advertisements and sponsorships agreements, whereby the e-zine posts links to other sites.

A major competitor to *Slate, Salon* publishes news, features, interviews, and other content, with revenue coming chiefly from advertising and subscription fees. *Salon* was created in 1995 to cover political and cultural issues, and garners six million unique visitors a month. The once-free site piled up losses throughout the 2000s. Consequently, *Salon* began to limit access to content with the launch of a subscription-based Salon Premium service. Subscribers paid $29 to $45 annually for ad-free content.

Another well-known e-zine, *TheStreet,* was created in response to predictions that the number of U.S. households trading stocks electronically would grow exponentially throughout the late 1990s. Hedge fund manager and *New York* magazine columnist James J. Cramer and *New Republic* editor-in-chief and chairman Martin Peretz created TheStreet.com in 1996. The site is supported by advertising and operates a sister subscription site, Real Money.com, which features commentary from market experts. In 2011, *TheStreet* introduced a new graphic design and identity, including an updated corporate logo, ticker symbol, and corporate Web address.

PRESENT CONDITIONS

According to the Association of Magazine Media, the number of consumer magazine Web sites rose by nearly 50% between 2006 and 2010. As of 2012, subscriptions that originated online accounted for more than 20% of new sales. E-zines were increasingly used by traditional publishers as effective tools for offering subscribers additional Web-only content. Digital subscriptions comprised as much as 15% of overall circulation at some publications, according to BPA Worldwide.

A growing number of e-zines transitioned or debuted in digital format in the late 2000s. Digital versions were not necessarily Web sites, but downloadable data files with software tools that enabled readers to navigate content. This enabled traditional magazine publishers to input text into digital e-zines without any additional writing or editing required. In addition, publishers increasingly introduced titles that were available exclusively on the Apple App Store. News Corp. debuted *The Daily,* an iPad-based newsstand, in 2011.

The proliferation of iOS apps, or mobile applications that enabled content to work on devices such as the iPad and iPhone, gave publishers a vast new audience. Device users who signed up for the *Wired* iOS app, for example, could purchase a subscription from the App Store and have new issues downloaded to their mobile devices automatically when they were published with no interaction required.

Boasted as the "first 'all media' product," *The Daily* sprang to life as a subscription system that included text, photos, and video, all at a cost of 99 cents per week or $39.99 per year. "There's no paper, no multimillion dollar presses, no trucks, and we're passing on these savings to the reader," News Corp. chief Rupert Murdoch said at the announcement. "The target audience is the 50 million Americans expected to own tablets in the next year." *The Daily* featured a layout similar to a magazine with text columns and dotted with media-rich video, audio, and photos.

E-ZINES AND MOBILE COMMERCE

The proliferation of mobile devices such as the Apple iPad and Amazon Kindle created both challenges and new opportunities for e-zine publishers. Such devices were anticipated to sell more than 200 million units by 2014, according to the Audit Bureau of Circulations (ABC). Nearly 90% of digital magazine publishers, including e-zine publishers, expected readers to rely more on mobile devices for content. Publishers further listed Apple as the top e-reader manufacturer that would have an impact on the digital publishing segment, although Google's Android products were also expected to have an impact.

A natural result of the mobile device explosion has been an increasingly insatiable demand among American consumers for information on the go. For instance, 85% of U.S. residents owned a cell phone in 2010, according to the Pew Research Center's Internet & American Life Project. "Publishers are clearly becoming better at multitasking and producing content for both print and digital distribution," according to the Audit Bureau of Circulations.

SEE ALSO *E-books; Electronic Publishing; Mobile E-Commerce.*

BIBLIOGRAPHY

Audit Bureau of Circulations. *Going Mobile: How Publishers Are Solidifying Strategies and Adapting to the Mobile Market.* Arlington Heights, IL, November 2010. Available from http://www.accessabc.com/pdfs/mobile2010.pdf.

Black, Jane. "On the Web, Small and Focused Pays Off." *BusinessWeek Online,* August 28, 2001. Available from http://www.businessweek.com/bwdaily/dnflash/aug2001/nf20010828_333.htm.

Cheng, Jacqui. "With The Daily Launch, iOS Developers Can Also Offer Subscriptions." *Ars Technica,* February 2011. Available from http://arstechnica.com/apple/news/2011/02/with-the-daily-launch-ios-developers-can-also-offer-subscriptions.ars.

———. "iPad Newsstand 'The Daily' Finally Makes Debut at 99¢ per Week." *Ars Technica,* February 2011. Available from http://arstechnica.com/apple/news/2011/02/ipad-newsstand-the-daily-finally-makes-debut-at-99-per-week.ars.

"Company Profiles." Austin, TX, Hoover's, 2011. Available from http://www.hoovers.com.

"Magazine Publishers Industry Profile." Austin, TX: First Research. Available from http://www.firstresearch.com/industry-research/Magazine-Publishers.html.

Pack, Thomas. "Slate's Moore Has Faith in Online Ads." *EContent,* September 2001.

Peterson, Thane. "The Wolf at Salon's Door." *BusinessWeek Online,* August 7, 2001. Available from http://www.businessweek.com/bwdaily/dnflash/aug2001/nf2001087_180.htm.

Slate. "About Us." New York, June 9, 2009. Available from http://www.slate.com/id/2147070.

Stern, Gary M. "TheStreet.com: Gaining the Competitive Edge." *Link-Up,* February 1998.

Taylor, Cathy. "Takin' It to the Street." *Mediaweek,* November 18, 1996.

F

FACEBOOK

Facebook, the largest social network in the world, had more than 750 million active users as of July 2011. Facebook began in 2004 as a small private network connecting Harvard University students. By the end of that decade, it had grown to become one of the world's most visited Web sites, reaching an estimated 43% of Internet users around the world. It was considered one of the "four titans of technology," alongside Google, Apple, and Amazon.com.

Facebook describes itself as a "social utility that helps people communicate more efficiently with their friends, family, and coworkers." Users can register for a free account and then create a personal page. They can post text messages about the events in their lives or personal opinions, as well as photographs, videos, and links to other Web sites. They can share their personal page with other Facebook users and play online games together. In order to connect with another user, Facebook users must send an automated request to that user inviting him or her to become their "friend" on Facebook. That request must then be approved by the receiving user before the connection is effective. The ability to "friend" and "unfriend" other users lets individuals determine whether they share their personal updates with a specific person. Facebook's privacy control settings also allow users to restrict who can see what on their site. For example, users can share different details of their personal life with a group of coworkers than those seen by family members or close friends.

Facebook has also become an attractive site for marketing and advertising campaigns, drawing significant dollars away from competing Web sites and from traditional advertising outlets. Facebook has banner ads and sponsored links that are tailored toward each user's online usage patterns and history. However, Facebook is most useful for referral marketing programs, relying on users to share with their "friends" links they find of interest. Users can also "like" fan pages that are set up for certain products, services, companies, celebrities, and events. This endorsement is visible to other members of their personal network. Facebook hosted an estimated four million fan pages as of August 2011.

HISTORY AND GROWTH OF FACEBOOK

Facebook was founded in February 2004 by Mark Zuckerberg, a Harvard University student. Zuckerberg had previously developed or worked on several similar sites, most notably Facemash, the direct predecessor of Facebook. The site, which was originally called "TheFacebook," was first available only to other Harvard students. The site was an immediate success at Harvard. By March 2004, three other Harvard students joined Facebook as cofounders to help to spread the concept to other universities—first to other Ivy League colleges and to Stanford University in California, and later to virtually all educational institutions in the United States and Canada. A high school network was added in 2005, and employees of certain companies—such as Microsoft and Apple—were also able to join.

By September 2006, Facebook was open to anyone above the age of 12 with a valid e-mail address. Once the platform was available to the general public, Facebook quickly grew into the largest social network in the world, passing MySpace in 2009 for the top position. Among all Web destinations, advertising statistical service DoubleClick AdPlanner estimated Facebook had one trillion page views in June 2011 (although experts said a July 2011, 467 billion measurement by pageview service comScore was probably more accurate). Both studies showed Facebook leading second-place Google by a substantial margin.

Zuckerberg founded Facebook as a private company in Massachusetts. In June 2004, he moved the headquarters to Palo Alto, California. Sean Parker, a cofounder of the music file-sharing service Napster and social networking site Plaxo, was the first president of Facebook. The company moved again in 2011 to a new headquarters in Menlo Park, California. The company had more than 2,000 employees at that time, with a number of other offices around the world.

Facebook remained privately held through 2011. Its first round of funding came in the summer of 2004, when Peter Thiel, the cofounder of PayPal, invested $500,000. A second round of $12.7 million came in April 2005 from Accel Partners. The third round of $27.5 million followed in 2006, with Greylock Partners leading the funding and Meritech Capital Partners, Accel Partners, and Thiel also participating. In 2007, Microsoft paid $240 million for a 1.6% stake, which implied a $15 billion value for Facebook. Goldman Sachs and other investors put in another $1.5 billion in January 2011, which boosted Facebook's implied value to $50 billion. By June 2011, that value was estimated at $85 billion.

Facebook was widely expected to go public once the economic downturn and market uncertainly that began in 2008 ended. The company had $1.86 billion in revenues for 2010, with most of that generated by advertising revenues. Facebook was expected to fetch $100 billion when its initial public offering (IPO) hit the market, possibly in 2012.

During its brief history, Facebook fended off several takeover attempts. Rival site Friendster offered $10 million to buy the company in 2004. Yahoo offered $1 billion in mid-2006, an offer Zuckerberg turned down. Viacom had also offered $750 million for Facebook in March 2006.

ISSUES AND CONCERNS

With its dramatic growth and wide social impact, Facebook also met with controversy over the years. Concerns about privacy—specifically, how much personal data Facebook shared with its advertising partners—and how much control users had over their own information were a frequent issue. Facebook was continually making changes to its product, so each change in features (such as news feeds and privacy controls) typically brought resistance from long-time users. Parents faced continual dilemmas over the age at which they should let their children join Facebook, and how much time youngsters should spend in a virtual social world. Facebook has also been banned in a number of countries, including fundamentalist Muslim states and China. Its role in facilitating the Arab Spring uprisings in 2011 against authoritarian regimes brought it favorable media attention. However, the United Kingdom also looked at limiting the impact of social media after looters and arsonists used it to organize riots that same summer.

Facebook's history included litigation and legal issues since its earliest days. Only a week after the company was launched, three Harvard seniors claimed Zuckerberg had stolen their ideas for a college-based networking site to start Facebook. Their lawsuit against Zuckerberg was settled out of court. Another lawsuit, by Eduardo Saverin, an early Facebook cofounder, was also settled. Parker, the company's first president, was forced out in 2005 over personal legal troubles. These disputes were documented in such books as *The Accidental Billionaires* (2009), and were fictionalized in the 2010 film, *The Social Network.*

GAMING AND OTHER APPLICATIONS

From its beginning, Facebook relied on a variety of applications to set itself apart from rival online destinations. Its core applications were developed by Facebook itself, while others were created by external companies as "plug-ins" that run on Facebook's open platform. While the initial role of Facebook was simply connecting individuals in an online environment, that goal was enhanced by such capabilities as playing games and sharing photographs with friends, family, and coworkers. Facebook users were able to stay in touch during virtually any waking moment by using a computer, cellular phone, smartphone, tablet PC, or various other devices.

The role of casual gaming in the Facebook strategy illustrated how successful the platform has been in attracting and retaining users. Playing games keeps visitors on the site longer, thus boosting its appeal to advertisers and marketers.

A major beneficiary of the Facebook gaming platform was its leading game developer, Zynga, which provided such popular games as *Mafia Wars, Farmville,* and *Zynga Poker.* By mid-2011, Zynga had more than 264 million active users on Facebook, a number exceeding the combined total for the next largest 15 gaming firms. Almost all of Zynga's revenues came through Facebook. When Zynga filed for its IPO, it reported 2010 profits of $90 million on $597 million in sales.

Among in-house developed products, Facebook's photo-sharing application (or "app") has been among its most successful services. The app was launched in

2005, making it one of the platform's first enhancements. By 2007, Facebook had passed such popular photo-sharing sites as Flickr and Picassa to become the top online photo site, with 23.9 million monthly visitors. By 2008, Facebook had grown to 10 billion photos, and it was storing 100 billion photos by the summer of 2011.

DIVERSIFICATION

As Facebook continued to grow, it moved from being only a social networking site: It aimed to be a different way to organize online information. In 2011, it formed a partnership with Warner Brothers to stream certain movies to its users for a modest fee. Facebook also added Reed Hastings, CEO of video distributor Netflix, to its board, sparking speculation of a further move into the streaming movie business. Also that year, Facebook added free one-on-one video chat through a new partnership with Skype, which had 145 million regular users of its own.

In the early 2010s, Facebook was expected to challenge online job sites like Monster.com with expanded career pages for professional recruitment. LinkedIn, the social networking site geared for professionals, was also apparently a target for Facebook as it introduced its new Branchout service. Facebook stated it had three million jobs and 20,000 internships when it introduced Branchout to its users in July 2011.

FACEBOOK'S ROLE IN E-COMMERCE

Online games, photo sharing, and other applications were all forces in the growth and success of Facebook. Compared to other online destinations, the average time a user spent on Facebook and the frequency of visits was far greater than for other platforms, including both social media and nonsocial networking sites. This made Facebook a more appealing destination for advertisers—and a more favorable marketing platform for e-commerce campaigns. As a result, Facebook has been able to supplant older sites like MySpace; draw advertising dollars from both traditional media and online competitors like Yahoo; and introduce such innovations as its own virtual currency.

Factors such as lower costs and more targeted results led a number of companies to move their print, television, and radio advertising to online outlets in the early years of the twenty-first century. Due to Facebook's popularity, the cost-per-click for its ads rose 74% from 2010 to 2011 in major global media markets, while display advertising prices rose 45%. Facebook was projected to generate $2.2 billion in advertising revenues in the United States for 2011, increasing its graphical display ad market share from 12.2% to 17.7% during a 12-month span. The numbers moved Facebook past Yahoo (13.3% market share) as the top online advertising destination, with Google, Microsoft, and AOL rounding out the top five sites. Meanwhile, Yahoo, which had rejected a $47.5 billion takeover offer from Microsoft in 2008, was only valued at $14 billion by August 2011.

While Facebook was not the first major social networking site, it surpassed MySpace for the top ranking in 2008. News Corp. paid $580 million for MySpace in 2005 but was unable to match fierce competition from Facebook. From January to August 2011, for example, MySpace lost about half of its 73 million unique visitors in the United States alone. News Corp. eventually took a $254 million write-off when it sold MySpace for $35 million in June 2011. The new owners, advertising firm Specific Media, then announced plans to change MySpace from a social network into a music site that would compete with iTunes.

Another area where Facebook was just beginning to make an impact was virtual currency, which is used to support the sale of both virtual goods and "real world" products and services. The virtual goods market was expected to grow from $600 million in 2009 to $2.4 billion by 2012, according to the firm Javelin Strategy & Research. Gamers such as Zynga had already offered virtual currency in their games, with which users could purchase various premium upgrades (such as new furniture for their virtual homes). Facebook moved a step further in 2011 with Facebook Credits that could be used in many areas of the Facebook platform. For roughly 10 cents per credit, users could buy Facebook Credits that were good for streaming movies, gaming enhancements, Facebook gifts to friends, and other purposes. Facebook was criticized for requiring game developers to accept Facebook Credits, as Facebook received 30% of all sales. Facebook Credits were also expected to challenge PayPal as the top online payment processing mechanism.

SEE ALSO *Social Media.*

BIBLIOGRAPHY

Baloun, Karel. *Inside Facebook.* San Francisco, CA: Karel Baloun, 2006.

Bockmier, Zack. "Zynga Likely to Benefit from Facebook-Google+ Competition." *Seeking Alpha,* August 17, 2011. Available from http://seekingalpha.com/article/287885-zynga-likely-to-benefit-from-facebook-google-competition.

Bradshaw, Tim. "Facebook Ad Prices Soar as Big Brands Shift from TV and Print." *Financial Express,* July 19, 2011. Available from http://www.financialexpress.com/news/Facebook-ad-prices-soar-as-big-brands-shift-from-TV-and-print/819642/.

Bruner, Jon. "What's a 'Like' Worth?" *Forbes,* August 8, 2011. Available from http://www.forbes.com/forbes/2011/0808/technology-social-media-facebook-google-like-worth.html.

Deaux, Joe. "Facebook Board Adds Netflix CEO Hastings." *TheStreet,* June 23, 2010. Available from http://www.thestreet.com/story/11163943/1/facebook-board-adds-netflix-ceo-hastings.html.

Facebook. "Factsheet." Menlo Park, CA, 2011. Available from http://www.facebook.com/press/info.php?factsheet.

"Facebook to Surpass Yahoo in Display Ad Dollars." *Dayton Business Journal,* June 21, 2011. Available from http://www.bizjournals.com/dayton/news/2011/06/21/facebook-to-surpass-yahoo-in-display.html.

Faiola, Anthony. "After Riots, British Government Weighs Social Media Restraints." *Washington Post,* August 12, 2011. Available from http://www.thewashingtonpost.newspaperdirect.com.

"Google+ and Facebook." *Live Trading News,* August 19, 2011. Available from http://www.livetradingnews.com/google-and-facebook-50571.htm.

Hackman, Mark. "Google's Google+ Adds Games, but Wants Data in Return." *PC Magazine,* August 11, 2011. Available from http://www.pcmag.com/article2/0,2817,2390952,00.asp.

Hampp, Andrew. "Revamped MySpace Will Have iTunes, Spotify and Vevo in Its Crosshairs." *Advertising Age,* August 23, 2011. Available from http://adage.com/article/digital/revamped-myspace-itunes-spotify-vevo/229418.

Hernandez, Vittorio. "Facebook Reaches One Trillion Hits." *All Headline News,* August 26, 2011. Available from http://www.allheadlinenews.com/articles/90058221.

Horn, Leslie. "News Corp. Lost $254 Million on MySpace." *PC Magazine,* August 11, 2011. Available from http://www.pcmag.com/article2/0,2817,2390915,00.asp.

Kirkpatrick, David. *The Facebook Effect.* New York: Simon & Schuster, 2010.

McCarthy, Caroline. "Facebook's Follies: A Brief History," *CNET,* May 13, 2010. Available from http://news.cnet.com/8301-13577_3-20004853-36.html.

Mezrich, Ben. *The Accidental Billionaires: The Founding of Facebook.* New York: Random House, 2009.

Oreskovic, Alexei. "Facebook Launches Video Chat with Skype." *Reuters,* July 7, 2011. Available from http://www.reuters.com/article/2011/07/07/us-facebook-idUSTRE76559120110707.

Phillips, Sarah. "A Brief History of Facebook." *Guardian,* July 25 2007. Available from http://www.guardian.co.uk/technology/2007/jul/25/media.newmedia.

Sengupta, Somini. "New Control Over Privacy on Facebook." *New York Times,* August 24, 2011. Available from http://www.nytimes.com/2011/08/24/technology/facebook-aims-to-simplify-its-privacy-settings.html.

Takahashi, Dean. "Why Game Developers Hate the Facebook-Zynga Marriage, and How Google+ Can Benefit." *VentureBeat,* July 29, 2011. Available from http://venturebeat.com/2011/07/29/facebook-zynga-google-games.

Ulanoff, Lance. "Facebook Is Bigger Than All of Us." *PC Magazine,* July 22, 2010. Available from http://www.pcmag.com/article2/0,2817,2366875,00.asp.

———. "Facebook Won't Replace Netflix Any Time Soon." *PC Magazine,* March 9, 2011. Available from http://www.pcmag.com/article2/0,2817,2381706,00.asp.

"United States Internet and Facebook Usage State by State." Internet World Stats, 2010. Available from http://www.internetworldstats.com/stats26.htm.

"Virtual Currency and Social Network Payments — The New Gold Rush: How Emerging Virtual Transactions Will Alter the Payments Landscape Forever" Pleasanton, CA: Javelin Strategy & Research. June 29, 2011. Available from https://www.researchandmarkets.com/reportinfo.asp?cat_id=0&report_id=1837996&q=Virtual%20Currency%20and%20Social%20 Network%20Payments%20&p=1.

Walmsley, Andrew. "Facebook Dominates but the Social Network Reigns Supreme." *Marketing,* August 3, 2011. Available from http://www.mareketingmagazine.co.uk.

Wortham, Jenna. "Sims Move In on Facebook." *New York Times,* August 22, 2011. Available from http://query.nytimes.com/gst/fullpage.html?res=9900E6DC1339F931A1575BC0A9679D8B63.

"Yahoo Value Plummets to $14bn in Three Years." *AllBusiness.com,* August 10, 2011. Available from http://www.allbusiness.com/marketing-advertising/marketing-advertising/16648709-1.html.

Yang, Jia Lynn. "Four Titans of Tech Are Racing to Be King of Digital Age." *Washington Post,* August 17, 2011. Available from http://www.washingtonpost.com/business/economy/four-titans-of-tech-are-racing-to-be-king-of-digital-age/2011/08/16/gIQA51i8JJ_story.html.

Zieminski, Nick, and Bijoy Koyitty. "Facebook, LinkedIn Threaten to Slay Monster.com." *Reuters,* August 24, 2011. Available from http://www.reuters.com/article/2011/08/24/us-monster-socialmedia-idUSTRE77N6QW20110824.

FEDEX CORP

With a workforce of nearly 275,000 worldwide, FedEx Corp. is one of the world's premier providers of shipping, e-commerce, and business services. In 2009, FedEx Express and FedEx Ground, two of the company's segments, combined for an average daily volume of over seven million delivered packages. FedEx is the clear leader by share in the international express delivery market, and it also maintains a leading 49% share of ground freight shipping in the United States. So dominant is the company in the shipping market, and the market in shipping so strongly correlated to economic activity, economists frequently use FedEx volumes as a surrogate for overall economic activity. FedEx maintains a fleet of delivery vehicles, trucks, and aircraft located in over 220 countries and territories throughout the world.

EARLY HISTORY

In 1971, Frederick W. Smith raised $91 million in venture capital, added $4 million of inherited money to this funding, and purchased a used aircraft company in Little Rock, Arkansas. He began using the aircraft to provide overnight delivery services for envelopes and small packages being shipped within the United States. Smith eventually named his business Federal Express.

Through various highs and lows, Smith's tenacity finally paid off in 1976, when the firm achieved profitability for the first time. With roughly 19,000 packages delivered every day, sales in that year reached $3.6 million.

By the 1980s, package delivery rates for the company had reached 65,000 per day, while the firm operated units in nearly 90 U.S. cities. That year, the firm also launched its "FedEx Overnight Letter" and began international service to Canada. By then, Federal Express had become the leading airfreight services provider in the United States. Sales reached $1 billion in 1983. International expansion continued in 1985 when Federal Express established a European headquarters in Brussels, Belgium, while sales grew to $2 billion.

Federal Express began an aggressive expansion policy in the 1980s which included acquisitions such as Cansica and Island Courier Companies. The firm added to its international holdings in 1988, with the purchase of Italy's SAMIMA and three freight carriers based in Japan.

In 1989, in its largest purchase to date, Federal Express paid roughly $885 million for Tiger International Inc. Tiger operated an air cargo delivery service known as the Flying Tigers, which held runway rights in major metropolitan airports in Asia, Europe, and South America. The purchase allowed the firm to strengthen its airfreight services, particularly overseas, where sales nearly doubled.

By the start of the 1990s, Federal Express held 43% of the express transportation market, compared to the 26% market share of its largest rival, United Parcel Service (UPS).

Express packages delivered daily averaged 1.4 million in 1993. By then, Federal Express had grown into the largest overnight delivery service on the globe. To compete with the same-day delivery and early morning delivery services offered by UPS, FedEx began offering similar services for both packages and letters in 1995. The firm also began making deliveries to eight countries located in the former Soviet Union. The firm also became the first U.S. cargo carrier allowed to fly in China. A 15-day strike at UPS allowed FedEx to capture market share from its rival. By then, the firm's fleet had grown to 590 airplanes and 38,500 vehicles.

MOVE TO THE INTERNET

According to a November 1997 article in *Fortune,* FedEx had been engaged in e-commerce since the 1970s with its COSMOS and DADS systems. Its PC-based automated shipping system, known as FedEx PowerShip, had first been implemented in 1984. The company's handheld bar code scanner system, known as SuperTracker, had been in place since 1986. "Smith figured out two decades ago that FedEx was in the information business, so he stressed that knowledge about cargo's origin, present whereabouts, destination, estimated time of arrival, price, and cost of shipment was as important as its safe delivery." The firm also began offering supply chain consulting services in the 1990s, using its state-of-the-art technology to help clients streamline order fulfillment processes electronically.

In 1994, FedEx launched its Web site, which allowed clients to track package shipments online. Software known as FedEx Ship permitted shipment processing via desktop terminals. It was two years later that FedEx made its first major move toward conducting operations on the Internet. The company released its first version of FedEx interNetShip, the first service that permitted clients to manage shipping via the Internet. interNetShip also allowed users—both shippers and recipients—to access shipping information via the Internet and print shipping documentation. FedEx began offering e-business tools related to FedEx shipping and tracking processes in 1997. One year later, the firm launched FedEx Logistics to oversee its growing supply chain services operations.

Despite the firm's early e-business savvy, most analysts believed that rival UPS had gotten the upper hand in Internet-based shipping. This partly was because it focused on deliveries to residences, which began dramatically increasing as businesses and consumers alike started to purchase everything from books and CDs to computers and software on the World Wide Web. Hoping to compete with UPS and its leading domestic ground delivery service, FedEx paid $2.4 billion for Caliber System, a trucking company with a fleet of 13,500 trucks, in January 1999. The deal was designed to strengthen FedEx's small foothold in the business-to-business ground shipping market and also allowed it to launch business-to-consumer delivery services. FedEx established FedEx Home Delivery to handle its new residential ground delivery operations. At that time, the company handled shipping for only 10% of all goods sold online, compared to the 55% handled by UPS, which had forged alliances with the likes of e-tailing giant Amazon.com. The FedEx Marketplace was designed that year as a hub for e-merchants using Federal Express shipping.

FEDEX IN THE NEW MILLENIUM

In early 2000, FedEx diversified into customs brokerage with the purchase of Tower Group International, a unit that eventually formed the core of a new subsidiary, FedEx Trade Networks Inc. The trading unit also provided trade consulting and international transportation and logistics services.

In February 2001, the U.S. Postal Service agreed to put FedEx boxes in roughly 10,000 post offices across the nation. A month later, in conjunction with w-Technologies Inc., FedEx began making its FedEx.com Web site available on most wireless devices.

In 2004, FedEx acquired office supply and copy retailer Kinko's for $2.4 billion and renamed the operation FedEx Kinko's Office and Print Centers. Less than a year later, in a further expansion of its global shipping operations, FedEx announced the development of a new Asia Pacific shipping hub in Guangzhou, China.

Continuing its policy of growth and acquisition in the trucking and express transport arena, between 2004 and 2007 FedEx acquired ANC, a U.K. express company; Flying-Cargo Hungary Kft, an Eastern European express deliverer; and PAFEX, an India-based air freight company.

Seemingly at the height of its success in 2008, FedEx announced disappointing earnings and future earnings estimates. Hit with a double whammy of a declining economy and rising fuel prices, FedEx was experiencing a profitability squeeze in both its Ground and Express shipping components. Corporate revenues for 2009 were down to $35.5 billion from $38 billion in 2008, while operating margin declined from a peak of 9.3% in 2007, to only 2.1% in 2009. In response FedEx announced plans to significantly increase operating efficiency through its new "20/20" plan. Under the plan FedEx would reduce aircraft emissions by 20%, increase trucking fleet fuel efficiency by 20%, and accomplish both of these goals by 2020. U.S. salaried personnel received a base pay reduction, and 401K matching contributions were suspended. The company also reduced other employee costs and adjusted routes to improve efficiency.

In 2010, company profitability growth was renewed as some of the efficiency efforts begun in 2009 began to bear fruit. Introduction of the more fuel-efficient Boeing 777F aircraft was part of the reason for these gains. Although revenues for the year continued to decline, falling to $34.7 billion, the lowest since 2006, operating margins improved to 5.8%. By the end of the year, softening fuel prices and increasing volumes were cause for the company to issue favorable forecasts for the future.

In 2011, the company was organized into seven segments:

- FedEx Express—the familiar air express delivery arm
- FedEx Ground—the lower-cost, day-definite ground shipment alternative
- FedEx Office—the business printing, publishing, and document service
- FedEx Freight—the less-than-load world low-cost freight hauler
- FedEx Custom Critical—the expedited surface and air hauler for shipments requiring increase security or temperature control
- FedEx Trade Networks—a worldwide freight forwarding company, utilizing whatever means or methods of transport might best meet customer needs
- FedEx Supply Chain—providing integrated services for customers with high-value products or complex supply chain requirements

In 2011, FedEx, now a leaner, stronger, more efficient company, saw record revenues of nearly $40 billion, a 13% increase over 2010 levels, while earnings per share improved nearly 20%. The company reinstituted 401K matching compensation and salary increases that had been suspended in 2009. Perhaps appropriately for this aggressive and well-managed company, the title of the *2011 Annual Report* was "You Ain't Seen Nothing Yet."

SEE ALSO *Fulfillment Problems; Order Fulfillment; Shipping and Shipment Tracking; United Parcel Service, Inc. (UPS).*

BIBLIOGRAPHY

"FedEx Assists Online Deployments." *InfoWorld,* July 31, 2000.

FedEx Corp. "Company Information." Memphis, TN, 2011. Available from http://about.van.fedex.com/our_company/company_information.

———. "FedEx Annual Report 2011." Memphis, TN, 2011. Available from http://fedexannualreport2011.hwaxis.com.

———. "FedEx Timeline." Memphis, TN. Available from http://about.van.fedex.com/our_company/company_information/fedex_history/fedex_timeline.

"FedEx Moves Ahead with Wireless Plans." *eWeek,* April 2, 2001.

"FedEx Picks Up American Freightways." *Mergers & Acquisitions,* January 2001.

Fonseca, Brian. "FedEx Readies Online Returns Program for the Holiday Rush." *InfoWorld,* October 16, 2000.

Frook, John Evans. "FedEx, Orbit Offer E-commerce Help; Late to the Party, Shipping Giant to Offer Web-Building Services for Small Businesses." *B to B.* June 19, 2000.

Grant, Linda. "Why Fed-Ex Is Flying High." *Fortune,* November 10, 1997.

Gutierrez, Carl. "FedEx's Package of Problems." *Forbes,* June 18, 2008.

O'Reilly, Brian. "They've Got Mail! The Growth of Internet Commerce Has Raised the Stakes in the Boxing Match Between UPS and FedEx." *Fortune,* February 7, 2000.

Robinson, Sean. "E-Commerce Delivers Growth in Shipping Industry." *Puget Sound Business Journal,* May 12, 2000.

Rynecki, David. "Net Effects: Why E-commerce Makes UPS a Complete Package, but Not FDX." *Fortune,* February 7, 2000.

Tatge, Mark. "Going Postal" *Forbes,* February 5, 2001.

FIBER OPTICS

Fiber optics is the transmission of data via light waves passed through glass threads. Most major telephone companies have replaced traditional copper telephone lines with fiber optic cables. Additionally, local-area networks often use fiber optic technology. Single-mode fiber is used in conjunction with laser light to transfer data more than five miles in distance. Multimode fiber is used with a lower frequency light-emitting diode (LED) for shorter transmissions.

THE BEGINNING OF FIBER OPTICS

Fiber optic cables can carry significantly more data at a much greater speed than metal cables. For this reason, companies across the globe became interested in the technology, starting as early as the 1970s. For example, several Japanese companies, including Furukawa Electric Company Ltd., worked cooperatively to develop fiber optic cables capable of transmitting more information faster and more reliably than conventional microwave cable. Furukawa's developments throughout the 1980s included the first single-mode fiber optic connector using high-heat fusion splicing methods; a stronger, more heat resistant fiber optic cable; and a flexible fiber optic scope for use in examining the inside of pipes.

Western Electric engineers started experimenting with fiber optics in 1979. In 1980, AT&T Corp. sought permission from the Federal Communications Commission to build a 611-mile fiber optic network connecting major cities in the northeastern United States. By 1984, fiber cables in the United States had reached 250,000 miles. Other leading telecommunications players, such as Nippon Telegraph and Telephone Corp., also began to focus on fiber optic technologies in the early 1980s. Williams Telecommunications developed a fiber optic cable network that could be run inside unused steel pipelines; AMP Inc. spent more than $100 million in the development of fiber optics technology; and NYNEX Corp. entered the international long distance business by forming a $400 million joint venture to lay a transatlantic fiber optic cable. In 1988, GTE Laboratories developed the first fiber optic amplifier, and Bell Laboratories sent light pulses over fiber optic cables for 2,480 miles, setting a distance record. That year, the first transatlantic fiber optic cable was completed. In 1989, AT&T and Kokusai Denshin Denwa brought the first transpacific fiber optic cable into use.

Advances in fiber optics continued into the next decade as an increasing number of telecommunications companies, as well as firms in other industries, began embracing the technology. MCI Communications Corp. and British Telecom began working together to lay a transatlantic fiber optic cable in 1990. In 1992, Nynex Corp. revealed its intent to lay a fiber optic cable connecting the eastern United States with Japan via England and the Middle East. LDDS Communications, the predecessor to WorldCom, gained access to its first nationwide fiber optic network in 1995 when it paid $2.5 billion for WilTel Network Services, a unit of the Williams Companies. Simplex Technologies Inc. partnered with Tyco into 1997 to form Tyco Submarine Systems Ltd., an undersea fiber optic telecommunication cable system. The following year, ADC Telecommunications Inc. introduced the EtherRing switch, which allowed less expensive implementation of Ethernet technology over fiber optic networks.

Fiber optic developments continued to improve telecommunications in the early 2000s. To improve the speed and quality of their networks, many organizations began upgrading to optical Ethernet systems. Nortel Networks, for example, converted its North American ATM systems to optical Ethernet networks. According to an October 2001 article in *Business Communications Review,* "the rationale for these activities is straightforward: simpler, faster, and more reliable networking opportunities for rethinking server and storage distribution, and increased knowledge-worker productivity. The reason these are taking place now is the maturing of Ethernet transmission and switching, and the increased investment in metropolitan optical networking."

FIBER OPTICS IN THE 2010s

By 2010, fiber optic networks had spread throughout much of the developed world, as even the Vatican boasted an optical network within its ancient walls. Most of the remaining opportunities for expanding optical services were in the "last miles" sector, where the global recession that began in 2008 and cost advantages for existing copper lines had slowed the conversion of shorter, local networks to fiber optics.

With the fiber optics market maturing in most developed economies, many companies were looking at emerging markets for their future expansion. In July 2010, Fujitsu and NSW of Germany announced completion of a $100 million underwater network in Indonesia that provided several islands in that nation with their first high-bandwidth access to Internet, e-commerce, and voice and data services. Fiber optics was also a major factor in the growth of e-commerce in Kenya, where the technology helped support a boom in payment portal and online retailers. Another submarine project, the 14,000-kilometer West African Cable System (WACS), was installed in April 2011, providing the continent's third international fiber gateway. WACS officials said the direct link between Europe and South Africa was expected to meet the country's e-commerce and data needs for the next 25 years after it became fully operational in mid-2012.

Also in Africa, FTS, a billing and control systems provider, stated that fiber optics would provide a cost-effective revenue source for telecommunications providers to support e-banking, e-commerce, and similar services in areas better accessed by fiber optic networks than by mobile telephone systems. In India, K. S. Rao, the chief operating officer of Sterlite Technologies, said fiber optic-based wireline systems complement the exploding wireless networks, which are constrained by a "severe spectrum crunch, especially in cities."

The companies competing in the fiber optic space had also evolved by the early 2010s. Many of the major players were diversified multinational firms such as Fujistu, 3M, Nortel, Corning, Tyco, Siemens AG, and Sumitomo Electric, which provided fiber optics along with other technological products.

Despite the global economic slowdowns that hurt the fiber optics sector in 2000 and 2008–2009, analysts generally expected the industry to rebound in the 2010s. Global Industry Analysts (GIA) announced in early 2011 that it expected the world fiber optics components market would reach $31.3 billion by 2015. GIA stated, "Continued migration from copper to fiber network in the post-recession period, and the need to offer attractive service packages and capture large volume of subscribers, will witness service providers continuing to invest heavily to replace the traditional last mile networks with an end-to-end fiber access network, thus translating into increased demand for fiber optic components." Similarly, a January 2011 study by BCC Research put the global value of the fiber optic connector market alone at $1.9 billion the previous year, and forecast the market would grow by 9.6% annually to $3.1 billion in 2016.

SEE ALSO *Bandwidth; Connectivity, Internet; Internet Infrastructure; Photonics.*

BIBLIOGRAPHY

The Fiber Optic Association (FOA). "The FAO Reference to Fiber Optics." Fallbrook, CA, September 2011. Available from http://www.thefoa.org/tech/ref/index.html.

"Fiber Optic Connectors: Global Market." Wellesley, MA: BCC Research, January 2011. Available from http://www.report linker.com/p0363460-summary/Fiber-Optic-Connectors-Global-Markets.html.

"Fiber Optics." In *Webopedia.* Darien, CT: Internet.com, 2011. Available from http://www.webopedia.com/TERM/F/fiber_optics.html.

"Fiber Optics to the Fore." Washington, DC: National Academy of Sciences, 2009. Available from http://www.beyonddis covery.org/content/view.page.asp?I=456.

"Five Fiber Optics Stocks Worth a Look." *Seeking Alpha,* September 7, 2011. Available from http://seekingalpha.com/article/292094-5-fiber-optic-stocks-worth-a-look.

"Fixed Line Still a Revenue Opportunity in Africa." *Billing World,* September 14, 2011. Available from http://www.billingworld.com/news/2011/09/fixed-line-remains-revenue-opportunity-in-africa.aspx.

Fujitsu. "Fujitsu and NSW Complete Indonesian Submarine Fiber-Optic Network." Tokyo, Japan, May 28, 2010. Available from http://www.fujitsu.com/global/news/pr/archives/month/2010/20100528-02.html.

Glatz, Carol. "In Centuries-Old Building, Some Vatican Workers Have Techie Paradise." *Catholic Review,* September 24, 2011. Available from http://www.catholicnews.com/data/stories/cns/1103765.htm.

"Global Fiber Optic Components Market to Reach US $31.3 Billion by 2015, According to New Report by Global Industry Analysts Inc." *PRWeb,* January 12, 2011. Available from http://www.prweb.com/releases/fiber_optic_components/fiber_optic_products/prweb8058160.htm.

Kinyanjui, Kul. "Payment Portal Promises Major E-commerce Shift." *Business Daily,* January 25, 2010. Available from http://www.businessdailyafrica.com/Corporate+News/-/539550/849548/-/xrb45w/-/index.html.

"Maturing Fiber Optics Market Has Finisar, JDS Uniphase and Others Poised for Growth." *Ticker Spy,* February 16, 2011. Available from http://www.tickerspy.com/newswire/?p=4046.

Rao, K. S. "Fiber Optics in a 3G World." *Communications Today,* August 6, 2011. Available from http://www.communi cationstoday.co.in/index.php?option=com_content& task=view&id=4116&Itemid=48.

Rasool, Farzana. "WACS Lands Near Cape Town." *ITWeb,* April 19, 2011. Available from http://www.itweb.co.za/index.php?option=com_content&view= article&id=43042:wacs-lands-near-cape-town&catid=147.

Rybczynski, Tony. "Optical Ethernet—Preparing for the Transition." *Business Communications Review,* October 2001.

FILO, DAVID

David Filo cofounded Yahoo! Inc. with fellow Stanford University doctoral student Jerry Yang in March 1995. Initially a search tool for the World Wide Web, Yahoo! grew into the leading Internet portal, with more than 100 million surfers using the site every month by 2000. While Yahoo! has seen many ups and downs since then, Filo continues to oversee the technological development of Yahoo! in his capacity as Chief Yahoo. In 2011, the 45-year old Filo was number 375 on *Forbes* magazine's list of the 400 richest Americans, with a net worth estimated at $1.1 billion.

THE EARLY YEARS

Filo earned a bachelor's degree in computer engineering from Tulane University. After completing his master's degree in electrical engineering at Stanford University, Filo elected to stay at Stanford to begin working on a doctoral degree in electrical engineering. It was there that he and Yang became friends in 1989. After having difficulty keeping track of his growing list of favorite sites with the new Mosaic software that allowed users to browse the World

Wide Web, Filo enlisted Yang's help to develop a program that would let him group these pages together by subject. Filo and Yang then posted the organized list of sites, named "Jerry's Guide to the World Wide Web," on the Web. After receiving e-mail from Web users across the globe about the usefulness of the list, Filo and Yang decided to catalog the entire Web, using several layers of categories and subcategories.

As traffic on the site grew, Stanford began experiencing bottlenecks and eventually asked Filo and Yang to move the site to the commercial sector. After turning down buyout offers from the likes of Netscape and America Online (AOL), Filo and Yang decided to postpone their dissertations and cofound Yahoo!, an acronym for "Yet Another Hierarchical Officious Oracle." Recognizing their limitations, the pair hired Tim Koogle to run the business, focusing their efforts instead on developing the technology (Filo's area of expertise), and creating a household brand name (a task well suited to the outgoing Yang). When the company conducted its initial public offering in 1996, Filo and Yang both became millionaires. Their shares would eventually be worth billions.

In 1998, when fellow Stanford students Larry Page and Sergey Brin were debating whether to continue their studies or focus on developing their own search engine, Google, they approached Filo to see if Yahoo! would buy the fledgling business. Yahoo! did not buy Google, but Filo encouraged Page and Brin to find private funding and concentrate on building their site. Around this time, Filo and Yang decided to save money on upgrade costs by hiring AltaVista and Inktomi to run Yahoo!'s search functions. This freed up funds to spend on content and other services designed to get users to spend more time on the site.

UPS AND DOWNS

In 2001, Yahoo! CEO Timothy Koogle stepped down in the face of declining revenue, although Filo and Yang retained their roles as Chief Yahoos. Koogle was replaced by Terry Semel, who focused on expanding Yahoo's search capability. As Google widened its share of searchers in the following years, Yahoo's share in the American search market fell from about one-third in 2004 to about one-fifth in 2008. At the same time, Facebook and MySpace supplanted Yahoo's social networking capabilities. Semel resigned in 2008 and was replaced as CEO by Yang, while Filo retained his role as Chief Yahoo.

In 2008, Yahoo rejected a buyout offer from Microsoft, largely based on Filo and Yang's strong opposition to Microsoft. The fallout led to Yang's ouster as CEO. Filo, as head of technology, concentrated on developing a new social network-like environment for both developers and consumers called Yahoo Open Strategy. The strategy allowed Yahoo users to develop new applications, using open-source software, and to control their e-mail, photo, and bookmark management, instant messaging, and calendar planning from one command center.

While the strategy directed by Filo helped somewhat, the company continued to flounder as a result of a series of missteps. In 2011, CEO Carol Bartz was fired and Yahoo! began to search for a plan that would save it from breakup. Private equity firms circled with an eye toward snapping up the company's most profitable areas, namely its 43% stake in Chinese Internet company Alibaba and 35% stake in Yahoo! Japan. In the fourth quarter of 2011, Yang began an attempt to retake control of Yahoo!, while chairman of the board Roy Bostock attempted to keep him out. At the time, Yang owned 3.63% of Yahoo!, while Filo owned 5.80%.

In the early 2010s, it seemed likely that any future moves by Yang to regain control of Yahoo! would require Filo's cooperation. The future of Yahoo! is unclear, but it is certain that Filo, as Chief Yahoo, will play a large part in whatever happens.

SEE ALSO *Yahoo! Inc.; Yang, Jerry.*

BIBLIOGRAPHY

Davidoff, Stephen. "A Weak Board at Yahoo Stumbles in a Series of Missteps." *New York Times,* September 20, 2011. Available from http://dealbook.nytimes.com/2011/09/20/weak-board-at-yahoo-stumbles-in-a-series-of-missteps.

May, Patrick. "Lack of Corporate Focus Leaves Yahoos in Limbo." *Silicon Valley Mercury News,* September 18, 2011. Available from http://www.mercurynews.com/business/ci_18925804.

Mangalindan, Mylene, and Suein L. Hwang. "Yahoo!'s Isolation Plays into Downfall; The Coteries of Early Hires Made the Company a Hit, but an Insular Place." *Contra Costa Times,* March 11, 2001.

Schlender, Brent. "How a Virtuoso Plays the Web: Eclectic, Inquisitive, and Academic, Yahoo's Jerry Yang Reinvents the Role of the Entrepreneur." *Fortune,* March 6, 2000.

Sen, Chiranjoy. "Yahoo! Back to Doing What It Started Out to Do: Cofounder." *Economic Times,* April 24, 2009. Available from http://economictimes.indiatimes.com/yahoo-back-to-doing-what-it-started-out-to-do-co-founder/articleshow/4447393.cms.

Stross, Randall E. "How Yahoo! Won the Search Wars." *Fortune,* March 2, 1998.

"Web Crawlers." *Forbes,* October 9, 2000.

"Yahoo Comes Full Circle with Retreat from Search." *Associated Press,* July 30, 2009. Available from http://articles.nydailynews.com/2009-07-30/news/17929012_1_yahoo-terry-semel-search-engine.

FINANCING, SECURING

All new companies need financing of some sort to launch operations. In some cases, entrepreneurs are able to simply dip into their personal savings accounts. In other cases, entrepreneurs will ask a friend or relative for funding. Most often, though, new businesses will turn to outside sources such as banks and venture capital firms for start-up funding. Since venture capital firms actually purchase a portion of the company they are funding, quite often they help to steer the firm's strategic development.

Funding for firms that have not yet launched operations is known as seed money or seed investing, while funding for fledgling upstarts that have already opened for business is called early-stage investing. Banks and venture capitalists also loan money to established businesses seeking additional growth; this process is known as expansion-stage financing. Wealthy individuals who fund start-ups are sometimes called angel investors. To gain access to outside funding, entrepreneurs typically submit a business plan, which details exactly how a new or existing company will accomplish goals like launching operations, finding customers, making money, and expanding into new markets. The most successful business plans, at least in terms of securing funding, are those with a clearly defined target market. In many cases, once officials at a bank or other funding institution determine that a business plan warrants further consideration, they expect the individuals requesting the funding to pitch their ideas in person as well.

VENTURE CAPITAL

Venture capital firms focus almost exclusively on companies developing significant innovations, such as new software, a life-saving cancer drug, or a new model for consumer sales. Unless a company can demonstrate that it is poised for significant growth, a venture capitalist will typically not invest. As venture capitalists assume high risk alongside the company founders, they provide capital in exchange for an equity position in the company.

Most venture capital firms raise their funds from institutional investors such as pension funds, insurance companies, endowments, foundations, and high-net-worth individuals. Their return on investment, which can vary from nothing to millions, is usually realized when the company goes public with its initial public offering (IPO). As opposed to banks, which usually receive their income through regular interest and payments, venture capital companies may have to wait five-to-ten years to see any return on their initial investment.

In 2010, there were 462 active venture capital firms in the United States. In the same year, venture capitalists invested approximately $22 billion in almost 2,749 companies. Of these, 1,001 received financing for the first time. A 2011 Global Insight study, referred to on the National Venture Capital Association's Web site, noted that companies receiving venture capital financing accounted for nearly 12 million jobs and $3.1 trillion in revenues in the United States alone.

OTHER PRIVATE FINANCING OPTIONS

Similar to venture capitalists, angel investors provide start-up financing for entrepreneurs. The difference is usually in the size of the loan. Whereas venture capital firms make loans in the millions or even billions of dollars, angels, who are investing from their own personal net worth, generally finance less than $1 million. According to the National Angel Capital Organization (NACO), angels invest "personal after-tax assets in exchange for equity in a start-up company." Such companies tend to be small and medium-size enterprises (SMEs).

Also similar to venture capitalists, the investing mood of angels is subject to market conditions. In a 2009 article, the *New York Times* reported that the global economic crisis left angel investors feeling "skittish." They invested in fewer tech start-ups and demanded more of those that they did consider. In November 2009, half of the investors surveyed by the Angel Capital Association stated that they had invested about half of what they had predicted in 2008.

PEER-TO-PEER LENDING

For small-business owners or entrepreneurs, peer-to-peer lending may be an option. Prosper.com is a large peer-to-peer lending market place and matches borrowers with requests between $2,000 and $25,000 with investors. All loans are given to the individual entrepreneur, rather than the business itself, meaning that repayment of the loan is required independent of whether the business is successful or fails. Loans require no collateral, and approval is primarily based on an individual's credit rating.

SEE ALSO *Angel Investors; Business Plan; Due Diligence.*

BIBLIOGRAPHY

Benoit, David. "Bank Boon: Business Loans?" *Wall Street Journal,* July 20, 2011. Available from http://online.wsj.com/article/SB10001424052702303795304576456393921821486.html.

Blakey, Elizabeth. "Venture Capital Oasis: Luxury E-tailers." *E-Commerce Times,* September 27, 2001. Available from http://www.ecommercetimes.com/story/13640.html.

Cawley, Rusty. "Angel Investors Look for More Than a Business Plan." *Dallas Business Journal,* December 10, 1999.

Elstrom, Peter. "The Great Internet Money Game." *BusinessWeek Online,* April 16, 2001. Available from http://www.businessweek.com/magazine/content/01_16/b3728602.htm.

Evans, Matt. "Market Volatility Dampens Angel Investors' Moods." *Business Journal,* August 19, 2011. Available from http://www.bizjournals.com/triad/print-edition/2011/08/19/market-volatility-dampens-angel.html.

Forsman, Theresa. "The New VC Style: Deep Pockets, Short Arms." *BusinessWeek Online,* October 15, 2001. Available from http://www.businessweek.com/smallbiz/content/oct2001/sb20011015_903.htm.

Himselstein, Linda. "Robert C. Kagle." *BusinessWeek Online,* September 27, 1999. Available from http://www.businessweek.com/1999/99_39/b3648024.htm.

Macaluso, Nora. "Raising Capital: Dos and Don'ts for Small E-businesses." *E-Commerce Times,* November 20, 2001. Available from http://www.ecommercetimes.com/story/14857.html.

Miller, Claire Cain, and Brad Stone. "Angels Flee from Tech Start-Ups." *New York Times,* February 2, 2009. Available from http://www.nytimes.com/2009/02/03/technology/start-ups/03angel.html?pagewanted=all.

National Angel Capital Organization. "About Us." Toronto, Canada, 2011. Available from http://www.angelinvestor.ca/About_Us.asp.

National Venture Capital Association. "VC Industry Overview." Arlington, VA, 2011. Available from http://www.nvca.org/index.php?option=com_content&view=article&id=141&Itemid=589.

Prosper Marketplace, Inc. "About Us." San Francisco, CA, 2011. Available from http://www.prosper.com/about.

Shook, David. "VCs Go Back to the Future." *BusinessWeek Online,* November 14, 2001. Available from http://www.businessweek.com/technology/content/nov2001/tc20011114_7189.htm.

U.S. Small Business Administration. "What SBA Offers to Help Small Businesses Grow." Washington, DC, 2011. Available from http://www.sba.gov/content/what-sba-offers-help-small-businesses-grow.

FIREWALL

A firewall protects a computer network or personal computer (PC) from attacks from hackers or malicious software, known as malware. In e-commerce, a hacker may try to access customers' financial information or disrupt the business in some way. Firewall software may be integrated into a router or other piece of hardware, or it may be installed on a server or PC. The firewall acts like a gateway through which all Internet traffic must flow. It decides whether to open a port and let the data through or block it based on certain rules, such as who initiated the request and where it is from. The firewall also logs all activity so that in the event of a breach, there is an audit trail. Although a firewall (when properly implemented) provides protection from attacks via the Internet, it does not protect against internal attacks.

ROLE OF A FIREWALL

The purpose of a firewall it to protect company information, including customer records. However, even with the implementation of a firewall, security breaches commonly occur. According to statistics compiled by the nonprofit Identity Theft Resource Center, there were 371 high-profile security breaches during 2010. Of these, 108 were against medical or health care companies, 60 were against government or military networks, 39 targeted the financial industry, and 34 were aimed at educational institutions. The remaining 130 attacks were against other types of businesses. The attacks that exposed the greatest number of records were against financial institutions.

When a security network breach occurs that exposes personal data, it usually makes headlines. In 2011, one top hacker story involved several denial-of-service attacks against Sony Corp. A denial-of-service attack overwhelms the network in such a way that legitimate users cannot gain access. The April attack against PlayStation Network involved the theft of 75 million customers' financial data and caused the company to shut down this service for over a month. Next, a breach at Sony Online Entertainment involved financial data for another 25 million customers. Together with the class-action lawsuit filed by customers for Sony's failure to secure its data, Sony estimated the attacks and necessary measures to increase security would cost the company more than $170 million.

Another type of serious breach to occur in April 2011 was at the e-mail marketing firm Epsilon. Hackers stole personal e-mail information belonging to the mailing lists of dozens of retailers, banks, hotels, and other companies that use Epsilon's services. Consumer e-mail information is often the target of hackers who wish to launch phishing attacks. A phishing scam sends an e-mail that appears to be from a familiar source and tricks the recipient into entering personal information at a fraudulent Web site.

HOW A FIREWALL WORKS

Firewalls can be installed either on the network or on a PC. A network-level firewall protects the perimeter of the network by filtering all traffic flowing between the network and the Internet. This type of firewall may be software bundled with a router or other hardware to create a "security appliance," or it may be installed on a server. An application-level firewall is installed on an individual PC to provide protection regardless of which network the PC is attached to. Windows XP operating system, for example, includes firewall software. If an application tries to communicate over the network, the software sends an alert, so the user can assess the danger and either give permission or block it. Many businesses use both types of firewalls to provide more than one layer of protection.

All firewalls use "packet filtering" to monitor traffic flowing to and from the Internet. Internet traffic is broken into packets that contain the IP address of the source and the intended recipient. When a PC on the network requests data, such as a particular Web page, the network-level firewall examines the IP addresses of the packet and decides whether to forward it or block it. If a hacker sends a data packet that was not requested on the network and does not follow the predetermined rules, the firewall will block it. An application-level firewall is able to look more closely at the contents of the packet and forward or block it based on complex rules. For example, a Web page containing objectionable keywords might be blocked.

Another, newer type of firewall technology offers dynamic packet filtering, referred to as a stateful packet inspection. This type of firewall creates a state table with the properties of all established connections so that it can tell whether a packet is part of an existing connection. It can quickly confirm a packet as valid if it has the properties stored in the state table. This make a network less vulnerable to attacks from hackers; however, the firewall will not work if the hacker tricks a network user into soliciting an outside connection.

Enhanced firewall protection can include stateful filtering and an application gateway. An application gateway is sometimes referred to as a proxy, because it stands between the network server and an Internet host and prevents direct contact between the two. While the stateful inspection looks at what is being sent over each port, the application gateway examines the contents. The downside of a firewall with more stringent filtering is that it is more expensive and may slow down the network.

FIREWALL LIMITATIONS

A common warning from security systems experts is that a firewall's effectiveness is only as good as its implementation. Most security breaches are not a result of failed security technology but rather the complete lack of a firewall or the improper use of the technology. The latest technology could still lead to a security breach if servers do not require passwords or firewall software is still set to the default password. Another mistake that network administrators make is to reduce the filtering rules of intrusion detection technology to a level that diminishes the firewall's effectiveness.

Firewalls cannot protect against attacks from within the organization. Another potential threat is a mobile user who connects to the network with an infected PC. E-mail with an attached file containing a virus poses another threat. A virus worm, Trojan horse, or spyware that begins to work from within the PC can destroy files or create a breach in the firewall. If the firewall does not have an antivirus feature that scans e-mail for malicious attachments, antivirus software should be installed that alerts the user to a suspicious attachment before it is opened.

SEE ALSO *Hacking.*

BIBLIOGRAPHY

Avolio, Frederic. "Firewalls and Internet Security, the Second Hundred (Internet) Years." *Internet Protocol Journal* 2, no. 2 (June 1999). Available from http://www.cisco.com/web/about/ac123/ac147/ac174/ac200/about_cisco_ipj_archive_article09186a00800c85ae.html.

Goldman, David. "Mass E-mail Breach: Just How Bad Is It?" *CNN Money,* April 6, 2011. Available from http://money.cnn.com/2011/04/06/technology/epsilon_breach/index.htm.

"High Profile Data Breaches." *Focus,* 2011. Available from http://www.focus.com/fyi/high-profile-data-breaches.

Northrup, Tony. "Firewall." Microsoft TechNet. Available from http://technet.microsoft.com/en-us/library/cc700820.aspx.

Zetter, Kim. "FBI Arrests U.S. Suspect in LulzSec Sony Hack; Anonymous Also Targeted." *Wired,* September 22, 2011. Available from http://www.wired.com/threatlevel/2011/09/sony-hack-arrest.

FISCHER, ADDISON

Addison Fischer is considered by many to be a trailblazer in the computer security industry. He has founded and made major investments in several firms that specialize in authentication and encryption software. Up until 1996, Fischer served as a board member for RSA Data Security Inc., maker of the world's leading data encryption software. As of 2011, his board seats included Surety Technologies and Xcert International. Fischer is also chairman of SmartDisk Corp., which he spun off in 1998 from Fischer International Systems Corp., a firm he founded in 1982. In the early 2010s, he continues to service as chairman of Fischer International.

EARLY HISTORY

After graduating from West Virginia University with both a bachelor's and master's degree in mathematics, Fischer began working on his doctorate. As a college student, he worked for the university's computer center, where he gained his first experience with the development of mainframe computer security systems. Hooked by the seemingly limitless possibilities computer technology afforded to nearly all business sectors, Addison postponed his doctoral studies to work on an electronic stock predictor for the financial industry, which he completed in 1980. That year, he was named partner at Duquesne Capital Management. Two years later, when Fischer founded Fischer International, his goal was to create security software for data housed on personal computers, as well as for a technology that was just beginning to grow in popularity: e-mail. Tao, one of the new firm's first products, used IBM mainframes as a platform for electronic messaging.

One of Fischer's best-known developments is Smarty, a hardware device that allows personal computers to decipher smart cards—small cards with computer chips that allow the holder to access data such as financial records, gain access to restricted areas, and purchase goods and services. In 1998, Fischer spun Smarty off into SmartDisk Corp. He initially retained a 60% stake in SmartDisk but later reduced his holdings considerably.

The National Institute of Standards and Technology (NIST) and the U.S. Department of Defense's National Computer Security Center both formally recognized Fischer for his government report titled "Electronic Document Authorization" in the early 1990s. In 1996, Fischer became the major investor in public-key encryption technology vendor Xcert and one of the original investors in Certco, an electronic certification software provider spun off by Bankers Trust Corp. The chief investor in RSA Data Security in the late-1980s, Fischer also contributed capital when RSA spun off its digital authentication technology holdings into publicly held VeriSign Inc. in 1998.

OTHER AWARDS AND VENTURES

Along with his many business commitments, Fischer also serves on various computer security committees established by the U.S. government to address issues related to electronic commerce. He has made presentations on such topics as digital signature methodology and digital telephony to the U.S. Congress. In June 2009, Fischer was awarded the Hero of Privacy Award by the Electronic Privacy Information Center, recognizing his efforts to focus public attention on emerging civil liberties issues and protecting privacy, the First Amendment, and constitutional values.

Since the early 2000s, Fischer has focused his efforts on venture capital investing and providing seed money for emerging technology companies. He also became involved in promoting the environment, establishing several nongovernmental organizations (NGOs) dedicated to preserving rainforests around the world, and educating people on the need for conservation.

Fischer cofounded two small private Silicon Valley venture capital firms, Tierra del Oro and Camino del Oro, specializing in funding high-tech start-up companies. In 2000, these funds were brought under the umbrella of the Zenerji Fund, where Fischer served as managing director. (He continued to serve in that position as of 2011.) Fischers' other ventures (including Fischer International Identity LLC, Fischer International Systems Corporation, and Surety) were also brought into Zenerji.

Zenerji has two functions. One is to provide venture capital, asset management, and operational support to technology-based companies. In 2011, its portfolio included Actify, a company providing affordable product design visualization to various industries; and Audible Magic, which provides tools to detect, monitor, and manage copyrighted content use. Zenerji also owns properties in Central and South America and manages these properties to provide environmental stewardship and preservation. Zenerji works to support the development of sustainable communities and multidisciplinary research in ecology, waste management, forestry, economics, business, anthropology, engineering, architecture and agriculture. Through Zenerji, Fisher works to combine his venture capital work and his work on privacy issues with philanthropic endeavours.

CONSERVATION EFFORTS

Since 2003, Fischer has served on the board of the Amazon Conservation Team, a private nonprofit organization that works to protect the ancestral lands of indigenous South American tribes. In 2008, Fischer cofounded the Planet Heritage Foundation. Planet Heritage works with other NGOs and philanthropic organizations to promote marine conservation, biodiversity conservation, and climate change solutions, such as the large-scale promotion of electric vehicles. Fischer has also served as a director of the Jane Goodall Institute since 2005, and in 2009 he became director of the EastWest Institute, an NGO working to resolve and prevent international conflicts. He also serves on the advisory boards of Electronic Privacy Information Center (EPIC), the Amazon Conservation Team, and the Sylvia Earle Foundation, which works to preserve the marine environment.

SEE ALSO *Computer Security; Cryptography, Public and Private Key; Digital Certificate Authority; Encryption; RSA Data Security.*

BIBLIOGRAPHY

"Addison Fischer." Morgantown, WV: West Virginia University Alumni Association, 2011. Available from http://alumni.wvu.edu/awards/academy/addison_fischer.

Fischer International Systems Corp. "About Us." Naples, FL, 2011. Available from http://www.fisc.com/about.asp?pid=58.

———. "Addison Fischer." Naples, FL, 2011. Available from http://www.fischerinternational.com/company/team.htm.

Kane, Brad. "The Mysteries Behind the Shangri-La Hotel: The Five-Star Tour." *Naples News,* September 7, 2006. Available from http://www.naplesnews.com/news/2006/sep/07/mysteries_behind_shangrila_hotel_fivestar_tour.

Planet Heritage Foundation. "Addison Fischer, Founder and President." Naples, FL, 2011. Available from http://www.planetheritage.org/team/addison-fischer.

Souccar, Miriam K. "Smart Cards: 'Building the Future' Drives E-commerce Pioneer." *American Banker,* February 24, 1999.

FLOW

For some people, surfing the Web brings on a light, trance-like state of mind that stems from being totally focused on viewing information online. Known as flow, this state of mind can make people oblivious to surroundings and to the amount of time that passes while they are online. This is similar to what happens when one becomes completely absorbed in a book or article. The concept of flow has been around for some time. Mihaly Csikszentmihalyi, a University of Chicago psychologist whose interests include creativity and socialization, began using the term during the 1970s when he conducted research in the field. In 1990, Csikszentmihalyi wrote a book titled *Flow: The Psychology of Optimal Experience.*

Although flow has been studied in a number of areas, including sports, games, and work, it has especially powerful implications for companies engaging in e-commerce. Vanderbilt University professors Donna Hoffman and Thomas Novak have conducted research on the concept of flow as it relates to the Internet. In an interview in the *Los Angeles Times* conducted by John Geirland and Eva Sonesh-Kedar, Hoffman explained: "The implications of flow go beyond advertising and are even broader for online transactions and purchases. If the online experience isn't compelling, people aren't going to stay very long on the Web in general, and your site in particular. A consequence of flow is the reinforcement of a good feeling, so much so that it may be important for encouraging repeat visits or repeat purchase behavior."

In their research, Novak, Hoffman, and Yiu-Fai Yung of the SAS Institute indicated that flow was of importance to Web site designers and online marketing professionals. Creating Web sites that provide ample excitement for a wide audience was a major challenge for designers. If users find a site uninteresting, boredom can break a pattern of flow and they will move on to another site or an offline task. This defeats one of the central marketing tactics of e-commerce, to keep consumers on a company's site as long as possible, increasing the chance they will purchase goods or services or view online advertising.

Research conducted in 2006 by Ming-Hui Huang suggests that the degree of flow depends in part on the personal relevance of a particular site. Huang's research indicated that consumers tend to become bored or anxious when searching through a site that does not focus their attention, and will quickly navigate away to a more challenging or interesting site. This may suggest that flow is most relevant when talking about particular Web sites, rather than about the Internet itself. Huang's earlier work, in 2003, suggested that sites can increase flow by satisfying both the informational and entertainment needs of consumers. Improving content and staging may be more important for flow that navigating content.

In 2007, Maria Sicilia and Salvador Ruiz suggested that achieving a high state of flow enhances consumers' ability to process information. This suggests that Web sites should incorporate more demanding information and interactive operations without making the site too complicated to navigate. Research also suggests that flow is encouraged by site features that are challenging and competitive, stimulate control, and include interactive activities such as discussion groups, uploading and downloading options, and reading and posting capacities for newsgroups, e-mail, and games.

FLOW AND DESIGN

One example for how these design elements work together to produce flow is the Web site of photographer Yann Arthus-Bertrand, author of the *World from Above* photography series. The site was analysed in 2003 for *Optimization Week* by flow specialist Andy King. King suggested the site increases flow by immersing the viewer in an interactive experience that includes the use of feedback and transitions to make the site appear faster than it actually is. Linear progress bars and countdown timers are used as pictures load, to keep anticipation high and stress low. "The feeling of depth, the limited stimulus field (the non-scrolling window), the immediate feedback and responsiveness, and the sense of control all contribute to what Csikszentmihalyi calls the flow state."

Research reported in the *Journal of Consumer Psychology* in 2010 supports the idea that complex design can enhance both flow and the amount of time a consumer spends on a site. Generally, consumers tend to prefer brands that are easier to choose. However, when consumers are more immersed in narrative processing, such as when they achieve flow on a Web site, they are more likely to develop a preference for that brand, site, or product. In other words, once they achieve flow on a site, they are more likely to return to that site.

SEE ALSO *Attention Economy.*

BIBLIOGRAPHY

Berkun, Scott. "The Role of Flow in Web Design" *Microsoft MSDN,* January/February, 2001. Available from http://msdn.microsoft.com/en-us/library/ms993280.aspx.

"The Creative Flow of Change Makers." *Futurist,* May/June 1997.

"Flow in Web Design." Ann Arbor, MI: Website Optimization, 2008. Available from http://www.websiteoptimization.com/speed/2.

Geirland, John, and Eva Sonesh-Kedar. "Cyberculture Q&A. What Is This Thing Called Flow? Think Nirvana on the Web." *Los Angeles Times,* July 6, 1998. Available from http://articles.latimes.com/1998/jul/06/business/fi-1160.

Huang, Ming-Hui. "Designing Web Site Attributes to Induce Experiential Encounters." *Computers in Human Behavior* 19, no. 4 (2003): 425–42.

———. "Flow, Enduring, and Situational Involvement in the Web Environment: A Tripartite Second-Order Examination." *Psychology & Marketing* 23, no. 5 (2007): 383–411.

"Internet Users Go with the Flow" *USA Today,* April 29, 1996. Available from http://www.usatoday.com/life/cyber/tech/lcs 073.htm.

King, Andy. "Flowing with Yann Arthus-Bertrand." *Optimization Week,* 2004. Available from http://www.optimizationweek. com/reviews/yab.

McMahon, Kay. "An Exploration of the Importance of Website Usability from a Business Perspective." *Flow Theory,* 2011. Available from http://www.flowtheory.com/KTMDissertation. pdf.

Nielson, Jesper, and Jennifer Escalas. "Easier Is Not Always Better: The Moderating Role of Processing Type on Preference Fluency." *Journal of Consumer Psychology* 20, no. 3 (July 2010): 295–305.

Novak, Thomas P., Donna L. Hoffman, and Yiu-Fai Yung. "Measuring the Customer Experience in Online Environments: A Structural Modeling Approach." *Marketing Science* 19, no. 1 (Winter 2000): 22–42. Available from http://mktsci.journal.informs.org/content/19/1/22.short.

Sicilia, Maria, and Salvador Ruiz. "The Role of Flow in Web Site Effectiveness." *Journal of Interactive Advertising* 8, no. 1 (Fall 2007). Available from http://jiad.org/article97.

FORECASTING, BUSINESS

Business forecasting has always been one component of running an enterprise. However, forecasting traditionally was based less on concrete and comprehensive data than on face-to-face meetings and common sense. Since then, business forecasting has developed into a much more scientific endeavor, with a host of theories, methods, and techniques designed for forecasting certain types of data. The development of information technologies and the Internet propelled this development into overdrive, as companies not only adopted such technologies into their business practices but into forecasting schemes as well. In the 2000s, projecting the optimal levels of goods to buy or products to produce involved sophisticated software and electronic networks that incorporate mounds of data and advanced mathematical algorithms tailored to a company's particular market conditions and line of business.

Business forecasting involves a wide range of tools, including simple electronic spreadsheets, enterprise resource planning (ERP) and electronic data interchange (EDI) networks, advanced supply chain management systems, and other Web-enabled technologies. The practice attempts to pinpoint key factors in business production and extrapolate from given data sets to produce accurate projections for future costs, revenues, and opportunities. This normally is done with an eye toward adjusting current and near-future business practices to take maximum advantage of expectations.

FACTORS INFLUENCING BUSINESS FORECASTING

In the Internet age, the field of business forecasting was propelled by three interrelated phenomena. First, the Internet provided a new series of tools to aid the science of business forecasting. Second, business forecasting had to take the Internet itself into account in trying to construct viable models and make predictions. Finally, the Internet fostered vastly accelerated transformations in all areas of business that made the job of business forecasters that much more exacting. By the 2000s, as the Internet and its myriad functions highlighted the central importance of information in economic activity, more and more companies came to recognize the value, and often the necessity, of business forecasting techniques and systems.

Business forecasting is indeed big business, with companies investing tremendous resources in systems, time, and employees aimed at bringing useful projections into the planning process. According to a survey by the Hudson, Ohio-based AnswerThink Consulting Group, which specializes in studies of business planning, the average U.S. company spends more than 25,000 person-days on business forecasting and related activities for every billion dollars of revenue.

Companies have a vast array of business forecasting systems and software from which to choose, but choosing the correct one for their particular needs requires a good deal of investigation. According to the *Journal of Business Forecasting Methods & Systems,* any forecasting system needs to be able to facilitate data-sharing partnerships between businesses, accept input from several different data sources and platforms, operate on an open architecture, and feature an array of analysis techniques and approaches.

Forecasting systems draw on several sources for their forecasting input, including databases, e-mails, documents, and Web sites. After processing data from various sources, sophisticated forecasting systems integrate all the necessary data into a single spreadsheet, which the company can then manipulate by entering in various projections—such as different estimates of future sales—that the system will incorporate into a new readout.

One of the distinguishing characteristics of forecasting systems is the mathematical algorithms they use to take various factors into account. For example, most forecasting systems arrange relevant data into hierarchies, such as a consumer hierarchy, a supply hierarchy, a geography hierarchy, and so on. To return a useful forecast, the system cannot simply allocate down each hierarchy separately but must account for the ways in which those dimensions interact with each other. Moreover, the degree of this interaction varies according to the type of business in which a company is engaged. Thus, businesses need to fine-tune their allocation algorithms in order to receive useful forecasts.

Traditional forecasting methods used analysis such as time series and explanatory analysis to anticipate sales. In the time-series model, data simply is projected forward based on an established method—of which there are several, including the moving average, the simple average, exponential smoothing, decomposition, and Box-Jenkins. Each of these methods applies various formulas to the same basic premise: data patterns from the recent past will continue more or less unabated into the future. To conduct a forecast using the time-series model, one need only plug available historical data into the formulas established by one or more of the above methods. Obviously, the time-series model is the most useful means for forecasting when the relevant historical data reveals smooth and stable patterns. Where jumps and anomalies do occur, the time-series model may still be useful, providing those jumps can be accounted for.

Explanatory models of forecasting are more often used for new businesses, or where there is scant historical data to draw on. Models of explanatory analysis, such as a regression analysis, measure the relationship between two variables. In this method, the variables are compared to each other in order to determine the strength of their relationship. For example, one might compare sales to national GDP to determine if GDP is likely to affect sales and by how much.

DATA MINING

With the rise of the Internet, data mining became a powerful tool of forecasting. Data mining involves using algorithms to find patterns in digital data. As computer processing power has increased, and greater sources of data have become available, the uses of data mining have grown. Data mining is particularly useful for forecasting in the retail industry. For example, retail grocer Tesco credits its success to its ability to manage and mine huge amounts of data, giving the retailer the ability to operate multiple retail formats and the market knowledge to offer an optimized range of brands and products. Tesco also uses data mining to create new shop formats, arrange store layout, target sales promotions, and develop new products.

According to Stephen Brock at IBM, as the economy became more volatile beginning in 2007, businesses began moving to more frequent forecasting. He suggests that companies in an especially volatile area, such as retail fashion, could forecast weekly, or even daily, and should be prepared to reforecast immediately if conditions should change, such as on the release of a similar product by a competitor.

The use of a forecast range, or forecasts made under a variety of scenarios, is another innovation in forecasting. Companies have also been moving more toward rolling forecasts. Rather than a traditional approach—in which a forecast is made at fixed points in the year, such as quarterly—a rolling forecast looks at conditions at a fixed point in the future, such as one month ahead. This allows companies to project and plan around a fixed point.

Business forecasting systems often work hand-in-hand with supply chain management systems. In such systems, all partners in the supply chain can electronically oversee all movement of components within that supply chain and gear the chain toward maximum efficiency. The Internet has proven to be a panacea in this field, and business forecasting systems allow partners to project the optimal flow of components into the future so that companies can try to meet optimal levels rather than continually catch up to them.

SEE ALSO *Data Mining; Electronic Data Interchange (EDI); Enterprise Resource Planning (ERP); Forecasting, Technological.*

BIBLIOGRAPHY

Allen, David. "Looking Forwards." *Management Accounting,* March 2000.

Capell, Kerry. "Tesco: 'Wal-Mart's Worst Nightmare'." *Bloomberg Businessweek,* December 29, 2008. Available from http://www.businessweek.com/globalbiz/content/dec2008/gb20081229_497909.htm.

Culberston, Scott, Jim Burruss, and Lee Buddress. "Control System Approach to E-commerce Fulfillment." *Journal of Business Forecasting Methods & Systems,* Winter 2000/2001.

Greenberg, Andy. "Mining Human Behavior at MIT" *Forbes,* August 30, 2010. Available from http://www.forbes.com/forbes/2010/0830/e-gang-mit-sandy-pentland-darpa-sociometers-mining-reality.html.

"IBM Better Forecasting—Sat Nav for Your Business." Sheffield, UK: Insight Direct. Available from http://www.youtube.com/watch?v=koANXHpAWes.

Jain, Chaman L. "Which Forecasting Model Should We Use?" *Journal of Business Forecasting Methods & Systems,* Fall 2000.

Krause-Traudes, Maike, Simon Scheider, Stefan Rüping and Harald Meßner. "Spatial Data Mining for Retail Sales Forecasting." 11th AGILE International Conference on Geographic Information Science, University of Girona, Spain, 2008. Available from http://www.techrepublic.com/whitepapers/spatial-data-mining-for-retail-sales-forecasting/1126155.

Lapide, Larry. "New Developments in Business Forecasting: The Internet Does Not Eliminate the Need to Forecast." *Journal of Business Forecasting Methods & Systems,* Fall 2000.

McKeefry, Hailey Lynne. "Adding More Science to the Art of Forecasting." *Ebn,* March 5, 2001.

Safavi, Alex. "Choosing the Right Forecasting Software and System." *Journal of Business Forecasting Methods & Systems,* Fall 2000.

"Squeeze the Process." *CMA Management,* October 1999.

FORECASTING, TECHNOLOGICAL

In order to effectively prepare business strategies in the technologically fast-paced worlds of e-commerce, information technology, and the global economy, it has become important for companies and policy makers to look into the future with sophisticated models for determining the course of technological change. The field of technological forecasting, more commonly referred to as foresight studies, emerged as an energetic and vibrant area of study and practice in the 1960s. Although its methods and purposes have shifted, it has continued to develop and change into the twenty-first century.

While the 1960s witnessed the coalescence of various practices and techniques into a coherent and systematic field of study, the roots of technological forecasting reach back even further. According to *Technological Forecasting and Social Change,* perhaps the first organized and systematic attempt at comprehensive technological forecasting was the study—conducted under the auspices of President Franklin D. Roosevelt's National Resource Commission in 1935—of the likely social and economic impacts of 13 major inventions. In the 1960s, when post-World War II economic development produced rapid and influential technological innovations, researchers began to organize the field systematically and devise a number of standard observations and techniques.

TECHNIQUES

The S-Shaped Logistic Curve is a forecasting technique that highlights an S-shaped technological development curve divided into three stages: the relatively slow period of initial growth, in which the emergent technology struggles to distinguish and assert itself as a viable force against its competitors; the subsequent period of accelerated growth once the technology has proven superior and begins to edge out existing technologies; and the maturation stage, characterized by a leveling off of growth patterns as the technology reaches an equilibrium with its economy. To take maximum advantage of the S-shaped curve, businesses employ sophisticated mathematical models. These pinpoint the most advantageous strategy of exploiting the technology's natural growth.

Envelope curves involve a series of S-curves based on the development of successive generations of particular technologies. In this scenario, each generation improves upon its predecessor, creating an overall envelope curve of the generations' individual S-shaped curves. In this way, analysts can study the development of technologies over time and devise methods for the extrapolation of knowledge into the future.

At the heart of foresight studies is the Delphi Method, which takes its name from the prophetic oracle of Greek antiquity. First developed by the RAND Corporation, the Delphi Method assumes that the best source of predictive information for any given technological field is the technical experts in that field. Thus, building a technological forecast begins with querying a committee of experts as to where they believe the technology is headed. To avoid biases and pressure from dominant players in the field, the Delphi Method insists that experts participate anonymously. Once panel members are assembled—by virtue of peer selection, honors and awards, involvement and rank in a professional society, or other qualifications—members are queried individually on the course of development for that particular technology. For instance, an expert may be asked his or her opinion as to the likely timing and impact of certain technological breakthroughs. After each round of questioning, the project analysts examine the information derived and organize it for panel members to consider in the next round. Panel members analyze the reasoning behind other members' predictions and reconsider their own views; through an iterative process, members come to reach a viable consensus in their predictions. After a satisfactory consensus is achieved, the findings are organized into a final report, on which a company bases its own technological forecast and accordant strategies.

THIRD GENERATION

For years, the thrust of technological forecasting was on assessing the likely development and characteristics of useful inventions, and forecasts were measured by the extent to which predictions proved accurate. In the 1990s, forecasting began to extend beyond mere technical aspects to include more comprehensive views of particular market conditions and the effects of technological development thereon. This market focus is now referred to as "second generation" foresight studies. Beginning in the early 2000s, a "third generation" of foresight studies was developed which focused on using a multidisciplinary, multieconomy approach to understand the effect that different technologies will have on society as a whole. Foresight mapping was seen as a way to prepare for changes to society brought about by technology and increased globalization.

Third-generation foresight studies are more often used by planners and civil servants, rather than companies, to determine where to direct national resources for the best prospect of future growth and well-being. Goals of third-generation foresight studies include identification of key or emerging technologies, improvement of national competitiveness, vision building, creation of intergovernmental networks, improved information dissemination and education, and development of a forward-looking culture.

Propelled in no small part by growing concerns over the environmental effects of technological developments, the 2000s and early 2010s have witnessed an expansion in the range of individuals consulted for useful forecasting information. Going beyond technical experts, foresight studies may consult individuals or groups that are likely to be affected by particular courses of development. For instance, a government undertaking a social impact analysis as an element of a national foresight study might consult with environmental and consumer groups to gauge the likely effect of development on their interests, behavior, and attitudes. Meanwhile, a corporation may choose to bring in customers and academics to balance the opinions of the fields' scientific experts.

In the late 1990s and 2000s, many countries began to carry out regular or ongoing national foresight studies, as well as bilateral and multinational studies, using a variety of techniques, with the goal of incorporating foresight into policy and planning decisions. For example, the European Commission, through the Institute for Prospective Technological Studies, conducts foresight projects with a European scope on a wide range of topics—sectoral, infrastructural, and regional. The Center for Technology Foresight was established under the umbrella of the Asia-Pacific Economic Cooperation Council to conduct a number of multilateral foresight projects, including studies of megacities, water supply and management, smart transport, education, and nanotechnology. The International Panel on Climate Control (IPCC) also uses multinational foresight studies to examine different scenarios of effects of various factors on global warming and their consequences.

SEE ALSO *Forecasting, Business; Scenario Planning; Simulation Software.*

BIBLIOGRAPHY

Alsan, Alper, and M. Atilla Oner. *Comparison of National Foresight Studies by Integrated Foresight Management Model.* Elsevier, 2004. Available from http://www.maoner.com/2004_futures.pdf.

Coates, Vary, Mahmud Farooque, et al. "On the Future of Technological Forecasting." *Technological Forecasting and Social Change,* May 2001.

du Preez, Gert T., and Carl W. I. Pistorius. "Technological Threat and Opportunity Assessment." *Technological Forecasting and Social Change,* July 1999.

Georghiou, Luke. "Third Generation Foresight – Integrating the Socio-economic Dimension." *Proceedings of the International Conference on Technology Foresight, NISTEP,* Japan, 2001. Available from http://www.nistep.go.jp/achiev/ftx/eng/mat077e/html/mat077oe.html.

Johnson, Ron. "The State and Contribution of International Foresight." In *The Role of Foresight in the Selection of Research Policy Priorities. Conference Proceedings,* 98–113. Seville, Spain: European Commission, 2002.

Vasquez, Jabier Medina. "Map of Levels of Complexity and Indetermination for Foresight Studies." *Second International Seville Seminar on Future-Oriented Technology Analysis (FTA).* September 2006. Available from http://foresight.jrc.ec.europa.eu/fta/presentations.html.

FORRESTER RESEARCH INC.

With roughly 2,700 business clients, more than 1,200 employees, and sales of $250 million in 2010, Cambridge, Massachusetts-based Forrester Research Inc. is one of the leading market research firms covering the Internet and technology. Its early focus on Internet technology, which began in 1995, helped to bolster the firm's image as an Internet industry expert capable of predicting future trends in technology, business practices, and customer behavior. By 2011, the company was focusing its business on providing research, consulting, programs, and consumer insight to executives at companies across the globe. In addition to its locations in the United States, the company's international locations, as of 2012, included Australia, Dubai, Germany, India, Israel, the Netherlands, Portugal, Switzerland, and the United Kingdom.

Forrester offers a wide variety of services and products, including online communities for IT, marketing and strategy, and technology industry professionals; teleconferences; business data; consumer data; events; executive programs; and consulting. The communities offer Forrester clients and registered and nonregistered guests a format in which they can discuss common issues and problems, as well as share techniques and advice. While nonregistered guests can take part in the communities, only Forrester clients and registered guests are given full access to all content and tools.

Forrester also offers Business and Consumer Technographics. To obtain its Consumer Technographics, the firm has surveyed more than two million households worldwide to gain insight into how technology impacts the way consumers research, select, purchase, use, and communicate about products and services. For businesses, the company offers Forrester Tech Marketing Navigator, and Forrsights for Business Technology. Tech Marketing Navigator uses input from 20,000 influencers in tech markets across the globe to help its clients make marketing decisions. Forrsights for Business Technology helps its business clients understand how businesses budget for, purchase, and use technology.

Forrester's consulting business is targeted toward IT professionals, marketing professionals, and technology industry professionals and executives. These clients can work one-on-one with an analyst, who will provide the client with the specific information and recommendations he or she needs based on existing Forrester research.

In the early 2010s, founder and CEO George Forrester Colony controlled about one-third of the company's stock.

FOUNDING

Forrester got its start in 1983 when, after a five-year stint at rival Yankee Group conducting telecommunications and office automation market research, Harvard University graduate George Forrester Colony decided to open his own market research firm. The new company, operated out of Colony's basement, first focused on telecommunications market research. Forrester eventually moved into the PC and networking markets. According to an October 1996 article in *Marketing Computers,* "Colony, credited with coining the term 'client/server' practically defined the course of network technology in the late '80s and '90s, and led many through its dark alleyways as the technology developed." The need for market research grew as new technology continued to emerge, and by the mid-1990s Forrester had evolved into a "leading prognosticator on Internet computing, having recognized early the effects that the Internet would have on business." Employees Mary Modahl and Bill Bluestein recognized the Internet's importance in 1993. Within two years, they convinced Colony, CEO, to create the New Media Research Group to devote resources to analyzing Web site operations, new Internet-based technologies, and the demographics of Web surfers.

In 1996, Forrester was focused on three markets: strategic management; corporate information technology (IT); and new media research, which included the Internet. Sales grew 71% to roughly $25 million, and clients exceeded the 1,000 mark. By then, the firm had expanded domestically into both the Midwest and the West Coast. Internationally, it served both the United Kingdom and Australia. Worldwide employees totaled 135. *Business Week* ranked Forrester 13th on its "Hot Growth" list.

Forrester set itself apart from competitors by making bold predictions about emerging technologies. For example, the firm accurately predicted the integral role intranets would come to play for corporations. That willingness to make proclamations about the future of technology was not without risk, however. For example, Forrester incorrectly favored IBM Corp.'s OS/2 operating system over Windows NT, which later emerged as the clear winner in the networking industry. In the early 1990s, Forrester also forecasted the success of the System 10 database developed by Sybase Inc., which turned out to fare poorly. After much speculation about whether or not the firm would succeed if it were required to answer to shareholders who might want to tone down predictions in the interest of profits, Forrester conducted its initial public offering in November 1996.

Earnings in 1998 grew to $7.5 million on sales of $61.6 million. Forrester launched its PowerRankings service, which listed the best e-commerce sites among different categories of online retailers, the following year. To compile its list, Forrester surveyed nearly 20,000 online customers and also conducted its own anonymous shopping tests at the busiest Web sites in the following categories: airline; apparel; books, music and video; brokerage; computer hardware and software; educational; general merchandise; health care; flowers; and toys and games. The e-tailers were evaluated for six different criteria: cost, customer service, delivery, features, transacting, and usability. (This site and the PowerRankings were later discontinued.) In November, to bolster its international operations, Forrester acquired London, England-based Fletcher Research, a two-year-old market analysis firm covering Internet usage in the United Kingdom.

Forrester teamed up with Information Resources Inc. in June 2000 to create Netquity, a brand marketing research service targeting brand managers selling products on the Internet. A few months later, BuyerZone.com and Forrester began offering market analysis reports to small and medium-sized businesses. In November, the firm began working with the National Association of Purchasing Management to monitor the utilization of Internet-based procurement by various businesses. Also that year, Forrester developed its eBusiness TechRankings. Sales grew from $87.3 million to $157.1 million, and net income nearly doubled from $11 million to $21.6 million. European research centers were located in London, England; Frankfurt, Germany; and Amsterdam, the Netherlands.

FORRESTER IN THE 2010S

By 2011, the company's business model and focus had changed dramatically from its early days, and it had discontinued many of the earlier service offerings that had led to its success. Sales figures in 2011, however, testified to the fact that its nimbleness in changing with the maturing Internet industry and corresponding business client needs was working. As of the second quarter of 2011, sales were $73.5 million, an increase of nearly $10 million from the same quarter in 2010.

Forrester's revised business model makes full use of its nearly 500 analysts who are available to work with business clients. The company is also working to develop its business in emerging economies, purchasing companies in Russia and the Asia-Pacific to do so. It announced the purchase of Asia-Pacific-based Springboard Research in May 2011, and in July of that year it announced that it was expanding its Technographics business into Russia.

Forrester hit many important milestones and received worldwide attention and accolades throughout the first decade of the twenty-first century and continuing into the

2010s. The company was ranked 80th on *Forbes* magazine's America's 200 Best Small Companies in 2008 and was named one of the 100 Fastest Growing Companies by *Fortune Small Business* in 2007.

SEE ALSO *E-commerce Consultants.*

BIBLIOGRAPHY

"BuyerZone.com and Forrester Research Form Channel Partnership." *PR Newswire,* October 3, 2000.

Fattah, Hassan. "Would Wall Street Muzzle George Colony?" *Marketing Computers,* October 1996.

"Forrester Research Inc. Company Information." *New York Times,* 2011. Available fromhttp://topics.nytimes.com/top/news/business/companies/forrester-research-inc/index.html.

Forrester Research Inc. "Corporate Fact Sheet." Cambridge, MA, 2011. Available from http://a964.g.akamaitech.net/7/964/714/0b70497c3d1161/www.forrester.com/imagesV2/uplmisc/FOR_CM_FactSheet_Q211.pdf.

"Forrester Research and the National Association of Purchasing Management Collaborate to Generate a Quarterly Report on eBusiness." *Business Wire,* November 6, 2000.

"Forrester Research's Creative Thinker." *InformationWeek,* November 15, 1999.

Judge, Paul C. "Forrester Research: Sassy, Quirky, and Rich." *BusinessWeek Online,* May 26, 1997. Available from http://www.businessweek.com/1997/21/b35289.htm.

Konicki, Steve. "Economic Slowdown Hits Hard at Analyst Firms." *InformationWeek,* September 10, 2001.

Violino, Bob, and Rich Levin. "Analyzing the Analysts." *InformationWeek,* November 17, 1997.

FORTRAN

FORTRAN (FORmula TRANslating) is a programming language historically used in math, science, and engineering programs. It is recognized as the first high-level programming language. High-level programming languages are much closer to human language than machine language, through which computer hardware accepts commands. High-level languages eventually get translated to a primary, numeric machine language consisting of zeros and ones.

FORTRAN was developed by John Backus at IBM's world headquarters in 1954, and it was released in 1957 after three years of development. IBM was trying to make computers more user friendly to increase sales. FORTRAN achieved this goal because the language was easy to learn in a short period of time and required no previous computer knowledge. It eliminated the need for engineers, scientists, and other users to rely on assembly programmers in order to communicate with computers. Assembly code is a form of programming language that is closer to, and more complicated than, high-level languages.

FORTRAN's strength lies in its ability to perform numeric computations. However, in *Computer Languages,* Backus explained that most people incorrectly assumed FORTRAN's main contribution was that it allowed programmers to replace machine code with algebraic formulas, while in reality the language's main benefit was that it mechanized the organization of loops within programs, a device that became critical to many scientific applications.

After its initial release, FORTRAN evolved through several different versions. FORTRAN II was introduced about one year after the original, followed by FORTRAN III in 1958 and FORTRAN IV in 1962. To avoid confusion, the American National Standards Institute (ANSI) issued a standardized version of FORTRAN in 1966. As this version had some limitations, Canada's University of Waterloo developed a version for students called WATFOR (WATerloo FORtran), followed by an enhanced version known as WATFIV. ANSI later introduced FORTRAN 77 around 1977, which cleared up some of the uncertainties surrounding its 1966 version and improved its compatibility as well as its ability to manipulate nonnumeric data and process files stored on removable disk and magnetic tape. In the early 1990s, ISO and ANSI developed FORTRAN-90.

FORTRAN IN THE TWENTY-FIRST CENTURY

Although FORTRAN is often referred to as being somewhat of a relic, it was still being used in a number of applications throughout the 2000s and into the 2010s. New standardizations continued to be released on a regular basis between the mid-1990s through the 2000s. These versions were introduced in 1995, 2003, and 2008, according to the British Computer Society (BCS). BCS noted how a number of government organizations in the United Kingdom as well as some private businesses continued to use FORTRAN despite the emergence of numerous competitors. C+ and C++ were the primary contenders, but many users have remained loyal to FORTRAN due to its unmatched mathematical capabilities.

On January 15, 2007, FORTRAN's longevity and continued use was challenged by Sun Microsystems, which launched Fortress, a language that was developed to replace it. This was also the year that FORTRAN developer John Backus died at the age of 82. However, the introduction of Fortress has not meant the end of FORTRAN. In 2010, ANSI voted to publish the standardized version FORTRAN 2008, which was released in November of that year. It included enhancements to aid optimization, bit manipulation procedures, and execution of command line commands, among other improvements.

As of early 2012, BCS says FORTRAN is still being used for applications such as weather forecasting and climate prediction, financial analysis, and computational fluid dynamics.

SEE ALSO *Programming Language.*

BIBLIOGRAPHY

Appleman, Daniel. *How Computer Programming Works.* Berkeley, CA: Apress, 2000.

Computer Languages. Alexandria, VA: Time-Life Books, 1986.

"FORTRAN 1957–2008: A Language with a Past, Present, and Future." British Computer Society, May 19, 2008. Available from http://www.fortran.bcs.org/2008/Fortran_1957_2008.pdf.

"FORTRAN." *Techencyclopedia,* 2001. Available from www.techweb.com/encyclopedia.

"FORTRAN." *Webopedia,* 2001. Available from http://www.webopedia.com/TERM/F/FORTRAN.html.

Leff, Lawrence F., and Arlene Podos. *Computer Programming in FORTRAN the Easy Way.* Woodbury, NY: Barron's Educational Series Inc., 1985.

Savvas, Antony. "Sun Unveils Fortress as a Replacement for Fortran." *ComputerWeekly.com,* January 15, 2007. Available from http://www.computerweekly.com/Articles/2007/01/15/221192/Sun-unveils-Fortress-as-replacement-for-Fortran.htm.

Woods, Bob. "ComputerLiteracy.com Inks E-commerce Pacts." Utica, NY: The Data & Analysis Center for Software (DACS), March 8, 1999. Available from http://www.thedacs.com/techs/abstract/242977.

FOURSQUARE

Foursquare is a location-based social networking application that works on three levels. It acts as a friend finder, showing where in the city a person (and his or her friends) is at any given time. Foursquare also allows users to leave each other tips and suggestions about favorite places—such as the best food to order at a particular restaurant. Foursquare also works as a social game. Users compete to win deals based on how often they visit a particular retailer or check in at a particular site. Foursquare takes advantage of the GPS chip in smartphones to allow users to broadcast their location to others in the Foursquare community. Users who check in at certain locations can earn points towards free meals or other deals. It is this third level that allows Foursquare to monetize by partnering with merchants and other businesses.

FOUNDATION

Foursquare founders Dennis Crowley and Naveen Selvadurai were not neophytes in the social networking app scene when they created Foursquare. Crowley attended New York University's Interactive Telecommunications Program, where he designed a location-based social networking application called Dodgeball. Google purchased Dodgeball in 2005, and Crowley continued to develop the app for Google. Dodgeball allowed users to text their current location to the Dodgeball service. The service would then send that information to other Dodgeball members in the area. Crowley left Google in 2007 and met Selvadurai when the two shared office space while working for different companies. When Google mothballed Dodgeball at the beginning of 2009, Crowley realized this created a gap in the location-based social networking market. He and Selvadurai teamed up to create Foursquare. They wrote the initial programming for Foursquare over a six-week period, working at a kitchen table in Crowley's apartment. The program was launched in March 2009 at the South by Southwest conference in Austin, Texas.

Once users open the Foursquare application, it notifies them of the locations of friends in the city, and also of participating locations nearby. When users visit a location listed with Foursquare, they can update their status by "checking-in" and earn points toward a badge. There are many different badges, such as the Local Badge (for visiting the same location several times a month), an Animal House badge (for visiting places popular with fraternities), and the Mayor's Badge, for visiting a location more times than any other Foursquare user in a given period. At the same time, friends can follow the users' progress around the city.

RAPID GROWTH

Crowley and Selvadurai worked alone on Foursquare for around six months, placing the application on the iTunes store and conducting preliminary tests with people in the fashion, music, and creative industries in New York. In September 2009, they raised $1.35 million from venture capitalists and angel investors, including Union Square Ventures, O'Reilly Alphatech Ventures, Digg founder Kevin Rose, and Twitter cofounder Jack Dorsey. At the time of the initial round of financing, the company had no employees and did not even have a bank account.

Following the investment, Crowley and Selvadurai began rapidly growing the business. They added employees, office space, and new cities to the Foursquare format. They also began to find new merchant partners to monetize the company and take greater advantage of the application's social game aspects. Local businesses could pay to advertise deal offers on Foursquare and to become a location where users could earn badges. In 2009, Yahoo reportedly offered $100 million for Foursquare, but Crowley and Selvadurai decided not to sell, and instead, in June 2010, they raised an additional $20 million from another round of investment, led by venture capital firm Andreessen Horowitz and including additional investments by Union Square and AlphaTech. This round of funding gave Foursquare a pre-money valuation of $95 million.

By mid-2011, Foursquare had ten million registered users, more than 166 different badges on offer, and a growing number of merchant deals and platforms. In June 2011, Foursquare announced a partnership with American Express in which American Express offered discounts to cardholders when they checked in on their cellphone at certain shops and restaurants. By using an application programming interface, Foursquare also allows companies to add applications onto the Foursquare platform. For example, in August 2011 Foursquare partnered with ESPN to allow users who check in at sports venues to receive facts, stats, and up-to-the-minute news on ESPN-branded venue detail pages on Foursquare. This deal joined partnerships with Movietickets.com, Condé Nast, HBO, Marc Jacobs, Bravo, Warner Brothers, Zagat, and Texas A&M University. By October 2011, Foursquare had more than 500,000 businesses signed up to use the merchant platform and had logged more than one billion check-ins.

Many large retailers have found Foursquare a useful tool to build a local following. Cable television network Bravo partners with Foursquare to allow Bravo viewers to "unlock" badges by checking in at locations linked to Bravo shows, such as restaurants favored by the celebrities on *Top Chef* or retailers popular with the women on *Real Housewives.* Participants can get tips on what to do or buy at the locations and earn prizes for getting there first. In December 2010, Pepsi teamed up with Foursquare for a charity drive in New York. Every time someone checked in within the city limits, Pepsi donated four cents to a nonprofit called CampInteractive.

MONEY AND SOCIAL MEDIA

Foursquare joins the ranks of social applications such as Groupon, Gowalla, and BrightKite that are attempting to monetize by offering a new marketing platform for merchants and deals for consumers and app users. Although not yet declaring a profit in 2011, Foursquare's model for monetizing location-based social networking has proved popular. With GPS chips making their way into more and more phones and devices, there are possibilities for Foursquare to expand. Crowley envisages his application being used to remind people of things they want to do and to recommend activities based on location and on what friends have done in the same place in the past. "If you think of the phone as a bunch of sensors stuck in this device connected to the network, how can I walk around the city and have the phone come alive and remind me, 'Oh this is a place you should go to lunch' or 'this is the place you read an article about 6 months ago'?" He sees the future Foursquare as a way to keep people plugged in and updated without overloading them. For example, users could download an article with a list of the 50 best sandwiches in New York, and then Foursquare will alert them whenever they approach one of the places selling a sandwich on the list. Users would not even need to read the article.

Foursquare also has its downsides. There are several cases of people using Foursquare to stalk others, and the application is useless outside of major cities that participate in Foursquare. It may also only be a matter of time before sites such as Facebook and Twitter add check-in and games to their service and compete with Foursquare on its own turf. As with other social applications, users may tire of Foursquare and move on before the company finds a way to build profits and sustain its business model. The key to Foursquare's success may well lie in its ability to insert itself into the daily fabric of people's lives and as a feature that is inserted into marketing campaigns as a matter of course.

SEE ALSO *Location-Based Services.*

BIBLIOGRAPHY

Brady, Diane. "Social Media's New Mantra: Location, Location, Location." *Bloomberg Businessweek,* May 6, 2010. Available from http://www.businessweek.com/magazine/content/10_20/b4178034154012.htm.

Hesseldahl, Arik. "Foursquare Tries Broadening Its Appeal." *Bloomberg Businessweek,* April 19, 2010. Available from http://www.businessweek.com/technology/content/apr2010/tc20100416_027539.htm.

Kennerly, John. "Leveraging Location-Based Social Apps: A Foursquare Example." *Speaking of Information,* August 3, 2010. Available from http://johnkennerly.wordpress.com/2010/08/03/leveraging-location-based-social-apps-a-foursquare-example.

Schoenfeld, Erick. "(Founder Stories) Foursquare's Crowley: 'Now Is Our Best Shot to Invent the Future'." *Tech Crunch,* March 4, 2011. Available from http://techcrunch.com/2011/03/04/founder-stories-foursquare-crowley-invent-future.

Wortham, Jenna. "A Start-Up Matures, Working With AmEx." *New York Times,* June 22, 2011. Available from http://www.nytimes.com/2011/06/23/technology/23locate.html.

FRAUD, INTERNET

According to the U.S. National Consumers League (NCL), Internet-related fraud cost individuals and businesses roughly $3 billion annually. In many ways, the Internet seems tailor-made for engaging in fraudulent activity. A single individual can perpetrate elaborate, low-cost schemes while enjoying anonymity and a platform from which to reach potential victims all over the world. Among the crimes the Internet facilitates are identity theft and the generation of false, but valid, credit card numbers. The most frequently reported scam in 2010 involved merchandise purchased over the Internet. The NCL reported that almost 30% of all reported complaints were related to Internet purchases.

VARIETIES OF ONLINE FRAUD

Internet scams come in a wide range of guises. In the 2000s, the most common online fraud concerned the compromise of shoppers' personal financial information when released to complete a sale on the Internet. Even well-known retailers seem prone to security breaches and hacking. A variety of sensitive personal information is revealed in such transactions, including a person's name, address, e-mail account, phone and social security numbers, passwords, and credit card data. In response to the number of identity thefts and fraud related to credit cards (including online fraud), five of the largest credit card companies—American Express, Discover Financial Services, JCB International, MasterCard Worldwide, and Visa Inc.—formed the Payment Card Initiative (PCI) Security Standards Council in 2006. The council's purpose is to assist merchants, vendors, and security consulting companies in preventing payment cardholder data fraud.

Online auction sites have historically presented prime breeding grounds for online fraud. The Internet Crime Complaint Center (IC3)—a joint effort between the National White Collar Crime Center (NW3C), which is part of the Bureau of Justice Assistance (BJA), and the Federal Bureau of Investigation (FBI)— noted in its 2010 Internet fraud report that 71.2% of its referrals to law-enforcement agencies in 2004 were related to Internet auction fraud. However, in 2010 Internet auction fraud represented slightly more than 10% of the referrals. IC3 speculates that the drop could demonstrate the growing diversification of crimes related to the Internet.

The IC3 report described how 372 complaints about the same company triggered an investigation. The company was offering "free" samples of various products, for which the purchaser was to pay the shipping costs. Once in receipt of the consumer's credit card information, the company then proceeded to charge a number of unauthorized transactions. In May 2011, the Canadian Broadcasting Corporation (CBC) reported that an Alberta man had been accused by the Federal Trade Commission of $450 million in Internet fraud using a similar ruse.

Two relatively new types of cyberattacks and fraud were included in the Computer Security Institute's (CSI) annual survey of merchants: the exploitation of client Web browsers and the exploitation of a user's social network profile. In 2009, 11% of the survey respondents reported Web browser exploitation, compared to 10% in 2010. Social network profile abuse was reported by 7% of respondents in 2009 and 5% in 2010.

PROTECTION AGAINST E-FRAUD

Most industry-standard encryption technologies only protect customer data during its actual transmission. An equally vulnerable point—the Web site's storage of personal data after the transaction occurs—often remains unprotected. Many hackers break into the servers that store customer data collected from past e-commerce transactions. Third-party sites that process credit card information also may furnish weak links. Thus, most online merchants rely on secure sockets layer (SSL) encryption technology to protect e-commerce data while in transit.

Retailers also can require the three-digit card verification value (CVV or CVV2), which is printed above the signature on the back of credit cards, to prevent unauthorized use of credit card numbers that have been obtained over the Web. Finally, transaction-risk scoring software exists that can spot deviations from customers' usual shopping patterns. One of the more recent developments is a smart card payment option, which has become popular in Europe.

THE EXTENT OF E-FRAUD

In its 2010/2011 Internet Crime Report, IC3 noted that it received and processed 303,809 complaints in 2010, over 25,000 complaints per month. In 2010, IC3 received the highest number of complaints since its inception in 2000 and reached a landmark—it processed its two-millionth complaint.

SEE ALSO *Computer Crime; Computer Security; Hacking; Misinformation Online; Payment Card Industry Data-Security Standard (PCI/DSS).*

BIBLIOGRAPHY

"2010/2011 CSI Computer Crime and Security Survey." New York: Computer Security Institute, 2011. Available from http://gocsi.com/survey.

Abaya, Carol. "Top Money Scams of 2010." *Newsroom Jersey,* December 23, 2010. Available from http://www.newjersey newsroom.com/economy/top-money-scams-of-2010.

"Alta Man Accused of $450 Million Internet Fraud." *CBC News,* May 19, 2011. Available from http://www.cbc.ca/news/canada/edmonton/story/2011/05/19/edmonton-jesse-willms-ftc-complaint.html.

Atanasov, Maria. "The Truth about Internet Fraud." *Ziff Davis Smart Business for the New Economy,* April 2001.

Carbonara, Peter. "The Kid and the Con Man." *Money,* March 2001.

Feldman, Amy. "A Classic Scam Takes to the Internet." *Money,* July 2001.

Haney, Clare. "Auction Sites Hit Hard by Electronic Crime." *InfoWorld,* January 15, 2001.

Internet Crime Complaint Center. "2010 Internet Crime Report." Washington, DC, 2011. Available from http://www.ic3.gov/media/annualreport/2010_ic3report.pdf.

Kandra, Ann. "The Myth of Secure E-shopping." *PC World,* July 2001.

PCI Security Standards Council. "About Us." Wakefield, MA, 2011. Available from https://www.pcisecuritystandards.org/organization_info/index.php.

Smith, Hilary. "Internet Opens New Avenues for Wireless Fraud." *RCR Wireless News,* November 20, 2000.

Wallerstein, Lisa. "Fraud in the 'New Economy.'" *Business Credit,* November/December 2000.

FUCHS, IRA H.

Ira Fuchs is credited with cofounding Because It's Time Network (BITNET), the world's first computer messaging network for liberal arts professors, in 1981. His work played a crucial role in the early development of the Internet and e-mail technology, and he continues to pioneer information technology projects in the academic world, championing the use of open-source software in the 2010s to meet the technology needs of educational institutions of all levels.

BEGINNING OF BITNET

As an undergraduate student majoring in physics at Columbia University, where he later earned a master's degree in computer science, Fuchs was approached by Kenneth King, director of the Thomas Watson computer laboratory, which had been funded by IBM Corp. Fuchs agreed to take on some systems programming work, and when King accepted a position with the City University of New York (CUNY), he took Fuchs with him. At the age of 24, Fuchs became director of CUNY's computing center. It was there that Fuchs began to see a need among liberal arts scholars for messaging capabilities similar to those offered to math and physics researchers on ARPAnet, a messaging network established by the U.S. Department of Defense in 1969.

Fuchs began discussing his idea with Yale scholar Greydon Freeman. Recognizing that most campuses already were equipped with the remote spooling communications system (RSCS) built into IBM computers, Fuchs and Freeman began researching ways to use RSCS in conjunction with a mainframe system, a modem, and a phone line to allow messages and files to pass back and forth between universities. Hoping to generate additional support for their ideas, Fuchs and Freeman headed up a consortium of technology representatives from several universities in the Northeast that would soon serve, under Fuchs's guidance, as the executive committee to BITNET.

CUNY and Yale were linked on May 5, 1981, marking the birth of BITNET. By 1984, BITNET had connected more than 150 campuses. Interested in the potential of such a network, IBM began working with Fuchs and agreed to fund BITNET's expansion into Europe, Asia, and the Middle East, and also to pay for the establishment of a headquarters facility. In 1986, Eric Thomas created LISTSERV, mailing list software specifically designed to work with BITNET. As a result, BITNET users were able to send e-mail messages to a special LISTSERV address and then see their message automatically forwarded to multiple people whose names were on the list. While BITNET is no longer used today, LISTSERV evolved into a popular commercial mailing list software program.

In the mid-1990s it became apparent to Fuchs and the rest of BITNET's managerial board—by then known as the Corporation for Research and Educational Networking (CREN)—that BITNET, in its original form, had been rendered virtually obsolete by the Internet. However, despite his network's short life, Fuchs's impact on messaging technology has been profound. According to Internet researcher Paul Gilster, as quoted by Barbara Fox in a *U.S. 1 Newspaper* article, "Fuchs and Freeman were the ones who took networking out of the technical and made it available as a practical daily tool."

Fuchs left City College in 1986 for Princeton University, where he accepted the position of vice president for computing and information technology. After spearheading the development of the university's Web site, he began working on getting the entire campus, including students living in dormitories, hooked up to the Internet. While working for Princeton, Fuchs also became the chief scientist for Journal Storage (JSTOR), a program funded by the Andrew W. Mellon Foundation that catalogs out-of-print academic journals and makes articles accessible online.

In July 2000, Fuchs accepted the post of vice president for research in information technology at the Mellon Foundation, where he began working on a project to compile images of fine art works and make them accessible to online researchers. Fuchs held this position for ten years, and a direct result of his efforts at Mellon Foundation was the development of collaborative, open-source software now being used by more than ten million people at colleges, universities, museums, libraries, and performing arts institutions.

NEXT GENERATION

In September 2010, Fuchs left the Mellon Foundation to become executive director of Next Generation Learning Challenges in Boulder, Colorado, a collaborative initiative whose goal is to address the barriers to educational innovation and utilize the potential of technology to produce a significant positive impact on college readiness and completion in the United States. The program is administered by EDUCAUSE, a nonprofit association with offices in Washington, D.C. and Boulder, Colorado. The mission of EDUCAUSE is similar to Next Generation: to advance higher education by promoting the intelligent use of information technology.

As executive director of Next Generation Learning Challenges, Fuchs is continuing his decades-long championship of open-source solutions for learning institutions through collaborations. In an interview published in *EDUCAUSE Review Magazine* Fuchs stated, "We focus on technology that can support student achievement from kindergarten through the senior year in college, with an emphasis on helping low-income students, who often face the most significant barriers to college readiness and completion."

SEE ALSO *ARPAnet; BITNET; History of the Internet and World Wide Web (WWW).*

BIBLIOGRAPHY

"Collaboration for a Positive-Sum Outcome: An Interview with Ira H. Fuchs." *EDUCAUSE Review Magazine* 46, no. 3 (May-June 2011). Available from http://www.educause.edu/EDUCAUSE+Review/EDUCAUSEReviewMagazine Volume46/CollaborationforaPositiveSumOu/228656.

Fox, Barbara. "Making the Internet Work for Princeton." *U.S. 1 Newspaper,* November 27, 1996. Available from http://161.58.97.168/irafuchs.html.

Grier, David Alan, and Mary Campbell. "A Social History of Bitnet and Listserv, 1985–1991." In *IEEE Annals of the History of Computing* 22, no. 2, (April-June 2000): 32–41, doi:10.1109/85.841135. Available from http://www.computer.org/portal/web/csdl/doi?doc=doi/10.1109/85.841135.

Next Generation Learning Challenges. Boulder, CO: EDUCAUSE, 2011. Available from http://nextgenlearning.org.

Olsen, Florence. "Mellon Foundation Hires Princeton's Ira Fuchs for a New Technology Post." *Chronicle of Higher Education,* April 17, 2000.

FULFILLMENT PROBLEMS

Online fulfillment is a cornerstone of e-commerce, encompassing all of the steps involved in purchasing and receiving a product, from order placement and billing to packaging, shipping, and beyond. Fulfillment problems arise when a breakdown or bottleneck occurs at some point in the process. Before the advent and wide use of the Internet, companies could often hide inefficient fulfillment systems, but with e-commerce this is not possible.

Online fulfillment differs considerably from fulfillment models used for brick-and-mortar stores. Rather than shipping relatively small numbers of large orders to retail chains or distributors, high volumes of smaller orders for individual consumers must be processed. This presents a new set of requirements for retailers, especially in the areas of speed, connectivity, and customer service.

KINDS OF FULFILLMENT PROBLEMS

Most fulfillment problems stem from companies not being able to make good on promises of product availability and fast shipping as made in their advertisements. While accepting orders is quite simple, filling them quickly and efficiently is another matter. Among the factors that cause problems are a lack of real-time connectivity and integration, poor planning or forecasting, and trouble with warehouse operations.

Lack of real-time connectivity—either between businesses and consumers or businesses and other businesses—is a primary cause of fulfillment problems. Generally speaking, e-commerce happens very quickly. The amount of time that elapses between the sales transaction process and when a product is actually shipped can literally be a matter of minutes. To achieve this high rate of speed, a company's Web site must be integrated with its other back-end systems, such as accounting or inventory, and the information must be made available to all trading partners. This creates confidence in the fulfillment system and allows potential problems to be identified before they develop.

If a company's Web site is not integrated with its other systems, orders may come in via the World Wide Web and sit for days or weeks until they are manually reentered by someone into another system. Not only does this cause fulfillment to move at a very slow pace, it also makes it difficult for companies to monitor the status of their operations and introduces the opportunity for human error. Product codes, prices, shipping addresses, and more can be accidentally altered during manual reentry.

Whether fulfillment occurs between businesses and individual consumers or businesses and other businesses, effective fulfillment systems are built from the inside out, instead of from the outside in. What this means is that they need to be flexible enough to work with and accept data in various formats from computer systems at other organizations. In the world of e-commerce, companies frequently change relationships with other manufacturers, suppliers, and distributors. Having a fulfillment system that can accommodate different trading partners, no matter what system they use, is attractive because it reduces the need for making special arrangements.

Poor forecasting and planning also creates problems in the fulfillment process. Forecasting involves using information from a variety of different sources to predict business fluctuations, sometimes with the use of special software programs. When this is not done, companies lose their ability to deliver goods or services on time due to inventory shortages, inadequate warehouse staffing, and so on. Besides forecasting consumer demand for their own products and services, companies also may need to consider production forecasts from suppliers they rely on during the manufacturing process.

Finally, because of the need for constant, real-time information about the status of products and shipments, modern warehouses are a requirement for successful e-tailers. When warehouses are operated under manual systems, inefficiencies and mistakes often occur, such as shipping items to the wrong address and long delays. In the early 2010s, companies now rely on warehouse management software (WMS), overhead scanners, conveyor belt systems, wireless computer networks, wearable computers, handheld bar code scanners, and portable printers to streamline operations and automate the movement of goods through their warehouses. The way such technologies were used was complex and varied depending on the warehouse or distribution center.

SOLVING FULFILLMENT ISSUES

According to Sucharita Mulpuru's Forrester blog, more than 5.5 million people shopped online for the first time in 2010. With the reality that consumers have embraced online shopping, it behooves e-tailers to review and fix any fulfillment issues they may have.

A helpful aspect of the shipping and tracking of orders is that this process can be handed over to postal and courier services. The U.S. Postal Service and the Canadian Post, as well as the courier companies, have systems that allow for various pieces of information to be inserted on a form—reference number, tracking number, and so forth—to keep consumers informed of the progress of their shipment. E-mail notifications can be requested to save the consumer the tiresome exercise of constantly checking Web sites.

Third-party companies have begun to emerge that can handle the entire process from ordering to inventory stocking, sourcing packaging materials, and shipping for the e-tailer. This enables traditional wholesalers, as well as retailers, to take orders over the Internet and ship directly to consumers. For example, BTB Mailflight, established in 1969, is one of the U.K.'s leading international mailing, fulfillment, and print companies. The company, which became a member of the La Poste Group in March 2008, offers full or partial service to its clients, including order processing, a contact center (for payment processing, customer service, refunds, upselling and cross-selling), a paperwork division, packing, shipping, and stock management.

SEE ALSO *Order Fulfillment; Shipping and Shipment Tracking.*

BIBLIOGRAPHY

BTB Mailflight. "Fulfilment Services and International Postal Solutions." Bedfordshire, UK, 2011. Available from www.btbmf.co.uk.

Cruz, Mike, and David Jastrow. "Christmas Fulfillment." *Planet IT,* December 15, 2000.

Johnson, John R. "Fulfilling Web Expectations." *Warehousing Management,* March 2001.

Kontzer, Tony. "Ignoring Your Fulfillment Systems? Bad Move." *Planet IT,* July 28, 2000. Available from www.planetit.com.

Leon, Mark. "Online Retail Success Lies Behind the Scenes." *InfoWorld,* June 12, 2000.

Mulpuru, Sucharita. "Forrester's U.S. Online Retail Forecast Reports 12.6% Growth in 2010." *Forrester Blogs,* February 28, 2011. Available from http://blogs.forrester.com/category/forecast.

Patsuris, Penelope. "FTC Demands Dot-Com Christmas Delivery." *Forbes,* September 29, 2000.

Terreri, April. "Bar Code Gold." *Warehousing Management,* March 2001.

Tiernan, Bernadette. *e-Tailing.* Chicago: Dearborn Financial Publishing, 2000.

Verton, Dan. "Tis the Season to Build Long-Term Loyalty Online." *Computerworld,* October 30, 2000.

G

GARTNER, INC.

With roughly 4,500 employees, Gartner, Inc., is one of the largest information technology (IT) consulting firms in the United States. Its client base includes approximately 11,600 businesses, institutions, and other organizations that prefer to let outside experts advise them on decisions regarding computer hardware and software, communications devices, and other technology-related topics. In 2010, sales were more than $1.2 billion and operations spanned 85 countries.

COMPANY BEGINNINGS

Gartner was established in 1979 by partners Gideon Gartner and David Stein to offer research and analysis regarding the information technology (IT) industry to buyers and sellers of computers and related devices. Six years later, the firm founded Gartner Group Securities, a unit serving the investment community with IT recommendations and information. Sales reached $40 million in 1988, and earnings exceeded $2 million. Britain's Saatchi & Saatchi paid $90 million for Gartner Group that year. However, Saatchi & Saatchi found itself struggling with cash flow problems, and less than a year later it announced plans to divest Gartner Group. Gideon Gartner revealed his intent to buy the company himself and threatened to resign if anyone else purchased the firm.

Gartner Group's managers conducted a leveraged buyout in 1990 with the help of Dun & Bradstreet. The firm was placed under ownership of a new company called Information Partners Capital Fund L.P., and Manny Fernandez was named president and CEO. A few years later, Gideon Gartner sold his stake in Gartner, breaking all ties with the company he had founded.

In 1993, sales reached $123 million and net income neared the $7 million mark. By then, operations spanned 20 countries. Gartner Group conducted its initial public offering, listing its shares on NASDAQ. The firm then used its fresh capital to begin making acquisitions, including IT system evaluator Real Decisions and IT research and analysis provider New Science. Profits more than doubled in 1994 to $15 million, and sales grew to $170 million. In 1995, Gartner Group bought IT market researcher Dataquest Inc. and MZ Projekte, an IT research and recommendation firm serving Germany, Switzerland, and Austria. International expansion continued with the creation of Gartner Group Japan, K.K.

In 1996, Gartner paid $2.5 million for project management software consultant Productivity Management Group Inc. The $4.3 million acquisition of health care industry technology consultant C.J. Singer & Co. marked Gartner's first foray into the health care industry. Gartner also purchased a 40% stake in Web content provider EC Cubed. In 1997, the company acquired a 32% stake in Jupiter Communications, LLC, a consumer online and interactive industry researcher that would grow to be one of Gartner's largest competitors. Additional acquisitions included Swedish management consultant Informatics MCAB, Singapore-based IT product and vendor database compiler Datapro Information Services, and French IT information publisher Bouhot and Le Gendre. Earnings grew to $73 million on revenues of $511 million.

In 1999, the firm's largest shareholder, IMS Health Inc., sold its 47% stake in Gartner. CEO William Clifford also resigned to join a fledgling dot-com firm. Perhaps most damaging was the perception that Gartner had lost ground to competitors by not paying enough attention to the emerging e-business industry. As a result, new president and CEO Michael Fleisher announced the firm's intention to invest millions of dollars in developing Gartner's e-business services. To this end, Gartner acquired INTECO Corp., a research firm focused on Internet and e-commerce technology. The company also bought a 70% stake in cPulse, LLC, which had developed an e-business application that tracked the satisfaction level of online customers.

Gartner hired 441 new employees, including 24 e-business consultants, in the first half of 2000 as part of a $10 million employee recruitment and retention program. Silver Lake Partners L.P. paid $300 million for a 20% stake in Gartner. In March, Gartner paid $80 million for TechRepublic Inc., a Web site for IT professionals. Four months later, the firm launched its eMetrix service, a real-time e-business monitor that cautioned IT managers and other executives if a major supply chain problem appeared imminent.

EVOLVING IN THE TWENTY-FIRST CENTURY

The general downturn in technology investing that began with the dot-com crash in 2000 had a direct impact on Gartner, but the company did experience an 11% growth in revenue in 2001, reaching $952 million, due mainly to the continuing success of its research business.

By 2004, Gartner was seeking to add to its revenue by diversifying its product offerings, and so it increased the number of events it held that were centered on IT professionals. (In its annual report, Gartner stated that event revenue grew 16% from the previous year.) This was also the first year the company was under the leadership of its new CEO, Eugene (Gene) Hall, a former executive with Automatic Data Processing (ADP), and the year the company acquired Meta Group, an international IT consulting firm.

Revenues for Gartner were more than $1 billion by 2006, and it had expanded its service offerings to chief information officers (CIO)s and other IT leaders. The goal of the company moving forward was to differentiate itself from other consulting firms. It accomplished this by focusing on its ability to provide customized research and recommendations through its army of research analysts positioned across the globe.

Despite the global recession of 2008 and 2009, Gartner was able to grow its revenue and expand its profit margin by focusing on the two areas in which it excelled, research and consulting for IT professionals and leaders. The company ended 2010 with research contracts valued at $978 million. While the company's other segments continued to grow, research continued to be Gartner's primary strength.

As of 2012, Gartner's business was separated into four distinct segments: research, contract review, IT key metrics data, and networking. Gartner offered research products specific to two groups of clients: IT professionals and executives. Contract review service, as it sounds, offered an objective review of IT sales contracts between Gartner clients, while IT metrics offered clients up-to-date data on IT market buying patterns. Gartner also provided networking opportunities through online communities and events.

Despite Gartner's business segmentation, research was by far the service that brought in the most revenue, earning $865 million of the company's $1.2 billion total in 2010. Consulting generated the next highest revenue figure at $302 million, and Gartner events generated $121 million. As of 2012, Eugene Hall remained the company's CEO.

SEE ALSO *E-commerce Consultants.*

BIBLIOGRAPHY

Ferranti, Mark. "Gartner, Align Thyself." *CIO*, November 15, 2001.
"Gartner, Inc." Austin, TX: Hoover's, 2011. Available from http://www.hoovers.com/company/Gartner_Inc/rjhsxi-1.html.
"Tech Consulting Firm Rankings 2011: Prestige." *Vault*, 2011. Available from http://www.vault.com/wps/portal/usa/rankings/individual?rankingId1=143&rankingId2=-1&rankings=1&regionId=0&rankingYear=2011.

GATES, WILLIAM H. (BILL)

William H. (Bill) Gates is the founder and chairman of Microsoft Corp., the world's leading software company. In 2000, revenues at Microsoft reached approximately $23 billion, with 39,000 total employees. By 2011, the company had revenues of $69.9 billion, up almost 12% from 2010 levels, and had over 90,000 employees. Gates's firm is best known for its two landmark products: the Windows operating system, which in 2011 held a 89.7% share of the global personal computer (PC) market, and the Microsoft Office suite, which has sold over 100 million licenses through 2010, making it the firm's best-selling product. In 2000, Gates handed managerial control of the firm over to president Steve Ballmer, opting instead to focus on technology development. In 2008, Gates transitioned out of a day-to-day role with the company to spend more time on his global health and education work with the foundation he started with his wife Melinda in 2000.

Due in large part to his share of Microsoft, Gates is one of the wealthiest men in the world, with assets totaling over $56 billion in 2011.

FOUNDING A NEW COMPANY

A native of Seattle, Washington, Gates became interested in computer programming when he was in high school. In 1973, he began his undergraduate studies at Harvard, where he lived in the same dormitory as Steve Ballmer. In February 1975, at the age of 19, Gates and Honeywell employee Paul Allen, a childhood friend of Gates, began tinkering with a computer language known as BASIC (Beginner's All-Purpose Symbolic Instruction Code). The partners soon developed a version of BASIC for Albuquerque, New Mexico-based MITS, manufacturer of Altair, the world's first personal computer (PC). Since the creators of BASIC, two mathematics professors at Dartmouth College, had never copyrighted or patented the language, programmers throughout the world had customized BASIC to meet their needs. Gates and Allen used variations of BASIC as the basis for their new company, Microsoft, formally founded on April 4, 1975. Eventually, Gates also created DiskBASIC, a disk management program. Other variations of BASIC eventually formed the core of many of Microsoft's most successful products. For example, Visual BASIC was created in the early 1990s to serve an object-oriented language for Microsoft Windows applications.

In 1976, Gates dropped out of Harvard in order to devote more time to his new business. He moved the headquarters to Albuquerque, New Mexico, and began to build the company. Aside from his innovations with BASIC, Gates's first major impact on the computer industry came in the form of a legal contract. Gates devised an agreement which allowed hardware developers to use and sell variations of proprietary software languages. This contract eventually served as a model for future software licensing deals.

In the late 1970s, Gates oversaw the development and release of software products which led to Microsoft becoming the leading microcomputer language distributor in the United States. Believing that international markets were just as important as North American ones, Gates launched operations in Japan and moved corporate headquarters to Bellevue, Washington.

When Gates and Allen incorporated their company on June 25, 1981, Gates took over as president and chairman of the board, while Allen adopted the role of executive vice president. Two months later, Microsoft completed its MS-DOS operating system, allowing IBM to begin selling its new PCs. More than 50 microcomputer manufacturers had signed MS-DOS licensing agreements with Microsoft by the end of the year. Microsoft's major product release that year, the Multiplan Electronic Worksheet, was named software product of the year by *InfoWorld* magazine.

STEERING MICROSOFT'S GROWTH AS A SOFTWARE MANUFACTURER

Gates oversaw the release of several flagship products in 1983. Among other products the firm shipped its first version of Microsoft Word, a word processing program that eventually would compete with Novell Inc.'s popular WordPerfect program. In November, Gates unveiled his firm's new Windows operating system, the success of which would be key in Microsoft's eventual dominance of the PC industry.

Gates moved his growing firm to Redmond, Washington, in February 1986. He completed Microsoft's initial public offering (IPO) one month later, selling shares for $21 apiece and raising $61 million in fresh capital. In less than one year, when shares began selling for more than $84 each, Gates found himself a billionaire at the age of 31. Product releases in the late 1980s included Microsoft Word 3.0, which quickly became the top seller at Microsoft, and a Windows-based spreadsheet program called Excel.

In 1988, Apple Computer Inc. brought charges against Microsoft, asserting that Gates and his cohorts had cribbed the "look and feel" of the Macintosh operating system when developing Windows. Microsoft would eventually prevail in the suit against Apple, following an appeal which went all the way to the U.S. Supreme Court.

Revenues at Microsoft reached $1 billion in 1990, and roughly 90% of worldwide PCs used either MS-DOS or Windows as a platform.

Gates's dominance of the PC industry continued to grow, and Microsoft's market valuation reached a whopping $25 billion by 1993. Multimedia efforts paid off when Microsoft's Encarta CD-ROM earned the distinction of being named consumer disc product of the year. Gates also oversaw his firm's diversification into network servers, which culminated in the launch of Windows NT, a platform for the network servers increasingly used by large enterprises. Gates had been working on Windows NT since 1990. According to David Kirkpatrick in a May 1997 issue of *Fortune,* the development of NT was part of a long-term goal of Gates, Allen, and other technology gurus: "shunting the world's biggest computing tasks from mainframes to cheaper, smaller machines." Like most of Microsoft's earliest versions of its products, the first release of NT needed quite a bit of tweaking. In fact, it was not until the launch of Windows 2000 that NT had evolved into the system Gates had envisioned.

While Gates's decision to push Microsoft into as many new PC-related industries as possible allowed his company's brand to become one of the most recognized in the world by the mid-1990s, it also compounded the firm's legal troubles. Several competitors filed complaints against Microsoft, alleging that the firm repeatedly used anticompetitive tactics to gain market share. As a result, the U.S. Department of Justice began scrutinizing Microsoft. Hoping to bring the investigation to an end once and for all, Microsoft offered to alter its marketing practices in 1994.

Work began in the mid-1990s on Windows 95, an upgrade to Microsoft's operating system that would completely alter the look of most desktop machines. In September 1994, upstart Netscape Communications Corp.'s Web browser, which served as a graphic user interface (GUI) for the Internet much in the same way Windows served as a GUI for PCs, caught Gates's attention. As a result, he licensed technology from Spyglass and ordered the quick development of a product that would compete with Netscape's Navigator. Gates also unveiled Microsoft's BackOffice, a Windows NT suite that combined various server applications. In early 1995, Gates saw his plans to acquire Intuit Inc. for $2.1 billion quashed by the Justice Department, which raised various antitrust concerns regarding the deal.

REFOCUSING MICROSOFT ON INTERNET TECHNOLOGY

As work on Windows 95 was winding down, Gates began to realize that his firm was lagging behind rivals like Sun Microsystems, America Online, and Netscape in the burgeoning Internet arena. With the long-awaited Windows 95 operating system near completion, Gates changed Microsoft's focus from PC operating systems to Internet technology. When the company launched Windows 95 in August, in one of technology industry's most highly anticipated product releases, it included the Internet Explorer browser, a direct competitor to Netscape's Navigator, which had secured 80% of the Internet browser market. The new operating system also included the Microsoft Network, an online service competing with America Online, Compuserve, and other Internet service providers.

In November 1995, Gates published *The Road Ahead,* which went on to become a *New York Times* best-seller. He also recruited Michael Kinsley to create *Slate,* an online magazine first published the following June. Microsoft introduced Internet Explorer 2.0 to compete with the second version of Netscape's Navigator, and what became known as the "browser wars" began in earnest. Gates also began working with NBC on the online news source that eventually became known as MSNBC.

While Gates put considerable resources into Windows NT and its related BackOffice suite, he also preserved the firm's other Internet initiatives. For example, the firm released Internet Explorer 4.0 in mid-1997. By that time, Microsoft had reduced Netscape's browser market share to roughly 40%. Complaints regarding Microsoft's bundling of its Internet Explorer with Windows 95 to allegedly undermine Netscape's ability to compete led to yet another Justice Department investigation. It was at this time that reports began to emerge about alleged threats by Gates and his higher-ups to cancel the Windows licenses of PC makers not willing to install Explorer on their machines in place of Netscape's Navigator. The litigation resulted in a U.S. District Court ruling that Microsoft must sell a version of Windows 95 unbundled from Internet Explorer. Gates initially resisted the decree, insisting that his programmers would be unable to separate the programs without damaging the operating system. However, to avoid contempt of court charges, Gates eventually decided to allow computer manufacturers to sell Windows 95 without Internet Explorer.

Early in 1998, Microsoft bought Hotmail, a free Web-based e-mail system. Sales that year surged by 30% to $14.5 billion. Although the firm had trounced Netscape in the browser wars, the fact remained that many of Gates's Internet endeavors had simply fallen short of expectations, leaving Microsoft reliant on the nearly saturated PC operating system and PC applications suite industries. As a result, growth at Gates's software behemoth began to decelerate in the late 1990s. Adding to the downturn were delays in the release of Windows NT 5.0, a product Gates needed to pursue his plan to storm the network server market. Recognizing that a major company overhaul was in order, Gates named longtime Microsoft employee Steven Ballmer president in 1998.

Early in 1999, Ballmer and Gates launched a major client-focused reorganization at Microsoft. The company reorganized around five customer-based divisions: corporate systems clients; knowledge workers; ordinary Windows customers; programmers; and consumers interested in digitized content, entertainment, and shopping. Ballmer and Gates recognized that to lure the large corporate accounts it aimed to target with Windows NT, Microsoft needed to be more in tune with its clients. Larger enterprises typically demanded from their technology providers a high level of service, something that even Microsoft admitted was not its strong suit.

That year, Gates published his second best-selling book, *Business @ the Speed of Thought.* The book, on the *New York Times* best-seller list for seven weeks, has been translated into 25 languages and is available in 60 countries worldwide. Proceeds from both of Gates's books were donated to nonprofit organizations which foster the use of technology in education and skill development.

In January 2000, Gates appointed Ballmer CEO, retaining his own role as chairman and taking on the additional role of chief software architect. In a letter to employees detailing the management changes, Gates pointed to Microsoft's success in altering the way individuals interacted with computers as a metaphor for his firm's new focus: "Today we must make a similar bet on using software to improve the way people experience the Internet—an even more important revolution than the GUI." One month later, the firm shipped its long-awaited new version of Windows NT, renamed Windows 2000, which was designed to serve as the operating platform for large enterprises, including leading e-commerce players like Buy.com and BarnesandNoble.com.

A lengthy antitrust investigation of Microsoft climaxed in April 2000, when the court ruled that the firm had aggressively monopolized the PC operating systems industry. Along with 17 states, the Justice Department proposed that Gates separate Microsoft into two companies, one overseeing the firm's Office software applications and the other handling its Windows-based operating systems. As predicted, Microsoft's lawyers appealed the judgment. Finally in 2002, the U.S. District Court approved a final judgment between the federal government and nine remaining states, which left the company largely intact.

MICROSOFT AND GATES IN THE NEW MILLENIUM

Over the course of the next six years, until Gates's separation from the daily operations of the company in 2008, Microsoft continued to update its core products while launching new products geared primarily toward mobility and digital entertainment. In 2003, the company launched Windows Mobile for pocket PC's and smartphones. In October 2004, Gates announced Windows XP Media Center, Microsoft's vision of the future of digital entertainment everywhere. In 2008, as Gates readied his departure from Microsoft daily operations, he and other executives briefed company employees and the press on strategy for the company going forward. They outlined four key themes for the future. First, the company will respond to growing interest in virtualization, whereby software tools migrate to servers which create virtual desktop environments. The second theme was a continuation of the first, concerning operations in cloud computing or software-as-a-service (SaaS), with customers to be given more flexibility in the types of services they receive from Microsoft. Third, Microsoft would promote (through Windows Mobile) unified communications and mobility, the capacity to connect video, voice, and data communications over mobility devices. Fourth, the company would aggressively pursue computer-based collaboration through the development of Share Point and folder-sharing software technologies.

In 2000, Gates had begun to transition his life away from Microsoft toward a new focus for his talents. The William H. Gates Foundation, and the Gates Learning Foundation, begun in earlier years, became the Bill & Melinda Gates Foundation, started with an additional $16 billion of Gates's vast fortune for the purpose of promoting global health, education, and libraries. In 2005, Bill and Melinda Gates, along with U2 singer Bono, were named *Time Magazine* Persons of the Year. In January 2006, Gates announced a foundation investment of $900 million in an effort to eradicate tuberculosis.

In 2008, Gates made the foundation the central focus of his efforts by leaving daily operational management of Microsoft. Since then the foundation has built a new headquarters funded by Bill and Melinda in downtown Seattle, Washington. By 2009, the Gates Foundation made grants totaling $3 billion and had a staff of 800. In 2010, Bill and Melinda announced a pledge of $10 billion over the next 10 years, in a call for a "decade of vaccinations." Recognizing the good efforts and prodigious management talents of both Bill and Melinda Gates, other wealthy business leaders, such as Warren Buffet, have come forward and pledged additional billions to the foundation.

SEE ALSO *Allen, Paul; Ballmer, Steve; Microsoft Corp.; Microsoft Network (MSN); Microsoft Windows.*

BIBLIOGRAPHY

"At War with Microsoft." *Economist,* May 23, 1998.

Baker, Sharon M. "Microsoft Pushing Ahead on Many Fronts." *Puget Sound Business Journal,* March 12, 1999.

Bill and Melinda Gates Foundation. "About the Foundation." Seattle, WA, 2011. Available from http://www.gatesfoundation.org/about/Pages/overview.aspx.

"Bill's Big Roll-Out." *Economist,* September 18, 1999.

Kirkpatrick, David. "He Wants All of Your Business—and He's Starting to Get It." *Fortune,* May 26, 1997.

———. "Microsoft: Is Your Company Its Next Meal?" *Fortune,* April 27, 1998.

———. "The New Face of Microsoft: The Management Change Is Just the First Step." *Fortune,* February 7, 2000.

"Microsoft: The Beast Is Back." *Fortune,* June 11, 2001.

"Microsoft Company 15 September 1975." The History of Computing Project. Available from http://www.thocp.net/companies/microsoft/microsoft_company.htm.

"Microsoft Corp." In *Notable Corporate Chronologies.* Farmington Hills, MI: Gale Group, 1999.

"William H. Gates." Redmond, WA, 2011. Available from http://www.microsoft.com/presspass/exec/billg.

Mitchell, Russ. "Microsoft's Midlife Crisis." *U.S. News & World Report,* October 19, 1998.

Nocera, Joseph. "The Men Who Would Be King: Case Has Content. Gates Has Software. The Internet Will Be Their Battleground." *Fortune,* February 7, 2000.

Wailgum, Thomas. "What's Driving Microsoft's Strategy." *PC World,* April 27, 2008. Available from http://www.pcworld.com/businesscenter/article/145175/whats_driving_microsofts_strategy.html.

GATEWAY, INC.

Gateway, Inc., is a wholly owned subsidiary of the Taiwan-based Acer Group, a leading personal computer (PC) maker with a 13.4% share of the world computer sales market and 11.4% share of the U.S. computer sales market as of 2010. Acer purchased Gateway in 2007.

In 1991, Gateway was an early pioneer of the business-to-business (B2B) market. By 1997, with the launch of its E-series line of PCs, Gateway targeted larger corporations, government, and professionals in the health care and education industries. Shortly prior to the sale of its Professional Service business unit to MPC Inc., Gateway entered into discussions with Acer, a Taiwanese PC maker wanting to acquire the company. It became clear after the acquisition by Acer that the Taiwanese company desired to focus its energies and investment in the consumer retail sector as opposed to the corporate and nonprofit sector.

EARLY HISTORY

Gateway was founded in 1985 when partners Ted Waitt, who dropped out of the business management program at the University of Iowa, and Mike Hammond launched TIPC Network, a computer mail-order business, in the Waitt family farmhouse in Sioux City, Iowa. The upstart was funded by a $10,000 loan from Waitt's grandmother. Initially, customers were charged a $20 membership fee to gain access to TIPC's mail-order inventory, which included peripheral hardware and software for Texas Instruments computers. Within four months, TIPC generated $100,000 in sales. In 1986, the company began assembling its own computers; however, sales of these machines accounted for only a small percentage of annual revenues, which reached $1 million.

In 1987, Gateway developed an IBM-compatible personal computer (PC) using components from other PC makers. Although Gateway's PC was similar to one sold by Texas Instruments, with two floppy disk drives and a color monitor, it cost only $1,995, roughly half the price of Texas Instruments' machine. The firm changed its name to Gateway 2000 in 1988, which proved to be a pivotal year for the direct-sales PC company as its low-cost machines, powered with 286 processors, began to garner attention. Increased growth prompted Gateway to move headquarters from the Waitt ranch to a 5,000-square-foot building. The firm also launched its first major advertising campaign, running a full-page ad in which a photo of the Waitt family cattle herd appeared above a caption reading, "Computers from Iowa?" In addition, Waitt launched a performance incentive program for his staff, rewarding hourly employees with monthly cash bonuses that were tied to profits. Efforts paid off as sales skyrocketed from $1.5 million to $12 million in less than 12 months.

Sales grew nearly sixfold in 1989, exceeding $70 million. In 1990, Gateway relocated to South Dakota, a state with no income taxes. The firm also launched several light-hearted advertisements that poked fun at its rural location and portrayed a Holstein cow as Gateway's mascot. Continued growth prompted Waitt to bolster his management team with six executives from large PC firms. Sales jumped to $275 million that year as the firm shipped roughly 225 PCs per day. Employees totaled 185. Gateway was named the fastest-growing private company in America by *Inc.* magazine in 1991. To house its expanding operations, Gateway built a new 44,000-square-foot headquarters building. The firm also began targeting corporate markets for the first time. Sales continued to soar, reaching $626 million.

In 1992, Gateway unveiled its first notebook computer, the Handbook, which weighed less than three pounds. The Handbook proved to be one of the few Gateway products that sold poorly in the early 1990s. Although the recession at that time had taken a toll on other PC makers, Gateway found its sales exploding as people in the market for a new PC began seeking out less expensive models. As a result, revenues exceeded $1 billion for the first time. Earnings of $1.1 million boosted Gateway into the first-place spot among mail-order computer companies. However, as demand for its products was so high, Gateway found itself unable to fill orders. When clients began complaining about lengthy delays, as well as flaws in the computers that did finally arrive, the firm hired 200 new workers.

International growth took place for the first time in 1993, when Gateway opened a complex in Dublin, Ireland. That year, the firm completed its initial public offering (IPO), selling nearly 11 million shares for $150 million. Upon completion of the IPO, the Waitt family owned 85% of Gateway. In an effort to improve service to its business customers, Gateway increased its support staff more than twofold, hired additional technicians, and added a separate phone line dedicated to providing support services to companies using Gateway machines. Although many rivals had begun to levy fees for technical support, Gateway continued to offer its services for free. The firm created a sales and customer support unit in Kansas City, Missouri, in 1994. International expansion continued with the creation of showrooms—which allowed potential customers to examine Gateway merchandise prior to making a purchase—in France, Germany, Japan, and the United Kingdom. Sales reached $2.7 billion that year.

Gateway made its first foray into the Pacific Rim in 1995, creating a manufacturing plant in Malaysia to make PCs. The firm also moved into Australia with the purchase of Osborne Computer, based in Sydney. Steady demand prompted the firm to create a third U.S.

manufacturing plant, located in Hampton, Virginia, in 1996. To gain a foothold in Greece, the firm forged a distribution alliance with Dakos S.A. In a similar move, Gateway also inked a distribution deal with Al Yousuf Computers, based in the United Arab Emirates. Growth in Europe was bolstered with a new showroom in Sweden. New product developments included a large-screen PC and television set combo known as Destination; it was the first Gateway product to be marketed by traditional retailers. Also in the mid-1990s, Gateway established its Country Stores Inc. subsidiary. Gateway's 8,000-square-foot Country Stores, similar to the firm's European showrooms, gave customers the chance to examine Gateway merchandise before purchasing it via mail or telephone. The first Country Stores were based in Connecticut and North Carolina.

MOVE TO THE INTERNET

In 1996, Gateway was spending roughly $90 million on advertising annually to continue bolstering its name recognition. By then, the firm had become the world's tenth-largest computer company with earnings of $250 million on sales of $5 billion. It was second only to Dell Computer Corp. among direct sellers of PCs. According to a March 1997 issue of *Success,* the firm achieved that success because Waitt had made "a number of critical calls that put Gateway ahead of its industry. In 1988 it was the first to make EGA color monitors standard on all its systems. In 1990 it was the first to make Windows standard on all systems. In 1994, before anyone else, it made the Pentium chip standard. That same year Gateway was first to make CD-ROM drives standard on all its systems. And in July 1996 it became the first computer maker to allow customers to custom-order and pay for a new computer over the World Wide Web."

Clients could order customized PCs via the firm's World Wide Web site using a process similar to the one used by clients who placed telephone orders, which were typically filled in less than five days. Initially, some of the site's visitors would simply check prices and compare models before calling Gateway to formally place an order. Eventually, however, Web surfers became more comfortable with the idea of actually making the purchase online. Internet sales grew from $300 million to $700 million in 1997, as total annual revenues climbed to $6.3 billion.

The firm also began targeting business markets that year by launching its E-Series line of PCs for larger corporations. Designed to serve networked environments, each of the PCs offered in the E-Series line included Ethernet networking capabilities. To gain access to the server technology it needed to serve the networking needs of large enterprises, Gateway paid roughly $194 million in stock for Advanced Logic Research. The firm also diversified into Internet access with the launch of Gateway.net, a service it developed in conjunction with UUNet Technologies, the predecessor to WorldCom. For a flat fee of $12.95 per month, purchasers of new Gateway PCs were able to use Gateway.net software, which came bundled with the PC, to surf the Internet for up to 30 hours. These new activities reflected the firm's recognition that it needed to reduce its reliance on the PC market, which was nearing saturation. Price cuts by rivals like Dell and Compaq Computer Corp. forced Gateway to lower its prices by 12%.

With the millennium approaching, Gateway 2000 Inc. shortened its name to Gateway, Inc., in 1998. By mid-year, roughly 58 Country Stores spanning 26 states were in operation. Falling PC prices continued to hammer away at the firm's bottom line, prompting its relocation to San Diego, California, where it could access a larger pool of technological and managerial talent. In a major overhaul of operations, Waitt replaced 10 of 15 top executives.

In 1999, to attract new customers, Gateway began offering one year of free Internet access, with a limit of 150 hours per month, to those who purchased a Gateway machine costing more than $1,000. The firm also extended its e-commerce operations via an alliance with NECX Office and Personal Technology Center, one of the largest computer products e-tailers. According to the terms of the agreement, NECX and Gateway jointly operated SpotShop.com, which offered Gateway merchandise as well as peripheral equipment and software from other computer industry leaders. A deal with Yahoo! allowed Gateway.net users to customize their home pages via a new Gateway My Yahoo! application that operated as a news and shopping portal. In October, America Online (AOL) invested $800 million in Gateway to operate Gateway.net, the company's Internet service provider (ISP), which boasted 600,000 subscribers. Despite these efforts to diversify, PCs continued to account for 85% of earnings. However, Gateway made successful inroads into the corporate, education, and government sectors, as nearly half of total sales in 1999 came from these nonconsumer markets. By year's end, 200 Country Stores were operating in the United States, and Waitt had been succeeded as CEO by Gateway president Jeff Weitzen. Together, in the months prior to Waitt's resignation, Weitzen and Waitt had reshuffled Gateway's increasingly diverse operations into six segments: systems, software and peripherals, service and training, Internet access, portals and content, and financing. Waitt remained chairman and charged Weitzen with the task of developing Gateway's peripheral, or "beyond-the-box," efforts.

FALLING PROFITS AND LAYOFFS

Falling prices and near saturation in the PC industry forced Gateway to begin selling its PCs via traditional retail outlets in 2000. For example, the OfficeMax chain began carrying Gateway products that year. In an effort to cut costs, Gateway reached an agreement with rivals Compaq Computer Corp. and Hewlett-Packard Co. to create an independent Internet-based procurement operation for PC parts and supplies; each firm contributed $5 million to the new venture. Profits that year tumbled 26% to $316 million on revenues of roughly $10 billion; sales growth was just 7%, compared to an average of 20% over the previous five years.

Unhappy with the company's performance, Waitt resumed his role as CEO, ousting Weitzen in January 2001. In an effort to return Gateway to its core PC business, Waitt fired six of eight top executives and rehired several executives who had resigned during Weitzen's short tenure. He also closed 27 Country Stores and laid off 3,000 workers. While the firm continued to develop "beyond-the-box" products and services, PC sales once again became Gateway's key focus. Competition intensified when rival Dell Computer slashed its prices by roughly 20%, forcing Gateway to once again reduce its prices. Losses in the first half of the year reached $523.7 million on sales of $3.5 billion. Believing drastic action was in order, Waitt slashed Gateway's staff by one-fourth in September 2001, releasing 2,200 international workers and 2,500 domestic employees. The cuts, estimated to save $300 million annually, were an effort to offset the negative effects of the firm's lowered prices. However, Gateway also shuttered several international operations, which reduced revenues another 14%. After reducing its size, Gateway also began to look to its Country Stores, which offered services like online bill payment and small business technical support, as potential growth areas.

In March 2004, Gateway acquired e-Machines, one of the world's fastest-growing PC makers. E-Machines mostly sold its PCs in third-party retail stores, such as Best Buy and Costco, rather than in specialty stores that Gateway had invested heavily in, thus avoiding the overhead costs associated with expensive real estate and staff.

STORE CLOSURES

In April 2004, shortly after acquiring e-Machines, which preferred to sell through third-party retail stores, Gateway announced its intention to close all 188 of its retail stores and lay off 2,500 employees. A company spokesman said the company was looking for any way to reduce costs. Gateway continued to sell its computers and peripherals over the Internet and by phone.

At the time, Gateway was the only major computer maker to have its own stores. Gartner Group analyst Martin Reynolds told *USA Today* contributor Michelle Kessler that Gateway's overhead was almost double that of Dell's, which made it difficult for Gateway to compete with its rivals, such as Dell and Hewlett-Packard, who were not encumbered with real estate and store employee costs. Gateway's shares rose by 4% to $5.63 after the news of the closures was announced.

ACQUISITIONS AND MERGERS

In September 2007, MPC Corporation, a PC distributor in the professional business sector including government, health care, and education, announced that it had signed a deal with Gateway to acquire the latter's Professional Service business unit for approximately $90 million. The unit comprised Gateway's small, medium, and large business customers and its government and education operations.

The acquisition was not a success for MPC, which filed for Chapter 11 bankruptcy in November 2008. "Unforeseen issues surrounding our integration of the Gateway Professional business unit, combined with adapting the operations of our manufacturing partner.. .have proven more challenging than originally anticipated, and have contributed to extensive losses," MPC CEO John Yeros said in a statement quoted by Agam Shah in *PCWorld.*

Around the same time as Gateway was negotiating with MPC to purchase its professional market, Taiwan-based PC maker Acer announced its intention to acquire Gateway. At the time, Gateway was the fourth-largest computer seller in the United States, while Acer was the third-largest in the world, behind Hewlett-Packard and Dell.

"Of the various mergers [in the past few years] this one is one of the more sensible ones," said Roger Kay, principal at Endpoint Technologies, as quoted by Chloe Albaneusius in *PC Magazine.* Indeed, in a January 2008 blog for *CNET News,* reporter Erica Ogg's headline was: "Acer and Gateway, One Big Happy Family." In 2011, the Acer/Gateway company was the second-largest PC seller in the world, selling its brands through retailers, e-tailers, and partners in the United States, Canada, Mexico, and a number of South American and Asia-Pacific markets.

SEE ALSO *Waitt, Ted.*

BIBLIOGRAPHY

Albaneusius, Chloe. "Acer Buys, Will Preserve Gateway, eMachine Brands." *PC Magazine,* August 27, 2007. Available from http://www.pcmag.com/article2/0,2817,2176056,00.asp.

Allen, Mike. "Gateway's 'Retrenching' Continues." *San Diego Business Journal,* September 3, 2001.

Brooker, Katrina. "I Built This Company, I Can Save It: Retired Gateway CEO Ted Waitt Shocked the Computer World When He Ousted His Successor and Seized Control." *Fortune,* April 30, 2001.

Conlin, Michelle. "For Whom the Dell Tolls." *Forbes,* August 10, 1998.

Gateway, Inc. "Company Background." Irvine, CA, 2011. Available from http://us.gateway.com/gw/en/US/content/company-background.

Gordon, Joanne. "Green Pastures for Gateway." *Chain Store Age Executive,* November 1997.

Holstein, William J. "Gateway Gets Citified." *U.S. News & World Report,* May 3, 1999.

"Internet Access: Gateway Breaks Ground with Internet Strategy." *EDGE: Work-Group Computing Report,* March 1, 1999.

Kessler, Michelle. "Gateway to Close All Stores, Fire 2,500." *USA Today,* April 1, 2004. Available from http://www.usatoday.com/tech/news/2004-04-01-gateway-stores_x.htm.

Kirkpatrick, David. "New Home. New Ceo. Gateway Is Moo and Improved." *Fortune,* December 20, 1999.

Loro, Laura. "Gateway Raking in Online PC Orders." *Business Marketing,* October 1997.

"New PCs: Gateway 2000 Launches E-series PCs Designed for the Corporate Market." *EDGE: Work-Group Computing Report,* May 26, 1997.

Ogg, Erica. "Acer and Gateway, One Big Happy Family." *CNET News,* January 7, 2007. Available from http://news.cnet.com/8301-10784_3-9843390-7.html.

Popovich, Ken. "Gateway Moves to Stem Wounds—But High Inventory and Weak Consumer Demand Dog Faltering PC Maker." *eWeek,* February 5, 2001.

Shah, Agam. "Gateway Unit Acquisition Still Haunting MPC." *PCWorld,* November 7, 2008. Available from http://www.pcworld.com/businesscenter/article/153491/gateway_unit_acquisition_still_haunting_mpc.html.

Warshaw, Michael. "Guts and Glory: From Farm Boy to Billionaire: Ted Waitt's Inspiring Story of Incredible Growth." *Success,* March 1997.

Weintraub, Arlene. "Can Gateway Survive in a Smaller Pasture?" *BusinessWeek Online,* September 10, 2001. Available from http://www.businessweek.com/magazine/content/01_37/b3748053.htm.

GENERAL PACKET RADIO SERVICE

General Packet Radio Service (GPRS) was the network protocol that made Internet access feasible on cell phones and other mobile devices. GPRS greatly improved data transfer rates, enabled users to have a permanent connection to the Internet on cell phones, and helped telecommunication companies transition from second-generation to third-generation networks. As GPRS was released after the introduction of 2G networks and implemented before 3G networks were launched, it was termed a 2.5G technology.

GSM

The European Technology Standards Institute (ETSI) popularized several major telecommunications standards, including the Global System for Mobile Communications (GSM) standard, and later the GPRS standard. GSM was originally developed by the European Telecommunication Standards Institute, and ETSI took over the project in 1989. The GSM standard was announced in 1990, and its commercial launch in 1991 initiated the second generation of wireless network technology. European telecommunications companies adopted the standard, ensuring that a cell phone user in Europe would be able to use networks in multiple nations.

The main issue with the GSM standard was the connection speeds it offered. A cell phone user could connect to a local network, but a telecommunications firmneeded to set up specialized sites that could provide snippets of information using the small amount of bandwidth that was available. A specialized protocol was also necessary to reach these sites, which was known as the Wireless Application Protocol (WAP). This system was suitable for reporting news headlines, local weather conditions, and other brief bits of information, but more complex services such as online banking were difficult to provide. According to *Network* magazine, GSM data transfer adoption was limited to a small number of specialized users, such as traveling sales representatives, and 95% of bandwidth remained voice traffic in 2000.

GPRS RELEASE

When GPRS was launched, the protocol was added to existing network services,including the established GSM network. According to a white paper from Usha Communications Technology, the initial GPRS upgrade improved data transfer rates from 9.6 kilobits per second (kbps) to around 56 kbps. This was still not enough bandwidth for heavily graphics-oriented applications, but it did provide enough bandwidth to load mostly text-based Web pages conveniently, so the use of WAP was no longer necessary. Major telecommunications firms started to offer GPRS service to their subscribers in 2001.

GPRS was also a packet-switched service, and it could operate under the standard Internet Protocol (IP). Previous wireless networks had been circuit switched, which made their use inconvenient because callers had to dial in to the network to use it, and the connection continued to use up the telecommunication company's bandwidth until the callers ended their call. Using packet switching, the telecommunication company saved enough bandwidth to provide much higher transfer speeds using its existing GSM network. Cell phone users could also be billed based on the amount of data they downloaded under a GPRS system, instead of based on the number of minutes they used.

GPRS SIGNIFICANCE

GPRS did not remain the fastest wireless protocol for very long, as faster 3G services were launched shortly after its arrival. The BBC reported that the first telecom to offer a 3G network was the Japanese firm DoCoMo in October 2001. GPRS still gained acceptance in the early 2000s because of its availability. Early 3G networks were typically only offered in a few major cities, such as Tokyo and London, and GPRS was more widespread because it was compatible with the 2G GSM infrastructure.

The 2G network was not originally designed to handle Internet traffic, and it took several years for many telecommunications firms to complete the upgrade to 3G networks. In the meantime, GPRS made Internet sites that targeted mobile phone users worth creating.

Some consumers had a choice between GPRS and an alternative service. In a 2003 article, *ZDNet* reported that GPRS was typically about half as fast as the Code Division Multiple Access (CDMA) service, but telecommunications firms charged similar subscription fees for each service. Some consumers chose GPRS anyway because their local CDMA coverage was insufficient.

GPRS was still in use in the 2010s. A carrier with 3G capability often continued to operate its GPRS service so that network access was still available if its 3G network crashed. 3G networks were still unavailable in some places, especially less populated areas.

SEE ALSO *Mobile E-commerce; Smartphone.*

BIBLIOGRAPHY

Berlind, David. "Which Network—CDMA or GPRS? No Easy Answers." *ZDNet,* January 12, 2003. Available from http://www.zdnet.com/news/which-network-cdma-or-gprs-no-easy-answers/296408.

European Telecommunications Standards Institute. "Our Role in Europe." Sophia-Antipolis Cedex, France, 2011. Available from http://www.etsi.org/WebSite/AboutETSI/RoleinEurope/OurroleinEurope.aspx.

"First 3G Mobiles Launched in Japan."*BBC,* October 1, 2001. Available from http://news.bbc.co.uk/2/hi/business/1572372.stm.

"General Packet Radio Service." Usha Communications Technology White Paper, June 26, 2000. Available from http://wenku.baidu.com/view/e9fb71d850e2524de5187eed.html?from=related.

Rysavy, Peter. "Emerging Technology: Clear Signals for General Packet Radio Service." *Network Magazine,* December 2000. Available from http://www.rysavy.com/Articles/GPRS2/gprs2.html.

Scourias, John. "Overview of the Mobile System for Global Communications." Waterloo, Ontario, Canada: University of Waterloo, October 14, 1997. Available from http://big.uwaterloo.ca/~jscouria/GSM/gsmreport.html.

Segan, Sascha. "The First 3G Phones for T-Mobile." *PC Mag,* July 17, 2008. Available from http://www.pcmag.com/article2/0,2817,2325743,00.asp.

GENERAL USAGE FOR INTERNATIONAL DIGITALLY ENSURED COMMERCE (GUIDEC)

E-commerce is powerful because it enables companies and individuals from across the globe to engage in business transactions. However, this same advantage also can be a roadblock. Business standards that are deemed acceptable in one part of the world may be viewed quite differently in another region. Furthermore, when business transactions occur between parties on opposite sides of the globe, matters of security become major concerns. Determining the honesty and integrity of a business partner becomes more difficult. It was for reasons such as these that the International Chamber of Commerce (ICC) developed General Usage for Digitally Ensured Commerce (GUIDEC)—specific guidelines for ensuring the trustworthiness of digital transactions done via the Internet.

By the 2010s, digital signatures were commonplace, especially in e-commerce and business to business transactions, and GUIDEC had been used by most businesses to ensure that practices relating to them met these standards. However, by 2006, the Internet Governance Forum, an initiative of the United Nations, had largely replaced GUIDEC when it came to international e-commerce.

THE ICC

The ICC has been working to promote cooperation between businesses on a global basis since its inception in 1919. Although it is a voluntary organization, many companies that do business internationally become members (there were companies from more than 120 countries as of 2012) and follow its recommendations to stay in good standing. ICC recognized the need for international guidance of Internet transactions as early as the mid-1990s.

Developed by experts in the legal, software, commercial banking, and certification authority fields, GUIDEC was first drafted in 1995, when it was called Uniform International Authentication and Certifications Practices (UIACP). Two years later, in November 1997, GUIDEC was unveiled to the world at the ICC's international conference, the World Business Agenda for Electronic Commerce. The document took different legal systems across the globe (both civil and common law) into consideration as related to e-commerce, and provided a glossary of core concepts and different best-practice examples companies could look to for clarification. Legal firms around the globe quickly incorporated GUIDEC's standards into their e-commerce legal practices. The goal of this first version of GUIDEC was to provide a framework for ensuring that digital signatures and messages could be legally binding. The committee that developed it looked at all relevant laws in countries around the world in order to present its own guidance that its members could use when conducting e-commerce.

Due to continuing changes in e-commerce as well as its format as a living document (meaning it could be modified), the ICC published a second version of GUIDEC in October 2001. According to the ICC, GUIDEC I covered global legal aspects of e-commerce, both civil and common law aspects, as well as inherent international principles associated with e-commerce. GUIDEC II added to the information already presented in GUIDEC I by including information on new technologies of e-commerce such as biometrics. The primary focus of GUIDEC II was to provide a guideline that international businesses could use to authenticate digital messages through the use of new technologies. GUIDEC II was also written to provide a legal framework for message authentication as well as information on basic e-commerce principles such as information system security issues, public key cryptographic techniques, and biometric capabilities.

No further updates of GUIDEC have been published since GUIDEC II. The ICC has since created a new committee, Business Action to Support the Information Society (BASIS). The goal of BASIS, which formed in 2006, is to discover ways that information and communication technologies can improve social development and economic growth on a global basis. In a presentation at the 2011 Internet Governance Forum, BASIS said it was confident that there were no Internet governance issues that were being overlooked.

SEE ALSO *Global E-commerce Regulation.*

BIBLIOGRAPHY

Essick, Kristi. "Internet & I-commerce: ICC Offers Guidelines to Standardize I-commerce Usage." *InfoWorld*, November 17, 1997.

International Chamber of Commerce. "Business Action to Support the Information Society." Paris, France, 2011. Available from http://www.iccwbo.org/basis.

———. "Task Forces on Security and Authentication." Paris, France. Available from http://www.iccwbo.org/policy/ebitt/id2340/index.html.

Tiernan, Bernadette. *e-tailing.* Chicago: Dearborn Financial Publishing, 2000.

United States Council for International Business. "Creating Trust in E-business – International Guidelines Updated." New York, November 28, 2001. Available from http://www.uscib.org/index.asp?DocumentID=1901.

GLASER, ROBERT

Once an employee at Microsoft Corp., Robert Glaser was the founder of Seattle-based RealNetworks. He turned himself and his company into a major competitor and bitter rival of Microsoft by the end of the twentieth century while simultaneously pioneering the market for streaming media, the technology that allows Internet surfers to download, listen to, or watch media clips online. However, by the end of the 2000s, RealNetworks had lost its competitive edge, primarily due to the introduction of Apple's iTunes in 2003.

In the early 2010s, Glaser continued in his role as RealNetworks's chairman, although he ceded his CEO position in 2010. In 2011, Glaser was also a venture development partner at Accel Partners, specializing in technology companies.

GLASER AND MICROSOFT

Glaser, a Yale graduate with degrees in computer science and economics, joined Microsoft in 1983 at the age of 21. He rose to the rank of vice president of multimedia and consumer systems within a decade, while also helping to develop popular Microsoft programs such as Excel and Word. However, as Microsoft grew into a commercial behemoth and its employee ranks grew from 250 to 15,000, Glaser grew restless, missing the excitement of a start-up company and the thrill of taking on established giants.

In 1993, Glaser decided to leave Microsoft and form his own company, originally called Progressive Networks, to highlight its ostensible mission of spreading progressive political ideas over the Internet. The company quickly invented the technology of streaming media. Following the release of its first product, RealAudio, the company changed its name to RealNetworks to more accurately reflect its line of work.

At one point, there seemed to be a harmonious relationship between RealNetworks and Microsoft, which purchased 10% of RealNetworks as an investment to improve its own Media Player and work toward greater interoperability between the two streaming media packages. However, as the U.S. government's case against Microsoft heated up in 1998, Glaser testified before the U.S. Senate that the Media Player deliberately shut out RealPlayer music files, thus bolstering the government's antitrust case against Microsoft. Microsoft, meanwhile, withdrew its investment from RealNetworks.

Despite such hitches, Glaser and RealNetworks continued to flourish throughout the 1990s. By the summer of 2001, RealNetworks maintained a registry of more than 170 million users, and radio stations, online record stores, and even major record labels all made their products available for download using the company's products. Glaser also served as the chairman and interim CEO of MusicNet, a subscription-based music delivery service that was created in 2001 by RealNetworks and three major record companies—Bertelsmann, EMI Group, and AOL Time Warner—to stream music packages over the Internet. This was a continuation of Glaser's fight against Napster, the free music-exchange network that panicked the record industry in the late 1990s and early 2000s.

Through the 1990s and early 2000s, RealNetworks, with its line of streaming audio products such as RealAudio and RealJukebox, dominated the streaming media market, which had grown into a $900 million industry, earning Glaser a sizable fortune. In 1999, *Forbes* placed him on its list of the richest individuals, with an estimated net worth of $2.4 billion.

AFTER THE DOT-COM CRASH

Following the dot-com crash in the early 2000s, RealNetworks struggled to regain its stock value. Glaser created new business segments and services in an effort to evolve the company and continue to provide value, innovation, and revenue. For example, in 2003, RealNetworks purchased Listen.com and built the company's Rhapsody music service. However, Apple and Microsoft products, as well as other competitors' products, continued to flourish in the markets that RealNetworks had first tapped into. Apple introduced iTunes the same year that Rhapsody launched and quickly overtook Rhapsody in popularity; in addition, RealNetworks' flagship product RealPlayer also lost significant ground throughout the 2000s thanks to products such as Apple's QuickTime. According to an article by Devin Leonard in *CNNMoney* in 2008, "as soon as Apple launched the iTunes Music Store the same year, it relegated Rhapsody to niche status." Leonard pointed out that RealPlayer had also lost ground in streaming media, citing statistics showing that by late 2007 RealPlayer had fallen to third place, with 27 million users, behind Microsoft (76 million users) and Apple (48 million users).

During 2004 and 2005, RealNetworks sued Microsoft for not including RealPlayer in Windows operating software. RealNetworks won the antitrust lawsuit and received $761 million from Microsoft. The company was not as fortunate in a subsequent lawsuit filed against the Motion Picture Association of America (MPAA) in 2008. RealNetworks was in the process of releasing a new product and software called RealDVD that would give users the ability to copy a DVD of a movie they had purchased, supposedly as a backup. The judge hearing the case immediately ordered RealNetworks to stop the sale of RealDVD, and in March 2010, nearly three months after Glaser had stepped down as CEO, the MPAA won the lawsuit. RealNetworks was ordered to pay the MPAA $4.5 million in legal fees.

As mentioned, Glaser resigned as CEO of RealNetworks in January 2010 but remained as chairman. The company reported that his resignation was part of an overall company reorganization that had been in development for several months prior to the announcement of Glaser's resignation. The company also announced that it planned to spin off the company's casual game business, Gamehouse, as a separate company, although as of fall 2011, this had not yet been done. As of 2011, RealNetworks had segmented its business into three areas: emerging products, core products, and Gamehouse.

After leaving RealNetworks, Glaser became a venture development partner at Accel Partners, a venture capital firm that funded RealNetworks in its early years. Glaser, known for his brash, no-holds-barred personality, stated that his leaving RealNetworks was a way for the company to attract "new blood" to its leadership. As of 2011, the interim CEO of RealNetworks was Mike Lunsford, who has been with the company since 2008. Previously, Lunsford served in executive positions with Earthlink.

In addition to Glaser's work with Accel Partners and RealNetworks, he is also the founder of the Glaser Progress Foundation, an organization that has as its goal the building of a more just, sustainable, and humane world. He is also president of the RealNetworks Foundation, which provides grants to charitable organizations.

SEE ALSO *RealNetworks, Inc.; Streaming Media.*

BIBLIOGRAPHY

Accel Partners. "Rob Glaser." Palo Alto, CA, 2011. Available from http://www.accel.com/bio/rglaser.php.

Bozza, Anthony, et. al. "Major Labels Go Online." *Rolling Stone,* May 19, 2001.

Careless, James. "Almost a Single Standard." *Broadcasting & Cable,* January 31, 2001.

Dudley, Brier. "Rob Glaser Resigns as CEO of Real Networks (Updated)." *Seattle Times,* January 13, 2010. Available from http://seattletimes.nwsource.com/html/technologybrierdudleysblog/2010785781_rob_glaser_resigns_as_ceo_of_r.html.

Essex, Andrew. "Robert Glaser: The Real Deal." *Rolling Stone,* October 12, 2000.

Kover, Amy. "Is Robert Glaser For Real?" *Fortune,* September 4, 2000.

Lenatti, Chuck. "Multimedia Gets Real." *Upside,* August 1999.

Leonard, Devin. "The Rise and Further Fall of RealNetworks." *CNNMoney,* October 8, 2008. Available from http://money.cnn.com/2008/10/07/technology/realnetworks.fortune.

Newcomb, Peter. "The Forbes 400: Microsoft Money." *Forbes,* October 11, 1999.

Sandoval, Greg. "RealNetworks Surrenders in RealDVD Case." *CNET,* March 3, 2010. Available from http://news.cnet.com/8301-31001_3-10463425-261.html.

Swisher, Kara. "RealNetworks' Rob Glaser Talks About Giving the Internet a Voice and, Yes, Woolly Mammoths!" *AllThingsD.com,* January 15, 2010. Available from http://allthingsd.com/20100115/realnetworks-rob-glaser-talks-about-giving-the-internet-a-voice-and-yes-woolly-mammoths.

Walker, Rob. "Between Rock and a Hard Drive." *New York Times Magazine,* April 23, 2000.

GLOBAL E-COMMERCE: AFRICA

While businesses covet the relatively untapped African e-commerce market and see tremendous opportunity there, Africa is facing a number of troubling obstacles to the development of e-commerce in the second decade of the twenty-first century. These problems are technical, social, and political. For instance, the continent is characterized by growing but inadequate telecommunications and business infrastructure, structural inequality, a number of severe armed conflicts, political upheaval, and massive public debt. In both Internet advancement and overall economic activity, Africa is marked by severe internal economic inequality both within and between nations. Although Africa had 14% of the world's population in 2006, it had just over 2% of gross domestic product (GDP). GDP per capita was only $1,079 in the region, versus $3,197 in Asia and $19,358 in North America. South Africa, accounting for 25% of African GDP in 2006, is the clear standout in terms of national economic performance and e-commerce activity.

Large-scale political changes—the Arab Spring of 2011—were aided by wireless social media, and these events eclipsed e-commerce progress and impacted local economies in a few Northern African nations in 2011. Meanwhile, the bulk of sub-Saharan Africa remains in dire poverty and faces a number of severe obstacles on the path to prosperity.

SLOW BEGINNINGS

Despite the continent's lackluster performance in overall Internet connectivity, African countries vastly improved their levels of Internet access through the 1990s and the first decade of the 2000s. Only 11 African nations were even connected to the Internet at the close of 1996. However, by 2010 all 54 countries maintained a permanent connection. Still, for the most part reliable broadband Internet connectivity was often limited to the national capitals and other major cities. Rural areas, where about 75% of the continent's population resides, often had little or no connectivity.

With 14% of the world's population in 2006, Africa had only 44 million or 3.8% of the world's Internet users. Furthermore, in 2006, with 281 million broadband subscribers worldwide, Africa accounted for only 1 million of those subscriptions. However, the pace of connectivity was quickening, and by 2007 another 6 million Internet subscribers had been added in just one year, increasing African Internet penetration to 5.3% of the total population. Much of the initial slow spread of Internet connectivity can be attributed to a lack of telecommunications infrastructure; Africa has lagged behind much of the rest of the world in this area, including fixed landline telephones.

TELECOMMUNICATIONS AND INFORMATION INFRASTRUCTURE

In telecommunications infrastructure, South Africa, Nigeria, Egypt, and Tunisia are well ahead of the rest of the continent, but Africa faced a massive degree of internal inequality in this area. In fact, most sub-Saharan African countries had little reliable telecommunications infrastructure at all in 2000, particularly in rural areas. This failure is often attributed to a combination of uncompetitive state-run telephone companies, which controlled 37% of the African market in 2006 (compared to a 7% share in Europe) and a general lack of available capital.

On the other hand, a lack of fixed infrastructure came with some key advantages as well. Most notably, the relative lack of telecommunications systems in Africa has accelerated the widespread installation of mobile telephone networks. Where fixed-line telephone penetration was often as low as 1 in a 100 in many areas on the continent just a decade ago, African mobile phone penetration had reached 22% by 2006, leaving little doubt where the future lay for telephone and internet in Africa.

A few countries, such as South Africa and Botswana, were already successful in laying down sophisticated fiber-optic and mobile networks that reached substantial portions of their populations by 2000. In South Africa, the number of mobile Internet users already surpassed that of fixed-line users by August 2000.

In 2004, the International Telecommunications Union (ITU), launched a regional project in connection with the European Union to help establish an integrated telecommunications market in West Africa. By 2007, many other sub-Saharan states had joined the project, and guidelines for the harmonization of these markets were established. Ministers for the countries represented pledged to promote rapid establishment of telecommunication networks. Nigeria's minister of communication, Chief Cornelius Adebayo, acknowledged the necessity of this when he said, "There is no doubt that ITU has the great potential for creating wealth in Africa and ridding our countries of the vestiges of poverty, hunger, diseases, and other elements of under-development." A key plank in ITU efforts has been assisting nations in dismantling noncompetitive national regulations supporting local telecommunication monopolies.

CHALLENGES TO INTERNET PENETRATION

There are many barriers to overcome in realizing increased penetration for broadband connectivity and e-commerce in Africa, particularly in the business-to-consumer (B2C) market. Many of these were discussed in a 2011 conference in Cape Town, South Africa, by Oliver Rippel, CEO of e-commerce for NIH Internet. Among the points covered by Rippel were:

1. Poor Internet Penetration. Despite progress, the continent still lags most other parts of the world, especially in the high-speed broadband services favored by sophisticated e-commerce companies.
2. Trust. African users are newer to Internet use and may require a period of time to develop levels of trust in e-commerce now enjoyed in many developed countries.
3. Poor Bank Account and Credit Card Penetration. Ninety-five percent of transactions in Africa are handled in cash, while 90% of e-commerce transactions are handled through credit cards. Some other system utilizing a form of "mobile cash" may need to be developed in Africa to overcome this economic and cultural distinction.

Other technical and social issues that have emerged include the often prohibitive expense of marketing for small African businesses. Shipping and trade barriers are still a problem in some countries, and competition from other low-cost producers in China and India have increased competitive pressure on continental producers.

As yet undetermined will be the political reaction in many African countries to the Internet- and social media-fueled revolutionary movements which occurred in Northern Africa in 2011. Leaders in other African countries, who have heretofore been receptive to broad dissemination of wireless Internet access, often viewing it as a new source of revenue, may have second thoughts as they fear for the stability of their own regimes.

More basic consumer problems still linger as well. Literacy, general education, and computer skill levels remain relatively low throughout Africa. While a growing middle class is emerging, and the technological developments occurring on the continent will offer tremendous opportunities in the years to come, the market will have its own quirks which e-marketers will need to adapt to in order to succeed in the African marketplace.

BRIGHT LIGHTS OF AFRICAN E-COMMERCE

By the second decade of the twenty-first century African e-commerce already had registered some clear successes. According to *African Business,* one business sector in which e-commerce gained a strong foothold was tourism. With the ability to set up a Web site and distribute tour information for minimal cost anywhere in the world, African tourism companies were able to promote themselves on a par with tourist packages globally. Tourism firms, now able to accept reservations directly via e-mail, are decreasingly dependent on foreign travel agencies, thereby significantly lowering the cost of business by eliminating the agents' fees.

South Africa can perhaps serve as a template for development in other African markets. While still small by international standards, the e-commerce market there exceeded $500 million in 2009 and was growing at a double-digit pace. Online merchants in South Africa have over a dozen payment service providers (PSP) to choose from, and while some difficulties still exist in cross-border funds transfer, international e-commerce merchants are increasingly regarding South Africa as a strong initial foothold on the continent.

Other African countries, notably Kenya, Uganda, Tanzania, and Ghana are also making progress, and along with South Africa completed a successful trial of mobile banking in 2009. Mobile banking was set for implementation in most African countries in 2010. Following this, e-commerce is expected to take off at a rapid pace, aided by rapid deployment of 3G broadband service.

Some leaders in African e-commerce in the early 2010s include Kalahari.com, an African version of Amazon.com., which retails books, e-books, readers, music, DVD's, games, and electronics throughout South Africa and recently launched a service in Kenya. Takealot.com, started by former Naspers executives, is a competitor of Kalahari.com, with a similar product mix. MallofAfrica provides a secure environment to purchase products not commonly available at African retail establishments.

BIBLIOGRAPHY

"5 Cool African eCommerce Websites." *Afrinovator,* August 29, 2011. Available from http://afrinnovator.com/blog/2011/08/29/5-cool-african-ecommerce-websites.

Banfield, Jessie. "Naidoo Message Spans Africa." *African Business,* June 1999.

Campbell, Anita. "eCommerce Gains Ground in Africa." *Small Business Trends,* September 6, 2004. Available from http://smallbiztrends.com/2004/09/ecommerce-gains-ground-in-africa.html.

Commey, Pusch. "Let the Telkom Games Begin!" *African Business,* April 2001.

Esterhuysen, Anriette. "The Comms Industry in Africa." *Communications International,* September 1999.

"International: Tapping into Africa." *Economist,* September 9, 2000.

International Telecommunications Union. "Africa, ITU Indicators 2007." Geneva, Switzerland, 2008. Available from http://www.itu.int/ITU-D/ict/statistics/at_glance/af_ictindicators_2007.html.

Mbogo, Steve. "Can Africa Exploit the Internet?" *Review of African Political Economy,* March 2000.

Moors De Giorgio, Emmanuelle. "The African Internet Revolution." *African Business,* April 2000.

"South Africa: Overview of E-commerce in South Africa." *Internet Business Law Services,* December 16, 2007. Available from http://www.ibls.com/internet_law_news_portal_view.aspx?s=sa&id=1098.

Twinomugisha, Alex. "African ICT Trends and Countries to Watch in 2010." *Africa Business Source,* February 5, 2010. Available from http://www.africabusinesssource.com/articles/africa-ict-trends-and-countries-to-watch-in-2010.

Vesely, Milan. "E-commerce Bonanza for African Firms." *African Business,* October 1999.

Williamson, Irving; and Stephen D'Alessandro. "New Prospects for Private Sector Led Trade, Investment, and Economic Development in Sub-Saharan Africa." *Law and Policy in International Business,* Summer 1999.

Wilson, David. "Somewhere Over the Rainbow." *Communications International,* March 2001.

GLOBAL E-COMMERCE: ASIA

According to Miniwatts Marketing group, in March 2011, there were over 922 million people who had access to the Internet in Asia, compared with 272 million in North America, and 476 million in Europe. According to Joe Ngyuen, vice president, Southeast Asia at comScore, increased Internet penetration in the region and positive forecasts are making it a lucrative market for global e-commerce.

ASIAN E-COMMERCE: A SLOW START WITH A DECADE OF GROWTH

In the early 2000s, despite the emerging possibilities, Asian businesses were slow to fully integrate e-commerce strategies into their overall business plans, according to *Far Eastern Economic Review.* They also were slow to overhaul the physical and network infrastructures necessary for Internet-based business. Though Asia was bursting with firms of all sizes using all manner of e-commerce software, only a tiny minority of Asian firms had radically transformed their internal and external operation to reflect a serious concern with, and involvement in, e-commerce. By the 2010s, this has changed in countries like China, Japan, and South Korea, but businesses in other countries in the region continued to struggle with the transformations needed to establish themselves online.

Meanwhile, without substantial investment in an online presence, many Asian businesses that had set up an online outlet did not establish an infrastructure capable of actually making sales over the Internet. Rather, many business Web sites tended to be little more than electronic brochures where the company and its products were introduced and explained, but without the kind of interactivity that allowed for sales, customer service, and so on. In 2008, Dion Wiggins, CEO of Asia Online, explained that 86% of Internet content was written in non-Asian languages. Of the remaining 14%, the majority of the content was in Chinese, Japanese, or Korean, which left all other Asian languages representing 0.03% of all online content.

A periodic analysis conducted by MasterCard's Intelligence group revealed that South Korea led the region in online shopping and in consumers who chose to make their purchases online, as opposed to brick-and-mortar establishments. China, however, was not far behind. The study found that in 2010, 93% of Chinese survey respondents intended to make an online purchase in the next six months. Eighty-six percent of South Koreans answered affirmatively, as did 86% of Indians and 83% Thai, the latter two being exponential growth areas for Internet penetration and e-commerce in the late 2000s and early 2010s. Interestingly, only 62% of Japanese intended to make online purchases in the near future, which was down from 85% in 2008.

While it was difficult to gauge the proportion of Asian businesses that had an Internet presence in 2011, the use of social networks and social media were seen as important benchmarks to companies' e-commerce savvy and their responsiveness to their customers' needs. A study by Burson-Marsteller found that of the leading Asian companies on the *Fortune* Global 100, only half were leveraging their brands within social networking and social media avenues, such as Facebook, LinkedIn, or Twitter. Of those, 60% allowed individual users to leave posts and comments on their Facebook page, but only 28% of fan posts were routinely responded to. This is in comparison to U.S. companies, where 89% allowed fan posts and 72% routinely responded.

However, Asian business-to-business (B2B) e-commerce enjoyed a significant boom in the early 2000s, beginning with the recovery from the Asian economic crisis of the late 1990s. Throughout the 2000s, B2B e-commerce expanded, especially in China, Japan, and South Korea. Even in face of a global recession in 2008 and 2009, brought on by the subprime mortgage crisis in the United States, Asian markets escaped relatively unscathed in comparison to many of their North American counterparts. Recovery was well underway by 2010, and in China alone, the value of the B2B e-commerce sector for that year was in excess of $576 billion. This was expected to rise to $735 billion in 2011 and $919 billion in 2012.

One segment of the business-to-business market that was exceptionally healthy in Asia in the early 2000s and into the 2010s was the digital marketplace—central Web locations that brought buyers and sellers of supplies together to haggle over prices and build new company relationships. Web sites like Alibaba and DIYTrade allowed Chinese wholesalers and manufacturers to enter into direct relationships with other businesses around the world, setting up purchase contracts and supply agreements.

A HISTORY OF E-COMMERCE HURDLES IN ASIA

Unfortunately, the explosion of e-commerce in the West, particularly in the United States, coincided fairly closely with the Asian economic crisis, which began in 1997 and continued for about two years. When one country after another saw its currency plummet, and other economic cracks widened into gaping holes, foreign investors divested from the region in a hurry. In turn, this accelerated the economic hardships. As a result, during e-commerce's developmental stage, most of the Asian region was too busy trying to hold existing economies together than to take the time or money to open up whole new business and technological strategies.

Timing was a factor in slowing Asia's e-commerce acceptance in another way as well. With the pace of e-commerce in the region trailing that of the United States, the dramatic stock market letdowns that affected the U.S. Internet market in 2000 and 2001 hit Asian e-commerce when the latter was in a far more precarious state of development. By the 2000s, e-commerce was a more or less established shopping medium in the United States. However, Asian companies and governments were only beginning to seriously dive in and reorganize business and technological infrastructures to accommodate e-commerce. When the boom in funding was pulled out from under the dot-com market, the Asian Internet economy could not recover as easily, and many Asian investors thought it was wise to pull back on their e-commerce ambitions, at least for the time being. In this way, the tech market bust was more devastating to the nascent "Asian New Economy" than it was to the more advanced Internet economy of the United States.

There were also cultural barriers to the mass proliferation of e-business, according to *Far Eastern Economic Review*. Throughout many regions of Asia, established, personal relationships confer a value of their own, something that is simply not accounted for in the purely cost- and efficiency-driven world of e-business.

Meanwhile, credit card use in Asia remains relatively light, and those who do use plastic to shop were largely uncomfortable using it online, much as many U.S. consumers were. While this remains a hurdle for Western companies wishing to penetrate the Asian market, many Asian intranational companies have successfully compensated for this by allowing customers a large selection of payment options, ranging from direct bank transfers, to cash-on-delivery, and even schemes that allow customers to print out a bar code and pay at any local convenience store.

Another hurdle that was as relevant in the early days of e-commerce as it was in the 2010s was that many consumers did not see the utility in shopping on the Internet, particularly in regions of bustling economic activity in which everything shoppers needed was available in a nearby store. Consumers, especially in Japan, preferred having the ability to see, handle, and examine the merchandise prior to purchase. Lingering security fears also continued to hinder the growth of e-commerce in the region.

Within Asia, the borderless world of the Internet did not translate well into the real world, where physical products still had to be shipped. With complex and rapidly fluctuating currency conversions, exorbitant shipping costs, and excessive delays in delivery, the added costs of shopping online at international business sites tended to be prohibitive. As a result, the majority of Internet businesses in Asia trafficked only within their own countries. Increasingly however, globalized companies have been addressing this issue by establishing distribution centers in Asia, thus leveraging bulk shipping rates and passing the savings along to their customers.

CONTINUED GROWTH INTO THE FUTURE

Despite certain persistent obstacles, analysts continued to be optimistic for the future of Asian e-commerce. By 2009, China had become the fastest-growing market for luxury brands like BMW and Bentley, and even in developing countries like Cambodia, Myanmar, Nepal, Pakistan, Philippines, and Sri Lanka, cellular phone usage was on the rise, with an increased number of consumers using these devices to access the Internet and e-commerce Web sites.

Even though Internet penetration in Asia continued to be fairly low, proportionally speaking, compared to North America and Europe, the raw number of Asian Internet users far surpassed those located anywhere else in the world.

The Chinese market was extremely receptive to e-commerce. Approximately 485 million individuals were online in China in March 2011. However, credit card penetration was exceptionally slight in the Chinese market, and most online transactions were paid for by alternative means, which also included regular checks or wire transfers. Moreover, China's markets were still under the tight control of governmental regulation, despite opening up considerably in recent years, and there were many technological shortcomings. On the other hand, the Chinese government was prepared to include e-commerce as a major part of its 12th Five-Year Plan (2011–2015). As part of this inclusion, Chinese officials intended to establish regulatory and supportive framework to bolster development in the e-commerce sector.

Korea benefited from a healthy infrastructure for, and widespread use of, broadband technology. This facilitated high-speed Internet access, which is a key component of online shopping. By 2011, South Korea had the largest number of broadband connections per capita than any other nation. About 35% of the entire population had broadband access, or 85% of all Internet subscribers. This was in part due to concerted efforts by both the government and broadband companies to provide these services to as many consumers as possible. MasterCard Intelligence group noted that through 2011, South Korea boasted the largest Asian e-commerce market in Asia and the proportion of online versus offline purchases was up to 50%, an all-time high for the country and one of the top in the region.

SEE ALSO *Digital Divide; Global Presence, Becoming a.*

BIBLIOGRAPHY

"Asia Online Speaks the Right Language to Attract Japanese Investment." *Asia Online,* April 14, 2008. Available from http://www.asiaonline.net/news.aspx?id=4.

"Asia Online: The Tiger and the Tech." *Economist,* February 5, 2000.

Bickers, Charles. "Back to Basics."*Far Eastern Economic Review,* August 24, 2000.

———. "Going Dotty Over Dot.coms."*Far Eastern Economic Review,* December 23, 1999.

Biers, Dan. "Asian Economic Forecast: United States—California's Bad Dream." *Far Eastern Economic Review,* February 1, 2001.

———. "Trading Up." *Far Eastern Economic Review,* August 10, 2000.

"BM Study Finds Asian Companies Missing Opportunities for Online Engagement." *Campaign India,* February 17, 2011. Available from http://www.campaignindia.in/Article/248404, bm-study-finds-asian-companies-missing-opportunities-for-online-engagement.aspx.

Burns, Simon. "E-business Special Report: A Look at the Data."*Far Eastern Economic Review,* November 23, 2000.

———. "E-business Special Report: The Winners." *Far Eastern Economic Review,* November 23, 2000.

Clark, Philip B. "Asia-Pacific Rim Surpasses Europe in E-transactions." *B to B,* February 5, 2001.

De Kruif, Bill. "Outsourcing May Be the Ticket for Taking Your E-business into Asia."*World Trade,* January 2001.

Goad, G. Pierre. "Riding the Net."*Far Eastern Economic Review,* March 23, 2000.

"Internet Usage in Asia." *Internet World Stats,* March 31, 2011. Available from http://www.internetworldstats.com/stats3.htm.

Kristiansson, Pontus. "Asian E-commerce–A Market Too Large to Ignore." Malmo, Sweden: Avail Intelligence, September 4, 2011. Available from http://www.avail.net/knowledge/blogs/asian-ecommerce-a-market-too-large-to-ignore.

Lewis, Steven. "Asia Embraces B2B E-commerce."*Asian Business,* April 2000.

Luk, Oliver. "Internet Economy to Hit $146bn by 2015." *Marketing Interactive,* May 5, 2011. Available from http://marketing-interactive.com/news/26152.

MasterCard Worldwide. "MasterCard Worldwide Insights Q4: APMEA Online Shopping Study 2010." Purchase, New York, 2010. Available from http://www.masterintelligence.com/ViewInsights.jsp?hidReportTypeId=1&hidReport=260&hidSectionId=181&hidUserId=null.

McKinsey, Kitty. "Asians Miss the E-biz Mark." *Far Eastern Economic Review,* March 15, 2000.

———. "Shoppers Lost in Cyberspace."*Far Eastern Economic Review,* February 22, 2001.

Messmer, Ellen. "Lessons from an Asian B2B Exchange." *Network World,* May 1, 2000.

Misra, Amit. "The Future of E-Commerce in Asia: A Promising Outlook," *Dazeinfo,* January 16, 2011. Available from http://www.dazeinfo.com/2011/01/16/the-future-of-e-commerce-in-asia-a-promising-outlook.

Mi-Young, Ahn. "Asia Awakes to E-commerce." *Industry Week,* May 1, 2000.

Nguyen, Joe. "E-commerce in Asia Pacific: Big Opportunity for a Growing Region." *ClickZ.asia,* December 21, 2010. Available from http://www.clickz.asia/2111/e-commerce-in-asia-pacific-big-opportunity-for-a-growing-region.

"Research and Markets: South Korea's Broadband Market – Overview, Statistics, and Forecasts Report 2011." *BusinessWire,* August 31, 2011. Available from http://www.businesswire.com/news/home/20110831005940/en/Research-Markets-South-Koreas-Broadband-Market–.

Shukla, Anuradha. "It's Boom Time for China's E-commerce Industry." *Business & Technology,* June 23, 2011. Available from http://biztechreport.com/story/1370-it%E2%80%99s-boom-time-china%E2%80%99s-e-commerce-industry.

Vashee, Kirti. "The Asian E-commerce Opportunity." *E-Commerce Times,* October 22, 2009. Available from http://www.ecommercetimes.com/story/emarketing/68438.html?wlc=1315895563.

Wilhelm, Kathy. "Ground Zero for a Data Explosion." *Far Eastern Economic Review,* November 16, 2000.

Zabala, Hector. "Time to Play Catch-Up." *Asian Business,* June 2000.

GLOBAL E-COMMERCE: AUSTRALIA

In the 1990s, when many American firms were rushing into e-commerce (often without a clear plan), Australians tended to be skeptical about the potential of e-commerce ventures, which meant that many existing businesses were in no rush to build Web sites. Indeed, lobby groups and retailers in Australia voiced concerns about the impact of online retail on traditional stores. As a result, e-commerce there grew at a slower pace. By the 2010s, however, Australians—like the rest of the world—were heading online to shop (and socialize) in ever greater numbers.

EARLY HISTORY OF INTERNET USAGE

The Australian Overseas Telecommunications Commission created an international dial-up service in the mid-1970s that allowed a few Australians to connect to ARPAnet, a U.S. Department of Defense network that proved to be the predecessor of the Internet. At roughly the same time, the Australian Computer Science Network (ACSNet), a modem-based network using the Unix-to-Unix

Copy Protocol (UUCP), was developed by computer science professors at the University of Melbourne and the University of Sydney.

It was in the early 1980s that Australia put in place a permanent e-mail connection to ARPAnet. A few years later, an e-mail gateway was added to ACSNet. ACSNet's storing, forwarding, and transferring features allowed Australia's computer scientists to engage in many of the same technologies, such as e-mail and file transfer protocol (FTP), that had recently been embraced by their colleagues around the world. Ironically, it was the success of this early network that many industry analysts blamed "for Australian computer scientists gaining access to the Internet about 5 years later than they should have," wrote Roger Clarke in May 2001.

Efforts to expand network access to noncomputer science areas of academia resulted in the creation of the South Pacific Education and Research Network (SPEARNet) by the Australian Vice-Chancellor's Committee (AVCC). In the late 1980s, work began on the creation of a national network for data, voice, and fax services. Eventually, this project evolved into what became known as the Australian Academic & Research Network (AARNet), which was officially launched in 1990 as an Internet protocol (IP) network without voice or fax capabilities. Like SPEARNet, AARNet was operated by AVCC. Melbourne University helped to oversee the development of Pegasus Networks, an early Internet service provider (ISP) that granted international Internet access via a connection to AARNet, in 1991. Within a year, several thousand Australians signed up for the service. Also in 1992, the Australian Public Access Network Association was created to offer hosting services to a growing number of bulletin boards and newsgroups; it eventually evolved into a noncommercial Internet access provider.

The Asia-Pacific Network Information Centre, which was created in 1993, began to oversee IP address registration in the Asia-Pacific region shortly after its formation. That year, ARPAnet decreed that acceptable use of the Internet could be expanded beyond research-oriented endeavors; this decision proved to be a major milestone in the transformation of the Internet into a commercial medium.

The advent of the World Wide Web sparked increased demand for Internet access across the globe. To better facilitate the growth of the Internet market in Australia, AARNet decided to implement a Value Added Reseller (VAR) program, through which it would allow ISPs to connect to its Internet backbone for a fee based on usage. In May 1994, Connect.com.au became the first ISP to sign up for the VAR program. That year, iinet Technologies, based in Perth, also began offering dial-up connections to the Internet. Australia's public telephone company, Telstra, launched its own ISP the following year. According to Clarke, "In mid-1995, AVCC transferred its commercial customers, associated assets, and the management of interstate and international links to Telstra. Telstra thereby acquired the whole of the infrastructure that at that stage constituted 'the Internet in Australia.'" Many analysts, including Clarke, believe that Telstra's sluggishness in responding to the demands of Internet growth worked to hinder the development of an Internet infrastructure, and thus e-commerce, on the continent. "During 1994–1997, the international linkage represented a serious bottleneck, but gradually Telstra started releasing additional capacity at something closer to the rate at which demand was growing."

It was in the mid-1990s that e-commerce efforts in Australia began in earnest. One of Australia's first CD e-tailers, SiteZero, emerged in 1996. That year, Melbourne IT secured a license to oversee administration of the com.au domain name registry. The firm began charging roughly $125 for domain name registration, prompting a surge in requests for net.au names, which were still free. Unable to keep up with demand, net.au registrar Connect.com began charging fees comparable to those of Melbourne IT.

Australians initially proved hesitant to embrace e-commerce. A mere 2.7% of Australian adults made online purchases in 1998; in 1999, that percentage grew to only 6%. A February 2000 study conducted by Australian law firm Freehill, Hollingdale & Page surmised that privacy issues were at least partly to blame. Although 80% of the online companies surveyed in the study adhered to some sort of a privacy protection standard, only 12% bothered to publish a privacy statement, which is a brief description of what a Web site does to protect the private information—such as credit card numbers and e-mail addresses—of its visitors. In addition, roughly 25% of the firms were unable to provide an online method of payment that was encrypted.

Unlike North America, where a multitude of dotcom upstarts saturated the e-commerce arena well before many traditional firms made their way online, most Australian e-tailers in 2000 were the online outlets of brick-and-mortar firms. According to a January 2001 article in *E-Commerce Times,* "Australian e-tailing is dominated by the traditional retailers who have entered the e-commerce realm. Currently, 50 percent of online stores in Australia are the e-tailing arms of traditional retailers. The next 35 percent of Australian e-commerce sites are online-only merchants, while the remaining 15 percent are wholesalers who use the Internet to sell directly to customers."

Early in 2001, in an effort to foster increased levels of e-commerce, the Australian government passed the

Commonwealth Government Privacy Act, a series of privacy stipulations that all online businesses were required to follow by the year's end. The requirements included publishing a privacy policy and making its location obvious to Web surfers. Other e-commerce efforts by Australia's government included continued deregulation of the telecommunications industry, a move designed to increase competition and thus drive down prices and foster the release of innovative products and services. In July, the government set aside $6.64 million in funding for B2B projects through 2006. Projects that secured grants from this program, dubbed Information Technology Online, included MarketBoomers, an online marketplace for the hotel and hospitality industry of Queensland, and Pharmaceutical Electronic Commerce and Communication, an online marketplace for health care products manufacturers.

CHALLENGES AND OPPORTUNITIES

By 2011, there were signs that Australia was catching up in e-commerce. The Electronic Transactions Amendment Bill 2011 updated electronic transactions in the country and ensured that such transactions met the guidelines of the UN Convention on the Use of Electronic Communications in International Contracts 2005. The bill updated Australia's Electronic Transactions Act of 1999. The 2011 bill verified the authority to apply traditional contract laws in electronic environments and outlined when such electronic contracts were binding. The bill passed both Houses and received royal assent in May 2011.

There was also some evidence that Australia was becoming an important player in the global ecommerce market. In 2011, market research company FiftyOne, Inc., identified "cross-border power shoppers." These consumers tended to make significantly more purchases than their peers and often shopped across borders using the Internet. According to FiftyOne, these shoppers accounted for up to half of online purchases in some countries. Australia was second, behind only Canada, for the number of cross-border power shoppers. In fact, power shoppers in Australia and New Zealand outnumbered those in the United Kingdom and Ireland by three to one, even though the combined population of New Zealand and Australia is one-third that of Ireland and the United Kingdom.

According to Google and the Deloitte Access Economics report, the Internet, including e-commerce, contributed $50 billion to the gross domestic product of Australia in 2010 and will contribute $70 billion by 2016. According to the report, Internet use in Australia more than doubled between 2008 and 2011. One factor that could boost e-commerce through 2016 and beyond is the building of the new National Broadband Network.

Quantium Online, operated by the former head of eBay Australia, reported in 2011 that the value of online purchases in Australia was increasing by 26% annually, with an annual jump of 20% in the number of Australians shopping online. Quantium also noted that most online shoppers in Australia—over 40%— were over the age of 45, while only 15% of online purchases were made by those under the age of 25. However, these numbers were in sharp contrast to findings by the Commonwealth Bank of Australia, which concluded that in 2010 Australian online shoppers under the age of 21 were the most heavy users of e-commerce, spending $4.2 billion on overseas retailers alone.

While consumers have flocked to e-commerce offerings in Australia, some groups have been critical of the success of electronic retail. In August 2011, the National Retail Association (NRA) submitted a report to the Australian government's Productivity Commission outlining the risks of e-commerce to Australian retailers. According to the group, Australia Post can only impose some delivery charges on international shipments and does not subject international shipments to scrutiny in cases where the shipment is considered as low risk. In addition, many goods shipped from e-retailers overseas are not subject to the 10% goods and services tax (GST). As a result, the NRA claims, international e-commerce retailers have an unfair advantage over local retailers. The NRA has proposed that more goods entering the country be scrutinized and subject to the GST. According to the NRA, e-commerce exports cost Australia AUD 1 billion ($1.04 billion) annually. Only imported parcels worth $1,000 or more are charged GST, and while the Productivity Commission agreed to lower the GST threshold in 2011, it noted that the change would not take place for a number of years, since new technology would need to be introduced to make the processing of imports and e-commerce purchases more cost-effective.

Technology changes after 2010 also affected online shopping in Australia. According to a 2011 article in trade publication *Inside Retail,* mobile phones will increasingly become the focus of e-commerce in Australia after 2011, as more and more consumers adopt smartphones and use them for new shopping experiences. Many consumers are already using shopping apps or taking part in "digital shoplifting," which involves scanning a bar code with a phone and using the information to instantly buy the product for less from an online business competitor.

SEE ALSO *Global Presence, Becoming a.*

BIBLIOGRAPHY

"AAPT and America Online Announce New AOL Australia Joint Venture." *Business Wire,* March 29, 2000.

"Aging Infrastructure Holding Back Australia." *Newsbytes,* July 25, 2001.

"Australian Users Turn Slowly to Broadband." *Newsbytes Asia,* September 21, 2001.

Clarke, Roger. "A Brief History of the Internet in Australia." May 5, 2001. Available from http://www.rogerclarke.com/II/OzIHist.html.

"Cross-Border Power Shoppers: Where They Live, How They Buy." New York: FiftyOne Inc., 2011. Available from http://www.fiftyone.com/resources/cross-border-power-shoppers.

"E-commerce Laws Modernised." *Herald Sun,* May 10, 2011. Available from http://www.heraldsun.com.au/news/breaking-news/e-commerce-laws-modernised/story-e6frf7ko-1226053406846.

Enos, Lori. "Australian Government Funds B2B E-commerce." *E-Commerce Times,* July 11, 2001. Available from http://www.technewsworld.com/story/11910.html.

Hammond, Michelle. "Commerce Uptake Higher Among Regional SMEs: Survey." *StartUpSmart,* August 2, 2011. Available from http://www.startupsmart.com.au/planning/2011-08-02/ecommerce-uptake-higher-among-regional-smes-survey.html.

———. "Internet Set to Contribute $70bn to Australian Economy by 2016: Report." *StartUpSmart,* August 3, 2011. Available from http://www.startupsmart.com.au/planning/2011-08-03/internet-set-to-contribute-$70bn-to-australian-economy-by-2016-report.html.

Hepworth, Annabel. "NBN Cost to 'Widen the Digital Divide'." *The Australian,* August 23, 2011. Available from http://www.theaustralian.com.au/national-affairs/nbn-cost-to-widen-the-digital-divide/story-fn59niix-1226120000176.

Kale, Neha. "CBA Report: Australians Under 21 the Most Prolific Online Shoppers." *Power Retail,* July 29, 2011. Available from http://www.powerretail.com.au/news/cba-report-australians-under-21-the-most-prolific-online-shoppers.

McLennan, David. "Online Shopping Tipped to Cost More." *Canberra Times,* August 5, 2011. Available from http://www.canberratimes.com.au/news/national/national/general/online-shopping-tipped-to-cost-more/2249201.aspx.

Nicholas, Katrina. "Survey Finds Cavalier Approach to Privacy." *Sydney Morning Herald,* April 10, 2001.

Pascoe, Michael. "Finally, A Clearer Picture of Online Shopping." *Sydney Morning Herald,* July 29, 2011. Available from http://www.smh.com.au/business/finally–a-clearer-picture-of-online-shopping-20110729-1i2yl.html.

"Retail Lobby Blasts Australia Post, Ecommerce Carriers." *Post and Parcel,* August 16, 2011. Available from http://postandparcel.info/41460/news/retail-lobby-blasts-australia-post-ecommerce-carriers.

"Statistics—E-Commerce in Australia Nov 1999." *AsiaPulse News,* March 1, 2000.

Stockdill, Robert. "Smartphones Retailers' Next Frontier Online." *Inside Retail,* August 22, 2011. Available from http://www.insideretailing.com.au/IR/IRNews/Smartphones-retailers-next-frontier-online-2092.aspx.

GLOBAL E-COMMERCE: CENTRAL AND SOUTH AMERICA

Throughout the 2000s and early 2010s, the development of e-commerce in Central and South America was several years behind similar development in North America and Europe. However, the region still represented a market with great promise. With a large and increasingly connected population, and markets that were ever more linked to those in the north, particularly those in the United States, business leaders both in the region and around the world were anxious to see the development of Central and South American e-commerce.

Complicating matters is the fact that there is little in the way of a defined "Latin American market." Rather, Central and South America are highly fragmented and every country—and often regions within countries—has to be considered on its own terms. This concept poses a great challenge to both outside investors and domestic entrepreneurs. On the one hand, those seeking to reap great financial rewards in Central and South America might want to push forward to develop a pan-regional market in which they could emerge as the standard bearer. On the other hand, an individual or company that is too aggressive risks losing sight of the nuances of the varying markets and thereby overextending its resources for diminishing returns.

CHALLENGES

The legal framework for e-commerce in South and Central America was fairly underdeveloped in the very early 2000s, thus inhibiting the possibilities for growth. By the late 2000s, Latin American countries started acknowledging the importance of the burgeoning e-commerce industry, and in 2011, a number of regulatory and legal framework projects were underway across the region. Central and South American governments derive their greatest share of revenue from value-added taxes, which are those levied on the sale of imported goods. When the various players involved in a transaction are all located in different countries, which often is the case with e-commerce, the assessment of a value-added tax becomes increasingly difficult. As a result, efforts such as *Mercado Común del Sur,* or *Mercosur* (Southern Common Market) have endeavored to harmonize tariffs and encourage free trade of goods between member nations. *Mercosur,* as part of its focus, dedicated special efforts to expanding regulatory and legal incentives for member states.

For the most part, e-commerce taxation throughout the region has been tied to the existing rules for physical-world taxation. However, the difficulty in enforcing such taxation and the resulting decline in tax revenues spurred the region's governments into action to coordinate with governments elsewhere, particularly in Europe, to implement taxation schemes geared specifically toward e-commerce. Several countries, including Argentina, Brazil, Chile, and Venezuela have negotiated tax treaties with the Organisation for Economic Cooperation and Development (OECD). Additionally, a number of Latin American countries have entered into multilateral agreements through the Latin American Integration Association (ALADI), the Latin American and Caribbean Economic System (SELA), and the Organiztion of American States (OAS).

Other regulatory developments in the region included Argentina and Dominican Republic both developing strategies for promoting and facilitating telework. This was seen as a growing sector of the labor force and yet was not specifically dealt with or covered by existing regulation and legislation. New efforts were undertaken to help guarantee legal status and protection of teleworkers under labor law, equal access to the Internet, and incentives given to both companies and workers engaged in telework in order to promote the practice, which has proven to have numerous advantages such as contributing to a cleaner environment, lessening reliance on fossil fuels, and reducing traffic congestion in busy South American cities from commuting workers.

Increased Popularity and Internet Penetration. A great deal of social and economic disparity, both within and between countries, plagued much of Central and South America, inhibiting the spread of e-commerce. Because Internet access throughout the region was so expensive and presented so many technical problems, Internet penetration hovered at around 3% in the early 2000s. However, through both public and private sector investments in infrastructure, the region was marked by rapid expansion throughout the 2000s, making Latin America the fastest-growing Internet population in the world. By 2011, there were nearly 216 million Internet users in Latin America and the Caribbean, equating to a 36.2% penetration. While still lower than North America (78.3%) and Europe (58.3%), in the eyes of many e-merchants, the time was ripe to jump into the Central and South American market in order to capture the eyes of those users as they come online, thereby building early customer loyalty.

Early in the 2000s, one important consideration for e-commerce was the relative lack of personal computer ownership compared to other regions in the world. This meant that those accessing the Internet were far less likely than those to the north to engage in e-commerce, since they did not enjoy access in the privacy of their own homes. Undeterred, by the early 2010s, consumers had many more ways to access the Internet than ever before. Cellular phones, tablet PCs, and netbooks all represented a growing list of ways that users could get connected and go online, some of which were available at reasonable cost. As the popularity of such non-PC devices grew, so did Internet penetration in many remote regions of Central and South America.

At the same time, broadband penetration remained very low, with Puerto Rico representing an anomalous 33%, with the next leading countries, Argentina and Uruguay, having only 12.6 and 12.3% broadband penetration, respectively.

Historically, computer ownership in Latin America was a hobby for elites, and therefore business-to-consumer e-commerce has been fairly limited in its possibilities. According to *Payments News,* e-commerce in Latin America grew 39% in 2009, bringing with it $21 billion in value. Analysts at Capture Commerce reported in 2011 that the forecasted rate of growth for this region was 204%, and e-commerce spending by 2014 would be $27.1 billion.

Infrastructure The biggest early obstacle to Central and South American e-commerce was the lack of a comprehensive telecommunications infrastructure throughout the region. This problem did not go unnoticed by outside investors eyeing the region's explosive potential, by way of new phone lines, computers, information technology, Internet service providers (ISPs), and wireless technology.

Some structural difficulties in the region were deeply rooted. For instance, in 1999, a lack of phone lines, combined with an average gross domestic product per capita of less than $4,000, were of particular concern to investors and e-commerce companies. Fortunately, the situation was addressed throughout the 2000s with a number of physical infrastructure projects targeted at overall economic development. A consortium of public and private bodies were most interested in helping countries in the Caribbean and Latin America catch up with their northern neighbors in terms of both infrastructure and economic development. In a 2011 report, the Inter-America Development Bank (IDB) provided $5.4 billion in financing (of which $2.6 billion was loaned and $2.8 billion was financed) to enhance infrastructure projects in the region. Many of the projects aided by these funds were rooted in renewable energy and roads that would improve the flow of goods and services as well as improve the tourism industry. In theory, these improvements would, in turn, enhance the overall economy and by extension, e-commerce as well.

In the early 2000s, a major concern for e-commerce was the lack of credit card penetration in Latin America. Studies showed that credit card penetration was as low as 10% in many areas, with even the most affluent parts of Brazil not exceeding 50%. Over the 2000s decade, however, credit card penetration skyrocketed, and toward the end of 2009, there were 205 million credit card users, or a 37% penetration. At the same time, debit cards had a 70% penetration (381 million users), but the problem was that these latter cards could frequently not be used in online transactions. Rather than forcing a credit card purchase model, it has become the goal of the e-commerce industry in Latin America to develop and improve systems that would allow debit card use online.

Even where users did have credit cards, they were more hesitant to use them over the Internet in Central and South America, where merchants generally assume little responsibility for their products—"where 'caveat emptor' is the conventional wisdom," as *Brandweek* put it. Security fears, big enough problems in the United States, were greatly magnified in Latin America and highlighted another challenge for e-commerce in the region: overcoming consumers' reluctance to shop online in the first place. These fears were faced in North America and Europe, and have been largely dealt with through implementation of improved encryption technologies to safeguard credit card numbers, along with the establishment of formal government-sponsored frameworks designed to address such issues. This battle was largely fought on the front of improving perceptions of security by consumers. A 2010 study by VISA and America Economia showed this to have improved dramatically in many countries, compared to two years prior. Brazilians, for instance, when polled whether they had high confidence in the security of their transactions, responded affirmatively, from about 55% in 2008 to over 75% in 2010, and Costa Rica's confidence went from 70 to 80% in the same timespan. Setbacks were seen in some countries, though. Paraguay's confidence in security decreased from just over 60% in 2008 to just 51% in 2010.

THE OVERALL MARKET: BRIGHT SPOTS AND FUTURE OUTLOOK

Latin America was seen as one of the fastest-growing regions for e-commerce in the world. Euromonitor International estimated a 204% growth rate and e-commerce spending of $27.1 billion by 2014. The *Latin Business Chronicle* echoed this sentiment, presenting highly optimistic compound annual growth rate (CAGR) figures for the region. A 17% CAGR from 2010 to 2015 would mean sales reaching $25 billion, but only 4% of global sales.

Some analysts were especially optimistic about the prospects for e-commerce in particular countries, such as Brazil. Brazil harbored the highest percentage of South or Central American Internet shoppers. In 2011, there were over 81 million Internet users, and 27.4 million Brazilians reported making an online purchase in 2011. And, while still paltry, credit card use was rising more quickly in Brazil than in any other country in the region. As might be expected, Brazil also had the most online merchants, according to *Business Week*. Brazil, in fact, faced a glut of ISPs in the early 2000s, with more than 500 providers. In addition to this, a rapidly developing middle class and increasing GDP contributed to the number and value of purchases made by Brazilians in the early 2010s. Forrester Research estimated Brazilian e-commerce sales to reach $22 billion by 2016, representing a 178% growth. Much of this growth was predicted to come from consumer electronics, but home appliances and health and beauty products would also contribute.

SEE ALSO *Digital Divide; Global Presence, Becoming a.*

BIBLIOGRAPHY

"10 Myths About Internet Business in Latin America." *Tetuan Valley*, June 27, 2011. Available from http://blog.tetuanvalley.com/2011/06/10-myths-about-internet-business-in-latin-america.html.

Cleaver, Joanne. "Online Explosion."*Marketing News*, June 21, 1999.

Disabatino, Jennifer. "U.S., Latin America Blending E-commerce." *Computerworld*, May 29, 2000.

Ebenkamp, Becky. "Manana's Opportunities."*Brandweek*, February 28, 2000.

"Ecommerce Grew 39% in Latin America and the Caribbean in 2009." *Payment News*, August 5, 2010. Available from http://www.paymentsnews.com/2010/08/ecommerce-grew-39-in-latin-america-and-the-caribbean-in-2009.html.

"Ecommerce Stock Outlook & Review." *Zacks Equity Research*, June 16, 2011. Available from http://www.zacks.com/commentary/17989/eCommerce+Stock+Outlook+%26+Review.

"E-readiness in Latin America." *America Economia VISA*, 2010. Available from http://www.ecommerceday.mx.

Fattah, Hassan. "Latin Crowd."*MC Technology Marketing Intelligence*, August 2000.

Gross, Jorge A., Nicasio del Castillo, Manuel Solano, and Eduardo Pupo German Jimenez. "Latin America Explores Cyberspace."*International Tax Review*, December 2000/January 2001.

Heim, Anna. "How E-commerce Is Growing in Brazil." *TNW*, August 29, 2011. Available from http://thenextweb.com/la/2011/08/29/how-e-commerce-is-growing-in-brazil.

"Hypergrowth for E-commerce?"*Futurist*, September/October 2000.

Inter-American Development Bank. "IDB Backs Large Infrastructure and Natural Resource Projects in Latin America and the Caribbean." Washington, DC, March 25, 2011. Available from http://www.iadb.org/en/annual-meeting/2011/annual-meeting-article,2836.html?amArticleID=9177.

Katz, Ian, and Elisabeth Malkin. "Battle for the Latin American Net." *Business Week*, November 1, 1999.

Kennard, William E. "Connecting the Globe: The Latin American Initiative." *Presidents and Prime Ministers*, March/April 2000.

Latev, Daniel. "Latin America: E-commerce Leader." *Latin Business Chronicle*, May 13, 2011. Available from http://www.latinbusinesschronicle.com/app/article.aspx?id=4909.

"Latin American Internet Usage Statistics." *Internet World Stats,* March 31, 2011. Available from http://www.internetworldstats.com/stats10.htm.

Moore, Stefany. "Brazilian E-commerce Spending Set to Jump 178% by 2016, Forrester Says." *Internet Retailer,* April 7, 2011. Available from http://www.internetretailer.com/2011/04/07/brazilian-e-commerce-spending-set-jump-178-2016.

NL Agency Ministry of Economic Affairs, Agriculture and Innovation. "Chili: E-business." The Hague, The Netherlands, February 16, 2011. Available from http://www.agentschapnl.nl/onderwerp/chili-e-business.

Patino, Martha. "Focus on Latin America." *World Trade,* February 2001.

Pereiera, Pedro. "E-business Washes into Latin America." *Computer Reseller News,* December 13, 1999.

Piper, Mark. "Dot Coms Discover Another Eden." *Euromoney,* July 2000.

Rospigliosi, Guillermo. "E-commerce Status and Trends in Latin America." VISA Inc., Presentation for CTST the Americas, May 4, 2009, New Orleans. Available from http://www.sourcemediaconferences.com.

Saba, Jennifer. "O Brazil!" *MC Technology Marketing Intelligence,* November 1999.

Shivers, Tom. "Forecast for Global Ecommerce: Growth." *Capture Commerce,* January 20, 2011. Available from http://www.capturecommerce.com/blog/general/forecast-for-global-ecommerce-growth.

GLOBAL E-COMMERCE: EUROPE

The development of e-commerce across the globe varies widely depending on factors such as an area's technological infrastructure; the technological expertise of residents, which is related to both the ability of e-commerce companies to find qualified workers and the ability of citizens to engage in Internet-related transactions; funding available for e-commerce ventures; and national, regional, and local commerce regulations. Globally, e-commerce has been experiencing tremendous growth around the world since the late 1990s. A 2011 Capture Commerce report set e-commerce growth at 84% and predicted a value of $193.5 billion by 2014.

In spite of these impressive growth figures, compared to North America, e-commerce grew more slowly in Europe for a variety of reasons. In general, Europeans were initially more skeptical about the potential of e-commerce ventures, which meant funding was more difficult for start-up companies to obtain. E-commerce players also faced many more regulatory hurdles than in the United States for several main reasons. First, taxation and cross-border trade regulations overseen by the European Union were changing to keep up with improvements in technology. Second, online commerce laws varied widely across the different countries within Europe, a fact that not only dissuaded some traditional European firms from engaging in e-commerce, but also slowed the European expansion of some worldwide e-commerce giants. Other hurdles cited by analysts included issues tied to culture and perception, where a sales campaign targeting German consumers would have little or no impact in the United Kingdom or France, for instance. In addition, questions of reliability, trust, and security complicated many cross-border transactions as many Europeans preferred to deal within their own countries' borders. All of this created a virtual obstacle course for businesses that did not yet see the significance or importance in engaging in e-commerce. Even in 2011, the great majority of e-commerce transactions were centered in five western European countries, with other, smaller nations representing only a small fraction of the remaining pie. These five, in order of value of sales were the United Kingdom, Germany, France, Spain, and Italy. The top three alone accounted for 70% of all online sales in Europe.

CONNECTIVITY

Beginning in the late 1990s, Europe began to experience a similar revolution in Internet providers and broadband access that was seen in North America and Asia. At first, free Internet providers began to crop up, with companies such as Dixons Group in the United Kingdom, who offered Freeserve. This was a no-cost way to access the Internet (with the exception of the local telephone line charges, which still applied). An estimated 16 million Europeans got their first taste of the Internet in this manner.

It was not long however, before broadband access saw increased penetration in the region. With only 1.6% penetration in 2002, broadband access in the United Kingdom grew to 30.6% by 2010. Likewise, Germany went from 3.2% to 31.3%, France from 1.2 to 31.1%, Spain from 2.0 to 22.5%, and Italy from 1.0 to 21.3%. Most technologies were still based on digital subscriber lines (DSL), however, and in 2010, new technologies such as Fiber to the Home (FTTH) connections lagged far behind those in Asia or North America.

That being said, Europe led the world in mobile broadband penetration in 2011. Europe's mobile broadband penetration was 46.3%, while that of the Americas was only 24.2%. The world average was 13.4%. In some areas of Europe such as the Commonwealth of Independent States (CIS), and northern European countries like Finland, where land line infrastructure has always been very limited, cellular phone subscriptions were at near-saturated levels.

The estimated value of e-commerce in Europe by 2013 was $283 billion, according to a report by J.P. Morgan. In addition, the compound annual growth rate (CAGR) was estimated at 13.2% for the region. In a report by the Centre for Retail Research, e-commerce in Europe totaled $230 billion in 2010, of which the United Kingdom represented about $70 billion, Germany represented $52.6 billion, and France represented $41.8 billion.

REGIONALISM

Although Europe is often treated as a single economic entity, it is clear that regional disparity makes any sort of generalization when it comes to trends difficult, and interpretable results and predictions spurious. For instance, even though Poland represented a mere $4.7 billion in sales, it was also was one of the fastest-growing e-commerce countries in 2010, with 36% growth from 2009. In an attempt to make some sense of the high degree of regionalism in European e-commerce, some analysts have taken a regional approach, choosing to treat Western Europe, Southern Europe, Central Europe, Northern Europe, and the CIS as separate entities.

While in 2011, an estimated 90% of U.K. residents had at least visited an online shopping Web site, only 25% of Spaniards and 20% of Italians had done so. According to e-marketing analyst Karin von Abrams, these latter two countries had no tradition of home shopping by ordering products from catalogs, unlike the United Kingdom. As a result, for some countries this style of shopping simply crossed over and translated directly into online shopping, but in regions where this was all new, acceptance was low and met with general skepticism.

E-COMMERCE EFFORTS IN THE UNITED KINGDOM

Since the late 1990s, the United Kingdom has been a leading European e-commerce arena, and it continued to lead the continent in the 2010s. By March 2011, 82% of adult U.K. citizens accessed the Internet regularly. According to the Organisation for Economic Co-Operation and Development (OECD), the United Kingdom was ranked fifth in the world for number of fixed broadband connections, or just over 19.6 million subscriptions. Likewise, in wireless broadband, the United Kingdom had 22.6 million subscriptions, which also ranked fifth.

In terms of e-commerce performance, analysts reported that the United Kingdom exceeded growth expectations in 2010 and continued to be high on the radar for e-retailers. In a 2011 survey conducted by IMRG and *eDigitalResearch,* 61% of U.K. respondents from a sample of 6,000 indicated that they would be making online purchases using their mobile devices in the coming year. However, in the larger sense, e-commerce sales only represented 10% of the total share of retail sales in the United Kingdom. As e-commerce in the United Kingdom matured, mere function and simple online presence were overshadowed by user experience as the dominant force for investment and improvement. Many companies strove to improve the appearance and functionality of their e-commerce sites in order to attract consumers who were already online and used to making purchases in a virtual environment.

E-COMMERCE EFFORTS IN GERMANY

Germany was Europe's second-largest e-commerce market in 2011. Representing 65 million users in March 2011, more than three-fourths of them reported having made online purchases in 2010. Broadband penetration in Germany was ranked third in the world by OECD, with 26 million subscriptions. For wireless broadband, Germany ranked seventh, behind both the United Kingdom and France, with over 21 million subscriptions. Several powerhouse companies dominated the German e-commerce arena, including Otto Group, which owned many retail companies; Amazon; and Bertelsmann AG. According to analysts, the buzzword for future development in German e-commerce was *m-commerce* (or mobile commerce), capitalizing on ever-increasing mobile broadband connections in the country. Clothing and sporting goods were the most shopped for items, as were books, music, home electronics, and other household goods.

E-COMMERCE EFFORTS IN FRANCE

When Socialist Party candidate Francois Mitterand took control of France in the early 1980s, the country embarked on its first real online effort. The government-owned France Telecom distributed a set-top appliance, known as the Minitel, which was Europe's first e-commerce channel—a sort of precursor to the modern-day Internet, offering travel packages, concert tickets, hotel reservations and *messageries,* the precursor to the present-day chat room. According to a December 2000 article in *DSN Retailing Today,* "Although France made early use of online technology, its widespread adoption of the Minitel was seen by many as a long-term liability that prevented the nation from embracing newer e-commerce technology. By distributing the Minitel to virtually all of France, France Telecom had created a market standard within the country—and a limited one at that—which for better or worse was in large part responsible for the late arrival of the World Wide Web in that country."

In spite of Minitel and France Telecom's dominance in the early e-commerce arena, the country has not lagged far behind other European countries in its adoption of Internet and broadband technologies. To the contrary, the country's early exposure to e-commerce may have eased the transition into more modern systems and services. In 2010, the OECD reported France to have the world's fourth-largest broadband penetration, with over 21 million subscribers, and sixth-largest mobile broadband penetration, with over 22 million subscribers. In all, there were about 45 million French Internet users in March 2011. Like their German and British counterparts, nearly three quarters of all those online had made some kind of online purchase in 2010.

France's love affair with fashion and clothing persisted into the online arena, with online efforts by major French companies such as Louis Vuitton S.A. continuing to bolster e-commerce throughout the nation. In addition to this, travel Web sites proved to be enormously popular, with over six million French users visiting a travel-related Web site each day.

E-COMMERCE EFFORTS IN SPAIN

While Spain was one of the top five European e-commerce countries, its online sales, Internet and broadband penetration, and likelihood of making future online purchases lagged far behind the top three. The OECD's 2010 report put Spain in ninth place worldwide in terms of broadband penetration, with just under 11 million subscriptions, and the same ranking for mobile broadband, or just under 13 million subscriptions. The total number of Internet users was 29 million in March 2011. Unlike their British, German, or French counterparts, however, only 25 to 50% of Spaniards made any sort of Internet purchase in 2010, a number that analysts hoped would rise quickly. In 2008, e-commerce represented only 2.9% of the country's total retail sales. In addition, rather than shopping through online retail shops, Spaniards seemed to prefer to go directly to manufacturers' Web sites and to companies that specialized solely in online sales, versus companies that had brick-and-mortar outlets as well. In 2010, major Spanish e-tailer BuyVIP was bought out by Amazon, giving the global book and consumer goods giant a significant toehold in Spain.

E-COMMERCE EFFORTS IN ITALY

Like Spain, Italy was a minor player in comparison with the top three e-commerce giants (United Kingdom, Germany, and France). From a demographic perspective, Italy ranked seventh in the world for broadband penetration, with over 13 million subscriptions, according to the 2010 OECD report. It ranked fourth in the world for mobile broadband penetration, with over 23 million subscriptions. Italy had a total of 30 million Internet users in March 2011. Despite low historic results, analysts remained optimistic for Italy to show high e-commerce growth rates. Some of the more popular e-shopping areas for consumers revolved around apparel, which saw a growth rate of 41% from previous years, books and music (growing by 30%), and computers or consumer electronics, which grew by 20%. Unlike France's high desire for travel-related content, the online Italian tourism market only posted a 13% growth.

THE FUTURE OF EUROPEAN E-COMMERCE

While the future of European e-commerce was seen as very positive by most analysts, with impressive growth rates promised well into the mid-2010s, there were also numerous challenges and hurdles that remained unconquered. National markets, regulations, and norms (outside of the European Commission's scope of standardization and normalization) posed problems that made cross-border transactions troublesome in certain situations. A 2010 *Economist* article gave the example of French company Carrefour, which was unable to purchase wheels of Dutch cheese from itself (under its own house brand), because the Dutch government mandated a different size of cheese wheel than the French government did. Likewise, a French chair manufacturer with a presence in both France and Italy must not only pass safety certification in France but in Italy as well. Other, far more basic disparities, such as pricing differences and distribution travails, created cross-border shipping nightmares and hindered sales. While intra-European sales and trade were largely encumbered by such regulatory difficulties, many foreign-owned and operated firms like Apple, eBay, Amazon, and Dell were able to successfully reach the European market with fewer issues, further emphasizing the need for increased harmonization among European legislators.

SEE ALSO *Global E-commerce Regulation.*

BIBLIOGRAPHY

Addison, Dominick. "Free Web Access Business Model Is Unsustainable in the Long Term." *Marketing,* August 9, 2001.

"B2C Ecommerce in Western Europe Will Grow by Over 12% in 2011, to Reach $235 Billion." *Hi-Media Group,* July 2011. Available from http://blog.hi-media.com/b2c-ecommerce-in-western-europe-will-grow-by-over-12-in-2011-to-reach-235-billion.

Centre for Retail Research. "Online Retailing: Britain and Europe." Newark, UK, 2011. Available from http://www.retailresearch.org/onlineretailing.php.

Dembeck, Chet. "Internet Gold Rush Grips Europe."*E-Commerce Times,* August 17, 1999. Available from http://www.ecommerce times.com/story/1016.html.

"E-commerce Growth Quickens."*Europe,* October 1999.

"E-commerce in Southern Europe Still Has a Long Way to Go." *Ecommerce Facts,* July 5, 2011. Available from http://e-commercefacts.com/background/2011/07/e-commerce-trend.

"E-commerce on 2010 in Italy." *E-Business Consulting,* May 24, 2011. Available from http://www.e-businessconsulting.it/en/home/dettaglio-news/hash/78039fded26312358950887dff6354ab/news/e-commerce-2010-in-italia-1/?tx_ttnews[year]=2011&tx_ttnews[month]=05&tx_ttnews[day]=24.

"E-commerce Trends 2011." Windsor, UK: Immediasite, 2011. Available from http://www.immediasite.com/Ecommerce_Trends_2011.htm.

European Commission. Eurostat. "Broadband Penetration Rate." Brussels, Belgium, 2010. Available from http://epp.eurostat.ec.europa.eu/tgm/table.do?tab=table&init=1&language=en&pcode=tsiir150&plugin=1.

"Europe's Need for E-freedom." *Economist,* October 28, 2010. Available from http://www.economist.com/node/17361454?story_id=17361454&fsrc=rss.

"France: Online Travel Market." *NewMediaTrendWatch,* August 22, 2011. Available from http://www.newmediatrendwatch.com/markets-by-country/10-europe/52-france?start=4.

Fry, Andy. "Online Shockwaves." *Campaign,* April 13, 2001.

Greenberg, Paul A. "Blurring the Borders of E-commerce." *E-Commerce Times,* July 3, 2001. Available from http://www.ecommercetimes.com/story/11674.html.

———. "Europe Struggles to Standardize E-commerce Laws." *E-Commerce Times,* November 1, 1999. Available from http://www.ecommercetimes.com/story/1607.html.

"German B2C E-Commerce Market Continues Strong Upward Trend." *PR.com,* August 11, 2011. Available from http://www.pr.com/press-release/344906.

Gwin, Peter. "AOL's European Expansion." *Europe,* June 2001.

Hewitt, Patricia, and Andrew Pinder. "Online Strategy Is Back on Schedule." *Computer Weekly,* March 29, 2001.

"Internet Usage in Europe." *Internet World Stats,* March 31, 2011. Available from http://www.internetworldstats.com/stats4.htm.

King, Andy. "European Mobile Broadband Penetration Nearly Twice the Americas–February 2011 Bandwidth Report." *PRLog,* March 1, 2011. Available from http://www.prlog.org/11343477-european-mobile-broadband-penetration-nearly-twice-the-americas-february-2011-bandwidth-report.html.

Mahoney, Michael. "Europe Learns Its E-commerce Dos and Don'ts." *E-Commerce Times,* April 20, 2001. Available from http://www.ecommercetimes.com/story/9139.html.

Milmo, Sean. "E-commerce Gains Speed as Europe Evolves." *Chemical Market Reporter,* October 25, 1999.

Organisation for Economic Co-Operation and Development. "OECD Broadband Portal." Paris, France, June 23, 2011. Available from http://www.oecd.org/document/54/0,3746,en_2649_34225_38690102_1_1_1_1,00.html#Penetration.

"Positive B2C E-commerce Trend in Western Europe Reports yStats.com GmbH & Co. KG." *Mobile Commerce Trends,* June 30, 2011. Available from http://www.mobilecommercetrends.org/positive-b2c-e-commerce-trend-in-western-europe-reports-ystats-com-gmbh-co-kg.

Rao, Leena. "J.P. Morgan: Global E-commerce Revenue to Grow by 19 Percent in 2011 to $680B." *TechCrunch,* January 3, 2011. Available from http://techcrunch.com/2011/01/03/j-p-morgan-global-e-commerce-revenue-to-grow-by-19-percent-in-2011-to-680b.

Shivers, Tom. "Forecast for Global Ecommerce: Growth." *Capture Commerce,* January 20, 2011. Available from http://www.capturecommerce.com/blog/general/forecast-for-global-ecommerce-growth.

Spiegel, Rob. "Europe Closing E-commerce Gap with U.S." *E-Commerce Times,* December 21, 1999. Available from http://www.ecommercetimes.com/story/2047.html.

"UK and Europe Falling Behind on Superfast Broadband Penetration." *ISPReview,* May 27, 2010. Available from http://www.ispreview.co.uk/story/2010/05/27/uk-and-europe-falling-behind-on-superfast-broadband-penetration.html.

"UK Consumer Trends Revealed for Christmas." Stockton-on-Tees, UK: Visualsoft, August 24, 2011. Available from http://www.visualsoft.co.uk/ecommerce-blog/2011/uk-consumer-trends-revealed.

Weihbold, Ulf. "E-commerce: Is Europe Behind or Just Different?" *TechCrunch Europe,* August 26, 2010. Available from http://eu.techcrunch.com/2010/08/26/e-commerce-is-europe-behind-or-just-different.

Yates, Karen. "Dixons Provides Free Internet Access to Gain Retail Foothold." *Campaign,* October 30, 1998.

GLOBAL E-COMMERCE: NORTH AMERICA

The development of e-commerce varies widely in different regions across the globe. Factors that impact e-commerce include the technological expertise of residents, which affects both the ability of e-commerce companies to find qualified workers and the ability of citizens to engage in Internet-related transactions; funding available for e-commerce ventures; and the technological infrastructure of an area. In the late 1990s, e-commerce grew most quickly in North America, particularly in the United States, due to the increasing number of Internet-savvy shoppers there, as well as the world's largest base of technical experts, who not only were available to work for e-commerce ventures, but who also, in many cases, launched their own firms. Also fueling the North American e-commerce boom was the unprecedented level of funding available from a variety of sources. Moreover, many analysts believed that the time savings afforded by shopping online appealed to U.S. residents, who were considered more time-conscious than individuals in other parts of the world, such as Europe or Asia.

By 2011, much of the world was still playing catch-up with North America in terms of e-commerce technology, Internet and broadband penetration, and growth in online sales. Yet North America was not the largest growth region—that honor belonged to Central and South America, with expected growth of 204% into 2014, followed by Europe and the Commonwealth of Independent States (CIS), with 184%. However, in terms of e-commerce spending, North America was still the leader, expected to tip the scales at $202.8 billion in 2014, with Europe a close second at $166.5 billion, and Asia in third place at $93.2 billion.

EARLY HISTORY

The rise of e-commerce in North America has its roots in the founding of several key companies, including online services provider America Online, Inc. (AOL), online retailing giant Amazon.com, online auction powerhouse eBay, Internet portal Yahoo!, and World Wide Web browser developer Netscape Communications Corp. The success of each of these firms played a pivotal role in the North American Internet revolution and the subsequent growth of e-commerce across the continent.

America Online The first of these firms was founded in May 1985, when 26-year-old Steven Case partnered with Jim Kimsey to establish the predecessor to AOL, Quantum Computer Services, in conjunction with Commodore International, Ltd. By 1987, believing that a mass market for interactive online services and content existed, Case put together a nationwide online network for PC owners called America Online in 1989, and eventually changed Quantum's name to America Online, Inc. (AOL). The new AOL service included games, e-mail, and real-time chat capabilities.

Case spent the early 1990s honing AOL's focus to IBM-compatible and Macintosh computer markets and growing its subscribers with offers such as giving AOL software away free. Throughout the 1990s AOL pursued strategic alliances with computing giants like Microsoft, Apple, Sun Microsystems, AT&T, Hewlett-Packard, and Netscape Communications, and it was not long before AOL's value skyrocketed. Revenues exceeded $1 billion in 1997, and membership grew to more than ten million subscribers. Despite highly publicized technical problems surrounding the firm's inability to handle traffic surges resulting from a new $19.95 per month unlimited access program launched in 1997, the flat fee pushed AOL's subscriber base even higher. By then, AOL had solidified its position as a leading Internet player. According to *Businessweek Online* writer Catherine Yang, "more than any other leader in e-business, the 41-year-old chairman of America Online Inc. is responsible for bringing the Internet revolution to the masses."

Netscape At roughly the same time as AOL was developing its portal to the Web, Silicon Graphics cofounder Jim Clark partnered with 22-year-old Marc Andreessen, one of the developers of the Mosaic graphic user interface (GUI) program for the Web, to create Mosaic Corp. The company was formed in 1994 and its Web browser was called Mosaic Netscape, which was renamed Netscape Navigator later that year. Clark and Andreessen's launch of Netscape's free Web browser, Navigator, is viewed by many industry analysts as a key reason for the advent of the Internet revolution.

Less than a year after Netscape's initial public offering (IPO), Navigator had secured roughly 80% of the Web browser market. This success attracted the attention of Microsoft Corp., which decided to include a version of its own browser, Internet Explorer, with its Windows 95 platform. By giving this software away free, both Netscape and Microsoft made Internet access even easier for PC users to obtain.

Yahoo! Less than a year after Netscape's inception, Stanford University doctoral students David Filo and Jerry Yang cofounded Yahoo! Inc. In the early 1990s, the two began using Mosaic to browse the Web. After having difficulty keeping track of his growing list of favorite sites, Filo sought Yang's help to develop a program that would allow him to group Web sites into subject categories. The partners named the resulting list of sites "Jerry's Guide to the World Wide Web" and posted it on the Web. When Web surfers across the globe e-mailed positive feedback regarding Jerry's Guide, Yang and Filo decided to begin indexing all Web sites. They set a goal of cataloging 1,000 sites per day; when subject categories became unwieldy, they added layers of subcategories to improve organization. The site's popularity grew rapidly, and Stanford's server began struggling under the increased traffic load. As a result, the university asked Yang and Filo to find another organization to host what they renamed Yahoo!, an acronym for "Yet Another Hierarchical Officious Oracle." Buyout offers emerged from executives at Netscape, AOL, and what would become other leading Internet firms, but Yang and Filo turned them down. Instead, they agreed to take a leave of absence from their studies to cofound Yahoo! Inc. in March 1995. After securing financial backing from Sequoia Capital, Yang and Filo hired Tim Koogle to run their business. When the company went public in 1996, Yang and Filo became overnight millionaires.

Amazon.com Within months of Yahoo!'s official launch, Amazon.com appeared on the Web. Amazon's founder, 30-year-old Jeff Bezos, resigned as a Wall Street executive in 1994 to pursue his dream of creating an Internet retailer. After deciding to focus on the book market, he hired four employees and began working in the garage of his new home in Seattle, Washington, to build the retail site. Bezos chose the name Amazon, believing the title of the largest river in the world expressed his site's ability to reach vast numbers of customers. When Amazon.com went online in July 1995, the site allowed visitors to search for books by author or title, as well as subject or keyword. Book prices, considerably lower than those of traditional book retailers, coupled with free shipping, attracted many users to the site. In fact, in just three months Amazon achieved its first 100-order day.

During Amazon's second year of operation, Bezos began focusing on increasing the firm's growth. One of his most lauded moves, the creation of the "associates" program in July 1996, allowed individual Web site owners and operators to offer links to Amazon from their site.

The associate then received a commission any time a visitor clicked on that link and bought a book. Amazon conducted its IPO in May 1997. In October of that year, Amazon became the Internet's first retail operation with one million customers. Amazon's success left traditional book retailers scrambling to retain customers. Amazon also helped fuel the e-commerce boom in North America by prompting many Web surfers to make their first online purchase.

ebay eBay.com also emerged on the Web scene in 1995 when Pierre Omidyar's girlfriend, a Pez candy dispenser collector, began looking to contact other nearby collectors. Omidyar—a Tufts University computer science graduate who worked for communications software maker General Magic Inc.—realized that the Internet could help make this possible. He created Auction Web, an online auction site that let sellers post items for sale by describing the merchandise, setting a minimum bid, and choosing the length of the auction, which could range anywhere from three to ten days. Buyers could then bid on an object, and the highest bidder at the end of the auction was able to purchase the object for the bid price. Payment and delivery were handled by the buyer and seller. Site traffic grew well beyond Omidyar's expectations in 1996, prompting his resignation from General Magic. Seeing the potential to make money, Omidyar decided that Auction Web—renamed eBay in September 1997—would start charging a small fee, including a commission based on the final price, for each item listed for sale. Since the entire auctioning process was automated, overhead costs remained minimal; as a result, Omidyar's business became profitable very quickly, setting it apart from other Internet ventures and validating the Internet as a viable business medium.

EXPLOSIVE GROWTH

As the number of North American Internet users began to climb and e-commerce sales continued to grow, the stock prices of Internet-based firms began to soar. Amazon.com's shares, which originally listed on the NASDAQ for $18 apiece, rose in value to nearly $100 in less than a year, leaving founder Bezos near billionaire status. Yahoo!'s stock prices also skyrocketed in the late 1990s, and both Yang and Filo became billionaires. In September 1997, eBay conducted its IPO; eBay stock jumped from $18 to $50 in a matter of minutes, and within two months, share prices reached $100.

eBay's registered users reached 1.2 million by the end of 1998, and sales soared 724% to $47.4 million. In December of that year, more than one million new customers shopped online at Amazon.com for holiday gifts. Total customers exceeded 6.2 million, securing Amazon.com's position as the number three U.S. bookseller, behind Barnes & Noble and Borders. (Borders went bankrupt in 2011.) In addition, Yahoo! became one of the few Web-based ventures to make money via online advertising. In fact, the only one of the five major Internet pioneer firms facing difficulty was Netscape, which struggled to hang onto its browser market share in the face of stiff competition from Microsoft. In November 1998, Netscape agreed to be purchased by America Online for roughly $4.2 billion. Stock prices soared on news of the deal, and by the buyout's completion in March 1999, the price tag exceeded $10 billion. These success stories prompted venture capital firms to fund hordes of e-commerce startups. At the end of 1999, despite significant e-commerce growth across both Europe and Asia, North America accounted for 67% of the worldwide B2B e-commerce market and 76% of the worldwide B2C market.

DOT-COM FALLOUT

Total North American online consumer sales in 2000 reached an unprecedented $38.3 billion. However, concerns regarding the performance of many Internet-based firms, including leaders like Amazon.com, caused stock prices to plummet during the second half of the year. Amazon.com lost $720 million on sales of $1.6 billion in 1999. By August 2000, Amazon.com's stock prices plummeted to $28 per share.

Dot-com funding started to dry up when stock prices began to fall, leaving many upstarts short of cash. When dot-coms like Pets.com and X.com began closing their doors, Yahoo! found itself scrambling to find advertising customers to take their place. As a result, Yahoo!'s stock also took a drastic nosedive. By the end of 2000, it was clear to even the most bullish analysts that the North American "Netcraze" had come to an abrupt halt. While some companies like Amazon.com were able to withstand the sudden drop, hundreds were not, and subsequently shut their doors soon. The dot-com debacle was further exacerbated by recessionary economic conditions in North America. Despite the downturn, however, companies like AOL and eBay continued to thrive.

PRIVACY AND SECURITY CONCERNS WITH E-COMMERCE

Despite many companies shuttering their doors, e-commerce as a whole continued to grow in North America throughout the 2000s. However, e-commerce brought with it the threat of cybercrime and problems related to security on the Internet. Already burdened by some well-publicized cases of identity theft and stolen credit card information used to make illegal online purchases, both businesses and consumers quickly realized the critical importance of having secure systems in place in order to use the Internet for monetary transactions and to store securely the identity information of thousands, and even millions, of people.

Solutions were sought in various ways. While companies turned to privacy technology such as data encryption and secure communication channels for the task, many legislators saw the need to regulate who was allowed to do what with peoples' private information. Privacy laws started being enacted or modernized to include electronically transmitted information, with the intent of making companies more aware and responsible for how they handled private information.

In the United States, because of the popularity of credit and debit cards for the majority of financial transactions, much of the regulation of e-commerce fell under the Consumer Credit Protection Act of 1968, and more specifically, Title I, being the Truth in Lending Act (Section Z), commonly referred to as TILA/Z. Under TILA/Z, consumers are afforded protection from unauthorized credit card charges through limited liability. Also outlined are specific procedures allowing for the resolution of billing disputes and errors. The second major piece of legislation critical in e-commerce in the United States was Regulation E of the Electronic Funds Transfer Act of 1978, or EFTA/E. This gives individuals recourse in the event of errors in electronic fund transfers. Both legislations were overseen by the Federal Reserve Board until 2011, when TILA's authority was transferred to the Consumer Financial Protection Bureau.

In Canada, broad-sweeping federal legislation known as the Personal Information Protection and Electronic Documents Act (PIPEDA) was established for this precise purpose. It was passed in 2000 and implemented in three phases. In the first, 2001 phase, the law covered only regulated industries such as airlines and banks. The next year, the law's coverage expanded to include the health care sector, and in 2004 it covered any and all companies and businesses in Canada. The government itself was excluded from this legislation, as information held by the public sector is dealt with under the Canadian Privacy Act. Under PIPEDA, consumers are given specific protection and rights, such as the ability to demand access to the personal information an organization has collected about them, to view this information, and to make corrections to it if necessary. Consumers are also guaranteed the right to know what information is being collected and disclosed and why. In addition, the act states that individuals have the right to expect that organizations will treat their private information with appropriate security and privacy, and that it will not be used in any other way but that for which the individual has given consent.

Secure Sockets Layer One of the most important technologies to emerge in the 1990s that revolutionized Internet security and the confidence and trust people had in online transactions was the development of SSL (secure sockets layer) protocol in 1994. SSL is a form of data encryption that ensures information is scrambled while it is being sent, and that only the intended, authorized recipient can decode the message on the other end. When an individual accesses an e-commerce site, his or her Web browser requests the company's Web server to identify itself. In response, the server sends back a copy of its SSL certificate, which certifies their true identity and that the information to be exchanged will be secure. The individual's browser checks the certificate and decides whether or not to trust it, based on a list of rules stored within the browser. If there is a problem, such as the certificate being outdated, the individual will see an error message. If all checks out, it sends a message back to the server that everything is okay. The server then sends a digitally signed acknowledgement, and a secure, encrypted session is started between the individual's browser and the company's Web server. All of this happens quickly, automatically, and behind the scenes. From the customer's viewpoint, the only visible difference between an SSL-secured connection and a regular one is an icon indicator in the Web browser, often represented by a picture of a closed padlock, or a highlight in another color. Seeing this, the customer may be reasonably certain that sensitive information is being sent and received securely.

According to analysts, the number of people who felt comfortable using their credit cards for online transactions has fluctuated during the twenty-first century. A 2011 survey conducted by Rasmussen Reports found that 57% of Americans felt somewhat confident in the security of their transactions, versus 36% who were not confident. Since 2008, this confidence level has ranged between 49 and 65%. Interestingly, the number of Americans banking online diminished from 49% in 2008 to 41% in 2011.

The burgeoning e-commerce industry, combined with concerns over online security, gave birth to a new type of service, allowing individuals to make purchases without divulging their credit or debit card information to the ever-increasing number of companies that sprung up to offer their products and services over the Internet. PayPal was such a company, established in 1998 in Palo Alto, California, but quickly becoming a global presence. PayPal was purchased in 2002 by eBay and has operated as a wholly owned subsidiary since then. By becoming a central intermediary, individuals only had to give their bank account or credit card information to PayPal instead of each company with which they wanted to do business. Then, when a customer wanted to make a purchase on a company's Web site, as part of the checkout process, they would be sent to Paypal's Web site where they would log in using their PayPal credentials and authorize the correct amount of money for the purchase to be sent to the company, using either a credit card, debit card, or bank account as a funding source. PayPal would then take care of the background work of electronically transferring the funds quickly and appropriately.

Another company, mainly popular in Europe, was Moneybookers, (rebranded as Skrill in 2010), which used similar operating principles, and served as competition to PayPal's services. While these intermediary services were not perfect and were still susceptible to security holes and leaks, they were seen by many as a vast improvement over giving out credit and debit card information directly to potentially unknown and untrusted organizations. Virtually all such funds transfer or escrow companies also had their own internal procedures in place for mediation and dispute resolution, and complying with appropriate regional and national consumer protection laws, in the event of problems with the goods or services that were exchanged. In 2011, there were over 30 different companies offering these services to customers around the world. Some services acted as an "e-wallet" where customers would deposit money first (through conventional or electronic means) which they could then withdraw on demand when making online purchases.

In spite of governments' and organizations' best efforts to establish secure operating procedures that are resistant to attempts at intercepting or misappropriating information, one technique known as phishing was in common use in 2011. Phishing is when a malicious individual or group attempts to fool people into giving up personal information such as user names, passwords, bank or credit card numbers, and other data that could be used to commit cybercrime. One common technique was to send e-mails that—through authentic-looking appearance, logos, and writing—purported to originate from the intended victim's bank, credit card company, or other organization where such information might be stored (such as PayPal). The e-mail would ask the victim to confirm his or her personal information by clicking on a Web link enclosed in the e-mail, in order to prevent a disruption to services or termination of an account. By clicking on the link, the victim would then be taken to a cleverly masked look-alike site, where any personal information entered in by the victim would get harvested for criminal purposes. The most effective defense against these types of attacks has been public awareness, and consumer education in teaching users how to differentiate between legitimate and bogus e-mail communications with organizations. According to one security specialist, in one year from May 2004 to May 2005, over 1.2 million U.S. users were affected by phishing scams, at a cost of about $929 million.

FORGING AHEAD INTO THE 2010S

According to Forrester Research, U.S. online sales were expected to see a compound annual growth rate (CAGR) of 10% into 2015. By then, the value of e-commerce was expected to reach $278.9 billion. Canada represented a smaller market, consumers having spent $16 billion online in 2010, and was expected to grow to $30 billion by 2015.

Canada and the United States were both listed at about 77% Internet penetration. In Canada, the largest sectors for e-commerce were in travel-related products and services, books, magazines, online newspapers, clothing, jewelry, accessories, music, and consumer electronics. In the United States, leading e-commerce categories were consumer electronics, event tickets, and computer hardware, all of which grew by 15% in 2011, according to comScore. In 2010, 42% of American Internet users made some kind of online purchase.

One of the newest buzzwords in the early 2010s was *m-commerce,* "m" meaning mobile. Although the term itself was not new (having been coined as early as 1997 by Kevin Duffy of Group Telecom), its usability was greatly limited by high cost and limited availability of Internet service on mobile devices. As the popularity of mobile broadband Internet connections grew, so did the desire to make mobile online transactions. In 2010, 86 million Americans used some form of mobile Internet service, using devices like smartphones. M-Commerce transactions in the United States were worth around $2.4 billion in 2010. Globally, m-commerce was expected to reach $119 billion in sales by 2015, or 8% of all e-commerce transactions.

SEE ALSO *Amazon.com; eBay Inc.; Global Presence, Becoming a; Netscape Communications Corp.; Safe Harbor Privacy Framework; Shake-Out, Dot-com; Yahoo! Inc..*

BIBLIOGRAPHY

"57% Are Still Confident in Online Security." *Rasmussen Reports,* April 14, 2011. Available from http://www.rasmussenreports.com/public_content/lifestyle/general_lifestyle/april_2011/57_are_still_confident_in_online_security.

"At the Epicenter of the Revolution." *BusinessWeek Online,* September 16, 1999.

"ComScore Reports $37.5 Billion in Q2 2011 U.S. Retail E-Commerce Spending, Up 14 Percent vs. Year Ago." *comScore,* August 8, 2011. Available from http://www.comscore.com/Press_Events/Press_Releases/2011/8/comScore_Reports_37.5_Billion_in_Q2_2011_U.S._Retail_E-Commerce_Spending.

Demery, Paul. "Online Sales Will Average 10% Growth Over Next Five Years." *Internet Retailer,* January 26, 2011. Available from http://www.internetretailer.com/2011/01/26/online-sales-will-average-10-growth-over-next-five-years.

Dunlap, Charlotte. "5 Biggest Investors: Jim Clark—The Man with the Midas Touch—Integral to the Launch of Three Billion-Dollar Start-Up Companies." *Computer Reseller News,* September 20, 1999.

Eads, Stephani. "Will Jeff Bezos Be the Next Tim Koogle?" *BusinessWeek Online,* March 12, 2001. Available from http://www.businessweek.com/bwdaily/dnflash/mar2001/nf20010312_979.htm.

Elstrom, Peter. "The Great Internet Money Game." *Business Week Online,* April 16, 2001. Available from http://www.businessweek.com/magazine/content/01_16/b3728602.htm.

Hazleton, Lesley. "Jeff Bezos: How He Built a Billion-Dollar Net Worth Before His Company Even Turned a Profit." *Success,* July 1998.

Heun, Christopher T. "Online Retailers Stick to the Basics." *InformationWeek,* October 29, 2001.

Jaffe, Sam. "Online Extra: eBay: From Pez to Profits." *BusinessWeek Online,* May 14, 2001. Available from http://www.businessweek.com/magazine/content/01_20/b3732616.htm.

Lee, Jeanne. "Why eBay Is Flying." *Fortune,* December 7, 1998.

Mahoney, Michael. "Report: Global E-commerce to Hit $550B in 2001." *E-Commerce Times,* March 21, 2001. Available from http://www.ecommercetimes.com/story/8331.html.

———. "Report: North American E-commerce to Grow 46 Percent in 2001." *E-Commerce Times,* May 3, 2001. Available from http://www.ecommercetimes.com/story/9440.html.

"Navigating the Canadian Ecommerce Landscape." *Elastic Path,* February 24, 2011. Available from http://www.getelastic.com/navigating-the-canadian-ecommerce-landscape.

Office of the Privacy Commissioner of Canada. "The Personal Information Protection and Electronic Documents Act (PIPEDA)." Ottawa, Ontario, Canada, April 24, 2009. Available from http://www.priv.gc.ca/leg_c/leg_c_p_e.cfm.

"Phishing." *Nigerian Spam.* Available from http://www.nigerianspam.com/Phishingpge.html.

"Research and Markets: North America B2C E-commerce Report 2011." *BusinessWire,* March 7, 2011. Available from http://www.businesswire.com/news/home/20110307006291/en/Research-Markets-North-America-B2C-E-Commerce-Report.

Shivers, Tom. "Forecast For Global Ecommerce: Growth." *Capture Commerce,* January 20, 2011. Available from http://www.capturecommerce.com/blog/general/forecast-for-global-ecommerce-growth.

Verisign. "Secure Sockets Layer (SSL): How It Works." Dulles, VA, 2011. Available from http://www.verisign.com/ssl/ssl-information-center/how-ssl-security-works/index.html.

Vogelstein, Fred. "The Talented Mr. Case." *U.S. News & World Report,* January 24, 2000.

Yang, Catherine. "Stephen M. Case." *BusinessWeek Online,* September 27, 1999. Available from http://www.businessweek.com/1999/99_39/b3648006.htm?scriptFramed.

GLOBAL E-COMMERCE REGULATION

In the early days, when the Internet was mainly a tool for government, military, and academic personnel, regulation was barely an issue, outside of the basic requirements for and restrictions on access. Once the World Wide Web came along and the Internet was opened to commercial activity, however, cyberspace became tied to the conflict-ridden world of national and international economic policies and regulations, to the chagrin of many interested parties, among them businesses, industry groups, legislators, governments, and issue advocates. By the early 2010s, Internet regulation became an important enough discussion topic to warrant the first "e-G8" summit in Paris, in May 2011. Topics that were discussed ranged from regulatory impacts on social networking, freedom of speech and the Arab revolutions, and the need for policing of cybercrime.

Regulating the Internet was a contentious issue, coming at a time when the trend throughout much of the world was toward deregulating markets. While many civil libertarians viewed the Internet as a distinctly new medium that should remain free of the hands of government, the reality, according to the *Economist,* was that "the Internet is neither as different nor as 'naturally' free as wired utopians claim." Along with the Internet's possibilities for democratization and the unleashing of creative and empowering forces came new opportunities for mischief, such as the invasion of privacy and theft, not to mention legal concerns relating to contracts, transactions, and trade. In these areas there were increasing calls for regulation to sort out the various considerations and, in a sense, free the Internet from ambiguity. Indeed, the outcomes of the 2011 e-G8 summit resulted in little consensus among participants and even fewer concrete recommendations and plans of action.

JURISDICTION

Many Internet pioneers hoped to keep the medium more or less free from government controls. Tim Berners-Lee (inventor of the World Wide Web) and the World Wide Web Consortium (W3C) that he heads were committed to keeping the Web as open as possible, allowing for the widest range of input and choices. The standards and protocols they sponsored had a tremendous impact toward this end, but the group was a private nonprofit organization, not a government regulatory body. The W3C worked with business leaders, citizen groups, and others to reach a wide consensus, and drew praise for this laid-back and cooperative approach.

As the Internet proliferated further around the globe, many saw a need for a single body that could act as a global regulator of one sort or another. The nature of such a regulatory body, however, was much disputed. Questions abounded over how much power it should or could have, how it should enforce regulations, and how it would be structured. Some proposed that either the W3C or the Internet Corporation for Assigned Names and Numbers (ICANN) take on a broader regulatory function, but as of the early 2010s it seemed unlikely that either organization could or would assume such a role. Other likely prospects included more established government forums such as the Organisation for Economic Cooperation and Development (OECD) and the World Trade Organization (WTO), but critics warned that these bodies lacked the kind of openness, accountability, and consensus-based decision making that would be required to negotiate competing global interests.

Meanwhile, even attempts within countries to establish areas of jurisdiction often ended in a jumble or in court. In the United States, the Federal Communications Commission (FCC) assumed some authority over American Internet service provider (ISP) practices. In 2007, the FCC ruled against Internet provider Comcast for disrupting peer-to-peer traffic on its networks. In 2010, the D.C. Circuit Court of Appeals ruled that the FCC overstepped its bounds and overturned the FCC's 2007 decision.

In Canada, while the Canadian Radio–Television and Telecommunications Commission (CRTC) held close regulatory oversight over the Internet and Internet service providers, it was not above reproach. In 2010, after having forced Internet providers to institute a bandwidth cap on consumers, thus effectively banning unlimited usage, public outrage caused the prime minister to promise to overturn the CRTC's decision if it did not rescind it itself.

In Germany, laws prohibiting the propagation of Nazi ideology included Internet censorship, regardless of where it was hosted or located. As a result, since 2005, 76 German ISPs were forced to block access to Web sites containing forbidden materials, in spite of falling outside of German jurisdiction. Yet even in 2011, the bans remained in place in spite of lawsuits and public demonstrations against the practice.

SELF-REGULATION

While debates over regulation and jurisdiction continued, calls were growing for the creation of an international e-commerce regulating body, not to impose new regulations from above but to see to it that the increasing number of national regulations did not wind up impeding global e-commerce. These sentiments were shared by industry groups and others who felt that the best way to foster e-commerce was to impose as little regulation from above as possible, and to allow industries to meet their own specific challenges and coordinate with other industries to achieve a common end.

The Software and Information Industry Association (SIIA) was one industry group that promoted and implemented self-regulatory measures rather than relying on governmental bodies to impose regulations from the outside. The group created comprehensive membership guidelines requiring member companies to abide by clear standards of behavior to protect consumer privacy, and it conducted industry-wide educational and policy forums to address issues important to members.

NET NEUTRALITY AND COMPETITION

One of the most significant arguments against industry self-regulation revolved around the question of net neutrality. Many experts have asserted that if Internet service providers were left to regulate themselves, they might introduce a system of discriminating network traffic based on amount or nature of usage. For instance, if a customer wanted to watch videos online, companies could block access to streaming video Web sites unless a premium package were purchased that would allow access. Another example might involve a shopping Web site that would enter into an exclusivity agreement with an Internet provider. Then the shopping site would show lower prices to customers from that particular ISP and higher prices to everybody else.

The issues surrounding net neutrality were hotly debated in countries all around the world, with many proponents voicing their opinions both for and against this principle. Some countries had already enacted rudimentary net neutrality laws, including the United States through the FCC. However, as with the 2007 Comcast case, the FCC's authority and jurisdiction has continued to be disputed, and even though U.S. lawmakers have attempted to pass net neutrality legislation, strong lobbies on both sides of the issue have threatened with lawsuits or legislative reversals of any rules governing the issue.

In 2010, Chile became the first country to pass specific net neutrality legislation that would make it illegal for any company to "block, interfere with, discriminate against, hinder, or arbitrarily restrict the right of any Internet user to use, send, receive or offer any content, application, or legal service." On the other side of the globe, the Netherlands became the first European country to pass similar net neutrality laws.

The argument for net neutrality naturally segued into a discussion of free competition and antitrust legislations. Many economists, legislators, and industry experts warned that unless the Internet were assured a state of neutrality, situations would arise where companies could establish unfair barriers to entry for competitors by creating agreements with Internet providers or telecommunications companies, or such companies might merge entirely to form monopolistic entities.

Business leaders were by no means universally opposed to regulations, especially in the area of net neutrality. Such regulation was often strongly encouraged by businesses and industry groups as a way of clarifying rules and processes and removing ambivalence about the path of e-commerce. Notable corporate supporters of net neutrality included Google, Verizon, Amazon.com, Twitter, and Facebook, as well as many small-business owners across the United States and beyond.

REGULATING A CYBERSPACE WITHOUT BORDERS

A regulatory problem of mounting concern was how to implement national regulations in a borderless Internet world. Most regulations of the Internet largely applied existing, physical-world rules to cyberspace, and did not address the possibility that essential parts of an electronic transaction might lie outside national borders. The Internet increasingly made borders superfluous, and the full potential of the Internet, particularly for commerce, was based on this characteristic. This fueled the growing calls for international regulatory bodies to oversee developments in cyberspace.

For instance, online shoppers in the United States might still be vulnerable to compromised security of their financial information when shopping at foreign Web sites due to the uneven nature of international privacy and security measures. The Federal Trade Commission (FTC) encouraged the U.S. government to be proactive in working with other countries toward harmonization and stronger enforcement of international consumer protection laws.

Countries with more closed economic systems, such as China, were mixed in their reactions to and regulation of e-commerce. While the Chinese government encouraged e-commerce and was investing in the infrastructure to make China competitive in the online marketplace, it continued to maintain tight controls on the development of Chinese e-commerce, strictly implementing a legal framework for e-commerce to reflect the nation's interest. One major development was the inclusion of e-commerce as a major part of the Chinese government's 12th Five-Year Plan (2011–2015). As part of this inclusion, Chinese officials intended to establish a regulatory and supportive framework to bolster development in the e-commerce sector. However, well into 2011, there seemed to be no end in sight to what many have nicknamed, "The Great Firewall of China" (the official Chinese term is "the Golden Shield Project"), a state-run system that filters and blocks Web sites, content, or information that could be seen as subversive, harmful, or contrary to the goals of China's Communist leadership. The existence of this firewall effectively continued to limit China's participation in global e-commerce by prohibiting access to many search engines, social media, and e-commerce Web sites.

SEE ALSO *Internet Tax Freedom Act; Legal Issues, Overview of; Privacy: Issues, Policies, Statements; Taxation and the Internet.*

BIBLIOGRAPHY

Allan, Alex. "The E-business of the House."*Director,* September 2000.

Assange, Julian. "Wikileaks: About." *Internet Archive,* September 28, 2007. Available from http://web.archive.org/web/20080216000537/ http://www.wikileaks.org/wiki/Wikileaks: About.

Banham, Russ, and Charles Wesley Orton. "A Taxing Problem." *World Trade,* June 2000.

Carr, Austin. "Google, Verizon Team Up to Support Net Neutrality, but with Wires (and Strings) Attached." *Fast Company,* August 9, 2010. Available from http://www.fastcompany.com/1679583/google-and-verizons-open-internet-policy-revealed.

Chase, Steven. "CRTC Will Rescind 'UnlimitedUse' Internet Decision — Or Ottawa Will Overturn It." *Globe and Mail,* February 2, 2011. Available from http://www.theglobeandmail.com/news/politics/crtc-will-rescind-unlimited-use-internet-decision-or-ottawa-will-overturn-it/article1892522.

"ChilePublica Su Ley QueGarantiza la Neutralidad de la Red." *El Mundo,* August 27, 2010. Available from http://www.elmundo.es/elmundo/2010/08/27/navegante/1282907501.html.

European Commission. Taxation and Customs Union. "VAT on Electronic Services." Brussels, Belgium. Last modified March 10, 2011. Available from http://ec.europa.eu/taxation_customs/taxation/vat/traders/e-commerce/index_en.htm.

"Europe: Hate Speech." *OpenNet Initiative.* Available from http://opennet.net/research/regions/europe.

"Europe's Need for E-freedom." *Economist,* October 28, 2010. Available from http://www.economist.com/node/17361454?story_id=17361454&fsrc=rss.

"Internet Regulation Makes G8 Agenda." *Al Jazeera,* May 26, 2011. Available from http://english.aljazeera.net/news/europe/2011/05/201152692413757852.html.

Jarvis, Steve. "FTC Report Is Net Security 'Wish List'." *Marketing News,* November 20, 2000.

Kang, Cecilia. "Web Giants Facebook, Amazon, Twitter Join Support for Net Neutrality." *Washington Post,* October 19, 2009. Available from http://voices.washingtonpost.com/posttech/2009/10/internet_heavyweights_are_weig.html.

Kennedy, Gabriela. "China Rushes to Catch Up with the Internet." *International Financial Law Review,* July 2000.

———. "E-commerce: The Taming of the Internet in China."*China Business Review,* July/August 2000.

"Leaders: Regulating the Internet."*Economist,* June 10, 2000, 18.

L'Hoest, Raphael. "The European Dimension of the Digital Economy."*Intereconomics,* January/February 2001.

Litan, Robert E. "The Internet Economy." *Foreign Policy,* March/April 2001.

MacAskill, Ewen. "US Blocks Access to WikiLeaks for Federal Workers." *Guardian,* December 3, 2010. Available from http://www.guardian.co.uk/world/2010/dec/03/wikileaks-cables-blocks-access-federal.

McGraw, Harold III. "Monetizing Digital Content."*Executive Speeches,* February/March 2001, 26.

Patel, Ajay, and Allison Lindley. "Resolving Online Disputes: Not Worth the Bother?"*Consumer Policy Review,* January/February 2001.

Lynch, Grahame. "Nationalizing the 'Net." *America's Network,* July 1, 2000.

Piazza, Peter. "Companies Steer Toward a Safe Harbor."*Security Management,* February 2001.

Prem, Richard, Ned Maguire, and Jeff Clegg. "United States."*International Tax Review,* September 1999.

Rashid, Fahmida Y. "BlackBerry Ban Averted, as RIM, UAE Strike Deal on Encryption." *eWeek.com,* October 10, 2010.

Available from http://www.eweek.com/c/a/Security/BlackBerry-Ban-Averted-as-RIM-UAE-Strike-Deal-on-Encryption-435456.

Rosenberg, Dave. "U.S. Inches Closer to Taxation of Virtual Goods." *CNET,* January 9, 2009. Available from http://news.cnet.com/8301-13846_3-10138800-62.html.

Segan, Sascha. "Life Behind the Great Firewall of China." *PCMag,* June 27, 2011. Available from http://www.pcmag.com/slideshow/story/266213/life-behind-the-great-firewall-of-china#fbid=vR3YEoCgeaf.

Shukla, Anuradha. "It's Boom Time for China's E-commerce Industry." *Business & Technology,* June 23, 2011. Available from http://biztechreport.com/story/1370-it%E2%80%99s-boom-time-china%E2%80%99s-e-commerce-industry.

Sinrod, Eric J. "Looking for a Cyberlaw Legacy." *Computerworld,* March 5, 2001. Available from http://www.computerworld.com/s/article/58260/Looking_for_a_Cyberlaw_Legacy

Tamrin, Shahrim. "No BlackBerry Ban for Malaysia." *Malay Mail,* September 27, 2010. Available from http://www.mmail.com.my/content/50531-no-blackberry-ban-malaysia.

Thompson, Bill. "Meet the Regulators." *New Statesman,* July 10, 2000.

Truedson, Misty Perez. "Small Business Owners Support Net Neutrality in Letters to FCC." *Save the Internet,* January 14, 2010. Available from http://www.savetheinternet.com/blog/10/01/14/small-business-owners-support-net-neutrality-letter-fcc.

Vogel, Peter S. "Net Neutrality in a Nutshell." *E-Commerce Times,* May 11, 2011. Available from http://www.ecommercetimes.com/story/Net-Neutrality-in-a-Nutshell-72425.html?wlc=1305574787&wlc=1317011693.

GLOBAL POSITIONING SYSTEM (GPS)

The Global Positioning System (GPS) is a U.S.-owned network of 24 satellites that provides users with positioning, navigation, and timing services. Originally developed for military use, GPS was made available for civilian use in the 1980s. It remains, however, under the management of the U.S. Air Force. GPS works in any weather, anywhere on Earth, 24 hours a day, to provide highly accurate three-dimensional location information and precision timing, accessible to military, civilian, and commercial users around the globe.

TECHNOLOGY

GPS satellites are in constant motion, orbiting the Earth twice a day at an altitude of approximately 12,000 miles. They are powered by solar energy, and small rocket boosters keep them flying in the correct path. Satellites in the GPS network are positioned in six equally-spaced orbital planes surrounding the Earth, an arrangement ensuring that there are at least four satellites in view from almost any point on the planet.

As the satellites circle the Earth, they transmit radio signals to a GPS receiver that calculates its position based on the information it receives. According to Garmin.com, "Essentially, the GPS receiver compares the time a signal was transmitted by a satellite with the time it was received. The time difference tells the GPS receiver how far away the satellite is. Now, with distance measurements from a few more satellites, the receiver can determine the user's position and display it on the unit's electronic map." A satellite's low-power radio waves travel by line of sight, which means that solid objects can affect transmissions. For example, a signal will not pass through a building or a mountain, though it can travel through clouds and glass.

In order to calculate a two-dimensional position (latitude and longitude), a GPS receiver must be locked onto the signal of at least three satellites. Signals from four or more satellites must be received for a GPS to determine a user's three-dimensional position (latitude, longitude, and altitude). Once the user's location has been established, the GPS unit can determine additional information, including speed, trip distance, sunrise and sunset time, and distance to destination. If the GPS receiver cannot gather information from enough satellites to provide accurate location data, it will notify the user.

ASSISTED GPS

Assisted GPS, or A-GPS, was developed for mobile devices in the mid-2000s. A hybrid solution that incorporates both satellite and network-based features, this technology sends additional data for a GPS receiver through mobile networks, such as nearby Wi-Fi stations or cellular towers. Previously, GPS for mobile phone applications did not work well because signals were too weak inside buildings—or anywhere the view of a satellite was obstructed. The time for the mobile GPS receiver to determine a location could be more than ten minutes, and battery power was drained quickly. With A-GPS, users within range of a mobile network can have their locations locked in faster using less power.

E-COMMERCE APPLICATIONS

As the cost of GPS chips dropped over the course of the 2000s, more mobile devices were equipped with GPS technology. In 2007, over half of all new mobile phones had GPS capability. Marketers were quick to determine ways in which GPS technology could be used to target consumers, and location-based marketing became a new norm in mobile e-commerce. Besides increasing point-of-sale transactions, GPS-based mobile e-commerce can save businesses money. Direct marketing targets the most promising potential customers, and materials are delivered electronically and often on demand, thereby eliminating printing and distribution expenses.

Coupons and local ads can be delivered easily to a mobile device through GPS. As a result, retailers have the opportunity to increase foot traffic by advertising instant offers based on a user's location: "Come within the next 30 minutes and enjoy 20% off your purchase," for example. The closer a person is to a business, the more likely he or she is to enter the place. Additionally, a consumer can receive detailed product information while actually standing in front of the product in a store.

GPS-enabled smartphones and location-based social networking services allow users to share, meet, and recommend places based on their physical coordinates. Foursquare, an app for mobile devices that allows users to share their locations with friends by "checking in," is a popular location-based retail service. Foursquare displays restaurants, bars, businesses, parks, and other attractions in a city. After checking in at any of these locations, people can write reviews and tips about the places. Users can earn points every time they check in, which can lead to loyalty perks, such as food and drink discounts. Loopt is a similar service that lets users see where their friends are on a map and provides real-time answers to common questions regarding a business.

SEE ALSO *Foursquare; Smartphone.*

BIBLIOGRAPHY

Evans, Liana. "Location-Based Marketing: The Convergence of Social and Mobile." *ClickZ Marketing News & Expert Advice,* May 18, 2011. Available from http://www.clickz.com/clickz/column/2071614/location-marketing-convergence-social-mobile.

Garmin Ltd. "What Is GPS?" Olathe, KS, 2011. Available from http://www8.garmin.com/aboutGPS.

Keohane, Ellen. "Is GPS Technology the Next Marketing Breakthrough?" *Direct Marketing News,* December 27, 2007. Available from http://www.dmnews.com/is-gps-technology-the-next-marketing-breakthrough/article/100222.

McCourty, Robert. "Location Based Marketing and Web Site Optimization." *The Mender,* May 14, 2003. Available from http://www.metamend.com/article-location-search.html.

U. S. National Coordination Office for Space-Based Positioning, Navigation, and Timing. "The Global Positioning System." Washington, DC, September 8, 2011. Available from http://www.gps.gov/systems/gps.

GLOBAL PRESENCE, BECOMING A

With the world's disparate economies increasingly integrating into one global economy, and with the Internet affording more companies the ability to extend their reach overseas, the competitive pressures to establish a global presence—and the opportunities that abound therein—have taken on great importance. Indeed, what was seen as a simple possibility in the early 2000s became a strategic imperative by the 2010s; the Internet was propelling the business climate in that direction, and companies were compelled to stake a claim to this new economic environment in order to remain competitive and profitable. The boom in e-commerce coincided with the dissolving of international borders in the business world, thereby heating competition both domestically and internationally. Companies that may have traditionally been restricted to local niches rapidly found themselves in direct competition with companies from across the globe.

While the United States was by far the largest e-commerce market from the late 1990s well into 2011, analysts estimated that the proportion of online shoppers based in countries other than the United States would expand dramatically through the 2010s. According to some analysts, the fastest region for e-commerce growth was Central and South America, estimated to grow by 204% into 2014. Another high-growth area was expected to be Europe, specifically the region of the Commonwealth of Independent States (CIS), with an anticipated growth of 184%. To put this into a global perspective, North America was expected to grow 98%, and Asia, 71%.

In spite of Asia's relatively lackluster growth estimate, many investors flocked to the region for other reasons. In March 2011, there were over 922 million Asians with Internet access, far higher than North America and Europe, but with only 24% penetration. As penetration would only increase, and with countries like China seeing exponential rises in gross domestic product, Asian e-commerce was viewed very positively by companies engaged in e-commerce.

COOPERATIVE EFFORTS

To facilitate global e-commerce and to ease the trepidation many companies may have toward negotiating the various obstacles to establishing a global e-commerce presence, several standards organizations from around the world, including the American National Standards Institute (ANSI) and the International Organization for Standardization (ISO) Committee on Consumer Policy (COPOLCO), work on the creation and implementation of international e-commerce standards. The main thrust of these standardization efforts is the goal to protect consumers.

Obtaining ISO certification has been an important goal for many global firms, but especially in Asia. A 2011 study by Japanese researcher Tsunehiro Otsuki at the Osaka School of International Public Policy concerned the effects of ISO on exports of Eastern European and Central Asian companies. The study revealed an average increase of 44.9% in sales performance, giving further credence to the practice of international standardization.

LANGUAGE AND CULTURE

Well into the 2010s, English has been the dominant language on the Web, but that lopsided balance is not expected to continue as countries upgrade their online access and telecommunications infrastructure. One change in particular signified this shift and very quickly began to take root in countries that did not utilize the Roman alphabet. In 2009 ICANN (Internet Corporation for Assigned Names and Numbers), the regulatory body that governs URLs (web addresses), began to allow top-level domain names to contain non-Roman characters. For example, a Japanese company, rather than applying for a domain name written in Roman letters and ending in ".jp," could opt for a name written in kanji characters, and the suffix for the word "Japan," (Nippon), could be written in Japanese kanji as well. As a result of this trend, and to take advantage of key foreign markets, globalizing companies increasingly designed their Web sites to facilitate all the major languages for those countries in which they do business. The easiest way to establish a multilingual Web site was to outsource translation work to a third party, although machine-based translation services continue to improve in quality and accuracy and increased in popularity.

LOGISTICS

After taking advantage of the Web's global reach, companies face the challenge of getting their products to their destinations. International logistics operations can be extraordinarily tricky to implement, particularly at the level of speed and efficiency that the Internet promises. Companies must weigh the cost of maintaining inventory against the cost of shipping for their various markets. A number of information technology vendors created software and other products to aid companies in cross-country logistics, including applications designed to tie together various business processes into a simple, integrated enterprise system. Other applications merge operations with databases designed to help firms navigate various tax laws and shipping concerns.

Perhaps the greatest obstacle to establishing efficient logistics operations was the red tape involved in getting goods into different countries. According to analysis firm Benchmarking Partners, the average company maintains about 25% of its internationally sourced inventory at distribution warehouses, which adds significant costs. In addition, according to *InformationWeek,* the duties and other costs levied on companies that do not efficiently negotiate a country's trading environments can make or break a company trying to achieve a global presence. Companies were not blind to this problem, however, and innovations in this area were expected well into the future. Many shipping experts and analysts have provided a bevy of resources to help in the battle against shipping costs. The U.S. government even provided e-commerce advice to businesses on its export.gov Web site. One consulting company in 2011 specialized in freight auditing services, promising to reduce costs, accelerate cycle times, and still enhance customer service. Another company chose to outsource their international shipping to third-party vendors, also resulting in quantitatively boosting sales abroad.

SEE ALSO *Global E-commerce: Africa; Global E-commerce: Asia; Global E-commerce: Australia; Global E-commerce: Central and South America; Global E-commerce: Europe; Global E-commerce: North America; Global E-commerce Regulations.*

BIBLIOGRAPHY

Adhikari, Richard. "ICANN's 'Tower of Babel' Decision May Prevent Net Schism." *TechNewsWorld,* October 30, 2009. Available from http://www.technewsworld.com/story/68522.html?wlc=1317103931.

Asmus, Carl W. "Revamping the Supply Chain for a Global Economy." *World Trade,* November 2000.

Baker, Sunny. "Global E-commerce, Local Problems." *Journal of Business Strategy,* July/August 1999.

"Business Poses New Challenges for IT Architectures." *InformationWeek,* February 7, 2000.

Byrnes, Brian. "Latin America Lures Chinese Tourists." *CNN,* September 26, 2011. Available from http://edition.cnn.com/2011/09/26/travel/latin-china-tourism.

Cooper, Cameron. "The Dollar Also Rises: The Strong Dollar Can Make Life Difficult for Exporters." *Australian,* November 26, 2010. Available from http://www.theaustralian.com.au/business/small-business/the-dollar-also-rises-the-strong-dollar-can-make-life-difficult-for-exporters/story-e6frg9hf-1225954583021.

DePalma, Donald. "Think Globally, Act Consistently." *e-Business Advisor,* June 2001.

Enright, Allison. "Going Global? A Commerce Department Guide Aims to Smooth the Way." *Internet Retailer,* January 26, 2011. Available from http://www.internetretailer.com/2011/01/26/going-global-commerce-department-guide-aims-smooth-way.

European Commission. Taxation and Customs Union. "VAT on Electronic Services." Brussels, Belgium. Last modified March 10, 2011. Available from http://ec.europa.eu/taxation_customs/taxation/vat/traders/e-commerce/index_en.htm.

"Freight Auditing Companies Needed in Global eCommerce." *Source Consulting,* July 8, 2011. Available from http://www.sourceconsulting.com/blog/freight-auditing-companies-needed-in-global-ecommerce.

Hohenstein, Peter C. "Crossing E-commerce Borders Like a Diplomat."*Afp Exchange,* Fall 2000.

Kershner, Donald. "Protect Your Transactions with Currency Forward Contracts." *WorkOnInternet,* June 22, 2011. Available from http://www.workoninternet.com/business/investment-financial-strategy/future-exchange/150048-foreign-exchange.html.

"Internet Law — Free Trade Agreements and their Relevance for E-commerce." *Internet Business Law Services,* March 3, 2008. Available from http://www.ibls.com/internet_law_news_portal_view.aspx?s=latestnews&id=1998.

Otsuki, Tsunehiro. "Effect of ISO Standards on Exports of Firms in Eastern Europe and Central Asia: An Application of the Control Function Approach." OSIPP Discussion Paper DP–2011–E–005, June 8, 2011. Available from http://www.osipp.osaka-u.ac.jp.

Portnoy, Sandy. "Language Is No Barrier." *CRN,* March 12, 2001. Available from http://www.crn.com/news/channel-programs/18813157/language-is-no-barrier.htm;jsessionid=fY9F9SFuma7r2T1wE8lB2Q**.ecappj02.

Shivers, Tom. "Forecast for Global Ecommerce: Growth." *Capture Commerce,* January 20, 2011. Available from http://www.capturecommerce.com/blog/general/forecast-for-global-ecommerce-growth.

Shukla, Anuradha. "It's Boom Time for China's E-commerce Industry." *Business & Technology,* June 23, 2011. Available from http://biztechreport.com/story/1370-it%E2%80%99s-boom-time-china%E2%80%99s-e-commerce-industry.

Sweat, Jeff. "Ship It." *InformationWeek,* January 22, 2001.

Tellez, Sonia. "Think Globally When Designing a PM Solution." *Computing Canada,* December 10, 1999.

U.S. Department of the Treasury. Internal Revenue Service. "Tax Laws and Issues — E-business & E-commerce." Washington, DC, July 11, 2011. Available from http://www.irs.gov/businesses/small/industries/article/0,,id=209348,00.html.

Winder, Davey. "Tapping into a New Customer Base Is Simply a Case of Minding Your Language." *Network News,* October 25, 2001.

Zuckerman, Amy. "Hot Global Standards and Testing Trends." *World Trade,* October 2000.

GOMEZ APPLICATION PERFORMANCE MANAGEMENT

Since 2009, Gomez Inc. has been a wholly owned subsidiary of the Compuware Corporation. First named Gomez Advisors, Gomez was founded in 1997 by Julio Gomez, John Robb, and Alexander Stein. Just four years later, Gomez had secured the leading position among Internet research firms that served both consumers and e-business firms. The company evaluated over 6,000 e-commerce sites using its "Internet Scorecard," which ranked the performance and quality of World Wide Web sites in various industries such as finance and banking, travel, airline, and other retail-based sites. The firm also developed GomezPro, a subscription-based Web site that catered to businesses, and GomezNetworks, a division that offered real-time Web site and transaction performance measurement and diagnostic services. Through its Internet Quality Measurement (IQM) Program, the company helped its customers evaluate and compare its offerings, measure and monitor its performance against others in its industry, and develop online strategies.

DEVELOPMENT OF THE INTERNET SCORECARD

In 1997, Gomez, Robb, and Stein created Gomez Advisors as part of the Ashton Technology Group. Operating as a subsidiary of the group, Gomez first focused on evaluating the online services provided by brokers. With a goal of improving the online experience for consumers, the company established its Internet Scorecard in June 1997 and began rating various Web sites. Gomez ratings—rankings based on various criteria—soon became quite popular in the brokerage industry. Receiving top accolades from Gomez was considered a coup among industry players. A 1999 *BusinessWeek Online* article claimed that "for online brokers, getting a top rating from Gomez Advisors Inc. is like winning an Oscar."

The Internet Scorecard ranking consisted of roughly 150 different criteria points. Gomez collected data on those points by visiting Web sites, conducting business and using customer service on those Web sites, and monitoring performance. The online sites were then ranked by Scorecard categories, which included ease of use, customer confidence, on-site resources, relationship services, and overall cost. Ease of use, for example, used between 30 and 50 criteria points such as functionality, simplicity of opening an account or making a purchase, and ease of Web site navigation. Customer confidence used criteria such as the availability and depth of customer service options, and the ability to resolve customer service issues. The on-site resources category was rated based on criteria such as product availability, and relationship services were based on criteria such as online help, advice, frequent buyer incentives, and personalized data. The overall cost category was ranked using criteria such as average cost for typical services and additional fees related to shipping and handling.

The Scorecards were then listed on the Gomez Web site. For example, a consumer who wanted to find information on different full-service broker Web sites could go to the Gomez site and peruse the broker Internet Scorecards that the firm had listed. The consumer could view the ranking listed by overall score, or view the ranking by individual category such as Ease of Use. A profile of each company was listed as well and offered information on the pros and cons of the site and how the company performed in each category.

EXPANSION

In April 1999, Gomez sold 1.1 million shares as part of a private placement effort; Ashton kept a 28% interest in the firm. Using the $5.5 million it raised, Gomez began to broaden its marketing efforts and also started to develop new products. During that year, Gomez expanded into rating the online efforts of companies in other industries. Touting itself as the "E-Commerce Authority," the company launched scorecards for airlines, apparel retailers, consumer electronics and computers retailers, drug stores, furniture stores, grocery delivery services, hotels, loan and insurance providers, pet stores, sporting goods retailers, and toy stores.

As Gomez entered the new millennium, it began to focus on providing services to businesses as well as consumers. In March 2000, the firm launched GomezPro.com, a business-to-business site created to help companies in their e-commerce efforts. Through its IQM Program, the site offered e-commerce tools, quarterly Internet Scorecard reports, custom advisory services, and market research studies. That same month, Gomez also developed a Merchant Certification program designed to reward the efforts of online merchants in over 25 different industries, as well as foster consumer confidence among online shoppers. Merchants that met eight different criteria, such as having customer support access and published privacy policies, received a Gomez PASS seal. If the merchant met more advanced criteria, it received a PASS PLUS seal. By May 2000, over 2,000 online merchants were part of the program.

In order to strengthen its foothold in the business services market, Gomez announced the formation of GomezNetworks in September 2000. This new division was developed to provide real-time Internet site and transaction performance measurement and diagnostic services. The firm hoped to use the network division in conjunction with GomezPro to capture increased business from online firms looking to compare their e-business initiatives against others in their industry.

SURVIVING THE TECHNOLOGY BUST

Gomez continued to grow while many technology companies failed after the turn the century. The company added services to its GomezNetworks division with strategic alliances and also grew beyond its U.S. borders.

New product offerings included partnerships designed to enhance its business services. In 2001, Gomez and Empirix partnered to deliver real-time Web site monitoring. This allowed companies to isolate performance issues with their Web sites more easily, thereby improving transaction times and avoiding downtime. In 2002, Gomez partnered with Akamai Technologies Inc. to license Akamai's proprietary software, EdgeScape, to add IP intelligence to its products. (IP intelligence can identify connection speed, location, and other characteristics associated with an IP address.) Other product debuts included the Usability Benchmark Assessment and the Experience Benchmark, both designed to measure aspects of the customer experience with client Web sites.

Gomez found a lucrative market in GomezNetworks division, now named Internet Performance Management division (IPMD). In 2004, Gomez sold its Gomez Pro Scorecard and Website Assessment Business Unit to Watchfire Corporation to focus on IPMD. In addition, the company hired Bruce Reading to oversee global sales, marketing, and customer service.

GLOBAL GROWTH

In 2002, Gomez Inc. expanded to Europe by utilizing reseller ActualIT Solutions Ltd. Gomez acquired ActualIT Solutions one year later. In early 2003, Gomez acquired WebPerform, a U.K.-based company that provided consultation services for commercial clients to improve Web services. With this acquisition, Gomez formed Gomez Europe. In 2004, Gomez opened subsidiary Gomez Deutschland GmbH. In 2007, the company expanded its European presence to Zurich.

LEADERSHIP TURNOVER

Having survived the dot-com recession that left other technology companies defunct, Gomez appeared to be an example of how a technology company could succeed. Its business model provided a valuable service to its clients, and the company's revenues continued to grow. However, turmoil at the top seemed to indicate that all was not as it should be.

CEO Alex Stein won the Ernst & Young Entrepreneur of the Year Award in 2004 in the Information Technology category. Under Stein's leadership, the company booked a record-setting 2003. Stein was credited with key strategic movements to focus the company's market and ensure financial soundness. However, Stein left in the second half of 2004 for undisclosed reasons. After that, Jill Smith was hired and ran the company for seven months before leaving for personal reasons. In 2006, Jaime Ellertson was recruited from S1 Corporation to take over the role.

Indeed, although Gomez continued to grow, it had yet to earn a profit. In 2007, the company reported a net loss of $2.3 million on revenue of $32.6 million. In the first half of 2009, Gomez reported its first-ever profit, earning $1.9 million in the first six months of the year. However, while things had gotten better, profitability was not consistent.

COMPUWARE ACQUISITION

By the late 2000s, Gomez looked to earn a return on its investment. However, this proved difficult in another challenging market environment.

In May 2007, Gomez announced that it had filed a registration statement for an initial public offering (IPO) on the NASDAQ Global Market. The company hoped to earn $80.5 million. However, the recession of 2008–2009 kept the IPO on hold.

In October 2009, Gomez announced its intention to become a wholly owned subsidiary of the Compuware Corporation. The deal closed in November of that year. Under Compuware, Gomez's software-as-a service (SaaS) platform was combined with Compuware's Vantage Application Performance Management (APM) solutions. Under the unified brand name Gomez, Compuware's Gomez APM services provided Web cross-browser testing, Web load and performance testing, Web performance management, and Web performance business analysis.

Compuware continued to invest heavily in its APM services. In 2011, *Retailer* magazine cited Gomez APM as the number one Web performance monitoring solution to Internet retailers for the fifth year in a row. In July of that year, the company acquired dynaTrace, adding its PurePath solutions to its APM portfolio. PurePath helps developers optimize Web performance through different computing environments, including private, cloud, and hybrid environments.

SEE ALSO *E-commerce Consultants.*

BIBLIOGRAPHY

"Akamai and Gomez Align to Enhance Web Performance Measurement." *Internet Retailer,* March 4, 2002. http://www.internetretailer.com/2002/03/04/akamai-and-g-mez-align-to-enhance-web-performance-measurement.

"Empirix and Gomez Partner to Deliver New Standards in Web Site Monitoring; Partnership to Address Industry Need for Real-Time Performance Testing Service." *Business Wire,* February 27, 2001.

Gomez Inc. "About Gomez." Waltham, MA, 2001. Available from www.compuware.com/application-performance-management.

"Gomez CEO Dr. Alex Stein Wins Ernst & Young Entrepreneur of the Year Award." *Business Wire,* June 30, 2004. Available from http://www.businesswire.com/news/home/200406300 05130/en/Gomez-CEO-Dr.-Alex-Stein-Wins-Ernst.

"Gomez Introduces Quantifiable Usability Measurement Offering." *Business Wire,* February 11, 2003. Available from http://www.thefreelibrary.com/Gomez+Introduces+Quantifiable+Usability+Measurement+Offering.-a097458366.

"Gomez Launches GomezNetworks." *Business Wire,* September 29, 2000.

"Gomez Solidifies International Presence with Purchase of UK Reseller." *Business Wire,* February 19, 2003. Available from http://www.thefreelibrary.com/Gomez+Solidifies+International+Presence+With+Purchase+of+UK+Reseller.-a097819998.

"Gomez Taps Industry Veteran to Extend Internet Performance Management Leadership." *Business Wire,* March 22, 2004. Available from http://www.businesswire.com/news/home/20040322005579/en/Gomez-Taps-Industry-Veteran-Extend-Internet-Performance.

Haley, Colin C. "Gomez Advisors to Make National Push." *InternetNews,* February 21, 2000. Available from http://www.internetnews.com/ec-news/article.php/307541/Gomez+Advisors+to+Make+National+Push.htm.

Smith, Geoffrey. "How Good Are the Gomez Ratings?" *BusinessWeek Online,*October 25, 1999. Available from http://www.businessweek.com/1999/99_43/b3652131.htm.

"Watchfire Acquires Gomez Pro Scorecard and Website Assessment Business Unit." *Business Wire,* March 8, 2004. Available from http://www.businesswire.com/news/home/20040308005561/en/Watchfire-Acquires-Gomez-Pro-Scorecard-Website-Assessment.

Young, Vicki M. "IPOS Stunted in Harsh Climate." *WWD,* November 17, 2000.

GOOGLE INC.

Google Inc. is a publicly held corporation that provides Internet search, online, and mobile advertising platforms, and a host of search-related products and services. The most widely used search engine in the world, Google passed the one billion mark in monthly visitors in May 2011. In the early 2010s Google is generally considered the most successful Internet company in history.

Based in Mountain View, California, Google was founded in 1998 by two Stanford University graduate students. The company went public in 2004, raising $1.67 billion in its initial public offering (IPO). By December 2010, the multinational company had more than 24,400 employees and annual revenues exceeding $29.3 billion.

Through the early years of the twenty-first century, Google dominated the Internet search engine market. Net Applications reported that in August 2011, the Google Search product had an 83% market share globally for desktop search, and 92% of the market for mobile phone and PC tablet searches.

The company earns the vast majority of its income through its Internet advertising products. Income from its AdWords and AdSense programs are used to support a wide variety of free products, including Google Search, Gmail (e-mail application), Google Product Search (comparison shopping), Google Chrome (Web browser), Google Maps, YouTube (video sharing site), Picasa (photo sharing), and Google+ (social networking).

In the late 2000s, Google expanded its role in mobile commerce. Google introduced its Android mobile phone operating system in November 2007, a competitor to Apple's popular iPhone. By August 2011, Google reported more than 150 million Android devices had been activated worldwide. Also that month, Google announced an agreement to acquire Motorola Mobility for $12.5 billion and move into cellular phone manufacturing. The company previously paid $750 million in 2009 to acquire mobile advertising firm AdMob.

HISTORY AND GROWTH OF GOOGLE

Google began as a research project in 1996 by Stanford University graduate students Larry Page and Sergey Brin. The two created an Internet search engine known as "BackRub" in their dorm room, later moving their operations to a garage in Menlo Park, California. "BackRub" was different from most search engines at that time because it ranked sites based on the links between Web pages rather than the number of times a search term appeared on a site. After Andy Bechtolsheim, the cofounder of Sun Microsystems, invested $100,000 in the search engine, Page and Brin incorporated Google in August 1998. (The name is a variation of the term "googol," a mathematical term for the number 1 followed by 100 zeros.) By mid-1999, Google received another $25 million in funding by such investors as Sequoia Capital and Kleiner Perkins Caufield & Byers. In June 2000, Google became the default search engine for Yahoo!, which accelerated its expansion across the Web. Google's IPO in 2004 raised $1.67 billion. With most of Google's shares retained by employees and executives, the IPO gave Google a market capitalization exceeding $23 billion. By the fall of 2011, the company's market cap was more than $172 billion.

Google's growth is a result of a combination of products and services the company built, along with numerous acquisitions during the early part of the twenty-first century. Since its earlier days, the company has stated that "Google's mission is to organize the world's information and make it universally accessible and useful." Search remains the centerpiece of Google's strategy. While the majority of its revenues come from paid advertising tied to search results, most of its Web-based applications are free. Such products as the Gmail e-mail service, YouTube, and the Chrome Web browser are closely integrated with its advertising platforms.

Google has also made a number of acquisitions to support its strategy. Many were relatively small deals of niche web developers and other services to expand its offerings. One example was the September 2011 acquisition of restaurant rating service Zagat to complement Google's local mapping and location services. Major deals included the 2007 acquisition of digital marketing firm DoubleClick for $3.1 billion in cash; $1.65 billion in stock for video-sharing site YouTube in 2006; a $750 million stock deal for AdMob, the mobile advertising company, in 2009; a $676 million purchase of airline fare tracker ITA Software in 2010; and the 2011 announcement of a $12.5 billion stock purchase of Motorola Mobility Holdings, the cell phone manufacturer.

However, Google's size and market dominance has also brought a number of regulatory probes in the United States and Europe. A proposed Internet advertising union with Yahoo! was dropped in 2008 after U.S. and Canadian regulators announced plans to file an antitrust suit. The company also announced in August 2011 a $500 million settlement over a federal probe into Google's distribution of online ads for Canadian pharmacies that made illegal sales to U.S. consumers.

Major competitors for Google in the Internet search space include Yahoo!, Microsoft, and Baidu. While Facebook is not a search engine, it surpassed Google in late 2010 as the world's most popular site and is driving more traffic to top Web sites. Google also challenged Facebook in the social media network field with its 2011 Google+ product. In mobile e-commerce, Google competes with Apple with its Android phones.

In early 2011, Google announced a streamlined management structure. After 10 years as chief executive officer, Eric Schmidt was named executive chairman. Cofounder Page assumed the duties of CEO while the other cofounder, Brin, focused on strategic initiatives and new products.

GOOGLE'S ADVERTISING PLATFORM AND OTHER PRODUCTS

Google has long been one of the dominant players in the Web advertising market, which was estimated at $12.3 billion for the United States in 2011. More than 95% of Google's revenues were generated through its advertising programs, which are highly integrated with its search engine and a huge variety of free products. In the second quarter of 2011, Google reported $9 billion in revenue. "Google-owned sites generated revenues of $6.23 billion, or 69% of total revenues," the company stated in its quarterly financial announcement. "Google's partner sites generated revenues, through [the] AdSense program, of $2.48 billion, or 28% of revenues, in the second quarter of 2011.%" Some 54% of total revenues ($4.87 billion) were generated outside the United States during that quarter.

Google has two primary advertising programs: AdWords and AdSense. Under AdWords, advertisers pay Google so that their ads show up next to search results when an online user enters certain keywords. The cost can be based on how many times a company's ad is seen by a user (cost-per-view) or by how often a view follows the ad link to the advertiser's site (cost-per-click). Google AdSense pays the owners of various Web sites to include relevant Google ads on their sites on a cost-per-click basis. A free product, Google Analytics, provides Web site owners with tools to track visitors and determine advertising efficiency.

However, the programs have not been without controversy. AdWords was the target of several lawsuits claiming that Google should not be allowed to sell keywords based on trademarked brands to those brand's competitors. Google has settled some of those cases out of court but had not lost any court cases as of early 2012. However, Rosetta Stone was appealing its loss to the U.S. Court of Appeals in 2011. Despite objections and more potential lawsuits, Google expanded the practice to Europe.

Google made a number of acquisitions to directly support its advertising platforms. In 2007, it announced a $3.1 billion cash deal to acquire DoubleClick, which provides digital marketing technology and services. The 2009 acquisition of mobile advertising platform AdMob for $750 million was designed to help expand Google's reach into both the iPhone and Android smartphone market.

While its search engine and advertising platform are the center of its business model, Google also offers a wide variety of free products that are available to the general public. The company had more than 180 other Google domains in 2012, including news, stock, and sports updates in numerous languages. Most of these products are heavily integrated with display advertising and search engine-based marketing. The offerings include the Gmail e-mail service, the Chrome Web browser, the Blogger platform for blogging, and Google Calendar for sharing appointments. Other products include:

- GOOGLE MAPS. This search feature displays maps and directions for a given address, along with advertising relevant to the location (such as local hotels). Graphical maps can be seen as well as satellite images of the area through the Google Earth product.
- GOOGLE PRODUCT SEARCH. Originally known as "Froogle," Google Product Search is an online price comparison offering that shows products available from a variety of online and brick-and-mortar vendors.
- GOOGLE DOCS/GOOGLE CLOUD. Based on several earlier products, Google Docs was introduced in early 2007, providing customers a free online suite of word processing, spreadsheet, and presentation software. The ability to share and update documents through the Internet posed a direct challenge to the proprietary Microsoft Office suite of products. Microsoft later introduced a Web-based version of its products as Microsoft Office Live. Google Docs (and the similar Google Apps for businesses) were closely tied to cloud computing, which provides software and data storage remotely through the Internet rather than on local machines. Google offered cloud computing capabilities to business and introduced such products as Google Cloud Print and Cloud Connect.
- YOUTUBE. Google acquired YouTube, the video sharing/social networking service, in 2006. Users can post videos for free and share them with their friends.
- GOOGLE+. Google picked up 25 million users in two months after launching this social networking site in June 2011. The competitor to Facebook—which with 750 million users had surpassed Google as the most visited site in 2010 and was cutting into Google's advertising revenues—debuted to generally favorable reviews.
- GOOGLE BOOKS. This ambitious project aims to load every book in the world into a digital format and make them available around the world. However, Google Books continued to battle a number of legal challenges over copyright issues that could prevent it from building a true global library.
- GOOGLE OFFERS. Google began rolling out this service in mid-2011 as a competitor to such daily bargain sites as Groupon, LivingSocial, and similar local sites.
- GOOGLE HOTEL FINDER. Google rolled out this product in 2011 to compete with such online leisure sites as Kayak and Priceline. The company acquired ITA Software in 2010 to obtain its product for airline flight searches. Hotel Finder is a similar service, offering location-based searches for discounted hotel rooms.

GOOGLE AND MOBILE COMMERCE

While Google was formed about personal computer searches, it soon expanded into mobile e-commerce as the market exploded in the early years of the twenty-first century. Cellular phones, smartphones like Apple's iPhone and tablet computers like the iPad provided new methods for individuals to connect with the Internet outside their home or office. Google made most of its applications available on mobile platforms, following both the customer numbers and the advertising dollars that continue to grow with mobile e-commerce.

Google acquired Android, an operating software system for mobile phones, in 2005. In November 2007, it launched the Open Handset Alliance, a consortium of more than 80 companies that wanted an open platform to compete with Apple's popular iPhone. Google made most of the Android software available as open source, and manufacturers such as Samsung, Motorola, LG, and HTC created devices for the platform.

By the second quarter of 2011, Android accounted for 52% of the U.S. smartphone market. Apple was second with a 29% market share, with Blackberry accounting for 11%. In August 2011, Google stated more than 150 million Android devices had been activated around the world. The Android network included 39 manufacturers and 231 carriers in 123 countries. However, the Android's popularity and its open architecture also brought it a new notoriety: in mid-2011, computer security firm McAfee said that Android had become the mobile software most frequently targeted by hackers.

Also in August 2011, Google announced it would acquire Motorola Mobility Inc. for $12.5 billion in cash. Google stated the deal will enable it to "supercharge the Android ecosystem and will enhance competition in mobile computer. Motorola Mobility will remain a licensee of Android and Android will remain open." The announcement brought immediate criticism over Google's move into the manufacturing arena. However, Google executives also stated they were acquiring Motorola to get access to its 17,000 patents, which would help it protect Android from continuing litigation from various telecommunications competitors.

In addition to its Android development, Google had also carved out a significant slice of the mobile advertising market across all platforms. In 2009, the company acquired AdMob, which sells mobile ads that appear on iPhones and other platforms, for $750 million in stock.

SEE ALSO *Brin, Sergey; Page, Larry; Search Engine Strategy; Web 2.0.*

BIBLIOGRAPHY

Bedecarre, Tom. "It's Time to Stop Worrying and Start Loving Google." *Campaign,* August 26, 2011. Available from http://campaignlive.co.uk/analysis/1086692/Its-time-stop-worrying-start-loving-Google.

Bockmier, Zack. "Zynga Likely to Benefit from Facebook-Google+ Competition." *Seeking Alpha,* August 17, 2011. Available from http://seekingalpha.com/article/287885-zynga-likely-to-benefit-from-facebook-google-competition.

Chatterjee, Surojit. "Top 5 Reasons Why Google-Motorola Deal Will Shake Up Technology Industry." *International Business Times News,* August 20, 2011. Available from http://sanfrancisco.ibtimes.com/articles/201063/20110820/top-5-reasons-why-google-motorola-deal-will-shake-up-technology-industry-patents-android-google-tv-g.htm.

Claburn, Thomas. "Gmail Makes You 80 Times Greener, Says Google." *InformationWeek,* September 7, 2011. Available from http://www.informationweek.com/news/cloud-computing/software/231600934.

Denison, D. C. "Google Joins the Group on Bargain Hunts." *Boston Globe,* September 7, 2011. Available from http://articles.boston.com/2011-09-07/business/30123850_1_discount-sites-deal-site-daily-deal.

Goldman, David. "Facebook Hits 1 Trillion Page Views? Nope." *CNNMoney,* August 26 2011. Available from http://money.cnn.com/2011/08/26/technology/facebook_1_trillion_page_views/index.htm.

Google. "Corporate Information." Mountain View, California, 2011. Available from http://www.google.com/intl/en/about/corporate/company.

———. "Introducing the Google+ Project: Real-Life Sharing, Rethought for the Web." *The Official Google Blog,* June 18, 2011. Available from http://googleblog.blogspot.com/2011/06/introducing-google-project-real-life.html.

———. "Supercharging Android: Google to Acquire Motorola Mobility." *The Official Google Blog,* August 15, 2011. Available from http://googleblog.blogspot.com/2011/08/supercharging-android-google-to-acquire.html.

"Google+ and Facebook." *Live Trading News,* August 19, 2011. Available from http://www.livetradingnews.com/google-and-facebook-50571.htm.

"Google Hotel Finder Rocks the Boat for Kayak, Priceline." *Forbes,* September 7, 2011. Available from http://www.forbes.com/sites/greatspeculations/2011/09/07/google-hotel-finder-rocks-the-boat-for-kayak-priceline/.

"Google's Interactions with Federal Regulators." *Forbes.com,* August 24, 2011. Available from http://www.forbes.com/feeds/ap/2011/08/24/technology-broadcasting-amp-entertainment-us-tec-google-glance_8640203.html.

Hachman, Mark. "Google's Google+ Adds Games, but Wants Data in Return." *PC Magazine,* August 11, 2011. Available from http://www.pcmag.com/article2/0,2817,2390952,00.asp.

Helft, Miguel. "Federal Judge Rejects Google's Negotiated Deal to Digitize Books." *New York Times,* March 22, 2011. Available from http://www.nytimes.com/2011/03/23/technology/23google.html.

"The History of Google." *Web Hosting Report,* September 2011. Available from http://www.webhostingreport.com/learn/google.html.

Kaine, Cameron. "Google's Expensive Attempt to Be Apple's Clone." *Seeking Alpha,* September 7, 2011. Available from http://seekingalpha.com/article/292043-google-s-expensive-attempt-to-be-apple-s-clone.

Metz, Rachel. "Google Buys Restaurant Review Service Zagat." *Forbes.com,* September 8, 2011. Available from http://www.forbes.com/feeds/ap/2011/09/08/technology-business-and-professional-services-us-google-zagat_8666222.html.

Miller, Claire Cain. "Google to Pay $500 Million to Settle Illegal Ad Charges." *New York Times,* August 25, 2011. Available from http://query.nytimes.com/gst/fullpage.html?res=9406EFD91238F936A1575BC0A9679D8B63.

Morrissey, Brian. "Google to Acquire AdMob for $750 Mil." *AdWeek,* November 9, 2009. Available from http://www.adweek.com/news/advertising-branding/google-acquire-admob-750-mil-100852.

Murray, Andrew Conry. "The Basics About Chrome OS." *InformationWeek,* July 20, 2009. Available from http://www.informationweek.com/news/windows/operatingsystems/218501041?queryText=chrome.

Net Applications. "Market Share for Mobile and Desktop." Aliso Viejo, CA, September 2011. Available from http://www.marketshare.com.

Scott, Virginia. *Google*. Santa Barbara, CA: ABC-CLIO/Greenwood, 2008.

Sorkin, Andrew Ross. "Is Google Turning into a Mobile Phone Company? No, It Says." *New York Times,* August 15, 2011. Available from http://dealbook.nytimes.com/2011/08/15/google-turning-into-a-mobile-phone-company-no-it-says/.

Stross, Randell E. *Planet Google: One Company's Audacious Plan to Organize Everything We Know*. New York: Free Press, 2008.

Takahashi, Dean. "Why Game Developers Hate the Facebook-Zynga Marriage, and How Google+ Can Benefit." *VentureBeat,* July 29, 2011. Available from http://venturebeat.com/2011/07/29/facebook-zynga-google-games.

Turner, Debbie. "Google Birthday — 13 Years Old Today: Key Moments in History." *Online Social Media,* September 4, 2011. Available from http://www.onlinesocialmedia.net/20110904/google-birthday-13-years-old-today-key-moments-in-history.

Vivek, Wadhwa. "Google, Twitter and the Best Regulator." *Washington Post,* July 8, 2011. Available from http://www.washingtonpost.com.

"Yahoo Value Plummets to $14bn in Three Years." *AllBusiness.com,* August 10, 2011. Available from http://www.allbusiness.com/marketing-advertising/marketing-advertising/16648709-1.html.

Yang, Jia Lynn. "Four Titans of Tech Are Racing to Be King of Digital Age." *Washington Post,* August 17, 2011. Available from http://www.washingtonpost.com/business/economy/four-titans-of-tech-are-racing-to-be-king-of-digital-age/2011/08/16/gIQA51i8JJ_story.html.

Yin, Sara. "Report: Schmidt Says Google+ Is For 'Real Names' Only." *PC Magazine,* August 29, 2011. Available from http://www.pcmag.com/article2/0,2817,2392013,00.asp.

GREENBERG, JERRY

Jerry Greenberg is the cofounder of Sapient Corp., a firm that provides information technology (IT) services to customers ranging from the U.S. Marine Corps to AT&T Mobility. In 2001, the company made more than $860 million in revenues and employed approximately 9,000 people. Along with cofounder J. Stuart Moore, Greenberg served as co-CEO and cochairman of the board from 1991 to 2006. Greenberg returned to Sapient's board as a non-independent director in 2010.

FOUNDING SAPIENT

A native of rural New Jersey, Greenberg studied philosophy at Harvard University before switching his major to economics. After graduation, he began working for various information technology consulting firms, eventually ending up at Cambridge Technology Partners, where he met Moore. In 1991, 25-year-old Greenberg and 29-year-old Moore cofounded Sapient Corp. in Cambridge, Massachusetts. Rather than seek outside funding, the partners used $40,000 of their own savings and charged nearly $70,000 on their credit cards.

Initially, Sapient focused on offering client-server integration services. Greenberg and Moore set out to differentiate their firm from its many competitors not only by helping customers figure out how technology could eliminate difficulties or enhance operations, but also by creating, executing, and supporting whatever applications they decided to use. Also unlike many other consultancies, Greenberg and Moore offered predetermined prices and deadlines, and linked employee pay, including their own, to client satisfaction.

Sapient grew from 95 employees in 1994 to 213 in 1995, and sales and profits both more than doubled. By then, offices had been opened in San Francisco and New York. Sapient was listed publicly in April 1996, raising $33 million that was earmarked for expansion efforts. Initially, Greenberg and Moore each retained roughly 36% of the firm's stock. (Combined, the two owned around one-fifth of the company stock in 2011.) Recognizing that many of Sapient's clients were growing increasingly interested in e-commerce, Greenberg began repositioning the firm to offer e-business integration services. He oversaw four small acquisitions—including Adjacency and Studio Archetype, two World Wide Web design firms—that enhanced Sapient's technology and services without overwhelming the firm.

Eventually, Sapient was able to offer a full range of e-commerce services that included the planning and creation of online stores. Unlike many CEOs of e-business service firms, Greenberg also kept a tight rein on advertising spending and promotional hype, careful not to make promises his firm could not keep. Greenberg's efforts translated into something that eluded so many e-commerce players in the late 1990s: profits. In 1998, Sapient earned $9.4 million on sales of $165 million. Those numbers were upped to $30.3 million in profits and $277 million in sales in 1999. According to a November 2000 article in *Computer Reseller News,* "In an industry screaming with hype and larger-than-life personalities, Sapient co-CEO Jerry A. Greenberg stands out quietly." The article credits Greenberg and Moore for transforming "a nine-year-old consulting and integration company grounded in client/server computing into one of the foremost Web integrators on the scene."

By the end of 2000, the firm had 2,600 employees working in 18 offices around the world. However, despite the strength of Sapient's position, the North American economic slowdown, particularly in the e-commerce sector, did undercut Sapient's profits in the first quarter of 2001. As a result, Greenberg and Moore announced that the workforce would be reduced by

20%, the office in Sydney, Australia, closed, and U.S. operations consolidated.

SURVIVING THE DOT-COM BUST

Sapient survived through the turn of the century, a time when many technology companies failed, although it did not emerge unscathed. Between 2000 and 2003, the company eliminated about 1,600 jobs and reported a net loss of $185 million in 2001 and $225 million in 2002.

Sapient opened a Global Services Division in Bangalore in 2004. Having lost most of its U.S. workforce, the company took advantage of the labor cost savings in India. By 2004, over half of Sapient's workforce was in India.

Finally, Sapient began to grow again. In 2005, the company established a Government Services division, an independent subsidiary in Arlington, VA. Acquisitions included the 2006 purchase of the Planning Group International (PGI) and the 2008 purchase of the Derivatives Consulting Group Limited (DCG) out of London. In 2009, Sapient acquired Nitro Group, LLC, for $50 million. Nitro specialized in digital commerce, marketing technology, and social media.

SCANDAL FOLLOWS HONOR

Greenberg was named one of the Top 25 Most Influential Consultants by *Consulting Magazine* in 2005. The recognition was due to his leadership in implementing Sapient's unique business model. However, Greenberg and Moore both came under suspicion of insider trading in 2006, and this led to their ouster from the company they had founded. Investigators uncovered discrepancies in the company's granting of stock options between 1997 and 2001. Greenberg resigned, as did Moore. While it was clear the two left due to these circumstances, Greenberg said that he had planned to leave the company, and that they decided to "accelerate the CEO succession plan."

A NEW VENTURE

After leaving Sapient, Greenberg turned to a venture less technical but one he was just as passionate about. He loved cooking at home and particularly loved sushi. He had been friends with famed sushi chef Kazunori Nozawa. The two came together with a business model that offered exacting and authentic sushi accessible to the masses. Together, Nozawa, his son Tom, and Greenberg founded Sugarfish Sushi, a group of restaurants that made traditional but high-quality sushi Sugarfish Sushi served simplified and authentic Japanese sushi. Sugarfish Sushi has consistently won food critic acclaim with its traditional sushi made from the finest ingredients.

RETURN TO SAPIENT

In 2010, Greenberg rejoined Sapient, this time as a member of the board of directors. As reported on *TMCnet.com,* he stated, "I'm delighted to be rejoining the board during this period of tremendous growth and opportunity for Sapient."

SEE ALSO *Sapient Corp..*

BIBLIOGRAPHY

"Jerry A. Greenberg Rejoins Board of Directors at Sapient." *TMCnet.com,* October 27, 2010. Available from http://www.tmcnet.com/usubmit/2010/10/27/5095558.htm.

Mulqueen, John T. "Young Company Flourishes." *Communications Week,* June 17, 1996.

Rosa, Jerry. "Eleven—JerryGreenberg—The Stalwart." *Computer Reseller News,* November 13, 2000, 145.

"Sapient's Co-CEO Recognized for Leadership, Innovation and Commitment to Client Success; Jerry Greenberg Named One of Top 25 Most Influential Consultants." *Business Wire,* May 23, 2005. Available from http://www.businesswire.com/news/home/20050523005772/en/Sapients-Co-CEO-Recognized-Leadership-Innovation-Commitment-Client.

"Sapient Corp." *Advertising Age,* June 19, 2000.

"Sapient's New Hub in B'lore Soon, to Hire More." *India Times,* May 15, 2004. Available from http://archives.infotech.indiatimes.com/articleshow/676804.cms

Swarts, Will. "Shakeup at Sapient." *SmartMoney,* October 17, 2006.

Walsh, Tom. "Sapient Continues Thinning Its Ranks." *Boston Herald,* March 11, 2003.

Whitford, David. "The Two-Headed Manager: Sapient Co-CEOs Jerry Greenberg and Stuart Moore Have (Almost) Nothing in Common. That Helps Explain Why Their Relationship Works." *Fortune,* January 24, 2000.

"U.S. Business Brief: Sapient Cuts 720 Jobs, Warns of Losses." *Futures World News,* May 7, 2001.

GROSSMAN'S PARADOX

Information has long been a cornerstone of business strategy. Firms need to know where they fit into the broader market, what the competitive openings are, what their customers' tastes and needs are, and how to manipulate all this information to their advantage. In the Information Age, particularly with the proliferation of the Internet, data moves at hyperspeed and is ever more critical as businesses try to seek out exclusive information before their competitors can do so. As information gathering, processing, and application accelerates, it steadily bears out an interesting theory of market efficiency known as Grossman's paradox.

Under traditional market theory, it is assumed that markets function best when market players have full and complete knowledge of all information relevant to the market. In this way, actors can predict the consequences of their behavior—and that of their competitors—and adjust their strategies accordingly, leading to the greatest overall efficiency for the market. Economist Sanford Grossman pointed out an inherent flaw in such market assumptions while he was at the University of Pennsylvania's Wharton School: Perfectly efficient markets would provide no incentive to seek out new information. In other words, no profit could be gained by such activity. But if there is no profit, no business would gather information, and no one could possibly be perfectly informed, thus undoing the market equilibrium. This is to say, firms that had ceased gathering new information about the market could not possibly make informed decisions about prices or allocation of resources, and the market's efficiency would be destroyed. Grossman suggested that perfect information, or anything close to it, was purely fiction and was a contradiction in the efficient market theory. As a result, according to Grossman, no player in a market could ever be perfectly informed, and thus the drive to obtain more information than the next competitor would always be a component of market economics.

INFORMATION ECONOMICS

Several economists agreed with Grossman, and Grossman' paradox is studied in a branch of microeconomics known as "Information Economics." A good deal of work in this branch is based on an article by Austrian-born economist Friedrich Hayek in 1945, titled "The Use of Knowledge in Society." Hayek hypothesized that the lack of perfect and complete information was the primary reason that centrally planned economies were doomed to fail. This led to the study of "information asymmetry."

The study of information asymmetry examines interactions in the market where one party has more information than another. For example, when a buyer and seller haggle over the price of a home, the primary resident (seller) is the only one who truly knows the history of the house. The buyer can try to obtain this information by hiring an inspector and researching public records, but the information gathered will likely be incomplete. Similarly, only the buyer knows if he can afford the monthly payments required to purchase the house. Again, the seller can obtain this information by requesting a copy of the buyer's credit report, but it may also contain incomplete or erroneous information.

PARADOX APPLIED

The application of Grossman's paradox can also be observed with the emergence of the Internet as a source of information for market participants. The Internet provides ample evidence of imperfect information. First, the Internet provides more information than could possibly be absorbed by a single person. A simple search on Google for the term "IBM Stock" returns over 67 million results. This "information overload" may be reduced using specified search parameters, but results are imperfect.

The second issue with information accessed on the Internet is that it is often not credible. For example, a search for "narcotics overdose" may return both useful information from reputable medical experts on how to react in such a situation, or a personal diary (blog) about a unknown person's suicide attempt.

Indeed, until a reliable categorization system such as the Dewey Decimal System can be found for the Internet, the organization, accumulation, and dissemination of information is a profitable venture, a fact that supports Grossman's paradox. Database management, software that accumulates and organizes data, is an industry that employed 293,000 in 2008 and is expected to grow 17% by 2018.

ABOUT GROSSMAN

Grossman went on to found QFS Asset Management, a fund management company. In 2009, the CME Group and the Mathematical Sciences Research Institute (MSRI) awarded Grossman the CME Group-MSRI Prize in Innovative Quantitative Applications.

SEE ALSO *Data Mining.*

BIBLIOGRAPHY

"2009 CME Group-MSRI Prize in Innovative Quantitative Applications Awarded to Sanford Grossman for Innovative Approaches to Asset Pricing Models." *PR Newswire,* September 11, 2009. Available from http://www.prnewswire.com/news-releases/2009-cme-group-msri-prize-in-innovative-quantitative-applications-awarded-to-sanford-grossman-for-innovative-approaches-to-asset-pricing-models-62145962.html.

Encyclopedia of the New Economy. Waltham, MA: Wired Digital, 2001.

"Grossman's Paradox." In *The Devil's Derivatives Dictionary,* March 2002. Available from http://www.margrabe.com/Devil/DevilF_J.html#sectG.

Stelzer, Irwin M. "Why They Call It the Dismal Science; Everything You Need to Know About the Mortgage Crisis in Three Economics Buzzwords." *Weekly Standard,* November 26, 2007. Available from http://www.weeklystandard.com/Content/Public/Articles/000/000/014/369xpsgs.asp.

GROUPON INC.

Groupon Inc. (the name was created by combining "group" and "coupon") was the first Web site to establish local daily deals as a lucrative e-commerce business. The notion behind the site was to help people experience more of the interesting things a city has to offer, rather than just relying on familiar places to go. Groupons offer steep discounts of 50% to 90% at stores, restaurants, salons, theaters, and more. Based in Chicago, Illinois, the company had expanded to 43 countries by 2011, just three years after its wildly successful launch. In the fall of that year, it launched Groupon Goods to compete in the e-tail market space.

After registering on the site, subscribers receive a daily e-mail or notification through their mobile device with the deal of the day. Most deals also have a limit on the number that subscribers can purchase for themselves or as a gift for someone else, and subscribers must act before the deal expires at midnight. Since Groupon deals are essentially volume discounts, it only goes into effect if the pre-set minimum number of people buy it. At that point, all buyers are charged the cost of the Groupon and receive an e-mail the following day with a link to redeem it. Groupon makes money by retaining typically 50% of proceeds from the sale of the Groupon. Deals that are not particularly lucrative for a vendor can still pay off by providing much needed exposure to a wide audience.

UNOBTRUSIVE ORIGINS

Groupon was founded in November 2008 by 27-year-old Andrew Mason. He had launched a Web site called the Point one year prior. The premise behind the Point was that it was easier to get people to commit to something when they do not have to actually follow through until the campaign has enough support to likely be successful. Creating a campaign was free, but once a certain number of people committed to it, referred to as the "tipping point," the Point collected 5% of fund-raising activities that occurred through the site.

The Point could be used to organize group discounts, which led to the idea of a Web site devoted to collective buying power. Subsequently, Groupon was launched in November 2008 as a side project to get deals in Chicago, where Mason lived. Particularly for small businesses with limited marketing budgets, Groupon offered a novel way to gain exposure without having to pay anything. In addition, businesses received proceeds from the sale of the Groupon upfront, while weeks might pass before a Groupon buyer decided to redeem it.

RECORD-SETTING SUCCESS

Although YouTube held the record for reaching a valuation of $1 billion faster than any other dot-com, Groupon was the first to reach $1.35 billion in under a year and a half. This occurred in April 2010 after Groupon raised $170 million from Moscow-based Digital Sky Technologies and other investors. The underwriting report Morgan Stanley had put together to attract investors estimated the company would surpass $500 million that year. Another notable accomplishment was Groupon's ability to turn a profit after only seven months of operations. (YouTube still remained unprofitable five years after its launch.)

Part of Groupon's success can be attributed to its compatibility with mobile devices, which offer a huge growth opportunity for e-commerce. A free app is available for nearly any mobile device, including the iPhone, iPad, Android, and BlackBerry. Not only can mobile users receive the daily deal and purchase it on their mobile device, it can be redeemed that way as well. Another big selling point on the site is that it makes a concerted effort to notify subscribers upfront about any restrictions on deals, such as it only applying to a specific location, which might be perceived as "catches."

In 2010, Google Inc. made a bid at acquiring Groupon for cash and management incentives worth $6 billion. Google hoped to use Groupon to target the local-ad market, estimated at $133 billion in the United States. Google could use the data it gathered on Groupon's 35 million members to target them with relevant ads. As the CEO and largest shareholder, Mason evidently did not like what the acquisition might mean to the company's direction and 7,000 employees, because the deal was rejected before the year ended.

Amidst Google's bid attempt, Amazon.com confirmed it had invested $175 million in Groupon rival LivingSocial.com. Based in Washington, D.C., the social shopping site had ten million subscribers in the United States, Canada, United Kingdom, Ireland, and Australia. As with Groupon, subscribers receive a daily deal for their area. After purchasing a deal, subscribers can notify friends about the offer and if three also buy it, the referring user gets the deal for free. (Groupon's strategy for rewarding subscribers who make a referral through e-mail or social networking channels is to give a $10 credit after a referral buys a Groupon.)

EXPANSION INTO E-TAILING

Groupon began filing for an initial public offering (IPO) in June 2011, which led to a significant reduction in 2010 reported revenues, from $713 to $313 million, in accordance with the U.S. Security and Exchange Commission's (SEC's) accounting practices. Things began to look up for the social shopping site when it launched Groupon Goods three months later to compete with Amazon.com and other e-tailers. Available only to U.S. subscribers, the new site sends daily deals on discounted merchandise, such as sunglasses, TVs, and mattresses. At this time, LivingSocial was reportedly considering raising capital through private funding rather than following Groupon's lead in filing for an IPO.

SEE ALSO *Mobile E-commerce.*

BIBLIOGRAPHY

Groupon. "About Us." Chicago, IL, 2011. Available from http://www.groupon.com/about.

LivingSocial. "How It Works." Washington, DC, 2011. Available from http://livingsocial.com/deals/how_it_works.

Locke, Laura. "Groupon Gets into Direct E-commerce with Groupon Goods." *CNET*, September 28, 2011. Available from http://news.cnet.com/8301-1023_3-20113081-93/groupon-gets-into-direct-e-commerce-with-groupon-goods.

MacMillan, Douglas, and Joseph Galante. "Google's Groupon Bid Said Rejected." *Bloomberg Businessweek*, December 4, 2010. Available from http://www.businessweek.com/technology/content/dec2010/tc2010124_281295.htm.

The Point. "Frequently Asked Questions." Chicago, IL, 2011. Available from http://www.thepoint.com/doc/faq.

Steiner, Chistopher. "Meet the Fastest Growing Company Ever." *Forbes*, August 12, 2010. Available from http://www.forbes.com/forbes/2010/0830/entrepreneurs-groupon-facebook-twitter-next-web-phenom.html.

Tsotsis, Alexia. "LivingSocial Confirms $175 Million Amazon Investment." *TechCrunch*, December 2, 2010. Available from http://techcrunch.com/2010/12/02/livingsocial-confirms-175-million-amazon-investment.

GROVE, ANDREW (ANDY) S.

Andrew S. Grove is best known for his leadership of Intel Corp. He served the firm as president from 1979 to 1987, when he replaced Gordon Moore as CEO. During Grove's 11-year tenure at the helm of Intel, he orchestrated the firm's pivotal shift from memory chips to microprocessors and grew Intel into the world's leading microprocessor maker, as well as one of the most profitable manufacturers on the globe. In May 1998, Grove was succeeded as CEO by Craig Barrett.

Grove subsequently served as Intel's chairman of the board until 2005, and as of 2011 he continued to work at Intel as a senior advisor. As chairman, Grove actively participated in the firm's shift from central processing units (CPUs) to networking technology, including flash memory chips and cell phone processors, and Internet services, such as World Wide Web hosting.

STARTING INTEL

A native of Budapest, Hungary, Grove earned his bachelor's degree in chemical engineering from City College of New York and his doctoral degree from the University of California at Berkeley. In 1967, Grove took a position as an assistant director in the research and development laboratory of Fairchild Semiconductor. The following year, when Robert Noyce and Gordon Moore established NM Electronics—later renamed Intel, from the first syllables of the words "integrated electronics"—Grove helped the partners secure an office and set up manufacturing facilities. His official title was vice president of operations. Although Grove was not technically a founder of the firm, he was an instrumental player from the start, according to *Fortune* writer Brent Schlender. "It was he who masterminded Intel's pivotal 11th-hour marketing victory of Motorola to get the contract to supply microprocessors for IBM's landmark PC in 1979. Six years later, he was the one who made the gutsy and prescient decision to pull Intel out of the memory chip business, firing 6,000 employees in the process, and to focus the company on more lucrative microprocessors."

ACADEMIC PURSUITS

While driving Intel's growth as a CPU manufacturer, Grove also taught at Stanford and the University of California, Berkeley. He received honorary degrees from the City College of New York, Harvard University, and the Worcester Polytechnic Institute. In addition, Grove holds many patents on the semiconductor. He is a prolific author, having published over 40 technical papers, and the following books:

- *Physics and Technology of Semiconductor Devices*—Published in 1967, Grove wrote this textbook used by many university professors prior to his role in founding Intel.
- *High Output Management*—First published in 1983 and again in 1995, this book is a guidebook on management science. The book is written for managers who are tasked with leading others toward a goal.
- *One-on-One with Andy Grove*—First published as a series of articles for the local newspaper, the articles were picked up for publication in 1987. They are a question-and-answer type of format, much like "Dear Abby" for the business workplace.
- *Only the Paranoid Survive*—First published in 1996 and reprinted in 1999, Grove wrote about the business strategy of managing and adapting to massive change. Called "strategic inflection points," these moments are those that can be game-changers: change in government policy, a seemingly innocuous invention, or a new competitor that threatens a company's product.
- *Swimming Across: A Memoir*—In 2002, Grove wrote of his early life as a Jew under Hitler's regime and, after the war, under the Soviet Union's communist regime. Unlike many Jews, his family survived, and not until 1956 did his family flee communism and come to America.

- *Strategy Is Destiny: How Strategy-Making Shapes a Company's Future*—In 2002, Grove partnered with Robert Burgelman to write another textbook, this time about corporate strategy and how strategy can impose order on a chaotic environment. In 2006, the two authors followed up with *Strategic Dynamics: Concepts and Cases.*

RECOGNITION AND AWARDS

TIME magazine named Grove "Man of the Year" in 1997; that year he also earned *Industry Week*'s "Technology Leader of the Year" award and *CEO* magazine's "CEO of the Year" distinction. By then, more than 80% of all personal computers (PCs) housed Intel CPUs. In 2004, Grove was recognized by the Wharton School of Business as the "Most Influential Business Person of the Last 25 Years."

By 2006, Grove agreed to have his biography written. Richard S. Tedlow, a professor at the Harvard Business School, approached Grove regarding the project. He was given open access to Grove and his life. The book not only detailed Grove's experience as an escapee from two authoritarian regimes, it also devoted chapters to subjects previously unwritten about Grove, including Hungarian politics and his struggles with prostate cancer and Parkinson's disease.

In 2009, Andrew Grove joined George Lucas, Harvey Milk, and Carol Burnett for induction into the California Hall of Fame. According to Maria Shriver, who conceived and presented the award, inductees are "remarkable individuals who embody the innovative spirit of the Gold State and who have changed the world by pursuing their dreams."

Grove has been cited in many books about immigrant success stories, American business leaders, and economic theory. He has also been cited in books about protecting religious rights in America by maintaining the separation of church and state.

INTEL SUCCESSION

In 1998, Grove stepped down from the CEO position, remaining as chairman of the board. Craig Barrett stepped into the role just as personal computer growth began to slow. Although the Internet revolution played a major role in fueling Intel's success as growing numbers of consumers purchased PCs to access the Internet, it also eventually sparked technological developments that offered consumers alternative means of accessing the Internet. As a result, Intel began to reposition itself as a networking technology and Internet services provider.

Grove remained as chairman of the board until 2005. Although it was Barrett who oversaw nearly $8.5 billion in acquisitions of communications and networking enterprises and the launch of World Wide Web hosting services, Grove continued to help steer the firm he is credited for parlaying into an industry powerhouse.

Under Grove's leadership, the company navigated the dot-com bust when other technology companies were failing near the turn of the century. However, the company did suffer during these years. Intel's sales decreased 21% in 2001, and its stock price had dropped by two-thirds by 2003. In addition, the company and its leadership watched as many of their fellow executives were discovered to have defrauded investors. In 2002, amid scandals such as WorldCom and Enron, Grove said, "The same way the market sentiment shifted toward unbridled exuberance, the values of a lot of people managing companies in this market environment drifted toward 'me, me, me.'" However, by the first quarter of 2003, the company grew 13% and the stock price increased 54%.

In November 2004, Grove announced that he would retire effective May 2005. As before, Barrett replaced him (this time as chairman). As of 2011, Grove continued to offer his expertise to Intel and to the public, often taking the less popular opinion. He teaches his concepts at Stanford University in a course titled "Strategy and Action in Information Technology." In July 2010, he wrote an essay in *Bloomberg BusinessWeek* advocating stiff tariffs on products made overseas to aid in American job recovery. While Grove's intelligence is unchallenged, his opinions were met with ridicule by some economists, who largely agree that globalization is beneficial.

SEE ALSO *Intel Corp.*.

BIBLIOGRAPHY

Intel Corp. "Andrew S. Grove." Santa Clara, CA: Intel Corp., 2011. Available from http://newsroom.intel.com/community/intel_newsroom/bios?n=Andrew%20S.%20Grove&f=FormerCEO.

Johnson, Judy. "Andrew Grove: He Hid from Hitler Then Changed the World. " *World and I,* October 2009.

Lagos, Marisa. "Milk, Lucas among 13 Inducted in Hall of Fame." *SFGate.com,* December 2, 2009. Available fromhttp://articles.sfgate.com/2009-12-02/bay-area/20872231_1_harvey-milk-day-stuart-milk-gay-rights.

Race, Tim. "New Economy; Scandals Appall Some Longtime Corporate Chiefs." *New York Times,* July 1, 2002. Available from http://www.nytimes.com/2002/07/01/business/new-economy-scandals-appall-some-longtime-corporate-chiefs.html.

Rivlin, Gary. "Intel's President Is Promoted to Chief Executive." *New York Times,* November 13, 2004. http://www.nytimes.com/2004/11/12/technology/12intel.html.

Roth, Daniel. "Craig Barrett Inside." *Fortune,* December 18, 2000.

Schlender, Brent. "The Incredible, Profitable Career of Andy Grove." *Fortune,* April 27, 1998.

———. "Their Reign Is Over." *Fortune,* October 16, 2000.

Weber, Jonathan. "Looking Beyond Economic Orthodoxy to Create American Jobs." *New York Times,* July 11, 2010. Available from http://www.nytimes.com/2010/07/11/us/11bcweber.html.

H

HACKING

Hacking is a popular term for the act of breaking in, tampering with, or maliciously destroying private information contained in computer networks. It can also be used more broadly to refer to any illegal attempt to get information through electronic means. For example, while hacking originally referred to tampering with computer information, the advent of more advanced cell phones and mobile devices in the late 2000s and early 2010s have made these devices more vulnerable to hacking as well. For example, in 2011, the *News of the World* tabloid in the United Kingdom decided to cease publication after a phone hacking scandal was uncovered. (Editors at the newspaper were accused of hacking into the cell phones of celebrities and royalty.)

EARLY HISTORY

During the 1960s, the word "hacker" became prominent as a description of a person with strong computer skills, an extensive understanding of how computer programs worked, and a driving curiosity about computer systems. Hacking, however, soon became nearly synonymous with illegal activity. While the first incidents of hacking dealt with breaking into phone systems, hackers also began diving into computer systems as technology advanced.

In the 1980s, the Computer Fraud and Abuse Act was passed, imposing more severe punishments for those caught abusing computer systems. In the early 1980s, the Federal Bureau of Investigation (FBI) made one of its first arrests related to hacking. A Milwaukee-based group known as the 414s were accused of breaking into 60 different computer systems, including the Memorial Sloan-Kettering Cancer Center and the Los Alamos National Laboratory. As negative publicity surrounding hackers continued to grow, those who considered themselves true hackers—computer programming enthusiasts who pushed computer systems to their limits without malicious intent and followed a hacker code of ethics—grew weary of the media's depiction of hackers. As a result, several hacker groups coined the term 'cracker' in 1985 to define a person who broke into computer systems and ignored hacker ethics; however, the media continued to use the word hacker despite the fact that most early hackers, although they believed technical information should be freely available to any person, abided by a code of ethics that looked down upon destroying, moving, or altering information in a way could cause injury or expense.

In the 1990s, a number of government sites were attacked by hackers. During 1995 alone, U.S. Defense Department computers dealt with 250,000 hacker attacks. As technology advanced and business transactions conducted over the Internet increased, malicious hackers became even more destructive. Popular Web sites such as Yahoo!, America Online, eBay, and Amazon.com were hacked, costing millions and leaving online shoppers doubtful about security on these sites.

HACKING DEFINITIONS

Hacking activity can be defined by its intent. "White hat" hacking, sometimes also known as ethical hacking, involves hacking into computer systems in order to find flaws so that businesses and companies can fix the problems. There are white hat hacking conferences, events, firms, and even courses; governments and security experts rely on white hat hackers to uncover vulnerabilities so that these flaws can be corrected before they can be exploited by "black hat" hackers. Black hat hackers exploit computer vulnerabilities and engage in online criminal activities.

A growing number of hacking activities were more ambiguous—difficult to describe as either malevolent or helpful. For example, in 2010 and 2011, law enforcement agencies reported increased instances of so-called hacktivism. This type of hacking is politically motivated and often organized in order to raise awareness about specific issues. In 2011, the hacker collective Anonymous was one of the more established hacktivist collectives. Hacktivisim and similar hacking activities became part of popular culture after 2010 with the popularity of author Stieg Larsson's fictional hacker Lisbeth Salander and the widespread news coverage of hacker Julian Assange and his Web site WikiLeaks.

Hacking also became an international, politicized activity in the early 2010s. Many nations, including the United States, China, and Brazil, reported an increase of hacking attacks on government Web sites. In 2011, China was accused of being the point of origin of many hacking attacks. The Chinese government responded by claiming 493,000 cyber attacks were directed at China in 2010, with over half of those attacks coming from foreign nations such as the United States and India. According to China, about 10% of government Web sites in China were targeted in 2010, an increase of more than 67% when compared with 2009.

DIFFERENT TYPES OF HACKING ACTIVITY

As the cost of hacking attacks continues to rise, businesses have been forced to increase spending on network security. However, hackers have also developed new skills that allow them to break into more complex systems. Hacking typically involves compromising the security of networks, breaking the security of application software, or creating malicious programs such as viruses.

Hackers have different tools in order to access information and carry out hacking activity. Denial-of-service (DoS) attacks are designed to swamp a computer network, causing it to crash. Mail bombs act in a similar fashion but attack the network's mail servers. Network hackers also try to break into secure areas to find sensitive data. Once a network is hacked, files can be removed, stolen, or erased.

Hackers that create viruses, logic bombs, worms, and Trojan horses are involved in perhaps the most malicious hacking activities. Collectively, these types of programs are known as malware. A virus is a program that has the potential to attack and corrupt computer files by attaching itself to a file to replicate itself. It can also cause a computer to crash by utilizing all of the computer's resources. Similar to viruses, logic bombs are designed to attack when triggered by a certain event like a change in date. Worms attack networks in order to replicate and spread. A Trojan horse is a program that appears to do one thing but really does something else. While a computer system might recognize a Trojan horse as a safe program, upon execution it can release a virus, worm, or logic bomb.

Some types of malware, including worms, allow hackers to remotely access a computer and even remotely control groups of computers to carry out attacks on networks. Some hackers use remote access of computers in order to steal information from specific systems. Malware known as key loggers are designed specifically to record every keystroke made on a computer. This allows hackers to get passwords and other sensitive information entered at a compromised computer.

While in the early days of hacking, computer professionals were the only ones with the technological knowhow to hack into computers and mobile devices, in the 2010s almost any computer user could hack into a computer or mobile device. Indeed, there were online videos and articles showing the average user how to do just that. As of 2012, there are also many types of malware and hacking or spyware software available online. Some of these software systems even offered support for users. This software was designed specifically to help users hack into other computers and even cell phone accounts. In some cases, the software was marketed at parents concerned about what their children were doing online.

PREVENTING HACKING ACTIVITY

While preventing all hacking activity is deemed nearly impossible by many computer experts, businesses spend billions of dollars on protecting computer networks. The most popular method of protection against hacking among personal home computer users is anti-malware software. Many companies provide antivirus software that scans a computer's hard drive for infected material, alerting customers when bad files are found. Software offering a high degree of protection comes with antispyware, antispam, and other anti-malware software, all designed to target the different types of malware threats. Firewalls, also often included in complete anti-malware software packages, act as a deterrent to hacking by protecting private networks and computer ports from the public, thus keeping most outsiders from tampering with computer systems.

Some home users and companies opt to set up virtual private networks (VPNs). There are services offering VPN services for a monthly charge. The more popular services include VyprVPN and HotSpotVPN. VPNs work by encrypting all communication sent from a computer, so that hackers trying to see the data access only a nonsensical collection of letters and numbers.

Unfortunately, many malicious hackers eye security systems not as a deterrent but as a mere obstacle to overcome. However, as long as hacking attacks persist, both individuals and businesses will continue to invest in programs and software designed to protect systems from unwanted visitors.

SEE ALSO *Computer Crime; Computer Security; Denial-of-Service Attack; Fraud, Internet; Viruses.*

BIBLIOGRAPHY

Ashford, Warwick. "Almost Every Organisation Is Being Targeted by Sophisticated Malware Attacks, McAfee Study Reveals." *Computer Weekly,* August 3, 2011. Available from http://www.computerweekly.com/Articles/2011/08/03/247508/Almost-every-organisation-is-being-targeted-by-sophisticated-malware-attacks-McAfee-study.htm.

———. "China Blames US for Cyber Attacks." *Computer Weekly,* August 10, 2011. Available from http://www.computerweekly.com/Articles/2011/08/10/247582/China-blames-US-for-cyber-attacks.htm.

Blakey, Elizabeth. "Commit a Cybercrime? You're Hired!" *E-Commerce Times,* July 17, 2000. Available from http://www.ecommercetimes.com/story/3789.html.

Dunn, John E. "Mobile Phone Hacking — Can You Stop It?" *PC World,* January 25, 2011. Available from http://www.pcworld.com/article/217647/mobile_phone_hacking_can_you_stop_it.html.

Farrell, Greg, and Michael A. Riley. "Hackers Take $1 Billion a Year as Banks Blame Their Clients." *Bloomberg,* August 4, 2011. Available from http://www.bloomberg.com/news/2011-08-04/hackers-take-1-billion-a-year-from-company-accounts-banks-won-t-indemnify.html.

The Internet Crime Complaint Center (IC3). "2010 Internet Crime Report." Washington, DC, 2011. Available from http://www.ic3.gov/media/annualreport/2010_IC3Report.pdf.

Johnson, Chris. "Attack of the Cyber Insider." *Sydney Morning Herald,* July 30, 2011. Available from http://www.smh.com.au/technology/technology-news/attack-of-the-cyber-insider-20110729-1i4do.html.

"Joint Efforts Needed to Battle Hackers." *China Daily,* August 10, 2011. Available from http://www.chinadaily.com.cn/china/2011-08/10/content_13088968.htm.

Mandeville, David. "Hackers, Crackers, and Trojan Horses." *CNN In-Depth Reports,* March 29, 1999.

Murphy, Kate. "New Hacking Tools Pose Bigger Threats to Wi-Fi Users." *New York Times,* February 16, 2011. Available from http://www.nytimes.com/2011/02/17/technology/personaltech/17basics.html.

Trigaux, Robert. "A History of Hacking." *St. Petersburg Times,* 2000.

HARDWARE

The term hardware most often refers to computer machinery and equipment one can see and touch, such as central processing units (CPUs), storage drives, modems, memory chips, monitors, speakers, and printers. Memory and storage devices send data and instructions to the CPU. The type of hardware housed inside a computer determines how quickly the CPU can process these instructions. The software applications that reside on a computer—such as word processors, spreadsheets, databases, e-mail programs, and Web browsers—make the hardware useful to computer users in the same way that television programming makes televisions and remote controls useful to viewers.

The growth of the Internet forced many hardware companies to move into networking technology and World Wide Web services. For example, although the popularity of the Web helped fuel Intel's success when hordes of consumers bought PCs to gain access to the Internet from their homes, it also eventually sparked the development of hardware devices like cell phones and inexpensive Internet terminals that offered consumers alternative means of accessing the Internet. As a result, Intel began to restructure itself as a networking technology and Internet services provider. In fact, as the Internet made services more accessible, customers demanded more accessibility in the form of mobility. By 2011, over 45 million people in the United States owned smartphones. These are mobile devices with multiple capabilities including a Web browser, storage for computer and media files, GPS navigation, and personal planning.

One of the more popular pieces of hardware introduced in the late 2000s was the iPhone. Introduced by Apple in 2007, the iPhone is a smartphone with touchscreen capability and an intuitive interface that consumers responded to positively. The robust quality of the iPhone's hardware allowed third-party software applications (apps) to be installed onto it. Apple advertised this feature by announcing, "There's an app for that" with actors demonstrating using the iPhone to make restaurant reservations and unlock their car from miles away. Since 2007, thousands of apps have been developed for the iPhone and for other smartphones.

Other hardware devices allow users to connect to the Internet wirelessly using their laptop computer. Called "Wi-Fi" (short for wireless fidelity), a Wi-Fi-enabled device can connect to the Internet from a wireless access point, or "hotspot." A hotspot has a range of approximately 65 feet.

MODEMS AND STORAGE HARDWARE

Modems have evolved from dial-up modems using telephone lines to cable and satellite modems which allow for much faster connectivity. In addition, some wireless modems allow users to connect to the Internet wirelessly without needing to find a Wi-Fi hotspot, as these devices use the cellular telephone system for connectivity. Such modems can be embedded into a computer or mobile device, or they may be portable using a USB connection.

Since they are using the cell phone system, users of these devices typically pay a monthly rate, as they would a cell phone.

Storage and media hardware also continue to evolve. In the early 1990s, most computers were equipped with both a "floppy" disk drive and a 3.5-inch drive. By 2005, disk drives were mostly used for playing media using compact discs. Drives can be DVD-drives, Blu-ray disc drives, and CD-drives. These drives can read and write music, data, and video. For data storage, a USB flash drive is often used in the 2010s. USB flash drives are useful for both data storage and "plug-and-go" hardware such as speakers, a keyboard, mouse, or video camera.

SEE ALSO *Cloud Computing; Data Warehousing; Smartphone.*

BIBLIOGRAPHY

Cheng, Jacqui. "iPhone in Depth: The Ars Review." *ArsTechnica,* July 9, 2007. Available from http://arstechnica.com/apple/reviews/2007/07/iphone-review.ars.

"Gartner Says Sales of Mobile Devices in Second Quarter of 2011 Grew 16.5 Percent Year-on-Year; Smartphone Sales Grew 74 Percent." Stamford, CT: Gartner, August 11, 2011. Available from http://www.gartner.com/it/page.jsp?id=1764714.

"Hardware." In *Techencyclopedia.* Point Pleasant, PA: Computer Language Co., 2001. Available from http://www.techweb.com/encyclopedia.

"Hardware." In *Webopedia.* Darien, CT: Internet.com, 2001. Available from http://www.webopedia.com/TERM/H/hardware.html.

McDougall, Paul. "Intel Products Aim at Speeding E-commerce Transactions—Netstructure Line Designed to Keep Consumers from Giving Up on Online Orders." *Information-Week,* February 21, 2000.

Wireless Networking in the Developing World: A Practical Guide to Planning and Building Low-Cost Telecommunications Infrastructure. 2nd ed., 2007. Available from http://wndw.net/pdf/wndw2-en/wndw2-ebook.pdf.

HEWLETT-PACKARD CO.

Hewlett-Packard Co. (HP) is among the world's largest computer firms, posting $126.3 billion in revenues in 2010. Along with computers and printers, the firm also sells servers, calculators, televisions, storage devices, networking products, software, imaging products, and computer services to individual consumers and businesses.

Hewlett-Packard is a public company. Leo Apotheker was CEO, director, and president of the company from September 2010 to September 2011, when he was replaced as CEO and president by Meg Whitman. The executive chairman (as of 2012) is Raymond Lane.

CLIENTS AND MARKETPLACE

In May 2011, HP was ranked 11th on the *Fortune* 500. One reason the company is so large is that HP products can be found almost everywhere. Government agencies, small businesses, corporations, and students all use HP products.

Although HP does have a wide client base, it does face considerable competition. Other IT and computer competitors such as Dell and Microsoft, for example, capture a significant market share. In addition, HP has not fully developed mobile devices, so that competitors such as Apple and other makers of mobile devices have represented a larger threat to HP since 2010, especially given HP's unsuccessful foray into the increasingly important tablet market in 2011.

FINANCIAL GROWTH AND PERFORMANCE

Revenues for 2010 were $126.3 billion, up from $115 billion in 2009. In 2010, the Personal Systems Group accounted for 32% of revenues while the services sector accounted for 28%. That same year, the imaging and printing group accounted for 20% of the yearly revenues, and the Enterprise Storage and Servers division accounted for 15%.

EARLY HISTORY

In 1938, Stanford University electrical engineering graduates William Hewlett and David Packard started their own company in the garage of a home Packard was renting in Palo Alto, California. With a mere $538 in capital, the partners began marketing a resistance capacity audio oscillator (HP 200A), which was essentially a sound-equipment testing device that Hewlett created as a graduate student. The company's first break came when Walt Disney ordered eight of the new oscillators for the production of *Fantasia.* In January 1939, Hewlett and Packard named their new electronics manufacturing partnership Hewlett-Packard Co., after flipping a coin to decide the order of their names in the company's moniker.

Throughout the late 1940s, Hewlett and Packard devised and implemented management policies that would later lead to their recognition as pioneers in corporate management and employee relations. For example, they created an Open Door Policy, believing that all employees should feel empowered to approach management about issues and concerns. To facilitate this policy, employees worked in open cubicles, and managers worked in offices with no doors. The policies and philosophies which Hewlett and Packard developed came to be known as the HP Way.

HP completed its initial public offering (IPO) in November 1957. It was then that Packard created objectives for HP, believing that concrete goals would help to facilitate consistent choices by the firm's management team. The following year, HP completed its first acquisition when it purchased graphics recorder manufacturer F.L. Moseley. International expansion began in 1959 when a manufacturing plant was constructed in Germany and an office was established in Geneva, Switzerland, to serve as a headquarters for European operations. That year, HP became one of the first firms to add profit sharing to the compensation package it offered employees.

By the end of the 1960s, sales at HP exceeded $165 million, HP Laboratories was created to serve as the main research hub for the firm, and the firm invented the first scientific desktop calculator in the world, the HP 9100. Although divisions had been operating fairly independently since the late 1950s—with each department handling its own research and development, manufacturing, and marketing activities—this new structure granted the decision-making authority previously held by executive vice presidents to general managers, who oversaw divisions with similar product lines.

TRANSITION TO COMPUTER MANUFACTURING

After spending nearly three decades manufacturing various instruments for analysis and measurement, HP diversified into computers by developing the HP 2116A, a machine designed to control HP's test and measurement instruments. Even more instrumental in HP's shift to computers was its 1972 launch of the HP 35, the first scientific handheld calculator. The product is viewed by many industry analysts as a major stepping stone in the growth of the personal computing industry because it rendered obsolete the engineer's slide rule. HP also moved into the business computer market—dominated by IBM Corp. and Digital Equipment Corp.—when it introduced the HP 3000 minicomputer. Innovations in employee relations continued throughout the mid-1970s as flexible work hours were offered to employees and time clocks were eliminated.

HP unveiled its first personal computer in 1980. In 1982, the firm introduced its first desktop mainframe machine. In 1984, HP launched the ThinkJet printer and its most successful product to date, the LaserJet printer. That year, sales topped $6.5 billion as earnings reached a record $500 million. To handle its growing number of operating groups—each time a group reached 1,500 employees, it was split into two separate groups—HP created four broad sectors to oversee these units.

HP developed a line of computer systems using Reduced-Instruction-Set Computing (RISC), in place of Complex Instruction-Set Computing (CISC), in 1986. The group of machines, dubbed HP Precision Architecture, was able to execute programs two to three times faster than normal by excluding many routine instructions. Though RISC chips were denounced for their inflexibility, other computer firms soon began developing their own versions of the technology. The DeskJet printer, an inkjet printer for the mass market, was launched in 1988.

Although HP had succeeded in positioning itself as a leading computer maker by the late 1980s, each of its major computer lines, created for a specific purpose, was incompatible with the others. Recognizing that this strategy had resulted in redundant research and development efforts and limited expansion capabilities for consumers, HP began working to enhance the compatibility levels of its machines. As a result, all computer operations were placed in the same operating sector. Based on revenues of $9.8 billion, HP ranked 49th among *Fortune* 500 firms in 1988.

HP bought Apollo Computers, an engineering workstations vendor, for $500 million in 1989. In 1994, HP and Intel Corp. agreed to work together to create a computer chip able to run more than one operating system by the end of the decade. HP also moved into the home PC market with the launch of the HP Pavilion.

The mid-1990s were marked by price cuts for Hewlett-Packard as competition in the PC market intensified. In 1995, Hewlett-Packard reduced prices on its commercial PCs by up to 16%. The firm also launched its CopyJet color copier and printer, pricing it at roughly one-tenth the price of conventional color copiers. In an effort to enhance its share of the PC market in Europe, HP reduced prices there roughly 10% in 1996. Two years later, HP introduced the Pavilion home PC line, pricing the base model, the Pavilion 3260, at an unprecedented $800. By then, HP was the second-largest computer manufacturer in the world. After deciding to hone its focus to personal computers, printers, workstations, and servers, HP spun off its non-computer-related operations as Agilent Technologies in 1999.

MOVE TO THE INTERNET

One of the first major firms to engage in telecommuting, in 1994 HP developed a set of guidelines for employees who wished to work from home or at other offices. The firm's intranet, considered one of the largest in the world, allowed employees from all over the world to communicate with one another. Despite the firm's timeliness in this regard, however, it actually began a wholehearted embrace of the Internet much later that its competitors. The reason for this, ironically, was that the decentralized structure that had worked so well for HP since its inception had "become a recipe for inward focus and bureaucratic paralysis," according to the *Economist.*

The *Economist* also wrote that by the 1990s, "the company had become a collection of 130 independent product groups that tried harder to meet their own financial targets than to find any common thread. It was no surprise, then, that HP was late to the Internet party—even though it had the technology in its labs. While Sun Microsystems and IBM were busy marketing themselves as dot.com revolutionaries, HP was still focusing on hardware." It was not until Carly Fiorina took over as CEO in mid-1999 that the firm truly turned its focus to the Internet.

Fiorina launched a full-scale restructuring of HP, overhauling not only its internal organization by reshuffling operations into four major groupings—computer products, imaging products, consumer sales, and corporate sales—but also the firm's marketing strategies and corporate vision. By mid-2000 Amazon.com selected HP to provide roughly 90% of its Internet infrastructure, including Internet servers, storage devices, and PCs linked to the Internet. By then, HP had integrated its technology into various e-services solutions packages.

In January 2001, HP bought Bluestone Software Inc., a maker of e-business tools. Rapid integration of the acquisition allowed HP to release 25 software products the following month, including the Netaction e-services development and implementation suite, and the OpenView e-services systems management suite. In April, HP balanced out its new software releases with several new hardware products, namely 19 Internet server appliances.

THE MERGER WITH COMPAQ

In 2002, HP merged with Compaq Computer Corp. in a deal reportedly worth $25 billion. HP retained the Compaq brand and continued to sell computer products under both brands. In 2002, HP also earmarked $5 billion for research and development, partly as a result of newfound confidence in the future of the company. The merger transformed the new HP into a larger company, with 145,000 workers and locations in more than 160 countries.

The new HP formed as a result of the merger became one of the leading server, imaging, printing, and access device suppliers and an $87 billion global organization. The company also became among the top companies for IT services, storage solutions, and management software.

In 2005, Fiorina, one of the most powerful women in business at that time, was ousted, partly as a result of lower-than-expected profits from the Compaq Computer purchase and partly because shareholders were unhappy with the slow way that HP cut costs after the Compaq acquisition. Mark Hurd replaced Fiorina in March 2005, and the company began to experience a new growth and optimism. In May 2005, HP announced that earnings were 1% ahead of forecasts, and stocks for the company increased rapidly that same month.

DIGITAL EQUIPMENT

As part of the Compaq merger, HP was also able to access some of the remaining areas of expertise of the Digital Equipment Corporation (DEC). DEC had been a U.S. vendor of computer systems and peripherals since the 1950s, but the 1992 tech market downturn affected DEC severely, and the company sold off large portions of the business in an effort to stay afloat. By 1998, however, the company decided to sell the remainder of its organization. The company sold its customer support centers, some of its product lines, and multivendor global services sector to Compaq. HP acquired these parts of DEC during the Compaq acquisition. As a result, after the Compaq acquisition, HP began to sell what were once DEC products under its own logo and brand name.

PRETEXTING SCANDAL

During September 2006, HP faced one of the most notable public relations problems during its history when the media reported that HP chairperson Patricia Dunn had asked Ann Baskins, general counsel for HP, to hire independent security experts to look into the activities of journalists and HP board members. The aim was to find the source of a leak within HP pertaining to long-term HP strategy. The security experts hired private investigators, who used pretexting (essentially being less than honest or forthright) in order to obtain the phone records of journalists and board members. The media reports about Dunn's requests and especially the private investigators' activities angered board members and HP employees and generated a great deal of negative publicity for HP. Dunn denied knowing that private investigators would use pretexting, largely considered an illegal or suspect method of gathering information, but she eventually resigned from HP, as did Baskins. The pretexting case at HP prompted a U.S. House Committee on Energy and Commerce investigation as well as criminal charges.

EDS

In 2008, HP announced a plan to buy EDS, an IT services vendor, for $13.9 billion (about $25.00 per share). HP announced that the purchase would more than double services revenue for HP. After the merger, EDS retained its name and chairman as well as its executive offices, all now a part of the HP company. The purchase, according to analysts, was designed to help HP offer more support services, which could help them capture a larger market of consumers and purchasers, allowing HP to compete more effectively with IBM and other larger companies. At the time of the purchase in 2008, HP had customer support offerings, but the acquisition of EDS allowed HP to have access to EDS's data center management solutions, application outsourcing, and network management solutions.

In 2009, HP announced that EDS would be renamed HP Enterprise Services and would be overseen by the executive vice president of HP. By 2010, HPs efforts to merge the two companies had resulted in 100,000 layoffs and 200 offices closed.

2010 AND BEYOND

In early July 2010, HP finalized its $1.2 billion acquisition of Palm. Palm was a smartphone company, creating phones with the webOS platform. Palm had been struggling with hardware issues, and HP purchased the company in part to expand its offering of webOS mobile devices. After the acquisition, Palm became a global business unit within HP, reporting to the vice president of the HP Personal Systems Group. The new global business unit was tasked with developing webOS software and hardware for smartphones, tablets, and netbooks.

Although on the surface the acquisition seemed like a good fit for both companies, IDC research only gave the acquisition a 1 in 10 chance of succeeding. Writers at both *PC World* and *Information Week* predicted that Palm's struggling share of the mobile market and HP's small contribution to mobile devices would not be a good match, especially given the competitiveness of the mobile market. In July 2011, the first HP tablet computer using a webOS operating system went on sale.

The pessimism of analysts seemed well founded later in 2011, as HP tablets failed to sell. HP's TouchPad saw its price drop by 20%, as HP was willing to take a loss of $207 per tablet in an attempt to boost sales. The price drop did spark a huge boost in sales for HP as well as huge consumer demand in the products, but HP ultimately decided to close its mobile devices business and discontinue the tablets. By September 2011, the company started laying off employees in the mobile devices division. That month, company shares were down 45% from the beginning of 2011, trading at $22.78. That same month, a class-action lawsuit was filed by HP shareholder Richard Gammel and by other HP shareholders, alleging they were misled about the company's potential.

In September 2011, HP announced plans to spin off its PC division as it bowed out of mobile devices. The announcement was a surprise to many customers, especially given the predominance of HP computers on the marketplace. Somewhat confusingly, HP rushed to assure customers in 2011 that it was committed to the PC, leaving some consumers wondering whether HP personal computers will be phased out or not.

Adding to the chaos in September (or perhaps the cause of it), CEO Leo Apotheker was ousted by the board of HP and replaced by former eBay CEO Meg Whitman. While Whitman initially stated she would follow through with the strategies outlined by Apotheker, it is unclear in late 2011 just what direction HP will ultimately take in the early 2010s.

SEE ALSO *Hewlett, William R.; Packard, David.*

BIBLIOGRAPHY

Albanesius, Chloe. "HP Completes $1.2B Palm Acquisition." *PC Magazine,* July 1, 2010. Available from http://www.pcmag.com/article2/0,2817,2365993,00.asp.

Burrows, Peter. "The Radical: Carly Fiorina's Bold Management Experiment at HP." *BusinessWeek Online,* February 19, 2001. Available from http://www.businessweek.com/2001/01_08/b3720001.htm.

Conner, Deni. "Hewlett-Packard Unveils Bevy of Internet Appliances." *Network World,* April 23, 2001, 14.

Dubie, Denise. "What Does the HP-EDS Deal Really Mean?" *InfoWorld,* May 13, 2008. Available from http://www.infoworld.com/t/business/what-does-hp-eds-deal-really-mean-333.

Edwards, Cliff, and Aaron Ricadela. "HP's Plan to Make TouchPad a Hit." *PC World,* June 23, 2011. Available from http://www.businessweek.com/magazine/content/11_27/b4235040584134.htm.

Greenmeier, Larry. "How HP Carves Out the Magic—Hewlett-Packard Wants to Expand Its Service Offerings into the Product-Agnostic World of E-business." *Information Week,* November 13, 2000, 64.

Hamblen, Matt, and Nancy Gohring. "HP's Palm Acquisition Won't Be Easy." *PC World,* May 10, 2010. Available from http://www.pcworld.com/article/195935/hps_palm_acquisition_wont_be_easy.html.

Hamm, Steve, and Arik Hesseldahl. "HP and EDS Try a Tieup." *Business Week,* May 2008. Available from http://www.businessweek.com/technology/content/may2008/tc20080512_958875.htm.

"Hewlett-Packard Buys Bluestone in E-business Bid." *News-bytes,* October 16, 2000.

"Hewlett-Packard and Compaq Agree to Merge, Creating $87 Billion Global Technology Leader." Palo Alto, CA, September 3, 2001. Available from http://www.hp.com/hpinfo/newsroom/press/2001/010904a.html.

———. "HP History." Palo Alto, CA, 2011. Available from http://www8.hp.com/us/en/hp-information/about-hp/history/history.html.

"Hewlett-Packard Co." In *Notable Corporate Chronologies.* Farmington Hills, MI: Gale Research, 1999.

"Hewlett-Packard Debuts Super Server." *Xinhua News Agency,* September 13, 2000.

"Hewlett-Packard Ousts Female CEO; Compaq 'Fiasco' Doomed Fiorina." *Washington Times,* February 10, 2005.

Kessler, Michelle, and Jim Hopkins. "New HP Chief Makes the Best of a Bad Situation." *USA Today,* September 13, 2006.

Available from http://www.usatoday.com/tech/techinvestor/corporatenews/2006-09-12-hp-hurd-advantage_x.htm.
Lau, Kathleen. "HP Layoffs Final Chapter in EDS Integration." *Computer World,* June 2, 2010. Available from http://www.itworldcanada.com/news/hp-layoffs-final-chapter-in-eds-integration/140803.
Levine, Daniel S. "Hewlett-Packard Leaps into Software Market." *San Francisco Business Times,* February 16, 2001, 8.
Neel, Dan. "Amazon.com Becomes a Hewlett-Packard Shop." *Network World,* June 5, 2000.
"The New HP." *T H E Journal* 29, no. 11 (2002): 14.
Platt, Gordon. "Happy Honeymoon for New Head of Hewlett-Packard." *Global Finance,* June 2005.
"Rebuilding the Garage." *Economist,* July 15, 2000, 59. Available from http://www.economist.com/node/5938.
Sherr, Ian. "After Axing TouchPad, Hewlett-Packard Lays Off WebOS Employees." *Wall Street Journal,* September 20, 2011. Available from http://online.wsj.com/article/BT-CO-20110920-711292.html.
Simons, Mike. "Larry Ellison Outraged as HP Hands Top Job to Ex-SAP CEO." *Computerworld UK,* October 10, 2010. Available from http://www.computerworlduk.com/news/it-business/3242184/larry-ellison-outraged-as-hp-hands-top-job-to-ex–sap-ceo.
Wong, Grace. "Now, HP Is a Criminal Case." *CNN Money,* October 5, 2006. Available from http://money.cnn.com/2006/10/04/news/companies/hp_california/index.htm?cnn=yes.
Worthen, Ben. "Hewlett-Packard Faces Shareholder Suit." *Wall Street Journal,* September 15, 2011. Available from http://online.wsj.com.
Zeman, Eric. "Analysis of HP-Palm Acquisition." *Information Week,* April 29, 2010. Available from http://www.informationweek.com/news/mobility/smart_phones/224700269.

HEWLETT, WILLIAM R.

William R. Hewlett was the cofounder of Hewlett-Packard Co. (HP). Along with partner David Packard, Hewlett was instrumental in growing the California-based firm from a small manufacturer of measurement instruments into a personal computer, printer, and IT services powerhouse that reached $126 billion in sales in 2010. Lauded for their innovative management style, which fostered creativity and open communications between employees and managers, Hewlett and Packard are considered two of the fathers of Silicon Valley.

A native of Ann Arbor, Michigan, Hewlett earned his bachelor's degree from Stanford University, where he first met Packard, in 1934. After completing his master's degree in electrical engineering at the Massachusetts Institute of Technology, Hewlett returned to California, earning an additional engineering degree from Stanford in 1939. The previous year, he and Packard started a business in the garage of a home Packard was renting in Palo Alto. The partners launched operations with just $538 in capital. Their first major product was a resistance capacity audio oscillator (HP 200A), essentially a sound equipment testing device, that Hewlett devised as a graduate student. Hewlett's advisor at Stanford, Frederick Terman, encouraged the partners to market the oscillator, and this advice proved well heeded when Walt Disney ordered eight of the new oscillators for the production of *Fantasia.* Hewlett and Packard officially established their firm in January 1939 as Hewlett-Packard Co. Hewlett's name was positioned first because he won a coin toss that he and Packard agreed would decide the issue.

When Hewlett returned to Palo Alto after serving in World War II, he was named vice president of HP. It was at this time that he and Packard began setting in motion the innovative management policies that would later earn them accolades. For example, HP's Open Door Policy was designed to help all employees feel comfortable enough to communicate their ideas and concerns to management. To this end, Hewlett placed employees in open cubicles and created offices without doors for executives. He also oversaw HP's decision to become one of the first firms to add profit sharing to the compensation package it offered employees. After working as executive vice president from 1957 to 1964, Hewlett took over as president. By then, Hewlett's and Packard's management style had become known as the "HP Way." According to Jeff Bliss, writer for *Computer Reseller News,* it was the HP Way that fueled the growth of Silicon Valley, because it began attracting East Coast technology experts to California. "The best talent at Eastern institutions such as the Massachusetts Institute of Technology and Bell Labs took notice, and the Western migration of the country's technological brain trust began. The environment awaiting these scientists, teachers, and engineers could not have been more conducive to encouraging technology."

Hewlett added CEO to his list of titles in 1969, when Packard left the firm to serve as Secretary of Defense in the Nixon administration. One of Hewlett's first decisions at the helm of HP was to further decentralize the firm. The divisions had been operating fairly autonomously since the late 1950s. Each department oversaw its own research and development, manufacturing, and marketing operations. Wanting to preserve the company's entrepreneurial spirit, Hewlett and Packard also decided that each time a group reached 1,500 employees, it would be split in two. To decentralize this structure even further, Hewlett pushed decision-making authority down the executive chain, granting the control previously held by executive vice presidents to the general managers who supervised divisions with associated product lines.

With Hewlett at the reins, HP unveiled its first blockbuster product, the world's first handheld scientific calculator, known as the HP 35, in 1972. Hewlett also oversaw HP's move into the business computer market with the launch of the HP 3000 minicomputer and the decision to eliminate time clocks and offer flexible work hours to employees. Hewlett served as both president and CEO until 1977 and as CEO only until 1978; between 1978 and 1983, Hewlett acted as chairman. HP created its first personal computer, the HP-85, in 1980, and its first desktop mainframe machine, the HP 9000, in 1982.

Hewlett reduced his activity in the firm in 1983, when he took on the role of vice chairman. The following year, HP launched its LaserJet printer, which became its most successful product ever. While Hewlett was no longer in charge of day-to-day operations when the printer was unveiled, he certainly played a role in fostering the environment out of which such a product was conceived. For his contributions to science and technology, Hewlett was awarded the National Medal of Science by President Ronald Reagan in 1985. In 1987, he was named chairman emeritus, a role he retained until his death in January 2001.

OTHER PURSUITS

Starting in 1950, Hewlett took on an array of roles and responsibilities to give back to his community. He joined the board of directors of the Institute of Electrical and Electronics Engineers (IEEE), which was called the Institute of Radio Engineers at the time. He served as president in 1954. In addition to his contributions to IT, Hewlett also took an active role in California's education and medical systems. A trustee of Mills College and Stanford University, he also served as board president and, subsequently, director of Stanford Hospital in Palo Alto. In addition, he was a member of a regional panel of the Commission on White House Fellows for two years, director of the Kaiser Foundation Hospital and Health Plan for six years, and director of the Drug Abuse Council in Washington, D.C. for two years.

Hewlett's legacy grew after his death. HP tripled its revenues in the 2000s, overtaking Dell Inc. as the largest computer retailer in the world. Growth of the William and Flora Hewlett Foundation was not as rapid as that of the private firm, but the organization did increase its grant-giving from under $200 million in 2002 to a disbursement of approximately $358 million in 2010. With $7.4 billion in assets, the foundation funded programs in education, the environment, global development, and the performing arts, with a mission to improve quality of life.

SEE ALSO *Hewlett-Packard Co.; Packard, David.*

BIBLIOGRAPHY

Akin, David. "Hewlett Helped Define Silicon Valley Success." *National Post,* January 13, 2001, D6.

Bliss, Jeff. "William Hewlett." *Computer Reseller News,* November 16, 1997, 45.

Hausman, Eric. "HP Co-founder William Hewlett Dies." *CRN,* January 12, 2001. Available from http://www.crn.com/news/channel-programs/18812119/hp-co-founder-william-hewlett-dies.htm;jsessionid=-Vcu8T8y2tEMxd4K9fapmg**.ecappj02.

Hewlett-Packard Co. "2010 Annual Report." Palo Alto, CA, 2011 Available from http://h30261.www3.hp.com.

Hewlett-Packard Co. "HP History." Palo Alto, CA, 2011. Available from http://www8.hp.com/us/en/hp-information/about-hp/history/history.html.

———. "William R. Hewlett." Palo Alto, CA, 2011. Available from http://www8.hp.com/us/en/company-information/executive-team/hewlett.html?jumpid=reg_R1002_USEN.

"Hewlett-Packard Co." In *Notable Corporate Chronologies.* Farmington Hills, MI: Gale Research, 1999.

The William and Flora Hewlett Foundation. "About the William and Flora Hewlett Foundation." Menlo Park, CA, 2011. Available from http://www.hewlett.org/about.

HIGHER EDUCATION, E-COMMERCE AND

Since its inception, university and college faculty have used the Internet as a powerful research tool and a vehicle for the dissemination of information. By the mid-1990s, many instructors communicated with students and colleagues via e-mail and incorporated Web-based materials into their courses. As the twenty-first century began, educators and administrators positioned the Internet as a central component of learning. By the 2010s, virtually every college course had an online component, and some entire college systems were completely "virtual."

HISTORY

During the 1950s and 1960s, computers on campuses were employed primarily for scientific research. By the late 1960s, computer technology was adopted for instructional and administrative purposes. With the personal computer revolution of the 1980s, more departments provided individual computers for faculty, and computing resources became increasingly integrated into humanities and arts teaching and research. When they appeared in the 1990s, courses delivered over the Web represented a new development in distance learning. They continued an educational trend dating back to the nineteenth century, when mail correspondence courses first offered access to higher education for much of America's widely scattered population.

The first schools to adopt online education as a teaching vehicle frequently designed and generated their own software platforms for course delivery, since user-ready products were not commercially available. Colleges and universities experimented with various forms of online education. Some institutions required even residential students to complete a portion of their coursework online. Others formed consortia of several schools, making their pooled course offerings available via online portals. The University of California, Los Angeles (UCLA) was the first university to mandate that all of its arts and sciences classes develop Web sites.

While such online businesses as Full Sail and the University of Phoenix remained at the top of the market through much of the 2000s, advancements during the first decade of the twenty-first century provided the technology and means for many other colleges to join the online industry and offer at least select degrees to students through a Web-based teaching program. Quality began to vary widely, between projects set up by accredited institutions of higher learning that were expanding into Web solutions, and diploma mills that focused on making profit but not providing a worthwhile educational experience. Businesses like Straighterline and Learning Counts became popular institutions that focused on businesslike pricing strategies and marketing plans not usually pursued by the nonprofit universities.

By the late 2000s, online classes had become widely accepted, and where a degree came from became as important as the degree itself. The for-profit businesses that could offer credit transfers to traditional universities and colleges began to have an edge over their competitors. Normal colleges began to embrace a wide variety of online techniques for teaching. With the varied options available for getting a degree, students began to develop buying power similar to consumers in many other markets. Colleges began to aim for convenience and expanded features in order to compete with online options, which entered into fiercer competition between themselves. Hybrid classes started to become an option for busy students. For classes like biology, students could attend online courses for most of the information, but come in to key classes for labs, examples, and special lessons.

These developments on the whole benefited higher education as a facet of e-commerce. In 2011, the top online programs in the United States included the Penn State University World Campus, which earned the highest distance learning ratings from organizations like TheBestColleges.org. Boston University Online became another popular choice, as did Full Sail (for its specialty in film) and Saint Joseph's University Online. Many schools, like Saint Joseph's, specialized in a wide variety of masters degrees, which were in general much easier to offer in hybrid and online environments. In the early 2010s it was unusual for colleges not to have at least one or two degrees available through primarily online courses. While quality issues made many studies unreliable, retention rates averaged around 95% for many online learners, while traditional learners stayed at around 74% retention.

ASSOCIATED SERVICES

As online components fused successfully with higher education, a number of online companies began filling the provider gap for universities and students, offering needed services. By the late 2000s, e-commerce companies not directly involved in higher education could still make a profit supplementing it. Study aids like Cliff's Notes began to focus on its online presence, where students could consult them more quickly and cheaply than purchasing book-bound versions. Other study guides and exam preparation materials became available online as universities posted their own information on dedicated sites.

Students, university administrators, and professors also took advantage of social media. It became easy for students to share class information and links via Twitter, and some professors found it efficient to answer questions via Facebook and Twitter. Facebook fan pages and Flickr photo albums both depended on college student participation in their early days.

Online news agencies, journalism sites, and blogs also became important for students seeking key information on a variety of topics, and some businesses started specifically to collate this information for useful reference. Cloud computing was often a part of these varied ventures and was a source of profit for many large providers. For example, in 2010 Arkansas Tech University used Tegrity as a provider for cloud-based lecture capturing tools, where lecture information could be saved in provider servers and accessed when necessary.

SEE ALSO *Intellectual Property; Legal Issues.*

BIBLIOGRAPHY

"Back to the Future with Peter Thiel." *National Review,* January 20, 2011. Available from http://www.nationalreview.com/articles/257531/back-future-peter-thiel-interview?page=5.

Barker, Jacquelyn. "Sophisticated Technology Offers Higher Education Options." *Technological Horizons In Education Journal,* November 2000.

Birchard, Karen. "European Nations Promote Online Education." *Chronicle of Higher Education,* April 27, 2001. Available from http://chronicle.com.

Blumenstyk, Goldie. "Colleges Get Free Web Pages, but with a Catch: Advertising." *Chronicle of Higher Education,* September 3, 1999.

Bollag, Burton. "Developing Countries Turn to Distance Education." *Chronicle of Higher Education.* June 15, 2001.

Carnevale, Dan, and Jeffrey Young. "Who Owns On-Line Courses? Colleges and Professors Start to Sort It Out." *Chronicle of Higher Education,* December 17, 1999.

Carr, Sarah. "With National E-university, Britain Gets in the Online-Education Game." *Chronicle of Higher Education,* August 17, 2001.

Charp, Sylvia. "E-learning." *Technological Horizons in Education Journal,* April 2001.

Clayton, Mark. "Click 'n Learn." *Christian Science Monitor,* August 15, 2000.

"Cloud-Based Lecture Capture Makes Immdiate Impact at Arkansas Tech University." *University Business,* September 22, 2011. Available from http://www.universitybusiness.com/webseminar/cloud-based-lecture-capture-makes-immediate-impact-arkansas-tech-university.

Cohen, David. "In Cyberuniversities, a Place for South Korea's Women." *Chronicle of Higher Education,* April 6, 2001. Available from http://chronicle.com.

Driscoll, Emily. "Top Education Trends for 2011." *Fox Business,* February 3, 2011. Available from http://www.foxbusiness.com/personal-finance/2011/02/03/education-trends.

Dobeneck, Monica Von. "Online Test: Higher-Education Institutions Are Adding Options for Flexible Learning." *Patriot-News,* August 8, 2011. Available from http://blog. pennlive.com/business/2011/08/online_test_higher-education_i.html.

Dunn, Samuel. "The Virtualizing of Education." *The Futurist,* March/April 2000.

Farrington, Gregory, and Stephen Bronack. "Higher Education Online: How Do We Know What Works—And What Doesn't?" *Technological Horizons in Education Journal,* May 2001.

Green, Joshua. "The Online Education Bubble." *American Prospect,* October 23, 2000.

Grossman, Wendy. "On-Line U." *Scientific American,* July 1999. Available from http://www.sciam.com.

"Higher Education and Digital Marketing–Joining the Party." *Webcredible,* September 2010. Available from http://www.webcredible.co.uk/user-friendly-resources/marketing/higher-education.shtml.

Hobart, Byrne. "How to Short the Bubble in Higher Education." *Business Insider,* February 15, 2011. Available from http://www.businessinsider.com/how-to-short-the-bubble-in-higher-education-2011-2.

Johnston, Chris. "The Information Age Draws Nearer." *Times Educational Supplement,* January 5, 2001.

Katz, Stanley. "In Information Technology, Don't Mistake a Tool for a Goal." *Chronicle of Higher Education,* June 15, 2001.

Lewin, Tamar. "Online Enterprises Gain Foothold as Path to College Degree." *New York Times,* August 25, 2011. Available from http://www.nytimes.com/2011/08/25/education/25future.html2.

Marcus, David. "A Scholastic Gold Mine." *U.S. News & World Report,* January 24, 2000.

Michaels, James W., and Dirk Smillie. "Webucation." *Forbes,* May 15, 2000. Available from http://www.forbes.com/forbes/2000/0515/6511092a.html.

Morris, Kathleen. "Wiring the Ivory Tower." *Business Week,* August 9, 1999.

Noble, David F. "Digital Diploma Mills: The Automation of Higher Education." *First Monday,* January 5, 1998. Available from http://outreach.lib.uic.edu/www/issues/issue3_1/noble.

Stross, Randall. "The New Mailbox U: Discarding Standards in Pursuit of a Buck." *U.S. News & World Report,* January 15, 2001.

"Top 25 Online Colleges of 2011." *The Best Colleges,* 2011. Available from http://www.thebestcolleges.org/top-online-schools.

Weiss, Stefanie. "Virtual Education 101." *Washington Post,* April 9, 2000.

HISTORY OF THE INTERNET AND WORLD WIDE WEB

The Internet has had a revolutionizing effect, not only on communications and computing, but also on broader areas of life such as economics, culture, language, and social relations. In that same time, however, the Internet and, subsequently, the World Wide Web, have undergone a number of permutations, and the intentions of its developers have not always coincided with the ways in which the technology has been realized. As the technology and its influence spread, of course, the designs of the original planners were diluted. From its origins as a military-based, Pentagon-funded networking architecture for experimental communications, the Internet flowered into perhaps the most sweeping revolution in the history of communications technology. The World Wide Web, meanwhile, grew from a vehicle designed to universalize the Internet and democratize electronically based information to a commercial juggernaut that transformed the way business is conducted.

THE PREHISTORY OF THE INTERNET

Although in the popular imagination the Internet is a feature of the 1990s, the earliest inklings of the possibilities of networked computers can be traced to the early 1960s. In 1962, J.C.R. Licklider at the Massachusetts Institute of Technology (MIT) first elucidated his dream of a "Galactic Network" connecting computers across the globe for the distribution and access of data and programs. Licklider went on to become the first director of the Defense Advanced Research Projects Agency (DARPA), an arm of the U.S. Department of Defense and the body that funded and coordinated the original research into what became the Internet.

Licklider's MIT colleagues Leonard Kleinrock and Lawrence G. Roberts performed the groundbreaking work toward the development of the Internet's architecture. First, Kleinrock published a revolutionary paper touting the plausibility of using packet switching rather than circuits for communications, thereby paving the way for the necessary computer networking. Roberts built on Kleinrock's theories to devise the first wide-area computing network, using a regular, circuit-based telephone line to allow computers in Massachusetts and California to communicate directly. While the computers were indeed able to run programs and exchange data, Roberts was convinced that Kleinrock's insistence on the superiority of packet switching was correct.

Having joined DARPA, Roberts in 1967 presented a paper outlining his vision for the original version of the Internet, known as ARPANET, the specifications of which were set by the following fall. Roberts's main position was that the network DARPA was building could be expanded and put to greater use once it was completed. Kleinrock relocated to the University of California, Los Angeles (UCLA) just in time for DARPA to send a proposal for the further development of his packet-switching ideas for the network DARPA was constructing. Kleinrock and a handful of other interested scholars at UCLA established the Network Measurement Center for the ARPANET project.

ARPANET's first host computer was set up at Kleinrock's Network Measurement Center at UCLA in 1969, and other nodes, at Stanford Research Institute (SRI), University of California, Santa Barbara (UCSB), and the University of Utah in Salt Lake City, were connected shortly afterward. As computers were added to ARPANET, the Network Working Group worked to devise a communication protocol that would enable different networks to talk to each other, resulting in the host-to-host Network Control Protocol (NCP), which was rolled out in 1970. Thus the Internet as it is known today began to bloom.

OPENING THE INTERNET

Still, for the first few years of its existence, ARPANET was largely unknown outside of the relatively esoteric group of technologists that was developing it. That changed in 1972, when Robert Kahn of Bolt Beranek and Newman (BBN), one of the chief figures in the development of the ARPANET architecture, organized a conference at the International Computer Communication Conference (ICCC), where ARPANET was first demonstrated publicly. That same year, the first major Internet application, called electronic mail, or e-mail, was introduced. Over the next decade, e-mail was the most widely used network application in existence.

The early years of ARPANET saw the network grow slowly, as nodes were gradually added, and the vast array of computers plugged into it demanded software and interface hardware so as to adequately interact with ARPANET. As ARPANET expanded into what is now referred to as the Internet, it was grounded on what is known as an open architecture network. In such an environment, other networks could connect to and interact with the Internet and all other networks to which it is connected, but the technology used to build each network could be decided by that network's provider and did not need to be dictated by any particular architecture. Packet switching, pioneered by Kleinrock, allowed for such architectural freedom to connect networks on a peer, rather than hierarchical, basis. In fact, open-architecture networking was originally referred to as "Internetting" when it was introduced to DARPA in 1972.

While this greatly expanded the uses of the Internet in its limited environment of the day, it resulted in the lack of a common user interface on the Internet. In fact, most of the early networks connected to the Internet were designed for a closed community of researchers and scholars, so the issue of cross-network capacity was a very low priority. For academics, military officials, and scientists, this was satisfactory on the whole as the Internet was geared toward very specialized users. It limited the overall availability of the Internet, however, in a manner that would not be remedied until the 1990s and the introduction of the World Wide Web.

For several years, the bulk of the research involving Internet communications, including work on the various networking and transmission logistical concerns, was funded primarily by the U.S. Department of Defense, and thus was primarily designed around and translated into military concerns. Network Control Protocol, however, proved limited in an open-architecture environment since it was dependent on the ARPANET network design for end-to-end reliability, and any transmission packets that were compromised could bring the protocol to an abrupt stop. To get multiple packet networks to communicate with each other regardless of the underlying networking technology, a common communication protocol was needed. The first effort toward this end was the work on the Transmission Control Protocol (TCP) by Vinton Cerf at the Stanford Research Institute and Robert Kahn at BBN. The design called for gateways, or routers, to connect networks to the Internet without calling for any network reconfiguration. After several years of research and design, the first TCP specification was published in December 1974. Just a few months later, DARPA transferred ARPANET as a fully operational Internet to the Defense Communications Agency (later renamed the Defense Information Systems Agency).

By the late 1970s, the U.S. military became interested in Internet technology not just as an experimental and theoretical tool, but as an actual, extant military communications system. As a result, the military began to use Internet communications protocols in packet radio systems and various ground-satellite stations in Europe. The transfer of voice messages highlighted complications in these radio-based networks and led to the development of a complementary Internet Protocol (IP), which was combined with TCP to produce the TCP/IP protocol suite. TCP/IP quickly emerged as the standard for all military Internet systems, and, by extension, the Internet itself.

Through the early 1980s, various Internet products consolidated into the TCP/IP protocol, setting the stage for the opening of commercial applications. In large part this was due to the National Science Foundation Net

(NSFNet) Initiative. This program, which was born of a network designed to link supercomputers together based on software designed by David Mills of the University of Delaware, and which was led by Dennis Jennings at the National Science Foundation (NSF), quickly generated supporting software and systems by IBM, MCI, and others to accommodate the quickly escalating networking demand. Thanks to the outgrowth of technologies stemming from NSFNet, the number of computers connected to the Internet jumped from only several hundred in 1983 to over 1.3 million in 1993, while the number of networks leapt from a tiny handful to over 10,000. By 1990, the NSFNet, in fact, had generated such a profound transformation in the Internet's backbone and reach that ARPANET itself was decommissioned.

Soon commercial e-mail carriers, already devising systems and software for use in intranets, began exploiting the possibilities of Internet-based e-mail; commercial Internet service providers came along in their wake, sprouting up from the original handful of networks brought to life under NSFNet. For several years, however, these services were still primarily geared toward researchers and businesses, those few groups that already had a need for and access to the Internet. The Internet as a household resource was still largely unheard of.

The rapid expansion of the Internet in the 1980s necessitated new methods of management such as the Domain Name System (DNS). In its earliest incarnations, users had to memorize numerical addresses to access the fairly limited number of host networks, but that became unfeasible as the number of connected networks expanded. With the proliferation of local area networks (LANs), Internet managers designed the DNS to create easily identifiable hierarchies of hosts to facilitate easy Internet navigation.

In the late 1980s and early 1990s, a series of policy initiatives, including a forum at the Harvard Kennedy School of Government on "The Commercialization and Privatization of the Internet" and a National Research Council committee report titled "Towards a National Research Network," paved the way for the next steps of Internet evolution, including the sponsorship by the U.S. government of high-speed computer networks that would serve as the backbone for the explosion of the information superhighway and e-commerce in the 1990s.

THE WORLD WIDE WEB

Perhaps the invention that most facilitated the growth of the Internet as a global information-sharing system is the World Wide Web. Unlike the Internet, however, the early design and development of the World Wide Web was primarily the work of just one person: Tim Berners-Lee. Working as a contract programmer at the Geneva, Switzerland-based Centre Européen de la Recherche Nucléaire (European Laboratory for Particle Physics, or CERN), Berners-Lee repeatedly proposed to develop a global interactive interface for use on the Internet so as to turn the fragmented and relatively exclusive Internet into a popular and seamless whole. After several rejections, Berners-Lee simply developed a prototype using the laboratory's phone book entries in 1989. Called Enquire Within Upon Everything, the prototype was designed to link and connect elements much in the way that the brain makes random connections and associations. Unlike the average database system, according to Berners-Lee, the Web was to be designed to make random associations between arbitrary objects in the files.

Just as the Internet evolved to ensure the greatest possible flexibility and interoperability, so the Web's original architectural design specifically minimized the degree of specification so as to minimize constraints on the user. In this way, the design could be modified and updated while leaving the basic architecture undisturbed. Thus, for instance, users could enter the existing File Transfer Protocol (FTP) in the address space and it would be as workable as the new Hypertext Transfer Protocol (HTTP). HTTP was the communications protocol that allowed the Web to transfer data to and from any computer connected to the Internet, and was designed as an improvement on the FTP standard in that it took advantage of the Web's capacity to read and translate intricate features.

The intermixing of these protocols and file formats was the key, for Berners-Lee, to ensuring the widest proliferation as well as the greatest durability of his creation. Not only would the Web in this way be able to evolve with changing systems and protocols, but the early adoption would be made smoother in that users could adopt the Web from whatever systems they were currently using as a parallel or supplementary system. Shortly after the successful demonstration of the phonebook prototype, the Internet community, still relatively esoteric, began experimenting with browser platforms for viewing the Web. One of the early successes was the Mosaic program written by Marc Andreessen, later the founder of Netscape.

Taking advantage of the Internet's gateways and bypassing centralized registries, Berners-Lee devised the uniform resource locators (URLs) that are the basis for Web addresses under the DNS. URLs were built to highlight the central power of the Web: that any link can connect to any other document or resource anywhere on the Internet, or in the "universe of information," as Berners-Lee put it. URLs are structured to identify the kind of space that is being accessed (for instance, by the prefixes "http:" or "ftp:") followed by the specific address within that information space.

The last piece of the WWW puzzle was the medium's lingua franca: Hypertext Markup Language (HTML), a language of codes, built on hypermedia principles dating back to the 1940s, that informed the browser how to interpret the files for the Web. By 1991, all the elements were in place, and the World Wide Web was released from Berners-Lee's laboratory to the public free of any charge.

COMMERCIALIZATION

Beginning in the mid-1990s, the World Wide Web helped propel the Internet to a new stage of mass consumption, and in the process both were radically transformed, as was the society that used them. The Internet and World Wide Web opened new fields of debate over social and cultural concerns, including the right to privacy, the protection of children from harmful or inappropriate materials, freedom of speech as it pertains to electronic networks, intellectual property, issues of social equality, the security of financial and personal data online, and a host of other issues.

As businesses grew increasingly interested in the Internet and the Web for their own strategies, the race to take advantage of the emerging e-commerce markets highlighted the needs of commercial interests in the Internet architecture, in Web- and e-mail-based security measures, and in business models structured on Internet communications and technology. In turn, businesses used these technologies as tools to enter and take advantage of new markets throughout the world, thus furthering the proliferation of the Internet and the globalization of the world's economies. In the process, the range of social and cultural concerns connected to the Web and the Internet were intensified.

By the mid-1990s, the Internet and the World Wide Web had evolved into critical components of the national—and international—infrastructure, components with which the rest of economic and social life were increasingly intertwined. As a result, the spate of questions, concerns, cautions, and enthusiasm about these technologies required careful negotiation to ensure that these forces served the good of everyone they affected. Several organizations sprouted up for just that purpose, including the World Wide Web Consortium and the Internet Society, which brought together diverse interests to attempt to oversee the development of these technologies within the context of the overall common good.

ADAPTATION

The Internet quickly became the home of business ventures, and by the mid-1990s a new industry had opened up: Internet providers, companies that specialized not only in providing Internet capabilities but in making available tools and software that the average user could use to access the Internet. It was, in fact, the age of the browser. Some browsers that began in popularity were doomed to obscurity within several years, such as Netscape, Opera, and the earliest major browser, Mosaic. But a number of browsers begun in the early days continued to develop and were still popular 20 years later, such as Internet Explorer, released for the first time in 1995. (By the early 2000s other popular browsers had been developed after years of experience in the market, and people also began to use Safari and Firefox.) The earliest browsers quickly began a browser war, and the market did not appear roomy enough for multiple browsers at that time, and Microsoft competed intensely with Netscape.

The year 1998 saw the appearance of Google. By this time, the Internet and e-commerce in general were in a highly hyped phase, with a large amount of positive activity and the introduction of myriad new businesses attempting to take advantage of the trend. The bursting of the tech bubble had not yet occurred, and online business thrived. Web developers worked to expand their abilities and usher in the Internet age. A variety of different languages and development structures that became standard were made in these years, such as XML, a newer standard for encoding documents. JavaScript was developed around the same time as the first major browsers, leading to Java programming abilities in general. Web cookies that sent information between Web sites and browsers and CSS, or cascading style sheets for Web site creation, were also developed during this period. Flash programming arose in 1997, and what businesses could use the Internet for became—increasingly—an open question.

COMMERCIAL CHANGES

By 1999, Internet Explorer had become the browser of choice, and the America Online (AOL) model of charging for services had fallen out of favor in the face of free services providers for Internet users. Google searches were up to 3 million each day, and by 2000 more than 70 million computers had been connected to the Internet, with international growth that in many cases was just beginning. Google searches, within a single year, had jumped up to 18 million. Unfortunately, the wave that online businesses were riding was about to crash.

The dot-com bust of 2000 and 2001, often referred to as the bursting of the tech bubble, was the result of misplaced and investor overexuberance. A large number of businesses obtained funding merely on speculation, and the market could not support such growth without actual viable business models. As a result, a vast number of Internet companies failed, tech stocks plummeted, and the market learned a valuable lesson about what sort of companies the Internet could sustain. Future attempts were planned and executed with much greater care, and investors began to learn how to spot sound online business strategies.

As the market began to recover in the early 2000s, a number of other important developments occurred. Digital sales, for example, became a viable industry, beginning with digital music and moving on to digital downloads for a variety of media. Internet speeds and download capabilities for the common user had diversified away from the dial-up option and reached a point where movies and games could be downloaded directly to computers. At the same time, digital piracy became an ongoing problem for Internet regulators.

The Internet Protocol language had gone through several iterations by this time. Throughout most of the 2000s, IPv4 was used for most data transfers. IPv6 was available by this time, but adopting required a massive switch to different data transfer capabilities, a move the market was not ready to consider until the early 2010s, when IPv6 became necessary to bolster the shrinking supply of IPv4 Web site addresses. Data also became much more malleable during this time. Tim Berners-Lee coined the term "Semantic Web" to refer to the rise of metadata, or data about data that is used within Web programming to collate and distribute information. The Semantic Web was seen as a new version of the World Wide Web, but one that operated in the background and was accessed only via machine, with data being linked by programs for the sake of efficiency although users never even saw it.

SOCIETY AND CONVERGENCE

By the 2010s, the Internet had become an accepted part of every industry and was used for a vast number of purposes by both businesses and individuals. Social media, in the form of social networking, blogs, microblogs, forums, and advanced search engines, were very common. Facebook and Flickr, both created in 2004, had become worldwide phenomena by 2011. Twitter, created in 2006, became the microblog of choice. Businesses and individuals began to choose online communication methods over traditional methods because of the enhanced ability for rich, two-way communication.

As the World Wide Web adopted more and more advancements that made displaying media easier, it started to take market share away from more traditional industries. The process was called convergence, an event where developments in one technology render another technology unnecessary. Convergence in wireless development was responsible for making PDAs (Personal Digital Assistant devices) unnecessary when a smartphone could do the same work. When videos could be easily stored on servers and shared online, the convergence trend began to eat away at the television and telephone industries. By 2010, online news consumers used between two and five Web sites per day to collect news instead of traditional newspapers.

By 2011, HTML5 was being adopted by many major online companies, including YouTube and Twitter. The latest iteration of HTML allowed for even more flexibility in arranging and displaying data, increasing the efficiency of Web sites. The third version of CSS was also adopted. By this time Google had released a browser of its own, Google Chrome, and the market was becoming increasingly complex and diverse. Increased growth was expected in China, India, Russia, Indonesia, and Brazil, which had the potential to double current Internet users between 2011 and 2015.

SEE ALSO *ARPAnet; Berners-Lee, Tim; Three Protocols, The; URL (Uniform Resource Locator); World Wide Web (WWW); World Wide Web Consortium (W3C).*

BIBLIOGRAPHY

Berners-Lee, Tim. "The World Wide Web: Past, Present, and Future." Cambridge, MA: World Wide Web Consortium, August 1996. Available from http://www.w3.org/People/Berners-Lee/1996/ppf.html.

Berners-Lee, Tim, and Mark Fischetti. *Weaving the Web: The Original Design and Ultimate Destiny of the World Wide Web by Its Inventor.* San Francisco, CA: HarperCollins, 1999.

Bryant, Martin. "20 Years Ago Today, the World Wide Web Opened to the Public." *The Next Web,* June 8, 2011. Available from http://thenextweb.com/insider/2011/08/06/20-years-ago-today-the-world-wide-web-opened-to-the-public.

Case, Steve. "Steven Case: The Complete History of the Internet's Boom, Bust Boom Cycle." *Business Insider,* January 14, 2011. Available from http://www.businessinsider.com/what-factors-led-to-the-bursting-of-the-internet-bubble-of-the-late-90s-2011-1.

Cerf, Vinton. "How the Internet Came to Be." In *The Online User's Encyclopedia,* edited by Bernard Aboba. Boston, MA: Addison-Wesley, 1993.

Curtis, Anthony R. "A Brief History of the World Wide Web." University of North Carolina at Pembroke, 2011. Available from http://www.uncp.edu/home/acurtis/Courses/ResourcesForCourses/WebHistory.html.

"Evolution of the Web." *Appspot,* 2011. Available from http://evolutionofweb.appspot.com.

Ghosh, Rahul. "New Possibilities with the Internet in 2011." *Technorait,* March 30, 2011. Available from http://technorati.com/blogging/article/new-possibilities-with-the-internet-in.

"The History of the Internet." *iTok Blog,* March 23, 2011. Available from http://www.itok.net/blog/index.php/2011/03/history-of-the-internet.

Internet Society (ISOC). "Histories of the Internet." Reston, VA: Internet Society, 2011. Available from http://www.isoc.org/internet/history/.

"IPv6 Marks the Next Chapter in the History of the Internet." *The Official Google Blog,* February 3, 2011. Available from http://googleblog.blogspot.com/2011/02/ipv6-marks-next-chapter-in-history-of.html.

HOME NETWORKING

Home networking is the connection of several electronic devices, such as personal computers (PCs) and printers, to a single network. Although proponents of the technology initially claimed that future home networks would link all sorts of appliances (like microwaves and refrigerators), most of the home networks in existence in 2011 comprised desktop computers, laptop computers, modems, audio/video equipment, gaming consoles, mobile devices, and printers. This type of technology allows home computer users with more than one PC to do things like share files between multiple machines, use a single Internet connection, and send documents from various PCs to a single printer.

In the late 1990s, many research firms predicted that home networking would become a billion-dollar market within a couple of years. For example, Dataquest Inc. forecasted $2 billion in U.S. home networking sales by 2002 and $4 billion in sales by 2004. However, the technology caught on less quickly than anticipated and sales had only reached $290 million by 2000. This changed dramatically during the 2000s due to the widespread acceptance and use of various technical standards, such as 802.11x, that were designed to aid in the creation of wireless home networks. Once 802.11x and other technologies expanded bandwidth, the home networking market began to cross into visual media and home entertainment industries, because one Internet connection could disseminate media-streaming services to devices in any room of the house. With these market entrants considered, the home networking market was estimated at $74 billion in 2009.

WI-FI

Since large bundles of cables snaking throughout a house was not a desired feature for many home owners, people were slow to adopt wired home networks. In contrast, wireless home networking products began to garner recognition in 2001. That year, EarthLink, a leading Internet service provider (ISP), began selling 2Wire home networking products, known as residential gateways, which allowed multiple PCs in a single home to share a DSL Internet connection. 2Wire's HomePortal 1000 allowed customers to create a home network using the Wi-Fi wireless standard. (Wireless connections were abbreviated to Wi-Fi, a wireless standard officially known as 802.11x.)

A number of 802.11x technologies were developed in the 2000s. Each was a particular technology whose standards were devised by the Institute of Electrical and Electronic Engineers (IEEE). 802.11b was the first frequency used to establish Internet connectivity throughout the home. It used a 2.4 GHz frequency and capped out at an 11 Mbps bandwidth. 802.11a allowed for a thicker bandwidth (54 Mbps), but it implemented a higher frequency, which was significantly hampered by walls and other barriers. 802.11g solved this problem by offering the same data delivery at the 2.4 GHz frequency originally used by 802.11b. 802.11n systems, which implemented both 5 GHz and 2.4 GHz at the same time, could reach speeds of up to 450 Mbps.

In terms of broadband connectivity and speed, the United States was a middle-of-the-pack performer in comparison to other developed nations. By 2011, many considered distribution of the Internet to be a contributor to economic growth, due to the increasing preponderance of e-commerce. Therefore, the mediocre performance of the United States, in terms of household penetration, average speed, and price for medium or large bandwidths, was an area of concern, especially considering that the United States had lost considerable ground over the preceding decade, prior to which it had been a top performer. One possible explanation for U.S. broadband lagging behind was because it relied on governmental policy established in the first half of the decade, which turned away from "open access" policies and toward privatization. Open access would entail making Internet infrastructure widely accessible. Under such policies, any company would be able to provide Internet access by sharing the established infrastructure without the significant upfront costs associated with laying down wires and towers. In theory, open access would increase competition between Internet providers, lowering costs of service and increasing innovations in the field.

A study spearheaded by Harvard University's Berkman Center for Internet & Society found a strong correlation between countries with open access policies and high-performance, cheap, and plentiful household broadband access. However, privatization of telecommunications infrastructure was not likely to be repealed in the 2010s.

SEE ALSO *Connectivity, Internet.*

BIBLIOGRAPHY

"Cisco's Plan to Pop Up in Your Home." *Fortune,* February 1, 1999.

Costello, Sam. "Earthlink Offers Home Networking to DSL Users." *Network World,* April 2, 2001.

"Home Networking: Broadcom Enters Home Networking Market; Broadcom Announces MediaShare Technology Providing More than 10 Times the Performance of Existing HomePNA Solutions." *EDGE: Work-Group Computing Report,* February 15, 1999.

"Household Networking Takes Up Residence." *Computer Dealer News,* January 15, 1999.

Lee, Kevin. "Researchers Develop 'Duplex' Wireless, Double Your Mobile Broadband Fun." *PCWorld,* September 7, 2011. Available from http://www.pcworld.com/article/239624/

researchers_develop_duplex_wireless_double_your_ mobile_ broadband_fun.html.

"Media Networking Shines Brightly in $74 Billion Home Networking Market." Scottsdale, AZ: ABI Research, April 6, 2009. Available from http://www.abiresearch.com/press/ 3175-Media+Networking+Shines+Brightly+in+$74 +Billion+ Home+Networking+Market.

"Next Generation Connectivity." Cambridge, MA: Berkman Center for Internet & Society at Harvard University, February 16, 2011. Available from http://cyber.law. harvard.edu/pubrelease/broadband/.

Wi-Fi Alliance. "Discover and Learn." Austin, TX, 2011. Available from http://www.wi-fi.org/discover_and_learn.php.

Wilson, Tracy V., and John Fuller. "How Home Networking Works." HowStuffWorks. Available from http://www.how stuffworks.com/home-network.htm.

HOOVER'S, INC.

Hoover's Inc., a subsidiary of Dun & Bradstreet (D&B), is an online business information resource and portal. Headquartered in Austin, Texas, Hoover's also offers information, including analytical information, through its blogs and index pages. The company also distributes information through third-party licensing and data feeds. The target audience includes business professionals as well as sales and marketing professionals in need of business and industry information and statistics.

Hoover's offers a wide range of business information, some of which is available for free and some to paid subscribers only. The site includes proprietary information developed by Hoover's as well as content from third-party providers. According to the Hoover's profile on its own Web site, the company had information on about 65 million entities and 85 million people as of early 2012.

The Hoover's Online site is organized into the following channels as of 2012: Companies, Directories, Industries, Resources, Products, IPO Central, Lead Builder, Hoover's Books, Hoover's API, and Hoover's Mobile. The site also features an easy-to-use site search where users can search for company names, personal names, and more. Additional links are provided at the home page for sales professionals, small-business users, marketing professionals, and researchers. The Web site also provides fast links for IPO Central, business advice and resources, videos, Webinars, and network sites.

HOOVER'S STRUCTURE

Hoover's core asset is its database of information on public and private companies and industry segments. Some of this information can be accessed for free. Premium subscribers have access to ConnectMail, list building solutions, The D&B Standard Marketing Prescreen Score, company hierarchies, First Research offerings (with up-to-date industry trends and information), alerts and notifications, Hoover's social media offerings, industry profiles, and more.

Hoover's other channels organize links and information targeted at individuals and companies looking for business-related information. Available links and content at the Company Directory channel include links to company details, grouped by sales, jobs, industry, and location. The IPO Central channel offers information about recent offering performance, filings, and upcoming events. The Lead Generation channel allows marketing and sales professionals to build lists of leads. In 2011, Hoover's updated this service, offering users a free preview as well as providing additional information about costs and record counts of each list before purchase. The service also allowed businesses to build a list and save it for later purchase. The Hoover's Books channel allows users to review and purchase Hoover's handbooks about businesses and industries.

In 2011, Hoover's signed an agreement with social media company LinkedIn Corporation that was designed to allow users of Hoover's business platform to enjoy LinkedIn functionality. Hoover's also offers a First Research product and mobile apps.

HOOVER'S HISTORY

The company that became Hoover's Inc. was established in 1990 as the Reference Press by entrepreneur Gary Hoover and former University of Chicago classmates Alta Campbell and Patrick Spain. The company's flagship publication was a reference directory called *Hoover's Handbook*. First published in 1991, the book contained profiles of more than 500 major corporations. It was aimed at general readers as well as professionals and was available in bookstores. When Gary Hoover left the company in 1992 to start a chain of travel superstores, Patrick Spain became CEO.

From the start the company was interested in exploring the electronic delivery of its informational database. Through a partnership with Sony, information from the *Hoover's Handbook* was made available in electronic form. In 1993, the company began licensing information from its database to America Online. In 1994, Time Warner, through its subsidiary Warner Books, took a significant minority position in the Reference Press and assumed responsibility for bookstore distribution of its titles. In 1995, the Reference Press launched Hoover's Online, a Web-based business reference service. By the end of 1996, the company had more than 20 online services and was on *Inc.* magazine's list of the 500 fastest-growing private companies. In August 1996, the Reference Press changed its name to Hoover's Inc., in recognition of the strong brand it had created. In November

1996, the company published *Cyberstocks: An Investor's Guide to Internet Companies* and launched a companion Web site that contained the full text of the book at no charge, along with other financial information and interactive services, including daily updates of the 100 stocks profiled in the book.

During 1997, the company gained two equity investors, Internet search engine InfoSeek and Media General, Inc., a provider of news, information, and entertainment services. Both companies gained seats on Hoover's board of directors. In 1998, Hoover's Online redesigned its site to create a portal that provided visitors with a variety of free, subscription, and personalized online services and databases. The focus of Hoover's portal was information about companies. By March 1998, the company's subscriber base had more than doubled over a six-month period. During 1998, the company partnered with Amazon.com to launch the Store at Hoover's, where visitors to Hoover's Online could purchase books, magazines, and CDs.

Hoover's Inc. went public on July 21, 1999, with an initial public offering that netted $42 million for the company. For its fiscal year ending March 31, 1999, Hoover's reported revenue of $9.2 million and a net loss of $2.2 million. During that year, Hoover's formed new strategic partnerships and alliances and expanded existing ones. It signed agreements with AltaVista Search Service and Reuters. The company also agreed to license some of its company information to CNBC.com and began coproducing exclusive editorial content for use at CNBC.com and on-air at CNBC. CNBC parent NBC purchased a minority interest in Hoover's, as did Knowledge Net Holdings and Nextera Enterprises. Hoover's also gained access to additional content through agreements with Media General Financial Services, Dow Jones & Co., and News Alert, Inc.

In 2003, after a few challenging years, the company was sold for $119 million to Dun & Bradstreet. In 2009, Hyune Hand became president of Hoover's, a position she retained as of late 2011.

SEE ALSO *Content Provider.*

BIBLIOGRAPHY

"Austin, Texas, Online Business Information Company to Take New CEO." *Knight-Ridder/Tribune Business News,* May 4, 2001.

Dun & Bradstreet (D&B). "D&B 2010 Annual Report." Short Hills, NJ, March 23, 2011. Available from http://files.shareholder.com/downloads/DNB/1356468713x0x453612/E95015D3-0AF0-40C6-8BE1-2B973026DB6C/148032_009_The_Dun_and_Bradstreet_Corporation_BMK1.pdf.

Dzinkowski, Ramona. "Creating New Revenue Streams at Hoover's Online." *Strategic Finance,*January 2001.

Hoover's Online. "About Hoover's." Austin, TX, 2011. Available from http://www.hoovers.com/about/100000489-1.html#.

"Hoover's Upgrades Online List Service for B2B." *BtoB,* August 4, 2011. Available fromhttp://www.btobonline.com/article/20110804/DIRECT0201/308049998/hoovers-upgrades-online-list-service-for-b-to-b.

"Internet Software and Services: Hoover's, Inc." *Bloomberg Business week,* August 13, 2011. Available from http://investing.businessweek.com/research/stocks/private/snapshot.asp?privcapId=9545.

Martin, Nicole. "Capitalizing on Content." *E Content,* May 2001.

Milliot, Jim. "Hoover's Has New Investor, Will Boost Online." *Publishers Weekly,* September 22, 1997.

Rivkin, Jacqueline. "Reaching the Business Book Buyer via the Mass Market." *Publishers Weekly,* January 11, 1991.

Tudor, Jan Davis. "Hoover's Online: Data Worth Paying For." *EContent,* December 1999.

Vonder Haar, Steven. "Web Portals Give Users the Business." *Inter@ctive Week,* September 13, 1999.

HTML (HYPERTEXT MARKUP LANGUAGE)

Hypertext markup language (HTML) is an authoring or presentation language (not a programming language) used for creating pages on the World Wide Web. The language consists of special codes or tags that determine a page's visible appearance when read by a Web browser. In addition to defining the overall structure and layout of a Web page, HTML also is used to denote links to other Web pages, the placement of graphics or pictures on a page and the appearance of text, including bold or italicized type and different fonts.

According to the National Center for Supercomputing Applications (NCSA), Tim Berners-Lee invented HTML at CERN, the European Laboratory for Particle Physics in Geneva. As of result of Berners-Lee's work, it became possible for entrepreneurs, small businesses, and large corporations to post information about their products and services onto the Internet in a visual format.

HTML PROTOCOLS AND VARIANTS

Among the protocols that have been developed in HTML are hypertext transfer protocol (HTTP) and secure hypertext transfer protocol (S-HTTP or HTTPS). HTTP is the standard Web page protocol, which presents information on the Web page to the user. It does not involve the transfer of data from user to website. HTTPS, on the other hand, is a secure delivery vehicle, which takes confidential information from the user, such as passwords and user names, encrypts the data, and then unencrypts the data after it has been successfully transferred to the Web site. HTTPS functions by using secure sockets layer (SSL) protocols to create and verify encryption codes. It differentiates senders and receivers from each other, establishing channels between the two. The protocol then leaves the encryption and decryption process to SSL.

HTML is closely related to another language called Standard Generalized Markup Language (SGML). In the early 2000s a subset of SGML known as Extensible Markup Language (XML) led to the development of XHTML, a hybrid language that combines HTML with XML. XHTML has powerful implications for e-commerce because the language's XML component allows users to share information in a universal, standard format without making the kinds of special arrangements required by Electronic Data Interchange (EDI), the protocol in which many large companies exchange electronic data with suppliers and other entities. According to *ABA Banking Journal,* "XML is a set of simple rules for converting the meaning of a document written in any software into a globally standardized format that any other software can understand." According to the journal, online banking pioneer Wells Fargo was among the first financial institutions to use XML.

By contrast, other spin-offs of HTML, such as HTML5, took more time for widespread, universal adoption. HTML5 was a simpler, more efficient set of protocols that allowed Web sites to present more complex data, such as high-resolution, three-dimensional images, and animations. Prior to HTML5, Web sites relied on graphics plug-ins, such as Flash Player, to present complex images. Due to HTM5's increased power, browsers chose to adopt HTML5 extremely quickly, but there were other problems. For one, the main browser companies/organizations (Apple, Mozilla, Google, and Microsoft) came into conflict over the markup language used to translate the code. Without a single markup language, the same Web site would look different, depending upon the browser that was accessing it. As a result, when Google posted a new Web site for the musical group, Arcade Fire, to demonstrate the power of HTML5, complete with cutting edge visuals and animations, only Google's browser, Chrome, could correctly interpret the site.

As a result of such incompatibilities, the Web was thrown into a brief state of confusion, as companies scuffled over the markup language to be adopted. The general manager of Internet Explorer, Dean Hachamovitch, pointed out to *TechCrunch* that the Internet was experiencing the same kind of fragmentation as it had during the browser wars of the late 1990s. By 2011, however, this brief, second flare-up of the browser wars was at an end. Meanwhile, Adobe's Flash team, realizing that it would not be able to compete with HTML5, prepared to specialize in online gaming. The company was given some extra time to adapt, as the World Wide Web Consortium (WC3) slated HTML5 to replace HTML as the Web standard in 2014.

SEE ALSO *Berners-Lee, Tim; Electronic Data Interchange (EDI); XML.*

BIBLIOGRAPHY

Blank, Christine. "Beating the Banner Ad." *American Demographics,* June 2000.

Clarke, Gavin. "Adobe Bets on Flash 11 to Fend Off HTML5 Invasion." *The Register,* September 21, 2011. Available from http://www.theregister.co.uk/2011/09/21/adobe_flash_11_uncertain_future.

Dotson, Jeremy. "HTTP vs. HTTPS." *Biztech,* June 2007. Available from http://www.biztechmagazine.com/article/2007/07/http-vs-https.

"HTML." *Tech Encyclopedia,* February 10, 2001. Available from www.techweb.com/encyclopedia.

"HTML." *Webopedia,* February 10, 2001. Available from http://www.webopedia.com/TERM/H/HTML.html.

Schonfeld, Erick. "In the Coming HTML5 Browser Wars, the Markup Should Remain the Same." *Tech Crunch,* September 2, 2010. Available from http://techcrunch.com/2010/09/02/html5-browser-wars/.

Schwartz, Matthew. "Spreading the Word on XHTML." *Computer World,* June 19, 2000.

Winder, Davey. "Is the Browser War Over?" *PC Pro,* July 16, 2010. Available from http://www.pcpro.co.uk/features/359542/is-the-browser-war-over.

I

IBM CORP.

International Business Machines (IBM) Corporation is the largest provider of computer products and services in the world. The company employs more than 420,000 people globally and generated almost $100 billion in sales in 2010. While IBM was initially a company that made computer hardware such as mainframes, by the 2010s it had expanded from this manufacturing base to include a massive variety of computer software products and information technology services.

EARLY HISTORY

In 1911, Charles R. Flint oversaw the formation of Computing-Tabulating-Recording Co. (C-T-R) by merging three companies: Hollerith's Tabulating Machine Co.; the Computing Scale Co. of America, established in 1901; and International Time Recording Co., founded in 1889. A manufacturer of industrial time recorders, scales, tabulating machines, and more, C-T-R formed the core of what would become International Business Machines (IBM). Clients included railroads, chemical companies, utilities, and life insurance companies. Based in New York, the new firm employed 1,300 workers.

Flint hired National Cash Register Co. executive Thomas J. Watson, Sr., to run C-T-R as general manager in 1914. He laid the groundwork for what would become a key factor in IBM's long-term success—excellent customer service. Watson also focused on fostering employee loyalty by putting in place programs that offered rewards for meeting sales goals and by hosting various events for the families of employees. He was appointed president in 1915. That year, at the firm's first sales convention, Watson began to recognize that C-T-R's tabulating machines were its most promising products. He shifted focus from clocks and scales to tabulators and other basic office gadgets.

The firm launched an electric synchronized time clock system, which was quickly followed by the release of a printing tabulator and an electric accounting machine in 1920. C-T-R bought Chicago, Illinois-based Ticketograph Co. in 1921. In February 1924, C-T-R changed its name to International Business Machines Corp. New product releases included the Carroll Rotary Press, which produced punched cards at a high rate of speed; a self-regulating time clock system; and a horizontal sorting machine.

Although the stock market crash of 1929 left many businesses floundering, IBM was able to pay a 5% stock dividend. In fact, throughout the Great Depression, IBM hired new employees and continued growing operations and building inventory. In 1931, the firm launched its 400 series alphabetical accounting machines and 600 series calculating machines.

The firm faced its first legal battle in 1932 when the U.S. Justice Department filed an antitrust suit against IBM after finding that its cross-licensing agreement with rival Remington Rand—a deal that was put in place in the 1910s—was anticompetitive. Four years later, after determining that IBM held 85% of the U.S. keypunch, tabulating, and accounting equipment markets, the Supreme Court ordered IBM to nullify its restrictive agreements.

The Social Security Act of 1935 offered an unprecedented opportunity to IBM as the government needed calculating machines that could maintain employment records for more than 26 million citizens. Since IBM had bolstered its inventory throughout the Depression, it was able to fulfill the landmark contract for more than 400 accounting machines and 1,200 keypunchers. The firm continued making new product releases, including its first successful electric typewriter and a proof machine to clear bank checks.

In 1936, IBM became one of the first U.S. companies to offer employees paid holidays and vacations. That year, the firm released a collator and a test-scoring machine. Employees exceeded more than 10,000. By the start of World War II, IBM was posting earnings in excess of $9 million, or roughly one-quarter of sales. With revenues nearing the $50 million mark, IBM had become the leading office machine maker in the United States. Analysts pointed to three major practices that enhanced IBM's performance: its policy of leasing its machines to clients; its focus on large-scale, customized systems; and its cross-licensing deals with rivals.

MOVE TO COMPUTING

It was during the World War II years that IBM made its first move toward computing. In 1944, in conjunction with Harvard University, IBM created the Automatic Sequence Controlled Calculator, the first large-scale device that could process lengthy calculations. Over eight feet tall, the five-ton machine, known as Mark I, housed nearly 500 miles of wire and 765,000 parts.

In 1946, IBM introduced its first small, electronic calculator, known as the 603 Multiplier, and pocket-sized braille writing devices. The following year, IBM introduced its Selective Sequence Electronic Calculator, its first large-scale digitized calculator. The Card-Programmed Electronic Calculator, unveiled in 1949, was the firm's first product built exclusively for computing centers. The 407 Accounting Machine and the IBM Model A "Executive" Electric Typewriter were also shipped that year.

Thomas Watson, Jr., took over as IBM president in 1952. Believing IBM should focus its efforts on computers, Watson launched a large-scale research program with the goal of bypassing competitors like Remington Rand. The U.S. Justice Department filed its second antitrust suit against IBM the same year; the litigation eventually resulted in a consent decree between IBM and the government. Shortly thereafter, the firm launched a computer designed for scientific calculations, the IBM 701. The vacuum tubes used in the 701 were smaller and easier to replace than the switches used in earlier machines. Product introductions in 1953 included the IBM 702, the 650, and the Model A Toll Biller.

The IBM 705 machine, launched in 1955, was the firm's first general purpose business computer; its success helped to oust Remington Rand from its first-place spot in the new computer market. In 1958, Control Data and Sperry Rand launched computers using new transistor technology in place of vacuum tubes. As a result, IBM began working on the IBM 7090, a transistor-based machine that could perform nearly 230,000 calculations per second. IBM also divested its time equipment operations. The following year, IBM created its Advanced Systems Development unit to experiment in emerging markets.

Thomas J. Watson, Jr., took over as chairman of the board in 1961, and Albert L. Williams was appointed president. In April 1964, IBM introduced the System/360, which used software and peripheral equipment compatible with each of the five models in IBM's line of computers. This interchangeability was a new concept in the computer industry, and it proved to be one of IBM's most important moves. In 1965, the firm used a computer-based communications network to connect its U.S. and European engineering, manufacturing, and administrative facilities to coordinate work on System/360.

Throughout the 1970s, the firm successfully defended itself against antitrust cases by Xerox Corp., Memorex, Transamerica, and others. In 1979, the field engineering division began offering 24-hour telephone assistance for customers with software problems. The first IBM retail shops, called IBM Product Centers, opened in London and Buenos Aires.

In 1981, IBM changed its marketing practices to allow marketing teams to sell and distribute an entire product line to clients. John R. Opel took over as CEO. The firm introduced its landmark IBM Personal Computer (PC), which helped to launch the PC revolution, in August of that year. The machine was the firm's smallest and least expensive computer system to date. It used a processor chip from Intel Corp. and the DOS operating system of Microsoft Corp.

To sell its PCs, IBM began authorizing retailers like Sears, Roebuck & Co. and Computerland. The firm also expanded its sales channels to include manufacturers who integrated IBM products into their systems. In 1984, dealer outlets across the globe totaled 10,000. Sales reached $46 billion, with net income growing to $6.6 billion.

THE PC REVOLUTION

John F. Akers took over as CEO in 1985. After several decades of considerable growth, the firm faced a slowdown in both earnings and sales. One factor in the firm's plateau was stiff competition from rivals like Compaq Computer Corp., which was able to develop its own IBM-compatible PC. In fact, makers of these IBM "clones" were able to outsell IBM in the retail PC market. In 1985, IBM developed the token-ring local area network (LAN), which allowed employees working at desktop PCs to share files and peripheral equipment like printers with other desktop PC users. Ironically, the PC revolution that IBM had played a major role in sparking also eventually forced the computing giant to reinvent itself. Used to selling large-scale systems to businesses, IBM was ill prepared to target the fastest- growing segment of the burgeoning PC market: individual consumers. By the end of the decade, IBM had made plans to cut thousands of jobs through attrition and take a $2.3 billion charge against earnings for restructuring.

Although the firm spent the early part of the 1990s pursuing new markets and forging joint product development agreements with other firms, it continued to flounder. The accelerating rate of technological advancements in the data processing industry had eroded IBM's dominant position, which depended on businesses using very large and expensive mainframes designed essentially for number crunching. As increasingly powerful semiconductor chips allowed for smaller computers able to handle a broader range of functions, minicomputers, microcomputers, and work stations had undercut the value of huge mainframes.

Believing that IBM needed a major overhaul to best respond to these market changes, Akers announced his intention to divide IBM into nine semi-autonomous divisions, each accountable for its own corporate decisions and performance. In 1992, IBM launched its first laptop computer. Losses reached $8 billion the following year.

SHIFT TO E-BUSINESS SERVICES

RJR Holdings executive Louis V. Gerstner, Jr., was hired to take over as CEO and chairman on April 1, 1993. He canceled Akers's plan to divide IBM into separate entities, believing that the firm's ability to offer comprehensive business solutions to clients would prove beneficial in the long run. He also began reining in IBM's research and development spending, which had reached $6 billion by 1992. In June 1995, IBM bought Lotus Development Corp., hoping to strengthen its foothold in the computer software market and use the Lotus Notes messaging software to offer integrated e-mail, data processing, and Internet services to clients. The firm also folded its software operations into a single unit to simplify purchasing and support services for customers. Sales that year totaled $71 billion. In 1996, IBM added network software maker Tivoli Systems Inc. to its holdings.

By mid-1997, services had become the fastest-growing segment of IBM's operations. The firm began touting itself as an e-business products and services provider. In 1998, IBM increased its advertising budget by 21%, pushing its e-business servers, software, hardware, technology, and services in an effort to target business managers expected to use the Internet to streamline processes and improve profitiability. IBM's first e-Business Innovation Center was launched in Santa Monica, California, in January 2000 with 16 employees. Central to the firm's e-business services was its WebSphere server software, which IBM used to support the e-commerce initiatives, including retail Web sites, of clients.

Rather than targeting dot-com upstarts, as many e-business service providers had done, IBM peddled its services to traditional businesses. As a result, when the dot-com fallout in 2000 left many in the e-business services industry floundering, IBM continued to grow. However, trends in the market and strategic decisions within the company began to signal major changes for the corporation as it began to adapt to the needs of the new computer market.

BUSINESS DEVELOPMENT AND CHANGES

By 2001, IBM was producing the first major models of its eServer line, UNIX servers that were designed for a variety of purposes but especially focused on small business and organizational use. The eServers could be connected together to create computers with exponentially greater processing power. IBM also released products in its monitor and ThinkPad laptop lines, but this old business model was about to change.

By 2002, Samuel J. Palmisano had become CEO, president, and chairman of IBM. Under his direction, the corporation led the world in the creation of the most U.S. patents of any entity. While the 20 millionth ThinkPad was sold in 2003, Palmisano was more interested in innovation and the unique prospective of partnerships with other industries around the world. While the company continued to update and sell its eServer line, it also began to work on additional projects, like the 2003 IBM On Demand Community, an effort to sustain corporate philanthropy by providing businesses with software to aid volunteer and donation efforts across the world.

Then, in 2005, the corporation went through a drastic permanent change. Competition in the consumer market had become too intense for IBM to maintain acceptable levels of profitability. The solution was to cut consumer products from the core business model of the company, and by 2005 IBM had completed a deal to sell its computer product lines, including the ThinkPad line, to Lenovo, an electronics company based in Hong Kong. IBM focused on producing processor components for the manufacturing industry while keeping business-oriented lines such as its data servers active. In 2006, the company launched a z9 Business Class mainframe, sporting a starting price of $100,000, and focused on automated service capabilities with room for scalability and security additions for growing businesses.

By 2008, IBM had repositioned itself fully as a producer of middleware and as a provider of the software and data intelligence necessary for end products and services but not directly connected to the consumer market. Between 2000 and 2008 IBM acquired 50 smaller software companies. In 2008, it added Telelogic and Cognos to the list. Along with its new focus on data management and software capabilities, the company began to focus even more on innovation and new projects.

The results could soon be seen in a variety of industries. IBM advocated inventory management systems and new scanning technologies to track products through a store more efficiently and automate related ordering procedures. The corporation always had a connection to the health care industry with its creation of the heart-lung bypass machine and other designs. It followed these up by producing lasers for Lasik eye surgery and creating software used for drug design in the pharmaceutical industry, as well as pioneering DNA transistor chips and biological computing fields.

INNOVATIONS

In 2011, IBM celebrated its official centennial. By then, IBM was continuing its habit of innovation with several projects. One of the most notable was the creation of the Watson supercomputer, which beat the best *Jeopardy* game show players in the world. IBM immediately aimed for a practical application with a contract with WellPoint, which began using the supercomputer to help doctors diagnose patients and create treatment plans through a combination of expert systems, data management, and data transfer.

In May 2011, IBM and ETH Zurich, a European science university, opened the new Binnig and Rohrer Nanotechnology Center, located on the IBM campus in Zurich. The goal was to create a center to research nanoelectromechanical systems, organic electronics, and carbon-based devices. IBM planned to use the center as a new source of innovation for future markets, including the growth of fields still in their infancy.

SEE ALSO *E-commerce Solutions; History of the Internet and World Wide Web.*

BIBLIOGRAPHY

Bartholomew, Doug. "Can It Weather the Storm?" *Industry Week,* March 19, 2001.

Foley, Mary Jo. "Second Chance for IBM?" *Datamation,* July 1996.

Frook, John Evan. "Big Blue Boosts Ad Spending 21% to Spread E-business Message to the Web-Challenged." *Business Marketing,* December 1, 1999.

———. "IBM Pushes Product into Whole New Sphere." *B to B,* February 5, 2001.

IBM Corp. "Our History of Progress." Armonk, New York, 2011. Available from http://www-03.ibm.com/ibm/history/.

———. "IBM and ETH Zurich Open Collaborative Nanotechnology Center." Armonk, NY, May 17, 2011. Available from http://www-03.ibm.com/press/us/en/pressrelease/34539.wss.

———. "IBM Archives: 2000s." Armonk, NY, 2011. Available from http://www-03.ibm.com/ibm/history/history/decade_2000.html.

"IBM Turns 100: Marks Numerous Contributions to Healthcare." *eHealthNews,* June 16, 2011. Available from http://www.ehealthnews.eu/ibm/2659-ibm-turns-100-marks-numerous-contributions-to-healthcare.

Ibold, Hans. "IBM's Internet Arm Grows Despite Market Downturn." *Los Angeles Business Journal,* January 29, 2001.

"International Business Machines Corp." In *Notable Corporate Chronologies.* Farmington Hills, MI: Gale Group, 1999.

Lohr, Steve. "IBM Reports Strong Second-Quarter Earnings." *New York Times,* July 18, 2011. Available from http://www.nytimes.com/2011/07/19/technology/ibm-reports-strong-second-quarter-earnings.html?_r=1&ref=internationalbusinessmachines.

Mand, Adrienne. "All About E: New IBM Site Targets E-business Market." *MEDIAWEEK,* February 15, 1999.

Moschella, David. "IBM: Your One-Stop E-commerce Shop?" *Computerworld,* October 27, 1997.

Nusca, Andrew. "IBM at 100: 15 Inflection Points in History." *ZD Net,* June 16, 2011. Available from http://www.zdnet.com/blog/btl/ibm-at-100-15-inflection-points-in-history/50486.

Smith, Rich. "IBM to the ER–Stat!" *Motley Fool,* September 13, 2011. Available from http://www.fool.com/investing/general/2011/09/13/ibm-to-the-er-stat.aspx.

Songini, Mare. "IBM Rolling Out New E-commerce Software." *Network World,* January 31, 2000.

Thackray, John. "IBM Act II: Can Lou Really Execute?" *Electronic Business,* July 1998.

ICANN (INTERNET CORPORATION FOR ASSIGNED NAMES AND NUMBERS)

ICANN (Internet Corporation for Assigned Names and Numbers) oversees the distribution of Internet domain names, or site addresses, and other identifiers that distinguish one Internet site from another. The nonprofit entity handles the assignment of IP addresses, which identify computers that are connected to a TCP/IP network; port numbers, which identify the type of port being used to ensure that data is connected to the proper service; and other protocol parameters that allow the Internet to operate as it does. While ICANN is a nonprofit organization it does operate in many ways like a business, paying its top executives salaries commensurate with those of private enterprise, as well as generating enough revenues to pay its operating costs without outside contributions. In 2010, the organization posted $65 million in revenues and claimed $64 million in total assets.

As mandated by the U.S. Department of Commerce, ICANN was founded in 1998 by Dr. Jon Postel as a private, nonprofit association to handle Internet addressing policies and procedures. The growing number of Web sites, particularly those engaged in commerce, had resulted in a number of skirmishes between domain name holders. Incorporated in the United States, ICANN was the end result of an effort launched in July 1997 by the Clinton administration to facilitate the formulation of standard international policy regarding domain name assignation and dispute resolution procedures. ICANN supplanted the governmentally operated IANA (Internet Assigned Numbers Authority), which was established by the Internet Society and Federal Network Council to handle the assignment of domain names and other Internet protocol parameters.

ICANN was also established to eliminate the monopoly on domain name registration held by Network Solutions Inc. (NSI), the first private organization to register domain names. Founded in 1979, NSI began charging a fee for the service in 1995. VeriSign bought NSI in March 2000, and took over NSI's joint business of both selling domain names and controlling the registries, or master lists, of .com, .org, and .net addresses. Once established, ICANN implemented a number of strategies to take market share from VeriSign. To start, ICANN oversaw production of a number of new generic top-level domain (gTLD) extensions, such as .info, .biz, and country code extensions. In addition, a number of lawsuits arose between the two organizations, as ICANN accused VeriSign of taking advantage of its .com monopoly, while VeriSign pointed fingers at the earnings of ICANN executives. By 2011, VeriSign's .com and .net extensions accounted for 110 million top-level domains, representing over half of the total domains on the Internet. However, according to a VeriSign report, growth of registrations using .com and .net extensions was below average, indicating a reduction of market control in the future.

MORE TOP-LEVEL DOMAINS

ICANN also released a plan to create private extensions in 2012. For example, companies such as Burger King could register the gTLD, .kingofburgers. Verizon could register the extension .verizon. Private extensions were slated to cost $185,000, with an annual upkeep of $25,000 and additional costs for start-up fees, and so forth. Contested extensions, such as .money, would be auctioned to the highest bidder.

DotBrand, a company that was initiated to consult with businesses regarding the lengthy application process for private gTLDs, estimated that between 300 and 3,000 businesses were interested in applying for their own extensions. DotBrand's CEO Ben Crawford pointed out to *ITP.net* that businesses that owned their extensions would be given full control of all domain names registered under their private extension, which would entail providing employees or franchises Web sites of their own with the company extension. With a private extension, a company would also have the right to take back the employee/franchise's Web site, should a dispute occur, regaining control of all online traffic. This was a contrast to registrants of the .com gTLD, who could not retain control of IP addresses. Franchises often purchased their own IP addresses. Not only were ICANN's revenues likely to increase substantially, VeriSign's market control was likely to slip.

SEE ALSO *Cybersquatting; Domain Name; Internet Society (ISOC); URL (Uniform Resource Locator).*

BIBLIOGRAPHY

"Domain Strain; Internet Governance; ICANN's Unwelcome Rival." *Economist,* March 10, 2001.

Enzer, Georgina. "DotBrand Opens in UAE." *ITP.net,* September 21, 2011. Available from http://www.itp.net/586306-dotbrand-opens-in-uae.

"ICANN." In *Techencyclopedia.* Point Pleasant, PA: Computer Language Co., 2001. Available from http://www.techweb.com/encyclopedia.

"ICANN." In *Webopedia.* Darien, CT: Internet.com, 2001. Available from http://www.webopedia.com/TERM/I/ICANN.html.

"Icann's Latest Gaffe." *Computer Weekly,* April 5, 2001.

Internet Corporation for Assigned Names and Numbers (ICANN). "About ICANN." Marina del Rey, CA, 2001. Available from http://www.icann.org/en/about.

———. "Annual Report 2010." Marina del Rey, CA, June 10, 2011. Available from http://www.icann.org/en/annualreport.

———. "ICANN's Major Agreements and Related Reports." Marina del Rey, CA, June 10, 2011. Available from http://www.icann.org/en/general/agreements.htm.

VeriSign. "Domain Name Industry Brief." Mountain View, CA, August 2011. Available from http://www.verisigninc.com/en_US/why-verisign/research-trends/domain-name-industry-brief/index.xhtml.

INCUBATORS, E-COMMERCE

Incubators are the nurseries in which Internet start-ups can develop their business plans, products, services, and infrastructures, secured with plenty of financial capital, physical space, and on-hand expertise. In short, incubators are companies in business to support and bring to life new companies, often dot-coms.

HOW INCUBATORS WORK

Even before start-up entrepreneurs are ready to seek out a first round of venture capital, they need the time and resources to develop their businesses into models that venture capitalists will find attractive. This is especially true for companies seeking to attain venture capital from the leading VC funds, which typically gravitate toward larger projects and have less time for seed investment for the initial development stage. Incubators thus saw a market niche in the business development market to provide an economy of scale unavailable to early-stage companies. Business acceleration is their line of work, in that they take a concept under their wings and nurture it through its early growth period and turn it into a living company. They exchange their initial capital investment and expertise for equity in the start-up company.

Incubators are full-service company accelerators, offering everything from finance capital and management expertise to marketing analysis and legal advice. They tend to provide their e-commerce companies with office space, ample facilities and infrastructure, and recruitment services so as to attract executives capable of making the business stand on its own. Typically, incubator firms maintain their own staff to comb over the companies' business plans and implement Web sites and technological infrastructure, while at the same time seeking out venture capital funding and creating equity pools for each client. Once the companies are prepared to stand on their own, they are turned loose to generate their own later-stage venture capital and move toward an initial public offering (IPO). Incubators generate their own profits primarily by reaping returns on their initial investment, as the formerly incubating firm grows and its stock price soars, the value of the incubator's original stake grows as well.

Incubators vary considerably in the degree of control they exercise over their incubating companies. Some incubators concentrate primarily on sheer volume, and therefore have less time and resources to devote to the development of their firms. Others, however, exercise extensive authority over the direction of the companies' development, since the incubator's success depends on the eventual success of their companies and because bringing start-ups to life is, after all, the incubator's area of expertise. In general, this is the main feature distinguishing incubators from venture capitalists. While some VC firms take an active role in guiding a company's development, incubators' activities often border on cofounding firms, and even the most hands-off incubators have more direct participation in the company's early gestation and growth than do venture capitalists.

Successful incubators require more than just a thick wallet and high-powered connections, a fact many incubators in the early 2000s discovered to their dismay. In addition to ample capital, for an incubator to truly generate a sustainable business model, it must be able to provide the kind of hands-on support that will generate excitement about the product or service the business is offering. It also must be able to put the firm directly into contact with its potential customer base. Most importantly, the business must have a long-term plan for profitability and a route toward repaying its benefactor's initial investments. This seemingly obvious rule was often lost during the height of dot-com mania in the 1990s and early 2000s, which had some enthusiasts insisting that the laws of business were forever changed by the new economy.

INCUBATORS' RAPID RISE AND FALL, AND BEYOND

The incubator concept was largely popularized, according to *Fortune,* in 1996, when Bill Gross founded the incubator firm Idealab, which went on to become one of the leading incubators through the dot-com craze. Idealab claimed Internet firms like eToys, NetZero, and GoTo.com as alumnae of its incubation. Another incubator called CMGI quickly emerged as Idealab's major rival, and between them those two companies defined the basic incubator paradigm that others adopted. For a while, in the thick of the excitement over the new economy, and Internet start-ups in particular, the incubator concept was hailed by many dot-com enthusiasts as a central innovation for company creation in the Internet age. The result was an extremely rapid pace of company development at incubators such as Idealab, where ideas were transformed into viable start-ups at a remarkable pace, and in great quantity.

Through the Internet market heyday of the late 1990s, incubators were all the rage, and new ones cropped up at an astonishing rate. Even major venture capital firms set up their own incubator operations or partnered with existing incubators, recognizing that many of the dot-com start-ups they wished to back required a good deal more hand holding than they were used to providing. Other businesses outside of the traditional equity-funding field also took advantage of the emerging field to spin off incubator outfits. These organizations included the likes of Andersen Consulting, Dell Computer, Hewlett-Packard, Panasonic, IBM, and even a number of business schools at universities such as the University of North Carolina and the University of California, Berkeley.

After the dot-com boom fizzled in the early 2000s, many skeptics eyed incubators suspiciously, seeing them as among the more garish excesses of the dot-com craze. Indeed, following the bust of the technology stock market beginning in March 2000, incubators rapidly disappeared as investors rushed to liquidate their capital investments. Thus, by 2001 the incubator model had largely fallen out of favor, with few investors ready to sink money into risky start-ups following the drubbing many took at the tail end of the dot-com craze, and with the U.S. economy slowing considerably.

The sudden crash of the incubator sector in the early 2000s partly mirrored, and was directly related to, many of the features that led to the abrupt shift in fortune for the Internet industry in general. With investors pouring money into Internet stocks and valuations soaring through the roof, many incubators became convinced that their time was at hand, and that just about any Internet idea could generate enormous returns. As a result, they tended to go overboard by financing shaky ideas and accumulating far too many start-up hopefuls under their umbrellas. Once the tech market began to falter, incubators suddenly found themselves with far too many companies to incubate, and realized that they had invested a great deal of money that would never be seen again. These realities scared investors away from the incubators themselves. Ultimately, once the Internet industry fell to earth, there were too few good ideas to sustain the incubators and their bloated portfolios.

Like the Internet market in general, the success enjoyed by many incubators in the late 1990s encouraged hordes of imitators to join the field. Not only were these imitators ill-equipped for the business, they also contributed to a market glut that demanded a shakeout. In October 2000, *Business Week* reported that less than one-third of all incubators had managed to turn out even one company, while just under half nursed a company that had proved attractive enough to generate financing from outside the incubator itself.

By fall 2000, just before the industry shakeout really took hold, there were some 350 incubators growing at least ten businesses under their shell, according to a study by Harvard Business School. The primary survival method for the bulk of these firms was to attempt to merge their struggling companies—especially those in which they had invested substantial resources—with already successful companies. Another strategy was to shut down less promising start-ups and concentrate their portfolios on those companies with the most thoroughly developed and viable business plans.

However, this did not mean that incubators were creatures of the exuberant 1990s, on their way to extinction. Many investors with a more sober-minded analysis of the potential of Internet-based companies, and typically with more thoroughly devised business plans, still clung to the idea of providing breathing room for companies at the seed stage as a valuable and profitable venture.

THE REINVENTION OF INCUBATORS

By 2005, many assumed that incubators were gone. In fact, the National Business Incubation Association estimated that by 2005 more than one in four incubators in the United States had closed. About 1,100 remained open across the country, but many changed their model and became virtual incubators. Unlike traditional incubators, virtual business incubators did not rely on the physical presence of shareholders and business leaders. Instead, the incubators offered mentoring and a host of business services for entrepreneurs across local and state boundaries. Virtual incubators had low overhead and were able to secure government funding in the 2000s since they promoted business growth and employment growth. For entrepreneurs, virtual incubators offered important services and help at low cost.

In addition to these changes, incubators after 2005 welcomed many types of businesses, rather than just focusing on dot-coms. Incubators such as Idea Village, the Mason Enterprise Center, and the Colorado Springs Technology Incubator made it easier for entrepreneurs to join, when compared to the incubators of the 1990s.

According to the National Business Incubation Association, by October 2006, there were more than 1,115 business incubators in the United States, 191 in Mexico, and 120 in Canada. That year, the National Business Incubation Association reported that there were more than 7,000 incubators globally. In North America, about 95% were nonprofit organizations. Most incubators—54%—worked with entrepreneurs across industries while 39% focused on helping technology companies, and 4% focused on other niche industries.

One trend in the 2010s was the presence of boutique start-up incubators and accelerators. These incubators included companies such as TechStars. The main feature of boutique incubators was that they focused on one type of business and created networks of assistance to help those businesses. These incubators tended to give dedicated support to a smaller number of businesses, to ensure that these businesses had all the resources needed for success.

In 2011, there was a growing interest in incubators as a possible way to improve the U.S. economy. For example, the incubator One Million by One Million was established to help one million entrepreneurs reach $1 million in annual profits by 2020. The stated aim of One Million by One Million was to create ten million jobs internationally and to contribute a trillion dollars to the world economy.

SEE ALSO *Angel Investors; Financing, Securing; Start-Ups.*

BIBLIOGRAPHY

Adkins, Dinah. "What Are the New Seed or Venture Accelerators?" Athens, OH: National Business Incubation Association, June 2011. Available from http://www.nbia.org/resource_library/review_archive/0611_01a.php.

Christopher, Alistair. "Incubators Lose Favor, Some Still See Potential." *Venture Capital Journal,* May 1, 2001.

Dahl, Darren. "Percolating Profits: A New Generation of 'Virtual' Business Incubators Is Jump-Starting Start-Ups

Nationwide." *Inc.,* February 1, 2005. Available from http://www.inc.com/magazine/20050201/getting-started.html.

"FAQ." One Million by One Million, 2011. Available from http://1m1m.sramanamitra.com/what-to-expect-from-the-premium-program/faq.

Guglielmo, Connie. "Bringing Up Baby." *Upside,* October 2000.

Kolle, Claudine. "Wanted: Fresh Ideas." *Asian Business,* January 2001.

McCarty, Brad. "Boutique Startup Accelerators: Natural Progression, or Impending Danger?" *The Next Web,* August 21, 2011. Available from http://thenextweb.com/insider/2011/08/21/boutique-startup-accelerators-natural-progression-or-impending-danger.

National Business Incubation Association. "Resource Library." Athens, OH, 2011. Available from http://www.nbia.org/resource_library/faq/index.php#3.

Nicolle, Lindsay. "Nurtural Selection." *Director,* November 2000.

Nocera, Joseph. "Bill Gross Blew Through $800 Million in 8 Months (and He's Got Nothing to Show for It). Why Is He Still Smiling?" *Fortune,* March 5, 2001.

Sanborn, Stephanie. "Incubators Endure." *InfoWorld,* December 18, 2000.

Vizard, Michael, and Eugene Grygo. "Start-Up Incubator Firms Pulling the Plug." *InfoWorld,* October 30, 2000.

Weisul, Kimberly. "Incubators Lay an Egg." *Business Week,* October 9, 2000.

INDEPENDENT SALES ORGANIZATION (ISO)

Since the overwhelming majority of e-commerce transactions involve credit cards, the ability to accept credit cards as a form of payment is essential for e-commerce proprietors (PayPal and other alternate forms of payment notwithstanding). In order to obtain this capability, merchants had to apply for special merchant accounts with acquiring banks. After such an account was established, acquiring banks accepted funds from card-holding consumers on behalf of the merchant. Although a number of different steps and variables were involved in this process, this essentially involved monies being transferred (from the bank that issued the credit card to the consumer) to the acquiring bank, and ultimately to the merchant.

For good reason, acquiring banks are selective about the businesses to which they provide merchant accounts. Some kinds of businesses—such as online wagering or adult entertainment sites and those that are small, home-based, or not yet established—are more prone to risk and credit-card fraud than others. For these kinds of businesses, obtaining merchant accounts directly from acquiring banks can be difficult. Independent sales organizations (ISOs) are third-party organizations that partner with acquiring banks to find, open, and manage merchant accounts on behalf of such businesses in exchange for a higher fee, or for a percentage of the merchant's sales. ISOs also are called merchant service providers (MSPs) when they offer financial transaction processing services. ISOs are able to offer merchant accounts to riskier merchants, and charge higher fees, because they do not fall under the same laws and regulations that actual banks do. Along with the acquiring banks they work with, ISOs also assume much of the liability and risk that comes with this service.

AuctionWatch explained that in the early 2000s, merchant account industry sources indicated ISOs and MSPs were responsible for opening roughly 80% of all merchant accounts, with banks accounting for the remainder. Although the exact number of ISOs and MSPs was hard to come by due to lack of regulation within the merchant account industry, *Auction Watch* placed the figure between 700 on the low end to as many as several thousand, with fewer than 200 representing legitimate operations. This latter point indicated a cause for concern and caution on the part of merchants. It was not uncommon for businesses to file complaints against malicious ISOs that advertised low rates to get their business and then levied additional excessive fees or inflated charges for credit-card processing equipment. Although it generally cost merchants more to obtain merchant accounts through ISOs, the fees and other costs involved varied considerably, which caused confusion. Additionally, according to Workz.com, "To confuse matters further, ISOs often refer to themselves as merchant account providers even though they do not provide the account. This is a matter of semantics which has not been clarified or enforced by any governing body."

Nonetheless, ISOs' less-than-ethical business practices were addressed in the 2000s. In 2004, Certified Merchant Services (CMS), an ISO based in Texas, settled a complaint made by the Federal Trade Commission (FTC) for $23.5 million. In addition to being forced to sell its assets for distribution to aggrieved clients and administration fees, the FTC barred the company from continuing to use underhanded tactics, such as "...falsifying merchants' signatures; altering or adding to signed documents relating to merchant accounts; certain billing and debiting practices; and misrepresenting the savings that merchants would achieve by doing business with CMS." The CMS case was the first complaint the FTC made against any ISO, though it was not the last.

In large part, the unethical business practices of ISOs were due to easy entry to the market, as well as increasing competition for merchant services. According to *Digital Transactions,* many ISO entrants were small companies or professional, single proprietors that worked with merchants in other areas, such as accounting. These companies typically saw an opportunity to add a transaction processing service to their services catalog, hoping to make their professional services more convenient and, thus, more attractive. In other words, merchant services became, like many other e-commerce markets, increasingly vertical to accommodate competition.

Another, more innovative fork of the same trend was exemplified by a partnership between As Seen on TV, Inc., and PowerPay in 2011. PowerPay, a large ISO, looked to expand its services to mobile devices, and As Seen on TV, Inc., agreed to collaborate on a mobile app, allowing merchant transaction processing to be conducted on mobile devices. In turn, this would provide PowerPay with a competitive advantage.

Without regulation, it is unlikely that ISOs will consolidate as other IT industries did in the 2000s, though more prominent organizations, such as PowerPay, will most likely continue to grow their market share through partnerships and other increased service options.

SEE ALSO *Mobile E-commerce.*

BIBLIOGRAPHY

"As Seen on TV, Inc. Partners with PowerPay to Offer a Mobile App." *Business Wire,* September 1, 2011. Available from http://www.businesswire.com/news/home/20110901006650/en/TV-Partners-PowerPay-Offer-Mobile-App.

Federal Trade Commission. "Federal Trade Commission Garners $23.5 Million In Settlement of Certified Merchant Services Case." Washington, DC, January 15, 2004. Available from http://www.ftc.gov/opa/2004/01/cmsjudgment.shtm.

"MPI Case May Not Be the Last ISO Action, FTC Says." *Digital Transactions,* May 29, 2007. Available from http://www.digitaltransactions.net/index.php/news/story/1389.

Roe, Andy. "Merchant Beware." *AuctionWatch,* February 18, 2000.

Rosen, Ellen. "Merchants Pay (and Pay) for Right to Use Credit Cards." *New York Times,* September 30, 2004. Available from http://www.nytimes.com/2004/09/30/business/30sbiz.html.

INFOMEDIARY MODEL

In order to understand the definition of an infomediary model, it is helpful to first understand the concept of a basic business model.

WHAT IS A BUSINESS MODEL?

Whether a company sells products or services to consumers, other businesses, or both, there are many different ways to approach the marketplace and make a profit. Business models are used to describe how companies go about this process. They spell out the main ways in which companies make profits by identifying a company's role during commerce and describing how products, information, and other important elements are structured. Just as there are many different industries and types of companies, there are many different kinds of business models. While some are simple, others are very complex. Even within the same industry, companies may rely on business models that are very different from one another, and some companies may use a combination of several different models.

General business models by themselves do not necessarily map out a company's specific strategy for success. Strategic marketing plans, which are a specialized type of business model, are used for that purpose. They identify the specific situation in which a company finds itself in a particular marketplace, the differentials that set a company apart from its competitors, the marketing tactics used to accomplish strategic objectives, and so on.

Business models involve different levels in what are known as supply/value chains. Value chains outline the activities involved in creating value from the supply side of economics, where raw materials are used to manufacture a product, to the demand side when finished products or components are marketed and shipped to resellers or end-users. Companies review and analyze different steps in value chains to create optimal and effective business models.

Some long-established business models have been adopted on the Internet with varying degrees of success. Among these are mail-order models, advertising models, free-trial models, subscription models, and direct-marketing models. Other business models originated with the Internet and e-commerce and focus heavily on the movement of electronic information. These include digital-delivery models, information-barter models, and freeware models.

Every business model has its own inherent strengths and weaknesses, and online business models are no exception; they vary in their suitability for different enterprises. Business models themselves are not enough to guarantee success. As Jeffrey F. Rayport explains, "Every e-commerce business is either viable or not viable. They hardly qualify for the paint-by-number prescriptions that business people seem to expect. Business models themselves do not offer solutions; rather, how each business is run determines its success. So the success of e-commerce businesses will hinge largely on the art of management even as it is enabled by the science of technology."

THE INFOMEDIARY MODEL

A major Internet business model, the infomediary model is characterized by the capture and/or sharing of information. The simplest form of an infomediary model is the registration model. In this scenario, companies require users to register before gaining access to information on their Web sites, even if the information itself is provided at no charge. One possible scenario for this example involves companies that offer white papers, or expert articles containing valuable advice, to Web site visitors. These white papers usually are written by the company's experts, who are available as consultants. Registration is a condition for viewing or downloading the articles so the company can capture contact information and other data from the interested party and use it to make sales calls and potentially acquire new clients for its consultants.

Companies using an infomediary model also may be third parties that provide products like free computers or services such as free Internet access to consumers in exchange for information about themselves. This information is then sold to other companies who use it to develop more sophisticated, successful marketing campaigns. The information collected commonly includes things like product and service preferences; buying habits; and demographic details like age, sex, and income level.

The idea of an infomediary was first suggested in the book *Net Worth: Shaping Markets When Customers Make the Rules,* written by John Hagel III and Marc Singer, two consultants. The book, published in 1999, highlighted the value of a consumer's information to businesses and spelled out ways that companies could get that information more easily and with the consumers' consent.

In an interview with *OneWWWorld,* Hagel explained the term as follows: "The infomediary maximizes the value of the information by being helpful to the customer in locating products and services that are most relevant to the customer based on who they are and what their preferences are."

AllAdvantage was a company that pioneered some aspects of the infomediary model. Launched in 1999, the company paid users part of the advertising revenue generated by the pages they looked at on the Internet. The company's slogan was "Get Paid to Surf the Web." Unfortunately, many of the users of AllAdvantage used spamming methods to increase the number of income-generated referrals they obtained. After the burst of the dot-com bubble, there was a dramatic decrease in advertising revenue that negatively impacted AllAdvantage. The company shuttered the consumer part of its business in 2001.

In the early 2000s, NetZero was another example of a third-party infomediary. The company offered 40 hours of monthly Internet access to more than eight million consumers in exchange for their marketing information. As part of the deal, consumers were required to allow a special browser called the ZeroPort to remain on their screen while online. The ZeroPort displayed ads that, based on the marketing information they provided to NetZero, were likely to interest them. It also served as a Web navigation tool and displayed customized information like sports, e-mail, news, and stock prices. Using technology from marketing software manufacturer Amazing Media, NetZero also allowed small businesses to reach local or regional consumers through the ZeroPort and view the daily results of their online ad campaigns.

Since those early ventures, eBay, the Internet auction site, has become a successful infomediary by bringing together buyers and sellers in a central, trusted location. The auction site has no vested interest in any of the transactions, but rather acts as a safe vehicle for people and companies to share information about goods for sale.

By the early 2010s social media and networking sites such as Facebook, Twitter, LinkedIn, and Google+ were also acting as infomediaries, though not always with companies. Instead, users were able to control the personal information they shared with different groups of friends, family members, work colleagues, and acquaintances. Increasingly, however, these sites were working as an infomediary between users and some types of businesses as more companies saw the value of creating a social media presence as a way to connect with customers.

Trust is a key component of an infomediary. If customers learn that the company is not using the information as originally intended, there can be a backlash. For this reason infomediaries need to be "customer-facing" not "vendor-facing," according to a 2004 paper by Bethany L. Leickly titled "Infomediaries in Information Economies." Trusted infomediaries like eBay have suffered when fraudulent transactions diminished their reputation among consumers. And while part of the mission of the infomediaries is to keep information private and safe, some have been subject to privacy concerns. However, in order to make money these infomediaries still must provide enough value to the companies that seek customer information to make the services worth paying for. Success at striking that balance will be key for the success of infomediaries in the future.

SEE ALSO *Business Models; Social Media.*

BIBLIOGRAPHY

Bambury, Paul. "A Taxonomy of Internet Commerce." *First-Monday,* 1998.

"Biz—QuickStudy." *Computerworld,* November 1, 1999.

Leickly, Bethany L. *Intermediaries in Information Economies.* Washington, DC: Georgetown University, MA Thesis, 2004. Available from http://extrafancy.net/bethany/index.php.

Levin Consulting. "The Network Is the Infomediary: A Critique of Net Worth: Shaping Markets When Customers Make the Rules." New York, 1999. Available from http://www.alevin.com/infomediary7.htm.

McDowell, Dagen. "Dear Dagen: Business Models Explained." *TheStreet,* September 13, 1999. Available from http://www.thestreet.com/story/782926/1.html.

"Most Viral Companies, Industries Emerge as Consumers Share Opinions with Others." *PRNewswire,* March 29, 2001. Available from http://www.thefreelibrary.com/Most+Viral+

Companies,+Industries+Emerge+as +Consumers+Share+Opinions...-a072428800.

Rappa, Michael. "Business Models on the Web." *Managing the Digital Enterprise,* January 17, 2010. Available from http://digitalenterprise.org/models/models.html.

Rayport, Jeffrey F. "The Truth about Internet Business Models." *Strategy & Business* 16, Third Quarter, 1999. Available from http://www.strategy business.com.

Sarkar, Christian. "Interview with John Hagel." *OneWWWorld,* June 2002. Available from http://www.onewwworld.com.

Sviokla, John. "Listen Up!" *CIO Magazine,* April 15, 2001.

Timmers, Paul. "Business Models for Electronic Markets." *Electronic Markets,* April 1998.

INFORMATION ARCHITECTURE

Before the widespread adoption of computers, individuals were limited to some degree by the physical space needed to store paper-based information. With digital information, this is not the case, and the volumes of information to which users have access can be enormous. Furthermore, people have many different options when it comes to the ways in which they access information, ranging from closed private systems to open Web-based systems, wireless networks, online communities, and social media. As diverse as these many different systems are the interfaces individuals use to select and retrieve data.

Information architecture (IA) is an important field in the Information Age. At the core of IA is the concept of creating information systems (including applications, databases, and complex Web sites) based on the unique needs of those who use them. Therefore, effective information architecture involves professionals—who may or may not officially carry the title of information architect—focusing on the needs of customers or users first, and then on the information used to create an application or system. This allows for the development of systems that are logical and useful.

The term "information architect" was coined by Richard Saul Wurman in the 1970s while speaking at the American Institute of Architects National Convention. In a 2004 interview with *InfoDesign* magazine, Wurman said, "I thought the explosion of data needed an architecture, needed a series of systems, needed systemic design, a series of performance criteria to measure it." In that same interview he also said that 90% of the time when people use the term they are not using it as he envisioned.

Although IA pertains to Web sites used during e-commerce, it also applies to other valuable systems including intranets (private areas of the Internet), digital libraries, and knowledge management systems. Due to its broad scope, information architects often bring varying degrees of different skills to the table, and no one job title (like Web designer) adequately covers all of the responsibilities these elements require. According to Louis Rosenfeld, who at one time operated a leading IA consulting firm, the field of IA draws on the skills and abilities of a wide variety of different fields, including design, anthropology, computer science, library science, information retrieval, human-computer interface engineering, interface and interaction design, markup and data modeling, and technical communications. In addition to skills in one or more of these areas, common sense, logical thinking, and good communication skills are critical for information architects.

Along with coauthor Peter Morville, Rosenfeld wrote one of the seminal texts of the information architecture discipline, *Information Architecture for the World Wide Web.* The book explains the basics of information architecture as well as how it is incorporated into many of the functions people use regularly to organize and find information on the Internet.

For example, search engines such as Google make use of information architecture as a way to organize data about Web pages to present the most likely target of a user's search terms. At the same time, savvy Web designers looking for search engine "hits" have been able to get their Web pages to the top of Google's lists of search results by understanding and using the information architecture of the search engine.

PROFESSIONAL IA ORGANIZATION

The Information Architecture Institute, formerly known as the Asilomar Institute for Information Architecture, was founded in November 2002 as a nonprofit organization intended to support people and groups that specialize in the design and construction of shared information environments. The group provides education, advocacy, networking opportunities and other services to people in the field of information architecture. The group, based in Beverly, Massachusetts, attracted 163 charter members representing 120 organizations in 13 countries, demonstrating the far reach of the information architecture field. By the end of 2010, the group had 1,449 members in 48 countries.

According to the Institute's Web site, "as information proliferates exponentially, usability is becoming the critical success factor for Web sites and software applications. Good IA lays the necessary groundwork for an information system that makes sense to users."

SEE ALSO *Business-to-Business (B2B) E-commerce; Electronic Data Interchange (EDI); Google.*

BIBLIOGRAPHY

Dillon, Andrew. "Practice Makes Perfect: IA at the End of the Beginning?" *Bulletin of the American Society for Information Science,* April/May 2001.

Knemeyer, Dirk. "Richard Saul Wurman: The InfoDesign Interview." *Infodesign,* January, 2004. Available from http://www.informationdesign.org/special/wurman_interview.htm.

Morville, Peter, and Louis Rosenfeld. *Information Architecture for the World Wide Web.* 2nd ed. Sebastopol, CA: O'Reilly Media, 2002.

"Our Mission." Beverly, MA: Information Architecture Institute, January 16, 2007. Available from http://www.iainstitute.org/en/about/our_mission.php.

Peek, Robin. "Defining Information Architecture." *Information Today,* June 2000.

Wiggins, Richard W. "Argus Associates, Inc. Closes Shop." *Information Today,* May 2001.

INFORMATION MANAGEMENT SYSTEMS

If businesspeople in the early twentieth century had been able to look ahead and foresee the twenty-first century corporate landscape, it is likely they would have been amazed by the role information plays in today's economy. Not only does the world rely more heavily on information than ever before, the speed at which it must travel and the ways in which it must be organized and accessed are critical. This stands in stark contrast to the days before e-mail, database systems, and fax machines, when it was acceptable to wait weeks for a letter to travel between business partners in different cities.

As information began to take center stage in the business world, systems were required to manage its many uses. Information management systems evolved for this purpose. These systems involve the collection, identification, analysis, storage, presentation, and distribution of information. They play central roles in many business processes, including transactions and communication within organizations, and between companies and their many business partners (suppliers, manufacturers, distributors, vendors, and customers).

RISE OF INFORMATION MANAGEMENT

Information management began as a formal discipline in the late 1960s and early 1970s when computer programmers began studying the problems businesses and governments encountered managing information and began devising ways to solve them. Some of the first applications of information management technology were implemented at the National Aeronautics and Space Administration (NASA) during the Apollo program designed to land people on the Moon. Decades later, the development of faster and more efficient computers (able to process information at record speeds) and the development of the Internet (which allowed real-time access to data) made the management of information using computer systems even more important to the day-to-day operations of most businesses by the 2010s.

According to the Association for Information and Image Management (AIIM), "the center of an effective business infrastructure in the digital age is the ability to capture, create, customize, deliver, and manage enterprise content to support business processes." AIIM identified several information management technologies that play key roles in the success and development of e-business, including content and document management, enterprise portals, business process management, image and knowledge management, data mining, and data warehousing.

One of the common applications of an information management system is as a transaction processing system (TPS). In this system, information regarding various kinds of transactions are recorded and managed. TPSs are important components of many companies because they are the backbone of the sales, payment, and inventory management processes that allow a business to run smoothly. For a transaction processing system to work all aspects of the transaction must be completed—for example, if a bill is being paid, the money must both be removed from the payer's account and then also deposited and credited to the payee. Transaction processing is considered a real-time application, compared with batch processing.

Another example of using a TPS might be when someone makes a purchase using a debit card. The expectation is that all of the components of the process will happen quickly and seamlessly. TPSs are also used to manage tasks such as payroll or hotel reservations.

Another important information management system used by many businesses is the management information system, or MIS. With this type of system, managers in a business can get regular reports on data related to the business, such as a summary of certain types of transactions. A retail business might use these types of reports to study sales trends, for example, or to predict inventory needs by understanding historical customer demand.

Businesses engaged in certain kinds of service operations may use a customer relationship management system, or CRM. With these type of information systems the business is able to track all facets of the customer relationship and keep everything current. An example might be a financial advisory firm that wants to make sure every phone call with a customer is logged for all of the people who deal with that customer to see.

Supply chain management systems (SCMs) bring together information from all the companies in a supply chain, including manufacturers, wholesalers, retailers, and even customers. By managing a supply chain in this way, businesses can make sure the right goods are at the right place at the right time, without having excess inventory or delays. Businesses using "just in time" supply chain management use a SCM to track supply and demand closely enough to avoid as much waste as possible.

In addition to facilitating many different processes, information management systems are often used for specific global uses or applications. For example, organizations use human resource information systems (HRIS) to manage important employee data such as job classifications, pay ranges, salaries, income tax withholdings, benefit information, and so on. In the health care industry, physician practices, hospitals, health care systems, and insurance companies use these systems to manage information about patients, including medical records and data that can be used to tailor communications with them based on medical conditions or interest areas. In the realm of e-commerce, information management systems are used to organize and process complex arrays of data regarding products and customers. Information about a company's inventory of available items might be stored in an information management system, along with specific data regarding customer orders.

The huge amount of information available in the world and the many ways in which people and businesses want to use it has created enormous demand for systems that manage information well.

SEE ALSO *Data Mining; Data Warehousing; Database Management; Knowledge Management.*

BIBLIOGRAPHY

Association for Information Systems. "About AIS." Atlanta, GA, 2011. Available from http://home.aisnet.org/displaycommon.cfm?an=3.

Hain, Robert, Mark Harrington, Rick Long, Dean Meltz, and Geoff Nicholls. *IBM's Information Management System: Then and Now.* London: Pearson plc, 2005.

Waltz, Mitzi. "Oracle E-business Suite Draws Cautious Interest." *InformationWeek,* October 16, 2000.

INFORMATION REVOLUTION VS. INDUSTRIAL REVOLUTION

The domination of the Internet as a source of information in the 1990s and 2000s led to the conception of the Information Revolution, akin in its historical importance and impact to previous economic revolutions, particularly the Industrial Revolution.

INDUSTRIAL REVOLUTION

The initial step in attempting to compare social epochs is to locate them historically and sketch a broad outline of what they entailed. At the most basic level, the Industrial Revolution calls to mind a succession of breakthrough inventions: the steam engine, the cotton gin, railroads, and so on. More broadly, the Industrial Revolution saw economic production shift from small-scale, relatively localized production based on individual skills and craftsmanship by artisans to large-scale, centralized production incorporating heavy, mechanized machinery and mass numbers of wage workers. In addition, the Industrial Revolution shifted the center of economic activity from agriculture to industry and manufacturing. This created a series of sweeping social and economic transformations that upended existing paradigms.

The Industrial Revolution can be broken into three major phases. The first phase, in the late eighteenth and early nineteenth centuries, saw the development of textiles, coal, and iron into modern industries. The second occurred in the mid-nineteenth century, with the opening of new territories to economic development and the overhauling of transportation via the large-scale implementation of railroad systems, aided by developments such as the steam engine. The third epoch came in the early twentieth century, when the development of the mass-factory and industrial machinery transformed the industrial and social landscape. Through the first half of the twentieth century, the economic center was dominated by science-based technologies, particularly those related to steel, chemicals, the internal combustion engine, and electricity, such as automotive technologies and petroleum-based industries. While each of these epochs ushered in sweeping changes and innovations, they also produced profound social disruptions, as individuals and groups readjusted their places in society, often resulting in great upheaval.

INFORMATION REVOLUTION

Like the Industrial Revolution and most historical periods, the Information Revolution was not as abrupt a cataclysm as the name might suggest. Rather, what became known as the Information Revolution, although largely associated with the closing decades of the twentieth century, had direct roots in the thick of the Industrial Age. The most direct forebears to the Information Revolution appeared around World War II in the 1940s. This period was marked by heavy government investment in new technologies, particularly those used by the military for the war effort. Among these technologies were electronics and computers, which shortly after the war began to be applied more broadly in the business world. By the late twentieth century, the leading economic sectors, particularly in the United States, were those involving electronics, computers, high technology, telecommunications, and related service sectors. In the process, these technologies ushered in the information economy, centered on knowledge-based industries.

Like previous economic revolutions, the Information Revolution is marked most noticeably by a series of technological breakthroughs. In this case, the developments in electronics and computer technologies, along with dramatic changes in telecommunications, provided the basis for economic change. One of the central dates for the Information Revolution was 1959, when two scientists working separately—Jack Kilby at Texas Instruments and Robert Noyce at Fairchild Semiconductor—arrived almost simultaneously at the invention of the silicon chip, the device that inscribes electronic information in a microscopic space, allowing for the mass production—and mass dissemination—of computers. With the vastly enhanced powers of memory, calculation, and control placed in a microscopic chip, computers were poised to assume a central role in economic life. Following this breakthrough, computers came to constitute the central infrastructure of everything from office telephone networks to transportation control systems to industrial production facilities, setting the stage for further information breakthroughs once the vastly enhanced communication powers of the Internet were unleashed.

Of course, one of the preeminent—and least expected—hallmarks of the Information Revolution is electronic commerce. E-commerce propelled commercial activity into the borderless world of hyperspace, where transactions for everything from groceries to industrial equipment took place with little regard for geography and with nearly instantaneous satisfaction of commercial wants. Even in its earliest versions seen in the 1990s, e-commerce altered conceptions of business strategy and relationships, and on the consumer side e-commerce overhauled customer expectations of speed and convenience, pushing the field of business competition to new grounds.

GLOBALIZATION

The Information Revolution also features a new era of economic globalization as geography gradually disappears as a barrier to economic activity. The world economy has undergone enormous globalization processes before, particularly in the late nineteenth and early twentieth centuries, but the process was continually ebbing and flowing with the winds of political and social change. The level of globalization fostered by the Information Revolution, however, is altogether unprecedented in human history, as the speed with which information, transactions, and capital can travel virtually anywhere in the world render distance almost obsolete, at least in certain key economic sectors.

SOCIAL RELATIONS, WORK, AND DEMOGRAPHICS

The Industrial Revolution changed where and how people lived. For instance, while the early stages of the Industrial Revolution gave birth to the modern metropolis—huge cities acting as economic and social centers—the later stages of the Industrial Revolution, such as that involving the development of the internal combustion engine, gave rise to suburbs, highways, and dramatically increased personal mobility.

It was unclear just what the overall effects of the Information Revolution would be in changing social relationships and geography. The creation of the information superhighway, for instance, could conceivably have effects on demographics as dramatic as—but very different in character from—those caused by the Industrial Revolution. For instance, with geographic location diminishing in importance to the production process, people may be freer to live in remote locations; at the least, people may be less bound by their work lives to certain locations, potentially leading to vastly new kinds of communities and other social organizations.

In terms of social relationships and relationships to the production process, the Information Revolution has indeed led to radical transformations. The mass-scale, centralized-factory paradigm of the Industrial Revolution featured a production process in which individual workers were relatively "de-skilled" compared to their predecessors, and had only to perform minute functions requiring little training and with little overall understanding of the production process as a whole. As a result, companies were able to produce at vastly accelerated rates while keeping costs down, leading to tremendous profits that, in boom times, afforded them the option of paying higher wages in order to quell labor unrest. On the one hand, this created an economic environment in which centralized, hierarchical managerial bureaucracies were essential to organize production and maintain control over the production process. On the other hand, the centralized factory created an atmosphere in which it was relatively easy for workers to organize themselves for greater remuneration for their labors.

In comparison, the Information Revolution created an opposite effect. With computers, information technology, and high-tech communication systems dominating the business environment, production can be scattered across diverse locations and coordinated at high speed with great precision. This allows businesses to concentrate their particular production facilities where they are optimally efficient—for example, where labor costs and regulatory red tape are minimal—leading to greater profit margins. Moreover, the movement toward computer controls creates a less egalitarian environment for wage workers than the mass assembly-line model. Educated workers with technical skills and the accompanying career mobility became more common, and flat organizations became possible with the adoption of new communication and data management techniques. However, the Information Revolution also led to a large number of automated systems that reduced the need for worker input and focused control on the higher levels of organizational hierarchy.

COMMON ISSUES

Both the Industrial and Information Revolution created specific problems in the economies that they affected. These problems could still be seen in emerging markets around the world in the early 2010s (as part of the Industrial Revolution) and were also manifesting in advanced markets due to the Information Revolution. One of the key issues was education. Education models are a central part of society, but they depend on a number of different factors, among them what skills students need to make a living, and what technology students use to learn material. Both factors changed once during the Industrial Age and again in the Information Age.

In the Information Age, the skills that students were taught were primarily oriented toward working in an Industrial Age as educational systems were slow to meet the new requirements the market demanded. What was interpreted as a lowering of educational standards could also be understood as a simple reaction to new educational needs. This included new communication needs. Attention spans shifted. Students became more used to absorbing information at high speeds through social networking, blogs, and a variety of applications. These became the new tools of education, and the result was a tension between old education models, new education needs, and the political forces that drive education systems in most markets.

Another common issue seen in both the Industrial and Information Revolutions was the change in workforce roles. As mentioned, labor needs changed and technical skills became more popular in the Information Age. This led to a dearth of simplistic labor positions in many industries, as they were replaced with automation and robotic applications. Essentially, this removed an entire category of roles from the workforce, or at the least outsourced them to other markets. Some job loss is always associated with such revolutions, and while a negative aspect of the change, this is often balanced by the creation of new classes of jobs, albeit occupations requiring a higher degree of education and experience.

Other issues can be more insidious. The Industrial Age created a variety of environmental problems, including long-term issues of pollution that technology and businesses were not yet prepared to deal with. Even well into the Information Age, the pollution problems created by the Industrial Age are still posing issues for current and future generations. Analysts predict the possibility of similar forms of pollution created in the Information Revolution, which the market is currently unaware of, but will become problems in later years. In this case the problem is not environmental pollution, but pollution of information. The Internet has produced massive amounts of information, much of it biased, misleading, or blatantly incorrect. This may lead to future pollution problems as people attempt to find pure, worthwhile information.

FUTURE TRENDS

The Information Age was not over by the early 2010s, although studies were rife with ideas on how it would progress in coming years. Many agreed that data management was becoming increasingly important, not only as a way to manage information pollution but also as a way to create entirely new uses for data. New data management techniques began to grow in popularity as businesses sought to connect all the data available through complex analysis and data mining techniques. Statistics became an increasingly important part of strategic decisions on nearly every level. Data became more immediate, more useful, and even more self-aware, a trend that was expected to continue with time. Like the assembly line had sped up manufacturing and improved production quality, new processing techniques in data management and sharing were expected to create similar benefits for information that entered companies.

The concept of a third Industrial Revolution also became a significant concept in the face of changes begun in the 2000s. The second Industrial Revolution was considered the subtle but widespread move from manufacturing to service industries that had heralded the start of the Information Revolution. But a third Industrial Revolution would be made possible by the tools created during the Information Age, specifically the new communication and development methods created.

This third Industrial Revolution had two expected parts. The first part was the outsourcing of tasks. Rather than have tasks based on the location of the business, tasks were expected to become more market-based, moving around the world with widespread offshoring to find a market most suited for them. The outsourcing to China, India, and Indonesia in the 2000s was considered the beginning of this process. As the job market became more fluid, another round of job losses were expected in some nations just as job increases were expected in many emerging markets—all this due in large part to the communication tools that the Information Age furnished.

The second part of this third revolution was expected to be composed of environmental changes. The Information Age gave businesses the ability to discover potential environmental problems and fix them, just as it gave governments the ability to study ecological issues and quickly spread the results so that new regulations could be created. Environmental considerations, sustainable manufacturing, and ecological mindfulness appeared to be requirements for the new Industrial Age, changing not only how products are made but also how businesses approach product development and marketing.

SEE ALSO *History of the Internet and World Wide Web; Knowledge Worker; Society, Culture, and the Internet.*

BIBLIOGRAPHY

Castells, Manuel. *The Information Age: Economy, Society and Culture.* Blackwell, 1996.

Cote, Marcel. "Reinventing Our Jobs." *CA Magazine,* April 2000.

Drucker, Peter F. "Beyond the Information Revolution." *Atlantic,* October 1999. Available from http://www.theatlantic.com/magazine/archive/1999/10/beyond-the-information-revolution/4658/1/.

——— "Knowledge Work." *Executive Excellence,* April 2000.

European Commission. "Internet Ecology, Here and Now." Europa.eu, 2011. Available from http://ec.europa.eu/information_society/events/cf/bud11/item-display.cfm?id=6386.

Gerstner, John. "The Other Side of Cyberspace." *Communication World,* March 1999.

Giles, Jim. " Big Data: The Next Chapter for the Information Revolution." *Smarter Computing Blog,* August 22, 2011. Available from http://www.smartercomputingblog.com/2011/08/22/big-data-the-next-phase-of-the-information-revolution.

"The Industrial Revolution of Data." New Orleans, LA: The Olinger Group, June 22, 2011. Available from http://www.olingergroup.com/2011/recent-news/the-industrial-revolution-of-data.

"Is Information Management an Evolution or a Revolution?" *Smart Data Collective,* May 14, 2011. Available from http://smartdatacollective.com/mike20/36213/information-management-evolution-or-revolution.

Johnson, Brad. "Nicholas Stern: We Need a New Industrial Revolution." *Grist,* March 14, 2011. Available from http://www.grist.org/climate-change/2011-03-14-nicholas-stern-we-need-a-new-industrial-revolution.

Krauss, Michael. "Visionaries Don't Take Technology for Granted." *Marketing News,* June 19, 2000.

Matthews, Jessica T. "The Information Revolution." *Foreign Policy,* Summer 2000.

Sennholtz, Hans F. "The Third Industrial Revolution." Auburn, AL: Ludwig von Mises Institute, April 3, 2006. Available from http://mises.org/daily/2105.

Taylor, Timothy. "Thinking About a 'New Economy.'" *Public Interest,* Spring 2001.

Watson, Max. "Golden Age of Customers and IT." *Information Week,* April 24, 2000.

INFORMATION TECHNOLOGY (IT)

Information technology (IT) broadly describes the processing and management of data in computer systems. Within IT's wide parameters are the hardware (including hard drives, modems, monitors, servers, mainframe systems, and routers) and software (word processing and spreadsheet programs, Web browsers, and databases) that make the movement, manipulation, and storage of information possible. Thus, IT also gives life to the Internet, the World Wide Web, and e-commerce. Emerging fields in IT include the development of new Web and mobile technologies as well as the application of IT to other branches of science, such as biology and medicine.

From the early 1970s onward, computers and electronic information were increasingly critical elements of the corporate landscape. Large companies devoted entire departments to information technology. These IT departments went by a variety of names, including information systems (IS) and management information systems (MIS). E-commerce created additional demand for IT workers.

As the Internet and e-commerce exploded in popularity, many companies spent hefty sums on IT in an effort to keep up with or exceed the competition. While the bursting of the dot-com bubble in the early 2000s and the recession of 2008–2009 both negatively impacted IT spending, by 2011 it had stabilized again, and a report by Wells Fargo Securities senior analyst Jason Maynard predicted that spending would hold steady into 2012. In January 2011, research firm Gartner predicted that global IT spending would be $3.6 trillion in 2011, an increase of 5.1% from the previous year. The largest percentage of that spending was expected to be on telecommunication services, thanks to the proliferation of mobile devices used for many business and personal applications.

The term IT includes a mind-boggling number of different brands, variations, and kinds of computer systems, platforms, devices, applications, and products. As consumers and businesses purchase these products over time, issues of integration and compatibility frequently arise. Due to issues like this, companies rely on relationships with the vendors from whom they purchase products for technical advice and support. In addition to hiring IT professionals of their own, organizations also rely heavily on consultants to improve the functionality of systems and processes.

IT CONSULTING

Although consultants often provide strategic value to companies, such is not always the case. Like other business practices, there are advantages and drawbacks to using consultants. As explained in *Computerworld,* "IT has always depended on strategic relationships with vendors and its heavy use of consultants to a degree that's unmatched in any other field of business. That's because no company can go it alone. The best consultants either provide special skills, handle the ever-growing IT workload and provide development and integration capabilities or take on the management of large-scale projects."

The importance of IT for many businesses and the rapid development of new technologies has also led to an explosion in the need for IT education. Companies expect IT professionals to be well-versed in the latest technological innovations, and for many long-term computer programmers that means going back to school to learn new programming languages and computer systems. Specialized schools, online universities, and community colleges have joined more traditional four-year schools in offering education in IT and related fields. In some cases companies seeking well-educated IT professionals have partnered with schools in other countries to provide the appropriate coursework for future IT workers in those nations. The focus on education outside the United States is part of a major trend in IT since the end of the 1990s, namely, outsourcing.

IT OVERSEAS

A major development in IT during the late twentieth and early twenty-first centuries was a shift to moving IT functions to personnel in other countries. IT outsourcing became popular after the identification of the Y2K bug, which required the use of thousands of programmers to rewrite code. Many firms turned to programmers in other countries— especially India— as a source of cheap labor for this task. As the IT industry dramatically grew in the early 2000s, more and more companies outsourced functions to people in Asian countries such as Vietnam and China, as well as emerging nations in Eastern Europe. (India has remained a major player in outsourced IT, with an estimated 25% of the nation's workforce employed in the IT industry, and with export revenues of $59 billion in 2011.)

With the development of new communications technologies (such as video conferencing and project sharing software), it has become even easier for companies to situate their IT operations abroad, where they find a multitude of trained English-speaking professionals who are willing to work for far less money than is expected by IT workers in the United States.

SEE ALSO *Database Management; Knowledge Management.*

BIBLIOGRAPHY

Bernasek, Anna. "Buried in Tech." *Fortune,* April 16, 2001.

Dignan, Larry. "Gartner Raises IT Spending Forecast for 2011." *ZDNet,* January 6, 2011. Available from http://www.zdnet.com/blog/btl/gartner-raises-it-spending-forecast-for-2011/43316.

India Brand Equity Foundation. "Information Technology." Gurgaon, Haryana, India, May 2011. Available from http://www.ibef.org/industry/informationtechnology.aspx.

"Information Technology." *Techencyclopedia,* May 7, 2001. Available from http://www.techweb.com/encyclopedia.

"IT." *Webopedia,* May 7, 2001. Available from http://www.webopedia.com/TERM/I/IT.html.

Joachim, David. "Report: IT Workers Still in Short Supply." *InternetWeek,* April 30, 2001.

Keen, Peter G. "Consultant, Anyone?" *Computerworld,* March 12, 2001.

Prencipe, Loretta W. "Management Briefing—The Job Market: Are IT Professionals Working in a Time of Feast or Famine?" *InfoWorld,* April 9, 2001.

Rosenberg, Dave. "IT Spending Update: 2011 Budgets Intact." *CNET,* September 15, 2011. Available from http://news.cnet.com/8301-13846_3-20106858-62/it-spending-update-2011-budgets-intact.

Whiteley, Philip, and Max McKeown. "The Human Face of IT." *Computer Weekly,* April 12, 2001.

World Economic Forum. "The Global Information Technology Report 2010–2011." Geneva, Switzerland, March 2011. Available from http://www.weforum.org/reports/global-information-technology-report-2010-2011-0.

INFORMATION THEORY

Information theory posits that information is simply data that reduces the level of uncertainty on a given subject or problem, and can be quantified by the extent to which uncertainty is diminished. More importantly for the practical uses of information theory, however, is that it fits the concept of information and communication into mathematical theory. All content, no matter what its form—music, text, or video—can be reduced to a simple string of ones and zeros, thereby allowing tremendous flexibility in the mode of interpretation of that information. The application of information theory has had a tremendous impact on telecommunications and information technology and, by implication, the Internet, since it deals expressly with information-carrying capacities.

CLAUDE SHANNON

Information theory is the product of the renowned scientist Claude Shannon. Born in 1916 in Petoskey, Michigan, Shannon grew up in an era when telecommunications were primarily limited to the telegraph and the telephone. From an early age, Shannon displayed an affinity for electronic equipment and radios and a penchant for devising his own inventions, much in the spirit of his hero and distant relative Thomas Edison.

Shannon attended the University of Michigan and later the Massachusetts Institute of Technology (MIT), studying electrical engineering and mathematics, in which he excelled. After college, he went to work for Bell Telephone Laboratories, where he worked on cryptographic systems using early computers. In 1948, on the strength of his work and research, Shannon published his "A Mathematical Theory of Communication," a breakthrough paper that for the first time demonstrated that all information exchanges could be expressed digitally in terms of ones and zeros, based on mathematical reductions.

Shannon redefined the traditional concept of entropy to mean, in the realm of information theory, the amount of uncertainty in a given system. Information was simply anything that reduced the level of uncertainty, and hence the degree of entropy. To measure the amount of information, Shannon devised a mathematical theory in which capacities could be expressed in terms of bits per second. In fact, many historians of science insist Shannon was the first to employ the term "bit," which is shorthand for "binary digit." All information, Shannon claimed, could ultimately be understood as a string of bits, and could therefore be stored and transmitted as such. Shannon also developed theories on the practical transmission of digital information. He surmised that when information is sent over "noisy" or compromised channels, simply adding redundant bits to the message can smooth out and correct the corruption in the information.

INFORMATION THEORY TODAY

As the foundation upon which modern telecommunications systems, technologies, and theories are built, information theory was of central importance to the Internet era; it was ultimately responsible for most of the revolutionary breakthroughs in digital communication and information storage. Compact discs and digital television, not to mention the Internet, are everyday items that owe their existence to information theory. Information theory holds that all channels of information transmission and storage can also be expressed and analyzed in terms of bits, thereby providing the link that allowed for perfecting physical methods of information transmission, including how to send highly encoded Internet signals over simple telephone wires.

One practical application of information theory is the development of lossless data compression. With lossless data compression, the exact original data can be rebuilt from a compressed file without any loss of information. An example would be the ZIP file format, which allows users to compress files to a smaller size but then allow them to be expanded to full size at a later time or by another user. This type of data compression contrasts with "lossy" compression, which compromises some of the data in the process of compressing a file. Photo compression formats can either be lossless, like GIF, or lossy, like TIF, depending on the goals of the user. Data compression formats of both types were developed using the foundations of information theory, especially coding theory.

In the Internet world, information theory proved tremendously important not only for the basics of Internet telecommunications but also for cryptography, another field in which Shannon worked. Cryptography, in the contemporary sense, refers to protecting electronic information from compromise by applying mathematical algorithms consisting of a series of bits that scrambles the information and later decodes it when necessary. Cryptography was a key component of the development of e-commerce, since it lay at the heart of privacy and transaction protection.

Telecommunications have benefited from Shannon's theory because of the greater understanding it provided of the way information is transmitted through channels, and how the capacity of the channel and any "noise" provided by the channel can potentially corrupt the information as it travels.

Surprising beneficiaries of the study of information theory have been gamblers. The application of information theory to investing and gambling is called "proportional betting" or Kelly betting, after John Larry Kelly, Jr. Kelly was a scientist at Bell Labs and an associate of Shannon. He was also an expert in game theory. Kelly developed a strategy using information theory that has become a major component of many investment strategies and was used by a team of students from MIT to win at casinos, as detailed in the book *Bringing Down the House* by Ben Mezrich.

In addition to its role as the bedrock of modern telecommunications, information theory also washed over fields as disparate as biology, ecology, medicine, mathematics, psychology, linguistics. Information theory has played a role in the development of missions to deep space and in the study of black holes, as well as in the study of seismic information to pinpoint the locations of oil wells.

In a 2001 obituary, published in the *New York Times* after Shannon's death at age 84, MIT professor Robert G. Gallager said, "Shannon was the person who saw that the binary digit was the fundamental element in all of communication. That was really his discovery, and from it the whole communications revolution has sprung."

SEE ALSO *Cryptography; Encryption.*

BIBLIOGRAPHY

"Claude Shannon." *Times* (London), March 12, 2001.

Golomb, Solomon W. "Retrospective: Claude E. Shannon (1916–2001)." *Science,* April 20, 2001.

Hirschberg, Daniel S., and Debra A. Lelewer. "Data Compression." *ACM Computing Surveys,* September 1987. Available from http://citeseerx.ist.psu.edu/viewdoc/summary?doi=10.1.1.39.9148&rank=1.

Johnson, George. "Claude Shannon, Mathematician, Dies at 84." *New York Times,* February 27, 2001. Available from http://www.nytimes.com/2001/02/27/nyregion/claude-shannon-mathematician-dies-at-84.html?pagewanted=all&src=pm.

Pierce, John Robinson. *An Introduction to Information Theory: Symbols, Signals and Noise.* 2nd ed. Mineola, NY: Dover Publications, 1980.

Poundstone, William. *Fortune's Formula: The Untold Story of the Scientific Betting System That Beat the Casinos and Wall Street.* New York: Hill and Wang, 2005.

INITIAL PUBLIC OFFERING (IPO)

An initial public offering (IPO) takes place when a privately held company goes public and makes its first offering of shares to the public. It is a significant stage in the growth of a business. It provides the business with access to capital, not only through the IPO but also through subsequent secondary stock offerings. For the company's founders and venture capital backers, an IPO can provide the opportunity to realize a substantial cash return on their early investments. IPOs also tend to generate a lot of publicity and create more interest in a company. Once a company has gone public, it can use its stock in acquisitions and mergers. Stock can also be offered to key employees and used to attract new talent.

Investors were attracted to the IPOs of high-tech and e-commerce companies in the last half of the 1990s. Many of those companies had yet to turn a profit, yet their IPOs were successful beyond all expectations. Investors appeared more interested in a firm's potential for success in the online world, as indicated by its market position or market share, and seemed willing to overlook its losses. This displacement of profitability by market potential in the eyes of investors was one phenomenon that led observers to develop the concept of the New Economy.

Although America Online went public in 1992, it was the hugely successful IPO of Netscape Communications in August 1995 that was credited with starting the investor craze for Internet start-ups that lasted until the end of the decade. Netscape's stock was first offered at $28 a share; it was worth $75 after one day of trading, and it peaked at $171 on December 5, 1995. The company's first-day market capitalization was $2.2 billion.

In 1996, it was the IPOs of Internet search engines that attracted the interest of investors. Yahoo!, Lycos, and Excite all went public in April 1996. From mid-1996 through mid-1997, however, investors began to view electronic commerce companies more realistically, and relatively few high-tech or e-commerce IPOs were executed. Weak first-quarter earnings in 1997 from established firms made investors more selective about buying new technology stocks.

MORE E-COMMERCE COMPANIES GO PUBLIC: 1997–1999

More well-known e-commerce companies began to go public in 1997. Online bookseller Amazon.com held its IPO in May 1997. The company sold eight million shares at $18 a share after the market closed. The next day the stock opened at $27 a share and rose to $80 before closing at $25.50.

High-speed Internet access provider @Home filed for an initial public offering in May 1997 and went public in July. Its stock more than doubled on the first day of trading, from its initial $10.50 price to a high of $25.50 before settling at $19. The IPO gave @Home proceeds of $94.5 million and a market capitalization of more than $2 billion.

The success of Amazon.com's and @Home's IPOs created an air of exuberance around high-tech and Internet IPOs that lasted for a couple of years. Neither Amazon.com nor @Home had shown any profits at the time of their IPOs, yet their stock increased in value following their IPOs.

Online auction site eBay went public in September 1998 with an IPO that raised more than $60 million. When eBay held its IPO, investors quickly bid up the initial offering price of $18 to more than $54. After the stock settled down to around $47 a share, analysts noted that the valuation reflected consumer excitement over online auctions and investor awareness of the potential for profit. At the time most Internet ventures were losing money, but eBay managed to show a positive net income of $348,000 for the first six months of 1998.

IPO SLOWDOWN BEGAN IN 2000

The IPO market remained strong in the first quarter of 2000. According to figures cited in *Business Week,* 33 Internet firms went public in January and February, with average first-day gains of 160% in January and 144% in February. IPO.com projected there would be more than 500 high-tech IPOs in the coming year, compared to 387 in 1999. The research firm did not know that conditions for high-tech and e-commerce IPOs would change dramatically during the year.

While the IPO market remained strong through the first quarter of 2000, it finally cooled off in the second quarter of the year. Buy.com and other Internet companies that had gone public saw their stock prices fall to their IPO levels and below. Investors were becoming more concerned about the cash-flow problems and high cash-burn rates of online retailers. For the rest of 2000, a shakeout of dot-com companies took place, with many going out of business for lack of funding. In November 2000, approximately 27 companies withdrew their IPO filings because of the weak market for IPOs, including PetSmart.com and CarsDirect.com.

Conditions for high-tech IPOs had not improved much when Loudcloud, an e-commerce solutions company started by Netscape cofounder Marc Andreessen, held its initial public offering on March 9, 2001. The unfavorable investment climate for Internet-based companies forced the company to lower its initial offering price. Instead of selling 10 million shares at $10 to $12 a share, Loudcloud had to sell 25 million shares at an offering price of $6 in order to raise the $150 million it needed.

IPO MARKET COOLING CONTINUES THROUGH THE 2000s

In 2002, the Sarbanes-Oxley Act was passed to enforce stricter rules for businesses and for accounting. The act was meant to increase transparency to prevent scandals such as Enron from occurring again. However, according to Professor Jay Ritter of the University of Florida, the legislation may also have slowed interest in IPOs. According to Ritter, once the Sarbanes-Oxley Act passed, the number of IPOs dropped, and as of early 2012 has not yet rebounded to pre-2002 levels.

According to an article by John Berlau in the *Financial Post,* the act may be especially challenging for smaller companies hoping to go public, since accounting regulations for IPOs can place a larger burden on small companies due to the cost of compliance. According to one study, companies with valuations of $75–$250 million may spend up to 77% of their assets for first-year compliance and 41% of total assets after four years. Berlau reported that such costs mean that smaller and midsize companies can no longer raise money reliably through IPOs, the way they would have in the 1980s and 1990s.

In fact, the costs of compliance are so high that President Obama announced in 2011 that he would reduce the barriers that prevent more companies from going public and raising capital. The Obama administration also announced in 2011 that it would review Sarbanes-Oxley and other legislation, in cooperation with the Securities and Exchange Commission.

Another factor which slowed IPO market growth in the 2000s was the bursting of the dot-com bubble. After many companies went public with little capital and planning, venture capital as well as the IPO market became less welcoming to newcomers. From the early 2000s to 2011, in fact, the Asian market for IPOs outstripped the U.S. market. In 2011, for example, the top market for IPOs in terms of closed deals was China, with 103 deals. The United States lagged behind with 64 closed deals. The United States bested China in the IPO market in 2011, with $27.3 billion in total volume, compared to $23.1 billion for China. However, 2011 statistics showed that the Asia-Pacific region had 55% of worldwide IPO deals as well as 44% of IPO market proceeds. North America, in contrast, had 25% of worldwide deals and 25% of proceeds.

GOING PUBLIC AFTER THE RECESSION OF 2008

The recession and credit crisis which began in 2008 shook investor and public confidence and affected the willingness of companies to go public. In 2008, the United States saw 31 IPO transactions, according to an article in the *Washington Times.* In 2009, there were 63 such transactions, and by 2010 there were 150.

In 2010, amid market concerns and economic instability, several companies planning to go public delayed their plans. Chinese gas company MIE Holdings, for example, postponed its planned May 2010 offering after the Dow Jones Industrial Average dropped 1,000 points on May 6. Swire Properties also planned to raise $2.7 billion but decided not to go public after world equity markets teetered. Some companies that did go public in 2010 saw their offerings drop. Essar Energy, for example, slid 7.4% after being listed on the London Stock Exchange, and Niska Gas Storage Partners dropped 6.8% during its first day on the New York Stock Exchange in May 2010.

Despite such delays and challenges, some IPOs succeeded. PZU, a Polish insurer, successfully went public in 2010, and enjoyed 15% increases during its first day on the market. South Korean company Samsung Life went ahead with an IPO that raised $4.4 billion in 2010.

According to the *Wall Street Journal,* however, IPOs were not out of trouble after 2010. In fact, the number of killed IPOs in 2011 was higher than the number in any other year since 1996, when such numbers were first tracked by Dealogic. According to Dealogic, about $44.1 billion worth of IPOs, or about 215 IPOs, were killed in 2011. Many more companies delayed IPO plans in early stages, and were thus not reported in these numbers. Weak Asian markets and the poor performance of some debuted IPOs contributed to the trend. According to the *Wall Street Journal,* more than 50% of U.S. companies going public in 2011 dipped below their offer price.

Statistics such as these may have helped to postpone anticipated IPOs, such as Groupon and Zynga, in 2011. Facebook was anticipated to go public in April 2012, with a valuation of $100 billion. However, tech investors were disappointed when the *Financial Times* reported in September 2011 an announcement by Facebook CEO Mark Zuckerberg that the company would not go public as soon as initially reported. Citing sources claiming that

Zuckerberg wanted to focus on development, the *Financial Times* reported that the transaction could occur late in 2012.

While many companies hesitated to trade publicly in 2011, there were some larger IPOs planned. China's Beijing Jingdong Century Trading Co., for example, planned to go public in 2011 and announced plans to raise up to $5 billion from its IPO by June 2012. The company owns an online retailer similar to Amazon.com.

In 2011, investors were also pegging hopes on tech IPOs. Some IPOs in the tech sector continued to do well. For example, social media company LinkedIn Corp. reported 2011 revenue growth that was above expectations. Shares of the company increased almost 80% higher than the IPO price only three months after the IPO.

SEE ALSO *New Economy; Volatility.*

BIBLIOGRAPHY

Baldwin, Clare. "Tech IPOs Could Lead the Way Post-Labor Day." *Reuters,* September 7, 2011. Available from http://www.reuters.com/article/2011/09/07/us-markets-stocks-ipos-idUSTRE7831IQ20110907.

Berlau, John. "Is Obama Ready to Drop Sarbanes?" *Financial Post,* September 15, 2011. Available from http://opinion.financialpost.com/2011/09/15/is-obama-ready-to-drop-sarbanes.

Bruton, Garry D., Salim Chahine, and Igor Filatotchev. " Founders, Private Equity Investors and Underpricing in Entrepreneurial IPOs." *Entrepreneurship: Theory and Practice* 33, no. 4 (2009): 909–12.

Chao, Loretta, and Laurie Burkitt. "The Biggest IPO You Haven't Heard Of: Chinese Online Retailer Hopes to Raise Up to $5 Billion in U.S." *Wall Street Journal,* September 16, 2011. Available from http://online.wsj.com/article/SB10001424053111904491704576570612044417314.html.

Clancy, Heather. "Linux Lovefest on Wall Street." *Computer Reseller News,* August 16, 1999.

Dembeck, Chet. "Has the IPO Bubble Burst?" *E-Commerce Times,* August 6, 1999. Available from http://www.technewsworld.com/story/939.html?wlc=1317223009.

"E-investors Embrace Business-to-Business." *Business Week,* March 6, 2000.

Grocer, Stephen. "Record Year for Scrapped IPOs." *Wall Street Journal,* September 16, 2011. Available from http://blogs.wsj.com/deals/2011/09/16/record-year-for-scrapped-ipos.

Hersch, Warren S. "IPO Market Shows Robust Performance." *Computer Reseller News,* July 28, 1997.

"IPO Market Starts to Pep Up Again." *Washington Times,* February 4, 2011.

Lang, Brent. "Facebook Delays IPO." *Reuters,* September 14, 2011. Available from http://www.reuters.com/article/2011/09/14/idUS215727425020110914.

Macaluso, Nora. "E-commerce IPO Market Falls to Earth." *E-Commerce Times,* April 7, 2000. Available from http://www.ecommercetimes.com/story/2918.html?wlc=1317223164.

Marjanovic, Steven. "Internet Commerce Stocks Seen Headed for a Hard Landing." *American Banker,* May 18, 1998.

Platt, Gordon. "IPOs Pulled Following Market Declines." *Global Finance,* June 2010.

Regan, Keith. "PayPal to End IPO Drought." *E-Commerce Times,* October 1, 2001. Available from http://www.ecommercetimes.com/story/13856.html.

———. "Tech Stock Rally Raises Hopes for IPO Revival." *E-Commerce Times,* May 21, 2001. Available from http://www.ecommercetimes.com/story/9871.html.

Sanibel, Michael. "Top IPO Nations." *San Francisco Chronicle,* September 12, 2011. Available from http://www.sfgate.com/cgi-bin/article.cgi?f=/g/a/2011/09/12/investopedia59692.DTL.

Sloan, Allan. "Step Right Up." *Newsweek,* April 29, 1996.

——. "Trains You Can Miss." *Newsweek,* June 2, 1997.

Tracey, Brian. "Wall St. Throws Cold Water on Internet Commerce." *American Banker,* March 18, 1997.

Wigglesworth, Robin. "German Listing Delays Add to IPO Gloom." *Financial Times,* September 16, 2011. Available from http://www.ft.com/cms/s/0/ea6921dc-e04f-11e0-ba12-00144feabdc0.html.

Zhou, Haiyan, and Sanjay Varshney. "The Economic Profitability of Pre-IPO Earnings Management and IPO Underperformance." *Journal of Economics and Finance* 34, no. 3 (2010): 229–31.

INNOVATION

As a relatively new way of conducting business, e-commerce itself is a technological innovation. Within the e-commerce industry are also multiple and varied examples of businesses using innovative ideas to attract new customers and increase sales. For example, the decision by Lands' End Inc. to add to its World Wide Web site "Your Personal Model," an application that allows users to create a three-dimensional model of their body shape and then suggests appropriate clothing, was an innovation that attracted new customers. In many cases, the simple act of creating an Internet-based company—such as eBay or Amazon.com—is also an innovation.

Amazon.com The world's largest online retailer, Amazon.com, is the result of an innovative idea aggressively pursued by founder Jeff Bezos. In 1994, the 30-year-old Bezos moved to Seattle, Washington, to take advantage of the anticipated surge in Internet use many analysts were predicting for the mid-1990s. Bezos perused roughly 20 different products, including magazines, CDs, and computer software, that he deemed appropriate for sale on the Internet. Eventually, Bezos decided to pursue books, believing that the electronic searching and organizing capabilities of an online site could help to organize the industry's sizable and varied offerings. At the same time, the small size of most books would simplify distribution efforts. Bezos also believed that customers would be more likely to make their first online purchase if the risk was minimal; an inexpensive object like a book might prove less intimidating than something more costly, like computer equipment.

After building one of the first viable online retail operations, Bezos continued to use innovative ideas to build his customer base. His "associates" program, established in July 1996, permitted individual Web site owners and operators to offer links to Amazon.com from their site. In return, the associate earned a commission any time a user clicked on the link to Amazon.com and purchased a book. Within two years, this associates program secured 30,000 members. Another major innovation was the one-click shopping technology developed by Amazon in 1997. According to *Electronic Business* writer Marc Brown, Amazon.com developed the technology in an effort to reduce the number of sales lost to customers frustrated with online checkout processes that included completing lengthy personal information forms. "Amazon.com captures the buying impulse immediately by storing this information in a database, assigning the customer a unique I.D., and storing the I.D. in a cookie on the customer's computer. The next time the customer visits, the I.D. is automatically read and used to locate the customer's record." Thanks to the one-click innovation, for which Amazon secured a patent in October 1999, any returning Amazon.com customer is able to make a purchase simply by clicking on the "Buy Now" icon located next to each product.

Amazon has continued to be an innovator in the bookselling industry, introducing the Kindle e-book reader in November 2007. Since then the company has added hundreds of thousands of e-books on its Web site that can be purchased and downloaded for reading on the Kindle.

Ebay Another key e-commerce innovator is Pierre Omidyar, founder of eBay.com. When Omidyar's girlfriend, a Pez candy dispenser aficionado, expressed her desire to interact with other nearby collectors, the 31-year-old Omidyar created Auction Web, a basic online auction site that permitted sellers to post items for sale by describing the object, setting a minimum bid, and selecting the auction's length, which could extend from three to ten days. Buyers were able to bid on an object at any time during the auction, and the highest bidder won the right to purchase the object for the bid price. Omidyar stipulated that payment and delivery were to be handled by the buyer and seller. Despite the fact that the site offered no search engine, no guarantees of any type regarding the merchandise sold, and no dispute resolution services, it attracted an immediate following. Eventually, Auction Web evolved into eBay, which became the world's largest online auction site, with more than 94 million registered users.

InnoCentive In the early twenty-first century one of the biggest forces in innovation was a move toward more open models that allowed people from a wide variety of disciplines to work together to develop new ideas. Called by a number of names, this type of innovation allowed businesses to tap previously unused sources of information and ideas.

One model for this open innovation approach was InnoCentive, a research and development company based in Waltham, Massachusetts, that offered "challenge problems" to anyone who could solve them, in areas ranging from computer science and math to engineering, business, and the sciences. The company was founded in 2001 by a group of scientists backed by funding from Eli Lilly and Co. The challenge problems are shared with a community of as many as 250,000 solvers from all over the world who can earn cash prizes ranging from $10,000 to $100,000 for their solutions. According to the company, more than $7 million has already been awarded. In an article in *Wired* magazine, Jill Panetta, InnoCentive's chief scientific officer, said over 30% of the problems posted on the site have been solved, "which is 30 percent more than would have been solved using a traditional, in-house approach."

In addition to providing a place where businesses with research problems can find potential solvers, InnoCentive also has science experts who consult with the solvers and give feedback on solutions as they progress. The company also provides the legal framework to handle intellectual property issues between the solver and the company seeking a solution.

Crowdsourcing Another variation of this open innovation idea is "crowdsourcing," an approach that reaches out to an undefined group of people to solve problems, develop new technology, or provide input on a design. The word crowdsourcing was coined by Jeff Howe in an article in *Wired* magazine in June 2006. Crowdsourcing has led to phenomenon such as user-generated television, Wikipedia, and stock photo companies that provide thousands of images from photographers all over the world.

Unfortunately, as innovation has increased, so have mechanisms that oppose it. The new openness of innovation models and the rapid pace of change can cause problems in many arenas for people and companies attempting to create something new. For example, the U.S. Patent Office has a ten-year backlog in processing patents, with 1.2 million of them sitting unprocessed due to lack of staff and funding. Without patents, many new companies are unable to secure the funding to get off the ground, and new technologies have languished.

The patent backlog has been blamed for stifling innovation and for hurting the economic recovery by holding back the job creation that could come with all these new companies. Congress has repeatedly cut funding for the Patent Office, which was operating at a $1 million per business day deficit by 2011.

Another major issue for innovators is the rise of "patent trolls." This term is used to refer to people or companies that own patents on inventions they have no intention of using for anything other than to file patent infringement cases against other firms. Patent trolls often buy patents cheap from bankrupt companies and then seek out and sue other firms, claiming patent infringement. In some cases the patent is actually not being infringed, but the cost of defending against a lawsuit is so high that the target company is forced to settle or pay a high licensing fee. A suit by a patent troll can be devastating to a new company with little capital and can keep innovators from using their new ideas in the marketplace. A 2011 Boston University study estimated patent trolls have cost innovators $500 billion.

SEE ALSO *Affiliate Model; Amazon.com; Bezos, Jeff; eBay Inc.*.

BIBLIOGRAPHY

"An Amazonian Survival Strategy: The E-tailer Is Long on Web Savvy, Short on Profits. The World is Full of Companies with the Opposite Problem. Will the Two Tango?" *Newsweek,* April 9, 2001.

Brown, Marc E. "'One-Click Shopping' Still Risky to Implement." *Electronic Business,* May 2001.

Govidarajan, Vijay. "Strategic Innovation: A Conceptual Road-Map." *Business Horizons,* July 2001.

Hazleton, Lesley. "Jeff Bezos: How He Built a Billion-Dollar Net Worth Before His Company Even Turned a Profit." *Success,* July 1998.

Howe, Jeff. "The Rise of Crowdsourcing." *Wired,* June 2006. Available from http://www.wired.com/wired/archive/14.06/crowds.html.

InnoCentive. "What We Do." Waltham, MA, 2011. Available from http://www.innocentive.com/about-innocentive.

Jaffe, Sam. "Online Extra: eBay: From Pez to Profits." *BusinessWeek Online,* May 14, 2001. Available from http://www.businessweek.com/magazine/content/01_20/b3732616.htm.

Lee, Timothy B. "Study: Patent Trolls Have Cost Innovators Half a Trillion Dollars." *Ars Technica,* September 2011. Available from http://arstechnica.com/tech-policy/news/2011/09/study-patent-trolls-have-cost-innovators-half-a-trillion-bucks.ars.

Schmid, John. "Patent Backlong Hinders Nation's Job Creation." *Milwaukee-Wisconsin Journal Sentinel,* January 29, 2011. Available from http://www.jsonline.com/business/114839694.html.

INSTINET GROUP LLC

Instinet Group is the oldest and largest of the electronic communication networks (ECNs)—privately owned systems that post the buy and sell prices of stock. Rather than purchasing large chunks of stocks and holding them until it can sell them at a better price—a practice known in the industry as seeking a favorable spread—Instinet makes its money by charging a fee for each trade it completes. Instinet's service distinguishes itself by keeping confidential the name of the company buying or selling the stock, which allows a firm to place orders without impacting the market.

In 2011, Instinet was controlled by the Japanese bank Nomura.

BACKGROUND

Instinet was founded with six subscribers in 1969 as Institutional Networks Corp. by Jerome Pustilnik, once a director of research at Spingarn Heine. Bill Lupien purchased the company in the 1980s and continued to develop the computer-based trading system that served large institutions. By conducting transactions electronically, the firm was able to offer its clients, mainly large institutions, anonymity in their stock purchases and sales. However, it was not until Reuters acquired it for $120 million after the stock market crash in 1987 that Instinet began to attract widespread attention. The firm's technology eliminated the need for a team of in-house brokers and allowed it to charge lower transaction fees and stay open 24 hours a day, seven days a week. More importantly, Instinet offered anonymity. Since traditional traders would quite often have to deal with several other brokers before closing a deal, the potential for information leaks was high.

The increasing growth of ECNs brought intensified scrutiny to the burgeoning ECN industry. Concerned that the lines between brokers and actual exchanges were becoming a bit too blurred, and leery about the unregulated exchange activity conducted by ECNs, the SEC decided in 1999 to allow ECNs to apply for permission to operate as official stock exchanges.

PART OF NASDAQ

Instinet's 2001 public offering garnered $464 million in its first day of trading and helped legitimize electronic trading for investors. Four years later, NASDAQ acquired Instinet for $1.88 billion to better compete against the New York Stock Exchange, which merged with ECN Archipelago Holdings. Under the deal, Instinet's electronic marketplace, Inet, was combined with NASDAQ's operations. Its other major unit—Instinet, the Institutional Broker—was acquired by private equity firm Silver Lake Partners, which paid $207 million for its piece of the deal. In late 2006, Silver Lake struck a $1 billion deal with Japanese bank Nomura to purchase Instinet. Nomura viewed the acquisition as an effective play at expanding its business to U.S. institutional investors.

INSTINET IN THE 2010S

By 2011, Instinet was a wholly owned subsidiary of Nomura and offered a number of services to investors. Its main broker-dealer subsidiary, Instinet LLC, boosted its market share to 4.3% of the overall U.S. equities market and 1.5% of the U.S. listed-options market. In addition, Instinet was ranked among the top five firms in August 2011 for the New York Stock Exchange's agency program trading volume, and was a top-ten liquidity provider for NASDAQ-listed securities.

Capitalizing on its notoriety as the world's first major ECN, Instinet expanded its breadth of offerings with such services as sales trading, algorithmic trading, liquidity sourcing, transaction analysis, multi-asset trading, commission management, and research. Its Chi-X Global subsidiary provided market infrastructure technologies and trading venues that hinged on a high-speed, cost-efficient trading model.

Instinet's sales trading segment included 14 sales trading desks worldwide as well as a global portfolio trading group that formulated strategy, represented orders, and executed single stocks or portfolios. Its algorithmic trading operations utilized advance algorithms within a risk-controlled framework that allowed investors to exploit event-driven trading opportunities. Its liquidity sourcing offerings were available to clients in 46 countries.

SEE ALSO *Day Trading; Electronic Communications Networks (ECNs); Investing, Online.*

BIBLIOGRAPHY

Dwyer, Paula. "Rethinking Wall Street." *BusinessWeek Online,* October 11, 1999. Available from http://www.businessweek.com/archives/1999/b3650168.arc.htm.

Celarier, Ian S. "The ECN Dilemma: Blasting Fragmentation, Wall Street Calls for a Centralized Market Structure That Threatens the Upstarts." *Investment Dealers Digest,* March 6, 2000.

Ceron, Gaston F. "Tales of the Tape: ECNs Face a Fork in the Road." *Dow Jones News Service,* March 8, 2001.

Gelsi, Steve, and David Weidner. "Nasdaq to Acquire Instinet for $1.88B." *Market Watch,* April 22, 2005. Available from http://www.marketwatch.com/story/group-led-by-nasdaq-to-buy-instinet-for-188-billion.

Horowitz, Jed. "Nasdaq Dealers Push for ECN Status Under New Rules." *Investment Dealers Digest,* March 31, 1997.

Instinet Group LLC. "About Instinet." New York, 2011. Available from http://www.instinet.com/includes/index.jsp?thePage=/html/ab_index.txt.

Labate, John. "Companies & Finance International: Instinet Puts Off Plan." *Financial Times,* December 21, 2000.

Lacey, Stephen. "Instinet Instigates ECN IPO Battle." *Red Herring,* February 12, 2001.

Lewis, Mark. "Instinet IPO Soars on Debut." *Forbes,* May 18, 2001. Available from http://www.forbes.com/2001/05/18/0518instinet.html.

McNamee, Mike. "Still King of the E-bourses?" *Business Week,* June 21, 1999.

Quinn, James. "Sale of Instinet Lands Silver Lake a Fivefold Return." *Telegraph,* November 3, 2006. Available from http://www.telegraph.co.uk/finance/2950079/Sale-of-Instinet-lands-Silver-Lake-a-fivefold-return.html.

Pedrosky, Paul. "Big Brother vs. Big Broker." *Forbes,* August 26, 1996.

Weinberg, Neil. "Darwinism on Wall Street." *Forbes,* November 13, 2000.

INTANGIBLE ASSETS

In the corporate world, companies possess many different tangible assets with real marketplace value. Real estate, office equipment and furniture, computers, cash, and accounts receivable are assets that, if necessary, can be exchanged in trade or used to pay off debts. Such assets normally carry established market values, which vary depending on different economic and geographic factors. They are relatively easy to quantify and include on financial reports.

However, tangible assets are only part of the total picture. Companies also possess vast arrays of intangible assets. Intangible assets have real value and are important to a company's success but are much harder to measure and quantify. These assets can be customer-, technology-, or market-based. Examples include organizational ability, research and development, brand equity, customer databases, exclusivity within a particular market or geographic area, software, drawings, special expertise, customer satisfaction, the speed at which companies are able to bring new products and services to market, and more. Such assets usually involve information and are knowledge-based, focusing on products, services, and organizational systems. Knowledge-based, intangible assets are sometimes referred to as intellectual capital.

CAPTURING INTANGIBLE ASSETS

Although they may not be visible to the naked eye the same way tangible assets are, it is important for companies to take stock of the intangible assets they have and find ways to capture and preserve them. Many ways of accomplishing this existed in the 2010s. One approach was to keep employees with special knowledge, skills, and abilities happy so that they did not leave and seek employment with competing organizations. Another approach involved storing intangible assets in computerized "expert systems." Based on artificial intelligence technology, expert systems are databanks of human knowledge that users can query in order to receive answers to common problems or challenges. Such systems have been used in the finance and insurance fields, where information is key, as well as in retail settings.

As information and knowledge play increasingly prominent roles in the business world, identifying and managing intangible assets are issues that all retailers, brick-and-mortar as well as online, must deal with. According to *Investor Relations Business,* Wayne Upton of the Financial Accounting Standards Board indicated this was a challenge for all companies, regardless of size. "The issue of intangible assets is just as important for a company like Pfizer Corp. as it is for a start-up, although Pfizer may do a better job," he explained.

One of the reasons intangible assets are so important is because they can be converted to tangible assets, ultimately generating revenue. Books, software products, equipment, patents, and inventions are prime examples. Intangible assets also are of considerable interest to investors. In the past, a company's book value often was closely associated with its market value. However, by the 2000s market values often exceeded book values, and the difference was often attributable to the value of a company's intangible assets. The dollar value of such assets is considerable. *Futurist* cited the Harvard Business School's newsletter, *Harvard Management Update,* which indicated that intangible assets were worth "an average of three times more than the physical assets a company may possess, such as equipment and buildings."

VALUING INTANGIBLE ASSETS

The valuation of intangible assets can be a tricky prospect. However, as Kelvin King of the World Intellectual Property Organization noted, three basic methods exist: market-based valuation, cost-based valuation, and valuation based on estimates of past and future economic benefits. The challenge with market-based valuation is that identifying a comparable market transaction can become a hopeless pursuit. An intangible like intellectual property is not typically developed as an item to be sold. King suggested that cost-based valuation was equally difficult, because the approach assumes some relationship between the cost and value of an intangible asset. Meanwhile, it ignores such things as maintaining such an asset over a period of time. Using estimates of past and future economic benefits takes into account four specific criteria when valuating intangible assets: capitalization of historic profits, gross profit differential methods, excess profit methods, and a relief-from-royalty method. While impediments abound, King conceded that such valuation methods are sometimes necessary to a business since intangibles can, indeed, generate revenue to varying degrees.

INTANGIBLES WORLDWIDE

While they may be difficult to value, intangible assets can have a momentous impact on the business community at large, from local independent retailers to multinational conglomerates. In fact, intangibles are valuable to not just businesses, but people and countries. For instance, New Zealand capitalized on an opportunity to create a new intangible asset when it hosted the World Cup rugby finals in 2011. Since the event was expected to generate $700 million for the country, the government invested in infrastructure upgrades and other improvements to prepare for tens of thousands of visitors from around the world. Part of that investment included $50 million in grants as part of the country's technology development grant program. "It turns out that in order for companies to receive the grant, the money has to be spent on research and development here in New Zealand. Many of the awardees, including Mako Networks and Xero, have definite plans to add R&D staff as a result," wrote Simon Eskow in *Reseller News.* "So the benefits to New Zealand of this investment are tangible—money is filtered back into the economy through domestic employment and expenditures; semi-tangible—the tech industry gets resources to attract engineers and perhaps develop technology that will spur new businesses; and intangible—that New Zealand increases its goodwill as a technology innovator and exporter of products."

SEE ALSO *Intellectual Capital; Intellectual Property; World Intellectual Property Organization.*

BIBLIOGRAPHY

Boulton, Richard E. S., Barry D. Libert, and Steve M. Samek. "A Business Model for the New Economy." *Journal of Business Strategy,* July/August 2000.

Eskow, Simon. "The Warm Glow of Intangible Assets." *Reseller News,* September 23, 2011. Available from http://reseller.co.nz/reseller.nsf/opinion/the-warm-glow-of-intangible-assets.

King, Kelvin. "The Value of Intellectual Property, Intangible Assets and Goodwill." Geneva, Switzerland: World Intellectual Property Organization. Available from http://www.wipo.int/sme/en/documents/value_ip_intangible_assets.htm.

Stewart, Thomas A. "Accounting Gets Radical." *Fortune,* April 16, 2001.

Wagner, Cynthia G. "Making Intangible Assets More Tangible." *Futurist,* May/June 2001.

"You're Not Special, FASB Tells Dotcoms." *Investor Relations Business,* April 30, 2001.

INTEGRATION

Connectivity is a main element of e-commerce. It is a requirement for engaging in electronic transactions between two or more parties, be they businesses or consumers. However, companies that excel at e-commerce do more than simply connect with customers, suppliers, and other business partners; they find ways to integrate the many different computer systems and databases that are part of their operations with each other (internal integration), or with parties on the outside (external integration) so they function together seamlessly.

EXTERNAL INTEGRATION

External integration focuses on the sharing of data through standardized industry systems rather than using tailored interfaces in business systems applications. The business has to comply with certain industry interoperability standards that guarantee the compatibility of its IT systems with those of external players. The successful integration of application platforms for credit card transactions, for example, is dictated by specific compatibility standards of the industry.

External integration is especially important in the realm of business-to-business (B2B) e-commerce, where companies can realize significant cost savings and increased efficiencies by integrating their systems. Companies and business partners may integrate systems at different points in a supply chain, which encompasses all of the different levels involved in manufacturing products. Supply chains include everything from raw materials to finished products, which can be used by other companies in their manufacturing processes or purchased by consumers.

The B2B online transactions segment stimulated growth of electronic retailing (e-tailing) through the 2000s. A report by BuddeComm, "2010 World Digital Economy—E-Commerce and M-Commerce Trends," observed that the Internet's overall share of total U.S. retail sales grew from 1.5% in 2003 to less than 4% in 2010, and the growth trend was likely to continue, with sales expected to reach $240 billion by 2014. Confirming this trend, Mark Brohan in *Internet Retailer* quoted statistics from the U.S. Department of Commerce showing that total U.S. e-commerce sales grew by 14.8% from $144.2 billion in 2009 to $165.4 billion in 2010.

INTERNAL INTEGRATION

Successful e-commerce companies also make sure the many different systems they use within their enterprises are integrated. This internal integration allows many different pieces of relevant information about transactions and other business activities to be shared with appropriate divisions or departments. For example, in business-to-consumer commerce, when a customer orders a product online via an order form on a company's Web site, data about the order is instantly sent to the accounting department for billing and financial reporting purposes, to the warehouse for packing and shipping purposes, and to customer service in the event of questions or concerns regarding the status of the order.

When e-commerce exploded in popularity, many companies rushed in by putting up Web sites and accepting online orders. However, these front-end elements represented only half of the equation. Many organizations failed to think through processes and systems on the back end, namely how they would connect systems together.

When companies took this approach, bottlenecks arose in what should have been a seamless process. Orders that came in via the Web would be billed quickly to a customer's credit card but were then printed out on paper and held for days or weeks in the warehouse before being filled. Practices like these hindered the growth of successful e-commerce.

As Mark Leon explained in *InfoWorld,* "Retail success hinges on what happens behind that fabulous Web site: logistics and fulfillment, payment systems, systems and policies to handle returns, customer service, and, running through it all, integration. Without these the site won't scale, and customers who once loved the Web store will quickly turn fickle and point their browsers elsewhere."

TYPES OF INTERNAL INTEGRATION

Unlike external integration, internal integration focuses on the interfaces that define the enterprise applications of the business. Internal integration provides more flexibility for organizations to tailor the designs and interfaces of their applications to suit their specific needs. This is because the organization does not need to comply with specific industry standards required to make its applications compatible with those of external partners or stakeholders. A white paper prepared by Enterprise Integration Incorporated in 2006 identified point-to-point integration, database-to-database integration, and enterprise application integration as some of the main categories of internal integration.

Point-to-point integration is based on the modeling of data on the basis of known source and target systems with developed source codes for transmitting information within a system. Database-to-database integration, on the other hand, is based on achieving internal systems interoperability through inbuilt architectural replications designed to transmit information across databases. Enterprise application integration is based on message-oriented middleware (MOM) that shares data and guides business processes by interconnecting various applications or databases. The MOM is usually managed by third-party vendors such as WebMethods, Oracle, or IBM.

SEE ALSO *Enterprise Application Integration (EAI).*

BIBLIOGRAPHY

"2010 World Digital Economy—E-commerce and M-commerce Trends." Bucketty, New South Wales, Australia: BuddeComm, October 29, 2010. Available from https://www.budde.com.au/Research/World-Digital-Economy-E-Commerce-and-M-Commerce-Trends.html?r=51.

"Amazon.com Announces Second Quarter Sales up 41% to $6.57 Billion." *Business Wire,* July 22, 2010. Available from http://phx.corporate-ir.net/phoenix.zhtml?c=97664&p=irol-newsArticle&ID=1451041&highlight=.

Baum, David. "Middleware." *InfoWorld,* November 30, 1992.

Borck, James R. "Web Commerce from the Ground Up." *InfoWorld,* August 2, 1999.

Brohan, Mark. "The New Top 500." *Internet Retailer,* May 4, 2011. Available from http://www.internetretailer.com/2011/05/03/top-500-return-double-digit-annual-growth.

Champy, Jim. "New Infrastructure." *Computerworld,* February 26, 2001.

Deatsch, Katie. "2 Million Holiday Shoppers Get a Bar Code Scanning App in Hopes of Shopping Smarter." *Internet Retailer,* December 8, 2010. Available from http://www.internetretailer.com/2010/12/08/2-million-holiday-shoppers-get-bar-code-scanning-app.

Dias, D. M., S. L. Palmer, J. T. Rayfield, H. H. Shaikh, and T. K. Sreeram. "E-commerce Interoperability with IBM's WebSphere Commerce Products." *IBM Systems Journal* 41, no. 2 (2002).

"Global Mobile Statistics 2011: All Quality Mobile Marketing Research, Mobile Web Stats, Subscribers, Ad Revenue, Usage Trends..." *Mobi Thinking,* July 2011. Available from http://mobithinking.com/mobile-marketing-tools/latest-mobile-stats.

Grygo, Eugene. "Bringing Web Exchanges into the Back End—Companies Consider Connecting Digital Exchange Transactions with Internal Apps." *InfoWorld,* March 27, 2000.

Leon, Mark. "Online Retail Success Lies Behind the Scenes." *InfoWorld,* June 12, 2000.

Meehan, Michael. "Vendors Try to Make Middleware More User-Friendly." *Computerworld,* May 15, 2000.

———. "Middleware to the Rescue." *Computerworld,* May 10, 1993.

O'Neill, Mark. "XML and Security." *XML-Journal,* December 8, 2001. http://www.vordel.com/news/articles/01-12-08.html.

Sollish, Fred B. "An Introduction to Open Standards." Available from http://www.ftc.gov/bc/b2b/comments/obi.pdf.

"White Paper: What Is Integration?" Alexandria, VA: Enterprise Integration Incorporated, 2006. Available from http://www.abs-europe.com/assets/Image/FAQ/What_Is_Integration.pdf.

INTEL CORP.

The world's largest maker of microprocessors, Santa Clara, California-based Intel Corp. posted earnings of $11.4 billion on revenues of $43.6 billion. Although Intel spent considerable effort attempting to move into new markets—such as communications and networking equipment and Internet hosting services in the late 1990s—it returned to its core business as a PC chip maker in the 2000s, commanding 80% of the market in 2011. That year Jane Shaw was chairwoman of the board, while Paul Otellini held the positions of CEO, president, and director.

HISTORY

In 1968, three engineers from Fairchild Semiconductor—then the world's largest semiconductor company—founded Intel. The name came from the first syllables of "integrated electronics." Gordon E. Moore, Dr. Robert Noyce (co-inventor of the integrated circuit), and Andy Grove initially led the company in the production of memory chips and quickly began to revolutionize the electronics industry.

In 1971, Intel introduced the 4004 microprocessor, marketed as "a micro-programmable computer on a chip." Ten years later, IBM selected the 8088 chip for its new personal computer line, which helped to launch the PC revolution when it was shipped.

While the 1970s were profitable years for Intel, aggressive pricing by Japanese rivals forced the company to refocus on microprocessors in the mid-1980s. During the second half of that decade, the company had moved up from the tenth-largest to the third-largest maker of semiconductors.

Intel's aggressive advertising campaign, centered around the "Intel Inside" logo, proved successful as the company's earnings exceeded $1 billion for the first time in 1992. It also fought—and litigated—vigorously for market share with chief rival Advanced Micro Devices (AMD). The company released its Pentium processor in 1993, which executed more than 100 million instructions per second and was five times more powerful than its previous microprocessor. By the mid-1990s, roughly 80% of worldwide PCs ran on Intel processors.

The end of the 1990s brought a string of problems for Intel. After a decade of over 30% compound annual growth, the company stumbled as its attempts to expand into such areas as modems and video conferencing were unsuccessful. Falling PC prices, product recalls, computer industry consolidation, and increased competition added to its woes, causing Intel's revenue growth to slow to 5%, while earnings declined for the first time in a decade. Nonetheless, the company continued developing faster microprocessors, such as the Pentium III, a 1 gigahertz (GHz) processor introduced in early 2000. AMD briefly unseated Intel as the maker of the world's fastest chip with its less expensive 1.2 GHz Athlon processor before Intel released the Pentium IV, a 1.5 GHz chip. Meanwhile, the company continued to grow through the 2000s via a series of strategic acquisitions, including Denmark-based GIGA A/S ($1.25 billion); Basis Communications ($450 million); and Wind River Systems ($884 million).

INTEL IN THE 2010s

In a development that echoed the late 1990s, Intel encountered a number of obstacles in the late 2000s. In particular, the company was hobbled by a number of factors, such as a recession that saw slumping demand for PCs; lawsuits; and yet more problem-riddled forays into niche markets. The company once again refocused on developing advanced microprocessors and targeted specific applications beyond PCs, including cloud computing, virtualization, and data center platforms. Intel also attempted to broaden its reach into smartphones, tablet PCs, televisions, cars, and other products.

Intel's renewed focus produced record sales in 2010, surpassing $40 billion for the first time ever, marking a 24% improvement over 2009. Reinvigorated sales came in large part from a surge in demand for business and consumer PCs as the world economy steadily improved. The company created product groups for specific markets, such as PC Client, Data Center, Embedded and Communications, Digital Home, Ultra-Mobility, NAND Solutions, and Wind River Software. Intel also ramped up research and development with a goal of releasing a new microarchitecture for its bread-and-butter processors every two years, and next-generation silicon processes in intervening years. To further that end, the company planned to invest $9 billion in capital improvements in 2011 to boost manufacturing capacity.

In addition to core-product sales growth, Intel also continued to grow through acquisitions. In 2011, the company purchased Infineon's wireless unit for $1.4 billion and security software provider McAfee for $7.6 billion. The Asia-Pacific region accounted for a third of 2010 sales, followed by China (16%), the United States (15%), and Europe (13%). Microprocessors reigned as Intel's primary revenue generator, accounting for nearly 60% of company sales in the PC client group and 17% of sales in the data center group.

SEE ALSO *Grove, Andrew; Microprocessor; Moore, Gordon; Noyce, Robert.*

BIBLIOGRAPHY

"Company Profiles." Austin, TX: Hoover's, 2011. Available from http://www.hoovers.com.

Edwards, Cliff. "Can Craig Barrett Reverse Intel's Slide?" *Business Week Online,* October 4, 2001. Available from http://www.businessweek.com/magazine/content/01_42/b3753001.htm.

"Intel—Chipzilla Takes a Beating." *Economist,* November 11, 2000.

Intel Corp. "Company Facts." Santa Clara, CA, 2011. Available from http://www.intel.com/content/www/us/en/company-overview/company-facts.html.

"Intel Corp." *Notable Corporate Chronologies.* Farmington Hills, MI: Gale Group, 1999.

"The New Intel." *Business Week,* March 13, 2000.

Roth, Daniel. "Craig Barrett Inside: Can This Nature-Loving Onetime Professor Lead Intel out of the Woods? One Thing's for Sure: He's Got Awfully Big Hiking Boots to Fill." *Fortune,* December 18, 2000.

Schlender, Brent. "Intel Unleashes Its Inner Attila." *Fortune,* October 15, 2001.

INTELLECTUAL CAPITAL

The term "intellectual capital"—also known as organizational capital or knowledge capital—defines a range of intangible assets that are quantified differently than its physical and financial assets. It is knowledge that "transforms raw materials and makes them more valuable," according to Thomas Stewart in *Business: The Ultimate Resource.* Such raw materials can be either physical or intangible, like information. Generally, knowledge must be an asset to be considered intellectual capital. Among these assets are intellectual property and patents; employees' and managers' collective knowledge; and the internal information infrastructure, systems, and software that enable the dissemination, sharing, manipulation, and optimization of that knowledge.

Perhaps as important as what intellectual capital includes is what it excludes. Knowledge or information not involved in production or wealth creation is not included in intellectual capital. "Just as raw material such as iron ore should not be confused with an asset such as a steel mill, so knowledge materials such as data or miscellaneous facts ought not to be confused with knowledge assets," writes Stewart.

The Organisation for Economic Co-operation and Development (OECD) defines intellectual capital as "the economic value of two categories of intangible assets of a company: (a) organizational (structural) capital; and (b) human capital." Structural capital, according to *Financial Management,* covers supply chains, distribution networks, and proprietary software systems. Such features have assumed unprecedented importance in the information age.

In part, the concept of intellectual capital grew out of a rising dissatisfaction among many academics, accountants, and—perhaps especially—investors with standard accounting methods. Such methods poorly assessed the actual value of firms, particularly firms in the fields of information technology (IT) or other knowledge-intensive sectors. In order to assess the value and prospects of such firms accurately, these critics contended, it was necessary to somehow quantify and account for the collective knowledge and the organization of that knowledge within a firm.

The major factors contributing to the growth and importance of intellectual capital included economic globalization, which greatly intensified global competition and trade; market deregulation, particularly in such IT-heavy sectors as telecommunications; and technological innovation in knowledge-related fields, particularly the growth in IT and computers. These changes forced a shift in corporate organization toward a less centralized and vertical model of corporate organization, greater outsourcing of operations, and more fluid channels of interaction within and between firms, all of which enhanced the importance of intellectual capital.

FIRMS TAKE STOCK OF THEIR INTELLECTUAL CAPITAL

The concept of intellectual capital took hold in the late 1990s when the Internet and IT helped drive a U.S. economic boom. While quantification techniques were debated, intellectual capital became a field ripe for management concerns. Companies that wanted a competitive edge in an information-centered economy required an accurate assessment of their inherent intellectual value.

As intellectual capital became central to a firm's operations and value, managers took steps to protect it from compromise. The task of keeping knowledge, including knowledge inside employees' heads, within the purview of the firm at all times was a concern throughout the 2000s and into the 2010s. Confidentiality agreements were one result of this trend, guaranteeing that while employees worked at a firm and even after they left, they would not divulge information and company secrets to other parties.

ASSESSING VALUE IN THE INFORMATION AGE

Knowledge management consultant Karl-Erik Sveiby was one of the first to analyze the impact of intellectual capital on organizations. When he noticed that one of his country's oldest business magazines employed a proprietary model for valuing initial public offerings that often broke down for high-tech companies, Sveiby concluded that such companies possessed assets not described in financial documents.

As the global economy entered the 2000s, firms endeavored to establish meaningful measures for intellectual capital. Some divided intellectual capital into multiple categories, based on Sveiby's original model, which posited, among other things, that:

- Human capital was capital entrenched in individuals' minds.
- Structural capital embodied processes, information systems, databases, and other systems.
- Relationship capital derived from customer relationships, brands, and trademarks, among others.

In some countries, government agencies have stepped in to try and bridge the gap. For instance, the Danish Agency for Trade and Industry published a *Guideline for Intellectual Capital Statements* that helps companies state their resource bases and what activities they pursue to develop them. As part of the guideline, Danish firms examine a collection of indicators, or metrics, used to count intangibles. These might include proportion of staff with a university degree; training investment per employee; staff turnover; social events, including theme days; cooperative agreements with universities and business schools; number of approved patents; shared knowledge documents online; and the rate of product innovation.

Using these indicators, a firm can then determine income that is attributable to projects that came about from one of those indicators—such as university connections—compared to income that is generated in-house.

SEE ALSO *Intellectual Property; Knowledge Management.*

BIBLIOGRAPHY

Bernhut, Stephen. "Measuring the Value of Intellectual Capital." *Ivey Business Journal,* March/April, 2001.

Cohen, Jeffrey A. *Intangible Assets: Valuation and Economic Benefit.* Hoboken, NJ: John Wiley & Sons, 2005.

David Skyrme Associates. "Measuring Knowledge: A Plethora of Methods." Newbury, UK, October 2005. Available from http://www.skyrme.com/insights/24kmeas.htm.

Duffy, Jan. "Managing Intellectual Capital." *Information Management Journal,* April, 2001.

Guthrie, James. "Measuring Up to Change." *Financial Management,* December 2000.

Koenig, Michael. "The Resurgence of Intellectual Capital." *Information Today,* September 2000.

Stewart, Thomas A. "Accounting Gets Radical." *Fortune,* April 16, 2001.

———. *Business: The Ultimate Resource.* 3rd ed. London: A&C Black, 2011.

Taylor, Christie. "Intellectual Capital." *Computerworld,* March 12, 2001.

INTELLECTUAL PROPERTY

Few fields of law faced more rapid transformation from the effects of Internet and e-commerce than the realm of intellectual property. Intellectual property (IP) is considered to be the intangible result of intellectual work, such as inventions, literary and artistic works, and commercial symbols, names, images, and designs. Advances in communication and information technology have dramatically affected intellectual property rights.

Intellectual property laws concern the rights and protections pertaining to copyright, patents, trademarks, and trade secrets. Copyright and patent law debates often bring society's desire for free access to information into conflict with creators' and inventors' wishes to profit from and protect their creations. Businesses have intellectual property interests in safeguarding their identities and competitiveness through trademark and trade-secret protections.

The resolution of intellectual property questions was generating large-scale transformations in many Internet-related industries, as well as in fundamental legal issues such as privacy and freedom of information and expression. Since many online transactions transcend national borders, some observers predict that the challenges created by the Internet will result in the wholesale revision of both U.S. and international intellectual property laws.

COPYRIGHTS

Copyright protects a creator's or copyright owner's rights to control the publication, performance, duplication, and profitability of created works. Such works include literature, musical compositions, choreography, graphic and fine arts, motion pictures, and sound recordings. U.S. copyright protects the expression of ideas, rather than ideas themselves; it arises automatically when a creative work is expressed (or "fixed") in a tangible medium. Though registration for copyright is optional, creators cannot file suit for infringement without having registered. Copyright owners can sue for damages and courts can issue injunctions to prevent further infringement.

Limitations on copyright protection include the unauthorized "fair use" of a work by others for noncommercial purposes such as criticism, comment, news reporting, teaching, or research. Under the "first sale doctrine," libraries and archives may generate one copy of a work for archival conservation, and the owner of a copy of a work may sell, lend, or dispose of that copy. Finally, all works in the public domain may be freely duplicated, performed, and distributed.

The basic provisions of American copyright law are set forth in the Copyright Act of 1976. In addition to traditionally recognized creative works, the act also protects online text, image, and sound files. Copyright holders may bring civil suits or the federal government may prosecute the intentional infringement of copyright committed for commercial advantage or financial gain. Besides direct infringement, contributory infringement and vicarious liability, through which one person aids another in carrying out copyright infringement, can constitute criminal liability.

Several subsequent copyright laws affect copyright in cyberspace. In 1992, the Copyright Felony Act targeted computer software piracy; earlier, only unauthorized copying of sound recordings, motion pictures, or audiovisual works constituted federal copyright felonies. The Digital Performance Right Act of 1996 required that anyone wishing to use nonoriginal music for public digital performance on a Web site obtain license from the copyright owner.

In 1997, the No Electronic Theft (NET) Act abandoned the requirement that intentional infringement be committed for financial gain in order to be prosecutable. This criminalized infringement carried out simply to harm another. Some commentators suggested that henceforth, since online browsing involves copying in the statutory sense, anyone who browses copyrighted content without permission could be guilty of actionable copyright infringement.

Congress enacted the Digital Millennium Copyright Act (DMCA) of 1998 to further amend U.S. copyright law in light of Internet-related concerns. The act aligned U.S. legislation more closely with international copyright legislation as embodied in the World Intellectual Property Organization's (WIPO) Copyright Treaty. In addition, it prohibited anyone from circumventing technology intended to block unauthorized access to copyrighted material on the Web, such as decrypting protected content. The DMCA does permit authorized institutions to make up to three digital copies for preservation and to electronically "loan" those copies to other institutions.

The Copyright Office The policy roles of the Copyright Office were redefined when the DCMA became operational in 2000. The act effectively expanded the regulatory responsibilities of the Copyright Office to intellectual property rights that are related to electronic commerce. This development saw the Copyright Office transform its work performance approaches throughout the 2000s from the traditional bureaucracy to more flexible, accessible, and interactive online channels.

The gradual transformation of the Copyright Office culminated in the opening of the New Copyright Public Records Reading Room to the public and the posting of the electronic registration on the organization's Web site in December 2006 and July 2008, respectively. The tremendous transformation of the Copyright Office was achieved under the stewardship of Marybeth Peters, who served as the register of copyrights between 1994 and 2010. Peters was replaced by Maria Pallante in 2011 in an acting capacity.

LEGAL DEVELOPMENTS IN THE TWENTY-FIRST CENTURY

The enactment of electronic intellectual property rights laws that commenced in the late 1990s were continued in the 2000s. The United States Congress enacted the Technology, Education, and Copyright Harmonization Act (TEACH) in November 2002, a statute that effectively allowed accredited, nonprofit educational institutions to use copyrighted works in distance education.

In 2004, major realignments were introduced in the federal copyright agencies following the enactment of the Copyright Royalty and Distribution Reform Act that replaced the Copyright Arbitration Panel with the Copyright Royalty Board. The Artists' Rights and Theft Preservation Act of 2005 was the other major legal advancement in intellectual property rights. This act granted authors the rights to file advance registration of certain categories of works in progress that were destined for distribution in the market.

RealDVD Case The RealDVD case that was filed in September 2008 was one of the conspicuous anticircumvention court cases that occurred during the 2000s. The Electronic Frontier Foundation (EFF) reported that the Hollywood studios sued RealNetworks over its RealDVD software, which "was designed to allow consumers to copy their DVDs to their computers for later playback. Real also had intended to launch a line of consumer electronics devices that would have combined a DVD player with a hard drive." RealNetworks' plan, however, was suspended in August 11, 2009, the day that it was to officially launch its program, through a preliminary court injunction issued by a federal judge.

The litigation was finally settled on March 3, 2010, when RealNetworks offered to drop its bid to distribute its RealDVD copying software. The *New York Times* reported that RealNetworks agreed to pay Hollywood studios $4.5 million in legal costs in addition to agreeing to refund all the 2,700 customers who had purchased the RealDVD.

The "Jailbreaking" Controversy Another major controversy emerged in July 2010 when the U.S. Copyright Office released its triennial rulemaking on section 1201 of the copyright law. The rulemaking was made as a follow-up to the 2009 triennial hearings on anticircumvention laws. The controversy was sparked by the Copyright Office's decision to include "jailbreaking" among the six classes of works that were granted selective exemptions from the anticircumvention laws. "Jailbreaking" refers to the use of different applications in a phone in which a manufacturer has imposed the use of applications other than its own. Apple Inc., for example, designed its iPhones with advanced technologies that restrict users to running applications from the iTunes App Store only.

During the 2009 triennial hearings on the DCMA, Apple Inc. filed a petition that sought to convince the Copyright Office to recognize jailbreaking as an infringement of copyrights. The 2010 ruling of the Copyright Office, therefore, effectively legalized the jailbreaking of Apple iPhones and Apple apps in circumstances that amounted to fair use of copyrighted works. This particular exemption attracted the ire of Apple Inc. and also generated publicity, accolades, and condemnations of varied proportions from different industry players such as the EFF. In his article titled "Fair Use and the DCMA Triennial Rulemaking," Bill Rosenblatt lamented that the exemption "shows best how TCMs and the DCMA have evolved beyond their original intended purposes."

IMPLICATIONS OF DIGITAL RIGHTS MANAGEMENT

The emergence of Web 2.0 tools such as blogs, live chats, live video streaming, and YouTube have also influenced the transformation of digital rights management (DRM). DRM refers to the technological encryptions that are imposed on digital files to restrict accessibility to content or functionality of applications. The electronic media has increasingly been exposed to hackers who decode software security encryptions to break DRM restrictions and gain unauthorized access to online content.

BMG, RCA, and Arista were among the first companies to use DRM in 2002. These record companies used DRM technology to restrict their audio compact discs (CDs) from playing in computers. Publishers, however, experienced many technical setbacks because the audio CDs that were DRM-protected introduced software complications in the computers of users. In 2005, for example, Sony BMG recalled millions of its DRM-protected audio CDs because they installed unsolicited software on the computers of users, a situation that exposed computers to hackers. The application of DRM in audio CDs was finally abolished in 2007 following the realization by record companies that the DRM protection was expensive to maintain and upgrade regularly.

Microsoft Microsoft has been a victim of frequent hacking by individuals who seek free and unauthorized access to its Windows software products. The company has therefore been involved in numerous litigation proceedings concerning the infringement of its software copyrights. In September 2006, for example, the company sued a group of hackers for breaking into its DRM technology and gaining unauthorized access to its proprietary source code. In March 2010, Ubisoft, an online gaming company, fell victim to similar machinations of hackers who gained unauthorized access to its games by taking down its "always on" DRM servers.

E-books and Kindle The growth of the e-book audience and the subsequent emergence of the Kindle have tremendously influenced the dimension of intellectual property with respect to DRM of online content. Kindle is a wireless reading device for e-books. The first version of Kindle—Kindle 1—was released by Amazon in November 2007, and its user numbers had grown to 275,000 by the end of 2008. Kindle 2 and Kindle 3 were released in October 2009 and July 2010, respectively. The number of books in Amazon's Kindle store exceeded 725,000 in 2011.

The significance of DRM in the use of e-books was best demonstrated by Amazon in July 2009 when the company erased digital editions of George Orwell's novels *Nineteen Eighty-Four* and *Animal Farm* from its Kindle store after it became known that the e-books had been added by a company that did not own the copyrights of the two books.

Patent Trolling Patent trolls are significant components of intellectual property rights. A patent troll is a business that models its activities on acquiring ownership rights for a particular technology for purposes of licensing the use of the patented rights to other parties rather than inventing the technology. The holder of a patent gains the right to seek compensation or file litigation against any party that infringes the patented technology unknowingly.

Patent trolls intellectual portfolios involve acquiring multiple patented technologies for product development and holding onto them over a given duration until they mature into lucrative opportunities. During this period of maturation, the patent trolls monitor, observe and scan various sources of information to identify companies that infringe on the patented technology. The patents are acquired cheaply from companies experiencing financial difficulties, such as bankruptcy and liquidation. Patent trolls particularly target small and mid-size patent-infringing companies that may lack adequate litigation defenses and are therefore likely to opt for early settlement. Patent trolls are regarded as an affirmation of the shortcomings of patent laws.

CREATIVE COMMONS VERSUS IP MONETIZATION

The creative commons license was established by the Creative Commons Nonprofit Organization for purposes of promoting the sharing of copyrighted works without infringing the copyright laws. Creative commons licenses basically allow the content creator to retain copyrights but permit others to use their works. The main categories of the creative common licenses include:

- Attribution, Noncommercial, No Derivatives license that allows the owners of copyrights to share their work with others, but they must give credit to the owner, and they are not allowed to make any changes or make money from it.
- Attribution, Noncommercial Share Alike license that allows others to use and change the interpretation of the author's work, but users are required to give credit to the author and the resulting new work must be licensed the same way as the original and should not be used for profit.
- Attribution, Noncommercial license that allows parties to give a different interpretation of the work, but they must acknowledge the original creator, and the work should not be used for any commercial purposes.
- Attribution, No Derivatives license that allows the author's work to be used by others for commercial and noncommercial purposes, but the work cannot be changed, and the author must be acknowledged.
- Attribution, Share Alike license that states that the author's work can be used for commercial purposes, but the author must be acknowledged and any subsequent licensing must be exactly the same as the original license.
- Attribution license that allows other parties to use the author's work in any way, but the author's work must be acknowledged.

The establishment of the creative commons license counteracted IP monetization because it enabled the free use of copyrighted content.

SEE ALSO *Enterprise Rights Management; Higher Education and the Internet; Intellectual Capital; World Intellectual Property Organization (WIPO).*

BIBLIOGRAPHY

Creative Commons. "About the Licenses." Mountain View, CA, 2011.http://creativecommons.org/licenses.

"Digital Rights and Wrongs." *Economist,* July 17, 1999.

Electronic Frontier Foundation. "RealNetworks v. DVD-CCA (RealDVD Case)." San Francisco, CA, 2011. Available from https://www.eff.org/cases/universal-city-studios-v-realnetworks.

Ellis, Davis. "Cyberlaw and Computer Technology: A Primer on the Law of Intellectual Property Protection." *Florida Bar Journal,* January 1998.

Gladney, Henry. "Digital Intellectual Property: Controversial and International Aspects." *Columbia-VLA Journal of Law & the Arts,* Fall 2000.

Goel, Vindu. "RealNetworks Drops Fight to Sell DVD Copying Software." *Bits* (blog), *New York Times,* March 3, 2010. Available from http://bits.blogs.nytimes.com/2010/03/03/realnetworks-drops-fight-to-sell-dvd-copying-software.

Kirk, Jeremy. "Microsoft Files Lawsuit against DRM Hackers." *IDG News Service,* September 27, 2006. Available from http://www.networkworld.com/news/2006/092706-microsoft-files-lawsuit-against-drm.html?ap1=rcb.

Legal Advantage. "What Is Patent Trolling?" Washington, DC, 2011. Available from http://www.scribd.com/doc/15601305/Legal-Advantage-What-is-Patent-Trolling.

Lohmann, Fred von. "Apple Says iPhone Jailbreaking Is Illegal." San Francisco, CA: Electronic Frontier Foundation, February 12, 2009. Available from https://www.eff.org/deeplinks/2009/02/apple-says-jailbreaking-illegal.

Marechal, Sander. "DRM on Audio CD's Abolished." *LXer,* January 9, 2007. Available from http://lxer.com/module/newswire/view/78008/index.html.

Mutchler, John. & "Will the Digital Millennium Copyright Act Stunt Global Electronic Commerce?" *Intellectual Property Today,* October 2000.

Rosenblatt, Bill. "Fair Use and the DMCA Triennial Rulemaking." *Copyright and Technology,* July 29, 2010. Available from http://copyrightandtechnology.com/2010/07/29/fair-use-and-the-dmca-triennial-rulemaking.

Samuelson, Pamela. "The Digital Rights War." *Wilson Quarterly,* Autumn 1998.

Stone, Brad. "Amazon Erases Orwell Books from Kindle." *New York Times,* July 17, 2009. http://www.nytimes.com/2009/07/18/technology/companies/18amazon.html.

Tennant, Roy. "Copyright and Intellectual Property Rights." *Library Journal,* August 1999.

U.S. Copyright Office. "A Brief Introduction and History." Washington, DC, 2011. Available from http://www.copyright.gov/circs/circ1a.html.

INTELLIGENT AGENTS

Intelligent agents are a member of the bot family—software programs that operate unattended, usually on the Internet. Therefore, agents are sometimes referred to as bots. Individuals or organizations use intelligent agents to perform functions or tasks that otherwise would involve human interaction or repetition. Operating independently on behalf of their users, some intelligent agents mimic human behavior and thought processes and are able to make decisions, learn, and interact with other intelligent agents. Intelligent agents come in stationary and mobile varieties, meaning that they can either reside on individual computer systems or travel from server to server across the Internet to carry out different tasks.

INTELLIGENT AGENTS IN BUSINESS

In the world of e-commerce, consumers use intelligent agents known as shopping bots to search for product and pricing information on the Web. Each shopping bot operates differently, depending on the business model used by its operator. In one scenario, shopping bots direct users to retailers who, by subscribing for a fee, are part of a closed system. Open systems are a more common arrangement and involve agents that include the entire Web in their searches.

Shopping bots have become very popular with consumers. However, they are not popular with some companies because of their ability to initiate bidding wars and eat away profits in the process.

Heavy industry has also taken advantage of the automation benefits offered by intelligent agents. For instance, the mining industry has utilized the technology to improve the processes of drilling, blasting, and transporting material. Mining companies constantly look for ways to automate their processes, and intelligent agents enable them to do so by identifying faults within various processes and streamlining operations among overlapping responsibilities. "The concept of associating functional system elements with an intelligent agent provides the basis for excellent system operation, and performance even when unexpected component failure, environmental changes, workload changes, or altered system operating objectives occur," wrote Paul McRoberts in *Australian Mining.*

The marketing industry additionally utilizes intelligent agents, sometimes to a controversial degree. Marketers were able to use script-reading bots to make evening phone calls to residences. The practice encountered stiff consumer resistance in the mid-2000s, resulting in the national "Do Not Call" list that enabled consumers to opt out of receiving such calls.

Be that as it may, marketers are able to use embedded and nonembedded bots to track consumer behavior. For instance, bots would appear online when users visited certain Web sites; a bot might offer alternative airline fares to a user booking a future flight online. Again, the use of such bots occasionally crossed ethical lines, according to Paul Smith and Ze Zook, who wrote in *Marketing Communications: Integrating Offline and Online with Social Media,* "Some are programmed to be polite, aggressive, or even abusive. All are programmed to be intrusive whenever anything is being bought."

OTHER BOT APPLICATIONS

Intelligent agents also provide varying levels of customer service on the Web. In addition to providing direct answers to common questions, they can save companies money by helping customers narrow down their problem before speaking to a live customer service representative. One such intelligent agent was able to provide round-the-clock customer service to subscribers and prospective customers in English and Spanish. Cloud and on-site customer interaction software maker eGain unveiled its eGain Chatbot in 2011 to help answer questions on mobile phone models, plans, billing, product issues, and procedures. The bot was designed to behave like a human customer service agent, interacting with users in a conversational style.

By maximizing efficiency and convenience, intelligent agents will likely play increasingly important roles in the world of e-commerce. According to the Gartner Group, nonhuman entities including bots were projected to account for 10% of Internet users' total online "friends" by 2015. As that vision becomes reality, security will become a concern for buyers and sellers alike. When consumers send agents out with strategic objectives and the ability to negotiate terms and conditions and make purchases on their behalf, they will need assurances that the agents cannot be manipulated or compromised by other agents. Likewise, companies will need to watch for agents that are used for malicious purposes.

The proliferation of malware in the late 2000s and early 2010s was just one example of the dangerous side of intelligent agents. As intelligent agents continued to grow exponentially in ability, the computing industry increasingly saw the need to secure information and computer resources from unauthorized access. Technology such as behavior-based profiling of software agents helped users to separate helpful bots from more dangerous malware.

SEE ALSO *Shopping Bots.*

BIBLIOGRAPHY

Allen, Maryellen Mott. "The Myth of Intelligent Agents." *Online,* November/December 2000.

Baumohl, Bernard. "Can You Really Trust Those Bots?" *TIME,* December 11, 2000.

Clancy, Heather. "Bots on Parade for ISVs." *Computer Reseller News,* November 20, 2000.

Gavrilova, Marina L., and C. J. Kenneth Tan. *Transactions on Computational Science XII: Special Issue on Cyberworlds.* Berlin: Springer-Verlag, 2011.

Mandry, Torsten, Gunther Pernul, and Alexander W. Rohm. "Mobile Agents in Electronic Markets: Opportunities, Risks, Agent Protection." *International Journal of Electronic Commerce,* Winter 2000–2001.

McRoberts, Paul. "Automation: Leading the Way." *Australian Mining,* October 14, 2011. Available from http://www.miningaustralia.com.au/news/automation–leading-the-way.

Plummer, Daryl. "Gartner Top Predictions for 2011: IT's Growing Transparency and Consumerization." Stamford, CT: Gartner, 2010. Available from http://www.gartner.com/it/content/1462300/1462334/december_15_top_predictions_for_2011_dplummer.pdf.

"Premier Wireless Operator in the US Selects eGain Virtual Assistant Technology to Provide Innovative, Multilingual Customer Self-Service." *Market Watch,* October 6, 2011. Available from http://www.marketwatch.com/story/premier-wireless-operator-in-the-us-selects-egain-virtual-assistant-technology-to-provide-innovative-multilingual-customer-self-service-2011-10-06?reflink=MW_news_stmp.

Schwartz, Ephraim. "Web Bots Enhance Self-Service Experience." *InfoWorld,* February 7, 2000.

Smith, Paul R., and Ze Zook. *Marketing Communications: Integrating Offline and Online with Social Media.* 5th ed. London: Kogan Page, 2011.

"Special Issue: Intelligent Agents for Electronic Commerce." *International Journal of Electronic Commerce,* Spring 2000.

Trott, Bob. "Online Agents Evolve for Customer Service." *InfoWorld,* December 11, 2000.

Ulfelder, Steve. "Undercover Agents." *Computerworld,* June 5, 2000.

INTERCHANGE AND INTERCHANGE FEE

The vast majority of financial transactions that happen during e-commerce involve credit cards, especially those between consumers and companies that sell goods and services. The credit cards that consumers use are issued by different card-issuing banks throughout the world, to which one must apply and be approved before receiving a card. In general, when credit cards are used to make purchases, several different parties are usually involved. These include the cardholder, card-issuing bank, merchant, and the acquiring bank that handles credit card transactions for the merchant.

Interchange is the process by which a card-issuing bank transfers monies to a merchant's acquiring bank in order to cover a cardholder's purchase. During interchange, the card-issuing bank deducts an interchange fee for every transaction. The interchange fee eventually is passed along to the merchant, along with other "discount fees" that make it possible for acquiring banks to profit from the transactions. The income that card-issuing banks received by charging interchange fees grew in the 2000s. According to credit card information Web site Card Hub, interchange income increased 65% between 2006 and 2010, rising from $16.8 billion to $27.7 billion.

INTERCHANGE FEE CONTROVERSY

Interchange fees have courted controversy, especially in the area of antitrust violations. Howard H. Chang and David S. Evans argued in *Antitrust Bulletin* that "interchange fees for modern payment card systems are part of a long historical line of vertical price restrictions that have reflected the exercise of market power. When new payment systems require the cooperation of large segments of the banking industry, it naturally gives rise to the concern that those banks will enact systems and rules that are not necessary to the success of the payment system, but that result in a significant reduction in the benefits that will flow to the public from the new technology."

Throughout the 2000s, banks and credit card companies were investigated for the way they determined and set interchange fees. In the United States, Congress tried to stem unnecessarily high fees through the Dodd-Frank Financial Reform and Consumer Protection Act of 2010. In 2011, an addendum to the act, the Durbin Amendment, enabled merchants to give customers discounts for using alternative payment services that contained lower or no processing fees, such as cash and checks. Furthermore, the amendment tasked the Federal Reserve with regulating interchange fees for debit cards to ensure they remain reasonable and proportional. The legislation initially capped fees at 12 cents per transaction. Banks and credit card companies that were concerned over the drastic fee decline lobbied successfully to increase the cap to 21 cents, approved in late 2011.

Despite what many hailed as progress in regulating interchange fees, the Durbin Amendment had its fair share of criticism. For instance, while it restricted how much large banks could charge merchants for debit card transactions, it placed no restrictions on credit card networks like VISA and MasterCard. Also exempted from the regulations were sellers of prepaid cards and banks and credit unions with less than $10 billion in assets. "Although the Durbin Amendment will decrease the amount that large banks can charge in interchange fees, loopholes within the legislation will significantly diminish its impact for both merchants and banks over time," according to Card Hub. Meanwhile, some critics contended that consumers would see no price relief as a result of the new legislation, citing a previous effort in Australia as having little impact on individual consumers. Large banks that were subject to regulations were expected to make up for the lost income by increasing monthly fees and minimum balance requirements, thus making debit card reward programs less appealing.

Prior to the Durbin Amendment, fees averaged roughly 44 cents per transaction, amounting to about $2 of every $100 paid to credit card companies and banks. Interchange fees were double the amount of late fees paid by Americans to credit companies and banks, and triple the amount of ATM fees, according to Tim Parker in *Investopedia.* "The interchange fee is supposed to cover the cost of processing your credit card payment," wrote Parker. "However, according to the Merchant's Payment Coalition, 'only 13% of the credit card interchange fee goes to processing credit card transactions; much of the rest goes to pay for billions of pieces of unsolicited junk mail annually, among other dubious credit card marketing activities aimed at students or those with bad credit histories.'"

SEE ALSO *Transaction Issues.*

BIBLIOGRAPHY

Chang, Howard H., and David S. Evans. "The Competitive Effects of the Collective Setting of Interchange Fees by Payment Card Systems." *Antitrust Bulletin,* Fall 2000.

Daly, James J. "Many Happy Returns." *Credit Card Management,* May 2000.

"Interchange Fee Study—Durbin Amendment." *Card Hub,* 2010. Available from http://education.cardhub.com/interchange-fee-study-2010.

Parker, Tim. "The Truth About Credit Card Swipe Fees." *Investopedia,* July 14, 2011. Available from http://financialedge.investopedia.com/financial-edge/0711/The-Truth-About-Credit-Card-Swipe-Fees.aspx#axzz1b3dTujTl.

INTERNATIONAL CHAMBER OF COMMERCE (ICC)

The International Chamber of Commerce (ICC), which also describes itself as the world business organization, was founded in 1919 to promote peace among countries through trade and prosperity. The ICC grew to become the leading body of representation for enterprises around the globe. Its rules and guidelines, while being voluntary, govern international business actions and have become a standard used by ICC members, which include businesses and associations in over 130 countries involved in international trade. The ICC was given the highest level of consultative status with the United Nations shortly after its formation.

LEADERSHIP

In March of 2011, Gerard Worms became chairman of the ICC, and Harold McGraw III was vice chairman. Secretary general for the organization was Jean-Guy Carrier. Victor K. Fung was ICC honorary chairman.

In addition to these members, the executive board of the ICC also includes elected members from all over the world, who serve for three years per term. As of October 2011, elected executive board members included Jose Luiz Alqueres (Brazil), Pedro Aspe (Mexico), Abdul Rahman Attar (Syria), John Buchanan (United Kingdom), Manfred Gentz (Germany), Martin Granholm (Finland), Khalifa bin Jassim bin Mohammad Al-Thani (Qatar), Young Tae Kim (Korea), Peter Mihok (Slovak Republic), Yogendra Modi (India), Mikio Sasaki (Japan), Andreas Schmid (Switzerland), Oren Shachor (Israel), Andrea Tomat (Italy), Kees van der Waaij (the Netherlands), and Chen Yuan (China). The executive board also includes three ex officio members. As of 2011, these members included Jorma Ollila (chairman of the World Business Council for Sustainable Development), John Beechey (chairman of the Court of Arbitration), and Rona Yircali (chairman of ICC World Chambers Federation).

The ICC council oversees much of the work of the ICC and meets twice annually most years. The executive board of the ICC creates and oversees ICC policies, programs, and strategies. The board also takes care of the finances, approves policy documents, and recommends ICC chairmanship and secretary general appointments. In addition to the council and board, there are also national committees and groups in different countries. These groups and committees have two tasks: they represent the ICC in their nations, and they ensure that their own nation's interests are represented when the ICC develops policies.

MAJOR DEVELOPMENTS

The ICC is involved in business-related issues such as trade and investment policy, financial services, information technologies, telecommunications, marketing ethics, the environment, transportation, competition law, and intellectual property. As an increasing number of business transactions began taking place on the World Wide Web throughout the 1990s, the ICC began focusing on Internet-related issues and formed the Commission on Telecommunications and Information Technologies. The commission was founded to "formulate policy on issues such as electronic business, information security, telecommunications, and competition," according to the ICC. Upon its formation, its agenda included advising governments on competition in the telecommunications industry and pushing for the implementation and increased development of the World Trade Organization telecommunications agreement, along with aiding developing countries in meeting telecommunications objectives.

Along with the development of the commission, the ICC also created the Electronic Commerce Project (ECP). The ECP consisted of experts from various other ICC commissions including Banking Technique and Practice, Telecommunications and Information Technologies, Financial Services and Insurance, Transport, and International Commercial Practice. According to the ICC, the ECP was developed "to create global trust in electronic trade transactions by defining best business practices for the digital age." In 2001, the project was divided into areas including the General Usage for International Digitally Ensured Commerce (GUIDEC) and the Electronic Trade Practices Working Group.

GUIDEC, a set of international rules, definitions, and guidelines for the use of electronic authentication techniques, was the first ECP initiative. It became available on the ICC Web site in November 1997 and was considered to be one of the first sets of global regulations for electronic commerce. GUIDEC was created to promote a global understanding of techniques used in electronic commerce and business transactions on the Internet, and to "establish a general framework for the ensuring and certification of digital messages, based upon existing law and practice in different legal systems."

The Electronic Trade Practices Working Group (ETP) was also developed to establish a set of rules regarding electronic trade and settlement. The ETP was formed to make trade more efficient on the Internet by setting guidelines for buyers and sellers who negotiate, making contracts, and arranging for financing, transport, and insurance on the Web. The ETP has worked to integrate international trade regulations that typically related to transactions in the physical world with those taking place with more frequency on the Web.

Throughout the 2000s, the ICC was involved in addressing technological changes and advertising using new technologies. In 2006, the ICC established the Business Action to Support the Information Society (BASIS) initiative to promote companies to develop Internet policies. That same year, the ICC published new guidelines to help businesses promote fair advertising for the food and beverage industry.

In 2011, the ICC introduced a Consolidated ICC Code of Advertising and Marketing Communications in order to help promote self-regulation that would protect customers. The new code outlined consumer rights online, company responsibilities in terms of advertising, and set up new parameters to protect minors online. The code also established rules for protecting private information online and set up standards for online advertising.

In 2011, the ICC also announced changes to its rules of arbitration for international issues. The new rules went into effect at the start of 2012 and aimed to reduce the costs and the delays associated with international arbitration. According to ICC representatives, the new rules will address current information technology issues that affect international arbitration, as well as new arbitration practices.

SEE ALSO *General Usage for Internationally Digitally Ensured Commerce (GUIDEC).*

BIBLIOGRAPHY

Brown, Jennifer. "New ICC Rules of Arbitration Aim to Cut Costs and Time."*Legal Feeds,* September 23, 2011. Available from http://www.canadianlawyermag.com/legalfeeds/467/New-ICC-rules-of-arbitration-aim-to-cut-costs-and-time.html.

"ICC G20 Advisory Group and Top CEOs Gather in Hong Kong." *Arbitrage Magazine,* September 24, 2011. Available from http://www.arbitragemagazine.com/topics/finance/icc-1g20-advisory-group-2top-ceos-gather-3hong-kong.

International Chamber of Commerce. "GUIDEC." Paris, 2001. Available from www.iccwbo.org/home/guidec.

———. "ICC's New Business Chief to Focus on Developing World." Paris, February 15, 2001. Available from http://www.iccwbo.org/policy/environment/iccbidg/index.html.

———. "Public Policies Enable the Internet to Create Opportunity and Jobs." Paris, September 26, 2011. Available from http://www.iccwbo.org/basis/index.html?id=45819.

Mahoney, Michael. "Europeans Crack Down on $3.9B Internet Banking Scam." *E-Commerce Times,* April 12, 2001. Available from http://www.ecommercetimes.com/story/8901.html.

"New Marketing Code Raises Consumer Protection Standards Around the World." *Utah Pulse,* October 2, 2011. Available from http://utahpulse.com/bookmark/15871816-New-Marketing-Code-Raises-Consumer-Protection-Standards-Around-the-World.

INTERNATIONAL COMMITTEE FOR INFORMATION TECHNOLOGY STANDARDS (INCITS)

The need for common standards is obvious to anyone who has ever traveled with an electric hair dryer and learned that it needed a special adapter to be used in Europe, or who once tried to purchase a printer cartridge only to find 30 or 40 incompatible types from which to choose. The need for standards is even more apparent in electronic commerce, which presupposes the rapid, accurate, technically problem-free exchange of data between computers via the World Wide Web. The International Committee for Information Technology Standards (INCITS) takes a leading role in establishing IT standards for the United States and in representing American interests in groups that set international standards, including the International Organization for Standardization (ISO).

The mission of INCITS—pronounced "insights"—is to establish standards in the areas of: "Information and Communication Technologies (ICT), encompassing storage, processing, transfer, display, management, organization, and retrieval of information." Multimedia, such as JPEG and MPEG, intercommunication among various computers and information systems, storage media such as portable hard disks, memory chips, database technology, security, and programming languages were always a primary focus of the group. In early 2001, the organization added electronic commerce to its agenda of interests.

The organization's moniker also went through a series of transformations, starting with its formation in 1961 as the Accredited Standards Committee X3. In 1997, it was renamed the National Committee for Information Technology Standards (NCITS), which was upgraded to the International Committee for Information Technology Standards (INCITS) in 2002.

Some 1,700 organizations around the world are members of INCITS. They include leading companies from the computer, telecommunications, and Internet industries, defense industries, and governmental bodies and universities. The highest level of membership, the executive board, is composed of companies and organizations, such as the U.S. Department of Defense, U.S. Department of Homeland Security, Adobe, Apple, EMC Corporation, Farance, Hewlett-Packard, IBM, Institute of Electrical and Electronics Engineers (IEEE), Intel, Microsoft, Oracle, and Sony.

COMMITEE WORK

Members pay an annual membership fee, plus an additional fee to procure voting rights on any of INCITS' 22 Technical Committees (TCs). The TCs are where the main work of NCITS is accomplished. They research, study, and hammer out standards for the IT industry. There are TCs devoted to most conceivable categories of the IT realm, ranging from the apparently mundane, like computer paper and forms, office equipment, and storage media (such as optical digital data disks), to high-level specialties such as the various programming languages, character sets, security, I/O interfaces, text processing, and database technologies.

TCs carry out three main functions. First, within the limits of their assigned technical scope, they study and draft proposed new standards for hardware and software. Second, they recommend new standards-related projects for study to INCITS. Third, they act as technical advisors for or on behalf of INCITS at meetings of international standards-setting organizations.

Establishing a new standard at INCITS is a process that can take from 6 to 18 months at its most rapid, or years and years at its slowest. Once INCITS accepts a standard, compliance is strictly voluntary, even by the group's members. A critical standard in which INCITS had a hand at establishing was the size of floppy disks. The five-inch floppy was universal in its day, and the easy transfer of data between computers was a fact of life.

In the wake of the terrorist attacks on the World Trade Center and the Pentagon in September 2001, INCITS turned its attention to the establishment of common standards for biometrics—the measurement and analysis of biological data. If an international standard for taking and transmitting electronic fingerprints had been in place before the attack, for example, it would have been much easier to track terrorists across international borders because fingerprints could have been exchanged by law enforcement agencies instantaneously. Four years after the Biometrics TC was established, it generated significant results. INCITS' biometric standards were adopted in a number of governmental organizations, including the U.S. Department of Homeland Security. Among the standards utilized was the template for face recognition data storage. The Biometrics TC continues to develop standards for data interchange formats, application program interfaces profiles, and performance testing for physical identification software to be used across the globe.

SEE ALSO *Biometrics.*

BIBLIOGRAPHY

InterNational Committee for Information Technology Standards (INCITS). "INCITS Technical Committee M1, Biometrics, Takes Steps to Enhance the Usability of Its Family of Open Systems Standards for Biometric Data Interchange and Interoperability." Washington, DC, August 24, 2006. Available from http://www.incits.org/press/2006/pr200606.pdf.

———. " What Is INCITS?" Washington, DC, 2011. Available from http://www.incits.org/geninfo.htm.

Ryan, Paul. "ISO OOXML Convener: Microsoft's Format 'Heading for Failure'." *Ars Technica,* April 2, 2010. Available from http://arstechnica.com/microsoft/news/2010/04/iso-ooxml-convener-microsofts-format-heading-for-failure.ars.

Yasin, Rutrell. "Open XML Voted Down but Not Out." *Government Computer News,* September 8, 2007. Available from http://gcn.com/articles/2007/09/08/open-xml-voted-down-but-not-out.aspx.

INTERNATIONAL DATA CORP. (IDC)

With more than 60 offices around the world, work in 110 countries worldwide, and roughly 1,500 employees as of 2012, International Data Corp. (IDC) is an information technology (IT) market research, analysis, and consulting firm. IDC's wide-ranging research covers all aspects of the IT industry, including operating systems, PCs, peripheral equipment, semiconductors, software, services, telecommunications products, distribution channels, and the Internet. IDC's clients—mainly IT professionals, IT suppliers, e-business executives, service suppliers, investment professionals, investors, and corporate managers—have access to various information services, conferences, and research documents, many of which are available for purchase at IDC's online store. Those who opt for customized consulting appointments with IDC analysts may seek assistance with business strategy development, product development, assessment of competition, creation and achievement of marketing goals, and evaluation of potential alliances and purchases.

In addition to consulting, custom research, market research, and advisory services, IDC also organizes information technology events and conferences. Based in Framingham, Massachusetts, IDC operates as a subsidiary of International Data Group, which had 2010 revenues of $3.16 billion.

COMPETITION

According to Hoover's Online, companies such as Aberdeen Group, Inc., Forrester Research, Inc., and Gartner, Inc., represent the largest competition for IDC. Forrester Research had a reported $7.3 million in sales in 2010. Gartner was one of IDC's largest competitors, with 4,461 employees and $100.4 million in sales as of 2010, according to Hoover's market research.

DEVELOPMENT

IDC was founded in 1964 by Patrick J. McGovern, a biophysics graduate from the Massachusetts Institute of Technology (MIT), to offer IT statistics to the fledgling computer industry. While earning his degree at MIT, McGovern had worked as the associate editor for *Computers and Automation,* the first computer magazine published in the United States. When he graduated in 1959, McGovern had been promoted to associate publisher, a position he held for the next five years.

In 1967, IDC began publishing *Computerworld,* a weekly newspaper covering the computer industry. Eventually, publishing became the firm's main focus. By 1970, McGovern had moved his publishing activities—which eventually would include industry giants like *PC World, MacWorld, Network World,* and *CIO*—into a new entity called International Data Group (IDG). It was under this parent that IDC began to operate as a subsidiary.

The firm conducted its first industry briefing session in 1968. IDC expanded internationally for the first time in 1969, when it established an office in the United Kingdom. Six years later, the firm moved into both Germany and Japan. IDC bought Link Resources Corp. in 1980. Within three years, 13 offices were in operation, including units in Spain, France, Italy, Sweden, and Norway. IDC created IDC China Ltd. in 1986. By the end of the decade, the firm also had moved into Canada, Korea, and Latin America.

Kirk Campbell was named IDC president and CEO in 1990, two positions he continued to hold as of 2011. IDC held its first European IT Forum in Venice, Italy, in 1991; roughly 200 industry professionals attended. International expansion continued the following year with the establishment of new offices in Greece, Nigeria, Turkey, South Africa, and Egypt. The firm conducted its Global New Media survey for the first time in 1995. Participants from 13 different countries were queried. That year, IDC created a subsidiary in Brazil. Aggressive growth efforts persisted in 1996 with the creation of a market research office in Moscow, Russia, and a Latin American research center in Miami, Florida. Sales that year reached roughly $100 million. By then, the firm was operating offices in 400 countries, employing 300 market researchers, and generating more than 2,000 IT market surveys each year.

Wanting to grant clients 24-hour access to its information, IDC launched its Internet-based IDCNet service in 1997. The firm conducted its first forum for Internet executives the following year. Sales in 1999 grew another 22%, and the firm's workforce grew by 17% to nearly 600. The firm's rapid growth finally came to a halt in the early 2000s as the dot-com meltdown undercut the need for e-commerce market research, prompting IDC to lay off numerous e-commerce analysts in 2001.

DISPUTED CLAIMS

In the 2000s, IDC also faced some criticism over the information it was distributing. For example, in 2005, an article in the *Economist* disputed the findings of study data released by the Business Software Alliance (BSA) and the IDC about the extent and costs of software piracy. The IDC determined the rate of piracy by estimating the amount of software installed in each country and comparing that to the known amount of software sold in each country. The resulting amount after subtracting the two numbers was supposed to yield the amount of pirated software. The IDC then multiplied that number by the cost per software unit to determine the economic cost of the software. However, the article claimed that this approach was problematic as it did not address the complexities of software piracy. In 2002, IDC was criticized for releasing a study, sponsored by Microsoft, which concluded that Linux servers were more expensive than newly released Microsoft ones.

IDC continued expanding in the 2000s, especially as information technology became less focused in a small number of countries. After establishing offices in Africa and the Middle East in the 1990s, IDC opened a new office in Dubai in 2001 and began an expansion run in those two regions, expanding into Casablanca, Lagos, Istanbul, Johannesburg, and Nairobi in the early 2000s. In 2011, IDC announced a new dedicated office in Riyadh, Saudi Arabia.

In 2011, IDC decided to host that year's CIO Summit in Saudi Arabia. The CIO summits began in 2008 and are customized events that address the local needs of businesses and attendees. In addition to the summits, IDC also organizes online conferences, interactive panels, briefings, and other events for managers, analysts, and PR professionals.

SEE ALSO *Information Technology.*

BIBLIOGRAPHY

"BSA or Just BS?" *Economist,* May 19, 2005. Available from http://www.economist.com/node/3993427.

"IDC Steps Up Presence in Saudi Arabia with New Country Office Financial." *Financial,* October 4, 2011. Available from http://finchannel.com/Main_News/Business/95888_IDC_Steps_Up_Presence_in_audi_Arabia_with_New_Country_Office.

International Data Corp. "About IDC." Framingham, MA, 2011. Available from http://www.idc.com/about/about.jsp?t=1321192940902.

"International Data Corp." Austin, TX: Hoover's, 2011. Available from http://www.hoovers.com/company/IDC_Research_Inc/ryykrki-1-1njea3.html.

Konicki, Steve. "Economic Slowdown Hits Hard at Analyst Firms." *InformationWeek,* September 10, 2001.

Lettice, John. "Windows Costs Less Than Linux. A Bit. Sometimes – MS Study." *The Register,* December 3, 2002. Available from http://www.theregister.co.uk/2002/12/03/windows_costs_less_than_linux.

Violino, Bob, and Rich Levin. "Analyzing the Analysts." *InformationWeek,* November 17, 1997.

INTERNATIONAL TELECOMMUNICATIONS UNION (ITU)

The International Telecommunications Union (ITU) is a United Nations (UN) agency charged with overseeing international cooperation regarding information and communication technologies (ICTs), including satellite orbits, the radio spectrum, broadband Internet, cell phones, and other communication and information technology. The ITU also establishes worldwide ICT standards and policies and helps provide access to telecommunications in developing nations. In addition, the ITU hosts events to bring together telecommunication companies, world leaders, and others involved in information technologies. The ITU is part of the United Nations Development Group and is based in Geneva.

As of 2012, the ITU has members that include more than 700 academic institutions and private-sector organizations, as well as 193 countries. The ITU had 12 offices around the world that same year. Dr. Hamadoun Touré of Mali was reelected for a four-year term as ITU secretary-general in 2010.

HISTORY

The International Telecommunications Union dates back to 1865, when 20 countries jointly signed the framework agreement at the International Telegraph Convention, establishing common rules and standard equipment for transmitting telegraph messages across international lines. The International Telegraph Union was launched to provide a forum to turn this agreement into a living framework through the evolution of international communications technologies, facilitating dialogue and enabling amendments to the initial agreement. Within a matter of years, the International Telegraph Union was busily devising legislation aimed at developing international standards for telephony and radio communications, further solidifying its role as the primary body governing and promoting international communications.

In 1932, the Telegraph Union merged the 1865 International Telegraph Convention and the 1906 International Radiotelegraph Convention into one agreement called the International Telecommunications Convention, and in 1934 changed its name to the International Telecommunications Union (ITU), assuming responsibility for promoting and standardizing all international communications. The ITU moved under the auspices of the United Nations in 1947 under an agreement aimed at modernizing the union.

In 1989, at a Plenipotentiary Conference held in Nice, France, the ITU took responsibility for spearheading technical telecommunications assistance to developing countries, placing such activities on a par with their traditional standardization and coordination activities. Through the Telecommunications Development Bureau, established the following year, technological developments in telecommunications were met with new initiatives from the ITU aimed at integrating these innovations into the infrastructures of developing countries, thereby connecting them to a broader world network.

DEVELOPMENT IN THE 2000s AND NEW CONCERNS

In 2002, the Marrakesh Plenipotentary Conference addressed the need for the ITU to focus on accessibility by creating interconnected services and networks. That same year, the ITU began planning the World Summit on the Information Society (WSIS).

The WSIS was the first time national leaders and policymakers met to address information technologies in the emerging information age. The first part of the WSIS, in late 2003, was attended by 11,000 representatives from 175 nations. A large concern at that WSIS summit was the Internet. Specifically, some countries were concerned about the role that the Internet Corporation for Assigned Names and Numbers (ICANN) played in regulating the Internet. ICANN is a nonprofit company that has an agreement with the U.S. government to oversee the addressing system online. Many nations at the 2003 summit felt that ICANN did not reflect their interests and wanted that organization replaced with a UN agency or group that would be more international in scope and would be better able to regulate issues such as taxes for online purchases and problems such as online security. The second part of the WSIS took place in 2005; 19,000 people from 174 nations took part.

The Connect Africa Summit took place in 2007, organized partly by the ITU. That event was designed to increase ICT access across the continent and generated promised investments of more than $55 billion from the ICT, national leaders, and private organizations. The summit also addressed the ITU's Millennium Development Goals (MDGs), which would improve access and connectivity around the world by the year 2015. The ITU established the World Information Society Award and presented the first recipient during the 2007 summit.

In 2011, the ITU recommended getting rid of Greenwich Mean Time (GMT) because that system, according to the ITU, was no longer accurate enough for information and communications technology. GMT is a system used to set international clocks. It measures time according to the sun's movement over a line located in Greenwich, England. The system measures time by the movement of the Earth, but researchers have concluded that the rotation of the planet slows down slightly every year and is therefore not perfectly reliable. ITU recommended using Coordinated Universal Time (UTC) as the new system for international clocks. UTC uses atomic clocks to establish time, and the ITU suggested in 2011 that the International Bureau of Weights and Measures (BIPM) could oversee the new system of UTC.

The ITU has also been involved in establishing standards and policies concerning the environmental impact of ICTs. In September 2011, the ITU announced a new set of standards and methods to measure the environmental effect of ICTs and developed a set of guidelines concerning the use of minerals in ICTs. At issue also was the use of minerals from conflict areas in information and communications technology. Some minerals used in the production of cell phones and other devices are so-called conflict minerals, derived from countries engaged in wars or from countries with poor human rights records. The 2011 announcement also included plans to increase both recycling and the life of cell phone batteries in order to minimize their environmental impact.

BIBLIOGRAPHY

International Telecommunications Union. "About ITU." Geneva, Switzerland, 2011. Available from http://www.itu.int/en/about/Pages/default.aspx.

Malim, George. "E-commerce a Priority." *Telecommunications,* August 1999.

McGuire, David. "U.N. Summit to Focus on Internet." *Washington Post,* December 5, 2003. Available from http://www.washingtonpost.com/ac2/wp-dyn/A36852-2003Dec4?language=printer.

Todd, Tony. "World Telecoms Body Recommends Scrapping GMT." *France 24,* 5 October 2011. Available from http://www.france24.com/en/20111004-world-telecoms-body-recommends-scrapping-gmt.

"UN Reports Agreement on Ways to Assess Green Impact of Information Technologies." *UN News Centre,* September 28, 2011. Available from http://www.un.org/apps/news/story.asp?NewsID=39877&Cr=information+ technology&Cr1=.

Yarbrough, Tanya L. "Connecting the World: The Development of the Global Information Infrastructure." *Federal Communications Law Journal,* March 2001.

INTERNET

A collection of networks linking billions of computers throughout the world, the Internet is used by more than two billion people as of March 2011, according to Miniwatts Marketing Group, for things like research, communication, and commerce transactions. Via technology that spawned the "information age," the Internet has become a tool for professional, educational, and personal exchanges. As the Internet's popularity has increased, so have the opportunities for making money online. According to Miniwatts Marketing Group, Internet usage grew more than 480% globally between 2001 and 2011.

The Internet works by connecting individual computers or devices through an Internet service provider (ISP). When a device connects to the Internet through an ISP, that device becomes part of the ISP's network. The ISP then may link to a larger network. Larger ISPs may rent fiber optic lines from other companies in order to provide Internet service to customers. ISPs allow their customers to share information by connecting to Network Access Points (NAPs). NAPs allow for immense amounts of data to travel all over the world.

WHO IS ONLINE?

According to Miniwatts Marketing Group and the Web site Internet World Stats, world Internet penetration rates are highest for North America, Oceania, and Europe. The rates are 78.3% for North America, 60.1% for Oceania and Australia, 58.3% for Europe, 37% for Latin America and the Caribbean, 31.7% for the Middle East, 23.8% for Asia, and 11.4% for Africa. The worldwide Internet penetration rate is 30.2%, considerably lower than the rate in North America, Oceania, and Europe.

According to the same source, as of March 2011, the largest number of world Internet users (44%) were located in Asia, followed by Europe (22.7%), North America (13%), Latin America and the Caribbean (10.3%), Africa (5.7%), the Middle East (3.3%), and Oceania and Australia (1%). Internet usage over the decade 2001 to 2011 has risen fastest, in terms of percentage growth, in Africa, which had 118,609,620 Internet users in 2011, with usage growing 2,527.4% between 2001 and 2011. The next highest growth rate was in the Middle East, which had 68,553,666 Internet users in March 2011, a 1,987.0 % increase over those same years. Other regions were as follows (2011 figures and growth rates since 2001): Latin America and the Caribbean (215,939,400 Internet users; 1,037.4% increase); Asia (922,329,554 Internet users; 706.9% increase;) Europe (476,213,935 Internet users; 353.1% increase;); Oceania and Australia, with a comparatively smaller population (21,293,830 Internet users; 179.4% increase), and North America (272,066,000 Internet users; 151.7% increase). The low growth rate in North America was because that region was one of the first to enjoy widespread use of the Internet among its population.

HISTORY

The precursor of the Internet, ARPAnet, was created in 1969 by the Advanced Research Projects Agency (ARPA) at the directive of the U.S. Department of Defense, which sought a means for governmental communication in the event of nuclear war. To create what would become the world's largest wide area network (WAN), ARPA chose Interface Message Processors (IMPs) to connect host computers via telephone lines. To create the underlying network needed to connect the IMPs, ARPA hired Bolt Beranek and Newman, a Cambridge, Massachusetts-based research and development firm. The last component needed was a protocol, or a set of standards, that would facilitate communication between the host sites. This was developed internally by the Network Working Group. ARPAnet's Network Control Protocol allowed users to access computers and printers in remote locations and exchange files between computers. This protocol eventually was replaced by the more sophisticated Transmission Control Protocol/Internet Protocol (TCP/IP), which allowed ARPAnet to be connected with a several other networks that had been launched by various institutions. It was this group of networks that eventually formed the core of what later became known as the Internet. No longer useful, ARPAnet was shut down in 1990.

A National Science Foundation decree that prevented commercial use of the Internet was dissolved in 1991, the same year the World Wide Web came into existence. By then, personal computer use by businesses, institutions, and individuals had increased dramatically. When the graphics-based Web browsing program known as Mosaic was released in 1993, the Internet's growth exploded. Firms like Netscape and Yahoo! were founded soon after, making access to the Internet even easier. By 1996, an estimated 40 million individuals were accessing the Internet, and by 1999, that number had grown to 200 million.

In 1997, the search engine Google was created by Stanford students Sergey Brin and Larry Page. Within a few years, this search engine became one of the most popular ways to search the Internet for relevant content and allowed more Internet users to search for data more easily. It is difficult to overstate the importance of Google to Internet use in the early 2000s and into the 2010s. Google made the Internet accessible and made it easier to access data. Google's paid advertising also changed the way that businesses advertised online.

USES OF THE INTERNET

The Internet became a powerful sales tool and a place to do business in the 2000s, with e-commerce often touted as one of the rapidly growing areas online. According to BuddeComme, a research and consultancy company, less than 4% of retail sales in the United States in 2010 were made online. Nevertheless, online sales were a multibillion-dollar business in 2011 and were forecast to account for more than $240 billion in U.S. sales by 2014.

As the Internet has grown in importance in the twenty-first century, many countries have been striving to bring accessibility to more potential Internet users. National and international investment in fiber optics and broadband technologies is designed to help with this issue, as is the promotion of newer, inexpensive browsing devices. In 2010, for example, India's human resource development minister Kapil Sibal announced plans for a $35 computing device. The device, Aakash, was launched in 2011 and the government even subsidized the item for students. The device was made by Datawind, a Canadian-based company.

After the early 2000s, the Internet became so ubiquitous in individual lives that many people chose to work, socialize, and do business online. The Internet allowed for the rise of teleworking, online marketing, purely online businesses, e-mail, and social media. Use of the Internet became not only more widespread but also more interactive. Social media sites and blogs encouraged communication and not just information sharing online.

After the first decade of the 2000s, another change to the Internet took place. While in the 1990s and early 2000s, most people accessed the Internet through computers, by 2011 many people were using mobile devices to go online. According to a 2011 Global Consumer Survey (GCS) report by MEF, 18% of polled Internet users in five continents use mobile Internet exclusively, no longer relying on fixed line Internet connections. The switch meant that more users were doing online banking, online shopping (now dubbed m-commerce rather than e-commerce), and other tasks through mobile devices, despite concerns about the security of mobile Internet connections.

NATIONS AND THE INTERNET

One issue that has always affected the Internet is freedom. From companies to universities to nations, there are many people and groups who wish to control how the Internet is used. There are also many people who wish to protect the essential freedom of the Internet, which allows anyone to share and use information online. In 2011, U.S. secretary of state Hillary Clinton spoke out about the importance of Internet freedom. After 2009 and through 2011, however, an increasing number of countries began to worry about the impact of the Internet on domestic security. As more and more individuals were able to share information and opinions via social networking sites and blogs, some nations began using Internet surveillance and filtering tools to restrict the amount of information their citizens were able to access.

SEE ALSO *ARPAnet; History of the Internet and World Wide Web (WWW).*

BIBLIOGRAPHY

"2010 World Digital Economy – E-commerce and M-commerce Trends." Bucketty, New South Wales, Australia: BuddeComm, October 2011. Available from https://www.budde.com.au/Research/2010-World-Digital-Economy-E-Commerce-and-M-Commerce-Trends.html?r=51.

"Aakash, the World's Cheapest Tablet PC, Is Here." *Tribune,* October 5, 2011. Available from http://www.tribuneindia.com/2011/20111006/main4.htm.

Briggs, Helen. "Internet 'May Be Changing Brains.'" *BBC,* October 19, 2011. Available from http://www.bbc.co.uk/news/health-15353397.

Dreyfus, Hubert L. *On the Internet.* New York: Routledge, 2009.

Green, Lelia. *The Internet: An Introduction to New Media.* New York: Berg Publishers, 2010.

"Internet." In *Techencyclopedia.* Point Pleasant, PA: Computer Language Co., 2001. Available from www.techweb.com/encyclopedia.

"Internet." In *Webopedia.* Darien, CT: Internet.com, 2001. Available from http://www.webopedia.com/TERM/I/Internet.html.

"An Internet Time Line." *PC Week,* November 18, 1996.

Miriri, Duncan. "Europe Plans Charter to Safeguard Internet Users." *Reuters,* September 27, 2011. Available from http://www.reuters.com/article/2011/09/27/us-internet-governance-europe-idUSTRE78Q3RP20110927.

"Mobile Internet Access Grows Despite Security Concerns." *Biz Community,* October 25, 2011. Available from http://www.bizcommunity.com/Article/196/78/66129.html.

National Museum of American History. "Birth of the Internet: ARPANET: General Overview." Washington, DC: Smithsonian Institution. Available from http://smithsonian.yahoo.com/birthoftheinternet.html.

Roberts, Hal, Ethan Zuckerman, Jillian York, Rob Faris, and John Palfrey. "International Bloggers and Internet Control." Cambridge, MA: Berkman Center for Internet and Society at Harvard University, August 18, 2011. Available from http://cyber.law.harvard.edu/publications/2011/International_Bloggers_Internet_Control.

Roberts, Hal, Ethan Zuckerman, and John Palfrey. "2011 Circumvention Tool Evaluation." Cambridge, MA: Berkman Center for Internet and Society at Harvard University, August 18, 2011. Available from http://cyber.law.harvard.edu/publications/2011/2011_Circumvention_Tool_Evaluation.

"World Internet Stats." Internet World Stats, 2011. Available from http://www.internetworldstats.com/stats.htm.

INTERNET ACCESS, TRACKING GROWTH OF

The tracking of Internet accessibility in the 2010s has largely been based on Web analytics measurement tools. Web analytics refers to the process of measuring the performance of a Web site in terms of the behavior of online visitors, with the objective of establishing user accessibility trends. Web analytics profiles the frequencies and online behaviors of individual Web site visitors and enables Web site tracking firms or Web site owners to determine the effectiveness of their content and navigation systems. Web analytics is mainly carried out through two forms of measurement, off-site analytics and on-site analytics.

OFF-SITE ANALYTICS

Off-site Web analytics focuses on the measurement of the likely Internet browsing trends of potential visitors to a Web site. This measurement tool operates on a macro basis, such that it seeks to establish a bigger picture and relationship between past, current, and likely future Web site visitor behaviors and trends. Panels and Internet service providers (ISPs) are the two main sources of data applied in the measurement technique applied in off-site analytics procedures.

Panel Measurement Technique The panel-based measurement technique involves a combination of phone calls and the recruitment of a number of people of varied demographic characteristics from targeted geographical regions in order to convert them into panelists or panel participants. Nielsen Ratings and comScore are some of the leading measurement companies that use this mode of Web measurement. The size of the panel may range from hundreds of thousands to millions. comScore, for example, is the Internet measuring company that is known to have the highest number of panelists, as many as two million people spread globally.

The tracking company then installs monitoring software in the computers of these panelists for purposes of measuring their Internet browsing activities and trends. The data obtained from the panelists, however, is treated merely as a sample and not representative data. The data is taken through an extrapolation process to derive a representative estimate of the behavioral trends of the overall Internet population.

ISP Technique The ISP technique involves gathering Internet usage information on the off-site activities of users through sampling anonymous data generated by ISPs. The data generated by ISPs is not subjected to extrapolation because it is characterized by a wide and more comprehensive coverage adequate enough to serve as representative sample. In his article "Improving the Web with Web Analytics," Brian Clifton identified the company Hitwise "as one of the leading Web analytics firms that use the ISP technique, boasting a representative data of over 25 million anonymous people." Although the technique does not provide the demographic characteristics of the data because of its anonymous nature, it provides analytics vendor firms with general categories of users in terms of channel of Internet access, home users, and working users.

ON-SITE ANALYTICS

On-site Web analytics utilizes measuring tools that track the actual traffic and activities of visitors streaming into a Web site. This type of Web analytics monitors the entire process of the activities of a visitor right from the first click into a browser all the way to conversion of a lead. As such, on-site Web analytics provide a detailed account of visitor activities including the points at which a visitor abandons a process.

Page tagging is the technique that is widely applied by vendor firms in on-site Web analytics processes. The page tagging technique involves integrating java script codes in the form of small snippets on Web pages. These java script codes record the activities of visitors in the browsers before storing them as cookies. These cookies track the browsing history and trends of individuals to establish their search preferences. The cookies are then streamed in real time to a server that has been designated to collect this data.

On-site Web analytics is cheaper than off-site Web analytics and can be applied in any Web site regardless of size or traffic volumes. Unlike off-site Web analytics, however, on-site Web analytics has certain drawbacks: it cannot be applied in tracking competitor activities, it is exposed to cookies deletions, and it provides demographic details only on request. Third-party cookies are particularly considered to be infringements to the privacy of Internet users and many people secure their Web sites from cookies. This situation inhibits the effectiveness and accuracy of the data collected through on-site Web analytics tools.

Web Analytics vendor firms have been striving to overcome the challenges associated with on-site Web analytics. Google Analytics, for example, endeavored to overcome some of these challenges when in December 2009 it introduced the Asynchronous Tracking Code, a technologically enhanced Web tracking snippet. In his article "Google Analytics Launches Asynchronous Tracking," Brian Kuhn reported that the Asynchronous Tracking Code eliminates tracking errors, enhances the accuracy of on-site data collection, and accelerates the load times for tracking codes.

TRACKING MOBILE PHONES BROWSING TRENDS

The measurement of Internet browsing accessed through mobile phones has been one of the most prevalent trends in the 2010s. Like the PC-targeted Internet accessibility measurement, the measurement of Internet accessibility through mobile phone is usually based on metrics such as average time spent on a Web site and average pages viewed per visit, all presented as averages of visitations to all the tracked sites. In her article "Smartphone Market Drives 600% Growth in Mobile Web Usage," Vanessa Daly quoted statistics of the Bango Annual Mobile Usage Study of 2010 that reported a 600% surge in traffic to mobile Web sites. Daly reported that Bango gathered the data by "sampling 50 million phone users worldwide who had accessed third party mobile sites through the company's platform." The findings of Bango's study demonstrated just how significant mobile usage in browsing has become to Internet measuring and analytics firms.

Surveys that are based on representative samples are also commonly used to track mobile phone usage trends in Internet browsing. comScore, for example, runs the MobiLens, a research unit that derives its data of the use of mobile phones in Internet browsing from an intelligent online survey of a nationally representative sample that comprises mobile subscribers aged above 13 years. MobiLens's data collection process, however, leaves out additional mobile phones of respondents who own multiple phones because it focuses only on the primary mobile phones of the respondents.

MAJOR INTERNET TRACKING FIRMS

Many internet tracking firms have emerged over the years following the accelerated growth in Internet usage that has been triggered by globalization. comScore, Coremectrics, Nielsen Ratings, Google Analytics, WebTrends, Omniture, Hitwise, Yahoo Web Analytics, and Nedstat are some of the leading Web analytics in the 2010s. The profiles of some of these companies are summarized below.

comScore comScore is a company that measures accessibility and trends of Internet usage. Headquartered in Reston, Virginia, the company enjoys a global presence and ranks among the leading industry players in e-commerce surveys and data analytics. comScore was founded in 1999 through a collaboration between Dr. Magid Abraham and Gian Fulgoni. The founding objective of comScore was premised on the need to establish a customizable measuring company for consumer online buying behaviors, a research segment that had been neglected by the leading market research companies at the time. Abraham and Fulgoni identified this gap after observing that the leading measuring companies of the time such as Nielsen NetRatings restricted their tracking of Internet usage metrics to the demographics of Web site visitors.

comScore officially launched its commercial services in January 2001, although it experienced some financial difficulties in the next two years following the dot-com bust that occurred between 2001 and 2002. comScore, nonetheless, demonstrated resilience when it acquired Media Metrix in June 2002, a feat that was followed by the acquisition of Q2 Brand Intelligence and Survey Site in 2004 and 2005, respectively. The company was converted into a public company in 2007 through a successful initial public offering (IPO). The company has since been listed at NASDAQ Stock Exchange under the SCOR ticker symbol.

In 2008, comScore expanded its business profile to measuring behavioral aspects Internet usage through mobile media when it acquired M:Metrics. ARS Group Nexius Products Division, and Nedstat were the other major acquisitions that were made by the company in 2010. comScore has particularly demonstrated online measuring success through its trademarked Unified Digital Measurement, a platform that combines the use of Web analytic solutions with other forms measurement such as panels and ISPs. The company tracking activities were extended to Web sites exceeding three million with a panel that comprises consumers from 170 countries.

COREMETRICS

Coremetrics is the other leading player in the Internet usage measurements and analytics industry. Founded in 1999, the company was headquartered in San Mateo, California, before its 2010 acquisition by IBM. Coremetrics has made a name for itself as the dominant provider of on-demand Web analytics. Coremetrics was particularly recognized for its innovative Lifetime Individual Visitor Experience (LIVE), a Web analytics technology that captures and stores the clickstream activities of visitors to Web sites. The unique technology creates individual profiles of the visitors from the stored information. The individual visitor profiles are used in online target marketing applications such as e-mails and search engine marketing. The company won the Best Web Analytics Software award in June and August 2011.

SEE ALSO *Internet Metrics; Tracking Web Site Analytics.*

BIBLIOGRAPHY

Albanesius, Chloe. "Opt Out of Google Analytics Data Gathering with New Beta Tool." *PC Mag,* May 25, 2010. Available from http://www.pcmag.com/article2/0,2817,2364174,00.asp.

"Appraising Your Investment in Enterprise Web Analytics." Cambridge, MA: Forrester Consulting, September 2009.

Available from http://static.googleusercontent.com/external_content/untrusted_dlcp/www.google.com/en/us/analytics/case_studies/Appraising-Investments-In-Enterprise-Analytics.pdf.

Clifton, Brian. "Improving the Web with Web Analytics." *Measuring Success* (blog), February 22, 2009. Available from http://www.advanced-Web-metrics.com/blog/2009/02/22/improving-the-Web-with-Web-analytics.

comScore. "About comScore." Reston, VA, 2011. Available from http://www.comscore.com/About_comScore.

———. "comScore Reports July 2011 U.S. Mobile Subscriber Market Share." Reston, VA, August 30, 2011. Available from http://www.comscore.com/Press_Events/Press_Releases/2011/8/comScore_Reports_July_2011_U.S._Mobile_Subscriber_Market_Share.

Coremetrics Inc. "Company Profile." San Mateo, CA, June 21, 2011. Available from http://coremetrics-inc.topseos.com.

Daly, Venessa. "Smartphone Market Drives 600% Growth in Mobile Web Usage." *Bango,* February 16, 2010. Available from http://news.bango.com/2010/02/16/600-percent-growth-in-mobile-Web-usage.

"E-commerce Web Analytics Market Share." *Istobe,* January 2010. Available from http://istobe.com/papers/Istobe%20E-Commerce%20Web%20Analytics%20Market%20Share%20Jan%202010.pdf.

Enge, Eric. "2007 Web Analytics Shootout – Final Report." Stone Temple Consulting, August 27, 2007. Available from http://www.stonetemple.com/articles/analytics-report-august-2007.shtml.

Kuhn, Brian. "Google Analytics Launches Asynchronous Tracking." *The Official Google Code Blog,* December 1, 2009. Available from http://googlecode.blogspot.com/2009/12/google-analytics-launches-asynchronous.html.

Mortensen, Dennis R. "EU and US JavaScript Disable Index Numbers + Web Analytics Data Collection Impact." New York: Visual Revenue, August 18, 2007. Available from http://visualrevenue.com/blog/2007/08/eu-and-us-javascript-disabled-index.html.

"Omniture, Inc., Company Profile." Yahoo! Finance, September 2011. Available from http://biz.yahoo.com/ic/106/106239.html.

INTERNET INFRASTRUCTURE

Generally speaking, infrastructures are the frameworks or architectures that systems are made of. For example, a nation's transportation infrastructure consists of roadways, railroads, airports, ocean ports, and rivers. Although not as visible to the naked eye, the Internet also has an infrastructure consisting of many different elements, each of which plays a critical role in the delivery of information from one point to another.

EVOLUTION OF THE INTERNET INFRASTRUCTURE

Simply defined, the Internet is a very large network of many other computer networks. The U.S. government played an important role in creating what eventually became the Internet during the 1960s. The Department of Defense Advanced Research Projects Agency (DARPA) funded early research into packet switching technology, which computer systems use to communicate. This approach differed from the way telephone systems transmitted data. Packet switching technology led to the development of ARPAnet, the Internet's predecessor.

DARPA, the Defense Communications Agency, and Stanford University supported the development of important communication protocols—called Transmission Control Protocol and Internet Protocol (TCP/IP)—that defined the way information is transmitted on the Internet. TCP/IP became the standard communication protocol used on ARPAnet in January 1983. Generally speaking, communication protocols like TCP/IP are the means by which devices understand and agree upon how and when they will share information with one another.

In 1990, ARPAnet was succeeded by NSFNET, which the National Science Foundation (NSF) created in 1987 to link university computer science departments across the United States. The NSF established regional networks that aggregated traffic from the universities and accordingly fed it into the "backbone" of NSFNET. The universities that connected to the NFSNET backbone further connected other networks of colleges and individuals.

In 1995, the NSF did away with its backbone and turned what had been NSFNET over to the commercial sector. It created network access points (NAPs) that made it possible for telecommunication companies like MCI and Sprint to establish Internet backbones of their own, to which national or regional Internet service providers (ISPs) could connect. Organizations or individuals seeking Internet access then had to obtain it directly from a NAP, or subscribe to ISPs like America Online (AOL) with NAP access.

The process used to send and receive information across the world is more or less hidden to the user and occurs in just seconds. In order for this to happen, a user on one ISP's network must be able to connect to users on another ISP's network, which may be located across the nation or across the globe. Devices known as routers make sure that the packets of data sent from a computer on one ISP's network are sent to the intended machine on another local or wide-area network via the quickest, most efficient route, in accordance with communication protocols like TCP/IP.

INFRASTRUCTURE ADEQUACY

By the early 2000s, the amount of traffic on the Internet had grown significantly. Research from Telcordia revealed that the number of Internet hosts, which includes routers, mail servers, workstations, Web servers and so forth, increased 45% during 2000, reaching 100 million. At that time, the global population of Internet users was estimated to be 350 million. Furthermore, the kinds of services, including e-commerce, being performed on the Internet were growing in sophistication and complexity. Corresponding to this were increasing demands in the areas of network quality and performance.

Legislation and Telecommunications Infrastructure Issues In 2002, the U.S. Congress enacted the Critical Infrastructure Information Act (CII Act) that established a guiding framework through which the Department of Homeland Security (DHS) would secure the country's telecommunication infrastructure network. The act was passed following the Code Red worm that caused the shutdown of Web sites through a denial-of-service attack in 2001 and another denial-of-service attack that targeted root servers in the Domain Name System in 2002. These two attacks denied Web site accessibility to millions of users.

The CII Act particularly formed the backbone against which the Protected Critical Infrastructure Information (PCII) Program was established. The PCII program mandated the DHS to receive voluntarily submitted confidential information from the private sector that concerned the critical infrastructure of the country.

The CII Act 2002, however, has been criticized as having been ineffective in protecting the nation's critical infrastructure from exposure to potential security threats. The telecommunications infrastructure has particularly been identified as one of the weakest points in the critical information infrastructure. The continued leakage of the country's critical diplomatic and security cables to Julian Assange's WikiLeaks hacking network in 2010 is one such example of the insufficiencies of the U.S. critical information infrastructure.

FUTURE GROWTH PROSPECTS

A report summary of the "Communications and Network Services Outlook, 2010–2015" identified "three core areas that will remain critical towards achieving enhanced federal communications and network infrastructure in future." The three core areas were as follows:

- integration of voice and data systems into a unified communications architecture
- enhanced mobility and facilitation for federal telecommunications networks
- adoption of cloud computing with emphasis on cloud communications

The report summary further recommended the increased adoption of seamless integration of mobile telephony to Internet infrastructure to facilitate the fast-growing segment of remote Internet accessibility using mobile communication devices. The report summary projected that the "federal communications and network services market would experience a compound annual growth rate of 4.9 percent to increase from $21.8 billion in 2010 to 27.6 billion in 2015."

SIGNIFICANCE OF CLOUD COMPUTING INTERNET INFRASTUCTURE

Cloud computing is the manipulation, storage, and security of data and information in a virtual server platform that transforms computing from a product into a service that is accessed in real time through the Internet. The concept behind cloud computing is aided by the flexibility of adjusting the capacity or capabilities of IT infrastructure without incurring additional costs for acquiring new IT infrastructure, software licenses, or employee training costs. The development of cloud computing has been synonymous with the development of the Internet infrastructure.

The commercial impact of cloud computing, however, became prominent in 1999 when Salesforce.com launched its cloud application that allowed users to process transactions online. Amazon.com followed suit in 2002 when it launched the Amazon Web Services, a cloud-based application that stored data and processed computing tasks. This was followed by the launch of Amazon Elastic Compute Cloud (EC2) in 2006 that featured e-commerce services that were compatible with business-based and individual-based computer applications.

The advent of Amazon EC2 and the subsequent release of the Amazon S3 were considered to have opened up the browser-based cloud computing infrastructure to widespread use and served as a pacesetting trend for Web cloud infrastructure development. A cloud infrastructure is mainly driven by a variety of applications that include, but are not limited to, utility-based cloud infrastructure, software as a service (SaaS), and infrastructure as a service (IaaS).

Utility-Based Cloud Infrastructure This type of cloud infrastructure involves storing information and data in virtual servers that provide accessibility to an organization's IT systems on demand. IBM has been the leading player in this segment for many years. Sun, through its SunSystems accounting software, has also been a leading corporate vendor of the utility-based cloud infrastructure.

Software as a Service Software as a service is a cloud application that uses a browser to distribute a single application to many users. Extensive commercial use of cloud computing was pioneered by Salesforce.com in 1999 when it introduced the distribution of enterprise applications through its Web site. Other SaaS applications such as Google desktop apps have since been launched as competitors to Salesforce.com. The launch of Google apps in 2009 added to the growing list of SaaS applications in the cloud computing segment. Google apps premiered as an enterprise application that is based on browser distribution.

Infrastructure as a Service Infrastructure as a service is an application that allows users to develop their own applications but use the infrastructure of a service provider to deliver and run the applications through the internet. IaaS is considered to be more flexible than SaaS because it enables the organization to take control of its data, information processing, and storage. The applications of the users, however, must comply with the design limitations of the cloud services vendors. Salesforce.com has also been the dominant player in this segment, although the entry of the Google App Engine in the cloud services segment in 2008 introduced stiff competition. Google App Engine is offered as a free cloud hosting infrastructure over the Internet.

SEE ALSO *ARPAnet; Connectivity, Internet.*

BIBLIOGRAPHY

"About Us." American Registry for Internet Numbers, 2011. Available from https://www.arin.net/about_us/index.html.

Diversity Limited. "Moving Your Infrastructure to the Cloud: How to Maximize Benefits and Avoid Pitfalls." Christchurch, New Zealand, 2010. Available from http://resources.idgenterprise.com/original/AST-0041546_MovingyourInfrastructuretotheCloud-HowtoMaximizeBenefitsandAvoidPitfalls.pdf.

INPUT. "Report Summary: Federal Communications and Network Services Outlook, 2010–2015." Reston, VA: Deltek Information Systems, 2011. Available from http://www.input.com/corp/downloads/INPUT-Federal-Communications-Network-Services-Summary.pdf.

Internet Corporation for Assigned Names and Numbers (ICANN). "About ICANN." Marina del Rey, CA, 2011. Available from http://www.icann.org/en/about.

Internet Society. "About the Internet Society." Reston, VA, 2011. Available from http://www.isoc.org/isoc.

———. "Infrastructure: Infrastructure Description." 2011. Available from http://www.isoc.org/internet/infrastructure.

Kleeman, Michael. "Perspective: Fixing Our Fraying Internet Infrastructure." *CNET,* October 11, 2007. Available from http://news.cnet.com/Fixing-our-fraying-Internet-infrastructure/2010-1034_3-6212819.html.

Knorr, Eric, and Galen Gruman. "What Cloud Computing Really Means." *InfoWorld,* 2011. Available from http://www.infoworld.com/d/cloud-computing/what-cloud-computing-really-means-031?page=0,0.

Lawler, Ryan. "If Netflix Is Right, Amazon Already a Cloud Champ." *Infrastructure,* August 31, 2011. Available from http://gigaom.com/cloud/netflix-amazon-openstack.

Marsan, Carolyn Duffy. "Faster 'Net Growth Rate Raises Fears about Routers." *Network World,* April 2, 2001. Available from http://www.networkworld.com/news/2001/0402routing.html.

Mohamed, Arif. "A History of Cloud Computing." *Computer Weekly,* March 27, 2009. Available from http://www.computerweekly.com/Articles/2009/06/10/235429/A-history-of-cloud-computing.htm.

"Number of Internet Hosts Reaches 100 Million." *DataWeek,* February 14, 2001. Available from http://www.dataweek.co.za/article.aspx?pklarticleid=835.

RIPE NCC. "The Internet Registry System." Amsterdam, The Netherlands, September 16, 2011. Available from www.ripe.net.

Thareja, Ashok K. "Enabling a Faster Global Internet Via Satellite." *Telecommunications,* February 2001.

Thyfault, Mary E. "Developing Nations Schooled in Quality, Reliability, Speed." *InformationWeek,* March 26, 2001.

Tyson, Jeff. "How Internet Infrastructure Works." *How Stuff Works,* May 15, 2001. Available from http://computer.howstuffworks.com/internet/basics/internet-infrastructure.htm.

U.S. Government Accountability Office. "Internet Infrastructure: Challenges in Developing a Public/Private Recovery Plan." Testimony Before the Subcommittee on Information Policy, Census, and National Archives, House Committee on Oversight and Government Reform.October 23, 2007. Available from http://www.gao.gov/new.items/d08212t.pdf.

Weinberg, Neal. "Here's a Quiz: Can You Name the Top Five ISPs?" *Network World,* April 16, 2001.

INTERNET METRICS

In general, Internet metrics encompass a wide variety of measurements or assessments made on the Internet. These can be very broad measurements, applying to the traffic patterns and usage of the Internet as a whole, or they can apply specifically to an organization's Internet infrastructure, which might include the network connections, cables, workstation computers, servers (computers used to host Web sites, shared software applications, and e-mail systems), and e-commerce software.

On the broader scale, Internet metrics refers to any number of Internet aspects that can be measured or presented in a statistical format, including online advertising industry revenue reports and projections, trends about the preferences of Web site users, or other statistics about the Internet economy. Global Internet metrics also apply to different technical aspects of the Internet's infrastructure, including the miles of cable that connect the world's computers, and routers (computers that relay information between devices on the Internet and different Internet service providers).

USES AND LIMITS

After the early 2000s, Internet metrics was used almost synonymously with "Web site analytics," or the accumulation of data about specific Web sites and blogs. Webmasters used this information to optimize their Web sites in order to present content that would attract new Web site visitors. Web analytics tells Webmasters specific things, including the type of visitors to a Web site, how they came to the site (i.e., from a search engine or an incoming link), visitors are located geographically, what pages visitors visit when on the Web site, and how long visitors remain on the site. This information is key to Webmasters making decisions about online marketing and content creation. Internet metrics also helps online marketers and Web site owners determine their conversion rates. That is, if Internet metrics show that many people are visiting a Web site but few people are making purchases or making other desired choices online, marketers can use this feedback to adjust their conversion strategy.

Internet metrics is sometimes categorized into off-site and on-site Internet metrics. On-site analysis refers to the data collected about visitors to a specific site. The aim of this type of data gathering is to determine how effectively a Web site is performing. Off-site metrics refers to data collection about possible demographics and possible trends or topics online. This type of metric can help identify topics and target audiences of interest.

There are limitations to Web analytics and Internet metrics applications, such as the fact that gathered information can be misleading. Web analytics tools and other Internet metrics tools designed to keep track of Web site users are limited by processes of gathering information. For example, Web analytics tools typically measure the number of unique visitors by using cookies. If a visitor clears cookies after every visit or uses multiple devices to access the Web site, analytics tools will count that one visitor as multiple visitors. In addition, Internet metric tools cannot capture the reasons why an Internet user behaves in a certain way on a Web site. To determine why visitors leave the Web site quickly, for example, more intensive polls or market research may be needed to determine whether users are not finding relevant information or are facing other issues on the site.

HISTORY

In the 1990s, Web sites used counters, which were images that refreshed each time they were accessed. These counters visibly kept track of an estimated number of visitors to the Web site. However, the counters were limited. Repeated visits by the same visitor were often counted as multiple visitors. In the 2000s, Internet metrics became more important as e-commerce and online business applications increased. More sophisticated tools were developed in order to help Webmasters and Internet users gather data.

In the early 2000s, the Cooperative Association for Internet Data Analysis (CAIDA) was one organization devoted to Internet metrics on a large scale. CAIDA collected, monitored, analyzed, and visualized data about the Internet in four broad areas. Topology measurements helped to reveal global characteristics about the Internet, describing the ways in which the many networks that constitute the Internet are joined together, and revealing information about the size and constituency of the Internet's core. Workload measurements monitored the distribution and flow of Internet traffic. Performance measurements provided a means for, in the words of KC Claffy, "isolating global problems within the infrastructure, as well as assessing service quality by country or other granularity of interest." Finally, routing data provided details about "relationships between individual Autonomous Systems at a given point in time."

Internet metrics also play critical roles at the organizational level. Just as companies use Internet metrics to measure, monitor, and report on their financial performance, successful ones also take steps to measure the electronic elements of their business efforts. This involves monitoring performance and statistics at the user (client) level, on the back end (different computer systems and databases that may be used during the company's e-commerce activities), and at a level in between these that includes things like network performance and servers.

MAJOR APPLICATIONS

In 2005, Google launched Google Analytics, a free Internet metrics tool. By 2011, this Internet metrics tool was the most popular Internet metrics tool used by Web sites. According to the BuiltWith Web site, 13,926,809 Web sites use Google Analytics (as of 2012). The Google Analytics tool could be used on blogs, Web sites, and other online spaces, calculating the number of new visits, the visits per month, the bounce rate, and other statistics Webmasters required in order to optimize their Web site. In 2011, Google announced plans to add an interactive mapping feature, known as flow visualization, to Google Analytics. This feature would allow Web site owners to view where visitors to a site or blog went online and how long they stayed on specific pages on a specific site or blog. The interactive map also allowed Web site owners to compare visitor experience by country.

Metrics related to Web site traffic can be used to lure potential advertisers to a company's site, to understand how customers use a Web site, and to improve or streamline processes that make a Web site experience better. However, as with any statistic, the meaning of Internet metrics varies depending on how they are calculated, the context in which they are used, and the value or weight users assign to them.

SEE ALSO *Internet Access, Tracking Growth of; Web Site Analytics.*

BIBLIOGRAPHY

Bhatnagar, Alka. "Web Analytics for Business Intelligence." *Online* 33, (November/December 2009): 32.

Bilton, Nick, and Claire Cain Miller. "Google Announces New Data Visualization Tools for Analytics." *New York Times,* October 19, 2011. Available from http://bits.blogs.nytimes.com/2011/10/19/google-announces-new-data-visualization-tools-for-analytics/?scp=1&'sq=web%20analytics&st=cse.

Claffy, KC. "Tracking a Metamorphic Infrastructure." Cooperative Association for Internet Data Analysis (CAIDA), April 13, 2000. Available from http://lists.ufl.edu/cgi-bin/wa?A2=ind0004&L=CCC&P=2536.

"Google Analytics." Builtwith.com, October 2011. Available from http://trends.builtwith.com/Web sitelist/Google-Analytics.

Jeffery, Mark. *Data-Driven Marketing: The 15 Metrics Everyone in Marketing Should Know.* Hoboken, NJ: John Wiley and Sons, 2010.

Kaushik, Avinash. *Web Analytics: An Hour a Day.* Indianapolis, IN: Wiley Publishing, 2007.

Levine, Shira."Tracking the Packets." *America's Network,* March 1, 2000.

NetIQ Corp. "About Us," Houston, TX, 2011. Available from http://www.netiq.com/about_netiq/default.asp.

Plaza, Beatriz. "Google Analytics: Intelligence for Information Professionals." *Online,* 34, no. 5 (September/October 2010): 33.

"Sizing Up Internet Benchmarking Tools." *Folio,* Winter 2000/2001.

Stanhope, Joe. "Google Shakes Up Web Analytics, Again." *Forbes,* September 29, 2011. Available from http://www.forbes.com/sites/forrester/2011/09/29/google-shakes-up-web-analytics-again.

INTERNET PAYMENT PROVIDER

As they are widely used to pay for goods and services online, credit cards are an important part of e-commerce. According to the Online Retail Payments Forecast 2010–2014, published by Javelin Strategy and Research, 70% of online customers used a credit card for online shopping in 2009. In Canada in 2009, online shoppers purchased $15 billion worth of items, with 84% of purchasers paying directly for their purchases, generally by credit card. Although companies can establish merchant accounts directly with banks, it also is possible for this service to be handled by Internet payment providers. In addition to setting up merchant accounts, Internet payment providers also provide additional services that fill companies' needs related to the processing of financial transactions.

HISTORY

CyberCash Inc. was one leading Internet payment provider during the early 2000s. Besides offering merchant accounts to companies so they could accept credit card payments from consumers, CyberCash provided solutions in the area of business-to-business transactions. These transactions extended beyond credit cards to include electronic fund transfer (EFT) and purchasing cards. The company also provided services in the area of fraud detection and risk management via FraudPatrol. Despite its early entrance to the market, the company filed for bankruptcy in 2001 and was purchased by VeriSign.

VeriFone was another leading Internet payment provider in the early 2000s. The company provided payment solutions to consumers, merchants, and banks throughout the world. Its products included the point-of-sale terminals used at physical retail locations to process credit-card transactions, as well as software that accomplished the same for companies doing business on the Internet. VeriFone also provided installation, repair, and consulting services. VeriFone Systems, Inc., generated $1 billion in sales in 2010.

Besides VeriFone and CyberCash, there were many other Internet Payment Providers in the early 2000s. Some catered to small and midsize companies that experienced difficulty obtaining merchant accounts directly from banks. Others specialized in servicing companies in industry segments like adult entertainment, which were considered to carry a higher-than-average risk for fraud or disputes. Many banks were leery of offering merchant accounts to e-commerce companies because of concerns over fraud and high charge-back rates, especially those in high-risk categories.

TWENTY-FIRST CENTURY DEVELOPMENTS

In the 2000s, one of the most popular forms of payments online was through online payment providers. These companies, including PayPal and Google Checkout, allow vendors to process payments without having a merchant account and also allow customers to pay for purchases online without the use of a credit card, although the systems allow for credit card payments as well.

In 2011, PayPal was one of the largest e-commerce solutions providers, reporting revenues of $2.23 billion in 2009. The company was established in 1998 and became a subsidiary of eBay in 2002. As PayPal became the primary way for vendors and buyers of the eBay auction site to handle transactions, PayPal grew, and eventually many retailers and vendors outside of eBay also adopted PayPal as a way of taking care of e-commerce payment transactions. However, PayPal has been involved in lawsuits and has been widely criticized for freezing accounts. In 2011, PayPal announced PayPal Access, a program that would allow customers visiting participating Web sites to log in and pay for purchases without having to log in to their accounts at the end of the transaction.

In 2006, Google launched Google Checkout, an online payment system allowing customers to make purchases at participating vendor sites. With a structure similar to that of PayPal, Google Checkout, also allows charities to accept online donations using its system.

Moneybookers is another online payment provider. Established in 2001, the company has approximatley 16 million customers, as of 2012. The U.K.-based company was purchased by Investcorp Technology Partners in 2007 and announced plans in 2011 to rename itself Skrill.

RISK CONCERNS

In the early 2010s, one emerging trend with payment providers was increased consumer interest in mobile payments. According to PayPal Australia, payments made from mobile devices were increasing at a rate of 430% annually, with more than 1,000 transactions taking place from mobile phones every hour. The switch from e-commerce to mobile-device-based commerce (m-commerce) has meant that Internet providers have had to offer apps and options for customers who wish to pay through mobile devices. The rise in mobile purchases and financial transactions made through mobile devices has also increased concerns about security.

Indeed, security has been an ongoing concern for Internet payment providers. As online services, they are susceptible to denial-of-service (DoS) attacks as well as hacking attempts. Consumers of these services are also susceptible to phishing scams, in which criminals send e-mails to customers and to random e-mail addresses with the payment provider logo. The e-mails appear to be from the Internet payment provider and ask customers to visit a Web site to enter their account information. Criminals can then access this information and use it for identity theft or simply to remove money from consumer accounts.

SEE ALSO *M-commerce Security; Mobile E-commerce.*

BIBLIOGRAPHY

Botha, J., C. Bothma, and Pieter Geldenhuys. *Managing E-commerce in Business.* 2nd ed. Cape Town, South Africa: Juta and Company, 2008.

"Canada Online Shopping Statistics." *Online Marketing Trends,* January 21, 2011. Available from http://www.onlinemarketing-trends.com/2011/01/canada-online-shopping-statistics.html.

"Google Unveils UK Payments System." *BBC,* April 12, 2007. Available from http://news.bbc.co.uk/2/hi/business/6549643.stm.

Grzybek, Eva. "PayPal Access—Is This the Future of Online Payments?" *Huffington Post,* October 20, 2011. Available from http://www.huffingtonpost.co.uk/eva-grzybek/paypal-access-is-this-the_b_1021328.html.

Hisey, Pete. "At War Over Merchant Risk." *Credit Card Management,* July 2000.

Kamildjanov, Ozdobek. "Moneybookers–Company Profile." *FX Compared,* March 2, 2011. Available from http://www.fxcompared.com/blog/foreign-currency-companies/moneybookers-company-profile.

Loechner, Jack. "Consumers Comfortable Shopping Online with Credit Cards." *Media Post,* March 10, 2010. Available from http://www.mediapost.com/publications/article/123814.

Messmer, Ellen. "Credit Crunch for E-comm Wannabes." *Network World,* May 31, 1999.

Methananda, Nirosha. "PayPal–Smartphone Payments on 430% Year-on-Year Trajectory."; *Power Retail,* October 18, 2011. Available from http://www.powerretail.com.au/news/paypal-smartphone-payments-to-grow.

"Online Retail Payments Forecast 2010–2014: Alternative Payments Growth Strong but Credit Card Projected for Comeback." Pleasanton, CA: Javelin Strategy and Research, 2011. Available from https://www.javelinstrategy.com/Brochure-171.

Sisk, Michael. "Enabling On-Line Credit Card Use in Minutes, Not Weeks." *US Banker,* April 2000.

INTERNET SERVICE PROVIDER (ISP)

Internet service providers (ISPs) provide access to the Internet through telephone dial-up connections as well as through permanent or "always-on" connections. Prior to ISPs, access to the Internet required an account at a university or government agency and a working knowledge of Unix.

EARLY HISTORY

At the beginning of 1995 there were approximately 160 commercial Internet access providers in the United States. According to *PC Magazine,* average monthly fees were about $17.50, with connect time billed at $3 per hour. Some ISPs could only be reached through a long-distance telephone call. ISPs offered Internet access through three basic types of accounts. Shell or terminal-emulation accounts connected the user to a Unix system with either a command-line interface or a proprietary GUI (graphical user interface). SLIP or PPP dial-up accounts used a modem to make a temporary direct Internet connection and required TCP/IP software. Permanent direct connections for LANs over leased lines were provided primarily for business customers. At the time America Online, CompuServe, and other online services offered limited Internet access. IBM and Microsoft were in the process of building Internet software into new versions of Windows and OS/2.

During 1995 the ISP market became more competitive. The dominant ISPs in 1995 were UUNet Technologies (annual revenue of $94 million), Netcom Online Communications Services ($52 million), and PSINet ($39 million). UUNet was focused on business and corporate customers, while Netcom pioneered flat-rate pricing for the consumer market. In addition to these national and international ISPs, the ISP market included large interexchange carriers, such as AT&T and MCI Communications Corp., and regional ISPs, which numbered in the thousands and were growing daily by mid-1996. Netcom began providing Internet service in 1995 and had 400,000 subscribers after one year in business. AT&T also entered the ISP market in 1995 and claimed it signed up 200,000 subscribers in the first few weeks. Both AT&T and MCI offered unlimited Internet access to consumers for a flat rate of $20 per month, while Netcom charged a flat fee of $20 for 400 hours per month. Sprint Corp. followed with a plan similar to its long-distance competitors, AT&T and MCI. UUNet, on the other hand, charged businesses an average of $1,000 a month for Internet service. Consumers were more interested in low-cost access, while reliability and speed were priorities for corporate customers.

At this stage the Internet was growing rapidly, and ISPs were challenged to build out their infrastructure, improve their router technology, and increase their access points. By 1996 regional Bell operating companies (RBOCs) and long-distance carriers were forming new subsidiaries to provide Internet service. After AT&T rolled out its WorldNet service in 1995, the RBOCs saw Internet service as a way to leverage their large networks. Pacific Bell, through its newly formed subsidiary Pacific Bell Internet, began offering Internet access in April 1996 to 75% of its residential customers in the San Francisco Bay area, Los Angeles, Sacramento, and San Diego, as well as dedicated frame relay access for businesses. Bell Atlantic's Internet Solutions began offering dedicated Internet service to businesses and flat-rate dial-up services to residential users in mid-1996.

ISPs also formed alliances to network and share their customers with other ISPs, so that users who traveled abroad could save on long-distance connect charges. Peering arrangements were established between ISPs who agreed to carry each other's traffic. By 1998 it was more common for bandwidth wholesalers who operated their own networks, such as UUNet and PSINet, to sell access to their shared-use modem pools and other equipment to local ISPs. That made it easier for start-up ISPs to go into business without investing in equipment, while fast-growing ISPs could lease infrastructure from a larger provider. UUNet and other providers also offered turnkey ISP services to smaller telecommunications companies and others interested in entering the ISP market.

LEGISLATIVE DEVELOPMENT

The Digital Millennium Copyright Act 1998 (DCMA) that became operational in 2000 granted ISPs a reprieve by limiting their liabilities for fair use of copyrighted content or functionalities by third parties in the internet. These exemptions were granted under the "safe harbors" provisions as contained in section 512 of the DCMA. The "safe harbors" provisions outline the conditions that must be fulfilled by ISPs to qualify for the exemptions for third-party copyrights infringements.

One such condition as stipulated by section 512 of the DCMA is the requirement that ISPs provide accessible procedures of "notice and takedown" that copyright holders can use to report or block infringements on their copyrighted content. Google, for example, provides an online link for reporting and removing copyright infringement for its online products comprising AdSense, AdWords, Android Market, Blogger, Gmail, Image Search, Orkut, Picasa, Web Search, and YouTube. Many other ISPs have also been keen at observing the "safe harbors" provisions to avoid willful infringement of copyright laws. This enables them to take full advantage of the protection offered by the "safe harbors" to avoid the liabilities that would have otherwise prevented them from providing hosting and transmission channel to user-generated content online.

In November 2007, The U.S. House of Representatives passed the Broadband Census of America Act that provided the regulatory framework for reporting and measuring broadband availability and uptake. The act, which was signed into law by President George W. Bush in October 2008, required the Federal Communications Commission (FCC) to narrow down its procedures of measuring broadband from general formats such as average speeds or geographic percentage coverage to specific metrics such as exact speed in terms of kilobytes per second or specific ZIP code areas.

The Broadband Census of America Act 2010 was enacted following concerns about the accuracy and credibility of FCC broadband measurement reports by industry stakeholders. In January 2007, for example, FCC reported that broadband services covered 99% of U.S. ZIP codes, a statistic that was obviously far from the truth. The bill also extended $20 million and $50 million for broadband maps and broadband demand assessments in states, respectively.

Internet Uptake Trends The 2008–2009 global economic crisis did not affect the overall growth in the number of Internet users. ISPs continued to strengthen their bandwidth capabilities to meet the demand that was created by the accelerated growth in the number of Internet users and vendors. The growth of demand for Internet services was boosted by the increased use of portable mobile communication devices such as Apple iPhones, Apple iPads, and Google's Android open software smartphones. The release of Apple iPad in January 2010, for example, boosted this trend because the portable mobile device was fitted with advanced features that enabled users to browse the Web, read e-books, stream live videos, send e-mails and chat online. Apple Inc. unveiled the iPad 2, a more advanced version of the iPad that came with additional user functionalities, in March 2011.

In the 2000s there was a remarkable increase in the number of Internet users in the United States among homes, small businesses, and corporate organizations. An article titled "Internet Users in the World: Distribution by World Regions—2011" quoted statistics from Nielsen Online that showed "internet usage in North America experienced a 151.7 percent growth in the period between 2000 and 2011, a growth rate that represented a 78.3 percent penetration in the population."

There was expanded use of the wireless broadband network in e-commerce following technological advancements in the wireless telecommunications during the 2000s. Indeed, the scope of activities of many ISPs was redefined in October 1, 2001, when the first-ever commercial use of third-generation (3G) network was launched in Japan. The 3G network later spread to the United States in 2003 when it was introduced by Monet Mobile Networks and later by Verizon Wireless.

ISPs were revolutionized further with the unveiling of the fourth-generation (4G) network platform. Sweden's TeliaSonera is on record as having been the first company worldwide to launch the 4G network on December 14, 2009. These developments, together with the accelerated integration of Internet applications in wireless mobile communication devices, influenced the expanded activities of ISPs.

MAJOR PROVIDERS FOR CONSUMERS AND BUSINESSES

ISPs continued to experience tremendous growth from 2005 through to 2011. The increase in the number of customers of Time Warner Cable (TWC) during this period stands out as clear testimony of the accelerated growth of ISPs. In his article titled "Time Warner Cable Hits 10 Million ISP Customers," Ray Wellington reported that "TWC signed its ten millionth high-speed internet user in April 2011." This was commendable growth considering that the company was ranked fifth in 2008. TWC's competitive market performance effectively cemented its position as the third-largest ISP in the United States as of mid-2011, trailing only AT&T and Comcast.

SEE ALSO *Internet Infrastructure.*

BIBLIOGRAPHY

105th Congress Report. "Digital Millennium Copyright Act." 2nd Session House of Representatives,105–796. October 8, 1998. Available from http://www.copyright.gov/legislation/hr2281.pdf.

Addison, Dominick. "Free Web Access Business Model Is Unsustainable in the Long Term." *Marketing,* August 9, 2001.

Beattie, Andrew. "Market Crashes: The Dotcom Crash." *Investopedia.* Available from http://www.investopedia.com/features/crashes/crashes8.asp#axzz1VphKS0j3.

Christensen, Nick. "Ranking Internet Service Providers by Size." *Jet Café,* November 20, 2005. Available from http://www.jetcafe.org/~npc/isp/large.html.

Dunlap, Charlotte. "Internet Service Providers." *Computer Reseller News,* June 3, 1996.

Free ISP Report. "Another One Bites the Dust—FreeInternet.com Files for Bankruptcy." *Addlebrain,* October 9, 2000. Available from http://www.addlebrain.com/articles/freei.html.

Freeman, Paul. "How to Choose the Right Internet Service Provider." *Washington Business Journal,* June 15, 2001.

Gerber, Cheryl. "Where David and Goliath Clash." *Telephony,* November 18, 1996.

Gonzalez, Sean. "Routes to the Net." *PC Magazine,* February 21, 1995.

Google Inc. "Google History." Mountain View, CA, 2011. Available from http://www.google.com/about/corporate/company/history.html.

———. "Removing Content from Google." Mountain View, CA, August 2011. Available from http://www.google.com/support/bin/static.py?page=ts.cs&ts=1114905.

Gross, Grant. "Update: House Passes Broadband Statistics Bill." *InfoWorld,* November 14, 2007. Available from http://www.infoworld.com/t/networking/update-house-passes-broadband-statistics-bill-209.

"Internet Users in the World: Distribution by World Regions—2011." *Internet World Stats,* August 2011. Available from http://www.internetworldstats.com/stats.htm.

Kopf, David. "So You Want to Be an ISP?" *America's Network,* May 15, 1996.

McDonald, Tim. "ISP Survey: Bigger Is Not Necessarily Better." *E-Commerce Times,* August 9, 2001.

Rhine, Jon. "Not Easy Being Free." *San Francisco Business Times,* December 15, 2000.

Weil, Nancy. "Owning the Net." *InfoWorld,* March 20, 2000.

Weinberg, Neil. "Backbone Bullies." *Forbes,* June 12, 2000.

Wellington, Ray. "Time Warner Cable Hits 10 Million ISP Customers." *Hot Hardware,* April 30, 2011. Available from http://hothardware.com/News/Time-Warner-Cable-Hits-10-Million-ISP-Customers.

INTERNET SOCIETY (ISOC)

By the 2000s, there were countless societies, taskforces, initiatives, and organizations in place to guide or regulate myriad facets of e-commerce and the Internet. One of the most prolific and respected was the Internet Society (ISOC), a nonprofit corporation based in Reston, Virginia. To facilitate global Internet access, communication, security, and privacy, the group supported a principle-based methodology. In 2011, Raúl Echeberría, an ISOC board member, described the organization's overarching stance as follows: "What we learn, time and again, is that the best and most lasting solutions are the ones that we arrive at through cooperation and mutual respect, that are rooted in principle, and that open the door to innovation."

A holistically oriented body, the ISOC addresses the broader framework of how the Internet fits into and serves society and how best to shape it. It sees the proliferation and development of the Internet as an end in itself, as well as a mechanism by which companies, individuals, and governments around the world can cooperate in and enhance their respective fields of interest.

The ISOC specifically addresses several diverse areas of concern.

- It helps to devise and implement technical standards for the Internet and its internetworking technologies and applications.
- It harmonizes policies and developments at the international level.
- It devises and contributes to administrative policies and processes.
- It leads educational and research efforts to promote better understanding of and dialogue about the Internet.
- It collects and stores data for archiving and disseminating the history of the Internet.
- It performs hands-on work in helping developing countries to implement a viable Internet infrastructure.

The proposed formation of the Internet Society was formally announced at an international networking conference in Copenhagen in June 1991. The society was officially launched in January of the following year. By the early 2000s, its professional membership consisted of more than 150 organizational and 6,000 individual members from more than 100 countries around the world, including government agencies, nonprofit organizations, leading corporations, and start-up entrepreneurs. Its guiding principles call for an Internet that is free of direct or indirect censorship (such as restrictive governmental or private control of Internet technology), free of discrimination in any form, and free of the misuse of personal information. Its principles also call for self-regulation and the cooperative development of technical standards, as well as greater networking between individuals and organizations.

One of the ISOC's greatest concerns at the start of the 2000s was the management of the global Domain Name System (DNS). Its most ambitious proposals, generated under its Council of Registrars (CORE), would have transformed the International Corporation for Assigned Names and Numbers (ICANN) into a governing body with the power to set—and the teeth to enforce—its own rules governing domain name accreditation. The ISOC also worked to promote the commercial potential of the Internet, and its input helped to shape the U.S. White House strategy paper on global e-commerce.

Throughout the 2000s, the ISOC continued to amend DNS protocols in order to make the Internet safer. For example, the organization worked to promote the adoption of domain name system security extensions (DNSSEC). DNSSEC made it extremely difficult for hackers to falsify domain names in order to steal private information from users. The ISOC's Web site was the first .org domain to begin using the extra security extensions in 2010, and by 2011, the .com domain was the only generic top-level domain (gTLD) remaining not to provide DNSSEC as an option.

IPV6

IPv6 was one of ISOC's important initiatives throughout the 2000s, and this program was designed to replace IPv4 as the type of file that would house a site's IP address. ISOC was concerned as early as 1998 that the small, 32-bit, IPv4 files would not be able to support as many IP addresses as the Internet would require. Being a significantly larger file (with 128 bits), IPv6 would allow an inexhaustible supply of IPs, thereby allowing the Internet to expand to its full potential. Initially, companies were slow to integrate IPv6; however, as the Internet came closer and closer to exhausting all remaining IPv4 addresses, an increasing number of private publications started to promote IPv6's adoption.

In an article written in the form of a cost-benefit analysis of IPv6, Ken Salchow in *Network World* pointed out that IP addresses were scarce in 2011, which had driven costs up. Earlier in the same year, Microsoft purchased a grouping of IPs from Nortel Networks for $7.5 million. This demonstrated the increasing demand for IP addresses, as well as the increasing financial reasons for choosing IPv6.

In the 2010s, ISOC planned to continue spreading its principled vision of the Web by facilitating global access, trust/privacy, and communication. To achieve this end, it planned on opening additional regional bureaus in order to promote the agency. By the end of 2010, the organization had five bureaus around the world, in North America (Reston, Virginia), Africa (Addis Ababa, Ethiopia), Europe (Brussels, Belgium), Asia (Suva, Fiji), and the Caribbean and Latin America (Montevideo, Uruguay). These bureaus helped support 85 different national chapters of the ISOC, which had 44,000 individual members.

SEE ALSO *Global E-Commerce Regulation); ICANN (Internet Corporation for Assigned Names and Numbers); Internet Infrastructure; World Wide Web Consortium (W3C).*

BIBLIOGRAPHY

Gittlen, Sandra. "Recycled Domain Naming Plan Still Misses the Mark." *Network World*, March 8, 1999.

"The IETF Home Page." Reston, VA: Internet Engineering Task Force, 2011. Available from http://www.ietf.org.

"Internet Architecture Board Home Page." Reston, VA: Internet Architecture Board, 2011. Available from http://www.iab.org.

Internet Society (ISOC). "About the Internet Society." Reston, VA, 2011. Available from http://www.isoc.org/isoc.

———. "Internet Society 2010 Annual Report." Reston, VA, September, 2011. Available from http://www.isoc.org/isoc/reports/ar2010.

Rudich, Joe. "Private Standards for Public Web." *Computer User*, March 2000.

Salchow, Ken. "IPv6 migration: Do It for the Right Reasons." *Network World*, September 6, 2011. http://www.networkworld.com/news/tech/2011/090211-ipv6-migration-250395.html.

Thomas, Keir. "Are You Ready for the Net's Biggest Security Upgrade?" *PCWorld*, April 5, 2011. Available from http://www.pcworld.com/businesscenter/article/224256/are_you_ready_for_the_nets_biggest_security_upgrade.html.

INTERNET TAX FREEDOM ACT

The U.S. Congress addressed the controversial issue of taxation and e-commerce with the passage of the Internet Tax Freedom Act (ITFA), which took effect in October 1998. ITFA, through a number of extensions, has prohibited the imposition of new e-commerce taxation since October 1, 1998, with the last extension to reach 2014. According to the legislation's sponsors, ITFA was enacted to create a tax-free period that would allow for the unfettered growth of Internet commerce during its formative stages. At the same time, a clear and efficient national e-commerce tax policy could be developed. Although this last goal was not effectively reached by 2011, debate in the early 2010s increasingly centered around whether to make ITFA permanent.

Interest in the burgeoning world of e-commerce boomed as the financial stakes involved became more apparent. J.P. Morgan estimated that e-commerce in the United States generated $572 billion in the 2010 fiscal year, representing a huge potential source of sales, and possibly tax, revenues. The majority of states, as well as the District of Columbia, levied sales taxes on commercial transactions that occurred within their borders. They also imposed use taxes on goods and services that customers bought out-of-state but consumed in their home state. Under the Commerce and Due Process Clauses, states or localities traditionally could only claim tax jurisdiction if they could demonstrate that a "substantial nexus" existed between vendor and purchaser, which generally was understood to mean that the seller had a physical presence, such as a store or warehouse, in the state in which the item was purchased. Part of the dilemma concerning the taxing of e-commerce transactions is that in many cases such a substantial nexus does not exist, because an online customer can buy items over the Internet regardless of where he or she and the seller are physically located. For this reason, Amazon.com was extremely careful in the 2000s not to place distribution centers in certain states, so as to avoid having to charge sales tax to its customers in those states.

POSTRECESSION BUDGETS

States increasingly looked for ways to charge sales tax for Internet purchases. This was due to two main factors. According to Geoffrey Fowler, writing in the *Wall Street Journal*, more often than not, the recession of 2008–2009 left state governments with debt and decreased income, causing them to look for additional sources of revenue. Secondly, e-commerce sales rose dramatically in the latter half of the 2000s, becoming a larger and larger prospective source of revenue. Consequently, states began to pass legislature that allowed sales tax to apply to more Internet purchases. For instance, in 2010 Colorado passed a law requiring e-commerce sites to either charge sales tax on purchases made by Colorado residents or inform the state government of all purchases, thereby enabling the state to charge consumers directly. The State of New York passed a law in 2008 that deemed local affiliate marketers as sales agents, enabling sales taxation on e-tailers that depended upon New York affiliate marketers for customers. A number of other states also considered passing similar laws in the early 2010s.

The question was further complicated by the fact that sales taxes can be more easily applied to transactions involving the transfer of tangible goods. However, many of the items sold online are intangible, such as downloaded songs, information services, and other goods that traditionally have been exempt from sales taxes. Finally, the United States contains more than 30,000 independent state and local tax jurisdictions. Thus, the duty of sellers to collect and remit sales and use taxes is vastly more challenging if they must be able to calculate the appropriate tax rates for each jurisdiction, rather than only that of the state and locality in which they are located.

ITFA CONTINUANCE

As mentioned earlier, the Internet Tax Freedom Act has been extended a number of times. President George W. Bush extended the moratorium until 2014 when he signed the Internet Tax Freedom Amendments Act of 2007. The extension received a unanimous vote by Congress, and the act's seven-year term was interpreted by Roger Cochetti, group director of U.S. Public Policy for CompTIA, as a sign of "Congress's firm belief that the Internet is a priceless engine for economic, social, and civic advancement in the United States that must not be burdened with discriminatory and abusive tax schemes." Even with Congressional acknowledgement that the Internet should remain free of abusive taxes, it was impossible to know how certain areas of e-commerce taxation, such as state sales taxes, would develop in the 2010s.

SEE ALSO *Taxation and the Internet.*

BIBLIOGRAPHY

Cox, Christopher. "Internet Tax Freedom at One: No Net Taxes, More Sales Tax Revenue." Washington, DC: Office of U.S. Representative Christopher Cox, 1998.

———. "'PlainEnglish' Summary of the Internet Tax Freedom Act (P.L. 105-277)." Washington, DC: Office of U.S. Representative Christopher Cox, 1998.

Fallaw, Timothy. "The Internet Tax Freedom Act: Necessary Protection or Deferral of the Problem?" *Journal of Intellectual Property Law,* Fall 1999.

Fowler, Geoffrey. "States Pressure E-tailers to Collect Sales Tax." *Wall Street Journal,* March 18, 2010. Available from http://online.wsj.com/article/SB10001424052748704059004575128003135531516.html.

Huddleson, Joe. "Internet Taxation Issues Remain Unanswered." *Tax Adviser,* February 2001.

Jones, K. C. "President Bush Signs Internet Tax Freedom Act." *InformationWeek,* November 1, 2007. Available from http://www.informationweek.com/news/202801131.

McLaughlin, Matthew. "The Internet Tax Freedom Act: Congress Takes a Byte Out of the Net." *Catholic University Law Review,* Fall 1998.

Rao, Leena. "J.P. Morgan: Global E-commerce Revenue to Grow by 19 Percent in 2011 to $680B." *TechCrunch,* January 3, 2011. Available from http://techcrunch.com/2011/01/03/j-p-morgan-global-e-commerce-revenue-to-grow-by-19-percent-in-2011-to-680b.

INTRANETS AND EXTRANETS

INTRANETS

Intranets combine all the features of the Internet, including e-mail, Web sites, interactivity, and cross-network uploading and downloading, but are specifically for use inside a particular organization, such as a business, research facility, or school. In other words, an intranet is a sort of bordered, limited-access Internet that allows for more comprehensive and efficient passageways to company information. Intranets find their most prolific use in the business world, where they help to streamline company operations by providing access to corporate data—everything from meeting schedules to sales projections to product-development reports—to those inside the firm. Many companies even build portals on their intranets to provide a central point of access and navigation scheme for company information and news.

Typically, intranets grow out of the need to address specific problems within a firm or department that requires data to be readily available to a number of separate users. From these initial steps, the network grows to incorporate more company information and provide access to more and more members of the firm. Corporate applications and software also are geared toward integration with the internal network. The intranet really begins to pay off, however, when it graduates from a massive information storage device to a tool for knowledge creation.

GLOBAL INTRANETS

The concept of virtual private network has been applied widely in the intranets of many organizations to facilitate remote accessibility of their databases across geographic regions. Companies achieve this feat by integrating their databases with secured content management systems. Deloitte & Touche, for example, has a worldwide intranet that connects its employees across the globe.

Content management systems (CMS) applications are generally extended through a partial cloud that involves hosting the Web server of a user in a remote application, with the user retaining the rights to control the server functionalities in terms of managing contents or altering source codes. A company may adopt either proprietary CMS software or open-source CMS software. Proprietary CMS software is usually tailor-made to suit the specific needs of a company and is offered at a fee by enterprise solutions vendors, whereas open-source CMS is offered free through user community portals or third parties and is customizable to specific user requirements.

The concept of mobile intranets has also taken root following the widespread use of mobile device applications such as tablets and smartphones in day-to-day business administration activities. The remote accessibility to a company's intranet provides employees with the flexibility to pursue their duties and enhance their knowledge capabilities.

The Nielsen Norman Group has been rating companies with the best-designed intranets since 2000. Cisco Systems won in 2001 and 2005, while Deloitte & Touche and Wal-Mart won in 2009 and 2010, respectively. In a summary of the *Nielsen Norman Group Report 2011,* Jacob Nielsen reported that "AMP Limited of Australia was ranked as having had the best intranet design in 2011." Duke Energy and Verizon were the only U.S. companies that ranked among the top 10, in positions 5 and 10, respectively.

Legal Challenges Content licensing has remained a major concern in the use of intranets for many companies. Intellectual property rights require users of licensed content in an intranet to observe caution when using such content. As such, any organization that provides a remotely accessible intranet must always seek a balance between work performance, knowledge management, and intellectual property rights management to avoid litigations.

EXTRANETS

Extranets operate on the same general principle as intranets but link an enterprise's internal networks to those of strategic business partners. That is, extranets link two or more businesses in an exclusive network open only to those parties. Extranets include everything from simple intrafirm electronic ordering systems to more complex and comprehensive information-sharing networks. Extranets became increasingly common as the move to digitally integrate data pertinent to sales and joint development blossomed. Business-to-business e-commerce pushed extranets to the forefront of business planning in the early 2000s.

Often referred to as business-to-business Webs, extranets typically evolve from intranets when the latter are opened up to suppliers and trading partners to eliminate inefficiencies in their business channels. By opening up the company's internal network to suppliers, for instance, corporate databases are rendered transparent so as to ensure adequate inventory control and optimal delivery schedules.

However, this arrangement is not without its complications. While businesses enjoy clear advantages by integrating portions of their networks with those of partnering firms, that integration can cause sticky problems between businesses that partner in some lines of business but compete in others. There is always the worry that the other firm may try to gain a bit more information and advantage from the arrangement. As a result, companies increasingly institute internal safeguards, in the form of security checks and network firewalls, to keep partnering firms confined to only those areas of the network that are pertinent to the partnership. To avoid the appearance of acting in bad faith, the establishment of security measures, proper use guidelines, and clear access limits is increasingly a part of the initial negotiating process when establishing an extranet partnership. The owners of data typically maintain control over, and set policies regarding, the level of protection their information requires.

By integrating suppliers, partners, and even customers into a cohesive network, extranets allow for quicker and more efficient responses to subtle or rapid shifts in market opportunities and phenomena. Extranets ideally put all parties into seamless contact with each other, regardless of their respective locations. More contentiously, extranets connect partners to such an extent that middlemen, such as wholesalers, are often cut out of the transaction process altogether, resulting in significant cost savings. Alternatively, extranets force such intermediaries to broaden their focus and offer value-added services in order to keep their businesses worthwhile to clients.

Managed Service Providers Managed service providers (MSPs) have become an important component of Internet security. MSPs develop and operate applications that reduce or eliminate the exposure of extranets to security threats on behalf of organizations. Established MSPs such as IBM and SecureWorks extend various cloud-based security services to their customers. These advancements enable the MSPs to conduct real-time tracking and scanning of the extranet activities of their customers to prevent security threats such as scams, hacking, and viruses. Google entered the MSP market segment in July 2007 when it acquired Postini, a leading MSP.

Hybrid Protection Hybrid protection is a concept of Internet security that combines elements of the cloud with computer security features to achieve maximum protection against online security threats. Cloud-based applications are used to monitor online activities, and they block any harmful computer attacks such as spyware, viruses, and phishing immediately after they are detected. The hybrid protection has particularly been applied in securing online shopping and online banking transactions from threats such as phishing and malware attacks. The transformation of phishing into one of the biggest threats to safe online banking and shopping transactions prompted many online-based businesses to secure their extranets using advanced hybrid protection packages.

The security of extranets has been enhanced through the emergence of various nonprofit organizations that were founded through collaborations by different stakeholders seeking to promote responsible use of the internet. Such organizations and events include the Anti-

Phishing Working Group (APWG) and the National Cybersecurity Awareness Month (NCSAM).

APWG came into existence in 2003 following the efforts of a group of industry players comprising internet service providers (ISPs), financial institutions such as PayPal and Visa, and enterprise solutions providers. The membership of the organization had grown to more than 1,800 public and private institutions in 2011. The NCSAM was also founded in 2003 through a partnership of the National Cyber Security Alliance (NCSA) and the Department of Homeland Security. The NCSAM has since been held in October every year, with the NCSA having reached out to approximately 175,000 participants in 2010 alone.

SEE ALSO *Business-to-Business (B2B); E-commerce; Channel Conflict/Harmony; Channel Transparency; Data Mining; Digital Certificates; Intellectual Capital; Knowledge Management.*

BIBLIOGRAPHY

Baker, Sunny. "Getting the Most from Your Intranet and Extra-net Strategies." *The Journal of Business Strategy,* July/August 2000.

Boss, Richard W. "Intranets and Extranets." Chicago: American Library Association, 2011. Available from http://www.ala.org/ala/mgrps/divs/pla/tools/technotes/intranets.cfm.

"Content Management Systems: The Different Types of Content Management System." Business Link, 2011. Available from http://businesslink.gov.uk/bdotg/action/detail?itemId=1087352295&r.l1=1073861197&r.l2=1074448623&r.l3=1087336342&r.s=sc &type=RESOURCES.

"Interact Releases Interact Answers for Intranet." *Intranets,* March 22, 2011. Available from http://www.intranetstoday.com/Articles/Editorial/News-26-Tools/Interact-Releases-Interact-Answers-for-Intranet-74505.aspx.

Krill, Paul. "Portals Play Key Role as Intranets and Extranets Evolve." *InfoWorld,* May 7, 2001.

Moch, Chrissy. "Everything You Always Wanted to Know About Extranets, but Were Afraid to Ask." *Telephony,* September 13, 1999.

National Cyber Security Alliance. "Cybersecurity Is Your Business: How Small/Medium-Sized Businesses Can Participate in National Cyber Security Awareness Month," August 31, 2011. Available from http://www.staysafeonline.org/blog/cybersecurity-your-business-how-smallmedium-sized-businesses-can-participate-national-cyber-sec.

Nielsen, Jacob. "10 Best Intranets of 2011." *Alertbox,* January 4, 2011. Available from http://www.useit.com/alertbox/intranet_design.html.

Schwarzwalder, Robert. "The Extraordinary Extranet." *Econ-tent,* December 1999.

Wierzbicki, Karl. "Extended Intranets Add to Your Business' Reach. " *Computing Canada,* October 29, 1999.

Yasin, Rutrell. "Tools, Policies Make Good Security Mix—Companies Aim to Build Safer Internet." *InternetWeek,* October 30, 2000.

INVESTING, ONLINE

After the Internet opened to the mass public in the 1990s, it did not take long for investors to see the potential for buying and selling securities online. While forms of online investing existed before the Internet became popular, the proliferation of Internet access and the coinciding stock market boom ushered in a vast industry catering to all kinds of investors. The Internet had something to offer for individual bidders, those who worked through brokers, and both aggressive and defensive investors.

Online investing generally is well within the reach of any Internet user with enough cash to risk in the market. In addition, entering buy and sell orders to online brokers typically carries lighter commissions, thereby allowing the investor to hold on to more of what he or she earns in the market.

THE ACTORS

The convenience, low barriers to entry, and technical ease of trading over the Internet spurred a massive influx of individuals taking control of their own financial investment schemes. With a fantastic wealth of financial information only a mouse-click away, the Internet fosters the idea that becoming an investor is well within reach of the average Internet user. In addition to keen market insight, experienced online investors boast sophisticated software for charting and technical and fundamental analysis.

The online investing boom also launched its own breed of individual investor: the day trader. Day traders generally were nontraditional investors, often fancying themselves as rebels in the investment world, with few or no ties to large brokerages or market makers. Day trading and electronic trading were a perfect match, with the latter pitched as a vehicle by which the market was democratized and wrested from the exclusive hands of traditional market players. Day traders worked by sheer volume and speed, purchasing a flurry of securities early in the day and unloading them all by the time the markets closed, with the goal of profiting from the incremental price movements of those securities throughout the day. While on average these fluctuations were miniscule for individual securities, by purchasing mountains of securities day traders hoped that the tiny gains would combine to reap tremendous rewards.

Inevitably, this unorthodox investment practice turned out to be controversial. Analysts chalked up no small amount of the market volatility in the late 1990s to the day traders, who critics claimed undermined the ability of public companies to maintain steady projections of cash flow and thus effectively plan for the future. In addition, employers feared that day trading was eating into their employees' work hours, prompting many businesses to install software designed to block employees out of day-trading sites.

Brokerages, Old and New At first, major traditional brokerages such as Merrill Lynch and Morgan Stanley were slow to adopt online trading as part of their services. However, after watching the explosive growth of electronic communications networks and individual online investing, they too jumped online to catch up to the upstarts.

Having received an order, electronic brokers have a variety of procedures for processing the transaction. For instance, the brokerage may pass the order through an approval process verifying that the client is authorized to trade in particular securities. Then, once approval is met, brokerages transfer the order to either an electronic trading system such as NASDAQ or to their own agents located on the floors of exchanges like the New York Stock Exchange, depending on where the particular security is listed.

THE ONLINE INVESTING PHENOMENON

Electronic trading had its genesis in the desire by institutional investors to be able to trade after hours. In 1969, Reuters Group PLC founded Instinet Corp. for just this purpose. Thus, while online trading eventually would come to prominence as a populist practice, its origins lay in the demands of a relatively exclusive club of established investors.

The three primary advantages attributed to online investing are the lower commissions levied on trades, around-the-clock portfolio access, and greatly enhanced access to and control over the investment process. However, simply giving individuals greater access and control means that those same individuals, to truly take advantage, must familiarize themselves with the wealth of global market information available on the Internet. They also must become familiar with the subtle techniques—and enormous potential risks—involved in playing the securities markets.

The availability of the Internet as a convenient and relatively democratic investment vehicle helped to transform the nature of financial markets by stimulating vastly greater movement of securities prices and resultant market fluctuations. For instance, analysts frequently noted the decline of the buy-and-hold mentality among the investor pool, whereby investors purchased stocks with the intention of holding onto them for some length of time, thereby providing longer-term financial streams to the companies. Instead, online investors were more likely to purchase stocks and unload them in a relatively short period of time, simultaneously contributing to and hoping to profit from rapid market fluctuations. This certainly was true of day traders, who operated under this logic by definition. However, other online investors also helped to shrink the average period of time that an individual investor held on to a particular security.

ONLINE DIVERSIFICATION

After the market recovered from the dot-com bust, online companies in general began to diversify. Constantly increasing connectivity speeds and more advanced Web architecture allowed companies to offer an increasing number of multimedia services and products. The result of these changes was a broadening of many online industries, including online investment. The ability to trade securities online became expected: in order to add value to their services, online trading companies began adding extra tools to help investors out. Intelligent asset allocators, financial analysis applications, interest and income calculators, and a variety of other tools helped online investors make their decisions, all at a lower cost than a consultation with a financial advisor would cost.

These new abilities also spawned new problems. By 2010, many investors depended on an online trading tool to seek out other traders and react quickly to market changes. However, server crashes and data delays could easily render such systems ineffective and led to unavoidable losses for many investors. For the less-serious day traders, the lack of information of more complex investment tactics led to unwise choices, and investment scams became increasingly successful.

As the industry began to adjust to these new problems, new online investment options rose up, and traditional centers began focusing even more on their online sectors. Online news agencies like Yahoo! began to devote significant resources to develop their investment news and advice sections in order to meet the growing demand. Unfortunately, by 2006 and 2007 another crash had created widespread problems in the investment market, this time with real estate and mortgage-backed securities. The effects were not limited to online investments, and the investment houses that fell (like Lehman Brothers) did so because of their investment choices and strategies, not their dependence on online resources. As the overall market suffered, however, online investment also dwindled.

As the market attempted to recover in the early 2010s from the housing market crash, the use of online resources and the accuracy of those resources became even more important. Investors preparing to venture into a market (especially the housing market) wanted greater assurances than were previously available. Online research of investments, especially investment property, became more common, and the amount of data available increased in accordance with demand.

By 2011, several major online companies had risen to the front of the investment market. Charles Schwab, after weathering the market crash, managed one of the largest online investing directories available, using tools like an online chat function to bring value to customers. TD Ameritrade became a widely used online broker specializing in exchange-traded funds (ETFs), especially among investors with larger budgets. The Motley Fool grew into an online hub of investment research, news, advice, and directories. ING Direct and Fidelity Investments also provided a number of services for online investors.

In 2011, Scottrade Bank offered a mobile app so that investors could trade on-the-go using tablet computers and smartphones, a move that many online investment firms had made or were making so that investors could monitor market changes on the move.

The 2010s also saw the rise of new trends in the online investment market. One such trend was international investing. In order to compete globally and provide more services, online trading companies began to offer international trading and international mutual fund services.

SEE ALSO *NASDAQ Stock Market; New Economy.*

BIBLIOGRAPHY

Beliakov, Victor, and Thomas Barnwell. "Investigative Investing." *Asian Business,* April 2000.

Cagan, Michele. "Is There a Downside?" *Netplaces,* 2011. Available from http://www.netplaces.com/investing/diy-investing/is-there-a-downside.htm.

Carey, Theresa W. "The Electronic Investor: Direct Connections." *Barron's,* April 17, 2000.

Crockett, Roger O., "Netting Those Investors." *Business Week,* September 18, 2000.

Hunsberger, Brent. "It's Only the Money: Online Investing Tools Often Sharp, Don't Always Quite Cut It." *Oregon Live,* February 5, 2011. Available from http://blog.oregonlive.com/finance/2011/02/online_tools_often_sharp_dont.html.

Konana, Prabhudev, Nirup M. Menon, and Sridhar Balasubramanian. "The Implications of Online Investing." *Communications of the ACM,* January 2000.

Koretz, Gene. "Shootout at the Online Corral." *Business Week,* May 15, 2000.

Lohr, Steve. "Investing Online $10 at a Time." *Bits* (blog), *New York Times,* June 1, 2011. Available from: http://bits.blogs.nytimes.com/2011/06/01/investing-online-10-at-a-time.

"Online Investing Directory." *Shrewd Investments,* 2011. Available from http://shrewd-investment.com/online-investing-directory/.

"Online Investors Deserve Better." *Business Week,* May 22, 2000.

"Online Stock Trading Review." *Top Ten Reviews,* 2011. Available from http://online-stock-trading-review.topten reviews.com.

Rafalaf, Andrew. "Full-Service Brokerages Begin to Embrace the Internet ... Finally." *Wall Street & Technology,* August 1999.

"Real Estate Market Analysis." La Jolla, CA: Lyons Realty, May 6, 2011. Available from http://lyonsrealty.com/tag/market-trends.

Scottrade. "Company History and Timeline." St. Louis, MO, 2011. Available from http://about.scottrade.com/who-we-are/history.html.

Smith, Geoffrey, and Anne Tergesen. "Your Guide to Online Investing." *Business Week,* May 24, 1999.

Tergesen, Anne. "Readin', Writin', and Stockpickin'." *Business Week,* September 25, 2000.

Thornton, Emily. "Why E-brokers Are Broker and Broker." *Business Week,* January 22, 2001.

ISLAND ECN

Island ECN played a key role in redefining how stocks and other securities are traded. Island was an electronic marketplace that enabled market professionals to display limit orders for stocks and other securities, directly matching buyers and sellers, and in doing so it eliminated many of the traditional stock market middlemen and their fees. Before the company merged with Instinet in 2002, thousands of market participants entered over 2 billion shares into Island every trading day, averaging over 400 million shares traded on a daily basis.

As an Electronic Communication Network (ECN), Island was part of the NASDAQ. The NASDAQ functions as a collection of marketplaces, offering a quotation service, which lists the best price for the stocks traded, and connectivity services that enable participants to interact with each other. The NASDAQ, however, does not offer trading services. Therefore market professionals must ensure that their orders for NASDAQ securities are posted in a marketplace that offers best liquidity, that is, the best chances of getting an execution quickly at low cost. Island ECN proved that it could meet all these needs. In 2001, Island was the second-largest ECN, after Instinet Inc. Instinet acquired Island in 2002 for $508 million, and three years later Instinet was purchased by NASDAQ.

THE EMERGENCE OF ISLAND

The groundwork for Island ECN was laid by Joshua Levine, who in the mid-1990s wrote the software that would become the basis for its electronic trading system. Levine's system grew out of NASDAQ's SOES—small order execution system—which was introduced after the 1987 stock market crash. SOES automatically matched trades of 1,000 shares or less, making it possible for investors to deal with one another directly, without the intervention of the traditional middlemen.

Island was founded in 1997 by Jeff Citron and Levine with funding from Datek Online Holdings Corporation. Island was an immediate hit, its popularity driven in part by the day trading fad of the late 1990s. The effects were felt throughout the stock world. Competing ECNs were soon opening their virtual doors, and the New York Stock Exchange (NYSE) and NASDAQ were compelled to look for ways to simplify their business in order to meet the challenge. Levine himself fueled the competition with his outspoken criticisms of NYSE and NASDAQ as anticompetitive monopolies. Thanks to Levine's efforts, the NYSE eventually repealed its rule prohibiting its members from trading substantial amounts of NYSE-listed stock off the trading floor. The repeal made it possible for Island to begin trading in stock listed on the NYSE.

Levine stepped aside in 1998 and was replaced as Island's president and CEO by Matthew Andresen, who was also fueled by a passion to change the way securities were traded. Under Andresen, in June 1999 Island applied to the SEC to become the nation's first for-profit exchange, enabling it to compete head-to-head with NYSE and NASDAQ for orders. Some critics speculated that acquiring market status would impose on Island the crippling costs of instituting and enforcing a complex set of SEC rules. Island maintained that its electronic form and the high degree of transparency that form entailed—providing, for example, an easy-to-follow audit trail for every order—would make enforcement far easier than in traditional securities markets. It would also provide Island with the opportunity to make millions of dollars in earnings every year from the sale of its market data.

After being fined for several trading violations, Island's parent Datek sold a 90% interest in Island to a group composed of Bain Capital, TA Associates, and Silver Lake Partners. The sale was seen by some as an attempt to distance Island from Datek's problems while its exchange application was being considered. In one case, the company was accused of trading on a NASDAQ system meant for small investors. Allegedly, Datek created more than 100 dummy accounts to invest over $50 million in the 1990s. Datek settled for $6.3 million in 2002 without claiming guilt or innocence.

MEASURING UP TO COMPETITION

Island ECN offered investors a variety of advantages. It provided the flexibility of the longest trading session available at the time. Island began matching orders at 7:00 a.m., before the market opened, and continued until 8:00 p.m., hours after the market closed. It was able to do business much faster than traditional markets, with a speed as fast as 3/100ths of a second, compared to several seconds for traditional markets, a speed that the NYSE finally caught up to in the late 2000s. That speed was the difference between executing or failing to execute an order, which added a significant amount of value to using the Island system. Finally, ECNs such as Island cut the cost of trading significantly, charging fractions of a cent per share instead of five to six cents charged by traditional middlemen.

Despite the competitive advantages of Island's ECN, 2002 promised to be difficult for the young company. NASDAQ was set to release its SuperMontage system, a Web-based trading portal that facilitated exchange with many of the same advantages of the other ECNs. When the older, larger ECN, Instinet, began to court Island, the company was not averse to joining forces. Instinet acquired Island later in the year. Ed Nicoll, Island chairman, became CEO of the new, larger Instinet. Mathew Andresen shifted position to chief operating officer of the ECN division, while Andre Villeneuve continued in his role as chairman of Instinet. All signs pointed to the merger's purpose as an alliance for the upcoming competition with NASDAQ.

Three years later, the new joint company was acquired by NASDAQ for $934 million. This last deal was conducted to give NASDAQ an edge on NYSE, demonstrating the continued trend toward consolidation and competition in e-commerce, which continued to pervade the industry through the twenty-first century.

SEE ALSO *Day Trading; Electronic Communications Networks (ECNs); NASDAQ Stock Market; NYSE Arca.*

BIBLIOGRAPHY

Andresen, Matthew. "Don'tCLOBber ECNs." *Wall Street Journal,* March 27, 2000.

"Datek Abused SOES for Five Years in 1990s, SEC Charges." *The Street,* January 24, 2002. Available from http://www.thestreet.com/markets/marketfeatures/10007355.html.

"Island ECN Calls on Congress to Revamp National Market System, Eliminating ITS." *Daily Report for Executives,* April 18, 2001.

"Island Won't Strand Traders." *Active Trader,* October 2001.

Joyce, Erin. "Instinet Acquires Island ECN." *InternetNews,* June 10, 2002. Available from http://www.internetnews.com/bus-news/article.php/1355751/Instinet+Acquires+Island+ECN.htm.

Kolbert, Elizabeth. "The Last Floor Show." *New Yorker,* March 20, 2000.

Marlin, Steve. "Nasdaq Buying Instinet Group, Setting Up E-trading Showdown with NYSE." *InformationWeek,* April 22, 2005. Available from http://www.informationweek.com/news/161501151.

Moyer, Liz. "NYSE Set to Go Public Mar. 8." *Forbes,* February 28, 2006. Available from http://www.forbes.com/2006/02/28/nyse-archipelago-0228markets05.html.

Pegg, Jonathan. "Driving Harder in a Bear Market to Pump Up Volume." *Fortune Banker,* April 2001.

Ponczak, Jeff. "Super, or Just So (es)-so?" *Active Trader,* October 2001.

Santini, Laura. "A Rebel's Gamble." *Investment Dealers' Digest,* January 29, 2001.

iVILLAGE

iVillage was the first site on the Web devoted to the concerns and interests of women in the prime of their lives. Besides the Web site iVillage.com, the iVillage extensions included NBC Digital Health Network, GardenWeb, Astrology.com, and iVillageUK. The Web site offered content and message boards in Pregnancy & Parenting, Health, Entertainment, Beauty & Style, Food, Home & Garden, and Love & Sex.

After weathering the dot-com crash, the company managed to survive dangerously low stock prices and the threat of bankruptcy, due to its high number of unique visitors. The site's reputation as the go-to Web site for women gathered enough advertisers and investors to keep the company afloat despite low revenues. Then, in the middle of a surge in the Web site's popularity, NBC acquired iVillage for $600 million in 2006 and led the site through a number of different versions in the attempt to make it a profitable acquisition. By 2011, iVillage was receiving over 30 million unique visitors every month, serving as an integral piece of NBC's Women and Lifestyle Entertainment Networks Group. Profitability, however, was still around the corner.

CONCEPTION AND EARLY YEARS

Candice Carpenter (now Olsen) conceived of iVillage in 1995. A graduate of Stanford and Harvard, Carpenter was hired as a consultant by the fledgling America Online (AOL). She knew next to nothing about computers or the developing Web culture, but she was immediately impressed by the various online communities she found lurking under the surface at AOL: a community for pet-owners, another for quilters, and so on. Carpenter's insight was that such communities would be a determining factor for the Internet's future; her genius was to take that realization and create a business brand around it.

With New York media veterans Nancy Evans and Robert Levitan, Carpenter sketched out her ideas about Web community. In September 1995, they planned out three online communities centered on health, family, and careers. They took the name iVillage because "i" as in "Internet," was the online prefix of choice at the time. iVillage's first incarnation was not aimed at women Web surfers in particular. However, it was soon apparent that Carpenter, Evans, and Levitan had found the bait to lure an elusive audience—women in the prime of their lives made up about 80% of iVillage traffic. AOL was interested in those numbers; so were the Tribune Company and Kleiner Perkins, a venture capital firm. All put up money for iVillage. AOL's backing represented its first investment in an independent company.

Parent Soup, iVillage's first interactive community, went online on AOL in January 1996. The site's content included articles and polls on a broad spectrum of parenting topics, as well as chat rooms where parents could exchange advice or consult experts. At the same time, the company began forging deals with product manufacturers, like KidSoft, a maker of software for parents and children. Products were featured on the Web site and could be purchased at iVillage's Parent Soup General Store. A second community, At Work, devoted to career and work issues, debuted later in 1996, followed by Better Health & Medical, and a general community for women, Life Soup. Life Soup was designed as a site where women could exchange ideas on a broad range of interesting topics, including finance, fitness, food, sex, and relationships.

By fall 1997 iVillage boasted an average of 51 million page views per month. It represented, according to iVillage, a bloc of women more than twice as big as any other on the Web. With experts at the time predicting that 34 million women were about to begin using the Web, iVillage's prospects looked bright indeed. Soon it was attracting established advertisers, such as Polaroid, Compaq Computer, and Astra-Merck. Other companies wanted to partner with iVillage. In May 1998, it was the beneficiary of a $32.5 million infusion from one group of companies. AT&T partnered with iVillage in November 1998 to launch an Internet service provider targeted specifically at women. Shortly thereafter, NBC was given a stake in iVillage in return for promotion on its regular and cable networks. By the end of 1998, iVillage had 14 channels online, one million registered users, and was reporting nearly three million visitors every month. It was by far the most popular site for women on the Internet.

Nonetheless, there were skeptics when iVillage announced in March 1999 that it would go public. Some said the company was not well known enough to generate interest among investors; others said its business was not sufficiently rooted in the "real world" of the traditional economy; that is, it was seen as too heavily tied to the virtual New Economy. At first shares were to be offered for about $13 a piece. Then, just before the offering, iVillage's underwriter upped the price to $23. That would have given the company a market value of about $556 million. Against most expectations, though, the stock opened at a blockbusting $95.875 a share. At the end of the first day of trading, iVillage was worth over $2 billion and its share price continued to climb, eventually topping off at $130 a share.

LIFE AFTER THE IPO

It was a bubble waiting to burst. By mid-1999 the company had yet to earn a penny of profit. By design or default, iVillage had begun shifting its focus away from its original business plan. No longer was it a pure community—nearly 30% of its revenue was coming from e-commerce, mainly its online shops. On other fronts, it was sued by ex-employees who charged, among other things, that they had been bilked out of promised stock options. Worst of all, from an investor's point of view, was the fact that iVillage was still hemorrhaging cash. It lost $86.7 million in the first nine months of 1999 alone. By the end of the year, iVillage's share price had plunged to $9.50.

In April 2000, in an attempt to stabilize the company's fortunes, Doug McCormick, a member of the iVillage board, was named president. Three months later McCormick replaced founder Candice Carpenter as CEO. Shortly after, Carpenter resigned her board position—or was pushed out—and left iVillage altogether. Various reasons were put forward for Carpenter's surprising and rapid departure. Some blamed her abrasive management style, which allegedly was responsible for the high turnover among iVillage staff. iVillage's five CFOs in just four years, coupled with charges that Carpenter fired one CFO after she had questioned Carpenter about irregularities in the company's books, gave rise to questions about Carpenter's handling of company finances. The most important factor, however, was undoubtedly iVillage's poor showing on Wall Street, a downturn Carpenter was unable to turn around. By spring 2001 the firm's shares were hovering around the $1 mark and were threatened with delisting by NASDAQ.

McCormick's appointment raised questions of its own, most prominently about the wisdom of installing a man as the head and public face of a Web site aimed at women. However, McCormick made changes right away. He signaled a move away from e-commerce by selling off iBaby, iVillage's online baby shop. In early 2001, he oversaw iVillage's purchase of its main competitor, Women.com, for $25 million in cash. Publicly it was referred as a merger because the Hearst Corporation, Women.com 's primary shareholder, made a $20 million investment in iVillage. The move created a women's megasite and made iVillage the default choice of advertisers looking to reach women through the Web.

SURVIVING THE BUST

In late 2001, one of iVillage's subsidiaries received a boon that helped to keep the company afloat. After the terrorist attacks on September 11, an increasing percentage of online activity was devoted to religious or spiritual Web sites, and Astrology.com benefited. According to *Forbes,* 25% of Internet users found information on spiritual matters online, showing a 4% increase over 2000. After the attacks, over 40% of people reported sending prayers via e-mail, for instance, and roughly one-quarter reported searching for information on the Islamic faith. Consequently, Astrology.com received 870,000 visitors per week, outstripping the iVillage site itself, as well as adding a considerable amount of clout and fame to the iVillage brand.

By 2006, the site was still gaining visitors but not recording a profit. Revenue in 2005 grew by one-third of the revenue earned in 2004. When NBC bought iVillage in 2006, the company reported to *Forbes* that it expected to post $200 million in digital revenues from the site by the end of 2006. Robert Wright, chairman and executive at NBC Universal, shelled out $600 million to integrate the iVillage brand with his company's digital strategy, despite the continued operating loss recorded by the company.

NBC made a number of significant changes to give the site more focus, leading to increased readership and optimism. One major revision was conducted throughout 2009, when NBC completely reworked the outlook, focus, and integration of iVillage with its parent company. At that time, the site welcomed over 20 million unique visitors per month. During the process, a number of topics were eliminated, including Love, Go Green, and Weddings, though some of these topics were joined with other subjects. An entertainment section was added and emphasis was turned to "newsy" articles and member involvement. Discussion groups supported conversation in any number of trending topics. The more than 30 million unique visitors per month in 2011 was considered a healthy number for a Web site.

SEE ALSO *Community Model; Evans, Nancy; Olsen, Candice Carpenter; Women and the Internet.*

BIBLIOGRAPHY

Barlas, Pete. "Investors Find Way to 'Women's' Web." *Investor's Business Daily,* August 5, 1998.

———. "It Takes NBC to Build iVillage." *Investor's Business Daily,* November 30, 1998.

iVillage. "About iVillage." New York, 2011. Available from http://www.ivillage.com/about-ivillage/8-a-257165.

"iVillage."*IPO Reporter,* March 15, 1999.

"iVillage and AT&T to Launch First Women's Internet." *Business Wire,* November 18, 1998.

"iVillage Announces Online Network for Women." *PR Newswire,* September 8, 1997.

Jensen, Elizabeth. "At NBC's Site for Women, a True Makeover." *New York Times,* September 6, 2009. Available from http://www.nytimes.com/2009/09/07/business/media/07village.html.

Kaufman, Joanne. "iVillage: Learning the Hard Way." *Fortune Small Business,* March 2001.

Olsen, Parmy. "Wright's NBC Universal to Buy IVillage for $600M." *Forbes,* March 6, 2006. Available from http://www.

forbes.com/2006/03/06/ivillage-nbc-universal-cx_po_0306 autofacescan07.html.

Patsuris, Penelope. "You've Got God." *Forbes,* January 2, 2002. Available from http://www.forbes.com/2002/01/02/0102 religion.html.

Scheier, Rachel. "Working on a Cure for iVillage's Ills." *Daily News,* July 17, 2000.

Seo, Diane. "Rivals Battle to Be New Online Force." *Los Angeles Times,* July 23, 1999.

Siwolop, Sana. "A Shifting Landscape at the iVillage Offering." *New York Times,* March 21, 1999.